# Educational Psychology

### FIFTH EDITION

## John W. Santrock

*University of Texas at Dallas*

Mc Graw Hill

*Connect Learn Succeed*™

The McGraw-Hill Companies

Connect
Learn
Succeed™

Educational Psychology, FIFTH EDITION

Published by McGraw-Hill, an imprint of The McGraw-Hill Companies, Inc., 1221 Avenue of the Americas, New York, NY 10020. Copyright © 2011, 2009, 2004, 2001 by The McGraw-Hill Companies, Inc. All rights reserved. No part of this publication may be reproduced or distributed in any form or by any means, or stored in a database or retrieval system, without the prior written consent of The McGraw-Hill Companies, Inc., including, but not limited to, in any network or other electronic storage or transmission, or broadcast for distance learning.

Some ancillaries, including electronic and print components, may not be available to customers outside the United States.

This book is printed on acid-free paper.
Printed in USA

2 3 4 5 6 7 8 9 0 QVS / QVS 17 16 15 14

ISBN: 978-0-07-131496-1
MHID: 0-07-131496-2

# About the **Author**

**John W. Santrock** John Santrock received his Ph.D. from the University of Minnesota in 1973. He taught at the University of Charleston and the University of Georgia before joining the program in Psychology and Human Development at the University of Texas at Dallas, where he currently teaches a number of undergraduate courses.

John has been a member of the editorial boards of *Child Development* and *Developmental Psychology*. His research on father custody is widely cited and used in expert witness testimony to promote flexibility and alternative considerations in custody disputes. John also has authored these exceptional McGraw-Hill texts: *Children* (11th edition), *Adolescence* (13th edition), *Life-Span Development* (13th edition), and *Child Development* (13th edition).

For many years John was involved in tennis as a player, a teaching professional, and a coach of professional tennis players. He has been married for more than 35 years to his wife, Mary Jo, who is a realtor. He has two daughters—Tracy, who also is a realtor, and Jennifer, who is a medical sales specialist. He has one granddaughter, Jordan, age 19, and two grandsons, Alex, age 6, and Luke, age 4. In the last decade, John also has spent time painting expressionist art.

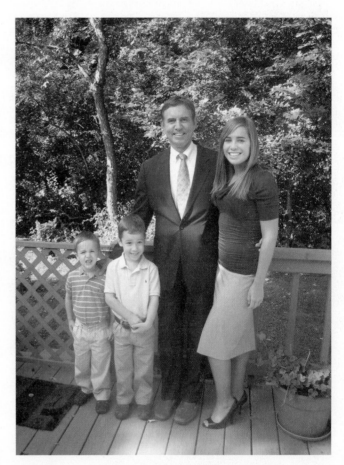

John Santrock with his grandchildren Luke, Alex, and Jordan.

*For the educators in my family:*
*My wife, Mary Jo, a teacher; my father,*
*John F. Santrock, Jr., a teacher,*
*principal, and superintendent of*
*schools; my mother, Ruth Smith*
*Santrock, an administrative*
*assistant; my grandmother, Della*
*Karnes Santrock, who taught*
*all grades in a one-room*
*school; and John F. Santrock,*
*Sr., a principal.*

# Brief **Contents**

# Contents

CHAPTER 3

# Social Contexts and Socioemotional Development  70

CHAPTER 4

# Individual Variations  110

## CHAPTER 7

# Behavioral and Social Cognitive Approaches   216

## CHAPTER 10

# Social Constructivist Approaches   332

## CHAPTER 11

# Learning and Cognition in the Content Areas   360

CHAPTER  12

# Planning, Instruction, and Technology   398

**CHAPTER 15**

# Standardized Tests and Teaching  514

CHAPTER 16

# Classroom Assessment and Grading   547

# List of **Features**

# Expert **Consultants**

Educational psychology has become an enormous, complex field, and no single author, or even several authors, can possibly keep up with the rapidly changing content in the main areas of the field. To solve this problem, John Santrock sought the input of leading experts about content in many different areas of educational psychology. The experts provided detailed evaluations and recommendations for chapters or content in their areas of expertise. The biographies and photographs of the experts, who literally are a Who's Who in the field of educational psychology, follow.

 **Dale Schunk** Dr. Schunk is a leading expert on children's learning and motivation in educational settings. He is dean of education and professor of curriculum at the University of North Carolina at Greensboro. He received his Ph.D. from Stanford University and previously was a faculty member at the University of Houston, the University of North Carolina at Chapel Hill, and Purdue University (where he was head of the Department of Educational Studies). Dr. Schunk has published over ninety-five articles and chapters, is the author of *Learning Theories: An Educational Perspective* (5th ed., 2008), coauthor with Paul Pintrich and Judith Meece of *Motivation in Education* (3rd ed., 2008), and has edited several books on education and self-regulation. His awards include the Distinguished Service Award from Purdue University School of Education, the Early Contributions Award in Educational Psychology from the American Psychological Association, and the Albert J. Harris Research Award from the International Reading Association.

*"My overall evaluation is that these are excellent chapters (Chapter 7, "Behavioral and Social Cognitive Approaches," and Chapter 13, "Motivation, Teaching, and Learning") in an outstanding educational psychology text. The chapters contain a nicely integrated mix of theory, research, and practice. Important topics are included, and topical coverage represents material of greatest use to beginning teachers. The material is very clearly written and liberally exemplified; the writing style and applications will be readily comprehended by undergraduates. References are current and are excellent sources for students to consult. I also like the way the text is personalized; John Santrock presents the material as if he is talking directly to students. Chapters are highly readable, engaging, and interesting. Organization throughout the chapters is strong. I like the chapter organization around connections: teaching, research, developmental, personal, diversity, and technology . . . The Learning Goals framework is very clear; it helps students focus on the major points in the chapters. This is most helpful in educational psychology because there is so much content to cover. . . . I highly recommend this text for course adoption."* –Dale Schunk

 **Carolyn Evertson** Dr. Evertson is widely recognized as one of the world's leading experts in classroom management. She is professor of education Emerita at Peabody College, Vanderbilt University, where she is also director of *COMP: Creating Conditions for Learning*, a nationally disseminated program for helping teachers to become more effective classroom managers. Her program has provided classroom management support for more than 70,000 teachers. Dr. Evertson obtained her Ph.D. from the University of Texas at Austin and has published more than 100 articles and chapters on classroom management and supporting students' social and academic learning in school environments. She has coauthored two leading texts: *Classroom Management for Elementary Teachers* (8th ed., 2009) and *Classroom Management for Middle and High School Students* (8th ed., 2009). In addition, she coauthored (with Carol Weinstein) another important text, the *Handbook of Classroom Management* (2006).

*"This has been a particularly strong chapter in the past editions as well as here. One of the author's strong points is simplifying the complexities of teaching without losing the important concept, thus demystifying the tasks and ideas without dumbing down the content. Good job! Helping students make the connections between teaching and learning in the classroom, students at different developmental levels, cultural diversity, the learning materials, and so on, is a great organizational feature."* –Carolyn Evertson

 **Richard Mayer** Richard E. Mayer is professor of psychology at the University of California, Santa Barbara (UCSB), where he has served since 1975. He received a Ph.D. in psychology from the University of Michigan in 1973 and served as a visiting assistant professor of psychology at Indiana University from 1973 to 1975. His research interests are in educational and cognitive psychology. His current research involves the intersection of cognition, instruction, and technology with a special focus on multimedia learning and computer-supported learning. He is past president of the Division of Educational Psychology of the American Psychological Association, former editor of the *Educational Psychologist* and former co-editor of *Instructional Science*, former chair of the UCSB Department of Psychology, and the year 2000 recipient of the E. L. Thorndike Award for career achievement in educational psychology. Currently he is vice president for Division C (Learning and Instruction) of the American Educational Research Association and is on the editorial boards of twelve journals, mainly in educational psychology. In addition, since 1981 he has served on a local school board in Goleta, California. He is the author of more than 400 publications, including 25 books.

*". . . the chapters (Chapter 8, "The Information-Processing Approach"; Chapter 9, "Complex Cognitive Processes"; and Chapter 11, "Learning and Cognition in the Content Areas") are well-written, well-organized, engaging, and fun to read. John Santrock provides many concrete examples from classroom settings, which are intended to help the reader connect the material with practical teaching situations. He cites some up-to-date sources and shows a broad knowledge of the field."* –Richard Mayer

**Bill Howe** Dr. William A. Howe is the education consultant for multicultural education, gender equity, and civil rights at the Connecticut State Department of Education.

He is the founder of the New England Conference on Multicultural Education (NECME) and past president of the National Association for Multicultural Education (NAME). He is on the boards of several organizations, including the STEM National Advisory Board, Advisory Board for Native Village, Asian Pacific American Coalition of CT (APAC), University of Connecticut Asian American Studies Institute, Advisory Board of Programs in International Educational Resources of the Yale Center for International and Area Studies, Education Advisory Committee for the Mashantucket Pequot Museum and Research Center, Hartford Public Library Center for the Book and the editorial board of Multicultural Perspectives, the official journal of the National Association for Multicultural Education (NAME). Over the past fifteen years, Dr. Howe has trained over 14,000 educators in multicultural education.

Dr. Howe is coauthoring a textbook on multicultural education and a book of inspirational stories about teachers. He was a coauthor of the second edition of *Handbook for Achieving Gender Equity through Education*.

*"I wish I had this kind of textbook when I took psych courses as an undergraduate. I remember pages of boring, dense text that induced sleep within minutes of opening the book. John Santrock provides not only a lively and interesting, but immensely useful text that should be a how-to manual on every teacher's bookshelf. I would have been a better beginning teacher had I had this kind of resource.* –Bill Howe

**Karen Swan** Karen Swan is the James J. Stukel Distinguished Professor of Educational Leadership at the University of Illinois–Springfield. Her research has focused primarily on the general area of electronic media and learning, and she has authored over seventy journal articles and book chapters in this area, as well as producing several hypermedia programs and co-editing two books on educational technology topics. Her current research concerns online learning, and she has published and presented extensively on learning effectiveness, interactivity, and the development of online communities of inquiry. In recognition of such efforts, she was awarded the Sloan-C award for Most Outstanding Achievement in Online Learning by an Individual.

*"The technology sections, which are now nicely and quite rightly integrated into the text, are both relevant and current."* –Karen Swan

**James McMillan** Dr. McMillan is one of the leading experts on educational assessment. He currently is professor and chair of the Department of Educational Foundations at Virginia Commonwealth University and director of the Metropolitan Educational Research Consortium, a university/public school partnership that conducts and disseminates applied research. Dr. McMillan obtained his Ph.D. at Northwestern University. He is the author of *Classroom Assessment* (4th ed., 2007) and *Assessment Essentials for Standards-Based Education* (2008), and coauthor of *Research in Education* (7th ed., 2010) and *Understanding and Evaluating Research* (4th ed., 2010). He has published extensively in leading educational journals, including *Educational Measurement*, *Educational Psychology*, *American Educational Research Journal*, and *Psychological Measurement*. Currently he is investigating links between classroom assessment, grading practices, and student motivation. For the past several years he also has been active in Virginia's state testing and accountability program.

*"John Santrock's text presents essential content in a student-friendly manner for undergraduate classes. I continue to be impressed with the thoughtful revisions that provide updated references and content where appropriate."* –James McMillan

**Nancy DeFrates-Densch** Dr. DeFrates-Densch is an expert in translating theory into practice. She is currently an Instructor of Educational Psychology at Northern Illinois University, where she has taught since 1991 and from which she earned her doctoral degree in educational psychology. She regularly provides in-service training for practicing teachers and seminars for pre-service teachers regarding developmentally appropriate classroom management practices and gifted learners. Her research interests focus on academic motivation, and pre-service teacher beliefs and attitudes.

*"John Santrock's* Educational Psychology *(5th ed.) provides a comprehensive overview of the field for undergraduate students. The research presented in the text is an appropriate balance of current and classic. The text is pedagogically sound and is student-friendly. It strikes a great balance among theory, research and practice, which will help students to make that connection to their own teaching experiences."* –Nancy DeFrates-Densch

**Ken Kiewra** Kenneth A. Kiewra is professor of educational psychology at the University of Nebraska–Lincoln. He is a graduate of the State University of New York at Oneonta and is certified in elementary and secondary English education. Upon graduation, he taught third grade in Miller Place, New York. Dr. Kiewra later earned his Ph.D. from Florida State University and was also on the faculty at Kansas State University and Utah State University. His research pertains to study strategies in general and to the SOAR study method in particular. He has authored numerous articles along with two books for students—*Learning to Learn: Making the Transition from Student to Life-Long Learner* and *Learn How to Study and SOAR to Success*—and one book for teachers—*Teaching How to Learn*. Dr. Kiewra is the former director of the University of Nebraska's Academic Success Center and the former editor of *Educational Psychology Review*.

*"Thank you for inviting me to review John Santrock's fifth edition of* Educational Psychology. *It is an honor to do so. His many books are highly visible and have made substantial contributions to the domain of educational psychology and to the students and prospective teachers served. . . . Overall, I found the two chapters (Chapter 8, "The Information-Processing Approach," and Chapter 9, "Complex Cognitive Processes") that I reviewed clear, well-written, current, and informative. They are, in my opinion, good chapters that especially strive to make important connections to teaching."* –Ken Kiewra

# Preface

It is gratifying that the first four editions of *Educational Psychology* have been so well received. Preparing the fifth edition has been both highly rewarding and challenging: rewarding because I continue to learn so much more about educating students and because the feedback from students and instructors has been consistently enthusiastic; a challenge because of the need to continue meeting or exceeding instructors' expectations and keeping the material fresh and up to date.

One of my goals for each edition of *Educational Psychology* has been to write a book that students say this about:

*"I love this book."*

*"I am using many of the ideas from my educational psychology text in my teaching, and they are working great!"*

*"I teach in the inner city, and my educational psychology text is a great resource for me. The focus on diversity and technology have been extremely useful. I am enriched by the book."*

These comments come from Jennifer Holliman-McCarthy, Richard Harvell, and Greg Hill, who have used this text in their educational psychology course and are now public school teachers.

Another goal I have had for each edition of *Educational Psychology* has been to write a book that instructors say this about:

*"I wasn't prepared to like this text. In general, ed psych texts are all too predictable. While people claim to be innovative, in the end they are not. In contrast, John Santrock's text is a big WOW! His book is different. It is written for the prospective teacher and not the future educational psychologist."*

*"Those who are not using Santrock have not seen it. Please communicate my sincere enjoyment of this quality text to John Santrock."*

These comments come from educational psychology instructors Randy Lennon, University of Northern Colorado, and Robert Brown, Florida Atlantic University–Boca Raton. Such comments speak to the hallmarks of *Educational Psychology*: the thorough **connection of theory to practice,** the emphasis on **expert contributors and cutting-edge research,** and a time-tested **learning system** that permeate each chapter.

## CONNECTING THEORY AND PRACTICE

I've been teaching an undergraduate educational psychology course every year for a number of years. Each year I ask the students to tell me what they like about the course and the text, and what they think could be improved. I have incorporated many of their suggestions in the text.

In talking with students, it became clear that they needed an explicit framework for connecting theory and practice. Three aspects of *Educational Psychology* now emphasize this connection: (1) "Teaching Connections: Best Practices and Strategies for . . . ," (2) "Connecting with the Classroom: Crack the Case," and (3) "Teaching Stories."

## Teaching Connections: Best Practices and Strategies for . . .

A feature formerly titled "Best Practices" that appears numerous times in each chapter is now titled "Teaching Connections: Best Practices and Strategies for . . . " The purpose behind Teaching Connections is to provide recommendations that students can use when they become teachers themselves. The feature includes many new examples of "Best Practices and Strategies" in every chapter of the book. For example, Chapter 8's "Teacher Connections" feature focuses on the importance of consolidation and reconsolidation in memory through variation on an instructional theme.

A special aspect of "Teaching Connections" is "Through the Eyes of Teachers," which is embedded in "Best Practices and Strategies," presenting the strategies that leading teachers—many of them award-winning—use related to the topic(s) discussed in text preceding the feature.

In addition, extensive examples of teaching appear throughout the text. Teaching examples and strategies are embedded throughout the text. For virtually every main topic, introduction of a new concept is followed by examples and strategies for best teaching practices.

## Connecting with the Classroom: Crack the Case

At the end of each chapter, a full-page case study related to the chapter's content appears. The case study in this feature, titled "Connecting with the Classroom: Crack the Case," provides students an opportunity to apply what they have learned in the chapter to a real-world teaching issue or problem. At the end of the case study, a series of questions—in some cases, PRAXIS™-type multiple-choice items—are presented for reflection and critical thinking. For example, the case study in Chapter 3's "Connecting with the Classroom" concerns a fight among fifth graders.

## Teaching Stories

Each chapter opens with a high-interest teaching story that is linked to the chapter's content. Many of these stories were written especially for this text by outstanding teachers. For example, Chapter 2 opens with Donene Polson's story about collaborative learning in Washington Elementary School in Salt Lake City, Utah.

---

### Connecting with the Classroom: Crack the Case

#### The Fight

Many schools, including the one in which Miss Mahoney teaches, emphasize character education as a strategy for preventing violence. The basic idea is to promote empathy among students and to disallow behaviors such as teasing, name-calling, and threats of any kind. Miss Mahoney has included character education in the curriculum of her fifth-grade class. However, many of her students, especially the boys, continue to display the very behaviors she is trying to eliminate.

Two students in Miss Mahoney's class, Santana and Luke, are on the same club soccer team and often get into verbal conflicts with each other, although they appreciate each other's talents on the field. Tuesday night at practice, in violation of the team's rules, Santana told Luke that he "sucks." Luke decides to let it go. He doesn't want Santana to suffer a one-game suspension, recognizing Santana's value to the team in light of facing a tough opponent that weekend.

Thursday in class, Luke accuses Santana of stealing the cards he was using to organize a project. Luke is very angry. Santana also gets infuriated, claiming he did not steal them. He then finds them on the floor and hands them to Luke. "Here's your dumb cards, Luke," he says. "See? I didn't steal them."

In anger, Luke says, "Fine. Then how come they're all crinkled? You know, I could beat you up, and maybe I just will."

"Yeah, right. You and who else?" asks Santana with a sneer.

Two other boys working nearby overhear the altercation and begin contributing their perspectives.

"Yeah, Santana, Luke would kick your rear," says Grant.

"I think Santana would win," chimes in Peter.

"Meet me at the park tomorrow after school, and let's just see!" demands Santana.

"No problem," retorts Luke.

Thursday evening, they are both at soccer practice. Nothing is said about the fight that is to take place the next day after school.

Friday morning Santana's mother calls Miss Mahoney to tell her that Santana is afraid to come to school because Luke has threatened to beat him up. Obviously, Miss Mahoney is concerned and realizes she must address the situation. Luke's mother also talks to the principal about the situation. However, all Santana's mother told either of them is that Luke had threatened to beat up her son. She didn't know why and did not think the reason mattered in the least. She wanted her son protected and the other boy punished.

That morning, Luke's mother was in the school for another purpose. The principal stopped her to talk about the situation, telling her that Santana had told his mother he was afraid to come to school because Luke was going to beat him up. Luke's mother asked for more information. On hearing Santana's side of the story, which was simply that Luke had threatened him, she told the principal that this didn't sound right—that Luke was impulsive enough that if he'd wanted to beat up Santana, he probably would have just hit him, not planned a fight for a later date. She wanted to talk to Luke before she jumped to any conclusions and asked that Miss Mahoney and the principal talk to both of the boys and any other children involved.

Both Miss Mahoney and the principal did as Luke's mother asked. The story that came out is the one you read. They decided that Luke should serve an in-school suspension the following day and miss recess all week "because it is the third 'incident' we've had with him this year." Santana received no punishment and walked away from the meeting grinning.

- What are the issues in this case?
- At what stage of moral development would you expect these boys to be, based on the information you have? What predictions can you make regarding each boy's sense of self and emotional development?
- What can you say about the boys' mothers?
- What do you think about the punishment that Luke received? How would you have handled this situation?
- What impact do you think this will have on the boys' future relationship? What impact on their attitudes toward school?

# EXPERT CONTRIBUTORS AND CURRENT RESEARCH

This fifth edition of *Educational Psychology,* is characterized by the contributions of the leading experts in the field and the most current research.

## Expert Content and Research Consultants

Educational psychology has become such an enormous, complex field that no single author, or even several authors, can possibly be expert in many different areas. To solve this problem, I have sought the input of leading experts in many different areas of educational psychology. They provided me with detailed evaluations of the first draft of this latest edition and recommendations in their area of expertise. Among the individuals who have served in this capacity on past editions are Albert Bandura, Joyce Epstein, Karen Harris, Kenji Hakuta, Barbara McCombs, Carlos Diaz, Daniel Hallahan, Micki Chi, Michael Pressley, Valerie Pang, Erik Anderman, Algea Harrison, Robert Siegler, and James Kauffman. The collective expertise of the consultants on the first four editions and on the new fifth edition have immensely improved the quality of this text.

The expert consultants for the fifth edition of *Educational Psychology,* whose photographs and biographies appear on pages xix and xx are:

**Dale Schunk** *University of North Carolina–Greensboro*
**Carolyn Evertson** *Vanderbilt University*
**Richard Mayer** *University of California–Santa Barbara*
**Bill Howe** *Connecticut State Department of Education*
**Nancy DeFrates-Densch** *Northern Illinois University*
**James McMillan** *Virginia Commonwealth University*
**Karen Swan** *University of Illinois–Springfield*
**Ken Kiewra** *University of Nebraska–Lincoln*

## Recent Content and Research

The fifth edition of *Educational Psychology* presents the latest content and research, including more than 1,000 citations from the years 2008–2011. In a number of places in each chapter, a research icon signals the presence of a research discussion related to the topic. Pages xxviii–xxxiv highlight the main content and research additions on a chapter-by-chapter basis.

## Expert **Consultants**

Educational psychology has become an enormous, complex field, and no single author, or even several authors, can possibly keep up with the rapidly changing content in the main areas of the field. To solve this problem, John Santrock sought the input of leading experts about content in many different areas of educational psychology. The experts provided detailed evaluations and recommendations for chapters or content in their areas of expertise. The biographies and photographs of the experts, who literally are a Who's Who in the field of educational psychology, follow.

**Dale Schunk** Dr. Schunk is a leading expert on children's learning and motivation in educational settings. He is dean of education and professor of curriculum at the University of North Carolina at Greensboro. He received his Ph.D. from Stanford University and previously was a faculty member at the University of Houston, the University of North Carolina at Chapel Hill, and Purdue University (where he was head of the Department of Educational Studies). Dr. Schunk has published over ninety-five articles and chapters, is the author of *Learning Theories: An Educational Perspective* (5th ed., 2008), coauthor with Paul Pintrich and [...]ation in Education (3rd ed., 2008), and has edited [...]ation and self-regulation. His awards include the [...] Award from Purdue University School of Education, [...]ons Award in Educational Psychology from the [...]al Association, and the Albert J. Harris Research [...]national Reading Association.

[...]n is that these are excellent chapters (Chapter 7, [...] Cognitive Approaches," and Chapter 13, "Motivation, [...]g") in an outstanding educational psychology text. [...] nicely integrated mix of theory, research, and prac[...]re included, and topical coverage represents material [...]ning teachers. The material is very clearly written [...]d; the writing style and applications will be readily [...]rgraduates. References are current and are excellent [...] consult. I also like the way the text is personalized; [...] the material as if he is talking directly to students. [...]readable, engaging, and interesting. Organization [...]s is strong. I like the chapter organization around [...]esearch, developmental, personal, diversity, and tech[...]ing Goals framework is very clear; it helps students [...]ts in the chapters. This is most helpful in educational [...]re is so much content to cover. . . . I highly recom[...]se adoption." –Dale Schunk

**[Caroly]n Evertson** Dr. Evertson is widely recogn[...] one of the world's leading experts in classroom [...]ent. She is professor of education Emerita at [...] College, Vanderbilt University, where she is also [...] of COMP: Creating Conditions for Learning, a [...]d program for helping teachers to become more [...]nagers. Her program has provided classroom man[...]more than 70,000 teachers. Dr. Evertson obtained [...]versity of Texas at Austin and has published more

than 100 articles and chapters on classroom management and supporting students' social and academic learning in school environments. She has coauthored two leading texts: *Classroom Management for Elementary Teachers* (8th ed., 2009) and *Classroom Management for Middle and High School Students* (8th ed., 2009). In addition, she coauthored (with Carol Weinstein) another important text, the *Handbook of Classroom Management* (2006).

*"This has been a particularly strong chapter in the past editions as well as here. One of the author's strong points is simplifying the complexities of teaching without losing the important concept, thus demystifying the tasks and ideas without dumbing down the content. Good job! Helping students make the connections between teaching and learning in the classroom, students at different developmental levels, cultural diversity, the learning materials, and so on, is a great organizational feature."* –Carolyn Evertson

**Richard Mayer** Richard E. Mayer is professor of psychology at the University of California, Santa Barbara (UCSB), where he has served since 1975. He received a Ph.D. in psychology from the University of Michigan in 1973 and served as a visiting assistant professor of psychology at Indiana University from 1973 to 1975. His research interests are in educational and cognitive psychology. His current research involves the intersection of cognition, instruction, and technology with a special focus on multimedia learning and computer-supported learning. He is past president of the Division of Educational Psychology of the American Psychological Association, former editor of the *Educational Psychologist* and former co-editor of *Instructional Science,* former chair of the UCSB Department of Psychology, and the year 2000 recipient of the E. L. Currently he is vice president for Division C (Learning and Instruction) of the American Educational Research Association and is on the editorial boards of twelve journals, mainly in educational psychology. In addition, since 1981 he has served on a local school board in Goleta, California. He is the author of more than 400 publications, including 25 books. *Multimedia Learning* (editor, 2005), and *Applying the Science of Learning* (in press).

*". . . the chapters (Chapter 8, "The Information-Processing Approach"; Chapter 9, "Complex Cognitive Processes"; and Chapter 11, "Learning and Cognition in the Content Areas") are well-written, well-organized, engaging, and fun to read. John Santrock provides many concrete examples from classroom settings, which are intended to help the reader connect the material with practical teaching situations. He cites some up-to-date sources and shows a broad knowledge of the field."* –Richard Mayer

---

### CONTROVERSIES AND ISSUES IN INTELLIGENCE

The topic of intelligence is surrounded by controversy. Is nature or nurture more important in determining intelligence? Are intelligence tests culturally biased? Should IQ tests be used to place children in particular schooling tracks?

> **Thinking Back/Thinking Forward**
>
> The nature-nurture issue is one of developmental psychology's main issues. Chapter 2, p. 32

**Nature and Nurture** The **nature-nurture issue** (discussed in Chapter 2) involves the debate about whether development is primarily influenced by nature or by nurture. *Nature* refers to a child's biological inheritance, *nurture* to environmental experiences.

"Nature" proponents argue that intelligence is primarily inherited and that environmental experiences play only a minimal role in its manifestation (Rushton & Ankney, 2009). The emerging view of the nature-nurture issue is that many complicated qualities, such as intelligence, probably have some genetic loading that gives them a propensity for a particular developmental trajectory, such as low, average, or high intelligence. The actual development of intelligence, however, requires more than just heredity.

Most experts today agree that the environment also plays an important role in intelligence (Grigorenko & Takanishi, 2010; Preiss & Sternberg, 2010). This means that improving children's environments can raise their intelligence. It also means that enriching children's environments can improve their school achievement and the acquisition of skills needed for employment. Craig Ramey and his associates (1988) found that high-quality early educational child care (through 5 years of age) significantly raised the tested intelligence of young children from impoverished backgrounds. Positive effects of this early intervention were still evident in the intelligence and achievement of these students when they were 13 and 21 years of age (Ramey, Ramey, & Lanzi, 2009).

RESEARCH

Another argument for the importance of environment in intelligence involves the increasing scores on IQ tests around the world. Scores on these tests have been increasing so fast that a high percentage of people regarded as having average intelligence in the early 1900s would be considered below average in intelligence today (Flynn, 1999, 2007) (see Figure 4.5). If a representative sample of today's children took the Stanford-Binet test used in 1932, about one-fourth would be defined as very superior, a label usually accorded to less than 3 percent of the population. Because

# LEARNING GOALS SYSTEM

Using the Learning Goals System will help students understand and retain the text material. Key aspects of the system are the "Learning Goals" list; the graphic of "Chapter Maps"; and the features titled "Review, Reflect, and Practice" and "Reach Your Learning Goals," which are all linked together.

At the beginning of each chapter is a page that includes both a chapter outline and three to six learning goals that preview the chapter's main themes and underscore the most important ideas in the chapter. Then, at the beginning of each major section of a chapter is a mini-chapter map that provides a visual organization of the key topics in the section. At the end of each section is "Review, Reflect, and Practice," in which the learning goal for the section is restated, a series of review questions related to the mini-chapter map are asked, a question that encourages critical thinking about a topic related to the section is posed, and PRAXIS™ Practice items are presented. At the end of the chapter is a section titled "Reach Your Learning Goals." This includes an overall chapter map that visually organizes all of the main headings, a restatement of the chapter's learning goals, and a summary of the chapter's content that is directly linked to the chapter outline at the beginning of the chapter and the questions asked in the "Review" part of "Review, Reflect, and Practice" within the chapter. The "Reach Your Learning Goals" summary essentially answers the questions asked in the within-chapter "Review" sections.

Two other important learning connections for students are (1) "Portfolio Activities" and (2) "Study, Practice, and Succeed." At the end of each chapter, "Portfolio Activities" related to the chapter's content are presented. They are organized into three categories for instructors' ease of use: Independent Reflection, Collaborative Work, and Research/Field Experience. Each Portfolio Activity is coded to a specific INTASC standard.

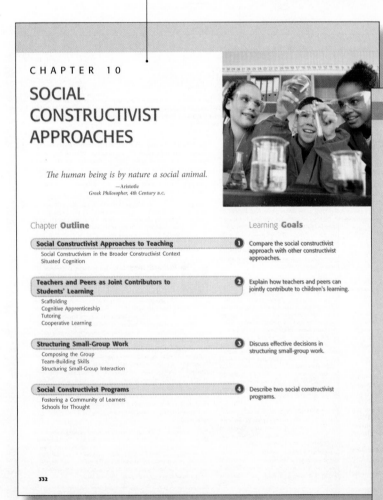

CHAPTER 10

# SOCIAL CONSTRUCTIVIST APPROACHES

*The human being is by nature a social animal.*
—Aristotle
*Greek Philosopher, 4th Century B.C.*

Chapter **Outline**

**Social Constructivist Approaches to Teaching**
Social Constructivism in the Broader Constructivist Context
Situated Cognition

**Teachers and Peers as Joint Contributors to Students' Learning**
Scaffolding
Cognitive Apprenticeship
Tutoring
Cooperative Learning

**Structuring Small-Group Work**
Composing the Group
Team-Building Skills
Structuring Small-Group Interaction

**Social Constructivist Programs**
Fostering a Community of Learners
Schools for Thought

Learning **Goals**

❶ Compare the social constructivist approach with other constructivist approaches.

❷ Explain how teachers and peers can jointly contribute to children's learning.

❸ Discuss effective decisions in structuring small-group work.

❹ Describe two social constructivist programs.

332

Reach Your **Learning Goals**

Social Constructivist Approaches

❶ **SOCIAL CONSTRUCTIVIST APPROACHES TO TEACHING:** Compare the social constructivist approach with other constructivist approaches.

Social Constructivism in the Broader Constructivist Context

Piaget's and Vygotsky's theories are constructivist. Piaget's theory is a cognitive constructivist theory, whereas Vygotsky's is social constructivist. The implication of Vygotsky's model for teaching is to establish opportunities for students to learn through social interactions with others—with the teacher and peers—in constructing knowledge and understanding. In Piaget's view, students construct knowledge by transforming, organizing, and reorganizing previous knowledge and information. In both Piaget's and Vygotsky's models, teachers are facilitators, not directors. Distinctions between cognitive and social constructivist approaches are not always clear-cut. All social constructivist approaches emphasize that social factors contribute to students' construction of knowledge and understanding.

Situated Cognition

Situated cognition is the idea that thinking occurs (is situated) in social and physical contexts.

❷ **TEACHERS AND PEERS AS JOINT CONTRIBUTORS TO STUDENTS' LEARNING:** Explain how teachers and peers can jointly contribute to children's learning.

Scaffolding

Scaffolding is the technique of providing changing levels of support over the course of a teaching session, with a more skilled individual—a teacher or a more advanced peer of the child—providing guidance to fit the student's current performance.

Cognitive Apprenticeship

A cognitive apprenticeship involves a novice and an expert. The expert stretches and supports the novice's understanding of and use of a culture's skills.

Tutoring

Tutoring involves a cognitive apprenticeship between an expert and a novice. Tutoring can take place between an adult and a child or a more skilled child and a less skilled child. Individual tutoring is effective. Classroom aides, volunteers, and mentors can serve as tutors to support teachers and classroom learning. Reading Recovery and Success for All are two examples of effective tutoring programs. In many cases, students benefit more from cross-age tutoring than from same-age tutoring. Tutoring can benefit both the tutee and the tutor.

Cooperative Learning

Cooperative learning occurs when students work in small groups to help each other learn. Researchers have found that cooperative learning can be an effective strategy for improving students' achievement, especially when group goals and individual accountability are instituted. Cooperative learning works better for complex than simple tasks. It often improves intrinsic motivation, encourages student interdependence, and promotes deep understanding. Cooperative learning approaches include STAD (Student-Teams-Achievement Divisions), the jigsaw classroom (I and II), learning together, group investigation, and cooperative scripting. Such learning approaches generally recommend heterogeneous groupings with diversity in ability, ethnicity, socioeconomic status, and gender. Creating a cooperative community involves developing positive interdependence at a number of levels: a small group within a classroom, the class as a whole, between classrooms, the entire school, between parents and the school, and between the school and the neighborhood. Cooperative learning has a number of strengths, but there also are some potential drawbacks to its use.

# WHAT'S NEW IN THE FIFTH EDITION

In addition to the increased emphasis on connecting theory to practice, the presentation of expert contributors and research, and the use of the hallmark Learning Goals System, the latest edition of *Educational Psychology* includes the following changes:

## Integrating Diversity, Development, and Technology

This edition includes fewer boxed features as the material on a number of topics is now integrated seamlessly into the text discussion. Three aspects of educational psychology that appear in the natural flow of the text that previously were separated from the text in boxes are diversity, development, and technology.

## Diversity

For this new edition, which includes a strong emphasis on diversity, I deleted the "Diversity in Education" boxes in previous editions and reworked the material into the main text. A number of adopters and reviewers have commented that they like this more seamless integration of diversity in the text. In addition, Chapter 5, "Sociocultural Diversity," is devoted to a number of diversity topics that are central to understanding connections of educational psychology and diversity. Further, every edition of *Educational Psychology* has included one or more leading experts on diversity and education to ensure that the text's diversity material is current and provides prospective teachers with effective strategies related to diversity issues. Diversity is discussed in every chapter, and the appearance of the diversity material is signaled by an icon in the margin.

DIVERSITY

## Development

Prospective teachers who take a course in educational psychology will be teaching at different grade levels. Therefore, they benefit from learning about developmental changes in students and the best way to teach students at specific grade levels. I have included a strong emphasis on development in this fifth edition of *Educational Psychology*. Chapters 2 ("Cognitive and Language Development") and 3 ("Socioemotional Development") focus exclusively on developmental changes in children and adolescents. Chapter 2 also presents very contemporary information about the development of the brain and its connections to learning.

DEVELOPMENT

In addition, I asked a number of outstanding teachers at four different levels of schooling (early childhood, elementary school, middle school, and high school) to provide their recommendations of the best teaching practices related to the topic being discussed at that point in the text. Their comments are embedded seamlessly in the flow of the text with developmental icons in the margin signaling the appearance of the material.

Developmental content is also included in the discussion of many topics throughout the text, again signaled by a developmental icon.

## Technology

The new edition also has a strong emphasis on technology, and, with the guidance of leading expert Karen Swan, I expanded and updated many of the technology discussions to include recent programs and research. As with the material on diversity, I have deleted boxed features, in this case those titled "Technology and Education," and reworked that material into the text as part of my effort to make the text a more seamless presentation. Chapter 12, "Planning, Instruction, and Technology," presents extensive information about the use of technology in teaching and learning. Also, as with diversity, every edition of *Educational Psychology* has included one or more expert consultants on technology, a topic that is discussed in every chapter of the text. The appearance of the technology material is signaled by a technology icon in the margin.

TECHNOLOGY

## Teaching **Stories** Verna Rollins

Verna Rollins teaches language arts at West Middle School in Ypsilanti, Michigan, and has developed a reputation for effectively dealing with so-called hard to teach or difficult students. She has found that the best strategy to use with these students is to find out what they need, decide how to provide it, provide it, and constantly evaluate whether it is working. A challenge for many regular education classroom teachers is how to effectively teach children with disabilities. In many instances, the education of children with disabilities in the regular education classroom is carried out in coordination with a special education teacher or staff. Here is Verna Rollins' description of her contribution in the coordinated effort to teach a student with a severe disability:

Jack was in a special education classroom for children with physical disabilities. He has twisted legs, cerebral palsy, seizures, and some other brain damage from birth. He also has a comparatively short attention span. Since he drools, speaks in a loud monotone, stutters when he is excited, and has so little motor control that his penmanship is unreadable, people often think he is mentally retarded.

My strategies included making sure that he had all the equipment he needed to succeed. I gave him tissues for the drooling and mutually agreed-upon reminders to wipe his mouth. I found that he could speak softly and without stuttering if he calmed down. We developed a signaling plan in which I would clear my throat when he talked too loudly and I would prompt him with the phrase "slow speech" when he was too excited to speak in a smooth voice.

He used a computer to take quizzes and needed a little more time to complete any task, but he was so excited about being "out in the real world" that his attention span improved, as did his self-worth. In fact, his mother wrote a letter to me expressing her gratitude for the "most positive influence you have been on him! You have re-instilled and greatly increased his love of reading and writing. You have given my child a wonderful gift."

## Thinking Back, Thinking Forward

Based on my students' desire for more information about connections with content across different educational psychology topics, I have substantially increased the number of these connections in the text. I also created a new feature, "Thinking Back, Thinking Forward," that appears multiple times in each chapter with a backward connecting arrow to inform students where the topic was discussed in earlier chapters or a forward connecting arrow to indicate where the topic will appear again in future chapters. Included in the "Thinking Back, Thinking Forward" feature is a brief description of the backward or forward connection.

## Practice with PRAXIS™

A number of learning features in the text will help the student learn extensive strategies for becoming an effective teacher and preparing for state standards-based tests, such as PRAXIS™.

## Teaching Stories

Each chapter opens with a high-interest teaching story that is linked to the chapter's content.

---

## TEACHING CONNECTIONS: Best Practices
### Strategies for Working with Children Who Are Gifted

Here are some recommended strategies for working with children who are gifted:

1. *Identification: How do you know if a student is gifted?* Traditional single-measure evaluations of potential have given way to broader-spectrum identification procedures that include nominations by parents, peers, and community members, as well as teachers. While intelligence and achievement tests may be part of the identification process, they should not be the only means by which gifted students are identified. Not all gifted students earn good grades; not all are well-behaved. In fact, because of boredom, many earn poor marks and become disruptive in class. Some gifted students also have learning disabilities.

2. *Remember that giftedness is often domain-specific.* Don't expect a student to be gifted across most domains. While some students are gifted across many domains, others have narrower areas of special aptitude or talent.

3. *Remember that gifted students often learn material faster and retain more than other students.* This means that a gifted student whose needs are being met is likely to progress more than one grade level in an academic year.

4. *Think in terms of student readiness rather than ability.* As discussed in Chapter 2, students are ready to learn material at different times. Gifted students are often ready earlier than their non-gifted classmates. Consider Alex's readiness in the case at the end of the chapter.

5. *Provide your gifted students with challenges based on their readiness.* This can be done by differentiating instruction in a number of ways, among them curriculum compacting, tiered assignments, learning contracts, and independent study (Tomlinson, 2001). Parents should be involved in decisions regarding how to meet the needs of their gifted children, just as they are in the creation of IEPs for students with disabilities.

One example of such differentiation would be for students to all be studying a particular unit in science, say the solar system. While the majority of students read material written at-grade-level, students gifted in science and reading might read material intended for students at a much higher grade level, even the college level, perhaps. To read about some ways talented teacher Margaret (Peg) Cagle accomplishes this, see *Through the Eyes of Teachers.*

### THROUGH THE EYES OF TEACHERS
**Passionate About Teaching Math to Students Who Are Gifted**

Margaret (Peg) Cagle teaches gifted seventh- and eighth-grade math students at Lawrence Middle School in Chatsworth, California. She especially advocates challenging students who are gifted to take intellectual risks. To encourage collaboration, she often has students work together in groups of four, and frequently tutors students during lunch hour. As 13-year-old Madeline Lewis commented, "If I don't get it one way, she'll explain it another and talk to you about it and show you until you do get it." Peg says it is important to be passionate about teaching math and open up a world for students that shows them how beautiful learning math can be. (*Source:* Wong Briggs, 2007, p. 6D)

Margaret (Peg) Cagle with some of the gifted seventh- and eighth-grade math students she teaches at Lawrence Middle School in Chatsworth, California.

6. *Understand that for some students acceleration is the only viable option.* For young students with broad spectrum high abilities, this may mean skipping a grade or joining the class above for particular content area instruction. For middle-school students, it may mean taking some courses at the high school, and for high school students, it may mean taking college courses in order to be adequately challenged. Contrary to popular myth, acceleration does not often have negative results (Colangelo, Assouline, & Gross, 2004). Again, parents should be involved in this decision.

## Teaching Connections: Best Practices and Strategies

Numerous times in each chapter, this important feature provides recommendations for effective ways to educate students related to the content that has just been discussed. Also, embedded in many "Best Practices and Strategies" are "Through the Eyes of Teachers" inserts that present the strategies used by outstanding, in many cases award-winning, teachers.

# CONNECTING WITH THE CLASSROOM: CRACK THE CASE

This feature presents a full-page case study related to the chapter's content after the last "Review, Reflect, and Practice" section and before the chapter summary. The case study gives the student an opportunity to apply what was learned in the chapter to a real-world teaching issue or problem. At the end of the case study is a series of questions—in some cases, PRAXIS™-type multiple-choice items—for reflection and critical thinking.

### Connecting with the Classroom: Crack the Case

#### The Test

George has a test next week in his eighth-grade history class. He is having considerable difficulty remembering terms, names, and facts. On his last test, he identified General Sherman as a Vietnam War hero and Saigon as the capital of Japan. Historical dates are so confusing to him that he does not even try to remember them. In addition, George has difficulty spelling.

The test will consist of 50 objective test items (multiple-choice, true/false, and fill-in-the-blank) and 2 essay items. In general, George does better on essay items. He purposely leaves out any names about which he is uncertain and always omits dates. Sometimes he mixes up his facts, though, and often loses points for misspelled words. On objective items he has real problems. Usually, more than one answer will appear to be correct to him. Often he is "sure" he is correct, only to discover later that he was mistaken.

Before the last test, George tried to design some mnemonic devices to help him understand. He used acronyms, such as *HOMES* (for *Huron, Ontario, Michigan, Erie,* and *Superior*).

Although he remembered his acronyms quite well, he could not recall what each letter stood for. The result was a test paper filled with acronyms. Another time a classmate suggested that George try using concept maps. This classmate lent George the concept maps she had designed for her own use. George looked at them and found them to be very busy and confusing—he couldn't figure out what they even meant. They were not at all useful to him.

George has decided he is in need of some serious help if he is to pass this class. He has sought you out for help.

1. What are the issues in this case?
2. With what type of learning is George having difficulty?
3. What type of learning is easier for George?
4. Design a study-skills program for George drawing on principles of the cognitive information-processing approach.

# PRAXIS™-TYPE MULTIPLE-CHOICE QUESTIONS IN "REVIEW, REFLECT, AND PRACTICE"

At the end of each "Review, Reflect, and Practice" feature in every chapter, the student will have an opportunity to practice answering PRAXIS™-type multiple-choice questions related to the material immediately preceding the feature.

## Portfolio Items

Activities related to chapter content are presented at the end of the chapter. Depending on the instructor's requirements, students can be asked to write about these educational circumstances in a portfolio and/or discuss them with other students.

## Self-Assesment

This box appears once in each chapter and is closely related to the content of the chapter. It is a powerful tool that helps students to evaluate and understand themselves in their efforts to become an outstanding teacher.

### Review, Reflect, and Practice

**1** Describe the information-processing approach.

**REVIEW**
- What view does the information-processing approach take of children as learners?
- What are two important cognitive resources and how do they contribute to developmental changes in children's information processing?
- What are some key mechanisms of change in the information-processing approach?

**REFLECT**
- In terms of your ability to learn, are there ways that you wish you were more like a computer? Or are you better than any computer in all aspects of processing information? Explain.

**PRAXIS™ PRACTICE**
1. Information processing is most closely aligned with
   a. behaviorism.
   b. cognitive psychology.
   c. social cognitive theory.
   d. ecological theory.
2. According to the information-processing approach, a 15-year-old can compute faster than a 10-year-old because the
   a. 15-year-old's brain has had more time to develop, and the 15-year-old has had more experience working with numbers.
   b. 15-year-old has had more experiences of both positive and negative reinforcement.
   c. 15-year-old's brain has lost many of its original connections and undergone demyelinization.
   d. 15-year-old has had much more time to develop rote memory skills.
3. Ms. Parks wants her students to know their basic math facts without having to stop to think about them. Therefore, Ms. Parks plays many math games with her second-grade students, such as addition and subtraction bingo, math bees, and card games. What is Ms. Parks' goal in playing these games with her students?
   a. to help her students to develop automaticity in knowing their math facts
   b. to encourage strategy construction
   c. to foster encoding skills
   d. to improve metacognitive skills, such as self-awareness

*Please see the answer key at the end of the book.*

### PORTFOLIO ACTIVITIES

Now that you have a good understanding of this chapter, complete these exercises to expand your thinking.

#### Independent Reflection
1. Select the general age of the child you expect to teach one day. Make a list of that child's characteristic ways of thinking according to Piaget's theory of cognitive development. List other related characteristics of the child based on your own childhood. Then make a second list of your own current ways of thinking. Compare the lists. In what important cognitive ways do you and the child differ? What adjustments in thinking will you need to make when you set out to communicate with the child? Summarize your thoughts in a brief essay.
2. How might thinking in formal operational ways rather than concrete operational ways help students develop better study skills?

3. What is the most useful idea related to child development that you read about in this chapter? Write the idea down in your portfolio and explain how you will implement this idea in your classroom.

#### Research/Field Experience
4. Find an education article in a magazine or on the Internet that promotes "left-brained" and "right-brained" activities for learning. In a brief report, criticize the article based on what you read in this chapter about neuroscience and brain education.

*Go to the Online Learning Center for downloadable portfolio templates.*

# CHAPTER-BY-CHAPTER CHANGES

Following are the main chapter-by-chapter content changes that were made in this new edition of *Educational Psychology*.

## CHAPTER 1
## EDUCATIONAL PSYCHOLOGY: A TOOL FOR EFFECTIVE TEACHING

- Extensive citation updating, including many 2010 and 2011 references
- Editing and updating based on feedback from leading expert James McMillan
- More seamless integration of the discussions of diversity, technology, best practices, and teachers' recommendations for working with students at different developmental levels
- New section, "Thinking Skills," that emphasizes the importance of teachers engaging in critical and reflective thinking skills, as well as guiding students in developing these thinking skills
- Expanded and enhanced emphasis on caring as an important ingredient of being a successful teacher, including new title, "Commitment, Motivation, and Caring," for main section formerly titled "Commitment and Motivation"
- Expanded coverage of "Teaching Connections: Best Practices and Strategies for Becoming an Effective Teacher," including "Stay committed and motivated."
- New section, "Quantitative Research and Qualitative Research," that focuses on a widely used categorization of research (McMillan & Wergin, 2010; Plano Clark & Creswell, 2010)
- New discussion of mixed-methods research that describes the increasing interest on the part of educational psychologists in using multiple research designs and/or measures in the same study (McMillan & Wergin, 2010; Plano Clark & Creswell, 2010)

## CHAPTER 2
## COGNITIVE AND LANGUAGE DEVELOPMENT

- Expanded and updated discussion of connecting biological, cognitive, and socioemotional processes (Diamond, Casey, & Munakata, 2011)
- New description of the rapidly emerging fields of developmental cognitive neuroscience and developmental social neuroscience to illustrate the interface of biological, cognitive, and socioemotional processes (de Haan & Gunnar, 2009; Diamond, Casey, & Munakata, 2011)
- New final paragraph on the interaction of nature and nurture that emphasizes development as a co-construction of biology, culture, and the individual (Myers, 2010)

- Updated coverage of the development of the brain based on feedback from expert consultants Charles Nelson and Martha Ann Bell
- New material on Mark Johnson and his colleagues' (2009) view of the powerful neural leadership, organizational role of the prefrontal cortex during development
- Expanded coverage of the pruning of synapses and what this means by the end of adolescence (Kuhn, 2009)
- Description of recent research indicating that rather than perceiving themselves to be invulnerable, adolescents see themselves as vulnerable, with some studies even indicating that adolescents envision that they are vulnerable to experiencing a premature death (Fischhoff & others, 2010)
- New section, "Piaget, Constructivism, and Technology," that describes Piaget's influence on Seymour Papert and early applications of technology to education, then provides information about some excellent Web sites for students that have a constructivist foundation, including Scratch, LifeLong Kindergarten, and Computer Clubhouse
- Coverage of recent research on the effectiveness of the Tools of the Mind curriculum to improve at-risk young children's self-regulatory and cognitive control skills (Diamond & others, 2007)
- Modifications and updates of the discussion of language development based on comments by experts Barbara Pan and Gigliana Melzi
- New section, "Early Literacy Development," including a number of recent research studies that highlight the types of early experiences that enhance young children's literacy development (Barbarin & Aikens, 2009)
- Coverage of a recent study of key factors in young children's early literacy experiences in low-income families (Rodriquez & others, 2009)
- Discussion of a recent longitudinal study that connected early home environment with early language skills, which in turn predicted school readiness (Forget-Dubois & others, 2009)

## CHAPTER 3
## SOCIAL CONTEXTS AND SOCIOEMOTIONAL DEVELOPMENT

- Updated commentary about the positive aspects of Bronfenbrenner's theory (Gauvain & Parke, 2010)
- New material on the important role that peers have in the transition to the first grade
- Inclusion of NAEYC's (2009) extensively revised and updated guidelines for developmentally appropriate practice, including new Figure 3.4 (NAEYC, 2009)
- Expanded and updated discussion of developmental-appropriate education's characteristics and goals (Barbarin & Miller, 2009)

- New material on the critical role the teacher plays in children's school success, including research on how the child's current relationship with a teacher can compensate for earlier difficult relationships
- Expanded and updated material on the new movement to combine pre-K through third-grade students in the same public school (Barbarin & Miller, 2009)
- Inclusion of a recent physical activity intervention study that increased the self-image of adolescent girls (Schneider, Dunton, & Cooper, 2008)
- Coverage of a recent study indicating the importance of exploration in ethnic identity development (Whitehead & others, 2009)
- Discussion of a recent study of Latino youth indicating a link between growth in identity exploration and an increase in self-esteem (Umana-Taylor, Gonzales-Backen, & Guimond, 2009)
- Updated conclusions about whether gender differences in moral orientation are as strong as Gilligan suggests (Blakemore, Berenbaum, & Liben, 2009)
- Expanded and updated discussion of why students cheat (Anderman & Anderman, 2010)
- New section: "Prosocial Behavior"
- New "Teaching Connections: Best Practices and Strategies for Increasing Children's Prosocial Behavior" (Barbarin & Odom, 2009)
- New discussion of gratitude, including a recent study of its link with a number of positive aspects of adolescent development (Froh, Yurkewicz, & Kashdan, 2009)
- Coverage of a recent study on African American and Latino adolescents' beliefs about the importance of service learning in keeping adolescents from dropping out of school (Bridgeland, DiIulio, & Wulsin, 2008)
- Updated and expanded coverage of children's outcomes following a disaster (Kar, 2009)

**CHAPTER 4**
## INDIVIDUAL VARIATIONS

- New section, The Neuroscience of Intelligence (Dreary, Penke, & Johnson, 2010; Glascher & others, 2010)
- Discussion of the link between overall brain size and intelligence
- Coverage of recent research on a distributed neural network that involves the frontal and parietal lobes and the neural network's link to intelligence (Colom & others, 2009)
- New conclusion to the section on heredity/environment and intelligence and tying of this conclusion to the nature-nurture issue first discussed in Chapter 2
- New material on three main criticisms of learning and thinking styles based on a recent international assessment

of researchers in the field (Peterson, Rayner, & Armstrong, 2009)

- Updated coverage of temperament based on feedback from leading expert John Bates
- Discussion of a recent study of effortful control and children's adjustment problems in China and the United States (Zhou, Lengua, & Yang, 2009)
- New discussion of developmental changes in temperament styles, such as effortful control, and the importance of considering the individual differences that emerge from these developmental changes (Bates, 2008)
- New material on the importance of considering the multiple temperament dimensions of children rather than classifying them on a single dimension (Bates, 2008)
- New discussion of the greater stability of personality traits in adulthood than in adolescence (Roberts, Wood, & Caspi, 2008)
- Description of a recent study indicating that agreeableness and emotional stability increase from early through late adolescence (Klimstra & others, 2009)
- New coverage of the concept of goodness of fit in temperament

**CHAPTER 5**
## SOCIOCULTURAL DIVERSITY

- New discussion of a recent cross-cultural comparison of U.S. and Chinese 7th and 8th graders' academic and motivational behavior (Yang & Pomerantz, 2009)
- Update on the Eisenhower Foundation's (2010) Quantum Opportunities Program and its continuing expansion in the United States
- New material on the adjustment problems of children and adolescents from affluent families (Ansary & Luthar, 2009; Luthar & Goldstein, 2008)
- Expanded and updated coverage of technological connections around the world, including new discussion of the *Global Challenge Award* in which middle and high school students can participate with peers around the world
- Updated statistics on the percentage of U.S. children under 18 years of age living in poverty (Childstats.gov, 2009)
- New discussion of how adolescents in poverty likely are more aware of their social disadvantage and its associated stigma than are children (McLoyd & others, 2009)
- New discussion of the myth of Asian American students as the "model minority" (Yoo, Burrola, & Steger, 2010; Zhou, Siu, & Xin, 2009)
- New information about the current trend in multicultural education not to focus exclusively on ethnicity but rather cover a diversity of differences, including religion, sexual orientation, disability, and others (Howe, 2010)

- New coverage of the view that too often individuals think that multicultural education is reserved only for students of color; rather, all students, including non-Latino White students can benefit from multicultural education (Howe, 2010)

- Expanded discussion of strategies teachers can use to prevent or reduce ethnic group discrimination (Barbarin & Odom, 2009)

- Coverage of a recent research review indicating that bilingual children have lower formal language proficiency than monolingual children (Bialystok & Craik, 2010)

- Expanded introduction to different aspects of gender, including new material on gender identity

- New commentary about boys having more rigid gender stereotypes than girls do (Blakemore, Berenbaum, & Liben, 2009)

- New description of a recent study of 3- to 10-year-old boys' and girls' gender stereotyping (Miller & others, 2009)

- New material on no gender differences in overall intelligence but gender differences in some cognitive areas (Blakemore, Berenbaum, & Liben, 2009; Galambos, Berenbaum, & McHale, 2009)

- Inclusion of information about an increase in relational aggression in middle and late childhood (Dishion & Piehler, 2009)

- Inclusion of information from a recent research review that girls engage in more relational aggression than boys in adolescence but not in childhood (Smith, Rose, & Schwartz-Mette, 2010)

- Updated description of gender differences in emotion (Blakemore, Berenbaum, & Liben, 2009)

- Coverage of a recent study of same-sex education and its benefits for girls (Kessels & Hannover, 2008)

### CHAPTER 6
## LEARNERS WHO ARE EXCEPTIONAL

- Description of a recent study of gender differences in handwriting impairment (Berninger & others, 2009)

- New coverage of neurotransmitters, such as serotonin and dopamine, and their possible link to ADHD (Levy, 2009; Rondou & others, 2010; Zhou & others, 2010)

- Description of a recent meta-analysis indicating that behavior management treatments are effective in reducing the effects of ADHD (Fabiano, 2009)

- Significantly updated and expanded discussion of autism spectrum disorders (Anderson & others, 2009).

- New information about the recent increase in the estimate of the number of children with autistic spectrum disorders

- Expanded discussion of gender and autism, including Baron Cohen's (2008) argument that autism reflects an extreme male brain

- New material on recent research using animated faces and emotions to improve autistic children's ability to recognize faces, including a new figure (Baron-Cohen & others, 2007)

- New commentary about the reason children who are gifted don't always become adults who are gifted

- New section, "Nature-Nurture, Developmental Changes, and Domain-Specific Giftedness," in the discussion of "Children Who Are Gifted"

- New material on developmental changes in giftedness in childhood and adolescence with increased emphasis on domain-specific giftedness (Keating, 2009; Matthews, 2009)

- Inclusion of commentary by Bill Gates about domain-specific giftedness

- Expanded description of "Teaching Connections: Best Practices and Strategies for Working with Children Who Are Gifted" to include the domain-specific aspects of giftedness

### CHAPTER 7
## BEHAVIORAL AND SOCIAL COGNITIVE APPROACHES

- New section on "Models in the Classroom"

- New section on "Models in the Media"

- New coverage of a recent study that found a link between experiencing harsh corporal punishment as children and reduced prefrontal cortex volume as young adults (Tomoda & others, 2009)

- Expanded discussion of the effects of punishment on children, including the current conclusion of some experts that adequate research evidence has not yet been obtained about the effects of abusive physical punishment and mild physical punishment (Grusec, 2011; Knox, 2010; Thompson, 2009d)

- Expanded information about child abuse, including the teacher's responsibility of reporting reasonable suspicions of child abuse (Brodkin, 2009)

- Updated data on the percentage of U.S. freshman men who say they will major in elementary and secondary education (Pryor & others, 2008)

- New discussion of self-regulation as an important aspect of school readiness, including recent research (Graziano & others, 2007; Ponitz & others, 2009)

- New description of a recent study of adolescents in low-income families that linked a higher level of self-regulation to higher achievement and better grades (Buckner, Mezzacappa, & Bearsdlee, 2009)

## CHAPTER 8
## THE INFORMATION-PROCESSING APPROACH

- Discussion of a recent study that linked children's attention problems at 54 months of age with a lower level of social skills in peer relations in the first and third grades (NICHD Early Child Care Research Network, 2009)
- Expanded description of "Teaching Connections: Best Practices and Strategies for Helping Students Pay Attention"
- New material on using computer exercises to improve children's attention (Jaeggi, Berman, & Jonides, 2009; Tang & Posner, 2009), including recent research (Rabiner & others, 2010)
- Expanded coverage of the importance of attention in memory encoding (Ornstein, Coffman, & Grammer, 2009; Ornstein & Light, 2011; Ornstein & others, 2010)
- Inclusion of recent research linking working memory to children's attention (Alloway, Gathercole, & Elliott, 2010)
- New coverage of three recent studies of working memory that illustrate how important and wide ranging working memory capacity is for children's cognitive development and achievement (Andersson, 2010; Asian, Zellner, & Bauml, 2010; Welsh & others, 2010)
- New Figure 8.9 that compares eight different aspects of episodic and semantic memory
- New entry for "Teaching Connections: Best Practices and Strategies for Improving Students' Memory." This new entry involves memory development expert Patricia Bauer's (2009) emphasis on the importance of consolidation and reconsolidation in memory through variation on an instructional theme and frequent linking
- Expanded material included in "Teaching Connections: Best Practices and Strategies for Improving Students' Memory" that focuses on embedding memory-relevant language in teaching, including Peter Ornstein & his colleagues (Ornstein, Coffman, & Grammer, 2009; Ornstein & others, 2010) research on the extent to which teachers embed memory-relevant language, including strategies and metacognitive questions, in their classroom teaching
- New section, "Technology, Expertise, and Teaching," that focuses on Richard Mayer's (2008, 2009, 2010) recent views and research
- Description of recent longitudinal research on an increase in the frequency and quality of metacognitive skills in early adolescence (van der Stel & Veenman, 2010)

## CHAPTER 9
## COMPLEX COGNITIVE PROCESSES

- Clarification of the meaning of concepts
- New discussion of concept-mapping software that teachers can use in the classroom

- New section, "Technology and Critical Thinking," which includes updating of David Joanssen's (2006, 2010) *Mindtools*
- New section: "Decision Making in Adolescence"
- New material on how social contexts, especially the presence of peers, influence adolescent decision making (Steinberg, 2008)
- New discussion of the dual-process model of adolescent decision making
- Expanded coverage of "Teaching Connections: Best Practices and Strategies for Making Good Decisions for Yourself and Your Students" to included information and resources for improving adolescent decision making (Wargo, 2009)
- Expanded coverage of creative thinking
- New discussion of leading expert Mihaly Csikszentmihalyi's recommendations for leading a more creative life to help teachers become more creative and model creative thinking in the classroom for their students
- New photograph of Csikszentmihalyi in the setting where he gets his most creative thoughts
- Expanded "Teaching Connections: Best Practices and Strategies for Guiding Students to Become More Creative" to include engaging in creative thinking during the course of everyday teaching and naming four Web sites that enhance children's creative thinking (Wisenthal, 2010)
- Expanded coverage of problem-based learning, including new Figure 9.3

## CHAPTER 10
## SOCIAL CONSTRUCTIVIST APPROACHES

- New discussion of the increasing use of online peer tutoring (Thurston & others, 2009)
- New description of the recently introduced Microsoft Peer Coaching program for teachers (Barron, Dawson, & Yendol-Hoppey, 2009)
- New coverage of a recent large-scale evaluation of 110 studies on the Success for All peer tutoring program (What Works Clearinghouse, 2009)
- New material on the success of PALS in improving the literacy skills of pre-kindergarten and kindergarten children (McMaster & others, 2008; Townsend & Konold, 2010)
- Updated material on the Intercultural Development Research Association's (IDRA, 2010) Coca-Cola Valued Youth program
- Discussion of a recent study that found fifth- and sixth-grade students in FCL classrooms effectively reasoned and talked about complex biological concepts (Ash, 2008)

## CHAPTER 11
## LEARNING AND COGNITION IN THE CONTENT AREAS

- Deletion of section titled "Language Rule Systems," because this topic is now discussed in Chapter 2, and the deletion allows for expanded coverage of recent research on reading

- Inclusion of information about a recent study of a computer-based program that emphasizes the fact that phonics improved first-grade students' reading skills (Savage & others, 2009)

- New discussion of a study on teachers' knowledge about reading fluency and first- and second-grade students' fluency growth (Lane & others, 2009)

- Coverage of a recent study of reciprocal teaching and strategy instruction in reading comprehension (Sporer, Brunstein, & Kieschke, 2009)

- Discussion of a recent study of U.S. high school teachers' writing assignments that caused concern about the nature and frequency of the writing assignments students are required to do (Kluhara, Graham, & Hawken, 2009)

- Expanded material in "Teaching Connections: Best Practices and Strategies for Incorporating Writing into the Classroom" to include bringing writers and authors into the classroom to talk with students about their work

- New discussion of the significant shortage of qualified math teachers in U.S. middle and high schools (National Academies, Advisors to the Nation on Science, Engineering, and Social Policy, 2009)

- Expanded and updated coverage of young children's math education, including leading experts' recent conclusions about the key aspects of math children need to develop in the kindergarten years (Cross, Woods, & Schweingruber, 2009)

- Description of recent research on a link between early number competencies and math success later in the elementary school years (Jordan, Glutting, & Ramineni, 2010)

- New discussion of the Building Blocks for Math program that has been found to improve preschool children's math skills (Clements & Sarama, 2009; SRA/McGraw-Hill, 2010)

- New discussion of the significant shortage of qualified science teachers in middle and high school education in the United States (National Academies, Advisors to the Nation on Science, Engineering, and Medicine, 2009)

## CHAPTER 12
## PLANNING, INSTRUCTION, AND TECHNOLOGY

- Expanded coverage of "Teaching Connections: Best Practices and Strategies for Using Learner-Centered Instruction" to include using both direct instruction and learner-centered instruction rather than each one exclu-

sively to make the classroom a positive learning experience for students

- Description of a recent study on a link between students' taking responsibility for their homework, effort on homework, and achievement (Trautwein & others, 2009)

- Discussion of a recent study that found a link between the "big five" personality factor of conscientiousness and the effort put into homework, as well as gender differences in homework effort that fell along gender stereotypical lines (Trautwein & Ludtke, 2009)

- New discussion of interactive whiteboards and their use in both teacher-centered and student-centered instruction (Swan & others, 2009)

- New coverage of NASA for educators, an excellent Web site with a wide range of resources for teachers at all levels and professional development materials for using the resources effectively

- New section, "Graphics and Presentation," in the discussion of "Technology and Learning"

- Important new section, "Technological Pedagogical Content Knowledge (TPCK)," that focuses on the model created by Matthew Koehler and Punya Mishra (2010) that has recently been adopted by the American Association of Colleges of Teacher Education, including new Figure 12.7

- New material on the six stages teachers go through in effectively integrating a particular technology into their classroom instruction

## CHAPTER 13
## MOTIVATION, TEACHING, AND LEARNING

- New commentary about Ryan and Deci's (2009) description of teachers who create circumstances for students to engage in self-determination as autonomy-supportive teachers.

- Discussion of a recent study on extrinsic goal framing and lower levels of independent motivation and persistence (Vansteenkiste & others, 2008)

- Coverage of a longitudinal study linking children's intrinsic motivation in math and science from 9 to 17 years of age to their parents' motivational practices (Gottfried & others, 2009)

- Description of recent research on the contexts in which students show the most engagement (Shernoff, 2009)

- Coverage of a recent study of low/high self-efficacy and students' deep/surface approaches to studying (Part-Sala & Redford, 2010)

- Expanded material on "Teaching Connections: Best Practices and Strategies for Student Self-Determination and Choice" to include giving students choices that are personally meaningful to them (Anderman & Anderman, 2010)

- Expanded and updated coverage of *Quest Atlantis,* an increasingly popular learning activity engaged in by a community of 15,000 students worldwide; new material includes a photo of a *Quest Atlantis* computer screen (Barab & others, 2010a,b)

- Discussion of a recent Japanese study on the mastery and performance goal structure of classrooms and students' intrinsic motivation and academic self-concept (Murayama & Eliot, 2009)

- New coverage of Carol Dweck's recent research and ideas about improving students' growth mindset by teaching them about the brain's plasticity and how the brain changes when you put considerable effort into learning (Blackwell & others, 2007; Dweck & Masters, 2009)

- New material about Carol Dweck's recent development of computer modules, called "Brainology," that explain how the brain works and how through work and effort students can make their brain work better (Blackwell & Dweck, 2008; Dweck & Master, 2009)

- Expanded material in "Teaching Connections: Best Practices and Strategies for Improving Students' Self-Efficacy" to include helping students believe in their cognitive abilities (Anderman & Anderman, 2010)

- New discussion of personal goals and their importance in students' motivation (Boekaerts, 2009; Ford & Smith, 2009; Maehr & Zusho, 2009)

- New "Through the Eyes of Students: Hari Prabhakar, Student on a Path to Purpose"

- Inclusion of information about a recent study that linked students' perceptions of teachers' and peers' emotional support to students' self-regulation (Patrick, Ryan, & Kaplan, 2007)

- Coverage of a recent study on the influence of social goals on adolescent achievement (Kiefer & Ryan, 2008)

- Description of a recent study of how aggressive-disruptive friends influence the likelihood of adolescents graduating from high school (Veronneau & others, 2008)

- New material on a link between having academically oriented friends and achievement in adolescence (Crosnoe & others, 2008)

- Discussion of a recent study that revealed perceived racial discrimination by teachers was negatively related to African American and Caribbean Black adolescents' academic achievement (Thomas & others, 2009)

- Coverage of a recent large-scale longitudinal study focused on the importance of academic resources at home, especially in African American or low-SES students' achievement (Xia, 2010)

### CHAPTER 14
## MANAGING THE CLASSROOM

- Expanded emphasis on the importance of engaging in advanced planning before the school year starts for how

you are going to manage the classroom, including what you are going to say to students at the beginning of the school year (Sterling, 2009)

- New section: "Classroom Management and Diversity"

- Coverage of a recent study indicating the benefits of using clickers in a large lecture class because they increase students' cognitive engagement (Mayer & others, 2009)

- Description of a recent study linking behavioral control and caring with positive student outcomes, such as engagement in learning, which reflects Baumrind's concept of authoritative teaching (Nie & Lau, 2009)

- Coverage of a recent study linking an authoritative classroom climate to a higher level of safety, including less bullying and victimization (Gregory & others, 2010)

- Discussion of a recent study of classroom management strategies, teacher stress, and student misbehavior in Australian elementary schools (Clunies-Ross, Little, & Kienhuis, 2008)

- New material on a recent national survey of almost 3,500 U.S. schools (data for the 2007–2008 school year) regarding the scope of different types of aggression and violence (Neiman, DeVoe, & Chandler, 2009)

- Updated and expanded discussion of bullying, including the roles of social contexts and the larger peer group (Salmivalli & Peets, 2009)

- Coverage of recent research on the perspective taking and moral motivation of bullies (Gasser & Keller, 2009)

- New emphasis on the importance of contexts in the study of bullying (Salmivalli & others, 2009; Schwartz & others, 2010)

- Coverage of two recent studies of bullies' popularity in the peer group (Veenstra & others, 2010; Witvliet & others, 2010)

- Description of a recent study on peer victimization and the extent of its link to lower academic achievement (Nakamoto & Schwartz, 2010)

- Updated and expanded material on cyberbulling (Uhls & Greenfield, 2009)

- Description of a recent survey of the significant threat minors encounter with both online and offline bullying (Palfrey & others, 2009)

- Expanded discussion of strategies for dealing with bullies

### CHAPTER 15
## STANDARDIZED TESTS AND TEACHING

- Extensive updating and revisions based on leading expert James McMillan's (2010) feedback

- New commentary about benchmark and interim assessments that are used on a quarterly basis

- Inclusion of a recent analysis regarding the impossibility of NCLB reaching certain improvement targets in 2014 (Stecher & Vernez, 2010)
- Descriptiion of a recent analysis that in the 2008–2009 school year, approximately one-third of public schools did not make adequate yearly progress according to NCLB state standards (Dietz, 2010)
- Added criticism of the No Child Left Behind policy that it encourages a performance rather than a mastery achievement orientation
- Updated information about the limited progress being made in reducing the number of schools in high-poverty, high-minority locations in which students are taught by inexperienced, unqualified, or out-of-field teachers (Bumgardner, 2010)
- Expanded and updated material on the problem of narrowing the curriculum to cover only what is on state-mandated tests
- Added criticism of the No Child Left Behind policy regarding test score inflation produced by high-stakes testing (Koretz, 2009)
- New section on national assessments of educational progress using standardized test assessments in reading, math, and science (National Assessment of Educational Progress, 2008)
- New section on international comparisons using standardized tests in reading, math, and science, including the most recent assessments in three different studies of international comparisons (National Center for Education Statistics, 2009)
- New commentary about standard error of measurement in testing
- Added information about using challenging tasks that require critical thinking in preparing students to take standardized tests (Green & Johnson, 2010)
- Updated and expanded information about the difficulties in using performance assessments as part of large-scale testing

## CHAPTER 16
## CLASSROOM ASSESSMENT AND GRADING

- "Grading" added to the title of the chapter, which is now, "Classroom Assessment and Grading"
- Extensive updating and revision of chapter based on leading expert James McMillan's feedback
- Added commentary on use of reliability in classroom assessment
- Expansion of material on standards-based grading, including coverage of rubrics

# ACKNOWLEDGEMENTS

I am deeply indebted to many people at McGraw-Hill who have provided outstanding guidance and support for this text. I especially thank Beth Mejia, publisher for education and psychology, for the guidance and support she has provided. Thanks also to Allison McNamara, editor, who contributed knowledge and vision about the field of educational psychology that improved this edition. Sarah Kiefer, editorial assistant, did excellent work in coordinating many aspects of editing for this project. Dawn Groundwater, director of development, gave superb advice on the development of the manuscript. Erin Liedel Grelak, the developmental editor for this edition of the book, has been terrific to work with and did an excellent job in guiding and editing the revision of the manuscript. Maggie Jarpey did an excellent job of copyediting the manuscript. I also so much appreciate the excellent work that Aaron Downey has done in coordinating the production of this text. I thank Nancy DeFrates-Densch, Northern Illinois University, whose experience and understanding of translating theory into practice clearly came through in the new examples she created for "Teaching Connections: Best Practices and Strategies for . . ." in every chapter in the text. Nancy also contributed extensively to the book by writing the case studies, the PRAXIS™ Practice items, and creating many new examples of Best Practices. I also want to thank Laura Gaudet, Chadron State College; Nicholas Grecco IV, College of Lake County; Patricia Willems, Florida Atlantic University; and Samuel Zimmerman, Pace University, for their outstanding work in writing the material for the book's ancillaries.

On pages xix to xx of the preface the numerous expert content and research consultants for the book are profiled. As stated earlier, their feedback was invaluable in helping me to make the book's content superior to what I could have accomplished alone.

### Peer Reviewers for the Fifth Edition

In developing the fifth edition of *Educational Psychology,* we asked a number of educational psychology instructors to provide us with detailed information about the best ways to improve the text. Their recommendations were extremely helpful. Special thanks go to the following peer reviewers of the fifth edition:

**Lyanne Black,** *Indiana University of PA*
**Suzy Cox,** *Utah Valley University*
**Jayne Downey,** *Montana State University*
**Daniel Fasko,** *Bowling Green State University*
**Jaclyn Finkel,** *Anne Arundel Community College*
**Laura Gaudet,** *Chadron State College*
**Joyce Grohman,** *Atlantic Cape Community College*
**David Oxendine,** *University of North Carolina*
**Joseph Pizzillo,** *Rowan University*
**Catherine Polydore,** *Eastern Illinois University*
**Thomas Sepe,** *Community College of Rhode Island*
**Kenneth Tyler,** *University of Kentucky*
**Patricia Willems,** *Florida Atlantic University*
**Samuel Zimmerman,** *Pace University*

## Peer Reviewers from Previous Editions

In developing the fourth edition of *Educational Psychology*, we asked a number of educational psychology instructors to provide us with detailed information about the best ways to improve the text. Their recommendations were extremely helpful. Special thanks go to the following peer reviewers of previous editions:

**Frank Adams,** *Wayne State College*
**Irene Aiken,** *The University of North Carolina at Pembroke*
**Eric Anderman,** *University of Kentucky*
**James M. Applefield,** *University of North Carolina—Wilmington*
**Elizabeth C. Arch,** *Pacific University*
**Robert R. Ayres,** *Western Oregon University*
**Bambi Bailey,** *Midwestern State University*
**Jeffrey Baker,** *Rochester Institute of Technology*
**Melissa Lorenson Barstow,** *Community College of Rhode Island*
**Dorothy A. Battle,** *Georgia Southern University*
**Douglas Beed,** *University of Montana, Missoula*
**Richard Benedict,** *Madonna University*
**John T. Binfet,** *California State University—San Bernadino,*
**Christopher S. Boe,** *Pfeiffer University*
**Joseph Braun,** *California State University—Dominguez Hills*
**Roger Briscoe,** *Indiana University of Pennsylvania*
**Jonathan Brown,** *Clarion University*
**Kathy Brown,** *University of Central Oklahoma*
**Randy Brown,** *University of Central Oklahoma*
**Robert G. Brown,** *Florida Atlantic University*
**Alison Bryant,** *University of Missouri—Columbia*
**Kay Bull,** *Oklahoma State University*
**Mary D. Burbank,** *University of Utah*
**Melva M. Burke,** *East Carolina University*
**Russell N. Carney,** *Southwest Missouri State University*
**Chuck Catania,** *Miami University of Ohio*
**John Newman Clark,** *University of South Alabama*
**Sheryl Needle Cohn,** *University of Central Florida*
**Ellen Contopidis,** *Keuka College*
**Dorothy Valcarcel Craig,** *Middle Tennessee University*
**Rhoda Cummings,** *University of Nevada—Reno*
**Reagan Curtis,** *Northwestern State University*
**David Dalton,** *Kent State University*
**Nancy Defrates-Densch,** *Northern Illinois University*
**Rayne Sperling Dennison,** *Penn State*
**Gypsy Denzine,** *Northern Arizona University*
**Carlos F. Diaz,** *Florida Atlantic University*
**Jesse Diaz,** *Central Washington University*
**Ronna Dillon,** *Southern Illinois University—Carbondale*
**Joseph DiMauro,** *DeSales University*
**Peter Doolittle,** *Virginia Polytechnic University*
**Ruth Doyle,** *Casper College*
**Ronald Dugan,** *The College of St. Rose*
**David Dungan,** *Emporia State University*
**Kenneth Durgans,** *Xavier University*
**Audrey Edwards,** *Eastern Illinois University*

**Gordon Eisenmann,** *Augusta State University*
**Howard Epstein,** *Miami University of Ohio*
**Lena Ericksen,** *Western Washington University*
**Tsile Evers,** *Miami University—Oxford*
**Vicky Farrow,** *Lamar University*
**Sheryl Feinstein,** *Augusta College*
**Aubrey Fine,** *California Polytechnic University*
**Ericka Fisher,** *College of the Holy Cross*
**William R. Fisk,** *Clemson University*
**William L. Franzen,** *University of Missouri—St. Louis*
**Beth Gallihue,** *Towson University*
**M. Arthur Garmon,** *Western Michigan University*
**Patsy Garner,** *Crowder College*
**Susan Goldman,** *Vanderbilt University*
**Alyssa Gonzalez,** *Florida Atlantic University*
**Caroline Gould,** *Eastern Michigan University*
**Charles R. Grah,** *Austin Peay State University*
**Kim Grilliot,** *Bowling Green State University*
**Lynne A. Hammann,** *University of Akron*
**Felicia Hanesworth,** *Medaille College*
**Andrew Hanson,** *California State University—Chico*
**Walter Hapkiewicz,** *Michigan State University*
**Gregory Harper,** *State University of New York—Fredonia*
**Diane J. Harris,** *San Francisco State University*
**Algea Harrison,** *Oakland University*
**Jan Hayes,** *Middle Tennessee State University*
**William E. Herman,** *State University of New York—Potsdam*
**David Holliway,** *Marshall University*
**Alice S. Honig,** *Syracuse University*
**Sherri Horner,** *University of Memphis*
**Mara Huber,** *State University of New York—Fredonia*
**John H. Hummel,** *Valdosta State University*
**Judith Hughey,** *Kansas State University*
**Mona Ibrahim,** *Concordia College*
**Emilie Johnson,** *Lindenwood University*
**Steven Kaatz,** *Bethel College*
**Deborah Kalkman,** *Northern Illinois University*
**Susan Kelley,** *Lycoming College*
**Lee Kem,** *Murray State University*
**Elizabeth Kirk,** *Miami University of Ohio*
**Elaine Kisisel,** *Calumet College of Saint Joseph*
**Beverly Klecker,** *Morehead State University*
**Nancy Knapp,** *University of Georgia*
**Robert L. Kohn,** *University of Kansas*
**Becky Ladd,** *Illinois State University*
**William Lan,** *Texas Tech University*
**Marvin Lee,** *Shenandoah University*
**Randy Lennon,** *University of Northern Colorado*
**Bernie Les,** *Wayne State University*
**Edward Levinson,** *Indiana University*
**Dov Liberman,** *University of Houston*
**Kathryn W. Linden,** *emeritus, Purdue University*
**Kim Loomis,** *Kennesaw State University*
**Barbara F. Maestas,** *Towson University*
**P. Y. Mantzicopoulos,** *Purdue University*
**Julia M. Matuga,** *Bowling Green State University*

Richard E. Mayer *University of California—Santa Barbara*
Catherine McCartney, *Bemidji State University*
John R. McClure, *Northern Arizona University*
Rita McKenzie, *Northern Arizona University*
James H. McMillan, *Virginia Commonwealth University*
Sharon McNeely, *Northeastern Illinois University*
Lisa Mehlig, *Northern Illinois University*
John K. Meis, *Flager College*
Dorothy D. Miles, *Saint Louis University*
Barbara Milligan, *Middle Tennessee State University*
Connie M. Moss, *Duquesne University*
Beverly Moore, *Auburn University*
Ronald Mulson, *Hudson Valley Community College*
Peter Myerson, *University of Wisconsin—Oshkosh*
Joseph D. Nichols, *Indiana-Purdue University*
David Oxendine, *University of North Carolina—Pembroke*
Ernest Owen, *Western Kentucky University*
Ann Pace, *University of Missouri*
Karen Menke Paciorek, *Eastern Michigan University*
Nita A. Paris, *Kennesaw State University*
Peggy Perkins, *University of Nevada—Las Vegas*
Jim Persinger, *Emporia State University*
Barbara M. Powell, *Eastern Illinois University*
Geoff Quick, *Lansing Community College*
Barbara L. Radigan, *Community College of Allegheny County*
Sandra Nagel Randall, *Saginaw Valley State University*
Nan Bernstein Ratner, *University of Maryland—College Park*
Marla Reese-Weber, *Illinois State University*
Robert Rice, *Western Oregon University*
Lynda Robinson, *University of the Ozarks*
James Rodriquez, *San Diego State University*
Susan Rogers, *Columbus State Community College*
Lawrence R. Rogien, *Columbus State Community College*
Paul Rosenberg, *Muhlenberg College*
Deborah Salih, *University of Northern Iowa*
Jill Salisbury-Glennon, *Auburn University*
Ala Samarapungavan, *Purdue University*
Charles Jeff Sandoz, *University of Louisiana*
Rolando A. Santos, *California State University—Los Angeles*
Susan Sawyer, *Southeastern Louisiana University*
Gilbert Sax, *University of Washington*
Gayle Schou, *Grand Canyon University*
Dale Schunk, *University of North Carolina—Greensboro*
Marvin Seperson, *Nova Southeastern University*
Lisa Sethre-Hofstad, *Concordia College*
Alison Shook, *Albright College*
Jenny Singleton, *University of Illinois—Urbana-Champaign*
Michael Slavkin, *University of Southern Indiana*
Patricia Slocum, *College of DuPage*
Brian G. Smith, *Moorhead State University*
Michael Smith, *Weber State University*
Judith Stechly, *West Liberty State University*
Michael Steiff, *University of California—Davis*
Daniel Stuempfig, *California State University—Chico*
O. Suthern Sims, Jr., *Mercer University*
Gabriele Sweidel, *Kutztown University of Pennsylvania*

David E. Tanner, *California State University—Fresno*
Sara Tannert, *Miami University of Ohio*
David Tarver, *Angelo State University*
Karen Thierry, *Rutgers University*
Yuma I. Tomes, *Virginia Commonwealth University*
Donna Townsend, *Southwestern Assemblies of God University*
Julie Turner, *University of Notre Dame*
Atilano Valencia, *California State University—Fresno*
Eva G. Vandergiessen, *Fairmont State College*
David Vawter, *Wintrhop University*
Linda Veronie, *Slippery Rock University*
Libby Vesilind, *Bucknell University*
Penny Warner, *Winona State University*
Linda Weeks, *Lamar University*
Earl F. Wellborn, Jr., *Missouri Valley College*
David Wendler, *Martin Luther College*
Patricia Whang, *California State University—Monterey Bay*
Allan Wigfield, *University of Maryland—College Park*
Ryan Wilke, *Florida State University*
Glenda Wilkes, *University of Arizona,*
Patricia Willems, *Florida Atlantic University*
Tony L. Williams, *Marshall University*
Victor Willson, *Texas A&M University*
Ann K. Wilson, *Buena Vista University*
Steven R. Wininger, *Western Kentucky University*
Betsy Wisner, *Sate University of New York—Cortland*
Elizabeth F. Wisner, *Florida Community College at Jacksonville*
Jina Yoon, *Wayne State University*
Michael Young, *University of Connecticut*
Peter Young, *Southern Oregon University*
Steven Yussen, *University of Minnesota*

## Early Childhood, Elementary School, and Secondary School Teachers

Following are the outstanding teachers who provided descriptions of their real-world experiences in the classroom for the Developmental Focus feature that appears one or more times in each chapter.

Keren Abra, *School of the Sacred Heart, San Francisco, CA*
Connie Christy, *Aynor Elementary School (Preschool Program), Aynor, SC*
Maureen "Missy" Dangler, *Suburban Hills School, Chatham, NJ*
Mark Fodness, *Bemidji Middle School, Bemidji, MN*
Elizabeth J. Frascella, *Clinton Elementary, Chatham, NJ*
Susan M. Froelich, *Clinton School, Maplewood, NJ*
Valerie Gorham, *Kiddie Quarters, Union, NJ*
Jennifer Heiter, *Bremen High School, Bremen, IN*
Craig Jensen, *Cooper Mountain Elementary, Portland, OR*
Heidi Kaufman, *MetroWest YMCA Child Care and Educational Program, Framingham, MA*
Esther Lindbloom, *Cooper Mountain Elementary, Beaverton, OR*

**Casey Maass,** *Edison Middle School, West Orange, NJ*
**Karen L. Perry,** *Cooper Mountain Elementary, Portland, OR*
**Dennis Peterson,** *Deer River High School, Bemidji, MN*
**Felicia Peterson,** *Pocantico Hills School, Sleepy Hollow, NY*
**Janine Guida Poutre,** *Clinton Elementary, Chatham, NJ*
**Shane Schwarz,** *Clinton Elementary, South Orange, NJ*
**Sandy Swanson,** *Menomonee Falls High School, Menomonee Falls, WI*
**Heather Zoldak,** *Ridge Wood Elementary School, Northville, MI*

## Expert Consultants From Previous Editions

A number of leading experts in the field of educational psychology provided detailed comments about chapters and topics in their areas of expertise. Special thanks go to the following expert consultants who contributed to editions:

**Albert Bandura,** *Stanford University*
**Gary Bitter,** *Arizona State University*
**Joyce Epstein,** *Johns Hopkins University*
**Carlos Diaz,** *Florida Atlantic University*
**Eva Essa,** *University of Nevada, Reno*
**Carolyn Evertson,** *Vanderbilt University*
**Kenji Hakuta,** *Stanford University*
**Daniel Hallahan,** *University of Virginia*
**James Kauffman,** *University of Virginia*
**Richard Mayer,** *University of California—Santa Barbara*
**Barbara McCombs,** *University of Denver*
**James McMillan,** *Virginia Commonwealth University*
**Valerie Pang,** *San Diego State University*
**Michael Pressley,** *University of Notre Dame*
**Dale Schunk,** *University of North Carolina—Greensboro*
**Robert Siegler,** *Carnegie Mellon University*
**Karen Swan,** *Kent State University*

## Panel of Early Childhood, Elementary, Middle, and High School Teachers

A large panel of individuals who teach at the early childhood, elementary, middle, and high school levels provided me with the material about special teaching moments that they have experienced. These moments appear in the Teaching Stories and Best Practices boxes throughout the text. I owe these teachers a great deal of thanks for sharing the real world of their teaching experiences.

**Karen Abra,** *School of the Sacred Heart, San Francisco, CA*
**Mrs. Lou Aronson,** *Devils Lake High School, Devils Lake, ND*
**Daniel Arnoux,** *Lauderhill Middle Community School, Broward, FL*
**Lynn Ayres,** *East Middle School, Ypsilanti, MI*
**Fay Bartley,** *Bright Horizon Childrens Center, Bronx, NY*
**Barbara M. Berry,** *Ypsilanti High School, Ypsilanti, MI*
**Kristen Blackenship,** *Salem Church Elementary, Midlothian, VA*
**Wendy Bucci,** *Sugar Creek Elementary School, Verona, WI*

**Stella Cohen,** *Hackley School, Tarrytown, NY*
**Connie Christy,** *Aynor Elementary, Aynor, SC*
**Julie Curry,** *Hubbard Elementary School, Forsyth, GA*
**Alina Durso,** *PS 59-Beekman Hill International School, New York, NY*
**Andrea Fenton,** *Cortez High School, Glendale Union, AZ*
**Mark Fodness,** *Bemidji Middle School, Bemidji, MN*
**Kathy Fuchser,** *St. Francis High School, Humphrey, NE*
**Lawren Giles,** *Baechtel Grove Middle School, Bibb County, GA*
**Jerri Hall,** *Miller Magnet Middle School, Bibb County, GA*
**Jenny Heiter,** *Bremen High School, Bremen, IN*
**Anita Marie Hitchcock,** *Holley Navarre Primary, Santa Rosa Schools, FL*
**Laura Johnson-Brickford,** *Nordhoff High School, Ojai, CA*
**Heidi Kaufman,** *Associate Executive Director of Childcare, MetroWest YMCA, Framingham, MA*
**Juanita Kerton,** *Gramercy School/New York League for Early Learning, New York, NY*
**Chaille Lazar,** *Hedgecoxe Elementary, Plano, TX*
**Margaret Longworth,** *St. Lucie West Middle School, St. Lucie, FL*
**Adriane Lonzarich,** *Heartwood, San Mateo, CA*
**RoseMary Moore,** *Angelo State University, Angelo, TX*
**Therese Olejniczak,** *Central Middle School, East Grand Forks, MN*
**Dennis Peterson,** *Deer River High School, Bemidji, MN*
**Chuck Rawls,** *Appling Middle School, Bibb County, GA*
**Verna Brown Rollins,** *West Middle School, Ypsilanti, MI*
**Donna L. Shelhorse,** *Short Pump Middle School, Henrico County, VA*
**Michele Siegal,** *Brockton High School, Brockton, MA*
**Jason Stanley,** *Syracuse Dunbar Avoca, Syracuse, NE*
**Vicky Stone,** *Cammack Middle School, Huntington, VA*
**Sandy Swanson,** *Menomonee Falls High School, Menomonee Falls, WI*
**Tamela Varney,** *Central City Elementary, Cabell County, WV*
**Marlene Wendler,** *St. Paul's Lutheran School, New Ulm, MN*
**William Willford,** *Perry Middle School, Perry, GA*
**Yvonne Wilson,** *North Elementary School, Deer River, MN*
**Susan Youngblood,** *Weaver Middle School, Bibb County, GA*
**Heather Zoldak,** *Ridge Wood Elementary, Northville, MI*

## ANCILLARIES

The ancillaries listed here may accompany *Educational Psychology*, fifth edition. Please contact your McGraw-Hill representative for details concerning policies, prices, and availability.

**Student's Online Learning Center** (**www.mhhe.com/ santrockep5e**)
The online learning center includes:

- Study resources including multiple-choice, short-answer, and essay quizzes and Web links
- Portfolio Activities

- Crack the Case studies
- Self-assessment exercises
- Taking it to the Net activities
- The PRAXIS™ II study guide
- Bibliography Builder for easy and accurate citations and references

**Instructor's Online Learning Center (www.mhhe.com/santrockep5e)**
All of the materials on the Online Learning Center can be downloaded as complete documents. These include:

- The **Instructor's Manual**—authored by Nicholas Grecco IV at College of Lake County—a flexible planner with teaching suggestions, learning objectives, extended chapter outlines, lecture/discussion suggestions, video and film recommendations.
- The **Test Bank,** revised by Samuel Zimmerman, Pace University, has almost 1,000 questions specifically related to the main text, including multiple-choice, short-answer, critical thinking, and essay questions; many of which are applied assessment.
- **PowerPoint Slides,** by Laura Gaudet at Chadron State College, cover every chapter and concept presented in the text.
- **CPS questions,** by Patricia Willems at Florida Atlantic University, for every chapter in the text.

## Print Supplements and Related Texts

*A Guide to Observation, Participation, and Reflection in the Classroom* Arthea Reed and Verna Bergemann, ISBN 0-07-298553-4

This complete, hands-on guide to classroom observations provides detailed guides for observing the dynamics of the classroom, participating with the classroom teacher, and then reflecting on the experience. It also includes more than 50 practical blank forms that cover all aspects of observation, participation, and reflection, from the structured observation of a lesson to a checklist for determining teaching styles to reflections on small-group teaching.

*Teaching Portfolios: Presenting Your Professional Best,* 2e Patricia Rieman and Jeanne Okrasinski, ISBN 0-07-287684-0

This portfolio handbook includes authentic, student-generated artifacts as well as insights from administrators, teachers, and parents. Issues of classroom management, diversity, communication, planning, standards-based education, and reflection are all addressed in the context of how to approach these important aspects within a teaching portfolio and during interviews. The materials are designed for continued use as the students become in-service educators.

*Case Studies for Teacher Problem Solving* Rita Silverman, William Welty, and Sally Lyon

Choose from an online menu of eighty cases addressing core curriculum areas in teacher education—development, classroom management, leadership, special education, diversity, teaching methods, educational psychology, and more. Visit www.mhhe.com/primis to preview the cases, then order a printed and bound copy for your consideration. If you like your case book, placing an order is easy. If you don't, make changes—there is no obligation.

## Taking Sides and Annual Editions

Annual Editions: *Educational Psychology* 10/11, 25th Edition, Kathleen M. Cauley and Gina Pannozzo © 2011, ISBN 0-07-805060-X

Taking Sides: *Clashing Views in Educational Psychology,* 6th Edition, Leonard Abbeduto © 2010, ISBN 0-07-812754-8

Sources: *Notable Selections in Educational Psychology,* Rhett Diessner and Stacy Simmons, © 2000, ISBN 0-07-232334-5

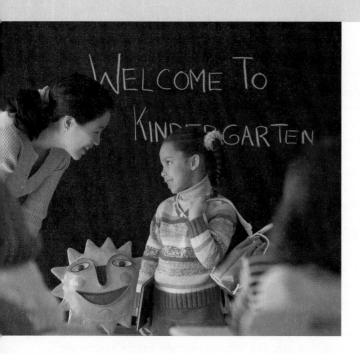

## CHAPTER 1

# EDUCATIONAL PSYCHOLOGY: A TOOL FOR EFFECTIVE TEACHING

*I touch the future. I teach.*

—Christa McAuliffe
*American Educator and Astronaut, 20th Century*

## Chapter **Outline**

## Learning **Goals**

**1** Describe some basic ideas about the field of educational psychology.

**2** Identify the attitudes and skills of an effective teacher.

**3** Discuss why research is important to effective teaching, and how educational psychologists and teachers can conduct and evaluate research.

# Teaching **Stories** Margaret Metzger

Effective teachers know that principles of educational psychology and educational research will help them guide students' learning. Margaret Metzger has been an English teacher at Brookline High School in Massachusetts for more than 25 years. Here is some advice she gave to a student teacher she was supervising that incorporates her understanding of basic principles of educational psychology, such as the importance of teaching how to learn and the need to apply educational research to teaching practice:

> Emphasize *how* to learn, rather than what to learn. Students may never know a particular fact, but they always will need to know how to learn. Teach students how to read with a genuine comprehension, how to shape an idea, how to master difficult material, how to use writing to clarify thinking. A former student, Anastasia Korniaris, wrote to me, "Your class was like a hardware store. All the tools were there. Years later I'm still using that hardware store that's in my head. . . ."
>
> Include students in the process of teaching and learning. Every day ask such basic questions as, "What did you think of this homework? Did it help you learn the material? Was the assign-ment too long or too short? How can we make the next assignment more interesting? What should the criteria for assessment be?" Remember that we want students to take ownership of their learning. . . .
>
> Useful research has been conducted lately on learning styles and frames of intelligence. Read that research. The basic idea to keep in mind is that students should think for themselves. Your job is to teach them how to think and to give them the necessary tools. Your students will be endlessly amazed at how intelligent they are. You don't need to show them how intelligent you are. . . .
>
> In the early years of teaching you must expect to put in hours and hours of time. You would invest similarly long hours if you were an intern in medical school or an associate in a law firm. Like other professionals, teachers work much longer hours than outsiders know. . . .
>
> You have the potential to be an excellent teacher. My only concern is that you not exhaust yourself before you begin. Naturally, you will want to work very hard as you learn the craft.

(*Source:* Metzger, 1996, pp. 346–351.)

## Preview

In the quotation that opens this chapter, twentieth-century teacher and astronaut Christa McAuliffe commented that when she taught, she touched the future. As a teacher, you will touch the future, because children are the future of any society. In this chapter, we explore what the field of educational psychology is all about and how it can help you contribute positively to children's futures.

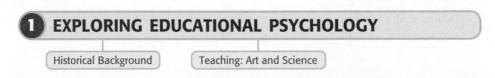

**1 EXPLORING EDUCATIONAL PSYCHOLOGY**

Historical Background    Teaching: Art and Science

Psychology is the scientific study of behavior and mental processes. **Educational psychology** is the branch of psychology that specializes in understanding teaching and learning in educational settings. Educational psychology is a vast landscape that will take us an entire book to describe.

### HISTORICAL BACKGROUND

The field of educational psychology was founded by several pioneers in psychology in the late nineteenth century. Three pioneers—William James, John Dewey, and E. L. Thorndike—stand out in the early history of educational psychology.

**William James**   Soon after launching the first psychology textbook, *Principles of Psychology* (1890), William James (1842–1910) gave a series of lectures called "Talks to Teachers" (James, 1899/1993) in which he discussed the applications of psychology to educating children. James argued that laboratory psychology experiments often can't tell us how to effectively teach children. He emphasized the importance of observing teaching and learning in classrooms for improving education. One of his

**educational psychology** The branch of psychology that specializes in understanding teaching and learning in educational settings.

2

William James　John Dewey　E. L. Thorndike

James, Dewey, and Thorndike created and shaped the field of educational psychology. *What were their ideas about educational psychology?*

recommendations was to start lessons at a point just beyond the child's level of knowledge and understanding to stretch the child's mind.

**John Dewey**　A second major figure in shaping the field of educational psychology was John Dewey (1859–1952), who became a driving force in the practical application of psychology. Dewey established the first major educational psychology laboratory in the United States, at the University of Chicago in 1894. Later, at Columbia University, he continued his innovative work. We owe many important ideas to John Dewey. First, we owe to him the view of the child as an active learner. Before Dewey, it was believed that children should sit quietly in their seats and passively learn in a rote manner. In contrast, Dewey (1933) argued that children learn best by doing. Second, we owe to Dewey the idea that education should focus on the whole child and emphasize the child's adaptation to the environment. Dewey reasoned that children should not be just narrowly educated in academic topics but should learn how to think and adapt to a world outside school. He especially thought that children should learn how to be reflective problem solvers. Third, we owe to Dewey the belief that all children deserve to have a competent education. This democratic ideal was not in place at the beginning of Dewey's career in the latter part of the nineteenth century, when high-quality education was reserved for a small portion of children, especially boys from wealthy families. Dewey pushed for a competent education for all children—girls and boys, as well as children from different socioeconomic and ethnic groups.

**E. L. Thorndike**　A third pioneer was E. L. Thorndike (1874–1949), who focused on assessment and measurement and promoted the scientific underpinnings of learning. Thorndike argued that one of schooling's most important tasks is to hone children's reasoning skills, and he excelled at doing exacting scientific studies of teaching and learning. Thorndike especially promoted the idea that educational psychology must have a scientific base and should focus strongly on measurement.

**Diversity and Early Educational Psychology**　The most prominent figures in the early history of educational psychology, as in most disciplines, were mainly White males, such as James, Dewey, and Thorndike. Prior to changes in civil rights laws and policies in the 1960s, only a few dedicated non-White individuals obtained the necessary degrees and broke through racial exclusion barriers to take up research in the field (Koppelman & Goodhart, 2011; Spring, 2010).

Two pioneering African American psychologists, Mamie and Kenneth Clark, conducted research on African American children's self-conceptions and identity (Clark & Clark, 1939). In 1971 Kenneth Clark became the first African American president of the American Psychological Association. In 1932 Latino psychologist George Sanchez conducted research showing that intelligence tests were culturally biased against ethnic minority children.

DIVERSITY

Mamie and Kenneth Clark

George Sanchez

Leta Hollingworth

Like other disciplines, educational psychology had few ethnic minority individuals and women involved in its early history. The individuals shown here were among the few from such backgrounds to overcome barriers and contribute to the field.

RESEARCH

Thinking Back/Thinking Forward

Self-efficacy plays an important role in motivation. Chapter 13, p. 450

Like ethnic minorities, women also faced barriers in higher education and so have only gradually become prominent contributors to psychological research. One often overlooked person in the history of educational psychology is Leta Hollingworth. She was the first individual to use the term *gifted* to describe children who scored exceptionally high on intelligence tests (Hollingworth, 1916).

**The Behavioral Approach**    Thorndike's approach to the study of learning guided educational psychology through the first half of the twentieth century. In American psychology, B. F. Skinner's (1938) view, which built on Thorndike's ideas, strongly influenced educational psychology in the middle of the century. Skinner's behavioral approach, which is described in detail in Chapter 7, involved attempts to precisely determine the best conditions for learning. Skinner argued that the mental processes proposed by psychologists such as James and Dewey were not observable and therefore could not be appropriate subject matter for a scientific study of psychology, which he defined as the science of observable behavior and its controlling conditions. In the 1950s, Skinner (1954) developed the concept of *programmed learning*, which involved reinforcing the student's behavior after each of a series of steps until the student reached a learning goal. In an early technological effort, he created a teaching machine to serve as a tutor and reinforce students' behavior for correct answers (Skinner, 1958).

**The Cognitive Revolution**    However, the objectives spelled out in the behavioral approach to learning did not address many of the actual goals and needs of classroom educators (Hilgard, 1996). In reaction, as early as the 1950s, Benjamin Bloom created a taxonomy of cognitive skills that included remembering, comprehending, synthesizing, and evaluating, which he suggested teachers should help students develop. The cognitive revolution in psychology began to take hold by the 1980s and ushered in a great deal of enthusiasm for applying the concepts of cognitive psychology—memory, thinking, reasoning, and so on—to helping students learn. Thus, toward the latter part of the twentieth century, many educational psychologists returned to an emphasis on the cognitive aspects of learning advocated by James and Dewey at the beginning of the century.

Both cognitive and behavioral approaches continue to be a part of educational psychology today (Anderman & Dawson, 2011; Veenman, 2011). We have much more to say about these approaches in Chapters 7 through 11.

More recently, educational psychologists have increasingly focused on the socioemotional aspects of students' lives. For example, they are analyzing the school as a social context and examining the role of culture in education (Campbell, 2010; Spring, 2010). We explore the socioemotional aspects of teaching and learning in many chapters of this book.

## TEACHING: ART AND SCIENCE

How scientific can teachers be in their approach to teaching? Both science and the art of skillful, experienced practice play important roles in a teacher's success. Educational psychology draws much of its knowledge from broader theory and research in psychology (Bonney & Sternberg, 2011; Danielson, 2010). For example, the theories of Jean Piaget and Lev Vygotsky were not created in an effort to inform teachers about ways to educate children, yet in Chapter 2 you will see that both of these theories have many applications that can guide your teaching. The field also draws from theory and research more directly created and conducted by educational psychologists, and from teachers' practical experiences. For example, in Chapter 13 you will read about Dale Schunk's (2008) classroom-oriented research on *self-efficacy* (the belief that one can master a situation and produce positive outcomes). Educational psychologists also recognize that teaching sometimes must depart from scientific recipes, requiring improvisation and spontaneity (Borich, 2011; Parkay & Stanford, 2010).

As a science, educational psychology's aim is to provide you with research knowledge that you can effectively apply to teaching situations and with research skills that will enhance your understanding of what impacts student learning (Alexander & Mayer, 2011; Harris, Graham, & Urdan, 2011). But your teaching will still remain an art. In addition to what you can learn from research, you will also continually make important judgments in the classroom based on your personal skills and experiences, as well as the accumulated wisdom of other teachers (Ryan & Cooper, 2010).

First-grade teacher, Zakia Sims, guiding her students' learning at William Lloyd Elementary School in Washington, D.C. Recognized as an outstanding teacher, Zakia has a master's degree from Howard University and a coveted National Board certificate. *To what extent is her teaching success likely art, and to what extent is it likely science?*

## Review, Reflect, and Practice

**①** Describe some basic ideas about the field of educational psychology.

### REVIEW

- How is educational psychology defined? Who were some key thinkers in the history of educational psychology, and what were their ideas?
- How would you describe the roles of art and science in the practice of teaching?

### REFLECT

- John Dewey argued that children should not sit quietly in their seats and learn in a rote manner. Do you agree with Dewey? Why or why not?

### PRAXIS™ PRACTICE

1. Mr. Smith believes that all children are entitled to an education and that this education should focus on the whole child. His views are most consistent with those of
   a. Benjamin Bloom.
   b. John Dewey.
   c. B. F. Skinner.
   d. E. L. Thorndike.

2. Four teachers are discussing influences on being an effective teacher. Which of their following four statements is likely to be most accurate?
   a. Applying information from scientific research is the most important factor in being an effective teacher.
   b. You can't beat a teacher's own personal experiences for becoming an effective teacher.
   c. Being an effective teacher is influenced by scientific research knowledge, teaching skills, and personal experiences.
   d. A teacher's innate skills trump all other factors in being an effective teacher.

*Please see the answer key at the end of the book.*

## 2 EFFECTIVE TEACHING

| Professional Knowledge and Skills | | Commitment, Motivation, and Caring |

Because of the complexity of teaching and individual variation among students, effective teaching is not "one size fits all." Teachers must master a variety of perspectives and strategies and be flexible in their application. Success requires the following key ingredients: (1) professional knowledge and skills, and (2) commitment, motivation, and caring.

## PROFESSIONAL KNOWLEDGE AND SKILLS

Effective teachers have good command of their subject matter and a solid core of teaching skills. They know how to use instructional strategies supported by methods of goal setting, instructional planning, and classroom management. In addition, they understand how to motivate students and how to communicate and work effectively with those of varying skill levels and culturally diverse backgrounds. Effective teachers also employ appropriate levels of technology in the classroom.

**Subject-Matter Competence**   In their wish lists of teacher characteristics, secondary school students increasingly have mentioned "teacher knowledge of their subjects" (NAASP, 1997). Having a thoughtful, flexible, conceptual understanding of subject matter is indispensable for being an effective teacher. Of course, knowledge of subject matter includes more than just facts, terms, and general concepts. It also includes knowledge about organizing ideas, connections among ideas, ways of thinking and arguing, patterns of change within a discipline, beliefs about a discipline, and the ability to carry ideas from one discipline to another. Clearly, having a deep understanding of the subject matter is an important aspect of being a competent teacher (Abruscato & DeRosa, 2010; Eby, Herrell, & Jordan, 2011).

**Instructional Strategies**   At a broad level, two major approaches characterize how teachers teach: constructivist and direct instruction. The constructivist approach was at the center of William James' and John Dewey's philosophies of education. The direct instruction approach has more in common with E. L. Thorndike's view.

The **constructivist approach** is a learner-centered approach that emphasizes the importance of individuals actively constructing their knowledge and understanding with guidance from the teacher. In the constructivist view, teachers should not attempt to simply pour information into children's minds. Rather, children should be encouraged to explore their world, discover knowledge, reflect, and think critically with careful monitoring and meaningful guidance from the teacher (Bonney & Sternberg, 2011; Lawson, 2010). Constructivists argue that for too long children have been required to sit still, be passive learners, and rotely memorize irrelevant as well as relevant information (Gredler, 2009).

Today constructivism may include an emphasis on *collaboration*—children working with each other in their efforts to know and understand (Slavin, 2011; Wentzel & Watkins, 2011). A teacher with a constructivist instructional philosophy would not have children memorize information rotely but would give them opportunities to meaningfully construct knowledge and understand the material while guiding their learning (Johnson, 2010).

By contrast, the **direct instruction approach** is a structured, teacher-centered approach characterized by teacher direction and control, high teacher expectations for students' progress, maximum time spent by students on academic tasks, and efforts by the teacher to keep negative affect to a minimum. An important goal in the direct instruction approach is maximizing student learning time (Estes, Mintz, & Gunter, 2011).

**constructivist approach** A learner-centered approach to learning that emphasizes the importance of individuals actively constructing knowledge and understanding with guidance from the teacher.

**direct instruction approach** A structured, teacher-centered approach characterized by teacher direction and control, high teacher expectations for students' progress, maximum time spent by students on academic tasks, and efforts by the teacher to keep negative affect to a minimum.

Some experts in educational psychology emphasize that many effective teachers use both a constructivist *and* a direct instruction approach rather than either exclusively (Darling-Hammond & Bransford, 2005). Further, some circumstances may call more for a constructivist approach, others for a direct instruction approach. For example, experts increasingly recommend an explicit, intellectually engaging direct instruction approach when teaching students with a reading or a writing disability (Berninger, 2006). Whether you teach more from a constructivist approach or more from a direct instruction approach, you can be an effective teacher.

*What characterizes constructivist and direct instruction approaches to educating students?*

**Thinking Skills** Effective teachers model and communicate good thinking skills, especially **critical thinking,** which involves thinking reflectively and productively and evaluating the evidence. Getting students to think critically is not easy; many students develop a habit of passively learning material and rotely memorizing concepts rather than thinking deeply and reflectively (Bonney & Sternberg, 2011). Thinking critically also means being open-minded and curious on the one hand, yet being careful to avoid key mistakes in interpretation on the other.

Throughout this book we will encourage you to think critically about topics and issues. At the end of each main section in a chapter, you will be asked "Reflect" questions related to the topic about which you have just read. In Chapter 9 you will read more extensively about critical thinking and other higher-level cognitive processes such as reasoning, decision making, and creative thinking, and you will learn how to encourage critical thinking in your students by building it into your lessons.

**Goal Setting and Instructional Planning** Whether constructivist or more traditional, effective teachers don't just "wing it" in the classroom. They set high goals for their teaching and organize plans for reaching those goals (Anderman & Dawson, 2011). They also develop specific criteria for success. They spend considerable time in instructional planning, organizing their lessons to maximize students' learning (Burden & Byrd, 2010). As they plan, effective teachers reflect and think about how they can make learning both challenging and interesting. Good planning requires consideration of the kinds of information, demonstrations, models, inquiry opportunities, discussion, and practice students need over time to understand particular concepts and develop particular skills. Although research has found that all of these features can support learning, the process of instructional design requires that teachers figure out which things students should do when, in what order, and how. (Darling-Hammond & others, 2005). Chapter 12 addresses planning in detail.

> **Thinking Back/Thinking Forward**
>
> In planning, teachers need to figure out which things students should do, when, in what order, and how. Chapter 12, p. 399

**Developmentally Appropriate Teaching Practices** Competent teachers have a good understanding of children's development and know how to create instruction materials appropriate for their developmental levels (Bredekamp, 2011; NAEYC, 2009). U.S. schools are organized by grade and to some degree by age, but these are not always good predictors of children's development.

At any grade level there is usually a two- or three-year span of ages with an even wider span of skills, abilities, and developmental stages. Understanding developmental

DEVELOPMENT

**critical thinking** Thinking reflectively and productively and evaluating the evidence.

"My mom told me to tell you that I am the educational challenge you were told about in college."

Reprinted by permission of Heiser Zedonek.

**Thinking Back/Thinking Forward**

The best teachers have very few discipline problems, not because they are great disciplinarians, but because they are great teachers. Chapter 14, p. 490

pathways and progressions is extremely important for teaching in ways that are optimal for each child (Follari, 2011; Marion, 2010).

Throughout this text, we call attention to developmental aspects of educating children and provide examples of teaching and learning that take into account a child's developmental level. Chapters 2 and 3 are devoted exclusively to development.

**Classroom Management Skills** An important aspect of being an effective teacher is keeping the class as a whole working together and oriented toward classroom tasks. Effective teachers establish and maintain an environment in which learning can occur (Jones & Jones, 2010; Mertler & Charles, 2011). To create this optimal learning environment, teachers need a repertoire of strategies for establishing rules and procedures, organizing groups, monitoring and pacing classroom activities, and handling misbehavior (ASCD, 2009).

**Motivational Skills** Effective teachers have good strategies for helping students become self-motivated and take responsibility for their learning (Anderman & Dawson, 2011). Educational psychologists increasingly stress that this is best accomplished by providing real-world learning opportunities of optimal difficulty and novelty for each student. Students are motivated when they can make choices in line with their personal interests. Effective teachers give them the opportunity to think creatively and deeply about projects.

In addition to guiding students to become self-motivated learners, teachers need to establish high expectations for students' achievement (Eccles & Roeser, 2009). Too often children are rewarded for inferior or mediocre performance with the result that they do not reach their full potential. When high expectations are created, however, a key aspect of education is to provide children—especially low-achieving children—with effective instruction and support to meet these expectations. Chapter 13 covers the topic of motivation in detail.

**Communication Skills** Also indispensable to teaching are skills in speaking, listening, overcoming barriers to verbal communication, tuning in to students' nonverbal communication, and constructively resolving conflicts (Hybels & Weaver, 2009). Communication skills are critical not only in teaching but also in interacting with parents (Weiss & others, 2010). Effective teachers use good communication skills when they talk "with" rather than "to" students, parents, administrators, and others; keep criticism at a minimum; and have an assertive rather than aggressive, manipulative, or passive communication style (Stewart, 2009). Effective teachers work to improve students' communication skills as well. Student communication skills are especially important because they have been rated as the skills most sought after by today's employers.

**Paying More Than Lip Service to Individual Variations** Virtually every teacher knows that it is important to take individual variations into account when teaching, but this is not always easy to do. Your students will have varying levels of intelligence, use different thinking and learning styles, and have different temperaments and personality traits (Martinez, 2010). You also are likely to have some students who are gifted and others with disabilities of various types (Darragh, 2010; Friend, 2011).

Consider Amber Larkin's challenges and experiences as a beginning teacher (Wong Briggs, 2007). Her classroom was a trailer, and her students included children who were homeless, non–English speaking, had disabilities, or were refugees who had never worn shoes or experienced any type of formal education. After four years of teaching, she was named one of *USA Today*'s 2007 National All-Star Teachers. Almost all of her students pass state-mandated No Child Left Behind (NCLB) tests, but she is just as pleased about her students' socioemotional growth. Her principal described her in the following manner: "There's an unspoken aura that great things are going to happen, and that's how she goes about her day" (Wong Briggs, 2007, p. 6D).

Amber Larkin, helping fifth-grade student Miya Kpa improve his academic skills. *What are some strategies for paying more than lip service to individual variation in students?*

Effectively teaching a class of students with such diverse characteristics requires much thought and effort (Rosenberg, Westling, & McLesky, 2011). **Differentiated instruction** addresses this challenge by recognizing individual variations in students' knowledge, readiness, interests, and other characteristics, then taking these differences into account in planning curriculum and engaging in instruction (Tomlinson, 2006). Thus, differentiated instruction aims to tailor assignments to meet students' needs and abilities. It is unlikely that a teacher can generate 20 to 30 different lesson plans to address the needs of each student in a classroom. However, differentiated instruction advocates discovering "zones" or "ball parks" in which students in a classroom cluster, thus providing three or four types/levels of instruction rather than 20 to 30. In Chapters 4 and 6 we provide strategies to help you guide students with different levels of skills and different characteristics to learn effectively.

### Working Effectively with Students from Culturally Diverse Backgrounds

Today one of every five children in the United States is from an immigrant family, and by 2040 one of every three U.S. children is projected to fit this description. Nearly 80 percent of the new immigrants are people of color from Latin America, Asia, and the Caribbean. Approximately 75 percent of the new immigrants are of Spanish-speaking origin, although children speaking more than 100 different languages are entering U.S. schools.

DIVERSITY

In this world of increasing intercultural contact, effective teachers must be knowledgeable about people from different cultural backgrounds and sensitive to their needs (Bennett, 2011; Shiraev & Levy, 2010). They should encourage students to have positive personal contact with other students of diverse backgrounds and think of ways to create settings in which such interaction can occur. Effective teachers will guide students in thinking critically about cultural and ethnic issues while taking actions to forestall or reduce student bias and cultivate acceptance. They need to serve as cultural mediators among students as well as, when necessary, between the culture of the school and the culture of the student, especially those who are unsuccessful academically (Darragh, 2010).

*What are some strategies effective teachers use regarding diversity issues?*

Here are cultural questions for teachers to ask themselves (Pang, 2005):

- Do I recognize the power and complexity of cultural influences on students?
- Are my expectations for my students culturally based or biased?
- Am I doing a good job of seeing life from the perspective of my students who come from different cultures than mine?
- Am I teaching the skills students may need to talk in class if their culture is one in which they have little opportunity to practice "public" talking?

### Assessment Knowledge and Skills

Competent teachers also have good assessment knowledge and skills. There are many aspects to effectively using assessment in the classroom (Drummond & Jones, 2010; Popham, 2011). You will need to decide what types of assessments you want to use to document your students' performance after instruction. You also will need to use assessment effectively before and during instruction (Green & Johnson, 2010; Nitko & Brookhart, 2011). For example, before teaching a unit on plate tectonics, you might decide to assess whether your students are familiar with terms like *continent, earthquake,* and *volcano.*

**Thinking Back/Thinking Forward**

Teachers can follow a number of guidelines for effective multicultural teaching. Chapter 5, p. 162

**differentiated instruction** Involves recognizing individual variations in students' knowledge, readiness, interests, and other characteristics, and taking these differences into account when planning curriculum and engaging in instruction.

**Thinking Back/Thinking Forward**

An important aspect of assessment is to make it compatible with contemporary views of learning and motivation. Chapter 16, p. 551

During instruction, you might want to use ongoing observation and monitoring to determine whether your instruction is at a level that challenges students and to detect which students need your individual attention (Cizek, 2010; McMillan, 2010). You will need to grade students to provide feedback about their achievement.

Other aspects of assessment involve state-mandated tests to assess students' achievement and teachers' knowledge and skills. The federal government's No Child Left Behind (NCLB) legislation requires states to test students annually in mathematics, English/language arts, and science, and holds states accountable for the success and failure of their students (Webb, Metha, & Jordan, 2010).

Because of NCLB, the extent to which instruction should be tied to standards, or what is called *standards-based instruction,* has become a major issue in educational psychology and U.S. classrooms (Yell & Drasgow, 2009). This issue is all about standards of excellence and what it takes to get students to pass external, large-scale tests. Many educational psychologists stress that the challenge is to teach creatively within the structure imposed by NCLB (McMillan, 2007). Much more information about NCLB is provided in Chapter 15.

Before you become a teacher, your subject-matter knowledge and teaching skills are also likely to be assessed by the state in which you plan to teach. A large majority of states now use the PRAXIS™ test to determine whether prospective teachers are qualified to teach (Shorall, 2009). Because of the increasing use of the PRAXIS™ test, this text includes a number of resources to help you prepare for it.

TECHNOLOGY

**Technological Skills** Technology itself does not necessarily improve students' ability to learn, but it can support learning (Lever-Duffy & McDonald, 2011; Maloy & others, 2011). Conditions that support the effective use of technology in education include vision and support from educational leaders; teachers skilled in using technology for learning; content standards and curriculum resources; assessment of effectiveness of technology for learning; and an emphasis on the child as an active, constructive learner (International Society for Technology in Education, [ISTE], 2007).

**Thinking Back/Thinking Forward**

Sample ISTE's Profiles for Being a Technology-Literate Student in Prekindergarten–Grade 2, Grades 3–5, Grades 6–8, and Grades 9–12. Chapter 12, p. 423

There is a profound gap between the technology knowledge and skills most students learn in school and those they need in the twenty-first-century workplace (Partnership for 21st Century Skills, 2008). Students will benefit from teachers who increase their technology knowledge and skills, and integrate computers appropriately into classroom learning (Newby & others, 2011; Roblyer & Doering, 2010). This integration should match up with students' learning needs, including the need to prepare for tomorrow's jobs, many of which will require technological expertise and computer-based skills. In addition, effective teachers are knowledgeable about various assistive devices to support the learning of students with disabilities (Turnbull, Turnbull, & Wehmeyer, 2010).

## COMMITMENT, MOTIVATION, AND CARING

Being an effective teacher requires commitment, motivation, and caring, qualities that include having a good attitude.

Beginning teachers often report that the investment of time and effort needed

*What are some important aspects of incorporating technology in the classroom?*

to be an effective teacher is huge. Some teachers, even experienced ones, say they have "no life" from September to June. Even putting in hours on evenings and weekends, in addition to all of the hours spent in the classroom, might still not be enough to get things done.

In the face of these demands, it is easy to become frustrated or to get into a rut and develop a negative attitude. Commitment and motivation help get effective teachers through the tough moments of teaching. Effective teachers have confidence in their own self-efficacy, don't let negative emotions diminish their motivation, and bring a positive attitude and enthusiasm to the classroom (Meece & Eccles, 2010). These qualities are contagious and help make the classroom a place where students want to be.

So, what is likely to nurture your own positive attitudes and continued enthusiasm for teaching? As in all fields, success breeds success. It's important to become aware of times when you've made a difference in an individual student's life. Consider the words of Carlos Diaz (1997), a professor of education at Florida Atlantic University, about Mrs. Oppel, his high school English teacher:

> To this day, whenever I see certain words (*dearth, slake*) I recognize them fondly as some of Mrs. Oppel's vocabulary words. As a teacher, she was very calm and focused. She also was passionate about the power of language and the beauty of literature. I credit her, at least partially, for my determination to try to master the English language and become a professor and writer. I wish I could bottle these characteristics and implant them in all of my students.

The better teacher you become, the more rewarding your work will be. And the more respect and success you achieve in the eyes of your students, the better you will feel about your commitment to teaching. With that in mind, stop for a moment and think about the images you have of your own former teachers. Some of your teachers likely were outstanding and left you with a very positive image. In a national survey of almost 1,000 students 13 to 17 years of age, having a good sense of humor, making the class interesting, and having knowledge of the subject matter were the characteristics students listed as the most important for teachers to have (NAASP, 1997). Characteristics secondary school students most frequently attributed to their worst teachers were having a boring class, not explaining things clearly, and showing favoritism. These characteristics and others that reflect students' images of their best and worst teachers are shown in Figure 1.1.

## THROUGH THE EYES OF STUDENTS

### "You Are the Coolest"

I just want to thank you for all the extra time you took to help me. You didn't have to do that but you did and I want to thank you for it. Thanks also for being straight up with me and not beating around the bush and for that you are the coolest. I'm sorry for the hard times I gave you. You take so much junk but through all that you stay calm and you are a great teacher.

*Jessica*
*Seventh-Grade Student*
*Macon, Georgia*
*Letter to Chuck Rawls, Her Teacher, at the End of the School Year*

© Glen Dines. Reprinted by permission of Ruth Dines.

| Characteristics of best teachers | % Total | | Characteristics of worst teachers | % Total |
|---|---|---|---|---|
| 1. Have a sense of humor | 79.2 | | 1. Are dull/have a boring class | 79.6 |
| 2. Make the class interesting | 73.7 | | 2. Don't explain things clearly | 63.2 |
| 3. Have knowledge of their subjects | 70.1 | | 3. Show favoritism toward students | 52.7 |
| 4. Explain things clearly | 66.2 | | 4. Have a poor attitude | 49.8 |
| 5. Spend time to help students | 65.8 | | 5. Expect too much from students | 49.1 |
| 6. Are fair to their students | 61.8 | | 6. Don't relate to students | 46.2 |
| 7. Treat students like adults | 54.4 | | 7. Give too much homework | 44.2 |
| 8. Relate well to students | 54.2 | | 8. Are too strict | 40.6 |
| 9. Are considerate of students' feelings | 51.9 | | 9. Don't give help/individual attention | 40.5 |
| 10. Don't show favoritism toward students | 46.6 | | 10. Lack control | 39.9 |

**FIGURE 1.1** STUDENTS' IMAGES OF THEIR BEST AND WORST TEACHERS

# SELF-ASSESSMENT 1.1
## The Best and Worst Characteristics of My Teachers

When you studied Figure 1.1, were you surprised by any of the characteristics listed by students to describe their best and worst teachers? Which of the top five characteristics students listed for the best teachers surprised you the most? Which of the top five characteristics of the worst teachers surprised you the most?

Now think about the top five characteristics of the best and the worst teachers you have had. In generating your lists, don't be constrained by the characteristics described in Figure 1.1. Also, after you have listed each characteristic, write down one or more examples of situations that reflected the characteristic.

### FIVE CHARACTERISTICS OF THE BEST TEACHERS I HAVE HAD

| Characteristics | Examples of Situations That Reflected the Characteristic |
|---|---|
| 1. _____ | _____ |
| 2. _____ | _____ |
| 3. _____ | _____ |
| 4. _____ | _____ |
| 5. _____ | _____ |

### FIVE CHARACTERISTICS OF THE WORST TEACHERS I HAVE HAD

| Characteristics | Examples of Situations That Reflected the Characteristic |
|---|---|
| 1. _____ | _____ |
| 2. _____ | _____ |
| 3. _____ | _____ |
| 4. _____ | _____ |
| 5. _____ | _____ |

## THROUGH THE EYES OF STUDENTS

### A Good Teacher

*Mike, Grade 2:*

A good teacher is a teacher that does stuff that catches your interest. Sometimes you start learning and you don't even realize it. A good teacher is a teacher that does stuff that makes you think. (Nikola-Lisa & Burnaford, 1994).

Think about the roles that a good sense of humor and your own genuine enthusiasm are likely to play in your long-term commitment as a teacher. Also, notice other characteristics in Figure 1.1 that relate to the caring nature of outstanding teachers. Effective teachers care for their students, often referring to them as "my students." They really want to be with the students and are dedicated to helping them learn. At the same time, they keep their role as a teacher distinct from student roles. Beyond their own caring, effective teachers also look for ways to help their students consider others' feelings and care about each other.

To think about the best and worst characteristics of the teachers you have had, complete Self-Assessment 1.1. Use the self-assessment to further explore the attitudes behind your commitment to become a teacher.

## TEACHING CONNECTIONS: Best Practices
### Strategies for Becoming an Effective Teacher

1. *Effective teaching requires teachers to wear many different hats.* It's easy to fall into the trap of thinking that if you have good subject-matter knowledge, excellent teaching will follow, but being an effective teacher requires many diverse skills. In Through the Eyes of Teachers, you can read about how Susan Bradburn, who teaches fourth and sixth grades at West Marian Elementary School in North Carolina, brings many dif-ferent skills to create effective lessons.

### THROUGH THE EYES OF TEACHERS
#### The "Turtle Lady"

Susan Bradburn teaches grades 4 to 6 at West Marian Elementary School in North Carolina. She created a school museum in which students conduct research and create exhibitions. She has put her school-museum concept

Susan Bradburn *(left)* with several students at West Marian Elementary School.

"on wheels" by having students take carts to other classes and into the community, and she has used award money to spread the use of mobile museums to other North Carolina schools. Nicknamed "the turtle lady" because of her interest in turtles and other animals, Susan takes students on three-day field trips to Edisto Island, South Carolina, to search for fossils and study coastal ecology. Her students sell calendars that contain their original poetry and art, and they use the proceeds to buy portions of a rain forest so it won't be destroyed.

2. *Engage in perspective taking.* You want to be the very best teacher you can possibly be. Think about what your students need from you to improve their academic and life skills. Also reflect on how you perceive your students and how they perceive you.

3. *Keep the list of characteristics of effective teachers we have discussed in this chapter with you throughout your teaching career.* Looking at the list and thinking about the different areas of effective teaching can benefit you as you go through your student teaching, your days as a beginning teacher, and even your years as an experienced teacher. By consulting this list from time to time, you might realize that you have let one or two areas slip and need to spend time improving yourself.

4. *Stay Committed and Motivated.* Being an effective teacher requires being committed and motivated even in the face of difficult and adverse circumstances. Work through your frustrations and develop good coping skills to face the tough times that come in any career. Remember that a positive attitude and a deep commitment to caring for children are key aspects of becoming a successful teacher.

## Review, Reflect, and Practice

**2** Identify the attitudes and skills of an effective teacher.

### REVIEW
- What professional knowledge and skills are required to be an effective teacher?
- Why is it important for teachers to be committed and motivated?

### REFLECT
- What is most likely to make teaching rewarding for you in the long run?

### PRAXIS™ PRACTICE
1. Suzanne spends a considerable amount of time writing lesson plans, developing criteria for student success, and organizing materials. Which professional skill is she demonstrating?
   a. classroom management
   b. communication

*(continued)*

## Review, Reflect, and Practice

### PRAXIS™ PRACTICE (CONTINUED)

    c. developmentally appropriate teaching practices

    d. goal setting and instructional management

2. Mr. Marcinello, who is midway through his first year of teaching, feels frustrated with his job. He is developing a negative attitude, and it is carrying over in his teaching. Which of the following areas does Mr. Marcinello need to work on the most at this point to become an effective teacher?

    a. classroom management and communication

    b. commitment and motivation

    c. technology and diversity

    d. subject-matter competence and individual variations

*Please see the answer key at the end of the book.*

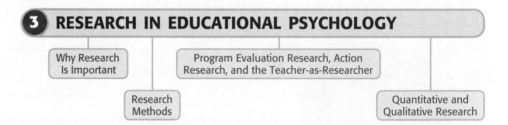

## ❸ RESEARCH IN EDUCATIONAL PSYCHOLOGY

Research can be a valuable source of information about teaching. We will explore why research is important and how it is done, including how you can be a teacher-researcher.

RESEARCH

## WHY RESEARCH IS IMPORTANT

It sometimes is said that experience is the best teacher. Your own experiences and experiences that other teachers, administrators, and experts share with you will make you a better teacher. However, by providing you with valid information about the best ways to teach children, research also can make you a better teacher (McMillan & Schumacher, 2010).

We all get a great deal of knowledge from personal experience. We generalize from what we observe and frequently turn memorable encounters into lifetime "truths." But how valid are these conclusions? Sometimes we err in making these personal observations, misinterpreting what we see and hear. Chances are, you can think of many situations in which you thought other people read you the wrong way, just as they might have felt that you misread them. When we base information only on personal experiences, we also aren't always totally objective because we sometimes make judgments that protect our ego and self-esteem (McMillan & Wergin, 2010).

We get information not only from personal experiences but also from authorities or experts. In your teaching career, you will hear many authorities and experts spell out a "best way" to educate students. The authorities and experts, however, don't always agree, do they? You might hear one expert one week tell you about a reading method that is absolutely the best, yet the next week hear another expert tout a different method. One experienced teacher might tell you to do one thing with your students, while another experienced teacher tells you to do the opposite. How can you tell which one to believe? One way to clarify the situation is to look closely at research on the topic.

## RESEARCH METHODS

Collecting information (or data) is an important aspect of research. When educational psychology researchers want to find out, for example, whether regularly playing video games detracts from student learning, eating a nutritious breakfast improves alertness in class, or getting more recess time decreases absenteeism, they can choose from many methods of gathering research information (Plano Clark & Creswell, 2010).

The three basic methods used to gather information in educational psychology are descriptive, correlational, and experimental.

**Descriptive Research** Descriptive research has the purpose of observing and recording behavior. For example, an educational psychologist might observe the extent to which children are aggressive in a classroom or interview teachers about their attitudes toward a particular type of teaching strategy. By itself, descriptive research cannot prove what causes some phenomenon, but it can reveal important information about people's behavior and attitudes (Stake, 2010).

*Observation* We look at things all the time. Casually watching two students interacting, however, is not the same as the type of observation used in scientific studies. Scientific observation is highly systematic. It requires knowing what you are looking for, conducting observations in an unbiased manner, accurately recording and categorizing what you see, and effectively communicating your observations (Langston, 2011; McBurney & White, 2010).

A common way to record observations is to write them down, often using shorthand or symbols. In addition, tape recorders, video cameras, special coding sheets, one-way mirrors, and computers increasingly are being used to make observation more accurate, reliable, and efficient.

Observations can be made in laboratories or in naturalistic settings (Babbie, 2011). A **laboratory** is a controlled setting from which many of the complex factors of the real world have been removed (Graziano & Raulin, 2010). Some educational psychologists conduct research in laboratories at the colleges or universities where they work and teach. Although laboratories often help researchers gain more control in their studies, they have been criticized as being artificial.

In **naturalistic observation,** behavior is observed out in the real world. Educational psychologists conduct naturalistic observations of children in classrooms, at museums, on playgrounds, in homes, in neighborhoods, and in other settings. Naturalistic observation was used in one study that focused on conversations in a children's science museum (Crowley & others, 2001). Parents were three times as likely to engage boys as girls in explanatory talk while visiting different exhibits at the science museum (see Figure 1.2). In another study, Mexican American parents who had completed high school used more explanations with their children as they were observed at a science museum than Mexican American parents who had not completed high school (Tennebaum & others, 2002).

**Participant observation** occurs when the observer-researcher is actively involved as a participant in the activity or setting (McMillan & Wergin, 2010). The participant observer will often participate in a context and observe awhile, then take notes on what she or he has viewed. The observer usually makes these observations and writes down notes over a period of days, weeks, or months and looks for patterns in the observations. For example, to study a student who is doing poorly in the class without apparent reason, the teacher might develop a plan to observe the student from time to time and record observations of the student's behavior and what is going on in the classroom at the time.

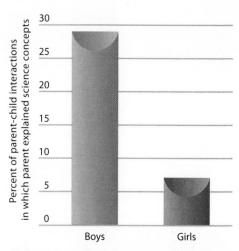

**FIGURE 1.2** PARENTS' EXPLANATIONS OF SCIENCE TO SONS AND DAUGHTERS AT SCIENCE MUSEUM

In a naturalistic observation study at a children's science museum, parents were three times more likely to explain science to boys than girls (Crowley & others, 2001). The gender difference occurred regardless of whether the father, the mother, or both parents were with the child, although the gender difference was greatest for fathers' science explanations to sons and daughters.

**laboratory** A controlled setting from which many of the complex factors of the real world have been removed.

**naturalistic observation** Observation in the real world rather than a laboratory.

**participant observation** Observation conducted at the same time the teacher-researcher is actively involved as a participant in the activity or setting.

Following are strategies recommended by teachers at different grade levels regarding how they use participant observation in their classroom:

**EARLY CHILDHOOD** We take notes, observe, and record the activities of our young children throughout the day. Taking notes on children at the preschool level  can be challenging because when children first notice that you are intently watching and taking notes, they may become curious and ask many questions, or become overly anxious and say things like, "Look at me!" to the teacher. As the year goes by, however, children get used to the recordings, and the questions are less frequent, allowing for a more accurate assessment of a child's needs.

—**Valarie Gorham,** *Kiddie Quarters, Inc.*

**ELEMENTARY SCHOOL: GRADES K–5** I meet with leveled reading groups, typically ranging from three to five students. Materials and texts that are at the group's  instructional level are used. As the lesson and activities are carried out, I take quick notes as I see the group or individuals grasping concepts, struggling in any way, or if a "teachable moment" presents itself. These notes help me later in my planning to make decisions about whether to reteach a certain lesson/concept, move on to new concepts/materials, or go to something other than originally planned because of a teachable moment or connection that has been discovered.

—**Susan Froelich,** *Clinton Elementary School*

**MIDDLE SCHOOL: GRADES 6–8** I once had a student who often came to class unprepared and late. Over time, I observed the student, took notes, and created a  chart for myself that listed the times the student did not come to class prepared or on time. Because I kept good records, I was able to find out that when the student had a physical education class just before my class, he was late. I then worked with the student and phys. ed. teacher to come up with a solution so that the student had time to get to my class with the necessary classroom materials.

—**Casey Maass,** *Edison Middle School*

**HIGH SCHOOL: GRADES 9–12** In the lab portion of my class, I have a chart that identifies when students are off-task and a notation for what they are doing instead  of the task, such as listening to an iPod, talking to their friends, and so on. After a pattern develops, I talk with the student and show them their pattern on the chart. High school students tend to understand graphs and data better than being reminded while they are being off-task. For me, charting provides a more positive environment than an interruption or reprimand.

—**Sandy Swanson,** *Menomonee Falls High School*

***Interviews and Questionnaires*** Sometimes the quickest and best way to get information about students and teachers is to ask them for it. Educational psychologists use interviews and questionnaires (surveys) to find out about children's and teachers' experiences, beliefs, and feelings. Most interviews take place face-to-face, although they can be done in other ways, such as over the phone or the Internet. Questionnaires usually are given to individuals in written form. They, too, can be transmitted in many ways, such as directly by hand, by mail, or via the Internet.

Good interviews and surveys involve concrete, specific, and unambiguous questions and some means of checking the authenticity of the respondents' replies. Interviews and surveys, however, are not without problems. One crucial limitation is that many individuals give socially desirable answers, responding in a way they think is most socially acceptable and desirable rather than how they truly think or feel. Skilled interviewing techniques and questions that increase forthright responses are crucial to obtaining accurate information (Babbie, 2011). Another problem with interviews and surveys is that the respondents sometimes simply are untruthful.

**Standardized Tests**   In **standardized tests,** uniform procedures are used for administration and scoring. They assess students' aptitudes or skills in different domains. Many standardized tests allow a student's performance to be compared with the performance of other students at the same age or grade level, in many cases on a national basis (Drummond & Jones, 2010). Students might take a number of standardized tests, including tests that assess their intelligence, achievement, personality, career interests, and other skills (Bart & Peterson, 2008). These tests can provide outcome measures for research studies, information that helps psychologists and educators make decisions about an individual student, and comparisons of students' performance across schools, states, and countries.

Standardized tests also play an important role in a major contemporary educational psychology issue—*accountability,* which involves holding teachers and students responsible for student performance. As we indicated earlier, both students and teachers increasingly are being given standardized tests in the accountability effort. The U.S. Government's NCLB Act is at the centerpiece of accountability; it mandated that in 2005 every state had to give standardized tests to students in grades 3 through 8 in language arts and math, with testing for science achievement added in 2007.

Brandi Binder is evidence of the brain's hemispheric flexibility and resilience. Despite having the right side of her cortex removed because of a severe case of epilepsy, Brandi at the age of 17 engaged in many activities often portrayed as only "right-brain" activities. She loved music and art and is shown here working on one of her paintings.

**Case Studies**   A **case study** is an in-depth look at an individual. Case studies often are used when unique circumstances in a person's life cannot be duplicated, for either practical or ethical reasons. For example, consider the case study of Brandi Binder (Nash, 1997). She developed such severe epilepsy that surgeons had to remove the right side of her brain's cerebral cortex when she was 6 years old. Brandi lost virtually all control over muscles on the left side of her body, the side controlled by the right side of her brain. At age 17, however, after years of therapy ranging from leg lifts to mathematics and music training, Brandi was an A student. Interestingly, she loved music and art, which usually are associated with the right side of the brain, the site of her surgery. Her recuperation was not 100 percent—for example, she did not regain the use of her left arm—but her case study shows that if there is a way to compensate, the human brain will find it. Brandi's remarkable recovery also provides evidence against the stereotype that the left side (hemisphere) of the brain is solely the source of logical thinking and the right hemisphere exclusively the source of creativity. Brains are not that neatly split in terms of most functioning, as Brandi's case illustrates.

Although case studies provide dramatic, in-depth portrayals of people's lives, we need to exercise caution when interpreting them (Leary, 2008). The subject of a case study is unique, with a genetic makeup and set of experiences that no one else shares. For these reasons, the findings do not always lend themselves to statistical analysis and may not generalize to other people.

**Ethnographic Studies**   An **ethnographic study** consists of in-depth description and interpretation of behavior in an ethnic or a cultural group that includes direct involvement with the participants (Plano Clark & Creswell, 2010). This type of study might include observations in naturalistic settings as well as interviews. Many ethnographic studies are long-term projects.

In one ethnographic study, the purpose was to examine the extent to which schools were enacting educational reforms for language minority students (U.S. Office of Education, 1998). In-depth observations and interviews were conducted in a number of schools to determine if they were establishing high standards and restructuring the way education was being delivered. Several schools were selected for intensive evaluation, including Las Palmas Elementary School in San Clemente,

**standardized tests** Tests with uniform procedures for administration and scoring. They assess students' performance in different domains and allow a student's performance to be compared with the performance of other students at the same age or grade level on a national basis.

**case study** An in-depth look at an individual.

**ethnographic study** In-depth description and interpretation of behavior in an ethnic or a cultural group that includes direct involvement with the participants.

**Observed correlation:** As permissive teaching increases, childrens' self-control decreases.

**Possible explanations for this correlation**

Permissive teaching → causes → Childrens' lack of self-control

Childrens' lack of self-control → causes → Permissive teaching

Other factors, such as genetic tendencies, poverty, and sociohistorical circumstances → cause both → Permissive teaching and Childrens' lack of self-control

FIGURE **1.3** POSSIBLE EXPLANATIONS FOR CORRELATIONAL DATA

An observed correlation between two events cannot be used to conclude that one event caused the other. Some possibilities are that the second event caused the first event or that a third, unknown event caused the correlation between the first two events.

California. The study concluded that this school, at least, was making the necessary reforms for improving the education of language minority students.

***Focus Groups***   In *focus groups* people are interviewed in a group setting, usually to obtain information about a particular topic or issue (Given, 2008). These groups typically consist of five to nine people in which a group facilitator asks a series of open-ended questions. Focus groups can be used to assess the value of a product, service, or program, such as a newly developed school Web site or the benefits of a recently instituted after-school program for middle school students.

***Personal Journals and Diaries***   Individuals may be asked to keep personal journals or diaries to document quantitative aspects of their activities (such as how frequently the individual uses the Internet) or qualitative aspects of their lives (such as their attitudes and beliefs about a particular topic or issue) (Given, 2008). Increasingly, researchers are providing digital audio or video recorders to participants in a study rather than have them write entries in a personal journal or diary.

**Correlational Research**   In **correlational research,** the goal is to describe the strength of the relation between two or more events or characteristics. Correlational research is useful because the more strongly two events are correlated (related or associated), the more effectively we can predict one from the other (Howell, 2010; Levin & Fox, 2011). For example, if researchers find that low-involved, permissive teaching is correlated with a student's lack of self-control, it suggests that low-involved, permissive teaching might be one source of the lack of self-control.

Correlation by itself, however, does not equal causation (Caldwell, 2010). The correlational finding just mentioned does not mean that permissive teaching necessarily causes low student self-control. It could mean that, but it also could mean that the student's lack of self-control caused the teachers to throw up their arms in despair and give up trying to control the out-of-control class. It also could be that other factors, such as heredity, poverty, or inadequate parenting, caused the correlation between permissive teaching and low student self-control. Figure 1.3 illustrates these possible interpretations of correlational data.

**Experimental Research**   **Experimental research** allows educational psychologists to determine the causes of behavior. Educational psychologists accomplish this

**correlational research** Research that describes the strength of the relation between two or more events or characteristics.

**experimental research** Research that allows the determination of the causes of behavior; involves conducting an experiment, which is a carefully regulated procedure in which one or more of the factors believed to influence the behavior being studied is manipulated and all others are held constant.

task by performing an *experiment,* a carefully regulated procedure in which one or more of the factors believed to influence the behavior being studied is manipulated and all other factors are held constant. If the behavior under study changes when a factor is manipulated, we say that the manipulated factor causes the behavior to change. *Cause* is the event that is being manipulated. *Effect* is the behavior that changes because of the manipulation. Experimental research is the only truly reliable method of establishing cause and effect (Jackson, 2011). Because correlational research does not involve manipulation of factors, it is not a dependable way to isolate cause (Mitchell & Jolley, 2010).

Experiments involve at least one independent variable and one dependent variable. The **independent variable** is the manipulated, influential, experimental factor. The label *independent* indicates that this variable can be changed independently of any other factors. For example, suppose we want to design an experiment to study the effects of peer tutoring on student achievement. In this example, the amount and type of peer tutoring could be an independent variable.

The **dependent variable** is the factor that is measured in an experiment. It can change as the independent variable is manipulated. The label *dependent* is used because the values of this variable depend on what happens to the participants in the experiment as the independent variable is manipulated. In the peer tutoring study, achievement is the dependent variable. This might be assessed in a number of ways. Let's say in this study it is measured by scores on a nationally standardized achievement test.

In experiments, the independent variable consists of differing experiences given to one or more experimental groups and one or more control groups. An **experimental group** is a group whose experience is manipulated. A **control group** is a comparison group that is treated in every way like the experimental group except for the manipulated factor. The control group serves as the baseline against which the effects of the manipulated condition can be compared. In the peer tutoring study, we need to have one group of students who get peer tutoring (experimental group) and one group of students who don't (control group).

Another important principle of experimental research is **random assignment,** in which researchers assign participants to experimental and control groups by chance. This practice reduces the likelihood that the experiment's results will be due to any preexisting differences between the groups (Stangor, 2011). In our study of peer tutoring, random assignment greatly reduces the probability that the two groups will differ on such factors as age, family status, initial achievement, intelligence, personality, health, and alertness.

To summarize the experimental study of peer tutoring and student achievement: (1) each student is randomly assigned to one of two groups, (2) one group (the experimental group) is given peer tutoring and the other (the control group) is not, (3) the independent variable consists of the differing experiences (tutoring or no tutoring) that the experimental and control groups receive, and (4) after the peer tutoring is completed, the students are given a nationally standardized achievement test (dependent variable). Figure 1.4 illustrates the experimental research method applied to time management and students' grades.

## PROGRAM EVALUATION RESEARCH, ACTION RESEARCH, AND THE TEACHER-AS-RESEARCHER

In discussing research methods so far, we have referred mainly to methods used to improve our knowledge and understanding of general educational practices. The same methods also can be applied to research whose aim is more specific, such as determining how well a particular educational strategy or program is working

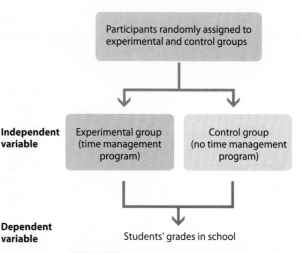

**FIGURE 1.4** EXPERIMENTAL RESEARCH STRATEGY APPLIED TO STUDY OF EFFECTS OF TIME MANAGEMENT ON STUDENTS' GRADES

**independent variable** The manipulated, influential, experimental factor in an experiment.

**dependent variable** The factor that is measured in an experiment.

**experimental group** The group whose experience is manipulated in an experiment.

**control group** The group whose experience is treated in every way like the experimental group except for the manipulated factor.

**random assignment** In experimental research, the assignment of participants to experimental and control groups by chance.

(Plano-Clark & Creswell, 2010). This more narrowly targeted work often includes program evaluation research, action research, and the teacher-as-researcher.

### Program Evaluation Research

Research designed to make decisions about the effectiveness of a particular program is called **program evaluation research.** (McMillan & Schumacher, 2010). It usually focuses on a specific school or school system, in which case its results are not intended to be generalized to other settings. A program evaluation researcher might ask questions like these:

- Has a gifted program started two years ago had positive effects on students' creative thinking and academic achievement?
- Has a technology program in place for one year improved students' attitudes toward school?
- Which of two reading programs being used in this school system has improved students' reading skills the most?

### Action Research

Research used to solve a specific classroom or school problem, improve teaching and other educational strategies, or make a decision at a specific location is called **action research** (Johnson, Mims-Cox, & Doyle-Nichols, 2010; Mills, 2011). The goal of action research is to improve educational practices immediately in one or two classrooms, at one school, or at several schools. Action research is carried out by teachers and administrators rather than educational psychology researchers. The practitioners, however, might follow many of the guidelines of scientific research described earlier, such as trying to make the research and observations as systematic as possible to avoid bias and misinterpretation. Action research can be carried out school-wide or in more limited settings by a smaller group of teachers and administrators; it can even be accomplished in a single classroom by an individual teacher (Hendricks, 2009).

**program evaluation research** Research designed to make decisions about the effectiveness of a particular program.

**action research** Research used to solve a specific classroom or school problem, improve teaching and other educational strategies, or make a decision at a specific level.

## TEACHING CONNECTIONS: Best Practices
### Strategies for Becoming an Effective Teacher-Researcher

1. *Collect many types of data in your classroom.* Students give us a wealth of data if we are willing to record it. Observation data, assessment data, and interview data might be particularly useful. You might enlist the aid of another teacher or assistant to help you record observation data. Keep the data organized. Electronic spreadsheets are particularly useful for organizing assessment data in a way that allows easy analysis.

2. *As you plan your lessons, think about the data you have collected.* Is one student struggling? Does another seem bored? Is the entire class having difficulty with a concept? You can use the data you collected to confirm or refute your impressions.

3. *Make your instructional decisions based on data.* If the student who seems bored is also achieving at a high level, you might consider differentiating instruction. If the assessment data indicate that the student who seems to be struggling is falling behind, s/he might benefit from differentiated instruction also. You might want to know if a different approach to teaching the concept the class mentioned above is struggling to understand would enhance learning. You can conduct an experiment to determine if a different strategy would be helpful to this particular group of students.

4. *Use the library or Internet resources to learn more about teacher-researcher skills.* This might include locating information about how to be a skilled clinical interviewer and a systematic, unbiased observer.

5. *Take a course in educational research methods.* This can improve your understanding of how research is conducted.

**The Teacher-as-Researcher**   The concept of **teacher-as-researcher** (also called teacher-researcher) is the idea that classroom teachers can conduct their own studies to improve their teaching practices (Plano Clark & Creswell, 2010). To obtain information, the teacher-researcher uses methods such as participant observation, interviews, and case studies. One widely used technique is the clinical interview, in which the teacher makes the student feel comfortable, shares beliefs and expectations, and asks questions in a nonthreatening manner. Before conducting a clinical interview with a student, the teacher usually will put together a targeted set of questions to ask. Clinical interviews not only can help you obtain information about a particular issue or problem but also can provide you with a sense of how children think and feel.

In addition to participant observation, the teacher might conduct several clinical interviews with a student, discuss the student's situation with the child's parents, and consult with a school psychologist about the student's behavior. Based on this work as teacher-researcher, the teacher may be able to create an intervention strategy that improves the student's behavior.

Thus, learning about educational research methods not only can help you understand the research that educational psychologists conduct but also has another practical benefit: the more knowledge you have about research in educational psychology, the more effective you will be in the increasingly popular teacher-researcher role (Thomas, 2005).

## QUANTITATIVE AND QUALITATIVE RESEARCH

Now that we have described a wide range of research methods, let's look at an increasingly common way of categorizing these methods: quantitative research and qualitative research (McMillan & Wergin, 2010; Plano Clark & Creswell, 2010). **Quantitative research** employs numerical calculations in an effort to discover information about a particular topic. Experimental and correlational research designs reflect quantitative research. So do many of the descriptive measures that were described earlier, such as observations, interviews, surveys, and standardized tests, when statistics are used to analyze the data collected. **Qualitative research** involves obtaining information using descriptive measures such as interviews, case studies, ethnographic studies, focus groups, and personal journals and diaries, but not statistically analyzing the information (Stake, 2010).

Recently there has been a push in educational psychology to conduct **mixed methods research,** which involves research that blends different research designs and/or methods (McMillan & Wergin, 2010; Plano Clark & Creswell, 2010). One combination of methods that can be adopted consists of using both quantitative and qualitative research designs. Thus, a researcher might use both a quantitative measure, such as an experimental design and statistically analyze the data, and also use a qualitative measure, such as a focus group or case study to obtain greater breadth and depth of information about a particular topic.

Now that we have explored many aspects of research designs and measures, let's examine how research might influence the strategies teachers use in the classroom. To find out, I asked the following teachers at different grade levels how their teaching had been influenced by research:

**EARLY CHILDHOOD**   Brain research has demonstrated the amazing amount of learning that takes place during the early years of life, in addition to the significant impact of high-quality early childhood education and care on the academic and long-term success of a child. Given the age of the children at our center—toddlers through pre–K—I find this research extremely motivating.

—HEIDI KAUFMAN, *MetroWest YMCA Child Care and Educational Program*

**teacher-as-resesarcher** Also called teacher-researcher, this concept involves classroom teachers conducting their own studies to improve their teaching practice.

**quantitative research** Employs numerical calculations in an effort to discover information about a particular topic.

**qualitative research** Involves obtaining information using descriptive measures such as interviews, case studies, personal journals and diaries, and focus groups but not statistically analyzing the information.

**mixed methods research** Involves research that blends different research designs and/or methods.

**ELEMENTARY SCHOOL: GRADES K–5** When adopting our new kindergarten reading curriculum, we conducted local assessments and collected data, read relevant  research of best practices, and worked cooperatively to come up with the policies and practices that will work in collaboration with our state expectations as well as our school vision and mission.

—**HEATHER ZOLDAK,** *Ridge Wood Elementary School*

**MIDDLE SCHOOL: GRADES 6–8** I attend Learning and the Brain conferences, and read associated research papers and books. These materials have helped me  understand brain development in middle school children, especially the considerable changes in early adolescence. This understanding has influenced my classroom management, enabled me to provide differentiated instruction, and helped me to appreciate and work with a range of students' learning styles and needs.

—**KEREN ABRA,** *Convent of the Sacred Heart School*

**HIGH SCHOOL: GRADES 9–12** The person who has most influenced my teaching is Nancie Atwell, a teacher who teaches teachers about teaching. Her lessons on how to get students to love reading are pragmatic and simple, yet extremely effective: Read what the students are reading, "sell" the books by talking about them to students, let students see you reading, read when they read, give time in class to read, make books easily available to students, and be excited and energetic when discussing new books in class. At the beginning of the year, nonreaders (who comprise the majority of the class) groan and roll their eyes when I say it is reading time. However, in just a few short weeks, students beg for daily reading time.

—**JENNIFER HEITER,** *Bremen High School*

## TEACHING CONNECTIONS: Best Practices
### Strategies for Being a Wise Consumer of Educational Research

1. *Go to the original source.* We often hear blurbs regarding research on the radio or TV news or read about them in teacher magazines. These sources often give only general or sensationalized versions of the actual results. Try to find the original source of the research.

2. *Consider the source.* Where are you finding the research? Is the source reliable? The gold standard for published research is that published in peer-reviewed journals by experts.

3. *Who funded the research?* Although this should certainly not be the case, the reported results of the research may be biased toward the funding source.

4. *Look at the sample.* A large sample is more likely to yield results that can be generalized than a small sample. To what degree does the sample match the population of children you are teaching? If you are teaching in an urban U.S. school, can the results of a study of rural Chilean students be generalized to your population?

5. *How was the research conducted?* Earlier we discussed several ways in which research can be conducted. Each has its advantages and disadvantages. Make certain that causation is not being inferred where it should not be (for instance from correlational data).

6. *Have other studies yielded similar results?* Once a ground-breaking result has been obtained, it is important that it is replicated. If several studies indicate the same conclusion, then we may begin to think about implementing in practice.

## Review, Reflect, and Practice

**3** Discuss why research is important to effective teaching, and how educational psychologists and teachers can conduct and evaluate research.

### REVIEW

- Why is research important in educational psychology?
- What are some types of research? What is the difference between correlational research and experimental research?
- What are some kinds of research that relate directly to effective classroom practices? What tools might a teacher use to do classroom research?
- What characterizes quantitative and qualitative research?

### REFLECT

- In your own K–12 education, can you remember a time when one of your teachers might have benefited from conducting action research regarding the effectiveness of his or her own teaching methods? What action research questions and methods might have been useful to the teacher?

### PRAXIS™ PRACTICE

1. Which of the following is more scientific?
   a. systematic observation
   b. personal experience
   c. a person's opinion
   d. a book written by a journalist

2. Mr. McMahon wants to know how much time his students spend off-task each day. To determine this, he carefully watches the students in class, keeping a record of off-task behavior. Which research approach has he used?
   a. case study
   b. experiment
   c. laboratory experiment
   d. naturalistic observation

3. Ms. Simon has been hired to determine how effective a school's health education program has been in reducing adolescent pregnancies. Which type of research will she conduct?
   a. action research
   b. experimental research
   c. program evaluation
   d. teacher-as-researcher

4. Mr. Nugerian wants to use qualitative research to discover why students are slacking off in their homework. Which of the following measures is he likely to use to obtain information about this problem?
   a. experimental research
   b. correlational research
   c. ethnographic study
   d. observation with statistical analysis of the data

*Please see the answer key at the end of the book.*

# The Classroom Decision

Ms. Huang teaches fourth grade at King Elementary School. Her class is comprised of 26 students, 16 girls and 10 boys. They are an ethnically and economically diverse group. They are also diverse in terms of their achievement levels. She has two students who have been identified as being gifted and three students with diagnosed learning disabilities. Overall, they are a cooperative group with a desire to learn.

Ms. Huang's school district recently purchased a new math curriculum that emphasizes conceptual understanding and application of mathematical principles to real-life situations. While Ms. Huang appreciates this, she also has some concerns. Many of her students have not yet mastered their basic math facts. She fears that without knowing their basic math facts very well, understanding mathematical principles will be useless to her students, and they still won't be able to work on application of these principles. She also worries that this will cause her students undue frustration and may decrease their interest and motivation in math.

In the past, Ms. Huang has had her students work on developing mastery of math facts using drill-and-practice methods such as flashcards, worksheets filled with fact problems, and a computer game that is essentially an electronic version of flashcards with graphics. She is comfortable with this method and says that it has helped prior students to develop the mastery she believes they need.

She voices her concern to her principal, who responds that the publisher's representative provided the district with evidence that the new program also helps students to develop mastery of basic facts. However, Ms. Huang is still skeptical. She wants to do the right thing for her students, but she isn't sure what that is. She decides that she needs to conduct some classroom research to determine which will benefit her students more—the new curricular approach or her more traditional approach.

1. What issues would need to be considered in conducting such a study?
2. What type of research would be most appropriate?
   a. case study
   b. correlational research
   c. experimental research
   d. naturalistic observation
3. Why?
4. If she compared the two different curricula and their outcomes, what would the independent variable be?
   a. student achievement relative to basic math facts
   b. the control group
   c. the experimental group
   d. which curricular approach was used
5. If Ms. Huang decided to conduct an experimental study in which she compared the two different curricula and their outcomes, what would the dependent variable be?
   a. student achievement relative to basic math facts
   b. the control group
   c. the experimental group
   d. which curricular approach was used
6. How should Ms. Huang go about conducting her study?

# Educational Psychology: A Tool for Effective Teaching

**1** **EXPLORING EDUCATIONAL PSYCHOLOGY:** Describe some basic ideas about the field of educational psychology.

Historical Background

Educational psychology is the branch of psychology that specializes in understanding teaching and learning in educational settings. William James and John Dewey were important pioneers in educational psychology, as was E. L. Thorndike. William James emphasized the importance of classroom observation to improve education. Among the important ideas in educational psychology that we owe to Dewey are these: the child as an active learner, education of the whole child, emphasis on the child's adaptation to the environment, and the democratic ideal that all children deserve a competent education. E. L. Thorndike, a proponent of the scientific foundation of learning, argued that schools should sharpen children's reasoning skills. There were few individuals from ethnic minority groups and few women in the early history of educational psychology because of ethnic and gender barriers. Further historical developments included Skinner's behaviorism in the mid–twentieth century and the cognitive revolution that had taken hold by the 1980s. Also in recent years, there has been expanded interest in the socioemotional aspects of children's lives, including cultural contexts.

Teaching: Art and Science

Teaching is linked to both science and art. In terms of art, skillful, experienced practice contributes to effective teaching. In terms of science, information from psychological research can provide valuable ideas.

**2** **EFFECTIVE TEACHING:** Identify the attitudes and skills of an effective teacher.

Professional Knowledge and Skills

Effective teachers have subject-matter competence, use effective instructional strategies, engage in good thinking skills and guide students in developing these thinking skills, pay more than lip service to individual variations, work with diverse ethnic and cultural groups, and have skills in the following areas: goal setting and planning, developmentally appropriate teaching practices, classroom management, motivation, communication, assessment, and technology.

Commitment, Motivation, and Caring

Being an effective teacher also requires commitment and motivation. This includes having a good attitude and caring about students. It is easy for teachers to get into a rut and develop a negative attitude, but students pick up on this, and it can harm their learning.

**3** **RESEARCH IN EDUCATIONAL PSYCHOLOGY:** Discuss why research is important to effective teaching, and how educational psychologists and teachers can conduct and evaluate research.

Why Research Is Important

Personal experiences and information from experts can help you become an effective teacher. The information you obtain from research also is extremely important. It will help you sort through various strategies and determine which are most and least effective.

*continued*

Research helps to eliminate errors in judgment that result from relying exclusively on personal experiences.

**Research Methods**

Numerous methods can be used to obtain information about various aspects of educational psychology. Research data-gathering methods can be classified as descriptive, correlational, and experimental. Descriptive methods include observation, interviews and questionnaires, standardized tests, case studies, ethnographic studies, focus groups, and personal journals and diaries. In correlational research, the goal is to describe the strength of the relation between two or more events or characteristics. An important research principle is that correlation does not equal causation. Experimental research allows the causes of behavior to be determined and is the only truly reliable method of establishing cause and effect. Conducting an experiment involves examining the influence of at least one independent variable (the manipulated, influential, experimental factor) on one or more dependent variables (the measured factor). Experiments involve the random assignment of participants to one or more experimental groups (the groups whose experience is being manipulated) and one or more control groups (comparison groups treated in every way like the experimental group except for the manipulated factor).

**Program Evaluation Research, Action Research, and the Teacher-as-Researcher**

Program evaluation research is research designed to make decisions about the effectiveness of a particular program. Action research is used to solve a specific classroom or social problem, improve teaching strategies, or make a decision about a specific location. The teacher-as-researcher (teacher-researcher) conducts classroom studies to improve his or her educational practices.

**Quantitative and Qualitative Research**

Quantitative research employs numerical calculations in an effort to discover information about a particular topic. Experimental and correlational research designs reflect quantitative research. Qualitative research involves obtaining information using descriptive measures such as interviews, case studies, and ethnographic studies but not statistically analyzing the data. Mixed methods research blends different research designs and/or methods.

# KEY TERMS

educational psychology 2
constructivist approach 6
direct instruction
   approach 6
critical thinking 7
differentiated instruction 9
laboratory 15

naturalistic observation 15
participant observation 15
standardized tests 17
case study 17
ethnographic study 17
correlational research 18
experimental research 18

independent variable 19
dependent variable 19
experimental group 19
control group 19
random assignment 19
program evaluation
   research 20

action research 20
teacher-as-researcher 21
quantitative research 21
qualitative research 21
mixed methods research 21

# PORTFOLIO ACTIVITIES

1. At the beginning of the chapter, you read teacher-astronaut Christa McAuliffe's quote: "I touch the future. I teach." Don your creative-thinking hat and come up with one or more brief statements that describe positive aspects of teaching.

2. After some thinking, write a personal statement about the following: What kind of teacher do you want to become? What strengths do you want to have? What kinds of potential weaknesses might you need to overcome? Either place the statement

in your portfolio or seal it in an envelope that you will open after your first month or two of teaching.

3. Think about the grade level you are planning to teach. Consider at least one way your classroom at that grade level is likely to be challenging. Write about how you will cope with this.

4. Information about educational psychology appears in research journals and in magazines and newspapers. Find an article in a research or professional journal (such as *Contemporary*

*Educational Psychologist, Educational Psychologist, Educational Psychology Review, Journal of Educational Psychology,* or *Phi Delta Kappan*) and an article in a newspaper or magazine on the same topic. How does the research/professional article differ from the newspaper or magazine account? What can you learn from this comparison? Write down your conclusions and keep copies of the articles.

*Go to the Online Learning Center for downloadable portfolio templates.*

## STUDY, PRACTICE, AND SUCCEED

Visit www.mhhe.com/santrockep5e to review the chapter with self-grading quizzes and self-assessments, to apply the chapter material to two more Crack the Case studies, and for suggested activities to develop your teaching portfolio.

# CHAPTER 2

# COGNITIVE AND LANGUAGE DEVELOPMENT

*Ah! What would the world be to us*
*If the children were no more?*
*We should dread the desert behind us*
*Worse than the dark before.*

—Henry Wadsworth Longfellow
*American Poet, 19th Century*

## Chapter **Outline**

### An Overview of Child Development

Exploring What Development Is
Processes and Periods
Developmental Issues
Development and Education

### Cognitive Development

The Brain
Piaget's Theory
Vygotsky's Theory

### Language Development

What Is Language?
Biological and Environmental Influences
Language Development

## Learning **Goals**

**1** Define development and explain the main processes, periods, and issues in development, as well as links between development and education.

**2** Discuss the development of the brain and compare the cognitive developmental theories of Jean Piaget and Lev Vygotsky.

**3** Identify the key features of language, the biological and environmental influences on language, and the typical growth of child's language.

# Teaching **Stories**   Donene Polson

In this chapter you will study Lev Vygotsky's sociocultural cognitive theory of development. Donene Polson's classroom reflects Vygotsky's emphasis on the importance of collaboration among a community of learners. Donene teaches at Washington Elementary School in Salt Lake City, an innovative school that emphasizes the importance of people learning together (Rogoff, Turkanis, & Bartlett, 2001). Children as well as adults plan learning activities. Throughout the day at school, students work in small groups.

Donene loves working in a school where students, teachers, and parents work as a community to help children learn (Polson, 2001). Before the school year begins, she meets with parents at each family's home to prepare for the upcoming year, getting acquainted and establishing schedules to determine when parents can contribute to classroom instruction. At monthly teacher-parent meetings, Donene and the parents plan the curriculum and discuss children's progress. They brainstorm about community resources that can be used to promote children's learning.

Many students come back to tell Donene that experiences in her classroom made important contributions to their development and learning. For example, Luisa Magarian reflected on how her experience in Donene's classroom helped her work with others in high school:

> From having responsibility in groups, kids learn how to deal with problems and listen to each other or try to understand different points of view. They learn how to help a group work smoothly and how to keep people interested in what they are doing. . . . As coeditor of the student news magazine at my high school, I have to balance my eagerness to get things done with patience to work with other students. (Rogoff, Turkanis, & Bartlett, 2001, pp. 84–85)

As Donene Polson's story shows, theories of cognitive development can form the basis of innovative instructional programs.

# Preview

Examining the shape of children's development allows us to understand it better. This chapter—the first of two on development—focuses on children's cognitive and language development. Before we delve into these topics, though, we need to explore some basic ideas about development.

**1  AN OVERVIEW OF CHILD DEVELOPMENT**

| Exploring What Development Is | Processes and Periods | Developmental Issues | Development and Education |

Twentieth-century Spanish-born American philosopher George Santayana once reflected, "Children are on a different plane. They belong to a generation and way of feeling properly their own." Let's explore what that plane is like.

## EXPLORING WHAT DEVELOPMENT IS

Why study children's development? As a teacher, you will be responsible for a new wave of children each year in your classroom. The more you learn about children's development, the more you can understand at what level it is appropriate to teach them.

Just what do psychologists mean when they speak of a person's "development"? **Development** is the pattern of biological, cognitive, and socioemotional changes that begins at conception and continues through the life span. Most development involves growth, although it also eventually involves decay (dying).

## PROCESSES AND PERIODS

The pattern of child development is complex because it is the product of several processes: biological, cognitive, and socioemotional. Development also can be described in terms of periods.

DEVELOPMENT

**development** The pattern of biological, cognitive, and socioemotional processes that begins at conception and continues through the life span. Most development involves growth, although it also eventually involves decay (dying).

**29**

PEANUTS: © United Features Syndicate, Inc.

*Children are the legacy we leave for the time we will not live to see.*

—Aristotle
*Greek Philosopher, 4th Century* B.C.

**Biological, Cognitive, and Socioemotional Processes**  *Biological processes* produce changes in the child's body and underlie brain development, height and weight gains, motor skills, and puberty's hormonal changes. Genetic inheritance plays a large part.

*Cognitive processes* involve changes in the child's thinking, intelligence, and language. Cognitive developmental processes enable a growing child to memorize a poem, figure out how to solve a math problem, come up with a creative strategy, or speak meaningfully connected sentences.

*Socioemotional processes* involve changes in the child's relationships with other people, changes in emotion, and changes in personality. Parents' nurturance toward their child, a boy's aggressive attack on a peer, a girl's development of assertiveness, and an adolescent's feelings of joy after getting good grades all reflect socioemotional processes in development.

Biological, cognitive, and socioemotional processes are inextricably intertwined (Diamond, Casey, & Munakata, 2011). Consider a child smiling in response to a parent's touch. This response depends on biological processes (the physical nature of touch and responsiveness to it), cognitive processes (the ability to understand intentional acts), and socioemotional processes (the act of smiling often reflects a positive emotional feeling, and smiling helps to connect us in positive ways with other human beings). Two rapidly emerging fields further explore this connection across biological, cognitive, and socioemotional processes:

- *developmental cognitive neuroscience,* which explores links between development, cognitive processes, and the brain (Diamond, Casey, & Munakato, 2011; Nelson, 2011), For example, later in this chapter you will learn about connections between developmental changes in regions of the brain and children's thinking.
- *developmental social neuroscience,* which examines connections between socioemotional processes, development, and the brain (Bell, Greene, & Wolfe, 2010; de Haan & Gunnar, 2009). For example, later in this chapter you will read about developmental changes in the brain and adolescents' decision making and risk-taking behavior.

DEVELOPMENT

**Periods of Development**  For the purposes of organization and understanding, we commonly describe development in terms of periods. In the most widely used system of classification, the developmental periods are infancy, early childhood, middle and late childhood, adolescence, early adulthood, middle adulthood, and late adulthood.

*Infancy* extends from birth to 18 to 24 months. It is a time of extreme dependence on adults. Many activities are just beginning, such as language development, symbolic thought, sensorimotor coordination, and social learning.

*Early childhood* (sometimes called the *preschool years*) extends from the end of infancy to about 5 years. During this period, children become more self-sufficient, develop school readiness skills (such as learning to follow instructions and identify

FIGURE **2.1** PERIODS AND PROCESSES OF DEVELOPMENT

Development moves through the infancy, early childhood, middle and late childhood, and adolescence periods. These periods of development are the result of biological, cognitive, and socioemotional processes.

letters), and spend many hours with peers. First grade typically marks the end of early childhood.

*Middle and late childhood* (sometimes called the *elementary school years*) extends from about 6 to 11 years of age. Children master the fundamental skills of reading, writing, and math, achievement becomes a more central theme, and self-control increases. In this period, children interact more with the wider social world beyond their family.

*Adolescence* involves the transition from childhood to adulthood. It begins around ages 10 to 12 and ends around 18 to 21. Adolescence starts with rapid physical changes, including height and weight gains and development of sexual functions. Adolescents intensely pursue independence and seek their own identity. Their thought becomes more abstract, logical, and idealistic.

Adult developmental periods have been described, but we have confined our discussion to the periods most relevant for children's and adolescents' education. The child and adolescent periods of human development are shown in Figure 2.1 along with the processes of development (biological, cognitive, and socioemotional). The interplay of these processes produces the periods of human development.

## DEVELOPMENTAL ISSUES

Despite all of the knowledge that developmentalists have acquired, debate continues about the relative importance of factors that influence the developmental processes and about how the periods of development are related. The most important issues in the study of children's development include nature and nurture, continuity and discontinuity, and early and later experience.

*Children are busy becoming something they have not quite grasped yet, something which keeps changing.*

—Alastair Reid
*American Poet, 20th Century*

**nature-nurture issue** Nature refers to an organism's biological inheritance, nurture to environmental influences. The "nature" proponents claim biological inheritance is the most important influence on development; the "nurture" proponents claim environmental experiences are the most important.

**continuity-discontinuity issue** The issue regarding whether development involves gradual, cumulative change (continuity) or distinct stages (discontinuity).

**early-later experience issue** The issue of the degree to which early experiences (especially infancy) or later experiences are the key determinants of the child's development.

**Nature and Nurture**    The **nature-nurture issue** involves the debate about whether development is primarily influenced by nature or by nurture (Cosmides, 2011; Eagly & Wood, 2011). *Nature* refers to an organism's biological inheritance, *nurture* to its environmental experiences. Almost no one today argues that development can be explained by nature or nurture alone. But some ("nature" proponents) claim that the most important influence on development is biological inheritance, and others ("nurture" proponents) claim that environmental experiences are the most important influence.

According to the nature proponents, the range of environments can be vast, but a genetic blueprint produces commonalities in growth and development (Mader, 2011). We walk before we talk, speak one word before two words, grow rapidly in infancy and less so in early childhood, and experience a rush of sexual hormones in puberty. Extreme environments—those that are psychologically barren or hostile—can stunt development, but nature proponents emphasize the influence of tendencies that are genetically wired into humans.

By contrast, other psychologists emphasize the importance of nurture, or environmental experiences, to development (Grusec, 2011; Kopp, 2011). Experiences run the gamut from the individual's biological environment (nutrition, medical care, drugs, and physical accidents) to the social environment (family, peers, schools, community, media, and culture). For example, a child's diet can affect how tall the child grows and even how effectively the child can think and solve problems.

Are children completely at the mercy of their genes and environment as they develop? Their genetic heritage and environmental experiences are pervasive influences on their development. However, children are more than the outcomes of their heredity and the environment they experience; they also can author a unique developmental path by changing the environment. As one psychologist recently concluded,

> In reality, we are both the creatures and creators of our worlds. We are . . . the products of our genes and environments. Nevertheless, . . . the stream of causation that shapes the future runs through our present choices. . . . Mind matters. . . . Our hopes, goals, and expectations influence our future. (Myers, 2010, p. 168)

**Continuity and Discontinuity**    The **continuity-discontinuity issue** focuses on the extent to which development involves gradual, cumulative change (continuity) or distinct stages (discontinuity). For the most part, developmentalists who emphasize nurture usually describe development as a gradual, continuous process, like the seedling's growth into an oak. Those who emphasize nature often describe development as a series of distinct stages, like the change from caterpillar to butterfly.

Consider continuity first. A child's first word, though seemingly an abrupt, discontinuous event, is actually the result of weeks and months of growth and practice. Puberty, another seemingly abrupt, discontinuous occurrence, is actually a gradual process occurring over several years.

Viewed in terms of discontinuity, each person is described as passing through a sequence of stages in which change is qualitatively rather than quantitatively different. A child moves at some point from not being able to think abstractly about the world to being able to. This is a qualitative, discontinuous change in development, not a quantitative, continuous change.

**Early and Later Experience**    The **early-later experience issue** focuses on the degree to which early experiences (especially in infancy) or later experiences are the key determinants of the child's development. That is, if infants experience harmful circumstances, can those experiences be overcome by later, positive ones? Or are the early experiences so critical—possibly because they are the infant's first, prototypical experiences—that they cannot be overridden by a later, better environment?

The early-later experience issue has a long history and continues to be hotly debated among developmentalists (Kopp, 2011; Schaie, 2011). Some developmentalists argue that, unless infants experience warm, nurturing care during the first year or so of life, their development will never quite be optimal (Sroufe, 2007). In contrast, later-experience advocates argue that children are malleable throughout development, and that later sensitive caregiving is just as important as earlier sensitive caregiving.

**Evaluating the Developmental Issues**    Most developmentalists recognize that it is unwise to take an extreme position on the issues of nature and nurture, continuity and discontinuity, and early and later experiences. Development is not all nature or all nurture, not all continuity or all discontinuity, and not all early or later experiences. However, there is still spirited debate about how strongly development is influenced by each of these factors (Goldsmith, 2011; Phillips & Lowenstein, 2011).

## DEVELOPMENT AND EDUCATION

In Chapter 1 we briefly described the importance of engaging in developmentally appropriate teaching practices. Here we expand on this important topic.

Developmentally appropriate teaching takes place at a level that is neither too difficult and stressful nor too easy and boring for the child's developmental level (Bredekamp, 2011). One of the challenges of developmentally appropriate teaching is that you likely will have children with an age range of several years and a range of abilities and skills in the classes you teach. Competent teachers are aware of these developmental differences. Rather than characterizing students as "advanced," "average," and "slow," they recognize that their development and ability are complex, and children often do not display the same competence across different skills.

**Splintered development** refers to the circumstances in which development is uneven across domains (Horowitz & others, 2005). One student may have excellent math skills but poor writing skills. Within the area of language, another student may have excellent verbal language skills but not have good reading and writing skills. Yet another student may do well in science but lack social skills.

Cognitively advanced students whose socioemotional development is at a level expected for much younger children present a special challenge. For example, a student may excel at science, math, and language but be immature emotionally. Such a child may not have any friends and be neglected or rejected by peers. This student will benefit considerably from having a teacher who helps her or him learn how to manage emotions and behave in more socially appropriate ways.

As we discuss development in this chapter and the next, keep in mind how the developmental changes we describe can help you understand the optimal level for teaching and learning. For example, it is not a good strategy to try to push children to read before they are developmentally ready—but when they are ready, reading materials should be presented at the appropriate level (Bredekamp, 2011; Jalongo, 2011).

> **Thinking Back/Thinking Forward**
>
> New guidelines exist for developmentally appropriate education (NAEYC, 2009). Chapter 3, p. 86

## Review, Reflect, and Practice

**1** Define development and explain the main processes, periods, and issues in development, as well as links between development and education.

**REVIEW**
- What is the nature of development?
- What three broad processes interact in a child's development? What general periods do children go through between birth and the end of adolescence?

*(continued)*

**splintered development** The circumstances in which development is uneven across domains.

## Review, Reflect, and Practice

### REVIEW (CONTINUED)

- What are the main developmental issues? What conclusions can be reached about these issues?
- What implications does the concept of development have for the notion of "appropriate" learning?

### REFLECT

- Give an example of how a cognitive process could influence a socioemotional process in the age of children you plan to teach. Then give an example of how a socioemotional process could influence a cognitive process in this age group.

### PRAXIS™ PRACTICE

1. Mr. Huxtaby is giving a talk on development to a parent-teacher organization. In his talk, which of the following is he most likely to describe as not being an example of development?
   a. pubertal change
   b. improvement in memory
   c. change in friendship
   d. an inherited tendency to be shy

2. Ms. Halle teaches third grade. Which period of development is likely to be of most interest to her?
   a. infancy
   b. early childhood
   c. middle childhood and late childhood
   d. adolescence

3. Piaget argued that children progress through a series of cognitive development stages. In contrast, Skinner stressed that individuals simply learn more as time goes on. Which developmental issue is highlighted in their disagreement?
   a. continuity and discontinuity
   b. early and later experience
   c. nature and nurture
   d. biological and socioemotional development

4. Alexander's scores on standardized mathematics achievement tests are always very high—among the highest in the nation. In contrast, his scores on reading achievement tests indicate that he is about average. This is an example of
   a. developmentally appropriate teaching.
   b. early versus later development.
   c. nature versus nurture.
   d. splintered development.

*Please see the answer key at the end of the book.*

**2 COGNITIVE DEVELOPMENT**

| The Brain | Piaget's Theory | Vygotsky's Theory |

Twentieth-century American poet Marianne Moore said that the mind is "an enchanting thing." How this enchanting thing develops has intrigued many psychologists. First, we explore increasing interest in the development of the brain and then turn to two major cognitive theories—Piaget's and Vygotsky's.

# THE BRAIN

Until recently little was known about how the brain changes as children develop. Not long ago scientists thought that genes determine how children's brains are "wired." Whatever brain heredity dealt them, children were essentially stuck with it. This view, however, turned out to be wrong. Instead, the brain has considerable *plasticity,* or the ability to change, and its development depends on experience (Nelson, 2011; Toga & Mazziotta, 2011). In other words, what children do can change the development of their brain.

**Development of Neurons and Brain Regions**   The number and size of the brain's nerve endings continue to grow at least into adolescence. Some of the brain's increase in size also is due to **myelination,** the process of encasing many cells in the brain with a myelin sheath (see Figure 2.2). This process increases the speed at which information travels through the nervous system (Schnaar & Lopez, 2009). Myelination in brain areas important in focusing attention is not complete until about 10 years of age. The implications for teaching are that children will have difficulty focusing their attention and maintaining it for very long in early childhood, but their attention will improve as they move through the elementary school years. The most extensive increase in myelination, which occurs in the brain's frontal lobes, where reasoning and thinking occur, takes place during adolescence (Giedd & others, 2009).

Another important aspect of the brain's development at the cellular level is the dramatic increase in connections between neurons (nerve cells) (Turrigiano, 2010). *Synapses* are tiny gaps between neurons where connections between neurons are made. Researchers have discovered an interesting aspect of synaptic connections. Nearly twice as many of these connections are made than ever will be used (Huttenlocher & Dabholkar, 1997). The connections that are used become strengthened and will survive, whereas the unused ones will be replaced by other pathways or disappear. That is, in the language of neuroscience, these connections will be "pruned." Figure 2.3 vividly shows the dramatic growth and later pruning of synapses in the visual, auditory, and prefrontal cortex areas of the brain. These areas are critical for higher-order cognitive functioning such as learning, memory, and reasoning.

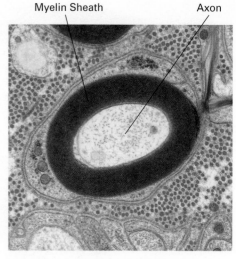

**FIGURE 2.2** MYELINATED NERVE

**Fiber.** The myelin sheath, shown in brown, encases the axon (white). This image was produced by an electron microscope that magnified the nerve fiber 12,000 times. *What role does myelination play in the brain's development?*

DEVELOPMENT

**myelination** The process of encasing many cells in the brain with a myelin sheath that increases the speed at which information travels through the nervous system.

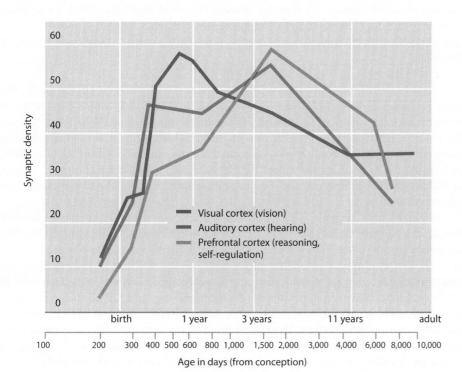

**FIGURE 2.3** SYNAPTIC DENSITY IN HUMAN BRAIN FROM INFANCY TO ADULTHOOD

The graph shows the dramatic increase and then pruning of synaptic density for three regions of the brain: visual cortex, auditory cortex, and prefrontal cortex. Synaptic density is believed to be an important indication of the extent of connectivity between neurons.

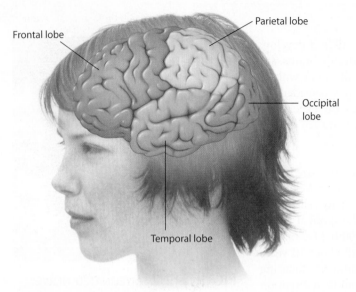

**FIGURE 2.4** THE BRAIN'S FOUR LOBES

Shown here are the locations of the brain's four lobes: frontal, occipital, temporal, and parietal.

Thinking Back/Thinking Forward

A surge of interest has occurred in discovering the aspects of the brain that are involved in intelligence. Chapter 4, p. 121

**corpus callosum** Where fibers connect the brain's left and right hemispheres.

**prefrontal cortex** The highest level in the frontal lobes; involved in reasoning, decision making, and self-control.

**amygdala** The seat of emotions in the brain.

Notice that in the prefrontal cortex (discussed further later on), where higher-level thinking and self-regulation take place, it is not until middle to late adolescence that the adult density of the synapses is achieved.

Figure 2.4 shows the location of the brain's four lobes. As just indicated, growth in the prefrontal cortex (the highest region of the frontal lobes) continues through adolescence. Rapid growth in the temporal lobes (language processing) and parietal lobes (spatial location) occurs from age 6 through puberty.

**Brain Development in Middle and Late Childhood**   Total brain volume stabilizes by the end of middle and late childhood, but significant changes in various structures and regions of the brain continue to occur (Gogtay & Thompson, 2010). In particular, the brain pathways and circuitry involving the prefrontal cortex continue to increase in middle and late childhood (Durston & Casey, 2006). These advances in the prefrontal cortex are linked to children's improved attention, reasoning, and cognitive control (Diamond, Casey, & Munakata, 2011).

Developmental neuroscientist Mark Johnson and his colleagues (2009) recently proposed that the prefrontal cortex likely orchestrates the functions of many other brain regions during development. As part of this neural leadership, organizational role, the prefrontal cortex may provide an advantage to neural connections and networks that include the prefrontal cortex. In their view, the prefrontal cortex likely coordinates the best neural connections for solving a problem.

Links between the changing brain and children's cognitive development involve activation of some brain areas so that they increase in activity while others decrease (Goswami, 2011; Nelson, 2011). One shift in activation that occurs as children develop in middle and late childhood is from diffuse, larger areas to more focal, smaller areas. This shift is characterized by the synaptic pruning mentioned earlier, in which areas of the brain not being used lose synaptic connections and those being used show an increase in connections. The increased focal activation is linked to improved cognitive performance, especially in *cognitive control,* which involves flexible and effective control in a number of areas (Durston & others, 2006). These areas include controlling attention, reducing interfering thoughts, inhibiting motor actions, and being flexible in switching between competing choices (Diamond, Casey, & Munakata, 2011).

**Brain Development in Adolescence**   Along with the rest of the body, the brain is changing during adolescence. Earlier we indicated that connections between neurons become "pruned" as children and adolescents develop. What results from this pruning is that by the end of adolescence individuals have "fewer, more selective, more effective connections between neurons than they did as children" (Kuhn, 2009, p. 153). And this pruning indicates that the activities adolescents choose to engage in and not to engage in influence which neural connections will be strengthened and which will disappear.

Scientists have recently discovered that adolescents' brains undergo significant structural changes (Giedd & others, 2009; Jackson-Newsom & Shelton, 2010). The **corpus callosum,** where fibers connect the brain's left and right hemispheres, thickens in adolescence, and this improves adolescents' ability to process information. We described advances in the development of the **prefrontal cortex**—the highest level of the frontal lobes involved in reasoning, decision making, and self-control—earlier in this section. However, the prefrontal cortex doesn't finish maturing until the emerging adult years, approximately 18 to 25 years of age, or later, but the **amygdala**—the seat of emotions such as anger—matures earlier than the prefrontal cortex. Figure 2.5 shows the locations of the corpus callosum, prefrontal cortex, and amygdala.

Leading researcher Charles Nelson (2011) points out that although adolescents are capable of very strong emotions, their prefrontal cortex hasn't adequately developed to the point at which they can control these passions. This means that the brain region for putting the brakes on risky, impulsive behavior is still under construction during adolescence (Giedd & others, 2009). Or consider this interpretation of the development of emotion and cognition in adolescence: "early activation of strong 'turbo-charged' feelings with a relatively unskilled set of 'driving skills' or cognitive abilities to modulate strong emotions and motivation" (Dahl, 2004, p. 18). This developmental disjunction may account for increased risk taking and other problems in adolescence (Steinberg, 2009). "Some things just take time to develop and mature judgment is probably one of them" (Steinberg, 2004, p. 56).

**Lateralization**   The cerebral cortex (the highest level of the brain) is divided into two halves, or hemispheres (see Figure 2.6). **Lateralization** is the specialization of functions in each hemisphere of the brain (van Ettinger-Veenstra & others, 2010). In individuals with an intact brain, there is a specialization of function in some areas.

The most extensive research on the brain's two hemispheres involves language. In most individuals, speech and grammar are localized to the left hemisphere (Carota & others, 2010; Gazzaniga, 2010). However, not all language processing is carried out in the brain's left hemisphere (Phan & Vicario, 2010). For example, understanding such aspects of language as appropriate use of language in different contexts, evaluation of the emotional expressiveness of language, and much of humor involves the right hemisphere (Kensinger & Choi, 2009). Also, when children lose much of their left hemisphere because of an accident, surgery for epilepsy, or other reasons, the right hemisphere in many cases can reconfigure itself for increased language processing (Staudt, 2010).

Because of the differences in functioning of the brain's two hemispheres, people commonly use the phrases "left-brained" and "right-brained" to say which hemisphere is dominant. Unfortunately, much of this talk is seriously exaggerated. For example, laypeople and the media commonly exaggerate hemispheric specialization by claiming that the left brain is logical and the right brain is creative. However, most complex functioning—such as logical and creative thinking—in normal people involves communication between both sides of the brain (Baars & Gage, 2010). Scientists who study the brain are typically very cautious with terms such as *left-brained* and *right-brained* because the brain is more complex than those terms suggest.

**Plasticity**   As we have seen, the brain has *plasticity* (Nelson, 2011; Toga & Mazziotta, 2011). What children do can change the development of their brain. By engaging students in optimal learning environments, you can stimulate the development of their brain (Goswami, 2010).

The remarkable case of Michael Rehbein illustrates the brain's plasticity. When Michael was 4½, he began to experience uncontrollable seizures—as many as 400 a day. Doctors said that the only solution was to remove the left hemisphere of his brain, where the seizures were occurring. Michael had his first major surgery at age 7 and another at age 10. Although recovery was slow, his right hemisphere began to reorganize and eventually took over functions such as speech that normally occur in

**Prefrontal cortex**
This "judgment" region reins in intense emotions but doesn't finish developing until at least emerging adulthood.

**Corpus callosum**
These nerve fibers connect the brain's two hemispheres; they thicken in adolescence to process information more effectively.

**Amygdala**
The seat of emotions such as anger; this area develops quickly before other regions that help to control it.

FIGURE **2.5**  CHANGES IN ADOLESCENT BRAIN

Left hemisphere        Right hemisphere

FIGURE **2.6**  HUMAN BRAIN'S HEMISPHERES

The two halves (hemispheres) of the human brain are clearly seen in this photograph.

**lateralization** The specialization of functions in each hemisphere of the brain.

(a)

(b)

## FIGURE **2.7** PLASTICITY IN BRAIN'S HEMISPHERES

(*a*) Michael Rehbein at 14 years of age. (*b*) Michael's right hemisphere (*right*) has reorganized to take over the language functions normally carried out by corresponding areas in the left hemisphere of an intact brain (*left*). However, the right hemisphere is not as efficient as the left, and more areas of the brain are recruited to process speech.

the brain's left hemisphere (see Figure 2.7). Individuals like Michael are living proof of the growing brain's remarkable plasticity and ability to adapt and recover from a loss of brain tissue.

**The Brain and Children's Education**  Unfortunately, too often statements about the implications of brain science for children's education have been speculative at best and often far removed from what neuroscientists know about the brain (Geake, 2010). We don't have to look any further than the hype about "left-brained" individuals being more logical and "right-brained" individuals being more creative to see that links between neuroscience and brain education are incorrectly made (Sousa, 1995).

Another commonly promoted link between neuroscience and brain education is that there is a critical, or sensitive, period—a biological window of opportunity—when learning is easier, more effective, and more easily retained than later in development. However, some experts on the development of the brain and learning conclude that the critical-period view is exaggerated (Blakemore & Choudhury, 2006). One leading neuroscientist even told educators that although children's brains acquire a great deal of information during the early years, most learning likely takes place after synaptic formation stabilizes, which is after the age of 10 (Goldman-Rakic, 1996).

A major issue involving the development of the brain is which comes first, biological changes in the brain or experiences that stimulate these changes (Lerner, Boyd, & Du, 2008)? Consider a recent study in which the prefrontal cortex thickened and more brain connections formed when adolescents resisted peer pressure (Paus & others, 2008). Scientists have yet to determine whether the brain changes come first or whether the brain changes are the result of experiences with peers, parents, and others. Once again, we encounter the nature-nurture issue that is so prominent in examining children's and adolescents' development.

Given all of the hype and hyperbole about brain education in the media, what can we conclude from the current state of knowledge in applying the rapidly increasing research on the brain's development to education?

- *Both early and later experiences, including educational experiences, are very important in the brain's development.* Significant changes occur at the cellular and structural level in the brain through adolescence (Paus, 2009).
- *Synaptic connections between neurons can change dramatically as a consequence of the learning experiences of children and adolescents* (Nelson, 2011). Connections between neurons that are used when children focus their attention, remember, and think as they are reading, writing, and doing math are strengthened; those that aren't used are replaced by other pathways or disappear.
- *Development at the highest level of the brain—the prefrontal cortex, where such important cognitive processes as thinking, reasoning, and decision making primarily occur—continues at least through the adolescent years* (Steinberg, 2009). This development in the prefrontal cortex moves from being more diffuse to more focal and involves increased efficiency of processing information (Diamond, Casey, & Munakata, 2011). As activation in the prefrontal cortex becomes more focused, cognitive control increases. This is exemplified in children being able to focus their attention more effectively and ignore distractions while they are learning as they become older.
- *Despite the increased focal activation of the prefrontal cortex as children grow older, changes in the brain during adolescence present a challenge to increased cognitive control.* In adolescence, the earlier maturation of the amygdala, which is involved in processing of emotions, and the more drawn-out development of the prefrontal cortex, provides an explanation of the difficulty adolescents have in controlling their emotions and their tendency to engage in risk taking (Steinberg, 2009).

- *Brain functioning occurs along specific pathways and involves integration of function.* According to leading experts Kurt Fischer and Mary Helen Immordino-Yang (2008),

    One of the lessons of educational neuroscience, even at this early point in its development, is that children learn along specific pathways, but they do not act or think in compartments. . . . On the one hand, they develop their learning along specific pathways defined by particular content, such as mathematics or history, but on the other hand they make connections between those pathways.

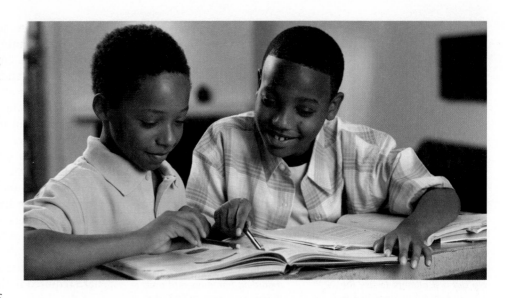

Reading is an excellent example of how brain functioning occurs along specific pathways and is integrated (Goswami, 2011). Consider a child who is asked by a teacher to read aloud to the class. Input from the child's eyes is transmitted to the child's brain, then passed through many brain systems, which translate the patterns of black and white into codes for letters, words, and associations. The output occurs in the form of messages to the child's lips and tongue. The child's own gift of speech is possible because brain systems are organized in ways that permit language processing.

These conclusions suggest that education throughout the childhood and adolescent years can benefit children's and adolescents' learning and cognitive development (Howard-Jones, 2010; Nelson, 2011). Where appropriate throughout the rest of the book, we will describe research on the development of the brain and children's education.

**schemas** In Piaget's theory, actions or mental representations that organize knowledge.

## PIAGET'S THEORY

Poet Noah Perry once asked, "Who knows the thoughts of a child?" More than anyone, the famous Swiss psychologist Jean Piaget (1896–1980) knew.

**Cognitive Processes**    What processes do children use as they construct their knowledge of the world? Piaget stressed that these processes are especially important in this regard: schemas, assimilation and accommodation, organization, and equilibration.

**Schemas**    Piaget (1954) said that as the child seeks to construct an understanding of the world, the developing brain creates **schemas.** These are actions or mental representations that organize knowledge. In Piaget's theory, *behavioral schemas* (physical activities) characterize infancy, and *mental schemas* (cognitive activities) develop in childhood. A baby's schemas are structured by simple actions that can be performed on objects, such as sucking, looking, and grasping. Older children have schemas that include strategies and plans for solving problems. For example, a 6-year-old might have a schema that involves the strategy of classifying objects by size, shape, or color. By the time we have reached adulthood, we have constructed an enormous number of diverse schemas, ranging from how to drive a car, to how to balance a budget, to the concept of fairness.

**Assimilation and Accommodation**    To explain how children use and adapt their schemas, Piaget offered two concepts: assimilation and accommodation.

*What are some applications of research on the brain's development to children's and adolescents' education?*

Assimilation occurs when people incorporate new information into their existing schematic knowledge. *How might this 8-year-old girl first attempt to use the hammer and nail, based on her preexisting schematic knowledge about these objects?*

Accommodation occurs when people adjust their knowledge schemas to new information. *How might the girl adjust her schemas regarding hammers and nails during her successful effort to hang the picture?*

FIGURE **2.8**  ASSIMILATION AND ACCOMMODATION

**assimilation** Piagetian concept of the incorporation of new information into existing knowledge (schemas).

**accommodation** Piagetian concept of adjusting schemas to fit new information and experiences.

**organization** Piaget's concept of grouping isolated behaviors into a higher-order, more smoothly functioning cognitive system; the grouping or arranging of items into categories.

**equilibration** A mechanism that Piaget proposed to explain how children shift from one stage of thought to the next. The shift occurs as children experience cognitive conflict, or disequilibrium, in trying to understand the world. Eventually, they resolve the conflict and reach a balance, or equilibrium, of thought.

**Assimilation** occurs when children incorporate new information into their existing schemas. **Accommodation** occurs when children adjust their schemas to fit new information and experiences.

Consider an 8-year-old girl who is given a hammer and nail to hang a picture on the wall. She has never used a hammer, but from observing others do this she realizes that a hammer is an object to be held, that it is swung by the handle to hit the nail, and that it usually is swung a number of times. Recognizing each of these things, she fits her behavior into this schema she already has (assimilation). But the hammer is heavy, so she holds it near the top. She swings too hard and the nail bends, so she adjusts the pressure of her strikes. These adjustments reflect her ability to slightly alter her conception of the world (accommodation). Just as both assimilation and accommodation are required in this example, so are they required in many of the child's thinking challenges (see Figure 2.8).

*Organization*  To make sense out of their world, said Piaget, children cognitively organize their experiences. **Organization** in Piaget's theory is the grouping of isolated behaviors and thoughts into a higher-order system. Continual refinement of this organization is an inherent part of development. A boy with only a vague idea about how to use a hammer also may have a vague idea about how to use other tools. After learning how to use each one, he relates these uses, organizing his knowledge.

*Equilibration and Stages of Development*  **Equilibration** is a mechanism that Piaget proposed to explain how children shift from one stage of thought to the next. The shift occurs as children experience cognitive conflict, or *disequilibrium,* in trying to understand the world. Eventually, they resolve the conflict and reach a balance, or *equilibrium,* of thought. Piaget pointed out that there is considerable movement between states of cognitive equilibrium and disequilibrium as assimilation and accommodation work in concert to produce cognitive change. For example, if a child believes that the amount of a liquid changes simply because the liquid is poured into a container with a different shape—for instance, from a container that is short and wide into a container that is tall and narrow—she might be puzzled by such issues as where the "extra" liquid came from and whether there is actually more liquid to drink. The child will eventually resolve these puzzles as her thought becomes more advanced. In the everyday world, the child is constantly faced with such counterexamples and inconsistencies.

Assimilation and accommodation always take the child to a higher ground. For Piaget, the motivation for change is an internal search for equilibrium. As old schemas are adjusted and new schemas are developed, the child organizes and reorganizes the old and new schemas. Eventually, the organization is fundamentally different from the old organization; it is a new way of thinking.

Thus, the result of these processes, according to Piaget, is that individuals go through four stages of development. A different way of understanding the world makes one stage more advanced than another. Cognition is *qualitatively* different in one stage compared with another. In other words, the way children reason at one stage is different from the way they reason at another stage.

**Piagetian Stages**  Each of Piaget's stages is age-related and consists of distinct ways of thinking. Piaget proposed four stages of cognitive development: sensorimotor, preoperational, concrete operational, and formal operational (see Figure 2.9).

**Sensorimotor Stage**

The infant constructs an understanding of the world by coordinating sensory experiences with physical actions. An infant progresses from reflexive, instinctual action at birth to the beginning of symbolic thought toward the end of the stage.

**Birth to 2 Years of Age**

**Preoperational Stage**

The child begins to represent the world with words and images. These words and images reflect increased symbolic thinking and go beyond the connection of sensory information and physical action.

**2 to 7 Years of Age**

**Concrete Operational Stage**

The child can now reason logically about concrete events and classify objects into different sets.

**7 to 11 Years of Age**

**Formal Operational Stage**

The adolescent reasons in more abstract, idealistic, and logical ways.

**11 Years of Age Through Adulthood**

FIGURE **2.9** PIAGET'S FOUR STAGES OF COGNITIVE DEVELOPMENT

**The Sensorimotor Stage**   The **sensorimotor stage,** which lasts from birth to about 2 years of age, is the first Piagetian stage. In this stage, infants construct an understanding of the world by coordinating their sensory experiences (such as seeing and hearing) with their motor actions (reaching, touching)—hence the term sensorimotor. At the beginning of this stage, infants show little more than reflexive patterns to adapt to the world. By the end of the stage, they display far more complex sensorimotor patterns.

DEVELOPMENT

**The Preoperational Stage**   The **preoperational stage** is the second Piagetian stage. Lasting approximately from about 2 to 7 years of age, it is more symbolic than sensorimotor thought but does not involve operational thought. However, it is egocentric and intuitive rather than logical.

Preoperational thought can be subdivided into two substages: symbolic function and intuitive thought. The **symbolic function substage** occurs roughly between 2 and 4 years of age. In this substage, the young child gains the ability to represent mentally an object that is not present. This stretches the child's mental world to new dimensions. Expanded use of language and the emergence of pretend play are other examples of an increase in symbolic thought during this early childhood substage. Young children begin to use scribbled designs to represent people, houses, cars, clouds, and many other aspects of the world. Possibly because young children are not very concerned about reality, their drawings are fanciful and inventive (Winner, 1986). One 3½ year-old looked at the scribble he had just drawn and described it as a pelican kissing a seal (see Figure 2.10a). In the elementary school years, children's drawings become more realistic, neat, and precise (see Figure 2.10b).

Even though young children make distinctive progress in this substage, their preoperational thought still has an important limitation: egocentrism. *Egocentrism is the inability to distinguish between one's own perspective and someone else's*

**sensorimotor stage**   The first Piagetian stage, lasting from birth to about 2 years of age, in which infants construct an understanding of the world by coordinating sensory experiences with motor actions.

**preoperational stage**   The second Piagetian stage, lasting from about 2 to 7 years of age, symbolic thought increases, but operational thought is not yet present.

**symbolic function substage**   The first substage of preoperational thought, occurring between about 2 to 4 years of age; the ability to represent an object not present develops and symbolic thinking increases; egocentrism is present.

(a)　　　　　　　(b)

**FIGURE 2.10** DEVELOPMENTAL CHANGES IN CHILDREN'S DRAWINGS

(*a*) A 3½-year-old's symbolic drawing. Halfway into this drawing, the 3½-year-old artist said it was "a pelican kissing a seal." (*b*) This 11-year-old's drawing is neater and more realistic but also less inventive.

*"I still don't have all the answers, but I'm beginning to ask the right questions."*

© Lee Lorenz/The New Yorker Collection/
www.cartoonbank.com

perspective. Piaget and Barbel Inhelder (1969) initially studied young children's egocentrism by devising the three-mountains task (see Figure 2.11). The child walks around the model of the mountains and becomes familiar with what the mountains look like from different perspectives. The child also can see that there are different objects on the mountains. The child then is seated on one side of the table on which the mountains are placed. The experimenter moves a doll to different locations around the table. At each location, the child is asked to select from a series of photos the one that most accurately reflects the view the doll is seeing. Children in the preoperational stage often pick the view that reflects where they are sitting rather than the doll's view.

What further cognitive changes take place in the preoperational stage? The **intuitive thought substage** is the second substage of preoperational thought, starting at about 4 years of age and lasting until about 7 years of age. At this substage, children begin to use primitive reasoning and want to know the answers to all sorts of questions. Piaget called this substage *intuitive* because the children seem so sure about their knowledge and understanding yet are unaware of how they know what they know. That is, they say they know something but know it without the use of rational thinking.

An example of young children's limitation in reasoning ability is the difficulty they have putting things into correct categories. Look at the collection of objects in Figure 2.12a. You would probably respond to the direction "Put the things together that you believe belong together" by grouping the objects by size and shape. Your sorting might look something like that shown in Figure 2.12b. Faced with a similar collection of objects that can be sorted on the basis of two or more properties, preoperational children seldom are capable of using these properties consistently to sort the objects into appropriate groupings.

Many of these preoperational examples show a characteristic of thought called **centration,** which involves focusing (or centering) attention on one characteristic to the exclusion of all others. Centration is most clearly present in preoperational children's lack of **conservation,** the idea that some characteristic of an object stays the same even though the object might change in appearance. For example, to adults it is obvious that a certain amount of liquid stays the same regardless of a container's

**Model of Mountains**

C

D　　　　　　　B

A
Child seated here

Photo 1
(View from A)

Photo 2
(View from B)

Photo 3
(View from C)

Photo 4
(View from D)

**FIGURE 2.11** THE THREE-MOUNTAINS TASK

The mountain model on the far left shows the child's perspective from view A, where he or she is sitting. The four squares represent photos showing the mountains from four different viewpoints of the model—A, B, C, and D. The experimenter asks the child to identify the photo in which the mountains look as they would from position B. To identify the photo correctly, the child has to take the perspective of a person sitting at spot B. Invariably, a child who thinks in a preoperational way cannot perform this task. When asked what a view of the mountains looks like from position B, the child selects Photo 1, taken from location A (the child's own view at the time) instead of Photo 2, the correct view.

FIGURE **2.12** ARRAYS

(*a*) A random array of objects. (*b*) An ordered array of objects.

**intuitive thought substage** The second substage of preoperational thought, lasting from about 4 to 7 years of age. Children begin to use primitive reasoning and want to know the answer to all sorts of questions. They seem so sure about their knowledge in this substage but are unaware of how they know what they know.

**centration** Focusing, or centering, attention on one characteristic to the exclusion of all others; characteristic of preoperational thinking.

**conservation** The idea that some characteristic of an object stays the same even though the object might change in appearance; a cognitive ability that develops in the concrete operational stage, according to Piaget.

shape. But this is not obvious at all to young children. Rather, they are struck by the height of the liquid in the container. In this type of conservation task (Piaget's most famous), a child is presented with two identical beakers, each filled to the same level with liquid (see Figure 2.13). The child is asked if the beakers have the same amount of liquid. The child usually says yes. Then the liquid from one beaker is poured into a third beaker, which is taller and thinner. The child now is asked if the amount of liquid in the tall, thin beaker is equal to the liquid that remains in the second original beaker. Children younger than 7 or 8 usually say no. They justify their answer

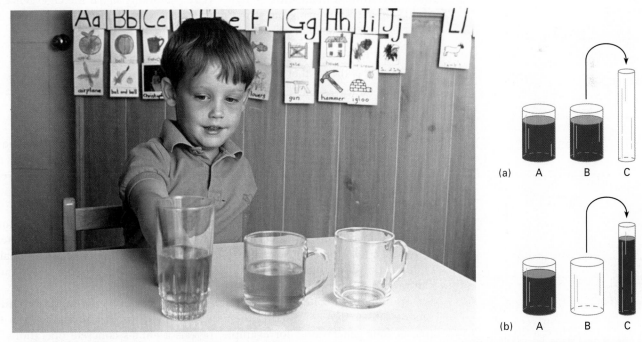

## FIGURE **2.13** PIAGET'S CONSERVATION TASK

The beaker test is a well-known Piagetian test to determine whether a child can think operationally—that is, can mentally reverse actions and show conservation of the substance. (*a*) Two identical beakers are presented to the child. Then, the experimenter pours the liquid from B into C, which is taller and thinner than A or B. (*b*) The child is asked if these beakers (A and C) have the same amount of liquid. The preoperational child says "no." When asked to point to the beaker that has more liquid, the preoperational child points to the tall, thin beaker.

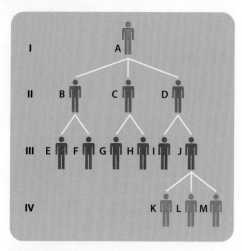

**FIGURE 2.14** CLASSIFICATION: AN IMPORTANT ABILITY IN CONCRETE OPERATIONAL THOUGHT

A family tree of four generations (*I to IV*): The preoperational child has trouble classifying the members of the four generations; the concrete operational child can classify the members vertically, horizontally, and obliquely (up and down and across). For example, the concrete operational child understands that a family member can be a son, a brother, and a father, all at the same time.

**concrete operational stage** Piaget's third cognitive developmental stage, occurring between about 7 to 11 years of age. At this stage, the child thinks operationally, and logical reasoning replaces intuitive thought but only in concrete situations; classification skills are present, but abstract problems present difficulties.

by referring to the differing height or width of the beakers. Older children usually answer yes. They justify their answers appropriately: If you poured the liquid back, the amount would still be the same.

In Piaget's view, failing the conservation of liquid task indicates that the child is at the preoperational stage of thinking. Passing the test suggests the child is at the *concrete operational stage* of thinking (discussed later on).

According to Piaget, preoperational children also cannot perform what he called *operations*—mental representations that are reversible. For example, in the beaker task, preschool children have difficulty understanding that reversing an action brings about the original conditions from which the action began. Two other examples should further help you understand Piaget's concepts of operations. A young child might know that $4 + 2 = 6$ but not understand that the reverse, $6 - 2 = 4$, is true. Or let's say a preschooler walks to his friend's house each day but always gets a ride home. If asked to walk home from his friend's house, he probably would reply that he didn't know the way because he never had walked home before.

Some developmentalists do not believe Piaget was entirely correct in his estimate of when conservation skills emerge. For example, Rochel Gelman (1969) trained preschool children to attend to relevant aspects of the conservation task. This improved their conservation skills.

Further, children show considerable variation in attaining conservation skills. Researchers have found that 50 percent of children develop conservation of mass at 6 to 9 years of age, 50 percent demonstrate conservation of length at 4 to 9 years of age, 50 percent show conservation of area at 7 to 9 years of age, and 50 percent of children don't attain conservation of weight until 8 to 10 years of age (Horowitz & others, 2005; Sroufe & others, 1992).

Yet another characteristic of preoperational children is that they ask a lot of questions. The barrage begins around age 3. By about 5, they have just about exhausted the adults around them with "Why?" "Why" questions signal the emergence of the child's interest in figuring out why things are the way they are. Following is a sampling of 4- to 6-year-olds' questions (Elkind, 1976):

> "What makes you grow up?"
> "Who was the mother when everybody was a baby?"
> "Why do leaves fall?"
> "Why does the sun shine?"

***The Concrete Operational Stage*** The **concrete operational stage,** the third Piagetian stage of cognitive development, lasts from about 7 to about 11 years of age. Concrete operational thought involves using operations. Logical reasoning replaces intuitive reasoning, but only in concrete situations. Classification skills are present, but abstract problems go unsolved.

A concrete operation is a reversible mental action pertaining to real, concrete objects. Concrete operations allow the child to coordinate several characteristics rather than focus on a single property of an object. At the concrete operational level, children can do mentally what they previously could do only physically, and they can reverse concrete operations.

An important concrete operation is classifying or dividing things into different sets or subsets and considering their interrelationships. Reasoning about a family tree of four generations, for example, reveals a child's concrete operational skills (Furth & Wachs, 1975). The family tree shown in Figure 2.14 suggests that the grandfather (A) has three children (B, C, and D), each of whom has two children (E through J), and one of these children (J) has three children (K, L, and M). Concrete operational thinkers understand the classification. For example, they can reason that person J can at the same time be father, brother, and grandson. A preoperational thinker cannot.

**TEACHING CONNECTIONS:** Best Practices
Strategies for Working with Preoperational Thinkers

As you have just read, young children think on a different plane than older children. Following are some effective strategies for advancing young children's thinking.

1. *Allow children to experiment freely with materials.* For example, give children various sizes of cups and a sand-box or water table. As they pour the sand or water back and forth between the cups, they will begin to understand the concepts of reversibility and conservation. If children are allowed to "play" with materials at a science table, they are likely to begin classifying objects.

2. *Ask children to make comparisons.* These might involve such concepts as bigger, taller, wider, heavier, and longer.

3. *Give children experience in ordering operations.* For example, have children line up in rows from tall to short and vice versa. Bring in various examples of animal and plant life cycles, such as several photographs of butterfly development or the sprouting of beans or kernels of corn.

4. *Have children draw scenes with perspective.* Encourage them to make the objects in their drawings appear to be at the same location as in the scene they are viewing. For example, if they see a horse at the end of a field, they should place the horse in the same location in the drawing.

5. *Construct an inclined plane or a hill.* Let children roll marbles of various sizes down the plane. Ask them to compare how quickly the different-size marbles reach the bottom. This should help them understand the concept of speed.

6. *Ask children to justify their answers when they draw conclusions.* For example, when they say that pouring a liquid from a short, wide container into a tall, thin container makes the liquid change in volume, ask, "Why do you think so?" or "How could you prove this to one of your friends?" This will help them to think more logically.

Some Piagetian tasks require children to reason about relations between classes. One such task is **seriation,** the concrete operation that involves ordering stimuli along some quantitative dimension (such as length). To see if students can serialize, a teacher might place eight sticks of different lengths in a haphazard way on a table. The teacher then asks the student to order the sticks by length. Many young children end up with two or three small groups of "big" sticks or "little" sticks rather than a correct ordering of all eight sticks. Another mistaken strategy they use is to evenly line up the tops of the sticks but ignore the bottoms. The concrete operational thinker simultaneously understands that each stick must be longer than the one that precedes it and shorter than the one that follows it.

**Transitivity** involves the ability to reason about and logically combine relationships. If a relation holds between a first object and a second object, and also holds between the second object and a third object, then it also holds between the first and third objects. For example, consider three sticks (A, B, and C) of differing lengths. A is the longest, B is intermediate in length, and C is the shortest. Does the child understand that if A is longer than B, and B is longer than C, then A is longer than C? In Piaget's theory, concrete operational thinkers do; preoperational thinkers do not.

***The Formal Operational Stage***   The **formal operational stage,** which emerges at about 11 to 15 years of age, is Piaget's fourth and final cognitive stage. At this stage, individuals move beyond reasoning only about concrete experiences and think in more abstract, idealistic, and logical ways.

The abstract quality of formal operational thinking is evident in verbal problem solving. The concrete operational thinker needs to see the concrete elements A, B, and C to make the logical inference that if A = B and B = C, then A = C. In contrast, the formal operational thinker can solve this problem when it is verbally presented.

Accompanying the abstract nature of formal operational thought are the abilities to idealize and imagine possibilities. At this stage, adolescents engage in extended

**seriation** A concrete operation that involves ordering stimuli along some quantitative dimension.

**transitivity** The ability to reason and logically combine relationships.

**formal operational stage** Piaget's fourth cognitive developmental stage, which emerges between about 11 and 15 years of age; thought is more abstract, idealistic, and logical in this stage.

## TEACHING CONNECTIONS: Best Practices
### Strategies for Working with Concrete Operational Thinkers

As you have just learned, for most of elementary school, children think at a concrete operational level, which is a different level than young children and adolescents. Following are some effective strategies for advancing children's thinking at the concrete operational level.

1. *Encourage students to discover concepts and principles.* Ask relevant questions about what is being studied to help them focus on some aspect of their learning. Refrain from telling students the answers to their questions outright. Try to get them to reach the answers through their own thinking.

2. *Involve children in operational tasks.* These include adding, subtracting, multiplying, dividing, ordering, seriating, and reversing. Make the reversibility of these operations explicit for the children. For instance, show them that subtracting is the reverse of adding. Use concrete materi-

als (i.e. manipulatives) for these tasks, possibly introducing math symbols later.

3. *Plan activities in which students practice the concept of ascending and descending classification hierarchies.* Have students list the following in order of size (such as largest to smallest): city of Atlanta, state of Georgia, country of United States, western hemisphere, and planet Earth.

4. *Include activities that require conservation of area, weight, and displaced volume.* Realize that there is considerable variation in children's attainment of conservation across different domains.

5. *Continue to ask students to justify their answers when they solve problems.* Help them to check the validity and accuracy of their conclusions.

speculation about the ideal qualities they desire in themselves and others. These idealistic thoughts can merge into fantasy. Many adolescents become impatient with their newfound ideals and the problems of how to live them out.

At the same time that adolescents are thinking more abstractly and idealistically, they also are beginning to think more logically. As formal operational thinkers, they think more like scientists. They devise plans to solve problems and systematically test

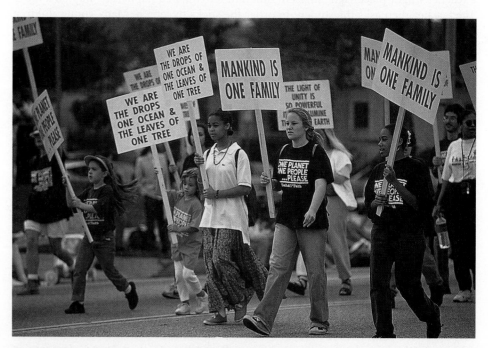

*Might adolescents' ability to reason hypothetically and to evaluate what is ideal versus what is real lead them to engage in demonstrations, such as this protest related to better ethnic relations? What other causes might be attractive to adolescents' newfound cognitive abilities of hypothetical-deductive reasoning and idealistic thinking?*

solutions. Piaget's term **hypothetical-deductive reasoning** embodies the concept that adolescents can develop hypotheses (best hunches) about ways to solve problems and systematically reach a conclusion. Formal operational thinkers test their hypotheses with judiciously chosen questions and tests. In contrast, concrete operational thinkers often fail to understand the relation between a hypothesis and a well-chosen test of it, stubbornly clinging to ideas that already have been discounted.

A form of egocentrism also emerges in adolescence (Elkind, 1978). *Adolescent egocentrism* is the heightened self-consciousness reflected in adolescents' beliefs that others are as interested in them as they themselves are. Adolescent egocentrism also includes a sense of personal uniqueness. It involves the desire to be noticed, visible, and "on stage."

Egocentrism is a normal adolescent occurrence, more common in the middle school than in high school years. However, for some individuals, adolescent egocentrism can contribute to reckless behavior, including suicidal thoughts, drug use, and failure to use contraceptives during sexual intercourse. Egocentricity may lead some adolescents to think that they are invulnerable.

However, reason to question the accuracy of the invulnerability aspect of the personal fable is provided by research that reveals many adolescents don't consider themselves invulnerable (Reyna & Rivers, 2008). Indeed, recent research suggests that rather than perceiving themselves to be invulnerable, most adolescents tend to portray themselves as vulnerable to experiencing a premature death (Fischoff & others, 2010).

I recently asked teachers to describe how they apply Piaget's cognitive stages to their classroom. Following are their comments:

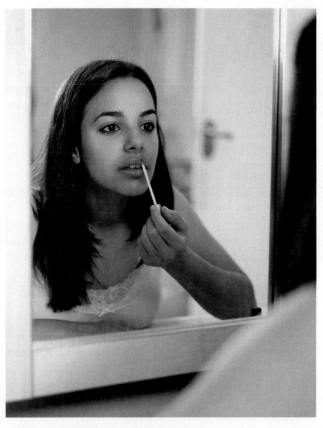

*What characterizes adolescent egocentrism?*

**EARLY CHILDHOOD**   When I teach songs to preschool students who are in the preoperational stage, I use PowerPoint slides projected on the board. The

slides have either all the words of the song included, or just key words. I also include corresponding clip art and pictures on the page borders.

RESEARCH

—**Connie Christy**, *Aynor Elementary School (Preschool Program)*

**ELEMENTARY SCHOOL: GRADES K–5**   In my second-grade science class, I use the following method to help students move from concrete thinking to more abstract

thinking: Children are given tasks and asked to discuss what happened (for example, the object sank or floated; when something is added to a system, the outcome changes). Then a theory or idea is developed from the actual observations. When children observe an occurrence and explain what was seen, they can more easily move from the concrete to the more abstract. Although these methods and others like it work well with my students, I need to repeat them often.

—**Janine Guida Poutre**, *Clinton Elementary School*

**MIDDLE SCHOOL: GRADES 6–8**   I challenge my seventh-grade students to share examples of how they've applied our classroom lessons to the real world. They can earn extra credit for doing so, but seem to care less about the points than they do about the opportunity to share their accomplishments. For example, after completing a unit on Progressivism, a student shared how he had gone online on his home computer and donated money to help Darfur refugees. He had previously planned to use this

**hypothetical-deductive reasoning** Piaget's formal operational concept that adolescents can develop hypotheses to solve problems and systematically reach (deduce) a conclusion.

## TEACHING CONNECTIONS: Best Practices
### Strategies for Working with Formal Operational Thinkers

As you have just learned, adolescents think on a different plane than children. Following are some effective strategies for working with adolescents who are formal operational thinkers.

1. *Realize that most adolescents are not full-fledged formal operational thinkers.* Thus, many of the teaching strategies discussed earlier regarding the education of concrete operational thinkers still apply to many young adolescents. As discussed in Through the Eyes of Teachers, Jerri Hall, a math teacher at Miller Magnet High School in Georgia, emphasizes that when a curriculum is too formal and too abstract, it will go over students' heads.

### THROUGH THE EYES OF TEACHERS
#### Piaget as a Guide

I use Piaget's developmental theory as a guide in helping children learn math. In the sixth, seventh, and eighth grades, children are moving from the concrete to the abstract stage in their cognitive processes; therefore, when I teach, I try to use different methods to aid my students to understand a concept. For example, I use fraction circles to help students understand how to add, subtract, multiply, and divide fractions, and the students are allowed to use these until they become proficient with the algorithms. I try to incorporate hands-on experiences in which students discover the rules themselves, rather than just teaching the methods and having the students

practice them with drill. It is extremely important for students to understand the why behind a mathematical rule so they can better understand the concept.

2. *Propose a problem and invite students to form hypotheses about how to solve it.* For example, a teacher might say, "Imagine that a girl has no friends. What should she do?"

3. *Present a problem and suggest several ways it might be approached.* Then ask questions that stimulate students to evaluate the approaches. For example, describe several ways to investigate a robbery, and ask students to evaluate which way is best and why.

4. *Demonstrate how to conduct experiments that require the separation and control of variables. Later ask students to conduct their own experiments.* These might involve science concepts or simple student-generated research questions, such as "which chewing gum retains its flavor the longest?"

5. *Encourage students to create hierarchical outlines when you ask them to write papers.* Make sure they understand how to organize their writing in terms of general and specific points. The abstractness of formal operational thinking also means that teachers with students at this level can encourage them to use metaphors.

money to buy himself a new guitar. This student took the theory of social activism from the Progressive era 100 years ago and applied it to his life today. This student's actions clearly demonstrate Piaget's formal operational stage in action.

—**Mark Fodness,** *Bemidji Middle School*

**HIGH SCHOOL: GRADES 9–12**   My high school art students take part in creativity competitions in which they build, create, explore, problem-solve, and perform

solutions to challenges presented to them. The competition—Destination Imagination—has challenged my students to brainstorm ideas and solutions to seemingly impossible tasks. As a result of their participation in this event, they have won regional and state titles along with the world championship.

—**Dennis Peterson,** *Deer River High School*

TECHNOLOGY

**Piaget, Constructivism, and Technology**   Recall from Chapter 1 that the basic idea of *constructivism* is that students learn best when they are actively constructing information and knowledge. Piaget's theory is a strong constructivist view. Early in the application of technology to children's learning, Seymour Papert (1980), who studied with Piaget for five years, created the Logo programming language for

Children at a Computer Clubhouse, one of 100 Computer Clubhouses worldwide, that provides students from low-income communities opportunities to creatively use technology to explore their ideas and develop their skills.

*Source:* www.computerclubhouse.org/

computers that was based on Piaget's constructivist view. A small robot labeled the "Logo Turtle" guided children in constructing solutions to problems. Today, all sorts of robotic kits are available, as well as Scratch (http://scratch.mit.edu/), an online programming and communication space for children, LifeLong Kindergarten (http://llk.media.mit.edu/projects.php), which has a number of creative projects for students of varying ages, and the Computer Clubhouse (www.computerclubhouse.org/), an international consortium of computer clubs linked over the Internet for 10–18-year-olds from low-income communities, providing a creative and safe out-of-school learning environment with adult mentors. Many others claim constructivism as their foundation and are used in schools worldwide.

**Evaluating Piaget's Theory** What were Piaget's main contributions? Has his theory withstood the test of time?

*Contributions* Piaget is a giant in the field of developmental psychology. We owe to him the present field of children's cognitive development. We also owe to him a long list of masterful concepts, including assimilation and accommodation, object permanence, egocentrism, conservation, and hypothetical-deductive reasoning. Along with William James and John Dewey, Piaget contributed to the current vision of children as active, constructive thinkers (Miller, 2011).

Piaget was a genius when it came to observing children. His careful observations showed us inventive ways to discover how children act on and adapt to their world. His work revealed some important things to look for in cognitive development, such as the shift from preoperational to concrete operational thinking, and showed us how children need to make their experiences fit their schemas (cognitive frameworks) while simultaneously adapting their schemas to experience.

Piaget is shown here with his family. Piaget's careful observations of his three children—Lucienne, Laurent, and Jacqueline—contributed to the development of his cognitive theory.

Having an outstanding teacher and gaining a good education in the logic of science and mathematics are important cultural experiences that promote the development of operational thought. *Might Piaget have underestimated the roles of culture and schooling in children's cognitive development?*

**Criticisms** Piaget's theory has not gone unchallenged. Questions have been raised in the following areas:

- *Estimates of children's competence.* Some cognitive abilities emerge earlier than Piaget thought, others later (Carpenter, 2011). Conservation of number has been demonstrated as early as age 3, although Piaget did not think it emerged until 7. Young children are not as uniformly "pre-" this and "pre-" that (precausal, preoperational) as Piaget thought (Flavell, Miller, & Miller, 2002). Other cognitive abilities can emerge later than Piaget thought. Many adolescents still think in concrete operational ways or are just beginning to master formal operations (Kuhn, 2009).

- *Stages.* Piaget conceived of stages as unitary structures of thought. Some concrete operational concepts, however, do not appear at the same time. For example, children do not learn to conserve at the same time as they learn to cross-classify.

- *Training children to reason at a higher level.* Some children who are at one cognitive stage (such as preoperational) can be trained to reason at a higher cognitive stage (such as concrete operational). However, Piaget argued that such training is only superficial and ineffective unless the child is at a maturational transition point between the stages (Gelman & Opfer, 2004).

- *Culture and education.* Culture and education exert stronger influences on children's development than Piaget envisioned. For example, the age at which children acquire conservation skills is related to the extent to which their culture provides relevant practice (Cole, 2006). An outstanding teacher can guide students' learning experiences that will help them move to a higher cognitive stage.

Despite the criticisms, some developmental psychologists conclude that we should not throw out Piaget altogether (Miller, 2011). These **neo-Piagetians** argue that Piaget got some things right although his theory needs considerable revision. In their revision of Piaget, neo-Piagetians emphasize how children process information through attention, memory, and strategies (Case, 2000). They especially stress that a more accurate vision of children's thinking requires more knowledge of strategies, how fast and how automatically children process information, the particular cognitive task involved, and the division of cognitive problems into smaller, more precise steps (Morra & others, 2008).

Despite such problems, Piaget's theory is a very useful one. As we see next, there are many ways to apply his ideas to educating children.

## VYGOTSKY'S THEORY

In addition to Piaget's theory, another major developmental theory that focuses on children's cognition is Russian Lev Vygotsky's theory. In Vygotsky's theory children's cognitive development is shaped by the cultural context in which they live (Gauvain & Parke, 2010).

**The Zone of Proximal Development** Vygotsky's belief in the importance of social influences, especially instruction, on children's cognitive development is reflected in his concept of the zone of proximal development. **Zone of proximal development (ZPD)** is Vygotsky's term for the range of tasks that are too difficult for the child to master alone but that can be learned with guidance and assistance of adults or more-skilled children. Thus, the lower limit of the ZPD is the level of skill reached by the child working independently. The upper limit is the level of additional responsibility the child can accept with the assistance of an able instructor

---

**Thinking Back/Thinking Forward**

The information-processing approach emphasizes that children develop a gradually increasing capacity for processing information. Chapter 8, p. 254

DEVELOPMENT

**neo-Piagetians** Developmental psychologists who believe that Piaget got some things right but that his theory needs considerable revision; emphasize how to process information through attention, memory, and strategies.

**zone of proximal development (ZPD)** Vygotsky's term for the range of tasks that are too difficult for children to master alone but that can be mastered with guidance and assistance from adults or more-skilled children.

## TEACHING CONNECTIONS: Best Practices
### Strategies for Applying Piaget's Theory to Children's Education

Earlier in this chapter, you learned about applying Piaget's theory to teaching children at different stages of cognitive development. Following are five general strategies based on Piaget's theory for educating children.

1. *Take a constructivist approach.* In a constructivist approach, Piaget emphasized that children learn best when they are active and seek solutions for themselves. Piaget opposed teaching methods that treat children as passive receptacles. The educational implication of Piaget's view is that in all subjects students learn best by making discoveries, reflecting on them, and discussing them, rather than blindly imitating the teacher or doing things by rote.

2. *Facilitate rather than direct learning.* Effective teachers design situations that allow students to learn by doing. These situations promote students' thinking and discovery. Teachers listen, watch, and question students to help them gain better understanding. They ask relevant questions to stimulate students' thinking and ask them to explain their answers. As described in Through the Eyes of Teachers, Suzanne Ransleben creates imaginative classroom situations to facilitate students' learning.

## THROUGH THE EYES OF TEACHERS
### Stimulating Students' Thinking and Discovery

Suzanne Ransleben teaches ninth- and tenth-grade English in Corpus Christi, Texas. She designs classroom situations that stimulate students' reflective thinking and discovery.

Suzanne Ransleben, teaching English.

Suzanne created Grammar Football to make diagramming sentences more interesting for students and has students decipher song lyrics to help them better understand how to write poetry. When students first encounter Shakespeare, "they paint interpretations of their favorite line from *Romeo and Juliet*" (Source: Wong Briggs, 2004, p. 7D)

3. *Consider the child's knowledge and level of thinking.* Students do not come to class with empty heads. They have many ideas about the physical and natural world including concepts of space, time, quantity, and causality. These ideas differ from the ideas of adults. Teachers need to interpret what a student is saying and respond with discourse close to the student's level. Asking the children to do something for which they are not ready will not promote cognitive development. It will merely frustrate the children.

4. *Promote the student's intellectual health.* When Piaget came to lecture in the United States, he was asked, "What can I do to get my child to a higher cognitive stage sooner?" He was asked this question so often in the United States compared with other countries that he called it the American question. For Piaget, children's learning should occur naturally. Children should not be pushed and pressured into achieving too much too early in their development, before they are maturationally ready.

5. *Turn the classroom into a setting of exploration and discovery.* What do actual classrooms look like when the teachers adopt Piaget's views? Several first- and second-grade math classrooms provide some good examples (Kamii, 1985, 1989). The teachers emphasize students' own exploration and discovery. The classrooms are less structured than what we think of as a typical classroom. Workbooks and predetermined assignments are not used. Rather, the teachers observe the students' interests and natural participation in activities to determine what the course of learning will be. For example, a math lesson might be constructed around counting the day's lunch money or dividing supplies among students. Often games are prominently used in the classroom to stimulate mathematical thinking.

(see Figure 2.15). The ZPD captures the child's cognitive skills that are in the process of maturing and can be accomplished only with the assistance of a more-skilled person (Daniels, 2011).

Teaching in the ZPD reflects the concept of developmentally appropriate teaching we described earlier in the chapter. It involves being aware of "where students

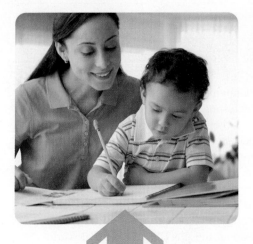

**Upper limit**

Level of additional responsibility
child can accept with assistance
of an able instructor

**Zone of proximal
development (ZPD)**

**Lower limit**

Level of problem solving
reached on these tasks by
child working alone

FIGURE **2.15** VYGOTSKY'S ZONE OF PROXIMAL DEVELOPMENT

Vygotsky's zone of proximal development has a lower limit and an upper limit. Tasks in the ZPD are too difficult for the child to perform alone. They require assistance from an adult or a more-skilled child. As children experience the verbal instruction or demonstration, they organize the information in their existing mental structures, so they can eventually perform the skill or task alone.

**scaffolding** A technique that involves changing the level of support for learning. A teacher or more-advanced peer adjusts the amount of guidance to fit the student's current performance.

are in the process of their development and taking advantage of their readiness. It is also about teaching to enable developmental readiness, not just waiting for students to be ready" (Horowitz & others, 2005, p. 105).

**Scaffolding** Closely linked to the idea of the ZPD is the concept of scaffolding. **Scaffolding** means changing the level of support. Over the course of a teaching session, a more-skilled person (a teacher or advanced peer) adjusts the amount of guidance to fit the child's current performance. When the student is learning a new task, the skilled person may use direct instruction. As the student's competence increases, less guidance is given. Scaffolding is often used to help students attain the upper limits of their ZPD.

Asking probing questions is an excellent way to scaffold students' learning and help them to develop more sophisticated thinking skills. A teacher might ask a student such questions as "What would an example of that be?" "Why do you think that is so?" "Now, what's the next thing you need to do?" and "How can you connect those?" Over time, students should begin internalizing these kinds of probes and improve monitoring their own work (Horowitz & others, 2005).

Many teachers who successfully use scaffolding circulate around the classroom, giving "just-in-time" assistance to individuals, or detecting a class-wide misconception and then leading a discussion to correct the problem. They also give "children time to grapple with problems" and guide them when they observe that the child can no longer make progress (Horowitz & others, 2005, pp. 106–107).

**Language and Thought** In Vygotksy's view, language plays an important role in a child's development (Gredler, 2009). According to Vygotsky, children use speech not only for social communication, but also to help them solve tasks. Vygotsky (1962) further argued that young children use language to plan, guide, and monitor their behavior. This use of language for self-regulation is called *private speech*. For example, young children talk aloud to themselves about such things as their toys and the tasks they are trying to complete. Thus, when working on a puzzle, a child might say, "This piece doesn't go; maybe I'll try that one." A few minutes later she utters, "This is hard." For Piaget private speech is egocentric and immature, but for Vygotsky it is an important tool of thought during the early childhood years (John-Steiner, 2007).

Vygotsky said that language and thought initially develop independently of each other and then merge. He emphasized that all mental functions have external, or social, origins. Children must use language to communicate with others before they can focus inward on their own thoughts. Children also must communicate externally and use language for a long period of time before they can make the transition from external to internal speech. This transition period occurs between 3 and 7 years of age and involves talking to oneself. After a while, the self-talk becomes second nature to children, and they can act without verbalizing. When this occurs, children have internalized their egocentric speech in the form of *inner speech*, which becomes their thoughts.

Vygotsky argued that children who use private speech are more socially competent than those who don't. He believed that private speech represents an early transition in becoming more socially communicative. For Vygotsky, when young children talk to themselves, they are using language to govern their behavior and guide themselves.

Piaget held that self-talk is egocentric and reflects immaturity. However, researchers have found support for Vygotsky's view that private speech plays a positive role in children's development (Winsler, Carlton, & Barry, 2000). Researchers have revealed that children use private speech more when tasks are difficult, after they make mistakes, and when they are not sure how to proceed (Berk, 1994). They also have found that children who use private speech are more attentive and improve their performance more than children who do not use private speech (Berk & Spuhl, 1995).

I recently asked teachers how they apply Vygotsky's theory to their classroom. After reading their responses about Vygotsky, you might want to compare these responses with teachers' responses about how they apply Piaget's theory in their classroom that were described earlier in the chapter.

**EARLY CHILDHOOD**   In teaching music to preschoolers, I use private speech to help children learn unfamiliar rhythms. When my young students are learning a new

rhythm pattern on the African drums, for example, they don't count the eighth and quarter notes, because that is too difficult. Instead, I suggest certain words for them to repeat in rhythmic patterns to learn the beat, or they can come up with their own words to match the new rhythm. My guidance allows children to improve their understanding of musical rhythm.

—**CONNIE CHRISTY,** *Aynor Elementary School (Preschool Program)*

**ELEMENTARY SCHOOL: GRADES K–5**   One way to maximize students' zone of proximal development is by flexible grouping. In flexible grouping, groups change

often based on need, interest, and so on. I use different group styles—for example, whole class, small group, homogenous groups, and heterogeneous groups. Variance in group members and group styles allows all students to be instructed within their zone of proximal development. This may be on grade level in one area, above grade level in another, and below grade level in still another. The point is that flexible grouping allows me to give students of varying levels the instruction necessary to learn.

—**SUSAN FROELICH,** *Clinton Elementary School*

**MIDDLE SCHOOL: GRADES 6–8**   When I teach my students a new skill, it is important that I stay close to them while they are working. This way if they need my

assistance, I am there to help them master the new skill with some guidance. This practice works especially well when we are working on multistep projects.

—**CASEY MAASS,** *Edison Middle School*

**HIGH SCHOOL: GRADES 9–12**   Advanced art students and independent-study students have always been an active part of my classroom, especially when it comes

to helping other students maximize their zone of proximal development (and grow in their own skills as artists as well). In my ceramics class, for example, I have several advanced students—who have especially strong knowledge and skills on the ceramic wheel—help my first-year students, who are attempting to work on the wheel for the first time. This additional assistance from the advanced students allows me to help other students who need further instruction.

—**DENNIS PETERSON,** *Deer River High School*

We have discussed a number of ideas about both Piaget's and Vygotsky's theories and how the theories can be applied to children's education. To reflect on how you might apply their theories to your own classroom, complete Self-Assessment 2.1.

**Evaluating Vygotsky's Theory**   How does Vygotsky's theory compare with Piaget's? Although both theories are constructivist, Vygotsky's is a **social constructivist approach,** which emphasizes the  social contexts of learning and the construction of knowledge through social interaction.

**Thinking Back/Thinking Forward**

Collaborative learning and cognitive apprenticeships reflect Vygotsky's social constructivist approach. Chapter 10, p. 336

**social constructivist approach** Emphasizes the social contexts of learning and that knowledge is mutually built and constructed; Vygotsky's theory exemplifies this approach.

# SELF-ASSESSMENT 2.1
## Applying Piaget and Vygotsky in My Classroom

The grade level at which I plan to teach is _____

## PIAGET

The Piagetian stage of the majority of children in my classroom will likely be _____

The Piagetian concepts that should help me the most in understanding and teaching children at this grade level are

| Concept | Example |
|---------|---------|
| _____ | _____ |
| _____ | _____ |
| _____ | _____ |

## VYGOTSKY

The concepts in Vygotsky's theory that should help me the most in understanding and teaching children at this grade level are

| Concept | Example |
|---------|---------|
| _____ | _____ |
| _____ | _____ |
| _____ | _____ |

---

## TEACHING CONNECTIONS: Best Practices
### Strategies for Applying Vygotsky's Theory to Children's Education

Vygotsky's theory has been embraced by many teachers and has been successfully applied to education. Here are some ways Vygotsky's theory can be incorporated in classrooms:

1. *Assess the child's ZPD.* Like Piaget, Vygotsky did not think that formal, standardized tests are the best way to assess children's learning. Rather, Vygotsky argued that assessment should focus on determining the child's ZPD. The skilled helper presents the child with tasks of varying difficulty to determine the best level at which to begin instruction.

2. *Use the child's ZPD in teaching.* Teaching should begin toward the zone's upper limit, so that the child can reach the goal with help and move to a higher level of skill and knowledge. Offer just enough assistance. You might ask, "What can I do to help you?" Or simply observe the child's intentions and attempts and provide support when needed. When the child hesitates, offer encouragement. And encourage the child to practice the skill. You may watch and appreciate the child's practice or offer support when the child forgets what to do. In Through the Eyes of Teachers, you can read about John Mahoney's teaching practices that reflect Vygotsky's emphasis on the importance of the ZPD. In contrast to in-class work, homework should be aimed at the zone's lower limit so that the child will be capable of completing it. Keeping instruction in the ZPD is likely to require differentiation as children's zones of proximal development are not uniform.

### THROUGH THE EYES OF TEACHERS
**Using Dialogue and Reframing Concepts to Find the Zone of Proximal Development**

John Mahoney teaches mathematics at a high school in Washington, D.C. In Mahoney's view, guiding students' success in math is both collaborative and individual. He encourages dialogue about math during which he reframes concepts that help students subsequently solve problems on their own. Mahoney also never gives students the answers to math problems. As one student commented, "He's going to make you think." His tests always include a problem that students have not seen but have enough knowledge to figure out the problem's solution. (Source: Wong Briggs, 2005.)

John Mahoney, teaching math.

3. *Use more-skilled peers as teachers.* Remember that it is not just adults that are important in helping children learn. Children also benefit from the support and guidance of more-skilled children (Gredler, 2009). For example, pair a child who is just beginning to read with one who is a more advanced reader. It is also desirable to use cross-age tutoring.

4. *Monitor and encourage children's use of private speech.* Be aware of the developmental change from externally talking to oneself when solving a problem during the preschool years to privately talking to oneself in the early elementary school years. In the elementary school years, encourage children to internalize and self-regulate their talk to themselves.

5. *Place instruction in a meaningful context.* Educators today are moving away from abstract presentations of material, instead providing students with opportunities to experience learning in real-world settings. For example, instead of just memorizing math formulas, students work on math problems with real-world implications.

6. *Transform the classroom with Vygotskian ideas.* Tools of the Mind is a curriculum that is grounded in Vygotsky's (1962) theory with special attention given to cultural tools and developing self-regulation, the ZPD, scaffolding, private speech, shared activity, and play as important activity (Hyson, Copple, & Jones, 2006). Figure 2.16 illustrates how scaffolding was used in Tools of the Mind to improve a young child's writing skills. The Tools of the Mind curriculum was created by Elena Bodrova and Deborah Leong (2007) and has been implemented in more than 200 classrooms. Most of the children in the Tools of the Mind programs are at risk because of their living circumstances, which in many instances involve poverty and other difficult conditions such as being homeless and having parents with drug problems.

One study assessed the effects of the Tools of the Mind curriculum on at-risk preschool children (Diamond & others, 2007). The results indicated that the Tools of the Mind curriculum improved the self-regulatory and cognitive control skills (such as resisting distractions and temptations) of the at-risk children. Other research on the Tools of the Mind curriculum also has found that it improves young children's cognitive skills (Saifer, 2007).

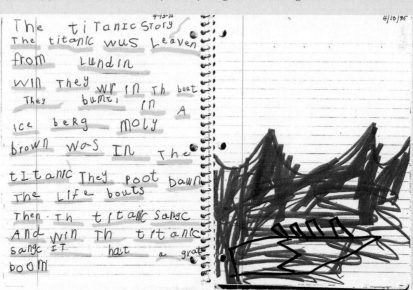

RESEARCH

(a) Five-year-old Aaron's independent journal writing prior to the scaffolded writing technique.

(b) Aaron's journal two months after using the scaffolded writing technique.

**FIGURE 2.16** WRITING PROGRESS OF A 5-YEAR-OLD BOY OVER TWO MONTHS USING THE SCAFFOLDING WRITING PROCESS IN TOOLS OF THE MIND

| | Vygotsky | Piaget |
|---|---|---|
| **Sociocultural Context** | Strong emphasis | Little emphasis |
| **Constructivism** | Social constructivist | Cognitive constructivist |
| **Stages** | No general stages of development proposed | Strong emphasis on stages (sensorimotor, preoperational, concrete operational, and formal operational) |
| **Key Processes** | Zone of proximal development, language, dialogue, tools of the culture | Schema, assimilation, accommodation, operations, conservation, classification |
| **Role of Language** | A major role; language plays a powerful role in shaping thought | Language has a minimal role; cognition primarily directs language |
| **View on Education** | Education plays a central role, helping children learn the tools of the culture | Education merely refines the child's cognitive skills that have already emerged |
| **Teaching Implications** | Teacher is a facilitator and guide, not a director; establish many opportunities for children to learn with the teacher and more-skilled peers | Also views teacher as a facilitator and guide, not a director; provide support for children to explore their world and discover knowledge |

FIGURE **2.17** COMPARISON OF VYGOTSKY'S AND PIAGET'S THEORIES

In moving from Piaget to Vygotsky, the conceptual shift is from the individual to collaboration, social interaction, and sociocultural activity (Gauvain & Parke, 2010). The endpoint of cognitive development for Piaget is formal operational thought. For Vygotsky, the endpoint can differ, depending on which skills are considered to be the most important in a particular culture (Daniels, 2011). For Piaget, children construct knowledge by transforming, organizing, and reorganizing previous knowledge. For Vygotsky, children construct knowledge through social interaction. The implication of Piaget's theory for teaching is that children need support to explore their world and discover knowledge. The main implication of Vygotsky's theory for teaching is that students need many opportunities to learn with the teacher and more-skilled peers (Rogoff & others, 2007). In both Piaget's and Vygotsky's theories, teachers serve as facilitators and guides, rather than as directors and molders of learning. Figure 2.17 compares Vygotsky's and Piaget's theories.

Criticisms of Vygotsky's theory also have surfaced. Some critics point out that Vygotsky was not specific enough about age-related changes (Gauvain, 2008). Another criticism focuses on Vygotsky not adequately describing how changes in socioemotional capabilities contribute to cognitive development (Gauvain, 2008). Yet another charge is that he overemphasized the role of language in thinking. Also, his emphasis on collaboration and guidance has potential pitfalls. Might facilitators be too helpful in some cases, as when a parent becomes too overbearing and controlling? Further, some children might become lazy and expect help when they might have done something on their own.

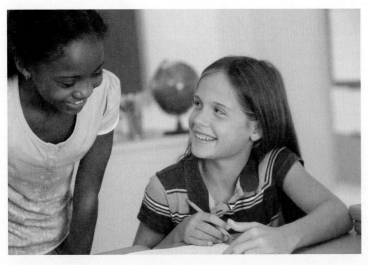

*What are some contributions and criticisms of Vygotsky's theory?*

In our coverage of cognitive development, we have focused on the views of two giants in the field: Piaget and Vygotsky. However, information processing also has emerged as an important perspective in understanding children's cognitive development (Martinez, 2010). It emphasizes how information enters the mind, how it is stored and transformed, and how it is retrieved to perform mental activities such as problem solving and reasoning. It also focuses on how automatically and quickly children process information. The subject of information processing is covered extensively in Chapters 8 and 9.

## Review, Reflect, and Practice

**②** Discuss the development of the brain and compare the cognitive developmental theories of Jean Piaget and Lev Vygotsky.

### REVIEW

- How does the brain develop, and what implications does this development have for children's education?
- What four main ideas did Piaget use to describe cognitive processes? What stages did he identify in children's cognitive development? What are some criticisms of his view?
- What is the nature of Vygotsky's theory? How can Vygotsky's theory be applied to education and his theory compared to Piaget's? What is a criticism of Vygotsky's theory?

### REFLECT

- Do you consider yourself to be a formal operational thinker? Do you still sometimes feel like a concrete operational thinker? Give examples.

### PRAXIS™ PRACTICE

1. Sander is a 16-year-old boy who takes many risks, such as driving fast and drinking while driving. Recent research on the brain indicates that a likely reason for this risk-taking behavior is that Sander's
   a. hippocampus is damaged.
   b. prefrontal cortex is still developing.
   c. brain lateralization is incomplete.
   d. myelination is complete.

2. Mrs. Gonzales teaches first grade. Which of her following strategies would Piaget most likely endorse?
   a. demonstrating how to perform a math operation and having students imitate her
   b. creating flash cards to teach vocabulary
   c. using a standardized test to assess students' reading skills
   d. designing contexts that promote student's thinking and discovery

3. Mr. Gould's fourth-grade students are learning about the relations among percentages, decimals, and fractions. He distributes an assignment requiring students to convert fractions to decimals and then to percentages. Christopher can do this assignment without help from Mr. Gould or his classmates. What would Vygotsky say about this task for Christopher?
   a. This task is appropriate for Christopher because it is within his zone of proximal development.
   b. This task is inappropriate for Christopher because it is above his zone of proximal development.
   c. This task is inappropriate for Christopher because it is below his zone of proximal development.
   d. This task is inappropriate for Christopher because it is within his zone of proximal development.

*Please see the answer key at the end of the book.*

## 3  LANGUAGE DEVELOPMENT

| What Is Language? | Biological and Environmental Influences | Language Development |

Think how important language is in children's everyday lives. They need language to speak with others, listen to others, read, and write. Their language enables them to describe past events in detail and to plan for the future. Language lets us pass down information from one generation to the next and create a rich cultural heritage.

## WHAT IS LANGUAGE?

**Language** is a form of communication—whether spoken, written, or signed—that is based on a system of symbols. Language consists of the words used by a community (vocabulary) and the rules for varying and combining them (grammar and syntax).

All human languages have some common characteristics (Berko Gleason, 2009). These include infinite generativity and organizational rules. *Infinite generativity* is the ability to produce an endless number of meaningful sentences using a finite set of words and rules.

When we say "rules," we mean that language is orderly and that rules describe the way language works (Berko Gleason & Ratner, 2009). Language involves five systems of rules: phonology, morphology, syntax, semantics, and pragmatics.

**Phonology**   Every language is made up of basic sounds. **Phonology** is the sound system of a language, including the sounds used and how they may be combined (Stoel-Gammon & Sosa, 2010). For example, English has the sounds *sp, ba,* and *ar,* but the sound sequences *zx* and *qp* do not occur.

A *phoneme* is the basic unit of sound in a language; it is the smallest unit of sound that affects meaning. A good example of a phoneme in English is /k/, the sound represented by the letter *k* in the word *ski* and the letter *c* in the word *cat.* The /k/ sound is slightly different in these two words, and in some languages such as Arabic these two sounds are separate phonemes.

**Morphology**   The **morphology** of a language refers to the units of meaning involved in word formation. A *morpheme* is a minimal unit of meaning; it is a word or a part of a word that cannot be broken into smaller meaningful parts. Every word in the English language is made up of one or more morphemes. Some words consist of a single morpheme (for example, *help*), whereas others are made up of more than one morpheme (for example, *helper,* which has two morphemes, *help* + *er,* with the morpheme *-er* meaning "one who"—in this case "one who helps"). Thus, not all morphemes are words by themselves; for example, *pre-, -tion,* and *-ing* are morphemes.

Just as the rules that govern phonology describe the sound sequences that can occur in a language, the rules of morphology describe the way meaningful units (morphemes) can be combined in words (Tager-Flusberg & Zukowski, 2009). Morphemes have many jobs in grammar, such as marking tense (for example, *she walks* versus *she walked*) and number (*she walks* versus *they walk*).

**Syntax**   The way words are combined to form acceptable phrases and sentences is their **syntax** (Naigles & Swensen, 2010). If someone says to you, "Bob slugged Tom" or "Bob was slugged by Tom," you know who did the slugging and who was slugged in each case because you have a syntactic understanding of these sentence structures. You also understand that the sentence "You didn't stay, did you?" is a grammatical sentence but that "You didn't stay, didn't you?" is unacceptable and ambiguous.

**language** A form of communication, whether spoken, written, or signed, that is based on a system of symbols.

**phonology** A language's sound system.

**morphology** Refers to the units of meaning involved in word formation.

**syntax** The ways that words must be combined to form acceptable phrases and sentences.

**Semantics**    The term **semantics** refers to the meaning of words and sentences. Every word has a set of semantic features, or required attributes related to meaning (Diesendruck, 2010). *Girl* and *women,* for example, share many semantic features, but they differ semantically in regard to age.

Words have semantic restrictions on how they can be used in sentences (Li, 2009). The sentence, *The bicycle talked the boy into buying a candy bar,* is syntactically correct but semantically incorrect. The sentence violates our semantic knowledge that bicycles don't talk.

**Pragmatics**    A final set of language rules involves **pragmatics,** the appropriate use of language in different contexts. Pragmatics covers a lot of territory. When you take turns speaking in a discussion, you are demonstrating knowledge of pragmatics (Siegal & Surian, 2010). You also apply the pragmatics of English when you use polite language in appropriate situations (for example, when talking to a teacher) or tell stories that are interesting.

Pragmatic rules can be complex, and they differ from one culture to another (Bryant, 2009). If you were to study the Japanese language, you would come face-to-face with countless pragmatic rules about conversing with individuals of various social levels and various relationships to you.

## BIOLOGICAL AND ENVIRONMENTAL INFLUENCES

Famous linguist Noam Chomsky (1957) argued that humans are prewired to learn language at a certain time and in a certain way. Some language scholars view the remarkable similarities in how children acquire language all over the world despite the vast variation in language input they receive as strong evidence that language has a biological basis.

Despite the influence of biology, children clearly do not learn language in a social vacuum (Gathercole & Hoff, 2010). Children are neither exclusively biological linguists nor exclusively social architects of language (Evans, 2009; Shatz, 2010). No matter how long you converse with a dog, it won't learn to talk, because it doesn't have the human child's biological capacity for language. Unfortunately, though, some children fail to develop good language skills even in the presence of very good role models and interaction. An interactionist view emphasizes the contributions of both biology and experience in language development. That is, children are biologically prepared to learn language as they and their caregivers interact.

In or out of school, encouragement of language development, not drill and practice, is the key (Sachs, 2009). Language development is not simply a matter of being rewarded for saying things correctly and imitating a speaker. Children benefit when their parents and teachers actively engage them in conversation, ask them questions, and emphasize interactive rather than directive language.

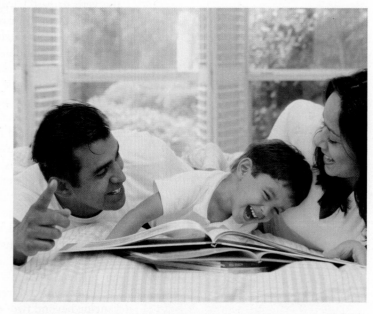

Both biological and environmental influences play important roles in children's language development.

## LANGUAGE DEVELOPMENT

What are some of the key developmental milestones in language development? We will examine these milestones in infancy, early childhood, middle and late childhood, and adolescence.

**Infancy**    Language acquisition advances past a number of milestones in infancy (Sachs, 2009). Because the main focus of this text is on children and adolescents

DEVELOPMENT

**semantics** The meaning of words and sentences.

**pragmatics** The appropriate use of language in different contexts.

rather than infants, we will describe only some of the many language milestones in infancy. Babbling occurs in the middle of the first year, and infants usually utter their first word at about 10 to 13 months. By 18 to 24 months, infants usually have begun to string two words together. In this two-word stage, they quickly grasp the importance of language in communication, creating phrases such as "Book there," "My candy," "Mama walk," and "Give Papa."

**Early Childhood** As children leave the two-word stage, they move rather quickly into three-, four-, and five-word combinations. The transition from simple sentences expressing a single proposition to complex sentences begins between 2 and 3 years of age and continues into the elementary school years (Bloom, 1998).

*Rule Systems of Language* Let's explore the changes in the five rules systems we described earlier—phonology, morphology, syntax, semantics, and pragmatics—during early childhood. In terms of phonology, most preschool children gradually become sensitive to the sounds of spoken words (Stoel-Gammon & Sosa, 2010). They notice rhymes, enjoy poems, make up silly names for things by substituting one sound for another (such as *bubblegum, bubblebum, bubbleyum*), and clap along with each syllable in a phrase.

As they move beyond two-word utterances, there is clear evidence that children know morphological rules. Children begin using the plural and possessive forms of nouns (*dogs* and *dog's*); putting appropriate endings on verbs (*-s* when the subject is third-person singular, *-ed* for the past tense, and *-ing* for the present progressive tense); and using prepositions (*in* and *on*), articles (*a* and *the*), and various forms of the verb *to be* ("I *was going* to the store"). In fact, they *overgeneralize* these rules, applying them to words that do not follow the rules. For example, a preschool child might say "foots" instead of "feet" or "goed" instead of "went."

Children's understanding of morphological rules was the subject of a classic experiment by children's language researcher Jean Berko (1958). Berko presented preschool and first-grade children with cards like the one shown in Figure 2.18. Children were asked to look at the card while the experimenter read the words on it aloud. Then the children were asked to supply the missing word. This might sound easy, but Berko was interested not just in the children's ability to recall the right word but also in their ability to say it "correctly" with the ending that was dictated by morphological rules. *Wugs* is the correct response for the card in Figure 2.18. Although the children were not perfectly accurate, they were much better than chance would dictate. Moreover, they demonstrated their knowledge of morphological rules not only with the plural forms of nouns ("There are two wugs") but also with the possessive forms of nouns and with the third-person singular and past-tense forms of verbs. Berko's study demonstrated not only that the children relied on rules, but also that they had *abstracted* the rules from what they had heard and could apply them to novel situations.

Preschool children also learn and apply rules of syntax (Lidz, 2010). After advancing beyond two-word utterances, the child shows a growing mastery of complex rules for how words should be ordered. Consider *wh-* questions, such as "Where is Daddy going?" or "What is that boy doing?" To ask these questions properly, the child must know two important differences between *wh-* questions and affirmative statements (for instance, "Daddy is going to work" and "That boy is waiting on the school bus"). First, a *wh-* word must be added at the beginning of the sentence. Second, the auxiliary verb must be inverted—that is, exchanged with the subject of the sentence. Young children learn quite early where to put the *wh-* word, but they take much longer to learn the auxiliary-inversion rule. Thus, preschool children might ask, "Where Daddy is going?" and "What that boy is doing?"

The speaking vocabulary of a 6-year-old child ranges from 8,000 to 14,000 words. Assuming that word learning began when the child was 12 months old,

RESEARCH

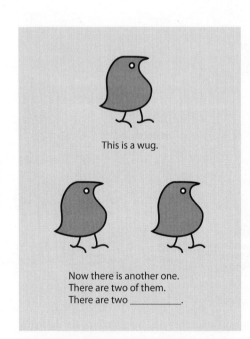

This is a wug.

Now there is another one.
There are two of them.
There are two _____.

**FIGURE 2.18** STIMULI IN BERKO'S STUDY OF YOUNG CHILDREN'S UNDERSTANDING OF MORPHOLOGICAL RULES

In Jean Berko's (1958) study, young children were presented cards such as this one with a "wug" on it. Then the children were asked to supply the missing word and say it correctly. "Wugs" is the correct response here.

this translates into a rate of five to eight new word meanings a day between the ages of 1 and 6.

What are some effective strategies for using technology to support children's vocabulary? Computers, of course, can be used in various strategies. CD-ROMs of stories, such as *Living Books*, can promote children's vocabulary development very effectively, especially when there is an option for students to find the meaning of unfamiliar words. Also, the program called Write: Outloud (2009) can help students build their vocabulary (www.donjohnston.com/products/write_outloud/index.html). Further, using the computer for listening to and watching stories can be part of a student's reading-center rotations, reading assignment, or an option during choice time. Learning new words can be enhanced if teachers plan a way for students to keep track of new words. For example, students can record new words in a portfolio for future reference.

TECHNOLOGY

Teachers also can create listening centers to support vocabulary development. Listening centers should include tape recorders, headphones, audiobooks, and corresponding literature. Audiobooks can be used to supplement printed materials, letting students enjoy the dramatization of stories and piquing their interest. Audiobooks may especially benefit students with special needs.

In addition to the remarkable advances young children make in semantics, substantial changes in pragmatics also occur during early childhood (Siegal & Surian, 2010). A 6-year-old is simply a much better conversationalist than a 2-year-old. What are some of the changes in pragmatics that are made in the preschool years? At about 3 years of age, children improve in their ability to talk about things that are not physically present. That is, they improve their command of the characteristic of language known as *displacement*. Children at this stage become increasingly removed from the "here and now" and are able to talk about things not physically present, as well as things that happened in the past or may happen in the future. Preschoolers can tell you what they want for lunch tomorrow, something that would not have been possible at the two-word stage in infancy. Preschool children also become increasingly able to talk in different ways to different people.

**Literacy in Early Childhood**    The concern about the ability of U.S. children to read and write has led to a careful examination of preschool and kindergarten children's experiences with the hope that a positive orientation toward reading and writing can be developed early in life (Otto, 2010). Indeed, early precursors of literacy and academic success include good language skills, phonological and syntactic knowledge, letter identification, and conceptual knowledge about print and its conventions and functions (Beatty & Pratt, 2011).

**Thinking Back/Thinking Forward**

Teachers can guide students in adopting a number of cognitive strategies for becoming better readers and writers. Chapter 11, p. 365

What should a literacy program for preschool children include? Instruction should be built on what children already know about oral language, reading, and writing. Parents and teachers also need to provide a supportive environment to help children develop literacy skills (Christie, Enz, & Vukelich, 2011; Tompkins, 2011). A recent study revealed that children's early home environment influenced their early language skills, which in turn predicted their readiness for school (Forget-Dubois & others, 2009). Another recent study found that literacy experiences (such as how often the child was read to), the quality of the mother's engagement with her child (such as attempts to cognitively stimulate the child) and provision of learning materials (such as age-appropriate learning materials and books) were important home literacy experiences in low-income families that were linked to the children's language development in positive ways (Rodriquez & others, 2009). In Chapter 11 we will further discuss many aspects of children's experiences that contribute to their literacy development.

RESEARCH

**Middle and Late Childhood**    Children gain new skills as they enter school that make it possible to learn to read and write. These include increased use of language

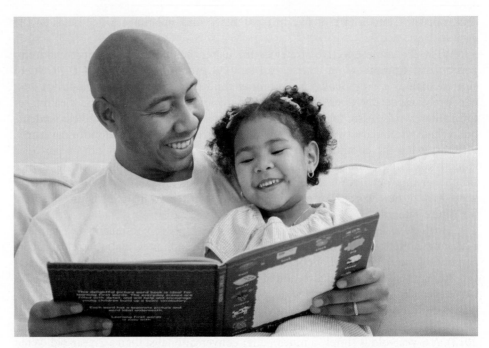

*What are some effective early literacy experiences that parents can provide young children?*

to talk about things that are not physically present, learning what a word is, and learning how to recognize and talk about sounds. They also learn the *alphabetic principle* that the letters of the alphabet represent sounds of the language.

Vocabulary development continues at a breathtaking pace for most children during the elementary school years (Pan & Uccelli, 2009). After five years of word learning, the 6-year-old child does not slow down. According to some estimates, elementary school children in the United States are moving along at the awe-inspiring rate of 22 words a day! The average U.S. 12-year-old has developed a speaking vocabulary of approximately 50,000 words.

During middle and late childhood, changes occur in the way mental vocabulary is organized. When asked to say the first word that comes to mind when they hear a word, preschool children typically provide a word that often follows the word in a sentence. For example, when asked to respond to *dog,* the young child may say "barks," or when asked to respond to the word *eat,* may say "lunch." At about 7 years of age, children begin to respond with a word that is the same part of speech as the stimulus word. For example, a child may now respond to the word *dog* with "cat" or "horse." To *eat,* they now might say "drink." This is evidence that children now have begun to categorize their vocabulary by parts of speech.

The process of categorizing becomes easier as children increase their vocabulary. Children's vocabulary increases from an average of about 14,000 words at age 6 to an average of about 40,000 words by age 11.

Children make similar advances in grammar (Tager-Flusberg & Zukowski, 2009). During the elementary school years, children's improvement in logical reasoning and analytical skills helps them understand such constructions as the appropriate use of comparatives *(shorter, deeper)* and subjectives ("If you were president . . ."). During the elementary school years, children become increasingly able to understand and use complex grammar, such as the following sentence: *The boy who kissed his mother wore a hat.* They also learn to use language in a more connected way, producing connected discourse. They become able to relate sentences to one another to produce descriptions, definitions, and narratives that make sense. Children must be able to do these things orally before they can be expected to deal with them in written assignments. In elementary school, defining words also becomes a regular part of classroom discourse, and children increase their knowledge of syntax as they study and talk about the components of sentences, such as subjects and verbs (Melzi & Ely, 2009).

These advances in vocabulary and grammar during the elementary school years are accompanied by the development of **metalinguistic awareness,** which is knowledge about language, such as knowing what a preposition is or being able to discuss the sounds of a language. Metalinguistic awareness allows children "to think about their language, understand what words are, and even define them" (Berko Gleason, 2009, p. 4). It improves considerably during the elementary school years. Defining words becomes a regular part of classroom discourse, and children increase their knowledge of syntax as they study and talk about the components of sentences such as subjects and verbs (Melzi & Ely, 2009).

During this period, children also make progress in understanding how to use language in culturally appropriate ways—pragmatics. By the time they enter adolescence, most know the rules for the use of language in everyday contexts— that is, what is appropriate and inappropriate to say.

*Adolescence*  Language development during adolescence includes increased sophistication in the use of words (Berko Gleason, 2009; Berman, 2010). As they develop abstract thinking, adolescents become much better than children at analyzing the function a word plays in a sentence.

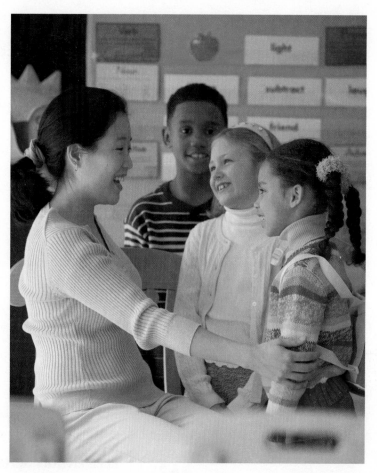

*What are some advances in language that children make during middle and late childhood?*

Adolescents also develop more subtle abilities with words (Berman, 2010). They make strides in understanding *metaphor,* which is an implied comparison between unlike things. For example, individuals "draw a line in the sand" to indicate a nonnegotiable position; a political campaign is said to be a "marathon, not a sprint." And adolescents become better able to understand and to use *satire,* which is the use of irony, derision, or wit to expose folly or wickedness. Caricatures are an example of satire. More advanced logical thinking also allows adolescents, from about 15 to 20 years of age, to understand complex literary works.

Most adolescents are also much better writers than children are. They are better at organizing ideas before they write, at distinguishing between general and specific points as they write, at stringing together sentences that make sense, and at organizing their writing into an introduction, body, and concluding remarks.

I recently asked teachers about the strategies they use to expand or advance children's and adolescents' language development in class. Following are their responses:

**EARLY CHILDHOOD**  My preschool students often listen to a piece of music and then describe what they heard in their own words. I use this opportunity to broaden their music vocabulary by expanding on what they've said. For example, a child listening to a recording might say, "I heard a low sound." I then respond by saying, "So what instrument do you think could have made that low *pitch*?"

—**Connie Christy,** *Aynor Elementary School (Preschool Program)*

**metalinguistic awareness** Knowledge of language.

## TEACHING CONNECTIONS: Best Practices
### Strategies for Vocabulary Development at Different Developmental Levels

In the discussion of semantic development, we described the impressive gains in vocabulary that many children make as they go through the early childhood, middle and late childhood, and adolescent years. However, there are significant individual variations in children's vocabulary, and a good vocabulary contributes in important ways to school success (Pan & Uccelli, 2009). In addition to ideas described earlier on using technology to improve children's vocabulary, here are other strategies to use in the classroom:

### Preschool and Kindergarten

1. *Explain new vocabulary in books that you read to young children.*

2. *Name, label, and describe all of the things in the classroom.*

3. *In everyday conversation with children, introduce and elaborate on words that children are unlikely to know about.* This activity can also be used at higher grade levels.

### Elementary, Middle, and High School

1. *If students have severe deficits in vocabulary knowledge, provide intense vocabulary instruction.*

2. *As a rule, don't introduce more than 10 words at a time.*

3. *Give students an opportunity to use words in a variety of contexts.* These contexts might include read-aloud, fill-in-the-blank sentences, and read-and-respond activities (students read short, information articles about a topic that includes targeted vocabulary words and then respond to questions about the articles).

4. *Writing can help students process word meanings actively.* For example, assign students a topic to write about using assigned vocabulary words

_____

Sources: Curtis & Longo, 2001; U.S. Department of Education, 2006.

DEVELOPMENT

**ELEMENTARY SCHOOL: GRADES K–5** I often tell my fifth-grade students rich, vivid stories about my childhood experiences growing up in eastern Oregon. It is during  these teaching moments that my students pay the most attention. I sometimes write these stories on a computer and project them onto a screen in the classroom. Then the students and I discuss the stories and the language used—for example, similes, metaphors, figures of speech. We revise and edit the stories as a group and discuss strengths and weaknesses. The students are then assigned a similar topic to write about. This transfer of knowledge is amazing as the students are entertained, exposed to a new way of writing as it happens—and they see how something can be improved on the spot.

—**CRAIG JENSEN,** *Cooper Mountain Elementary School*

**MIDDLE SCHOOL: GRADES 6–8** During classroom discussions with my seventh-grade students, I intentionally incorporate unfamiliar words that will encourage them  to ask, "What does that mean?" For example, when talking about John D. Rockefeller in class recently, I asked, "How many of you would like to become a philanthropist?" I urge students to use their newly learned word at home and to tell the class how they worked it into a conversation. This is a simple way to make vocabulary fun!

—**MARK FODNESS,** *Bemidji Middle School*

**HIGH SCHOOL: GRADES 9–12** My high school students often use slang words that I am unfamiliar with. When this happens, I ask the students what the word means and politely tell them that I want to expand my vocabulary. This dialogue often results in conversations about more appropriate words that the students can use in the workplace, classroom, or at home (and I learn something too!)

—**SANDY SWANSON,** *Menomonee Falls High School*

## Review, Reflect, and Practice

**③** Identify the key features of language, biological and environmental influences on language, and the typical growth of the child's language.

**REVIEW**

- What is language? Describe these five features of spoken language: phonology, morphology, syntax, semantics, and pragmatics.
- What evidence supports the idea that humans are "prewired" for learning language? What evidence supports the importance of environmental factors?
- What milestones does a child go through in the course of learning language, and what are the typical ages of these milestones?

**REFLECT**

- How have teachers encouraged or discouraged your own mastery of language?
- What experiences have done the most to expand your language skills?

**PRAXIS™ PRACTICE**

1. Josh has developed a large vocabulary. Which of the following language systems does this reflect?
   a. semantics
   b. pragmatics
   c. syntax
   d. morphology

2. Children raised in isolation from human contact often show extreme, long-lasting language deficits that are rarely entirely overcome by later exposure to language. This evidence supports which aspect of language development?
   a. biological
   b. environmental
   c. interactionist
   d. pragmatic

3. Tamara is discussing the birds she saw flying over her neighborhood. She says, "We saw a flock of gooses." If Tamara's language development is normal for her age, how old is Tamara likely to be?
   a. 2 years old
   b. 4 years old
   c. 6 years old
   d. 8 years old

*Please see the answer key at the end of the book.*

# The Book Report

Mr. Johnson assigned his high school senior American government students to read two books during the semester that had "something, anything to do with government or political systems" and to write a brief report about each of their chosen books.

One student in the class, Cindy, chose to read *1984* and *Animal Farm*, both by George Orwell. Written well before the year 1984, the book *1984* is about what could happen in "the future," given certain earlier political decisions. In essence, the world turns into a terrible place in which "Big Brother" monitors all of one's actions via two-way television-like screens. Infractions of minor rules are punished severely. *Animal Farm* is a brief novel about political systems portrayed as various farm animals such as pigs and dogs. Cindy enjoyed both books and completed them both before midterm. Her reports were insightful, reflecting on the symbolism contained in the novels and the implications for present-day government.

Cindy's friend, Lucy, put off reading her first book until the last minute. She knew Cindy enjoyed reading about government and had finished her reports. Lucy asked Cindy if she knew of a "skinny book" she could read to fulfill the assignment. Cindy gladly shared her copy of *Animal Farm* with her friend, but as Lucy began reading the book she wondered why Cindy had given her this book. It didn't seem to fit the requirements of the assignment at all.

The day before the first reports were due, Mr. Johnson overheard the girls talking. Lucy complained to Cindy, "I don't get it. It's a story about pigs and dogs."

Cindy responded, "They aren't really supposed to be farm animals. It's a story about the promises of communism and what happened in the Soviet Union once the communists took over. It's a great story! Don't you see? The pigs symbolize the communist regime that overthrew the czars during the Russian Revolution. They made all kinds of promises about equality for everyone. The people went along with them because they were sick and tired of the rich and powerful running everything while they starved. Once the czars were eliminated, the communists established a new government but didn't keep any of their promises—they controlled everything. Remember in the book when the pigs moved into the house and started walking on two legs? That's supposed to be like when the communist leaders began acting just like the czars. They even created a secret police force—the dogs in the story. Remember how they bullied the other animals? Just like the secret police in the Soviet Union."

Lucy commented, "I still don't get it. How can a pig or a dog be a communist or a cop? They're just animals."

Cindy looked at her friend, dumbfounded. How could she *not* understand this book? It was so obvious.

1. Drawing on Piaget's theory, explain why Cindy understood the book.
2. Based on Piaget's theory, explain why Lucy didn't understand the book.
3. What could Mr. Johnson do to help Lucy understand?
4. How could Mr. Johnson have presented this assignment differently, so that Lucy did not need to rush through a book?
5. At which of Piaget's stages of cognitive development is Cindy operating?
   a. sensorimotor
   b. preoperational
   c. concrete operational
   d. formal operational
   *[Explain your choice.]*
6. At which of Piaget's stages of cognitive development is Lucy operating?
   a. sensorimotor
   b. preoperational
   c. concrete operational
   d. formal operational
   *[Explain your choice.]*

# Cognitive and Language Development

**1 AN OVERVIEW OF CHILD DEVELOPMENT:** Define development and explain the main processes, periods, and issues in development, as well as links between development and education.

### Exploring What Development Is

Development is the pattern of biological, cognitive, and socioemotional changes that begins at conception and continues through the life span. Most development involves growth, but it also eventually includes decay (dying). The more you learn about children's development, the better you will understand the level at which to appropriately teach them. Childhood learning provides a foundation for learning in the adult years.

### Processes and Periods

Child development is the product of biological, cognitive, and socioemotional processes, which often are intertwined. Periods of development include infancy, early childhood, middle and late childhood, and adolescence.

### Developmental Issues

The main developmental issues are nature and nurture, continuity and discontinuity, and early and later experience. The nature-nurture issue focuses on the extent to which development is mainly influenced by nature (biological influence) or nurture (environmental influence). Although heredity and environment are pervasive influences on development, humans can author a unique developmental path by changing the environment. Some developmentalists describe development as continuous (gradual, cumulative change), others describe it as discontinuous (a sequence of abrupt stages). The early-later experience issue focuses on whether early experiences (especially in infancy) are more important in development than later experiences. Most developmentalists recognize that extreme positions on the nature-nurture, continuity-discontinuity, and early-later experience issues are unwise. Despite this consensus, these issues continue to be debated.

### Development and Education

Developmentally appropriate teaching takes place at a level that is neither too difficult and stressful nor too easy and boring for the child's developmental level. Splintered development occurs when there is considerable unevenness in development across domains.

**2 COGNITIVE DEVELOPMENT:** Discuss the development of the brain and compare the cognitive developmental theories of Jean Piaget and Lev Vygotsky.

### The Brain

An especially important part of growth is the development of the brain and nervous system. Myelination involving hand-eye coordination is not complete until about 4 years of age, and myelination involving focusing attention is not finished until about 10. Substantial synaptic pruning of the brain connections takes place, and the adult level of density of synaptic connections is not reached until some point in adolescence. Different regions of the brain grow at different rates. Changes in the brain in middle and late childhood included advances in functioning in the prefrontal cortex, which are reflected in improved attention, reasoning, and cognitive control. During middle and late childhood, less diffusion and more focal activation occurs in the prefrontal cortex, a change that is associated with an increase in cognitive control. Researchers have recently found a developmental disjunction between the early development of the amygdala, which is responsible for emotion, and the later development of the prefrontal cortex, which is responsible for reasoning and thinking. They argue that these changes in the brain may help to explain the risk-taking behavior and lack of mature judgment in adolescents. Changes in the brain during adolescence also involve the thickening of

*(continued)*

the corpus callosum. Lateralization in some verbal and nonverbal functions occurs, but in many instances functioning is linked to both hemispheres. There is considerable plasticity in the brain, and the quality of learning environments children experience influence the development of their brain. Too often links between neuroscience and education have been overstated. Based on recent research, what we do know indicates that educational experiences throughout childhood and adolescence can influence the brain's development.

**Piaget's Theory**

Jean Piaget proposed a major theory of children's cognitive development that involves these important processes: schemas, assimilation and accommodation, organization, and equilibration. In his theory, cognitive development unfolds in a sequence of four stages: sensorimotor (birth to about age 2), preoperational (from about ages 2 to 7), concrete operational (from about ages 7 to 11), and formal operational (from about ages 11 to 15). Each stage is a qualitative advance. In the sensorimotor stage, infants construct an understanding of the world by coordinating their sensory experiences with their motor actions. Thought is more symbolic at the preoperational stage, although the child has not yet mastered some important mental operations. Preoperational thought includes symbolic function and intuitive thought substages. Egocentrism and centration are constraints. At the concrete operational stage, children can perform operations, and logical thought replaces intuitive thought when reasoning can be applied to specific or concrete examples. Classification, seriation, and transitivity are important concrete operational skills. At the formal operational stage, thinking is more abstract, idealistic, and logical. Hypothetical-deductive reasoning becomes important. Adolescent egocentrism characterizes many young adolescents. We owe to Piaget a long list of masterful concepts as well as the current vision of the child as an active, constructivist thinker. Criticisms of his view focus on estimates of children's competence, stages, the training of children to reason at a higher cognitive level, and the neo-Piagetian criticism of not being precise enough about how children learn.

**Vygotsky's Theory**

Lev Vygotsky proposed another major theory of cognitive development. Vygotsky's view emphasizes that cognitive skills need to be interpreted developmentally, are mediated by language, and have their origins in social relations and culture. Zone of proximal development (ZPD) is Vygotsky's term for the range of tasks that are too difficult for children to master alone but that can be learned with the guidance and assistance of adults and more-skilled children. Scaffolding is an important concept in Vygotsky's theory. He also argued that language plays a key role in guiding cognition. Applications of Vygotsky's ideas to education include using the child's ZPD and scaffolding, using more-skilled peers as teachers, monitoring and encouraging children's use of private speech, and accurately assessing the ZPD. These practices can transform the classroom and establish a meaningful context for instruction. Like Piaget, Vygotsky emphasized that children actively construct their understanding of the world. Unlike Piaget, he did not propose stages of cognitive development, and he emphasized that children construct knowledge through social interaction. In Vygotsky's theory, children depend on tools provided by the culture, which determines which skills they will develop. Some critics say that Vygotsky overemphasized the role of language in thinking.

**3 LANGUAGE DEVELOPMENT:** Identify the key features of language, biological and environmental influences on language, and the typical growth of the child's language.

**What Is Language?**

Language is a form of communication, whether spoken, written, or signed, that is based on a system of symbols. Human languages are infinitely generative. All human languages also have organizational rules of phonology, morphology, syntax, semantics, and pragmatics. Phonology is the sound system of a language; morphology refers to the units of meaning involved in word formation; syntax involves the ways that words must be combined to form acceptable phrases and sentences; semantics refers to the meaning of words and sentences; and pragmatics describes the appropriate use of language in different contexts.

**Biological and Environmental Influences**

Children are biologically prepared to learn language as they and their caregivers interact. Some language scholars argue that the strongest evidence for the biological basis of language is that children all over the world reach language milestones at about the same age despite vast differences in their environmental experiences. However, children do not learn language in a social vacuum. Children benefit when parents and teachers actively engage them in conversation, ask them questions, and talk with, not just to, them. In sum, biology and experience interact to produce language development.

Language acquisition advances through stages. Babbling occurs at about 3 to 6 months, the first word at 10 to 13 months, and two-word utterances at 18 to 24 months. As children move beyond two-word utterances, they can demonstrate that they know some morphological rules, as documented in Jean Berko's study. Children also make advances in phonology, syntax, semantics, and pragmatics in early childhood. Young children's early literacy experiences enhance the likelihood children will have the language skills necessary to benefit from schooling. Vocabulary development increases dramatically during the elementary school years, and by the end of elementary school most children can apply appropriate rules of grammar. Metalinguistic awareness also advances in the elementary school years. In adolescence, language changes include more effective use of words; improvements in the ability to understand metaphor, satire, and adult literary works; and writing.

## KEY TERMS

development 29
nature-nurture issue 32
continuity-discontinuity
    issue 32
early-later experience issue 32
splintered development 33
myelination 35
corpus callosum 36
prefrontal cortex 36
amygdala 36
lateralization 37

schemas 39
assimilation 40
accommodation 40
organization 40
equilibration 40
sensorimotor stage 41
preoperational stage 41
symbolic function
    substage 41
intuitive thought substage 42
centration 42

conservation 42
concrete operational
    stage 44
seriation 45
transitivity 45
formal operational stage 45
hypothetical-deductive
    reasoning 47
neo-Piagetians 50
zone of proximal development
    (ZPD) 50

scaffolding 52
social constructivist
    approach 53
language 58
phonology 58
morphology 58
syntax 58
semantics 59
pragmatics 59
metalinguistic awareness 63

## PORTFOLIO ACTIVITIES

Now that you have a good understanding of this chapter, complete these exercises to expand your thinking.

### Independent Reflection

1. Select the general age of the child you expect to teach one day. Make a list of that child's characteristic ways of thinking according to Piaget's theory of cognitive development. List other related characteristics of the child based on your own childhood. Then make a second list of your own current ways of thinking. Compare the lists. In what important cognitive ways do you and the child differ? What adjustments in thinking will you need to make when you set out to communicate with the child? Summarize your thoughts in a brief essay.

2. How might thinking in formal operational ways rather than concrete operational ways help students develop better study skills?

3. What is the most useful idea related to children's language development that you read about in this chapter? Write the idea down in your portfolio and explain how you will implement this idea in your classroom.

### Research/Field Experience

4. Find an education article in a magazine or on the Internet that promotes "left-brained" and "right-brained" activities for learning. In a brief report, criticize the article based on what you read in this chapter about neuroscience and brain education.

*Go to the Online Learning Center for downloadable portfolio templates.*

## STUDY, PRACTICE, AND SUCCEED

Visit www.mhhe.com/santrockep5e to review the chapter with self-grading quizzes and self-assessments, to apply the chapter material to two more Crack the Case studies, and for suggested activities to develop your teaching portfolio.

# CHAPTER 3

# SOCIAL CONTEXTS AND SOCIOEMOTIONAL DEVELOPMENT

*In the end, the power behind development is life.*

—Erik Erikson
*European-born American Psychotherapist, 20th Century*

## Chapter **Outline**

### Contemporary Theories ①
Bronfenbrenner's Ecological Theory
Erikson's Life-Span Development Theory

### Social Contexts of Development ②
Families
Peers
Schools

### Socioemotional Development ③
The Self
Moral Development
Coping with Stress

## Learning **Goals**

**①** Describe two contemporary perspectives on socioemotional development: Bronfenbrenner's ecological theory and Erikson's life-span development theory.

**②** Discuss how the social contexts of families, peers, and schools are linked with socioemotional development.

**③** Explain these aspects of children's socioemotional development: self-esteem, identity, moral development, and coping with stress.

# Teaching **Stories**   Keren Abra

The socioemotional contexts of children's lives influence their ability to learn. Keren Abra teaches fifth grade in San Francisco. A student in her class, Julie, was very quiet, so quiet that in classroom discussions she whispered her responses. Her parents, who had gone through a bitter divorce, agreed that Julie needed a good therapist.

Julie was significantly underachieving, doing minimal work and scoring low on tests. A crisis of low grades and incomplete work brought her mother to school one evening, and her father to school the next morning, to talk with Keren. Later that week, Keren spoke with Julie, who looked terrified. Following are Keren's comments about her talk with Julie:

> I kept some objectives in mind. This child needed to know that she was a good student, that she was loved, that adults could be consistent and responsible, and that she didn't have to hide and

keep secrets. I told her that her parents had come in because we all were concerned about her and knew we needed to help her. I told her that her parents loved her very much and asked if she knew this (she and I agreed that nobody's perfect, least of all adults with their own problems). I explained that a tutor was going to help her with her work . . . I talked with Julie about how much I liked her and about coming forward more in class.

Change did not happen overnight with Julie, but she did begin to increasingly look me in the eye with a more confident smile. She spoke out more in class, and improved her writing efforts. Her best months were when she was seeing both a therapist and a tutor, although her grades remained a roller coaster. At the end of the school year, she commented that she and her mother both noticed that her best work was when she felt supported and confident. For an 11-year-old, that is a valuable insight.

# Preview

Divorce is just one of the many aspects of children's social contexts that can have profound effects on children's performance in school. In the chapter we will provide teaching strategies for helping students cope with the divorce of their parents. We will also explore how parents cradle their children's lives, as well as how children's development is influenced by successive waves of peers, friends, and teachers. Children's small worlds widen as they become students and develop relationships with many new people. In this second chapter on development, we will study these social worlds and examine children's socioemotional development.

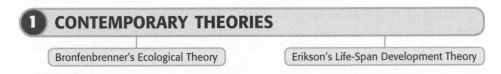

**1** CONTEMPORARY THEORIES

| Bronfenbrenner's Ecological Theory | Erikson's Life-Span Development Theory |

A number of theories address children's socioemotional development. In this chapter, we will focus on two main theories: Bronfenbrenner's ecological theory and Erikson's life-span development theory. These two theories were chosen for the comprehensive way they address the social contexts in which children develop (Bronfenbrenner) and major changes in children's socioemotional development (Erikson). In Chapter 7 we will discuss other theories (behavioral and social cognitive) that also are relevant to socioemotional development.

Thinking Back/Thinking Forward

Bandura's social cognitive theory also emphasizes the importance of social contexts. Chapter 7, p. 235

## BRONFENBRENNER'S ECOLOGICAL THEORY

The ecological theory developed by Urie Bronfenbrenner (1917–2005) primarily focuses on the social contexts in which children live and the people who influence their development.

DEVELOPMENT

**Five Environmental Systems** Bronfenbrenner's (1995, Bronfenbrenner & Morris, 2006) **ecological theory** consists of five environmental systems that range from close interpersonal interactions to broad-based influences of culture. The five systems are the microsystem, mesosystem, exosystem, macrosystem, and chronosystem (see Figure 3.1).

**ecological theory** Bronfenbrenner's theory that consists of five environmental systems: microsystem, mesosystem, exosystem, macrosystem, and chronosystem.

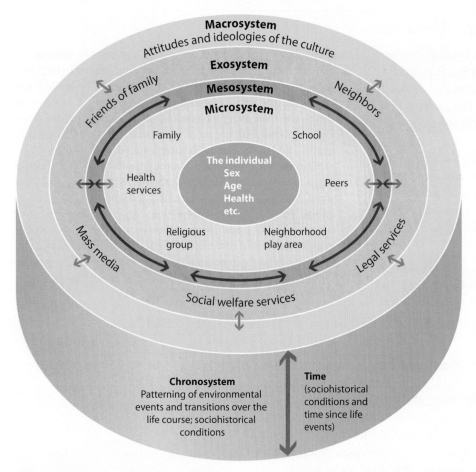

## FIGURE 3.1 BRONFENBRENNER'S ECOLOGICAL THEORY OF DEVELOPMENT

Bronfenbrenner's ecological theory consists of five environmental systems: microsystem, mesosystem, exosystem, macrosystem, and chronosystem.

Claire B. Kopp and Joanne B. Krakow, eds., The Child: Development in a Social Context, 1st ed., p. 648 (Figure 12.1). © 1982. Adapted and electronically reproduced by permission of Pearson Education, Inc., Upper Saddle River, New Jersey.

DIVERSITY

A *microsystem* is a setting in which the individual spends considerable time, such as the student's family, peers, school, and neighborhood. Within these microsystems, the individual has direct interactions with parents, teachers, peers, and others. For Bronfenbrenner, the student is not a passive recipient of experiences but is someone who reciprocally interacts with others and helps to construct the microsystem.

The *mesosystem* involves linkages between microsystems. Examples are the connections between family experiences and school experiences and between family and peers. We will have more to say about family-school connections later in the chapter.

The *exosystem* is at work when experiences in another setting (in which the student does not have an active role) influence what students and teachers experience in the immediate context. For example, consider the school and park supervisory boards in a community. They have strong roles in determining the quality of schools, parks, recreation facilities, and libraries, which can help or hinder a child's development.

The *macrosystem* involves the broader culture. *Culture* is a very broad term that includes the roles of ethnicity and socioeconomic factors in children's development. It's the broadest context in which students and teachers live, including the society's values and customs (Shiraev & Levy, 2010). For example, some cultures (such as rural China and Iran) emphasize traditional gender roles.

The *chronosystem* includes the sociohistorical conditions of students' development. For example, the lives of children today are different in many ways from when their parents and grandparents were children (Schaie, 2010, 2011). Today's children are more likely to be in child care, use computers, and grow up in new kinds of dispersed, deconcentrated cities that are not quite urban, rural, or suburban.

**Evaluating Bronfenbrenner's Theory** Bronfenbrenner's theory has gained popularity in recent years. It provides one of the few theoretical frameworks for systematically examining social contexts on both micro and macro levels, bridging the gap between behavioral theories that focus on small settings and anthropological theories that analyze larger settings. His theory has been instrumental in showing how different contexts of children's lives are interconnected. As we have just discussed, teachers need to consider not just what goes on in the classroom but also what happens in students' families, neighborhoods, and peer groups.

It should be mentioned that Bronfenbrenner (2000) added biological influences to his theory and subsequently described it as a *bioecological* theory. Nonetheless, ecological, environmental contexts still predominate in Bronfenbrenner's theory (Gauvain & Parke, 2010).

Criticisms of Bronfenbrenner's theory are that it gives too little attention to biological and cognitive factors in children's development and it does not address the step-by-step developmental changes that are the focus of theories such as Piaget's and Erikson's.

## TEACHING CONNECTIONS: Best Practices
### Strategies for Educating Children Based on Bronfenbrenner's Theory

1. *Think about the child as embedded in a number of environmental systems and influences.* These include schools and teachers, parents and siblings, the community and neighborhood, peers and friends, the media, religion, and culture.

2. *Pay attention to the connection between schools and families.* Build these connections through formal and informal outreach. There are a number of ways to do this, including inviting parents into the classroom for special occasions, such as open houses, asking parents to read with their children at home, bringing parents into the school as volunteers, speakers, or room parents, and holding parent/child activity nights.

3. *Recognize the importance of the community, socioeconomic status, and culture in the child's development.* These broader social contexts can have powerful influences on the child's development (Leventhal, Dupéré, & Brooks-Gunn, 2009). In Through the Eyes of Teachers, Juanita Kirton, an assistant principal at Gramercy Preschool in New York City, describes the community's value for her students.

### THROUGH THE EYES OF TEACHERS
#### The Community Is Full of Learning Opportunities and Supports for Students

Use of the community is very important. New York City is full of opportunities. I have been able to work closely with the Disabled Library in the neighborhood. They have been great at supplying the school with audiobooks for the children and lending special equipment for their use. The local fire department has been used for numerous trips. The firemen have been especially attentive to the students because of their various disabilities. The fire department has also come to visit the school, which was very exciting for the children. It was amazing to see how patient the firefighters were with the students. I am also encouraged to see many colleges and universities sending items and student teachers visiting the school. Donations from the Hasbro toy company during the holidays make a big difference in the way some students and families get to spend their holiday vacation. Our students are very visible in the New York City community, where we are located. This helps our neighbors get to know the staff and children and creates a safer environment.

## ERIKSON'S LIFE-SPAN DEVELOPMENT THEORY

Complementing Bronfenbrenner's analysis of the social contexts in which children develop and the people who are important in their lives, the theory of Erik Erikson (1902–1994) presents a developmental view of people's lives in stages. Let's take a journey through Erikson's view of the human life span.

DEVELOPMENT

**Eight Stages of Human Development**   In Erikson's (1968) theory, eight stages of development unfold as people go through the human life span (see Figure 3.2). Each stage consists of a developmental task that confronts individuals with a crisis. For Erikson, each crisis is not catastrophic but rather a turning point of increased vulnerability and enhanced potential. The more successfully an individual resolves each crisis, the more psychologically healthy the individual will be. Each stage has both positive and negative sides.

*Trust versus mistrust* is Erikson's first psychosocial stage. It occurs in the first year of life. The development of trust requires warm, nurturing caregiving. The positive outcome is a feeling of comfort and minimal fear. Mistrust develops when infants are treated too negatively or are ignored.

*Autonomy versus shame and doubt* is Erikson's second psychosocial stage. It occurs in late infancy and the toddler years. After gaining trust in their caregivers, infants begin to discover that their behavior is their own. They assert their independence and realize their will. If infants are restrained too much or punished too harshly, they develop a sense of shame and doubt.

*Initiative versus guilt* is Erikson's third psychosocial stage. It corresponds to early childhood, about 3 to 5 years of age. As young children experience a widening social

| Erikson's Stages | Developmental Period |
|---|---|
| **Integrity versus despair** | Late adulthood (60s onward) |
| **Generativity versus stagnation** | Middle adulthood (40s, 50s) |
| **Intimacy versus isolation** | Early adulthood (20s, 30s) |
| **Identity versus identity confusion** | Adolescence (10 to 20 years) |
| **Industry versus inferiority** | Middle and late childhood (elementary school years, 6 years to puberty) |
| **Initiative versus guilt** | Early childhood (preschool years, 3 to 5 years) |
| **Autonomy versus shame and doubt** | Infancy (1 to 3 years) |
| **Trust versus mistrust** | Infancy (first year) |

## FIGURE **3.2** ERIKSON'S EIGHT LIFE-SPAN STAGES

*What are the implications of saying that people go through stages of development?*

Erik Erikson with his wife, Joan, an artist. Erikson generated one of the most important developmental theories of the twentieth century. *Which stage of Erikson's theory are you in? Does Erikson's description of this stage characterize you?*

world, they are challenged more than they were as infants. To cope with these challenges, they need to engage in active, purposeful behavior that involves initiative. Children develop uncomfortable guilt feelings if they see themselves as irresponsible or are made to feel too anxious.

*Industry versus inferiority* is Erikson's fourth psychosocial stage. It corresponds approximately with the elementary school years, from 6 years of age until puberty or early adolescence. As they move into the elementary school years, children direct their energy toward mastering knowledge and intellectual skills. The danger in the elementary school years is that of developing a sense of inferiority, unproductiveness, and incompetence.

*Identity versus identity confusion* is Erikson's fifth psychosocial stage. It corresponds to the adolescent years. Adolescents try to find out who they are, what they are all about, and where they are going in life. They are confronted with many new roles and adult statuses (such as vocational and romantic). Adolescents need to be allowed to explore different paths to attain a healthy identity. If they do not adequately explore different roles and fail to carve out a positive future path, they can remain confused about their identity.

*Intimacy versus isolation* is Erikson's sixth psychosocial stage. It corresponds to the early adult years, the twenties and thirties. The developmental task is to form positive close relationships with others. The hazard of this stage is that one will fail to form an intimate relationship with a romantic partner or friend and become socially isolated.

*Generativity versus stagnation* is Erikson's seventh psychosocial stage. It corresponds to the middle adulthood years, the forties and fifties. Generativity means transmitting something positive to the next generation. This can involve such roles as parenting and teaching, through which adults assist the next generation in developing useful lives. Erikson described *stagnation* as the feeling of having done nothing to help the next generation.

*Integrity versus despair* is Erikson's eighth and final psychosocial stage. It corresponds to the late adulthood years, the sixties until death. Older adults tend to review their lives, reflecting on what they have done. If the retrospective evaluations are positive, they develop a sense of integrity. That is, they view their life as positively integrated and worth living. In contrast, older adults become despairing if their backward glances are mainly negative.

I recently asked teachers how they apply Erikson's life-span theory in their classrooms? Following are their comments:

**EARLY CHILDHOOD**   The initiative versus guilt stage of Erikson's theory characterizes my classroom as students are expected to become more responsible throughout the year. Children are assigned "jobs" to do for the day, such as being the door-holder, line leader, or messenger. The children are also expected to follow through with classroom and school rules. Uncomfortable, guilty feelings may arise if the children feel irresponsible as a result of breaking classroom rules or not fulfilling their responsibilities.

—**MISSY DANGLER**, *Suburban Hills School*

**ELEMENTARY SCHOOL: GRADES K–5**   The industry versus inferiority stage of Erikson's theory most applies to my second-grade students. As children enter this

stage, there is an energy to learn; however, the dangers at this stage are that children may feel incompetent if they are unsuccessful in their work. As a teacher of students at this developmental stage, [I find] it is important to give students opportunities to be successful. For example, if a second-grader is reading at a kindergarten level, and second-grade-level materials are given to this student, the student will develop feelings of incompetence. I use leveled reading materials in my classroom in reading and spelling. Each student is reading and being instructed with material at his or her reading level, which fosters feelings of confidence.

—SUSAN FROELICH, *Clinton Elementary School*

**MIDDLE SCHOOL: GRADES 6–8**   Erikson's identity versus identity confusion stage is evident in my sixth-grade students. At this stage, so many of my students

experience a decline in self-esteem. To address these negative feelings, I often have them become the teacher. That is, under my guidance, a student will conduct different classroom activities. Many times I select students who need to be recognized by their peers to be teacher for a day. Other times, I ask students—especially those most reluctant to participate in class—to have lunch with me. During lunch, I give them steps on how to overcome any fears or apprehensions they may have about taking part in class.

—MARGARET REARDON, *Pocantico Hills School*

**HIGH SCHOOL: GRADES 9–12**   As high school teachers dealing with students in the identity versus identity confusion stage, we need to especially value adolescents

as human beings. I know of so many teachers who roll their eyes at their students' petty squabbles and emotional curves. However, we need to remember that we went through the very same things, and these struggles helped to define who we are as adults. This came to me so vividly during my student teaching. The building was so similar in design to my own school. As I walked in the door, I immediately experienced every pimple on my chin and every tear shed in the girls' bathroom. Suddenly, I was the insecure girl listening to Lionel Richie at the dance, longing for John to ask me out.

—JENNIFER HEITER, *Bremen High School*

**Evaluating Erikson's Theory**   Erikson's theory captures some of life's key socioemotional tasks and places them in a developmental framework (Adams, 2008). His concept of identity is especially helpful in understanding older adolescents and college students. His overall theory was a critical force in forging our current view of human development as lifelong rather than being restricted only to childhood.

Erikson's theory is not without criticism (Coté, 2009). Some experts point out that his stages are too rigid. Life-span development pioneer Bernice Neugarten (1988) says that identity, intimacy, independence, and many other aspects of socioemotional development are not like beads on a string that appear in neatly packaged age intervals. Rather, they are important issues throughout most of our lives. Although much research has been conducted on some of Erikson's stages (identity versus identity confusion, in particular), the overall scope of his theory (such as whether the eight stages always occur in the order and according to the timetable he proposed) has not been scientifically documented. For example, for some individuals (especially females), intimacy concerns precede identity or develop simultaneously with it.

**TEACHING CONNECTIONS:** Best Practices

Strategies for Educating Children Based on Erikson's Theory

1. *Encourage initiative in young children.* Children in preschool and early childhood education programs should be given a great deal of freedom to explore their world. They should be allowed to choose most of the activities they engage in. If their requests for doing certain activities are reasonable, the requests should be honored. Children at this stage love to play. It not only benefits their socioemotional development but also is an important medium for their cognitive growth. Provide exciting materials that will stimulate their imagination. Especially encourage social play with peers and fantasy play. Help children assume responsibility for putting toys and materials back in place after they have used them. Criticism should be kept to a minimum so that children will not develop high levels of guilt and anxiety. Structure activities and environment for successes rather than failures by giving them developmentally appropriate tasks; for example, don't frustrate young children by having them sit for long periods of time doing academic paper-and-pencil tasks.

2. *Promote industry in elementary school children.* Teachers have a special responsibility for children's development of industry. It was Erikson's hope that teachers could provide an atmosphere in which children become passionate about learning. In elementary school, children thirst to know. Most arrive at elementary school steeped in curiosity and a motivation to master tasks. In Erikson's view, it is important for teachers to nourish this motivation for mastery and curiosity. Give students meaningful tasks to accomplish that are challenging, but not overwhelming. If students consistently have tasks to do that are too easy for them, they will not learn to be industrious. Be firm in requiring students to be productive, but don't be overly critical. Especially be tolerant of honest mistakes, allow students to correct these, and make sure that every student has opportunities for many successes.

3. *Stimulate identity exploration in adolescence.* Recognize that the student's identity is multidimensional. Ask adolescents to write essays about such dimensions, including vocational goals, intellectual achievement, and interests in hobbies, sports, music, and other areas, exploring who they are and what they want to do with their lives. Have people from different careers come and talk with your students about their work regardless of the grade you teach. Offer short exploratory courses or units that allow adolescents to explore a domain without making a long-term commitment to it. Encourage adolescents to think independently and to freely express their views by listening to, reading about, and participating in debates on religious, political, and ideological issues. This will stimulate them to examine different perspectives. Understand that adolescents often express their developing identities through their appearance, language choices, and peer group choices.

## THROUGH THE EYES OF TEACHERS
### Using Art to Explore Adolescents' Identities

My seventh-grade art students come to class the first day to read a list of classroom rules. I surprise them by passing out sheets of art paper, old magazines, and glue with the verbal directions to tell me about themselves—build a self-portrait—with torn paper. The students are inventive, enthusiastic, and excited to focus on their identities, and waste no time beginning. . . . After the opening project, my students are at ease knowing their creative expression is allowed and encouraged, and I am better able to understand their many changing attitudes and need to express them.

4. *Examine your life as a teacher through the lens of Erikson's eight stages* (Gratz & Bouton, 1996). Your successful career as a teacher could be a key aspect of your overall identity. Develop positive relationships with a partner, one or more friends, and with other teachers or mentors, all of which can be very rewarding and enhance your identity as a teacher.

5. *Benefit from the characteristics of some of Erikson's other stages.* Competent teachers trust, show initiative, are industrious and model a sense of mastery, and are motivated to contribute something meaningful to the next generation. In your role as a teacher, you can actively meet the criteria for Erikson's concept of generativity.

## Review, Reflect, and Practice

**1** Describe two contemporary perspectives on socioemotional development: Bronfenbrenner's ecological theory and Erikson's life-span development theory.

### REVIEW

- What are Bronfenbrenner's five environmental systems? What are some criticisms of his theory?
- What are the eight Eriksonian stages? What are some criticisms of his theory?

### REFLECT

- How well do you think your own socioemotional development can be described using Erikson's theory?

### PRAXIS™ PRACTICE

1. Which of the following is the best example of the mesosystem?
   a. Ike's parents monitor his behavior closely. They know where he is and with whom at all times.
   b. Ike's parents express concern about his grades. They attend parent-teacher conferences and belong to the PTA, as does John's teacher. They chaperone field trips.
   c. Ike attends church regularly, goes to religious school each week, and is preparing for his confirmation.
   d. Ike is quite adept with technology. His parents often ask him to program their electronic devices because of their lack of experience with these things when they were children.

2. Ms. Koslowsky teaches fourth grade. Understanding that it is important for her students to do well on the state-mandated achievement tests, she has high expectations for their daily work. Often her lessons frustrate some of her students because they don't understand the material. Rather than helping them to understand, she forges ahead. She is then frustrated by their performance on homework, frequently making caustic remarks on their papers. How would Ms. Rogers' teaching style be described from Erikson's perspective?
   a. Ms. Rogers' teaching style is closely aligned with the need to promote industry in elementary school children. Her high expectations will motivate the children to succeed.
   b. Ms. Rogers' teaching style is closely aligned with elementary-school-age children's need to discover who they are and establish an identity.
   c. Ms. Rogers' teaching style is unlikely to promote industry in elementary-school-age children. Instead, it is likely to make them feel inferior.
   d. Ms. Rogers' teaching style is likely to increase students' initiative. They will respond to her high expectations by taking initiative in their work.

*Please see the answer key at the end of the book.*

## **2** SOCIAL CONTEXTS OF DEVELOPMENT

| Families | Peers | Schools |

In Bronfenbrenner's theory, the social contexts in which children live are important influences on their development. Let's explore three of the contexts in which children spend much of their time: families, peers, and schools.

## FAMILIES

Although children grow up in diverse families, in virtually every family parents play an important role in supporting and stimulating children's academic achievement and attitudes toward school (Epstein, 2009). Our examination of parents' influence on children's schooling and achievement focuses on parenting styles, coparenting, the changing family in a changing society, and school-family linkages.

**Parenting Styles** There might be times when it is helpful for you to understand how parents are rearing their children and the effects this has on the children. Is there a best way to parent? Diana Baumrind (1971, 1996), a leading authority on parenting, thinks so. She states that parents should be neither punitive nor aloof. Rather, they should develop rules for children while at the same time being supportive and nurturing. Hundreds of research studies, including her own, support her view (Chen, 2009a,b). Baumrind says that parenting styles come in four main forms:

- **Authoritarian parenting** is restrictive and punitive. Authoritarian parents exhort children to follow their directions and respect them. They place firm limits and controls on their children and allow little verbal exchange. For example, an authoritarian parent might say, "Do it my way or else. There will be no discussion!" Children of authoritarian parents often behave in socially incompetent ways. They tend to be anxious about social comparison, fail to initiate activity, and have poor communication skills.

- **Authoritative parenting** encourages children to be independent but still places limits and controls on their actions. Extensive verbal give-and-take is allowed, and parents are nurturant and supportive. Children whose parents are authoritative often behave in socially competent ways. They tend to be self-reliant, delay gratification, get along with their peers, and show high self-esteem. Because of these positive outcomes, Baumrind strongly endorses authoritative parenting.

- **Neglectful parenting** is a parenting style in which parents are uninvolved in their children's lives. Children of neglectful parents develop the sense that other aspects of their parents' lives are more important than they are. They tend to behave in socially incompetent ways as a result of poor self-control and difficulty in handling independence. Such children are usually not achievement motivated.

- **Indulgent parenting** is a parenting style in which parents are highly involved with their children but place few limits or restrictions on their behaviors. These parents often let their children do what they want and get their own way because they believe the combination of nurturant support and lack of restraints will produce a creative, confident child. The result is that these children usually don't learn to control their own behavior. Indulgent parents do not take into account the development of the whole child.

Do the benefits of authoritative parenting transcend the boundaries of ethnicity, socioeconomic status, and household composition? Although some exceptions have been found, evidence links authoritative parenting with competence on the part of the child in research across a wide range of ethnic groups, social strata, cultures, and family structures (Shea & Coyne, 2008).

Nonetheless, researchers have found that in some ethnic groups, aspects of the authoritarian style may be associated with more positive child outcomes than Baumrind predicts. Elements of the authoritarian style may take on different meanings and have different effects depending on the context (McLoyd & others, 2009).

For example, Asian American parents often continue aspects of traditional Asian child-rearing practices sometimes described as authoritarian. Many Asian American parents exert considerable control over their children's lives. However, Ruth Chao

**authoritarian parenting** A restrictive and punitive parenting style in which there is little verbal exchange between parents and children; associated with children's social incompetence.

**authoritative parenting** A positive parenting style that encourages children to be independent but still places limits and controls on their actions; extensive verbal give-and-take is allowed; associated with children's social competence.

**neglectful parenting** A parenting style of uninvolvement in which parents spend little time with their children; associated with children's social incompetence.

**indulgent parenting** A parenting style of involvement but few limits or restrictions on children's behavior; linked with children's social incompetence.

(2005, 2007) argues that the style of parenting used by these parents is usually distinct from the domineering control of the authoritarian style as sometimes employed by other ethnic groups. Chao argues that for Asian American parents, the control reflects concern and involvement in children's lives and is best conceptualized as a type of training. The high academic achievement of Asian American children may be a consequence of the "training" provided by their parents.

DIVERSITY

An emphasis on requiring respect and obedience is also associated with the authoritarian style. In many African American and Latino families, especially in low-income neighborhoods, this type of child rearing may have positive outcomes. In these contexts, requiring obedience to parental authority may be an adaptive strategy to keep children from engaging in antisocial behavior that can have serious consequences for the victim or the perpetrator (McLoyd & others, 2009).

**Coparenting**    In *coparenting*, parents support one another in jointly raising a child. Lack of effective coparenting because of poor coordination between parents, undermining of the other parent, lack of cooperation and warmth, and disconnection by one parent are conditions that place children at risk for problems (Feinberg & Kan, 2008).

**The Changing Family in a Changing Society**    Increasing numbers of children are being raised in divorced families, stepparent families, and families in which both parents work outside the home. As divorce has become epidemic, a staggering number of children have been growing up in single-parent families. The United States has a higher percentage of single-parent families than virtually any other industrialized country (see Figure 3.3). Today, about one in every four children in the United States have lived a portion of their lives in a stepfamily by age 18. Also, more than two of every three mothers with a child from 6 to 17 years of age are in the labor force.

***Working Parents***    Work can produce positive and negative effects on parenting (Han, 2009). Recent research indicates that what matters for children's development is the nature of parents' work rather than whether one or both parents work outside the home (Clarke-Stewart, 2006). Ann Crouter (2006) recently described how parents bring their experiences at work into their homes. She concluded that parents who have poor working conditions, such as long hours, overtime work, stressful work, and lack of autonomy at work, are likely to be more irritable at home and engage in less effective parenting than their counterparts who have better work conditions in their jobs. A consistent finding is the children (especially girls) of working mothers engage in less gender stereotyping and have more egalitarian views of gender (Goldberg & Lucas-Thompson, 2008).

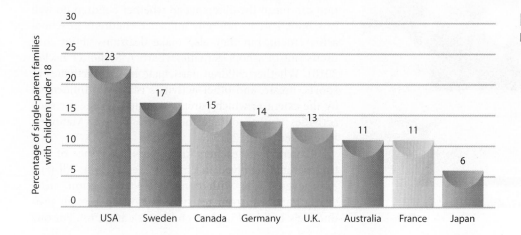

FIGURE **3.3** SINGLE-PARENT FAMILIES IN VARIOUS COUNTRIES

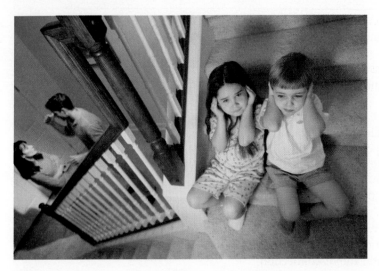

*What are some concerns about children in divorced families?*

***Children in Divorced Families*** Children from divorced families show poorer adjustment than their counterparts in nondivorced families (Amato & Dorius, 2011). Nonetheless, keep in mind that a majority of children in divorced families do not have significant adjustment problems (Ahrons, 2007). Note also that marital conflict may have negative consequences for children in the context of either marriage or divorce (Cummings & Merrilees, 2009). Indeed, many of the problems children from divorced homes experience begin during the predivorce period, a time when parents are often in active conflict with each other. Thus, when children from divorced homes show problems, the problems may be due not only to the divorce, but the marital conflict that led to it (Pruett & Barker, 2009a,b).

The effects of divorce on children are complex, depending on such factors as the child's age, the child's strengths and weaknesses at the time of the divorce, the type of custody, the socioeconomic status, and postdivorce family functioning (Ziol-Guest, 2009). The use of support systems (relatives, friends, housekeepers), an ongoing positive relationship between the custodial parent and the ex-spouse, the ability to meet financial needs, and good-quality schooling help children adjust to the stressful circumstances of divorce (Huurre, Junkkari, & Aro, 2006).

E. Mavis Hetherington's (1995, 2006) research documents the importance of schools when children grow up in a divorced family. Throughout elementary school, children in divorced families had the highest achievement and fewest problems when both the parenting environment and the school environment were authoritative (according to Baumrind's categorization). In the divorced families, when only one parent was authoritative, an authoritative school improved the child's adjustment. The most negative parenting environment occurred when neither parent was authoritative. The most negative school environment was chaotic and neglecting.

*What are some important parental influences on children's schooling and achievement?*

**School-Family Linkages** Even though parents typically spend progressively less time with their children as the children go through elementary and secondary school, they continue to have a strong influence on children's development (Pomerantz & Moorman, 2010). Parents can serve as gatekeepers and provide guidance as children assume more responsibility for themselves (Gauvain & Parke, 2010). Parents especially play an important role in supporting and stimulating children's academic achievement (Domina, 2009). The value parents place on education can mean the difference in whether children do well in school. Parents not only influence children's in-school achievement, but they also make decisions about children's out-of-school activities (Barber, Stone, & Eccles, 2010). Whether children participate in such activities as sports, music, and other activities is heavily influenced by the extent to which parents sign up children for such activities and encourage their participation (Mahoney, Parente, & Zigler, 2010).

Experienced teachers know the importance of getting parents involved in children's education. All parents, even those with considerable education, need yearly guidance from teachers in how to remain productively involved in their children's education. For one thing, education expert Joyce Epstein (2001, 2009) explains that almost all parents want their children to succeed in school, but need clear and useful information from their children's teachers and from other school and district leaders in order to help their children develop their full potential. For example, sometimes parents ask their child, "How was school today?" We know that conversation may end with the child responding, "Fine," or, "Okay," and not much more. Parents should be guided, instead, to ask their child, "Would you read to me something you wrote today?" or "Could you show me something you learned in math today?" or similar direct questions about work and projects in other content areas. Conversations or homework assignments that enable students to share ideas and celebrate successes are likely to promote positive school-related parent-child interactions.

For ways to develop effective school-family-community partnerships and programs, see the Web site of the National Network of Partnership Schools at Johns Hopkins University (NNPS): **www.partnershipschool.org.** Especially look at the section titled "In the Spotlight."

I recently asked teachers at different levels of schooling for the recommendations about getting parents/guardians involved in the schooling of their child. Following are their responses:

**EARLY CHILDHOOD**   Parents are an integral part of our classroom community; teachers cannot be successful without parental cooperation and participation. We

engage parents through ongoing conversation, home phone calls when needed, weekly newsletters, e-mails, parent-teacher conferences, and workshops every month where dinner is served.

—**Valarie Gorham,** *Kiddie Quarters, Inc.*

**ELEMENTARY SCHOOL: GRADES K–5**   Not all parents are available to volunteer in the classroom. For that reason, I provide alternative ways for parents to participate

in their child's schooling. For example, I sometimes ask parents to prepare materials at home that will be used in a classroom lesson. Additionally, each month we have a monthly homework calendar that parents complete with their child and fill out a response form on the back letting me know what the parent learned about their child, as well as how they helped their child complete the tasks.

—**Heather Zoldak,** *Ridge Wood Elementary School*

**MIDDLE SCHOOL: GRADES 6–8**   My team uses technology to communicate with parents daily. We post grades, homework, and daily announcements online. We also

require our students to use planners to write down assignments, missing work, and so on. We contact parents if there are concerns, but we also contact parents with positive news about their child.

—**Mark Fodness,** *Bemidji Middle School*

**HIGH SCHOOL: GRADES 9–12**   I teach 15 miles from my home in a small community, but I make it a point to be visible—this may mean shopping at the grocery

or drugstore in my school's community rather than frequenting the one closer to my home. When I shop within the vicinity of the school, I often see my students working and parents shopping, which makes me more approachable. I also try to go to school plays, competitions, and athletic events so that when parent-teacher conferences roll around, parents who have grown familiar with my face may be more inclined to attend the conference.

—**Jennifer Heiter,** *Bremen High School*

## TEACHING CONNECTIONS: Best Practices
### Strategies for Forging School-Family-Community Linkages

Joyce Epstein has developed six types of involvement that can be implemented to develop comprehensive school, family, and community partnerships in any elementary, middle, or high school. These goal-oriented and age-appropriate activities include the following:

1. *Provide assistance to families.* Schools can provide parents with information about child-rearing skills, the importance of family support, child and adolescent development, and home contexts that enhance learning at each grade level. Teachers are an important contact point between schools and families and need to become aware of whether the family is meeting the child's basic physical and health needs.

2. *Communicate effectively with families about school programs and their child's progress.* This involves both school-to-home and home-to-school communication. Encourage parents to attend parent-teacher conferences and other school functions (Eagle & Oeth, 2008). Set up times for parent meetings that are convenient for them to attend. Work on developing activities in which parents can get to know each other, not just know the teacher. Keep parents informed about what is happening in your class via newsletters—either paper or Web-based—or e-mail. Provide your contact information and availability to parents. Promptly return any phone calls or e-mail you receive from parents.

3. *Encourage parents to be volunteers.* Try to match the skills of volunteers to classroom needs. Remember from the opening teaching story in Chapter 2 that in some schools parents are extensively involved in educational planning and assisting teachers. Parents have different talents and abilities, just like children, which is reflected in comments by Heather Zoldak, a teacher at Ridge Wood Elementary School in Michigan, in Through the Eyes of Teachers.

### THROUGH THE EYES OF TEACHERS
#### Encouraging Parent Involvement

Understanding that parents come with different levels of comfort with the school environment is important when encouraging parent support for the classroom. Prepare a variety of opportunities for parents to become involved both inside the classroom and to support the classroom in other ways. Due to busy schedules, work restrictions, or comfort level based on their own experiences with school, some parents may be more involved if they can help outside the classroom on field trips or even prepare items at home for an upcoming project. Taking steps to build the comfort level and relationship with parents is a key factor in encouraging parents to be volunteers.

4. *Involve families with their children in learning activities at home.* This includes homework and other curriculum-linked activities and decisions (Epstein, 2009). Epstein (1998) coined the term *interactive homework* and designed a program that encourages students to go to their parents for help. In one elementary school that uses Epstein's approach, a weekly teacher's letter informs parents about the objective of each assignment, gives directions, and asks for comments.

5. *Include families as participants in school decisions.* Parents can be invited to be on PTA/PTO boards, various committees, councils, and other parent organizations. They might even serve as board of education members. At Antwa Elementary School in a rural area of Wisconsin, potluck supper parent-teacher organization meetings involve discussions with parents about school and district educational goals, age-appropriate learning, child discipline, and testing performance.

6. *Coordinate community collaboration.* Help interconnect the work and resources of community businesses, agencies, colleges and universities, and other groups to strengthen school programs, family practices, and student learning (Epstein, 2009). Schools can alert families to community programs and services that will benefit them.

## PEERS

In addition to families and teachers, *peers*—children of about the same age or maturity level—also play powerful roles in children's development and schooling (Lansford, Dishion, & Dodge, 2010; Rubin & Coplan, 2010; Wentzel & Watkins, 2011). For example, researchers have found that children who play well with others and have at least one close friend adjust better in the transition to first grade, achieve more in school, and are more mentally healthy (Ladd, Birch, & Buhs, 1999). One of the most important functions of the peer group is to provide a source of information and comparison about the world outside of the family.

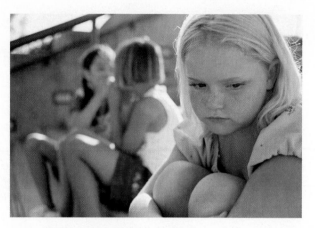

**Peer Statuses**    Developmentalists have pinpointed five types of peer status: popular children, average children, neglected children, rejected children, and controversial children (Asher & McDonald, 2009).

Many children worry about whether or not they are popular. *Popular children* are frequently nominated as a best friend and are rarely disliked by their peers. Popular children give out reinforcements, listen carefully, maintain open lines of communication with peers, are happy, act like themselves, show enthusiasm and concern for others, and are self-confident without being conceited (Hartup, 1983). *Average children* receive an average number of both positive and negative nominations from their peers. *Neglected children* are infrequently nominated as a best friend but are not disliked by their peers. *Rejected children* are infrequently nominated as someone's best friend and are often actively disliked by their peers. *Controversial children* are frequently nominated both as someone's best friend and as being disliked.

*What are some statuses that children have with their peers?*

Rejected children often have more serious adjustment problems than do neglected children, especially when rejected children are highly aggressive (Dodge, 2010; Prinstein & others, 2009). A social-skills intervention program was successful in increasing social acceptance and self-esteem and decreasing depression and anxiety in peer-rejected children (DeRosier & Marcus, 2005). Students participated in the program once a week (50 to 60 minutes) for eight weeks. The program included instruction in how to manage emotions, how to improve prosocial skills, how to become better communicators, and how to compromise and negotiate.

DEVELOPMENT

A special peer-relations problem involves bullying (Vernberg & Biggs, 2010). We will discuss bullying in Chapter 14 where we will provide strategies for dealing with bullies.

RESEARCH

**Friendship**    Friendships influence children's attitude toward school and how successful they are in the classroom (Thompson & Goodman, 2009). The importance of friendship was underscored in a two-year longitudinal study (Wentzel, Barry, & Caldwell, 2004). Sixth-grade students who did not have a friend engaged in less prosocial behavior (cooperation, sharing, helping others), had lower grades, and were more emotionally distressed (depression, low well-being) than their counterparts with one or more friends. Two years later, in the eighth grade, the students who did not have a friend in the sixth grade were still more emotionally distressed.

RESEARCH

Having friends can be a developmental advantage, but keep in mind that friendships are not all alike. Having friends who are academically oriented, socially skilled, and supportive is a developmental advantage. For example, one study revealed that friends' grade-point averages were consistent predictors of positive school achievement and also were linked to a lower level of negative behavior in areas such as drug abuse and acting out (Cook, Deng, & Morgano, 2007). But having certain types of friends can be a developmental disadvantage. For example, hanging out with friends who are delinquents greatly increases the risk of becoming delinquent (Farrington, 2010).

## SCHOOLS

In school, children spend many years as members of a small society that exerts a tremendous influence on their socioemotional development. How does this social world change as children develop?

## TEACHING CONNECTIONS: Best Practices
### Strategies for Improving Children's Social Skills

In every class you teach, some children will likely have weak social skills. One or two might be rejected children. Several others might be neglected. Here are some good strategies for improving children's social skills:

1. *Help rejected children learn to listen to peers and "hear what they say" instead of trying to dominate peers.* This includes learning to accurately read social cues. Rejected children often misinterpret the intentions of their peers, for instance assuming that an accidental bump was a purposeful shove, and act on the misinterpretation.

2. *Help neglected children attract attention from peers in positive ways and hold their attention.* They can do this by asking questions, listening in a warm and friendly way, and saying things about themselves that relate to the peers' interests. Also work with neglected children on entering groups more effectively. Establishing interest groups or clubs can help integrate neglected children in a positive way.

3. *Provide children low in social skills with knowledge about how to improve these skills.* In one study of sixth- and seventh-graders, knowledge of both appropriate and inappropriate strategies for making friends was related positively to peer acceptance (Wentzel & Erdley, 1993).

### Knowledge of Appropriate Strategies Includes Knowing

- How to initiate interaction, such as asking other children about their favorite activities or suggesting they do something together
- That it is important to be nice, kind, and considerate
- That it is necessary to show respect for others by being courteous and listening to what others have to say

### Knowledge of Inappropriate Strategies Includes Knowing

- Not to be aggressive, show disrespect, be inconsiderate, hurt others' feelings, gossip, spread rumors, embarrass others, or criticize others

*What are some appropriate and inappropriate strategies for improving social skills?*

- Not to present yourself negatively, be self-centered, care only about yourself, or be jealous, grouchy, or frequently angry
- Not to engage in antisocial behavior such as fighting, yelling at others, picking on others, making fun of others, being dishonest, breaking school rules, or taking drugs

4. *Read and discuss appropriate books on peer relations with students, and devise supportive games and activities.* Include these books as thematic units in your curriculum for young children. Make books on peer relations and friendship available to older children and adolescents. Ask students questions about how the characters in the book should react to various situations.

**Schools' Changing Social Developmental Contexts** Social contexts vary through the early childhood, elementary school, and adolescent years (Minuchin & Shapiro, 1983). The early childhood setting is a protected environment whose boundary is the classroom. In this limited social setting, young children interact with one or two teachers, usually female, who are powerful figures in their lives. Young children also interact with peers in dyads or small groups.

The classroom still is the main context in elementary school, although it is more likely to be experienced as a social unit than is the early childhood classroom. The teacher symbolizes authority, which establishes the climate of the classroom, the conditions of social interaction, and the nature of group functioning. Peer groups are more important now, and students have an increased interest in friendship.

As children move into middle and junior high school, the school environment increases in scope and complexity (Anderman & Mueller, 2010). The social field is now the whole school rather than the classroom. Adolescents interact with teachers and peers from a broader range of cultural backgrounds on a broader range of interests. More of the teachers are male. Adolescents' social behavior becomes weighted more strongly toward peers, extracurricular activities, clubs, and the community. Secondary school students are more aware of the school as a social system and might be motivated to conform to it or challenge it.

DEVELOPMENT

**Early Childhood Education**    There are many variations in how young children are educated (Marion, 2010; Morrison, 2011). However, an increasing number of education experts emphasize the importance of education being developmentally appropriate (Feeney & others, 2010; Follari, 2011).

*Developmentally Appropriate Practice*    In Chapters 1 and 2, we described the importance of engaging in developmentally appropriate teaching practices. Here we expand on this topic in reference to children from birth to 8 years of age. **Developmentally appropriate practice (DAP)** is based on knowledge of the typical development of children within an age span (age-appropriateness) as well as the uniqueness of the child (individual-appropriateness). DAP emphasizes the importance of creating settings that encourage children to be active learners and that reflect children's interests and capabilities (Kostelnik, Soderman, & Whiren, 2011). Desired outcomes for DAP include thinking critically, working cooperatively, solving problems, developing self-regulatory skills, and enjoying learning. The emphasis in DAP is on the process of learning rather than its content (Barbarin & Miller, 2009; Bredekamp, 2011). The most recent developmentally appropriate guidelines provided by the National Association for the Education of Young Children (NAEYC, 2009) are described in Figure 3.4.

Do developmentally appropriate educational practices improve young children's development? Some researchers have found that young children in developmentally appropriate classrooms are likely to have less stress, have better work habits, be more creative, and be more skilled socially than children in developmentally inappropriate classrooms (Hart & others, 2003; Stipek & others, 1995). However, not all studies show significant positive benefits for developmentally appropriate education (Hyson, Copple, & Jones, 2006). Among the reasons it is difficult to generalize about this research is that individual programs often vary, and the concept is an evolving one. Recent changes in this regard have given more attention to sociocultural factors, the teacher's active involvement, and implementation of systematic intentions, as well as how strongly academic skills should be emphasized and how they should be taught (NAEYC, 2009).

*The Montessori Approach*    Montessori schools are patterned after the educational philosophy of Maria Montessori (1870–1952), an Italian physician-turned-educator, who crafted a revolutionary approach to young children's education at the beginning of the twentieth century. Her approach has been widely adopted in private schools, especially those with early childhood programs, in the United States.

The **Montessori approach** is a philosophy of education in which children are given considerable freedom and spontaneity in choosing activities. They are allowed to move from one activity to another as they desire. The teacher acts as a facilitator rather than a director. The teacher shows the child how to perform intellectual

> **Thinking Back/Thinking Forward**
> Developmentally appropriate practice takes place at a level that is neither too difficult and stressful nor too easy and boring for the child's developmental level. Chapter 1, p. 7

RESEARCH

**developmentally appropriate practice**
Education based on knowledge of the typical development of children within an age span (age appropriateness) as well as the uniqueness of the child (individual appropriateness).

**Montessori approach**  An educational philosophy in which children are given considerable freedom and spontaneity in choosing activities and are allowed to move from one activity to another as they desire.

**Core Considerations in Developmentally Appropriate Practice**

**1 Knowledge to Consider in Making Decisions**

In all aspects of working with children, early childhood practitioners need to consider these three areas of knowledge: 1) What is known about child development and learning, especially age-related characteristics; 2) What is known about each child as an individual; and 3) What is known about the social and cultural contexts in which children live.

**2 Challenging and Achievable Goals**

Keeping in mind desired goals and what is known about the children as a group and individually, teachers plan experiences to promote children's learning and development.

**Principles of Child Development and Learning That Inform Practice**

**1** All the domains of development and learning—physical, cognitive, and social—are important, and they are linked.

**2** Many aspects of children's learning and development follow well-documented sequences, with later abilities, skills, and knowledge building on those already acquired.

**3** Development and learning proceed at varying rates from child to child, and at uneven rates across different areas of a child's individual functioning.

**4** Development and learning result from the interaction of biology and experience.

**5** Early experiences have strong effects—both cumulative and delayed—on children's development and learning; optimal periods exist for certain types of development and learning.

**6** Development proceeds toward greater complexity, self-regulation, and symbolic or representational capacities.

**7** Children develop best when they have secure, consistent relationships with responsive adults and opportunities for positive peer relations.

**8** Development and learning occur in and are influenced by multiple social and cultural contexts.

**9** Always mentally active in seeking to understand the world around them, children learn in a variety of ways; a wide range of teaching strategies can be effective in guiding children's learning.

**10** Play is an important context for developing self-regulation and for promoting language, cognition, and competence.

**11** Development and learning advance when children are challenged to achieve at a level just beyond their current mastery and when they are given opportunities to practice newly acquired skills.

**12** Children's experiences shape their motivation and approaches to learning, such as persistence, initiative, and flexibility; in turn, these characteristics influence their learning and development.

**Guidelines for Developmentally Appropriate Practice**

**1 Creating a Caring Community of Learners**

Each member of the community should be valued by the others; relationships are an important context through which children learn; practitioners ensure that members of the community feel psychologically safe.

**2 Teaching to Enhance Development and Learning**

The teacher takes responsibility for stimulating, directing, and supporting children's learning by providing the experiences that each child needs.

**3 Planning Curriculum to Achieve Important Goals**

The curriculum is planned to help children achieve goals that are developmentally appropriate and educationally significant.

**4 Assessing Children's Development and Learning**

In developmentally appropriate practice, assessments are linked to the program's goals for children.

**5 Establishing Reciprocal Relationships with Families**

A positive partnership between teachers and families benefits children's learning and development.

**FIGURE 3.4** RECOMMENDATIONS BY NAEYC FOR DEVELOPMENTALLY APPROPRIATE PRACTICE IN EARLY CHILDHOOD PROGRAMS SERVING CHILDREN FROM BIRTH THROUGH AGE 8

*Source:* Table excerpted and adapted from the NAEYC 2009 position statement Developmentally Appropriate Practice in Early Childhood Programs Serving Children from Birth through Age 8. Used with permission from the National Association for the Education of Young Children (NAEYC). Copyright © 2009 NAEYC. Full position statement text available at www.naeyc.org/files/naeyc/file/positions/PSDAP.pdf

activities, demonstrates interesting ways to explore curriculum materials, and offers help when the child requests it (Cossentino, 2008). A special emphasis in Montessori schools is to encourage children to make decisions at an early age and become self-regulated problem solvers who manage time effectively (Hyson, Copple, & Jones, 2006). The number of Montessori schools in the United States has expanded dramatically in recent years, from one school in 1959 to 355 schools in 1970 to approximately 4,000 in 2005 (Whitescarver, 2006).

Some developmentalists favor the Montessori approach, but others hold that it neglects children's social development. For example, although Montessori fosters independence and the development of cognitive skills, it deemphasizes verbal interaction between the teacher and child and peer interaction. Montessori's critics also

argue that it restricts imaginative play and that its heavy reliance on self-corrective materials may not adequately allow
for creativity and for a variety of learning styles (Goffin &
Wilson, 2001).

***Controversy in Early Childhood Education***    A current
controversy in early childhood education involves the curriculum (Bredekamp, 2011; Shonkoff, 2010). On one side are
those who advocate a child-centered, constructivist approach
much like that emphasized by the National Association for
the Education of Young Children (NAEYC), along the lines
of developmentally appropriate practice. On the other side
are those who advocate an academic, direct instruction
approach.

In reality, many high-quality early childhood education
programs include both academic and constructivist approaches. Many education experts like Lilian Katz (1999),
though, worry about academic approaches that place too
much pressure on young children to achieve and don't provide any opportunities to actively construct knowledge.
Also, competent early childhood programs should focus on
cognitive development *and* socioemotional development,
not exclusively on cognitive development (NAEYC, 2009).

Larry Page and Sergey-Brin, founders of the highly successful Internet search
engine, Google, recently said that their early years at Montessori schools
were a major factor in their success (International Montessori Council, 2006).
During an interview with Barbara Walters, they said they learned how to be
self-directed and self-starters at Montessori (ABC News, 2005). They commented that Montessori experiences encouraged them to think for themselves and allowed them the freedom to develop their own interests.

***Early Childhood Education for Children from Low-Income Families***    Beginning
in the 1960s, *Project Head Start* was designed to provide young children from
low-income families opportunities to acquire the skills and experiences that are
important for success in school (Zigler & Styfco, 2010). Funded by the federal
government, Project Head Start continues to serve children who are disadvantaged today. It is the largest federally funded program for U.S. children (Hagen
& Lamb-Parker, 2008).

DIVERSITY

In high-quality Head Start programs, parents and communities are involved
in positive ways. The teachers are knowledgeable about children's development and
use developmentally appropriate practices. Researchers have found that when
young children from low-income families experience a high-quality Head Start
program, there are substantial long-term benefits (Allen, 2008). These include
being less likely to drop out of school, or to be in a special education class, or to
be on welfare than their low-income counterparts who did not attend such a program (Lazar & others, 1982; Schweinhart & others, 2005). However, Head Start
programs are not all created equal. One estimate is that 40 percent of the 1,400
Head Start programs are inadequate (Zigler & Finn-Stevenson, 1999).

RESEARCH

**The Transition to Elementary School**    As children make the transition to
elementary school, they interact and develop relationships with new and significant
others. School provides them with a rich source of ideas to shape their sense of self.

A special concern about early elementary school classrooms is that they sometimes proceed primarily on the basis of negative feedback. I (your author) vividly
remember my first-grade teacher. Unfortunately, she never smiled; she was a dictator
in the classroom, and learning (or lack of learning) progressed more on the basis of
fear than of enjoyment and passion. Fortunately, I experienced some warmer, more
student-friendly teachers later on.

Children's self-esteem is higher when they begin elementary school than when
they complete it (Blumenfeld & others, 1981). Is that because they have experienced
so much negative feedback and were criticized so much along the way? We will say
more about the roles of reinforcement and punishment in children's learning in
Chapter 7 and about managing the classroom in Chapter 14.

As children make the transition to elementary school, they interact and develop relationships with new and significant others. School provides them with a rich source of new ideas to shape their sense of self. *What is a current concern about the transition to elementary school?*

RESEARCH

Teachers play an important role at every level of schooling, including elementary schools (Mashburn & others, 2008; Pianta & others, 2008). In a series of studies from infancy through third grade, positive teacher-child relationships were linked to a number of positive child outcomes (Howes & Ritchie, 2002). In this research, even when children evidenced a lack of trust in prior caregivers, their current relationship with a teacher was capable of being positive and compensating for earlier negative relationships. Children who have warm, positive relationships with their teachers have a more positive attitude toward school, are more enthusiastic about learning, and achieve more in school (Thompson & Goodman, 2009).

To help ease the transition to elementary school, a current trend is to increasingly place children in pre-K (prekindergarten) in the same school as children in first, second, and third grades (called "P-3") (Ritchie, Maxwell, & Bredekamp, 2009). However, there is concern that in such schools the child-centered emphasis of preschool and kindergarten will be replaced by emphasis on the higher-grade curricula that use standardized tests, workbooks, and ability grouping (Barbarin & Miller, 2009). The hope is that an integration of pre-K with P-3 will reflect the characteristics of developmentally appropriate education that were discussed earlier.

**The Schooling of Adolescents**    Three special concerns about adolescent schooling are (1) the transition to middle or junior high school, (2) effective schooling for young adolescents, and (3) the quality of high schools. How might the transition to middle or junior high school be difficult for many students?

*The Transition to Middle or Junior High School*    This transition can be stressful because it coincides with many other developmental changes (Anderman, 2011; Anderman & Anderman, 2010). Students are beginning puberty and have increased concerns about their body image. The hormonal changes of puberty stimulate increased interest in sexual matters. Students are becoming more independent from their parents and want to spend more time with peers. They must make the change from a smaller, more personalized classroom to a larger, more impersonal school. Achievement becomes more serious business, and getting good grades becomes more competitive (Kellough & Carjuzaa, 2009).

As students move from elementary to middle or junior high school, they experience the *top-dog phenomenon*. This refers to moving from the top position (in elementary school, being the oldest, biggest, and most powerful students in the school) to the lowest position (in middle or junior high school, being the youngest, smallest, and least powerful students in the school). Schools that provide more support, less anonymity, more stability, and less complexity improve student adjustment during this transition (Fenzel, Blyth, & Simmons, 1991).

There can also be positive aspects to the transition to middle or junior high school. Students are more likely to feel grown up, have more subjects from which to select, have more opportunities to spend time with peers and locate compatible friends, and enjoy increased independence from direct parental monitoring. They also may be more challenged intellectually by academic work.

*Effective Schools for Young Adolescents*    Educators and psychologists worry that junior high and middle schools have become watered-down versions of high schools, mimicking their curricular and extracurricular schedules. Critics argue that these

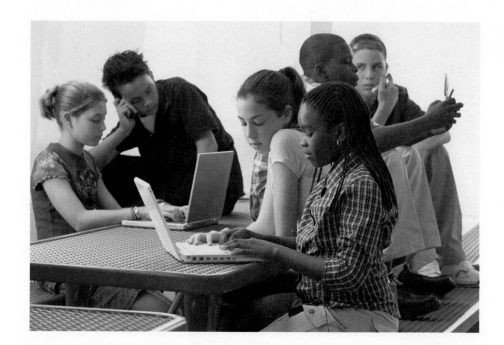

The transition from elementary to middle or junior high school occurs at the same time as a number of other developmental changes. *What are some of these other developmental changes?*

schools should offer activities that reflect a wide range of individual differences in biological and psychological development among young adolescents. The Carnegie Foundation (1989) issued an extremely negative evaluation of our nation's middle schools. It concluded that most young adolescents attended massive, impersonal schools; were taught from irrelevant curricula; trusted few adults in school; and lacked access to health care and counseling. It recommended that the nation develop smaller "communities" or "houses" to lessen the impersonal nature of large middle schools, have lower student-to-counselor ratios (10 to 1 instead of several-hundred to 1), involve parents and community leaders in schools, develop new curricula, have teachers team-teach in more flexibly designed curriculum blocks that integrate several disciplines, boost students' health and fitness with more in-school programs, and help students who need public health care to get it. Twenty-five years later, experts are still finding that middle schools throughout the nation need a major redesign if they are to be effective in educating adolescents (Eccles & Roeser, 2009).

**Improving America's High Schools** Just as there are concerns about U.S. middle school education, so are there concerns about U.S. high school education (Smith, 2009). Critics stress that in many high schools expectations for success and standards for learning are too low. Critics also argue that too often high schools foster passivity and that schools should create a variety of pathways for students to achieve an identity. Many students graduate from high school with inadequate reading, writing, and mathematical skills—including many who go on to college and have to enroll in remediation classes there. Other students drop out of high school and lack the skills that would allow them to obtain decent jobs, much less to be informed citizens (Jimerson, 2009).

In the last half of the twentieth century and the first several years of the twenty-first century, U.S. high school dropout rates declined (National Center for Education Statistics, 2008) (see Figure 3.5). In the 1940s more than half of U.S. 16- to 24-year-olds had dropped out of school; by 2006 this figure had decreased to 9.3 percent. The dropout rate of Latino adolescents remains high, although it is decreasing in the twenty-first century (from 28 percent in 2000 to 22.1 percent in 2006). The highest dropout rate in the United States, though, likely occurs for Native American youth—less than 50 percent finish their high school education.

Students drop out of schools for many reasons (Allensworth & Nagako, 2010; Jimerson, 2009). In one study, almost 50 percent of the dropouts cited school-related

DIVERSITY

FIGURE **3.5** TRENDS IN HIGH SCHOOL DROPOUT RATES

From 1972 through 2006 the school dropout rate for Latinos remained very high (22.1 percent of 16- to 24-year-olds in 2006). The African American dropout rate was still higher (10.9 percent) than the White non-Latino rate (5.8 percent) in 2006.

RESEARCH

reasons for leaving school, such as not liking school or being expelled or suspended (Rumberger, 1995). Twenty percent of the dropouts (but 40 percent of the Latino students) cited economic reasons for leaving school. One-third of the female students dropped out for personal reasons such as pregnancy or marriage.

According to a research review, the most effective efforts to discourage dropping out of high school provide early reading programs, tutoring, counseling, and mentoring (Lehr & others, 2003). They also emphasize the creation of caring environments and relationships, use block scheduling, and offer community-service opportunities.

Early detection of children's school-related difficulties, and getting children engaged with school in positive ways, are important strategies for reducing the dropout rate. Recently the Bill and Melinda Gates Foundation (2008) has funded efforts to reduce the dropout rate in schools where rates are high.

One strategy that is being emphasized in the Gates' funding is keeping students who are at risk for dropping out of school with the same teachers through their high school years. The hope is that the teachers will get to know these students much better, their relationship with the students will strengthen, and they will be able to monitor and guide the students toward graduating from high school.

Participation in extracurricular activities also is linked to reduced school dropout rates (Mahoney, Parente, & Zigler, 2010). Adolescents in U.S. schools usually have a wide array of extracurricular activities they can participate in beyond their academic courses. These adult-sanctioned activities typically occur in the after-school hours and can be sponsored either by the school or the community. They include such diverse activities as sports, academic clubs, band, drama, and service groups. In addition to lower school dropout rates, researchers have found that participation in extracurricular activities is linked to higher grades, better school engagement, improved likelihood of going to college, higher self-esteem, and lower rates of depression, delinquency, and substance abuse (Fredricks, 2008). Adolescents benefit from a breadth of extracurricular activities more than focusing on a single extracurricular activity (Mahoney & others, 2009). Also, the more years adolescents spend in extracurricular activities, the stronger the link is with positive developmental outcomes (Mahoney, Parente, & Zigler, 2010).

Of course, the quality of the extracurricular activities matters (Barber, Stone, & Eccles, 2010). High-quality extracurricular activities that are likely to promote positive adolescent development include competent, supportive adult mentors, opportunities for increasing school connectedness, challenging and meaningful activities, and opportunities for improving skills (Mahoney, Parente, & Zigler, 2010).

## Review, Reflect, and Practice

**2** Discuss how the social contexts of families, peers, and schools are linked with socioemotional development.

### REVIEW

- What four parenting styles did Baumrind propose, and which is likely to be the most effective? How do aspects of families such as working parents, divorce, and stepfamilies affect children's development and education? In what ways can school-family linkages be fostered?
- What are peers and the five peer statuses? What risks are attached to certain peer statuses? How do friendships matter?
- What are some characteristics and key aspects of schools at different levels of education—early childhood education, the transition to elementary school, and the schooling of adolescents?

### REFLECT

- What parenting style(s) have you witnessed and experienced? What effects did they have?

### PRAXIS™ PRACTICE

1. Which of the following teachers is most likely to encourage appropriate parental involvement in their children's education?
   a. Mr. Bastian sends home weekly progress notes to the parents who request them. He invites each parent to a conference at the end of the first grading period, and contacts parents if a child is in serious trouble at school.
   b. Ms. Washington contacts parents before the school year begins. She holds a meeting for parents to discuss her expectations for both children and parents and to answer questions. She requests volunteers to help in the classroom and chaperone field trips. She sends home weekly progress reports that include academic and social information.
   c. Ms. Jefferson tells parents that their children need to develop independence, which won't happen if they hover around at school and interfere with the educational process.
   d. Ms. Hernandez holds two parent-teacher conferences each year and e-mails parents if children fall behind in their work or present any problems in class. She occasionally e-mails a parent when a child has made marked improvement or accomplished something special.

2. Samuel is in fourth grade. He is large for his age, but not very mature. He is extremely sensitive to any kind of criticism—constructive or not. He cries when somebody teases him, which is often. Samuel often elicits teasing from his peers by engaging in it himself. Which peer status is most likely for Samuel?
   a. controversial
   b. neglected
   c. popular
   d. rejected

3. Which of the following is the best example of a developmentally appropriate unit on pioneer life for third-graders?
   a. Mr. Johnson's class has read about the daily lives of pioneers and is now constructing log cabins that demonstrate their understanding of the typical cabin of the period. Mr. Johnson moves around the room, giving help when needed, asking students why they are including certain features, and ensuring that all stay on task.

*(continued)*

## Review, Reflect, and Practice

### PRAXIS™ PRACTICE (CONTINUED)

b. In Ms. Lincoln's class, each student has read a different book about pioneer life and is now writing a book report. The students work quietly at their desks on their reports. She occasionally chastises students for talking or for daydreaming.

c. Mr. Roosevelt's class is taking turns reading aloud a book about pioneer life. Each student reads a paragraph of the book in turn. When they are finished with the book, they will be tested on the content.

d. Ms. Silver is lecturing to her students about pioneer life. She has gone over reasons for the westward migration, modes of transportation, and clearing the land and building a cabin. She will give them a test about pioneer life on Friday.

*Please see the answer key at the end of the book.*

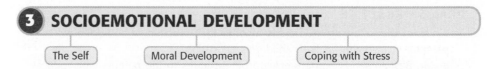

### ③ SOCIOEMOTIONAL DEVELOPMENT

| The Self | Moral Development | Coping with Stress |

So far we have discussed three important social contexts that influence students' socioemotional development: families, peers, and schools. In this section, we focus more on the individual students themselves as we explore the development of the self, morality, and coping with stress.

## THE SELF

*The living self has one purpose only: to come into its own fullness of being, as a tree comes into full blossom, or a bird into spring beauty, or a tiger into lustre.*

—D. H. Lawrence
*English Author, 20th Century*

RESEARCH

DEVELOPMENT

**self-esteem** Also called *self-image* and *self-worth,* the individual's overall conception of herself or himself.

According to twentieth-century Italian playwright Ugo Betti, when children say "I," they mean something unique, not to be confused with any other. Psychologists often refer to that "I" as the *self.* Two important aspects of the self are self-esteem and identity.

**Self-Esteem**    **Self-esteem** refers to an individual's overall view of himself or herself. Self-esteem also is referred to as *self-worth* or *self-image.* For example, a child with high self-esteem might perceive that she is not just a person but a *good* person.

For many students, periods of low self-esteem come and go. But for some students, persistent low self-esteem translates into other, more serious problems. Persistent low self-esteem is linked with low achievement, depression, eating disorders, and delinquency (Kaplan, 2009). A New Zealand longitudinal study assessed self-esteem at 11, 13, and 15 years of age and adjustment and competence of the same individuals when they were 26 years old (Trzesniewski & others, 2006). The results revealed that adults characterized by poorer mental and physical health, worse economic prospects, and higher levels of criminal behavior were more likely to have had low self-esteem in adolescence than their better-adjusted, more competent adult counterparts.

The seriousness of the problem depends not only on the nature of the student's low self-esteem but on other conditions as well. When low self-esteem is compounded by difficult school transitions (such as the transition to middle school) or family problems (such as divorce), the student's problems can intensify.

Researchers have found that self-esteem changes as children develop (Kaplan, 2009). In one study, both boys and girls had high self-esteem in childhood but their self-esteem dropped considerably in early adolescence (Robins & others, 2002). The

## TEACHING CONNECTIONS: Best Practices
### Strategies for Improving Children's Self-Esteem

A current concern is that too many of today's children and adolescents grow up receiving empty praise and as a consequence have inflated self-esteem (Graham, 2005; Stipek, 2005). Too often they are given praise for mediocre or even poor performances. Consequently, they may have difficulty handling competition and criticism.

However, it is possible to raise children's self-esteem constructively. Consider the following four strategies (Bednar, Wells, & Peterson, 1995; Harter, 2006):

1. *Identify the causes of low self-esteem and the areas of competence important to the self.* This is critical. Is the child's low self-esteem due to poor school achievement? Family conflict? Weak social skills? Students have the highest self-esteem when they perform competently in areas that they themselves feel are important. Thus, find out from students with low self-esteem what areas of competence they value. Do not jump to conclusions based on what you value.

2. *Provide emotional support and social approval.* Virtually every class has children who have received too many negative evaluations. These children might come from an abusive and demeaning family that constantly puts them down, or they might have been in prior classrooms that delivered too much negative feedback. Your emotional support and social approval can make a big difference in helping them value themselves more. In Through the Eyes of Teachers, Judy Logan, a middle school teacher in San Francisco, underscores the importance of providing emotional support. Understand that you cannot provide a student with social approval from his/her peers and trying to force it can backfire.

### THROUGH THE EYES OF TEACHERS
#### Listening, Explaining, and Supporting

I believe that a good teacher should passionately be on the side of her students. That does not mean I support them in everything they do. It means I demand the best of them and am willing to help them be their best selves. It means I listen, explain, support, and allow without judgment, sarcasm, or the need to impose the truth from the outside. The passage from childhood to adulthood we call adolescence is a very vulnerable journey. It is often a difficult time for students and for their families. It is an adolescent's "job" to rebel at times and to question the family environment that was such a comfortable cocoon during childhood. No matter how wonderful the parents, how loving the family, each adolescent needs to have other adults in whom to confide. . . .

3. *Help children achieve.* Achieving can improve children's self-esteem. Straightforward teaching of real academic skills often improves children's achievement, and subsequently their self-esteem. Often it is not enough to tell children they can achieve something; you also have to help them develop their academic skills. Make certain that the achievement is real—tasks must be challenging for this to have impact.

4. *Help children develop coping skills.* For students with low self-esteem, their unfavorable self-evaluations often trigger denial, deception, and avoidance. This type of self-generated disapproval makes a student feel personally inadequate. But when children face a problem and cope with it realistically, honestly, and nondefensively, it can raise their self-esteem.

---

self-esteem of girls dropped about twice as much as that of boys during adolescence (see Figure 3.6). Other studies have also found that female adolescents had lower self-esteem than male adolescents, and their lower self-esteem was associated with less healthy adjustment (McLean & Breen, 2009). However, note in Figure 3.6 that despite the drop in self-esteem among adolescent girls, their average self-esteem score (3.3) was still higher than the neutral point on the scale (3.0). In a recent study, a nine-month physical activity intervention with sedentary adolescent girls improved their self-image (Schneider, Dunton, & Cooper, 2008).

Variations in self-esteem are related to many aspects of development (Harter, 2006). For example, a recent study found that adolescents who had low self-esteem had lower levels of mental health, physical health, and economic prospects as adults than adolescents with high self-esteem (Trzesniewski & others, 2006). However, much of the research on self-esteem is *correlational* rather than experimental. Recall from Chapter 1 that correlation does not equal causation. Thus, if a correlational study finds an association between children's low self-esteem and low academic achievement, we know that low academic achievement could cause the low self-esteem as much as low self-esteem causes low academic achievement.

*How is school performance linked to children's self-esteem?*

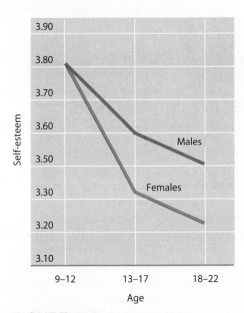

**FIGURE 3.6** THE DECLINE OF SELF-ESTEEM IN ADOLESCENCE

In one study the self-esteem of both boys and girls declined during adolescence, but it declined considerably more for girls than boys (Robins & others, 2002). The self-esteem scores represent the mean self-esteem scores on a 5-point scale, with higher scores reflecting higher self-esteem.

In fact, there are only moderate correlations between school performance and self-esteem, and these correlations do not suggest that high self-esteem produces better school performance (Baumeister & others, 2003). Efforts to increase students' self-esteem have not always led to improved school performance (Davies & Brember, 1999).

Students' self-esteem often varies across different domains, such as academic, athletic, physical appearance, social skills, and so on (Harter, 2006). Thus, a student might have high self-esteem in regard to schoolwork but have low self-esteem in the areas of athletic skills, physical appearance, and social skills. Even within the academic domain, a student might have high self-esteem in some subjects (math, for example) and low self-esteem in others (English, for example).

I recently asked teachers what strategies they use to promote self-esteem in their classrooms. Following are their recommendations.

**EARLY CHILDHOOD**   Our preschoolers feel really great when they receive stickers, stamps, and reward certificates for good behavior and work. In addition, each week  children are asked to come to school with one special item from home to discuss in class and say why the item is important to them.

—**MISSY DANGLER,** *Suburban Hills School*

**ELEMENTARY SCHOOL: GRADES K–5**   To help my second-graders improve self-esteem I focus on what they are doing correctly as opposed to what they are doing  incorrectly. I steer them to the correct answer rather than saying, "No, that's not right." Repeating or rephrasing the question also gives them another chance to try again in a nonthreatening environment. I also get on their eye level physically, sitting or bending down, so I can look them straight in the eyes, not down over them. These strategies help my young students feel important, valued, and part of the class, not just as a learner, but as a person.

—**JANINE GUIDA POUTRE,** *Clinton Elementary School*

**MIDDLE SCHOOL: GRADES 6–8**   I once had a student that did poorly on tests and quizzes. Every time there was a test, he would break down and start calling himself names because he could not answer the questions. However, this student was very good at drawing, and I used that skill to bolster his self-esteem. For example, I made sure that every time I needed some kind of diagram for a class assignment, I called on him for help. I would tell him that he had amazing artistic ability and tell him that everyone has strengths and weaknesses, and that it was important to work on his test-taking issues in order to improve them. I also told him about a few of my own weaknesses and what I do to improve them. And, I created review games that included drawing to help him study for quizzes. This did not help his self-esteem overnight, but over the course of the school year, he became prouder of his work and did not put himself down as much.

—**CASEY MAASS,** *Edison Middle School*

**HIGH SCHOOL: GRADES 9–12**   With my high school students, I make praise loud and clear, and I love to take the kids who have been labeled "loser" and relabel them  as "reader" or "grammar princess" or "best arguer in the school." Although these labels may seem silly, my high school students blossom under the praise. I also remember that the praise I give to one of my students may be the only praise that he or she has heard—indeed, that student may not get any praise at home. Praise not only improves self-esteem for students' in-class performance, but it also gives them *permission* to succeed and do well in general.

—**JENNIFER HEITER,** *Bremen High School*

**Identity Status**

| Position on Occupation and Ideology | Identity Diffusion | Identity Foreclosure | Identity Moratorium | Identity Achievement |
|---|---|---|---|---|
| **Crisis** | Absent | Absent | Present | Present |
| **Commitment** | Absent | Present | Absent | Present |

FIGURE **3.7** MARCIA'S FOUR STATUSES OF IDENTITY

**Identity Development**    Another important aspect of the self is identity. Earlier in the chapter, we mentioned that Erik Erikson (1968) argued that the most important issue in adolescence involves identity development—searching for answers to questions like these: Who am I? What am I all about? What am I going to do with my life? Not usually considered during childhood, these questions become nearly universal concerns during the high school and college years (Coté, 2009).

DEVELOPMENT

***Identity Statuses***    Canadian researcher James Marcia (1980, 1998) analyzed Erikson's concept of identity and concluded that it is important to distinguish between exploration and commitment. *Exploration* involves examining meaningful alternative identities. *Commitment* means showing a personal investment in an identity and staying with whatever that identity implies.

The extent of an individual's exploration and commitment is used to classify her or him according to one of four identity statuses (see Figure 3.7).

- **Identity diffusion** occurs when individuals have not yet experienced a crisis (that is, they have not yet explored meaningful alternatives) or made any commitments. Not only are they undecided about occupational and ideological choices, but they are also likely to show little interest in such matters.
- **Identity foreclosure** occurs when individuals have made a commitment but have not yet experienced a crisis. This occurs most often when parents hand down commitments to their adolescents, usually in an authoritarian manner. In these circumstances, adolescents have not had adequate opportunities to explore different approaches, ideologies, and vocations on their own.
- **Identity moratorium** occurs when individuals are in the midst of a crisis, but their commitments are either absent or only vaguely defined.
- **Identity achievement** occurs when individuals have undergone a crisis and have made a commitment.

To further consider identity, complete Self-Assessment 3.1. There you will be able to apply Marcia's identity statuses to a number of different areas of identity in your own life.

***Ethnic Identity***    A person's *ethnic identity* is an enduring aspect of the self that includes a sense of membership in an ethnic group, along with the attitudes and feelings related to that membership. The immediate contexts in which ethnic minority youth live also influence their identity development (Juang & Syed, 2010; Swanson, 2010). In the United States, many ethnic minority youth live in pockets of poverty, are exposed to drugs, gangs, and crime, and interact with youth and adults who have dropped out of school or are unemployed. Support for developing a positive identity is scarce. In such settings, programs for youth can make an important contribution to positive identity development.

Researchers are finding that a positive ethnic identity is related to positive outcomes for ethnic minority adolescents (Umana-Taylor, Gonzales-Backen, &

DIVERSITY

**identity diffusion**  The identity status in which individuals have neither explored meaningful alternatives nor made a commitment.

**identity foreclosure**  The identity status in which individuals have made a commitment but have not explored meaningful alternatives.

**identity moratorium**  The identity status in which individuals are in the midst of exploring alternatives but have not yet made a commitment.

**identity achievement**  The identity status in which individuals have explored meaningful alternatives and made a commitment.

Your identity is made up of many different parts, and so too will your students' identities be comprised of many different dimensions. By completing this checklist, you should gain a better sense of your own identity and the different aspects of your future students' identities. For each component, check your identity status as diffused, foreclosed, in a moratorium, or achieved.

| Identity Component | IDENTITY STATUS | | | |
|---|---|---|---|---|
| | Diffused | Foreclosed | Moratorium | Achieved |
| Vocational identity | | | | |
| Religious identity | | | | |
| Achievement/intellectual identity | | | | |
| Political identity | | | | |
| Sexual identity | | | | |
| Gender identity | | | | |
| Relationship identity | | | | |
| Lifestyle identity | | | | |
| Ethnic and cultural identity | | | | |
| Personality characteristics | | | | |
| Interests | | | | |

If you checked "Diffused" or "Foreclosed" for any areas, take some time to think about what you need to do to move into a "Moratorium" identity status in those areas, and write about this in your portfolio.

RESEARCH

DEVELOPMENT

Guimond, 2009). For example, one study revealed that ethnic identity was linked with higher school engagement and lower aggression (Van Buren & Graham, 2003). A recent study of Latino youth indicated that growth in identity exploration was linked with a positive increase in self-esteem (Umana-Taylor, Gonzales-Backen, & Guimond, 2009). Exploration is an important aspect of establishing a secure sense of one's own identity, which in turn is linked to a positive attitude toward one's own group and other groups (Whitehead & others, 2009).

## MORAL DEVELOPMENT

As children develop a sense of self and an identity, they also develop a sense of morality.

**Domains of Moral Development**   A person's **moral development** concerns rules and conventions about just interactions between people. These rules can be studied in three domains: cognitive, behavioral, and emotional. In the *cognitive domain* the key issue is how students reason or think about rules for ethical conduct. In the *behavioral domain* the focus is on how students actually behave rather than on the morality of their thinking. In the *emotional domain* the emphasis is on how students morally feel. For instance, do they associate strong enough guilt feelings with an immoral action to resist performing that action? Do they show empathy toward others?

**Kohlberg's Theory**   Lawrence Kohlberg (1976, 1986) stressed that moral development primarily involves moral reasoning and occurs in stages. Kohlberg arrived at his theory after interviewing children, adolescents, and adults (primarily males) about their views on a series of moral dilemmas. A key concept in understanding progression through the levels and stages is that their morality becomes more internal or mature. That is, their reasons for their moral decisions or values begin to go beyond the external or superficial reasons they gave when they were younger. Let's further examine Kohlberg's stages.

### Identity Exploring

Michelle Chin, age 16, reflecting on her identity, commented, "Parents do not understand that teenagers need to find out who they are, which means a lot of experimenting, a lot of mood swings, a lot of emotions and awkwardness. Like any teenager, I am facing an identity crisis. I am still trying to figure out whether I am a Chinese American or an American with Asian eyes."

Michelle Chin

**Kohlberg's Level 1: Preconventional Reasoning**   The lowest level of reasoning in Kohlberg's theory is **preconventional reasoning,** which consists of two stages: punishment and obedience orientation (stage 1) and individualism, instrumental purpose, and exchange (stage 2).

- Stage 1. *Punishment and obedience orientation* is the first Kohlberg stage of moral development. At this stage, moral thinking is often tied to punishment. For example, children and adolescents obey adults because adults tell them to obey.

- Stage 2. *Individualism, instrumental purpose, and exchange* is the second stage of Kohlberg's theory. At this stage, individuals pursue their own interests but also let others do the same. Thus, what is right involves an equal exchange. People are nice to others so that others will be nice to them in return.

**Kohlberg's Level 2: Conventional Reasoning**   The second, or intermediate, level in Kohlberg's theory of moral development is **conventional reasoning.** Individuals at this level abide by certain standards (internal), but they are the standards of others (external), such as parents or the laws of society. Conventional reasoning consists of two stages: mutual interpersonal expectations, relationships, and interpersonal conformity (stage 3) and social systems morality (stage 4).

- Stage 3. *Mutual interpersonal expectations, relationships, and interpersonal conformity* is Kohlberg's third stage of moral development (occurring at the second level). At this stage, individuals value trust, caring, and loyalty to others as a basis of moral judgments. Children and adolescents often adopt their parents' moral standards at this stage, seeking to be thought of by their parents as a "good girl" or a "good boy."

- Stage 4. *Social systems morality* is the fourth stage in Kohlberg's theory of moral development (occurring, like stage 3, at the second level). At this stage, moral judgments are based on understanding the social order, law, justice, and duty. For example, adolescents may say that for a community to work effectively, it needs to be protected by laws that are adhered to by its members.

Lawrence Kohlberg, the architect of a provocative cognitive developmental theory of moral development. *What is the nature of his theory?*

**moral development**   Development with respect to the rules and conventions of just interactions between people.

**preconventional reasoning**   The lowest level in Kohlberg's theory. At this level, morality is often focused on reward and punishment. The two stages in preconventional reasoning are punishment and obedience orientation (stage 1) and individualism, instrumental purpose, and exchange (stage 2).

**conventional reasoning**   The second, or intermediate, level in Kohlberg's theory of moral development. At this level, individuals abide by certain standards (internal), but they are the standards of others such as parents or the laws of society (external). The conventional level consists of two stages: mutual interpersonal expectations, relationships, and interpersonal conformity (stage 3) and social systems morality (stage 4).

| LEVEL 1 | LEVEL 2 | LEVEL 3 |
|---|---|---|
| **Preconventional Level** **No Internalization** | **Conventional Level** **Intermediate Internalization** | **Postconventional Level** **Full Internalization** |
| **Stage 1** Heteronomous Morality | **Stage 3** Mutual Interpersonal Expectations, Relationships, and Interpersonal Conformity | **Stage 5** Social Contract or Utility and Individual Rights |
| *Individuals pursue their own interests but let others do the same. What is right involves equal exchange.* | *Individuals value trust, caring, and loyalty to others as a basis for moral judgments.* | *Individuals reason that values, rights, and principles undergird or transcend the law.* |
| **Stage 2** Individualism, Purpose, and Exchange | **Stage 4** Social System Morality | **Stage 6** Universal Ethical Principles |
| *Children obey because adults tell them to obey. People base their moral decisions on fear of punishment.* | *Moral judgments are based on understanding of the social order, law, justice, and duty.* | *The person has developed moral judgments that are based on universal human rights. When faced with a dilemma between law and conscience, a personal, individualized conscience is followed.* |

**FIGURE 3.8** KOHLBERG'S THREE LEVELS AND SIX STAGES OF MORAL DEVELOPMENT

Kohlberg argued that people everywhere develop their moral reasoning by passing through these age-based stages.

***Kohlberg's Level 3: Postconventional Reasoning*** The third and highest level in Kohlberg's theory is **postconventional reasoning.** At this level, morality is more internal. The postconventional level of morality consists of two stages: social contract or utility and individual rights (stage 5) and universal ethical principles (stage 6).

- Stage 5. *Social contract or utility and individual rights* is the fifth Kohlberg stage (occurring at the third level). At this stage, individuals reason that values, rights, and principles undergird or transcend the law. A person evaluates the validity of actual laws and examines social systems in terms of the degree to which they preserve and protect fundamental human rights and values.
- Stage 6. *Universal ethical principles* is the sixth and highest stage in Kohlberg's theory of moral development (occurring at the third level). At this stage, the person has developed a moral standard based on universal human rights. When faced with a conflict between law and conscience, the person will follow conscience, even though the decision might involve personal risk.

RESEARCH

A summary of Kohlberg's three levels and six stages, along with examples of each of the stages, is presented in Figure 3.8. In studies of Kohlberg's theory, longitudinal data show a relation of the stages to age, although few people ever attain the two highest stages, especially stage 6 (Colby & others, 1983). Before age 9, most children reason about moral dilemmas at a preconventional level. By early adolescence, they are more likely to reason at the conventional level.

Kohlberg stressed that underlying changes in cognitive development promote more advanced moral thinking. He also said that children construct their moral thoughts as they pass through the stages—that they do not just passively accept a cultural norm for morality. Kohlberg argued that a child's moral thinking can be advanced through discussions with others who reason at the next higher stage. He thought that the mutual give-and-take of peer relations promotes more advanced moral thinking because of the role-taking opportunities it provides children.

***Kohlberg's Critics*** Kohlberg's provocative theory has not gone unchallenged (Gibbs, 2010; Walker & Frimer, 2011). One criticism centers on the idea that moral thoughts don't always predict moral behavior. The criticism is that Kohlberg's theory

**postconventional reasoning** The third and highest level in Kohlberg's theory of moral development. At this level, morality is more internal. The postconventional level consists of two stages: social contract or utility and individual rights (stage 5) and universal ethical principles (stage 6).

places too much emphasis on moral thinking and not enough on moral behavior. Moral reasons sometimes can be a shelter for immoral behavior. Bank embezzlers and U.S. presidents endorse the loftiest of moral virtues, but their own behavior can prove to be immoral. No one wants a nation of stage-6 Kohlberg thinkers who know what is right yet do what is wrong.

Another line of criticism is that Kohlberg's theory is too individualistic. Carol Gilligan (1982, 1998) distinguishes between the justice perspective and the care perspective. Kohlberg's is a **justice perspective** that focuses on the rights of the individual, who stands alone and makes moral decisions. The **care perspective** views people in terms of their connectedness. Emphasis is placed on relationships and concern for others. According to Gilligan, Kohlberg greatly underplayed the care perspective—possibly because he was a male, most of his research was on males, and he lived in a male-dominant society.

In extensive interviews with girls from 6 to 18 years of age, Gilligan and her colleagues (Gilligan, 1992; Gilligan & others, 2003) found that girls consistently interpret moral dilemmas in terms of human relationships and base these interpretations on listening and watching other people. A recent review concluded that girls' moral orientations are "somewhat more likely to focus on care for others than on abstract principles of justice, but they can use both moral orientations when needed (as can boys . . .)," suggesting that gender differences are small at best (Blakemore, Berenbaum, & Liben, 2009, p. 132).

Carol Gilligan. *What is Gilligan's view of moral development?*

**Cheating**  A moral development concern of teachers is whether students cheat and how to handle the cheating if they discover it (Anderman & Anderman, 2010). Academic cheating can take many forms, including plagiarism, using "cheat sheets" during an exam, copying from a neighbor during a test, purchasing papers, and falsifying lab results. A 2006 survey revealed that 60 percent of secondary school students said they had cheated on a test in school during the past year and one-third of the students reported that they had plagiarized information from the Internet in the past year (Josephson Institute of Ethics, 2006).

Why do students cheat? Among the reasons students give for cheating include the pressure for getting high grades, time pressures, a self-perception that one doesn't have the ability to succeed, poor teaching, lack of interest, and perceiving a low likelihood of being caught and punished for cheating (Anderman & Anderman, 2010; Stephens, 2008). In terms of pressure for getting high grades, students are more likely to cheat if their goal is simply to get a high grade; they are less likely to cheat if their goal is to master the material being studied (Anderman & Anderman, 2010). In terms of having a self-perception that one doesn't have the ability to succeed, their doubts about their ability and failure-related anxiety may lead them to cheat. In terms of perceiving a low likelihood of being caught and punished for cheating, students may weigh the risk of getting a good grade by cheating as less costly than that of getting a failing grade by not cheating (Anderman & Anderman, 2010). In terms of poor teaching, students are more likely to cheat when they perceive their teacher to be incompetent, unfair, and uncaring (Stephens, 2008).

**justice perspective**  A moral perspective that focuses on the rights of the individual; Kohlberg's theory is a justice perspective.

**care perspective**  A moral perspective that focuses on connectedness and relationships among people; Gilligan's approach reflects a care perspective.

A long history of research also implicates the power of the situation in determining whether students cheat or not (Anderman & Anderman, 2010; Hartshorne & May, 1928–1930). For example, students are more likely to cheat when they are not being closely monitored during a test, when they know their peers are cheating, whether they know if another student has been caught cheating, and when student scores are made public (Anderman & Murdock, 2007; Carrell, Malmstrom, & West, 2008).

Strategies for decreasing academic cheating include making sure students are aware of what constitutes cheating and what the consequences will be if they cheat, closely monitoring students' behavior while

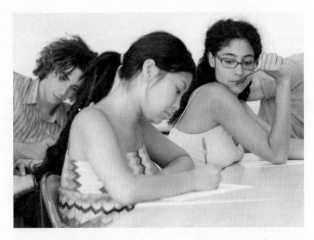

*Why do students cheat? What are some strategies teachers can adopt to prevent cheating?*

Learning to share is an important aspect of altruism. *What are some ways teachers can encourage students to be more altruistic?*

RESEARCH

Thinking Back/Thinking Forward

Girls are better at regulating and controlling their emotions than boys are. Chapter 5, p. 168

**altruism**  An unselfish interest in helping another person.

**gratitude**  A feeling of thankfulness and appreciation, especially in response to someone doing something kind or helpful.

**hidden curriculum**  Dewey's concept that every school has a pervasive moral atmosphere even if it does not have a program of moral education.

**character education**  A direct approach to moral education that involves teaching students basic moral literacy to prevent them from engaging in immoral behavior and doing harm to themselves or others.

they are taking tests, and conveying to them the importance of being a moral, responsible individual who engages in academic integrity. In promoting academic integrity, many colleges have instituted an honor code that emphasizes self-responsibility, fairness, trust, and scholarship (Narváez & others, 2008). However, few secondary schools have developed an honor code. The Center for Academic Integrity (**www .academicintegrity.org**) has extensive materials available to help schools develop such academic-integrity policies.

**Prosocial Behavior**    Caring about the welfare and rights of others, feeling concern and empathy for them, and acting in a way that benefits others are all components of *prosocial behavior,* which involves transcending narrow self-interest and valuing the perspectives of others (Barbarin & Odom, 2009). The purest forms of prosocial behavior are motivated by **altruism,** an unselfish interest in helping another person (Eisenberg & others, 2009).

Learning to share is an important aspect of prosocial behavior. It is important that children develop a belief that sharing is an obligatory part of a social relationship and involves a question of right and wrong. It is also important that children experience **gratitude,** a feeling of thankfulness and appreciation, especially in response to someone doing something kind or helpful. A recent study of young adolescents revealed that gratitude was linked to a number of positive aspects of development, including satisfaction with one's family, optimism, and prosocial behavior (Froh, Yurkewicz, & Kashdan, 2009).

Gender differences characterize prosocial behavior. Females view themselves as more prosocial and empathic, and they also engage in more prosocial behavior than males (Eisenberg & others, 2009).

**Moral Education**    Is there a best way to educate students so they will develop better moral values? Moral education is hotly debated in educational circles (Narváez & Lapsley, 2009). We will study one of the earliest analyses of moral education, then turn to some contemporary views.

***The Hidden Curriculum***    Recall from Chapter 1 that John Dewey was one of educational psychology's pioneers. Dewey (1933) recognized that even when schools do not have specific programs in moral education, they provide moral education through a "hidden curriculum." The **hidden curriculum**—conveyed by the moral atmosphere that is a part of every school—is created by school and classroom rules, the moral orientation of teachers and school administrators, and text materials. Teachers serve as models of ethical or unethical behavior (Sanger, 2008). Classroom rules and peer relations at school transmit attitudes about cheating, lying, stealing, and consideration for others. Through its rules and regulations, the school administration infuses the school with a value system.

***Character Education***    Currently 40 of 50 states have mandates regarding **character education,** a direct approach to moral education that involves teaching students basic moral literacy to prevent them from engaging in immoral behavior and doing harm to themselves or others (Arthur, 2008). The argument is that behaviors such as lying, stealing, and cheating are wrong, and that students should be taught this fact throughout their education (Berkowitz, Battistich, & Bier, 2008). According to the character education approach, every school should have an explicit moral code that is clearly communicated to students. Any violations of the code should be met with sanctions. Instruction in moral concepts with respect to specific behaviors, such as cheating, can take the form of example and definition, class discussions and role-playing, or rewards to students for proper behavior. More recently, an emphasis on the importance

## TEACHING CONNECTIONS: Best Practices
### Strategies for Increasing Children's Prosocial Behavior

Parents and teachers can play important roles in promoting prosocial behavior in children by modeling it and providing children with opportunities to engage in it. For example, teachers can do the following (Barbarin & Odom, 2009; Eisenberg, Fabes, & Spinrad, 2006; Witmer & Honig, 1994):

1. *Encourage children to be accountable for their own behavior and treat others with kindness and respect.*

2. *Model being helpful, cooperative, and showing concern for others, and encourage these behaviors in children.* For example, a teacher who comforts a child in times of stress is likely to observe other children imitating her comforting behavior.

3. *Valuing and emphasizing considerations of others' needs encourages children to engage in more helping behaviors.*

4. *Tell the child after he or she has engaged in prosocial behavior how pleased you are with the child's prosocial action.* Go beyond just saying, "That's good," or, "That's nice." Be specific in identifying prosocial behaviors. You might say, "You are being helpful." Or, you might say, "You shared because you like to help others."

5. *Develop class and school projects that foster altruism.* Let children come up with examples of projects they can do that will help others. These projects might include cleaning up the schoolyard, writing to children in troubled

*What can teachers do to encourage prosocial behavior, such as this girl providing assistance?*

lands, collecting toys or food for individuals in need, and making friends with older adults during visits to a nursing home.

Remember to do the above in a developmentally appropriate manner. While the comment above regarding sharing is appropriate for young children, you would state it differently for adolescents, "It was nice of you to share your supplies with Sue. I'm sure she appreciated it. I know I did."

of encouraging students to develop a *care perspective* (discussed earlier in this chapter) has been accepted as a relevant aspect of character education (Noddings, 2008). Rather than just instructing adolescents in refraining from engaging in morally deviant behavior, a care perspective advocates educating students in the importance of engaging in prosocial behaviors, such as considering others' feelings, being sensitive to others, and helping others. Critics argue that some character education programs encourage students to be too passive and noncritical.

**Values Clarification** Values clarification means helping people to clarify what their lives are for and what is worth working for. Students are encouraged to define their own values and to understand others' values. Values clarification differs from character education in that students are not told what their values should be. In values clarification exercises, there are no right or wrong answers. The clarification of values is left up to the individual student. Advocates of values clarification praise it for being "value-free." Critics, however, argue that it can lead

**values clarification** An approach to moral education that emphasizes helping people clarify what their lives are for and what is worth working for; students are encouraged to define their own values and understand the values of others.

### Jewel Cash, Teen Dynamo

Jewel Cash, seated next to her mother, is participating in a crime watch meeting at a community center. A junior at Boston Latin Academy, Jewel was raised in one of Boston's housing projects by her mother, a single parent. Today she is a member of the Boston Student Advisory Council, mentors children, volunteers at a women's shelter, manages and dances in two troupes, and is a member of a neighborhood watch group—among other activities. Jewel told an interviewer from the *Boston Globe,* "I see a problem and I say, 'How can I make a difference?' . . . I can't take on the world, even though I can try. . . . I'm moving forward but I want to make sure I'm bringing people with me" (Silva, 2005, pp. B1, B4).

RESEARCH

**cognitive moral education** An approach to moral education based on the belief that students should value things such as democracy and justice as their moral reasoning develops; Kohlberg's theory has served as the foundation for many cognitive moral education efforts.

**service learning** A form of education that promotes social responsibility and service to the community.

to controversial content offending community standards. Because of its relativistic nature, they say, values clarification undermines accepted values and fails to stress morally correct behavior.

***Cognitive Moral Education*** Cognitive moral education is an approach based on the belief that students should learn to value ideals such as democracy and justice as their moral reasoning develops. Kohlberg's theory has been the basis for a number of cognitive moral education programs. In a typical program, high school students meet in a semester-long course to discuss a number of moral issues. The instructor acts as a facilitator rather than as a director of the class. The hope is that students will develop more advanced notions of such concepts as cooperation, trust, responsibility, and community. Toward the end of his career, Kohlberg (1986) recognized that the school's moral atmosphere is more important than he initially envisioned. For example, in one study, a semester-long moral education class based on Kohlberg's theory was successful in advancing moral thinking in three democratic schools but not in three authoritarian schools (Higgins, Power, & Kohlberg, 1983). The hope of cognitive moral education is that students will develop more advanced notions of such concepts as cooperation, trust, responsibility, and community (Enright & others, 2008).

***Service Learning*** In **service learning,** a form of education that promotes social responsibility and service to the community, students engage in activities such as tutoring, helping older adults, working in a hospital, assisting at a child-care center, or cleaning up a vacant lot to make a play area. An important goal of service learning is for students to become less self-centered and more strongly motivated to help others (Eisenberg & others, 2009). Service learning is often more effective when two conditions are met (Nucci, 2006): (1) giving students some degree of choice in the service activities in which they participate, and (2) providing students opportunities to reflect about their participation.

Service learning takes education out into the community. Adolescent volunteers tend to be extraverted, committed to others, and have a high level of self-understanding (Eisenberg & others, 2009). A recent study revealed that adolescent girls participated in service learning more than adolescent boys (Webster & Worrell, 2008).

Researchers have found that service learning benefits adolescents in a number of ways (Hart, Matsuba, & Atkins, 2008). These improvements in adolescent development related to service learning include higher grades in school, increased goal setting, higher self-esteem, an improved sense of being able to make a difference for others, and an increased likelihood of serving as volunteers in the future (Benson & others, 2006). A recent study of more than 4,000 high school students revealed that those who worked directly with individuals in need were better adjusted academically, and those who worked for organizations had better civic outcomes (Schmidt, Shumow, & Kacar, 2007). And in a recent study, students themselves saw the benefit of participating in service learning programs—74 percent of African American and 70 percent of Latino adolescents reported that service learning programs could have a "fairly or very big effect" on keeping students from dropping out of school (Bridgeland, DiIulio, & Wulsin, 2008).

I recently asked teachers what strategies they use to advance their students' moral development, values, and prosocial behavior in their classrooms. Following are their recommendations.

**EARLY CHILDHOOD**   One prosocial rule that we establish with our preschoolers is zero tolerance for fighting. However, this is a difficult concept to teach some young children because when they are angry, the first thing they want to do is hit. A way to address hitting is to constantly teach children self-control. For example, we say things to children like "When we are walking in the hallway, we have control of our own body and can make it walk a certain way." Our goal is to make self-control second nature in our children.

—**VALARIE GORHAM,** *Kiddie Quarters, Inc.*

**ELEMENTARY SCHOOL: GRADES K–5**   My fifth-graders take on at least two community service projects a year. This year, we went on a field trip to the Oregon Food Bank. My students learned about hungry families in Oregon, what each child can do to help, and were given a task to do at the food bank. We bagged around 1,600 pounds of carrots, and this equated to feeding about 57 families. It was hard work, but my students saw the results and felt good about themselves.

—**CRAIG JENSEN,** *Cooper Mountain Elementary School*

**MIDDLE SCHOOL: GRADES 6–8**   As my seventh-graders study history, I like to present them with discussion questions in the form of moral dilemmas: "What would you do if . . ." types of questions. A teacher can ask an endless number of questions that relate to a students' everyday life. For instance, Robert E. Lee had to decide if he would be loyal to his state or his country. In this lesson, I ask students questions such as, "Is your loyalty ever tested? If so, how did you make your decision?" These questions make for great discussions and get students thinking about their own values and morals.

—**MARK FODNESS,** *Bemidji Middle School*

**HIGH SCHOOL: GRADES 9–12**   I sometimes discuss my own moral dilemmas with my students and tie them to classroom topics so that they have a role model. For example, I once told them the story of when my infant daughter and I were in Walmart and she somehow grabbed a jar of baby food off the shelf and tucked it into her car seat. I didn't notice the jar until I lifted her out of the car when we arrived home. Although the value of the jar of food was only 37 cents, I returned it to the store. I share this story with my students when we discuss plagiarism and Modern Language Association (MLA) citation style to emphasize the importance of being honest.

—**JENNIFER HEITER,** *Bremen High School*

## COPING WITH STRESS

In service learning and integrative ethical education, an important theme is getting students to help others. There are times, though, when students need help themselves, especially when they experience stressful events (Kopp, 2009). As children get older, they more accurately appraise a stressful situation and determine how much control they have over it. Older children generate more coping alternatives to stressful conditions and use more cognitive coping strategies (Saarni & others, 2006). They are better than younger children at intentionally shifting their thoughts to something that is less stressful, and at reframing, or changing one's perception of a stressful situation. For example, a younger child may be very disappointed that a teacher did

DEVELOPMENT

*What are some effective strategies teachers can use to help children cope with traumatic events such as the terrorist attacks on the United States on 9/11/2001 and Hurricane Katrina in August 2005?*

not say hello when the child arrived in the classroom. An older child may reframe the situation and think, "My teacher may have been busy with other things and just forgot to say hello."

By 10 years of age, most children are able to use these cognitive strategies to cope with stress (Saarni, 1999). However, in families that have not been supportive and are characterized by turmoil or trauma, children may be so overwhelmed by stress that they do not use such strategies (Frydenberg, 2008).

Disasters can especially harm children's development and produce adjustment problems. Children who experience disasters often display acute stress reactions, depression, panic disorder, and post-traumatic stress disorder (Kar, 2009). Proportions of children developing these problems following a disaster depend on such factors as the nature and severity of the disaster, as well as the support available to the children. The terrorist attacks on the World Trade Center in New York City and the Pentagon in Washington, D.C., on September 11, 2001, and hurricanes Katrina and Rita in September 2005, raised special concerns about how to help children cope with such stressful events (Osofsky, 2007). Following are some strategies teachers can use to help students cope with stressful events (Gurwitch & others, 2001, pp. 4–11):

- Reassure children (numerous times, if necessary) of their safety and security.
- Allow children to retell events and be patient in listening to them.
- Encourage children to talk about any disturbing or confusing feelings, reassuring them that such feelings are normal after a stressful event.
- Protect children from reexposure to frightening situations and reminders of the trauma—for example, by limiting discussion of the event in front of the children.
- Help children make sense of what happened, keeping in mind that children may misunderstand what took place. For example, young children "may blame themselves, believe things happened that did not happen, believe that terrorists are in the school, etc. Gently help children develop a realistic understanding of the event" (p. 10).

In Chapters 2 and 3 we examined how students develop, focusing mainly on the general pattern. In Chapter 4, we will explore how individual students vary with regard to intelligence and other personal characteristics.

## Review, Reflect, and Practice

**③** Explain these aspects of children's socioemotional development:
self-esteem, identity, moral development, and coping with stress.

### REVIEW

- What is self-esteem, and what are some ways to increase students' self-esteem? What is the nature of identity development, and what are the four statuses of identity?
- What is moral development? What levels of moral development were identified by Kohlberg, and what are two criticisms of his theory? Contrast the justice and care perspectives. What characterizes academic cheating? What are some forms of moral education?
- How can children be helped to cope with stress?

### REFLECT

- What is the level of moral development likely to be among the children you intend to teach? How might this affect your approach to how you manage students' relations with others in the class.

### PRAXIS™ PRACTICE

1. Teachers can have the most positive impact on students' self-esteem and achievement by
   a. making academic tasks easy.
   b. having children who often receive negative feedback from peers work in groups with these peers to foster social approval.
   c. helping children succeed by teaching them appropriate learning strategies.
   d. intervening in children's problems so that they don't get frustrated.

2. Marika sees Jamal take Yosuke's snack. Soon afterward, she sees Yosuke retaliate by taking Jamal's favorite pen. Marika does not report these incidents to the teacher, because they involve equal exchanges. According to Kohlberg, which stage of moral development has Marika reached?
   a. stage 1
   b. stage 2
   c. stage 3
   d. stage 4

3. Ms. Delgado teaches third grade in a community in which a gunman opened fire on the patrons of a store in the local mall. Her students are understandably upset by the news and by the fact that the gunman has not, as of yet, been apprehended. According to Gurwitch and colleagues (2001), which of the following would be the *least* appropriate thing for Ms. Delgado to do?
   a. Allow her students to talk about what happened and their fears that it could happen at the school.
   b. Disallow conversation about the shootings.
   c. Reassure her students that they are safe at school, including a brief discussion of appropriate emergency procedures.
   d. Listen to the students' accounts to ensure that they have no misconceptions about themselves being in some way responsible for the shootings.

*Please see the answer key at the end of the book.*

# The Fight

Many schools, including the one in which Miss Mahoney teaches, emphasize character education as a strategy for preventing violence. The basic idea is to promote empathy among students and to disallow behaviors such as teasing, name-calling, and threats of any kind. Miss Mahoney has included character education in the curriculum of her fifth-grade class. However, many of her students, especially the boys, continue to display the very behaviors she is trying to eliminate.

Two students in Miss Mahoney's class, Santana and Luke, are on the same club soccer team and often get into verbal conflicts with each other, although they appreciate each other's talents on the field. Tuesday night at practice, in violation of the team's rules, Santana told Luke that he "sucks." Luke decides to let it go. He doesn't want Santana to suffer a one-game suspension, recognizing Santana's value to the team in light of facing a tough opponent that weekend.

Thursday in class, Luke accuses Santana of stealing the cards he was using to organize a project. Luke is very angry. Santana also gets infuriated, claiming he did not steal them. He then finds them on the floor and hands them to Luke. "Here's your dumb cards, Luke," he says. "See? I didn't steal them."

In anger, Luke says, "Fine. Then how come they're all crinkled? You know, I could beat you up, and maybe I just will."

"Yeah, right. You and who else?" asks Santana with a sneer.

Two other boys working nearby overhear the altercation and begin contributing their perspectives.

"Yeah, Santana, Luke would kick your rear," says Grant.

"I think Santana would win," chimes in Peter.

"Meet me at the park tomorrow after school, and let's just see!" demands Santana.

"No problem," retorts Luke.

Thursday evening, they are both at soccer practice. Nothing is said about the fight that is to take place the next day after school.

Friday morning Santana's mother calls Miss Mahoney to tell her that Santana is afraid to come to school because Luke has threatened to beat him up. Obviously, Miss Mahoney is concerned and realizes she must address the situation. Luke's mother also talks to the principal about the situation. However, all Santana's mother told either of them is that Luke had threatened to beat up her son. She didn't know why and did not think the reason mattered in the least. She wanted her son protected and the other boy punished.

That morning, Luke's mother was in the school for another purpose. The principal stopped her to talk about the situation, telling her that Santana had told his mother he was afraid to come to school because Luke was going to beat him up. Luke's mother asked for more information. On hearing Santana's side of the story, which was simply that Luke had threatened him, she told the principal that this didn't sound right—that Luke was impulsive enough that if he'd wanted to beat up Santana, he probably would have just hit him, not planned a fight for a later date. She wanted to talk to Luke before she jumped to any conclusions and asked that Miss Mahoney and the principal talk to both of the boys and any other children involved.

Both Miss Mahoney and the principal did as Luke's mother asked. The story that came out is the one you read. They decided that Luke should serve an in-school suspension the following day and miss recess all week "because it is the third 'incident' we've had with him this year." Santana received no punishment and walked away from the meeting grinning.

- What are the issues in this case?
- At what stage of moral development would you expect these boys to be, based on the information you have? What predictions can you make regarding each boy's sense of self and emotional development?
- What can you say about the boys' mothers?
- What do you think about the punishment that Luke received? How would you have handled this situation?
- What impact do you think this will have on the boys' future relationship? What impact on their attitudes toward school?

# Social Contexts and Socioemotional Development

**1 CONTEMPORARY THEORIES:** Describe two contemporary perspectives on socioemotional development: Bronfenbrenner's ecological theory and Erikson's life-span development theory.

**Bronfenbrenner's Ecological Theory**

Bronfenbrenner's ecological theory seeks to explain how environmental systems influence children's development. He described five environmental systems that include both micro and macro inputs: microsystem, mesosystem, exosystem, macrosystem, and chronosystem. Bronfenbrenner's theory is one of the few systematic analyses that includes both micro and macro environments. Critics say the theory lacks attention to biological and cognitive factors. They also point out that it does not address step-by-step developmental changes.

**Erikson's Life-Span Development Theory**

Erikson's life-span development theory proposes eight stages, each centering on a particular type of challenge or dilemma: trust versus mistrust, autonomy versus shame and doubt, initiative versus guilt, industry versus inferiority, identity versus identity confusion, intimacy versus isolation, generativity versus stagnation, and integrity versus despair. Erikson's theory has made important contributions to understanding socioemotional development, although some critics say the stages are too rigid and that their sequencing lacks research support.

**2 SOCIAL CONTEXTS OF DEVELOPMENT:** Discuss how the social contexts of families, peers, and schools are linked with socioemotional development.

**Families**

Baumrind proposed four parenting styles: authoritarian, authoritative, neglectful, and indulgent. Authoritative parenting is associated with children's social competence and is likely to be the most effective. Children benefit when parents engage in coparenting. The nature of parents' work can affect their parenting quality. A number of factors are linked to children's adjustment in divorced families. An important aspect of school-family linkages focuses on parental involvement. Fostering school-family partnerships involves providing assistance to families, communicating effectively with families about school programs and student progress, encouraging parents to be volunteers, involving families with their children in learning activities at home, including families in school decisions, and coordinating community collaboration.

**Peers**

Peers are children of about the same age or maturity level. Parents influence their children's peer worlds in a number of ways. Peer relations are linked to children's competent socioemotional development. Children can have one of five peer statuses: popular, average, rejected, neglected, or controversial. Rejected children often have more serious adjustment problems than do neglected children. Friendship is an important aspect of students' social relations. Students who have friends engage in more prosocial behavior, have higher grades, and are less emotionally distressed.

**Schools**

Schools involve changing social developmental contexts from preschool through high school. The early childhood setting is a protected environment with one or two teachers, usually female. Peer groups are more important in elementary school. In middle school, the social field enlarges to include the whole school, and the social system becomes more complex. Controversy characterizes early childhood education curricula. On one side are the advocates of the developmentally appropriate, child-centered, constructivist approach; on the other are the advocates of an instructivist, academic approach. An increasingly popular early childhood program is the Montessori approach. Head Start has provided early childhood education for children from low-income families. High-quality Head Start programs are effective educational

*(continued)*

interventions, but up to 40 percent of these programs may be ineffective. A special concern is that many early elementary school classrooms rely mainly on negative feedback. The transition to middle or junior high is stressful for many students because it coincides with so many physical, cognitive, and socioemotional changes. It involves going from the top-dog position to the lowest position in a school hierarchy. A number of recommendations for improving U.S. middle schools have been made. An increasing number of educational experts also believe that substantial changes need to be made in U.S. high school education. Participation in extracurricular activities has a number of positive outcomes for adolescents.

**③ SOCIOEMOTIONAL DEVELOPMENT:** Explain these aspects of children's socioemotional development: self-esteem, identity, moral development, and coping with stress.

**The Self**

Self-esteem, also referred to as *self-worth* or *self-image*, is the individual's overall conception of himself or herself. Self-esteem often varies across domains and becomes more differentiated in adolescence. Four keys to increasing students' self-esteem are to (1) identify the causes of low self-esteem and the domains of competence important to the student, (2) provide emotional support and social approval, (3) help students achieve, and (4) develop students' coping skills. Marcia proposed that adolescents have one of four identity statuses (based on the extent to which they have explored or are exploring alternative paths and whether they have made a commitment): identity diffusion, identity foreclosure, identity moratorium, identity achievement. Ethnic identity is an important dimension of identity for ethnic minority students.

**Moral Development**

Moral development concerns rules and conventions about just interactions between people. These rules can be studied in three domains: cognitive, behavioral, and emotional. Kohlberg stressed that the key to understanding moral development is moral reasoning and that it unfolds in stages. Kohlberg developed a provocative theory of moral reasoning. He argued that development of moral reasoning consists of three levels—preconventional, conventional, and postconventional—and six stages (two at each level). Kohlberg reasoned that these stages were age related. Two main criticisms of Kohlberg's theory are (1) that it does not give enough attention to moral behavior, and (2) that it gives too much power to the individual and not enough to relationships with others. In this regard, Gilligan argued that Kohlberg's theory is a male-oriented justice perspective. She proposed that what is needed in moral development is a female-oriented care perspective. Academic cheating is pervasive and can occur in many ways. A long history of research indicates the power of the situation in influencing whether students cheat or not. An important aspect of prosocial behavior is altruism, an unselfish interest in helping another person. Sharing and gratitude are two aspects of prosocial behavior. The hidden curriculum is the moral atmosphere that every school has. Three types of moral education are character education, values clarification, and cognitive moral education. Service learning is becoming increasingly important in schools.

**Coping with Stress**

As children get older, they use a greater variety of coping strategies and more cognitive strategies. Teachers can guide students in developing effective strategies for coping with stressful events, such as terrorist attacks and hurricanes, by providing reassurance, encouraging children to talk about disturbing feelings, and helping them make sense of what happened.

## KEY TERMS

ecological theory 71
authoritarian parenting 78
authoritative parenting 78
neglectful parenting 78
indulgent parenting 78
developmentally appropriate
    practice 85

Montessori approach 85
self-esteem 92
identity diffusion 95
identity foreclosure 95
identity moratorium 95
identity achievement 95
moral development 97

preconventional
    reasoning 97
conventional reasoning 97
postconventional
    reasoning 98
justice perspective 99
care perspective 99

altruism 100
gratitude 100
hidden curriculum 100
character education 100
values clarification 101
cognitive moral education 102
service learning 102

# PORTFOLIO ACTIVITIES

**Independent Reflection Meeting the Socioemotional Needs of Students.** Think about the age of students you intend to teach. Which of Erikson's stages is likely to be central for them? What, if anything, does Bronfenbrenner's theory suggest about important resources for students at that age? Does his system suggest particular challenges to students or ways that you as a teacher might facilitate their success? Write down your ideas in your portfolio.

**Collaborative Work the Role of Moral Education in Schools.** Which approach to moral education (character education, values clarification, or cognitive moral education) do you like the best? Why? Should schools be in the business of having specific moral education programs? Get together with several other students in this class and discuss your perspectives. Then write a brief statement that reflects your own perspective on moral education.

**Research/Field Experience Foster Family-School Linkages.** Interview several teachers from local schools about how they foster family-school linkages. Try to talk with a kindergarten teacher, an elementary teacher, a middle school teacher, and a high school teacher. Summarize your discoveries.

*Go to the Online Learning Center for downloadable portfolio templates.*

# STUDY, PRACTICE, AND SUCCEED

Visit www.mhhe.com/santrockep5e to review the chapter with self-grading quizzes and self-assessments, to apply the chapter material to two more Crack the Case studies, and for suggested activities to develop your teaching portfolio.

# CHAPTER 4

# INDIVIDUAL VARIATIONS

*Individuals play out their lives in different ways.*

—Thomas Huxley,
*English Biologist, 19th Century*

## Learning **Goals**

**1** Discuss what intelligence is, how it is measured, theories of multiple intelligences, the neuroscience of intelligence, and some controversies and issues about its use by educators.

**2** Describe learning and thinking styles.

**3** Characterize the nature of personality and temperament.

# Teaching **Stories**  Shiffy Landa

Shiffy Landa, a first-grade teacher at H. F. Epstein Hebrew Academy in St. Louis, Missouri, uses the multiple-intelligences approach of Howard Gardner (1983, 1993) in her classroom. Gardner argues that there is not just one general type of intelligence but at least eight specific types.

Landa (2000, pp. 6–8) believes that the multiple-intelligences approach is the best way to reach children because they have many different kinds of abilities. In Landa's words:

> My role as a teacher is quite different from the way it was just a few years ago. No longer do I stand in front of the room and lecture to my students. I consider my role to be one of a facilitator rather than a frontal teacher. The desks in my room are not all neatly lined up in straight rows . . . students are busily working in centers in cooperative learning groups, which gives them the opportunity to develop their interpersonal intelligences.

Students use their "body-kinesthetic intelligence to form the shapes of the letters as they learn to write. . . . They also use this intelligence to move the sounds of the vowels that they are learning, blending them together with letters, as they begin to read."

Landa states that "intrapersonal intelligence is an intelligence that often is neglected in the traditional classroom." In her classroom, students "complete their own evaluation sheets after they have concluded their work at the centers. They evaluate their work and create their own portfolios," in which they keep their work so they can see their progress.

As she was implementing the multiple-intelligences approach in her classroom, Landa recognized that she needed to educate parents about it. She created "a parent education class called the Parent-Teacher Connection," which meets periodically to view videos, talk about multiple intelligences, and discuss how they are being introduced in the classroom. She also sends a weekly newsletter to parents, informing them about the week's multiple-intelligences activities and students' progress.

# Preview

Shiffy Landa's classroom techniques build on Howard Gardner's multiple-intelligences theory, one of the theories of intelligence that we will explore in this chapter. You will see that there is spirited debate about whether people have a general intelligence or a number of specific intelligences. Intelligence is but one of several main topics in this chapter. We also will examine learning and thinking styles, as well as personality and temperament. For each of these topics, an important theme is students' individual variations and the best strategies for teachers to use related to these variations.

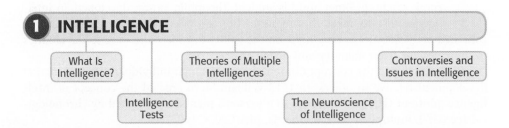

Intelligence is one of our most prized possessions. However, even the most intelligent people have not been able to agree on how to define and measure the concept of intelligence.

## WHAT IS INTELLIGENCE?

What does the term *intelligence* mean to psychologists? Some experts describe intelligence as the ability to solve problems. Others describe it as the capacity to adapt and learn from experience. Still others argue that intelligence includes characteristics such as creativity and interpersonal skills.

The problem with intelligence is that—unlike height, weight, and age—it cannot be directly measured. We can't peel back a person's scalp and see how much intelligence

**Thinking Back/Thinking Forward**

Vygotsky's social-constructivist approach emphasizes that intelligence is constructed through interactions with more-skilled individuals, which is reflected in his concept of the zone of proximal development. Chapter 2, p. 50

Alfred Binet constructed the first intelligence test after being asked to create a measure to determine which children would benefit from instruction in France's schools.

**Thinking Back/Thinking Forward**

The most common way of classifying a child as gifted is that the child scores 130 or higher on an intelligence test. Chapter 6, p. 204

**intelligence** Problem-solving skills and the ability to adapt to and learn from experiences.

**mental age (MA)** An individual's level of mental development relative to others.

**intelligence quotient (IQ)** A person's mental age (MA) divided by chronological age (CA), multiplied by 100.

**normal distribution** A symmetrical distribution, with a majority of scores falling in the middle of the possible range of scores and few scores appearing toward the extremes of the range.

he or she has. We can evaluate intelligence only *indirectly* by studying and comparing the intelligent acts that people perform.

The primary components of intelligence are similar to the cognitive processes of memory and thinking that we will discuss in Chapters 8 and 9. The differences in how these cognitive processes are described, and how we will discuss intelligence, lie in the concepts of individual differences and assessment. *Individual differences* are the stable, consistent ways in which people are different from one another. Individual differences in intelligence generally have been measured by intelligence tests designed to tell us whether a person can reason better than others who have taken the test (Neukrug & Fawcett, 2010).

We will use as our definition of **intelligence** the ability to solve problems and to adapt and learn from experiences. But even this broad definition doesn't satisfy everyone. As you will see shortly, Robert Sternberg (2009, 2010a,b) proposes that practical know-how should be considered part of intelligence. In his view, intelligence involves weighing options carefully and acting judiciously, as well as developing strategies to improve shortcomings. Also, a definition of intelligence based on a theory such as Lev Vygotsky's, which we discussed in Chapter 2, would have to include the ability to use the tools of the culture with help from more-skilled individuals. Because intelligence is such an abstract, broad concept, it is not surprising that there are different ways to define it.

## INTELLIGENCE TESTS

In this section, we will first describe individual intelligence tests. Then, we will examine group intelligence tests.

**Individual Intelligence Tests**   The two main intelligence tests that are administered to children on an individual basis today are the Stanford Binet test and the Wechsler scales.

***The Binet Tests***   An early version of the Binet was the first well-known intelligence test developed. In 1904 the French Ministry of Education asked psychologist Alfred Binet to devise a method of identifying children who were unable to learn in school. School officials wanted to reduce crowding by placing in special schools students who did not benefit from regular classroom teaching. Binet and his student Theophile Simon developed an intelligence test to meet this request. The test was called the 1905 Scale. It consisted of 30 questions, ranging from the ability to touch one's ear to the abilities to draw designs from memory and define abstract concepts.

Binet developed the concept of **mental age (MA),** an individual's level of mental development relative to others. In 1912 William Stern created the concept of **intelligence quotient (IQ),** which refers to a person's mental age divided by chronological age (CA), multiplied by 100. That is, MA/CA × 100.

If mental age is the same as chronological age, then the person's IQ is 100. If mental age is above chronological age, then IQ is more than 100. For example, a 6-year-old with a mental age of 8 would have an IQ of 133. If mental age is below chronological age, then IQ is less than 100. For example, a 6-year-old with a mental age of 5 would have an IQ of 83.

The Binet test has been revised many times to incorporate advances in the understanding of intelligence and intelligence testing. These revisions are called the *Stanford-Binet tests* (because the revisions were made at Stanford University). By administering the test to large numbers of people of different ages from different backgrounds, researchers have found that scores on a Stanford-Binet test approximate a normal distribution (see Figure 4.1). As described more fully in Chapter 15, a **normal distribution** is symmetrical, with a majority of the scores falling in the middle of the possible range of scores and few scores appearing toward the extremes of the range.

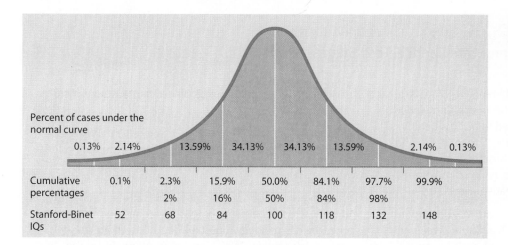

FIGURE **4.1** THE NORMAL CURVE AND STANFORD-BINET IQ SCORES

The distribution of IQ scores approximates a normal curve. Most of the population falls in the middle range of scores. Notice that extremely high and extremely low scores are very rare. Slightly more than two-thirds of the scores fall between 84 and 116. Only about 1 in 50 individuals has an IQ of more than 132, and only about 1 in 50 individuals has an IQ of less than 68.

The current Stanford-Binet test is administered individually to people aged 2 through adult. It includes a variety of items, some of which require verbal responses, others nonverbal responses. For example, items that reflect a typical 6-year-old's level of performance on the test include the verbal ability to define at least six words, such as *orange* and *envelope,* as well as the nonverbal ability to trace a path through a maze. Items that reflect an average adult's level of performance include defining such words as *disproportionate* and *regard,* explaining a proverb, and comparing idleness with laziness.

The current version of the Stanford-Binet is the fifth edition. An important addition to the fourth edition that has been continued and expanded on in the fifth edition is analysis of five aspects of cognitive ability and two aspects of intelligence (Bart & Peterson, 2008). The five aspects of cognitive ability are *fluid reasoning* (abstract thinking), *knowledge* (conceptual information), *quantitative reasoning* (math skills), *visual-spatial reasoning* (understanding visual forms and spatial layouts), and *working memory* (recall of new information). The two aspects of intelligence assessed by the fifth edition of the Stanford-Binet are *verbal intelligence* and *nonverbal intelligence.* A general composite score is still obtained to reflect overall intelligence. The Stanford-Binet continues to be one of the most widely used tests to assess students' intelligence.

**The Wechsler Scales**   Another set of tests widely used to assess students' intelligence is called the *Wechsler scales,* developed by psychologist David Wechsler. They include the Wechsler Preschool and Primary Scale of Intelligence–Third Edition (WPPSI-III) to test children from 2 years 6 months to 7 years 3 months of age; the Wechsler Intelligence Scale for Children–Fourth Edition (WISC-IV) for children and adolescents 6 to 16 years of age; and the Wechsler Adult Intelligence Scale–Third Edition (WAIS-III).

The Wechsler scales not only provide an overall IQ score and scores on a number of subtests but also yield several composite indexes (for example, the Verbal Comprehension Index, the Working Memory Index, and the Processing Speed Index). The subtest and composite scores allow the examiner to quickly determine the areas in which the child is strong or weak. Three of the Wechsler subscales are shown in Figure 4.2.

Intelligence tests such as the Stanford-Binet and Wechsler are given on an individual basis. A psychologist approaches an individual assessment of intelligence as a structured interaction between the examiner and the student. This provides the psychologist with an opportunity to

**Verbal Subscales**

**Similarities**

A child must think logically and abstractly to answer a number of questions about how things might be similar.

Example: "In what way are a lion and a tiger alike?"

**Comprehension**

This subscale is designed to measure an individual's judgment and common sense.

Example: "What is the advantage of keeping money in a bank?"

**Nonverbal Subscales**

**Block Design**

A child must assemble a set of multicolored blocks to match designs that the examiner shows.
Visual-motor coordination, perceptual organization, and the ability to visualize spatially are assessed.

Example: "Use the four blocks on the left to make the pattern on the right."

FIGURE **4.2** SAMPLE SUBSCALES OF THE WECHSLER INTELLIGENCE SCALE FOR CHILDREN–FOURTH EDITION (WISC-IV)

Simulated items similar to those in the Wechsler Intelligence Scale for Children–Fourth Edition. The Wechsler includes 11 subscales, 6 verbal and 5 nonverbal. Three of the subscales are shown here.

## TEACHING CONNECTIONS: Best Practices
### Strategies for Interpreting Intelligence Test Scores

Psychological tests are tools (Anastasi & Urbino, 1997). Like all tools, their effectiveness depends on the user's knowledge, skill, and integrity. A hammer can be used to build a beautiful kitchen cabinet or to break down a door. Similarly, psychological tests can be used well or badly abused. Here are some cautions about IQ that can help teachers avoid using information about a student's intelligence in negative ways:

1. *Avoid unwarranted stereotypes and negative expectations about students based on IQ scores.* Too often, sweeping generalizations are made on the basis of an IQ score. Imagine that you are in the teachers' lounge on the second day of school in the fall. You mention one of your students, and another teacher remarks that she had him in her class last year. She says that he was a real dunce and that he scored 83 on an IQ test. How hard is it to ignore this information as you go about teaching your class? Probably difficult. But it is important that you not develop the expectation that because Johnny scored low on an IQ test, it is useless to spend much time teaching him (Weinstein, 2004). An IQ test should always be considered a measure of current performance. It is not a measure of fixed potential. Maturational changes and

enriched environmental experiences can advance a student's intelligence.

2. *Don't use IQ tests as the main or sole characteristic of competence.* A high IQ is not the ultimate human value. Teachers need to consider not only students' intellectual competence in areas such as verbal skills, but also their creative and practical skills. It is generally advisable to have at least three data sources regarding student competence before making important decisions about students, such as placement. While one of these might be the results of an intelligence test, others might include classroom performance, achievement test scores, observation data, and parental reports.

3. *Especially be cautious in interpreting the meaningfulness of an overall IQ score.* It is wiser to think of intelligence as consisting of a number of domains. Many educational psychologists stress that it is important to consider the student's strengths and weaknesses in different areas of intelligence. Intelligence tests such as the Wechsler scales can provide information about those strengths and weaknesses.

sample the student's behavior. During the testing, the examiner observes the ease with which rapport is established, the student's enthusiasm and interest, whether anxiety interferes with the student's performance, and the student's degree of tolerance for frustration.

**Group Intelligence Tests** Students also may be given an intelligence test in a group. Group intelligence tests include the Lorge-Thorndike Intelligence Tests and the Otis-Lennon School Ability Test (OLSAT). Group intelligence tests are more convenient and economical than individual tests, but they do have their drawbacks. When a test is given to a large group, the examiner cannot establish rapport, determine the student's level of anxiety, and so on. In a large-group testing situation, students might not understand the instructions or might be distracted by other students.

Because of such limitations, when important decisions are made about students, a group intelligence test should always be supplemented with other information about the student's abilities. For that matter, the same strategy holds for an individual intelligence test despite its superior accuracy. But certainly a decision to place a student in a class for students who have mental retardation, a special education class, or a class for students who are gifted should not be based on a group test alone. In such instances, an extensive amount of relevant information about the student's abilities should be obtained outside the testing situation.

## THEORIES OF MULTIPLE INTELLIGENCES

Is it more appropriate to think of a student's intelligence as a general ability or as a number of specific abilities? Psychologists have thought about this question since early in the twentieth century and continue to debate the issue.

**Sternberg's Triarchic Theory**   According to Robert J. Sternberg's (1986, 2004, 2010a,b, 2011a,b) **triarchic theory of intelligence,** intelligence comes in three forms: analytical, creative, and practical. *Analytical intelligence* involves the ability to analyze, judge, evaluate, compare, and contrast. *Creative intelligence* consists of the ability to create, design, invent, originate, and imagine. *Practical intelligence* focuses on the ability to use, apply, implement, and put into practice.

To understand what analytical, creative, and practical intelligence mean, let's look at examples of people who reflect these three types of intelligence:

- Consider Latisha, who scores high on traditional intelligence tests such as the Stanford-Binet and is a star analytical thinker. Latisha's *analytical intelligence* approximates what has traditionally been called intelligence and what is commonly assessed by intelligence tests.
- Todd does not have the best test scores but has an insightful and creative mind. Sternberg calls the type of thinking at which Todd excels *creative intelligence.*
- Finally, consider Emanuel, a person whose scores on traditional IQ tests are low but who quickly grasps real-life problems. He easily picks up knowledge about how the world works. Emanuel's "street smarts" and practical know-how are what Sternberg calls *practical intelligence.*

Sternberg (2010a,b, 2011a,b) says that students with different triarchic patterns look different in school. Students with high analytic ability tend to be favored in conventional schools. They often do well in classes in which the teacher lectures and gives objective tests. These students typically get good grades, do well on traditional IQ tests and the SAT, and later gain admission to competitive colleges.

Students high in creative intelligence often are not in the top rung of their class. Creatively intelligent students might not conform to teachers' expectations about how assignments should be done. They give unique answers, for which they might get reprimanded or marked down.

Like students high in creative intelligence, students who are practically intelligent typically do not relate well to the demands of school. However, these students frequently do well outside the classroom's walls. Their social skills and common sense may allow them to become successful managers or entrepreneurs despite undistinguished school records.

Sternberg (2010a,b) stresses that few tasks are purely analytic, creative, or practical. Most tasks require some combination of these skills. For example, when students write a book report, they might analyze the book's main themes, generate new ideas about how the book could have been written better, and think about how the book's themes can be applied to people's lives. Sternberg argues that it is important for classroom instruction to give students opportunities to learn through all three types of intelligence.

Sternberg (2010c, 2011c) believes that *wisdom* is linked to both practical and academic intelligence. In his view, academic intelligence is a necessary but in many cases insufficient requirement for wisdom. Practical knowledge about the realities of life also is needed for wisdom. For Sternberg, balance between self-interest, the interests of others, and context produces a common good. Thus, wise individuals don't just look out for themselves—they also need to consider others' needs and perspectives, as well as the particular context involved. Sternberg assesses wisdom by presenting problems to individuals that require solutions which highlight various intrapersonal, interpersonal, and contextual interests. He also emphasizes that such aspects of wisdom should be taught in schools (Sternberg, 2010c, 2011c; Sternberg, Jarvin, & Reznitskaya, 2011).

**Gardner's Eight Frames of Mind**   As we indicated in the Teaching Stories introduction to this chapter, Howard Gardner (1983, 1993, 2002) argues that there are many specific types of intelligence, or frames of mind. They are described here

Robert J. Sternberg, who developed the triarchic theory of intelligence.

*"You're wise, but you lack tree smarts."*
© Donald Reilly/The New Yorker Collection/ www.cartoonbank.com

**triarchic theory of intelligence** Sternberg's view that intelligence comes in three main forms: analytical, creative, and practical.

Howard Gardner, here working with a young child, developed the view that intelligence comes in the forms of these eight kinds of skills: verbal, mathematical, spatial, bodily-kinesthetic, musical, intrapersonal, interpersonal, and naturalist.

along with examples of the occupations in which they are reflected as strengths (Campbell, Campbell, & Dickinson, 2004):

- *Verbal skills:* The ability to think in words and to use language to express meaning (authors, journalists, speakers)
- *Mathematical skills:* The ability to carry out mathematical operations (scientists, engineers, accountants)
- *Spatial skills:* The ability to think three-dimensionally (architects, artists, sailors)
- *Bodily-kinesthetic skills:* The ability to manipulate objects and be physically adept (surgeons, crafts people, dancers, athletes)
- *Musical skills:* A sensitivity to pitch, melody, rhythm, and tone (composers, musicians, and music therapists)
- *Intrapersonal skills:* The ability to understand oneself and effectively direct one's life (theologians, psychologists)
- *Interpersonal skills:* The ability to understand and effectively interact with others (successful teachers, mental health professionals)
- *Naturalist skills:* The ability to observe patterns in nature and understand natural and human-made systems (farmers, botanists, ecologists, landscapers)

Gardner argues that each form of intelligence can be destroyed by a different pattern of brain damage, that each involves unique cognitive skills, and that each shows up in unique ways in both the gifted and *idiot savants* (individuals who have mental retardation but have an exceptional talent in a particular domain, such as drawing, music, or numerical computation).

At various times, Gardner has considered including *existential intelligence,* which involves concern and reasoning about meaning in life, as a ninth intelligence (McKay, 2008). However, as yet, he has not added it as a different form of intelligence.

Although Gardner has endorsed the application of his model to education, he has also witnessed some misuses of the approach. Here are some cautions he gives about using it (Gardner, 1998):

- There is no reason to assume that every subject can be effectively taught in eight different ways to correspond to the eight intelligences, and attempting to do this is a waste of effort.
- Don't assume that it is enough just to apply a certain type of intelligence. For example, in terms of bodily-kinesthetic skills, random muscle movements have nothing to do with cultivating cognitive skills.
- There is no reason to believe that it is helpful to use one type of intelligence as a background activity while children are working on an activity related to a different type of intelligence. For example, Gardner points out that playing music in the background while students solve math problems is a misapplication of his theory.

Technology can be used to facilitate learning in each area of intelligence (Dickinson, 1998, pp. 1–3):

- *Verbal skills.* Computers encourage students to revise and rewrite compositions; this should help them to produce more competent papers. Many aspects of computer-mediated communication, such as e-mail, chat, and text messaging, provide students with opportunities to practice and expand their verbal skills.
- *Logical/mathematical skills.* "Students of every ability can learn effectively through interesting software programs that provide immediate feedback and go far beyond drill-and-practice exercises." Formula manipulation software such as *Mathematica* (2008) (**www.wolfram.com/products/mathematica/index.html**) and Flash mathematics applets can help students improve their logical/mathematics skills.

- *Spatial skills.* Computers allow students to see and manipulate material. Virtual-reality technology can also provide students with opportunities to exercise their visual-spatial skills,
- *Bodily-kinesthetic skills.* "Computers rely mostly on eye-hand coordination for their operation—keyboarding and the use of a mouse or touch-screen. This kinesthetic activity . . . makes the student an active participant in the learning." For example, Nintendo Wii (2008) (**http://www.nintendo.com/wii**) can be used to improve students' bodily-kinesthetic skills.
- *Musical skills.* "The Musical Instrument Digital Interface (MIDI) makes it possible to compose for and orchestrate many different instruments through the computer." Apple Computer's GarageBand (2008) (**www.apple.com/ilife/ garageband**) software is also a good musical skills source.
- *Intrapersonal skills.* "Technology offers the means to explore a line of thought in great depth" and to have extensive access to a range of personal interests. "The opportunity for students to make such choices is at the heart of giving them control over their own learning and intellectual development."
- *Interpersonal skills.* "When students use computers in pairs or small groups, their comprehension and learning are facilitated and accelerated. Positive learning experiences can result as students share discoveries, support each other in solving problems, and work collaboratively on projects."
- *Naturalist skills.* Electronic technologies can "facilitate scientific investigation, exploration, and other naturalist activities." For example, National Geographic Online allows students to go on expeditions with famed explorers and photographers. Zoo Cams Worldwide (2008) provides live footage to help students learn more about animals (**www.zoos-worldwide.de/ zoocams.html**).

I recently asked teachers how they apply Gardner's theory of multiple intelligence in their classrooms. Following are their recommendations.

**EARLY CHILDHOOD**    Since each one of my preschoolers is different, I recognize that they have different skills and different needs. For example, we had a child who  was very good at physical activities, such as bouncing a ball and tossing it into a net, but who struggled with learning how to count. To improve her counting skills, we had her count the number of times she bounced the ball and how many times the ball went into the net.

—**Heidi Kaufman,** *Metro West YMCA Child Care and Educational Program*

**ELEMENTARY SCHOOL: GRADES K–5**    Students need choices. Some need to move around regularly in the classroom, sit on the floor, or write on the board.  Some need a nondistracting, edge-of-the-room seat. If instruction is given, or a question is asked, partner-talk can help to reinforce learning, but some students need a quiet, personal prompt from the teacher. I also provide choices for final assignments—for example, oral presentation, graphic representation, an essay or poem, and PowerPoint slides.

—**Keren Abra,** *Convent of the Sacred Heart Elementary School*

**MIDDLE SCHOOL: GRADES 6–8**    Group projects offer great opportunities to incorporate Gardner's theory into the classroom. I try to develop group projects that  require participants to read, do artwork, do math, think creatively, speak in public, and so on. By including these various skills, group members are able to express their knowledge in a way that meets their individual style of learning.

—**Casey Maass,** *Edison Middle School*

## TEACHING CONNECTIONS: Best Practices
### Strategies for Implementing Each of Gardner's Multiple Intelligences

Applications of Gardner's theory of multiple intelligences to children's education continue to be made (Campbell, 2008). Following are some specific strategies that teachers can use related to Gardner's eight types of intelligence (Campbell, Campbell, & Dickinson, 2004):

1. *Verbal skills.* Read to children and let them read to you, visit libraries and bookstores with children, and have children summarize and retell a story they have read.

2. *Mathematical skills.* Play games of logic with children, be on the lookout for situations that can inspire children to think about and construct an understanding of numbers, and take children on field trips to computer labs, science museums, and electronics exhibits.

3. *Spatial skills.* Have a variety of creative materials available for children to use, take children to art museums and hands-on children's museums, and go on walks with children. When they get back, ask them to visualize where they have been and then draw a map of their experiences.

4. *Bodily-kinesthetic skills.* Provide children with opportunities for physical activity and encourage them to participate, provide areas where children can play indoors and outdoors, and encourage children to participate in dance activities.

5. *Musical skills.* Give children an opportunity to play musical instruments, create opportunities for children to make music and rhythms together using voices and instruments, and take children to concerts.

6. *Intrapersonal skills.* Encourage children to have hobbies and interests, listen to children's feelings and give them sensitive feedback, and have children keep a journal or scrapbook of their ideas and experiences.

7. *Interpersonal skills.* Encourage children to work in groups, help children to develop communication skills, and provide group games for children to play.

8. *Naturalist skills.* Create a naturalist learning center in the classroom, engage children in outdoor naturalist activities, such as taking a nature walk or adopting a tree, and have children make collections of flora or fauna and classify them.

In Through the Eyes of Teachers, Joanna Smith, a high school English teacher, describes how she implements Gardner's multiple intelligences into her classroom.

### THROUGH THE EYES OF TEACHERS
#### Giving Students a Choice of Which Type of Intelligence They Want to Use for a Project

I try to draw on Gardner's eight frames of mind throughout the year by giving a variety of assignments. My students sometimes have a choice about which "type of intelligence" to use, depending on their project. For example, at the end of the first semester, students do an outside reading project based on a self-selected book. They create a project based on the book's themes and characters. For example, students might give a monologue from a character's perspective, create a family tree, make a CD of thematic songs, or give a "tour" of the book's setting live or on tape. This type of project is always successful because it allows students to choose in what mode, in what frame of mind, they will present their knowledge.

We have discussed a number of ideas about Gardner's concept of multiple intelligences. To evaluate your strengths and weaknesses on his eight types of intelligence, see Self-Assessment 4.1.

**HIGH SCHOOL: GRADES 9–12**   I often give my students the power of choice when it comes to how a project can be completed. For example, they can complete a project as an artistic piece, a written project, or a demonstration so that students can choose the mode that best fits their comfort level.

—**JENNIFER HEITER,** *Bremen High School*

**Emotional Intelligence**   Both Gardner's and Sternberg's theories include one or more categories related to the ability to understand one's self and others and to get

# SELF-ASSESSMENT 4.1
## Evaluating Myself on Gardner's Eight Types of Intelligence

Read these items and rate yourself on a 4-point scale. Each rating corresponds to how well a statement describes you: 1 = not like me at all, 2 = somewhat unlike me, 3 = somewhat like me, and 4 = a lot like me.

| | 1 | 2 | 3 | 4 |
|---|---|---|---|---|

**Verbal Thinking**

1. I do well on verbal tests, such as the verbal part of the SAT.

2. I am a skilled reader and read prolifically.

3. I love the challenge of solving verbal problems.

**Logical/Mathematical Thinking**

4. I am a very logical thinker.

5. I like to think like a scientist.

6. Math is one of my favorite subjects.

**Spatial Skills**

7. I am good at visualizing objects and layouts from different angles.

8. I have the ability to create maps of spaces and locations in my mind.

9. If I had wanted to be, I think I could have been an architect.

**Bodily-Kinesthetic Skills**

10. I have great hand-eye coordination.

11. I excel at sports.

12. I am good at using my body to carry out an expression, as in dance.

**Musical Skills**

13. I play one or more musical instruments well.

14. I have a good "ear" for music.

15. I am good at making up songs.

**Insightful Skills for Self-Understanding**

16. I know myself well and have a positive view of myself.

17. I am in tune with my thoughts and feelings.

18. I have good coping skills.

**Insightful Skills for Analyzing Others**

19. I am very good at "reading" people.

20. I am good at collaborating with other people.

21. I am a good listener.

**Naturalist Skills**

22. I am good at observing patterns in nature.

23. I excel at identifying and classifying objects in the natural environment.

24. I understand natural and human-made systems

*(continued)*

## SCORING AND INTERPRETATION

Total your score for each of the eight types of intelligence and place the total in the blank that follows the label for each kind of intelligence. Which areas of intelligence are your strengths? In which are you the least proficient? It is highly unlikely that you will be strong in all eight areas or weak in all eight areas. By being aware of your strengths and weaknesses in different areas of intelligence, you can get a sense of which areas of teaching students will be the easiest and most difficult for you. If I (your author) had to teach musical skills, I would be in big trouble because I just don't have the talent. However, I do have reasonably good movement skills and spent part of my younger life playing and coaching tennis. If you are not proficient in some of Gardner's areas and you have to teach students in those areas, consider getting volunteers from the community to help you. For example, Gardner says that schools need to do a better job of calling on retired people, most of whom likely would be delighted to help students improve their skills in the domain or domains in which they are competent. This strategy also helps to link communities and schools with a sort of "intergenerational glue."

along in the world. In Gardner's theory, the categories are interpersonal intelligence and intrapersonal intelligence; in Sternberg's theory, practical intelligence. Other theorists who emphasize interpersonal, intrapersonal, and practical aspects of intelligence focus on what is called *emotional intelligence,* which was popularized by Daniel Goleman (1995) in his book *Emotional Intelligence.*

The concept of emotional intelligence was initially developed by Peter Salovey and John Mayer (1990). They conceptualize **emotional intelligence** as the ability to perceive and express emotion accurately and adaptively (such as taking the perspective of others), to understand emotion and emotional knowledge (such as understanding the roles that emotions play in friendship and other relationships), to use feelings to facilitate thought (such as being in a positive mood, which is linked to creative thinking), and to manage emotions in oneself and others (such as being able to control one's anger).

There continues to be considerable interest in the concept of emotional intelligence (Fiori, 2009). Critics argue that emotional intelligence broadens the concept of intelligence too far and has not been adequately assessed and researched (Humphrey & others, 2007).

**emotional intelligence** The ability to perceive and express emotion accurately and adaptively, to understand emotion and emotional knowledge, to monitor one's own and others' emotions and feelings, to discriminate among them, and to use this information to guide one's thinking and action.

### Do Children Have One Intelligence or Many Intelligences?

Figure 4.3 provides a comparison of Gardner's, Sternberg's, and Salovey/Mayer's views. Notice that Gardner includes a number of types of intelligence not addressed by the other views, and that Sternberg is unique in emphasizing creative intelligence. These theories of multiple intelligences have much to offer. They have stimulated us to think more broadly about what makes up people's intelligence and competence (Moran & Gardner, 2006). And they have motivated educators to develop programs that instruct students in different domains (Winner, 2006).

Theories of multiple intelligences also have many critics. They conclude that the research base to support these theories has not yet developed. In particular, some argue that Gardner's classification seems arbitrary. For example, if musical skills represent a type of intelligence, why don't we also refer to chess intelligence, prizefighter intelligence, and so on?

A number of psychologists still support the concept of *g* (general intelligence) (Lubinski, 2009; Veselka & others, 2009). For example, one expert

| Gardner | Sternberg | Salovey/Mayer |
|---------|-----------|---------------|
| Verbal Mathematical | Analytical | |
| Spatial Movement Musical | Creative | |
| Interpersonal Intrapersonal | Practical | Emotional |
| Naturalistic | | |

**FIGURE 4.3** COMPARING GARDNER'S, STERNBERG'S, AND SALOVEY/MAYER'S INTELLIGENCES

on intelligence, Nathan Brody (2007), argues that people who excel at one type of intellectual task are likely to excel at other intellectual tasks. Thus, individuals who do well at memorizing lists of digits are also likely to be good at solving verbal problems and spatial layout problems. This *general intelligence* includes abstract reasoning or thinking, the capacity to acquire knowledge, and problem-solving ability (Brody, 2007; Carroll, 1993).

Advocates of the concept of general intelligence point to its success in predicting school and job success (Deary & others, 2007). For example, scores on tests of general intelligence are substantially correlated with school grades and achievement test performance, both at the time of the test and years later (Strentze, 2007).

Intelligence tests are moderately correlated with job performance (Lubinski, 2009). Individuals with higher scores on tests designed to measure general intelligence tend to get higher-paying, more prestigious jobs (Lubinsky, 2009). However, general IQ tests predict only about one-fourth of the variation in job success, with most variation being attributable to other factors, such as motivation and education (Wagner & Sternberg, 1986). Further, the correlations between IQ and achievement decrease the longer people work at a job, presumably because as they gain more job experience they perform better (Hunt, 1995).

Some experts who argue for the existence of general intelligence nevertheless conclude that individuals also have specific intellectual abilities (Brody, 2007). In sum, controversy still characterizes whether it is more accurate to conceptualize intelligence as a general ability, specific abilities, or both (Lubinski, 2009; Sternberg, 2010a,b, 2011a,b). Sternberg (2009) actually accepts that there is a *g* for the kinds of analytical tasks that traditional IQ tests assess but thinks that the range of tasks those tests measure is far too narrow.

## THE NEUROSCIENCE OF INTELLIGENCE

In the current era of extensive research on the brain, interest in the neuroscience underpinnings of intelligence has increased (Dreary, Penke, & Johnson, 2010; Glascher & others, 2009; Neubauer & Fink, 2009). Questions about the brain's role in intelligence include whether having a big brain is linked to higher intelligence and whether intelligence is located in certain brain regions?

Are individuals with a big brain more intelligent than those with a smaller brain? Recent studies using MRI scans to assess total brain volume indicate a moderate correlation (about +.3 to +.4) between brain size and intelligence (Luders & others, 2009; Rushton & Ankney, 2009).

Is intelligence linked to specific regions of the brain? Early consensus was that the frontal lobes were the likely location of intelligence. However, researchers recently have found that intelligence is distributed more widely across brain regions (Glascher & others, 2010; Haier & others, 2009; Karama & others, 2009). The most prominent finding from brain imaging studies reveals that a distributed neural network involving the frontal and parietal lobes is related to higher intelligence (Colom & others, 2009) (see Figure 4.4). For example, Albert Einstein's total brain size was average but a region of his brain's parietal lobe (an area active in processing math and spatial information) was 15 percent larger than average (Witelson, Kigar, & Harvey, 1999). Other brain regions that have been linked to higher intelligence (although at a lower level of significance than the frontal/parietal lobe network) include the temporal and occipital lobes, as well as the cerebellum (Luders & others, 2009).

As the technology to study the brain's functioning continues to improve, we are likely to see more specific conclusions about the brain's role in intelligence. As this research proceeds, keep in mind that both heredity and environment likely contribute to links between the brain and intelligence. For example, even brain size depends on environmental factors such as nutrition.

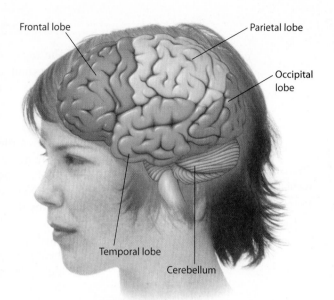

**FIGURE 4.4** INTELLIGENCE AND THE BRAIN

Researchers recently have found that a higher level of intelligence is linked to a distributed neural network in the frontal and parietal lobes. To a lesser extent than the frontal/parietal network, the temporal and occipital lobes, as well as the cerebellum, also have been found to have links to intelligence. The current consensus is that intelligence is likely to be distributed across brain regions rather than being localized in a specific region, such as the frontal lobes.

RESEARCH

# CONTROVERSIES AND ISSUES IN INTELLIGENCE

The topic of intelligence is surrounded by controversy. Is nature or nurture more important in determining intelligence? Are intelligence tests culturally biased? Should IQ tests be used to place children in particular schooling tracks?

**Nature and Nurture** The **nature-nurture issue** (discussed in Chapter 2) involves the debate about whether development is primarily influenced by nature or by nurture. *Nature* refers to a child's biological inheritance, *nurture* to environmental experiences.

"Nature" proponents argue that intelligence is primarily inherited and that environmental experiences play only a minimal role in its manifestation (Rushton & Ankney, 2009). The emerging view of the nature-nurture issue is that many complicated qualities, such as intelligence, probably have some genetic loading that gives them a propensity for a particular developmental trajectory, such as low, average, or high intelligence. The actual development of intelligence, however, requires more than just heredity.

Most experts today agree that the environment also plays an important role in intelligence (Grigorenko & Takanishi, 2010; Preiss & Sternberg, 2010). This means that improving children's environments can raise their intelligence. It also means that enriching children's environments can improve their school achievement and the acquisition of skills needed for employment. Craig Ramey and his associates (1988) found that high-quality early educational child care (through 5 years of age) significantly raised the tested intelligence of young children from impoverished backgrounds. Positive effects of this early intervention were still evident in the intelligence and achievement of these students when they were 13 and 21 years of age (Ramey, Ramey, & Lanzi, 2009).

Another argument for the importance of environment in intelligence involves the increasing scores on IQ tests around the world. Scores on these tests have been increasing so fast that a high percentage of people regarded as having average intelligence in the early 1900s would be considered below average in intelligence today (Flynn, 1999, 2007) (see Figure 4.5). If a representative sample of today's children took the Stanford-Binet test used in 1932, about one-fourth would be defined as very superior, a label usually accorded to less than 3 percent of the population. Because

**Thinking Back/Thinking Forward**

The nature-nurture issue is one of developmental psychology's main issues. Chapter 2, p. 32

RESEARCH

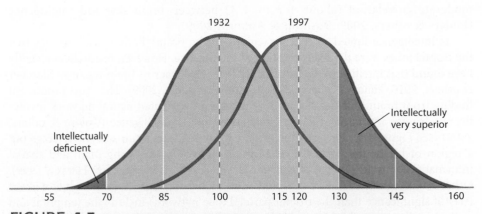

## FIGURE **4.5** THE INCREASE IN IQ SCORES FROM 1932 TO 1997

As measured by the Stanford-Binet intelligence test, American children seem to be getting smarter. Scores of a group tested in 1932 fell along a bell-shaped curve with half below 100 and half above. Studies show that if children took that same test today, half would score above 120 on the 1932 scale. Very few of them would score in the "intellectually deficient" end, on the left side, and about one-fourth would rank in the "very superior" range.

**nature-nurture issue** Issue that involves the debate about whether development is primarily influenced by nature (an organism's biological inheritance) or nurture (environmental experiences).

the increase has taken place in a relatively short period of time, it can't be due to heredity but, rather, might result from such environmental factors as the explosion in information people are exposed to and the much higher percentage of the population receiving education. This worldwide increase in intelligence test scores over a short time frame is called the *Flynn effect,* after the researcher who discovered it— James Flynn.

Studies of schooling also reveal effects on intelligence (Sternberg, Jarvin, & Grigorenko, 2008). The biggest effects occur when large groups of children are deprived of formal education for an extended period, resulting in lower intelligence.

One analysis of studies on schooling and intelligence concluded that schooling and intelligence influence each other (Ceci & Williams, 1997). For example, individuals who finish high school are more intelligent than those who drop out of school. This might be because brighter individuals stay in school longer, or because the environmental influence of schooling contributes to their intelligence.

Researchers increasingly are interested in manipulating the early environment of children who are at risk for impoverished intelligence (Ramey, Ramey, & Lanzi, 2009; Sternberg, 2009). The emphasis is on prevention rather than remediation. Many low-income parents have difficulty providing an intellectually stimulating environment for their children. Programs that educate parents to be more sensitive caregivers and better teachers, as well as support services such as high-quality child-care programs, can make a difference in a child's intellectual development.

DEVELOPMENT

It is extremely difficult to tease apart the effects of nature or nurture, so much so that psychologist William Greenough (1997, 2000) says that asking which is more important is like asking what's more important to a rectangle, its length or its width. We still do not know what, if any, specific genes actually promote or restrict a general level of intelligence. If such genes exist, they certainly are found both in children whose families and environments appear to promote the development of children's abilities and in children whose families and environments do not appear to be as supportive. Regardless of one's genetic background, growing up "with all the advantages" does not guarantee high intelligence or success, especially if those advantages are taken for granted. Nor does the absence of such advantages guarantee low intelligence or failure, especially if the family and child can make the most of whatever opportunities are accessible to them.

**Ethnicity and Culture**   Are there ethnic differences in intelligence? Are conventional tests of intelligence biased, and if so, can we develop culture-fair tests?

DIVERSITY

***Ethnic Comparisons***   In the United States, children from African American and Latino families score below children from White families on standardized intelligence tests. On the average, African American schoolchildren score 10 to 15 points lower on standardized intelligence tests than White American schoolchildren do (Brody, 2000). These are *average scores,* however. About 15 to 25 percent of African American schoolchildren score higher than half of White schoolchildren do, and many Whites score lower than most African Americans. The reason is that the distribution of scores for African Americans and Whites overlap.

As African Americans have gained social, economic, and educational opportunities, the gap between African Americans and Whites on standardized intelligence tests has begun to narrow (Ogbu & Stern, 2001). This gap especially narrows in college, where African American and White students often experience more similar environments than in the elementary and high school years (Myerson & others, 1998). Also, when children from disadvantaged African American families are adopted into more-advantaged middle-socioeconomic-status families, their scores on intelligence tests more closely resemble national averages for middle-socioeconomic-status children than for lower-socioeconomic-status children (Scarr & Weinberg, 1983).

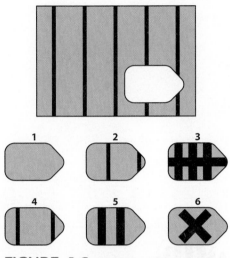

## FIGURE 4.6 SAMPLE ITEM FROM THE RAVEN'S PROGRESSIVE MATRICES TEST

Individuals are presented with a matrix arrangement of symbols, such as the one at the top of this figure, and must then complete the matrix by selecting the appropriate missing symbol from a group of symbols, such as the ones at the bottom.

Simulated item similar to those found in the *Raven's Progressive Matrices* (Standard, Sets A–E). Copyright © 1976, 1958, 1938 by NCS Pearson, Inc. Reproduced with permission. All rights reserved. "Ravens Progressive Matrices" is a trademark, in the U.S. and/or other countries, of Pearson Education, Inc. or its affiliate(s).

RESEARCH

**stereotype threat** The anxiety that one's behavior might confirm a negative stereotype about one's group.

**culture-fair tests** Tests of intelligence that are intended to be free of cultural bias.

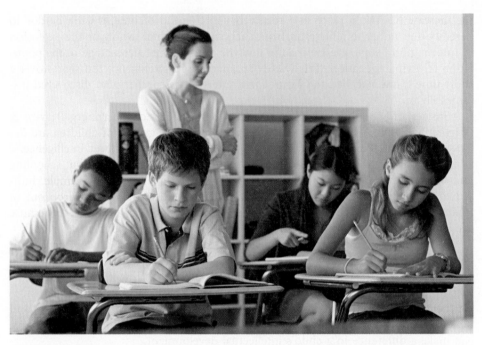

*How might stereotype threat be involved in ethnic minority students' performance on standardized tests?*

***Cultural Bias and Culture-Fair Tests*** Many of the early tests of intelligence were culturally biased, favoring urban children over rural children, children from middle-income families over children from low-income families, and White children over minority children (Miller-Jones, 1989). The standards for the early tests were almost exclusively based on non-Latino White, middle-socioeconomic-status children. Contemporary intelligence tests attempt to reduce such cultural bias (Merenda, 2004).

One potential influence on intelligence test performance is **stereotype threat,** the anxiety that one's behavior might confirm a negative stereotype about one's group (Schmader & others, 2009; Steele & Aronson, 2004). For example, when African Americans take an intelligence test, they may experience anxiety about confirming the old stereotype that Blacks are "intellectually inferior." Some studies have confirmed the existence of stereotype threat (Beilock, Rydell, & McConnell, 2007). For example, African American students do more poorly on standardized tests if they perceive that they are being evaluated. If they think the test doesn't count, they perform as well as White students (Aronson, 2002). However, critics argue that the extent to which stereotype threat explains the testing gap has been exaggerated (Sackett, Borneman, & Connelly, 2009).

**Culture-fair tests** are intelligence tests that aim to avoid cultural bias. Two types of culture-fair tests have been developed. The first includes questions familiar to people from all socioeconomic and ethnic backgrounds. For example, a child might be asked how a bird and a dog are different, on the assumption that virtually all children are familiar with birds and dogs. The second type of culture-fair test contains no verbal questions. Figure 4.6 shows a sample question from the Raven's Progressive Matrices Test. Even though tests such as the Raven's Progressive Matrices are designed to be culture-fair, people with more education still score higher than those with less education do (Shiraev & Levy, 2010).

Why is it so hard to create culture-fair tests? Most tests tend to reflect what the dominant culture thinks is important (Shiraev & Levy, 2010). If tests have time limits, that will bias the test against groups not concerned with time. If languages differ, the same words might have different meanings for different language groups. Even pictures can produce bias because some cultures have less experience with drawings and photographs. Within the same culture, different groups could have different attitudes, values, and motivation, and this could affect their performance on intelligence tests. Because of such difficulties in creating culture-fair tests, Robert Sternberg and his colleagues (Sternberg, 2011d; Zhang & Sternberg, 2011) conclude that there are no culture-fair tests, only *culture-reduced tests.*

**Revisiting the Nature/Nurture Issue**   In sum, there is a consensus among psychologists that both heredity and environment influence intelligence. This consensus reflects the nature-nurture issue that was highlighted in Chapter 2 and discussed earlier in this chapter. Recall that the nature-nurture issue focuses on the extent to which development is influenced by nature (heredity) and nurture (environment). Although psychologists agree that intelligence is the product of both nature and nurture, there is still disagreement about how strongly each influences intelligence (Brans & others, 2010; Irvine & Berry, 2010).

**Ability Grouping and Tracking**   Another controversial issue is whether it is beneficial to use students' scores on an intelligence test to place them in ability groups. Two types of ability grouping have been used in education: between-class and within-class.

*"You can't build a hut, you don't know how to find edible roots and you know nothing about predicting the weather. In other words, you do terribly on our I.Q. test."*
© Sidney Harris. ScienceCartoonsPlus.com

***Between-Class Ability Grouping (Tracking)***   In **between-class ability grouping (tracking),** students are grouped based on their ability or achievement. Tracking has long been used in schools as a way to organize students, especially at the secondary level (Gustafson, 2007; Slavin, 1995). The positive view of tracking is that it narrows the range of skill in a group of students, making it easier to teach them. Tracking is said to prevent less-able students from "holding back" more talented students.

A typical between-class grouping involves dividing students into a college preparatory track and a general track. Within the two tracks, further ability groupings might be made, such as two levels of math instruction for college preparatory students. Another form of tracking takes place when a student's abilities in different subject areas are taken into account. For example, the same student might be in a high-track math class and a middle-track English class.

Critics of tracking argue that it stigmatizes students who are consigned to low-track classes (Banks, 2010). For example, students can get labeled as "low-track" or "the dummy group." Critics also say that low-track classrooms often have less-experienced teachers, fewer resources, and lower expectations (Wheelock, 1992). Further, critics stress that tracking is used to segregate students according to ethnicity and socioeconomic status because higher tracks have fewer students from ethnic minority and impoverished backgrounds (Banks, 2008, 2010). In this way, tracking can actually replay segregation within schools. The detractors also argue that average and above-average students do not get substantial benefits from being grouped together.

Does research support the critics' contention that tracking is harmful to students? Researchers have found that tracking does harm the achievement of low-track students (Kelly, 2008). However, it seems to benefit high-track students (such as those in a gifted program). Also, researchers have found that "students who are 'tracked-up' or who are exposed to a more rigorous curriculum learn more than the same-ability students who are 'tracked-down' or offered a less challenging course of study (Gamaron, 1990; Hallinan, 2003) . . ." (Banks & others, 2005, p. 239).

One variation of between-class ability grouping is the **nongraded (cross-age) program,** in which students are grouped by their ability in particular subjects regardless of their age or grade level (Fogarty, 1993). This type of program is used far more in elementary than in secondary schools, especially in the first three grades. For example, a math class might be composed of first-, second-, and third-graders

RESEARCH

**between-class ability grouping (tracking)** Grouping students based on their ability or achievement.

**nongraded (cross-age) program** A variation of between-class ability grouping in which students are grouped by their ability in particular subjects regardless of their age or grade level.

These students participate in the Advancement Via Individual Determination (AVID) program in San Diego. Rather than being placed in a low track, they are enrolled in rigorous courses and provided support to help them achieve success. *What types of support are they provided?*

grouped together because of their similar math ability. The **Joplin plan** is a standard nongraded program for instruction in reading. In the Joplin plan, students from second, third, and fourth grade might be placed together because of their similar reading level.

We mentioned that tracking has negative effects on low-track students. When tracks are present, it is especially important to give low-achieving students an opportunity to improve their academic performance and thus change tracks. In the San Diego County Public Schools, the Advancement Via Individual Determination (AVID) program provides support for underachieving students. Instead of being placed in a low track, they are enrolled in rigorous courses but are not left to achieve on their own. A comprehensive system of support services helps them succeed. For example, a critical aspect of the program is a series of workshops that teach students note-taking skills, question-asking skills, thinking skills, and communication skills. The students also are clustered into study groups and urged to help each other clarify questions about assignments. College students, many of them AVID graduates, serve as role models, coaches, and motivators for the students. At each AVID school, a lead teacher oversees a team of school counselors and teachers from every academic discipline. In recent years the dropout rate in AVID schools has declined by more than one-third, and an amazing 99 percent of the AVID graduates have enrolled in college.

In sum, tracking is a controversial issue, especially because of the restrictions it places on low-track students. Too often, scores on a single-group IQ test are used to place students in a particular track. Researchers have found that group IQ tests are not good predictors of how well students will do in a particular subject area (Garmon & others, 1995).

***Within-Class Ability Grouping*** The program of **within-class ability grouping** involves placing students in two or three groups within a class to take into account differences in students' abilities. A typical within-class ability grouping occurs when elementary school teachers place students in several reading groups based on their reading skills. A second-grade teacher might have one group using a third-grade, first-semester reading program; another using a second-grade, first-semester program; and a third group using a first-grade, second-semester program. Such within-class grouping is far more common in elementary than in secondary schools. The subject area most often involved is reading, followed by math. Although many elementary school teachers use some form of within-class ability grouping, there is no clear research support for this strategy.

**Joplin plan** A standard nongraded program for instruction in reading.

**within-class ability grouping** Placing students in two or three groups within a class to take into account differences in students' abilities.

## TEACHING CONNECTIONS: Best Practices
### Strategies for the Use of Tracking

As you have read, if tracking is used, a number of cautions need to be exercised. Following are some strategies teachers can adopt to successfully implement ability or skill grouping.

1. *Use other measures of student knowledge and potential in particular subject areas to place students in ability groups rather than a group-administered IQ test.* For instance, if you want to have reading-skill groups, use current reading achievement to group the children.

2. *Avoid labeling groups as "low," "middle," and "high."* Also avoid comparisons of groups. Many teachers allow children to name their own groups. Others use colors as group names.

3. *Don't form more than two or three ability groups.* It is more difficult to give adequate attention to a larger number of groups. One possible exception to this would be guided-reading groups for younger children. In this case, the teacher works with a small number of students while the rest of the class works on a related activity.

4. *Consider the students' placements in various ability groups as subject to review and change.* Carefully monitor students' performance, and if a student in a lower-achieving group progresses adequately, move the student to a higher group. If a student in a higher-achieving group is struggling, evaluate whether the higher-achieving group is the right one for the student and decide what supports the student might need to improve performance. The key is to consider group placement to be very flexible and based on current or recent past performance.

5. *Especially consider alternatives to tracking for low-achieving students.* Throughout this book, we will describe instructional strategies and support services for low-achieving students, such as those being used in the AVID program. Lower-achieving students will likely benefit from increased teacher attention and scaffolding.

## Review, Reflect, and Practice

**1** Discuss what intelligence is, how it is measured, theories of multiple intelligences, the neuroscience of intelligence and some controversies and issues about its use by educators.

### REVIEW

- What does the concept of intelligence mean?
- What did Binet and Wechsler contribute to the field of intelligence? What are some pros and cons of individual versus group tests of intelligence?
- What is Sternberg's triarchic theory of intelligence? What is Gardner's system of "frames of mind"? What is Mayer, Salovey, and Goleman's concept of emotional intelligence? How is each theory relevant to education? What are some aspects of the controversy about whether intelligence is better conceptualized as general intelligence or multiple intelligences?
- How is the brain linked to intelligence?
- What are three controversies related to intelligence?

### REFLECT

- Suppose that you were about to teach a particular group of children for the first time and were handed intelligence test scores for every child in the class. Would you hesitate to look at the scores? Why or why not?

*(continued)*

## Review, Reflect, and Practice

**PRAXIS™ PRACTICE (CONTINUED)**

1. Which of the following is the best indicator of high intelligence?
   a. scoring 105 on an IQ test
   b. reciting the Gettysburg Address from memory
   c. not making the same mistakes twice when given the opportunity to repeat a task after receiving feedback
   d. earning high grades

2. Susan took the Otis-Lennon School Ability Test to determine if she qualified for her school's gifted program. Based on her score of 125, she did not qualify for the program. Which of the following is a valid statement regarding this screening procedure?
   a. Because this was an individual test, the psychologist was able to ensure that rapport had been established and that anxiety did not interfere with her performance. Thus, the decision should stand.
   b. Because this was a group test, the psychologist was unable to ensure that rapport had been established and anxiety did not interfere with her performance. Thus, the decision should not stand. More information is needed.
   c. Because her score was well above average, she should be included in the gifted program.
   d. Because her score is just average, she should not be included in the gifted program.

3. Which of these students best exemplifies Sternberg's practical intelligence?
   a. Jamal, who writes wonderful science fiction stories
   b. Chandra, who is able to understand *The Great Gatsby's* symbolism at a complex level
   c. Mark, who is the most talented athlete in the school
   d. Jessica, who gets along well with others and is good at "reading" others' emotions

4. Which of these statements best reflects what is currently known about the brain's role in intelligence?
   a. The total size of a child's brain is strongly correlated with intelligence.
   b. Intelligence is likely distributed widely across brain regions.
   c. Intelligence is located almost entirely in the brain's prefrontal lobes.
   d. The most consistent finding about the brain and intelligence is that higher intelligence is linked to a lower volume of gray matter.

5. Which of these statements is most consistent with current research on the nature-nurture issue in intelligence?
   a. Because intelligence is mainly inherited, there is little room to improve students' intelligence.
   b. Because intelligence is influenced by both heredity and environment, providing students with an enriched classroom environment might have a positive influence on their intelligence.
   c. Students who delay schooling tend to score higher on intelligence tests than those who do not, which suggests that environment is more important for intelligence than heredity.
   d. Recent steep increases in intelligence indicate that intelligence is mainly determined by heredity.

*Please see the answer key at the end of the book.*

## ② LEARNING AND THINKING STYLES

> Impulsive/Reflective Styles          Deep/Surface Styles

*Intelligence* refers to ability. **Learning and thinking styles** are not abilities but, rather, preferred ways of using one's abilities (Zhang & Sternberg, 2009). In fact, teachers will tell you that children approach learning and thinking in an amazing variety of ways. Teachers themselves also vary in their styles of learning and thinking. None of us has just a single learning and thinking style; each of us has a profile of many styles. Individuals vary so much that literally hundreds of learning and thinking styles have been proposed by educators and psychologists.

Yet, criticisms have been leveled at the concept of learning and thinking styles (Rayner & Peterson, 2009). A recent survey of researchers in this field revealed the three most common criticisms to be (1) the low reliability of the styles (lack of consistency when they are assessed), (2) low validity of the styles (whether the tests that are used actually measure the styles purportedly being assessed), and (3) confusion in the definitions of styles (Peterson, Raynor, & Armstrong, 2009). Our coverage of learning and thinking styles is not meant to be exhaustive but introduces two widely discussed sets of styles: impulsive/reflective and deep/surface.

### IMPULSIVE/REFLECTIVE STYLES

**Impulsive/reflective styles,** also referred to as *conceptual tempo,* involve a student's tendency either to act quickly and impulsively or to take more time to respond and reflect on the accuracy of an answer (Kagan, 1965). Impulsive students often make more mistakes than reflective students.

Research on impulsivity/reflection shows that reflective students are more likely than impulsive students to do well at these tasks (Jonassen & Grabowski, 1993): remembering structured information; reading comprehension and text interpretation; and problem solving and decision making.

Reflective students also are more likely than impulsive students to set their own learning goals and concentrate on relevant information. Reflective students usually

**learning and thinking styles** Individuals' preferences in how they use their abilities.

**impulsive/reflective styles** Also referred to as *conceptual tempo,* they involve a student's tendency either to act quickly and impulsively or to take more time to respond and reflect on the accuracy of the answer.

---

## TEACHING CONNECTIONS: Best Practices
### Strategies for Working with Impulsive Children

You are likely to have some children in your classroom who are impulsive. You can help them become less impulsive by adopting the following strategies.

1. *Monitor students in the class to determine which ones are impulsive.* Who blurts out answers? Who always raises his/her hand first? Who finishes tasks quickly, but makes careless mistakes?

2. *Don't encourage such impulsivity by using assessments that require great speed, such as completing 30 math fact problems in a minute.*

3. *Talk with them about taking their time to think through an answer before they respond.* Then in class when you ask questions, wait before you call on students instead of calling on the first student to raise his/her hand.

4. *Encourage them to label new information as they work with it.*

5. *Model the reflective style as a teacher.* Take time to think before you respond and let the students know that this is what you are doing.

6. *Help students set high standards for their performance.* Encourage students to review their work before turning it in. Encourage them to revise their errors.

7. *Recognize when impulsive students start to take more time to reflect.* Compliment them on their improvement.

8. *Guide students in creating their own plan to reduce impulsivity.*

**Thinking Back/Thinking Forward**

Self-regulation, which involves self-gener-ation and self-monitoring of thoughts, feelings, and behaviors to reach a goal, is increasingly recognized as a key aspect of learning. Chapter 7, p. 243

**Thinking Back/Thinking Forward**

In one view of memory, deeper processing of information is predicted to produce bet-ter memory than shallow processing of information. Chapter 8, p. 264

**deep/surface styles** Involve whether students approach learning materials in a way that helps them understand the meaning of the materials (deep style) or to learn only what needs to be learned (surface style).

have higher standards for performance. The evidence is strong that reflective students learn more effectively and do better in school than impulsive students.

In thinking about impulsive and reflective styles, keep in mind that although most children learn better when they are reflective rather than impulsive, some chil-dren are simply fast but accurate learners and decision makers. Reacting quickly is a bad strategy only if you come up with wrong answers. Also, some reflective children ruminate forever about problems and have difficulty finishing tasks. Teachers can encourage these children to retain their reflective orientation but arrive at more timely solutions. In Chapter 7 we will discuss a number of other strategies for help-ing students self-regulate their behavior.

## DEEP/SURFACE STYLES

**Deep/surface styles** involve how students approach learning materials. Do they do this in a way that helps them understand the meaning of the materials (deep style) or as simply what needs to be learned (surface style) (Marton, Hounsell, & Entwistle, 1984)? Students who approach learning with a surface style fail to tie what they are learning into a larger conceptual framework. They tend to learn in a passive way, often rotely memorizing information. Deep learners are more likely to actively con-struct what they learn and give meaning to what they need to remember. Thus, deep learners take a constructivist approach to learning. Deep learners also are more likely to be self-motivated to learn, whereas surface learners are more likely to be motivated to learn because of external rewards, such as grades and positive feedback from the teacher (Snow, Corno, & Jackson, 1996).

## TEACHING CONNECTIONS: Best Practices
### Strategies for Helping Surface Learners Think More Deeply

In addition to having children in your classroom who are im-pulsive, you also are likely to teach children who are surface learners. Following are some effective strategies for turning sur-face learners into learners who think more deeply.

1. *Monitor students to determine which ones are surface learners.*

2. *Discuss with students the importance of going beyond rote memorization.* Encourage them to connect what they are learning now with what they have learned in the past.

3. *Ask questions and give assignments that require students to fit information into a larger framework.* For example, instead of just asking students to name the capital of a particular state, ask them if they have visited the capital and what their experiences were, what other cities are located in that section of the United States, or how large or small the city is.

4. *Be a model who processes information deeply rather than just scratching the surface.* Explore topics in depth, and talk about how the information you are discussing fits within a larger network of ideas.

5. *Avoid using questions that require pat answers.* Instead, ask questions that require students to deeply process infor-mation. Connect lessons more effectively with children's

existing interests. In Through the Eyes of Teachers, Therese Olejniczak, a middle school teacher in East Grand Forks, Minnesota, describes how she gets students to slow down so they won't gloss over important material.

### THROUGH THE EYES OF TEACHERS
**Paying Attention to the Details**

Seventh-graders are in a hurry, no matter which intelli-gences they favor or use. I often teach study skills to students to help them slow down and gather details they might miss in their haste to complete assignments.

One method I use is to have the entire class silently read an article on a topic I've selected with their interests in mind. Then I ask the students to list details of the article on the black-board. I call on students one at a time as they raise their hands enthusiastically, and each student—in his or her adolescent need to belong—participates by contributing details to the list.

Afterward, the students and I review the details, marvel-ing at the depth of information they have found. Unplanned peer-tutoring occurs when students discover obscure items that others have skimmed past, revealing to one another their need to slow down. Small groups then create final re-ports that include a written summary and illustration.

I recently asked teachers to identify the strategies they use to influence their students' learning and thinking styles. Following are their recommendations.

**EARLY CHILDHOOD**   Preschoolers can be very eager to answer a question or take part in an activity, which means they often talk over others so that they can be heard

by the teacher. While we are always happy to have enthusiastic students, we also teach them to wait to be called on and to take their time before answering a question.

—**MISSY DANGLER,** *Suburban Hills School*

**ELEMENTARY SCHOOL: GRADES K–5**   We use a "think time" procedure in which students think and respond to a question on signal after an adequate time for

reflection. And we incorporate a think-pair-share procedure that gives all students an opportunity to think about a question, pair up with a partner, and then share their ideas. I also ask students what their partner said to encourage listening skills.

—**HEATHER ZOLDAK,** *Ridge Wood Elementary School*

**MIDDLE SCHOOL: GRADES 6–8**   I try to provide differentiated learning opportunities to suit all of my students' learning styles. For example, the students who are gifted can work on extensive independent research projects, and students who enjoy technology are allowed to complete a research project using a PowerPoint presentation. I give hands-on projects to students who enjoy drawing or developing creative projects.

—**FELICIA PETERSON,** *Pocantico Hills School*

**HIGH SCHOOL: GRADES 9–12**   As an art teacher, I foster an attitude of openness and acceptance in my classroom, which helps to promote my students' learning. When students feel that their ideas will be respected and heard, they are not afraid to try something different.

—**DENNIS PETERSON,** *Deer River High School*

## Review, Reflect, and Practice

**2** Describe learning and thinking styles.

**REVIEW**

- What is meant by learning and thinking styles? Describe impulsive/reflective styles.
- How can deep/surface styles be characterized?

**REFLECT**

- Describe yourself or someone else you know well in terms of the learning and thinking styles presented in this section.

**PRAXIS™ PRACTICE**

1. Ms. Garcia has her students read passages from a novel and then gives them 30 minutes to describe the gist of what they have read. Which students are likely to do well on this task?
   a. students with an impulsive style of thinking
   b. students with a reflective style of thinking

*(continued)*

## Review, Reflect, and Practice

**PRAXIS™ PRACTICE (CONTINUED)**

    c. students with practical intelligence

    d. students with average intelligence

2. Which question encourages a deep style of thinking?

    a. What is the inverse of one-half?

    b. What is the lowest prime number?

    c. How much flour would you use to make half of the cookie recipe?

    d. What does it mean to say that addition is the opposite of subtraction?

*Please see the answer key at the end of the book.*

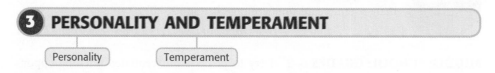

## ③ PERSONALITY AND TEMPERAMENT

    Personality    Temperament

We have seen that it is important to be aware of individual variations in children's cognition. It also is important to understand individual variations in their personality and temperament.

### PERSONALITY

We make statements about personality all the time and prefer to be around people with certain types of personality. Let's examine just what the term *personality* means.

    **Personality** refers to distinctive thoughts, emotions, and behaviors that characterize the way an individual adapts to the world. Think about yourself for a moment. What is your personality like? Are you outgoing or shy? Considerate or caring? Friendly or hostile? These are some of the characteristics involved in personality.

    How stable are personality traits in adolescence? Some researchers have found that personality is not as stable in adolescence as in adulthood (Roberts, Wood, & Caspi, 2008). The greater degree of change in personality during adolescence may be linked to the exploration of new identities.

**The "Big Five" Personality Factors**  As with intelligence, psychologists are interested in identifying the main dimensions of personality (Engler, 2009; Olson & Hergenhahn, 2011). Some personality researchers argue that they have identified the **"Big Five" factors of personality,** the "supertraits" thought to describe personality's main dimensions: openness, conscientiousness, extraversion, agreeableness, and neuroticism (emotional stability) (see Figure 4.7). (Notice that if you create an acronym from these trait names, you get the word *OCEAN*.)

**personality** Distinctive thoughts, emotions, and behaviors that characterize the way an individual adapts to the world.

**"Big Five" factors of personality** Openness, conscientiousness, extraversion, agreeableness, and neuroticism (emotional stability).

**FIGURE 4.7** THE "BIG FIVE" FACTORS OF PERSONALITY

Each column represents a broad "supertrait" that encompasses more narrow traits and characteristics. Using the acronym *OCEAN* can help you to remember the Big Five personality factors (openness, conscientiousness, and so on).

| **O**penness | **C**onscientiousness | **E**xtraversion | **A**greeableness | **N**euroticism (emotional stability) |
|---|---|---|---|---|
| • Imaginative or practical | • Organized or disorganized | • Sociable or retiring | • Softhearted or ruthless | • Calm or anxious |
| • Interested in variety or routine | • Careful or careless | • Fun-loving or somber | • Trusting or suspicious | • Secure or insecure |
| • Independent or conforming | • Disciplined or impulsive | • Affectionate or reserved | • Helpful or uncooperative | • Self-satisfied or self-pitying |

Much of the research on the Big Five factors has used adults as the participants in studies (McCrae & Costa, 2006; Noftle & Fleeson, 2010). However, an increasing number of such studies focus on children and adolescents (Heaven & Ciarrochi, 2008; Selfhout & others, 2010; Soto & others, 2008). A recent study of the Big Five factors found that agreeableness and emotional stability increased from early through late adolescence (Klimstra & others, 2009).

DEVELOPMENT

The major finding in the study of the Big Five factors in childhood and adolescence is the emergence of conscientiousness as a key predictor of adjustment and competence (Roberts & others, 2009). Following are examples of recent research that document this link:

RESEARCH

- A study of the Big Five factors revealed that conscientiousness was the best predictor of both high school and college grade-point average (Noftie & Robins, 2007). In this study, openness was the best predictor of SAT verbal scores.

- A study of fifth- to eighth-graders found that conscientiousness was linked to better interpersonal relationships: higher-quality friendships, better acceptance by peers, and less victimization by peers (Jensen-Campbell & Malcolm, 2007).

The Big Five factors can give you a framework for thinking about your students' personality traits. Your students will differ in their emotional stability, how extraverted or introverted they are, how open to experience, how agreeable, and how conscientious they are.

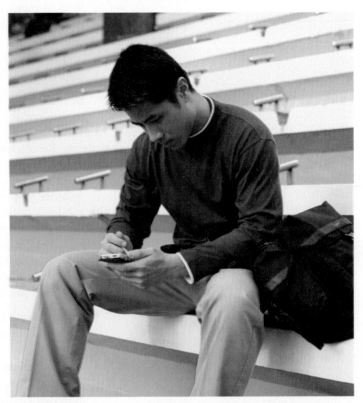

An adolescent with a high level of conscientiousness organizes his daily schedule and plans how to use his time effectively. *What are some characteristics of conscientiousness? How is it linked to adolescents' competence?*

**Person-Situation Interaction**   In discussing learning and thinking styles, we indicated that a student's style can vary according to the subject matter the student is learning or thinking about. The same is true for personality characteristics. According to the concept of **person-situation interaction,** the best way to characterize an individual's personality is not in terms of personal traits or characteristics alone, but also in terms of the situation involved. Researchers have found that students choose to be in some situations and avoid others depending on their personality traits (Cervone & Pervin, 2010; Schultz & Schultz, 2009).

Suppose you have an extravert and an introvert in your class. According to the theory of person-situation interaction, you can't predict which one will show the best adaptation unless you consider the situation they are in. The theory of person-situation interaction predicts that the extravert will adapt best when asked to collaborate with others and that the introvert will adapt best when asked to carry out tasks independently. Similarly, the extravert likely will be happier when socializing with lots of people at a party, the introvert when in a more private setting alone or with a friend.

In sum, don't think of personality traits as always dooming a student to behave in a particular way across all situations. The context or situation matters (Berecz, 2009; Larsen & Buss, 2010). Monitor situations in which students with varying personality characteristics seem to feel most comfortable and provide them with opportunities to learn in those situations. If a particular personality trait is detrimental to the student's school performance (perhaps one student is so introverted that she or he fears working in a group), think of ways you can support the student's efforts to change.

**person-situation interaction** The view that the best way to conceptualize personality is not in terms of personal traits or characteristics alone, but also in terms of the situation involved.

## TEMPERAMENT

Closely related to personality and to learning and thinking styles, **temperament** is a person's behavioral style and characteristic ways of responding. Some students are

**temperament** A person's behavioral style and characteristic ways of responding.

active; others are calm. Some respond warmly to people; others fuss and fret. Such descriptions involve variations in temperament.

**Temperament Classifications**    Scientists who study temperament seek to find the best ways to classify temperaments. The most well-known classification was proposed by Alexander Chess and Stella Thomas (Chess & Thomas, 1977; Thomas & Chess, 1991). They conclude that there are three basic styles, or clusters, of temperament:

- An **easy child** is generally in a positive mood, quickly establishes regular routines in infancy, and adapts easily to new experiences.
- A **difficult child** reacts negatively and cries frequently, engages in irregular daily routines, and is slow to accept change.
- A **slow-to-warm-up child** has a low activity level, is somewhat negative, and displays a low intensity of mood.

RESEARCH

In their longitudinal investigation, Chess and Thomas found that 40 percent of the children they studied could be classified as easy, 10 percent as difficult, and 15 percent as slow to warm up. Notice that 35 percent did not fit any of the three patterns. Researchers have found that these three basic clusters of temperament are moderately stable across the childhood years. A difficult temperament, or a temperament that reflects a lack of control, can place a student at risk for problems.

Another way of classifying temperament focuses on the differences between a shy, subdued, timid child and a sociable, extraverted, bold child. Jerome Kagan (2002, 2010) regards shyness with strangers (peers or adults) as one feature of a broad temperament category called *inhibition to the unfamiliar*.

RESEARCH

Mary Rothbart and John Bates (2006) emphasize that three broad dimensions best represent what researchers have found to characterize the structure of temperament. Here are descriptions of these three temperament dimensions (Rothbart, 2004, p. 495):

- *Extraversion/surgency* includes "positive anticipation, impulsivity, activity level, and sensation seeking." Kagan's uninhibited children fit into this category.
- *Negative affectivity* consists of "fear, frustration, sadness, and discomfort." These children are easily distressed; they may fret and cry often. Kagan's inhibited children fit this category.
- *Effortful control (self-regulation)* involves "attentional focusing and shifting, inhibitory control, perceptual sensitivity, and low-intensity pleasure." Children high on effortful control show an ability to keep their arousal from getting too high and have strategies for soothing themselves. By contrast, children low on effortful control are often unable to control their arousal; they become easily agitated and intensely emotional. A recent study of school-age children in the United States and China revealed that in both cultures low effortful control was linked to externalizing problems, such as lying, cheating, being disobedient, and being overly aggressive (Zhou, Lengua, & Wang, 2009).

From Rothbart's perspective (2004, 2007), early views of temperament emphasized that children's behavior is energized by their positive and negative emotions or arousal level. The more recent emphasis on effortful control, however, stresses that children can engage in a more cognitive, flexible approach to stressful circumstances.

Individual differences emerge in the development of children's temperament styles (Eisenberg & others, 2010). In the case of effortful control, for example, although maturation of the brain's prefrontal lobes must occur for any child's attention to improve and the child to achieve effortful control, some children develop it and others do not (Bates, 2008). These individual differences in children are at the heart of what characterizes temperament (Bates, 2008).

**easy child**  A temperament style in which the child is generally in a positive mood, quickly establishes regular routines, and easily adapts to new experiences.

**difficult child**  A temperament style in which the child tends to react negatively, cries frequently, engages in irregular routines, and is slow to accept new experiences.

**slow-to-warm-up child**  A temperament style in which the child has a low activity level, is somewhat negative, and displays a low intensity of mood.

## TEACHING CONNECTIONS: Best Practices
### Strategies for Teaching Children with Different Temperaments

Here are some teaching strategies related to students' temperaments (Keogh, 2003; Sanson & Rothbart, 1995):

1. *Show attention to and respect for individuality* (Sanson & Rothbart, 1995). Teachers need to be sensitive to the student's signals and needs. The goal of good teaching might be accomplished in one way with one student, in another way with another student, depending on the students' temperaments.

2. *Consider the structure of the students' environment* (Sanson & Rothbart, 1995). Crowded, noisy classrooms often pose greater problems for a "difficult" child than for an "easy" child. Fearful, withdrawn students often benefit from slower entry into new contexts.

3. *Be aware of problems that can emerge by labeling a child "difficult" and by using packaged programs for "difficult children"* (Sanson & Rothbart, 1995). Acknowledging that some children are harder to teach than others often is helpful. Advice on how to handle a particular temperament also can be useful. However, whether a particular characteristic is truly "difficult" depends on its fit with the environment, so the problem does not necessarily rest with the child. Labeling a child as "difficult" has the same danger of becoming a self-fulfilling prophecy as exists with labeling in regard to intelligence. Also keep in mind that temperament can be modified to some degree (Sanson & Rothbart, 2002). Packaged programs rarely take individual differences into account.

4. *Use effective strategies for dealing with difficult children in the classroom.* Following are some of these strategies (Keogh, 2003):
   - Try to avoid confrontations and power struggles by anticipating problem situations for the student; if the student engages in disruptive behavior, intervene at the first instance of the disruption.
   - Evaluate the physical context of the classroom, such as where the difficult child sits, who sits near her, and so on for clues about reducing disruptive behavior.
   - Minimize delay times between activities and standing in line, which gives a difficult child less time to be disruptive.

5. *Use effective strategies with shy and slow-to-warm-up students.* Keep in mind that it is easy to overlook shy, slow-to-warm-up children because they are unlikely to cause problems in the classroom. Following are some strategies for helping these children (Keogh, 2003):
   - Don't place this type of student immediately into group activities; let the student become involved in groups at his own pace initially. If over time, shy students are still reluctant to actively participate in groups, encourage them but don't push them.
   - Assign students' work partners with their temperaments in mind; for example, don't pair an intense, difficult child with a shy, slow-to-warm-up child. Beware of putting two intense, difficult children together.
   - Help shy, slow-to-warm-up students get started on activities that they appear hesitant about beginning, and be available to provide help during these activities.

6. *Help children with problems controlling their emotions to regulate their behavior.* In this regard, you can
   - Control your emotions when interacting with students. By observing how you handle difficult situations, students may be prompted to model your calm behavior.
   - Recognize that you are an important person in being able to guide children to regulate their emotions. Instruct children to talk to themselves in ways that may help to reduce their frustration and arousal. For example, if children have difficulty controlling their anger, they can learn to distract themselves from arousing events or stop and take a series of deep breaths. Many teachers have "chill out" areas in their classrooms—a place to which students can retreat for a few minutes to calm themselves if they are feeling overwhelmed.
   - Teach students appropriate ways to express their emotions. While we certainly don't want students hitting one another or screaming, they still need a way to let others know that something is bothering them.

An important point about temperament classifications such as Chess and Thomas' and Rothbart and Bates' is that children should not be pigeonholed as having only one temperament dimension, such as "difficult" or "negative affectivity." A good strategy when attempting to classify a child's temperament is to think of temperament as consisting of multiple dimensions (Bates, 2008). For example, a child might be extraverted, show little emotional negativity, and have good self-regulation.

DEVELOPMENT

Another child might be introverted, show little emotional negativity, and have a low level of self-regulation.

**Goodness of Fit** The match between an individual's temperament and the environmental demands the individual must cope with, called **goodness of fit,** can be important to a child's adjustment (Miller, Tserakhava, & Miller, 2010). In general, the temperament characteristics of effortful control, manageability, and agreeableness reduce the effects of adverse environments, whereas negative emotionality increases their effects (Rothbart & Bates, 2006).

## Review, Reflect, and Practice

**③** Characterize the nature of personality and temperament.

### REVIEW

- What is meant by the concept of personality? What are the Big Five factors of personality? What does the idea of person-situation interaction suggest about personality? How is temperament different from personality? Describe an easy child, a difficult child, and a slow-to-warm-up child. What are other categorizations of temperament? What are some good teaching strategies related to children's temperament?

### REFLECT

- Describe yourself in terms of the Big Five personality factors. In your K–12 education, how aware do you think your teachers were of your personality strengths and weaknesses? Might things have been different if they had known you better?

### PRAXIS™ PRACTICE

1. Maria is an outgoing, agreeable, fun-loving child. According to the concept of person-situation interaction, which of the following is likely to characterize Maria?
   a. Maria enjoys working independently on detail-oriented tasks.
   b. Maria likes to work on tasks that involve interaction with other students.
   c. Maria prefers to read by herself in a corner.
   d. Maria needs to be taught to control her impulses.

2. Stanton has been a challenging student. His frustration tolerance is low, and when he gets frustrated he often disrupts the class with angry outbursts. His teacher has difficulty handling him. What advice is most likely to help her deal with Stanton?
   a. She should show her frustration in dealing with him because once he realizes the impact of his behavior on others, he will learn to control his behavior.
   b. She should be calm with Stanton so he can observe a more adaptive response to frustration.
   c. She should send him out of the classroom every time he gets angry.
   d. She should separate him from his classmates and make him do his classwork by himself so that they won't imitate his behavior.

*Please see the answer key at the end of the book.*

**goodness of fit** The match between a child's temperament and the environmental demands the child must cope with.

# Workshops

Mr. Washington and his colleague, Ms. Rosario, had just attended a workshop on adapting instruction to children's learning styles. Ms. Jacobson and her colleague, Mr. Hassan, had just attended a workshop on adapting instruction to cover multiple intelligences. The four met in the teachers' workroom and were discussing what they had learned.

"Well," said Mr. Washington, "this certainly explains why some students seem to want to sit and listen to me talk, while others like to be more actively involved. Joe's obviously an executive type. He likes lectures. Martha, on the other hand, must be legislative. She just loves to work on projects and can't stand it when I tell her how to do things."

"No, I don't think so," Ms. Jacobson replies. "I think Joe's high in verbal intelligence. That's why he can make sense out of your lectures. He writes well, too. Martha likes to do things with her hands. She's higher in spatial and bodily-kinesthetic intelligence."

Mr. Washington responds, "No, no, no. Learning styles explain their differences much better. Here, look at this."

At this point, Mr. Washington shows Ms. Jacobson the handouts from the workshop he and Ms. Rosario had attended. Mr. Hassan gets out the handouts from the workshop he and Ms. Jacobson had attended as well. They begin comparing notes. They all recognize students in each of the schemes in the handouts. In fact, they can recognize the same student in both sets of handouts.

At this point, two other teachers—Mrs. Peterson and Mrs. Darby—walk into the room. They are very excited about a graduate class they are taking at a nearby university.

Mrs. Peterson says, "You know, I never thought about personality when considering teaching methods. It's no wonder Martha doesn't behave terribly well in my class. She's just too impulsive for the kind of structure I have."

Ms. Jacobson is dismayed. "You mean they're telling you we have to adapt our classrooms to the students' personalities now, too?" she asks.

Mr. Hassan is also upset. "Gee," he says, "just when I thought I had it all figured out. Used to be we just had to consider IQ. Now all this. We have 25 kids in our classes. How can we possibly adapt to all these differences? What are we supposed to do, have 25 different lesson plans? Maybe we should do some kind of profile on them and then group them by profile. What do you think, guys?"

1. What are the issues in this case?

2. To what extent should teachers adapt their instruction to the strengths, learning styles, and personalities of their students? Why?

3. What will you do in your classroom to accommodate individual differences such as students' strengths, learning styles, and personalities?

4. What other individual differences do you think you might have to accommodate? How will you do this?

5. On which theory is Ms. Jacobson basing her comments regarding Joe and Martha?
   a. Gardner's eight frames of mind
   b. general intelligence
   c. Sternberg's triarchic theory of intelligence
   d. Vygotsky's sociocultural theory

6. What type of grouping is Mr. Adams most likely discussing?
   a. between-class ability grouping
   b. Joplin plan
   c. nongraded program
   d. within-class ability grouping

# Reach Your **Learning Goals**

## Individual Variations

**① INTELLIGENCE:** Discuss what intelligence is, how it is measured, theories of multiple intelligences, the neuroscience of intelligence, and some controversies and issues about its use by educators.

### What Is Intelligence?

Intelligence consists of problem-solving skills and the ability to adapt to and learn from experiences. Interest in intelligence often focuses on individual differences and assessment.

### Intelligence Tests

Binet and Simon developed the first intelligence test. Binet developed the concept of mental age, and Stern created the concept of IQ as MA/CA $\times$ 100. The Stanford-Binet scores approximate a normal distribution. The Wechsler scales also are widely used to assess intelligence. They yield an overall IQ plus scores on a number of subscales and composite indexes. Group tests are more convenient and economical than individual tests, but group tests have a number of drawbacks (lack of opportunities for the examiner to establish rapport, distraction occurring from other students). A group intelligence test should always be supplemented with other relevant information when decisions are made about students. This also holds for an individual intelligence test.

### Theories of Multiple Intelligences

According to Sternberg's triarchic theory of intelligence, intelligence comes in three forms: analytical, creative, and practical. Gardner argues there are eight types of intelligence, or frames of mind: verbal, mathematical, spatial, bodily-kinesthetic, musical, intrapersonal, interpersonal, and naturalist. Project Spectrum and the Key School involve educational applications of Gardner's theory of multiple intelligences. The concept of emotional intelligence was initially developed by Salovey and Mayer. Goleman popularized the concept of emotional intelligence in his book, *Emotional Intelligence.* Mayer, Salovey, and Goleman stress that emotional intelligence is an important aspect of being a competent person. These approaches have much to offer, stimulating teachers to think more broadly about what makes up a student's competencies. However, they have been criticized along the lines of including some skills that should not be classified under intelligence and for the lack of a research base to support the approaches. Also, advocates of the concept of general intelligence argue that general intelligence is a reasonably good predictor of school and job performance.

### The Neuroscience of Intelligence

A substantial increase in interest in discovering links between the brain and intelligence has been stimulated by advances in brain imaging. Moderate correlation has been found between overall brain size and intelligence. Recent research has revealed a link between a distributed neural network in the frontal and parietal lobes and intelligence.

### Controversies and Issues in Intelligence

Three controversies and issues related to intelligence are (1) the nature-nurture question of how heredity and environment interact to produce intelligence, (2) how fairly intelligence testing applies across cultural and ethnic groups, and (3) whether students should be grouped according to ability (tracking). It is especially important to recognize that intelligence tests are an indicator of current performance, not fixed potential.

**② LEARNING AND THINKING STYLES:** Describe learning and thinking styles.

### Impulsive/Reflective Styles

Styles are not abilities but, rather, preferred ways of using abilities. Each individual has a number of learning and thinking styles. Impulsive/reflective styles also are referred to as *conceptual tempo.* This dichotomy involves a student's tendency to act quickly and impulsively or to take more time to respond and reflect on the accuracy of an answer. Impulsive students typically make more mistakes than reflective students.

| Deep/Surface Styles | Deep/surface styles involve the extent to which students approach learning—that is, whether to understand the meaning of materials (deep style) or to learn only what needs to be learned (surface style). Deep learners are more likely to be self-motivated to learn and take a constructivist approach to learning; surface learners are more likely to be motivated to learn because of external rewards. |

## 3 PERSONALITY AND TEMPERAMENT: Characterize the nature of personality and temperament.

**Personality**

Personality refers to distinctive thoughts, emotions, and behaviors that characterize the way an individual adapts to the world. Psychologists have identified the Big Five personality factors as openness, conscientiousness, extraversion, agreeableness, and neuroticism (emotional stability). The Big Five factors give teachers a framework for thinking about a student's personality characteristics. The Big Five factor of conscientiousness has increasingly been shown to be an important factor in children's and adolescents' development. The concept of person-situation interaction states that the best way to characterize an individual's personality is not in terms of traits alone but in terms of both the traits and the situations involved.

**Temperament**

Temperament refers to a person's behavioral style and characteristic way of responding. Chess and Thomas maintain that there are three basic temperament styles, or clusters: an easy child (generally in a positive mood), a difficult child (reacts negatively and cries easily), and a slow-to-warm-up child (low activity level, somewhat negative). A difficult temperament places a child at risk for problems. Other temperament categorizations have been proposed by Kagan (inhibition to the unfamiliar) and Rothbart and Bates (extraversion/surgency, negative affectivity, and effortful control [self-regulation]). In education involving students' temperaments, teachers should show attention to, and respect for, individuality; consider the structure of a student's environment; be aware of the problems involved when labeling a student as "difficult"; and use effective classroom strategies with difficult children, shy, slow-to-warm up children, and children who have difficulty regulating their emotions.

## KEY TERMS

intelligence 112
mental age (MA) 112
intelligence
     quotient (IQ) 112
normal distribution 112
triarchic theory of
     intelligence 115
emotional intelligence 120

nature-nurture issue 122
stereotype threat 124
culture-fair tests 124
between-class ability grouping
     (tracking) 125
nongraded (cross-age)
     program 125
Joplin plan 126

within-class ability
     grouping 126
learning and thinking styles 129
impulsive/reflective styles 129
deep/surface styles 130
personality 132
"Big Five" factors of
     personality 132

person-situation
     interaction 133
temperament 133
easy child 134
difficult child 134
slow-to-warm-up child 134
goodness of fit 136

## PORTFOLIO ACTIVITIES

Now that you have a good understanding of this chapter, complete these exercises to expand your thinking.

### Independent Reflection
**Your Multiple Intelligences.** Evaluate your own intelligence profile according to Gardner. In what frames of mind do you come out strongest? In which of Sternberg's three areas do you feel you

are the strongest? Write about your self-evaluation. (INTASC: Principles *2, 3*)

### Collaborative Work
**Personality Profiles.** Form a group of five or six students from your class, and have one person identify her or his personality and temperament traits. Have other members do the same, in turn.

After all have presented, discuss how the individuals in your group are similar or different. How will your personalities and temperaments translate into teaching styles? Write about this experience. (INTASC: Principles *2, 3*)

## Research/Field Experience

**Learning Styles in the Classroom.** Interview several teachers about students' different learning and thinking styles. Ask them what teaching strategies they use to accommodate these differences in students. Write a synopsis of your interviews. (INTASC: Principles *2, 3, 4, 9*)

*Go to the Online Learning Center for downloadable portfolio templates.*

# STUDY, PRACTICE, AND SUCCEED

Visit www.mhhe.com/santrockep5e to review the chapter with self-grading quizzes and self-assessments, to apply the chapter material to two more Crack the Case studies, and for suggested activities to develop your teaching portfolio.

## CHAPTER 5

# SOCIOCULTURAL DIVERSITY

*We need every human gift and cannot afford
to neglect any gift because of artificial barriers
of sex or race or class or national origin.*

—Margaret Mead
*American Anthropologist, 20th Century*

## Chapter **Outline**

## Learning **Goals**

**1** Discuss how variations in culture, socioeconomic status, and ethnic background need to be taken into account in educating children.

**2** Describe some ways to promote multicultural education.

**3** Explain various facets of gender, including similarities and differences in boys and girls; discuss gender issues in teaching.

# Teaching **Stories** Margaret Longworth

Margaret Longworth taught high school for a number of years and was a Teacher of the Year. She recently moved to the middle school level and currently teaches language arts at West Middle School in St. Lucie, Florida. When considering sociocultural diversity, she believes it is important for teachers to make schools "user friendly" for parents. In her words,

> Many parents—especially ethnic minority parents of color—are very intimidated by schools. They think teachers know everything. Principals know everything. And God forbid that they ever would need to approach the school board. To combat this intimidation, I became "user friendly." Many students and parents center their lives around the church in my community. So, to break the barriers between school and home, my Haitian paraprofessional began setting up meetings for me at the Haitian churches. The churches gave me their Sunday evening services. After they completed their preliminaries, they turned the service over to me. Through the assistance of an interpreter, I presented opportunities to help parents develop academic and life skills through education. I talked with them about special education classes, gifted classes, language programs, and scholarships, and encouraged them to keep their children in school. In turn, they felt confident enough to ask me about different happenings at school. Because of the parent-school-church connections that I was able to build up, I rarely had a discipline problem. If I did have to call parents, they would leave work or whatever they were doing and show up in my classroom. Many of these parents developed a relationship with the principal and guidance counselor and felt free to talk with school officials.

Margaret Longworth believes that in the classroom the key to improving children's interethnic relations is understanding. She comments,

> Understanding other persons' points of view requires spending time with them and getting to know them—how they think and feel. As students talk with each other and begin to appreciate each other, they soon learn that in many ways they aren't that different after all.

# Preview

Ours is a multicultural world of diverse backgrounds, customs, and values. Margaret Longworth's teaching story shows how teachers can improve students' lives and educational orientation by building bridges to their community. In this chapter we will explore many ways teachers have found to educate children from diverse cultural, socioeconomic, and ethnic backgrounds, including ways to make the classroom relevant for these children. We will also examine gender in schools and how teachers sometimes interact differently with boys and girls.

### ① CULTURE AND ETHNICITY

| Culture | Socioeconomic Status | Ethnicity | Bilingualism |

The students in the schools of Fairfax County, Virginia, near Washington, D.C., come from 182 countries and speak more than a hundred languages. Although the Fairfax County schools are a somewhat extreme example, they are harbingers of what is coming to America's schools. By the year 2025, 50 percent of all public school students are predicted to be from backgrounds that are currently classified as "minority." This challenges current definitions of the term. It also stresses the important educational goal of helping students develop respect for people from different cultural and ethnic backgrounds (Banks, 2010; Bennett, 2011; Campbell, 2010).

In this section, we will explore diversity in terms of cultures, socioeconomic status, and ethnicity. We'll also examine language issues, including the debate about bilingual education.

## CULTURE

**culture** The behavior patterns, beliefs, and all other products of a particular group of people that are passed on from generation to generation.

**Culture** refers to the behavior patterns, beliefs, and all other products of a particular group of people that are passed on from generation to generation. These products result from the interactions among groups of people and their environments over many years (Kitayama, 2011; Shiraev & Levy, 2010). A cultural group can be as large as the United States or as small as an isolated Amazon tribe. Whatever its size, the group's culture influences the behavior of its members (Bornstein, 2010; Irvine & Berry, 2010).

Psychologist Donald Campbell and his colleagues (Brewer & Campbell, 1976; Campbell & LeVine, 1968) found that people in all cultures often believe that what happens in their culture is "natural" and "correct" and what happens in other cultures is "unnatural" and "incorrect." Consequently, they tend to behave in ways that favor their cultural group and feel hostility toward other cultural groups.

Psychologists and educators who study culture are interested in comparing what happens in one culture with what happens in one or more other cultures (Goodnow, 2010; Zhang & Sternberg, 2011). **Cross-cultural studies** involve such comparisons, providing information about the degree to which people are similar and to what degree certain behaviors are specific to certain cultures (Kitayama, 2011; Shiraev & Levy, 2010). For example, a recent study revealed that from the beginning of the seventh grade through the end of the eighth grade, U.S. adolescents showed a decrease in the value they placed on academics and in their related motivational behavior (Wang & Pomerantz, 2009). No such decrease was shown in Chinese adolescents during the same time frame. In Chapters 12 and 15, we will further examine comparisons of U.S. and East Asian students.

DIVERSITY

RESEARCH

**Thinking Back/Thinking Forward**

Students in China, Japan, and Taiwan consistently outperform U.S. students in math achievement. Students in Singapore and Hong Kong recently had far greater gains in reading achievement than did U.S. students. Chapter 15, p. 527

### Individualist and Collectivist Cultures

One way that differences in cultures have been described involves individualism and collectivism (Triandis, 2007). **Individualism** refers to a set of values that give priority to personal goals rather than to group goals. Individualist values include feeling good, personal distinction, and independence. **Collectivism** consists of a set of values that support the group. Personal goals are subordinated to preserve group integrity, interdependence of the group's members, and harmonious relationships. Many Western cultures, such as those of the United States, Canada, Great Britain, and the Netherlands, are described as individualist. Many Eastern cultures, such as those of China, Japan, India, and Thailand, are labeled collectivist (Shwalb & others, 2010). Mexican culture also has stronger collectivist characteristics than U.S. culture. However, the United States has many collectivist subcultures, such as Chinese American and Mexican American.

A recent analysis proposed four values that reflect parents' beliefs in individualistic cultures about what is required for children's effective development of autonomy: (1) personal choice, (2) intrinsic motivation, (3) self-esteem, and (4) self-maximization, which consists of achieving one's full potential (Tamis-LeMonda & others, 2008). The analysis also proposed that three values reflect parents' beliefs in collectivistic cultures: (1) connectectness to the family and other close relationships, (2) orientation to the larger group, and (3) respect and obedience.

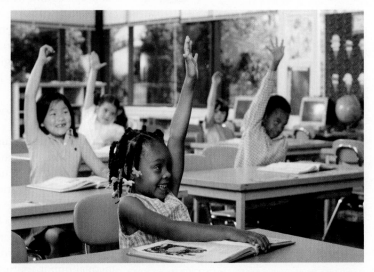

*What are some differences in individualist and collectivist cultures? What are some teaching strategies for working with students from these cultures?*

Critics of the individualistic and collectivistic cultures concept argue that these terms are too broad and simplistic, especially with globalization increasing (Kagitcibasi, 2007). Regardless of their cultural background, people demonstrate a need for both a positive sense of self and connectedness to others to develop fully as human beings. The analysis by Carolyn Tamis-LeMonda and her colleagues (2008, p. 204) emphasizes that in many families, children are not reared in environments that uniformly endorse individualistic or collectivistic values, thoughts, and actions. Rather, in many families, children are "expected to be quiet, assertive, respectful,

**cross-cultural studies** Studies that compare what happens in one culture with what happens in one or more other cultures; they provide information about the degree to which people are similar and to what degree behaviors are specific to certain cultures.

**individualism** A set of values that give priority to personal rather than to group goals.

**collectivism** A set of values that support the group.

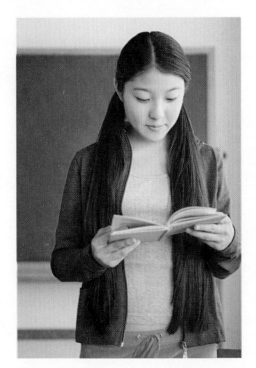

*How do East Asian and U.S. adolescents spend their time differently?*

DEVELOPMENT

RESEARCH

TECHNOLOGY

**Thinking Back/Thinking Forward**

Comparisons of U.S. and East Asian students reveal differences in math education, including time spent on learning tasks. Chapter 12, p. 401

RESEARCH

**socioeconomic status (SES)** A grouping of people with similar occupational, educational, and economic characteristics.

curious, humble, self-assured, independent, dependent, affectionate, or reserved depending on the situation, people present, children's age, and social-political and economic circles."

**Cross-Cultural Comparisons of Adolescents' Time Use** In addition to examining whether cultures are individualist or collectivist, another important cross-cultural comparison involves how children and adolescents spend their time (Larson, Wilson, & Rickman, 2009). Reed Larson and Suman Verma (1999) studied how adolescents in the United States, Europe, and East Asia spend their time in work, play, and developmental activities such as school. U.S. adolescents spent about 60 percent as much time on schoolwork as East Asian adolescents did, mainly because U.S. adolescents did less homework. U.S. adolescents also spent more time in paid work than their counterparts in most developed countries. And what U.S. adolescents had more of than adolescents in other industrialized countries was free time. About 40 to 50 percent of U.S. adolescents' waking hours (not counting summer vacations) was spent in discretionary activities, compared with 25 to 35 percent in East Asia and 35 to 45 percent in Europe. Whether this additional discretionary time is a liability or an asset for U.S. adolescents, of course, depends on how they use it.

The largest amounts of U.S. adolescents' free time were spent using the media and engaging in unstructured leisure activities, often with friends. U.S. adolescents spent more time in voluntary structured activities—such as sports, hobbies, and organizations—than East Asian adolescents.

According to Reed Larson (2007), U.S. adolescents may have too much unstructured time for optimal development. When adolescents are allowed to choose what they do with their time, they typically engage in unchallenging activities such as hanging out and watching TV. Although relaxation and social interaction are important aspects of adolescence, it seems unlikely that spending large numbers of hours per week in unchallenging activities fosters development. Structured voluntary activities may provide more promise for adolescent development than unstructured time, especially if adults give responsibility to adolescents, challenge them, and provide competent guidance in these activities (Larson, Wilson, & Rickman, 2009).

## SOCIOECONOMIC STATUS

**Socioeconomic status (SES)** refers to the grouping of people with similar occupational, educational, and economic characteristics. Socioeconomic status implies certain inequalities. Generally, members of a society have (1) occupations that vary in prestige, and some individuals have more access than others to higher-status occupations; (2) different levels of educational attainment, and some individuals have more access than others to better education; (3) different economic resources; and (4) different levels of power to influence a community's institutions. These differences in the ability to control resources and to participate in society's rewards produce unequal opportunities. Socioeconomic differences are a "proxy for material, human, and social capital within and beyond the family" (Huston & Ripke, 2006, p. 425). In the United States, SES has important implications for education. Low-SES individuals often have less education, less power to influence a community's institutions (such as schools), and fewer economic resources.

A parent's SES is likely linked to the neighborhoods and schools in which children live and the schools they attend (Huston & Bentley, 2010). Such variations in neighborhood settings can influence children's adjustment (Leventhal, Dupere, & Brooks-Gunn, 2009). For example, a recent study revealed that neighborhood disadvantage (involving such characteristics as low neighborhood income and unemployment) was linked to less consistent, less stimulating, and more punitive parenting, and ultimately to negative child outcomes (low verbal ability and behavioral problems) (Kohen & others, 2008).

So far we have focused on the challenges that many students from low-income families face. However, research by Souniya Luthar and her colleagues (Ansary & Luther, 2009; Luthar, 2006; Luthar & Goldstein, 2008) has found that adolescents from affluent families also face challenges. In their research, adolescents from affluent families were vulnerable to high rates of substance abuse and males from affluent families had more problems than females. Affluent female adolescents, on the other hand, were more likely to attain superior levels of academic success.

**The Extent of Poverty in America**   In a report on the state of America's children, the Children's Defense Fund (1992) described what life is like for all too many children. When sixth-graders in a poverty-stricken area of St. Louis were asked to describe a perfect day, one boy said that he would erase the world, then sit and think. Asked if he wouldn't rather go outside and play, the boy responded, "Are you kidding? Out there?"

Children who grow up in poverty represent a special concern (Tamis-LeMonda & McFadden, 2010). In 2007, 18 percent of U.S. children were living in families below the poverty line (Childstats.gov, 2009). The 18 percent figure represents an increase from 2001 (16.2 percent) but reflects a drop from a peak of 22.7 percent in 1993. The U.S. figure of 17 percent of children living in poverty is much higher than those from other industrialized nations. For example, Canada has a child poverty rate of 9 percent, and Sweden has a rate of 2 percent.

Poverty in the United States is demarcated along family structure and ethnic lines. In 2006, 42 percent of female-headed families lived in poverty compared with only 8 percent of married-couple families. In 2006, 33 percent of African American families and 27 percent of Latino families lived in poverty, compared with only 10 percent of non-Latino White families. Compared with non-Latino White children, ethnic minority children are more likely to experience persistent poverty over many years and live in isolated poor neighborhoods where social supports are minimal and threats to positive development abundant.

Because of advances in their cognitive growth, adolescents living in poverty conditions likely are more aware of their social disadvantage and the associated stigma than are children (McLoyd & others, 2009). Combined with the increased sensitivity to peers in adolescence, such awareness may cause them to try to hide their poverty status as much as possible from others.

**Educating Students from Low-SES Backgrounds**   Children in poverty often face problems at home and at school that compromise their learning (Huston & Bentley, 2010). A review of the environment of childhood poverty concluded that compared with their economically more-advantaged counterparts, poor children experience these adversities (Evans, 2004): more family conflict, violence, chaos, and separation from their families; less social support; less intellectual stimulation; more TV viewing; inferior schools and child-care facilities, as well as parents who are less involved in their school activities; more pollution and crowded, noisy homes; and more dangerous, deteriorating neighborhoods. Figure 5.1 shows the results of one study that illustrates these types of environmental differences that children from poor families and middle-income families experience (Evans & English, 2002). A recent study also revealed that the

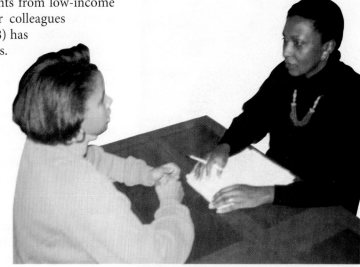

Vonnie McLoyd (*right*) has conducted a number of important investigations of the roles of poverty, ethnicity, and unemployment in children's and adolescents' development. She has found that economic stressors often diminish children's and adolescents' belief in the utility of education and their achievement strivings.

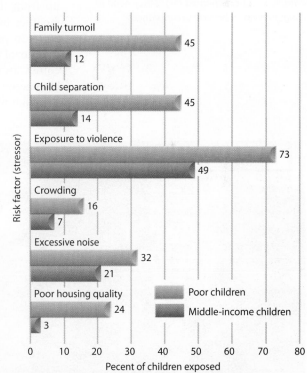

**FIGURE 5.1**   EXPOSURE TO SIX STRESSORS AMONG POOR AND MIDDLE-INCOME CHILDREN

One recent study analyzed the exposure to six stressors among poor children and middle-income children (Evans & English, 2002). Poor children were much more likely to face each of these stressors.

RESEARCH

Two boys who live in a poverty section of the South Bronx in New York City. *How does poverty affect the development of children like these? What types of experiences might they need to counter living in poverty circumstances?*

RESEARCH

In *The Shame of the Nation,* Jonathan Kozol (2005) criticized the inadequate quality and lack of resources in many U.S. schools, especially those in the poverty areas of inner cities, that have high concentrations of ethnic minority children. Kozol praises teachers like Angela Lively, who keeps a box of shoes in her Indianapolis classroom for students in need.

more years children spent living in poverty, the more their physiological indices of stress were elevated (Evans & Kim, 2007).

The schools that children from impoverished backgrounds attend often have fewer resources than schools in higher-income neighborhoods (Huston & Bentley, 2010). In low-income areas, students tend to have lower achievement test scores, lower graduation rates, and lower rates of college attendance. School buildings and classrooms are often old, crumbling, and poorly maintained. They are also more likely to be staffed by young teachers with less experience than schools in higher-income neighborhoods (Huston & Bentley, 2010). Schools in low-income areas are more likely to encourage rote learning, whereas schools in higher-income areas are more likely to work with children to improve their thinking skills (McLoyd & others, 2009). In sum, far too many schools in low-income neighborhoods provide students with environments that are not conducive to effective learning.

In *Savage Inequalities,* Jonathan Kozol (1991) vividly described some of the problems that children of poverty face in their neighborhood and at school. For example, Kozol observed that in East St. Louis, Illinois, which is 98 percent African American, there were no obstetric services, no regular trash collection, and few jobs. Blocks upon blocks of housing consist of dilapidated, skeletal buildings. Residents breathe the chemical pollution of nearby Monsanto Chemical Company. Raw sewage repeatedly backs up into homes. Child malnutrition is common. Fear of violence is real. The problems of the streets spill over into the schools, where sewage also backs up from time to time. Classrooms and hallways are old and unattractive, athletic facilities inadequate. Teachers run out of chalk and paper, and the science labs are 30 to 50 years out of date.

Kozol says that anyone who visits places like East St. Louis, even for a brief time, comes away profoundly shaken. Kozol also notes that although children in low-income neighborhoods and schools experience many inequities, these children and their families also have many strengths, including courage. Parents in such impoverished circumstances may intensely pursue ways to get more effective teachers and better opportunities for their children.

A downward trajectory is not inevitable for children and adolescents living in poverty (Philipsen, Johnson, & Brooks-Gunn, 2009). One potential positive path for youth who live in low-income circumstances is to become involved with a caring mentor. A program based on that idea was the Quantum Opportunities Program, funded by the Ford Foundation, providing year-round mentoring for minority students entering ninth grade at a high school with high rates of poverty and living in families that received public assistance (Carnegie Council on Adolescent Development, 1995). Each day for four years, mentors provided sustained support, guidance, and concrete assistance to their students.

The Quantum program required students to participate in (1) academic-related activities outside school hours, including reading, writing, math, science, and social studies, peer tutoring, and computer skills training; (2) community-service projects, including tutoring elementary school students, cleaning up the neighborhood, and volunteering in hospitals, nursing homes, and libraries; and (3) cultural enrichment and personal development activities, including life skills training, and college and job planning. In exchange for their commitment to the program, students were offered financial incentives that encouraged participation, completion, and long-range planning.

An evaluation of the Quantum project compared the mentored students with a nonmentored control group. Sixty-three percent of the mentored students graduated from high school, but only 42 percent of the control group did; 42 percent of the mentored students are currently enrolled in college, but only 16 percent of the control group are. Furthermore, control-group students were twice as likely as the mentored students to receive food stamps or welfare, and they had more arrests. Such programs clearly have the potential to overcome the intergenerational transmission of poverty and its negative outcomes.

The original Quantum Opportunities Program no longer exists, but the Eisenhower Foundation (2010) recently began replicating the Quantum program in Alabama, South Carolina, New Hampshire, Virginia, Mississippi, Oregon, Maryland, Washington, D.C., Ohio, and Iowa.

Children participating in the Quantum Opportunities Program at the Carver Center in Washington, D.C.

---

## TEACHING CONNECTIONS: Best Practices
### Strategies for Working with Children in Poverty

As we have seen, children living in poverty face challenges in school. Following are some effective strategies for working with children living in poverty circumstances.

1. *Improve thinking and language skills.* If you teach in a school in a low-income neighborhood, adopt the goal of helping children improve their thinking and language skills. As you will see in Through the Eyes of Teachers, this is an important goal in the classroom of Jill Nakamura, a first-grade teacher in Fresno, California.

### THROUGH THE EYES OF TEACHERS
#### Daily After-School Reading Club for Students in a High-Poverty School

Jill Nakamura teaches in a school located in a high-poverty area. She visits students at home early in the school year in an effort to connect with them and develop a partnership with their parents. "She holds daily after-school reading clubs for students reading below grade level . . . ; those who don't want to attend must call parents to tell them. In a recent school year (2004), she "raised the percent of students reading at or above grade level from 29 percent to 76 percent" (Wong, Briggs, 2004, p. 6D).

---

2. *Understand that students from impoverished families are not likely to have access to the same resources as those from middle-income families.*

Jill Nakamura, teaching in her first-grade classroom.

- For younger children this may mean they come to school without much experience with print media. This may result in their coming to school with fewer literacy skills.

- For older children and adolescents, this may mean they have very limited access to reference materials and computers. Therefore teachers need to understand what students can and cannot be expected to accomplish

*(continued)*

## TEACHING CONNECTIONS: Best Practices
### Strategies for Working with Children in Poverty

outside of the school environment (e.g., homework and projects). Access to these things should be provided to students beyond the school day.

3. *Don't overdiscipline.* Where poverty and other factors make it difficult to maintain safety and discipline, recognize the right, workable tradeoff between discipline and children's freedom. We will say more about classroom discipline in Chapter 14.

4. *Make student motivation a high priority.* Because many children from low-income backgrounds might come to your class not having experienced high parental standards for achievement, and thus might lack the motivation to learn, pay special attention to motivating these children to learn. We will address this topic further in Chapter 13.

5. *Think about ways to support and collaborate with parents.* Recognize that many parents in low-income areas are not able to provide much academic supervision or assistance to their children. This may be due to work schedules or lack of education themselves. Look for

ways to support the parents who can be trained and helped to do so.

6. *Look for ways to involve talented people from impoverished communities.* Recognize that parents in low-income areas can be quite talented, caring, responsive people in ways that teachers might not expect. Most impoverished communities have people whose wisdom and experience defy stereotypes. Find these people and ask them to volunteer their services to help support children's learning in your classroom, accompany children on field trips, and make the school more attractive.

7. *Observe the strengths of children from low-income backgrounds.* Many children from these circumstances come to school with considerable untapped knowledge, and teachers can access such richness (Pang, 2005). For example, these children may have substantial knowledge about how to use mass transit, whereas children in higher-income families are simply transported in cars.

## ETHNICITY

DIVERSITY

The word *ethnic* comes from the Greek word that means "nation." **Ethnicity** refers to a shared pattern of characteristics such as cultural heritage, nationality, race, religion, and language. Everyone is a member of one or more ethnic groups, and relations between people from different ethnic backgrounds, not just in the United States but in virtually every corner of the world, are often charged with bias and conflict.

**Immigration**    Nowhere is the changing tapestry of American culture more apparent than in the changing ethnic balances among America's citizens (Grigorenko & Takanishi, 2010; Hernandez, Denton, & Macartney, 2010). Relatively high rates of minority immigration have contributed to the growth in the proportion of ethnic minorities in the U.S. population (Kim & others, 2009; Rivera, 2010). Toward the end of the first decade of the twenty-first century, almost one-fourth of U.S. children are now Latino (Hernandez, Denton, & Macartney, 2010). And this growth of ethnic minorities is expected to continue (Healey, 2009). Asian Americans are expected to be the fastest-growing ethnic group of adolescents, with a growth rate of almost 600 percent by 2100. Latino adolescents are projected to increase almost 400 percent by 2100. By 2100 Latino adolescents are expected to outnumber non-Latino White adolescents.

An important point about any ethnic group is that it is diverse (De Feyter & Winsler, 2010; Short & others, 2010). There are many ready examples: Mexican Americans and Cuban Americans are Latinos, but they had different reasons for migrating to the United States, come from varying socioeconomic backgrounds, partake in different customs, and experience different rates and types of employment in the United States. Individuals born in Puerto Rico are distinguished from Latino individuals who have immigrated to the United States in that they are born U.S. citizens and are therefore not immigrants,

**ethnicity** A shared pattern of characteristics such as cultural heritage, nationality, race, religion, and language.

regardless of where they live in the United States. The U.S. government currently recognizes 511 different Native American tribes, each having a unique ancestral background with differing values and characteristics. Asian Americans include individuals of Chinese, Japanese, Filipino, Korean, and Southeast Asian origin, each group having distinct ancestries and languages. The diversity of Asian Americans is reflected in their educational attainment. Some achieve a high level of education; many others have little education. For example, 90 percent of Korean American males graduate from high school, but only 71 percent of Vietnamese males do.

Such diversity in Asian Americans is often overlooked because many Asian Americans are very successful in school achievement, don't take health risks, and don't engage in delinquent behavior. Because of these characteristics, they have been referred to as the "model minority" (Lee, 2009; Yoo, Burrola, & Steger, 2010). However, many Asian American students experience adjustment problems that include loneliness, anxiety, and depression (Zhou, Slu, & Xin, 2009).

Many of the families that have immigrated in recent decades to the United States, such as Asian Americans and Mexican Americans, come from collectivist cultures in which family obligation and duty to one's family are strong (Kim & others, 2009). The family obligation and duty may take the form of assisting parents in their occupations and contributing to the family's welfare (Fuligni, Hughes, & Way, 2009). These occupations are often service and manual-labor ones, such as in construction, gardening, cleaning, and restaurants. Many immigrant students serve as translators and negotiators for their families with the outside English-speaking world. Asian American and Latino families place a greater emphasis on family duty and obligation than do non-Latino White families.

**Ethnicity and Schools**   Educational segregation is still a reality for children of color in the United States (Banks, 2010). Almost one-third of African American and Latino students attend schools in which 90 percent or more of the students are from minority groups, typically their own minority group. The school experiences of students from different ethnic groups also depart in other ways (Spring, 2010). For example, African American and Latino students are much less likely than non-Latino White or Asian American students to be enrolled in academic, college preparatory programs and much more likely to be enrolled in remedial and special education programs. Asian American students are far more likely than students from other ethnic minority groups to take advanced math and science courses in high school. African American students are twice as likely as Latinos, Native Americans, or Whites to be suspended from school. Ethnic minorities of color constitute the majority of students in the largest school districts in the United States, a trend that is increasing (Banks, 2010). However, 90 percent of the teachers in America's schools are non-Latino White, and the percentage of minority teachers is projected to be even lower in coming years.

*(Top)* Immigrant Children from 12 countries participating in a U.S. citizenship ceremony in Queens, New York, on June 11, 2009. *What are some characteristics of immigrant children in the United States? (Bottom)* Latino immigrants in the Rio Grande Valley, Texas. *What are some cultural adaptations and educational challenges these immigrant children from Guadalajara, Mexico, might face in the United States?*

Further, just as the schools of students from low-income backgrounds have fewer resources than those of students from higher-income backgrounds, so too do the schools of students from ethnic minority backgrounds have fewer resources than the schools of their counterparts from largely non-Latino White backgrounds (Banks, 2010). For example, studies have found that students in California's predominantly minority schools had less access to every instructional resource surveyed, including textbooks, supplies, and computers, and were five times more likely to have uncertified teachers than students in predominantly non-Latino White schools (Oakes & Saunders, 2002; Shields & others, 2001).

In *The Shame of the Nation,* Jonathan Kozol (2005) described his visits to 60 U.S. schools in low-income areas of cities in 11 states. He saw many schools in which the minority population was 80 to 90 percent, concluding that school segregation is still present for many poor minority students. Kozol saw the inequities just summarized—unkempt classrooms, hallways, and restrooms; inadequate textbooks and supplies; and lack of resources. He also saw teachers mainly instructing students to rotely memorize material, especially as preparation for mandated tests, rather than engage in higher-level thinking. Kozol also frequently observed teachers using threatening disciplinary tactics to control the classroom.

**Prejudice, Discrimination, and Bias** The negative schooling experiences of many ethnic minority children that Kozol described may involve prejudice, discrimination, and bias (Rowley, Kurtz-Costes, & Cooper, 2010). **Prejudice** is an unjustified negative attitude toward an individual because of the individual's membership in a group. The group toward which the prejudice is directed might be defined by ethnicity, sex, age, or virtually any other detectable difference (Fuligni, Hughes, & Way, 2009). Our focus here is prejudice against ethnic groups of color.

People who oppose prejudice and discrimination often have contrasting views. Some value and praise the strides made in civil rights in recent years. Others criticize American schools and other institutions because they conclude that many forms of discrimination and prejudice still exist (Seaton, Yip, & Sellers, 2009).

**Diversity and Differences** Historical, economic, and social experiences produce both prejudicial and legitimate differences among various ethnic groups (Taylor & Whittaker, 2009). Individuals who live in a particular ethnic or cultural group adapt to that culture's values, attitudes, and stresses (Suyemoto, 2009). Their behavior might be different from one's own yet be functional for them. Recognizing and respecting these differences is an important aspect of getting along in a diverse, multicultural world (Cooper & others, 2008; McLoyd & others, 2009).

Recall also the point made earlier that another important dimension of every ethnic group is its diversity (Tewari & Alvarez, 2009). Not only is U.S. culture diverse—so is every ethnic group within the U.S. culture.

## BILINGUALISM

DIVERSITY

Throughout the world, many children speak more than one language. Some aspects of children's ability to learn a second language are transferred more easily to the second language than others (Pena & Bedore, 2009). A recent research review indicated that in learning to read, phonological awareness is rooted in general cognitive processes and thus transfers easily across languages; however, decoding is more language specific and needs to be relearned with each language (Bialystok, 2007).

DEVELOPMENT

**Learning a Second Language** U.S. students are far behind their counterparts in many developed countries in learning a second language. For example, in Russia schools have 10 grades, called *forms,* which roughly correspond to the 12 grades in American schools. Children begin school at age 7 in Russia and begin learning English in the third form. Because of this emphasis on teaching English, most Russian citizens under the age of 40 today are able to speak at least some English.

U.S. students who do not learn a second language may be missing more than the chance to acquire a skill. *Bilingualism*—the ability to speak two languages—has

**prejudice** An unjustified negative attitude toward an individual because of the individual's membership in a group.

a positive effect on children's cognitive development. Children who are fluent in two languages perform better than their single-language counterparts on tests of control of attention, concept formation, analytical reasoning, cognitive flexibility, and cognitive complexity (Bialystok, 2001, 2007; Bialystok & Craik, 2010). They also are more conscious of the structure of spoken and written language and better at noticing errors of grammar and meaning, skills that benefit their reading ability (Bialystok, 1997). However, a recent research review concluded that bilingual children have lower formal language proficiency (lower vocabulary, for example) than monolingual children (Bialystok & Craik, 2010).

In the United States, many immigrant children go from being monolingual in their home language to bilingual in that language and in English, only to end up monolingual speakers of English. This is called *subtractive bilingualism,* and it can have negative effects on children, who often become ashamed of their home language.

A first- and second-grade bilingual English-Cantonese teacher instructing students in Chinese in Oakland, California.

**Bilingual Education**   A current controversy related to bilingualism involves the millions of U.S. children who come from homes in which English is not the primary language (Echevarria & Graves, 2011; Herrera & Murry, 2011; Langdon, 2011). **English as a second language (ESL)** has now become a widely used term for bilingual education programs and classes that teach English to students whose native language is not English (Diaz-Rico & Weed, 2010; Haley, 2010). What is the best way to teach these children, who are referred to as *English-language learners (ELL)*?

The main ways used to teach ELL students are (1) English immersion, in which they are taught mainly or exclusively in English; (2) transitional bilingual education, in which they are taught reading or other subjects in their native

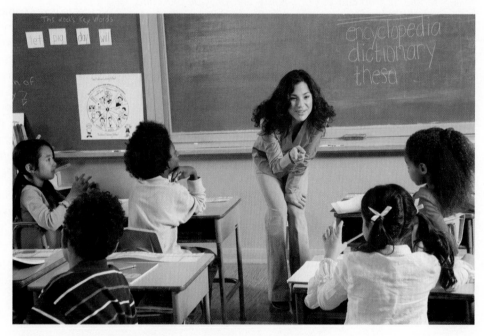

A Latina teacher works with students in a bilingual class on science.

language for several years and then moved into English classes; and (3) two-way, or dual, bilingual education, in which both native English-speaking students and ELL students are integrated in a bilingual classroom. In two-way bilingual education, a minimum of 30 percent of the students generally need to be ELL students.

Advocates of bilingual education argue that if children who do not know English are taught only in English, they will fall behind in academic subjects. How, they ask, can 7-year-olds learn arithmetic or history taught only in English when they do not speak the language?

Drawing general conclusions about the effectiveness of bilingual education is difficult—programs vary considerably in the number of years they are in effect, type of instruction, qualities of schooling other than bilingual education, teachers, school population, and other factors. Further, no effectively conducted experiments comparing bilingual to English-only education in the United States have been performed

**English as a second language (ESL)** A widely used term for bilingual education programs and classes that teach English to students whose native language is not English.

## TEACHING CONNECTIONS: Best Practices
### Strategies for Working with Linguistically and Culturally Diverse Children

Here are some classroom recommendations for working with linguistically and culturally diverse children:

1. *"Recognize that all children are cognitively, linguistically, and emotionally connected to the language and culture of their home."*

2. *"Acknowledge that children can demonstrate their knowledge and capacity in many ways.* Whatever language children speak, they should be able to show their capabilities and feel appreciated and valued."

3. *"Understand that without comprehensible input, second-language learning can be difficult.* It takes time to be linguistically competent in any language."

4. *"Model appropriate use of English, and provide the child with opportunities to use newly acquired vocabulary and language."* Learn at least a few words—more is better—in the child's first language to demonstrate respect for the child's culture.

5. *"Actively involve parents and families in the early-learning program and setting."* Encourage and assist parents in becoming knowledgeable about the value for children of knowing more than one language. Provide parents with strategies to support and maintain home language learning.

6. *"Recognize that children can and will acquire the use of English even when their home language is used and respected."* In Through the Eyes of Teachers, Daniel Arnoux, a middle school English teacher in Broward, Florida, describes how he seeks to make a difference in the lives of students whose natural first language is not English.

### THROUGH THE EYES OF TEACHERS
#### Giving Students a Sense of Pride

For the past seven years, I have been teaching ESOL (English for speakers of other languages) in addition to other middle-school subjects. I believe that I've made a difference in my students' lives by giving them a sense of pride in their heritage and by providing a learning environment in which they can grow.

To achieve equality, the educational system must recognize students' ethnic background and gender. The student's home culture isn't to be discarded but instead used as a teaching tool. What works best in improving children's interethnic problems is to confront the problem head-on. I create lessons that teach empathy and tolerance toward others. I've used my free time to talk to classes about human rights and prejudice toward students of different nationalities and cultures—in particular Haitian students, who are continually harassed and sometimes beaten in school.

Try always to know your students as human beings, and they will surely open up to you and learn. Tell them that you believe in them. If you believe they can achieve, they will.

7. *"Collaborate with other teachers to learn more about working with linguistically and culturally diverse children."*

8. *If students' parents speak a language other than English, be certain to have newsletters, permission slips, and other communication translated into their native language.*

*Source:* National Association for the Education of Young Children, 1996, pp. 7–11.

---

(Snow & Kang, 2006). Some experts argue that the quality of instruction is more important in determining outcomes than the language in which it is delivered (Lesaux & Siegel, 2003).

Some researchers have reported support for bilingual education in that children have difficulty learning a subject when it is taught in a language they do not understand, and when both languages are integrated in the classroom, children learn the second language more readily and participate more actively (Hakuta, 2000, 2001, 2005; Horowitz, 2008).

RESEARCH

Researchers have found that it takes ELL students approximately three to five years to develop speaking proficiency and seven years to develop reading proficiency in English (Hakuta, Butler, & Witt, 2000). Unfortunately, many bilingual education programs do not last this long.

It is important to note that immigrant children vary in their ability to learn English (Levine & McCloskey, 2009). For example, children from lower-socioeconomic backgrounds have more difficulty than those from higher-socioeconomic backgrounds (Rueda & Yaden, 2006). Thus, especially for low-SES immigrant children, more years of bilingual education may be needed than they currently receive.

## Review, Reflect, and Practice

**①** Discuss how variations in culture, socioeconomic status, and ethnic background need to be taken into account in educating children.

### REVIEW
- What is culture? How do individualistic and collectivistic cultures differ? How do U.S. adolescents spend their time compared with adolescents in Europe and East Asia?
- What is socioeconomic status? In what ways are children from impoverished backgrounds likely to have difficulty in school?
- How is ethnicity involved in children's schooling? What is the nature of second-language learning? What characterizes bilingual education?

### REFLECT
- In the context of education, are all ethnic differences negative? Come up with some differences that might be positive in U.S. classrooms.

### PRAXIS™ PRACTICE
1. Mr. Austin, who grew up in the midwestern United States, teaches math in a high school with students who have immigrated from Mexico, Korea, Vietnam, India, Pakistan, Poland, and the Czech Republic. He often uses competitive games as class activities, many of which involve individual races to solve problems on the whiteboard at the front of the classroom. Some of his students seem to immensely enjoy the games, but others get upset when they are unable to solve a problem. They become even more upset when Mr. Austin constructively criticizes them during the game. The most plausible explanation is that students who do *not* enjoy the games
   a. are not good athletes.
   b. have low self-esteem.
   c. grew up in a collectivist culture.
   d. grew up in an individualist culture.
2. Sally is a third-grade student at an economically diverse school. Sally lives in poverty, as do about one-fourth of her class. Another one-fourth of the class come from upper-middle-income families, and another half come from middle-income families. Sally's teacher, Ms. Roberts, has assigned a *diorama* (a scenic representation with sculpted figures and lifelike objects) project in lieu of a standard book report on *Charlotte's Web.*

   Kanesha, one of the more affluent children in the class, has created an elaborate diorama in a large shoe box. She placed plastic animals and small dolls in the diorama. The inside of her box is paneled with craft sticks to look like barn siding, and she used fine fishing line to create a web.

   Although Sally read, understood, and enjoyed the book, her diorama does not compare favorably to Kanesha's. First, she did not have a shoe box to use, so she used an old box she found at a grocery store. She made her animals out of paper because she could not afford plastic animals. She made her web out of an old shoelace.

*(continued)*

## Review, Reflect, and Practice

### PRAXIS™ PRACTICE (CONTINUED)

When Sally looked at her diorama next to Kanesha's, she almost cried. She did cry when Ms. Roberts gushed over how lovely Kanesha's diorama looked. What should Ms. Roberts have done differently?

a. She should have explained the income differences to the students before they began their project.

b. She should have had the students write traditional book reports.

c. She should have provided the materials and then had the students create the dioramas.

d. She should have praised Sally's diorama more than Kanesha's.

3. Robert teaches at an ethnically diverse elementary school. Since he decided to become a teacher, his goal has been to teach in a school like this one because he wants to help ethnic minority children. He makes considerable effort to ensure that all of his students are successful and feel part of the larger group. He is warm and caring toward his students, sometimes even providing lunch for those who forget to bring one or don't have enough money for the cafeteria. Often he praises minority students for work that he would deem only average from his majority students. What is Robert doing wrong?

a. He is substituting nurturance for academic standards.

b. He should provide a more nurturing environment for all students.

c. He should provide lunch for all of his students or none of them.

d. He is setting standards for minority students that are too high.

4. Mr. Williams teaches first grade and thinks his students will benefit from learning a second language, so he labels many of the items in his classroom in both English and Spanish. He chose Spanish because that is the second most common language in the area in which he teaches. What research supports Mr. Williams' approach?

a. First-graders are the right age to learn to read a second language but aren't too old to learn to speak a second language.

b. Because students in most countries do not learn to read a second language, Mr. Williams is giving his students an important advantage.

c. Children learn a second language better and more easily at this age than they will when they get older.

d. Mr. Williams should select a second language that is unfamiliar to most of his class.

*Please see the answer key at the end of the book.*

### 2 MULTICULTURAL EDUCATION

Empowering Students

Issues-Centered Education

Culturally Relevant Teaching

Improving Relationships Among Children from Different Ethnic Groups

**multicultural education** Education that values diversity and includes the perspectives of a variety of cultural groups on a regular basis.

The hope is that multicultural education can contribute to making our nation more like what the late civil rights leader Martin Luther King, Jr., dreamed of: a nation where children will be judged not by the color of their skin but by the quality of their character. **Multicultural education** is education that values diversity and includes the perspectives of a variety of cultural groups on a regular basis. Its proponents believe that children of color should be empowered and that multicultural education benefits all students (Banks, 2010). An important goal of multicultural education is equal educational opportunity for all students, with the result of closing the gap in academic achievement between mainstream students and students from underrepresented groups (Bennett, 2011; Florence, 2010).

Multicultural education grew out of the civil rights movement of the 1960s and the call for equality and social justice for women and people of color (Spring, 2010). As a field, multicultural education includes issues related to socioeconomic status, ethnicity, and gender. An increasing trend in multicultural education, though, is not to make ethnicity a focal point but to also include socioeconomic status, gender, religion, disabilitiy, sexual orientation, and other forms of differences (Howe, 2010). Another important point about contemporary multicultural education is that many individuals think that it is reserved for students of color. However, all students, including non-Latino White students, can benefit from multicultural education (Howe, 2010).

Because social justice is one of the foundational values of the field, prejudice reduction and equity pedagogy are core components (Banks, 2008, 2010). *Prejudice reduction* refers to activities teachers can implement in the classroom to eliminate negative and stereotypical views of others. *Equity pedagogy* refers to the modification of the teaching process to incorporate materials and learning strategies appropriate to both boys and girls and to various ethnic groups.

You and your students will benefit if you take a course or have some type of preparation involving multicultural education (Koppelman & Goodhart, 2011). For example, a study of math and science teachers revealed that their students' achievement was enhanced when their "teachers had a degree in the field in which they were teaching *and* had had preparation regarding multicultural education, special education, and English language development (Wenglinksy, 2002)" (Banks & others, 2005, p. 233).

Multicultural education expert James Banks (2008) recently described what should characterize a multicultural school:

- *The school staff's attitudes, beliefs, and actions.* The school's staff have high expectations for all students and are passionate about helping them learn.

- *The curriculum.* The course of study has been reformed so that students perceive events, concepts, and issues from the diverse views of different ethnic and socioeconomic groups.

- *Instructional materials.* Textbooks and learning materials represent the backgrounds and experiences of diverse ethnic and cultural views and are free from biases that marginalize the experiences of people of color, second-language minorities, women, and low-income individuals.

- *The school culture and the hidden curriculum.* The school culture reflects positive aspects of diversity and is supported by the "hidden curriculum"—the curriculum that is not explicitly taught but is nevertheless present and learned by students. The school's attitudes toward diversity can appear in

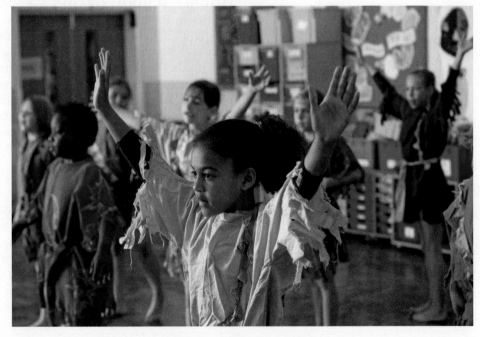

*What should be present if a school practices multicultural education?*

subtle ways, such as the types of photographs on school bulletin boards, the ethnic composition of the school's staff, and the fairness by which students from diverse backgrounds are disciplined or suspended.

- *The counseling program.* The school's counselors challenge students from diverse backgrounds to dream and provide them with strategies to reach those dreams. They guide students toward effective career choices and help them choose the appropriate courses that will enable them to pursue those choices.

I recently asked teachers how they promote diversity and acceptance of others in the classroom. Following are their responses.

**EARLY CHILDHOOD**   In all areas of my classroom, multicultural books in several languages, posters, and other items—for example, garments, dolls, and music—that  speak to diversity are displayed. The foods served to children during meal and snack times come from various cuisines and ethnic groups. At story time, books are read in different languages by parents and interpreted for the children to understand. Our philosophy is that we don't have to teach diversity, it already exists.

—**VALARIE GORHAM,** *Kiddie Quarters, Inc.*

**ELEMENTARY SCHOOL: GRADES K–5**   I teach the second-grade integrated ESL (English as a second language) class. At the beginning of the school year, as we are  establishing our classroom community, we take time to recognize each student by creating a bulletin board with a poster of the world at the center. The display is entitled, "We are the children . . . We are the World." Each child's photo is taken and then displayed with a string designating his or her country of origin. We use this map throughout the year as a springboard for many geography and social studies lessons as we explore and learn about the world and each other's cultural backgrounds.

—**ELIZABETH FRASCELLA,** *Clinton Elementary School*

**MIDDLE SCHOOL: GRADES 6–8**   I sometimes hear students call each other names in the halls and in the cafeteria. Instead of ignoring this behavior, I make  sure I use these incidents as teaching moments and explain to the students why it is wrong to call others names. I also use my classroom time to educate students on the beliefs and customs of different religions and cultural groups. And I am the advisor of our school's Unity Club, which celebrates the diversity within our school by showcasing different cultures. For example, the club recently created a special bulletin board—displaying the flags from each country represented within our school.

—**CASEY MAASS,** *Edison Middle School*

**HIGH SCHOOL: GRADES 9–12**   One-third of my school's population is Native American. As an art teacher, I present information on Native American art forms,  including pottery, beading, birchbark baskets, quillwork, and black ash baskets. All students learn what a Native American medicine wheel is (a circle of life) and what the various symbols—colors, directions, and animals—mean. Students make a medicine wheel for themselves and their own personal culture, whether they are Native American or not. Each piece is unique, which speaks to the diversity within the school.

—**DENNIS PETERSON,** *Deer River High School*

*What is involved in empowering students?*

## EMPOWERING STUDENTS

The term **empowerment** refers to providing people with the intellectual and coping skills to succeed and make this a more just world. In the 1960s to 1980s, multicultural education was concerned with empowering students and better representing minority and cultural groups in curricula and textbooks. Empowerment continues to be an important theme of multicultural education today (Hall, 2010). In this view, schools should give students the opportunity to learn about the experiences, struggles, and visions of many different ethnic and cultural groups (Banks, 2010). The hope is that this will raise minority students' self-esteem, reduce prejudice, and provide more equity in educational opportunities. The hope also is that it will help White students become more knowledgeable about minority groups and that both White students and students of color will develop multiple perspectives within their curricula.

Banks (2008, 2010) suggests that future teachers can benefit from writing a brief essay about a situation in which they felt marginalized (being excluded) by another group. Virtually everyone, whether from a minority or majority group, has experienced this type of situation at some point in her or his life. Banks suggests that you should be in a better position to understand the issues of sociocultural diversity after writing such an essay.

## CULTURALLY RELEVANT TEACHING

*Culturally relevant teaching* is an important aspect of multicultural education (Gollnick & Chinn, 2009). It seeks to make connections with the learner's cultural background (Pang, 2005).

Multicultural education experts stress that effective teachers are aware of and integrate culturally relevant teaching into the curriculum because it makes teaching more effective (Manning & Baruth, 2009). Some researchers have found that students from some ethnic groups behave in ways that may make certain educational tasks more difficult than others. For example, Jackie Irvine (1990) and Janice Hale-Benson (1982) observed that African American students are often expressive and high in energy. They recommended that, when students behave in this way, giving them

DIVERSITY

DIVERSITY

**empowerment** Providing people with intellectual and coping skills to succeed and make this a more just world.

Culturally relevant teaching is an important aspect of multicultural education. One aspect of culturally relevant teaching involves going into the community where parents live and work. Here a teacher visits a home of students who attend the Susan B. Anthony Elementary School in Sacramento.

opportunities to make presentations rather than always being required to perform on a written exam might be a good strategy. Other researchers have found that many Asian American students prefer visual learning more than their European American peers (Litton, 1999). Thus, with these students, teachers might want to use more three-dimensional models, graphic organizers, photographs, charts, and writing on the board.

Going into the community where your students live and their parents work can improve your understanding of their ethnic and cultural backgrounds (Banks & others, 2005). In the *funds of knowledge approach,* teachers visit students' households to develop social relationships with their students' family members to learn more about their cultural and ethnic background so that they can incorporate this knowledge into their teaching (Moll & Gonzáles, 2004). Through this approach, teachers can learn more about the occupations, interests, and community characteristics of their students' families. Examples of the funds of knowledge approach include guiding students to understand how their parents' carpentry skills relate to geometry and how the type of language students encounter outside of the classroom might help teachers in teaching students in English classes in school. Researchers have found that when the funds of knowledge approach is used, Latino students' academic performance improves (Gonzáles, Moll, & Amanti, 2005). The funds of knowledge approach acts as a bridge between the student's school and community.

Teachers need to have high achievement expectations for students from ethnic minority and low-income backgrounds and engage them in rigorous academic programs (Anderman & Anderman, 2010). When high achievement expectations and rigorous academic programs are combined with culturally relevant teaching and community connections, students from ethnic minority and low-income backgrounds benefit enormously. In one study of California students, a four-year evaluation found that Latino students who participated in a rigorous academic program that included community-based writing and study, academic advising, and time with community leaders were almost twice as likely to apply to and attend universities as their counterparts who did not participate in the program (Gandara, 2002).

## ISSUES-CENTERED EDUCATION

DIVERSITY

Thinking Back/Thinking Forward

Values clarification is one of several approaches to moral education. Chapter 3, p. 101

Issues-centered education also is an important aspect of multicultural education. In this approach, students are taught to systematically examine issues that involve equity and social justice. They not only clarify their values *(values clarification)* but also examine alternatives and consequences if they take a particular stance on an issue. Issues-centered education is closely related to *moral education,* which we discussed in Chapter 3. Consider the circumstance when some students were concerned with the lunch policy at a high school (Pang, 2005). The students who were on federally subsidized programs were forced to use a specific line in the cafeteria, which "labeled" them poor. Many of these low-income students felt humiliated and embarrassed to the point that they went without lunch. The students alerted teachers to the situation, and, together, the students and teachers developed a plan of action. They presented the plan to the school district, which revised its lunch line policy at the ten high schools affected by it.

# IMPROVING RELATIONSHIPS AMONG CHILDREN FROM DIFFERENT ETHNIC GROUPS

A number of strategies and programs are available to improve relationships among children from different ethnic groups (Short & others, 2010; Wright, 2011). To begin, we will discuss one of the most powerful strategies.

DIVERSITY

**The Jigsaw Classroom**    When social psychologist Elliot Aronson was a professor at the University of Texas at Austin, the school system contacted him for ideas to reduce the increasing racial tension in classrooms. Aronson (1986) developed the concept of the **jigsaw classroom,** which involves having students from different cultural backgrounds cooperate by doing different parts of a project to reach a common goal. Aronson used the term *jigsaw* because he saw the technique as much like a group of students cooperating to put different pieces together to complete a jigsaw puzzle.

How might this work? Consider a class of students, some White, some African American, some Latino, some Native American, and some Asian American. The lesson concerns the life of Joseph Pulitzer. The class might be broken up into groups of six students each, with the groups being as equally mixed as possible in terms of ethnic composition and achievement level. The lesson about Pulitzer's life is divided into six parts, and one part is assigned to each member of each six-person group. The parts might be passages from Pulitzer's biography, such as how the Pulitzer family came to the United States, Pulitzer's childhood, his early work, and so on. All students in each group are given an allotted time to study their parts. Then the groups meet, and each member works to teach his or her part to the group. Learning depends on the students' interdependence and cooperation in reaching the same goal.

*What are some features of a jigsaw classroom?*

Sometimes the jigsaw classroom strategy is described as "creating a superordinate goal or common task" for students. Team sports, drama productions, and music performances are additional examples of contexts in which students cooperatively and often very enthusiastically participate to reach a superordinate goal.

**Positive Personal Contact with Others from Different Cultural Backgrounds**    Contact by itself does not always improve relationships. For example, busing ethnic minority students to predominantly non-Latino White schools, or vice versa, has not reduced prejudice or improved interethnic relations (Frankenberg & Orfield, 2007). What matters is what happens after students arrive at a school.

Relations improve when students talk with each other about their personal worries, successes, failures, coping strategies, interests, and so on. When students reveal personal information about themselves, they are more likely to be perceived as individuals than simply as members of a group. Sharing personal information frequently produces this discovery: People from different backgrounds share many of the same hopes, worries, and feelings. Sharing personal information can help break down in-group/out-group and we/they barriers.

**jigsaw classroom** A classroom in which students from different cultural backgrounds cooperate by doing different parts of a project to reach a common goal.

**Perspective Taking** Exercises and activities that help students see other people's perspectives can improve interethnic relations. In one exercise, students learn certain proper behaviors of two distinct cultural groups, then attempt to interact with each other in accordance with those behaviors (Shirts, 1997). As a result, they experience feelings of anxiety and apprehension. The exercise is designed to help students understand the culture shock that comes from being in a cultural setting with people who behave in ways that are very different from what one is used to. Students also can be encouraged to write stories or act out plays that involve prejudice or discrimination. In this way, students "step into the shoes" of students who are culturally different from themselves and feel what it is like to not be treated as an equal.

Studying people from different parts of the world also encourages students to understand different perspectives. In social studies, students can be asked why people in certain cultures have customs different from their own. Teachers can also encourage students to read books on many different cultures.

TECHNOLOGY

**Technology Connections with Students Around the World** Traditionally, students have learned within the walls of their classroom and interacted with their teacher and other students in the classroom. With advances in telecommunications, students can learn with and from teachers and students around the world.

For example, in the Global Laboratory Project, an international, telecommunication-based project, students investigated local and global environments (Schrum & Berenfeld, 1997). After sharing their findings, students collaboratively identified various aspects of environments, discussed research plans, and conducted distributed studies using the same methods and procedures. Students from such diverse locations as Moscow, Russia; Warsaw, Poland; Kenosha, Wisconsin; San Antonio, Texas; Pueblo, Colorado; and Aiken, South Carolina, participated. As their data collection and evaluation evolved, students continued to communicate with their peers worldwide and to learn more, not only about science, but also about the global community.

The *Global Challenge Award* (**www.globalchallengeaward.org/display/public/ Home**), funded by the MacArthur Foundation, lets middle and high school students partner with international peers to form teams that cooperate to develop solutions to real-world problems (such as global warming). High-scoring teams win scholarships, travel awards, and cash prizes. More than 100,000 students had participated in the Global Challenge Award at the beginning of 2010.

New advances in telecommunication make it possible for students around the world to communicate through videoconferencing over the Internet. For example, at the Research Center for Educational Technology (RCET) at Kent State University, Ohio elementary students and their teachers are collaborating with their peers at the Instituto Thomas Jefferson in Mexico City on a variety of projects, including studies of plant biology, climate, and biography, using both Internet-based videoconferencing and e-mail (Swan & others, 2006). RCET researchers have found that projects that share common understandings but highlight local differences are especially productive.

An increasing number of schools are also using Internet-based videoconferencing for foreign language instruction. Instead of simulating a French café in a typical French language class, American students might talk with French students in a real café in France.

Such global technology projects can go a long way toward reducing American students' ethnocentric beliefs. The active building of connections around the world through telecommunications

Students in the Research Center for Educational Technology's AT&T classroom at Kent State University, studying plant biology with students at the Instituto Thomas Jefferson in Mexico City.

gives students the opportunity to experience others' perspectives, better understand other cultures, and reduce prejudice.

**Reducing Bias**   Children especially benefit if they learn early in their lives to show respect for individuals from ethnic groups other than their own. For example, in early childhood, teachers need to directly confront any hint of racism or discrimination in children's interactions. Teachers also should immediately stop peer interactions that are disrespectful of a child's ethnicity and talk about why he or she should not hurt the other child's feelings (Barbarin & Odom, 2009).

Louise Derman-Sparks and the Anti-Bias Curriculum Task Force (1989) created a number of tools to help young children reduce, handle, or even eliminate their biases. These are some of the antibias strategies recommended for teachers:

- Display images of children from a variety of ethnic and cultural groups. Select books for students that also reflect this diversity.
- Choose play materials and activities that encourage ethnic and cultural understanding. Use dramatic play to illustrate nonstereotypic roles and families from diverse backgrounds.
- Talk with students about stereotyping and discriminating against others. Make it a firm rule that no child is allowed to be teased or excluded because of ethnicity or race.
- Engage parents in discussions of how children develop prejudice, and inform parents about your efforts to reduce ethnic bias in your classroom.

**Increasing Tolerance**   Development of tolerance and respect for individuals from diverse ethnic groups is an important aspect of multicultural education (Barbarin, Mercado, & Jigjidsuren, 2010). The "Teaching Tolerance Project" provides schools with resources and materials to improve intercultural understanding and relationships between White children and children of color (Heller & Hawkins, 1994). The biannual magazine *Teaching Tolerance* is distributed to every public and private school in the United States (you can obtain a free copy by contacting Teaching Tolerance through **www.tolerance.org**). The magazine's purpose is to share views on and provide resources for teaching tolerance. For elementary school teachers, the "Different and Same" videos and materials (available through **www.fci.org**) can help children become more tolerant.

**The School and Community as a Team**   Yale psychiatrist James Comer (1988, 2006, 2010) stresses that a community team approach is the best way to educate children. Three important aspects of the Comer Project for Change are (1) a governance and management team that develops a comprehensive school plan, assessment strategy, and staff development program; (2) a mental health or school support team; and (3) a parents' program. The Comer program emphasizes a no-fault approach (the focus should be on solving problems, not blaming), no decisions except by consensus, and "no paralysis" allowed (that is, no naysayer can stand in the way of a strong majority decision). Comer says the entire school community should have a cooperative rather than an adversarial attitude. The Comer program is currently operating in more than 600 schools in 82 school districts in 26 states.

In his latest book, *Leave No Child Behind*, Comer (2004) agrees with the increased emphasis on higher standards and accountability in U.S. schools but argues that the emphasis on test scores and curriculum alone is inadequate. Comer says that children's socioemotional development and relationships with caregivers also need to be improved if educational reform is to be successful.

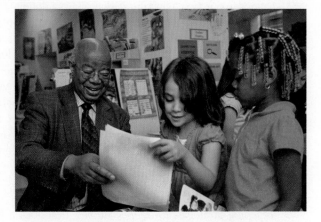

James Comer (*left*) is shown with some inner-city African American students who attend a school where Comer has implemented his community team approach.

## TEACHING CONNECTIONS: Best Practices
### Strategies for Multicultural Education

We already have discussed many ideas that will benefit children's relations with people from different ethnic and cultural backgrounds. Further guidelines for multicultural teaching include these recommendations from leading multicultural education expert, James Banks (2006, 2008):

1. *Be sensitive to racist content in materials and classroom interactions.* A good source for learning more about racism is Paul Kivel's (1995) book, *Uprooting Racism.*

2. *Learn more about different ethnic groups.* According to diversity expert Carlos Diaz (2005), only when you consider yourself "multiculturally literate" will you likely encourage students to think deeply and critically about diversity. Otherwise, says Diaz, teachers tend to see diversity as a "can of worms" that they don't want to open because they lack the background to explain it. To increase your multicultural literacy, read at least one major book on the history and culture of American ethnic groups. Two of Banks' books that include historical descriptions of these groups are *Cultural Diversity and Education* (2006) and *Teaching Strategies for Ethnic Studies* (2003). He also recently edited the *Handbook of Multicultural Education* (Banks, 2010).

3. *Be aware of students' ethnic attitudes.* Respond to students' cultural views in sensitive ways. In Through the Eyes of Teachers, Kathy Fucher, a high school teacher in Humphrey, Nebraska, describes some strategies for reducing students' prejudice.

### THROUGH THE EYES OF TEACHERS
#### Seeking to Reduce Prejudice Toward Latino Students in Nebraska

The meatpacking industry in Nebraska has brought many Latinos to our area. I find my students have a definite negative attitude toward them, usually as a result of their parents' influence. My effort to help them realize their prejudice is to teach David Gutterson's *Snow Falling on Cedars* to senior-level students. Though the fictional novel takes place off Puget Sound and deals with Japanese immigrants during World War II, I take students through discussion questions that provide striking similarity to their prejudice against Latinos. I have no way to measure the degree of prejudice, but I feel that education and awareness are key steps in decreasing the problem.

4. *Use trade books, films, videotapes, and recordings to portray ethnic perspectives.* Banks's (2003) book, *Teaching Strategies for Ethnic Studies,* describes a number of these. In Through the Eyes of Teachers, Marlene Wendler, a fourth-grade teacher in New Ulm, Minnesota, describes her teaching strategies in this regard.

### THROUGH THE EYES OF TEACHERS
#### Using Literature to Show How Minorities Have Been Treated

I use literature to help students understand other people and how they have sometimes been treated unfairly. During January, I focus on the southeastern United States in our social studies class and integrate language arts by having the whole class read *Meet Addy* and *Mississippi Bridge.* On Martin Luther King Day we read his biography. We get a little overview of how the Jews were treated in World War II through *Number the Stars.* We also get interested in learning more about Anne Frank. When the children read how these minorities were treated, they understand more fully that all people are more similar to them than different.

5. *Take into account your students' developmental status when you select various cultural materials.* In early childhood and elementary school classrooms, make the learning experience specific and concrete. Banks stresses that fiction and biographies are especially good choices for introducing cultural concepts to these students. Students at these levels can study such concepts as similarities, differences, prejudice, and discrimination but are not developmentally ready to study concepts such as racism. However, adolescents can read about and discuss racism and may benefit from doing so.

6. *Perceive all students in positive ways and have high expectations for them regardless of their ethnicity.* All students learn best when their teachers have high achievement expectations for them and support their learning efforts. We will have much more to say about the importance of high expectations for students' achievement in Chapter 13.

7. *Recognize that most parents, regardless of their ethnicity, are interested in their children's education and want them to succeed in school.* However, understand that many parents of color have mixed feelings about schools because of their own experiences with discrimination. People of different cultures may see the role of parents in their children's educations differently. Think of positive ways to get parents of color more involved in their children's education and to treat them as partners in their children's learning.

## Review, Reflect, and Practice

**2** Describe some ways to promote multicultural education.

### REVIEW

- What is multicultural education? What is the aim of "empowering" students?
- What is culturally relevant teaching?
- What is issues-centered education?
- How can teachers improve relationships among children from different ethnic groups?

### REFLECT

- In terms of multicultural education, what do you hope to do differently as a teacher than what your former teachers did?

### PRAXIS™ PRACTICE

1. According to Sonia Nieto, which of these is the best educational practice for empowering students?
   a. avoiding discussion of prejudice and discrimination
   b. teaching a second language to all non-Latino White students
   c. having separate weekly classes on multicultural topics
   d. encouraging all students to study culture critically

2. Which teacher's practice best exemplifies the concept of culturally relevant education?
   a. Mr. Lincoln, who does not allow any discussion of race or ethnicity in his class, deeming it irrelevant to his students' education
   b. Mr. Peters, who has differing expectations of his students based on gender, ethnicity, and SES
   c. Mr. Welch, who displays favoritism to members of ethnic minority groups
   d. Mr. Patterson, who recognizes that he comes from a different background than his students, but spends time in the community to help him to understand their culture

3. Which of the following is the best example of issues-centered education?
   a. As Mr. DeRosa's students study their history text, they look at events in terms of fairness to all groups and long-term social impact.
   b. Ms. Pang's students discuss historical facts and their impact on mainstream culture.
   c. Ms. Broadhouse's students are encouraged to debate issues, but debate winners always share the same views as Ms. Broadhouse.
   d. Mr. Taha's students are having a culture fair this Friday.

4. Middlesborough High School is an ethnically diverse school with considerable racial tension and conflict. When possible, the students self-select single-ethnicity groups. When forced to work in ethnically diverse groups, the students often argue and fail to cooperate. Several racially motivated violent episodes have occurred during this school year. Based on information in the text, which of these practices is most likely to improve relationships among the students from different ethnic groups?
   a. Assign the students to read books about various ethnic groups' history and contributions and discuss them in class in mixed ethnic groups.

*(continued)*

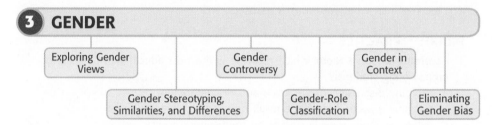

**3** **GENDER**

Exploring Gender Views

Gender Controversy

Gender in Context

Gender Stereotyping, Similarities, and Differences

Gender-Role Classification

Eliminating Gender Bias

*Gender* is a term extensively used throughout our everyday lives, including schools and education. What are some different views of gender?

## EXPLORING GENDER VIEWS

**Gender** refers to the characteristics of people as males and females. **Gender identity** involves a sense of one's own gender, including knowledge, understanding, and acceptance of being male or female (Blakemore, Berenbaum, & Liben, 2009). **Gender roles** are sets of expectations that prescribe how females or males should think, act, and feel. **Gender typing** refers to acquisition of a traditional masculine or feminine role. For example, aggression is more characteristic of a traditional masculine role, and nurturing is more characteristic of a traditional feminine role.

There are various ways to view gender development. Some views stress biological factors in the behavior of males and females; others emphasize social or cognitive factors. However, even gender experts with a strong environmental orientation acknowledge that girls and boys are treated differently because of their physical differences and their different roles in reproduction.

Social views of gender especially highlight the importance of the various social contexts in which children develop, especially families, peers, schools, and the media (Blakemore, Berenbaum, & Liben, 2009). Many parents encourage boys and girls to engage in different types of play and activities (Bronstein, 2006). Girls are more likely to be given dolls and, when old enough, are more likely to be assigned baby-sitting duties. Girls are encouraged to be more nurturing than boys. Fathers are more likely to engage in aggressive play with their sons than with their daughters. Parents allow their adolescent sons to have more freedom than their adolescent daughters.

Peers also reward and punish gender-related behavior (Rubin, Bukowski, & Parker, 2006). After extensive observations of elementary school classrooms, two researchers characterized the play settings as "gender school" (Luria & Herzog, 1985). In elementary school, boys usually hang out with boys and girls with girls. It is easier for "tomboy" girls to join boys' groups than for "feminine" boys to join girls' groups, because of our society's greater sex-typing pressure on boys. Developmental

**gender** The characteristics of people as males and females.

**gender identity** The sense of being male or female, which most children acquire by the time they are 3 years old.

**gender role** A set of expectations that prescribes how females or males should think, act, and feel.

**gender typing** Acquistion of a traditional masculine or feminine role.

psychologist Eleanor Maccoby (1998, 2007), who has studied gender for a number of decades, concludes that peers play an especially important gender-socializing role, teaching each other what is acceptable and unacceptable gender behavior.

Schools and teachers have important gender-socializing influences on boys and girls. Shortly, we will explore such topics as the gender differences related to schools and students' interactions with teachers, educational achievement, and gender bias in classrooms.

The media also play a gender-socializing role, portraying females and males in particular gender roles (Dubow, Huesmann, & Greenwood, 2007). Even with the onset of more diverse programming in recent years, researchers still find that television presents males as more competent than females (Strasburger, Wilson, & Jordan, 2008).

In addition to biological and social factors, cognitive factors contribute to children's gender development (Martin & Ruble, 2010). **Gender schema theory,** currently the most widely accepted cognitive theory of gender, states that gender typing emerges as children gradually develop gender schemas of what is gender-appropriate and gender-inappropriate in their culture. A *schema* is a cognitive structure, a network of associations that guides an individual's perceptions. A *gender schema* organizes the world in terms of female and male. Children are internally motivated to perceive the world and to act in accordance with their developing schemas. Bit by bit, children pick up what is gender-appropriate and gender-inappropriate in their culture, and develop gender schemas that shape how they perceive the world and what they remember. Children are motivated to act in ways that conform with these gender schemas (Martin & Ruble, 2010).

The playground in elementary school is like going to "gender school," as boys prefer to interact with boys and girls choose to interact with girls.

**Thinking Back/Thinking Forward**

Schema theories of memory state that when children reconstruct memory they fit it into information that already exists in their mind. Chapter 8, p. 270

## GENDER STEREOTYPING, SIMILARITIES, AND DIFFERENCES

What are the real differences between boys and girls? Before attempting to answer that question, let's consider the problem of gender stereotypes.

**Gender Stereotypes**  All stereotypes—whether they relate to gender, ethnicity, or other categories—refer to an image of what the typical member of a category is like. **Gender stereotypes** are broad categories that reflect impressions and beliefs about what behavior is appropriate for females and males. Many stereotypes are so general that they become ambiguous, and this is true for gender stereotypes. Consider the categories of "masculine" and "feminine." Diverse behaviors can be assigned to each category, such as scoring a touchdown or growing facial hair for "masculine," playing with dolls or wearing lipstick for "feminine." Stereotyping students as "masculine" or "feminine" can have significant consequences (Best, 2010). Labeling a male "feminine" or a female "masculine" can diminish her or his social status and acceptance in groups.

Recent research continues to find that gender stereotyping is pervasive (Blakemore, Berenbaum, & Liben, 2009). Researchers also have found that boys' gender stereotypes are more rigid than girls' (Blakemore, Berenbaum, & Liben, 2009).

Gender stereotyping changes developmentally (Zosuls, Lurye, & Ruble, 2008). By the time children enter elementary school, they have considerable knowledge about which activities are linked with being male or female. A recent study of 3- to 10-year old U.S. children revealed that older children used a higher percentage of gender stereotypes (Miller & others, 2009). In this study, appearance stereotypes were more prevalent in girls while activity (sports, for example) and trait (aggressive, for example) stereotyping was more common in boys.

**Gender Similarities and Differences in Academically Relevant Domains**
Many aspects of students' lives can be examined to determine how similar or different girls and boys are.

RESEARCH

DEVELOPMENT

**gender schema theory** States that gender typing emerges as children gradually develop gender schemas of what is gender-appropriate and gender-inappropriate in their culture.

**gender stereotypes** Broad categories that reflect impressions and beliefs about what behavior is appropriate for females and males.

## FIGURE **5.2** NATIONAL SCIENCE SCORES FOR BOYS AND GIRLS

In the National Assessment of Educational Progress, data collected in 2005 indicated that boys had slightly higher scores than girls in the fourth, eighth, and twelfth grades (Grigg, Lauko, & Brockway, 2006). The science scores could range from 0 to 300.

*"So according to the stereotype, you can put two and two together, but I can read the handwriting on the wall."*

Joel Pett, *The Lexington Herald-Leader*, CartoonArts International/CWS.

***The Brain*** Does gender matter when it comes to brain structure and activity? Human brains are much alike, whether the brain belongs to a male or a female (Hyde, 2007). However, researchers have found some differences:

- Female brains are smaller than male brains, but female brains have more folds; the larger folds (called *convolutions*) allow more surface brain tissue within the skulls of females than in males (Luders & others, 2004).
- An area of the parietal lobe that functions in visuospatial skills tends to be larger in males than in females (Frederikse & others, 2000).
- The areas of the brain involved in emotional expression tend to show more metabolic activity in females than in males (Gur & others, 1995).

Similarities and differences in the brains of males and females could be due to evolution and heredity, as well as social experiences.

***Physical Performance*** Because physical education is an integral part of U.S. educational systems, it is important to address gender similarities and differences in physical performance. In general, boys outperform girls in athletic skills such as running, throwing, and jumping. In the elementary school years, the differences often are not large; they become more dramatic in the middle school years (Smoll & Schutz, 1990). The hormonal changes of puberty result in increased muscle mass for boys and increased body fat for girls. This leads to an advantage for boys in activities related to strength, size, and power. Nonetheless, environmental factors are involved in physical performance even after puberty. Girls are less likely to participate in activities that promote the motor skills necessary to do well in sports (Thomas & Thomas, 1988).

Activity level is another area of physical performance in which gender differences occur. From very early in life, boys are more active than girls are in terms of gross motor movements (Blakemore, Berenbaum, & Liben, 2009). In the classroom, this means that boys are more likely than girls to fidget and move around the room, and they are less likely to pay attention. In physical education classes, boys expend more energy through movement than girls do.

***Intelligence*** No gender differences occur in overall intellectual ability, but gender differences do appear in some cognitive areas, such as math and verbal skills (Galambos, Berenbaum, & McHale, 2009).

***Math and Science Skills*** In the National Assessment of Educational Progress in the United States, fourth- and eighth-grade boys continued to slightly outperform girls in math through 2007 (National Assessment of Educational Progress, 2005, 2007). However, not all recent studies have shown differences. A recent very large scale study of more than 7 million U.S. students in grades 2 through 11 revealed no differences in math scores for boys and girls (Hyde & others, 2008).

One area of math that has been examined for possible gender differences is visuospatial skills, which include being able to rotate objects mentally and determine what they would look like when rotated. These types of skills are important in courses such as plane and solid geometry and geography. A recent research review revealed that boys have better visuospatial skills than girls (Halpern & others, 2007). For example, despite equal participation in the National Geography Bee, in most years all 10 finalists are boys (Liben, 1995). However, some experts argue that the gender difference in visuospatial skills is small (Hyde, 2007).

What about science? Are there gender differences? In one recent national study of science achievement, boys did slightly better in science than girls in the fourth, eighth, and twelfth grades (National Assessment of Educational Progress, 2005) (see Figure 5.2). In another study, this time focused on eighth- and tenth-graders, boys scored higher than girls on science tests, especially among average- and high-ability students (Burkham, Lee, & Smerdon, 1997). In science classes that emphasized hands-on lab activities, girls' science test scores improved considerably. This suggests the importance of active involvement of students in science classrooms, which may promote gender equity.

***Verbal Skills*** A major review of gender similarities and differences conducted in the 1970s concluded that girls have better verbal skills than boys do (Maccoby & Jacklin, 1974). However, more recent analyses suggest that in some instances there may be little or no differences in girls' and boys' verbal skills. For example, today boys score as high as girls on the verbal portion of the SAT test (Educational Testing Service, 2002).

During the elementary and secondary school years, however, girls outperform boys in reading and writing. In national studies of U.S. students, girls had higher reading achievement than boys in grades 4, 8, and 12, with the gap widening as students progressed through school (Coley, 2001; National Assessment of Educational Progress, 2007). Girls also have performed substantially better than boys in grades 4, 8, and 12 in writing skills (National Assessment of Educational Progress, 2007). Figure 5.3 shows the consistently higher writing scores of eighth-grade girls.

***Educational Attainment*** With regard to school achievement, girls earn better grades and complete high school at a higher rate than boys (Halpern, 2006). Boys are more likely than girls to be assigned to special/remedial education classes. Girls are more likely to be engaged with academic material, be attentive in class, put forth more academic effort, and participate more in class than boys are (DeZolt & Hull, 2001).

***Relationship Skills*** Sociolinguist Deborah Tannen (1990) says that boys and girls grow up in different worlds of talk—parents, siblings, peers, teachers, and others talk to boys and girls differently. In describing this talk, Tannen distinguishes between rapport talk and report talk:

- **Rapport talk** is the language of conversation and a way of establishing connections and negotiating relationships. Girls enjoy rapport talk and conversation that is relationship-oriented more than boys do.
- **Report talk** is talk that gives information. Public speaking is an example of report talk. Boys hold center stage through report talk with such verbal performances as storytelling, joking, and lecturing with information.

Some researchers criticize Tannen's ideas as being overly simplified and view communication between males and females as more complex (MacGeorge, 2004). For example, a meta-analysis confirmed the criticism that Tannen overemphasizes the size of gender differences in communication (Leaper & Smith, 2004). Gender differences did occur, but they were small, with girls only slightly more talkative and engaging in more affiliative speech than boys, and boys being more likely to use self-assertive speech.

***Prosocial Behavior*** Are there gender differences in prosocial behavior? Girls view themselves as more prosocial and empathic (Eisenberg & others, 2009). Across childhood and adolescence, girls engage in more prosocial behavior (Hastings, Utendale, & Sullivan, 2007). The biggest gender difference occurs for kind and considerate behavior, with a smaller difference in sharing.

***Aggression*** One of the most consistent gender differences is that boys are more physically aggressive than girls (Dodge, Coie, & Lynam, 2006). The difference is especially pronounced when children are provoked—this difference occurs across all cultures and appears very early in children's development (Ostrov, Keating, & Ostrov, 2004). Both biological and environmental factors have been proposed to account for gender differences in physical aggression (Blakemore, Berenbaum, & Liben, 2009). Biological factors include heredity and hormones; environmental factors include

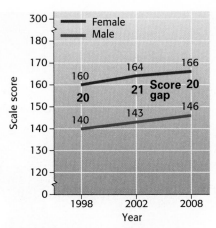

**FIGURE 5.3** TRENDS IN U.S. EIGHTH-GRADE BOYS' AND GIRLS' AVERAGE WRITING SCORES ON THE NATIONAL ASSESSMENT OF EDUCATIONAL PROGRESS

---

**Thinking Back/Thinking Forward**

Teachers can play important roles in promoting children's prosocial behavior and providing them with opportunities to engage in prosocial behavior. Chapter 3, p. 100

---

**rapport talk** The language of conversation and a way of establishing connections and negotiating relationships; more characteristic of females than males.

**report talk** Talk that gives information; more characteristic of males than females.

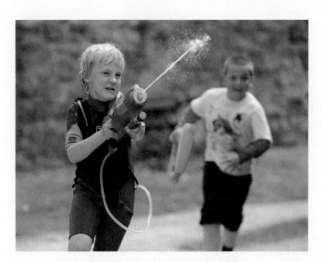

*What gender differences characterize aggression?*

Thinking Back/Thinking Forward

Serious, persistent problems in aggression can lead to children being classified as having an emotional and behavioral disorder. Chapter 6, p. 194

cultural expectations, adult and peer models, and the rewarding of physical aggression in boys.

Although boys are consistently more physically aggressive than girls, might girls show as much or more verbal aggression, such as yelling, than boys? When verbal aggression is examined, gender differences typically either disappear or are sometimes even more pronounced in girls (Eagly & Steffen, 1986).

Recently, increased interest has been shown in *relational aggression,* which involves harming someone by manipulating a relationship (Crick & others, 2009). Relational aggression includes such behaviors as trying to make others dislike a certain individual by spreading malicious rumors about the person. Relational aggression increases in middle and late childhood (Dishion & Piehler, 2009). Mixed findings have characterized research on whether girls show more relational aggression than boys, but one consistency in findings is that relational aggression comprises a greater percentage of girls' overall aggression than is the case for boys (Putallaz & others, 2007). And a research review revealed that girls engage in more relational aggression than boys in adolescence but not in childhood (Smith, Rose, & Schwartz-Mette, 2010).

***Emotion and Its Regulation*** Are there gender differences in emotion? Girls are more likely to express their emotions openly and intensely than are boys, especially in displaying sadness and fear (Blakemore, Berenbaum, & Liben, 2009). Girls also are better at reading others' emotions and are more likely to show empathy than are boys (Blakemore, Berenbaum, & Liben, 2009).

An important skill is to be able to regulate and control one's emotions and behavior. Boys usually show less self-regulation than girls (Eisenberg, 2010). This low self-control can translate into behavior problems. In one study, children's low self-regulation was linked with greater aggression, teasing of others, overreaction to frustration, low cooperation, and inability to delay gratification (Block & Block, 1980).

## GENDER CONTROVERSY

The previous sections described some substantial differences in physical performance, writing skills, aggression, self-regulation, and prosocial behavior of girls and boys but small or nonexistent differences in communication, math, and science. Controversy swirls about such similarities and differences. Evolutionary psychologists such as David Buss (2008) argue that gender differences are extensive and caused by the adaptive problems faced across evolutionary history. Alice Eagly (2001, 2009, 2010) agrees that gender differences are substantial but reaches a very different conclusion about their cause. She emphasizes that gender differences are due to social conditions that have resulted in women having less power and controlling fewer resources than men.

By contrast, Janet Shibley Hyde (2007) concludes that gender differences have been greatly exaggerated, especially fueled by popular books such as John Gray's (1992) *Men Are from Mars, Women Are from Venus* and Deborah Tannen's (1990) *You Just Don't Understand.* She argues that the research shows that females and males are similar in most psychological factors.

## GENDER-ROLE CLASSIFICATION

Not very long ago, it was accepted that boys should grow up to be masculine and girls to be feminine. In the 1970s, however, as both females and males became dissatisfied with the burdens imposed by their stereotypic roles, alternatives to femininity and masculinity were proposed. Instead of describing masculinity and femininity as a continuum in which more of one means less of the other, it was proposed that individuals could have both masculine and feminine traits.

This thinking led to the development of the concept of **androgyny,** the presence of positive masculine and feminine characteristics in the same person (Bem, 1977; Spence & Helmreich, 1978). The androgynous boy might be both assertive (masculine) and nurturant (feminine). The androgynous girl might be both powerful (masculine) and sensitive to others' feelings (feminine). Studies have confirmed that societal changes are leading girls to be more assertive (Spence & Buckner, 2000) and that sons are more androgynous than their fathers (Guastello & Guastello, 2003).

Gender experts such as Sandra Bem argue that androgynous individuals are more flexible, competent, and mentally healthy than their masculine or feminine counterparts. To some degree, though, which gender-role classification is best depends on context. For example, in close relationships, feminine and androgynous orientations might be more desirable. One study found that children high in femininity showed a stronger interest in caring than did children high in masculinity (Karniol, Groz, & Schorr, 2003). However, masculine and androgynous orientations might be more desirable in traditional academic and work settings because of the achievement demands in these contexts.

Despite talk about the "sensitive male," William Pollack (1999) argues that little has been done to change traditional ways of raising boys. He says that the "boy code" tells boys that they should show little if any emotion and should act tough. Boys learn the boy code in many contexts, especially peer contexts—sandboxes, playgrounds, schoolrooms, camps, hangouts. The result, according to Pollack, is a "national crisis of boyhood." Pollack and others suggest that boys would benefit from being socialized to express their anxieties and concerns and to better regulate their aggression. To think about your gender-role classification, see Self-Assessment 5.1.

## GENDER IN CONTEXT

Earlier we said that the concept of gender-role classification involves categorizing people in terms of personality traits. However, recall from our discussion of personality in Chapter 4, "Individual Variations," that it is beneficial to think of personality in terms of *person-situation interaction* rather than personality traits alone (Engler, 2009; Schultz & Schultz, 2009). Let's now further explore gender in context.

### Helping Behavior and Emotion
The stereotype is that females are better than males at helping. But it depends on the situation (Blakemore, Berenbaum, & Liben, 2009). Females are more likely than males to volunteer their time to help children with personal problems and engage in caregiving behavior. However, in situations where males feel a sense of competence or that involve danger, males are more likely to help (Eagly & Crowley, 1986). For example, a male is more likely than a female to stop and help a person stranded by the roadside with a flat tire.

She is emotional; he is not. That's the master emotional stereotype. However, like helping behavior, emotional differences in males and females depend on the particular emotion involved and the context in which it is displayed (Shields, 1991). Males are more likely to show anger toward strangers, especially male strangers, when they feel they have been challenged. Males also are more likely to turn their anger into aggressive action. Emotional differences between females and males often show up in contexts that highlight social roles and relationships. For example, females are more likely to discuss emotions in terms of relationships. They also are more likely to express fear and sadness.

### Culture
The importance of considering gender in context is most apparent when examining what is culturally prescribed behavior for females and males in different countries around the world (Shiraev & Levy, 2010). In the United States, there is now more acceptance of similarities in male and female behavior, but in many other countries roles have remained gender-specific (Best, 2010). For example, in many Middle Eastern countries the division of labor between males and females is dramatic.

A school in the Middle East with boys only. Many adolescents in the Middle East are not allowed to interact with the other sex, even in school. Although in the United States there now is more acceptance of similarities in schooling and work opportunities for males and females, many countries around the world remain more gender-specific.

**androgyny** The presence of positive masculine and feminine characteristics in the same individual.

# SELF-ASSESSMENT 5.1
## What Gender–Role Orientation Will I Present to My Students?

The items below inquire about what kind of person you think you are. Place a check mark in the column that best describes you for each item: 1 = Not like me at all, 2 = Somewhat unlike me, 3 = Somewhat like me, and 4 = Very much like me.

| Item | 1 | 2 | 3 | 4 |
| --- | --- | --- | --- | --- |
| 1. I'm independent. | _____ | _____ | _____ | _____ |
| 2. My emotional life is important to me. | _____ | _____ | _____ | _____ |
| 3. I provide social support to others. | _____ | _____ | _____ | _____ |
| 4. I'm competitive. | _____ | _____ | _____ | _____ |
| 5. I'm a kind person. | _____ | _____ | _____ | _____ |
| 6. I'm sensitive to others' feelings. | _____ | _____ | _____ | _____ |
| 7. I'm self-confident. | _____ | _____ | _____ | _____ |
| 8. I'm self-reflective. | _____ | _____ | _____ | _____ |
| 9. I'm patient. | _____ | _____ | _____ | _____ |
| 10. I'm self-assertive. | _____ | _____ | _____ | _____ |
| 11. I'm aggressive. | _____ | _____ | _____ | _____ |
| 12. I'm willing to take risks. | _____ | _____ | _____ | _____ |
| 13. I like to tell secrets to my friends. | _____ | _____ | _____ | _____ |
| 14. I like to feel powerful. | _____ | _____ | _____ | _____ |

## SCORING AND INTERPRETATION

Items 1, 4, 7, 10, 11, 12, 14 are masculine items. Items 2, 3, 5, 6, 8, 9, and 13 are feminine items. Look at the pattern of your responses. If you mainly checked 3 and 4 for the masculine items and mainly 1 and 2 for the feminine items, you likely are characterized by masculinity. If you mainly checked 3 and 4 for the feminine items and 1 and 2 for the masculine items, you likely are characterized by femininity. If you mainly checked 3 and 4 for both the masculine items and the feminine items, you likely are characterized by androgyny. If you mainly checked 1 and 2 for both the masculine and feminine items, your gender-role classification is likely undifferentiated.

DIVERSITY

In Iraq and Iran, males primarily are socialized and schooled to work in the public sphere; females are mainly socialized to remain in the private world of home and child rearing. Any deviations from this traditional masculine and feminine behavior are severely disapproved. Likewise, in rural China, although women have made some strides, the male role is still dominant.

Cultural and ethnic backgrounds also influence how boys and girls will be socialized in the United States. One study indicated that Latino and Latina adolescents were socialized differently as they were growing up (Raffaelli & Ontai, 2004). Latinas experienced far greater restrictions than Latinos in curfews, interacting with members of the other sex, getting a driver's license, getting a job, and involvement in after-school activities.

## ELIMINATING GENDER BIAS

How gendered are social interactions between teachers and students? What can teachers do to reduce or eliminate gender bias in their classrooms?

**Teacher-Student Interaction**   Gender bias is present in classrooms. Teachers interact more with boys than with girls at all levels of schooling (Blakemore, Berenbaum, & Liben, 2009). What evidence is there that this interaction is biased against boys? Here are some factors to consider (DeZolt & Hull, 2001):

- Complying, following rules, and being neat and orderly are valued and reinforced in many classrooms. These are behaviors that are typically associated with girls rather than boys.
- A large majority of teachers are females, especially in the elementary school. This may make it more difficult for boys than for girls to identify with their teachers and model their teachers' behavior.
- Boys are more likely than girls to be identified as having learning problems.
- Boys are more likely than girls to be criticized.
- School personnel tend to stereotype boys' behavior as problematic.

What evidence is there that the classroom is biased against girls? Consider the following factors (Sadker & Sadker, 1994, 2005):

- In a typical classroom, girls are more compliant, boys more rambunctious. Boys demand more attention; girls are more likely to quietly wait their turn. Educators worry that girls' tendency to be compliant and quiet comes at a cost: diminished assertiveness.
- In many classrooms, teachers spend more time watching and interacting with boys, whereas girls work and play quietly on their own. Most teachers don't intentionally favor boys by spending more time with them, yet somehow the classroom frequently ends up with this type of gendered profile.
- Boys get more instruction than girls and more help when they have trouble with a question. Teachers often give boys more time to answer a question, more hints at the correct answer, and further tries if they give the wrong answer.
- Girls and boys enter first grade with roughly equal levels of self-esteem, yet by the middle school years, girls' self-esteem is significantly lower than boys' (Robins & others, 2002).
- Although girls are identified for gifted programs more than boys in elementary school, by high school there are more boys than girls in gifted programs (U.S. Office of Education, 1999). There especially is a low number of African American and Latino girls in gifted programs (Banks & others, 2005).

Thus, there is evidence of gender bias against both boys and girls in schools. Many school personnel are not aware of their gender-biased attitudes. These attitudes are deeply entrenched in, and supported by, the general culture. Increasing awareness of gender bias in schools is clearly an important strategy in reducing such bias.

Might same-sex education be better for children than co-ed education? The research evidence related to this question is mixed (Blakemore, Berenbaum, & Liben, 2009). Some research indicates that same-sex education has positive outcomes for girls' achievement, whereas other research does not show any improvements in achievement for girls or boys in same-sex education (Mael, 1998; Warrington & Younger, 2003). A recent study revealed that girls who took a physics class in a same-sex education school had a more positive self-conception of their knowledge and understanding of physics than girls who took a physics class in a co-ed school (Kessels & Hannover, 2008).

**Curriculum Content and Athletics Content**   Schools have made considerable progress in reducing sexism and sex stereotyping in books and curriculum materials, largely in response to Title IX of the Educational Amendment Act of 1972, which states that schools must treat females and males equally. As a result, today's textbooks and class materials are more gender-neutral. Also, schools now offer girls far more opportunities to take vocational educational courses and participate in athletics than was the case when their parents and grandparents went to school (Gill, 2001). In 1972, 7 percent of high school athletes were girls. Today that figure has risen to nearly 40 percent. In addition, schools no longer can expel, or eliminate services for, pregnant adolescents.

Nonetheless, bias still remains at the curricular level. For example, school text adoptions occur infrequently, and therefore many students still are studying outdated, gender-biased books.

I recently asked teachers how they try to prevent gender bias in their classrooms. Following are their responses.

**EARLY CHILDHOOD**   The books we have in the classroom showcase men and women in various roles—for example, some of our books have female doctors and

male nurses. We also encourage boys to cook and girls to build. However, we often have concern from parents when their son expresses interest in playing with dolls or playing "dress up" with the girls. We had a parent workshop about these concerns in which we told parents that at this developmental stage, children are experimenting with roles and working out situations through play. This was a difficult workshop because although they listened, parents were not interested in breaking traditions.

—**Valarie Gorham**, *Kiddie Quarters, Inc.*

**ELEMENTARY SCHOOL: GRADES K–5**   To get my fifth-grade students to recognize gender bias, I do a short unit using old books I've collected over the years that

are very gender-biased. We talk about the historical aspect of these books and how roles have changed for both men and women. In addition to discussing how women's roles have changed, I also point out that men now have opportunities they didn't have in the past such as being nurses and early childhood education teachers.

—**Craig Jensen**, *Cooper Mountain Elementary School*

**MIDDLE SCHOOL: GRADES 6–8**   To prevent my sixth-grade students from sitting together by gender—that is, boys with boys and girls with girls—I have them

sit in mixed, cooperative groups with each group consisting of two boys and two girls. Another strategy I use in class is to never randomly pick students to participate. Instead, I go down my class list so that everyone gets a chance or I choose students in a boy-girl order.

—**Casey Maass**, *Edison Middle School*

**HIGH SCHOOL: GRADES 9–12**   I love to do exactly the opposite of what is traditional in my class when it comes to gender. For example, I ask girls to help me move

heavy books, or boys to help clean up a spill. Recently, I was telling my students how to address formal business letters, and we were talking about using "Miss," "Mr.," "Mrs.," or "Ms." I told them that I think it is silly that women are defined by marital status, whereas men are "Mr." regardless. Several students, boys and girls alike, had a faraway look that said, "I hadn't thought of that before." I may have planted a seed that will grow into their questioning the traditions that have very little merit in our modern world.

—**Jennifer Heiter**, *Bremen High School*

**Sexual Harassment**  Girls can encounter sexual harassment in many different forms—ranging from sexist remarks and covert physical contact (patting, brushing against bodies) to blatant propositions and sexual assaults (Martin, 2008). Literally millions of girls experience such sexual harassment each year in educational settings. A recent study of 12- to 18-year-old U.S. girls revealed that 90 percent reported having been sexually harassed at least once, with the likelihood increasing with age (Leaper & Brown, 2008).

The U.S. Office for Civil Rights (2008) publishes a guide on sexual harassment. In this guide, a distinction is made between quid pro quo and hostile environment sexual harassment:

- **Quid pro quo sexual harassment** occurs when a school employee threatens to base an educational decision (such as a grade) on a student's submission to unwelcome sexual conduct. For example, a teacher gives a student an *A* for allowing the teacher's sexual advances, or the teacher gives the student an *F* for resisting the teacher's approaches.

- **Hostile environment sexual harassment** occurs when students are subjected to unwelcome sexual conduct that is so severe, persistent, or pervasive that it limits the students' ability to benefit from their education. Such a hostile environment is usually created by a series of incidents, such as repeated sexual overtures.

Quid pro quo and hostile environment sexual harassment are illegal in educational settings, but potential victims are often not given access to a clear reporting and investigation mechanism where they can make a complaint.

Sexual harassment is a form of power and dominance of one person over another, which can result in harmful consequences for the victim. Sexual harassment can be especially damaging when the perpetrators are teachers, who have considerable power and authority over students (Ormerod, Collinsworth, & Perry, 2008).

**quid pro quo sexual harassment** Occurs when a school employee threatens to base an educational decision (such as a grade) on a student's submission to unwelcome sexual conduct.

**hostile environment sexual harassment** Occurs when students are subjected to unwelcome sexual conduct that is so severe, persistent, or pervasive that it limits the students' ability to benefit from their education.

## TEACHING CONNECTIONS: Best Practices
### Strategies for Reducing Gender Bias

Every student, female or male, deserves an education free of gender bias. Here are some strategies for attaining this desirable educational climate (Derman-Sparks & the Anti-Bias Curriculum Task Force, 1989; Pollack, 1999; Sadker & Sadker, 1994):

1. *Be aware that boys and girls are different from a very early age.* Be aware of the gender differences discussed above, but don't allow this knowledge to result in unfair bias in expectations or treatment.

2. *If you are given textbooks that are gender-biased, discuss this with your students.* By talking with your students about stereotyping and bias in the texts, you can help them think critically about such important social issues. If these textbooks are not gender-fair, supplement them with other materials that are. Many schools, libraries, and colleges have gender-fair materials that you can use.

### THROUGH THE EYES OF TEACHERS
**The Inclusive Quilt**

In my 25 years of teaching middle school, one of my goals has been for my classroom to be a blend of some of the things I know and some of the things my students know. The quilt experience serves as an example. My idea was to have the students feel connected not only to the women in the fields of science, politics, art, social reform, music, sports, literature, journalism, space, law, civil rights, education, humor, and so on, but also to the women in their own families.

I put a big piece of butcher paper on the blackboard, with the word *inclusive* at the top and asked the students to develop a list of what was needed to make our quilt truly inclusive. Hands popped up, and students volunteered categories

*(continued)*

# TEACHING CONNECTIONS: Best Practices
## Strategies for Reducing Gender Bias

first. We should have women in medicine. Sports. Civil rights. The list grew.

What else? How else can we make this quilt inclusive? What else do we know about diversity? Hands popped up again to create a second list. We should have Native American women. European American women. Latino women. Asian American women. Lesbian women. Again, our list grew. . . . We began to brainstorm a third list of individual women who were potential subjects for quilt squares. We created a long list of possibilities like Nancy Reagan, Jackie Kennedy, and Martha Washington, who did not end up on the final quilt itself, because the students decided they didn't want to have a lot of presidents' wives on the quilt. They ended up honoring Eleanor Roosevelt and Abigail Adams, who fit other categories on our list, such as social reform. . . .

I gave some thought to whom I wanted to honor on my patch. I decided to honor Brenda Collins, who is also named Eagle Woman. She is a member of the Bird Clan of the Cherokee Nation. She is a medicine woman, the first woman of her clan to get a Ph.D. and a teacher at Santa Rosa Junior College. She is also a friend and mentor. I have heard her speak several times, and I remember her saying that to be an educated Indian woman is like having a foot in each of two canoes, in rapid waters, always balancing two cultures. I decided to put two canoes and rapid water on her patch, with an eagle's wing by one canoe, and her doctoral degree by the other canoe. . . .

The finished quilt is colorful and diverse. No two patches are the same. I have provided the outline, the framework for the assignment, but each participant has created something uniquely their own. . . . (Source: Logan, 1997, pp. 1–23)

Judy Logan, in front of the inclusive quilt in her classroom.

Judy Logan, who has taught language arts and social studies for many years in San Francisco, describes one way that she helps students understand the contributions of females.

4. *Analyze the seating chart in your classroom and determine whether there are pockets of gender segregation.* When your students work in groups, monitor whether the groups are balanced by gender. However, understand that younger children, in particular, often prefer to work with same-sex peers and allow this on occasion as well.

5. *Enlist someone to track your questioning and reinforcement patterns with boys and girls or videotape your class so you can do this yourself.* Do this on several occasions to ensure that you are giving equal attention and support to girls and boys. In addition to logging the amount of attention you are giving to each gender, characterize the type of attention. According to Pollack (1999), while boys receive more attention in class, it is often negative attention.

6. *Use nonbiased language.* Don't use the pronoun *he* to refer to inanimate objects or unspecified persons. Replace words such as fireman, policeman, and mailman with words such as firefighter, police officer, and letter carrier. Don't use terms such as "male nurse" or "woman lawyer." Don't refer to all of your students as "you guys."

7. *Keep up-to-date on sex equity in education.* Read professional journals on this topic. Be aware of your own rights as a female or male and don't stand for sexual inequity and discrimination.

8. *Be aware of sexual harassment in schools and don't let it happen.* This is most likely to occur in middle-school hallways. Be a presence to help prevent such actions. Understand that boys can be victims of sexual harassment as well. Be willing to do something if a student comes to you about having been sexually harassed.

3. *Make sure that school activities and exercises are not gender-biased.* Assign students projects in which they find articles about nonstereotypical males and females, such as a female engineer or a male early childhood education teacher. Invite people from the community who have nonstereotypical jobs (such as a male flight attendant or a female construction worker) to come to your class and talk with your students. In Through the Eyes of Teachers,

## Review, Reflect, and Practice

**3** Explain various facets of gender, including similarities and differences in boys and girls; discuss gender issues in teaching.

### REVIEW

- What is gender, and what do the concepts of gender roles and gender typing mean? How have psychologists attempted to explain gender from biological, social, and cognitive perspectives?
- What are gender stereotypes? What problems are created by gender stereotypes? How are boys and girls similar and different?
- What characterizes gender-role classification?
- How might looking at behaviors in context reduce gender stereotyping?
- What evidence is there of gender bias in the classroom? What progress have schools made in reducing bias?

### REFLECT

- From your own K–12 education, come up with at least one instance in which your school or teacher favored either boys or girls. As a teacher, how would you try to correct that gender bias?

### PRAXIS™ PRACTICE

1. In Jack's family, the person who does the cooking does not do the dishes. Since Jack's mother generally cooks, his father generally does the dishes. One day in the "housekeeping" area of his kindergarten class, Jack was pretending to be the father of the family. His "wife" Emily pretended to cook dinner on the toy stove. After the family ate, Emily started to pretend to wash the dishes. Jack gasped and cried, "Hey, I'm the dad!" This example best supports which theory of gender development?
   a. biological
   b. cognitive developmental
   c. social cognitive
   d. psychoanalytic

2. Which teacher's opinion about gender differences is best supported by current research?
   a. Mr. Kain, who believes that girls are more talkative than boys
   b. Ms. Nash, who believes that boys are better at math than girls
   c. Ms. Kim, who believes that boys are more physically aggressive than girls
   d. Ms. Walter, who believes that boys are generally fairer and more law-abiding than girls

3. Which student would best be described as androgynous?
   a. Alex, who is sensitive to others' feelings, shares secrets with friends, and provides social support to others
   b. Chris, who is independent, competitive, patient, self-reflective, and provides social support to others
   c. Pat, who is kind, sensitive, self-reflective, and likes to tell secrets to friends
   d. Terry, who is independent, competitive, self-confident, aggressive, and willing to take risks

4. A male is most likely to display helping behavior in which situation?
   a. A friend's car battery has died and needs a jump.
   b. A small child needs help with writing a poem for language arts class.

*(continued)*

## Review, Reflect, and Practice

### PRAXIS™ PRACTICE (CONTINUED)

    c. A family member is ill and needs someone to provide care.

    d. A friend needs advice about a personal problem.

5. Ms. Vandt teaches fifth grade. Her class is comprised of approximately equal numbers of boys and girls. She often wonders why the boys can't behave more like the girls. The girls sit quietly, follow rules, and work well together. The boys have problems sitting still. They are rowdy and loud. Ms. Vandt tries to treat all of her students the same, but she often needs to reprimand the boys. What should she do?

    a. Allow the children time and space to move around and blow off steam. This will help the boys to attend better in class and the girls to socialize.

    b. Continue to reprimand the boys when they behave inappropriately. They will learn to sit quietly and be compliant.

    c. Divide the children into gender-specific groups so that the boys don't interfere with the girls' work.

    d. Point out the girls' compliant behavior as a model for the boys, so that they will understand what is expected of them.

*Please see the answer key at the end of the book.*

## Connecting with the Classroom: Crack the Case

# These Boys

Imagine that Larry is a 9-year-old boy in the fourth-grade class in which you are student teaching. You have heard him and a number of other students complaining about gender bias on the part of their teacher, Mrs. Jones. One day you overhear Larry being reprimanded by Mrs. Jones for an altercation he had with Annie, a female classmate.

"It isn't fair, Mrs. Jones," Larry says. "Annie took my homework and ripped it, and I get in trouble for taking it back."

"Now, Larry," admonishes Mrs. Jones. "You know Annie would never do that. You go apologize to her. I'll see you after school."

Larry walks away with a very angry look on his face, muttering, "The girls *never* get in trouble. It's always the boys."

You have heard this from students of Mrs. Jones in the past but have never really believed it. Over the course of the next three weeks you pay much closer attention to Mrs. Jones' behavior with a special sensitivity to gender bias. You notice that girls receive higher grades than boys, except in math. Boys are required to stay after school several times, girls not at all. When Mrs. Jones is on recess duty and there are altercations between boys and girls on the playground, the boys end up standing against the wall while the girls walk away smiling. In class, the girls are used as models of behaviors much more frequently than the boys. Their work receives more praise as well. You examine what students have been reading over the course of the year. Their required

reading thus far consists of *Little House on the Prairie, Charlotte's Web,* and *Little Women.*

The only thing you notice that appears to favor the boys is that they receive more of Mrs. Jones' attention. On further examination, however, you see that much of the attention is disciplinary in nature.

At one point, you overhear Mrs. Jones as she is walking down the hall, saying to a colleague, "These boys, I just don't know what I am going to do with them."

1. What are the issues in this case?

2. Based on the ideas and information presented in your text to this point, discuss what you believe to be happening in this classroom and the possible influences on Mrs. Jones' ideas of gender. Cite research and theories of gender development.

3. What influence do you believe Mrs. Jones' behavior will have on her students? Why?

4. What should Mrs. Jones do at this point? Why? What sort of outside assistance might help her?

5. If you were a student teacher in this classroom, what, if anything, would you do? Why?

6. What will you do in your own classroom to minimize gender bias?

# Sociocultural Diversity

**1 CULTURE AND ETHNICITY:** Discuss how variations in culture, socioeconomic status, and ethnic background need to be taken into account in educating children.

> Culture

Culture refers to the behavior patterns, beliefs, and all other products of a particular group of people that are passed on from generation to generation. The products result from the interaction among groups of people and their environment over many years. Cultures have been classified as individualistic (having a set of values that give priority to personal goals rather than group goals) and collectivistic (having a set of values that support the group). Many Western cultures are individualistic, many Eastern cultures collectivistic. U.S. adolescents spend less time in school and doing homework, more time in paid work, and have more discretionary time than their counterparts in Europe and East Asia. Concern is evidenced about what U.S. adolescents do with all of the discretionary time many of them have.

> Socioeconomic Status

Socioeconomic status (SES) is the categorization of people according to economic, educational, and occupational characteristics. The most emphasis is given to distinctions between individuals with low and middle socioeconomic status. Low-SES individuals usually have less education, less power to influence schools and other community institutions, and fewer economic resources than higher-SES individuals. Currently more than 17 percent of America's children live in poverty. Children in poverty face problems at home and at school that present barriers to their learning. Schools in low-income neighborhoods often have fewer resources and less-experienced teachers, and they are more likely to encourage rote learning rather than thinking skills.

> Ethnicity

The school population increasingly consists of children of color. School segregation is still a factor in the education of children of color. African American and Latino students are less likely than non-Latino White and Asian American students to be enrolled in college preparatory courses. Historical, economic, and social experiences produce legitimate differences among ethnic groups, and it is important to recognize these differences. However, too often the differences are viewed as deficits on the part of the minority group when compared with the mainstream non-Latino White group. It is important to recognize the extensive diversity that exists within each cultural group.

> Bilingualism

Researchers have found that bilingualism does not interfere with performance in either language. Success in learning a second language is greater in childhood than in adolescence. English as a second language (ESL) is a widely used term for programs and classes for students whose native language is not English. Bilingual education programs vary in terms of whether English-language learners (ELL) are taught primarily in English or in a two-way, dual immersion approach. Becoming proficient in English for ELL students is usually a very lengthy process.

**2 MULTICULTURAL EDUCATION:** Describe some ways to promote multicultural education.

> Empowering Students

Multicultural education is education that values diversity and includes the perspectives of a variety of cultural groups on a regular basis. Empowerment, which consists of providing people with the intellectual and coping skills to succeed and make this a more just world, is an important aspect of multicultural education today. It involves giving students the opportunity to learn about the experiences, struggles, and visions of many different ethnic and cultural groups. The hope is that empowerment will raise minority students' self-esteem, reduce prejudice, and provide more-equal educational opportunities.

| Culturally Relevant Teaching |

Culturally relevant teaching is an important aspect of multicultural education. It seeks to make connections with the learner's cultural background.

| Issues-Centered Education |

Issues-centered education also is an important aspect of multicultural education. In this approach, students are taught to systematically examine issues that involve equity and social justice.

| Improving Relationships Among Children from Different Ethnic Groups |

Among the strategies/related ideas for improving relationships between children from different ethnic groups are these: the jigsaw classroom (having students from different cultural backgrounds cooperate by doing different parts of a project to reach a common goal), positive personal contact, perspective taking, reduced bias, increased tolerance, and development of the school and community as a team.

## ❸ GENDER: Explain various facets of gender, including similarities and differences in boys and girls; discuss gender issues in teaching.

| Exploring Gender Views |

Gender refers to the characteristics of people as males and females. Among the components of gender are gender identity, gender roles, and gender typing. Biological, social, and cognitive views of gender have been proposed. Some views stress biological factors; other views emphasize social or cognitive factors. The most widely accepted cognitive view today is gender schema theory.

| Gender Stereotyping, Similarities, and Differences |

Gender stereotypes are broad categories that reflect impressions and beliefs about what behavior is appropriate for females and males. All stereotypes involve an image of what the typical member of a category is like. Some gender stereotypes can be harmful for children. Psychologists have studied gender similarities and differences in physical performance, the brain, math and science skills, verbal skills, school attainment, relationship skills (rapport talk and report talk), aggression/self-regulation, and prosocial behavior. In some cases, gender differences are substantial (as in physical performance, reading and writing skills, school attainment, physical aggression, and prosocial behavior); in others they are small or nonexistent (as in communication, math, and science). Today, controversy still swirls about how common or rare such differences really are.

| Gender Controversy |

Controversy continues to occur regarding how extensive gender differences are and what causes the differences. Buss argues for extensive gender differences that are evolutionary-based while Eagly also emphasizes considerable gender differences but concludes that they are the result of social conditions. Hyde states that there is considerable gender similarity in many areas.

| Gender-Role Classification |

Gender-role classification focuses on how masculine, feminine, or androgynous an individual is. In the past, competent males were supposed to be masculine (powerful, for example), females feminine (nurturant, for example). The 1970s brought the concept of androgyny, the idea that the most competent individuals have both masculine and feminine positive characteristics. A special concern involves adolescents who adopt a strong masculine role.

| Gender in Context |

Evaluation of gender-role categories and gender similarities and differences in areas such as helping behavior and emotion suggest that the best way to think about gender is not in terms of personality traits but instead in terms of person-situation interaction (gender in context). Although androgyny and multiple gender roles are often available for American children to choose from, many countries around the world still are male-dominant.

| Eliminating Gender Bias |

There is gender bias in schools against boys and girls. Many school personnel are unaware of these biases. An important teaching strategy is to attempt to eliminate gender bias. Schools have made considerable progress in reducing gender stereotyping in books and curriculum materials, but some bias still exists. Sexual harassment is a special concern in schools and is more pervasive than once believed. Recently, a distinction has been made between quid pro quo sexual harassment and hostile environment sexual harassment.

## KEY TERMS

culture 142
cross-cultural studies 143
individualism 143
collectivism 143
socioeconomic status
  (SES) 144
ethnicity 148

prejudice 150
English as a second language
  (ESL) 151
multicultural education 154
empowerment 157
jigsaw classroom 159
gender 164

gender identity 164
gender role 164
gender typing 164
gender schema theory 165
gender stereotypes 165
rapport talk 167
report talk 167

androgyny 169
quid pro quo sexual
  harassment 173
hostile environment sexual
  harassment 173

## PORTFOLIO ACTIVITIES

Now that you have a good understanding of this chapter, complete these exercises to expand your thinking.

**Independent Reflection Fostering Cultural Understanding in the Classroom.** Imagine that you are teaching a social studies lesson about the westward movement in U.S. history and a student makes a racist, stereotyped statement about Native Americans, such as "The Indians were hot-tempered and showed their hostility toward the White settlers." How would you handle this situation? (Banks, 1997). Describe the strategy you would adopt. (INTASC: Principles *1, 2, 4, 6, 7*)

**Collaborative Work Planning for Diversity.** With three or four other students in the class, come up with a list of specific diversity goals for your future classrooms. Also brainstorm and come up with some innovative activities to help students gain positive diversity experiences, such as the inclusive quilt discussed in this chapter. Summarize the diversity goals and activities. (INTASC: Principles *3, 4, 5, 6*)

**Research/Field Experience Equity in Action.** Observe lessons being taught in several classrooms that include boys and girls and students from different ethnic groups. Did the teachers interact with females and males differently? If so, how? Did the teachers interact with students from different ethnic groups in different ways? If so, how? Describe your observations. (INTASC: Principles *3, 6, 9*)

*Go to the Online Learning Center for downloadable portfolio templates.*

## STUDY, PRACTICE, AND SUCCEED

Visit www.mhhe.com/santrockep5e to review the chapter with self-grading quizzes and self-assessments, to apply the chapter material to two more Crack the Case studies, and for suggested activities to develop your teaching portfolio.

# CHAPTER 6

# LEARNERS WHO ARE EXCEPTIONAL

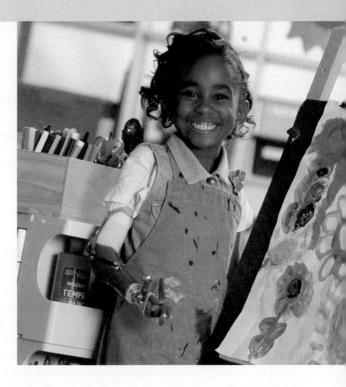

*Only the educated are free.*

—Epicurus
*Greek Philosopher, 4th Century* B.C.

Learning **Goals**

**1** Describe the various types of disabilities and disorders.

**2** Explain the legal framework and technology advances for children with disabilities.

**3** Define what gifted means and discuss some approaches to teaching children who are gifted.

# Teaching **Stories**  Verna Rollins

Verna Rollins teaches language arts at West Middle School in Ypsilanti, Michigan, and has developed a reputation for effectively dealing with so-called hard to teach or difficult students. She has found that the best strategy to use with these students is to find out what they need, decide how to provide it, provide it, and constantly evaluate whether it is working. A challenge for many regular education classroom teachers is how to effectively teach children with disabilities. In many instances, the education of children with disabilities in the regular education classroom is carried out in coordination with a special education teacher or staff. Here is Verna Rollins' description of her contribution in the coordinated effort to teach a student with a severe disability:

> Jack was in a special education classroom for children with physical disabilities. He has twisted legs, cerebral palsy, seizures, and some other brain damage from birth. He also has a comparatively short attention span. Since he drools, speaks in a loud monotone, stutters when he is excited, and has so little motor control that his penmanship is unreadable, people often think he is mentally retarded.
>
> My strategies included making sure that he had all the equipment he needed to succeed. I gave him tissues for the drooling and mutually agreed-upon reminders to wipe his mouth. I found that he could speak softly and without stuttering if he calmed down. We developed a signaling plan in which I would clear my throat when he talked too loudly and I would prompt him with the phrase "slow speech" when he was too excited to speak in a smooth voice.
>
> He used a computer to take quizzes and needed a little more time to complete any task, but he was so excited about being "out in the real world" that his attention span improved, as did his self-worth. In fact, his mother wrote a letter to me expressing her gratitude for the "most positive influence you have been on him! You have re-instilled and greatly increased his love of reading and writing. You have given my child a wonderful gift."

# Preview

Verna Rollins was challenged to find the best way to teach a child with multiple disabilities in her classroom and to coordinate this teaching with Jack's special education teacher. Like Verna Rollins, you will likely work with children with disabilities if you teach in a regular classroom. In the past, public school did little to educate these children. Today, however, children with disabilities must have a free, appropriate education—and increasingly they are educated in regular classrooms. In this chapter we will study children with many different types of disabilities, as well as another group of children who are exceptional—those who are gifted.

## ① CHILDREN WITH DISABILITIES

Approximately 14 percent of all children from 3 to 21 years of age in the United States received special education or related services in the 2006–2007 school year (National Center for Education Statistics, 2008). Figure 6.1 shows the four largest groups of students with a disability who were served by federal programs in the 2006–2007 school year (National Center for Education Statistics, 2008). As indicated in the figure, students with a learning disability were the largest group of students with a disability to be given special education.

Educators increasingly speak of "children with disabilities" rather than "disabled children" to emphasize the person, not the disability. Also, children with disabilities are no longer referred to as "handicapped," although the term *handicapping conditions* is still used to describe the impediments to the learning and functioning of

| Disability | Percentage of All Children in Public Schools |
|---|---|
| Learning disabilities | 5.6 |
| Speech and language impairments | 3.0 |
| Mental retardation | 1.1 |
| Emotional disturbance | 0.9 |

**FIGURE 6.1** THE FOUR HIGHEST PERCENTAGES OF STUDENTS WITH A DISABILITY SERVED BY A FEDERAL PROGRAM AS A PERCENTAGE OF ALL STUDENTS ENROLLED IN U.S. PUBLIC SCHOOLS (NATIONAL CENTER FOR EDUCATION STATISTICS, 2008)

individuals with a disability that have been imposed by society. For example, when children who use a wheelchair do not have adequate access to a bathroom, transportation, and so on, this is referred to as a handicapping condition.

## LEARNING DISABILITIES

Bobby's second-grade teacher complains that his spelling is awful. Eight-year-old Tim says reading is really hard for him, and a lot of times the words don't make much sense. Alisha has good oral language skills but has considerable difficulty in computing correct answers to arithmetic problems. Each of these students has a learning disability.

**Characteristics and Identification**   The U.S. government created a definition of learning disabilities in 1997 and then reauthorized the definition with a few minor changes in 2004. It states that a child with a **learning disability** has difficulty in learning that involves understanding or using spoken or written language, and the difficulty can appear in listening, thinking, reading, writing, and spelling. A learning disability also may involve difficulty in doing mathematics. To be classified as a learning disability, the learning problem cannot be primarily the result of visual, hearing, or motor disabilities; mental retardation; emotional disorders; or due to environmental, cultural, or economic disadvantage.

From the mid-1970s through the early 1990s, there was a dramatic increase in the percentage of U.S. students receiving special education services (from 1.8 percent in 1976–1977 to 12.2 percent in 1994–1995) (National Center for Education Statistics, 2008). Some experts say that the dramatic increase reflected poor diagnostic practices and overidentification. They argue that teachers sometimes are too quick to label children with the slightest learning problem as having a learning disability instead of recognizing that the problem may rest in ineffective teaching. Other experts say the increase in the number of children being labeled with a "learning disability" is justified (Hallahan, Kauffman, & Pullen, 2009).

About three times as many boys as girls are classified as having a learning disability. Among the explanations for this gender difference are a greater biological vulnerability among boys and *referral bias* (that is, boys are more likely to be referred by teachers for treatment because of their behavior).

Most learning disabilities are lifelong. Compared with children without a learning disability, children with a learning disability are more likely to show poor academic performance throughout their schooling, high dropout rates, and poor employment and postsecondary education records (Berninger, 2006). Children with a learning disability who are taught in the regular classroom without extensive support rarely achieve the level of competence of even children who are low achieving and do not have a disability (Hocutt, 1996). Still, despite the problems they encounter, many children with a learning disability grow up to lead normal lives and engage in productive work (Smith & Tyler, 2010).

Diagnosing whether a child has a learning disability is often a difficult task (Turnbull, Turnbull, & Wehmeyer, 2010). Because federal guidelines are just that, guidelines, it is up to each state, or in some cases school systems within a state, to determine how to define and implement diagnosis of learning disabilities. The same child might be diagnosed as having a learning disability in one school system and therefore receive services but not be diagnosed and not receive services in another school system. In such cases, parents sometimes will move to either obtain or avoid the diagnosis.

Initial identification of a possible learning disability usually is made by the classroom teacher. If a learning disability is suspected, the teacher calls on specialists. An interdisciplinary team of professionals is best suited to verify whether a student has a learning disability. Individual psychological evaluations (of intelligence) and educational assessments (such as current level of achievement) are required (Hallahan,

**learning disability** A child with a learning disability has difficulty in learning that involves understanding or using spoken or written language, and the difficulty can appear in listening, thinking, reading, writing, and spelling. A learning disability also may involve difficulty in doing mathematics. To be classified as a learning disability, the learning problem cannot be primarily the result of visual, hearing, or motor disabilities; mental retardation; emotional disorders; or due to environmental, cultural, or economic disadvantage.

Kauffman, & Pullen, 2009). In addition, tests of visual-motor skills, language, and memory may be used.

**Reading, Writing, and Math Difficulties**  The most common academic areas in which children with a learning disability have problems are reading, writing, and math.

**Dyslexia**  The most common learning disability is **dyslexia,** a severe impairment in the ability to read and spell (Ise & Schulte-Korne, 2010; Reid & others, 2009). Approximately 80 percent of children with a learning disability suffer from dyslexia. Such children have difficulty with phonological skills, which involve being able to understand how sounds and letters match up to make words, and also can have problems in comprehension.

**Dysgraphia**  A learning disability that involves difficulty in handwriting is **dysgraphia** (Rosenblum, Aloni, & Josman, 2010). Children with dysgraphia may write very slowly, their writing products may be virtually illegible, and they may make numerous spelling errors because of their inability to match up sounds and letters (Berninger, 2009). A recent study revealed that boys were more impaired in handwriting than were girls (Berninger & others, 2008).

**Dyscalculia**  Also known as *developmental arithmetic disorder,* **dyscalculia** is a learning disability that involves difficulty in math computation (Rykhlevskaia & others, 2010). It is estimated to characterize 2 to 6 percent of U.S. elementary school children (National Center for Learning Disabilities, 2006). Researchers have found that children with difficulties in math computation often have cognitive and neuropsychological deficits, including poor performance in working memory, visual perception, and visuospatial abilities (Shalev, 2004). A child may have both a reading and a math disability, and there are cognitive deficits that characterize both types of disabilities, such as poor working memory (Siegel, 2003).

**Causes and Intervention Strategies**  The precise causes of learning disabilities have not yet been determined (Hallahan, Kauffman, & Pullen, 2009; Rosenberg, Westling, & McLesky, 2011). However, some possible causes have been proposed. Learning disabilities tend to run in families with one parent being so affected, although the specific genetic transmission of learning disabilities is not known. Also, some learning disabilities are likely caused by problems during prenatal development or delivery. For example, a number of studies have found that learning disabilities are more prevalent in low birth weight infants (Litt & others, 2005).

Researchers have used brain-imaging techniques, such as magnetic resonance imaging (MRI), to reveal any regions of the brain that might be involved in learning disabilities (Shaywitz, Morris, & Shaywitz, 2008) (see Figure 6.2). This research indicates that it is unlikely learning disabilities reside in a single, specific brain location. They are more likely due to problems in integrating information from multiple brain regions or subtle difficulties in brain structures and functions (National Institutes of Health, 1993).

Many interventions have focused on improving the child's reading ability (Bursuck & Damer, 2011; Reid & others, 2009). Intensive instruction over a period of time by a competent teacher can help many children (Shaywitz, Morris, & Shaywitz, 2008). For example, in a recent brain-imaging study, 15 children with severe reading difficulties who had not shown adequate progress in response to reading instruction in the first grade were given an intensive eight weeks of instruction in phonological

**Thinking Back/Thinking Forward**

An increasing number of experts conclude that direct instruction in phonological training is a key aspect of learning to read. Chapter 11, p. 364

RESEARCH

**FIGURE 6.2** BRAIN SCANS AND LEARNING DISABILITIES

An increasing number of studies are using MRI brain scans to examine the brain pathways involved in learning disabilities. Shown here is 9-year-old Patrick Price, who has dyslexia. Patrick is going through an MRI scanner disguised by drapes to look like a child-friendly castle. Inside the scanner, children must lie virtually motionless as words and symbols flash on a screen and they are asked to identify them by clicking different buttons.

RESEARCH

**dyslexia** A severe impairment in the ability to read and spell.

**dysgraphia** A learning disability that involves difficulty in handwriting.

**dyscalculia** Also known as *developmental arithmetic disorder,* this learning disability involves difficulty in math computation.

RESEARCH

decoding skills and then another intensive eight weeks of word recognition skills (Simos & others, 2007). Significant improvement in a majority of the children's reading skills and changes in brain regions involved in reading occurred as a result of the intensive instruction.

I recently asked teachers how they work with students with a learning disability. Following are their responses.

**EARLY CHILDHOOD** To accommodate our children with learning disabilities, we have them sit close to teachers during work time at craft tables, we use more transition warnings so all students clearly know when we are moving to a different activity, and we prepare lessons that are visual and hands-on. Having children of different abilities in our school not only benefits the learning of children with disabilities, but it immensely helps their "typically" developing peers to accept others who are not like them.

—VALARIE GORHAM, *Kiddie Quarters, Inc.*

**ELEMENTARY SCHOOL: GRADES K–5** Learning disabilities come in all shapes and sizes and require adaptations to ensure that all students reach their full potential. An adaptation that helps a student with ADHD is not an adaptation that will help a student with dyslexia. Some of the adaptations and modifications I use in my class are visuals, modeling, graphic organizers, and mnemonic devices. Many students with learning disabilities have trouble learning information through one sense. Therefore, the more senses you engage while teaching, the more likely the children will learn.

—SHANE SCHWARZ, *Clinton Elementary School*

**MIDDLE SCHOOL: GRADES 6–8** When working with students with learning disabilities, I offer assistance with organization (by providing a notebook with color-coded individual folders for each subject); provide a structured classroom setting with high expectations; have private, open discussions concerning specific disabilities with the student; maintain a consistent classroom routine and schedule (students with learning challenges often have difficulty with change); and provide a daily overview of the day.

—FELICIA PETERSON, *Pocantico Hills School*

**HIGH SCHOOL: GRADES 9–12** With high school students, I find it extremely effective to pair the student with a learning disability with a concerned, helpful peer. Sometimes it is necessary to let the peer know what to expect or how to help the other student. However, there is a fine line to walk as you do not want other students to be aware of the student's disability. I also find that books on tape help students with a learning disability master information as does providing extra time to complete tests and quizzes.

—SANDY SWANSON, *Menomonee Falls High School*

## ATTENTION DEFICIT HYPERACTIVITY DISORDER

Matthew has attention deficit hyperactivity disorder, and the outward signs are fairly typical. He has trouble attending to the teacher's instructions and is easily distracted. He can't sit still for more than a few minutes at a time, and his handwriting is messy. His mother describes him as very fidgety.

## TEACHING CONNECTIONS: Best Practices
### Strategies for Working with Children Who Have Learning Disabilities

1. *Take the needs of the child with a learning disability into account during instructional time.* Clearly state the objective of each lesson. Present it visually on the board or with an overhead projector as well. Be sure directions are explicit. Explain them orally. Use concrete examples to illustrate abstract concepts. Provide clear, written directions for assignments and projects so students can refer to them later if needed.

2. *Provide accommodations for testing and assignments.* This refers to changing the academic environment so that these children can demonstrate what they know. An accommodation usually does not involve altering the amount of learning the child has to demonstrate. Common accommodations include reading instructions to children, highlighting important words in directions (such as by underlining), answering two of the three questions, using/giving untimed tests, testing in a place with fewer distractions, and allowing extra time on assignments.

3. *Make modifications.* This strategy changes the work itself, making it different from other children's work in an effort to encourage children's confidence and success. Asking a child with dyslexia to give an oral report while other children give written reports is an example of an appropriate modification.

4. *Improve organizational and study skills.* Many children with learning disabilities do not have good organizational skills. Teachers and parents can encourage them to keep long-term and short-term calendars and create "to-do" lists each day. Many teachers use assignment notebooks for this. This practice can begin as early as second grade. The teacher writes assignments on the board and reminds students to copy them into the assignment notebook. Projects should be broken down into their elements, with steps and due dates for each part. Apprising parents of important due dates is also helpful. One way to do this is via a Web-based calendar.

5. *Work with reading and writing skills.* As indicated earlier, the most common type of learning disability involves reading problems. Children with a reading problem often read slowly, so give them more advance notice of

outside reading assignments and more time for in-class reading. Many children with a learning disability that involves writing deficits find that a word processing program helps them compose their writing projects more quickly and competently, so make sure to provide them the opportunity to use a word processing program for their assignments. Some students find it helpful to dictate their thoughts while another person types. There are also computer programs that allow this. In Through the Eyes of Teachers, you can read about the unique strategy a second-grade teacher created for working with children who have a learning disability.

### THROUGH THE EYES OF TEACHERS
#### Creating a Character Named Uey Long and Using a Team Approach

Nancy Downing, a second-grade teacher at McDermott Elementary School in Little Rock, Arkansas, takes a multisensory approach to education, which she developed while working with her own child, who has learning difficulties. She created Downfeld Phonics using phonics, sign language, and lively jingles to make learning fun for students. She developed the character Uey Long (a uey is the sign over a short vowel) to demonstrate vowel rules.

6. *Challenge children with a learning disability to become independent and reach their full potential.* It is not only important to provide support and services for children with a learning disability but to also guide them toward becoming responsible and independent. Teachers need to challenge children with a learning disability to become all they can be. We will have more to say about the importance of challenging children with disabilities to reach their potential later in the chapter.

7. *Work closely with a special educator to design appropriate accommodations for your individual students.*

Using these seven main teaching strategies we have described is not meant to give children with a learning disability an unfair advantage, just an equal chance to learn. Balancing the needs of children with learning disabilities and those of other children is a challenging task.

---

**Characteristics**    **Attention deficit hyperactivity disorder (ADHD)** is a disability in which children consistently show one or more of these characteristics over a period of time: (1) inattention, (2) hyperactivity, and (3) impulsivity. For an ADHD diagnosis, onset of these characteristics early in childhood is required, and the characteristics must be debilitating for the child.

**attention deficit hyperactivity disorder (ADHD)**
A disability in which children consistently show one or more of the following characteristics over a period of time: (1) inattention, (2) hyperactivity, and (3) impulsivity.

- - - - - - - - - ▶

**Thinking Back/Thinking Forward**

Sustained attention is the ability to maintain attention over a period of time. Sustained attention is a very important aspect of cognitive development. Chapter 8, p. 258

◀ - - - - - - - - -

RESEARCH

DEVELOPMENT

Inattentive children have difficulty focusing on any one thing and may get bored with a task after only a few minutes. One study found that problems in sustaining attention were the most common type of attentional problem in children with ADHD (Tsal, Shalev, & Mevorach, 2005). Hyperactive children show high levels of physical activity, almost always seeming to be in motion. Impulsive children have difficulty curbing their reactions and don't do a good job of thinking before they act. Depending on the characteristics that children with ADHD display, they can be diagnosed as (1) ADHD with predominantly inattention, (2) ADHD with predominantly hyperactivity/impulsivity, or (3) ADHD with both inattention and hyperactivity/impulsivity.

**Diagnosis and Developmental Status** The number of children diagnosed and treated for ADHD has increased substantially, by some estimates doubling in the 1990s. A national survey found that 7 percent of U.S. children 3 to 17 years of age had ADHD (Bloom & Dey, 2006). The disorder occurs as much as four to nine times more in boys than in girls. There is controversy about the increased diagnosis of ADHD, however (Stolzer, 2009). Some experts attribute the increase mainly to heightened awareness of the disorder. Others are concerned that many children are being diagnosed without undergoing extensive professional evaluation based on input from multiple sources (Parens & Johnston, 2009).

Unlike learning disabilities, ADHD is not supposed to be diagnosed by school teams because ADHD is a disorder that appears in the classification of psychiatric disorders (called DSM-IV) with specific diagnostic criteria. Although some school teams may diagnose a child as having ADHD, this is incorrectly done and can lead to legal problems for schools and teachers. One reason that is given as to why a school team should not do the diagnosis for ADHD is that ADHD is difficult to differentiate from other childhood disorders, and accurate diagnosis requires the evaluation by a specialist in the disorder, such as a child psychiatrist.

Although signs of ADHD are often present in the preschool years, children with ADHD are not usually classified until the elementary school years. The increased academic and social demands of formal schooling, as well as stricter standards for behavioral control, often illuminate the problems of the child with ADHD (Daley, 2006). Elementary school teachers typically report that this type of child has difficulty in working independently, completing seatwork, and organizing work. Restlessness and distractibility also are often noted. These problems are more likely to be observed in repetitive or difficult tasks, or tasks the child perceives to be boring (such as completing worksheets or doing homework).

It used to be thought that children with ADHD improved during adolescence, but now it appears this improvement occurs in only about one-third of adolescents. Increasingly, it is being recognized that symptoms of ADHD may continue into adulthood (Miller, Nigg, & Faraone, 2007).

**Causes and Treatment** Definitive causes of ADHD have not been found. However, a number of causes have been proposed (Fararone & Mick, 2010; Stolzer, 2009). Some children likely inherit a tendency to develop ADHD from their parents (Durston, 2010; Tripp & Wickens, 2009). Other children likely develop ADHD because of damage to their brain during prenatal or postnatal development

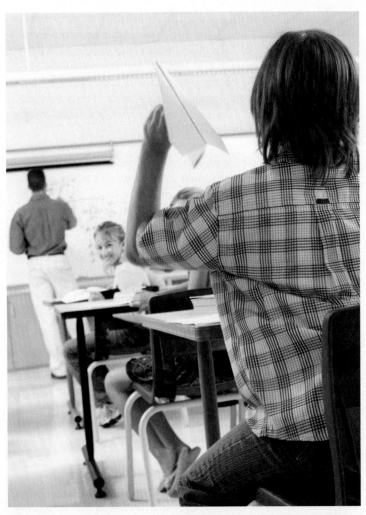

Many children with ADHD show impulsive behavior, such as this child who is throwing a paper airplane at other children. *How would you handle this situation if you were a teacher and this were to happen in your classroom?*

(Linblad & Hjern, 2010). Among early possible contributors to ADHD are cigarette and alcohol exposure during prenatal development and low birth weight (Knopik, 2009).

As with learning disabilities, the development of brain-imaging techniques is leading to a better understanding of the brain's role in ADHD (Hoeksema & others, 2010; Plomp, van Engeland, & Durston, 2009). A recent study revealed that peak thickness of the cerebral cortex occurred three years later (10.5 years) in children with ADHD than children without ADHD (peak at 7.5 years) (Shaw & others, 2007). The delay was more prominent in the prefrontal regions of the brain that are especially important in attention and planning (see Figure 6.3). Researchers also are exploring the roles that various neurotransmitters, such as serotonin and dopamine, might play in ADHD (Levy, 2009; Rondou, Haegeman, & Van Craenenbroeck, 2010; Zhou & others, 2010).

DEVELOPMENT

Stimulant medication such as Ritalin or Adderall (which has fewer side effects than Ritalin) is effective in improving the attention of many children with ADHD, but it usually does not improve their attention to the same level as children who do not have ADHD (Brams, Mao, & Doyle, 2009; Stray, Ellertson, & Stray, 2010). A recent meta-analysis concluded that behavior management treatments are effective in reducing the effects of ADHD (Fabiano & others, 2009). Researchers have found that a combination of medication (such as Ritalin) and behavior management often—but not always—improves the behavior of children with ADHD more than medication alone or behavior management alone (Parens & Johnston, 2009).

RESEARCH

Teachers play an important role in monitoring whether ADHD medication has been prescribed at the right dosage level. For example, it is not unusual for a student on ADHD medication to complete academic tasks in the morning, but in the afternoon, when the dosage has worn off, to be inattentive or hyperactive.

RESEARCH

Critics argue that many physicians are too quick to prescribe stimulants for children with milder forms of ADHD. Also, in 2006 the U.S. government issued a warning about the cardiovascular risks of stimulant medication to treat ADHD.

I recently asked teachers how they work with students who have ADHD. Following are their recommendations.

**EARLY CHILDHOOD**   Our preschoolers who have been diagnosed with ADHD work well within a very structured environment. Although our ADHD students  are treated just like any other student in the classroom, we take care to give them ample physical activity and sometimes receive extra time to gather their thoughts and calm down by taking a few deep breaths. If necessary, medication is given as prescribed by a pediatrician.

—**Missy Dangler**, *Suburban Hills School*

**ELEMENTARY SCHOOL: GRADES K–5**   I find that frequent breaks (such as asking the student to bring something to the school secretary or to put something away)  helps give the child an opportunity to move a bit and then refocus. In second grade, we play a lot of singing and movement games (such as "Simon Says") in the room between lessons, or when I see a lot of "itchiness." All of these games/songs allow standing up, moving, and singing or laughing and provide stretching and body awareness, which can help a child with ADHD to focus. Also, I don't have a problem with a child lying on the floor to work or standing at a desk, if that is how the child needs to focus. This is okay as long as the child is not bothering anyone else and completing the task at hand.

—**Janine Guida Poutre**, *Clinton Elementary School*

Prefrontal cortex                    Prefrontal cortex

◼ Greater than 2 years delay
◼ 0 to 2 years delay

**FIGURE 6.3** REGIONS OF THE BRAIN IN WHICH CHILDREN WITH ADHD HAD A DELAYED PEAK IN THE THICKNESS OF THE CEREBRAL CORTEX

*Note:* The greatest delays occurred in the prefrontal cortex.

## TEACHING CONNECTIONS: Best Practices
### Strategies for Working with Children Who Have ADHD

1. *Monitor whether the child's stimulant medication is working effectively.* Teachers are in a unique position to observe behavior over a long period of time. Make notes about times when the student is restless, non-attentive, or impulsive. Look for patterns. Share these data with the special educator and/or with parents.

2. *Repeat and simplify instructions about in-class and homework assignments.* Provide written directions to which students can refer later. Consider posting them on a Web site so homework or directions forgotten at school can be accessed—particularly important for older students.

3. *Involve a special education resource teacher.*

4. *State clear expectations and give the child immediate feedback.* Many older students can benefit from simple, agreed-upon cues to get them back on task. One might agree with the student to tap a student's desk unobtrusively to help refocus the student on work.

5. *Use proven, effective behavior management strategies, such as providing positive feedback for progress.* We will discuss these approaches in considerable detail in Chapter 7, "Behavioral and Social Cognitive Approaches."

6. *Provide structure and teacher-direction.* In many instances, a structured learning environment benefits children with ADHD. In Through the Eyes of Teachers, Joanna Smith, a high school English teacher, describes how she arranges her classroom to accommodate students with ADHD.

7. *Provide opportunities for students to get up and move around.* This can be in the form of recess for all students. Sadly, children with ADHD are often the first to

lose their recess privileges for either not getting their work finished or for inappropriate behavior. In addition, consider allowing students to learn while standing or sit at their desks on an exercise ball.

---

### THROUGH THE EYES OF TEACHERS
#### Structuring the Classroom to Benefit Students with ADHD

I have found success with these students when I seat them in the front row, make instructions explicit, break down larger tasks into smaller ones, write necessary information on the board and point out exactly where it is, allow extra time on tests (as specified on his or her plan), and check in with the students frequently. This frequent contact allows me to know how the student is doing, how much he understands, and gives him a welcomed opportunity to chat.

---

8. *Work closely with a special educator to design appropriate accommodations for your individual students.* Using these seven main teaching strategies we have described is not meant to give children with a learning disability an unfair advantage, just an equal chance to learn. Balancing the needs of children with learning disabilities and those of other children is a challenging task.

9. *Break assignments into shorter segments with interim due dates to ensure that students are staying on track.* Give feedback on each piece. Consider using the assignment notebook strategies described in the section regarding accommodations for students with learning disabilities.

10. *Allow students to take tests in a distraction-free environment.*

**MIDDLE SCHOOL: GRADES 6–8** Working with ADHD students requires organization and planning. My ADHD students sit in a strategic location in the room. I  usually pick a spot that allows them freedom to get up and move around if necessary. I also make sure that these students sit where I can easily access them. And I give directions clearly and ask the ADHD students to repeat the directions to me to make sure that they not only are listening but also understand.

—**CASEY MAASS**, *Edison Middle School*

**HIGH SCHOOL: GRADES 9–12** One of my biggest challenges in teaching is working with untreated ADHD students. One thing I do with my ADHD  students is to sit them in the front row. I may touch the student's shoulder as I walk by or gently knock on the desk to refocus the student's attention. When I am walking about the room, I will "loop" back to the student's desk or quietly ask for directions to be repeated back to me. I often check their assignment books to make sure that homework assignments are written down correctly. Of course, communication with parents also is very important.

—**Jennifer Heiter,** *Bremen High School*

## MENTAL RETARDATION

Increasingly, children with mental retardation are being taught in the regular class-room. The most distinctive feature of mental retardation is inadequate intellectual functioning (Friend, 2011). Long before formal tests were developed to assess intelligence, individuals with mental retardation were identified by a lack of age-appropriate skills in learning and in caring for themselves. Once intelligence tests were created, numbers were assigned to indicate how mild or severe the retardation was. A child might be only mildly retarded and able to learn in the regular classroom or severely retarded and unable to learn in that setting.

In addition to low intelligence, deficits in adaptive behavior and early onset also are included in the definition of mental retardation (Copeland & Luckasson, 2008). Adaptive skills include those needed for self-care and social responsibility, such as dressing, toileting, feeding, self-control, and peer interaction. By definition, **mental retardation** is a condition with an onset before age 18 that involves low intelligence (usually below 70 on a traditional individually administered intelligence test) and difficulty in adapting to everyday life. For an individual to be given a diagnosis of mental retardation, the low IQ and low adaptiveness should be evident in childhood, not following a long period of normal functioning that is interrupted by an accident or other type of assault on the brain.

**Classification and Types of Mental Retardation**   As indicated in Figure 6.4, mental retardation is classified as mild, moderate, severe, or profound. Approximately 89 percent of students with mental retardation fall into the mild category. By late adolescence, individuals with mild mental retardation can be expected to develop academic skills at approximately the sixth-grade level. In their adult years, many can hold jobs and live on their own with some supportive supervision or in group homes. Individuals with more severe mental retardation require more support.

If you have a student with mental retardation in your classroom, the degree of retardation is likely to be mild. Children with severe mental retardation are more likely to also show signs of other neurological complications, such as cerebral palsy, epilepsy, hearing impairment, visual impairment, or other metabolic birth defects that affect the central nervous system (Terman & others, 1996).

Most school systems still use the classifications of mild, moderate, severe, and profound. However, because these categorizations based on IQ ranges aren't perfect predictors of functioning, the American Association on Mental Retardation (1992) developed a new classification system based on the degree of support children require to function at their highest level (Hallahan, Kauffman, & Pullen, 2009). As shown in Figure 6.5, the categories used are intermittent, limited, extensive, and pervasive.

**Determinants**   Genetic factors, brain damage, and environmental factors are key determinants of mental retardation. Let's explore genetic causes first.

**Genetic Factors**   The most commonly identified form of mental retardation is **Down syndrome,** which is genetically transmitted. Children with Down syndrome have an extra (47th) chromosome. They have a round face, a flattened skull, an extra fold of skin over the eyelids, a protruding tongue, short limbs, and retardation of motor and mental abilities. It is not known why the extra chromosome is present, but the health of the male sperm or female ovum might be involved. Women between the ages of 18 and 38 are far less likely than younger or older women to give birth

| Type of Mental Retardation | IQ Range | Percentage |
|---|---|---|
| **Mild** | 55–70 | 89 |
| **Moderate** | 40–54 | 6 |
| **Severe** | 25–39 | 4 |
| **Profound** | Below 25 | 1 |

**FIGURE 6.4** CLASSIFICATION OF MENTAL RETARDATION BASED ON IQ

**Thinking Back/Thinking Forward**

The Stanford-Binet Test and the Wechsler Scales are the two most widely used individually administered intelligence tests. Chapter 4, pp. 112, 113

DEVELOPMENT

**mental retardation**  A condition with an onset before age 18 that involves low intelligence (usually below 70 on a traditional individually administered intelligence test) and difficulty in adapting to everyday life.

**Down syndrome**  A genetically transmitted form of mental retardation due to an extra (47th) chromosome.

A child with Down syndrome. *What causes a child to develop Down syndrome?*

| | |
|---|---|
| **Intermittent** | Supports are provided "as needed." The individual may need episodic or short-term support during life-span transitions (such as job loss or acute medical crisis). Intermittent supports may be low- or high-intensity when provided. |
| **Limited** | Supports are intense and relatively consistent over time. They are time-limited but not intermittent. Require fewer staff members and cost less than more-intense supports. These supports likely will be needed for adaptation to the changes involved in the school-to-adult period. |
| **Extensive** | Supports are characterized by regular involvement (for example, daily) in at least some setting (such as home or work) and are not time-limited (for example, extended home-living support). |
| **Pervasive** | Supports are constant, very intense, and are provided across settings. They may be of a life-sustaining nature. These supports typically involve more staff members and intrusiveness than the other support categories. |

**FIGURE 6.5** CLASSIFICATION OF MENTAL RETARDATION BASED ON LEVELS OF SUPPORT

*Mental Retardation: Definition, Classification, and Systems of Supports* by David L. Coulter, p. 26. Copyright © 1992 by American Association on Intellectual Developmental Disabilities. Reproduced with permission of American Association on Intellectual Developmental Disabilities in the format Textbook via Copyright Clearance Center.

DEVELOPMENT

to a child with Down syndrome. Down syndrome appears in about 1 in every 700 live births. African American children are rarely born with Down syndrome.

With early intervention and extensive support from the child's family and professionals, many children with Down syndrome can grow into independent adults

## TEACHING CONNECTIONS: Best Practices
### Strategies for Working with Children Who Have Mental Retardation

During the school years, the main goals of teaching children with mental retardation are to provide them with basic educational skills such as reading and mathematics, as well as vocational (Boyles & Contadino, 1997) and independent-living skills. Here are some positive teaching strategies for giving students who have mental retardation the best learning experience:

1. *Help students who have mental retardation to practice making personal choices and to engage in self-determination when possible.*

2. *Always keep in mind the student's level of mental functioning.* Students who have mental retardation will be at a considerably lower level of mental functioning than most other students in your class. If you start at one level of instruction, and the student is not responding effectively, move to a lower level.

3. *Work with a special educator to individualize your instruction to meet the student's needs.* Always follow the individual education plan (IEP) developed for the student.

4. *As with other students with a disability, make sure that you give concrete examples of concepts.* Make your instructions clear and simple.

5. *Give students opportunities to practice what they have learned.* Have them repeat steps a number of times and overlearn a concept to retain it.

6. *Have positive expectations for the student's learning.* It is easy to fall into the trap of thinking that the student with mental retardation cannot achieve academically. Set a goal to maximize his or her learning.

7. *Look for resource support.* Use teacher aides and recruit volunteers, such as sensitive retirees, to help you educate children with mental retardation. They can assist you in increasing the amount of one-on-one instruction the student receives.

8. *Consider using applied behavior analysis strategies.* Some teachers report that these strategies improve students' self-maintenance, social, and academic skills. If you are interested in using these strategies, consult a resource such as *Applied Behavior Analysis for Teachers,* by Paul Alberto and Anne Troutman (2009). The precise steps involved in applied behavior analysis can especially help you effectively use positive reinforcement with students who have mental retardation.

(Taylor, Brady, & Richards, 2005). Children with Down syndrome can fall into the mild to severe retardation categories (Terman & others, 1996).

***Brain Damage and Environmental Factors*** Brain damage can result from many different infections and environmental hazards (Hodapp & Dykens, 2006). Infections in the pregnant mother-to-be, such as rubella (German measles), syphilis, herpes, and AIDS, can cause retardation in the child. Meningitis and encephalitis are infections that can develop in childhood. They cause inflammation in the brain and can produce mental retardation. Environmental hazards that can result in mental retardation include blows to the head, malnutrition, poisoning, birth injury, and alcoholism or heavy drinking on the part of the pregnant woman (Berine-Smith, Patton, & Kim, 2006).

## PHYSICAL DISORDERS

Physical disorders in children include orthopedic impairments, such as cerebral palsy, and seizure disorders. Many children with physical disorders require special education and related services, such as transportation, physical therapy, school health services, and psychological services (Gargiulo, 2009; Heller & others, 2009).

**Orthopedic Impairments** Children with **orthopedic impairments** suffer restricted movement or lack of control over movement due to muscle, bone, or joint problems. The severity of problems ranges widely. Orthopedic impairments can be caused by prenatal or perinatal problems, or they can be due to disease or accident. With the help of adaptive devices and medical technology, many children with orthopedic impairments function well in the classroom (Hallahan, Kauffman, & Pullen, 2009).

   **Cerebral palsy** is a disorder that involves a lack of muscular coordination, shaking, or unclear speech. The most common cause of cerebral palsy is lack of oxygen at birth. Special computers are especially useful in helping children with cerebral palsy to learn.

**Seizure Disorders** The most common seizure disorder is **epilepsy,** a neurological disorder characterized by recurring sensorimotor attacks or movement convulsions. Children who experience seizures are usually treated with one or more anticonvulsant medications, which often are effective in reducing the seizures but do not always eliminate them. When they are not having a seizure, students with epilepsy show normal behavior. If you have a child in your class who has a seizure disorder, become well acquainted with the procedures for monitoring and helping the child during a seizure (Heller & others, 2009).

## SENSORY DISORDERS

Sensory disorders include visual and hearing impairments. Visual impairments include the need for corrective lenses, low vision, and being educationally blind. Children who are hearing impaired may be born deaf or experience a loss in hearing as they develop.

---

### THROUGH THE EYES OF STUDENTS

## It's Okay to Be Different

Why me? I often ask myself, why did I have to be the one? Why did I get picked to be different? It took more than ten years for me to find answers and to realize that I'm not *more* different than anyone else. My twin sister was born with no birth defects, but I was born with cerebral palsy.

   People thought I was stupid because it was hard for me to write my own name. So when I was the only one in the class to use a typewriter, I began to feel I was different. It got worse when the third-graders moved on to the fourth grade and I had to stay behind. I got held back because the teachers thought I'd be unable to type fast enough to keep up. Kids told me that was a lie and the reason I got held back was because I was a retard. It really hurt to be teased by those I thought were my friends. . . .

   I have learned that no one was to blame for my disability. I realize that I can do things and that I can do them very well. Some things I can't do, like taking my own notes in class or running in a race, but I will have to live with that. . . .

   There are times when I wish I had not been born with cerebral palsy, but crying isn't going to do me any good. I can only live once, so I want to live the best I can. . . . Nobody else can be the Angela Marie Erickson who is writing this. I could never be, or ever want to be, anyone else.

*—Angie Erickson*
***Ninth-Grade Student***
***Wayzata, Minnesota***

---

**orthopedic impairments** Restricted movements or lack of control of movements, due to muscle, bone, or joint problems.

**cerebral palsy** A disorder that involves a lack of muscle coordination, shaking, or unclear speech.

**epilepsy** A neurological disorder characterized by recurring sensorimotor attacks or movement convulsions.

## TEACHING CONNECTIONS: Best Practices
### Strategies for Working with Children Who Have a Hearing Impairment

1. *Be patient.*

2. *Speak normally (not too slowly or too quickly).*

3. *Don't shout, because this doesn't help.* Speaking distinctly is more helpful.

4. *Reduce distractions and background noises.*

5. *Face the student to whom you are speaking, because the student needs to see your gestures and your lips if he/she is going to read your lips.*

6. *Use an interpreter or stenographer.* Many deaf and hearing impaired students require an interpreter or stenographer. Interpreters will sign what you and others say for the student, while stenographers type what is said and create a transcript for the student.

7. *Be certain to give written as well as verbal instructions.*

## THROUGH THE EYES OF STUDENTS

### Eyes Closed

In kindergarten, children truly begin to appreciate, not fear or think strange, each other's differences. A few years ago, a child in my kindergarten class was walking down the hall with his eyes closed and ran into the wall. When I asked him what he was doing, he said, "I was just trying to do like Darrick. How come he does it so much better?" Darrick is his classmate who is legally blind. He wanted to experience what it was like to be blind. In this case, imitation truly was the greatest form of flattery.

*Anita Marie Hitchcock*
**Kindergarten Teacher**
**Holle Navarre Primary**
**Santa Rosa County, Florida**

**Visual Impairments** A small portion of students (about 1 in every 1,000 students) have very serious visual problems and are classified as visually impaired. This category includes students who have low vision and students who are blind. Children with *low vision* have a visual acuity of between 20/70 and 20/200 (on the familiar Snellen scale, in which 20/20 vision is normal) with corrective lenses. Children with low vision can read large-print books or regular books with the aid of a magnifying glass. Children who are *educationally blind* cannot use their vision in learning and must rely on their hearing and touch to learn. Approximately 1 in every 3,000 children is educationally blind. Many children who are educationally blind have normal intelligence and function very well academically with appropriate supports and learning aids.

An important task in working with a child who has visual impairments is to determine the modality (such as touch or hearing) through which the child learns best. Seating in the front of the class often benefits the child with a visual impairment.

**Hearing Impairments** A hearing impairment can make learning very difficult for children. Children who are born deaf or experience a significant hearing loss in the first several years of life usually do not develop normal speech and language. You also might have some children in your class who have hearing impairments that have not yet been detected (Gargiulo, 2009). If you have students who turn one ear toward a speaker, frequently ask to have something repeated, don't follow directions, or frequently complain of earaches, colds, and allergies, consider having the student's hearing evaluated by a specialist, such as an audiologist.

Many children with hearing impairments receive supplementary instruction beyond the regular classroom. Educational approaches to help students with hearing impairments learn fall into two categories: oral and manual. *Oral approaches* include using lip reading, speech reading (a reliance on visual cues to teach reading), and whatever hearing the student has. *Manual approaches* involve sign language and finger spelling. Sign language is a system of hand movements that symbolize words. Finger spelling consists of "spelling out" each word by signing.

**speech and language disorders** A number of speech problems (such as articulation disorders, voice disorders, and fluency disorders) and language problems (difficulties in receiving information and expressing language).

## SPEECH AND LANGUAGE DISORDERS

**Speech and language disorders** include a number of speech problems (such as articulation disorders, voice disorders, and fluency disorders) and language problems (difficulties in receiving information and expressing language) (Anderson & Shames, 2011; Norbury, Tomblin, & Bishop, 2008). Approximately 17 percent of all children who receive special education services have a speech or language impairment (National Center for Education Statistics, 2006).

DEVELOPMENT

**Articulation Disorders**    Problems in pronouncing sounds correctly are **articulation disorders.** A child's articulation at 6 or 7 years is still not always error-free, but it should be by age 8. Articulation problems can make communication with peers and the teacher difficult or embarrassing. As a result, the child might avoid asking questions, participating in discussions, or communicating with peers. Speech therapy usually reduces or resolves articulation problems, though it might take months or years (Dunkelberger, 2008; Owens, 2010).

**Voice Disorders**    Speech that is hoarse, harsh, too loud, too high-pitched, or too low-pitched reflects a **voice disorder.** Children with cleft palate often have a voice disorder that makes their speech difficult to understand. If a child speaks in a way that is consistently difficult to understand, refer the child to a speech therapist.

Speech therapist Sharla Peltier, helping a young child improve her language and communication skills. *What are some different types of speech problems children can have?*

**Fluency Disorders**    "Stuttering," in which a child's speech exhibits spasmodic hesitation, prolongation, or repetition, is caused by a **fluency disorder** (Ratner, 2009). The anxiety many children feel because they stutter often just makes their stuttering worse. Speech therapy is recommended (Kuder, 2009).

> **Thinking Back/Thinking Forward**
>
> Syntax is the language system that involves the way words are combined to form acceptable phrases and sentences. Chapter 2, p. 58

**Language Disorders**    **Language disorders** include a significant impairment in a child's receptive or expressive language (Anderson & Shames, 2011). **Receptive language** involves the reception and understanding of language. **Expressive language** involves using language for expressing one's thoughts and communicating with others. Language disorders can result in significant learning problems (Kuder, 2009). Treatment by a language therapist generally produces improvement in the child with a language disorder, but the problem is rarely eradicated. Language disorders include difficulties in phrasing questions properly to get the desired information, following oral directions, following conversation, especially when it is rapid and complex, and understanding and using words correctly in sentences.

DEVELOPMENT

**Specific language impairment (SLI)** involves language development problems with no obvious physical, sensory, or emotional difficulties involved (Monaco, 2008). In some cases the disorder is referred to as *developmental language disorder.*

Children with SLI have problems in understanding and using words in sentences (Pennington & Bishop, 2009). One indicator of SLI in 5-year-old children is their incomplete understanding of verbs (Leonard, 2007). They typically drop the –s from verb tenses (such as saying, "She walk to the store," instead of, "She walks to the store") and ask questions without "be" or "do" verbs (such as saying, "He live there?" instead of saying, "Does he live there?") (Marinis & van der Lely, 2007). These characteristics make children with SLI sound approximately two years younger than they are.

Early identification of SLI is important and can usually be accurately accomplished by 5 years of age and in some cases earlier. Intervention includes modeling correct utterances, rephrasing the child's incorrect utterances during conversation, and reading instruction (Ratner, 2009). Parents may also wish to send a child with SRI to a speech or language pathologist (Kuder, 2009).

**articulation disorders** Problems in pronouncing sounds correctly.

**voice disorders** Disorders producing speech that is hoarse, harsh, too loud, too high-pitched, or too low-pitched.

**fluency disorders** Disorders that often involve what is commonly referred to as "stuttering."

**language disorders** Significant impairments in receptive or expressive language.

**receptive language** The reception and understanding of language.

**expressive language** The ability to use language to express one's thoughts and communicate with others.

**specific language impairment (SLI)** Involves problems in language development that are not accompanied by other obvious physical, sensory, or emotional problems; in some cases, the disorder is called *developmental language disorder.*

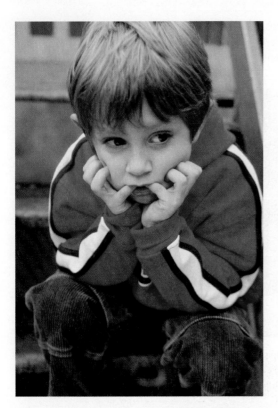

*What characterizes autism spectrum disorders?*

RESEARCH

**autism spectrum disorders (ASD)** Also called *pervasive developmental disorders,* they range from the severe disorder labeled *autistic disorder* to the milder disorder called *Asperger syndrome.* Children with these disorders are characterized by problems in social interaction, verbal and nonverbal communication, and repetitive behaviors.

**autistic disorder** A severe autism spectrum disorder (ASD) that has its onset in the first three years of life and includes deficiencies in social relationships, abnormalities in communication, and restricted, repetitive, and stereotyped patterns of behavior.

**Asperger syndrome** A relatively mild autism spectrum disorder (ASD) in which there is relatively good verbal language, mild nonverbal language problems, a restricted range of interests and relationships, and frequent repetitive routines.

# AUTISM SPECTRUM DISORDERS

**Autism spectrum disorders (ASD),** also called *pervasive developmental disorders,* range from the severe disorder labeled *autistic disorder* to the milder disorder called *Asperger syndrome* (each of which will be defined and discussed here). Autism spectrum disorders are characterized by problems in social interaction, problems in verbal and nonverbal communication, and repetitive behaviors (Boutot & Myles, 2011; Neuhaus, Beauchaire, & Bernier, 2010). Children with these disorders may also show atypical responses to sensory experiences (Centers for Disease Control and Prevention, 2010). Autism spectrum disorders can often be detected in children as early as 1 to 3 years of age.

**Autistic disorder** is a severe developmental autism spectrum disorder that has its onset in the first three years of life and includes deficiencies in social relationships, abnormalities in communication, and restricted, repetitive, and stereotyped patterns of behavior.

**Asperger syndrome** is a relatively mild autism spectrum disorder in which the child has relatively good verbal language, milder nonverbal language problems, and a restricted range of interests and relationships (Fernell & others, 2010). Children with Asperger syndrome often engage in obsessive repetitive routines and preoccupations with a particular subject. For example, a child may be obsessed with baseball scores or railroad timetables.

Recent estimates of autism spectrum disorders indicate that they are increasing in occurrence or are increasingly being detected and labeled (Liu, King, & Bearman, 2010). Once thought to affect only 1 in 2500 individuals, today's estimates suggest that they occur in about 1 in 150 individuals (Centers for Disease Control and Prevention, 2009).

What causes the autism spectrum disorders? The current consensus is that autism is a brain dysfunction with abnormalities in brain structure and neurotransmitters (Anderson & others, 2009). Genetic factors likely play a role in the development of the autism spectrum disorders (El-Fishawy & State, 2010; Shen & others, 2010). There is no evidence that family socialization causes autism. Mental retardation is present in some children with autism; others show average or above-average intelligence (Hoekstra & others, 2010).

Boys are four times more likely to have autism spectrum disorders (Gong & others, 2009). Simon Baron-Cohen (2008) recently argued that autism reflects an extreme male brain, indicated by males' reduced ability to show empathy and read facial expressions and gestures when compared with girls. In an attempt to improve these skills in 4- to 8-year-old boys with autism, Baron-Cohen and his colleagues (2007) showed the boys a number of animations on a DVD that put faces expressing different emotions on toy trains and tractor characters (see Figure 6.6). (See **www.thetransporters.com** for a look at a number of the facial expression animations in addition to the one shown in Figure 6.6.) After watching the animations 15 minutes every weekday for one month, the boys with autism were able to recognize real faces in different contexts the same way that children without autism could.

Children with autism benefit from a well-structured classroom, individualized instruction, and small-group instruction. Behavior modification techniques are sometimes effective in helping autistic children learn (Boutot & Myles, 2011; Kasari & Lawton, 2010). A recent research review concluded that when these behavior modifications are intensely provided and used early in the autistic child's life, they are more effective (Howlin, Magiati, & Charman, 2009).

# EMOTIONAL AND BEHAVIORAL DISORDERS

Most children have emotional problems sometime during their school years. A small percentage have problems so serious and persistent that they are classified as having an emotional or a behavioral disorder (Flick, 2011; Kauffman & Landrum, 2009).

**Emotional and behavioral disorders** consist of serious, persistent problems that involve relationships, aggression, depression, fears associated with personal or school matters, and other inappropriate socioemotional characteristics. Approximately 7 percent of children who have a disability and require an individualized education plan fall into this classification. Boys are three times as likely as girls to have these disorders (National Center for Education Statistics, 2003).

Various terms have been used to describe emotional and behavioral disorders, including *emotional disturbances, behavior disorders,* and *maladjusted children.* The term *emotional disturbance (ED)* recently has been used to describe children with these types of problems for whom it has been necessary to create individualized learning plans. However, critics argue that this category has not been clearly defined (Council for Exceptional Children, 1998).

FIGURE **6.6** A SCENE FROM THE DVD ANIMATIONS USED IN A STUDY BY BARON-COHEN AND OTHERS (2007)
*What did they do to improve autistic children's ability to read facial expressions?*
© Crown copyright MMVI, www.thetransporters.com, courtesy of Changing Media Development.

**Aggressive, Out-of-Control Behaviors** Some children classified as having a serious emotional disturbance engage in disruptive, aggressive, defiant, or dangerous behaviors and are removed from the classroom. These children are much more likely to be boys than girls and more likely to come from low-income than from middle- or high-income families (Dodge, Coie, & Lynam, 2006). When these children are returned to the regular classroom, both the regular classroom teacher and a special education teacher or consultant must spend a great deal of time helping them adapt and learn effectively.

In Chapter 3, we discussed rejected students and how to improve their social skills. Many of the comments and recommendations we made there apply to children with a serious emotional disturbance. In Chapter 7 and Chapter 14, we will discuss more strategies and plans for effectively dealing with children who show emotional and behavioral problems.

**Depression, Anxiety, and Fears** Some children turn their emotional problems inward, in which case their depression, anxiety, or fears may become so intense and persistent that their ability to learn is significantly compromised (Austin & Sciarra, 2010). All children feel depressed from time to time, but most get over their despondent, down mood in a few hours or a few days. For some children, however, the negative mood is more serious and longer lasting. *Depression* is a type of mood disorder in which the individual feels worthless, believes that things are not likely to get better, and behaves lethargically for a prolonged period of time. When children show these signs for two weeks or longer, they likely are experiencing depression. Having a poor appetite and not being able to sleep well also can be associated with depression.

Depression is much more likely to appear in adolescence than in childhood and has a much higher incidence in girls than in boys (Nolen-Hoeksema, 2011). Experts on depression say that this gender difference is likely due to a number of factors. Females tend to ruminate on their depressed mood and amplify it, whereas males tend to distract themselves from the negative mood; girls' self-images are often more negative than those of boys during adolescence; and societal bias against female achievement might be involved (Nolen-Hoeksema, 2011).

Because it is turned inward, depression is far more likely to go unnoticed than aggressive, acting-out behaviors. If you think that a child has become depressed, have the child meet with the school counselor (Kauffman & Landrum, 2009).

*Anxiety* involves a vague, highly unpleasant feeling of fear and apprehension. It is normal for children to be concerned or worried when they face life's challenges,

*What are some characteristics of students who show aggressive, out-of-control behaviors?*

**Thinking Back/Thinking Forward**

Rejected children are infrequently nominated as someone's best friend yet also actively disliked by their peers. Chapter 3, p. 83

Teachers can use effective strategies to deal with fighting, bullying, and hostility toward the teacher. Chapter 14, p. 135

**emotional and behavioral disorders** Serious, persistent problems that involve relationships, aggression, depression, fears associated with personal or school matters, and other inappropriate socioemotional characteristics.

# SELF-ASSESSMENT 6.1

## Evaluating My Experiences with People Who Have Various Disabilities and Disorders

Read each of these statements and place a check mark next to the ones that apply to you.

### 1. Learning Disabilities
_____ I know someone who has a learning disability and have talked with her or him about the disability.
_____ I have observed students with learning disabilities in the classroom and talked with teachers about their strategies for educating them.

### 2. Attention Deficit Hyperactivity Disorder
_____ I know someone with ADHD and have talked with him or her about the disability.
_____ I have observed students with ADHD in the classroom and talked with teachers about their strategies for educating them.

### 3. Mental Retardation
_____ I know someone who has mental retardation and have talked with her or his parents about their child's disability.
_____ I have observed students with mental retardation in the classroom and talked with their teachers about their strategies for educating them.

### 4. Physical Disorders
_____ I know someone with a physical disorder and have talked with him or her about the disability.
_____ I have observed students with physical disorders in the classroom and talked with their teachers about strategies for educating them.

### 5. Sensory Disorders
_____ I know someone with a sensory disorder and have talked with her or him about the disability.
_____ I have observed students with sensory disorders in the classroom and talked with their teachers about their strategies for educating them.

### 6. Speech and Language Disorders
_____ I know someone with a speech and language disorder and have talked with him or her about the disability.
_____ I have observed students with a speech and language disorder in the classroom and talked with their teacher about strategies for educating them.

### 7. Autism Spectrum Disorders
_____ I know someone with an autism spectrum disorder.
_____ I have observed students with an autism spectrum disorder in the classroom and talked with their teachers about strategies for educating them.

### 8. Emotional and Behavioral Disorders
_____ I know someone with an emotional and behavioral disorder and have talked with her or him about the disorder.
_____ I have observed students with emotional and behavioral disorders and talked with their teachers about strategies for educating them.

For those disabilities that you did not place a check mark beside, make it a point to get to know and talk with someone who has the disability and observe students with the disability in the classroom. Then talk with their teachers about their strategies for educating them.

DEVELOPMENT

**Thinking Back/Thinking Forward**

A number of programs have been developed to reduce students' high anxiety levels. Chapter 13, p. 466

but some children have such intense and prolonged anxiety that it substantially impairs their school performance (Rapee, Hudson, & Schniering, 2009). Some children also have personal or school-related fears that interfere with their learning. If a child shows marked or substantial fears that persist, have the child see the school counselor. More information about anxiety appears in Chapter 13.

At this point, we have explored many different disabilities and disorders. To evaluate your experiences with people who have these disabilities and disorders, complete Self-Assessment 6.1.

## Review, Reflect, and Practice

**1** Describe the various types of disabilities and disorders.

**REVIEW**

- What is the definition of a learning disability? What are some common learning disabilities? How are they identified? How are they best treated?
- What is attention deficit hyperactivity disorder? What are some important aspects of attention deficit hyperactivity disorder for teachers to know?
- What is the nature of mental retardation?
- What types of physical disorders in children are teachers likely to see?
- What are some common visual and hearing sensory disorders in children?
- What are the differences among articulation, voice, fluency, and language disorders? What characterizes autism spectrum disorders?
- What are the main types of emotional and behavioral disorders?

**REFLECT**

- Considering the age group of children and the subject that you plan to teach, which of the disabilities that we have discussed do you think will present the most difficulty for your teaching? Where should you focus your attention in learning more about this disability?

**PRAXIS™ PRACTICE**

1. Marty is in the fourth grade. Intelligence tests indicate that he is of average to above-average intelligence. However, his grades in reading, social studies, spelling, and science are very low. His math grades, on the other hand, are quite high and his writing skills are adequate. Achievement tests indicate that he reads at the first-grade level. When he reads aloud, it is apparent that he has difficulty matching sounds and letters. Marty most likely has
   a. ADHD.
   b. dyscalculia.
   c. dyslexia.
   d. dysgraphia.

2. Which of the following classroom environments is most likely to help students with ADHD learn?
   a. Ms. Caster's class, which is very loosely structured so that students will only have to attend to something for a short period of time
   b. Ms. Dodge's class, which is tightly structured and has explicit expectations, with student learning often supplemented by computer games and physical activity
   c. Ms. Ebert's class, in which students are expected to sit still for extended periods of time, working independently on seatwork
   d. Ms. Fish's class, in which students work at their own pace on self-selected tasks and receive sporadic feedback regarding their progress and behavior

3. Marci is a White non-Latino with mild mental retardation. In addition to cognitive deficits, she has poor motor skills. Her legs and arms are shorter than average. She has a round face, with an extra fold of skin over her eyelids. Her tongue protrudes. What is most likely the cause of Marci's mental retardation?
   a. Down syndrome
   b. fetal alcohol spectrum disorders
   c. fragile X syndrome
   d. maternal illness during pregnancy

*(continued)*

## Review, Reflect, and Practice

### PRAXIS™ PRACTICE (CONTINUED)

4. Mark is a middle school student in Ms. Walsh's language-arts class. Ms. Walsh observes that Mark often stares out the window. Sometimes calling his name redirects his attention to her; other times he continues to stare out the window for several seconds and appears oblivious to her reprimands. Mark's grades are suffering as a result of his inattention. What is the most likely explanation for Mark's inattention?
   a. ADHD
   b. absence seizure disorder
   c. tonic-clonic epilepsy
   d. cerebral palsy

5. Amiel's first-grade teacher notices that he squints a lot and holds books close to his face. Amiel most likely has which of the following disorders?
   a. physical disorder
   b. speech and language disorder
   c. sensory disorder
   d. autism spectrum disorder

6. Carrie's third-grade teacher, Ms. Brown, often gets frustrated when Carrie tries to answer questions in class. Carrie takes a long time to answer. Her sentence structure is not as good as that of other students in her class, and she often presents ideas in what sounds like a random manner. Ms. Brown should suspect that Carrie has
   a. articulation disorder.
   b. expressive language disorder.
   c. receptive language disorder.
   d. specific language impairment.

7. Mike is a seventh-grade boy of above-average intelligence. He has good language skills but does not interact well with other young adolescents. He has one friend and responds well to his mother and to the aide who works with him, although he shies away from contact with other people. He does fairly well in school as long as his routine is not disrupted. He especially enjoys math and anything to do with numbers. He has memorized the batting averages of the starting line-up of all major league baseball teams. Mike most likely has
   a. autistic disorder.
   b. Asperger syndrome.
   c. behavioral disorder.
   d. specific language disorder.

8. Which middle school student is at greatest risk of developing a serious emotional disturbance?
   a. Jill, the most popular girl in the seventh grade, who sometimes says demeaning things to less popular girls
   b. Kevin, an eighth-grader who gets good grades in most subjects, has difficulty interacting with classmates, and has memorized all of Shakespeare's sonnets
   c. Harriet, a sixth-grade girl whose ADHD symptoms are controlled well by medication
   d. Mark, a seventh-grade boy who gets poor grades in many classes and frequently acts out in angry, violent ways

*Please see the answer key at the end of the book.*

## ② EDUCATIONAL ISSUES INVOLVING CHILDREN WITH DISABILITIES

Legal Aspects    Technology

Public schools are legally required to serve all children with disabilities in the least restrictive environment possible. We will explore the legal aspects of working with children who have a disability and examine the role of technology in educating children with a disability.

## LEGAL ASPECTS

Beginning in the mid-1960s to mid-1970s, legislatures, the federal courts, and the U.S. Congress laid down special educational rights for children with disabilities. Prior to that time, most children with disabilities were either refused enrollment or inadequately served by schools. In 1975 Congress enacted **Public Law 94-142,** the Education for All Handicapped Children Act, which required that all students with disabilities be given a free, appropriate public education and which provided the funding to help implement this education.

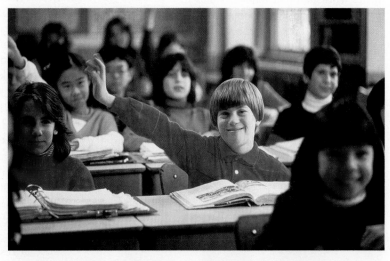

Increasingly, children with disabilities are being taught in the regular classroom, as is this child with mild mental retardation. *What are some legal aspects of educating children with disabilities?*

**Individuals with Disabilities Education Act (IDEA)** In 1990 Public Law 94-142 was recast as the **Individuals with Disabilities Education Act (IDEA).** IDEA was amended in 1997 and then reauthorized in 2004 and renamed the Individuals with Disabilities Education Improvement Act. IDEA spells out broad mandates for services to all children with disabilities (Friend, 2011). These include evaluation and eligibility determination, appropriate education and an *individualized education plan (IEP)* (discussed shortly), and education in the least restrictive environment (LRE) (Smith & Tyler, 2010; Taylor, Smiley, & Richards, 2009).

Children who are thought to have a disability are evaluated to determine their eligibility for services under IDEA. Schools are prohibited from planning special education programs in advance and offering them on a space-available basis. In other words, schools must provide appropriate education services to all children who are determined to need them (Friend, 2011).

Children must be evaluated and diagnosed with a disability before a school can begin providing special education services. However, because an assessment can take a long time, variations of prereferral interventions are in place in many schools. Parents must be invited to participate in the evaluation process. Reevaluation is required at least every three years (sometimes every year), when requested by parents, or when conditions suggest a reevaluation is needed. A parent who disagrees with the school's evaluation can obtain an independent evaluation, which the school is required to consider in providing special education services. If the evaluation finds that child has a disability and requires special services, the school must provide the child with appropriate services.

IDEA requires that students with disabilities have an **individualized education plan (IEP),** which is a written statement that spells out a program specifically tailored for the student with a disability. In general, the IEP should be (1) related to the child's learning capacity, (2) specially constructed to meet the child's individual needs and not merely copying what is offered to other children, and (3) designed to provide educational benefits.

**Public Law 94-142** The Education for All Handicapped Children Act, which required that all students with disabilities be given a free, appropriate public education and which provided the funding to help implement this education.

**Individuals with Disabilities Education Act (IDEA)** This act spells out broad mandates for services to all children with disabilities, including evaluation and determination of eligibility, appropriate education and an individualized education plan (IEP), and education in the least restrictive environment (LRE).

**individualized education plan (IEP)** A written statement that spells out a program specifically tailored for the student with a disability.

IDEA has many other specific provisions that relate to the parents of a child with a disability (Carter, Prater, & Dyches, 2009). These include requirements that schools send notices to parents of proposed actions, that parents be allowed to attend meetings regarding the child's placement or IEP, and that parents have the right to appeal school decisions to an impartial evaluator.

Amendments were made to IDEA in 1997. Two of these involve positive behavioral support and functional behavioral assessment.

*Positive behavioral support* focuses on culturally appropriate application of positive behavioral interventions to attain important behavior changes in children. "Culturally appropriate" refers to considering the unique and individualized learning histories of children (social, community, historical, gender, and so on). Positive behavioral support especially emphasizes supporting desirable behaviors rather than punishing undesirable behaviors in working with children with a disability or disorder.

*Functional behavioral assessment* involves determining the consequences (what purpose the behavior serves), antecedents (what triggers the behavior), and setting events (in which contexts the behavior occurs) (Heller & others, 2009). Functional behavioral assessment emphasizes understanding behavior in the context in which it is observed and guiding positive behavioral interventions that are relevant and effective.

A major aspect of the 2004 reauthorization of IDEA involved aligning it with the government's No Child Left Behind (NCLB) legislation, which was designed to improve the educational achievement of all students, including those with disabilities (Turnbull, Huerta, & Stowe, 2009). Both IDEA and NCLB mandate that most students with disabilities be included in general assessments of educational progress. This alignment includes requiring most students with disabilities "to take standard tests of academic achievement and to achieve at a level equal to that of students without disabilities. Whether this expectation is reasonable is an open question" (Hallahan & Kauffman, 2006, pp. 28–29). Alternative assessments for students with disabilities and funding to help states improve instruction, assessment, and accountability for educating students with disabilities are included in the 2004 reauthorization of IDEA.

**Least Restrictive Environment (LRE)** Under IDEA, the child with a disability must be educated in the **least restrictive environment (LRE).** This means a setting as similar as possible to the one in which children who do not have a disability are educated. And schools must make an effort to educate children with a disability in the regular classroom. The term **inclusion** means educating a child with special educational needs full-time in the regular classroom (Valle & Connor, 2011). Figure 6.7 indicates that in a recent school year slightly more than 50 percent of U.S. students with a disability spent more than 80 percent of their school day in a general classroom.

What is least restrictive likely depends to some degree on the child's disability (Carter, Prater, & Dyches, 2009). Some children with a learning disability or a speech impairment can be educated in the regular classroom, but children with severe hearing or vision impairments may need to be educated in separate classes or schools (Turnbull, Huerta, & Stowe, 2009).

In the last two decades, *collaborative teaming* has been increasingly advocated in educating children with disabilities (Hallahan, Kauffman, & Pullen, 2009). Here people with diverse expertise interact to provide services for children. Researchers have found that collaborative teaming often results in gains for children, as well as improved skills and attitudes for teachers (Snell & Janney, 2005).

**Thinking Back/Thinking Forward**

No Child Left Behind is the federal government's legislation that requires states to test students annually in various subjects. Chapter 1, p. 8; Chapter 15, p. 524

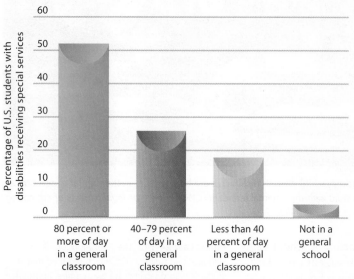

**FIGURE 6.7** PERCENTAGE OF U.S. STUDENTS WITH DISABILITIES 6 TO 21 YEARS OF AGE RECEIVING SPECIAL SERVICES IN THE GENERAL CLASSROOM

*Note:* Data for 2004–2005 school year; National Center for Education Statistics (2007).

**least restrictive environment (LRE)** A setting that is as similar as possible to the one in which children who do not have a disability are educated.

**inclusion** Educating children with special education needs full-time in the regular classroom.

Ideally, collaborative teaming encourages shared responsibility in planning and decision making. It also enables educators with diverse expertise to construct effective alternatives to traditional educational approaches. When collaborative teaming is used, many children remain in the regular classroom, and the regular classroom teacher is actively involved in planning the child's education.

Many legal changes regarding children with disabilities have been extremely positive (Rosenberg, Westling, & McLesky, 2011). Compared with several decades ago, far more children today are receiving competent, specialized services. For many children, inclusion in the regular classroom, with modifications or supplemental services, is appropriate (Friend, 2008). However, some leading experts on special education argue that the effort to use inclusion to educate children with disabilities has become too extreme in some cases. For example, James Kauffman and his colleagues (Kauffman & Hallahan, 2005; Kauffman, McGee, and Brigham, 2004) state that inclusion too often has meant making accommodations in the regular classroom that do not always benefit these children with disabilities. They advocate a more individualized approach that may not always involve full inclusion but rather allows for options such as special education outside the regular classroom. Kauffman and his colleagues (2004, p. 620) acknowledge that children with disabilities "*do* need the services of specially trained professionals to achieve their full potential. They *do* sometimes need altered curricula or adaptations to make their learning possible." However, "we sell students with disabilities short when we pretend that they are not different from typical students. We make the same error when we pretend that they must *not* be expected to put forth extra effort if they are to learn to do some things—or learn to do something in a different way." Like general education, an important aspect of special education should be to challenge students with disabilities "to become all they can be."

One concern about special education involves disproportionate representation of students from minority backgrounds in special education programs and classes. The U.S. Department of Education (2000) has three concerns about the overrepresentation of minority students in special education programs and classes: (1) students may be unserved or receive services that do not meet their needs, (2) students may be misclassified or inappropriately labeled, and (3) placement in special education classes may be a form of discrimination.

African American students are overrepresented in special education—15 percent of the U.S. student population is African American, but 20 percent of special education students are African American (National Center for Education Statistics, 2008). In some disabilities, the discrepancies are even greater. For example, African American students represent 32 percent of the students in programs for mild mental retardation, 29 percent in programs for moderate mental retardation, and 24 percent in programs for serious emotional disturbance.

However, it is not just a simple matter of overrepresentation of certain minority groups in special education. Latino children may be underidentified in the categories of mental retardation and emotional disturbance.

More appropriate inclusion of minority students in special education is a complex problem and requires the creation of a successful school experience for all students (Skidmore, 2009). Recommendations for reducing disproportionate representation in special education include the following (Burnette, 1998):

- Reviewing school practices to identify and address factors that might contribute to school difficulties
- Forming policy-making groups that include community members and promote partnerships with service agencies and cultural organizations
- Helping families obtain social, medical, mental health, and other support services
- Training more teachers from minority backgrounds and providing all teachers with more extensive course work and training in educating children with disabilities and diversity issues

Eighteen-year-old Chandra "Peaches" Allen was born without arms. Despite this disability, she has learned to write, eat, type, paint, and draw with her feet. She can even put on earrings. She is well-known for her artistic skills. She has won three grand-prize awards for her art in various shows. She is getting ready to enter college and plans to pursue a career in art and physical therapy. Chandra Allen's accomplishments reflect remarkable adaptation and coping. She is an excellent example of how adolescents can conquer a disability and pursue meaningful goals.

DIVERSITY

## TEACHING CONNECTIONS: Best Practices
### Strategies for Working with Children with Disabilities as a Regular Classroom Teacher

1. *Carry out each student's individualized education plan (IEP).* Work closely with a special educator to know and understand the needs of each of your students with disabilities.

2. *Encourage your school to provide increased support and training in how to teach students with disabilities.* In Through the Eyes of Teachers, Michelle Evans, a sixth-grade teacher, describes her relationship with resource personnel and some strategies that worked for her students.

### THROUGH THE EYES OF TEACHERS
#### Strategies for Working with Children Who Have a Disability

Support and resource personnel are invaluable. Communication with parents, student, and with anyone involved is essential. Make certain that you communicate with your entire class, too. . . . Because I want each student to feel successful, I create different levels of mastery or participation in learning objectives.

One student with cerebral palsy had difficulty standing, mental impairments, and other problems. She had little and often no short-term memory. As we sat together and talked, I found that her strength was that she loved to copy words, stories, and other things. Her hands were weak, but writing helped them. Her parents wanted her to do anything she could. By capitalizing on her fondness for copying and writing, she eventually learned math facts and spelling words. I assigned a poem about having a positive attitude as a memorization for everyone in the class. A few kids complained that the poem would be too hard to memorize when I presented it. She copied that poem so many times that three days after the assignment she stood and delivered it flawlessly to the class. I could see the complainers melt away as we all realized that she was the first to recite the poem. Her parents came to witness her accomplishment. There wasn't a dry eye in the room by the time she finished. She taught us a great deal.

3. *Become more knowledgeable about the types of disabilities students in your classroom have.* Read education journals, such as *Exceptional Children, Teaching Exceptional Children,* and *Journal of Learning Disabilities,* to keep up-to-date on the latest information about these children. Look into taking a class at a college or university or a continuing education course on topics such as exceptional children, mental retardation, learning disabilities, and emotional and behavioral disorders.

4. *Be cautious about labeling students with a disability.* It is easy to fall into the trap of using the label as an explanation of the child's learning difficulties. For example, a teacher might say, "Well, Larry has trouble with reading because he has a learning disability," when, in fact, the reason Larry is having trouble with reading is unknown or not yet identified. Also, labels have a way of remaining after the child has improved considerably. Remember that terms such as *mental retardation* and *learning disability* are descriptive labels for disorders, not for children. Always think of children with disabilities in terms of what the best conditions are for improving their learning and how they can be helped to make progress rather than in terms of unchanging labels.

5. *Remember that students with disabilities benefit from many of the same teaching strategies that benefit students without disabilities, and vice versa.* These include being caring, accepting, and patient; having positive expectations for learning; helping children with their social and communication skills as well as academic skills; and challenging children with disabilities to reach their full potential.

6. *Use person-first language.* Say "student with autism," not "autistic student." While it may seem like a little thing, it helps us to remember that people with disabilities are people first, their disabilities are a part of them, but do not define them.

7. *Help students without a disability to understand and accept children with a disability.* Provide children without a disability information about children with a disability and create opportunities for them to interact with each other in positive ways. *Peer tutoring* and *cooperative learning* activities can be used to encourage positive interaction between children without a disability and children with a disability (Fuchs, Fuchs, & Burish, 2000). We will discuss these activities further in Chapter 10.

TECHNOLOGY

## TECHNOLOGY

The Individuals with Disabilities Education Act (IDEA), including its 1997 amendments, requires that technology devices and services be provided to students with disabilities if they are necessary to ensure a free, appropriate education (Ulman, 2005).

Two types of technology that can be used to improve the education of students with disabilities are instructional technology and assistive technology (Blackhurst, 1997). *Instructional technology* includes various types of hardware and software combined with innovative teaching methods to accommodate students' learning needs in the classroom. Examples include videotapes, computer-assisted instruction, and complex hypermedia programs in which computers are used to control the display of audio and visual images stored on videodisc.

*Assistive technology* consists of various services and devices designed to help students with disabilities function within their environment. Examples include communication aids, alternative computer keyboards, and adaptive switches. To locate such services, educators can use computer databases such as the Device Locator System (Academic Software, 1996).

Special input devices can help students with physical disabilities use computers more effectively. Many students with physical disabilities such as cerebral palsy cannot use a conventional keyboard and mouse but can use alternative keyboards effectively.

## Review, Reflect, and Practice

**2** Explain the legal framework and technology advances for children with disabilities.

### REVIEW

- What is IDEA? How is it related to IEPs and LREs? What is the current thinking about inclusion?
- What is the difference between instructional and assistive technology?

### REFLECT

- What do you think will present the greatest challenges to you in teaching children with a disability?

### PRAXIS™ PRACTICE

1. Jenny has a moderate learning disability. She is educated in the special education classroom of her school, as she has been for the past two years. She and her classmates eat lunch in the resource room as well. Each of the students in the resource room works on different things, due to their very different abilities and disabilities. This placement was made because the regular education teachers in Jenny's school do not have the necessary skills to teach Jenny. Therefore, she was placed in the resource room with the school's sole special educator. What is the legal issue with this placement?
   a. Jenny's IEP does not specify a diagnosis.
   b. Jenny is not being educated in the least restrictive environment.
   c. Jenny's placement needs to be reconsidered at least every six months.
   d. The functional behavior assessment did not consider the use of technology.

2. Azel has cerebral palsy. His teacher has found an alternative computer keyboard to facilitate his learning. What type of technology is the teacher using?
   a. instructional technology
   b. computer-assisted instruction
   c. assistive technology
   d. complex hypermedia

*Please see the answer key at the end of the book.*

## 3 CHILDREN WHO ARE GIFTED

| Characteristics | Nature/Nurture, Developmental Changes, and Domain-Specific Giftedness | Educating Children Who Are Gifted |

**Thinking Back/Thinking Forward**

Robert J. Sternberg argues that creative thinking should be considered a different form of intelligence than the intelligence measured by traditional standardized tests of intelligence. Chapter 4, p. 115; Chapter 9, p. 310

At 2 years of age, art prodigy Alexandra Nechita colored in coloring books for hours and took up pen and ink. She had no interest in dolls or friends. By age 5 she was using watercolors. Once she started school, she would start painting as soon as she got home. At the age of 8, in 1994, she saw the first public exhibit of her work. In succeeding years, working quickly and impulsively on canvases as large as 5 feet by 9 feet, she has completed hundreds of paintings, some of which sell for close to $100,000 apiece. As a teenager, she continues to paint—relentlessly and passionately. It is, she says, what she loves to do. *What are some characteristics of children who are gifted?*

**children who are gifted** Children with above-average intelligence (usually defined as an IQ of 130 or higher) and/or superior talent in some domain such as art, music, or mathematics.

The final type of exceptionality we will discuss is quite different from the disabilities and disorders that we have described so far. **Children who are gifted** have above-average intelligence (usually defined as an IQ of 130 or higher) and/or superior talent in some domain such as art, music, or mathematics. Admissions standards for children who are gifted in schools are typically based on intelligence and academic aptitude, although there is increasing call to widen the criteria to include such factors as creativity and commitment (Horowitz, 2009; Winner, 2009). The U.S. government has described five areas of giftedness: intellectual, academic, creative, visual and performing arts, and leadership.

Some critics argue that too many children in "gifted programs" aren't really gifted in a particular area but are just somewhat bright, usually cooperative, and, usually, non-Latino White (Kaufman & Sternberg, 2008). They say the mantle of brilliance is cast on many children who are not that far from simply being "smart normal."

Although general intelligence as defined by an overall IQ score still remains as a key criterion in many states' decision of whether a child should be placed in a gifted program, changing conceptions of intelligence increasingly include ideas such as Gardner's multiple intelligences, and placement criteria are likely to move away from an IQ criterion in the future (Miller, 2008).

## CHARACTERISTICS

Ellen Winner (1996), an expert on creativity and giftedness, described three criteria that characterize children who are gifted:

1. *Precocity.* Children who are gifted are precocious when given the opportunity to use their gift or talent. They begin to master an area earlier than their peers. Learning in their domain is more effortless for them than for children who are not gifted. In most instances, children who are gifted are precocious because they have an inborn high ability in a particular domain or domains, although this inborn precocity has to be identified and nourished.

2. *Marching to their own drummer.* Children who are gifted learn in a qualitatively different way than children who are not gifted. One way they march to a different drummer is that they require less support, or *scaffolding* (discussed in Chapter 2), from adults to learn than their nongifted peers do. Often they resist explicit instruction. They also often make discoveries on their own and solve problems in unique ways within their area of giftedness. They can be normal or below normal in other areas.

3. *A passion to master.* Children who are gifted are driven to understand the domain in which they have high ability. They display an intense, obsessive interest and an ability to focus. They are not children who need to be pushed by their parents. They frequently have a high degree of internal motivation.

A fourth area in which children who are gifted excel involves information-processing skills. Researchers have found that children who are gifted learn at a faster pace, process information more rapidly, are better at reasoning, use better strategies, and monitor their understanding better than their nongifted counterparts (Davidson & Davidson, 2004).

## NATURE-NURTURE ISSUE, DEVELOPMENTAL CHANGES, AND DOMAIN-SPECIFIC GIFTEDNESS

Three important issues emerge in the education of children who are gifted: (1) What roles do nature and nurture play in giftedness? (2) What characterizes developmental changes in giftedness? (3) To what extent is giftedness domain-specific?

**Nature-Nurture Issue**   Is giftedness a product of heredity or environment (nature-nurture issue)? Likely both (Sternberg, 2009d). Individuals who are gifted recall that they had signs of high ability in a particular area at a very young age, prior to or at the beginning of formal training (Howe & others, 1995). This suggests the importance of innate ability in giftedness. However, researchers have also found that individuals with world-class status in the arts, mathematics, science, and sports all report strong family support and years of training and practice (Bloom, 1985). Deliberate practice is an important characteristic of individuals who become experts in a particular domain. For example, in one study, the best musicians engaged in twice as much deliberate practice over their lives as did the least successful ones (Ericsson, Krampe, & Tesch, 1993).

RESEARCH

**Developmental Changes and Domain-Specific Giftedness**   Do children who are gifted become gifted and highly creative adults? In Lewis Terman's (1925) classic research on children with superior IQs (average IQ = 150 in the Terman research), the children typically became experts in a well-established domain, such as medicine, law, or business. However, most did not become major creators (Winner, 2000). That is, they did not create a new domain or revolutionize an old domain.

One reason that some children who are gifted do not become gifted adults is that they have been pushed too hard by overzealous parents (Thomas, Ray, & Moon, 2007). As a result, they lose their intrinsic (internal) motivation (Winner, 1996, 2006). However, as we will discuss later, many children who are gifted have not been adequately challenged in school to develop their talent.

Research on giftedness is increasingly focused on domain-specific developmental trajectories (Liben, 2009; Matthews, 2009). During the childhood years, the child who is to become a gifted artist or the child who is to become a gifted mathematician begins to show expertise in that domain. However, individuals who are highly gifted are typically not gifted in many domains. Software genius Bill Gates (1998), the founder of Microsoft and one of the world's richest persons, for example, commented that sometimes you have to be careful when you are good at something to resist the urge to think that you will be good at everything. Gates says that because he has been so successful at software development, people expect him to be brilliant in other domains about which he is far from being a genius.

DEVELOPMENT

During adolescence, individuals who are talented become less reliant on parental support and increasingly pursue their own interests. Therefore, it is important to identify an individual's domain-specific talent and provide appropriate and optional educational opportunities by adolescence (Keating, 2009).

## EDUCATING CHILDREN WHO ARE GIFTED

Increasingly, experts argue that the education of children who are gifted in the United States requires a significant overhaul (Davis, Rimm, & Siegle, 2011; Sternberg, Jarvin, & Grigorenko, 2011; Winner, 2009). Underchallenged children who are gifted can become disruptive, skip classes, and lose interest in achieving. Sometimes these children just disappear into the woodwork, becoming passive and apathetic toward school (Moon, 2008). Teachers must challenge children who are gifted to reach high expectations (Webb & others, 2007).

Four program options for children who are gifted follow (Hertzog, 1998):

- *Special classes.* Historically, this has been the common way to educate children who are gifted. The special classes during the regular school day are called "pullout" programs. Some special classes also are held after school, on Saturdays, or in the summer.
- *Acceleration and enrichment in the regular classroom setting.* This could include early admission to kindergarten, grade skipping (also known as double promotion), telescoping (completing two grades in one year), advanced placement, subject-matter acceleration, and self-paced instruction (Cloud, 2007). *Curriculum compacting* is a variation of acceleration in which teachers skip over aspects of the curriculum that they believe children who are gifted do not need.
- *Mentor and apprenticeship programs.* These are important, underutilized ways to motivate, challenge, and effectively educate children who are gifted.
- *Work/study and/or community-service programs.* Educational reform has brought into the regular classroom many strategies that once were the domain of separate gifted programs. These include an emphasis on problem-based learning, having children do projects, creating portfolios, and critical thinking. Combined with the increasing emphasis on educating all children in the regular classroom, many schools now try to challenge and motivate children who are gifted in the regular classroom. Some schools also include after-school or Saturday programs or develop mentor apprenticeship, work/study, or community-service programs. Thus, an array of in-school and out-of-school opportunities is provided.

The Schoolwide Enrichment Model (SEM), developed by Joseph Renzulli (1998), is a program for children who are gifted that focuses on total school improvement. Renzulli says that when enrichment has a school-wide emphasis, positive outcomes are likely to occur, not only for children who are gifted but also for children who are not gifted and for classroom and resource teachers. When school-wide enrichment is emphasized, "us" versus "them" barriers often decrease, and classroom teachers are more willing to use *curriculum compacting* with the children who are most gifted. Instead of feeling isolated, resource teachers begin to feel more like members of a team, especially when they work with regular classroom teachers on enriching the entire classroom. Thus, important goals of SEM are to improve outcomes for both students who are gifted and those who are not gifted and to improve the contributions and relationships of classroom and resource teachers.

A number of experts argue that too often children who are gifted are socially isolated and underchallenged in the classroom (Davis, Rimm, & Siegle, 2011; Robinson, 2008; Winner, 2009). It is not unusual for them to be ostracized and labeled "nerds" or "geeks." A child who is truly gifted often is the only such child in the room and thus does not have the opportunity to learn with students of like ability. Many eminent adults report that school was a negative experience for them, that they were bored and sometimes knew more than their teachers (Bloom, 1985). Winner (2006) points out that American education will benefit when standards are raised for all children. When some children are still underchallenged, she recommends that they be allowed to

## THROUGH THE EYES OF STUDENTS

## Children Who Are Gifted Speak

James Delisle (1987) interviewed hundreds of elementary school children who are gifted. Here are some of their comments.

*In response to: Describe Your Typical School Day*

Oh what a bore to sit and listen,
To stuff we already know.
Do everything we've done and done again,
But we must still sit and listen.
Over and over read one more page
Oh bore, oh bore, oh bore.

Girl, Age 9, New York

I sit there pretending to be reading along when I'm really six pages ahead. When I understand something and half the class doesn't, I have to sit there and listen.

Girl, Age 10, Connecticut

*In response to: What Makes a Teacher a Gifted Teacher?*

She is capable of handling our problems and has a good imagination to help us learn.

Girl, Age 10, Louisiana

Will challenge you and let the sky be your limit.

Boy, Age 11, Michigan

Opens your mind to help you with your life.

Boy, Age 11, New Jersey

attend advanced classes in their domain of exceptional ability, such as allowing some especially precocious middle school students to take college classes in their area of expertise. For example, Bill Gates, founder of Microsoft, took college math classes and hacked a computer security system at age 13; Yo-Yo Ma, famous cellist, graduated from high school at 15 to attend Juilliard School of Music in New York City.

Some educators conclude that the inadequate education of children who are gifted has been compounded by the federal government's NCLB policy that seeks to raise the achievement level of students who are not doing well in school at the expense of enriching the education of children who are gifted (Clark, 2008). In the era of the NCLB policy, some individuals concerned about the neglect of students who are gifted argue that schools spend far more time identifying students' deficiencies than cultivating students' talents (Cloud, 2007). For example, U.S. schools spend approximately $8 billion a year educating students who are mentally retarded and only $800 million educating students who are gifted. In many cases, say the critics, U.S. education squanders the potential contributions of America's most talented young minds (Cloud, 2007).

I recently asked teachers how they work with students who are gifted. Following are their responses.

**EARLY CHILDHOOD**   Our preschoolers who are considered gifted are given more challenging projects to complete and given more responsibilities throughout the day. Parents are also contacted and given strategies and suggestions about extracurricular activities that will stimulate their child's strengths.

—**MISSY DANGLER,** *Suburban Hills School*

**ELEMENTARY SCHOOL: GRADES K–5**   When working with students who are gifted, it is important to remember that they don't need *more* work, but they do need work that will challenge them. Also, no matter how gifted students are, their work needs to always be checked to make sure that they haven't misunderstood something.

—**ESTHER LINDBLOOM,** *Cooper Mountain Elementary School*

**MIDDLE SCHOOL: GRADES 6–8**   It is important that you not bore students who are gifted in your classroom. For example, if children who are gifted are learning about the causes and effects of the Civil War, and they already know the information being covered, I would have them apply what they already know by having them create a journal about someone who lived during that time period.

—**CASEY MAASS,** *Edison Middle School*

**HIGH SCHOOL: GRADES 9–12**   Students who are gifted have a unique set of issues. They need to be challenged at a higher level, but they also need to accept the fact that other students who are not as gifted as they are also have worth. My homeroom is a prime example. Among the 18 students I have, one is the number-one student who never found a math or science problem that he couldn't solve; one is learning disabled with a seizure disorder; and three students have missed school time for jail.

In the three years that we have been together, we have worked on respecting differences in each other and on teamwork activities, and have won homeroom competitions. Relationships are key in getting students of all abilities to work together and feel part of a school or classroom community. Teachers need to build trust in order for this to happen.

—**SANDY SWANSON,** *Menomonee Falls High School*

# TEACHING CONNECTIONS: Best Practices
## Strategies for Working with Children Who Are Gifted

Here are some recommended strategies for working with children who are gifted:

1. *Identification: How do you know if a student is gifted?* Traditional single-measure evaluations of potential have given way to broader-spectrum identification procedures that include nominations by parents, peers, and community members, as well as teachers. While intelligence and achievement tests may be part of the identification process, they should not be the only means by which gifted students are identified. Not all gifted students earn good grades; not all are well-behaved. In fact, because of boredom, many earn poor marks and become disruptive in class. Some gifted students also have learning disabilities.

2. *Remember that giftedness is often domain-specific.* Don't expect a student to be gifted across most domains. While some students are gifted across many domains, others have narrower areas of special aptitude or talent.

3. *Remember that gifted students often learn material faster and retain more than other students.* This means that a gifted student whose needs are being met is likely to progress more than one grade level in an academic year.

4. *Think in terms of student readiness rather than ability.* As discussed in Chapter 2, students are ready to learn material at different times. Gifted students are often ready earlier than their non-gifted classmates. Consider Alex's readiness in the case at the end of the chapter.

5. *Provide your gifted students with challenges based on their readiness.* This can be done by differentiating instruction in a number of ways, among them curriculum compacting, tiered assignments, learning contracts, and independent study (Tomlinson, 2001). Parents should be involved in decisions regarding how to meet the needs of their gifted children, just as they are in the creation of IEPs for students with disabilities.

   One example of such differentiation would be for students to all be studying a particular unit in science, say the solar system. While the majority of students read material written at-grade-level, students gifted in science and reading might read material intended for students at a much higher grade level, even the college level, perhaps. To read about some ways talented teacher Margaret (Peg) Cagle accomplishes this, see *Through the Eyes of Teachers*.

## THROUGH THE EYES OF TEACHERS
### Passionate About Teaching Math to Students Who Are Gifted

Margaret (Peg) Cagle teaches gifted seventh- and eighth-grade math students at Lawrence Middle School in Chatsworth, California. She especially advocates challenging students who are gifted to take intellectual risks. To encourage collaboration, she often has students work together in groups of four, and frequently tutors students during lunch hour. As 13-year-old Madeline Lewis commented, "If I don't get it one way, she'll explain it another and talk to you about it and show you until you do get it." Peg says it is important to be passionate about teaching math and open up a world for students that shows them how beautiful learning math can be. (*Source:* Wong Briggs, 2007, p. 6D)

Margaret (Peg) Cagle with some of the gifted seventh- and eighth-grade math students she teaches at Lawrence Middle School in Chatsworth, California.

6. *Understand that for some students acceleration is the only viable option.* For young students with broad spectrum high abilities, this may mean skipping a grade or joining the class above for particular content area instruction. For middle-school students, it may mean taking some courses at the high school, and for high school students, it may mean taking college courses in order to be adequately challenged. Contrary to popular myth, acceleration does not often have negative results (Colangelo, Assouline, & Gross, 2004). Again, parents should be involved in this decision.

## TEACHING CONNECTIONS: Best Practices
### Strategies for Working with Children Who Are Gifted

7. *Continue to assess the students' readiness for advanced material.* Grouping should be flexible so that if a student no longer shows readiness for advanced work he/she can rejoin classmates who are functioning at grade level. Conversely, if a child shows readiness for advanced work in a different area, the opportunity for further advancement should be available.

8. *Learn about and use resources for students who are gifted.* Among these are National Research Center on Gifted and Talented Education at the University of Connecticut and the Belin-Blank Center at the University

of Iowa; *Gifted Child Quarterly* and *Gifted Child Today* journals; books on children who are gifted: The National Association for Gifted Children; *Genius Denied* by Jan Davidson and Bob Davidson (2004); *A Nation Deceived* by Nicholas Colangelo, Susan Assouline, and Miraca Gross (2004); and *Handbook of Gifted Education,* third edition, by Nicholas Colangelo and Gary Davis (2003).

9. *Consult the Pre-K–12 Gifted Program Standards (NAGC, 2000) to determine if your school is in alignment with standards for meeting the needs of gifted students.* **http://www.nagc.org/index.aspx?id=546**

## Review, Reflect, and Practice

**3** Define what gifted means and discuss some approaches to teaching children who are gifted.

### REVIEW

- What is the definition of being gifted? What are some criticisms of gifted programs? What characteristics does Winner ascribe to children who are gifted?
- What roles do nature-nurture, developmental changes, and domain specificity play in giftedness?
- What are some options for educating students who are gifted?

### REFLECT

- Suppose that you had several students in your class who were strikingly gifted. Might this lead to problems? Explain. What might you do to prevent such problems from developing?

### PRAXIS™ PRACTICE

1. Ms. Larson has a student in her kindergarten class who continuously surprises her. He requested that she allow him to play with a puzzle of the United States that no children had played with in years. She observed him expertly put each state in place, saying its name as he did so. Soon he was teaching the other students in the class each state's name, its capitol, and where it belonged in the puzzle. On a recent trip to the school learning center, he asked to check out a book of international flags that was written at an eighth-grade level. Her first instinct was to deny his request, but instead she asked him about the book. He told her "I know I can't read *all* of it, but I can read the names of the countries, and I want to learn more flags. See how many I already know?" He then flipped through the book, correctly identifying most of the flags. Which characteristics of giftedness is this student showing?
   a. numerical ability, highly developed social skills, and precocity
   b. verbal ability, intensity, and a passion to master

*(continued)*

## Review, Reflect, and Practice

**PRAXIS™ PRACTICE (CONTINUED)**

   c. high reading level, marching to his own drummer, and stubbornness

   d. precocity, marching to his own drummer, and a passion to master

2. Roberto is gifted in math but not in social studies and English. These characteristics of Roberto's giftedness are best described as

   a. due more to nature than nurture

   b. domain-specific

   c. reflecting deliberate practice

   d. domain-general

3. The kindergarten student in Ms. Larson's class (item 1) continued to progress in school. In fourth grade, he finished third in his K–8 school's geography bee. He finished first the next two years. In seventh grade he finally took his first course in geography. He received C's. He often complained to his parents that he already knew the material being taught, that he wanted to learn "new stuff, not just listen to the same old junk." His teacher put a great deal of emphasis on completing map worksheets, which he completed very quickly and sloppily. He often became disruptive in class. How should the geography teacher handle this situation?

   a. The teacher should punish the student for disrupting class. The student should continue to do the same assignments as the other students, because he needs to understand that not all work is fun.

   b. The teacher should consider curriculum compacting, because the student has already mastered the course content. Once challenged, his disruptive behavior is likely to diminish.

   c. The teacher should ask this student to become a co-teacher.

   d. The teacher should use the student's sloppy work as a negative example to the rest of the class.

*Please see the answer key at the end of the book.*

## Now What?

Before the school year starts, Ms. Inez always holds a "get acquainted meeting" with the parents of her incoming kindergartners. She does this so that she can explain what the children will be doing in kindergarten, her educational philosophy and expectations, the procedure for dropping students off at school the first day, and of course, to allow parents to ask any questions and share any concerns they might have. Inevitably, parents do have concerns and questions they would like addressed.

Here are some typical things she hears from parents:

"Joey still naps in the afternoon; can we have him changed to the morning class?"

"Ashley has severe asthma. She will need to have her nebulizer close in case she has an asthma attack. Do you know how to use one?"

"I just know that Steve won't be able to sit still for very long. Do you let the kids move a lot?"

"I hope you give the kids lots of active time. Bill won't be able to sit still for long either."

"Alex is very advanced for his age. What can you do to challenge him?"

"Amanda is advanced, too."

"So is my Timmy."

"Well, Peter seems to be behind. He doesn't speak very well."

Ms. Inez listens respectfully to each concern or question and assures the parents, "I'll do everything I can to ensure your children have a good year in my class. All children are different and learn at different rates, so don't be too worried about your child being a little bit behind or ahead. I think we'll all do fine together." As she is leaving for the evening, she chuckles at the number of parents who think their children are very advanced. It's the same every year—about a third of the parents are convinced that their child is the next Einstein.

The school year begins uneventfully. Ms. Inez uses the children's free-play time to observe them. Although there are obvious differences between the children, she doesn't notice that any of the children are truly exceptional, except perhaps for Harman and Rowan. Their lack of attention and inability to sit still during story time is beginning to be a bit disruptive. Ms. Inez makes a note to herself to talk to their parents about the possibility that they might have ADHD and recommend testing. Some other students might be candidates for this as well, including Alex. Although Ms. Inez has learned how to use Ashley's nebulizer, she hasn't needed to use it thus far.

Each day at the beginning of class, Ms. Inez marks off the day of the month on the calendar with a large *X*. She then writes a statement on the blackboard, describing the day's weather. On the tenth day of school she writes on the board, "Today is sunny and

hot." She then reads the statement to the students so that they can begin to make word associations.

"Today is sunny and warm." Alex shouts out. "That isn't what you wrote. You wrote today is sunny and hot."

Ms. Inez is astounded. Later, during free-play time she asks Alex to sit with her. Alex looks longingly at the puzzles, but grudgingly complies. "Alex, will you read this book to me?"

"Sure," replies Alex, and he does so flawlessly.

Ms. Inez queries, "Do you have this book at home?"

Alex: "Yep. Lots of others, too."

Ms. Inez: "How about this one? Do you have it?"

Alex: "Nope."

Ms. Inez: "Well then, suppose you try to read this one to me."

Alex: "OK, but then can I go play with the puzzles?"

Ms. Inez: "Certainly."

Alex reads the book to Ms. Inez, missing only a few words, and then rushes off to play with the puzzles, build towers of blocks and knock them down, and play with trucks. The next day during calendar time, Ms. Inez asks the class, "If today is the fifteenth day of the month and there are thirty days in the month, how could we find out how many days are left?"

The children call out, "We could count the days that don't have *X*'s on them."

"Very good," replies Ms. Inez.

Alex looks puzzled. "What's wrong, Alex?" asks Ms. Inez. "Why don't we just subtract?" he asks.

1. What are the issues in this case?

2. Why do you suppose Ms. Inez makes light of parents' perceptions of their children's strengths?

3. How should Ms. Inez approach the parents of the students she thinks might have ADHD?

4. Is it appropriate for her to recommend testing of any of the children? Why or why not? Would it be appropriate for her to recommend a particular doctor for this testing? Why or why not?

5. If Alex can already read and subtract, are there other skills he has likely mastered? If so, what might they be? How might this impact his experiences in kindergarten?

6. How should Ms. Inez address this?

7. Which of the following is most likely true about Alex?
   a. Alex has a fluency disorder.
   b. Alex has a learning disability.
   c. Alex has ADHD.
   d. Alex is gifted.

# Reach Your **Learning Goals**

## Learners Who Are Exceptional

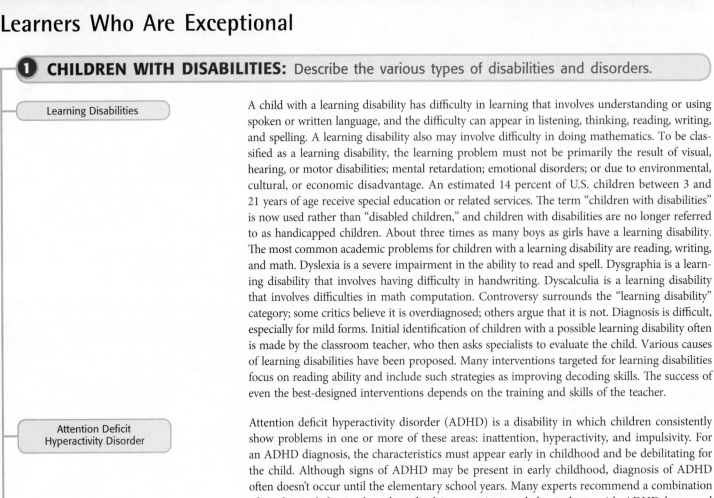

**❶ CHILDREN WITH DISABILITIES:** Describe the various types of disabilities and disorders.

**Learning Disabilities**

A child with a learning disability has difficulty in learning that involves understanding or using spoken or written language, and the difficulty can appear in listening, thinking, reading, writing, and spelling. A learning disability also may involve difficulty in doing mathematics. To be classified as a learning disability, the learning problem must not be primarily the result of visual, hearing, or motor disabilities; mental retardation; emotional disorders; or due to environmental, cultural, or economic disadvantage. An estimated 14 percent of U.S. children between 3 and 21 years of age receive special education or related services. The term "children with disabilities" is now used rather than "disabled children," and children with disabilities are no longer referred to as handicapped children. About three times as many boys as girls have a learning disability. The most common academic problems for children with a learning disability are reading, writing, and math. Dyslexia is a severe impairment in the ability to read and spell. Dysgraphia is a learning disability that involves having difficulty in handwriting. Dyscalculia is a learning disability that involves difficulties in math computation. Controversy surrounds the "learning disability" category; some critics believe it is overdiagnosed; others argue that it is not. Diagnosis is difficult, especially for mild forms. Initial identification of children with a possible learning disability often is made by the classroom teacher, who then asks specialists to evaluate the child. Various causes of learning disabilities have been proposed. Many interventions targeted for learning disabilities focus on reading ability and include such strategies as improving decoding skills. The success of even the best-designed interventions depends on the training and skills of the teacher.

**Attention Deficit Hyperactivity Disorder**

Attention deficit hyperactivity disorder (ADHD) is a disability in which children consistently show problems in one or more of these areas: inattention, hyperactivity, and impulsivity. For an ADHD diagnosis, the characteristics must appear early in childhood and be debilitating for the child. Although signs of ADHD may be present in early childhood, diagnosis of ADHD often doesn't occur until the elementary school years. Many experts recommend a combination of academic, behavioral, and medical interventions to help students with ADHD learn and adapt. ADHD is not supposed to be diagnosed by school teams because accurate diagnosis requires evaluation by a specialist, such as a psychiatrist. It is important for teachers to monitor whether ADHD medication has been prescribed at the right dosage, to involve a special education resource teacher, to use behavior management strategies, to supply immediate feedback to the child for clearly stated expectations, and to provide structure and teacher-direction.

**Mental Retardation**

Mental retardation is a condition with an onset before age 18 that involves low intelligence (usually below 70 on an individually administered intelligence test) and difficulty in adapting to everyday life. Mental retardation has been classified in terms of four categories based mainly on IQ scores: mild, moderate, severe, and profound. More recently, a classification system based on degree of support required has been advocated. Determinants of mental retardation include genetic factors (as in Down syndrome), brain damage (which can result from many different infections, such as AIDS), and environmental hazards.

**Physical Disorders**

Among the physical disorders that students might have are orthopedic impairments (such as cerebral palsy) and seizure disorders (such as epilepsy).

**Sensory Disorders**

Sensory disorders include visual and hearing impairments. Visual impairments include having low vision and being educationally blind. A child with low vision can read large-print books or regular books with a magnifying glass. An educationally blind child cannot use vision in learning, instead relying on hearing and touch. An important task is to determine which modality (such as touch or hearing) the student who is visually impaired learns best in. A number of technological devices help these students learn. Educational strategies for students with hearing impairments fall into two main categories: oral and manual. Increasingly, both approaches are used with the same student in a total-communication approach.

Speech and language disorders include a number of speech problems (such as articulation disorders, voice disorders, and fluency disorders) and language problems (difficulties in receiving and expressing language). Articulation disorders are problems in pronouncing words correctly. Voice disorders are reflected in speech that is too hoarse, loud, high-pitched, or low-pitched. Children with cleft palate often have a voice disorder. Fluency disorders often involve what we commonly call "stuttering." Language disorders involve significant impairments in children's receptive or expressive language. Receptive language involves the reception and understanding of language. Expressive language involves using language for expressing one's thoughts and communicating with others. Specific language impairment (SLI) is another type of speech and language disorder that children may have and involves problems in understanding and using words in sentences.

Autism spectrum disorder (ASD) is an increasingly popular term that refers to a broad range of autism disorders including the classical, severe form of autism, as well as Asperger syndrome. Autism is a severe autism spectrum disorder with an onset in the first three years of life, and it involves abnormalities in social relationships and communications. It also is characterized by repetitive behaviors. The current consensus is that autism involves an organic brain dysfunction.

Emotional and behavioral disorders consist of serious, persistent problems that involve relationships, aggression, depression, fears associated with personal or school matters, and other inappropriate socioemotional characteristics. The term emotional disturbance (ED) recently has been used to describe this category of disorders, although use of this term is not without criticism. In severe instances of aggressive, out-of-control behaviors, students are removed from the classroom. The problems are far more characteristic of boys than of girls. Problems involving depression, anxiety, and fear, involving turning problems inward, are much more likely to appear in girls than in boys.

## ❷ EDUCATIONAL ISSUES INVOLVING CHILDREN WITH DISABILITIES: Explain the legal framework and technology advances for children with disabilities.

### Legal Aspects

The educational rights for children with disabilities were laid down in the mid-1960s. In 1975 Congress enacted Public Law 94-142, the Education for All Handicapped Children Act, which mandated that all children be given a free, appropriate public education. Public Law 94-142 was recast in 1990 as the Individuals with Disabilities Education Act (IDEA), which spells out broad requirements for services to all children with disabilities. Children who are thought to have a disability are evaluated to determine their eligibility for services. The IDEA has many provisions that relate to the parents of children with disabilities. IDEA was amended in 1997, then reauthorized in 2004 and renamed the Individuals with Disabilities Improvement Act. The 2004 version especially focuses on its alignment with NCLB legislation, which has raised questions about whether students with disabilities can be expected to meet the same general education standards and achievement as students without disabilities. The IEP is a written plan of the program specifically tailored for the child with a disability. The plan should (1) relate to the child's learning capacity, (2) be individualized and not a copy of a plan that is offered to other children, and (3) be designed to provide educational benefits. The concept of least restrictive environment (LRE) is contained in the IDEA. It states that children with disabilities must be educated in a setting that is as similar as possible to the one in which children without disabilities are educated. This provision of IDEA has given a legal basis to making an effort to educate children with disabilities in the regular classroom. The term inclusion means educating children with disabilities full-time in the regular classroom. The trend is toward using inclusion more. Children's academic and social success is affected more by the quality of instruction they receive than by where they are placed.

Instructional technology includes various types of hardware and software, combined with innovative teaching methods, to accommodate children's needs in the classroom. Assistive technology consists of various services and devices to help children with disabilities function within their environment.

## ③ CHILDREN WHO ARE GIFTED: Define what gifted means and discuss some approaches to teaching children who are gifted.

### Characteristics

Children who are gifted have above-average intelligence (usually defined as an IQ of 130 or higher) and/or superior talent in some domain, such as art, music, or mathematics. Some critics argue that gifted programs include too many children who are just somewhat bright, usually cooperative, and, usually, non-Latino White. Winner described children who are gifted as having three main characteristics: precocity, marching to the tune of a different drummer, and a passion to master.

### Nature-Nurture Issue, Developmental Changes, and Domain-Specific Giftedness

Giftedness is likely a consequence of both heredity and environment. Developmental changes characterize giftedness. Deliberate practice is often important in the achievement of the gifted. In Terman's study, many gifted children became successful achievers in adulthood, but most did not become major creators. Increasingly the domain-specific aspect of giftedness is emphasized in adulthood.

### Educating Children Who Are Gifted

Educational programs available for children who are gifted include special classes ("pullout" programs), acceleration, enrichment, mentor and apprenticeship programs, as well as work/study or community-service programs. Debate focuses on whether acceleration or enrichment programs most benefit children who are gifted. Children who are gifted increasingly are being educated in the regular classroom. Some experts recommend that increasing the standards in the regular classroom will help children who are gifted, although programs such as mentoring and additional instruction might be needed for children who are still underchallenged. One concern is that the NCLB legislation has harmed the education of students who are gifted by focusing attention on students with deficiencies.

## KEY TERMS

learning disability 182
dyslexia 183
dysgraphia 183
dyscalculia 183
attention deficit hyperactivity
    disorder (ADHD) 185
mental retardation 189
Down syndrome 189
orthopedic impairments 191

cerebral palsy 191
epilepsy 191
speech and language
    disorders 192
articulation disorders 193
voice disorders 193
fluency disorders 193
language disorders 193
receptive language 193

expressive language 193
specific language impairment
    (SLI) 193
autism spectrum disorders
    (ASD) 194
autistic disorder 194
Asperger syndrome 194
emotional and behavioral
    disorders 195

Public Law 94-142 199
Individuals with Disabilities
    Education Act (IDEA) 199
individualized education
    plan (IEP) 199
least restrictive environment
    (LRE) 200
inclusion 200
children who are gifted 204

## PORTFOLIO ACTIVITIES

Now that you have a good understanding of this chapter, complete this exercise to expand your thinking.

**Independent Reflection Fostering Positive School-Home Linkages for Children with Disabilities.** Place yourself in the role of a parent. Imagine that the school has just notified you that your child has a learning disability. Write down answers to these questions: (1) What feelings are you likely to be having as a parent? (2) As a parent, what questions do you want to ask the teacher? (3) Now put yourself in the role of the teacher. How would you respond to these questions? (INTASC: Principles 3, 10)

**Research/Field Experience Inclusion in Action.** Interview elementary school, middle school, and high school teachers about their impressions of inclusion and other aspects of educating children with disabilities. Ask them what their most successful strategies are in working with children who have disabilities. Also ask what the biggest challenges are. Write a summary of the interviews. (INTASC: Principle *9*)

**Collaborative Work Technology Resources for Gifted Students.** Together with three or four other students in your class, come up with a list and description of software programs that you think would benefit gifted children. One good source of information on such software is the *Journal of Electronic Learning.* Write down the list and descriptions. (INTASC: Principles *3, 4, 9*)

# STUDY, PRACTICE, AND SUCCEED

Visit **www.mhhe.com/santrockep5e** to review the chapter with self-grading quizzes and self-assessments, to apply the chapter material to two more Crack the Case studies, and for suggested activities to develop your teaching portfolio.

# CHAPTER 7

# BEHAVIORAL AND SOCIAL COGNITIVE APPROACHES

*To learn is a natural pleasure.*

—Aristotle
*Greek Philosopher, 4th Century,* B.C.

## Chapter **Outline**

**What Is Learning?**

What Learning Is and Is Not
Approaches to Learning

**Behavioral Approach to Learning**

Classical Conditioning
Operant Conditioning

**Applied Behavior Analysis in Education**

What Is Applied Behavior Analysis?
Increasing Desirable Behaviors
Decreasing Undesirable Behaviors
Evaluating Operant Conditioning and Applied Behavior Analysis

**Social Cognitive Approaches to Learning**

Bandura's Social Cognitive Theory
Observational Learning
Cognitive Behavior Approaches and Self-Regulation
Evaluating the Social Cognitive Approaches

## Learning **Goals**

**1** Define learning and describe five approaches to studying it.

**2** Compare classical conditioning and operant conditioning.

**3** Apply behavior analysis to education.

**4** Summarize social cognitive approaches to learning.

# Teaching **Stories**   Ruth Sidney Charney

Ruth Sidney Charney has been a teacher for more than 35 years. She is one of the developers of the Responsive Classroom® approach to teaching and learning, a method that emphasizes positive reinforcement of students' good behavior. Following are some of her thoughts about reinforcing students' learning (Charney, 2005, pp. 1–2):

> We reinforce children when we notice. We notice the personal detail our children bring to school and we notice their efforts to behave and learn. . . . We applaud the five correct answers on the math paper (when last week there were only two), the extra sentence in writing, the crisp adjectives, the ten minutes of fair play in a game. . . .
>
> We reinforce by noticing the positive attempts children make to follow the rules and meet class expectations. We reinforce when children are practicing new skills or when they demonstrate behaviors recently modeled. . . .
>
> Examples of noticing and reinforcing students include
>
> - "Today's the day, isn't it?" the teacher whispers to Hector. He smiles at her, and they share a quick high-five salute,

acknowledging Hector's impending solo performance in the church choir.

- "Snazzy new boots?" the teacher asks Leila as she struts into class. . . .
- "Thanks for helping Tessa with her spelling. I notice you gave her good hints so she could spell some of the words herself."
- "I noticed it took much less time today to get in line. What did you notice . . . ?"
- "I noticed you got your math done this morning with no interruption. That took lots of concentration. . . ."
- "Thank you for your very efficient clean-up today. I noticed caps back on markers, pencils with points down in cans, paper off the floor. . . ."
- "You really found an interesting way to solve the problem and complete the project together."

# Preview

Virtually everyone agrees that helping students learn is an important function of schools. However, not everyone agrees on the best way to learn. We begin this chapter by examining just what learning involves, then turn to the main behavioral approaches to learning. Next we explore how behavioral principles are applied to educating students. In the final section we will discuss the social cognitive approaches to learning.

**1  WHAT IS LEARNING?**

What Learning Is and Is Not          Approaches to Learning

Learning is a central focus of educational psychology. When people are asked what schools are for, a common reply is, "To help children learn."

## WHAT LEARNING IS AND IS NOT

When children learn how to use a computer, they might make some mistakes along the way, but at a certain point they will get the knack of the behaviors required to use the computer effectively. The children will change from being individuals who cannot operate a computer into being individuals who can. Once they have learned how, they don't lose those skills. It's like learning to drive a car. Once you have learned how, you don't have to learn all over again. Thus, **learning** can be defined as a relatively permanent influence on behavior, knowledge, and thinking skills that comes about through experience.

Not everything we know is learned. We inherit some capacities—they are inborn, or innate, not learned. For example, we don't have to be taught to swallow, to flinch at loud noises, or to blink when an object comes too close to our eyes. Most human behaviors, however, do not involve heredity alone. When children use a computer

**learning** A relatively permanent influence on behavior, knowledge, and thinking skills that comes about through experience.

**217**

in a new way, work harder at solving problems, ask better questions, explain an answer in a more logical way, or listen more attentively, the experience of learning is at work.

The scope of learning is broad (Domjan, 2010; Klein, 2009). It involves academic behaviors and nonacademic behaviors. It occurs in schools and everywhere else that children experience their world.

## APPROACHES TO LEARNING

Approaches to learning can be categorized as behavioral or cognitive.

**Behavioral Approach** The learning approach that we discuss in the first part of this chapter is called *behavioral*. **Behaviorism** is the view that behavior should be explained by observable experiences, not by mental processes. For the behaviorist, behavior is everything that we do, both verbal and nonverbal, that can be directly seen or heard: a child creating a poster, a teacher explaining something to a child, one student picking on another student, and so on. **Mental processes** are defined by psychologists as the thoughts, feelings, and motives that each of us experiences but that cannot be observed by others. Although we cannot directly see thoughts, feelings, and motives, they are no less real. Mental processes include children thinking about ways to create the best poster, a teacher feeling good about children's efforts, and children's inner motivation to control their behavior.

For the behaviorist, these thoughts, feelings, and motives are not appropriate subject matter for a science of behavior because they cannot be directly observed (Shanks, 2009). *Classical conditioning* and *operant conditioning,* two behavioral views that we will discuss shortly, adopt this stance. Both of these views emphasize **associative learning,** which consists of learning that two events are connected or associated (Olson & Hergenhahn, 2009). For example, associative learning occurs when a student associates a pleasant event with learning something in school, such as the teacher smiling when the student asks a good question.

**Cognitive Approaches** *Cognition* means "thought," and psychology became more cognitive, or began focusing more on thought, in the last part of the twentieth century. The cognitive emphasis continues today and is the basis for numerous approaches to learning (Ashcraft & Radvansky, 2010; Martinez, 2010). We discuss four main cognitive approaches to learning in this book: social cognitive; information processing; cognitive constructivist; and social constructivist. The *social cognitive* approaches emphasize how behavior, environment, and person (cognitive) factors interact to influence learning (Bandura, 2009, 2010a). The *information-processing* approaches focus on how children process information through attention, memory, thinking, and other cognitive processes (Martinez, 2010). The *cognitive constructivist* approaches emphasize the child's cognitive construction of knowledge and understanding (Halford, 2008). The *social constructivist* approaches focus on collaboration with others to produce knowledge and understanding (Holzman, 2009).

Adding these four cognitive approaches to the behavioral approaches, we arrive at five main approaches to learning that we discuss in this book: behavioral, social cognitive, information processing, cognitive constructivist, and social constructivist. All contribute to our understanding of how children learn. A summary of the five approaches is presented in Figure 7.1.

As you read Chapters 7 through 11 on learning and cognition, keep in mind that students are more likely to learn in optimal ways in appropriate learning environments. Such learning environments should be tailored to specific learning goals, to the students' backgrounds and prior knowledge, and to the contexts in which learning will occur. Thus teachers not only need to understand the basic principles of learning but must also know how to use them to meet diverse learning goals in contexts where students' needs differ (Bransford & others, 2005, p. 78).

---

**Thinking Back/Thinking Forward**

Piaget's theory is a cognitive constructivist approach. Chapter 2, p. 39

Vygotksy's theory is a social constructivist approach. Chapter 2, p. 50; Chapter 10, p. 333

---

**behaviorism** The view that behavior should be explained by observable experiences, not by mental processes.

**mental processes** Thoughts, feelings, and motives that cannot be observed by others.

**associative learning** Learning that two events are connected (associated).

| Behavioral | Social Cognitive | Information-Processing | Cognitive Constructivist | Social Constructivist |
|---|---|---|---|---|
| Emphasis on experiences, especially reinforcement and punishment as determinants of learning and behavior | Emphasis on interaction of behavior, environment, and person (cognitive) factors as determinants of learning | Emphasis on how children process information through attention, memory, thinking, and other cognitive processes | Emphasis on the child's cognitive construction of knowledge and understanding | Emphasis on collaboration with others to produce knowledge and understanding |
| **First part of this chapter (7)** | **Last part of this chapter (7)** | **Chapters 8 and 9** | **Chapter 2 (Piaget) and some parts of Chapters 8 and 9** | **Chapter 2 (Vygotsky); and Chapter 10** |

FIGURE **7.1** APPROACHES TO LEARNING

## Review, Reflect, and Practice

**1** Define learning and describe five approaches to studying it.

**REVIEW**

- What is learning? Are there any behaviors that don't reflect learning?
- What essentially is behaviorism? What are four main cognitive approaches to learning?

**REFLECT**

- How do you learn? Think of a behavior you engage in and describe how you learned it.

**PRAXIS™ PRACTICE**

1. According to the psychological definition of learning, all of the following are examples of learning *except*
   a. writing.
   b. sneezing.
   c. swimming.
   d. washing dishes.

2. Mr. Zeller does not believe his students have learned anything unless they demonstrate it to him. This demonstration could be through assignments they turn in to him, answering questions in class, or the way they behave. Which approach to learning is most consistent with Mr. Zeller's ideas?
   a. cognitive
   b. behavioral
   c. social cognitive
   d. conditioning

   *Please see the answer key at the end of the book.*

## 2  BEHAVIORAL APPROACH TO LEARNING

Classical Conditioning     Operant Conditioning

The behavioral approach emphasizes the importance of children making connections between experiences and behavior. It includes two views: classical conditioning and operant conditioning.

**Before Conditioning**

**Conditioning**

**After Conditioning**

## FIGURE **7.2** PAVLOV'S CLASSICAL CONDITIONING

In one experiment, Pavlov presented a neutral stimulus (bell) just before an unconditioned stimulus (food). The neutral stimulus became a conditioned stimulus by being paired with the unconditioned stimulus. Subsequently, the conditioned stimulus (bell) by itself was able to elicit the dog's salivation.

## CLASSICAL CONDITIONING

**Classical conditioning** is a type of learning in which an organism learns to connect, or associate, stimuli so that a neutral stimulus (such as the sight of a person) becomes associated with a meaningful stimulus (such as food) and acquires the capacity to elicit a similar response. Classical conditioning was the brainchild of Ivan Pavlov (1927). To fully understand Pavlov's theory of classical conditioning, we need to understand two types of stimuli and two types of responses: unconditioned stimulus (UCS), unconditioned response (UCR), conditioned stimulus (CS), and conditioned response (CR).

Figure 7.2 summarizes the way classical conditioning works. An *unconditioned stimulus (UCS)* is a stimulus that automatically produces a response without any prior learning. Food was the UCS in Pavlov's experiments. An *unconditioned response (UCR)* is an unlearned response that is automatically elicited by the UCS. In Pavlov's experiments, the dog's salivation in response to food was the UCR. A *conditioned stimulus (CS)* is a previously neutral stimulus that eventually elicits a conditioned response after being associated with the UCS. Among the conditioned stimuli in Pavlov's experiments were various sights and sounds that occurred prior to the dog's actually eating the food, such as the sound of the door closing before the food was placed in the dog's dish. A *conditioned response (CR)* is a learned response to the conditioned stimulus that occurs after UCS-CS pairing.

Classical conditioning can be involved in both positive and negative experiences of children in the classroom. Among the things in the child's schooling that produce pleasure because they have become classically conditioned are a favorite song and feelings that the classroom is a safe and fun place to be. For example, a song could

**classical conditioning** A form of associative learning in which a neutral stimulus becomes associated with a meaningful stimulus and acquires the capacity to elicit a similar response.

be neutral for the child until he joins in with other classmates to sing it with accompanying positive feelings.

Children can develop fear of the classroom if they associate the classroom with criticism, so the criticism becomes a CS for fear. Classical conditioning also can be involved in test anxiety. For example, a child fails and is criticized, which produces anxiety; thereafter, she associates tests with anxiety, so they then can become a CS for anxiety (see Figure 7.3).

Some children's health problems also might involve classical conditioning (Chance, 2009). Certain physical complaints—asthma, headaches, and high blood pressure—might be partly due to classical conditioning. We usually say that such health problems can be caused by stress. Often what happens, though, is that certain stimuli, such as a parent's or teacher's heavy criticism, are conditioned stimuli for physiological responses. Over time, the frequency of the physiological responses can produce a health problem. A teacher's persistent criticism of a student can cause the student to develop headaches, muscle tension, and so on. Anything associated with the teacher, such as classroom learning exercises and homework, might trigger the student's stress and subsequently be linked with headaches or other physiological responses.

FIGURE **7.3** CLASSICAL CONDITIONING INVOLVED IN TEACHERS' CRITICISM OF CHILDREN AND TESTS

### Generalization, Discrimination, and Extinction

In studying a dog's responses to various stimuli, Pavlov rang a bell before giving meat powder to the dog. By being paired with the UCS (meat), the bell became a CS and elicited the dog's salivation. After a time, Pavlov found that the dog also responded to other sounds, such as a whistle. The more bell-like the noise, the stronger was the dog's response. *Generalization* in classical conditioning involves the tendency of a new stimulus similar to the original conditioned stimulus to produce a similar response (Pearce & Hall, 2009). Let's consider a classroom example. A student is criticized for poor performance on a biology test. When the student begins to prepare for a chemistry test, she also becomes very nervous because these two subjects are closely related in the sciences. Thus, the student's anxiety generalizes from taking a test in one subject to taking a test in another.

*Discrimination* in classical conditioning occurs when the organism responds to certain stimuli but not others. To produce discrimination, Pavlov gave food to the dog only after ringing the bell, not after any other sounds. Subsequently, the dog responded only to the bell. In the case of the student taking tests in different classes, she doesn't become nearly as nervous about taking an English test or a history test because they are very different subject areas.

*Extinction* in classical conditioning involves the weakening of the conditioned response (CR) in the absence of the unconditioned stimulus (UCS). In one session, Pavlov rang the bell repeatedly but did not give the dog any food. Eventually the dog stopped salivating at the sound of the bell. Similarly, if a student who gets nervous while taking tests begins to do much better on tests, his anxiety will fade.

### Systematic Desensitization

Sometimes the anxiety and stress associated with negative events can be eliminated by classical conditioning (Maier & Seligman, 2009). **Systematic desensitization** is a method based on classical conditioning that reduces anxiety by getting the individual to associate deep relaxation with successive visualizations of increasingly anxiety-producing situations. Imagine that you have a student in your class who is extremely nervous about talking in front of the class. The goal of systematic desensitization is to get the student to associate public speaking with relaxation, such as walking on a quiet beach, rather than anxiety. Using successive visualizations, the student might practice systematic desensitization two weeks before the talk, then a week before, four days before, two days before, the day before, the morning of the talk, on entering the room where the talk is to be given, on the way to the podium, and during the talk.

**systematic desensitization** A method based on classical conditioning that reduces anxiety by getting the individual to associate deep relaxation with successive visualizations of increasingly anxiety-provoking situations.

B. F. Skinner conducting an operant conditioning study in his behavioral laboratory. The rat being studied is in a Skinner box.

Desensitization involves a type of *counterconditioning*. The relaxing feelings that the student imagines (UCS) produce relaxation (UCR). The student then associates anxiety-producing cues (CS) with the relaxing feelings. Such relaxation is incompatible with anxiety. By initially pairing a weak anxiety-producing cue with relaxation and gradually working up the hierarchy (from two weeks before the talk to walking up to the podium to give the talk), all of the anxiety-producing cues should generate relaxation (CR).

Chances are you will have students who fear speaking in front of the class or have other anxieties, and there may be circumstances in your own life where you might benefit from replacing anxiety with relaxation. For example, it is not unusual for some teachers to feel comfortable when talking in front of their students but to get nervous if asked to give a presentation at a teaching conference. Counselors and mental health professionals have been successful at getting individuals to overcome their fear of public speaking using systematic desensitization. Should you be interested in adopting this strategy, do it with the help of a school psychologist rather than on your own.

**Evaluating Classical Conditioning** Classical conditioning helps us understand some aspects of learning better than others (Domjan, 2010). It excels in explaining how neutral stimuli become associated with unlearned, involuntary responses (Rescorla, 2009). It is especially helpful in understanding students' anxieties and fears (Klein, 2009). However, it is not as effective in explaining voluntary behaviors, such as why a student studies hard for a test or likes history better than geography. For these areas, operant conditioning is more relevant.

## OPERANT CONDITIONING

**Operant conditioning** (also called *instrumental conditioning*) is a form of learning in which the consequences of behavior produce changes in the probability that the behavior will occur. Operant conditioning is at the heart of B. F. Skinner's (1938) behavioral view. Consequences—rewards and punishments—are contingent on the organism's behavior.

**Reinforcement and Punishment** A **reinforcement (reward)** is a consequence that increases the probability that a behavior will occur. In contrast, **punishment** is a consequence that decreases the probability a behavior will occur. For example, you might tell one of your students, "Congratulations. I'm really proud of the story that you wrote." If the student works harder and writes an even better story the next time, your positive comments are said to reinforce, or reward, the student's writing behavior. If you frown at a student for talking in class and the student's talking decreases, your frown is said to punish the student's talking.

To reinforce behavior means to strengthen the behavior (Domjan, 2010). Two forms of reinforcement are positive reinforcement and negative reinforcement. In **positive reinforcement,** the frequency of a response increases because it is followed by a rewarding stimulus, as in the example in which the teacher's positive comments increased the student's writing behavior. Similarly, complimenting parents on being at a parent-teacher conference might encourage them to come back again.

Conversely, in **negative reinforcement,** the frequency of a response increases because it is followed by the removal of an aversive (unpleasant) stimulus. For example, a father nags at his son to do his homework. He keeps nagging. Finally, the son gets tired of hearing the nagging and does his homework. The son's response (doing his homework) removed the unpleasant stimulus (nagging).

One way to remember the distinction between positive and negative reinforcement is that in positive reinforcement something is added. In negative reinforcement, something is subtracted, or removed. It is easy to confuse negative reinforcement and

**operant conditioning** Also called *instrumental conditioning*, this is a form of learning in which the consequences of behavior produce changes in the probability that the behavior will occur.

**reinforcement (reward)** A consequence that increases the probability that a behavior will occur.

**punishment** A consequence that decreases the probability that a behavior will occur.

**positive reinforcement** Reinforcement based on the principle that the frequency of a response increases because it is followed by a rewarding stimulus.

**negative reinforcement** Reinforcement based on the principle that the frequency of a response increases because an aversive (unpleasant) stimulus is removed.

**Positive Reinforcement**

**Behavior:**
Student asks a good question

**Consequence:**
Teacher praises student

**Future behavior:**
Student asks more good questions

**Negative Reinforcement**

**Behavior:**
Student turns homework in on time

**Consequence:**
Teacher stops criticizing student

**Future behavior:**
Student increasingly turns homework in on time

**Punishment**

**Behavior:**
Student interrupts teacher

**Consequence:**
Teacher verbally reprimands
student

**Future behavior:**
Student stops interrupting teacher

Remember that reinforcement comes in positive and negative forms. In both forms,
the consequences increase behavior. In punishment, behavior is decreased.

**FIGURE 7.4**  REINFORCEMENT AND PUNISHMENT

punishment. To keep these terms straight, remember that negative reinforcement *increases* the probability a response will occur, whereas punishment *decreases* the probability it will occur. Figure 7.4 summarizes and presents examples of the concepts of positive reinforcement, negative reinforcement, and punishment.

**Generalization, Discrimination, and Extinction**    In our coverage of classical conditioning, we discussed generalization, discrimination, and extinction. These processes also are important dimensions of operant conditioning (Chance, 2009). Remember that in classical conditioning, *generalization* is the tendency of a stimulus similar to the conditioned stimulus to produce a response similar to the conditioned response. Generalization in operant conditioning means giving the *same* response to similar stimuli. Especially of interest is the extent to which behavior generalizes from one situation to another. For example, if a teacher praises the student for asking good questions related to English, will this generalize to stimulating the student to do harder work in history, math, and other subjects?

Remember that in classical conditioning, *discrimination* means responding to certain stimuli but not others. Discrimination in operant conditioning involves differentiating among stimuli or environmental events. For example, a student knows that the tray on the teacher's desk labeled "Math" is where she is supposed to place today's math work, whereas another tray labeled "English" is where today's English assignments are to be put. This might sound overly simple, but it is important because students' worlds are filled with many such discriminative stimuli. Around school these discriminative stimuli might include signs that say "Stay Out," "Form a Line Here," and so on.

In operant conditioning, *extinction* occurs when a previously reinforced response is no longer reinforced and the response decreases. In the classroom, the most common use of extinction is for the teacher to withdraw attention from a behavior that the attention is maintaining. For example, in some cases a teacher's attention inadvertently reinforces a student's disruptive behavior, as when a student pinches another student and the teacher immediately talks with the perpetrator. If this happens on a regular basis, the student might learn that pinching other students is a good way to get the teacher's attention. If the teacher withdraws his attention, the pinching might be extinguished.

## Review, Reflect, and Practice

**②** Compare classical conditioning and operant conditioning.

**REVIEW**

- What is classical conditioning? What are the UCS, UCR, CS, and CR? In the context of classical conditioning, what are generalization, discrimination, extinction, and systematic desensitization?
- What is operant conditioning? Explain the different types of reinforcement. Explain punishment. In the context of operant conditioning, what are generalization, discrimination, and extinction?

**REFLECT**

- Do you think that your emotions are the result of classical conditioning, operant conditioning, or both? Explain.

**PRAXIS™ PRACTICE**

1. Sylvia is participating in a class spelling bee. The teacher asks her to spell the word *mortgage*. "Don't forget the *t*, don't forget the *t*," Sylvia says to herself. "M-O-R-T-A-G-E," says Sylvia. "I'm sorry, that's incorrect, Sylvia," says her teacher. One of the students in the back of the class snickers and comments, "Gee, about time Miss Smarty-pants got one wrong. See, she's not so smart." Some other students join in the laughter. Sylvia begins to cry and runs out of the room. After that, Sylvia becomes very anxious about spelling bees. According to classical conditioning theory, what is the conditioned stimulus in this scenario?
   a. the teacher telling her she is incorrect
   b. the other students' laughter
   c. the word *mortgage*
   d. spelling bees

2. Tyler is a fourth-grade student. He loves to crack jokes, often at his teacher's expense. One day he called his teacher, Ms. Bart, "Ms. Fart." Ms. Bart quickly admonished him for his behavior and told him that name-calling was unacceptable. She made him stay after school to discuss his behavior. The other students in the class thought Tyler's nickname for Ms. Bart was hilarious, laughing along with Tyler and later telling him what a good name that was for Ms. Bart. The next day, Tyler again called Ms. Bart by the insulting nickname. According to operant conditioning theory, Tyler continued to use this name in spite of having to stay after school the day before because
   a. the behavior had continued for a lengthy period of time.
   b. he was positively reinforced by his classmates for the behavior.
   c. he was negatively reinforced by his teacher for his behavior.
   d. he was punished by his teacher for his behavior.

*Please see the answer key at the end of the book.*

# 3 APPLIED BEHAVIOR ANALYSIS IN EDUCATION

What Is Applied Behavior Analysis?

Decreasing Undesirable Behaviors

Increasing Desirable Behaviors

Evaluating Operant Conditioning and Applied Behavior Analysis

Many applications of operant conditioning have been made outside research laboratories in the wider worlds of classrooms, homes, business settings, hospitals, and other real-world settings (Moore Parten & others, 2010; Scarlett, Ponte, & Singh, 2009). This section describes how teachers can use *applied behavior analysis* to improve students' behavior and learning.

## WHAT IS APPLIED BEHAVIOR ANALYSIS?

**Applied behavior analysis** involves applying the principles of operant conditioning to change human behavior. Two uses of applied behavior analysis are especially important in education: increasing desirable behaviors and decreasing undesirable behaviors (Alberto & Troutman, 2009; Kraft, 2010). Applications of applied behavior analysis often use a series of steps (Reed & others, 2010). These typically begin with some general observations, then turn to determining the specific target behavior that needs to be changed, as well as observing its antecedent conditions. Next, behavioral goals are set, particular reinforcers or punishers selected, a behavior management program carried out, and the success or failure of the program evaluated (Dunlap & others, 2010).

*"Once it became clear to me that, by responding correctly to certain stimuli, I could get all the bananas I wanted, getting this job was a pushover."*

© Jack Ziegler/The New Yorker Collection/www.cartoonbank.com

## INCREASING DESIRABLE BEHAVIORS

Six operant conditioning strategies can be used to increase a child's desirable behaviors: choose effective reinforcers, make reinforcers contingent and timely, select the best schedule of reinforcement, consider contracting, use negative reinforcement effectively, and use prompts and shaping.

**Choose Effective Reinforcers**   Not all reinforcers are the same for every child. Applied behavior analysts recommend that teachers find out what reinforcers work best with which children—that is, individualize the use of particular reinforcers (Scarlett, Ponte, & Singh, 2009). For one student it might be praise, for another it might be getting to spend more time participating in a favorite activity, for another it might involve being a hall monitor for a week, and for yet another it could be getting to surf the Internet. To find out the most effective reinforcers for a child, you can examine what has motivated the child in the past (reinforcement history), what the student wants but can't easily or frequently get, and the child's perception of the reinforcer's value. Some applied behavior analysts recommend asking children which reinforcers they like best. Another recommendation is to consider novel reinforcers to reduce the child's boredom. Natural reinforcers such as praise and privileges are generally recommended over material rewards such as candy, stars, and money.

Activities are some of the most common reinforcers that teachers use. Named after psychologist David Premack, the **Premack principle** states that a high-probability activity can serve as a reinforcer for a low-probability activity. The Premack principle

Thinking Back/Thinking Forward

Applied behavior analysis can be used as part of managing the classroom effectively. Chapter 14, p. 493

**applied behavior analysis** Application of the principles of operant conditioning to change human behavior.

**Premack principle** The principle that a high-probability activity can serve as a reinforcer for a low-probability activity.

## "Watch Her, Mom"

One year a third-grade teacher at Salem Church Elementary School in Chesterfield County, Virginia, had an especially loud, active group of third-graders. The teacher, Kristen Blankenship, used a combination of individual and group positive reinforcement as a management strategy.

Not having a cafeteria, students ate their lunches in the classroom. While joining her son, Daniel, for lunch one day, his mother pulled Kristen aside, smiled, and said that Daniel had just whispered to her, "Watch her, Mom. She never yells, but she sure knows how to keep them in line."

is at work when an elementary school teacher tells a child, "When you complete your writing assignment, you can play a game on the computer" (but only effective if playing games on a computer is more desirable for the student than writing). The Premack principle also can be used with the entire class. A teacher might tell the class, "If all of the class gets their homework done by Friday, we will take a field trip next week."

**Make Reinforcers Contingent and Timely**  For a reinforcer to be effective, the teacher must give it only after the child performs the particular behavior. Applied behavior analysts often recommend that teachers make "If . . . then" statements to children—for example, "Tony, if you finish 10 math problems, then you can go out to play." This makes it clear to Tony what he has to do to get the reinforcer. It is important to make the reinforcer contingent on the child's behavior. That is, the child has to perform the behavior to get the reward. If Tony does not complete 10 math problems and the teacher still lets him go out to play, the contingency has not been established.

Reinforcers are more effective when they are given in a timely way, as soon as possible after the child performs the target behavior (Umbreit & others, 2007). This helps children see the contingency connection between the reward and their behavior. If the child completes the target behavior (such as doing 10 math problems by midmorning) and the teacher doesn't give the child playtime until late afternoon, he might have trouble making the contingency connection.

**Select the Best Schedule of Reinforcement**  Most of the examples given so far assume continuous reinforcement—that is, the child is reinforced every time he or she makes a response. In continuous reinforcement, children learn very rapidly, but when the reinforcement stops (for example, the teacher stops praising), extinction also occurs rapidly. In the classroom, continuous reinforcement is rare. A teacher with a classroom of 25 or 30 students can't praise a child every time he or she makes an appropriate response.

Partial reinforcement involves reinforcing a response only part of the time. Skinner (1957) developed the concept of **schedules of reinforcement,** which are partial reinforcement timetables that determine when a response will be reinforced. The four main schedules of reinforcement are fixed-ratio, variable-ratio, fixed-interval, and variable-interval.

On a *fixed-ratio schedule,* a behavior is reinforced after a set number of responses. For example, a teacher might praise the child only after every fourth correct response, not after every response. On a *variable-ratio schedule,* a behavior is reinforced after an average number of times, but on an unpredictable basis. For example, a teacher's praise might average out to being given every fifth response but be given after the second correct response, after eight more correct responses, after the next seven correct responses, and after the next three correct responses.

Interval schedules are determined by the amount of time elapsed since the last behavior was reinforced. On a *fixed-interval schedule,* the first appropriate response after a fixed amount of time is reinforced. For example, a teacher might praise a child for the first good question the child asks after two minutes have elapsed or give a quiz every week. On a *variable-interval schedule,* a response is reinforced after a variable amount of time has elapsed. On this schedule, the teacher might praise the child's question-asking after three minutes have gone by, then after fifteen minutes have gone by, after seven minutes have gone by, and so on. Giving a pop quiz at uneven intervals is another example of a variable-interval schedule.

What is the effect of using these schedules of reinforcement with children? Initial learning is usually faster with continuous rather than partial reinforcement. In other words, when students are first learning a behavior, continuous reinforcement works better. However, partial reinforcement produces greater persistence and greater

**schedules of reinforcement** Partial reinforcement timetables that determine when a response will be reinforced.

resistance to extinction than continuous reinforcement does. Thus, once children master a response, partial reinforcement works better than continuous reinforcement.

Children on fixed schedules show less persistence and faster response extinction than children on variable schedules (Waller & Higbee, 2010). Children show the most persistence on a variable-interval schedule. This schedule produces slow, steady responding because children don't know when the reward will come (Borrero & others, 2010). As we mentioned earlier, giving pop quizzes at uneven intervals is a good example of the variable-interval schedule. If the teacher starts making the quizzes more predictable (for example, once a week on Fridays), children will begin to show the stop-start work pattern that characterizes the fixed-interval schedule. That is, they won't work hard for most of the week; then toward the end of the week they will start cramming for the quiz. Thus, if your goal as a teacher is to increase children's persistence after the behavior has been established, variable schedules work best, especially the variable-interval schedule. Figure 7.5 shows the different response patterns associated with the different schedules of reinforcement.

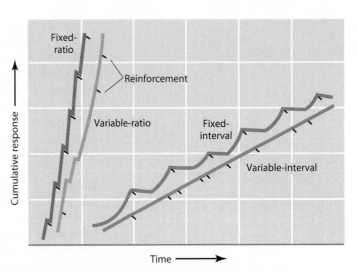

**FIGURE 7.5** SCHEDULES OF REINFORCEMENT AND DIFFERENT PATTERNS OF RESPONDING

In this figure, each hash mark indicates the delivery of reinforcement. Notice that ratio schedules (reinforcement is linked with number of responses) produce higher rates of responding than interval schedules (reinforcement is linked with the amount of time elapsed). The predictability of a reward also is important in that a predictable (fixed) schedule produces a higher response rate than an unpredictable (variable) schedule.

## Consider Contracting

In **contracting**, reinforcement contingencies are put in writing. If problems arise and children don't uphold their end of the bargain, the teacher can refer the children to the contract they agreed to. Applied behavior analysts suggest that a classroom contract should be the result of input from both the teacher and the student. Classroom contracts have "If . . . then" statements and are signed by the teacher and child, then dated. A teacher and child might agree on a contract that states that the child agrees to be a good citizen by doing _____, _____, and _____. As part of the contract, the teacher agrees to _____ if the student behaves in this manner. In some instances, the teacher asks another child to sign the contract as a witness to the agreement.

## Use Negative Reinforcement Effectively

Remember that in *negative reinforcement,* the frequency of response increases because the response removes an aversive (unpleasant) stimulus (Alberto & Troutman, 2009). A teacher who says, "Thomas, you have to stay in your seat and finish writing your story before you join the other students in making a poster," is using negative reinforcement. The negative condition of being left in his seat while the other children are doing something enjoyable will be removed if Thomas finishes the story he should have completed earlier.

Using negative reinforcement has some drawbacks. Sometimes when teachers try to use this behavioral strategy, children throw a tantrum, run out of the room, or destroy materials. These negative outcomes happen most often when children don't have the skills or capabilities to do what the teacher asks of them.

## Use Prompts and Shaping

Earlier in our discussion of operant conditioning, we indicated that discrimination involves differentiating among stimuli or environmental events. Students can learn to discriminate among stimuli or events through differential reinforcement. Two differential reinforcement strategies available to teachers are prompts and shaping (Alberto & Troutman, 2009).

**Prompts**  A **prompt** is an added stimulus or cue that is given just before a response that increases the likelihood that the response will occur. A reading teacher who holds up a card with the letters *w-e-r-e* and says, "Not was, but . . ." is using a verbal prompt. An art teacher who places the label "Watercolors" on one group of paints and "Oils" on another also is using prompts. Prompts help get behavior going. Once the students consistently show the correct responses, the prompts are no longer needed.

**contracting**  Putting reinforcement contingencies into writing.

**prompt**  An added stimulus or cue that is given just before a response, thus increasing the likelihood the response will recur.

Instructions can be used as prompts (Alberto & Troutman, 2009). For example, as the art period is drawing to a close, the teacher says, "Let's get started on reading." If the students keep doing art, the teacher adds the prompt, "Okay, put away your art materials and come with me over to the reading area." Some prompts come in the form of hints, as when the teacher tells students to line up "quietly." Bulletin boards are common locations for prompts, frequently displaying reminders of class rules, due dates for projects, the location of a meeting, and so on. Some prompts are presented visually, as when the teacher places her hand on her ear when a student is not speaking loudly enough.

***Shaping*** When teachers use prompts, they assume that students can perform the desired behaviors. But sometimes students do not have the ability to perform them. In this case, shaping is required (Peterson, 2008). **Shaping** involves teaching new behaviors by reinforcing successive approximations to a specified target behavior. Initially, you reinforce any response that in some way resembles the target behavior. Subsequently, you reinforce a response that more closely resembles the target, and so on until the student performs the target behavior, and then you reinforce it (Wildman, 2008).

Suppose you have a student who has never completed even 50 percent of her math assignments. You set the target behavior at 100 percent, but you reinforce her for successive approximations to the target. You initially might provide a reinforcer (some type of privilege, for example) when she completes 60 percent, then the next time only when she completes 70 percent, then 80, then 90, and finally 100 percent.

Shaping can be an important tool for the classroom teacher because most students need reinforcement along the way to reaching a learning goal (Chance, 2009). Shaping can be especially helpful for learning tasks that require time and persistence to complete. However, when using shaping, remember to implement it only if the other types of positive reinforcement and prompts are not working. Also remember to be patient. Shaping can require the reinforcement of a number of small steps en route to a target behavior, and these might take place only over an extended period of time.

## DECREASING UNDESIRABLE BEHAVIORS

When teachers want to decrease children's undesirable behaviors (such as teasing, hogging a class discussion, or smarting off to the teacher), what are their options? Applied behavior analysts Paul Alberto and Anne Troutman (2009) recommend using these steps in this order:

1. Use differential reinforcement.
2. Terminate reinforcement (extinction).
3. Remove desirable stimuli.
4. Present aversive stimuli (punishment).

Thus, the teacher's first option should be differential reinforcement. Punishment should be used only as a last resort and always in conjunction with providing the child information about appropriate behavior.

**Use Differential Reinforcement** In *differential reinforcement,* the teacher reinforces behavior that is more desired and different than what the child is doing (Pipkin, Vollmer, & Sloman, 2010). For example, the teacher might reinforce a child for doing learning activities on a computer rather than playing games with it, for being courteous rather than interrupting, for being seated rather than running around the classroom, or for doing homework on time rather than late.

**Terminate Reinforcement (Extinction)** The strategy of terminating reinforcement involves withdrawing positive reinforcement from a child's inappropriate behavior.

**shaping** Teaching new behaviors by reinforcing successive approximations to a specified target behavior.

Many inappropriate behaviors are inadvertently maintained by positive reinforcement, especially the teacher's attention. Applied behavior analysts point out that this can occur even when the teacher gives attention to an inappropriate behavior by criticizing, threatening, or yelling at the student.

Many teachers find it difficult to determine whether they are giving too much attention to inappropriate behavior. A good strategy is to get someone to observe your classroom on several occasions and chart the patterns of reinforcement you use with your students (Alberto & Troutman, 2009). If you become aware that you are giving too much attention to a student's inappropriate behavior, ignore that behavior and give attention to the student's appropriate behavior. Always combine taking attention away from inappropriate behavior with giving attention to appropriate behavior. For instance, when a student stops monopolizing the conversation in a group discussion after you withdraw your attention, compliment the student on the improved behavior.

## TEACHING CONNECTIONS: Best Practices
### Strategies for Using Time-Out

In using time-out, you have several options:

1. *Keep the student in the classroom, but deny the student access to positive reinforcement.* This strategy is most often used when the student misbehaves in some minor way. The teacher might ask the student to put his head down on the desk for a few minutes or might move the student to the periphery of an activity where he can still observe other students experiencing positive reinforcement. In Through the Eyes of Teachers, kindergarten teacher Rosemary Moore describes an innovative use of time-out.

### THROUGH THE EYES OF TEACHERS
#### The Peace Place

Resolving conflicts is always difficult for children. When my kindergartners engaged in power struggles, they often turned to me to referee. I thought it would be much more beneficial if they could arrive at their own compromise. Ownership of the plan would make it more acceptable to all parties. To accomplish this, I put two small chairs in a corner of the room. Above the chairs was a sign that said, "Peace Place." Then when I heard a struggle begin, I would send the parties to this corner. There they sat facing each other with their knees almost touching. Their task was to negotiate a "peace plan." When the plan was agreed upon, they were to come to me. I would listen to their plan and either approve it or send them back for another try. Initially, this took some time, but as the children began to realize that the time they spent arguing was time away from the activity they were arguing about, they arrived at their plan much more quickly. It was a pleasure to watch them grow in their negotiating abilities.

2. *For time-out to be effective, the setting from which the student is removed has to be positively reinforcing, and the setting in which the student is placed has to lack positive reinforcement.* For example, if you seat a student in the hall outside your classroom and students from other classes come down the hall and talk with the student, the time-out is clearly not going to serve its intended purpose.

3. *Before using time-out, be sure to tell the student what behaviors are responsible for the time-out.* For example, say to the student, "You tore up Corey's paper, so go to time-out right now for five minutes." Don't get into an argument with the student or accept lame excuses as to why the student should not get a time-out. If necessary, take the student to the time-out location. If the misbehavior occurs again, identify the behavior once again and repeat the time-out. If the student starts yelling, knocking over furniture, and so on, add time to time-out. Be sure to let the student out of time-out when the designated time away from positive reinforcement is up. Don't comment on how well the student behaved during time-out; just return the student to the prior activity.

4. *Positively reinforce the student's positive behavior when he or she is not in time-out.* Reinforce positive behavior during regular class time. For example, if a student got time-out for disruptive behavior, the teacher can praise her for quietly working on an assignment during class.

5. *Keep records of each time-out session, especially if a time-out room is used.* This will help you monitor effective and ethical use of time-outs.

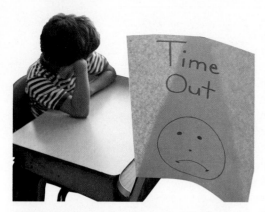

This second-grade student has been placed in "time-out" for misbehaving. *What is the nature of time-out?*

**Remove Desirable Stimuli** Suppose you have tried the first two options, and they haven't worked. A third option is to remove desirable stimuli from the student. Two strategies for accomplishing this are time-out and response cost.

***Time-Out*** The most widely used strategy for removing desirable stimuli is **time-out,** in which the student is taken away from positive reinforcement (Kazdin, 2008).

***Response Cost*** A second strategy for removing desirable stimuli involves **response cost,** which refers to taking a positive reinforcer away from a student, as when the student loses certain privileges. For example, after a student misbehaves, the teacher might take away 10 minutes of recess time or the privilege of being a class monitor. Response cost typically involves some type of penalty or fine. As with time-out, response cost should always be used in conjunction with strategies for increasing the student's positive behaviors.

I recently asked teachers how they use applied behavior analysis in their classroom. Following are their responses.

**EARLY CHILDHOOD** We use applied behavior analysis with our preschoolers by giving time-out to students who are misbehaving. For example, if a child throws a

toy across the room during free play, hits another student, or speaks disrespectfully, we explain why this behavior is inappropriate and give time-out. The child has to sit in a chair, away from other students, and misses five minutes of free-play time. As a result, the child learns that negative behavior will not be tolerated.

—**MISSY DANGLER,** *Suburban Hills School*

**ELEMENTARY SCHOOL: GRADES K–5** For my second-grade students, tangible or implied (a smile from me or attention) rewards work best. I also find that a com-

bination of individual and group rewards work well in my classroom. For example, I give each student a "Compliment Sheet" at the beginning of the school year. When I see behavior that I want to encourage, I tell the student publicly that he or she may have a compliment. The student fills in one of the circles on the compliment page, and the others in the class—seeing that this student's particular behavior has

been rewarded—imitate the student's behavior almost immediately. The rules are that no compliment may be removed and that a student may not ask for a compliment. When the Compliment Sheet is completed, a big deal is made of it, and the student can go to the prize box and choose a small token such as stickers. At first this is an external way of conditioning behavior, but the children seem to move rapidly from wanting the "thing" to wanting the compliment to wanting the positive attention to doing the right thing.

—**JANINE GUIDA POUTRE,** *Clinton Elementary School*

**MIDDLE SCHOOL: GRADES 6–8** I'm not big on rewards for my sixth-grade students. I think students who act inappropriately in class need to learn how to cope

and deal with controlling their behavior without expecting to receive something in return. Instead of rewards, I give students who turn from negative behavior to positive behavior more responsibility in the classroom. For example, students who engage in good behavior are given classroom jobs—for example, handing out pencils and paper, checking my mailbox in the main office, and turning on/shutting off computers. Students love responsibility and are happy when I depend on them to perform important duties in the classroom.

—**FELICIA PETERSON,** *Pocantico Hills School*

**time-out** Removing an individual from positive reinforcement.

**response cost** Taking a positive reinforcer away from an individual.

**HIGH SCHOOL: GRADES 9–12**   I set clear expectations for my high school students. For example, it is a classroom expectation that students  are in my classroom, ready to work, when the bell rings. Students soon learn that walking in late results in not knowing what is going on in class and may lower their grade if they cannot complete an activity. It is important to start class on time and not let the stragglers determine when class will start.

—SANDY SWANSON, *Menomonee Falls High School*

*What are some effective strategies for using reprimands?*

**Present Aversive Stimuli (Punishment)**   Most people associate the presentation of aversive (unpleasant) stimuli with punishment, as when a teacher yells at a student or a parent spanks a child. However, in accordance with the definition of punishment given earlier in the chapter, an aversive stimulus is punishment only if it decreases the undesirable behavior. All too often, though, aversive stimuli are not effective punishments in that they do not decrease the unwanted behavior and indeed sometimes increase the unwanted behavior over time (Bordin & others, 2009). A history of harsh physical discipline is linked to adolescent depression and externalized problems, such as juvenile delinquency, and is also related to poor school performance (Alyahri & Goodman, 2008; Bender & others, 2007). A recent study found that experiencing harsh corporal punishment in childhood was related to prefrontal cortex volume in young adults (Tomoda & others, 2009). Recall from Chapter 2 that the prefrontal cortex—where thinking, reasoning, and decision making take place—is the brain's highest level.

The most common types of aversive stimuli that teachers use are verbal reprimands. These are more effectively used when the teacher is near the student rather than across the room and when used together with a nonverbal reprimand such as a frown or eye contact. Reprimands are more effective when they are given immediately after unwanted behavior and when they are short and to the point. Such reprimands do not have to involve yelling and shouting, which often just raise the noise level of the classroom and present the teacher as an uncontrolled model for students. Instead, a firmly stated "stop doing that" with eye contact is often sufficient to stop unwanted behavior. Another strategy is to take the student aside and reprimand him in private rather than in front of the entire class.

Many countries, such as Sweden, have banned the physical punishment of schoolchildren (which usually involves school paddling) by principals and teachers (Durrant, 2008). However, in 2003, 23 U.S. states still allowed it, with the greatest prevalence in southern states. A study of college students in 11 countries found that the United States and Canada have more favorable attitudes toward corporal punishment than many other countries (Curran & others, 2001; Hyman & others, 2001) (see Figure 7.6). Use of corporal punishment by parents is legal in every state in America, and it is estimated that 70 to 90 percent of American parents have spanked their children (Straus, 1991). A national survey of U.S. parents with 3- and 4-year-old children found that 26 percent of parents reported spanking their children frequently, and 67 percent of the parents reported yelling at their children frequently (Regaldo & others, 2004).

In U.S. schools, male minority students from low-income backgrounds are the most frequent recipients of physical punishment. Many psychologists and educators argue that physical punishment of students should not be used in any circumstance.

Numerous problems are associated with using aversive stimuli, physical or otherwise, as intended punishment (Durrant, 2008):

• Especially when you use intense punishment such as yelling or screaming, you are presenting students with an out-of-control model for handling stressful situations.

**Thinking Back/Thinking Forward**

Authoritarian parenting is restrictive and punitive and so is an authoritarian classroom management style. Both are less effective styles than authoritative (rather than authoritarian) parenting and an authoritative classroom management style. Chapter 3, p. 78; Chapter 14, p. 489

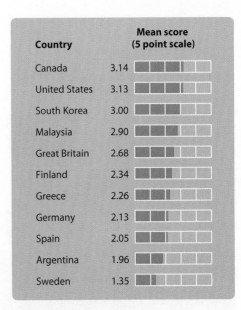

| Country | Mean score (5 point scale) |
|---|---|
| Canada | 3.14 |
| United States | 3.13 |
| South Korea | 3.00 |
| Malaysia | 2.90 |
| Great Britain | 2.68 |
| Finland | 2.34 |
| Greece | 2.26 |
| Germany | 2.13 |
| Spain | 2.05 |
| Argentina | 1.96 |
| Sweden | 1.35 |

**FIGURE 7.6** ATTITUDES ABOUT CORPORAL PUNISHMENT IN DIFFERENT COUNTRIES

A 5-point scale was used to assess attitudes toward corporal punishment, with scores closer to 1 indicating an attitude against its use and scores closer to 5 suggesting an attitude for its use.

- Punishment can instill fear, rage, or avoidance in students. Skinner's biggest concern was this: What punishment teaches is how to avoid something. For example, a student who experiences a punitive teacher might show a dislike for the teacher and not want to come to school.
- When students are punished, they might become so aroused and anxious that they can't concentrate clearly on their work for a long time after the punishment has been given.
- Punishment tells students what not to do rather than what to do. If you make a punishing statement, such as, "No, that's not right," always accompany it with positive feedback, such as, "but why don't you try this."
- What is intended as punishment can turn out to be reinforcing. A student might learn that misbehaving will not only get the teacher's attention but put the student in the limelight with classmates as well.
- Punishment can be abusive. When parents discipline their children, they might not intend to be abusive, but they might become so upset and angry when they are punishing the child that they become abusive. Teachers in all 50 states are legally required to report reasonable suspicions of child abuse to the police or local child protective services. Teachers should learn about their state's laws and their school district's policy regarding the reporting of child abuse (Brodkin, 2009).

A debate about punishment that is ongoing involves a distinction between mild punishment and more intense punishment (Grusec, 2011; Knox, 2010; Thompson, 2009d). A research review of 26 studies concluded that only severe or predominant use of spanking, not mild spanking, compared unfavorably with alternative discipline practices with children (Larzelere & Kuhn, 2005). Indeed, there are few longitudinal studies of punishment and few studies that distinguish adequately between moderate and heavy use of punishment. Thus, in the view of some experts, based on the research evidence available, it is still difficult to tell whether the effects of physical punishment are harmful to children's development—even though the idea that it might not be harmful is distasteful to some individuals (Grusec, 2009). One thing that is clear regarding research on punishment of children is that if physical punishment is used it needs to be mild, infrequent, age-appropriate, and used in the context of a positive parent-child relationship (Grusec, 2011). And also clear is that when physical punishment involves abuse, it can be very harmful to children's development (Cicchetti & Toth, 2011).

A final lesson related to using punishment less often is to spend more class time monitoring what students do right rather than what they do wrong. Too often disruptive behavior, not competent behavior, grabs a teacher's attention. Every day make it a point to scan your classroom for positive student behaviors that you ordinarily would not notice and give students attention for them.

*When used effectively, what are ways that operant conditioning and applied behavior analysis can be used to help teachers manage the classroom? What are some criticisms that have been leveled at these approaches?*

## EVALUATING OPERANT CONDITIONING AND APPLIED BEHAVIOR ANALYSIS

Operant conditioning and applied behavior analysis have made contributions to teaching practice (Kraft, 2010; Moore Parten & others, 2010). Reinforcing and punishing consequences are part of teachers' and students' lives. Teachers give grades, praise and reprimand, smile and frown. Learning about how such consequences affect students' behavior improves your capabilities as a teacher. Used effectively, behavioral techniques can help you manage your classroom. Reinforcing certain behaviors can improve some students' conduct and—used in conjunction with time-out—can increase desired behaviors in some incorrigible students.

## TEACHING CONNECTIONS: Best Practices
### Strategies for Using Applied Behavior Analysis to Change Behavior

1. *Focus on what you want students to do, rather than on what you want them not to do.* This will help you in using differential reinforcement. If you reinforce desirable behaviors that are incompatible with undesirable behaviors (for instance, being on-task, which is incompatible with being off-task), students will know what it is you want from them. In addition, tell students what they are doing right.

2. *Remember that one size does not fit all when it comes to reinforcement.* It is only reinforcement if the behavior increases. What is reinforcing to one student may be punishing to another. Extra recess may be highly valued by many children, but not by the child whose peers have rejected him/her. There are developmental differences in what students find to be reinforcing. What is reinforcing to first-graders is not likely to be reinforcing to middle school students. A very popular reinforcer among young children is lunch with the teacher. This is often used as punishment at the middle school level.

3. *Teachers often inadvertently reinforce behavior we do not want to continue.* As discussed above, this may be in the form of attention. For some students any attention (even negative) is better than no attention. However, we do it in other ways as well. We might inadvertently negatively reinforce a student's disruptive behavior by sending him/her out of the classroom, and thereby removing what the student considers to be an aversive stimulus (some content area, a test, reading aloud . . .).

4. *When using the Premack principle, we give students information about what they should find enjoyable.* "If you finish your math problems, then you may use the computer." This statement tells young children that using the computer is preferable to completing math problems. Is this a message you want to send?

5. *Teachers are not the only sources of reinforcement and punishment in the classroom.* Classmates often reinforce behavior that we are trying to extinguish. For instance, the class clown is reinforced by laughter from peers. As children develop peers have greater influence, thus reinforcement from peers may become more important than reinforcement from teachers.

6. *Punishment is not punishment unless the behavior decreases.* Just as reinforcement is not one-size-fits-all, neither is punishment. We see similar individual and developmental differences in what children see as punishing.

7. *Taking away recess as punishment (response cost) is a bad idea.* Children need unstructured time to engage in physical activity, play, and socialize (e.g., Pellegrini, 2005). Breaks such as recess can increase young children's attention to academic tasks (Pellegrini, Huberty, & Jones, 1995; Pellegrini & Smith, 1998). Older children and adolescents benefit from recess in similar ways.

8. *Given the problems associated with punishment, it should be a last resort.* Try other ways of getting students to do what it is you want them to do before you resort to punishment.

Critics of operant conditioning and applied behavior analysis argue that the whole approach places too much emphasis on external control of students' behavior; they say a better strategy is to help students learn to control their own behavior and become internally motivated (Eisenberger, 2009). Some critics argue that it is not the reward or punishment that changes behavior but, rather, the belief or expectation that certain actions will be rewarded or punished (Schunk, 2011). In other words, the behavioral theories do not give adequate attention to cognitive processes involved in learning (Anderson, 2009). Critics also point to potential ethical problems when operant conditioning is used inappropriately, as when a teacher immediately resorts to punishing students instead of first considering reinforcement strategies, or punishes a student without also giving the student information about appropriate behavior. Another criticism is that when teachers spend a lot of time using applied behavior analysis, they might focus too much on student conduct and not enough on academic learning. We will have much more to say about student conduct in Chapter 14.

### Thinking Back/Thinking Forward

The new trend in classroom management places more emphasis on guiding students toward self-discipline and less on externally controlling the student. Chapter 14, p. 477

## Review, Reflect, and Practice

**3** Apply behavior analysis to education.

### REVIEW
- What is applied behavior analysis?
- What are six ways to increase desirable behaviors?
- What are four ways to decrease undesirable behaviors?
- What are some effective and ineffective uses of operant conditioning and applied behavior analysis?

### REFLECT
- Come up with your own example for each of the six ways to increase desirable behavior in an educational setting.

### PRAXIS™ PRACTICE

1. The uses of applied behavior analysis in education include all of the following *except*
   a. asking a child to reflect about undesirable behavior.
   b. increasing desirable behavior.
   c. using prompts and shaping.
   d. decreasing undesirable behavior.

2. Ms. Sanders wants her students to be quiet and ready to learn as soon as possible after coming in from recess. Sometimes the children are so excited that they have difficulty quieting down. To help remind them that it is time to be quiet and listen, Ms. Sanders flicks the light switch on and off several times. The children immediately quiet and listen to her instructions. According to applied behavioral analysis, what is Ms. Sanders doing when she turns the lights on and off?
   a. prompting
   b. punishing
   c. coercing
   d. shaping

3. Sid is a real handful in class. He talks when he should be working quietly. He gets out of his seat without permission. He often disrupts class. His third-grade teacher, Ms. Marin, sends him out into the hall when he misbehaves as a form of time-out. However, Sid continues to misbehave. At one point, Ms. Marin checks on Sid in the hall and finds him quietly tossing a ball back and forth with a child from another class. Why has time-out been ineffective with Sid?
   a. Ms. Marin did not present an aversive enough stimulus to Sid.
   b. Ms. Marin did not use differential reinforcement effectively.
   c. Sid finds being in class to be reinforcing.
   d. Sid finds being in the hallway to be reinforcing.

4. Critics of applied behavior analysis techniques often point out that when these techniques are used in the classroom they
   a. lead to physical abuse of students.
   b. do not work effectively.
   c. take time away from academics.
   d. emphasize external control of behavior.

*Please see the answer key at the end of the book.*

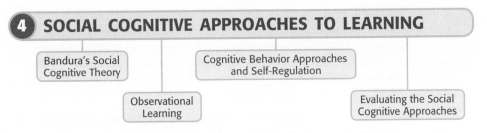

**Because** students' thoughts affect their behavior and learning, a number of cognitive approaches to learning have been proposed. In this section, we will explore several social cognitive approaches, beginning with social cognitive theory. This theory evolved out of behavioral theories but has become increasingly more cognitive (Spiegler & Guevremont, 2010).

## BANDURA'S SOCIAL COGNITIVE THEORY

**Social cognitive theory** states that social and cognitive factors, as well as behavior, play important roles in learning. Cognitive factors might involve the student's expectations for success; social factors might include students' observing their parents' achievement behavior. Social cognitive theory is an increasingly important source of classroom applications (Schunk, 2011).

Albert Bandura (1986, 1997, 2001, 2009, 2010a,b,c) is the main architect of social cognitive theory. He says that when students learn, they can cognitively represent or transform their experiences. Recall that in operant conditioning, connections occur only between environmental experiences and behavior.

Bandura developed a *reciprocal determinism model* that consists of three main factors: behavior, person/cognitive, and environment. As shown in Figure 7.7, these factors can interact to influence learning: Environmental factors influence behavior, behavior affects the environment, person (cognitive) factors influence behavior, and so on. Bandura uses the term *person,* but I have modified it to *person/cognitive* because so many of the person factors he describes are cognitive. The person factors Bandura describes that do not have a cognitive bent are mainly personality traits and temperament. Recall from Chapter 4 that such factors might include being introverted or extraverted, active or inactive, calm or anxious, and friendly or hostile. Cognitive factors include expectations, beliefs, attitudes, strategies, thinking, and intelligence.

Consider how Bandura's model might work in the case of the achievement behavior of a high school student we will call Sondra:

- *Cognition influences behavior.* Sondra develops cognitive strategies to think more deeply and logically about how to solve problems. The cognitive strategies improve her achievement behavior.
- *Behavior influences cognition.* Sondra's studying (behavior) has led her to achieve good grades, which in turn produce positive expectancies about her abilities and give her self-confidence (cognition).
- *Environment influences behavior.* The school Sondra attends recently developed a pilot study-skills program to help students learn how to take notes, manage their time, and take tests more effectively. The study-skills program improves Sondra's achievement behavior.
- *Behavior influences environment.* The study-skills program is successful in improving the achievement behavior of many students in Sondra's class. The students' improved achievement behavior stimulates the school to expand the program so that all students in the high school participate in it.
- *Cognition influences environment.* The expectations and planning of the school's principal and teachers made the study-skills program possible in the first place.

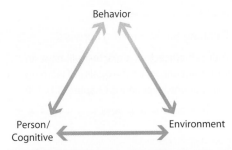

**FIGURE 7.7** BANDURA'S SOCIAL COGNITIVE THEORY

Bandura's social cognitive theory emphasizes reciprocal influences of behavior, environment, and person/cognitive factors.

**Thinking Back/Thinking Forward**

The Big Five Personality Factors are openness, conscientiousness, extraversion, agreeableness, and neuroticism (emotional stability). Chapter 4, p. 132

Albert Bandura, who developed social cognitive theory.

**social cognitive theory** Bandura's theory that social and cognitive factors, as well as behavior, play important roles in learning.

**Thinking Back/Thinking Forward**

Your self-efficacy as a teacher will have an important impact on the quality of learning your students' experience. Chapter 13, p. 450

• *Environment influences cognition.* The school establishes a resource center where students and parents can go to check out books and materials on improving study skills. The resource center also makes study-skills tutoring services available to students. Sondra and her parents take advantage of the center's resources and tutoring. These resources and services improve Sondra's thinking skills.

In Bandura's learning model, person/cognitive factors play important roles. The person/cognitive factor that Bandura (2009, 2010a) has emphasized the most in recent years is **self-efficacy,** the belief that one can master a situation and produce positive outcomes. Bandura (2009, 2010a) says that self-efficacy has a powerful influence over behavior. For example, a student who has low self-efficacy might not even try to study for a test because he doesn't believe it will do him any good. We will have much more to say about self-efficacy in Chapter 13.

Next we discuss the important learning process of observational learning, which is another of Bandura's main contributions. As you read about observational learning, note how person/cognitive factors are involved.

**FIGURE 7.8** BANDURA'S MODEL OF OBSERVATIONAL LEARNING

In Bandura's model of observational learning, four processes need to be considered: attention, retention, production, and motivation. *How might these processes be involved in this classroom situation in which a teacher is demonstrating how to tell time?*

## OBSERVATIONAL LEARNING

**Observational learning** is learning that involves acquiring skills, strategies, and beliefs by observing others. Observational learning involves imitation but is not limited to it. What is learned typically is not an exact copy of what is modeled but rather a general form or strategy that observers often apply in creative ways (Bandura, 2010b). The capacity to learn behavior patterns by observation eliminates tedious trial-and-error learning. In many instances, observational learning takes less time than operant conditioning.

**Thinking Back/Thinking Forward**

Four types of attention are selective, divided, sustained, and executive. Chapter 8, p. 258

**Thinking Back/Thinking Forward**

For memory to work, students have to take information in (encoding), store it or represent it (storage), and retrieve it for some purpose later (retrieval). Chapter 8, p. 263

**Processes in Observational Learning** Bandura (1986) describes four key processes in observational learning: attention, retention, production, and motivation (see Figure 7.8):

• *Attention.* Before students can produce a model's actions, they must attend to what the model is doing or saying. Attention to the model is influenced by a host of characteristics. For example, warm, powerful, atypical people command more attention than do cold, weak, typical people. Students are more likely to be attentive to high-status models than to low-status models. In most cases, teachers are high-status models for students.

• *Retention.* To reproduce a model's actions, students must code the information and keep it in memory so that they retrieve it. A simple verbal description or a vivid image of what the model did assists students' retention. For example, the teacher might say, "I'm showing the correct way to do this. You have to do this step first, this step second, and this step third," as she models how to solve a math problem. A video with a colorful character demonstrating the importance of considering other students' feelings might be remembered better than the teacher's instruction by itself. Such colorful characters are at the heart of the popularity of *Sesame Street* with children. Students' retention will be improved when teachers give vivid, logical, and clear demonstrations.

**self-efficacy** The belief that one can master a situation and produce positive outcomes.

**observational learning** Learning that involves acquiring skills, strategies, and beliefs by observing others.

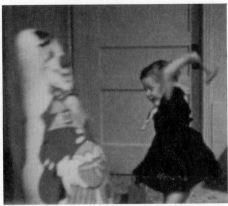

**FIGURE 7.9** BANDURA'S CLASSIC BOBO DOLL STUDY: THE EFFECTS OF OBSERVATIONAL LEARNING ON CHILDREN'S AGGRESSION

(*Left*) an adult model aggressively attacks the Bobo doll. (*Right*) a kindergarten-age girl who has observed the model's aggressive actions follows suit. *In Bandura's experiment, under what conditions did the children reproduce the model's aggressive actions?*

- *Production.* Children might attend to a model and code in memory what they have seen, yet because of limitations in their motor ability, not be able to reproduce the model's behavior. A 13-year-old might watch basketball player Lebron James and golfer Michelle Wie execute their athletic skills to perfection, or observe a famous pianist or artist, but not be able to reproduce their motor actions. Teaching, coaching, and practice can help children improve their motor performances.

- *Motivation.* Often children attend to what a model says or does, retain the information in memory, and possess the motor skills to perform the action but are not motivated to perform the modeled behavior. This was demonstrated in Bandura's (1965) classic Bobo doll study when children who saw the model being punished did not reproduce the punished model's aggressive actions (see Figure 7.9). However, when they subsequently were given a reinforcement or incentive (stickers or fruit juice), they did imitate the model's behavior.

Bandura argues that reinforcement is not always necessary for observational learning to take place. But if the child does not reproduce the desired behaviors, four types of reinforcement can help do the trick: (1) reward the model; (2) reward the child; (3) instruct the child to make self-reinforcing statements such as, "Good, I did it!" or, "Okay, I've done a good job of getting most of this right; now if I keep trying I will get the rest"; or (4) show how the behavior leads to reinforcing outcomes.

**Models in the Classroom**   As you can see, you will be an important model in students' lives. Your students will be observing your behavior countless times every day of the school year (Bandura, 2010b). An intentional way that teachers can use observational learning is through *modeled demonstrations,* in which the teacher describes and shows students how to solve problems and successfully complete academic tasks. For example, a teacher might demonstrate how to create an outline for a paper or do a PowerPoint presentation. Also students can become more reflective and think more critically by observing models.

In addition to being a key model yourself for children to observe and learn from, students learn from observing many other models, including parents, mentors, and peers. Students especially are likely to attend to and attempt to learn the behaviors of individuals who are competent and have prestige (Schunk, 2011). For example, a teacher might invite a well-known professional athlete to come to her class and talk about how important reading and doing well in school is. Because of the athlete's prestige, the students are likely to attend to what the athlete says and be motivated to adopt the behaviors she recommends.

Peers also can be important models in the classroom (Schunk, 2011). By observing peers successfully do school tasks, especially peers that a student likes or admires, the student's self-efficacy for performing well in school likely increases.

DIVERSITY

RESEARCH

Dr. Leonard Berry is a mentor in the 3-to-1 program in Dallas. He is shown here with Brandon Scarbough, 13 (*front*), and his own son, Leonard, 12 (*back*). Brandon not only has benefited from Dr. Berry's mentoring but also has become friends with his son.

One concern about the models that children and adolescents observe and interact with in the classroom is the lack of ethnic and gender diversity. As students in U.S. schools have become more ethnically diverse in recent decades, their teachers are still overwhelmingly non-Latino White females. In 2004 approximately 15 percent of U.S. public school students were African American, but just over 7 percent of their teachers were African American (National Center for Education Statistics, 2007). Only a small percentage of the African American teachers were males. In the same year, Latinos made up more than 19 percent of U.S. public school students, but just over 6 percent of their teachers were Latino. A majority of U.S. public schools still do not have a single ethnic minority teacher.

Men comprise about 10 percent of elementary school teachers but comprise nearly half of middle and high school teachers (many of whom are lured by additional incentives for coaching athletic teams). The situation is likely to get worse. In a recent national survey of college students, only .05 percent of males said their probable career would be as an elementary school teacher or administrator, and only 1.8 percent indicated that a similar career in secondary education was likely to be in their future (Pryor & others, 2008).

Regardless of your ethnic background, look around the community for possible mentors for students, especially students who come from low-income backgrounds and who lack positive role models. For example, the aim of the *3-to-1 mentoring program* is to surround each ethnic minority male student with three positive ethnic minority role models. The program began when several African American men were challenged by a sermon delivered by Zach Holmes at the St. Luke's Methodist Church in Dallas. In the sermon, Reverend Holmes urged his congregation to become more involved with children, both their own and children in the community, who don't have good role models. The 3-to-1 mentoring program has signed up more than 200 men and 100 boys (ages 4 to 18). That's far short of the goal of three mentors for each boy, but the men are working on increasing the number of mentors in the program. Some of the men in the mentoring program have their own children, like Dr. Leonard Berry, a physician, who has two sons and a daughter. He heeded the minister's challenge and regularly participates in the mentoring program, which involves academic tutoring as well as outings to activities such as sporting and cultural events. The mentors also take the students to visit the Johnson Space Center in Houston. To evaluate the roles that models and mentors have played in your own life and can play in your students' lives, complete Self-Assessment 7.1.

I recently asked teachers how they use observational learning in the classroom. Following are their responses.

**EARLY CHILDHOOD**   Preschool children spend a lot of time doing informal observation and may try to imitate what someone else has done to see if they can get similar results. For example, when a teacher tells a group of children to walk down the hall instead of running and praises those students who are walking, children who are running often slow down and walk, hoping they will be praised by the teacher.

—**HEIDI KAUFMAN**, *Metro West YMCA Child Care and Educational Program*

**ELEMENTARY SCHOOL: GRADES K–5**   My basic assumption with my elementary school students is that they learn appropriate behavior by observation and experience. Class rules are established and agreed upon at the beginning of the school year. I model effective learning behaviors, identify them when students use them, teach study skills, and end every class by stating one or two behavioral skills that were done well.

—**KEREN ABRA**, *Convent of the Sacred Heart Elementary School*

# SELF-ASSESSMENT 7.1
## Models and Mentors in My Life and My Students' Lives

Having positive role models and mentors can make an important difference in whether individuals develop optimally and reach their full potential. First, evaluate the role models and mentors who have played an important part in your life. Second, think about the type of role model you want to be for your students. Third, give some thought to how you will incorporate other models and mentors into your students' lives. Fourth, explore who your education mentor might be.

## MY MODELS AND MENTORS

List the most important role models and mentors in your life. Then describe what their positive modeling and mentoring have meant to your development.

Role Models and Mentors                     Their Contributions

1. _____    _____

2. _____    _____

3. _____    _____

4. _____    _____

5. _____    _____

### The Type of Role Model I Want to Be for My Students

Describe which characteristics and behaviors you believe are the most important for you to model for your students.

1. _____

2. _____

3. _____

4. _____

5. _____

### How Will I Incorporate Models and Mentors in My Classroom?

Describe a systematic plan for bringing models and mentors into your students' lives in one or more domain(s) you plan to teach, such as math, English, science, and music.

_____

_____

### Who Will Be My Education Mentor? What Would My Ideal Education Mentor Be Like?

Do you have someone in mind who might serve as an education mentor when you become a teacher? If so, describe the person.

_____

What would your ideal education mentor be like?

_____

_____

**MIDDLE SCHOOL: GRADES 6–8** I use observational learning with my sixth-grade students all the time. I make sure that they understand my expectations by not  only discussing them but also showing them what I expect. For example, I create checklists for my students at the beginning of the year so they can assess their work and monitor their progress. We then go over the checklists one-on-one and as a group and discuss ways that they can improve their work or behavior in order to reach their desired goals.

—**Casey Maass,** *Edison Middle School*

**HIGH SCHOOL: GRADES 9–12** As a high school art teacher, I am fortunate to work in an area that is visual, hands-on, and creative. Through one-on-one demon-strations, small-group and sometimes total class lectures/demonstrations, my students observe and learn artistic skills.

—**Dennis Peterson,** *Deer River High School*

TECHNOLOGY

DEVELOPMENT

*What educational lessons can be learned from Sesame Street?*

Thinking Back/Thinking Forward

Attention is a key aspect of processing information. Chapter 8, p. 254

Thinking Back/Thinking Forward

Gardner proposed that intelligence consists of eight different domains. Chapter 4, p. 115

**Models in the Media—the Example of Sesame Street** Children also are exposed to an extensive number of models in the media, so it's especially important that those experiences be positive. The television show *Sesame Street* is a very effective educational program that includes many positive observational learning opportunities for young children, and is designed to teach both cognitive and social skills (Bryant, 2007). The program began in 1969 and is still going strong. A fundamental message of *Sesame Street* is that education and entertainment work well together (Lesser, 1972). On *Sesame Street,* learning is exciting and entertaining. One study found that preschool children who watched the program were more likely to positively resolve conflicts, make positive comments about others, and engage in less stereotyping than their counterparts who did not watch it (Cole & others, 2003).

*Sesame Street* also illustrates the point that teaching can be done in both direct and indirect ways. Using the direct way, a teacher tells children exactly what they are going to be taught and then actually teaches it to them. This method is often used on *Sesame Street* to teach cognitive skills. But social skills usually are communicated in indirect ways on the show. Thus, rather than telling children, "You should cooperate with people," a sequence of events is shown to help them figure out what it means to be cooperative and what the advantages are.

Some of the attentional techniques used on *Sesame Street* are worthwhile to consider in the classroom. These involve first *catching* the child's attention, then *directing* it, and finally *sustaining* it. Music and sound are very effective in eliciting children's attention. For example, in teaching children to discriminate sounds, an automobile horn might be sounded or a computer's keyboard repeatedly pressed. Music is especially useful because it leads children to become actively involved in what they are watching or listening to. It is not unusual for children watching *Sesame Street* to get up out of their seats and start dancing and singing along with the jingles. Once the child's attention has been captured, it should be directed to something. Surprise and novelty are especially helpful in this regard; children's attention is directed because they begin to anticipate what is going to happen next. Once attention is directed, it then needs to be sustained. *Sesame Street* especially uses humor to accomplish this. Humor is judiciously placed: Ernie outsmarts Bert; the Cookie Monster annoyingly interrupts a lecture given by Kermit the Frog. For young children, physical gags often are funnier than verbal ones, and much of the humor that is effective involves physical acts that are surprising and incongruous.

## TEACHING CONNECTIONS: Best Practices
### Strategies for Effectively Using Observational Learning

1. *Think about what type of model you will present to students.* Every day, hour after hour, students will watch and listen to what you say and do. Just by being around you, students will absorb a great deal of information. They will pick up your good or bad habits, your expectations for their high or low achievement, your enthusiastic or bored attitude, your controlled or uncontrolled manner of dealing with stress, your learning style, your gender attitudes, and many other aspects of your behavior. A good strategy, then, is that you behave as you want your students to behave.

2. *Demonstrate and teach new behaviors.* Demonstrating means that you, the teacher, are a model for your students' observational learning. Demonstrating how to do something, from solving a math problem, reading, writing, thinking, to controlling anger or performing physical skills, is a common task for teachers. For example, a teacher might model how to diagram a sentence, develop a strategy for solving algebraic equations, or shoot a basketball. When demonstrating how to do something, you need to call students' attention to the relevant details of the learning situation. Your demonstrations also should be clear and follow a logical sequence.

3. *Think about ways to use peers as effective models.* The teacher is not the only model in the classroom. Children can also pick up their peers' good and bad habits, high or low achievement orientations, and so on, through observational learning. Remember that students are often motivated to imitate high-status models. Older peers usually have higher status than same-age peers. Thus, a good strategy is to have older peers from a higher grade model how to engage in the behaviors you want your students to perform. As children develop, peers increase in importance and therefore their influence increases as well. Older children and adolescents are much more likely to look to their peers as models. For students with low abilities or who are not performing well, another low-achieving student who struggles but puts considerable effort into learning and ultimately performs the behaviors can be a good model. More will be said in Chapter 10, "Social Constructivist Approaches," about peer collaboration and peers as tutors.

4. *Think about ways that mentors can be used as models.* Students and teachers benefit from having a mentor—someone they look up to and respect, someone who serves as a competent model, someone who is willing to work with them and help them achieve their goals. Just spending a few hours a week with a mentor can make a difference in a student's life, especially if the student's parents have not been good role models. As a teacher, a potential mentor for you is a more experienced teacher, possibly someone who teaches down the hall and has had a number of years of experience in dealing with some of the same problems and issues you will have to cope with.

5. *Evaluate which classroom guests will provide good models for students.* To change the pace of classroom life for you and your students, invite guests who have something meaningful to talk about or demonstrate. Recall what we said in Chapter 4 about Gardner's theory of multiple intelligences: There likely are some domains (physical, musical, artistic, or other) in which you don't have the skills to serve as a competent model for your students. When you need to have such skills demonstrated to your students, spend some time locating competent models in the community. Invite them to come to your classroom to demonstrate and discuss their skills. If this can't be arranged, set up field trips in which you take students to see them where they are working or performing. In Through the Eyes of Teachers, fourth-grade teacher Marlene Wendler describes a positive role model her school brings to teachers' classrooms.

## THROUGH THE EYES OF TEACHERS
### Here Comes the Judge

Our local judge has taken a proactive role in trying to eliminate teen behavioral problems. With a half dozen adults from the community, he comes to the fourth-grade classrooms in our areas and puts on skits about bullying. They show the whole group picking on a student in a bus situation. Then they do the skit again with someone in the group stopping the bullying. The students then role-play bullying situations, learning what to do if they are bullied and how to help someone who is bullied. Having the judge come to our school has made a lasting impression on our students.

6. *Consider the models children observe on television, videos, and computers.* Students observe models when they watch television programs, videos, films, or computer screens in your classroom. The principles of observational learning we described earlier apply to these media. For example, the extent to which the students perceive the media models as high or low in status, intriguing or boring, and so on will influence the extent of their observational learning.

TECHNOLOGY

| Poster 1 |
| :-- |
| **While listening** |

1. Does this make sense?
2. Am I getting this?
3. I need to ask a question before I forget.
4. Pay attention.
5. Can I do what the teacher is saying to do?

| Poster 2 |
| :-- |
| **While planning** |

1. Do I have everything together?
2. Do I have my friends tuned out so I can get this done?
3. I need to get organized first.
4. What order can I do this in?
5. I know this stuff.

| Poster 3 |
| :-- |
| **While working** |

1. Am I working fast enough?
2. Stop staring at my girlfriend (boyfriend) and get back to work.
3. How much time is left?
4. Do I need to stop and start all over?
5. This is hard for me but I can manage it.

| Poster 4 |
| :-- |
| **While checking** |

1. Did I finish everything?
2. What do I need to recheck?
3. Am I proud of this work?
4. Did I write all of the words?
5. I think I'm finished. I organized myself. Did I daydream too much, though?

**FIGURE 7.10** SOME POSTERS DEVELOPED BY A FIFTH-GRADE CLASS TO HELP THEM REMEMBER HOW TO EFFECTIVELY TALK TO THEMSELVES

From Brenda H. Manning and Beverly D. Payne, *Self-Talk for Teachers and Students*, "Four posters developed by a fifth grade class" p. 125, © 1996. Reproduced by permission of Pearson Education, Inc.

**cognitive behavior approaches** Changing behavior by getting individuals to monitor, manage, and regulate their own behavior rather than letting it be controlled by external factors.

**self-instructional methods** Cognitive behavior techniques aimed at teaching individuals to modify their own behavior.

# COGNITIVE BEHAVIOR APPROACHES AND SELF-REGULATION

Operant conditioning spawned applications and other real-world settings, and the interest in cognitive behavior approaches has also produced such applications. In the fifth century B.C., the Chinese philosopher Confucius said, "If you give a man a fish, you feed him for a day. If you teach a man to fish, you feed him for a lifetime." As you read about the cognitive behavior approaches and self-regulation, you will discover that they reflect Confucius' simple expression.

**Cognitive Behavior Approaches** In the **cognitive behavior approaches,** the emphasis is on getting students to monitor, manage, and regulate their own behavior rather than letting it be controlled by external factors. In some circles, this has been called *cognitive behavior modification* (Rait, Monsen, & Squires, 2010; Ryum & others, 2010). Cognitive behavior approaches stem from both cognitive psychology, with its emphasis on the effects of thoughts on behavior, and behaviorism, with its emphasis on techniques for changing behavior. Cognitive behavior approaches try to change students' misconceptions, strengthen their coping skills, increase their self-control, and encourage constructive self-reflection (Spiegler & Guevremont, 2010).

**Self-instructional methods** are cognitive behavior techniques aimed at teaching individuals to modify their own behavior by talking to themselves in positive ways. Following are some self-talk strategies that students and teachers can use to cope more effectively with stressful situations such as preparing to take a test (Meichenbaum, Turk, & Burstein, 1975):

- *Prepare for anxiety or stress.* "What do I have to do?" "I'm going to develop a plan to deal with it." "I'll just think about what I have to do." "I won't worry. Worry doesn't help anything." "I have a lot of different strategies I can use."

- *Confront and handle the anxiety or stress.* "I can meet the challenge." "I'll keep on taking just one step at a time." "I can handle it. I'll just relax, breathe deeply, and use one of the strategies." "I won't think about my stress. I'll just think about what I have to do."

- *Cope with feelings at critical moments.* "What is it I have to do?" "I knew my anxiety might increase. I just have to keep myself in control." "When the anxiety comes, I'll just pause and keep focusing on what I have to do."

- *Use reinforcing self-statements.* "Good, I did it." "I handled it well." "I knew I could do it." "Wait until I tell other people how I did it!"

In many instances, the strategy is simply to replace negative self-statements with positive ones. For example, a student might say to herself, "I'll never get this work done by tomorrow." This can be replaced with positive self-statements such as these: "This is going to be tough, but I think I can do it." "I'm going to look at this as a challenge rather than a stressor." "If I work really hard, I might be able to get it done." Or in having to participate in a class discussion, a student might replace the negative thought of "Everyone else knows more than I do, so what's the use of saying anything" with positive self-statements such as these: "I have as much to say as anyone else." "My ideas may be different, but they are still good." "It's okay to be a little nervous; I'll relax and start talking." Figure 7.10 shows posters that students in one fifth-grade class developed to help them remember how to talk to themselves while listening, planning, working, and checking.

Talking positively to oneself can help teachers as well as students reach their full potential. Uncountered negative thinking has a way of becoming a self-fulfilling prophecy. You think you can't do it, and so you don't. If negative self-talk is a problem for you, at random times during the day ask yourself, "What am I saying to myself right now?" Moments that you expect will be potentially stressful are excellent times to examine your self-talk. Also monitor your students' self-talk. If you hear students saying, "I can't do this" or "I'm so slow I'll never get this done," spend some time getting them to replace their negative self-talk with positive self-talk.

Cognitive behaviorists recommend that students improve their performance by monitoring their own behavior (Schunk, 2011). Such monitoring can involve getting students to keep charts or records of their behavior. When I (your author) wrote this book, I had a chart on my wall with each of the chapters listed. I planned how long it would take me to do each of the chapters, and then as I completed each one I checked it off and wrote down the date of completion. Teachers can get students to do some similar monitoring of their own progress by getting them to keep records of how many assignments they have finished, how many books they have read, how many homework papers they have turned in on time, how many days in a row they have not interrupted the teacher, and so on. In some cases, teachers place these self-monitoring charts on the walls of the classroom. Alternatively, if the teacher thinks that negative social comparison with other students will be highly stressful for some students, then a better strategy might be to have students keep private records (in a notebook, for example) that are periodically checked by the teacher.

Self-monitoring is an excellent strategy for improving learning, and one that you can help students learn to do effectively. By completing Self-Assessment 7.2, you should get a sense of the benefits of self-monitoring for your students.

**Self-Regulatory Learning**   Educational psychologists increasingly advocate the importance of self-regulatory learning (Winne & Nisbett, 2010). **Self-regulatory learning** consists of the self-generation and self-monitoring of thoughts, feelings, and behaviors in order to reach a goal. These goals might be academic (improving comprehension while reading, becoming a more organized writer, learning how to do multiplication, asking relevant questions) or they might be socioemotional (controlling one's anger, getting along better with peers).

As children become older, their capacity for self-regulation increases (McClelland & others, 2011; Thompson & Goodman, 2009). The increased capacity in self-regulation is linked to developmental advances in the brain's prefrontal cortex, which was discussed in Chapter 2 (Nelson, 2011).

Self-regulatory learners do the following (Winne, 2001, 2005):

- Set goals for extending their knowledge and sustaining their motivation
- Are aware of their emotional makeup and have strategies for managing their emotions
- Periodically monitor their progress toward a goal
- Fine-tune or revise their strategies based on the progress they are making
- Evaluate obstacles that may arise and make the necessary adaptations.

Self-regulation is an important aspect of school readiness (Ponitz & others, 2009). In a recent study, children who could regulate their emotions effectively in early childhood had better math and literacy scores in the early elementary school years than their counterparts who had poor emotion regulation (Graziano & others, 2007).

Researchers also have found that high-achieving students are often self-regulatory learners (Anderman & Anderman, 2010). For example, compared with low-achieving students, high-achieving students set more specific learning goals, use more strategies to learn, self-monitor their learning more, and more systematically evaluate their progress toward a goal. In one study of adolescents from low-income families, a higher level of self-regulation was linked to higher achievement and better grades (Buckner, Mezzacappa, & Beardslee, 2009).

Researchers have found that teaching students strategies as well as self-regulation skills is critical in many academic areas (Winne & Nesbitt, 2010). For example, most students with writing problems don't have adequate writing strategies to review and assess the quality of a story. Thus, to become better writers they not only need to

RESEARCH

**self-regulatory learning** The self-generation and self-monitoring of thoughts, feelings, and behaviors in order to reach a goal.

# SELF-ASSESSMENT 7.2
## Self-Monitoring

Self-monitoring can benefit you as well as your students. Many successful learners regularly self-monitor their progress to see how they are doing in their effort to complete a project, develop a skill, or perform well on a test or other assessment. For the next month, self-monitor your study time for this course you are taking in educational psychology. To achieve high grades, most instructors recommend that students spend two or three hours out of class studying, doing homework, and working on projects for every hour they are in class in college (Santrock & Halonen, 2009). The experience of self-monitoring your own study time should give you a sense of how important such skills are for your students to develop. You might adapt this form for students' homework, for example. Remember from our discussion of Bandura's social cognitive theory that self-efficacy involves your belief that you can master a situation and produce positive outcomes. One way to evaluate self-efficacy is your expectancy for attaining a particular score on an upcoming quiz or test. Determine what score or grade you want to achieve on your next quiz or test. Then each day you study, rate your self-efficacy for achieving the score you desire on a 3-point scale: 1 = not very confident, 2 = moderately confident, and 3 = very confident.

## FORM FOR SELF-MONITORING STUDY TIME

| Date | Assignment | Time Started | Time Finished | STUDY CONTEXT | | | |
| --- | --- | --- | --- | --- | --- | --- | --- |
| | | | | Where? | With Whom? | Distractions | Self-Efficacy |
| | | | | | | | |
| | | | | | | | |
| | | | | | | | |
| | | | | | | | |
| | | | | | | | |
| | | | | | | | |
| | | | | | | | |
| | | | | | | | |
| | | | | | | | |
| | | | | | | | |
| | | | | | | | |
| | | | | | | | |
| | | | | | | | |
| | | | | | | | |
| | | | | | | | |
| | | | | | | | |

learn self-regulation skills but also need training in writing strategy instruction (Harris & others, 2008).

Teachers, tutors, mentors, counselors, and parents can help students become self-regulatory learners. Barry Zimmerman, Sebastian Bonner, and Robert Kovach (1996) developed a model for turning low-self-regulatory students into students who engage in these multistep strategies: (1) self-evaluation and monitoring, (2) goal setting and strategic planning, (3) putting a plan into action and monitoring it, and (4) monitoring outcomes and refining strategies (see Figure 7.11).

Zimmerman and colleagues describe a seventh-grade student who is doing poorly in history and apply their self-regulatory model to her situation. In step 1, she self-evaluates her studying and test preparation by keeping a detailed record of them. The teacher gives her some guidelines for keeping these records. After several weeks, the student turns the records in and traces her poor test performance to low comprehension of difficult reading material.

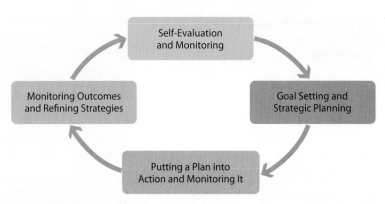

FIGURE **7.11** A MODEL OF SELF-REGULATORY LEARNING

In step 2, the student sets a goal, in this case of improving reading comprehension, and plans how to achieve the goal. The teacher assists her in breaking the goal into components, such as locating main ideas and setting specific goals for understanding a series of paragraphs in her textbook. The teacher also provides the student with strategies, such as focusing initially on the first sentence of each paragraph and then scanning the others as a means of identifying main ideas. Another support the teacher might offer the student if available is adult or peer tutoring in reading comprehension.

In step 3, the student puts the plan into action and begins to monitor her progress. Initially, she may need help from the teacher or tutor in identifying main ideas in the reading. This feedback can help her monitor her reading comprehension more effectively on her own.

In step 4, the student monitors her improvement in reading comprehension by evaluating whether it has had any impact on her learning outcomes. Most importantly, has her improvement in reading comprehension led to better performance on history tests?

Suppose that self-evaluations in this case reveal that the strategy of finding main ideas has only partly improved her comprehension, and only when the first sentence contains the paragraph's main idea. Consequently, the teacher recommends further strategies. Figure 7.12 describes how teachers can apply the self-regulatory model to homework.

The development of self-regulation is influenced by many factors, among them modeling and self-efficacy (Bandura, 2010a,b). Consider how modeling can be an effective strategy for building self-regulatory skills and self-efficacy in improving reading and writing in Zimmerman's four-phase model (Schunk & Zimmerman, 2006). Among the self-regulatory skills that models can engage in are planning and managing time effectively, attending to and concentrating, organizing and coding information strategically, establishing a productive work environment, and using social resources. For example, students might observe a teacher engage in an effective time management strategy and verbalize appropriate principles. By observing such models, students can come to believe that they also can plan and manage time effectively, which creates a sense of self-efficacy for academic self-regulation and motivates students to engage in those activities.

Self-efficacy can influence a student's choice of tasks, effort expended, persistence, and achievement (Bandura, 2010a). Compared with students who doubt their learning capabilities, those with high self-efficacy for acquiring a skill or performing a task participate more readily, work harder, persist longer in the face of difficulty, and achieve at a higher level. Yet self-efficacy is not the only influence on achievement. High self-efficacy will not result in competent performance when requisite

FIGURE **7.12** APPLYING THE SELF-REGULATORY MODEL TO HOMEWORK

**1. Self-evaluation and monitoring**

- The teacher distributes forms so that students can monitor specific aspects of their studying.

- The teacher gives students daily assignments to develop their self-monitoring skills and a weekly quiz to assess how well they have learned the methods.

- After several days, the teacher begins to have students exchange their homework with their peers. The peers are asked to evaluate the accuracy of the homework and how effectively the student engaged in self-monitoring. Then the teacher collects the homework for grading and reviews the peers' suggestions.

**2. Goal setting and strategic planning**

- After a week of monitoring and the first graded exercise, the teacher asks students to give their perceptions of the strengths and weaknesses of their study strategies. The teacher emphasizes the link between learning strategies and learning outcomes.

- The teacher and peers recommend specific strategies that students might use to improve their learning. Students may use the recommendations or devise new ones. The teacher asks students to set specific goals at this point.

**3. Putting a plan into action and monitoring it**

- The students monitor the extent to which they actually enact the new strategies.

- The teacher's role is to make sure that the new learning strategies are openly discussed.

**4. Monitoring outcomes and refining strategies**

- The teacher continues to give students opportunities to gauge how effectively they are using their new strategies.

- The teacher helps students summarize their self-regulatory methods by reviewing each step of the self-regulatory learning cycle. She also discusses with students the hurdles the students had to overcome and the self-confidence they have achieved.

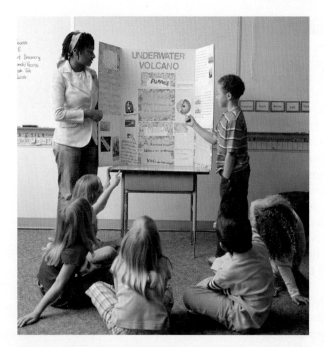

*What are some contributions of the social cognitive approaches to educating children? What are some criticisms of these approaches?*

knowledge and skills are lacking. We will further explore self-efficacy, goal setting, planning, and self-regulation in Chapter 13.

Teachers who encourage students to be self-regulatory learners convey the message that students are responsible for their own behavior, for becoming educated, and for becoming contributing citizens to society. Another message conveyed by self-regulatory learning is that learning is a personal experience that requires active and dedicated participation by the student.

## EVALUATING THE SOCIAL COGNITIVE APPROACHES

The social cognitive approaches have made important contributions to educating children (Spiegler & Guevremont, 2010). While keeping the behaviorists' scientific flavor and emphasis on careful observation, they significantly expanded the emphasis of learning to include social and cognitive factors. Considerable learning occurs through watching and listening to competent models and then imitating what they do. The emphasis in the cognitive behavior approach on self-instruction, self-talk, and self-regulatory learning provides an important shift from learning controlled by others to responsibility for one's own learning (Spiegler & Guevremont, 2010). These self-enacted strategies can significantly improve students' learning.

## TEACHING CONNECTIONS: Best Practices
### Strategies for Encouraging Students to Be Self-Regulated Learners

Following are some effective strategies for guiding students to engage in self-regulated learning:

1. *Gradually guide students to become self-regulated learners.* Helping students become self-regulated learners takes time and requires considerable monitoring, guidance, and encouragement on your part. High-achieving students are more likely to already be self-regulated learners than low-achieving students. All students can benefit from practicing their self-regulated learning skills, but recognize that low-achieving students will need more instruction and time to develop these skills. We should start this in very early elementary school and gradually increase the requirement and opportunity for self-regulation until in high school students are largely self-regulated. In early elementary years, we might do this by giving the children a week to complete all the learning center activities we have prepared, but allowing them to choose in what order they accomplish them. They would check them off as they complete them and we would monitor their progress throughout the week. Later, we might assign students to read a book and write a report about it. Students would determine how long they are going to allow for each piece of the assignment. Again, we would monitor their progress toward the goal of a completed book report, perhaps having interim due dates. Finally, at the high school level, students would be responsible for doing their own progress monitoring unless they request help.

2. *Make the classroom learning experience challenging and interesting for students.* When students are bored and uninterested in learning, they are less likely to become self-regulated learners. Instead of giving students one particular book to read, providing them with a choice from a variety of interesting books is likely to encourage their motivation to read. Giving students choices increases students' personal investment in their learning and increases their self-regulation (Blumenfeld, Kempler & Krajcik, 2006).

3. *Provide tips about thoughts and actions that will help students engage in self-regulation.* These might include specific guidelines, such as, "Planning for 30 minutes will help you . . ." and, "Every day stop and monitor where you are in what you want to accomplish." Other suggestions include encouraging students to reflect on their strengths and weaknesses in a learning situation and encouraging them to search for help and ways to use help effectively (All Kinds of Minds, 2009).

4. *Give students opportunities to experience the type of activities recommended by Zimmerman and his colleagues (1996).* That is, create projects for students in which they self-evaluate their current learning, set a goal to improve their learning and plan how to reach the goal, put the plan into action and monitor their progress toward the goal, and monitor the outcome and refine their strategies. Monitor students' progress through these steps and encourage their ability to engage in these learning activities independently. Provide scaffolding only as needed.

5. *Model self-regulated learning.* Verbalize effective self-regulation strategies for students, and tell them how you use self-regulation in your learning.

6. *Make sure that students don't just self-regulate but combine self-regulation with effective strategies for learning.* Students can self-regulate all they want, but if they don't have the "know-how," their self-regulation is unlikely to be beneficial.

Critics of the social cognitive approaches come from several camps. Some cognitive theorists point out that the approaches still focus too much on overt behavior and external factors and not enough on the details of how cognitive processes such as thinking, memory, and problem solving actually take place. Some developmentalists criticize them for being nondevelopmental, in the sense that they don't specify age-related, sequential changes in learning. It is true that social cognitive theory does not address development in great depth because it is mainly a theory of learning and social behavior. But labeling it as nondevelopmental is not accurate. Also, humanistic theorists fault social cognitive theorists for not placing enough attention on self-esteem and caring, supportive relationships. All of these criticisms also have been leveled at the behavioral approaches, such as Skinner's operant conditioning.

## Review, Reflect, and Practice

**4** Summarize social cognitive approaches to learning.

### REVIEW

- How does Figure 7.7 help to summarize Bandura's social cognitive theory? What does he mean by self-efficacy?
- What is Bandura's model of observational learning?
- What is the focus of self-instructional methods? What does self-regulatory learning involve?
- What are some contributions and criticisms of the social cognitive approaches?

### REFLECT

- Give some examples of how you use self-instructional and self-regulatory methods in your personal life. How effective are these methods? Should you use them more than you do? Explain.

### PRAXIS™ PRACTICE

1. Macy sits staring at her math homework. She has not attempted a single problem. "What's the use?" she says with a sigh. "I'll never get it right." According to Bandura's social cognitive theory, what is the most plausible explanation for Macy's response?
   a. Macy does not have the requisite language skills to do her homework.
   b. Macy has low self-efficacy.
   c. Macy has too much math anxiety.
   d. Macy's teacher has not provided enough negative feedback about her math homework.

2. Matt is the star of his high school's basketball team. The team is doing very well this year, in large part because of Matt's performance. This makes him a very popular student. About halfway through basketball season, Matt decides to shave his head. Soon other members of the basketball team shave their heads. Then the trend spreads to the rest of the school. By the end of February, 30 percent of the male students in the school have shaved heads. According to Bandura's social cognitive theory, what is the most plausible explanation for the students' behavior?
   a. Matt is a high-status role model.
   b. Matt was not punished.
   c. Matt was positively reinforced.
   d. Matt's self-efficacy was raised.

3. Marsha, a junior in high school, has debilitating test anxiety. She is particularly anxious about high-stakes tests, such as final exams. She often becomes so anxious that she "blanks out" and forgets everything that she has studied. What would a teacher using a cognitive behavior modification approach do to help her with her test anxiety?
   a. Help Marsha to develop anxiety management strategies and use self-instructions.
   b. Give her a study-skills book to read.
   c. Encourage her to think more about the consequences if she does do better on the tests.
   d. Tell Marsha to study until she has overlearned the material.

## Review, Reflect, and Practice

**PRAXIS™ PRACTICE (CONTINUED)**

4. An important way in which social cognitive theory builds on behavioral theory is its emphasis on
   a. personality.
   b. self-efficacy.
   c. attitudes.
   d. careful observation.

   *Please see the answer key at the end of the book.*

## Connecting with the Classroom: Crack the Case

# Consequences

Adam, a student in Mr. Potter's fourth-grade class, is disruptive from time to time although he is very bright. One day during language arts, Adam began talking loudly to other students in his area. He was also laughing and telling jokes. Mr. Potter chose to ignore Adam's behavior, hoping he would stop on his own. But Adam didn't stop. Instead, his behavior became more raucous. Still Mr. Potter ignored it. Soon Adam was making enough noise that Mr. Potter was afraid that students in the neighboring classrooms would be disturbed, so he verbally reprimanded Adam.

Adam was a bit quieter for the next few minutes. After that, however, he once again became loud and disruptive. Again Mr. Potter verbally reprimanded him. This time he also told Adam that if he continued with his disruptive behavior, he would have to go to the office. Adam's behavior became even more disruptive, so Mr. Potter sent him to the office. When Adam arrived at the office it was full of people—teachers getting their mail and making copies, volunteers signing in, students who were ill, students sent on errands, and other students who had been sent for disciplinary reasons. The school secretary told Adam to have a seat, which he did. He conversed with every person who entered the office as well as those who were there when he arrived. Half an hour after his arrival, he was sent back to class. He behaved quite well for the rest of the day, to Mr. Potter's relief.

The next day when students were assigned to write a paragraph, Adam once again became disruptive. He loudly told jokes to his classmates, laughed until tears were streaming down his face, and threw a paper airplane across the room. Mr. Potter reprimanded him and asked him to stop. When Adam didn't comply, Mr. Potter sent him to the office, which was once again bustling with activity.

Over the course of the next two weeks, Adam was sent to the office for disrupting class each day, always during a writing assignment. Mr. Potter was perplexed. Even more perplexing was that within three school days other children were becoming disruptive as well, requiring that they too be sent to the office.

1. What are the issues in this case?

Answer the following questions using principles of behavioral learning theories and correct terminology:

2. Why did Adam continue to disrupt class despite the consequences?

3. What has Adam learned?

4. Why did the other students join Adam in his disruptive behavior?

5. What should Mr. Potter do now?

6. What was Mr. Potter most likely trying to do when he initially ignored Adam's disruptive behavior?
   a. He was trying to extinguish the behavior by not reinforcing it.
   b. He was trying to negatively reinforce the behavior.
   c. He was trying to positively reinforce the behavior.
   d. He was trying to punish the behavior.

7. If Adam's goal was to escape writing assignments, which of the following best explains the consequences in operant conditioning terms?
   a. Adam was negatively reinforced for his behavior. An aversive stimulus was removed.
   b. Adam was positively reinforced for his behavior. A pleasant stimulus was presented.
   c. Adam was punished for his behavior. A pleasant stimulus was removed.
   d. Adam was punished for his behavior. An aversive stimulus was presented.

# Behavioral and Social Cognitive Approaches

**1 WHAT IS LEARNING?** Define learning and describe five approaches to studying it.

What Learning Is
and Is Not

Approaches to Learning

Learning is a relatively permanent change in behavior, knowledge, and thinking skills that occurs through experience. Learning is not involved in inborn, or innate, behaviors, such as blinking or swallowing.

Behaviorism is the view that behavior should be explained by experiences that can be directly observed, not by mental processes. Classical conditioning and operant conditioning are behavioral views that emphasize associative learning. Psychology became more cognitive in the last part of the twentieth century, and the cognitive emphasis continues today. This is reflected in four cognitive approaches to learning we discuss in this book: social cognitive, information processing, cognitive constructivist, and social constructivist. Social cognitive approaches emphasize the interaction of behavior, environment, and person (cognition) in explaining learning. Information-processing approaches focus on how children process information through attention, memory, thinking, and other cognitive processes. Cognitive constructivist approaches emphasize the child's cognitive construction of knowledge and understanding. Social constructivist approaches focus on collaboration with others to produce knowledge and understanding.

**2 BEHAVIORAL APPROACH TO LEARNING:** Compare classical conditioning and operant conditioning.

Classical Conditioning

Operant Conditioning

In classical conditioning, the organism learns to connect, or associate, stimuli. A neutral stimulus (such as the sight of a person) becomes associated with a meaningful stimulus (such as food) and acquires the capacity to elicit a similar response. Classical conditioning involves these factors: unconditioned stimulus (UCS), conditioned stimulus (CS), unconditioned response (UCR), and conditioned response (CR). Classical conditioning also involves generalization, discrimination, and extinction. Generalization is the tendency of a new stimulus similar to the original conditioned stimulus to produce a similar response. Discrimination occurs when the organism responds to certain stimuli and not to others. Extinction involves the weakening of the CR in the absence of the UCS. Systematic desensitization is a method based on classical conditioning that reduces anxiety by getting the individual to associate deep relaxation with successive visualizations of increasingly anxiety-producing situations. Classical conditioning is better at explaining involuntary behavior than voluntary behavior.

In operant conditioning (also called instrumental conditioning), the consequences of behavior produce changes in the probability that the behavior will occur. Operant conditioning's main architect was B. F. Skinner. Reinforcement (reward) is a consequence (either positive or negative) that increases the probability that a behavior will occur; punishment is a consequence that decreases the probability that a behavior will occur. In positive reinforcement, a behavior increases because it is followed by a rewarding stimulus (such as praise). In negative reinforcement, a behavior increases because the response removes an aversive (unpleasant) stimulus. Generalization, discrimination, and extinction also are involved in operant conditioning. Generalization means giving the same response to similar stimuli. Discrimination is differentiating among stimuli or environmental events. Extinction occurs when a previously reinforced response is no longer reinforced and the response decreases.

## ❸ APPLIED BEHAVIOR ANALYSIS IN EDUCATION: Apply behavior analysis to education.

**What Is Applied Behavior Analysis?**

**Increasing Desirable Behaviors**

**Decreasing Undesirable Behaviors**

**Evaluating Operant Conditioning and Applied Behavior Analysis**

Applied behavior analysis involves applying the principles of operant conditioning to change human behavior.

Strategies to increase desirable behaviors include choosing effective reinforcers, making reinforcers timely and contingent, selecting the best schedule of reinforcement, contracting, using negative reinforcement effectively, and using prompts and shaping. Find out which reinforcers work best with which students. The Premack principle states that a high-probability activity can be used to reinforce a low-probability activity. Applied behavior analysts recommend that a reinforcement be contingent—that is, be given in a timely manner and only if the student performs the behavior. "If . . . then" statements can be used to make it clear to students what they have to do to get a reward. Skinner described a number of schedules of reinforcement. Most reinforcement in the classroom is partial. Skinner described four schedules of partial reinforcement: fixed-ratio, variable-ratio, fixed-interval, and variable-interval. Contracting involves putting reinforcement contingencies in writing. Although negative reinforcement can increase some students' desirable behavior, exercise caution with students who don't have good self-regulatory skills. A prompt is an added stimulus or cue that increases the likelihood that a discriminative stimulus will produce a desired response. Shaping involves teaching new behaviors by reinforcing successive approximations to a specified target behavior.

Strategies for decreasing undesirable behaviors include using differential reinforcement, terminating reinforcement, removing desirable stimuli, and presenting aversive stimuli. In differential reinforcement, the teacher might reinforce behavior that is more appropriate or that is incompatible with what the student is doing. Terminating reinforcement (extinction) involves taking reinforcement away from a behavior. Many inappropriate behaviors are maintained by teacher attention, so taking away the attention can decrease the behavior. The most widely used strategy for removing desirable stimuli is time-out. A second strategy for removing desirable stimuli involves response cost, which occurs when a positive reinforcer, such as a privilege, is taken away from the student. An aversive stimulus becomes a punisher only when it decreases behavior. The most common forms of punisher in the classroom are verbal reprimands. Punishment should be used only as the last option and in conjunction with reinforcement of desired responses. Physical punishment should not be used in the classroom.

Used effectively, behavioral techniques can help you manage your classroom. Critics say that these approaches place too much emphasis on external control and not enough on internal control. They also argue that ignoring cognitive factors leaves out much of the richness of students' lives. Critics warn about potential ethical problems when operant conditioning is used inappropriately. And some critics say that teachers who focus too much on managing the classroom with operant techniques may place too much emphasis on conduct and not enough on academic learning.

## ❹ SOCIAL COGNITIVE APPROACHES TO LEARNING: Summarize social cognitive approaches to learning.

**Bandura's Social Cognitive Theory**

**Observational Learning**

Albert Bandura is the main architect of social cognitive theory. His reciprocal determinism model of learning includes three main factors: person/cognition, behavior, and environment. The person (cognitive) factor given the most emphasis by Bandura in recent years is self-efficacy, the belief that one can master a situation and produce positive outcomes.

Observational learning is learning that involves acquiring skills, strategies, and beliefs by observing others. Bandura describes four key processes in observational learning: attention, retention, production, and motivation. Observational learning is involved in many aspects of children's lives, including the classroom and the media.

Cognitive Behavior
Approaches and
Self-Regulation

Evaluating the Social
Cognitive Approaches

Self-instructional methods are cognitive behavior techniques aimed at teaching individuals to modify their own behavior. In many cases, it is recommended that students replace negative self-statements with positive ones. Cognitive behaviorists argue that students can improve their performance by monitoring their behavior. Self-regulatory learning consists of the self-generation and self-monitoring of thoughts, feelings, and behaviors to reach a goal. High-achieving students are often self-regulatory learners. One model of self-regulatory learning involves these components: self-evaluation and monitoring, goal setting and strategic planning, putting a plan into action, and monitoring outcomes and refining strategies. Self-regulation is an important aspect of school readiness. An important aspect of self-regulatory learning is that it gives students responsibility for their learning.

The social cognitive approaches have significantly expanded the scope of learning to include cognitive and social factors in addition to behavior. A considerable amount of learning occurs by watching and listening to competent models and then imitating what they do. The cognitive behavior emphasis on self-instruction, self-talk, and self-regulatory learning provides an important shift from learning controlled by others to self-management of learning. Critics of the social cognitive approaches say that they still place too much emphasis on overt behavior and external factors and not enough on the details of how cognitive processes such as thinking occur. They also are criticized for being nondevelopmental (although social cognitive advocates argue this label is not justified) and not giving enough attention to self-esteem and warmth.

## KEY TERMS

learning 217
behaviorism 218
mental processes 218
associative learning 218
classical conditioning 220
systematic desensitization 221
operant conditioning 222

reinforcement (reward) 222
punishment 222
positive reinforcement 222
negative reinforcement 222
applied behavior
    analysis 225
Premack principle 225

schedules of reinforcement 226
contracting 227
prompt 227
shaping 228
time-out 230
response cost 230
social cognitive theory 235

self-efficacy 236
observational learning 236
cognitive behavior
    approaches 242
self-instructional
    methods 242
self-regulatory learning 243

## PORTFOLIO ACTIVITIES

**Collaborative Work Decreasing Undesirable Behaviors.** Together with three or four other students in your class, consider the following students' undesirable behaviors. You want to decrease the behaviors. What is the best strategy for each? Discuss and compare your strategies with the group. (1) Andrew, who likes to utter profanities every now and then; (2) Sandy, who tells you to quit bugging her when you ask her questions; (3) Matt, who likes to mess up other students' papers; and (4) Rebecca, who frequently talks with other students around her while you are explaining or demonstrating something. (INTASC: Principles 2, 5)

**Independent Reflection Design a Self-Regulation Plan.** Letitia is a high school student who doesn't have adequate self-regulatory skills,

and this lack is causing her to have serious academic problems. She doesn't plan or organize, has poor study strategies, and uses ineffective time management. Using Zimmerman's four-step strategy, design an effective self-regulation program for Letitia. (INTASC: Principle 5)

**Research/Field Experience** *Sesame Street* **and Social Cognitive Learning.** *Sesame Street* uses many effective techniques to increase children's attention and help them learn. Watch an episode. Analyze the show. How were these techniques used on the show you watched? Describe any additional techniques you observed that you might be able to use in your classroom. (INTASC: Principles 2, 7, 9)

## STUDY, PRACTICE, AND SUCCEED

Visit **www.mhhe.com/santrockep5e** to review the chapter with self-grading quizzes and self-assessments, to apply the chapter material to

two more Crack the Case studies, and for suggested activities to develop your teaching portfolio.

# THE INFORMATION-PROCESSING APPROACH

*The mind is an enchanting thing.*

—Marianne Moore
*American Poet, 20th Century*

## Learning **Goals**

**1** Describe the information-processing approach.

**2** Characterize attention and summarize how it changes during development.

**3** Discuss memory in terms of encoding, storage, and retrieval.

**4** Draw some lessons about learning from the way experts think.

**5** Explain the concept of metacognition and identify some ways to improve children's metacognition.

# Teaching **Stories**   Laura Bickford

Laura Bickford chairs the English Department at Nordoff High School in Ojai, California. She recently spoke about how she encourages students to think:

> I believe the call to teach is a call to teach students how to think. In encouraging critical thinking, literature itself does a good bit of work for us, but we still have to be guides. We have to ask good questions. We have to show students the value in asking their own questions, in having discussions and conversations. In addition to reading and discussing literature, the best way to move students to think critically is to have them write. We write all the time in a variety of modes: journals, formal essays, letters, factual reports, news articles, speeches, or other formal oral presentations. We have to show students where they merely scratch the surface in their thinking and writing. I call these moments "hits and runs." When I see this "hit and run" effort, I draw a window on the paper. I tell them it is a "window of opportunity" to go deeper, elaborate, and clarify. Many students don't do this kind of thinking until they are prodded to do so.
>
> I also use metacognitive strategies all the time—that is, helping students know about knowing. These include asking students to comment on their learning after we have finished particular pieces of projects and asking them to discuss in advance what we might be seeking to learn as we begin a new project or activity. I also ask them to keep reading logs so they can observe their own thinking as it happens. For example, they might copy a passage from a reading selection and comment on it. Studying a passage from J. D. Salinger's *The Catcher in the Rye*, a student might write, "I've never thought about life the way that Holden Caulfield does. Maybe I see the world differently than he does. He always is so depressed. I'm not depressed. Salinger is good at showing us someone who is usually depressed. How does he manage to do that?" In addition, I ask students to comment on their own learning by way of grading themselves. This year a student gave me one of the most insightful lines about her growth as a reader that I have ever seen from a student. She wrote, "I no longer think in a monotone when I'm reading." I don't know if she grasps the magnitude of that thought or how it came to be that she made that change. It is magic when students see themselves growing like this.

# Preview

In the opening story, teacher Laura Bickford tells how she uses metacognitive strategies, one of the important aspects of cognitive learning and a major topic of this chapter. In addition to addressing metacognition, we'll explore what it means to take an information-processing approach in teaching, and we will examine three important aspects of cognition: attention, memory, and expertise.

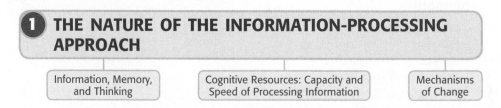

**1** **THE NATURE OF THE INFORMATION-PROCESSING APPROACH**

| Information, Memory, and Thinking | Cognitive Resources: Capacity and Speed of Processing Information | Mechanisms of Change |

How capable are children? Proponents of the information-processing approach to learning believe they are highly capable. Children attend to information being presented and tinker with it. They develop strategies for remembering. They form concepts. They reason and solve problems. These important skills are the topics of this section.

## INFORMATION, MEMORY, AND THINKING

The **information-processing approach** emphasizes that children manipulate information, monitor it, and strategize about it. Central to this approach are the processes of memory and thinking. According to the information-processing approach, children develop a gradually increasing capacity for processing information, which allows them to acquire increasingly complex knowledge and skills (Demetriou, Mouyi, & Spanoudis, 2011; Halford & Andrews, 2011; Siegler, 2009).

**information-processing approach** A cognitive approach in which people manipulate information, monitor it, and strategize about it. Central to this approach are the cognitive processes of memory and thinking.

Behaviorism and its associative model of learning was a dominant force in psychology until the 1950s and 1960s, when many psychologists began to acknowledge that they could not explain children's learning without referring to mental processes such as memory and thinking. The term *cognitive psychology* became a label for approaches that sought to explain behavior by examining mental processes. Although a number of factors stimulated the growth of cognitive psychology, none was more important than the development of computers. The first modern computer, developed by John von Neumann in the late 1940s, showed that inanimate machines could perform logical operations. This suggested that some mental operations might be carried out by computers, possibly telling us something about the way human cognition works. Cognitive psychologists often draw analogies to computers to help explain the relation between cognition and the brain (Martinez, 2010). The physical brain is compared with the computer's hardware, cognition with its software. Although computers and software aren't perfect analogies for brains and cognitive activities, nonetheless the comparison contributed to our thinking about the child's mind as an active information-processing system.

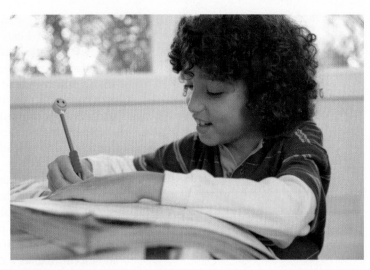

*What two characteristics of cognitive resources have an important influence on memory and problem solving?*

## COGNITIVE RESOURCES: CAPACITY AND SPEED OF PROCESSING INFORMATION

As children grow and mature, and as they experience the world, their information-processing abilities increase, influenced by concurrent increases in both capacity and speed of processing. These two characteristics of capacity and speed are often referred to as *cognitive resources* and are proposed to have an important influence on memory and problem solving.

Both biology and experience contribute to growth in cognitive resources (Bjorklund, 2011). Think about how much faster you can process information in your native language than in a second language. The changes in the brain we described in Chapter 2 provide a biological foundation for increased cognitive resources (Zelazo & Lee, 2011). As children grow and mature, important biological developments occur both in brain structures, such as changes in the frontal lobes, and at the level of neurons, such as the blooming and pruning of connections between neurons that produces fewer but stronger connections (Nelson, 2011). Also, as we discussed in Chapter 2, myelination (the process that covers the axon with a myelin sheath) increases the speed of electrical impulses in the brain. Myelination continues at least through adolescence (Paus, 2009).

Most information-processing psychologists argue that an increase in capacity as well as speed improves processing of information (Ashcraft & Radvansky, 2010; Siegler, 2009). For example, as children's information-processing capacity increases, they likely can hold in mind several dimensions of a topic or problem simultaneously, whereas younger children are more prone to focus on only one dimension. Adolescents can discuss how the varied experiences of the Founding Fathers influenced the Declaration of Independence and Constitution. Elementary-age children are more likely to focus on simple facts about the founders' lives.

What is the role of processing speed? How fast children process information often influences what they can do with that information. If an adolescent is trying to add up mentally the cost of items he is buying at the grocery store, he needs to be able to compute the sum before he has forgotten the price of the individual items. Children's speed in processing information is linked with their competence in thinking (Bjorklund, 2005, 2011). For example, how fast children can articulate a series of words affects how many words they can store and remember. Generally, fast processing is linked

### Thinking Back/Thinking Forward

Nearly twice as many synaptic connections between neurons are made than ever will be used. Connections that are used become strengthened and survive; unused ones become replaced by other pathways or disappear. Chapter 2, p. 35

with good performance on cognitive tasks. However, some compensation for slower processing speed can be achieved through effective strategies.

Researchers have devised a number of ways for assessing processing speed (Bonafacci & others, 2010). For example, it can be assessed through a *reaction-time task* in which individuals are asked to push a button as soon as they see a stimulus such as a light. Or individuals might be asked to match letters or numbers with symbols on a computer screen.

There is abundant evidence that the speed with which such tasks are completed improves dramatically across the childhood years (Kuhn, 2009). For example, a recent study of 8- to 13-year-old children revealed that processing speed increased with age, and, further, that the developmental change in processing speed preceded an increase in working memory capacity (Kail, 2007).

Controversy exists as to whether the increase in processing speed is due to experience or biological maturation. Experience clearly plays an important role. Think how much faster you could process the answer to a simple arithmetic problem as an adolescent than as a child. Also think about how much faster you can process information in your native language than in a second language. The role of biological maturation likely involves myelination.

DEVELOPMENT

RESEARCH

## MECHANISMS OF CHANGE

According to Robert Siegler (1998), three mechanisms work together to create changes in children's cognitive skills: encoding, automaticity, and strategy construction.

**Encoding** is the process by which information gets stored in memory. Changes in children's cognitive skills depend on increased skill at encoding relevant information and ignoring irrelevant information. For example, to a 4-year-old an *s* in cursive writing is a shape very different from an *s* that is printed. But a 10-year-old has learned to encode the relevant fact that both are the letter *s* and to ignore the irrelevant differences in their shape.

**Automaticity** refers to the ability to process information with little or no effort. Practice allows children to encode increasing amounts of information automatically. For example, once children have learned to read well, they do not think about each letter in a word as a letter; instead, they encode whole words. Once a task is automatic, it does not require conscious effort. As a result, as information processing becomes more automatic, we can complete tasks more quickly and handle more than one task at a time (Mayer, 2008). Imagine how long it would take you to read this page if you did not encode words automatically but instead focused your attention on each letter in each word.

**Strategy construction** is the creation of new procedures for processing information. For example, children's reading benefits when they develop the strategy of stopping periodically to take stock of what they have read so far. Developing an effective repertoire of strategies and selecting the best one to use on a learning task is a critical aspect of becoming an effective learner (Bjorklund, 2011; Scanlan, Anderson, & Sweeney, 2010).

In addition to these mechanisms of change, children's information processing is characterized by *self-modification* (Siegler, 1998, 2007, 2009). That is, children learn to use what they have learned in previous circumstances to adapt their responses to a new situation. For example, a child who is familiar with dogs and cats goes to the zoo and sees lions and tigers for the first time. She then modifies her concept of "animal" to include her new knowledge. Part of this self-modification draws on **metacognition,** which means "knowing about knowing" (Hacker, Dunlofsky, & Grasser, 2009). One example of metacognition is what children know about the best ways to remember what they have read. Do they know that they will remember what they have read better if they can relate it to their own lives in some way? Thus, in Siegler's application of information processing to development, children play an active role in their cognitive development when they develop metacognitive strategies.

**Thinking Back/Thinking Forward**

Teachers can help students to develop a number of effective strategies. Chapter 8, pp. 260 and 274

**encoding** The process by which information gets into memory.

**automaticity** The ability to process information with little or no effort.

**strategy construction** Creation of a new procedure for processing information.

**metacognition** Cognition about cognition, or "knowing about knowing."

## Review, Reflect, and Practice

**1** Describe the information-processing approach.

**REVIEW**

- What view does the information-processing approach take of children as learners?
- What are two important cognitive resources and how do they contribute to developmental changes in children's information processing?
- What are some key mechanisms of change in the information-processing approach?

**REFLECT**

- In terms of your ability to learn, are there ways that you wish you were more like a computer? Or are you better than any computer in all aspects of processing information? Explain.

**PRAXIS™ PRACTICE**

1. Information processing is most closely aligned with
   a. behaviorism.
   b. cognitive psychology.
   c. social cognitive theory.
   d. ecological theory.

2. According to the information-processing approach, a 15-year-old can compute faster than a 10-year-old because the
   a. 15-year-old's brain has had more time to develop, and the 15-year-old has had more experience working with numbers.
   b. 15-year-old has had more experiences of both positive and negative reinforcement.
   c. 15-year-old's brain has lost many of its original connections and undergone demyelinization.
   d. 15-year-old has had much more time to develop rote memory skills.

3. Ms. Parks wants her students to know their basic math facts without having to stop to think about them. Therefore, Ms. Parks plays many math games with her second-grade students, such as addition and subtraction bingo, math bees, and card games. What is Ms. Parks' goal in playing these games with her students?
   a. to help her students to develop automaticity in knowing their math facts
   b. to encourage strategy construction
   c. to foster encoding skills
   d. to improve metacognitive skills, such as self-awareness

*Please see the answer key at the end of the book.*

## **2** ATTENTION

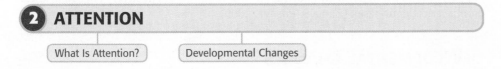

What Is Attention?     Developmental Changes

The world holds a lot of information that we need to perceive. What is attention and what effect does it have? How does it change developmentally?

## WHAT IS ATTENTION?

**Attention** is the focusing of mental resources. Attention improves cognitive processing for many tasks, from hitting a baseball, reading a book, or adding numbers

**attention** The focusing of mental resources.

*What attentional demands does multitasking place on children and adolescents?*

(Hanania & Smith, 2010; Tang & Posner, 2009). At any one time, though, children, like adults, can pay attention to only a limited amount of information. They allocate their attention in different ways (Rhodes, Gelman, & Brickman, 2010). Psychologists have labeled these types of allocation as selective attention, divided attention, sustained attention, and executive attention.

- **Selective attention** is focusing on a specific aspect of experience that is relevant while ignoring others that are irrelevant. Focusing on one voice among many in a crowded room or a noisy restaurant is an example of selective attention.

- **Divided attention** involves concentrating on more than one activity at the same time. If you are listening to music while you are reading this, you are engaging in divided attention.

- **Sustained attention** is the ability to maintain attention over an extended period of time. Sustained attention is also called *vigilance*. Staying focused on reading this chapter from start to finish without interruption is an example of sustained attention. Recall from our discussion in Chapter 6 that in one study difficulties in sustaining attention were the most common type of attentional problem characterizing children with ADHD (Tsal, Shalev, & Mevorach, 2005).

- **Executive attention** involves action planning, allocating attention to goals, error detection and compensation, monitoring progress on tasks, and dealing with novel or difficult circumstances. An example of executive attention is effectively deploying attention to effectively engage in the aforementioned cognitive tasks while writing a 10-page paper for a history course.

One trend involving divided attention is children's and adolescents' *multitasking,* which in some cases involves not just dividing attention between two activities, but even three or more (Bauerlein, 2008). A major influence on the increase in multitasking is the availability of multiple electronic media. Many children and adolescents have a range of electronic media at their disposal. It is not unusual for adolescents to simultaneously divide their attention among homework, instant messaging, surfing the Web, and looking at an iTunes playlist.

Is this multitasking beneficial or distracting? Since it expands the information children and adolescents attend to and forces the brain to share processing resources, multitasking can distract attention from what might be most important at the moment (Begley & Interlandi, 2008).

Sustained and executive attention are very important aspects of cognitive development. As children and adolescents are required to engage in larger, increasingly complex tasks that require longer time frames to complete, their ability to sustain attention is critical for succeeding on the tasks. An increase in executive attention supports the rapid increase in effortful control required to effectively engage in these complex academic tasks (Tang & Posner, 2009).

DEVELOPMENT

**selective attention** Focusing on a specific aspect of experience that is relevant while ignoring others that are irrelevant.

**divided attention** Concentrating on more than one activity at a time.

**sustained attention** Maintaining attention over an extended period of time; also called vigilance.

**executive attention** Involves action planning, allocating attention to goals, error detection and compensation, monitoring progress on tasks, and dealing with novel or difficult circumstances.

## DEVELOPMENTAL CHANGES

Some important changes in attention occur during childhood (Courage & Richards, 2008; Dixon, Zelazo, & De Rosa, 2010). Much of the research on attention has focused on selective attention. One study of 5- to 7-year-old children found that the older children and more socially advantaged children in a sample resisted the interference of competing demands and focused their attention better than the younger children and more socially disadvantaged children (Mezzacappa, 2004).

The length of time children can pay attention increases as they get older. The toddler wanders around, shifts attention from one activity to another, and seems to spend little time focused on any one object or event. In contrast, the preschool child might watch television for half an hour at a time. One study that observed 99 families in their homes for 4,672 hours found that visual attention to television dramatically increased in the preschool years (Anderson & others, 1985).

Preschool children's ability to control and sustain their attention is related to school readiness (Posner & Rothbart, 2007). For example, a study of more than 1,000 children revealed that their ability to sustain their attention at 54 months of age (4.5 years) was linked to their school readiness (which included achievement and language skills) (NICHD Early Child Care Research Network, 2005). In turn, children whose parents and teachers rated them higher on a scale of having attention problems at 54 months of age had a lower level of social skills in peer relations in the first and third grades than their counterparts who were rated lower on the attention problems scale at 54 months of age (NICHD Early Child Care Research Network, 2009). Sustained attention improves from 5 to 6 years to 11 to 12 years of age, and this increased attention is linked to better performance on cognitive tasks (Betts & others, 2006).

RESEARCH

Control over attention shows important changes during childhood (Posner & Rothbart, 2007). External stimuli are likely to determine the target of the preschooler's attention; what is salient, or obvious, grabs the preschooler's attention. For example, suppose a flashy, attractive clown presents the directions for solving a problem. Preschool children are likely to pay attention to the clown and ignore the directions, because they are influenced strongly by the salient features of the environment. After the age of 6 or 7, children pay more attention to features relevant to performing a task or solving a problem, such as the directions. Thus, instead of being controlled by the most striking stimuli in their environment, older children can direct their attention to more important stimuli. This change reflects a shift to *cognitive control* of attention, so that children act less impulsively and reflect more. Recall from Chapter 2 that the increase in cognitive control during the elementary school years is linked to changes in the brain, especially more focal activation in the prefrontal cortex (Durston & others, 2006).

DEVELOPMENT

**Thinking Back/Thinking Forward**

Researchers have found increased focal activation in the prefrontal cortex from 7 to 30 years of age. Chapter 2, p. 36

Attention to relevant information increases steadily through the elementary and secondary school years (Davidson, 1996). Processing of irrelevant information decreases in adolescence.

As children grow up, their abilities both to direct selective attention and to divide attention also improve. Older children and adolescents are better than younger children at tasks that require shifts of attention. For example, writing a good story requires shifting attention among many competing tasks—spelling the words, composing grammar, structuring paragraphs, and conveying the story as a whole. Children also improve in their ability to do two things at once. For example, in one investigation, 12-year-olds were markedly better than 8-year-olds and slightly worse than 20-year-olds at allocating their attention in a situation involving two tasks (divided attention) (Manis, Keating, & Morrison, 1980). These improvements in divided attention might be due to an increase in cognitive resources (through increased processing speed or capacity), automaticity, or increased skill at directing resources.

DEVELOPMENT

As we saw in Chapter 6, individual variations also characterize children, with some children having such significant attention problems that they are classified as having attention deficit hyperactivity disorder (ADHD). One study revealed that such attention problems in childhood are linked to information-processing difficulties in late adolescence (Friedman & others, 2007). In the study, 7- to 14-year-old children with attention problems (including inattention, disorganization, impulsivity, and hyperactivity) had difficulty inhibiting responses and working memory difficulties at 17 years of age.

RESEARCH

# TEACHING CONNECTIONS: Best Practices
## Strategies for Helping Students Pay Attention

With so many classroom tasks to complete and so many children in a class, it is easy to overlook working with children to improve their information-processing skills, such as attention. Following are some effective strategies to adopt in improving children's attention.

1. *Encourage students to pay close attention and minimize distraction.* Talk with children about how important it is to pay attention when they need to remember something. Give them exercises with opportunities to give their undivided attention to something. For example, in countries such as Hungary, kindergarten children participate in exercises designed to improve their attention (Mills & Mills, 2000; Posner & Rothbart, 2007). In one such exercise, the teacher sits in the center of a circle of children, and each child is required to catch the teacher's eye before being permitted to leave the group. In other exercises, teachers have children participate in stop-go activities during which they have to listen for a specific signal, such as a drumbeat or an exact number of rhythmic beats, before stopping the activity.

2. *Use cues or gestures to signal that something is important.* This might involve raising your voice, repeating something with emphasis, and writing the concept on the board or on a transparency. Sometimes it is helpful to be very explicit, "pay attention to this; it is important."

3. *Help students generate their own cue or catch phrase for when they need to pay attention.* Possibly vary this from month to month. Give them a menu of options to select from, such as "Alert," "Focus," or "Zero in." Teach them to say their word or pet phrase quietly but firmly to themselves when they catch their minds wandering.

4. *Make learning interesting.* Boredom can set in quickly for students, and when it does, their attention wanes. Relating ideas to students' interests increases their attention; in other words, what we teach should be relevant to students' lives. Infuse the classroom with novel, unusual, or surprising exercises. Start off a biology exercise on heredity and aging with a question such as "Can you live to be 100?" or "Might someone be able to live to be even 400 some day?" Think of relevant questions such as these to introduce various topics, as students will be more likely to pay attention to material that they can relate to.

5. *Use media and technology effectively as part of your effort to vary the pace of the classroom.* Video and television programs have built-in attention-getting formats, such as zooming in on an image; flashing a vivid, colorful image on the screen; and switching from one setting to another. Look for relevant videos and television programs that can help you vary the classroom's pace and increase students' attention. Unfortunately, too many teachers show videos only to keep students quiet, **TECHNOLOGY** which does not promote learning. However, if the curriculum is dull, it doesn't matter what kinds of "tricks" or "splashes" the teacher uses—students will not learn effectively. Make sure that the media and technology you use captures students' attention in meaningful ways that promote effective learning.

Computer exercises recently have been developed to improve children's attention (Jaeggi, Berman, & Jonides, 2009; Tang & Posner, 2009). For example, a recent study **RESEARCH** found that the attention exercises in Captain's Log (Braintrain), a commercially available program, were effective in reducing first-grade students' attention problems (Rabiner & others, 2009). Ten attention exercises that focus on training auditory and visual attention were used in the study. In one exercise, a student has to press the space bar on a computer each time that a symbol appears that matches one already on the screen. Other tasks require students to remember the locations of objects that have been recently presented. To advance through the program, students have to sustain their attention longer as tasks become more difficult.

6. *Focus on active learning to make learning enjoyable.* A different exercise, a guest, a field trip, and many other activities can be used to make learning more enjoyable, reduce student boredom, and increase attention. In *Through the Eyes of Teachers*, middle school English and drama teacher Lynn Ayres describes how games can add interest at all grade levels.

## THROUGH THE EYES OF TEACHERS
### Turning Boring Exercises into Active Learning Games

I have found that the most boring exercises (such as the kind you find on worksheets and textbooks) can be turned into an active learning game. One favorite game in my seventh-grade English class was "sit-set, rise-raise." I'd put two students in chairs next to tables and place a book on each table. If I said "rise," they were to stand. If I said "raise," they were to raise the book. They were to seat themselves if I said "sit," and they were to place the book on the table if I said "set." If I said "rise," and one of them stood up and the other student lifted the book, the student with the book held up was out and was replaced by a teammate. Or if they both

## TEACHING CONNECTIONS: Best Practices
### Strategies for Helping Students Pay Attention

stood up, the one who stood up first stayed, and the other student was replaced by a teammate. The students loved that game, and they really learned the difference between those two commonly confused pairs of verbs in the process.

That game taught me the effectiveness of getting students physically involved. I developed dozens of other games involving bells and timers and teams that had students running around the room, ringing bells, trying to beat a member of the opposing team in telling me if a word was a noun or an adjective. Almost any workbook or textbook exercise can be turned into a physical activity game if you put some thought into it, and middle school students learn so much more from doing an exercise that is both physical and mental.

7. *Don't overload students with too much information.* We live in an "information overload" society. Students who are given too much information too fast often have difficulty focusing their attention (Cowan & others, 2010).

8. *Be aware of individual differences in students' attentional skills.* Some students have severe problems in paying attention. You will need to take this into account when presenting material. You might develop a prompt to bring back students whose attention has waned. You might also use their wandering attention as a cue to you that students either need a break or a change in activity.

9. *Consider developmental changes in attention.* As discussed above, the length of time students are capable

of attending to something changes as they develop. Don't expect young children to sit and pay attention to a lesson for long periods of time. They need frequent changes in activity. As attention span develops, children can focus their attention for longer periods of time. However, even adolescents and adults benefit from frequent breaks. Be aware that young children have difficulty with selective attention.

10. *Minimize distractions.* Before you begin an exercise, look around the room for potential distractions, such as an open window to a playground where students are being noisy. Close the window and draw the shade to eliminate the distraction. This is particularly important for young children who have not yet developed selective attention.

11. *Occasionally accept the attentional hold of a distraction and incorporate it into your day.* Among children, the first snow of the school year is often a real attention-grabber. Construction going on outside the school is another. Rather than battling against their curiosity and excitement, it may be more prudent to stop what you are doing, acknowledge the distraction, and allow the students to spend a few minutes attending to it. Because their attention spans are not very long, young children in particular will not be likely to attend to the distraction very long either and you will be able to begin teaching again soon, with the distraction no longer a problem.

I recently asked teachers what they do to help students focus their attention in class. Following are their responses.

**EARLY CHILDHOOD**   Very young children are just developing their attention span. To help them along, we often use songs or instruments for transitions from

play time to work time. When material is introduced, we call out the children's names and ask questions, thus engaging them with the newly introduced item. During story time, we use exaggerated physical gestures and take on the voices of characters in the book to keep children motivated and listening.

—**VALARIE GORHAM,** *Kiddie Quarters, Inc.*

**ELEMENTARY SCHOOL: GRADES K–5**   One strategy I use to keep my fourth-grade students focused is to get into a role. For example, when I read *Bubba, the Cowboy Prince,* I put on a cowboy hat and create an accent. I also find that saying, "You will see this on your homework tonight," and, "This will be on your test," also grab their attention.

—**SHANE SCHWARZ,** *Clinton Elementary School*

**MIDDLE SCHOOL: GRADES 6–8**   My students especially stay focused when I let them teach each other—that is, I let them take turns playing the role of teacher.

—CASEY MAASS, *Edison Middle School*

**HIGH SCHOOL: GRADES 9–12**   High school students stay more focused when they know how events and information presented in class relate to their own lives. For example, the topic of food-borne illness is boring to most of my students, but when I tell them about how I got salmonella poisoning from a plate of chicken salad at a local restaurant, and the intense suffering I went through for many days, they become more intrigued with the topic of salmonella, its causes, prevention, and symptoms.

—SANDY SWANSON, *Menomonee Falls High School*

## Review, Reflect, and Practice

**2** Characterize attention and summarize how it changes during development.

**REVIEW**
- What is attention? What are four ways attention can be allocated?
- How does attention develop in childhood and adolescence?

**REFLECT**
- Imagine that you are an elementary school teacher and a child is having difficulty sustaining attention on a learning task. What strategies would you use to help the child sustain attention?

**PRAXIS™ PRACTICE**

1. Ms. Samson teaches first grade. Often while she is working with one group of children, she must monitor the behavior of the rest of the class, occasionally intervening in some manner. Sometimes she has three or four students at her desk, each needing something different from her. This does not seem to faze her in the least. She can talk to one student while tying another's shoes and monitoring the behavior of the rest with no problem. What skill has Ms. Samson mastered?
   a. divided attention
   b. selective attention
   c. sustained attention
   d. personal attention

2. Mark shifts his attention very quickly from one thing to another. The more colorful and noisy the thing, the more likely it is to draw his attention. He rarely attends to any one thing for more than a few minutes. From this description, Mark is most likely to be a
   a. toddler.
   b. preschooler.
   c. elementary-school-age child.
   d. adolescent.

*Please see the answer key at the end of the book.*

**3** **MEMORY**

| What Is Memory? | Encoding | Storage | Retrieval and Forgetting |

Twentieth-century playwright Tennessee Williams once commented that life is all memory except for that one present moment that goes by so quickly that you can hardly catch it going. But just what is memory?

## WHAT IS MEMORY?

**Memory** is the retention of information over time. Educational psychologists study how information is initially placed or encoded into memory, how it is retained or stored after being encoded, and how it is found or retrieved for a certain purpose later. Memory anchors the self in continuity. Without memory you would not be able to connect what happened to you yesterday with what is going on in your life at present. Today educational psychologists emphasize that it is important to view memory not in terms of how children add something to their memory but rather how they actively construct their memory (Ornstein & Light, 2010; Ornstein & others, 2010).

The main body of our discussion of memory will focus on encoding, storage, and retrieval. Thinking about memory in terms of these processes should help you to understand it better (see Figure 8.1). For memory to work, children have to take information in, store it or represent it, and then retrieve it for some purpose later.

As you learned earlier, *encoding* is the process by which information gets into memory, *storage* is the retention of information over time, and *retrieval* means taking information out of storage. Let's now explore each of these three important memory activities in greater detail.

## ENCODING

In everyday language, encoding has much in common with attention and learning (Reed, 2010). When a student is listening to a teacher, watching a movie, listening to music, or talking with a friend, he or she is encoding information into memory. Focusing attention—whether by visual inspection, physical manipulation, or using words—highlights features of an event or material being remembered and thus improves encoding (Ornstein, Coffman, & Grammer, 2009; Ornstein & Light, 2010). In addition to attention, which we just discussed, encoding consists of a number of processes: rehearsal, deep processing, elaboration, constructing images, and organization.

**Rehearsal**   The process of **rehearsal** is the conscious repetition of information over time to increase the length of time it stays in memory. For example, when you make a date to meet your best friend for lunch, you are likely to repeat, or rehearse, the date and time: "OK—Wednesday at 1:30." Rehearsal works best when you need to encode and remember a list of items for a brief period of time. When you must retain information over long periods of time, as when you are studying for a test you won't

**memory** The retention of information over time, which involves encoding, storage, and retrieval.

**rehearsal** The conscious repetition of information over time to increase the length of time it stays in memory.

| Encoding | Storage | Retrieval |
| Getting information into memory | Retaining information over time | Taking information out of storage |

**FIGURE 8.1** PROCESSING INFORMATION IN MEMORY

As you read about the many aspects of memory in this chapter, think about the organization of memory in terms of these three main activities: encoding, storage, and retrieval.

## The Cobwebs of Memory

I think the point of having memories is to share them, especially with close friends or family. If you don't share them, they are just sitting inside your brain getting cobwebs. If you have a great memory of Christmas and no one to share it with, what's the point of memories?

Before he
shares memories

After he
shares memories

X-ray

Cobwebs

No cobwebs

**Seventh-Grade Student**
West Middle School
Ypsilanti, Michigan

DEVELOPMENT

RESEARCH

**levels of processing theory** The theory that processing of memory occurs on a continuum from shallow to deep, with deeper processing producing better memory.

**elaboration** The extensiveness of information processing involved in encoding.

take until next week, other strategies usually work better than rehearsal. Rehearsal does not work well for retaining information over the long term because it often involves just rote repetition of information without imparting any meaning to it. When you construct your memory in meaningful ways, you remember better. As we will see next, you also remember better when you process material deeply and elaborate it.

**Deep Processing**   Following the discovery that rehearsal is not an efficient way to encode information for long-term memory, Fergus Craik and Robert Lockhart (1972) proposed that we can process information at a variety of levels. Their **levels of processing theory** states that the processing of memory occurs on a continuum from shallow to deep, with deeper processing producing better memory. Shallow processing means analyzing a stimuli's sensory, or physical, features at a shallow level. This might involve detecting the lines, angles, and contours of a printed word's letters or a spoken word's frequency, duration, and loudness. At an intermediate level of processing, you recognize the stimulus and give it a label. For example, you identify a four-legged, barking object as a dog. Then, at the deepest level, you process information semantically, in terms of its meaning. For example, if a child sees the word *boat,* at the shallow level she might notice the shapes of the letters, at the intermediate level she might think of the characteristics of the word (for instance, that it rhymes with *coat*), and at the deepest level she might think about the last time she went fishing with her dad on a boat and the kind of boat it was. Researchers have found that individuals remember information better when they process it at a deep level (Otten, Henson, & Rugg, 2001).

**Elaboration**   Cognitive psychologists soon recognized, however, that there is more to good encoding than just depth of processing. They discovered that memory benefits from the use of **elaboration,** which refers to extensiveness of information, in the process of encoding (Ashcraft & Radvansky, 2010). Thus, when you present the concept of democracy to students, they likely will remember it better if they come up with good examples of it. Examples based on self-reference are especially effective in elaborating information. If you are trying to get students to remember the concept of fairness, the more they can generate personal examples of inequities and equities they have personally experienced, the more likely they are to remember the concept.

The use of elaboration changes developmentally (Schneider, 2011). Adolescents are more likely to use elaboration spontaneously than children are. Elementary school children can be taught to use elaboration strategies on a learning task, but they are less likely than adolescents to use the strategies on other learning tasks in the future. Nonetheless, verbal elaboration can be an effective memory strategy even with young elementary school children. In one study, the experimenter told second- and fifth-grade children to construct a meaningful sentence for a keyword (such as "The postman carried a letter in his cart" for the keyword *cart*). As shown in Figure 8.2, both second- and fifth-grade children remembered the keywords better when they constructed a meaningful sentence containing the word than when just the keyword and its definition were told to the child (Pressley, Levin, & McCormick, 1980).

One reason elaboration works so well in encoding is that it adds to the distinctiveness of memory code (Hunt & Ellis, 2004). To remember a piece of information, such as a name, an experience, or a fact about geography, students need to search for the code that contains this information among the mass of codes in their long-term memory. The search process is easier if the memory code is unique (Hunt & Kelly, 1996). The situation is not unlike searching for a friend at a crowded airport—if your friend is 6 feet 3 inches tall and has flaming red hair, it will be easier to find him in the crowd than if he has more common features. Also, as a student elaborates information, more information is stored. And as more information is stored, it becomes easier to differentiate the memory from others. For example, if a student witnesses another student being hit by a car that speeds away, the student's memory of the car will be far better if she deliberately encodes her observations that the car is a red 2005 Pontiac with tinted windows and spinners on the wheels than if she observes only that it is a red car.

**Constructing Images** When we construct an image of something, we are elaborating the information. For example, how many windows are there in the apartment or house where your family has lived for a substantial part of your life? Few of us ever memorize this information, but you probably can come up with a good answer, especially if you reconstruct a mental image of each room.

Allan Paivio (1971, 1986) argues that memories are stored in one of two ways: as verbal codes or as image codes. For example, you can remember a picture by a label (*The Last Supper,* a verbal code) or by a mental image. Paivio says that the more detailed and distinctive the image code, the better your memory of the information will be.

Researchers have found that encouraging children to use imagery to remember verbal information works better for older children than for younger children (Schneider, 2011). In one study, experimenters presented twenty sentences to first- through sixth-grade children to remember (such as "The angry bird shouted at the white dog" and "The policeman painted the circus tent on a windy day") (Pressley & others, 1987). Children were randomly assigned to an imagery condition (make a picture in your head for each sentence) and a control condition (children were told just to try hard). Figure 8.3 shows that the imagery instructions improved memory more for the older children (grades 4 through 6) than for the younger children (grades 1 through 3). Researchers have found that young elementary school children can use imagery to remember pictures better than they can verbal materials, such as sentences (Schneider & Pressley, 1997).

**Organization** If students organize information when they are encoding it, their memory benefits. To understand the importance of organization in encoding, complete the following exercise: Recall the 12 months of the year as quickly as you can. How long did it take you? What was the order of your recall? Your answers are probably a few seconds and in natural order (January, February, March, and so on). Now try to remember the months in alphabetical order. Did you make any errors? How long did it take you? There is a clear distinction between recalling the months in natural order and recalling alphabetically. This exercise is a good one to use with your students to help them understand the importance of organizing their memories in meaningful ways.

Frank and Ernest

FRANK & ERNEST © Thaves/Dist. by United Feature Syndicate, Inc.

**FIGURE 8.2** VERBAL ELABORATION AND MEMORY

Both second- and fifth-grade children remembered words better when they constructed a meaningful sentence for the word (verbal elaboration group) than when they merely heard the word and its definition (control group). The verbal elaboration worked better for the fifth-graders than for the second-graders.

RESEARCH

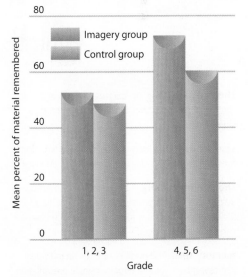

**FIGURE 8.3** IMAGERY AND MEMORY OF VERBAL INFORMATION

Imagery improved older elementary school children's memory for sentences more than younger elementary school children's memory for sentences.

The more you present information in an organized way, the easier your students will remember it. This is especially true if you organize information hierarchically or outline it. Also, if you simply encourage students to organize information, they often will remember it better than if you give them no instructions about organizing (Mandler, 1980).

**Chunking** is a beneficial organizational memory strategy that involves grouping, or "packing," information into "higher-order" units that can be remembered as single units. Chunking works by making large amounts of information more manageable and more meaningful. For example, consider this simple list of words: *hot, city, book, forget, tomorrow, smile.* Try to hold these in memory for a moment, then write them down. If you recalled all six words, you succeeded in holding 30 letters in your memory. But it would have been much more difficult to try to remember those 30 letters. Chunking them into words made them meaningful.

## STORAGE

After children encode information, they need to retain, or store, the information. Children remember some information for less than a second, some for about half a minute, and other information for minutes, hours, years, even a lifetime. The three types of memory, which correspond to these different time frames, are *sensory memory* (which lasts a fraction of a second to several seconds); *short-term memory* (lasts about 30 seconds), and *long-term memory* (lasts up to a lifetime).

**Sensory Memory**   **Sensory memory** holds information from the world in its original sensory form for only an instant, not much longer than the brief time a student is exposed to the visual, auditory, and other sensations.

Students have a sensory memory for sounds for up to several seconds, sort of like a brief echo. However, their sensory memory for visual images lasts only for about one-fourth of a second. Because sensory information lasts for only a fleeting moment, an important task for the student is to attend to the sensory information that is important for learning quickly, before it fades.

**Short-Term Memory**   **Short-term memory** is a limited-capacity memory system in which information is retained at least 30 seconds unless it is rehearsed or otherwise processed further, in which case it can be retained longer. Compared with sensory memory, short-term memory is limited in capacity but relatively longer in duration. Its limited capacity intrigued George Miller (1956), who described this in a paper with a catchy title: "The Magical Number Seven, Plus or Minus Two." Miller pointed out that on many tasks, students are limited in how much information they can keep track of without external aids. Usually the limit is in the range of 7 +/− 2 items.

The most widely cited example of the 7 +/− 2 phenomenon involves **memory span,** the number of digits an individual can report back without error from a single presentation. How many digits individuals can report back depends on how old they are. In one study, memory span increased from two digits in 2-year-olds, to five digits in 7-year-olds, to six to seven digits in 12-year-olds (Dempster, 1981) (see Figure 8.4). Many college students can handle lists of eight or nine digits. Keep in mind that these are averages and that individuals differ. For example, many 7-year-olds have a memory span of fewer than six or seven digits; others have a memory span of eight or more digits.

Related to short-term memory, British psychologist Alan Baddeley (2000, 2007) proposed that **working memory** is a three-part system that temporarily holds information as people perform tasks. Working memory is a kind of mental "workbench" where information is manipulated and assembled to help us make decisions, solve problems, and comprehend written and spoken language. Notice that working memory is not like a passive storehouse with shelves to store information until it moves

*"Can we hurry up and get to the test? My short-term memory is better than my long-term memory."*

© 2006; reprinted courtesy of Bunny Hoest and *Parade.*

DEVELOPMENT

**chunking** Grouping, or "packing," information into "higher-order" units that can be remembered as single units.

**sensory memory** Memory that holds information from the world in its original form for only an instant.

**short-term memory** A limited-capacity memory system in which information is retained at least 30 seconds unless it is rehearsed, in which case it can be retained longer.

**memory span** The number of digits an individual can report back without error in a single presentation.

**working memory** A three-part system that holds information temporarily as a person performs a task. A kind of "mental workbench" that lets individuals manipulate, assemble, and construct information when they make decisions, solve problems, and comprehend written and spoken language.

to long-term memory. Rather, it is a very active memory system (Ang & Lee, 2010; Baddeley, Eysenck, & Anderson, 2009; Martinez, 2010).

Figure 8.5 shows Baddeley's view of working memory and its three components: phonological loop, visuospatial working memory, and central executive. Think of them as an executive (central executive) with two assistants (phonological loop and visuospatial working memory) to help do your work.

- The *phonological loop* is specialized to briefly store speech-based information about the sounds of language. The phonological loop contains two separate components: an acoustic code, which decays in a few seconds, and rehearsal, which allows individuals to repeat the words in the phonological store.
- *Visuospatial working memory* stores visual and spatial information, including visual imagery. Like the phonological loop, visuospatial working memory has a limited capacity. The phonological loop and visuospatial working memory function independently. You could rehearse numbers in the phonological loop while making spatial arrangements of letters in visuospatial working memory.
- The *central executive* integrates information not only from the phonological loop and visuospatial working memory but also from long-term memory. In Baddeley's view, the central executive plays important roles in attention, planning, and organizing behavior. The central executive acts much like a supervisor who monitors which information and issues deserve attention and which should be ignored. It also selects which strategies to use to process information and solve problems. As with the other two components of working memory—the phonological loop and visuospatial working memory—the central executive has a limited capacity.

Working memory is linked to many aspects of children's development (Cowan & Alloway, 2009; Cowan & others, 2010). For example, children who have better working memory are more advanced in attentional skills, reading comprehension, math skills, and problem solving than their counterparts with less effective working memory (Alloway, Gathercole, & Elliott, 2010; Carretti & others, 2009; Hoffman & Schraw, 2009).

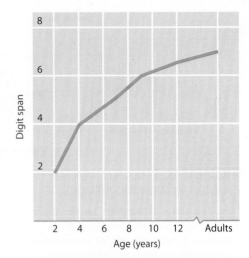

**FIGURE 8.4** DEVELOPMENTAL CHANGES IN MEMORY SPAN

In one study, memory span increased about three digits from 2 years of age to five digits at 7 years of age (Dempster, 1981). By 12 years of age, memory span had increased on average another one and a half digits.

**Working Memory**

**FIGURE 8.5** WORKING MEMORY

In Baddeley's working memory model, working memory consists of three main components: the phonological loop, visuospatial working memory, and the central executive. The phonological loop and visuospatial working memory serve as assistants, helping the central executive do its work. Input from sensory memory goes to the phonological loop, where information about speech is stored and rehearsal takes place, and to visuospatial working memory, where visual and spatial information, including imagery, is stored. Working memory is a limited-capacity system, and information is stored there for only a brief time. Working memory interacts with long-term memory, drawing information from long-term memory and transmitting information to long-term memory for longer storage.

**Verbal tasks**

Semantic Association

1.33 1.70 1.86 2.24 2.60

Digit/Sentence

1.75 2.34 2.94 2.98 3.71

**Visuospatial tasks**

Mapping/Directions

3.13 3.60 4.09 3.92 4.64

Visual Matrix

1.67 2.06 2.51 2.68 3.47

■ Age 8   ■ Age 10   ■ Age 13   ■ Age 16   ■ Age 24

## FIGURE 8.6 DEVELOPMENTAL CHANGES IN WORKING MEMORY

*Note:* The scores shown here are the means for each age group and the age also represents a mean age. Higher scores reflect superior working memory performance.

The following three recent studies illustrate how important working memory is in young children's cognitive development:

- Working memory and attention control predicted growth in emergent literacy and number skills in young children in low-income families (Welsh & others, 2010).
- Working memory capacity at 9 to 10 years of age predicted foreign language comprehension two years later at 11 to 12 years of age (Andersson, 2010).
- Working memory capacity predicted how many items on a to-be-remembered list that fourth-grade children forgot (Asian, Zellner, & Bauml, 2010).

Is the working memory of adolescents better than the working memory of children? One study found that it was (Swanson, 1999). Investigators examined the performances of children and adolescents on both verbal and visuospatial working memory tasks. As shown in Figure 8.6, working memory increased substantially from 8 through 24 years of age no matter what the task. Thus, the adolescent years are likely to be an important developmental period for improvement in working memory.

**Long-Term Memory**   **Long-term memory** is a type of memory that holds enormous amounts of information for a long period of time in a relatively permanent fashion. A typical human's long-term memory capacity is staggering, and the efficiency with which individuals can retrieve information is impressive. It often takes only a moment to search through this vast storehouse to find the information we want. Think about your own long-term memory. Who wrote the Gettysburg Address? Who was your first-grade teacher? You can answer thousands of such questions instantly. Of course, not all information is retrieved so easily from long-term memory.

**long-term memory** A type of memory that holds enormous amounts of information for a long period of time in a relatively permanent fashion.

**Atkinson-Shiffrin model** A model of memory that involves a sequence of three stages: sensory memory, short-term memory, and long-term memory.

**A Model of the Three Memory Stores**   This three-stage concept of memory we have been describing was developed by Richard Atkinson and Richard Shiffrin (1968). According to the **Atkinson-Shiffrin model,** memory involves a sequence of sensory memory, short-term memory, and long-term memory stages (see Figure 8.7). As we have seen, much information makes it no further than the sensory memories of sounds and sights. This information is retained only for a brief instant. However, some information, especially that to which we pay attention, is transferred to short-term

## FIGURE 8.7 ATKINSON AND SHIFFRIN'S THEORY OF MEMORY

In this model, sensory input goes into sensory memory. Through the process of attention, information moves into short-term memory, where it remains for 30 seconds or less, unless it is rehearsed. When the information goes into long-term memory storage, it can be retrieved over the lifetime.

FIGURE **8.8** CLASSIFICATION OF LONG-TERM MEMORY'S CONTENTS

memory, where it can be retained for about 30 seconds (or longer with the aid of rehearsal). Atkinson and Shiffrin claimed that the longer information is retained in short-term memory through the use of rehearsal, the greater its chance is of getting into long-term memory. Notice in Figure 8.7 that information in long-term memory also can be retrieved back into short-term memory.

Some contemporary experts on memory believe that the Atkinson-Shiffrin model is too simple (Bartlett, 2010). They argue that memory doesn't always work in a neatly packaged three-stage sequence, as Atkinson and Shiffrin proposed. For example, these contemporary experts stress that working memory uses long-term memory's contents in more flexible ways than simply retrieving information from it. Despite these problems, the model is useful in providing an overview of some components of memory.

**Long-Term Memory's Contents**  Different types of memory can be distinguished not only by how long they last but also on the basis of content. For long-term memory, many contemporary psychologists accept the hierarchy of contents described in Figure 8.8 (Bartlett, 2010). Here long-term memory is divided into the subtypes of declarative and nondeclarative memory, and one of those subtypes, declarative memory, is divided into episodic memory and semantic memory.

**Declarative and Nondeclarative Memory**  The long-term memory subtype of **declarative memory** is the conscious recollection of information, such as specific facts or events that can be verbally communicated. Declarative memory has been called "knowing that" (versus "knowing how") and more recently has been labeled "explicit memory" (versus "implicit memory"). Demonstrations of students' declarative memory could include recounting an event they have witnessed or describing a basic principle of math. However, students do not need to be talking to be using declarative memory. If students simply sit and reflect on an experience, their declarative memory is involved.

The long-term memory subtype of **nondeclarative memory** is procedural knowledge in the form of skills and cognitive operations. Nondeclarative memory cannot be consciously recollected, at least not in the form of specific events or facts. This makes nondeclarative memory difficult, if not impossible, to communicate verbally. Nondeclarative memory is sometimes called "knowing how," and it also has been described as "implicit memory." When students apply their abilities to perform a dance, ride a bicycle, or type on a computer keyboard, their nondeclarative memory is at work. It also is at work when they speak grammatically correct sentences without having to think about how to do it.

**Episodic and Semantic Memory**  Cognitive psychologist Endel Tulving (2000) distinguishes between two subtypes of declarative memory: episodic and semantic.

**declarative memory** The conscious recollection of information, such as specific facts or events that can be verbally communicated.

**nondeclarative memory** Procedural knowledge in the form of skills and cognitive operations. Nondeclarative memory cannot be consciously recollected, at least not in the form of specific events or facts.

| Characteristic | Episodic Memory | Semantic Memory |
| --- | --- | --- |
| Units | Events, episodes | Facts, ideas, concepts |
| Organization | Time | Concepts |
| Emotion | More important | Less important |
| Retrieval process | Deliberate (effortful) | Automatic |
| Retrieval report | "I remember" | "I know" |
| Education | Irrelevant | Relevant |
| Intelligence | Irrelevant | Relevant |
| Legal testimony | Admissible in court | Inadmissible in court |

FIGURE **8.9** SOME DIFFERENCES BETWEEN EPISODIC AND SEMANTIC MEMORY

These characteristics have been proposed as the main ways to differentiate episodic from semantic memory.

**episodic memory** The retention of information about the where and when of life's happenings.

**semantic memory** An individual's general knowledge about the world, independent of the individual's identity with the past.

**network theories** Theories that describe how information in memory is organized and connected; they emphasize nodes in the memory network.

**schema theories** Theories based on the premise that when we construct information, we fit it into information that already exists in our mind.

**schema** Information—concepts, knowledge, information about events—that already exists in a person's mind.

**Episodic memory** is the retention of information about the where and when of life's happenings. Students' memories of the first day of school, whom they had lunch with, or the guest who came to talk with their class last week are all episodic.

**Semantic memory** is a student's general knowledge about the world. It includes the following:

- Knowledge of the sort learned in school (such as knowledge of geometry)
- Knowledge in different fields of expertise (such as knowledge of chess, for a skilled 15-year-old chess player)
- "Everyday" knowledge about meanings of words, famous people, important places, and common things (such as what the word *pertinacious* means or who Nelson Mandela is)

Semantic memory is independent of the person's identity with the past. For example, students might access a fact—such as "Lima is the capital of Peru"—and not have the foggiest idea when and where they learned it. Figure 8.9 compares the characteristics of episodic and semantic memory.

**Representing Information in Memory** How do students represent information in their memory? Three main theories have addressed this question: network, schema, and fuzzy trace.

**Network Theories** The **network theories** describe how information in memory is organized and connected. They emphasize *nodes* in the memory network that stand for labels or concepts. Consider the concept "bird." One of the earliest network theories described memory representation as hierarchically arranged, with more-concrete concepts ("canary," for example) nestled under more abstract concepts (such as "bird"). However, it soon became clear that such hierarchical networks are too neat to accurately portray how memory representation really works. For example, students take longer to answer the question, "Is an ostrich a bird?" than to answer the question, "Is a canary a bird?" Thus, today memory researchers envision the memory network as more irregular and distorted (Ashcraft & Radvansky, 2010). A typical bird, such as a canary, is closer to the node, or center, of the category "bird" than is the atypical ostrich.

**Schema Theories** Long-term memory has been compared with a library of books. The idea is that our memory stores information just as a library stores books. In this analogy, the way students retrieve information is said to be similar to the process they use to locate and check out a book. The process of retrieving information from long-term memory, however, is not as precise as the library analogy suggests. When we search through our long-term memory storehouse, we don't always find the exact "book" we want, or we might find the "book" we want but discover that only "several pages" are intact—we have to reconstruct the rest.

**Schema theories** state that when we reconstruct information, we fit it into information that already exists in our mind. A **schema** is information—concepts, knowledge, information about events—that already exists in a person's mind. Unlike network theories, which assume that retrieval involves specific facts, schema theory claims that long-term memory searches are not very exact. We often don't find precisely what we want, and we have to reconstruct the rest. Thus, when asked to retrieve information, we may fill in the gaps between our fragmented memories with a variety of accuracies and inaccuracies.

We have schemas for all sorts of information (Martinez, 2010). If you tell virtually any story to your class and then ask the students to write down what the story was about, you likely will get many different versions. That is, your students won't remember every detail of the story you told and will reconstruct the story with their own particular stamp on it. Suppose you tell your class a story about two men and two women who were involved in a train crash in France. One student might reconstruct the story by saying the characters died in a plane crash, another might describe three men and three women, another might say the crash was in Germany, and so on. The reconstruction and distortion of memory is nowhere more apparent than in the memories given by courtroom witnesses. In criminal court trials such as that of O. J. Simpson, the variations in people's memories of what happened underscore how we reconstruct the past rather than take an exact photograph of it.

In sum, schema theory accurately predicts that people don't always store and retrieve bits of data in an accurate computer-like fashion. The mind can distort an event as it encodes and stores impressions of reality (Pipe & Salmon, 2009).

A **script** is a schema for an event. Scripts often contain information about physical features, people, and typical occurrences—the kind of information that is helpful when teachers and students need to figure out what is happening around them. In a script for an art activity, students likely will remember based on past experience that you will instruct them on what to draw, that they are supposed to put on smocks over their clothes, that they must get the art paper and paints from the cupboard, that they are to clean the brushes when they are finished, and so on. For example, a student who comes in late to the art activity likely knows much of what to do because he has an art activity script.

*"Why? You cross the road because it's in the script—that's why!"*
© Bernard Schoenbaum/The New Yorker Collection/www.cartoonbank.com

**Fuzzy Trace Theory** Another variation of how individuals reconstruct their memories is **fuzzy trace theory,** which states that when individuals encode information, it creates two types of memory representations: (1) a *verbatim memory trace,* which consists of precise details; and (2) a *fuzzy trace,* or gist, which is the central idea of the information (Brainerd & others, 2006; Reyna & Rivers, 2008). For example, consider a child who is presented with information about a pet store that has ten birds, six cats, eight dogs, and seven rabbits. Then the child is asked two different types of questions: (1) verbatim questions, such as "How many cats are in the pet store, six or eight?" and (2) gist questions, such as "Are there more cats or more dogs in the pet store?" Researchers have found that preschool children tend to remember verbatim information better than gist information, but elementary-school-age children are more likely to remember gist information (Brainerd & Gordon, 1994). So in fuzzy trace theory, the increased use of gist information by elementary-school-age children accounts for their improved memory, because fuzzy traces are less likely to be forgotten than verbatim traces.

## RETRIEVAL AND FORGETTING

After students have encoded information and then represented it in memory, they might be able to retrieve some of it but might also forget some of it. What factors influence whether students can retrieve information?

**Retrieval** When we retrieve something from our mental "data bank," we search our store of memory to find the relevant information. Just as with encoding, this search can be automatic or it can require effort. For example, if you ask your students what month it is, the answer will immediately spring to their lips. That is, the retrieval will be automatic. But if you ask your students to name the guest speaker who came to the class two months earlier, the retrieval process likely will require more effort.

An item's position on a list also affects how easy or difficult it will be to remember it. In the **serial position effect,** recall is better for items at the beginning and end

**script** A schema for an event.

**fuzzy trace theory** States that memory is best understood by considering two types of memory representations: (1) verbatim memory trace and (2) fuzzy trace, or gist. In this theory, older children's better memory is attributed to the fuzzy traces created by extracting the gist of information.

**serial position effect** The principle that recall is better for items at the beginning and the end of a list than for items in the middle.

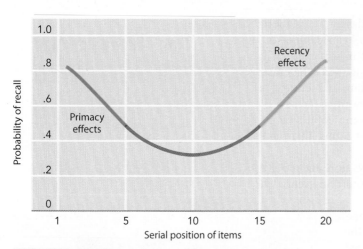

**FIGURE 8.10** THE SERIAL POSITION EFFECT

When a person is asked to memorize a list of words, the words memorized last usually are recalled best, those at the beginning next best, and those in the middle least efficiently.

of a list than for items in the middle. Suppose that when you give a student directions about where to go to get tutoring help, you say, "Left on Mockingbird, right on Central, left on Balboa, left on Sandstone, and right on Parkside." The student likely will remember "Left on Mockingbird" and "Right on Parkside" better than "Left on Balboa." The *primacy effect* is that items at the beginning of a list tend to be remembered. The *recency effect* is that items at the end of a list also tend to be remembered, even better than those at the beginning.

Figure 8.10 shows a typical serial position effect with a slightly stronger recency effect than primacy effect. The serial position effect applies not only to lists but also to events. If you spread out a history lesson over a week and then ask students about it the following Monday, they likely will have the best memory for what you told them on Friday of last week and the worst memory for what you told them on Wednesday of last week.

Another factor that affects retrieval is the nature of the cues people use to prompt their memory (Homa, 2008). Students can learn to create effective cues. For example, if a student has a "block" about remembering the name of the guest who came to class two months ago, she might go through the alphabet, generating names with each letter. If she manages to stumble across the right name, she likely will recognize it.

Another consideration in understanding retrieval is the **encoding specificity principle:** that associations formed at the time of encoding or learning tend to be effective retrieval cues. For example, imagine that a 13-year-old child has encoded this information about Mother Teresa: She was born in Albania, lived most of her life in India, became a Roman Catholic nun, was saddened by seeing people sick and dying in Calcutta's streets, and won a Nobel Prize for her humanitarian efforts to help the poor and suffering. Later, when the child tries to remember details about Mother Teresa, she can use words such as *Nobel Prize, Calcutta,* and *humanitarian* as retrieval cues.

The concept of encoding specificity is compatible with our earlier discussion of elaboration: The more elaboration children use in encoding information, the better their memory of the information will be. Encoding specificity and elaboration reveal how interdependent encoding and retrieval are.

Yet another aspect of retrieval is the nature of the retrieval task itself. *Recall* is a memory task in which individuals must retrieve previously learned information, as students must do for fill-in-the-blank or essay questions. *Recognition* is a memory task in which individuals only have to identify ("recognize") learned information, as is often the case on multiple-choice tests. Many students prefer multiple-choice items because they provide good retrieval cues, which fill-in-the-blank and essay items don't do.

**encoding specificity principle** The principle that associations formed at the time of encoding or learning tend to be effective retrieval cues.

**cue-dependent forgetting** Retrieval failure caused by a lack of effective retrieval cues.

**interference theory** The theory that we forget not because we actually lose memories from storage but because other information gets in the way of what we are trying to remember.

**Forgetting** One form of forgetting involves the cues we just discussed. **Cue-dependent forgetting** is retrieval failure caused by a lack of effective retrieval cues. The notion of cue-dependent forgetting can explain why a student might fail to retrieve a needed fact for an exam even when he is sure he "knows" the information. For example, if you are studying for a test in this course and are asked a question about a distinction between recall and recognition in retrieval, you likely will remember the distinction better if you possess the cues "fill-in-the-blank" and "multiple-choice," respectively.

The principle of cue-dependent forgetting is consistent with **interference theory,** which states that we forget not because we actually lose memories from storage but rather because other information gets in the way of what we are trying to remember.

For a student who studies for a biology test, then studies for a history test, and then takes the biology test, the information about history will interfere with remembering the information about biology. Thus, interference theory implies that, if you have more than one test to study for, you should study last what you are going to be tested on next. That is, the student taking the biology test would have benefited from studying history first and studying biology afterward. This strategy also fits with the *recency effect* we described earlier.

Another source of forgetting is memory decay. According to **decay theory**, new learning involves the creation of a neurochemical *memory trace*, which will eventually disintegrate. Thus, decay theory suggests that the passage of time is responsible for forgetting. Leading memory researcher Daniel Schacter (2001) now refers to forgetting that occurs with the passage of time as *transience*.

Memories decay at different speeds. Some memories are vivid and last for long periods of time, especially when they have emotional ties. We can often remember these "flashbulb" memories with considerable accuracy and vivid imagery. For example, consider a car accident you were in or witnessed, the events of your high school graduation, an early romantic experience, and where you were when you heard about the destruction of the World Trade Center towers. Chances are you will be able to retrieve this information many years afterward.

I recently asked teachers how they help their students improve their memory skills. Following are their responses.

**EARLY CHILDHOOD**   Repetition often helps preschoolers remember. For example, as a weekly theme, we focus on a letter of the week. Children are asked to write the same letter throughout the week. They also hear stories related to just that one letter and are asked to bring in something for "show and tell" that starts with the letter being highlighted that week.

—**MISSY DANGLER,** *Suburban Hills School*

**ELEMENTARY SCHOOL: GRADES K–5**   One strategy that works well with my students is to play the game *Jeopardy!* and use categories like math, grammar, science, social studies, and famous stories. The game keeps them excited and focused on the topics. Students receive bonus points for correct answers, which they can trade in for certain classroom privileges.

—**CRAIG JENSEN,** *Cooper Mountain Elementary School*

**MIDDLE SCHOOL: GRADES 6–8**   I use self-tests to help my seventh-graders improve their memory. Based on notes taken in class, students create their own quizzes and tests. Questions are on one side of the paper, answers on the other. When they study, they are seeing the questions, not the answers. This approach not only helps them remember, but also helps eliminate test anxiety for many students because they know what the test looks like before they get to class.

—**MARK FODNESS,** *Bemidji Middle School*

**HIGH SCHOOL: GRADES 9–12**   I find that mnemonic devices, silly little rhymes, and dances work best when helping my students remember information. Amazingly, as goofy as this may sound, my high school students remember information using these techniques.

—**JENNIFER HEITER,** *Bremen High School*

**decay theory** The theory that new learning involves the creation of a neurochemical *memory trace,* which will eventually disintegrate. Thus, decay theory suggests that the passage of time is responsible for forgetting.

# TEACHING CONNECTIONS: Best Practices
## Strategies for Helping Students Improve Their Memory

As with attention, memory skills in students can improve when teachers use certain strategies.

1. *Motivate children to remember material by understanding it rather than merely memorizing it.* Children will remember information better over the long term if they understand the information rather than just rehearsing and memorizing it (Bjorklund, 2011). Rehearsal works well for encoding information into short-term memory, but when children need to retrieve the information from long-term memory, it is much less efficient. For most information, encourage children to understand it, give it meaning, elaborate on it, and personalize it. Give children concepts and ideas to remember and then ask them how they can relate the concepts and ideas to their own personal experiences and meanings. Give them practice on elaborating a concept so they will process the information more deeply. Follow this by not expecting verbatim textbook responses on assessments.

2. *Repeat with variation on the instructional information and link early and often.* Memory development research expert Patricia Bauer (2009) recommends improving children's consolidation and reconsolidation of the information they are learning by two methods: (a) providing variations on a lesson theme to increase the number of associations in memory storage and (b) linking to expand the network of associations in memory storage. Both strategies expand the routes for retrieving information from storage.

3. *Assist students in organizing what they put into their memory.* Children will remember information better if they organize it hierarchically. Give them some practice arranging and reworking material that requires some structuring.

4. *Teach mnemonic strategies.* Memory aids for remembering information, *mnemonics,* can involve imagery and words (Homa, 2008). Different types of mnemonics include

   - For young children:
     - *Rhymes.* Examples of mnemonic rhymes for young children include the jar top/water faucet rule, "righty tighty; lefty loosey and
     - the spelling rule "*i before e except after c,*" the month rule, "Thirty days hath September, April, June, and November," the bolt-turning rule "Right is tight, left is loose,"
     - *Songs:* Examples include the alphabet song and *Head, Shoulders, Knees and Toes.*
     - *Phrases:* To use this strategy, form a sentence with each word beginning with the letter of the items to

be remembered. For example, young children would be able to remember cardinal directions using the mnemonic phrase *"Never eat soggy waffles."*

   - For older children:
     - *Rhymes:* Examples of mnemonic rhymes for older children include the spelling rule, "I before e except after c and when sounded like a as in neighbor and weigh;" and "Thirty days hath September, April, June, and November."
     - *Acronyms.* This strategy involves creating a word from the first letters of items to be remembered. For example, *HOMES* can be used as a cue for remembering the five original Great Lakes: *Huron, Ontario, Michigan, Erie,* and *Superior* and *ROY G. BIV* can be used for remembering the colors of the rainbow, *red, orange, yellow, green, blue, indigo,* and *violet.*
     - *Phrases:* Appropriate mnemonic phrases for older children include *"My very educated mother just served us noodles"* as a cue to remembering the planets in the solar system in order from the sun, *Mercury, Venus, Earth, Mars, Jupiter, Saturn, Uranus,* and *Neptune.* This phrase excludes Pluto due to its demotion in 2006.

   - For adolescents:
     - *Acronyms:* Appropriate mnemonic acronyms for adolescents include *FOIL* for the rule for multiplying the individual terms in two binomial quantities, *first terms, outside, inside, last.*
     - *Phrases:* Appropriate mnemonic phrases for adolescents include, *"Please excuse my dear aunt Sally,"* for the order of operations in math—*parentheses, exponents, multiplication, division, addition,* and *subtraction.*
     - *Method of loci.* Here children develop images of items to be remembered and mentally store them in familiar locations. Rooms of a house and stores on a street are common locations used in this memory strategy.
     - *Rhymes.* Examples of mnemonic rhymes are the spelling rule, "*I before e except after c,*" the month rule, "Thirty days hath September, April, June, and November," the bolt-turning rule "Right is tight, left is loose," and the alphabet song.
     - *Acronyms.* This strategy involves creating a word from the first letters of items to be remembered. For example, *HOMES* can be used as a cue for remembering the five original Great Lakes: *Huron, Ontario, Michigan, Erie,* and *Superior.*

## TEACHING CONNECTIONS: Best Practices
### Strategies for Helping Students Improve Their Memory

○ *Keyword method.* Another mnemonic strategy that involves imagery is the *keyword method,* in which vivid imagery is attached to important words. This method has been used to practical advantage in teaching students how to rapidly master new information such as foreign vocabulary words, the states and capitals of the United States, and the names of U.S. presidents. For example, in teaching children that Annapolis is the capital of Maryland, you could ask them to connect vivid images of Annapolis and Maryland, such as two apples getting married (Levin, 1980) (see Figure 8.11).

Some educators argue against teaching children to use mnemonics because they involve rote memorization. Clearly, as we said earlier, remembering for understanding is preferred over rote memorization. However, if children need to learn lists of concepts, mnemonic devices can do the trick. Think of mnemonic devices as a way for children to learn some specific facts that they might need to know to solve problems.

**FIGURE 8.11** THE KEYWORD METHOD

To help children remember the state capitals, the keyword method was used. A special component of the keyword method is the use of mental imagery. For example, to help children remember that Annapolis is the capital of Maryland, they were encouraged to envision two apples being married, thus associating *apple* with Annapolis and *marry* with Maryland.

5. *Embed memory-relevant language in your teaching.* Teachers vary considerably in how much they use memory-relevant language, such as strategies and metacognitive questions (questions related to students' knowledge of how memory works) that encourage students to remember information. In recent research that involved extensive observations of a number of first-grade teachers in the classroom, Peter Ornstein & his colleagues (Ornstein, Coffman, & Grammer, 2009; Ornstein & others, 2007, 2010) found that for the time segments observed, the teachers' use of strategy suggestions ranged from 1 to 14 percent, their use of metacognitive questions ranged from 1 to 10 percent, and their combined use of deliberate memory demands and cognitive structuring activities ranged from 10.0 to 35 percent. Further, when lower-achieving students were placed in classrooms in which teachers were categorized as "high-mnemonic teachers" who frequently embedded memory-relevant information in their teaching, their achievement increased (Ornstein & others, 2007).

## Review, Reflect, and Practice

**③** Discuss memory in terms of encoding, storage, and retrieval.

**REVIEW**

- What is memory? What is necessary for it to work?
- How are these five processes—rehearsal, deep processing, elaboration, constructing images, and organization—involved in encoding?
- What are the three time frames of memory? How are long-term memory's contents described? What are three theories about how they might be represented in memory? What makes a memory easier or harder to retrieve? What are some theories about why we forget?

**REFLECT**

- Which principles and strategies in our discussion of memory are likely to be useful for the subjects and grade levels at which you plan to teach?

*(continued)*

## Review, Reflect, and Practice

### PRAXIS™ PRACTICE

1. Natalie is playing a game called "Memory" at a birthday party. A covered tray with 15 objects is brought into the room. The cover is removed, and the children have 30 seconds to memorize the objects. They will then write down the objects they remember. The child who correctly remembers the most objects wins the game. Natalie notices that five of the objects are hair-related items—a comb, a brush, shampoo, a barrette, and a ponytail holder. She notices that another five objects are school supplies—a pencil, a pen, a ruler, a marker, and a glue stick. The final five objects appear to be random. Natalie has no problem remembering the items that she was able to group by type. She only remembers two of the other items. What memory strategy is Natalie using?
   a. chunking
   b. constructing images
   c. elaboration
   d. rehearsal

2. To test his students' memory skills, Mr. Watkins reads lists of nonsense words to them and asks them to recall as many as they can. Veronica can recall five words. If she performs as is expected for age, how old is Veronica most likely to be?
   a. 4
   b. 7
   c. 12
   d. 17

3. When asked to describe in detail how to make a peanut-butter-and-jelly sandwich, Maria skips several steps. When asked to make the sandwich, Maria does so flawlessly. Why is it that although Maria knows how to make the sandwich, she is unable to describe the process in detail?
   a. It is difficult to translate procedural memory into words.
   b. Maria has not encoded the process into long-term memory.
   c. It is difficult to translate episodic memory into semantic memory.
   d. Maria's episodic memory is faulty.

4. Mr. Madison wants his students to know the names of all of the states in the United States. To help them, he teaches them a song in which each state name is sung in alphabetical order. Most of his students learn the song with relative ease. They even sing the song to themselves when he gives them a quiz that requires them to write down the name of each state. However, when he gives them blank U.S. maps to fill in with state names, his students cannot complete them successfully. Why were they able to remember the names of the states, but not their locations?
   a. Mnemonic devices, such as the song Mr. Madison taught his students, are not effective for memorizing material.
   b. Mnemonic devices, such as the song Mr. Madison taught his students, increase the likelihood of cue-dependent forgetting.
   c. Mnemonic devices, such as the song Mr. Madison taught his students, increase the serial position effect.
   d. Mnemonic devices, such as the song that Mr. Madison taught his students, involve rote memorization and do not generalize to other memory tasks.

*Please see the answer key at the end of the book.*

## 4 EXPERTISE

| Expertise and Learning | Acquiring Expertise | Expertise and Teaching |

In the last section, we considered various aspects of memory. Our ability to remember new information about a subject depends considerably on what we already know about it (Ericsson, Krampe, & Tesch-Romer, 2009). For example, a student's ability to recount what she saw when she was at the library is largely governed by what she already knows about libraries, such as where books on certain topics are likely to be and how to check books out. If she knew little about libraries, the student would have a much harder time recounting what was there.

The contribution of prior content knowledge to our ability to remember new material is especially evident when we compare the memories of experts and novices in a particular knowledge domain (Nippold, 2009). An expert is the opposite of a novice (someone who is just beginning to learn a content area). Experts demonstrate especially impressive memory in their areas of expertise. One reason that children remember less than adults is that they are far less expert in most areas.

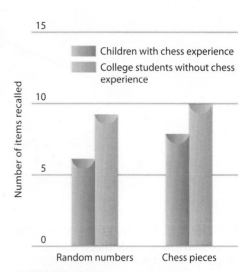

FIGURE **8.12** MEMORY FOR NUMBERS AND CHESS PIECES

### EXPERTISE AND LEARNING

Studying the behavior and mental processes of experts can give us insights into how to guide students in becoming more effective learners (Ericsson, Krampe, & Tesch-Romer, 2009; Papageorgi & others, 2010). What is it, exactly, that experts do? According to the National Research Council (1999), they are better than novices at the following:

- Detecting features and meaningful patterns of information
- Accumulating more content knowledge and organizing it in a manner that shows an understanding of the topic
- Retrieving important aspects of knowledge with little effort
- Adapting an approach to new situations
- Using effective strategies

In this section, we will consider various ways that you can help your students learn and remember these skills that experts use so effortlessly.

**Detecting Features and Meaningful Patterns of Organization**   Experts are better at noticing important features of problems and contexts that novices may ignore (Blair & Somerville, 2009; Bransford & others, 2006). Thus, the attentional advantage of experts starts them off at a more advantageous level than novices in a learning context. Experts also have superior recall of information in their area of expertise. The process of *chunking,* which we discussed earlier, is one way they accomplish this superior recall. For example, "Chess masters perceive chunks of meaningful information, which affects their memory of what they see. . . . Lacking a hierarchical, highly organized structure for the domain, novices cannot use this chunking strategy" (National Research Council, 1999, p. 21).

In areas where children are knowledgeable and competent, their memory is often extremely good. In fact, it often exceeds that of adults who are novices in that content area. This was documented in a study of 10-year-old chess experts (Chi, 1978). These children were excellent chess players but not especially brilliant in other ways. As with most 10-year-olds, their memory spans for digits were shorter than an adult's. However, they remembered the configurations of chess pieces on chessboards far better than did the adults who were novices at chess (see Figure 8.12).

Expert teachers recognize features and patterns that are not noticed by novice teachers (National Research Council, 1999, pp. 21, 25). For example, in one study,

RESEARCH

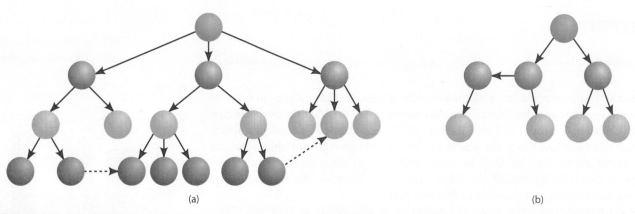

FIGURE **8.13** AN EXAMPLE OF HOW INFORMATION IS ORGANIZED IN THE MIND OF AN EXPERT AND A NOVICE

(*a*) An expert's knowledge is based on years of experience in which small bits of information have been linked with many other small pieces, which together are placed in a more general category. This category is in turn placed in an even more general category of knowledge. The dotted lines are used as pointers, associations between specific elements of knowledge that connect the lower branches and provide mental shortcuts in the expert's mind. (*b*) The novice's knowledge shows far fewer connections, shortcuts, and levels than an expert's knowledge.

expert and novice teachers had a very different understanding of the events in a videotaped classroom lesson in which three screens showed simultaneous events taking place throughout the classroom (left, center, and right areas) (Sabers, Cushing, & Berliner, 1991). One expert teacher said, "On the left monitor, the students' note taking indicates that they have seen sheets like this before; it's fairly efficient at this point because they're used to the format they are using." One novice teacher sparsely responded, "It's a lot to watch."

**Organization and Depth of Knowledge** Experts' knowledge is organized around important ideas or concepts more than novices' knowledge is (National Research Council, 1999). This provides experts with a much deeper understanding of knowledge than novices have (Bransford & others, 2006).

Experts in a particular area usually have far more elaborate networks of information about that area than novices do (see Figure 8.13). The information they represent in memory has more nodes, more interconnections, and better hierarchical organization.

The implications for teaching are that too often a curriculum is designed in a way that makes it difficult for students to organize knowledge in meaningful ways. This especially occurs when there is only superficial coverage of facts before moving on to the next topic. In this context, students have little time to explore the topic in depth in order to get a sense of what the important, organizing ideas are. This type of shallow presentation can occur in any subject area but is common in history and science texts that emphasize facts (National Research Council, 1999).

**Fluent Retrieval** The effort involved in retrieval of relevant information can vary greatly. Experts in a certain type of information can retrieve it almost effortlessly, or *fluently*, whereas novices must expend a great deal of effort in retrieving the same information (Posner & Rothbart, 2007).

The advantage of fluent retrieval is that it places fewer demands on conscious attention. Since the amount of information a student can attend to at one time is limited, ease of processing information in some aspects of a task frees up capacity to attend to other aspects of a task.

Consider expert and novice readers. Expert readers can quickly scan the words of a sentence and paragraph, which allows them to devote attention to understanding what they are reading. However, novice readers' ability to decode words is not yet fluent, so they have to allocate considerable attention and time to this task, which restricts the time they can give to understanding a passage. An important aspect of teaching is to help students develop the fluency they need to competently perform cognitive tasks (Beck & others, 1991).

**Adaptive Expertise** An important aspect of expertise "is whether some ways of organizing knowledge are better" than others for helping people to be "flexible and adaptive to new situations" (National Research Council, 1999, p. 33). *Adaptive experts* are able to approach new situations flexibly rather than always responding in a rigid, fixed routine (Gambrell, Malloy, & Anders-Mazzoni, 2007). An important theme in the book *Preparing Teachers for a Changing World* (Darling-Hammond & Bransford, 2005, p. 3) is to "help teachers become 'adaptive experts' who are prepared for effective lifelong learning that allows them to continually add to their knowledge and skills." In other words, teachers characterized by adaptive expertise are flexible and open to rethinking important ideas and practices to improve their students' learning (Hammerness & others, 2005).

Innovation and efficiency are the two main dimensions of one model of adaptive expertise (Bransford & others, 2006). Experts characterized by *efficiency* can quickly retrieve and apply information in skillful ways to explain something or solve a problem. Experts characterized by *innovation* are able to move away from efficiency, at least on a short-term basis, and unlearn previous routines. Innovation occurs when individuals "let go" and rethink their routine way of doing something.

In this model, adaptive experts possess a balance of efficiency and innovation (Bransford & others, 2006). For example, efficiency is at work when a teacher teaches students to speedily complete math computations, but this efficiency may limit the students' competence when they face new math problems. When this efficiency-oriented teacher adapts and adds teaching for understanding and application, innovation is taking place. The new skills she teaches are likely to increase the students' competence when they encounter new math problems.

Adaptive experts are motivated to learn from others (Hammerness & others, 2005). This may not be that difficult when the learning involves making a teacher's existing routines and practices more efficient. However, as we just indicated, adaptive expertise also includes innovation that requires sometimes replacing or transforming prior routines and practices, which is often not easy to do. Your teaching likely will benefit if you seek feedback from other competent teachers, even if their approaches are different than yours. This might occur when you watch a videotape of your teaching with other teachers who provide feedback about your teaching or invite a colleague to come to your classroom to observe your teaching.

In sum, adaptive expertise is a critical aspect of being an outstanding teacher. Teachers who are knowledgeable and adept at adapting different methods, practices, and strategies to meet the needs of different students are most likely to guide students to higher levels of learning and achievement (Gambrell, Malloy, & Anders-Mazzoni, 2007).

**Strategies**   Experts use effective strategies in understanding the information in their area of expertise and in advancing it (Ornstein, Coffman, & Grammer, 2009; Ornstein & Light, 2010). Earlier in the chapter we described a number of strategies that students can use to remember information, and later in the chapter we will further examine strategies in our discussion of metacognition.

Patricia Alexander (2003) uses the label *acclimation* to describe the initial stage of expertise in a particular domain (such as English, biology, or mathematics). At this stage, students have limited and fragmented knowledge that restricts their ability to detect the difference between accurate and inaccurate or between relevant and tangential information. To help students move beyond the acclimation stage, teachers need to guide students in determining what content is central and what is peripheral, as well as what is accurate and well supported and what is inaccurate and unsupported. In Alexander's (2003) view, students don't come to the classroom equipped with the strategies they need to move beyond the acclimation stage. Teachers must help students learn effective strategies and practice them in relevant situations before students can experience their value. Students also need to be encouraged to change and combine strategies to solve the problem at hand.

**Spreading Out and Consolidating Learning**   Students' learning benefits when teachers talk with them about the importance of regularly reviewing what they learn. Children who have to prepare for a test will benefit from distributing their learning over a longer period rather than cramming for the test at the last minute. Cramming tends to produce short-term memory that is processed in a shallow rather than deep

**Thinking Back/Thinking Forward**

Strategy construction refers to the creation of new procedures for processing information. Chapter 8, p. 256

Learning how to use strategies usually takes time. Chapter 8, p. 288

*What are some good study strategies?*

manner. A final, concentrated tune-up before the test is better than trying to learn everything at the last minute.

***Asking Themselves Questions*** When children ask themselves questions about what they have read or about an activity, they expand the number of associations with the information they need to retrieve. At least as early as the middle of elementary school, the self-questioning strategy can help children to remember. For example, as children read, they can be encouraged to stop periodically and ask themselves questions such as, "What is the meaning of what I just read?" "Why is this important?" and "What is an example of the concept I just read?" Students can use the same self-questioning strategy when they listen to you conduct a lesson, hear a guest give a talk, or watch a video. If you periodically remind children to generate questions about their experiences, they are more likely to remember the experiences.

***Taking Good Notes*** Taking good notes from either a lecture or a text benefits learning (Santrock & Halonen, 2009). When children are left to take notes without being given any strategies, they tend to take notes that are brief and disorganized. When they do write something down, it often is a verbatim record of what they have just heard. Give children some practice in taking notes and then evaluate their note taking. Encourage children not to write down everything they hear when they take notes. It is impossible to do this, anyway, and it can prevent them from getting the big picture of what the speaker is saying. Here are some good note-taking strategies:

- *Summarizing.* Have the children listen for a few minutes and then write down the main idea that a speaker is trying to get across in that time frame. Then have the child listen for several more minutes and write down another idea, and so on.
- *Outlining.* Show the children how to outline what a speaker is saying, using first-level heads as the main topics, second-level heads as subtopics under the first-level heads, and third-level heads under the second-level heads.
- *Using concept maps.* Help the children practice drawing concept maps, which are similar to outlines but visually portray information in a more spiderlike format (see Chapter 9).

All three note-taking strategies described so far—summarizing, outlining, and using concept maps—help children evaluate which ideas are the most important to remember. Outlining and concept maps also help children arrange the material hierarchically, which underscores an important theme of learning: it works best when it is organized.

***Using a Study System*** Various systems have been developed to help people to remember information that they are studying from a book. One of the earliest systems was called *SQ3R,* which stands for *Survey, Question, Read, Recite,* and *Review.* A more recently developed system is called *PQ4R,* which stands for *Preview, Question, Read, Reflect, Recite,* and *Review.* Thus, the PQ4R system adds an additional step, "Reflect," to the SQ3R system. From the later elementary school years on, students will benefit from practicing the PQ4R system. The system benefits students by getting them to meaningfully organize information, ask questions about it, reflect on it, and review it. Here are more details about the steps in the PQ4R system:

- *Preview.* Tell your students to briefly survey the material to get a sense of the overall organization of ideas—to look at the headings to see the main topics and subtopics that will be covered.
- *Question.* Encourage the children to ask themselves questions about the material as they read it.
- *Read.* Now tell the children to read the material. Encourage your students to be active readers—to immerse themselves in what they are reading and strive to understand what the author is saying. This helps students to avoid being

# SELF-ASSESSMENT 8.1

## How Effective Are My Memory and Study Strategies?

Teachers who themselves practice using good memory and study strategies are more likely to model and communicate these to their students than teachers who don't use such strategies. Candidly respond to these items about your own memory and study strategies. Rate yourself on this scale: 1 = never, 2 = some, 3 = moderate, 4 = almost, or 5 = always. Then total your points.

| 1 | 2 | 3 | 4 | 5 |
|---|---|---|---|---|
|   |   |   |   |   |
|   |   |   |   |   |
|   |   |   |   |   |
|   |   |   |   |   |
|   |   |   |   |   |
|   |   |   |   |   |
|   |   |   |   |   |
|   |   |   |   |   |
|   |   |   |   |   |
|   |   |   |   |   |
|   |   |   |   |   |

1. I'm a good time manager and planner.

2. I'm good at focusing my attention and minimizing distractions.

3. I try to understand material rather than rotely memorizing it.

4. I ask myself questions about what I have read or about class activities.

5. I take good notes in class and from textbooks.

6. I regularly review my notes.

7. I use mnemonic strategies.

8. I'm very organized in the way I encode information.

9. I spread out my studying to consolidate my learning.

10. I use good retrieval cues.

11. I use the PQ4R method or a similar study method.

## SCORING AND INTERPRETATION

If you scored 50–55 total points, you likely use good memory and study strategies. If you scored 45–49 points, you likely have some reasonably good memory and study strategies. If you scored below 45, spend some time working on improving your memory and study strategies.

If you would like to learn more about effective memory and study strategies, one resource is a book called *Your Guide to College Success* (Santrock & Halonen, 2009). Also, to gain more experience in developing good memory and study strategies, contact the study-skills center at your college or university; specialists there likely will be able to help you.

empty readers whose eyes just track the lines of text but whose minds fail to register anything important.

- *Reflect.* By occasionally stopping and reflecting on the material, students increase its meaningfulness. Encourage the children to be analytic at this point in studying. After they have read something, challenge them to break open the ideas and scratch beneath their surface. This is a good time for them to think out applications and interpretations of the information, as well as connecting it with other information already in their long-term memory.

- *Recite.* This involves children self-testing themselves to see if they can remember the material and reconstruct it. At this point, encourage the children to make up a series of questions about the material and then try to answer them.

- *Review.* Tell your students to go over the material and evaluate what they know and don't know. At this point, they should reread and study the material they don't remember or understand well.

To evaluate the extent to which you use good memory and study strategies, complete Self-Assessment 8.1.

## ACQUIRING EXPERTISE

What determines whether or not someone becomes an expert? Can motivation and practice get someone to expert status? Or does expertise also require a great deal of talent (Sternberg & Ben-Zeev, 2001)?

**Practice and Motivation** One perspective is that a particular kind of practice—*deliberate practice*—is required to become an expert (Rosenzweig & Bennett, 2009). Deliberate practice is at an appropriate level of difficulty for the individual, provides corrective feedback, and allows opportunities for repetition (Ericsson, Krampe, & Tesch-Romer, 2009).

RESEARCH

In one study of violinists at a music academy, the extent to which children engaged in deliberate practice distinguished novices from experts (Ericsson, Krampe, & Tesch-Romer, 1993). The top violinists averaged 7,500 hours of deliberate practice by age 18, the good violinists only 5,300 hours. Many individuals give up on becoming an expert because they won't put forth the effort it takes to engage in extensive deliberate practice over a number of years.

Such extensive practice requires considerable motivation. Students who are not motivated to practice long hours are unlikely to become experts in a particular area. Thus, a student who complains about having too much work, doesn't persevere, and doesn't extensively practice solving math problems over a number of years is not going to become an expert in math.

**Talent** A number of psychologists who study expertise stress that it requires not only deliberate practice and motivation but also talent (Hunt, 2006; Sternberg, 2009).

A number of abilities—music and athletic, for example—seem to have a heritable component (Plomin & others, 2009). For example, is it likely that Mozart could have become such an outstanding musical composer just because he practiced long hours? Is it likely that LeBron James became such a fantastic basketball player just because he was motivated to do so? Many talented individuals have attempted to become as great as Mozart or James but have given up trying after only mediocre performances. Clearly, heredity matters. Nonetheless, Mozart and James would not have developed expertise in their fields without being highly motivated and engaging in extensive deliberate practice. Talent alone does not make an expert.

## EXPERTISE AND TEACHING

Being an expert in a particular domain—such as physics, history, or math—does not mean that the expert is good at helping others learn it (Bransford & others, 2006). Indeed, "expertise can sometimes hurt teaching because many experts forget what is easy and what is difficult for students" (National Research Council, 1999, p. 32).

**Pedagogical Content Knowledge** Some educators have distinguished between the content knowledge required for expertise and the pedagogical content knowledge necessary to effectively teach it. *Pedagogical content knowledge* includes ideas about common difficulties that students have as they try to learn a content area, typical paths students must take to understand the area, and strategies for overcoming the difficulties they experience.

Expert teachers are good at monitoring students' learning and assessing students' progress. They also know what

An expert teacher monitoring students' learning. *What are some characteristics of expert teachers?*

types of difficulties students are likely to encounter, are aware of students' existing knowledge, and use this awareness to teach at the right level and to make new information meaningful. Some educational psychologists argue that in the absence of expert pedagogical awareness of their own students, inexpert teachers simply rely on textbook publishers' materials, which, of course, contain no information about the particular pedagogical needs of students in the teacher's classroom (Brophy, 2004).

**Technology, Expertise, and Teaching**   Richard Mayer (2008, 2009) has presented a number of ideas and conducted research on ways to incorporate expertise and technology in the classroom. In his cognitive theory of multimedia learning, Mayer (2009) highlights the following:

TECHNOLOGY

- There are two separate channels (auditory and visual) for processing information, which is sometimes referred to as *dual-coding theory*.
- Each channel has a limited (finite) capacity, similar to the concept of *cognitive load*.
- Learning is an active process of filtering, selecting, organizing, and integrating information based on prior knowledge.

Mayer's (2010) current interests in technology and expertise focus on (1) multimedia learning, such as discovering how illustrations influence the way students learn from scientific text and how students can learn to solve problems from videogames, and (2) human computer interaction, including how novices learn to interact with computers, strategies for designing e-learning environments that effectively promote learning, and how students learn from computer-based tutors.

## Review, Reflect, and Practice

**4** Draw some lessons about learning from the way experts think.

**REVIEW**

- What do experts do that novices often don't do in the process of learning?
- What does it take to become an expert?
- Is subject experience enough to make a good teacher? What else is needed?

**REFLECT**

- Choose an area in which you feel at least somewhat of an expert. Compare your ability to learn in that field with the ability of a novice.

**PRAXIS™ PRACTICE**

1. The case studies in this text are designed to help educational psychology students learn the material and begin to develop expertise. The first question of each case study asks students to identify the issues in the case. The author most likely included this question for each case because he understood that
   a. it is important for students to consolidate their learning.
   b. it is important for students to learn to determine what content is central and what is peripheral.
   c. in learning, it is important to strike a balance between efficiency and innovation.
   d. students need a great deal of help in developing fluent retrieval skills.

*(continued)*

## Review, Reflect, and Practice

### PRAXIS™ PRACTICE (CONTINUED)

2. Ryan is the best player on his soccer team. His coach thinks of him as a coach's dream player because he works so hard. It is rare for Ryan to perform a skill better than his teammates when it is initially introduced, but by the time the next practice comes, he will have mastered the skill. At one point, Ryan decided that he wanted to be able to score from a corner kick. He gathered up all the soccer balls he could find and kicked them one after another from the corner, trying to curl them into the goal. When he had finished, he gathered the balls and did it again. He continued this for an entire afternoon, and thereafter for at least an hour after school each day. His coach was very happily surprised when, in the next game, Ryan scored a goal from a corner kick. Why has Ryan developed expertise in soccer?

   a. He engages in extensive deliberative practice.
   b. He is relying on an inborn talent.
   c. He has an excellent teacher in his coach.
   d. He uses the PQ4R method 3.

3. Mr. Williams is a former college history professor who is now teaching high school American history. He discusses his research and writing with his students and tries to make history come alive by telling them about how historians find out about the past. After a month of teaching, he finds that his students seem confused during class discussions and perform poorly on tests of factual knowledge. The most likely explanation is that Mr. Williams lacks

   a. content expertise.
   b. pedagogical content knowledge.
   c. metacognition.
   d. cue-dependent knowledge.

*Please see the answer key at the end of the book.*

## 5 METACOGNITION

| Developmental Changes | The Good Information-Processing Model | Strategies and Metacognitive Regulation |
|---|---|---|

So far in this chapter, we have examined a number of ways that you help students improve their ability to process information as they learn, including how to improve their attention and memory, as well as strategies that can increase the likelihood that they will make the transition from being a novice to being an expert. Another way that you can help children process information more effectively is by encouraging them to examine what they know about how their mind processes information (Ghetti, Castelli, & Lyons, 2010). As you read at the beginning of this chapter, this involves *metacognition,* which involves cognition about cognition, or "knowing about knowing" (Flavell, 2004). A distinction can be made between metacognitive knowledge and metacognitive activity. *Metacognitive knowledge* involves monitoring and reflecting on one's current or recent thoughts. This includes both factual knowledge, such as knowledge about the task, one's goals, or oneself, and strategic knowledge, such as how and when to use specific procedures to solve problems. *Metacognitive activity* occurs when students consciously adapt and manage their thinking strategies during problem solving and purposeful thinking.

Metacognition helps children to perform many academic tasks more effectively (Williams & Atkins, 2009). Metacognitive skills also have been taught to students to help them solve problems (Serra & Metcalfe, 2009). In one study, in which each of 30 daily lessons involved math story problems, a teacher guided low-achieving students in learning to recognize when they did not know the meaning of a word, did not have all of the information necessary to solve a problem, did not know how to subdivide the problem into specific steps, or did not know how to carry out a computation (Cardelle-Elawar, 1992). After the 30 daily lessons, the students who were given this metacognitive training had better math achievement and better attitudes toward math.

One expert on children's thinking, Deanna Kuhn (2009), argues that metacognition should be a stronger focus of efforts to help children become better critical thinkers, especially at the middle school and high school levels. She distinguishes between first-order cognitive skills, which enable children to know about the world (and have been the main focus of critical-thinking programs), and second-order cognitive skills—meta-knowing skills—which involve knowing about one's own (and others') knowing.

## DEVELOPMENTAL CHANGES

How does metacognition change in childhood? Are there further changes in metacognition during adolescence?

DEVELOPMENT

**Childhood**    Many studies have focused on children's *metamemory,* or knowledge of how memory works (Ghetti, Castelli, & Lyons, 2010). In the last several decades, there has been extensive interest in children's theories about how the human mind works.

*Metamemory*    By 5 or 6 years of age, children usually know that familiar items are easier to learn than unfamiliar ones, that short lists are easier than long ones, that recognition is easier than recall, and that forgetting becomes more likely over time (Lyon & Flavell, 1993). In other ways, however, young children's metamemory is limited. They don't understand that related items are easier to remember than unrelated ones or that remembering the gist of a story is easier than remembering information verbatim (Kreutzer & Flavell, 1975). By fifth grade, students understand that gist recall is easier than verbatim recall.

RESEARCH

Preschool children also have an inflated opinion of their memory abilities. For example, in one study, a majority of preschool children predicted that they would be able to recall all ten items of a list of ten items. When tested, none of the young children managed this feat (Flavell, Friedrichs, & Hoyt, 1970). As they move through the elementary school years, children give more realistic evaluations of their memory skills (Schneider & Pressley, 1997).

Preschool children also have little appreciation for the importance of memory cues, such as, "It helps when you can think of an example of it." By 7 or 8 years of age, children better appreciate the importance of cueing for memory. In general, children's understanding of their memory abilities and their skill in evaluating their performance on memory tasks is relatively poor at the beginning of the elementary school years but improves considerably by age 11 or 12 (Bjorklund & Rosenblum, 2000).

*Theory of Mind*    Even young children are curious about the nature of the human mind. They have a **theory of mind,** which refers to awareness of one's own mental processes and the mental processes of others. Studies of theory of mind view the child as "a thinker who is trying to explain, predict, and understand people's thoughts, feelings, and utterances" (Harris, 2006, p. 847). Researchers are increasingly discovering that children's theory of mind is linked to cognitive processes and disabilities (Doherty, 2008; Wellman, 2011). For example, theory of mind competence at age 3 is related to a higher level of metamemory at age 5 (Lockl & Schneider, 2007). Researchers also have found that autistic children have difficulty in developing a theory of mind, especially in understanding others' beliefs and emotions (Hall, 2009). Sometimes this has been referred to as *mindblindness* (Jurecic, 2006).

**theory of mind** Awareness of one's own mental processes and the mental processes of others.

DEVELOPMENT

Children's theory of mind changes as they develop through childhood (Gelman, 2009; Wellman, 2011). The main changes occur at 2 to 3 years of age, 4 to 5 years of age, middle and late childhood, and adolescence.

- *Two to Three Years of Age.* In this time frame, children begin to understand three mental states: (1) perceptions, (2) emotions, and (3) desires. *Perceptions:* The child realizes that another person sees what is in front of his or her own eyes and not necessarily what is in front of the child's eyes. *Emotions:* The child can distinguish between positive (for example, happy) and negative (sad, for example) emotions. A child might say, "Tommy feels bad." *Desires:* The child understands that if someone wants something, he or she will try to get it. A child might say, "I want my mommy." Children refer to desires earlier and more frequently than they refer to cognitive states such as thinking, knowing, and beliefs (Rakoczy, Warneken, & Tomasello, 2007). Two- to three-year-olds understand the way that desires are related to actions and to simple emotions (Harris, 2006). For example, they understand that people will search for what they want and that if they obtain it, they are likely to feel happy, but if they don't they will keep searching for it and are likely to feel sad or angry.

- *Four to Five Years of Age.* Children come to understand that the mind can represent objects and events accurately or inaccurately. The realization that people can have *false beliefs*—beliefs that are not true—develops in a majority of children by the time they are 5 years old (Wellman, Cross, & Watson, 2001) (see Figure 8.14). In one study of false beliefs, young children were shown a Band-Aids box and asked what was inside (Jenkins & Astington, 1996). To the children's surprise, the box actually contained pencils. When asked what a child who had never seen the box would think was inside, 3-year-olds typically responded "pencils." However, the 4- and 5-year-olds, grinning at the anticipation of the false beliefs of other children who had not seen what was inside the box, were more likely to say "Band-Aids."

  Children's understanding of thinking has some limitations in early childhood (Wellman, 2011). They often underestimate when mental activity is likely occurring. For example, they fail to attribute mental activity to someone who is sitting quietly, reading, or talking (Flavell, Green, & Flavell, 1995).

- *Middle and Late Childhood.* It is only beyond the early childhood years that children have a deepening appreciation of the mind itself rather than just an understanding of mental states (Wellman, 2011). Not until middle and late childhood do children see the mind as an active constructor of knowledge or processing center (Flavell, Green, & Flavell, 1998). In middle and late childhood, children move from understanding that beliefs can be false to an understanding of beliefs and mind as "interpretive," exemplified in an awareness that the same event can be open to multiple interpretations (Carpendale & Chandler, 1996).

- *Adolescence.* Important changes in metacognition also take place during adolescence (Kuhn, 2009, 2011). Compared with children, adolescents have an increased capacity to monitor and manage cognitive resources to effectively meet the demands of a learning task. This increased metacognitive ability results in more effective cognitive functioning and learning. A recent longitudinal study revealed that from 12 to 14 years of age, young adolescents increasingly used metacognitive skills, and used them more effectively, in math and history classes (van der Stel & Veenman, 2010). For example, 14-year-olds monitored their own text comprehension more frequently and did so more effectively than their younger counterparts.

  Adolescents have more resources available to them than children (through increased processing speed, capacity, and automaticity), and they are more skilled at directing the resources. Further, adolescents have a better meta-level understanding of strategies—that is, knowing the best strategy to use and when to use it in performing a learning task (Kuhn, 2009).

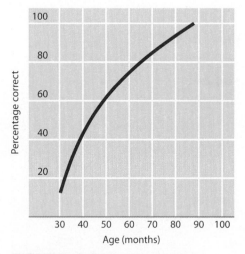

**FIGURE 8.14** DEVELOPMENTAL CHANGES IN FALSE-BELIEF PERFORMANCE

False-belief performance dramatically increases from 2½ years of age through the middle of the elementary school years. In a summary of the results of many studies, 2½-years-olds gave incorrect responses about 80 percent of the time (Wellman, Cross, & Watson, 2001). At 3 years, 8 months, they were correct about 50 percent of the time, and after that, gave increasingly correct responses.

Keep in mind, though, that there is considerable individual variation in adolescents' metacognition. Indeed, some experts argue that individual variation in metacognition is much more pronounced in adolescence than in childhood (Kuhn, 2009). Thus, some adolescents are quite good at using metacognition to improve their learning, others far less effective.

## THE GOOD INFORMATION-PROCESSING MODEL

Michael Pressley and his colleagues (Pressley, Borkowski, & Schneider, 1989; Schneider & Pressley, 1997) developed a metacognitive model called the *Good Information-Processing model*. It emphasizes that competent cognition results from a number of interacting factors. These include strategies, content knowledge, motivation, and metacognition. They argue that children become good at cognition in three main steps:

1. *Children are taught by parents or teachers to use a particular strategy.* With practice, they learn about its characteristics and advantages for learning *specific knowledge.* The more intellectually stimulating children's homes and schools are, the more specific strategies they will encounter and learn to use.

2. *Teachers may demonstrate similarities and differences in multiple strategies in a particular domain, such as math, which motivates students to see shared features of different strategies.* This leads to better *relational knowledge.*

3. *At this point, students recognize the general benefits of using strategies, which produces general strategy knowledge.* They learn to attribute successful learning outcomes to the efforts they make in evaluating, selecting, and monitoring strategy use *(metacognitive knowledge and activity).*

## STRATEGIES AND METACOGNITIVE REGULATION

In the view of Pressley and his colleagues (Pressley, 1983, 2007; Pressley & Harris, 2006; Pressley & Hilden, 2006), the key to education is helping students learn a rich repertoire of strategies that results in solutions of problems. Good thinkers routinely use strategies and effective planning to solve problems. Good thinkers also know when and where to use strategies (metacognitive knowledge about strategies). Understanding when and where to use strategies often results from the learner's monitoring of the learning situation.

Pressley and his colleagues argue that when students are given instruction about effective strategies, they often can apply strategies that they previously have not used on their own. They emphasize that students benefit when the teacher models the appropriate strategy and overtly verbalizes its steps. Then students should practice the strategy, guided and supported by the teacher's feedback until they can use it autonomously. When instructing students about employing a strategy, it also is a good idea to explain to them how using the strategy will benefit them. However, there are some developmental limitations to this approach. For instance, young children often cannot use mental imagery competently.

Just having students practice the new strategy is usually not enough for them to continue to use the strategy and transfer it to new situations. For effective maintenance and transfer, teachers should encourage students to monitor the effectiveness of the new strategy relative to their use of old strategies by comparing their performance on tests and other assessments (Harris & others, 2008). Pressley says that it is not enough to say, "Try it, you will like it"; you need to say, "Try it and compare."

An important aspect of metacognition is monitoring how well one is performing on a task (Graham & Olinghouse, 2009). This might involve becoming aware that one has not studied enough for a test or needs to reread a particular section of a chapter to understand it better. Mismonitoring is common. For example, elementary school students often think they are better prepared for a test than they actually are and think they understand text material better than they do. One

*What are some strategies for improving metacognitive regulation?*

## TEACHING CONNECTIONS: Best Practices
### Strategies for Helping Students Use Strategies

Following are some effective ways that teachers can guide students to develop strategies for helping students use strategies (Pressley, 1983, 2007; Pressley & McCormick, 2007):

1. *Recognize that strategies are a key aspect of solving problems.* Monitor students' knowledge and awareness of strategies for effective learning outcomes. Many students do not use good strategies and are unaware that strategies can help them learn. And after students learn a strategy, they tend to shorten and reduce it, in the process losing important components. Thus, be sure to monitor students who modify strategies in ways that make the strategies less effective.

2. *Model effective strategies for students.*

3. *Give students many opportunities to practice the strategies.* As students practice the strategies, provide guidance and support to the students. Give them feedback until they can use the strategies independently. As part of your feedback, inform them about where and when the strategies they used are most useful.

4. *Encourage students to monitor the effectiveness of their new strategy in comparison to the effectiveness of old strategies.* Students are much more likely to continue to use new strategies if they perceive them to be more effective than their old strategies. Help them to see the efficacy of their new strategies if they are unable to monitor the effectiveness themselves.

5. *Remember that it takes students a considerable amount of time to learn how to use an effective strategy.* Be patient and give students continued support during this tedious learning experience. Keep encouraging students to use the strategy over and over again until they can use it automatically.

6. *Understand that students need to be motivated to use the strategies.* Students are not always going to be motivated to use the strategies you want them to use. Especially important to students' motivation is their expectations that the strategies will lead to successful learning outcomes. Explicitly point out their successes in relation to strategy use. It can also help if students set goals for learning effective strategies. And when students attribute their learning outcomes to the effort they put forth, their learning benefits. Chapter 13 provides numerous recommendations for guiding students to become more motivated, which you can link to helping students become motivated to use strategies.

7. *Encourage children to use multiple strategies.* Most children benefit from experimenting with multiple strategies, finding out what works well, when, and where.

8. *Read more about strategy instruction.* Two good resources are *Best Practices in Literacy Instruction* (Gambrell, Morrow, & Pressley, 2007) and a chapter by Michael Pressley and Karen Harris (2006) titled "Cognitive strategies instruction: From basic research to classroom instruction," both of which include numerous helpful ideas about how to improve children's use of strategies. Especially good online sources are (a) **http://shop.ascd.org/ProductDisplay.cfm?ProductID=402086** (strategy instruction is shown in a video focusing on teaching in elementary and middle school classrooms), (b) **http://iris/peabody.vanderbilt.edu/index.html** (a free online interactive tutorial on strategy instruction), and (c) **www.unl.edu/csi** (Robert Reid's excellent Web site that is devoted to strategy instruction).

9. *Ask questions that help to guide students' thinking in various content areas.* These might include, "How can proofreading help me in writing a paper?" "Why is it important periodically to stop when I'm reading and try to understand what is being said so far?" and, "What is the purpose of learning this formula?"

10. *Recognize that low-achieving students and students with disabilities often need more support and time to become effective in independently using strategies.*

strategy is to encourage students who mismonitor to create practice tests and questions to assess how complete their understanding is.

Learning how to use strategies effectively often takes time (Bjorklund, 2011). Initially, it takes time to learn to execute the strategies, and it requires guidance and support from the teacher. With practice, students learn to execute strategies faster and more competently. *Practice* means that students use the effective strategy over and over again until they perform it automatically. To execute the strategies effectively, they need to have the strategies in long-term memory, and extensive practice makes this possible. Learners also need to be motivated to use the strategies. Thus, an important implication for helping students develop strategies such as organization is that once a strategy is learned, students usually need more time before they can use it efficiently (Schneider, 2004). Further, it is important for teachers to be aware that students may drop an effective strategy or continue to use a strategy that does not help them (Miller, 2000).

Do children use one strategy or multiple strategies in memory and problem solving? They often use more than one strategy (Bjorklund, 2011). Most children benefit from generating a variety of alternative strategies and experimenting with different approaches to a problem and discovering what works well, when, and where (Schneider & Bjorklund, 1998). This is especially true for children from the middle elementary school grades on, although some cognitive psychologists argue that even young children should be encouraged to practice varying strategies (Siegler, 2009).

Pressley and his colleagues (Pressley & others, 2001, 2003, 2004) have spent considerable time in recent years observing the use of strategy instruction by teachers and strategy use by students in elementary and secondary school classrooms. They conclude that teachers' use of strategy instruction is far less complete and intense than what is needed for students to learn how to use strategies effectively. They argue that education needs to be restructured so that students are provided with more opportunities to become competent strategic learners. Recall from earlier in the chapter in our discussion of memory that teachers vary considerably in how frequently they make suggestions for strategy use as well as how often they use metacognitive questions (Ornstein, Coffman, & Grammer, 2009; Ornstein & others, 2007, 2010).

A final point about strategies is that many strategies depend on prior knowledge. For example, students can't apply organizational strategies to a list of items unless they know the correct categories into which the items fall. The point about the importance of prior knowledge in strategy use coincides with the emphasis in our discussion earlier in the chapter of how experts use more effective strategies than novices.

## Review, Reflect, and Practice

**5** Explain the concept of metacognition and identify some ways to improve children's metacognition.

### REVIEW

- How do young children compare with older children in their metacognitive abilities? According to Pressley and colleagues' Good Information-Processing model, competent cognition results from what interacting factors?
- How can children be helped to learn metacognitive strategies and self-regulation?

### REFLECT

- How might the three steps in the Good Information-Processing model be part of teaching a topic to children? Select a topic that you might teach one day and try working through it as an example.

### PRAXIS™ PRACTICE

1. Sharmala's uncle has just played a trick on her. He presented her with a can that looked like a can of peanuts. However, when she opened the can, a cloth snake sprang out at her. Sharmala thought the trick was very funny and could hardly wait to play it on her brother. When her uncle asked her what she thought her brother would expect to be in the can, she giggled and responded, "Peanuts, but won't he be surprised." This is an example of Sharmala's development of
   a. the ability to allocate attention to different aspects of a problem.
   b. problem-solving expertise.

*(continued)*

## Review, Reflect, and Practice

### PRAXIS™ PRACTICE (CONTINUED)

c. metamemory skills.

d. theory of mind.

2. Marvel has learned to use strategies to solve math problems but does not use them to study for history exams or spelling quizzes. According to the Good Information-Processing model, the next step for Marvel's metacognitive development would most likely be to

a. ask his teacher for specific strategies for studying history.

b. ask his parents about the benefits of using strategies for math.

c. understand shared features of many different strategies.

d. learn to attribute successful learning to use of strategies.

3. Mr. Quinton has taught his students the PQ4R strategy for reading textbooks in hopes that it will help them on their next history test. The majority of his class improves their scores. Mr. Quinton is disappointed when in spite of improved performance, many of his students don't continue using the PQ4R strategy. What is the most plausible explanation for the students' behavior?

a. They did not compare the results of using the PQ4R with their prior strategies.

b. They don't have the requisite background knowledge to use the PQ4R strategy effectively.

c. They have not had enough practice to use the strategy effectively.

d. They have not yet developed expertise in using the strategy.

*Please see the answer key at the end of the book.*

## Connecting with the Classroom: Crack the Case

# The Test

George has a test next week in his eighth-grade history class. He is having considerable difficulty remembering terms, names, and facts. On his last test, he identified General Sherman as a Vietnam War hero and Saigon as the capital of Japan. Historical dates are so confusing to him that he does not even try to remember them. In addition, George has difficulty spelling.

The test will consist of 50 objective test items (multiple-choice, true/false, and fill-in-the-blank) and 2 essay items. In general, George does better on essay items. He purposely leaves out any names about which he is uncertain and always omits dates. Sometimes he mixes up his facts, though, and often loses points for misspelled words. On objective items he has real problems. Usually, more than one answer will appear to be correct to him. Often he is "sure" he is correct, only to discover later that he was mistaken.

Before the last test, George tried to design some mnemonic devices to help him understand. He used acronyms, such as *HOMES* (for *H*uron, *O*ntario, *M*ichigan, *E*rie, and *S*uperior).

Although he remembered his acronyms quite well, he could not recall what each letter stood for. The result was a test paper filled with acronyms. Another time a classmate suggested that George try using concept maps. This classmate lent George the concept maps she had designed for her own use. George looked at them and found them to be very busy and confusing—he couldn't figure out what they even meant. They were not at all useful to him.

George has decided he is in need of some serious help if he is to pass this class. He has sought you out for help.

1. What are the issues in this case?

2. With what type of learning is George having difficulty?

3. What type of learning is easier for George?

4. Design a study-skills program for George drawing on principles of the cognitive information-processing approach.

# The Information-Processing Approach

**① THE NATURE OF THE INFORMATION-PROCESSING APPROACH:** Describe the information-processing approach.

> Information, Memory, and Thinking

The information-processing approach emphasizes that children manipulate information, monitor it, and strategize about it. Central to this approach are the processes of memory and thinking.

> Cognitive Resources: Capacity and Speed of Processing Information

Capacity and speed of processing information, often referred to as cognitive resources, increase across childhood and adolescence. Changes in the brain serve as biological foundations for developmental changes in cognitive resources. In terms of capacity, the increase is reflected in older children being able to hold in mind several dimensions of a topic simultaneously. A reaction-time task is often used to assess speed of processing. Processing speed continues to improve in early adolescence.

> Mechanisms of Change

According to Siegler, three important mechanisms of change are encoding (how information gets into memory), automaticity (ability to process information with little or no effort), and strategy construction (creation of new procedures for processing information). Children's information processing is characterized by self-modification, and an important aspect of this self-modification involves metacognition—that is, knowing about knowing.

**② ATTENTION:** Characterize attention and summarize how it changes during development.

> What Is Attention?

Attention is focusing mental resources. Four ways that children and adolescents can allocate their attention are selective attention (focusing on a specific aspect of experience that is relevant while ignoring others that are irrelevant), divided attention (concentrating on more than one activity at the same time), sustained attention (maintaining attention over an extended period of time), and executive attention (involves action planning, allocating attention to goals, error detection and compensation, monitoring progress on tasks, and dealing with novel or difficult circumstances). Multitasking is an example of divided attention, and it can have possible harmful effects on children's and adolescents' attention when they are engaging in a challenging task.

> Developmental Changes

Salient stimuli tend to capture the attention of the preschooler. After 6 or 7 years of age, there is a shift to more cognitive control of attention. Selective attention improves through childhood and adolescence.

**③ MEMORY:** Discuss memory in terms of encoding, storage, and retrieval.

> What Is Memory?

Memory is the retention of information over time and involves encoding, storage, and retrieval.

> Encoding

In everyday language, encoding has much to do with attention and learning. Rehearsal, deep processing, elaboration, constructing images, and organization are processes involved in encoding, which is the mechanism by which information gets into memory. Rehearsal increases the length of time that information stays in memory. In deep processing, information is processed semantically, in terms of its meaning. Elaboration refers to the extensiveness of information processing. Constructing images helps to elaborate the information, and the more information is presented in an organized way, the easier it is to remember.

| | |
|---|---|
| **Storage** | One way that memory varies involves its time frames: sensory memory, short-term memory, and long-term memory. There is increasing interest in working memory, a kind of mental workbench. The Atkinson-Shiffrin model states that memory involves a sequence of three stages: sensory, short-term, and long-term memory. Long-term memory includes different types of content. Many contemporary psychologists accept this hierarchy of long-term memory's contents: division into declarative and nondeclarative memory, with declarative memory divided into episodic and semantic memory. Declarative memory (explicit memory) is the conscious recollection of information, such as specific facts or events. Nondeclarative memory (implicit memory) is knowledge of skills and cognitive operations about how to do something; it is hard to communicate verbally. Episodic memory is the retention of information about the where and when of life's happenings; semantic memory is a general knowledge about the world. |
| | Three major approaches to how information is represented are network theories (which focus on how information is organized and connected, with emphasis on nodes in the memory network); schema theories (which stress that students often reconstruct information and fit it into an existing schema); and fuzzy trace theory (which states that memory is best understood by considering two types of memory representation: (1) verbatim memory trace and (2) fuzzy trace, or gist. In this theory, older children's better memory is attributed to the fuzzy traces created by extracting the gist of information. A script is a schema for an event. |
| **Retrieval and Forgetting** | Retrieval is influenced by the serial position effect (memory is better for items at the beginning and end of a list than for items in the middle), the effectiveness of retrieval cues, encoding specificity, and the retrieval task (such as recall versus recognition). Forgetting can be explained in terms of cue-dependent forgetting (failure to use effective retrieval cues), interference theory (because information gets in the way of what we are trying to remember), and decay (losing information over time). |

## ④ EXPERTISE: Draw some lessons about learning from the way experts think.

| | |
|---|---|
| **Expertise and Learning** | Five important characteristics of experts are that they (1) notice features and meaningful patterns of information that novices don't, (2) have acquired a great deal of content knowledge that is organized in a manner that reflects deep understanding of the subject, (3) can retrieve important aspects of their knowledge with little effort, (4) are adaptive in their approach to new situations, and (5) use effective strategies. |
| **Acquiring Expertise** | Becoming an expert usually requires deliberate practice, motivation, and talent. |
| **Expertise and Teaching** | Being an expert in a particular area does not mean that the expert is good at helping others learn it. Pedagogical content knowledge is required to effectively teach a subject. |

## ⑤ METACOGNITION: Explain the concept of metacognition and identify some ways to improve children's metacognition.

| | |
|---|---|
| **Developmental Changes** | Children's metamemory improves considerably through the elementary school years. At 5 years of age, a majority of children understand that people can have false beliefs, and in middle and late childhood they understand that people actively construct knowledge. Adolescents have an increased capacity to monitor and manage resources to effectively meet the demands of a learning task, although there is considerable individual variation in metacognition during adolescence. |
| **The Good Information-Processing Model** | Developed by Michael Pressley and his colleagues, the Good Information-Processing model stresses that competent cognition results from several interacting factors including strategies, content knowledge, motivation, and metacognition. |

In the view of Pressley and his colleagues, the key to education is helping students learn a rich repertoire of strategies that result in solutions to problems. Most children benefit from using multiple strategies and exploring which ones work well, when, and where. For example, teachers can model strategies for students and ask questions that help guide students' thinking in various content areas.

# KEY TERMS

information-processing
   approach 254
encoding 256
automaticity 256
strategy construction 256
metacognition 256
attention 257
selective attention 258
divided attention 258
sustained attention 258

executive attention 258
memory 263
rehearsal 263
levels of processing
   theory 264
elaboration 264
chunking 266
sensory memory 266
short-term memory 266
memory span 266

working memory 266
long-term memory 268
Atkinson-Shiffrin model 268
declarative memory 269
nondeclarative memory 269
episodic memory 270
semantic memory 270
network theories 270
schema theories 270
schema 270

script 271
fuzzy trace theory 271
serial position effect 271
encoding specificity
   principle 272
cue-dependent
   forgetting 272
interference theory 272
decay theory 273
theory of mind 285

# PORTFOLIO ACTIVITIES

Now that you have a good understanding of this chapter, complete this exercise to expand your thinking.

**Independent Reflection Developing Expert Knowledge.** Think about the experts you know. Are your parents or instructors considered experts in their fields? How do you think they came to become experts and how long did it take? Based on what you know about how experts process information, which strategies do you think these experts use to organize, remember, and utilize their knowledge and skills? (INTASC: Principles *2, 4, 9*)

**Collaborative Work Strategies to Enhance Memory.** Get together with three or four other students in the class and brainstorm about the best ways to guide students in developing better memory and study strategies. Discuss how you might do this differently for children and adolescents at different grade levels. For example, at what

age should students start learning effective note-taking strategies? For children too young to be taking elaborate notes, are there gamelike activities that might help them begin to learn the concept and value of taking notes or keeping running records of some event? Write your conclusions. (INTASC: Principles *2, 4*)

**Research/Field Experience Capturing Students' Attention.** Observe a kindergarten, elementary, middle school, and high school classroom and focus on how the teacher maintains students' attention. How effective are each teacher's strategies? Would you do things differently to capture the students' attention? (INTASC: Principles *2, 9*)

*Go to the Online Learning Center for downloadable portfolio templates.*

# STUDY, PRACTICE, AND SUCCEED

Visit **www.mhhe.com/santrockep5e** to review the chapter with self-grading quizzes and self-assessments, to apply the chapter material to

two more Crack the Case studies, and for suggested activities to develop your teaching portfolio.

# CHAPTER 9

# COMPLEX COGNITIVE PROCESSES

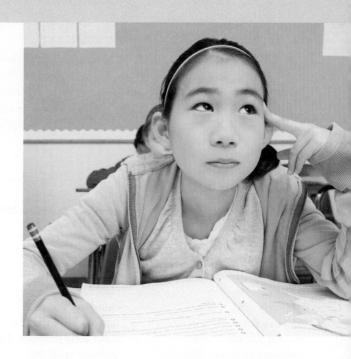

*I think, therefore I am.*

—René Descartes
*French Philosopher and Mathematician, 17th Century*

Learning **Goals**

**1** Discuss conceptual understanding and strategies for teaching concepts.

**2** Describe several types of thinking and ways that teachers can foster them.

**3** Take a systematic approach to problem solving.

**4** Define transfer and explain how to enhance it as a teacher.

# Teaching **Stories**   Marilyn Whirry

Marilyn Whirry is a twelfth-grade English teacher at Mira Costa High School in Manhattan Beach, California. In 1999 she was named Teacher of the Year in the United States and honored at a White House Reception. The following description of Marilyn's teaching appeared in a report by the Council of Chief State School Officers (2005, pp. 1–3).

> Marilyn's enthusiasm for life carries over into the classroom. Marilyn says about her life: "It is a canvas with swirling brush strokes that depict the motifs of my experience." According to Marilyn, teachers may never know how many students' lives they changed for the better because of their sense of responsibility and excitement for life.
>
> Marilyn's teaching philosophy centers around embracing and celebrating the act of learning. She says that teachers need to help students become motivated to search for knowledge and

to discover answers to questions of why and how. One of Marilyn's most important goals as a teacher is to get students to think deeply as they read and write. . . . Her teaching strategies include getting students to become aware of writing techniques in literary works that "promote dialogue and debate in group discussions."

> One of Marilyn's former students, Mary-Anna Rae, said that Marilyn's "intellectual engagement and her passion for life make her a powerful role model for students. In everything she does, she makes it clear that she is listening, attending to the students' deepest thinking." Mary-Anna, who now teaches herself, adds that Marilyn "enriched and expanded her world." Mary-Anna also says that Marilyn helped her to "grow more confident in what I had to say, finding my writer's voice and discovering that I could give my life purpose."

# Preview

One of Marilyn Whirry's major goals is to get her students to think deeply, an important emphasis in this chapter. In addition to exploring many aspects of thinking, we examine how teachers can guide students to engage in these other complex cognitive processes: understanding concepts, solving problems, and transferring what they learn to other settings.

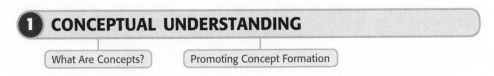

## WHAT ARE CONCEPTS?

**Concepts** group objects, events, and characteristics on the basis of common properties. Concepts help us to simplify, summarize, and organize information (Quinn, 2009, 2011).

Imagine a world in which we had no concepts: we would see each object as unique and would not be able to make any generalizations. If we had no concepts, we would find the most trivial problems difficult to formulate and even impossible to solve. Indeed, concepts help students make sense of the world (Chi & Brem, 2009; Oakes & others, 2010). Consider the concept of "book." If a student were not aware that a book is made of sheets of paper of uniform size, all bound together along one edge, and full of printed words and pictures in some meaningful order, each time the student encountered a new book she would have to figure out what it was. In a way, then, concepts keep us from "reinventing the wheel" each time we come across a new piece of information.

**concepts** They group objects, events, and characteristics on the basis of common properties.

*"Attention, everyone! I'd like to introduce the newest member of our family."*
© Jeff Kaufman/The New Yorker Collection/www.cartoonbank.com

Concepts also aid the process of remembering, making it more efficient (Racine, 2011). When students group objects to form a concept, they can remember the concept, then retrieve the concept's characteristics. Thus, when you assign math homework, you probably won't have to go through the details of what math is or what homework is. Students will have embedded in their memory a number of appropriate associations. In ways such as this, concepts not only help to jog memory but also make communication more efficient. If you say, "It's time for art," students know what you mean. You don't have to go into a lengthy explanation of what art is. Thus, concepts help students to simplify and summarize information, as well as improve the efficiency of their memory, communication, and use of time.

Students form concepts through direct experiences with objects and events in their world. For example, in constructing a sophisticated concept of "cartoons," children might initially experience TV cartoon shows, then read comic strips, and eventually look at some political caricatures. Students also form concepts through experience with symbols (things that stand for, or represent, something else). For example, words are symbols. So are math formulas, graphs, and pictures.

Some concepts are relatively simple, clear, and concrete, whereas others are more complex, fuzzy, and abstract. The former are easier to agree on. For example, most people can agree on the meaning of "baby." But we have a harder time agreeing on what is meant by "young" or "old." We agree on whether something is an apple more readily than on whether something is a fruit. Some concepts are especially complex, fuzzy, and abstract, like the concepts involved in theories of economic collapse or string theory in physics.

## PROMOTING CONCEPT FORMATION

Teachers can guide students to recognize and form effective concepts in a number of ways. The process begins with becoming aware of the features of a given concept.

**Learning About the Features of Concepts** An important aspect of concept formation is learning the key features, attributes, or characteristics of the concept (Madole, Oakes, & Rakison, 2010; Racine, 2011). These are the defining elements of a concept, the dimensions that make it different from another concept. For example, in our earlier example of the concept of "book," the key features include sheets of paper, being bound together along one edge, and being full of printed words and pictures in some meaningful order. Other characteristics such as size, color, and length are not key features that define the concept of "book." Consider also these critical features of the concept of "dinosaur": extinct and reptilian. In the case of the concept of "dinosaur," the feature "extinct" is important.

**Defining Concepts and Providing Examples**  An important aspect of teaching concepts is to clearly define them and give carefully chosen examples. The *rule-example strategy* is an effective way to do this (Tennyson & Cocchiarella, 1986). The strategy consists of four steps:

1. *Define the concept.* In addition to identifying the concept's key features or characteristics, link it to a *superordinate concept,* which is a larger class into which it fits. Thus, in specifying the key features of the concept of "dinosaur," you might want to mention the larger class into which it fits: "reptiles."

2. *Clarify terms in the definition.* Make sure that the key features or characteristics are well understood. Thus, in describing the key features of the concept of "dinosaur," it is important for students to know what a reptile is—usually an egg-laying vertebrate with an external covering of scales or horny plates that breathes by means of lungs.

3. *Give examples to illustrate the key features or characteristics.* With regard to dinosaurs, one might give examples and descriptions of different types of dinosaurs, such as a triceratops, an apatosaur, and a stegosaur. The concept can be further clarified by giving examples of other reptiles that are not dinosaurs, such as snakes, lizards, crocodiles, and turtles. Indeed, giving nonexamples of a concept as well as examples is often a good strategy for teaching concept formation. More examples are required when you teach complex concepts and when you work with less-sophisticated learners.

4. *Provide additional examples.* Ask students to categorize concepts, explain their categorization, or have them generate their own examples of the concept. Give examples of other dinosaurs, such as *Tyrannosaurus, Ornitholestes,* and *Dimetrodon,* or ask students to find more examples themselves. Also ask them to think up other nonexamples of dinosaurs, such as dogs, cats, and whales.

Do some children develop an intense, passionate interest in a particular category of objects or activities? A recent study of 11-month-old to 6-year-old children confirmed that they do (DeLoache, Simcock, & Macari, 2007). A striking finding was the large gender difference in categories, with an extremely intense interest in particular categories for boys as compared with girls. Categorization of boys' intense interests focused on vehicles, trains, machines, dinosaurs, and balls; girls' intense interests were more likely to involve dress-ups and books/reading but were not as extreme as boys' most intense interests were (see Figure 9.1).

**Hierarchical Categorization and Concept Maps**  Categorization is important because once a concept is categorized it can take on characteristics and features from being a member of a category (Chi & Brem, 2009). For example, students can infer that a triceratops is a reptile even if they have never been told that fact as long as they know that dinosaurs are reptiles and a triceratops is a dinosaur. Knowing

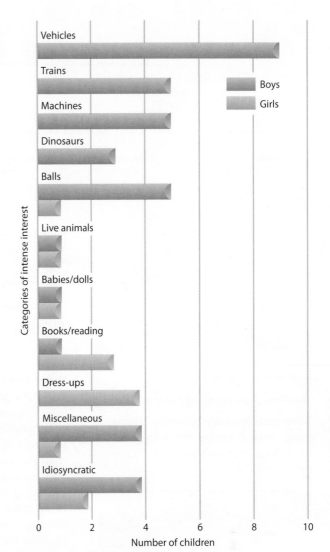

FIGURE **9.1**  CATEGORIZATION OF BOYS' AND GIRLS' INTENSE INTERESTS

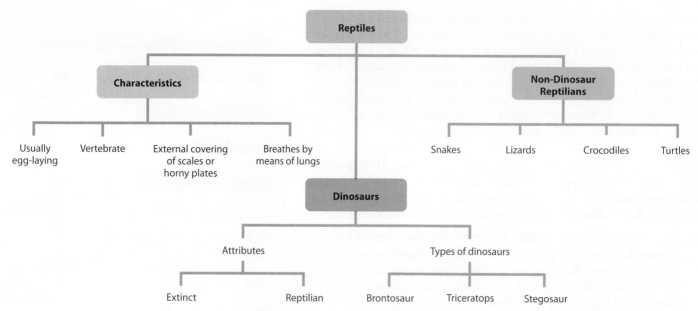

FIGURE **9.2** EXAMPLE OF A CONCEPT MAP FOR THE CONCEPT OF "REPTILE"

**Thinking Back/Thinking Forward**

When students contruct an image of something, they elaborate the information, which helps them to remember it. Chapter 8, p. 265

TECHNOLOGY

that a triceratops is a type of dinosaur lets students infer that a triceratops assumes the characteristics of dinosaurs (that they are reptiles).

A **concept map** is a visual presentation of a concept's connections and hierarchical organization. Getting students to create a map of a concept's features or characteristics can help them to learn the concept (Amadieu & others, 2009). The concept map also might embed the concept in a superordinate category and include examples and nonexamples of the concept (Ritchart, Turner, and Hadar, 2009). The visual aspects of the concept map relate to our Chapter 8 discussion of the use of imagery in memory. You might create a concept map with students' help, or let them try to develop it individually or in small groups. Figure 9.2 shows an example of a concept map for the concept of "reptile."

Teachers can access a number of concept mapping software programs to use in the classroom. Inspiration and Kidinspiration (**www.inspiration.com**) are good

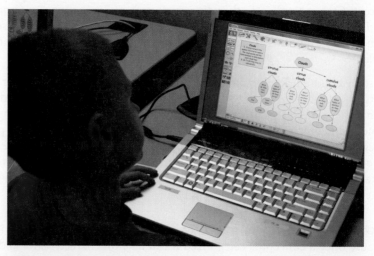

A student in the Research Center for Educational Technology's AT&T Classroom at Kent State University displaying the concept map he made in Kidspiration.

**concept map** A visual presentation of a concept's connections and hierarchical organization.

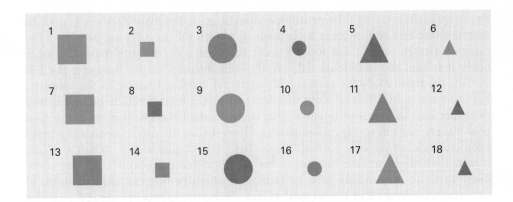

FIGURE **9.3**  GETTING STUDENTS TO GENERATE HYPOTHESES ABOUT A CONCEPT

ones. Wikipedia also has a linked list of concept mapping software that teachers can use: **http://en.wikipedia.org/wiki/List_of_concept_mapping_software.**

**Hypothesis Testing**    Students benefit from the practice of *hypothesis testing* in order to determine what a concept is and is not. *Hypotheses* are specific assumptions and predictions that can be tested to determine their accuracy. One way to develop a hypothesis is to come up with a rule about why some objects fall within a concept and others do not. Here is an example of how you can give your students practice in developing such hypotheses: Present your students with the picture of geometric forms shown in Figure 9.3. Then silently select the concept of one of those geometric forms (such as "circle" or "green circle") and ask your students to develop hypotheses about the concept you have selected. They can zero in on your concept by asking you questions related to the geometric forms and eliminating nonexamples. You might also let the students take turns selecting a concept and answering questions from the other students. Work with your students on developing the most efficient strategies for identifying the correct concept.

The concept of birds includes many different types of birds. *Which of these birds is likely to be viewed as the most typical bird?*

**Thinking Back/Thinking Forward**

In addition to outlining and constructing concept maps, summarizing is a good strategy for learning and remembering information. Chapter 8, p. 280

**prototype matching** Deciding if an item is a member of a category by comparing it with the most typical item(s) of the category.

**Prototype Matching**   In **prototype matching,** individuals decide whether an item is a member of a category by comparing it with the most typical item(s) of the category (Rosch, 1973). The more similar the item is to the prototype, the more likely it is that the individual will say the item belongs to the category; the less similar, the more likely the person will judge that it doesn't belong in the category. For example, a student's concept of a football player might include being big and muscular like an offensive lineman. But some football players, such as many field goal kickers, are not so big and muscular. However, an offensive lineman is a more prototypical example of a football player than a field goal kicker. When students consider whether someone belongs in the category "football player," they are more likely to think of someone who looks like an offensive lineman than to think of someone who looks like a field goal kicker. Similarly, robins are viewed as being more typical birds than ostriches or penguins. So members of a category can vary greatly yet still have qualities that make them a member of that category.

## TEACHING CONNECTIONS: Best Practices
### Strategies for Helping Students Form Concepts

1. *Use the rule-example strategy.* Remember that this involves four steps: (a) define the concept; (b) clarify the terms in the definition; (c) give examples to illustrate the key features or characteristics; and (d) provide additional examples and ask students to categorize these and explain their categorization, or have students generate their own examples of the concepts. Spend some time on this strategy, particularly with younger children. Consider the concept of "bird." Many young children will consider a key characteristic to be the ability to fly. However, not all birds fly and many animals that fly are not birds.

2. *Help students learn not only what a concept is but also what it is not.* Let's return to the concept "cartoon." Students can learn that even though they are humorous like a cartoon, clowns, jokes, and funny poems are not cartoons. If you are teaching the concept of "triangle," ask students to list the characteristics of "triangle" such as "three-sided," "geometric shape," "can be of any size," "can be of any color," "sides can vary in length," "angles can be different," and so on; also ask them to list examples of things that are not triangles, such as circles, squares, and rectangles.

3. *Make concepts as clear as possible and give concrete examples.* Spend some time thinking about the best way to present a new concept, especially an abstract one. Make it as clear as possible. If you want students to understand the concept "vehicle," ask them to come up with examples of it. They probably will say "car" and maybe "truck" or "bus." Show them photographs of other vehicles, such as a sled and a boat, to illustrate the breadth of the concept.

4. *Help students relate new concepts to concepts they already know.* In Chapter 8, we discussed the strategy of *outlining* for taking notes. Once students have learned this procedure, it is easier for them to learn how to construct concept maps, because you can show them how concept maps are linked with outlining in terms of hierarchical organization.

5. *Encourage students to create concept maps.* Getting students to map out the hierarchical organization of a concept can help them understand the concept's characteristics from more general to more specific. Hierarchical organization benefits memory. Students are likely to benefit more from concept maps they create themselves than those provided for them.

6. *Ask students to generate hypotheses about a concept.* Generating hypotheses encourages students to think and develop strategies. Work with students on developing the most efficient strategies for determining what a concept is.

7. *Give students experience in prototype matching.* Think of different concepts and then ask students what the prototypes of the concepts are. Then ask them for nonprototypical examples of the concept. Ask students to explain why they chose each example.

8. *Check for students' understanding of a concept and motivate them to apply the concept to other contexts.* Make sure that students don't just memorize a concept, but ask them how the concept can be applied in different contexts. For example, in learning the concept of fairness, ask students how fairness can make life smoother, not only at school but also at play, at home, and at work.

## Review, Reflect, and Practice

**1** Discuss conceptual understanding and strategies for teaching concepts.

### REVIEW
- What are concepts and why are they indispensable to thinking?
- What are some ways that students can be guided to construct effective concepts?

### REFLECT
- What might the concept "art" mean to a 3-year-old? To a 10-year-old? To a 16-year-old? To a professional artist? How do such changes come about?

### PRAXIS™ PRACTICE
1. Which of the following is the best example of a superordinate concept?
   a. collie
   b. dog
   c. German shepherd
   d. poodle
2. Ms. Peloti wants her students to learn about the concept "bird." She discusses the characteristics of birds with her students, including a defining characteristic: feathers. She then discusses irrelevant characteristics, such as flying—insects and bats fly too, but they are not birds; ostriches don't fly, but they are birds. Finally, the class discusses what a typical bird looks like. They finally agree that the most typical bird is a robin. Ms. Peloti then gives the children a list of animals and asks them to determine if they are birds by comparing them to the robin. What strategy of concept formation does this task represent?
   a. concept mapping
   b. hypothesis testing
   c. prototype matching
   d. relating concepts

*Please see the answer key at the end of the book.*

## **2** THINKING

What does it mean to think? How can teachers help students to become better thinkers? In this section, we will attempt to answer these important questions.

## WHAT IS THINKING?

**Thinking** involves manipulating and transforming information in memory. We think to form concepts, reason, think critically, make decisions, think creatively, and solve problems. Students can think about concrete things, such as a vacation at the beach or how to win at a video game, or about more abstract subjects, such as the meaning of freedom or identity. They can think about the past, such as what happened to them last month, or about the future, such as what their life will be like in the year

**thinking** Manipulating and transforming information in memory, which often is done to form concepts, reason, think critically, make decisions, think creatively, and solve problems.

## The Thinking Room

I recently talked with my granddaughter, Jordan Bowles, who is just beginning the second grade in Apex, North Carolina. I asked her what her classes were like this year.

She responded, "The usual stuff. Well, there is this one new class that I go to once a week. It's in the thinking room."

I then asked her what she was supposed to learn there.

Jordan said, "They are going to teach me not to jump to conclusions and my mom is happy about that."

RESEARCH

RESEARCH

MINDS AT WORK

**inductive reasoning** Reasoning from the specific to the general.

**analogy** A correspondence in some respects between otherwise dissimilar things.

2020. They can think about reality, such as how to do better on the next test, or about fantasy, such as what it would be like to meet Elvis Presley or land a spacecraft on Mars.

## REASONING

*Reasoning* is logical thinking that uses induction and deduction to reach a conclusion. We begin by focusing on inductive reasoning.

**Inductive Reasoning**  Reasoning from the specific to the general is **inductive reasoning.** It consists of drawing conclusions (forming concepts) about all members of a category based on observing only some of its members (Goswami, 2011; Heit, 2008). Researchers have found that inductive-reasoning skill is often a good predictor of academic achievement (Kinshuk & McNab, 2006).

What are some examples of the use of inductive reasoning in classrooms? When a student in English class reads only a few Emily Dickinson poems and is asked to draw conclusions from them about the general nature of Dickinson's poems, inductive reasoning is being requested. When a student is asked whether a concept in a math class applies to other contexts, such as business or science, again, inductive reasoning is being called for. Educational psychology research is inductive when it studies a sample of participants to draw conclusions about the population from which the sample is drawn. It is also inductive in that scientists rarely take a single study as strong enough evidence to reach a conclusion about a topic, instead requiring a number of studies on the same topic to have more confidence in a conclusion.

Indeed, an important aspect of inductive reasoning is repeated observation. Through repeated observation, information about similar experiences accumulates to the point that a repetitive pattern can be detected and a more accurate conclusion drawn about it. To study this aspect of inductive reasoning, researchers have examined whether inductive inferences are justified based on evidence about a single instance of two co-occurring events (Kuhn, Katz, & Dean, 2004). When two events occur together in time and space, we often conclude that one has caused the other, despite the possibility that other factors are involved. For example, a parent might conclude, "Harry is a bad influence on my daughter; Sharon didn't drink before she met him." The boy might be the cause, but the event may have been a coincidence. Of course, if there is repeated evidence (for example, every girl Harry has ever gone out with develops a drinking problem), then the argument becomes more persuasive.

Consider also a child who observes a black snake and concludes, "All snakes are black." The child's cousin sends him an e-mail about a pet snake she recently bought, and he concludes that the pet snake must be black. However, he clearly has not observed all of the snakes in the world—actually, only one in this case—so he has seen only a small sample of the world's snake population. Of course, he would be forced to change his mind if he saw a gray snake or a white snake. The conclusions drawn as a result of inductive reasoning are never finally certain, only more or less probable. But induction can provide conclusive *negative* results—for example, seeing a yellow snake proves that the assertion "All snakes are black" is *false.*

As just stated, inductive conclusions are never entirely certain—that is, they may be inconclusive. An inductive conclusion may be very likely, but there always is a chance that it is wrong, just as a sample does not perfectly represent its population (Kuhn, 2009). Teachers can help students improve their inductive reasoning by encouraging them to consider that the conclusion they reach depends on the quality and the quantity of the information available. Students often overstate a conclusion, making it more definitive than the evidence indicates.

Let's now consider another aspect of inductive reasoning: it is basic to analogies. An **analogy** is a correspondence between otherwise dissimilar things. Analogies can be used to improve students' understanding of new concepts by comparing them with already learned concepts.

One type of analogy involves formal reasoning and has four parts, with the relation between the first two parts being the same as, or very similar to, the relation between the last two. For example, solve this analogy: Beethoven is to music as Picasso is to _____. To answer correctly ("art"), you had to induce the relation between Beethoven and music (the former created the latter) and apply this relationship to Picasso (what did he create?).

How good are children and adolescents at inductive reasoning? Adolescents are better at many aspects of inductive reasoning than are children, including analogies and false inclusion when generalizing from a single event, but not as good as young adults (Kuhn, 2009).

**Deductive Reasoning**   In contrast to inductive reasoning, **deductive reasoning** is reasoning from the general to the specific. Figure 9.4 provides a visual representation of the difference between inductive and deductive reasoning.

When you solve puzzles or riddles, you are engaging in deductive reasoning. When you learn about a general rule and then understand how it applies in some situations but not others, you are engaging in deductive reasoning (Goswami, 2011; Johnson-Laird, 2008). Deductive reasoning is always certain in the sense that if the initial rules or assumptions are true, then the conclusion will be correct (Ricco, 2011). When educators and psychologists use theories and intuitions to make predictions, then evaluate these predictions by making further observations, they are using deductive reasoning.

Many aspects of deductive reasoning have been studied, including the occasions when knowledge and reasoning conflict. During adolescence, individuals are increasingly able to reason deductively even when the premises being reasoned about are false (Kuhn, 2009). Consider this deductive inference problem: *All basketball players are motorcycle drivers. All motorcycle drivers are women.* Assuming that these two statements are true, decide if the following statement is true or false: *All basketball players are women.*

Children rarely realize that such conclusions are valid deductions from the premises. From early adolescence through early adulthood, individuals improve in their ability to make accurate conclusions when knowledge and reasoning conflict. That is, they can "reason independently of the truth status of the premises" (Kuhn & Franklin, 2006).

## CRITICAL THINKING

Currently, there is considerable interest in critical thinking among psychologists and educators, although it is not an entirely new idea (Assaf, 2009; Bensley & others, 2010). **Critical thinking** involves thinking reflectively and productively and evaluating the evidence. Many of the "Reflect" questions that appear in every section of this book call for critical thinking.

**Mindfulness**   According to Ellen Langer (1997, 2005), mindfulness is a key to critical thinking. **Mindfulness** means being alert, mentally present, and cognitively flexible while going through life's everyday activities and tasks. Mindful students maintain an active awareness of the circumstances in their lives.

Mindful students create new ideas, are open to new information, and are aware of more than one perspective. In contrast, mindless students are entrapped in old ideas, engage in automatic behavior, and operate from a single perspective. Mindless students accept what they read or hear without questioning the accuracy of the information. Mindless students become trapped in rigid mindsets, not taking into account possible variations in contexts and perspectives. Langer emphasizes that asking good questions is an important ingredient of mindful thinking. She also stresses that it is

**Inductive Reasoning**

Specific

General

**Deductive Reasoning**

General

Specific

**FIGURE 9.4** INDUCTIVE AND DEDUCTIVE REASONING

The pyramid at the top (*right side up*) represents inductive reasoning—going from specific to general. The pyramid or triangle at the bottom (*upside down*) represents deductive reasoning—going from general to specific.

DEVELOPMENT

*"For God's sake, think! Why is he being so nice to you?"*

© Sam Gross/The New Yorker Collection/www .cartoonbank.com

**deductive reasoning**   Reasoning from the general to the specific.

**critical thinking**   Thinking reflectively and productively and evaluating the evidence.

**mindfulness**   Means being alert, mentally present, and cognitively flexible while going through life's everyday activities and tasks. Mindful students maintain an active awareness of the circumstances in their lives.

important to focus on the process of learning rather than the outcome. For example, Trisha didn't do well on her math test earlier this week. All she can think about is how poorly she did. If she were engaging in mindfulness, Trisha would evaluate why she did so poorly and think about what changes she could adopt to do better on the next test.

**Critical Thinking in Schools**  Here are some ways teachers can consciously build critical thinking into their lesson plans:

- Ask not only what happened but also "how" and "why."
- Examine supposed "facts" to determine whether there is evidence to support them.
- Argue in a reasoned way rather than through emotions.
- Recognize that there is sometimes more than one good answer or explanation.
- Compare various answers to a question and judge which is really the best answer.
- Evaluate and possibly question what other people say rather than immediately accepting it as the truth.
- Ask questions and speculate beyond what we already know to create new ideas and new information.

Jacqueline and Martin Brooks (1993, 2001) lament that few schools really teach students to think critically. In their view, schools spend too much time on getting students to give a single correct answer in an imitative way rather than encouraging students to expand their thinking by coming up with new ideas and rethinking earlier conclusions. They believe that too often teachers ask students to recite, define, describe, state, and list rather than to analyze, infer, connect, synthesize, criticize, create, evaluate, think, and rethink.

One way to encourage students to think critically is to present them with controversial topics or articles that present both sides of an issue to discuss. Some teachers shy away from having students engage in these types of critical-thinking debates or discussions because it is not "polite" or "nice" (Winn, 2004). However, critical thinking is promoted when students encounter conflicting accounts of arguments and debates because it can motivate them to delve more deeply into a topic and attempt to resolve an issue (Kuhn, 2009). In these circumstances, students often benefit when teachers refrain from stating their own views, allowing students to more freely explore different sides of issues and multiple perspectives on topics.

Getting students to think critically is not always an easy task (Willingham, 2008). Many students come into a class with a history of passive learning, having been encouraged to recite the correct answer to a question rather than put forth the intellectual effort to think in more complex ways (Noddings, 2008). By using more assignments that require students to focus on an issue, a question, or a problem instead of just reciting facts, teachers stimulate students' ability to think critically.

**Critical Thinking in Adolescence**  Adolescence is an important transitional period in the development of critical thinking (Kuhn, 2009). Several cognitive changes occur during adolescence that allow improved critical thinking, including the following (Keating, 1990):

- Increased speed, automaticity, and capacity of information processing, which frees cognitive resources for other purposes (See Chapter 8.)
- More knowledge in a variety of domains
- An increased ability to construct new combinations of knowledge
- A greater range and more spontaneous use of strategies or procedures such as planning, considering alternatives, and cognitive monitoring

Unfortunately, if a solid basis of fundamental skills (such as literacy and math skills) is not developed during childhood, critical-thinking skills are unlikely to mature in adolescence. For those adolescents who lack fundamental skills, potential gains in adolescent thinking are not likely.

**Technology and Critical Thinking** An increasing number of technology applications are available to improve students' critical thinking skills. David Jonassen (2006, 2010) argues that one of the best uses of technology in education involves computer applications that encourage students to think critically about the content they are studying. He calls such applications "mindtools," and sees them as constructivist tools that scaffold student creation of knowledge and reasoning about subject content. Jonassen distinguishes several categories of mindtools, including semantic organization tools, dynamic modeling tools, information interpretation tools, and conversation and collaboration tools.

TECHNOLOGY

*Semantic organization tools,* such as databases and concept mapping tools, help students organize, analyze, and visualize information they are studying. For example, students studying climate can query global databases to test their hypotheses concerning links between climate and population. Inspiration and Kidspiration are concept mapping tools for K–12 students that are relatively inexpensive and easy to use (see **www.inspiration.com**).

*Dynamic modeling tools* help students explore connections between concepts. These include spreadsheets, expert systems, systems modeling tools, and microworlds. For example, *spreadsheets* have been used in mathematics classes to help students explore mathematical relations between numbers. *Microworlds* simulate real-world phenomena, such as genetic combinations.

*Information interpretation tools* help learners access and interpret information, and include visualization and knowledge construction tools. For example, *visualization tools* are visual models of complex phenomena that make those phenomena more comprehensible. *Knowledge construction tools,* such as hypermedia, video editing, or Web design programs, scaffold student construction of knowledge in various forms. An example of a knowledge construction tool would be *WebQuests,* which are inquiry-oriented lessons with a particular format in which most of the information students

Students in the Research Center for Educational Technology's AT&T classroom at Kent State University studying energy by designing an energy-efficient home using *Better Homes and Gardens Home Designer* software.

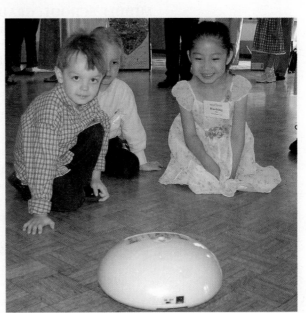

Kindergarten students in the Research Center for Educational Technology's AT&T classroom at Kent State University exploring patterns by programming the Logo Robotic Turtle.

work with comes from the Web (**http://webquest.org/**). WebQuests essentially provide scaffolding for critical inquiry using the Internet.

Finally, a variety of digital *conversation and collaboration tools,* such as e-mail, online discussion, chat, videoconferencing, and blogs, make it possible for students to interact and collaborate with experts and other students around the world. For example, students studying foreign languages can converse with native speakers using computer-mediated communication.

To read further about mindtools, visit Jonassen's Web site: **http://web.missouri .edu/jonassend/mindtools.html.** The examples and software sections are especially helpful. Perhaps you might want to select one mindtool and create a lesson plan that you can use in your teaching.

I recently asked teachers how they help their students improve their critical-thinking skills. What follows are their responses.

**EARLY CHILDHOOD**   One of the techniques we use to develop our preschoolers' critical-thinking skills is to have them put a favorite item into a mystery box. The  child then tells the class three clues about what is in the box, and the rest of the class guesses until they figure out what is inside the box. This game is rotated so that each child has a chance to put something in the box.

—**MISSY DANGLER,** *Suburban Hills School*

**ELEMENTARY SCHOOL: GRADES K–5**   One trait that is essential to critical thinking is intellectual courage. I teach this trait by asking my second-graders to consider such questions as "If everyone around you believes in 'such and such,' why is it hard to disagree?" or "When is it good to disagree?" or "Why do people get mad when they are questioned or doubted?" These questions help my students to think outside the box.

—**ELIZABETH FRASCELLA,** *Clinton Elementary School*

**MIDDLE SCHOOL: GRADES 6–8**   I always have the question: "What is the significance . . . ?" written on the classroom whiteboard. When we are covering any  topic in sixth-grade social studies class, I point to that question. I also have students write in a journal reflecting on a historical event and have them discuss what would be different today if the event never took place.

—**CASEY MAASS,** *Edison Middle School*

**HIGH SCHOOL: GRADES 9–12**   We have our psychology students compile a "personality scrapbook" that includes completed personality tests along with reflective  journals about the results as they relate to the student. Students then write a final paper entitled: "Who am I?" in which they "rethink" their own assumptions about themselves and their personality development. Students can also criticize and evaluate the effectiveness of personality tests in general.

—**JOSEPH MALEY,** *South Burlington High School*

## DECISION MAKING

Think of all the decisions you have to make in your life. Which grade level and subject should I teach? Should I go to graduate school right after college or get a job first? Should I establish myself in a career before settling down to have a family?

# TEACHING CONNECTIONS: Best Practices
## Strategies for Improving Children's Thinking

Twentieth-century German dictator Adolph Hitler once remarked that it was such good fortune for people in power that most people do not think. Education should help students become better thinkers. Every teacher would agree with that goal, but the means for reaching it are not always in place in schools. Here are some guidelines for helping students to become better thinkers.

1. *Be a guide in helping students to construct their own thinking.* You can't and shouldn't do students' thinking for them. However, you can and should be an effective guide in helping students construct their own thinking. Teachers who help students construct their own thinking (Brooks & Brooks, 1993, 2001)

   **Do**
   - Highly value students' questions.
   - View students as thinkers with emerging theories about the world.
   - Seek students' points of view.
   - Seek elaboration of students' initial responses.
   - Nurture students' intellectual curiosity.

   **Don't**
   - View students' minds as empty or see their role as a teacher as simply pouring information into students' minds.
   - Rely too heavily on textbooks and workbooks.
   - Simply seek the correct answer to validate student learning.

Alan Haskvitz with middle school students Simon Alarcon and Tracy Blozis, examining bones and trying to figure out where in the animal kingdom they belong.

2. *Use thinking-based questions.* One way to analyze your teaching strategies is to make sure you're using thinking-based questioning in addition to a lecture-based approach and fact-based questioning (Sternberg & Spear-Swirling, 1996). In the *lecture-based approach,* the teacher presents information in the form of a lecture. This is a helpful approach for quickly presenting a body of information, such as factors that led to the French Revolution. In *fact-based questioning,* the teacher asks questions primarily designed to get students to describe factual information. This is best used for reinforcing newly acquired information or testing students' content knowledge. For example, the teacher might ask, "When did the French Revolution occur? Who were the king and queen of France at that time?" In *thinking-based questioning,* the teacher asks questions that stimulate thinking and discussion. For example, the teacher might ask, "Compare the French and American revolutions. How were they similar? How were they different?" Make a point to include thinking-based questions in your teaching. They will help your

students construct a deeper understanding of a topic. In Through the Eyes of Teachers, Alan Haskvitz describes how he challenges students to think more independently and creatively. Questioning will also allow you to note and correct any misconceptions or flawed logic students might have.

## THROUGH THE EYES OF TEACHERS
### Challenging Students to Be Intellectual Risk-Takers

Alan Haskvitz, who teaches social studies at Suzanne Middle School in Walnut, California, believes in learning by doing and the importance of motivating students to improve the community. His students have rewritten voting instructions adopted by Los Angeles County, lobbied for a law requiring state government buildings to have rough-resistant landscaping, and created measures to reduce the city's graffiti. Alan has compiled thousands of teacher resources on this Web site: **www.reacheverychild.com.** He challenges students to be independent thinkers and intellectual risk-takers. He has students create an ideal island and discuss what everything from government to geography would be like on the island. (Sources: Briggs, 1999; Educational Cyber Playground, 2006).

3. *Provide positive role models for thinking.* Look around your community for positive role models who can demonstrate effective thinking, and invite them to come to your classroom and talk with your students. Also think about contexts in the community, such as museums, colleges and universities, hospitals, and businesses, where you can take students and they can observe and interact with competent thinkers.

4. *Be a thinking role model for students as a teacher.* Cultivate an active and inquiring mind yourself. Examine what we have said about thinking in this chapter. Work on being a positive thinking model for students by practicing these strategies.

5. *Keep up-to-date on the latest developments in thinking.* Continue to learn actively about new developments in teaching students to become more effective thinkers after you have become a teacher. Over the next decade there likely will be new technology programs through which you can improve students' thinking skills. Go to libraries to read educational journals, and attend professional conferences that include information about thinking.

*"You take all the time you need, Larry—this certainly is a big decision."*
© Eric Teitelbaum/The New Yorker Collection/www
.cartoonbank.com

RESEARCH

*"I'm happy to say that my final judgment of a case is almost always consistent with my prejudgment of the case."*
© Dana Fradon/The New Yorker Collection/www.cartoonbank.com

RESEARCH

**decision making** Evaluating alternatives and making choices among them.

**confirmation bias** The tendency to search for and use information that supports our ideas rather than refutes them.

**belief perseverance** The tendency to hold on to a belief in the face of contradictory evidence.

Should I buy a house or rent? **Decision making** involves thinking in which individuals evaluate alternatives and make choices among them.

In deductive reasoning, people use clear-cut rules to draw conclusions (Goswami, 2011; Rips, 2008). When we make decisions, however, the rules are seldom clear-cut and we may have limited knowledge about the consequences of the decisions (Gerrard & others, 2008). In addition, important information might be missing, and we might not trust all of the information we have.

In one type of decision-making research, investigators have studied how people weigh the costs and benefits of various outcomes (Redelmeier, 2005). They have found that people choose the outcome with the highest expected value (Smyth & others, 1994). For example, in choosing a college, a high school student might list the pluses and minuses of going to different colleges (related to such factors as cost, quality of education, and social life), then make a decision based on how the colleges fared on these criteria. In making a decision, the student might have weighted some of these factors more heavily than others (such as cost 3 points, quality of education 2 points, and social life 1 point).

**Biases and Flaws in Decision Making** Another fruitful subject of decision-making research is the biases and flawed heuristics (rules of thumb) that affect the quality of decisions (Baker, 2010; Pretz, 2008). In many cases, our decision-making strategies are well adapted to deal with a variety of problems. However, we are prone to certain flaws in our thinking (Stanovich, 2010). Common flaws involve confirmation bias, belief perseverance, overconfidence bias, hindsight bias, and the availability and representativeness heuristics. Decision making is improved when we become aware of these potential flaws.

**Confirmation Bias** One type of bias is **confirmation bias,** the tendency to search for and use information that supports our ideas rather than refutes them. Thus, in making a decision, a student might have an initial belief that a certain approach is going to work. He tests out the approach and finds out that it does work some of the time. He concludes that his approach is right rather than further exploring the fact that in a number of cases it doesn't work.

We tend to seek out and listen to people whose views confirm our own rather than listen to dissenting views (Kerschreiter & others, 2008). For example, you might have a particular teaching style, such as lecturing, that you like to use. If so, you probably have a tendency to seek advice from other teachers who use that style rather than from teachers who prefer other styles, such as collaborative problem solving by students.

In one study, Deanna Kuhn and her colleagues (1994) had participants listen to an audiotaped reenactment of an actual murder trial. Then, they were asked what their verdict would be and why. Rather than considering and weighing possibilities, drawing on all the evidence, many participants hurriedly composed a story that drew only from evidence that supported their earlier view of what happened. These participants showed a confirmation bias by ignoring evidence that ran counter to their version of events. Be aware of how easy it is for you and your students to become trapped by confirmation bias.

**Belief Perseverance** Closely related to confirmation bias, **belief perseverance** is the tendency to hold on to a belief in the face of contradictory evidence. People have a difficult time letting go of an idea or a strategy once they have embraced it (Stanovich, 2010). Consider Madonna. We might have a hard time thinking of her in a maternal role because of the belief perseverance that she is a wild, fun-loving rock star.

Another example of belief perseverance gives some college students trouble. They may have gotten good grades in high school by using the strategy of cramming for tests the night before. The ones who don't adopt a new strategy—spacing their study sessions more evenly through the term—often do poorly in college.

***Overconfidence Bias*** An **overconfidence bias** is the tendency to have more confidence in judgments and decisions than we should have, based on probability or past experience. People are overconfident about how long those with a fatal disease will live, which businesses will go bankrupt, whether a defendant is guilty in a court trial, and which students will do well in college. People consistently have more faith in their judgments than predictions based on statistically objective measures indicate they should (Finn, 2008).

In one study, college students were asked to make predictions about themselves in the coming academic year (Vallone & others, 1990). They were asked to predict whether they would drop any courses, vote in an election, and break up with their girlfriend or boyfriend. At the end of the year, the accuracy of their predictions was examined. The results: they were more likely to drop a class, not vote in an election, and break up with a girlfriend or a boyfriend than they had predicted.

*How do emotions and social contexts influence adolescents' decision making?*

***Hindsight Bias*** People not only are overconfident about what they predict will happen in the future (overconfidence bias), but also tend to overrate their past performances at prediction (Asa & Wiley, 2008). **Hindsight bias** is our tendency to falsely report, after the fact, that we accurately predicted an event.

As I write this chapter, baseball season is just beginning. Lots of people in different cities are predicting that their teams are going to make it to the World Series. Come October, after almost all of the teams have fallen by the wayside, many of the same people will say, "I told you our team wasn't going to have a good season."

**Decision Making in Adolescence** Adolescence is a time of increased decision making—which friends to choose, which person to date, whether to have sex, whether to choose immediate satisfaction or delay gratification for a positive outcome, whether to go to college, and so on (Galotti, Kozberg, & Gustafson, 2009). How competent are adolescents at making decisions? Older adolescents often make better decisions than younger adolescents, who in turn make better decisions than children.

Most individuals make better decisions when they are calm rather than emotionally aroused, which may especially be true for adolescents (Steinberg & others, 2009). Thus, the same adolescent who makes a wise decision when calm may make an unwise decision when emotionally aroused (Giedd, 2008; Halpern-Felsher, 2009).

Social contexts also play a key role in adolescent decision-making (Wray-Lake, Crouter, & McHale, 2010). For example, adolescents' willingness to make risky decisions is more likely to occur in contexts where mood-altering substances and other temptations are readily available (Reyna & Rivers, 2008). Also, recent research reveals that the presence of peers in risk-taking situations increases the likelihood that adolescents will make risky decisions (Steinberg, 2008). In one study of risk-taking involving a simulated driving task, the presence of peers increased an adolescent's decision to engage in risky driving by 50 percent but had no effect on adults (Gardner

DEVELOPMENT

RESEARCH

**Thinking Back/Thinking Forward**

The prefrontal cortex of the brain, which is an important region in higher-level thinking such as decision making, is not fully developed in adolescence. Chapter 2, p. 36

**overconfidence bias** The tendency to have more confidence in judgment and decisions than we should have, based on probability or past experience.

**hindsight bias** The tendency to falsely report, after the fact, that we accurately predicted an event.

**TEACHING CONNECTIONS:** Best Practices

Strategies for Making Good Decisions for Yourself and Your Students

Using these strategies explicitly allow you to become a good decision-making model for your students.

1. *Weigh the costs and benefits of various possible decisions.* You will encounter many circumstances in which you will benefit from pursuing this strategy. For example, will your students benefit more from examining a particular topic in a small-group format or a lecture format? One common way to do this with students is by making a "pros and cons" list. Another is to ask students to list various possible decisions they could make in a given situation and then the likely outcomes associated with each.

2. *Avoid confirmation bias.* Do you tend to only seek out people to talk with whose views confirm your own? Does a particular student avoid people with dissenting views and, if so, how can you help him or her? One way to combat this for older children and adolescents is to stage debates in class.

3. *Resist belief perseverance.* Are you holding on to some beliefs that might be outdated and need to be changed?

Do students have beliefs based on their past experiences that they are clinging to which don't fit their current situation? If so, how can you help them?

4. *Don't engage in overconfidence bias.* Do you have more confidence in your decisions than you should based on probability or your past experience? Might one of your future students gloss over the fact that he or she did poorly on the previous test in your class and be over-confident and not put in extra hours of study? Help students to examine evidence from the past when considering their actions.

5. *Avoid hindsight bias.* Be aware that people have a tendency to falsely report, after the fact, that they were able to predict an event.

6. *If you plan to teach in middle or high school, spend some time reading about and thinking further about how adolescents' make decisions and the factors that influence the decision making.* Especially for younger adolescents, occupy their time with positive activities to limit their opportunity to engage in risk-taking behavior (Wargo, 2009).

& Steinberg, 2005). One view is that the presence of peers activates the brain's reward system, especially dopamine pathways (Steinberg, 2008).

One proposal to explain adolescent decision making is the **dual-process model,** which states that decision making is influenced by two cognitive systems, one analytical and one experiential, which compete with each other (Reyna & Farley, 2006). The dual-process model emphasizes that it is the experiential system—monitoring and managing actual experiences—that benefits adolescents' decision making, not the analytical system. In this view, adolescents don't benefit from engaging in reflective, detailed, higher-level cognitive analysis about a decision, especially in high-risk, real-world contexts. In such contexts, adolescents just need to know that there are some circumstances that are so dangerous that they need to be avoided at all costs (Mills, Reyna, & Estrada, 2008). However, some experts on adolescent cognition argue that in many cases adolescents benefit from both analytical and experiential systems (Kuhn, 2009).

## CREATIVE THINKING

An important aspect of thinking is to be able to think creatively (Beghetto & Kaufman, 2010; Sternberg, 2009, 2010a,b). **Creativity** is the ability to think about something in novel and unusual ways and come up with unique solutions to problems.

J. P. Guilford (1967) distinguished between **convergent thinking,** which produces one correct answer and is characteristic of the kind of thinking required on conventional intelligence tests, and **divergent thinking,** which produces many answers to the same question and is more characteristic of creativity. For example, a typical convergent item on a conventional intelligence test is, "How many quarters will you get in return for 60 dimes?" The question has only one right answer. In contrast, divergent questions have many possible answers. For example, consider

**dual-process model** States that decision making is influenced by two systems, one analytical and one experiential, which compete with each other; in this model, it is the experiential system—monitoring and managing actual experiences—that benefits adolescent decision making.

**creativity** The ability to think about something in novel and unusual ways and come up with unique solutions to problems.

**convergent thinking** Thinking with the aim of producing one correct answer. This is usually the type of thinking required on conventional intelligence tests.

**divergent thinking** Thinking with the aim of producing many answers to the same question. This is characteristic of creativity.

these questions: "What image comes to mind when you sit alone in a dark room?" and "What are some unique uses for a paper clip?"

Are intelligence and creativity related? Although most creative students are quite intelligent (as measured by high scores on conventional intelligence tests), in other respects the reverse is not necessarily true. Many highly intelligent students are not very creative (Kaufman & Sternberg, 2010a,b; Sternberg, 2009, 2010c).

**Steps in the Creative Process** The creative process is often described as a five-step sequence:

1. *Preparation.* Students become immersed in a problem issue that interests them and their curiosity is aroused.
2. *Incubation.* Students churn ideas around in their head, a point at which they are likely to make some unusual connections in their thinking.
3. *Insight.* Students experience the "Aha!" moment when all pieces of the puzzle seem to fit together.
4. *Evaluation.* Now students must decide whether the idea is valuable and worth pursuing. They need to think, "Is the idea novel or is it obvious?"
5. *Elaboration.* This final step often covers the longest span of time and involves the hardest work. This step is what famous twentieth-century American inventor Thomas Edison was thinking about when he said that creativity is 1 percent inspiration and 99 percent perspiration.

Mihaly Csikszentmihalyi (pronounced ME-high-CHICK-sent-me-high-ee) (1996) argues that this five-step sequence provides a helpful framework for thinking about how to develop creative ideas. However, he emphasizes that creative people don't always go through the steps in a linear sequence. For example, elaboration is often interrupted by periods of incubation. Fresh insights may appear during incubation, evaluation, and elaboration. And insight might take years or only a few hours. Sometimes the creative idea consists of one deep insight. At other times, it is a series of small insights. To evaluate your creative thinking skills, see Self-Assessment 9.1.

**Teaching and Creativity** An important teaching goal is to help students become more creative (Kaufman & Sternberg, 2010; Sternberg, 2009, 2010a,b,c). Teachers need to recognize that students will show more creativity in some domains than others (Skiba & others, 2010). A student who shows creative-thinking skills in mathematics may not exhibit these skills in art, for example.

The design of schools and classrooms may influence the creativity of students (Beghetto & Kaufman, 2009). School environments that encourage independent work, are stimulating but not distracting, and make resources readily available are likely to encourage students' creativity.

Your students also will greatly benefit if you are a creative thinker yourself and engage in creative thinking in the course of your everyday teaching. Mihaly Csikszentmihalyi (1996) has recommended a number of strategies that might help you become a more creative thinker. He interviewed 90 leading figures in art, business, government, education, and science to learn how creativity works. He discovered that creative people regularly experience a state he calls *flow,* a heightened state of pleasure experienced when we are engaged in mental and physical challenges that absorb us. Csikszentmihalyi (2000) points out that everyone is capable of achieving flow. Based on his interviews with some of the most creative people in the world, the first step toward a more creative life is cultivating your curiosity and interest. How can you do this?

- *Try to be surprised by something every day.* Maybe it is something you see, hear, or read about. Become absorbed in a lecture or a book. Be open to what

*What do you mean, "What is it?" It's the spontaneous, unfettered expression of a young mind not yet bound by the restraints of narrative or pictorial representation.*
Sydney Harris. www.ScienceCartoonsPlus.com.

**Thinking Back/Thinking Forward**

In Sternberg's view, creative thinking is quite different than the analytical thinking that is at the core of traditional intelligence tests. Chapter 4, p. 115

# SELF-ASSESSMENT 9.1
## How Good Am I at Thinking Creatively?

Rate each of these activities as they apply to you in terms of how often you engage in them: 1 = never, 2 = rarely, 3 = sometimes, and 4 = a lot.

| | 1 | 2 | 3 | 4 |
|---|---|---|---|---|
| 1. I come up with new and unique ideas. | | | | |
| 2. I brainstorm with others to creatively find solutions to problems. | | | | |
| 3. I am internally motivated. | | | | |
| 4. I'm flexible about things and like to play with my thinking. | | | | |
| 5. I read about creative projects and creative people. | | | | |
| 6. I'm surprised by something and surprise others every day. | | | | |
| 7. I wake up in the morning with a mission. | | | | |
| 8. I search for alternative solutions to problems rather than giving a pat answer. | | | | |
| 9. I have confidence in my ability to create something innovative and worthwhile. | | | | |
| 10. I delay gratification and persist until I have developed creative ideas and products. | | | | |
| 11. I take risks in developing creative thoughts. | | | | |
| 12. I spend time around creative people. | | | | |
| 13. I spend time in settings and activities that stimulate me to be creative. | | | | |

Examine your overall pattern of responses. What are your strengths and weaknesses in creativity? Keep practicing your strengths and work on improving your weaknesses to provide students with a creative role model.

I asked Mihaly Csikszentmihalyi to send me a photograph of himself in the setting where he gets his most creative thoughts. Above is the photograph he sent. *When and where do you get your most creative thoughts? Do you think any of Csikszentmihalyi's recommendations would help you to become a more creative thinker?*

the world is telling you. Life is a stream of experiences. Swim widely and deeply in it, and your life will be richer.

- *Try to surprise at least one person every day.* In a lot of things you do, you have to be predictable and patterned, but in others you simply act out of habit. Do something different for a change. Ask a question you normally would not ask. Invite someone to go to a place you never have visited.

- *Write down each day what surprised you and how you surprised others.* Most creative people keep a diary, notes, or lab records to ensure that their experience is not fleeting or forgotten. Start with a specific task. Each evening record the most surprising event that occurred that day and your most surprising action. After a few days, reread your notes and reflect on your past experiences. After a few weeks, you might see a pattern of interest emerging in your notes, one that might suggest an area you can explore in greater depth.

- *When something sparks your interest, follow it.* Usually when something captures your attention, it is short-lived—an idea, a song, a flower. Too often we are too busy to explore the idea, song, or flower further. Or we think these areas are none of our business because we are not experts about them. Yet the world is our business. We can't know which part of it is best suited to our interests until we make a serious effort to learn as much about as many aspects of it as possible.

- *Wake up in the morning with a specific goal—something to look forward to.* Creative people wake up eager to start the day. Why? Not necessarily because they are cheerful, enthusiastic types but because they know that there is something meaningful to accomplish each day, and they can't wait to get started.

- *Spend time in settings that stimulate your creativity.* In Csikszentmihalyi's (1996) research, he gave people an electronic pager and beeped them randomly at different times of the day. When he asked them how they felt, they reported the highest levels of creativity when walking, driving, or swimming. I (your author) do my most creative thinking when I'm jogging. These activities are semiautomatic in that they take a certain amount of attention while leaving some time free to make connections among ideas.

Recall our discussion in Chapter 6 that a current concern is the education of children who are gifted in the face of standards-based education such as the No Child Left Behind legislation. So, too, is the mounting concern that this legislation has harmed the development of students' creative thinking by focusing attention on memorization of materials to do well on standardized tests (Kaufman & Sternberg, 2010).

I recently asked teachers how they help their students develop creative-thinking skills. Following are their responses

**Thinking Back/Thinking Forward**

Experts argue that the education of gifted students in the United States requires a significant overhaul. Chapter 6, p. 205

**EARLY CHILDHOOD**   When teaching music to my preschool students, I have them suggest an instrument from our instrument library to make the sound of a character in the book. Students also have to give a reason for why they selected the particular instrument.

—**Connie Christy,** *Aynor Elementary School (Preschool Program)*

**ELEMENTARY SCHOOL: GRADES K–5**   When I teach social studies, I have my students construct a mock travel agency. We start out by talking about traveling around the world, which emphasizes geography. We then discuss the business of travel agencies. The students brainstorm about what the travel agent's job entails and what would be found at a real travel agency. Students then become the travel agent, create travel brochures, book trips, and so on. This social studies project is fun and involves reading, writing, research, art, and marketing.

—**Craig Jensen,** *Cooper Mountain Elementary School*

**MIDDLE SCHOOL: GRADES 6–8**   When telling stories to my students, I often leave the last part of the story blank and have them create an ending. There is no right or wrong answer—just an opportunity for students to expand their creative thinking.

—**Margaret Reardon,** *Pocantico Hills School*

**HIGH SCHOOL: GRADES 9–12**   By providing an environment of freedom and safety, teachers can foster students' creative thinking. In particular, I find that having students brainstorm about various topics makes the creative juices flow.

—**Dennis Peterson,** *Deer River High School*

## TEACHING CONNECTIONS: Best Practices
### Strategies for Guiding Students to Think More Creatively

An important teaching goal is to guide students to become better creative thinkers (Runco, 2010; Skiba & others, 2010). Following are some effective strategies for helping students improve their creative-thinking skills:

### Engage in Creative Thinking During the Course of Everyday Teaching.
Students' creative thinking benefits when they are around teachers who think creatively and give the students opportunities to observe them thinking in creative ways. Periodically revisit Csikszentmihalyi's recommendations for becoming a creative thinker to improve your creative thinking skills.

### Encourage Creative Thinking on a Group and Individual Basis
*Brainstorming* is a technique in which people are encouraged to come up with creative ideas in a group, play off each other's ideas, and say practically whatever comes to mind that seems relevant to a particular issue. Participants are usually told to hold off from criticizing others' ideas at least until the end of the brainstorming session to encourage the free flow of ideas.

### Provide Environments That Stimulate Creativity
Some classrooms nourish creativity; others inhibit it (Beghetto & Kaufman, 2009). Teachers who encourage creativity often rely on students' natural curiosity. They provide materials and activities that stimulate students to find insightful solutions to problems, rather than ask many questions that require rote answers. Teachers also encourage creativity by taking students on field trips to locations where creativity is valued. Howard Gardner (1993) emphasizes that science, discovery, and children's museums offer rich opportunities to stimulate creativity.

### Don't Overcontrol Students
Teresa Amabile (1993) says that telling students exactly how to do things leaves them feeling that originality is a mistake and exploration is a waste of time. If, instead of dictating which activities they should engage in, you let your students select their interests and you support their inclinations, you will be less likely to destroy their natural curiosity. When ever possible, allow students choices in what to do, how to do it, or how to demonstrate what they have learned. Amabile also emphasizes that when teachers hover over students all of the time, they make them feel that they are constantly being watched while they are working. When students are under constant surveillance, their creative risk-taking and adventurous spirit diminish.

### Encourage Internal Motivation
Excessive use of prizes, such as gold stars, money, or toys, can stifle creativity by undermining the intrinsic pleasure students derive from creative activities. Creative students' motivation is the satisfaction generated by the work itself. Competition for prizes and formal evaluations often undermine intrinsic motivation and creativity (Amabile & Hennesey, 1992). However, this is not to rule out material rewards altogether. We will say more about internal and external motivation in Chapter 13.

---

## THROUGH THE EYES OF STUDENTS
### The Eight-Year-Old Filmmaker and Oozy Red Goop

Steven was 12 years old when he got his film-making badge in the Boy Scouts. He started imagining what he needed to do to make a movie, and his father bought him a Super-8 movie camera. Steven made a film called *The Last Gunfight.*

His mother gave him free reign of the house, letting him virtually turn it into a movie studio. When he was 16 years old as part of making a movie called *The Firelight,* he needed some "red, bloody-looking goop to ooze from the kitchen cabinets," so he got his mother to buy 30 cans of cherries. Steven dumped the cherries "into the pressure cooker and produced an oozy red goop."

Steven is Steven Spielberg, whose mother supported his imagination and passion for film making. Of course, Spielberg went on to become one of Hollywood's greatest directors with such films as *E.T., Jurassic Park,* and *Schindler's List.* (Source: Goleman, Kaufman, & Ray, 1993, p. 70.)

---

### Guide Students to Help Them Think in Flexible Ways
Creative thinkers are flexible in the way they approach problems in many different ways rather than getting locked into rigid patterns of thought. Give students opportunities to exercise this flexibility in their thinking (Sternberg, Jarvin, & Grigorenko, 2009).

### Build Students' Self-Confidence
To expand students' creativity, it helps when teachers encourage students to believe in their own ability to create something innovative and worthwhile. To this end, it is important not to be overly critical of their creations. Building students' confidence in their creative skills aligns with Bandura's (2009, 2010a) concept of *self-efficacy,* the belief that one can master a situation and produce positive outcomes. We will have much more to say about self-efficacy in Chapter 13.

### Guide Students to Be Persistent and Delay Gratification
Most highly successful creative products take years to develop. Most creative individuals work on ideas and projects for months and years without being rewarded for their efforts (Sternberg & Williams, 1996). As we discussed in Chapter 6

## TEACHING CONNECTIONS: Best Practices
### Strategies for Guiding Students to Think More Creatively

and Chapter 8, children don't become experts at sports, music, or art overnight. It usually takes many years working at something to become an expert at it; so it is with being a creative thinker who produces a unique, worthwhile product. To foster such perseverance, allow students to revise their work until they are satisfied with the result.

### Encourage Students to Take Risks
Creative individuals take risks and seek to discover or invent something never before discovered or invented (Sternberg, 2009, 2010c). They risk spending a lot of time on an idea or project that may not work. Creative people are not afraid of failing or getting something wrong (Sternberg, Jarvin, & Grigorenko, 2009). They often see failure as an opportunity to learn. They might go down twenty dead-end streets before they come up with an innovative idea. Make your classroom a safe one in which to take risks, be wrong, and even fail at something.

### Introduce Students to Creative People
A good strategy is to identify the most creative people in your community and ask them to come to your class and describe what helps them become creative or to demonstrate their

creative skills. A writer, a poet, a crafts person, a musician, a scientist, and many others can bring their props and productions to your class.

### Connect with Technology
An increasing number of Internet sites provide excellent resources for enhancing students' creative thinking. Following are some of these sites (Wisenthal, 2010):

- **www.shidonni.com**   At this Web site, appropriate for 5- to 12-year-olds, children can draw animals, name them, and design their environments.
- **www.makebeliefscomix.com**   Here children of all ages can write, read, and tell stories by creating comic strips, then print or e-mail them to friends or relatives.
- **www.scratch.mit.edu**   Designed by MIT Media Lab, children 8 years and older can create movies, video games, and music.
- **www.pbskids.org/Arthur/games/crankitup**   Children preschool age and older can create and record various musical pieces at this Web site

## Review, Reflect, and Practice

**2** Describe several types of thinking and ways that teachers can foster them.

### REVIEW
- What is thinking?
- How do inductive and deductive reasoning differ?
- What is the focus of critical thinking? Do most schools teach students to think critically? What is decision making? What are some flaws that can hinder effective decision making?
- What is creative thinking? How can teachers foster creative thinking?

### REFLECT
- Some experts lament that few schools teach students to think critically. Does your own experience support this view? If you agree with the experts, why do you think critical thinking is not more widely or effectively taught?

### PRAXIS™ PRACTICE
1. Ms. McDougal has a pet rabbit in her classroom. One day while Amari is petting the rabbit, it bites her. Amari decides that all rabbits are mean. This is an example of what kind of reasoning?
   a. analogy
   b. critical thinking

*(continued)*

## Review, Reflect, and Practice

### PRAXIS™ PRACTICE (CONTINUED)

    c. deductive

    d. inductive

2. Which teaching strategy is most likely to foster the development of critical-thinking skills in social studies?

    a. having students create timelines of important historical dates

    b. giving students worksheets that require them to recall the facts presented in their textbooks

    c. presenting students with statements such as "Lincoln was our greatest president" to defend or refute

    d. giving a multiple-choice test

3. Many students enter their educational psychology courses believing that when an authority figure presents an aversive stimulus to a child, and the child's misbehavior diminishes, the authority figure has negatively reinforced the child's behavior. Of course, we know that, actually, the authority figure has punished the child. Many of the students who entered your class with this misconception answer test questions on this subject incorrectly and will still have this misconception by the time they leave the class. What is the best explanation for this phenomenon?

    a. belief perseverance

    b. confirmation bias

    c. hindsight bias

    d. none of the above

4. All fifth-grade classes at Central School have just read *The Jungle Book.* Which assignment is most likely to foster creativity?

    a. The students write a story about how their lives would have been different if they had grown up in the wild like Mowgli.

    b. The students complete a story diagram, in which they describe the setting, characters, plot, climax, and theme of the book.

    c. The students create models of the temple where the monkeys lived, following a prototype that the teacher constructed.

    d. The students complete worksheets containing questions about the plot and characters of the book.

*Please see the answer key at the end of the book.*

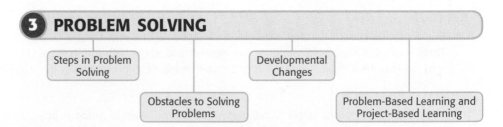

**3 PROBLEM SOLVING**

- Steps in Problem Solving
- Obstacles to Solving Problems
- Developmental Changes
- Problem-Based Learning and Project-Based Learning

Let's examine problem solving as a cognitive process, including the steps it involves, the obstacles to it, and how best to teach it.

    **Problem solving** involves finding an appropriate way to attain a goal. Consider these tasks that require students to engage in problem solving: creating a project for

**problem solving** Finding an appropriate way to attain a goal.

a science fair, writing a paper for an English class, getting a community to be more environmentally responsive, and giving a talk on the factors that cause people to be prejudiced. Although they seem quite different, each involves a similar series of steps.

## STEPS IN PROBLEM SOLVING

Efforts have been made to specify the steps that individuals go through in effectively solving problems. Following are four such steps (Bransford & Stein, 1993):

**Step 1. Find and Frame Problems**    Before you can solve a problem, you must recognize that it exists (Mayer, 2008). In the past, most problem-solving exercises in school involved well-defined problems that lent themselves to specific, systematic operations that produced a well-defined solution. Today educators increasingly recognize the need to teach students the real-world skill of identifying problems instead of just offering clear-cut problems to be solved (Chen, 2010; Laxman, 2010).

Consider a student whose broad goal is to create a science-fair project. What branch of science would it be best for her to present—biology, physics, computer science, psychology? After making this decision, she'll have to narrow the problem further: which domain within psychology should she choose—perception, memory, thinking, personality? Within the domain of memory, she might pose this question: How reliable are people's memories of traumatic events they have experienced? Thus, it may take considerable exploration and refinement for the student to narrow the problem down to a point of generating specific solutions. Exploring such alternatives is an important part of problem solving.

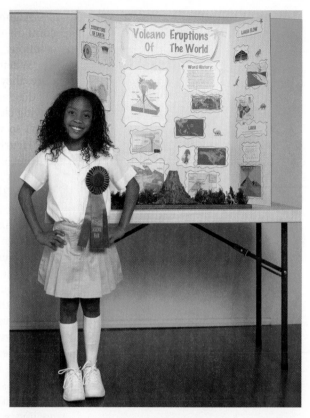

An important first step in solving many problems is finding and framing the various problems within the main problem. For example, in creating a science-fair project, certain problems have to be defined and solved before arriving at the final solution of a finished project.

**Step 2. Develop Good Problem-Solving Strategies**    Once students find a problem and clearly define it, they need to develop strategies for solving it (Quiamzade, Mugny, & Darnon, 2009; Yu, She, & Lee, 2010). Among the effective strategies are setting subgoals and using algorithms, heuristics, and means-end analysis.

**Subgoaling** involves setting intermediate goals that put students in a better position to reach the final goal or solution. Students might do poorly in solving problems because they don't generate subproblems or subgoals. Let's return to the science-fair project on the reliability of people's memory for traumatic events they have experienced. What might be some subgoaling strategies? One might be locating the right books and research journals on memory; another might be interviewing people who have experienced traumas in which basic facts have been recorded. At the same time as the student is working on this subgoaling strategy, she likely will benefit from establishing further subgoals in terms of what she needs to accomplish along the way to her final goal of a finished science project. If the science project is due in three months, she might set the following subgoals: finishing the first draft of the project two weeks before the project is due; having the research completed a month before the project is due; being halfway through the research two months before the project is due; having three trauma interviews completed two weeks from today; and starting library research tomorrow.

Notice that in establishing the subgoals, we worked backward in time. This is often a good strategy. Students first create a subgoal closest to the final goal and then work backward to the subgoal closest to the beginning of the problem-solving effort.

**subgoaling**  The process of setting intermediate goals that place students in a better position to reach the final goal or solution.

**Algorithms** are strategies that guarantee a solution to a problem. Algorithms come in different forms, such as formulas, instructions, and tests of all possible solutions.

When students solve a multiplication or long division problem by a set procedure, they are using an algorithm (Martin, 2009). When they follow the directions for diagramming a sentence, they are using an algorithm. Algorithms are helpful in solving clear-cut problems (Lau & Yuen, 2010). But since many real-world problems aren't so straightforward, looser strategies also are needed.

**Heuristics** are strategies or rules of thumb that can suggest a solution to a problem but don't ensure it will work. Heuristics help us to narrow down the possible solutions and help us find one that works (Acar, Turkmen, & Roychoudhury, 2010). Suppose that you go out on a day hike and find yourself lost in the mountains. A common heuristic for getting "unlost" is simply to head downhill and pick up the nearest tiny stream. Small streams lead to larger ones, and large streams often lead to people. Thus, this heuristic usually works, although it could bring you out on a desolate beach.

In the face of a multiple-choice test, several heuristics could be useful. For example, if you are not sure about an answer, you could start by trying to eliminate the answers that look most unlikely and then guess among the remaining ones. Also, for hints about the answer to one question, you could examine the statements or answer choices for other questions on the test.

A **means-end analysis** is a heuristic in which one identifies the goal (end) of a problem, assesses the current situation, and evaluates what needs to be done (means) to decrease the difference between the two conditions. Another name for means-end analysis is *difference reduction*. Means-end analysis also can involve the use of subgoaling, which we described earlier. Means-end analysis is commonly used in solving problems. Consider a student who wants to do a science-fair project (the end) but has not yet found a topic. Using means-end analysis, she could assess her current situation, in which she is just starting to think about the project. Then she maps out a plan to reduce the difference between her current state and the goal (end). Her "means" might include talking to several scientists in the community about potential projects, going to the library to study the topic she chooses, and exploring the Internet for potential projects and ways to carry them out.

**Step 3. Evaluate Solutions**   Once we think we have solved a problem, we might not know whether our solution is effective unless we evaluate it. It helps to have in mind a clear criterion for the effectiveness of the solution. For example, what will be the student's criterion for effectively solving the science-fair problem? Will it be simply getting it completed? Receiving positive feedback about the project? Winning an award? Winning first place? Gaining the self-satisfaction of having set a goal, planned for it, and reached it?

**Step 4. Rethink and Redefine Problems and Solutions over Time**   An important final step in problem solving is to continually rethink and redefine problems and solutions over time (Bereiter & Scardamalia, 2006). People who are good at problem solving are motivated to improve on their past performances and to make original contributions. Thus, the student who completed the science-fair project can look back at the project and think about ways the project can be improved. She might use feedback from judges or others who attended the fair in order to fine-tune the project for presentation again in some other venue.

## OBSTACLES TO SOLVING PROBLEMS

Some common obstacles to solving problems are fixation, a lack of motivation or persistence, and inadequate emotional control.

**algorithms** Strategies that guarantee a solution to a problem.

**heuristics** Strategies or rules of thumb that can suggest a solution to a problem but don't ensure that it will work.

**means-end analysis** A heuristic in which one identifies the goal (end) of a problem, assesses the current situation, and evaluates what needs to be done (means) to decrease the difference between the two conditions.

**Fixation**   It is easy to fall into the trap of becoming fixated on a particular strategy for solving a problem. **Fixation** involves using a prior strategy and failing to look at a problem from a fresh, new perspective. *Functional fixedness* is a type of fixation in which an individual fails to solve a problem because he views the elements involved solely in terms of their usual functions. A student who uses a shoe to hammer a nail has overcome functional fixedness to solve a problem.

A **mental set** is a type of fixation in which an individual tries to solve a problem in a particular way that has worked in the past. I (your author) had a mental set about using a typewriter rather than a computer to write my books. I felt comfortable with a typewriter and had never lost any sections I had written. It took a long time for me to break out of this mental set. Once I did, I found that books are much easier to write using a computer. You might have a similar mental set against using the new computer and video technology available for classroom use. A good strategy is to keep an open mind about such changes and monitor whether your mental set is keeping you from trying out new technologies that can make the classroom more exciting and more productive.

**Lack of Motivation or Persistence**   Even if your students already have great problem-solving abilities, that hardly matters if they are not motivated to use them (Perry, Turner, & Meyer, 2006). It is especially important for students to be internally motivated to tackle a problem and persist at finding a solution. Some students avoid problems or give up too easily.

An important task for teachers is to devise or steer students toward problems that are meaningful to them and then encourage and support them in finding solutions. Students are far more motivated to solve problems that they can relate to their personal lives than textbook problems that have no personal meaning for them. Problem-based learning takes this real-world, personal approach (Baturay & Bay, 2010; Kumar, 2010).

**Inadequate Emotional Control**   Emotion can hamper problem solving. Good problem solvers are not only highly motivated but also able to control their emotions and thus concentrate on a solution to a problem (Kuhn, 2009). Anxiety or fear can restrict a student's ability to solve a problem. Individuals who are competent at solving problems are usually not afraid of making mistakes.

## DEVELOPMENTAL CHANGES

Young children have some drawbacks that prevent them from solving many problems effectively. Especially notable is their lack of planning, which improves during the elementary and secondary school years. Among the reasons for the poor planning skills of young children is their tendency to try to solve problems too quickly at the expense of accuracy and their inability to inhibit an activity. Planning often requires inhibiting a current behavior to stop and think; preschool children often have difficulty inhibiting an ongoing behavior, especially if it is enjoyable (Bjorklund, 2005). Another drawback of young children's problem-solving ability is that even though they may know a rule, they fail to use it.

Other reasons that older children and adolescents become better problem solvers than young children involve *knowledge* and *strategies* (Bjorklund, 2011; Martinez, 2010). The problems that older children and adolescents must solve are often more complex than those young children face, and solving these problems accurately usually requires accumulated knowledge. The more children know about a particular topic, the better they will be able to solve a problem related to the topic. The increase in accumulated knowledge about a topic ties in with our discussion of experts and novices in Chapter 8.

Thinking Back/Thinking Forward

Motivation involves behavior that is energized, directed, and sustained. Chapter 13, p. 438

DEVELOPMENT

**fixation**   Using a prior strategy and thereby failing to examine a problem from a fresh, new perspective.

**mental set**   A type of fixation in which an individual tries to solve a problem in a particular way that has worked in the past.

| Phases | Teacher's Roles |
|---|---|
| **Phase 1:** Orient the student to the problem | Communicate clearly the goals of the lesson, inform students what is expected of them, and guide students to become motivated to engage in self-directed problem solving. |
| **Phase 2:** Organize students for study | Help students define and organize study tasks related to the problem. |
| **Phase 3:** Assist independent and group investigation | Encourage students to obtain appropriate information, conduct experiments, and search for explanations and solutions. |
| **Phase 4:** Develop and present artifacts and exhibits | Guide students' planning and creation of appropriate artifacts such as reports, videos, and help them to share their work with others. |
| **Phase 5:** Analyze and evaluate the problem-solving process | Encourage students to reflect on their investigations and the strategies and steps they used. |

**FIGURE 9.5** FIVE PHASES OF PROBLEM-BASED LEARNING

*Source:* After Arends (2004), Table 11.1.

**problem-based learning** Learning that emphasizes authentic problems like those that occur in daily life.

**project-based learning** Students work on real, meaningful problems beyond those of everyday life and create tangible products.

Older children and adolescents also are more likely than young children to have effective strategies that help them solve problems (Bjorklund, 2011; Kuhn, 2009, 2011). Recall our extensive discussion of metacognition and strategies in Chapter 8, where we explained how children's use of strategies improves as they get older. Especially important in using strategies to solve problems is to have a range of strategies from which to select, and this range increases during the elementary and secondary school years. Adolescents have an increased capacity to monitor and manage their resources to effectively meet the demands of a problem-solving task (Kuhn, 2009). Adolescents also are better than children at screening out information irrelevant to solving a problem (Kuhn, 2009).

## PROBLEM-BASED LEARNING AND PROJECT-BASED LEARNING

Now that we have discussed many aspects of problem solving, we turn our attention to two types of learning involving problems: problem-based learning and project-based learning.

**Problem-Based Learning** The emphasis in **problem-based learning** is on solving authentic problems like those that occur in daily life (Donnelly, 2010; Hung, 2009). Problem-based learning is used in a program called YouthALIVE! at the Children's Museum of Indianapolis (Schauble & others, 1996). There students solve problems related to conceiving, planning, and installing exhibits; designing videos; creating programs to help visitors understand and interpret museum exhibits; and brainstorming about strategies for reaching the wider community.

Unlike direct instruction in which the teacher presents ideas and demonstrates skills, in problem-based learning teachers orient students to a problem or problems and get students to explore and discover solutions on their own (Arends, 2004). Problem-based learning is especially effective in helping students develop confidence in generating their own thinking skills.

The general flow of problem-based learning consists of five phases: (1) orient students to the problem, (2) organize students for study, (3) assist with independent and group investigations, (4) develop and present artifacts and exihibits, and (5) analyze and evaluate work (Arends, 2004). Figure 9.5 provides more detailed information about the five phases of problem-based learning. We will further discuss problem-based learning in Chapter 12.

**Project-Based Learning** In **project-based learning,** students work on real, meaningful problems and create tangible products (Gutherie, 2010; van Rooij, 2009). Project-based learning and problem-based learning are sometimes treated as synonymous. However, while still emphasizing the process of learning in a constructivist manner, project-based learning gives more attention to the end product than problem-based learning (Bereiter & Scardamalia, 2006). The types of problems explored in project-based learning are similar to those studied by scientists, mathematicians, historians, writers, and other professionals (Bell, 2010; Kanter, 2010).

Project-based learning environment are characterized by five main features (Krajcik & Blumenfeld, 2006):

1. *A driving question.* The learning process begins with a key question or problem that needs to be solved.

## TEACHING CONNECTIONS: Best Practices
### Strategies for Improving Students' Problem Solving

1. *Give students extensive opportunities to solve real-world problems.* Make this a part of your teaching. Develop problems that are relevant to your students' lives. Such real-world problems are often referred to as "authentic," in contrast to textbook problems that too often do not have much meaning for students. These problem are, in general, ill-structured—that is, they do not have single, obvious solutions. The complexity of the problems should increase as children develop. For instance, considering environmental problems, young children might work together to clean up the playground at school, while older children might attempt to solve the problem of too much waste at the school by instituting a recycling program at the school, while adolescents could examine the causes of pollution of a nearby stream.

2. *Monitor students' effective and ineffective problem-solving strategies.* Keep the four problem-solving steps in mind when you give students opportunities to solve problems. Help students to work through the steps; make the process very salient to them. This may help them to focus on the process when they are solving problems independently. Also keep in mind such obstacles to good problem solving as becoming fixated, harboring biases, not being motivated, and not persisting. In Through the Eyes of Teachers, Lawren Giles, who teaches at Baechtel Grove Middle School in Willits, California, describes the different strategies she encourages students to use.

### THROUGH THE EYES OF TEACHERS
#### A Toolbox of Strategies

In teaching math, I use such problem-solving strategies as working backward, making a similar but simpler problem, drawing a diagram, making a table, and looking for patterns. We talk about what strategies make the most sense with different types of problems. When students successfully solve a problem, we look to see what methods were used, often finding more than one. I talk about multiple strategies in terms of carpenters having more than one kind of hammer in their toolboxes.

3. *Involve parents in children's problem solving.* The University of California at Berkeley has developed a program, called Family Math (Matematica Para la Familia, in Spanish) that helps parents experience math with their children in a positive, supportive way (Schauble & others, 1996). In the program, Family Math classes are usually taught by grade levels (K–2, 3–5, and 6–8). Many of the math activities require teamwork and communication between parents and children, who come to better understand not only the math but also each other. Family Math programs have served more than 400,000 parents and children in the United States.

4. *Work with children and adolescents to improve their use of rules, knowledge, and strategies in solving problems.* Recognize that young children may know a rule that enables them to solve a problem but not use it, so you may need to encourage them to use the rules they know. Set up situations in which use of a particular rule will greatly facilitate success in solving a problem. Encourage children to build up their knowledge base and to improve their knowledge of effective strategies that will help them solve problems.

5. *Use technology effectively.* Be motivated to incorporate multimedia programs into your classroom. Such programs can significantly improve your students' thinking and problem-solving skills.

2. *Authentic, situated inquiry.* As students examine the key question, they learn about the problem-solving process engaged in by experts in the discipline in relevant contexts.

3. *Collaboration.* Students, teachers, and community participants collaborate to find solutions to the problem.

4. *Scaffolding.* Learning technologies are used to challenge students to go beyond what they normally would in a problem-solving context.

5. *End product.* Students create tangible end products that address the key, driving question.

To evaluate your thinking and problem-solving skills, complete Self-Assessment 9.2.

# SELF-ASSESSMENT 9.2
## How Effective Are My Thinking and Problem-Solving Strategies?

Teachers who practice good thinking and problem-solving strategies themselves are more likely to model and communicate these to their students than teachers who don't use such strategies. Candidly respond to these items about your own thinking and problem-solving strategies. Rate yourself: 1 = very much unlike me, 2 = somewhat unlike me, 3 = somewhat like me, and 4 = very much like me; then total your points.

| | 1 | 2 | 3 | 4 |
|---|---|---|---|---|

1. I am aware of effective and ineffective thinking strategies.

2. I periodically monitor the thinking strategies I use.

3. I am good at reasoning.

4. I use good strategies for forming concepts.

5. I am good at thinking critically and deeply about problems and issues.

6. I construct my own thinking rather than just passively accepting what others think.

7. I like to use technology as part of my effort to think effectively.

8. I have good role models for thinking.

9. I keep up-to-date on the latest educational developments in thinking.

10. I use a system for solving problems, such as the four-step system described in the text.

11. I am good at finding and framing problems.

12. I make good decisions and monitor biases and flaws in my decision making.

13. When solving problems, I use strategies such as subgoaling and working backward in time.

14. I don't fall into problem-solving traps such as fixating, lacking motivation or persistence, and not controlling my emotions.

15. When solving problems, I set criteria for my success and evaluate how well I have met my problem-solving goals.

16. I make a practice of rethinking and redefining problems over an extended period of time.

17. I love to work on problem-solving projects.

18. I am good at creative thinking.

Total _____

## SCORING AND INTERPRETATION

If you scored 66–72 points, your thinking strategies likely are very good. If you scored 55–65 points, you likely have moderately good thinking strategies. If you scored below 54 points, you likely would benefit from working on your thinking strategies.

## Review, Reflect, and Practice

**3** Take a systematic approach to problem solving.

### REVIEW

- What is problem solving? What are the main steps in problem solving?
- What are three obstacles to problem solving?
- What are some developmental changes in problem solving?
- What is problem-based learning? What is project-based learning?

### REFLECT

- When you tackle a difficult problem, do you follow the four steps we described? What might you do to become a better model of a problem solver for your students?

### PRAXIS™ PRACTICE

1. Which of the following is the best example of the use of a heuristic?
   a. Betina needs to compute the average of a series of numbers. First she determines their sum and then divides the sum by the number in the series.
   b. Anders becomes separated from his mother at the store. He goes to a cashier and tells her that he is lost. The cashier takes him to the service counter and his mother is paged.
   c. Samarie needs to remember all five of the Great Lakes. He uses the acronym *HOMES.*
   d. Marjorie needs to know how much carpet she needs to cover the floor of her room. She uses the formula for the area of a rectangle and converts square feet to square yards.

2. Which of the following is the best example of functional fixedness?
   a. Zack needs to put in a screw, but he has no screwdriver. He has some change in his pocket, but he does not try to use a dime instead.
   b. Xavier continues to use the strategy of adding a number multiple times rather than learning his multiplication facts.
   c. Maria uses the formula for the area of a rectangle when solving a problem requiring her to find the area of a triangle.
   d. Sol is lost in the woods. He remembers his mother telling him that if he gets lost like this, he should "hug a tree." He stays in one spot and within 30 minutes his family finds him.

3. Jackson is 16 years old and is much better at problem solving than when he was younger. Which of the following is most likely to explain his improved problem solving as a teenager?
   a. His hormones are settling down better since he is no longer in puberty.
   b. He is better at monitoring the demands of a problem-solving task.
   c. He is more stimulus-driven, and that helps him to sort through more stimuli when he is given a problem to solve.
   d. He uses a minimum number of strategies that he knows well.

4. Which of the following is the best example of problem-based learning?
   a. Ms. Christian's science students use a shoe box to protect a raw egg from breaking when dropped off the school roof.
   b. Ms. Kohler's students solve word problems to help them see the application of math facts to everyday life.

*(continued)*

## Review, Reflect, and Practice

### PRAXIS™ PRACTICE (CONTINUED)

   c. Ms. Kringle's students solve a series of addition and multiplication problems of increasing difficulty.

   d. Ms. Randall's students answer the questions at the end of the chapter in their history book.

*Please see the answer key at the end of the book.*

### 4 TRANSFER

What Is Transfer?     Types of Transfer     Cultural Practices and Transfer

An important complex cognitive goal is for students to be able to apply what they learn in one situation to new situations (Banich & Caccamise, 2010; Stahl, 2010). An important goal of schooling is that students learn things that they can apply outside the classroom. Schools are not functioning effectively if students do well on tests in language arts but can't write a competent letter as part of a job application. Schools also are not effectively educating students if the students do well on math tests in the classroom but can't solve arithmetic problems on a job.

## WHAT IS TRANSFER?

**Transfer** occurs when a person applies previous experiences and knowledge to learning or problem solving in a new situation (Mayer, 2008). Thus, if a student learns a concept in math and then uses this concept to solve a problem in science, transfer has occurred. It also has occurred if a student reads and studies about the concept of fairness in school and subsequently treats others more fairly outside the classroom.

    Some experts argue that the best way to ensure transfer is to "teach for it" (Schwartz, Bransford, & Sears, 2005). They stress that transfer problems virtually are eliminated when teaching occurs in contexts where individuals need to perform. By preparing students so that the problems they are likely to encounter in real life are at worst near-transfer problems, the gap between students' present learning level and learning goals is significantly reduced (Bransford & others, 2005). Some other strategies that can improve transfer include giving two or more examples of a concept because one often is not enough; giving students representations or models, such as matrices, that help them structure a problem-solving activity; and encouraging students to generate more information themselves, which increases the likelihood they will remember what needs to be transferred (Sears, 2008). Yet another strategy to increase transfer is to give students well-structured contrasting cases and have them try to invent solutions for them before being given a lecture on the expert solution. The idea is that by first inventing a solution, students bring their prior knowledge to bear on the problem and make connections to the features of the problem. When they see the expert solution and how it relates the key features to each other, the students should be able to better understand how it works and thus transfer it better in the future.

## TYPES OF TRANSFER

What are some different types of transfer? Transfer can be characterized as (1) near or far and, (2) low-road or high-road (Schunk, 2011).

*"I don't get it! They make us learn reading, writing and arithmetic to prepare us for a world of videotapes, computer terminals and calculators!"*

Harley Schwadron from *Phi Delta Kappan.* Reprinted by permission of Harley Schwadron.

**transfer** Applying previous experiences and knowledge to learning or problem solving in a new situation.

**Near or Far Transfer**   In **near transfer** the classroom learning situation is similar to the one in which the initial learning took place. For example, if a geometry teacher instructs students in how to logically prove a concept, and then tests the students on this logic in the same setting in which they learned the concept, near transfer is involved.

**Far transfer** means the transfer of learning to a situation very different from the one in which the initial learning took place. For instance, if a student gets a part-time job in an architect's office and applies what he learned in geometry class to helping the architect analyze a spatial problem different from any problem he encountered in geometry class, far transfer has occurred.

**Low-Road or High-Road Transfer**   Gabriel Salomon and David Perkins (1989) distinguished between low-road and high-road transfer. **Low-road transfer** occurs when previous learning automatically, often unconsciously, transfers to another situation. This occurs typically with highly practiced skills in which there is little need for reflective thinking. For example, when competent readers encounter new sentences in their native language, they read them automatically.

By contrast, **high-road transfer** is conscious and effortful. Students consciously establish connections between what they learned in a previous situation and the new situation they now face. High-road transfer is mindful—that is, students have to be aware of what they are doing and think about the connection between contexts. High-road transfer implies abstracting a general rule or principle from previous experience and then applying it to the new problem in the new context. For example, students might learn about the concept of subgoaling (setting intermediate goals) in math class. Several months later, one of the students thinks about how subgoaling might help him complete a lengthy homework assignment in history. This is high-road transfer.

Salomon and Perkins (1989) subdivide high-road transfer into forward-reaching and backward-reaching transfer. **Forward-reaching transfer** occurs when students think about how they can apply what they have learned to new situations (from their current situation, they look "forward" to apply information to a new situation ahead). For forward-reaching transfer to take place, students have to know something about the situations to which they will transfer learning. **Backward-reaching transfer** occurs when students look back to a previous ("old") situation for information that will help them solve a problem in a new context.

To better understand these two types of high-road transfer, imagine a student sitting in English class who has just learned some writing strategies for making sentences and paragraphs come alive and "sing." The student begins to reflect on how she could use those strategies to engage readers next year, when she plans to become a writer for the school newspaper. That is forward-reaching transfer. Now consider a student who is at his first day on the job as editor of the school newspaper. He is trying to figure out how to construct the layout of the pages. He reflects for a few moments and thinks about some geography and geometry classes he has previously taken. He draws on those past experiences for insights into constructing the layout of the student newspaper. That is backward-reaching transfer.

## CULTURAL PRACTICES AND TRANSFER

Cultural practices may be involved in how easy or difficult transfer is. Prior knowledge includes the kind of knowledge that learners acquire through cultural experiences, such as those involving ethnicity, socioeconomic status, and gender (National Research Council, 1999). In some cases, this cultural knowledge can support children's learning and facilitate transfer, but in others it may interfere (Cole, 2006; Greenfield & others, 2006).

For children from some cultural backgrounds, there is a minimal fit or transfer between what they have learned in their home communities and what is required or taught by the school. For example, consider the language skill of storytelling. Euro-American children use a linear style that more closely approximates the linear

DIVERSITY

**near transfer** The transfer of learning to a situation that is similar to the one in which the initial learning took place.

**far transfer** The transfer of learning to a situation that is very different from the one in which the initial learning took place.

**low-road transfer** The automatic, often unconscious, transfer of learning to another situation.

**high-road transfer** The transfer of learning from one situation to another that is conscious and effortful.

**forward-reaching transfer** Occurs when the individual looks to apply learned information to a future situation.

**backward-reaching transfer** Occurs when the individual looks back to a previous situation for information to solve a problem in a new context.

expository style of writing and speaking taught in most schools (Lee & Slaughter-Defoe, 1995). This may involve recounting a series of events in a rigidly chronological sequence. By contrast, in some ethnic groups—such as Asian Pacific Island or Native American—a nonlinear, holistic/circular style is more common in telling a story, and Euro-American teachers may consider their discourse to be disorganized (Clark, 1993). Also, in African American children, a nonlinear, topic-associative storytelling approach is common (Michaels, 1986).

Methods of argumentation in support of certain beliefs also differ across cultures. Chinese speakers prefer to present supporting evidence first, leading up to a major point or claim (in contrast to a topic sentence followed by supporting details). Non-Chinese listeners sometimes judge this style as "beating around the bush" (Tsang, 1989). Rather than perceiving such variations in communication styles as being chaotic or as necessarily inferior to Euro-American styles, teachers need to be sensitive to them and aware of cultural differences. This is especially important in the early elementary school grades, when students are making the transition from the home environment to the school environment.

I recently asked teachers how they help their students transfer classroom knowledge to the outside world. Following are their responses.

**EARLY CHILDHOOD**   One way that we connect classroom knowledge with the outside world is to have instruments in class that make sounds similar to the music children hear when they are at home. For example, we have children from different cultures, and the music they and their families listen to features congas, steel drums, and guitars; we have these instruments in class and encourage children to play them.

—**VALARIE GORHAM,** *Kiddie Quarters, Inc.*

**ELEMENTARY SCHOOL: GRADES K–5**   When discussing immigration with my second-graders, I begin by asking them to think of a time when they moved to a new place, such as a new classroom or school, a new house or community, or a new country. I then ask them how they felt (for example, happy, sad, nervous) when they moved to this new place and why they felt this way. Then I ask them to take these thoughts and draw a picture of this time in their lives. This exercise helps students transfer information they have learned in class about immigration to similar experiences in their own lives.

—**ELIZABETH FRASCELLA,** *Clinton Elementary School*

**MIDDLE SCHOOL: GRADES 6–8**   When teaching social studies, I often have my students read newspaper articles about a particular topic and then write their own newspaper article that responds to what they have read. This gets them more personally involved in the topic.

—**CASEY MAASS,** *Edison Middle School*

**HIGH SCHOOL: GRADES 9–12**   High school students, especially juniors and seniors, are particularly interested in future careers. As a career and technical education teacher, I find that my students especially enjoy the unit on career awareness in which they identify personal skills and interests and identify careers in which those skills and interests would be best served.

—**SANDY SWANSON,** *Menomonee Falls High School*

## TEACHING CONNECTIONS: Best Practices
### Strategies for Helping Students Transfer Information

1. *Think about what your students need for success in life.*
We don't want students to finish high school with a huge
data bank of content knowledge but no idea how
to apply it to the real world. One strategy for
thinking about what students need to know is
to use the "working-backward" problem-solving
strategy we discussed earlier in this chapter. For example, what do employers want high school and college
graduates to be able to do? In a national survey of
employers of college students, the three skills that employers most wanted graduates to have were (1) oral communication skills, (2) interpersonal skills, and (3) teamwork
skills (Collins, 1996). The employers also wanted students
to be proficient in their field, have leadership abilities,
have analytical skills, be flexible, and be able to work
with computers. By thinking about and practicing the
competencies that your students will need in the future
and working with them to improve these skills, you will
be guiding them for positive transfer. This should begin
long before high school.

2. *Give students many opportunities for real-world learning.*
Too often, learning in schools has been artificial, with little consideration for transfer beyond the classroom or
textbook. This will be less true for your students if you
give them as many real-world problem-solving and thinking challenges as possible. You can bring the real world
into your classroom by inviting people from varying walks
of life to come and talk with your students. Or you can
take your students to the real world by incorporating relevant visits to parks, museums, businesses, colleges, and so
on in the curriculum. The places to which you take students and the activities in which they engage while there
will differ according to their age and the content you are
studying. Young children might visit a park as part of a
unit on plants, and collect and identify leaves from various trees. Adolescents might visit an amusement park as
part of a physics unit. In Through the Eyes of Teachers,
you can read about Chris Laster, an outstanding teacher,
who instructs students in ways that help them transfer
what they learn to the world outside the classroom.

### THROUGH THE EYES OF TEACHERS
#### Bringing Science Alive and Connecting Students to the Community

Chris Laster's students say that he brings science alive.
Among Laster's innovative real-world teaching strategies
that help students transfer their knowledge and understanding beyond the classroom are the following:

Chris Laster working with a student on the flight deck of the space
shuttle that Laster and other teachers built.

1. *Science Blasters.* Students write, direct, and produce
short videos for the school's closed-circuit TV station.

2. *Sci-Tech Safari.* Over the summer, students get hands-
on experience on field trips to intriguing places such
as the Okefenokee Swamp.

3. *Intrepid.* Students engage in vigorous training to prepare for a simulated 27-hour space mission aboard a
realistic-looking space shuttle built by Laster and other
teachers with parts from local businesses and a nearby
air force base. (Copeland, 2003)

3. *Root concepts in applications.* The more you attempt to
just pour information into students' minds, the less likely
it is that transfer will occur. When you present a concept, also define it (or get students to help you define it),
and then ask students to generate examples. Challenge
them to apply the concept to their personal lives or to
other contexts.

4. *Teach for depth of understanding and meaning.* Teaching
for understanding and meaning transfers more than does
teaching for the retention of facts. And students' understanding improves when they actively construct meaning
and try to make sense out of material themselves.

5. *Use prompts to encourage students to engage
in self-explanation.* Researchers have found
that generating explanations for oneself increases transfer (Siegler, 2002). For example,
one study revealed that encouraging third- to
fifth-grade students engaging in math problem-solving
exercises to explain how they arrived at their answers

*(continued)*

## TEACHING CONNECTIONS: Best Practices
### Strategies for Helping Students Transfer Information

was linked with improved transfer to new types of math problems (Rittle-Johnson, 2006). One way to do this is to have discussions in which students share how they arrived at their solutions.

6. *Teach strategies that will generalize.* Transfer involves not only skills and knowledge but also strategies (Schunk, 2011). Too often students learn strategies but don't understand how to apply them in other contexts. They might not understand that the strategy is appropriate for other situations, might not know how to modify it for use in another context, or might not have the opportunity to apply it (Pressley, 2007).

One model for teaching strategies that will generalize consists of three phases for improving transfer (Phye & Sanders, 1994). In an *initial acquisition* phase, students are given information about the importance of the strategy and how to use it as well as opportunities to rehearse and practice using it. In the second phase, called *retention*, students get more practice in using the strategy, and their recall of how to use the strategy is checked out. In the third phase, *transfer*, students are given new problems to solve. These problems require them to use the same strategy, but on the surface the new problems appear to be different.

---

**Thinking Back/Thinking Forward**

Teachers can engage in a number of strategies in helping students use more effective learning strategies. Chapter 8, p. 288

---

## Review, Reflect, and Practice

**4** Define transfer and explain how to enhance it as a teacher.

### REVIEW

- What is transfer? Why should teachers think about it?
- What are some different types of transfer?

### REFLECT

- Are there experiences from your own formal education that don't seem to transfer to outside school? What do you think is going on in such situations?

### PRAXIS™ PRACTICE

1. Which of the following is *not* an example of transfer?
   a. Maria reads a novel written in the eighteenth century and uses the information she gleans about marriage customs to answer a question in history class.
   b. Frank studies hard and learns an algorithm in math class.
   c. Danielle learns about endangered amphibians in science class and uses the information to research a science-fair project.
   d. Emma learns to use a dictionary in language-arts class and uses it to look up a social studies term.

2. Which of the following is the best example of far transfer?
   a. Cory uses the techniques she was taught in statistics class to analyze the data for a research project.
   b. Debbie drives her sister's car with little thought because of her experience driving her own car.
   c. Jason uses the trouble-shooting process that he was taught with regard to computers to successfully diagnose the problem with his car.
   d. Mike is able to read the Spanish word for television (*televisión*) because it looks like the English word.

*Please see the answer key at the end of the book.*

## The Statistics Test

Cassandra has a test in her math class this Friday. She has spent the last several evenings studying the statistical formulas for measures of central tendency and variability, as she knows they will be covered on the test. To do this she has quizzed herself repeatedly. In the beginning, she got them confused, but after repeated tries, she can now recite the formulas for each without fail. She is certain that she will have no problems on the test.

When she receives her test on Friday, the first thing she does is write down all of the formulas before she can forget them, certain that will be all she will need to do well on the exam. After writing down the formulas, she begins reading the test. The first question gives a list of scores and asks for the mean, median, mode, variance, and standard deviation.

Cassandra anxiously looks at her list of formulas. She knows which formula goes with which measure—for instance, she knows that the formula for the mean is $Sx/n$. The problem is that she doesn't know what $Sx$ means. She is reasonably sure that "/$n$" means she is to divide by $n$, but what is $n$? When looking at the rest of the formulas, she realizes that she has similar problems. She stares at the test in dismay. After all that studying and careful memorization, she can't complete a single problem on the test.

1. What are the issues in this case?
2. What went wrong for Cassandra?

3. What should she do differently if she wants to do better on her next test?
4. If you were the teacher of Cassandra's class, how would you help your students to prepare for this type of test?
5. Which of the following strategies is most likely to help Cassandra on her next statistics test?
   a. Concentrate on learning only one formula at a time.
   b. Forget about memorizing the formulas.
   c. Learn the definitions of *mean, median, mode, variance,* and *standard deviation.*
   d. Work practice problems of each type.
6. Which of the following teaching strategies would be most likely to help students to do well on this type of test?
   a. Make certain that students understand what the formulas mean by working many example problems in class.
   b. Quiz students on the definitions of *mean, median, mode, variance,* and *standard deviation.*
   c. Quiz students on the formulas.
   d. Teach students a mnemonic device to help them remember the formulas.

---

## Reach Your Learning Goals

# Complex Cognitive Processes

**1  CONCEPTUAL UNDERSTANDING:** Discuss conceptual understanding and strategies for teaching concepts.

> **What Are Concepts?**

> **Promoting Concept Formation**

Concepts group objects, events, and characteristics on the basis of common properties. They help us to simplify, summarize, and organize information. Concepts improve memory, communication, and time use.

In teaching concept formation to children, it is helpful to discuss with them the key features of concepts, definitions and examples of concepts (using the rule-example strategy), hierarchical categorization and concept maps, hypothesis testing, and prototype matching.

## 2 THINKING: Describe several types of thinking and ways that teachers can foster them.

**What Is Thinking?**

Thinking involves manipulating and transforming information in memory. Types of thinking include forming concepts, reasoning, thinking critically, making decisions, thinking creatively, and solving problems.

**Reasoning**

Inductive reasoning involves reasoning from the specific to the general. Analogies draw on inductive reasoning. Deductive reasoning is reasoning from the general to the specific. Both inductive and deductive reasoning improve during adolescence.

**Critical Thinking**

Critical thinking involves thinking reflectively and productively and evaluating evidence. Mindfulness is a concept that reflects critical thinking. Brooks and Brooks argue that too few schools teach students to think critically and deeply. They stress that too often schools give students a correct answer instead of encouraging them to expand their thinking by coming up with new ideas.

**Decision Making**

Decision making is thinking that involves evaluating alternatives and making choices among them. One type of decision making involves weighing the costs and benefits of various outcomes. Numerous biases (confirmation bias, belief perseverance, overconfidence bias, and hindsight bias) can interfere with good decision making. Older adolescents make better decisions than younger adolescents, who in turn are better at this than children are. Adolescents often make better decisions when they are calm than emotionally aroused. Social contexts, especially the presence of peers, influence adolescent decision making. The dual-process model has been advanced to explain the nature of adolescent decision making.

**Creative Thinking**

Creativity is the ability to think about something in novel and interesting ways and come up with unique solutions to problems. Guilford distinguished between convergent thinking (which produces one correct answer and is characteristic of the type of thinking required on conventional intelligence tests) and divergent thinking (which produces many answers to the same question and is characteristic of creativity). Although most creative students are quite intelligent, the reverse is not necessarily true. The creative process often involves five steps, although they don't always follow the same sequence. Here are some ways teachers can foster creativity in students: encourage creative thinking on a group and individual basis, provide environments that stimulate creativity, don't overcontrol students, encourage internal motivation, foster flexible thinking, build students' self-confidence, encourage students to take risks, guide students to be persistent and delay gratification, and introduce students to creative people.

## 3 PROBLEM SOLVING: Take a systematic approach to problem solving.

**Steps in Problem Solving**

Problem solving involves finding an appropriate way to attain a goal. Four steps in problem solving are (1) finding and framing problems; (2) developing good problem-solving strategies (such as using subgoaling, heuristics, algorithms, and means-end analysis); (3) evaluating solutions; and (4) rethinking and redefining problems and solutions over time.

**Obstacles to Solving Problems**

Obstacles to solving problems include fixedness (functional fixedness and mental set), lack of motivation or persistence, and not controlling one's emotions.

**Developmental Changes**

Developmental changes in problem solving occur. Accumulated knowledge and effectively using strategies improve older children's and adolescents' problem-solving ability.

**Problem-Based Learning and Project-Based Learning**

Problem-based learning emphasizes solving authentic problems like those that occur in daily life. In project-based learning, students work on real, meaningful problems beyond those of everyday life, and create tangible products.

**TRANSFER:** Define transfer and explain how to enhance it as a teacher.

What Is Transfer?

Types of Transfer

Cultural Practices and Transfer

Transfer occurs when a person applies previous experiences and knowledge to learning or problem solving in a new situation. Students especially benefit when they can apply what they learn in the classroom to situations in their lives outside of the classroom.

Types of transfer include near and far and low-road and high-road. Near transfer occurs when situations are similar; far transfer occurs when situations are very different. Low-road transfer occurs when previous learning automatically transfers to another situation. High-road transfer is conscious and effortful. High-road transfer can be subdivided into forward-reaching and backward-reaching transfer.

Cultural practices can influence how easy or difficult transfer is. For some children, there is minimal transfer between what they have learned in their home communities and what is taught in school.

## KEY TERMS

concepts 295
concept map 298
prototype matching 300
thinking 301
inductive reasoning 302
analogy 302
deductive reasoning 303
critical thinking 303
mindfulness 303

decision making 308
confirmation bias 308
belief perseverance 308
overconfidence bias 309
hindsight bias 309
dual-process model 310
creativity 310
convergent thinking 310
divergent thinking 310

problem solving 316
subgoaling 317
algorithms 318
heuristics 318
means-end analysis 318
fixation 319
mental set 319
problem-based learning 320
project-based learning 320

transfer 324
near transfer 325
far transfer 325
low-road transfer 325
high-road transfer 325
forward-reaching
transfer 325
backward-reaching
transfer 325

## PORTFOLIO ACTIVITIES

Now that you have a good understanding of this chapter, complete these exercises to expand your thinking.

**Independent Reflection: Evaluate Your Decision-Making Skills.**
Reflect on the ways that you make decisions. Are you able to make good-quality decisions regardless of opposition from others? Discuss to what extent your decisions are influenced by confirmation bias, belief perseverance, overconfidence bias, and hindsight bias. What can you do to strengthen your decision-making skills? (INTASC: Principles 4, 9)

**Collaborative Work: Create a Problem-Based Learning Project.**
Thinking creatively, get together with three or four other students

in the class and devise a problem-solving adventure in a subject area other than math, such as science, social science, or literature. Write it down. (INTASC: Principles 1, 4)

**Research/Field Experience: Creativity Research.** Read work by one of the leading researchers in the field of creativity, such as Teresa Amabile or Mark Runco. What are the key findings about creativity discussed in the research? To what extent can this research be implemented in the classroom? (INTASC: Principles 4, 9)

*Go to the Online Learning Center for downloadable portfolio templates.*

## STUDY, PRACTICE, AND SUCCEED

Visit www.mhhe.com/santrockep5e to review the chapter with self-grading quizzes and self-assessments, to apply the chapter material to

two more Crack the Case studies, and for suggested activities to develop your teaching portfolio.

## CHAPTER 10

# SOCIAL CONSTRUCTIVIST APPROACHES

*The human being is by nature a social animal.*

—Aristotle
*Greek Philosopher, 4th Century* B.C.

## Chapter **Outline**

## Learning **Goals**

**1** Compare the social constructivist approach with other constructivist approaches.

**2** Explain how teachers and peers can jointly contribute to children's learning.

**3** Discuss effective decisions in structuring small-group work.

**4** Describe two social constructivist programs.

# Teaching **Stories**  Chuck Rawls

Chuck Rawls teaches language arts at Appling Middle School in Macon, Georgia. He provides this teaching story about peer tutoring, a social constructivist approach to instruction:

> I was tricked into trying something different my first year of teaching. It was peer teaching in the guise of a schoolwide activity known as "Switch Day." This consists of having selected students switch places with members of the faculty and staff. Each student who wants to switch is required to choose a faculty or staff member and then write an essay explaining why he or she wants to switch with that particular person. To my surprise, Chris wrote a very good essay and was selected to switch with me.
>
> It worked wonderfully. Chris delivered the lesson very professionally, and the students were engaged because it was

something new and different. It was a riot to watch because Chris, both intentionally and unintentionally, used many of my pet phrases and mannerisms. He really did know his stuff, though, and demonstrated this as he helped students with their seatwork.

As the saying goes, "I didn't know he had it in him." Chris became my resident expert on subject-verb agreement, as that was the topic of the lesson and the students remembered what he taught them. I learned two lessons that day: (1) don't be afraid to try something different, and (2) peer tutoring works. However, it has to be the right student teaching the right material in the right setting.

# Preview

Children do some of their thinking by themselves, but because we are social beings, as Chuck Rawls' teaching story indicates, effective learning can also take place when children collaborate. Because of our American emphasis on the individual rather than the group, collaborative thinking only recently emerged as an important theme in American education. This chapter focuses on the collaborative thinking advocated by social constructivist approaches.

**1  SOCIAL CONSTRUCTIVIST APPROACHES TO TEACHING**

Social Constructivism in the Broader Constructivist Context        Situated Cognition

The social constructivist approaches involve a number of innovations in classroom learning. Before we study these innovations, let us first consolidate our knowledge about various constructivist perspectives and where the social constructivist approaches fit in the overall constructivist framework.

## SOCIAL CONSTRUCTIVISM IN THE BROADER CONSTRUCTIVIST CONTEXT

Recall from Chapter 1 that *constructivism* emphasizes how individuals actively construct knowledge and understanding. Early in this book (Chapter 2), we described Piaget's and Vygotsky's theories of development, both of which are constructivist. In Chapters 8 and 9, our main focus was on the information-processing approaches to learning, which included some ideas about how the individual child uses information-processing skills to think in constructivist ways. According to all of these constructivist approaches, students author their own knowledge.

In general, a **social constructivist approach** emphasizes the social contexts of learning and the idea that knowledge is mutually built and constructed. Involvement with others creates opportunities for students to evaluate and refine their understanding as they are exposed to the thinking of others and as they participate in creating shared understanding (Gauvain & Parke, 2010). In this way, experiences in social contexts provide an important mechanism for the development of students' thinking (Johnson & Johnson, 2010).

Vygotsky's social constructivist theory is especially relevant for the current chapter. Vygotsky's model is a social child embedded in a sociohistorical context. Moving from

**Thinking Back/Thinking Forward**

One of the main debates about educating students focuses on whether a constructivist or direct instruction is the better strategy. Chapter 1, p. 6; Chapter 12, p. 406

**social constructivist approach** Approach that emphasizes the social contexts of learning and the idea that knowledge is mutually built and constructed.

*What is the social constructivist approach to education?*

**Thinking Back/Thinking Forward**

Teachers can use a number of strategies linked to Vygotsky's theory in educating students. Chapter 2, p. 50

Piaget to Vygotsky, the conceptual shift is from the individual to collaboration, social interaction, and sociocultural activity (Daniels, 2011; Gredler, 2009). In Piaget's cognitive constructivist approach, students construct knowledge by transforming, organizing, and reorganizing previous knowledge and information. Vygotsky's social constructivist approach emphasizes that students construct knowledge through social interactions with others. The content of this knowledge is influenced by the culture in which the student lives, which includes language, beliefs, and skills (Holzman, 2009).

Piaget emphasized that teachers should provide support for students to explore and develop understanding. Vygotsky emphasized that teachers should create many opportunities for students to learn by coconstructing knowledge along with the teacher and with peers (Gauvain & Parke, 2010). In both Piaget's and Vygotsky's models, teachers serve as facilitators and guides rather than directors and molders of children's learning.

Notice that we speak about emphasis rather than a clear-cut distinction. Often there are no clear-cut distinctions between social constructivist and other constructivist approaches. For example, when teachers serve as guides for students in discovering knowledge, there are social dimensions to the construction. And the same is true for processing information. If a teacher creates a brainstorming session for students to come up with good memory strategies, social interaction is clearly involved.

Some sociocultural approaches, such as Vygotsky's, emphasize the importance of culture in learning—for example, culture can determine what skills are important (such as computer skills, communication skills, teamwork skills) (Gauvain & Parke, 2010). Other approaches focus more exclusively on the immediate social circumstances of the classroom, as when students collaborate to solve a problem.

RESEARCH

In one study of collaborative learning, pairs of children from two U.S. public schools worked together (Matusov, Bell, & Rogoff, 2001). One member of each pair was from a traditional school that provided only occasional opportunities for children to work together as they learned. The other member of the pair was from a school that emphasized collaboration throughout the school day. The children with the collaborative schooling background more often built on the partner's ideas in a collaborative way than the children with traditional schooling experience. The traditional school children predominately used a "quizzing" form of guidance based on asking known-answer questions and withholding information to test the partner's understanding. Collaborative learning often works best in classrooms with well-specified learning goals.

TECHNOLOGY

Increasing efforts are being made to connect collaborative learning and technology in the classroom. For example, one program, Computer-Supported Collaborative

Learning (CSCL), attempts to increase peer interaction and joint construction of knowledge through technology (Prinsen & others, 2009).

## SITUATED COGNITION

**Situated cognition** is an important assumption in the social constructivist approaches. It refers to the idea that thinking occurs (is situated) in social and physical contexts. In other words, knowledge is embedded in, and connected to, the context in which the knowledge developed (Langer, 2009). If this is so, it makes sense to create learning situations that are as close to real-world circumstances as possible. For example, to expand students' knowledge and understanding of volcanos, some students are placed in the role of scientists studying an active volcano, while other students are given the task of reporting what to expect to an emergency evacuation team (PSU, 2006). Using Internet resources, the "scientist" students examine news stories about active volcanos; the "evacuation team" students search for information about the impact that volcanos have on inhabitants and how they can be removed from the danger of an erupting volcano. Our discussion of problem-based learning and project-based learning in Chapter 9 demonstrated a similar emphasis on situated cognition.

TECHNOLOGY

**Thinking Back/Thinking Forward**

Problem-based learning emphasizes solving authentic problems like those that occur in everyday life. Project-based learning involves students working on real, meaningful problems and creating tangible products. Chapter 9, p. 320

## Review, Reflect, and Practice

**1** Compare the social constructivist approach with other constructivist approaches.

**REVIEW**

- Although they overlap, what is the basic difference between Piaget's and Vygotsky's approach?
- What is situated cognition?

**REFLECT**

- From what you learned in Chapter 2, do you think you would feel more at home with Piaget or Vygotsky? How might that be reflected in your own approach to classroom teaching?

**PRAXIS™ PRACTICE**

1. Which of the following is an example of a social constructivist approach?
   a. In Mr. Hanratty's class, students work together on social studies projects.
   b. In Ms. Baker's class, students work independently to discover basic principles of science.
   c. In Ms. Rinosa's class, students are assigned one hour of homework a day.
   d. In Mr. Francois' class, students engage in silent reading of their self-chosen books.
2. Which of the following best reflects situated cognition?
   a. Students read a book about the role of a justice of the peace in the legal system.
   b. The teacher arranges for students to visit a local justice of the peace office, talk with the justice of the peace, and observe a justice of the peace session.
   c. Students are given an assignment to collaborate with each other and write a report on the role of the justice of the peace in the legal system.
   d. The teacher assigns students the task of searching for articles about what a justice of the peace does and to do an oral report on what they have found.

*Please see the answer key at the end of the book.*

**situated cognition** The idea that thinking occurs (is situated) in social and physical contexts.

## ② TEACHERS AND PEERS AS JOINT CONTRIBUTORS TO STUDENTS' LEARNING

| Scaffolding | Cognitive Apprenticeship | Tutoring | Cooperative Learning |

Social constructivist approaches emphasize that teachers and peers can contribute to students' learning. Four tools for making this happen are scaffolding, cognitive apprenticeship, tutoring, and cooperative learning.

### SCAFFOLDING

**Thinking Back/Thinking Forward**

Scaffolding is closely linked to Vygotsky's concept of the zone of proximal development. Chapter 2, p. 52

In Chapter 2, we described *scaffolding* as the technique of changing the level of support over the course of a teaching session; a more skilled person (teacher or more-advanced peer of the child) adjusts the amount of guidance to fit the student's current performance. When the task the student is learning is new, the teacher might use direct instruction. As the student's competence increases, the teacher provides less guidance (Pawan, 2008). Think of scaffolding in learning like the scaffolding used to build a bridge. The scaffolding provides support when needed, but it is gradually removed as the bridge approaches completion. Researchers have found that when teachers and peers use scaffolding in collaborative learning, students' learning benefits (Nusbaum & others, 2009; Zydney, 2010).

Look for situations to use scaffolding in the classroom. For instance, good tutoring involves scaffolding, as we will see shortly. Also, scaffolding is increasingly used when technology is involved in learning (Prinsen & others, 2009). Work on giving just the right amount of assistance. Don't do for students what they can do for themselves. But do monitor their efforts and give them needed support and assistance.

### COGNITIVE APPRENTICESHIP

Developmental psychologist Barbara Rogoff (2003; Rogoff & others, 2007) stresses that an important tool of education is **cognitive apprenticeship,** a technique in which an expert stretches and supports a novice's understanding and use of a culture's skills. The term *apprenticeship* underscores the importance of active learning and highlights the situated nature of learning. In a cognitive apprenticeship, teachers often model strategies for students. Then teachers or more skilled peers support students' efforts at doing the task. Finally, they encourage students to continue their work independently.

To illustrate the importance of cognitive apprenticeships in learning, Rogoff describes the contrasting experiences of students from middle-income and poverty backgrounds. Many middle- and upper-income American parents involve their children in cognitive apprenticeships long before they go to kindergarten or elementary school. They read picture books with young children and bathe their children in verbal communication. In contrast, American parents living in poverty are less likely to engage their children in a cognitive apprenticeship that involves books, extensive verbal communication, and scaffolding (Heath, 1989).

**RESEARCH**

Cognitive apprenticeships are important in the classroom. Researchers have found that students' learning benefits from teachers who think of their relationship with a student as a cognitive apprenticeship, using scaffolding and guided participation to help the student learn (Grindstaff & Richmond, 2008).

### TUTORING

Tutoring is basically cognitive apprenticeship between an expert and a novice. Tutoring can take place between an adult and a child or between a more skilled child and a less skilled child. Individual tutoring is an effective strategy that benefits many students, especially those who are not doing well in a subject (Karsenty, 2010; Slavin & others, 2009).

**cognitive apprenticeship** A relationship in which an expert stretches and supports a novice's understanding and use of a culture's skills.

**Classroom Aides, Volunteers, and Mentors**  It is frustrating to find that some students need more individual help than you as their teacher can give them and still meet the needs of the class as a whole. Classroom aides, volunteers, and mentors can help reduce this frustration. Monitor and evaluate your class for students you believe could benefit from one-on-one tutoring. Scour the community for individuals with skills in the areas in which these students need more individual attention than you are able to give. Some parents, college students, and retirees might be interested in filling your classroom tutoring needs.

Several individual tutoring programs have been developed. The Reading Recovery program offers daily half-hour, one-on-one tutorial sessions for students who are having difficulty learning to read after one year of formal instruction. Evaluations of the Reading Recovery program have found that students who participated in the program in the first grade were still performing better in reading in third grade than their counterparts who did not participate (Sensenbaugh, 1995). However, some researchers have found that the key to whether a program like Reading Recovery is effective is the extent to which phonological-processing skills are included (Chapman, Tunmer, & Prochnow, 2001). A recent analysis with strict criteria for research success revealed that Reading Recovery has positive effects on students' alphabet skills and general reading achievement (What Works Clearinghouse, 2007a).

DEVELOPMENT

RESEARCH

Another program that uses tutoring is Success for All (SFA). Developed by Robert Slavin and his colleagues (1996; Slavin & others, 2009), this comprehensive program includes the following:

- A systematic reading program that emphasizes phonics, vocabulary development, and storytelling and story retelling in small groups
- A daily 90-minute reading period with students in the first through third grades being regrouped into homogeneous cross-age ability groups
- One-on-one tutoring in reading by specially trained certified teachers who work individually with students who are reading below grade level
- Assessments every eight weeks to determine students' reading progress, adjust reading group placement, and assign tutoring if needed
- Professional development for teachers and tutors, which includes three days of in-service training and guidelines at the beginning of the school year, then follow-up training throughout the year
- A family support team designed to provide parenting education and support family involvement in the school

Participants in the Success for All middle school program. *What is the nature of the Success for All program?*

First implemented during the 1987–1988 school year in five inner-city schools in Baltimore, Maryland, SFA has expanded to over 475 schools in 31 states. Some studies have found that students who have participated in the program have better reading skills and are less likely to be in special education classes than disadvantaged students who have not been involved in the program (Slavin & others, 2009; Weiler, 1998). A recent research review of 110 studies using strict criteria for evidence of research support revealed that SFA had positive affects in the alphabetic domain, such as phonological awareness (What Works Clearinghouse, 2009).

Mentors can play an important role in improving some students' learning (Bernstein & others, 2009; Crooks & others, 2010). Usually viewed as older and wiser, mentors guide, teach, and support younger individuals, who are sometimes called *mentees* or *protégés* (Linley, 2009). The guidance is accomplished through demonstration, instruction, challenge, and encouragement on a more or less regular basis over an extended period of time. In the course of this process, the mentor and the young person develop

RESEARCH

**Thinking Back/Thinking Forward**

Mentoring involves serving as a positive model for a student. There is a lack of male and minority role models and mentors in children's education. Chapter 7, p. 238

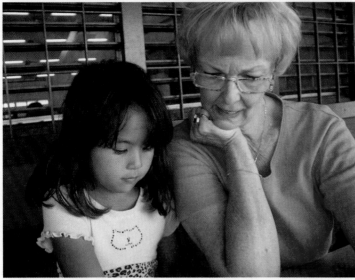

(*Top*) Shown here is a young man mentoring a child in the One on One Mentoring program, which involves the Salvation Army in Hennepin County, Minnesota. The goal of the problem is to provide every child in need an opportunity to succeed. (*Bottom*) Giving Back is a nonprofit organization that involves having individuals 50+ years of age serve as mentors for children to help them develop cognitive and interpersonal skills. Shown here a Giving Back mentor working with a young girl to improve her cognitive skills.

**Thinking Back/Thinking Forward**

Peers play an important role in many aspects of children's education. Chapter 3, p. 83; Chapter 12, p. 426; Chapter 13, p. 459

RESEARCH

a special bond of mutual commitment. In addition, the younger person's relationship to the mentor takes on an emotional character of respect, loyalty, and identification. (Hamilton & Hamilton, 2004, p. 396, based on a personal communication with ecological theorist Urie Bronfenbrenner.)

The majority of mentoring programs are outside the school and include such organizations as Big Brothers and Big Sisters, the largest formal mentoring program in the United States, as well as Boys and Girls Clubs of America and YMCA and YWCA. Recently schools have been the location of an increasing number of mentoring efforts, both for students and for beginning teachers who are mentored by experienced teachers (What Works Clearinghouse, 2009). The mentor comes to the school and works with the student, in many cases for an hour each week. Schools can be helpful in identifying students who might benefit from mentoring. A good strategy is to select not only high-risk, underachieving students for mentoring, but other students as well (DuBois & Karcher, 2006). Be aware that some mentoring relationships are more effective than others, and the matching of a student with a mentor requires careful selection and monitoring (Rhodes & Lowe, 2009).

**Peer Tutors** Fellow students also can be effective tutors (De Smet & others, 2010; McDuffle, Mastropieir, & Scruggs, 2009). In peer tutoring, one student teaches another. In *cross-age peer tutoring*, the peer is older. In *same-age peer tutoring*, the peer is a classmate. Cross-age peer tutoring usually works better than same-age peer tutoring. An older peer is more likely to be skilled than a same-age peer, and being tutored by a same-age classmate is more likely to embarrass a student and lead to negative social comparison.

Peer tutoring engages students in active learning and allows the classroom teacher to guide and monitor student learning as she or he moves around the classroom. Researchers have found that peer tutoring often benefits students' achievement (Slavin & others, 2009). In some instances, the tutoring benefits the tutor as well as the tutee, especially when the older tutor is a low-achieving student. Teaching something to someone else is one of the best ways to learn, although researchers have found that tutees' learning benefits more than tutors' learning (Roscoe & Chi, 2008).

In a study that won the American Educational Research Association's award for best research study, the effectiveness of a class-wide peer tutoring program in reading was evaluated for three learner types: low-achieving students with and without disabilities and average-achieving students (Fuchs & others, 1997). Twelve elementary and middle schools were randomly assigned to experimental (peer tutoring) and control (no peer tutoring) groups. The peer tutoring program was conducted in 35-minute sessions during regularly scheduled reading instruction three days a week. It lasted for 15 weeks. The training of peer tutors emphasized helping students get practice in reading aloud from narrative text, reviewing and sequencing the information that was read, summarizing large amounts of reading material, stating main ideas, predicting and checking story outcomes, and other reading strategies. Pretreatment and posttreatment reading achievement data were collected. Irrespective of the type of learner, students in the peer tutoring classrooms showed greater reading progress over the 15 weeks than their counterparts who did not receive peer tutoring.

***Peer-Assisted Learning Strategies (PALS)*** The peer tutoring program used in the study just described is called Peer-Assisted Learning Strategies (PALS). PALS was created by the John F. Kennedy Center and the Department of Special Education at Peabody College at Vanderbilt University. In PALS, teachers identify which children require help on specific skills and which children are most appropriate for helping other children learn those skills. Using this information, teachers pair children in the class so that partners work simultaneously and productively on different activities that address the problems they are experiencing. Pairs are changed regularly so that as students work on a variety of skills, all students have the opportunity of being "coaches" and "players."

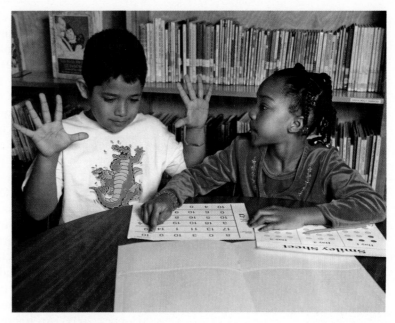

Students Participating in the PALS program.

PALS is a 25- to 35-minute activity that is used two to four times a week. Typically it creates 13 to 15 pairs in a classroom. It has been designed for use in the areas of reading and mathematics for kindergarten through sixth grade. It is not designed to replace existing curricula.

In PALS Math, students work on a sheet of problems in a skill area, such as adding, subtracting, using number concepts, or reading charts and graphs. PALS Math involves pairing students as a coach and a player. The coach uses a sheet with a series of questions designed to guide the player and provides feedback to the player. Students then exchange papers and score each other's practice sheets. They earn points for cooperating and constructing good explanations during coaching and for doing problems correctly during practice. PALS Math and PALS Reading are effective in developing students' mathematical and reading skills (Fuchs, Fuchs, & Burish, 2000; Mathes, Torgesen, & Allor, 2001).

The PALS program is highly effective with at-risk students, especially students in the early elementary grades, ethnic minority students, and students in urban schools (Rohrbeck & others, 2003). In one study, the reading comprehension of third- through sixth-grade native Spanish-speaking English language learners improved more when they were taught in a PALS format than in other reading instruction formats (Saenz, Fuchs, & Fuchs, 2005). A recent analysis involving strict criteria for evidence of research support confirmed that PALS has potentially positive outcomes for reading achievement (What Works Clearinghouse, 2007b). Further, PALS recently has been found to be effective with prekindergarten and kindergarten children in improving their literacy skills (McMaster & others, 2008; Townsend & Konold, 2010).

RESEARCH

DIVERSITY

Two other peer tutoring programs are Reciprocal Peer Tutoring (RPT) and Class Wide Peer Tutoring (CWPT) (Ginsburg-Block, 2005). RPT was initially developed for use with low-achieving urban elementary school students and provides opportunities for students to alternate in tutor and tutee roles. CWPT includes tutor training, reciprocal teaching, and motivational strategies such as team competition (Bowman-Perrott, 2009). A recent study found that over a three-year period CWPT was effective in improving middle school students' grades on weekly quizzes (Kamps & others, 2008).

The Valued Youth program is still another effective peer tutoring program. In 24 cities in the United States and Brazil, the Valued Youth program (now jointly sponsored by the Intercultural Development Research Association and Coca-Cola, and called the Coca-Cola Valued Youth program) gives secondary school students who are not achieving well or are at risk for school-related problems the responsibility of tutoring elementary school children (IDRA, 2010; Simons, Finlay, & Yang, 1991). The Valued Youth program began in 1984 and continues to expand today, with more than 540,000 students having participated in the program. The hope is that

Students in the Coca-Cola Valued Youth program. *What are some characteristics and outcomes of the program?*

the tutoring experience will improve not only the achievement of the students being tutored but also the achievement of the tutors. Over the course of its existence, less than 2 percent of students who participated in the Valued Youth program dropped out of school (IDRA, 2010).

One of the Valued Youth program tutors said, "Tutoring makes me want to come to school because I have to come and teach the younger kids." He also said that he did not miss many days of school, as he used to, because when he had been absent the elementary school children always asked him where he was and told him that they missed him. He said that he really liked the kids he taught, and that if he had not been a tutor he probably would have dropped out of school already.

TECHNOLOGY

***Online Peer Tutoring***   Online peer tutoring is increasingly being used in elementary schools, secondary schools, and colleges (Thurston & others, 2009). Online peer tutoring usually starts with the teacher engaging students in online tutoring; then, as students gain more experience in working together online, some of the online tutoring activities are conducted by trained, knowledgeable students. Of course, as with face-to-face tutoring, students will need training and guidance to become successful collaborators and peer tutors. One program, Microsoft Peer Coaching, combines technology and peer coaching for teachers themselves (Barron, Dawson, & Yendol-Hoppey, 2009). An important emphasis in the Microsoft program is having teachers coach other teachers in using technology to improve student learning.

I recently asked teachers how they use peer tutors and mentors in their classrooms. Following are their responses.

**EARLY CHILDHOOD**   We often have children lead various activities in the classroom—such as "show and tell"—giving them the opportunity to learn from each other.

—**MISSY DANGLER,** *Suburban Hills School*

**ELEMENTARY SCHOOL: GRADES K–5**   I use peer tutors in a variety of ways with my second-graders: "Buddy Readers" pairs strong readers with struggling readers; "Resident Experts" gives students showing full understanding of new skills in math, science, and social studies the opportunity to work with students who need extra help in these areas. In "Ask Three, Before Me," students who finish a writing task are expected to confer with three other students about their work (and make revisions as suggested) before sharing with me.

—**ELIZABETH FRASCELLA,** *Clinton Elementary School*

**MIDDLE SCHOOL: GRADES 6–8**   We first identify students who likely will be successful peer tutors and students who likely would benefit from having a tutor. We then  have peer tutors go through a training session; without this training, tutoring is much less likely to be successful. Tutoring not only helps the student who needs extra help, but also benefits the tutor because one of the best ways to learn a concept is by teaching it to someone else.

—**MARK FODNESS,** *Bemidji Middle School*

**HIGH SCHOOL: GRADES 9–12**   Students in my food service class are mentors to first-graders at the elementary school next door. My students do reading activities,  including acting out and making "Stone Soup" with the younger children. While these activities help the first-graders, they also reinforce important social skills for my high school students.

—**SANDY SWANSON,** *Menomonee Falls High School*

## TEACHING CONNECTIONS: Best Practices
### Strategies for Using Peer Tutoring

Here are some suggestions for how to best use peer tutoring (Goodlad & Hirst, 1989; Jenkins & Jenkins, 1987):

1. *Spend time training tutors.* For peer tutoring to be successful, you will have to spend some time training the tutors. To get peer tutors started off right, discuss competent peer tutoring strategies. Demonstrate how scaffolding works. Give the tutors clear, organized instructions and invite them to ask questions about their assignments. Divide the group of peer tutors into pairs and let them practice what you have just demonstrated. Let them alternately be tutor and tutee. Understand that not all students will want to act as tutors. Respect that choice.

2. *Use cross-age tutoring rather than same-age tutoring when possible.* This can be accomplished through cooperation between grade levels in the same building, or might involve bringing middle or high school students to an elementary school or high school students to a middle school. Students often look up to older students as role models. Use care in choosing appropriate students to act as such.

3. *Let students participate in both tutor and tutee roles.* This helps students learn that they can both help and be helped. Students are unlikely to be equally well-prepared in all subject areas, so while one might serve as a tutor in math, the same student might benefit from tutoring in social studies. Pairing of best friends often is not a good strategy because they have trouble staying focused on the learning assignment.

### THROUGH THE EYES OF TEACHERS
#### Cross-Age Peer Teaching at a Zoo

In Lincoln, Nebraska, several high school science teachers use the Folsum Zoo and Botanical Gardens as a context for guiding students' learning. The science classes are taught in two trailers at the zoo. The teachers emphasize the partnership of students, teachers, zoo, and community. One highlight of the program is the "Bug Bash," when the high school students teach fourth-grade students about insects.

4. *Don't let tutors give tests to tutees.* This can undermine cooperation between the students.

5. *Don't overuse peer tutoring.* It is easy to fall into the trap of using high-achieving students as peer tutors too often. Be sure that these students get ample opportunities to participate in challenging intellectual tasks themselves. Also ensure that students serving as tutors have enough time to complete their own work.

6. *Let parents know that their child will be involved in peer tutoring.* Explain to them the advantages of this learning strategy and invite them to visit the classroom to observe how the peer tutoring works.

7. *Monitor peer tutoring situations carefully.* Check frequently to ensure students are making progress. Also monitor the social aspects of peer tutoring to ensure that tutor and tutee are getting along and working well together.

## COOPERATIVE LEARNING

**Cooperative learning** occurs when students work in small groups to help each other learn. Cooperative learning has increasingly been used in recent years to improve student learning and skills (Thurston & others, 2010). Cooperative learning groups vary in size, although four is a typical number of students. In some cases, cooperative learning is done in dyads (two students). When students are assigned to work in a cooperative group, the group usually stays together for weeks or months, but most such groups occupy only a portion of the student's school day or year. In a cooperative learning group, each student typically learns a part of a larger unit of knowledge and then teaches that part to the group (Keramati, 2010; Moreno, 2009; White & Dinos, 2010). When students teach something to others, they tend to learn it more deeply.

**Research on Cooperative Learning**   Researchers have found that cooperative learning can be an effective strategy for improving achievement, especially when two conditions are met (Slavin, 1995):

- *Group rewards are generated.* Some type of recognition or reward is given to the group so that the group members can sense that it is in their best interest to help each other learn.

RESEARCH

**cooperative learning** Learning that occurs when students work in small groups to help each other learn.

- *Individuals are held accountable.* Some method of evaluating a student's individual contribution, such as an individual quiz or report, needs to be used. Without this individual accountability, certain students might do some *social loafing* (let other students do their work), and certain others might be left out because the rest of the group believes that they have little to contribute.

When the conditions of group rewards and individual accountability are met, cooperative learning improves achievement across different grades and in tasks that range from basic skills to problem solving (Johnson & Johnson, 2010).

RESEARCH

**Motivation**   Increased motivation to learn is common in cooperative groups (Blumenfeld, Kempler, & Krajcik, 2006; Jallifar, 2010). In one study, fifth- and sixth-grade Israeli students were given a choice of continuing to do schoolwork or going out to play (Sharan & Shaulov, 1990). Only when students were in cooperative groups were they likely to forgo going out to play. Positive peer interaction and positive feelings about making their own decisions were motivating factors behind students' choice to participate in the cooperative groups. In another study, high school students made greater gains and expressed more intrinsic motivation to learn algebraic concepts when they were in cooperative rather than individualistic learning contexts (Nichols & Miller, 1994).

**Interdependence and Teaching One's Peers**   Cooperative learning also promotes increased interdependence and connection with other students (Johnson & Johnson, 2010). In one study, fifth-graders were more likely to move to a correct strategy for solving decimal problems if their partners clearly explained their ideas and considered each other's proposals (Ellis, Klahr, & Siegler, 1994).

**Types of Tasks in Which Cooperative Learning Works Best**   Do some types of tasks work better in cooperative, collaborative efforts and others better on an individual basis? Researchers have found that cooperative learning implemented without rewards has little benefit in regard to simple tasks such as rote learning, memorization, or basic mathematics but produces better results with more complex tasks (Sears, 2006).

**Cooperative Learning Approaches**   A number of cooperative learning approaches have been developed. They include STAD (Student-Teams-Achievement Divisions), the jigsaw classroom (I and II), learning together, group investigation, and cooperative scripting. To read about these approaches, see Figure 10.1.

**Creating a Cooperative Community**   The school community is made up of faculty, staff, students, parents, and people in the neighborhood. More broadly, the school community also includes central administrators, college admissions officers, and future employers. To create an effective learning community, David and Roger Johnson (2002, pp. 144–146) conclude that cooperation and positive interdependence need to occur at a number of different levels: the learning group of children within a classroom (which we just discussed), the classroom, between classrooms, the school, school-parent interactions, and school-neighborhood interactions, as follows:

- *Class cooperation.* There are many ways to create cooperation and interdependence for the whole class. Class goals can be generated and class rewards given. This can be accomplished by adding bonus points to all class members' academic scores when all class members attain a goal "or by giving nonacademic rewards, such as extra free time, extra recess time, stickers, food, T-shirts, or a class party." Classroom cooperation can be promoted by "putting teams in charge of daily class cleanup, running a class bank or business, or

**STAD (Student-Teams-Achievement Divisions)**

STAD involves team recognition and group responsibility for learning in mixed-ability groups (Slavin, 1995). Rewards are given to teams whose members improve the most over their past performances. Students are assigned to teams of four or five members. The teacher presents a lesson, usually over one or two class periods. Next, students study worksheets based on material presented by the teacher. Students monitor their team members' performance to ensure that all members have mastered their material.

Teams practice working on problems together and study together, but the members take quizzes individually. The resulting individual scores contribute to the team's overall score. An individual's contribution to the team score is based on that individual's improvement, not on an absolute score, which motivates students to work hard because each contribution counts. In some STAD classrooms, a weekly class newsletter is published that recognizes both team and individual performances.

The STAD approach has been used in a variety of subjects (including math, reading, and social studies) and with students at different grade levels. It is most effective for learning situations that involve well-defined objectives or problems with specific answers or solutions. These include math computation, language use, geography skills, and science facts.

**The Jigsaw Classroom**

In Chapter 5, "Sociocultural Diversity," we described the jigsaw classroom, which involves having students from different cultural backgrounds cooperate by doing different parts of a project to reach a common goal. Here we elaborate on the concept.

Developed by Elliot Aronson and his colleagues (1978), *jigsaw I* is a cooperative learning approach in which six-member teams work on material that has been broken down into parts. Each team member is responsible for a part. Members of different teams who have studied the same part convene, discuss their part, and then return to their teams, where they take turns teaching their part to other team members.

Robert Slavin (1995) created *jigsaw II,* a modified version of *jigsaw I.* Whereas *jigsaw I* consists of teams of six, *jigsaw II* usually has teams of four or five. All team members study the entire lesson rather than one part, and individual scores are combined to form an overall team score, as in STAD. After they have studied the entire lesson, students become expert on one aspect of the lesson; then students with the same topics meet in expert groups to discuss them. Subsequently, they return to their teams and help other members of the team learn the material.

**Learning Together**

Created by David and Roger Johnson (1994), this approach has four components: (1) face-to-face interaction, (2) positive interdependence, (3) individual accountability, and (4) development of interpersonal group skills. Thus, in addition to Slavin's interest in achievement, the Johnsons' cooperative learning approach also focuses on socioemotional development and group interaction. In learning together, students work in four- or five-member heterogeneous groups on tasks with an emphasis on discussion and team building (Johnson & Johnson, 2009).

**Group Investigation**

Developed by Shlomo Sharan (1990; Sharan & Sharan, 1992), this approach involves a combination of independent learning and group work in two- to six-member groups), as well as a group reward for individual achievement. The teacher chooses a problem for the class to study, but students decide what they want to study in exploring the problem. The work is divided among the group's members, who work individually.

Then the group gets together, integrating, summarizing, and presenting the findings as a group project. The teacher's role is to facilitate investigation and maintain cooperative effort. Students collaborate with the teacher to evaluate their effort. In Sharan's view, this is the way many real-world problems are solved in communities around the world.

**Cooperative Scripting**

Students work in reciprocal pairs, taking turns summarizing information and orally presenting it to each other (Dansereau, 1988; McDonald and others, 1985). One member of the pair presents the material. The other member listens, monitors the presentation for any mistakes, and gives feedback. Then the partner becomes the teacher and presents the next set of material while the first member listens and evaluates it.

FIGURE **10.1**  COOPERATIVE LEARNING APPROACHES

engaging in other activities that benefit the class as a whole. Classroom interdependence may also be structured through dividing resources, such as having the class publish a newsletter in which each cooperative group contributes one article." In the case of a class studying geography, the ceiling was turned into a large world map. "The class was divided into eight cooperative groups. Each group was assigned a geographical location on which to do a report. The class then planned an itinerary for a trip to visit all eight places. Yarn was used to mark their journey. As they arrived at each spot, the appropriate group presented its report" about the location.

- *Interclass cooperation.* An interdisciplinary team of teachers may organize their classes into a "neighborhood" or "school within a school" in which classes work together on joint projects.
- *School-wide cooperation.* Cooperation at the level of the entire school can be attained in a number of ways. "The school mission statement may articulate the mutual goals shared by all members of the school and be displayed on the school walls" and highlighted on a school Web page. "Teachers can work in a variety of cooperative teams . . . and faculty/staff can meet weekly in teaching teams and/or study groups. . . . Teachers may be assigned to task forces to plan and implement solutions to school-wide issues. . . . Finally, school interdependence may be highlighted in a variety of school-wide activities, such as the weekly student-produced school news broadcast, . . . all-school projects, and regular school assemblies."
- *School-parent cooperation.* Cooperation is promoted between the school and parents "by involving parents in establishing mutual goals and strategic plans to attain the goals, . . . in sharing resources to help the school achieve its goals," and in creating activities that improve the likelihood that parents will develop a positive attitude toward the school.
- *School-neighborhood cooperation.* If the school is embedded in a neighborhood, a positive interdependence between the school and the neighborhood can benefit both. The school's mission "can be supported by neighborhood merchants who provide resources and financing for various events. Classes can perform neighborhood service projects, such as cleaning up a park."

**Evaluating Cooperative Learning** Among the positive aspects of cooperative learning are increased interdependence and interaction with other students, enhanced motivation to learn, and improved learning by teaching material to others (Johnson & Johnson, 2010; Williams, 2007). The possible drawbacks of cooperative learning are that some students prefer to work alone; low-achieving students may slow down the progress of high-achieving students; a few students may do most or all of the cognitive work while others do little (called *social loafing*); some students may become distracted from the group's task because they enjoy socializing; and many students lack the skills needed to collaborate effectively with others, engage in productive discussions, and explain their ideas or evaluate others' ideas effectively (Blumenfeld, Kempler, & Krajcik, 2006). Teachers who implement cooperative learning in their classrooms need to be attentive to these drawbacks and work to reduce them.

I recently asked teachers how they use cooperative learning in their classrooms. Following are their responses.

**EARLY CHILDHOOD** We often have our preschoolers work together by creating art projects or by cooking together. In these tasks, children are assigned different responsibilities and learn how to work together to reach a common goal.

—Missy Dangler, *Suburban Hills School*

**ELEMENTARY SCHOOL: GRADES K–5** I use base groups with learning partners on an ongoing basis in my classroom. These groups consist of four children who have established a feeling of trust with each other, work well together, and are balanced by gender, ability, and interest. The idea of learning partners is introduced as struggling readers are placed in these groups with students who are able to be supportive readers and empathetic to their classmates' needs.

—Elizabeth Frascella, *Clinton Elementary School*

**MIDDLE SCHOOL: GRADES 6–8**   The best group projects have a role for every participant; they all need to feel like they bring something to the table. I develop

group projects that require participants to read, do artwork, think creatively, speak in public, and so on. By including these skills, group members should be able to express their knowledge in a way that meets their style of learning.

—**MARK FODNESS,** *Bemidji Middle School*

**HIGH SCHOOL: GRADES 9–12**   I have learned that it is better not to have groups in which students select who will be included. Instead, I use a deck of cards for

random groups and change them for each project. Also, many students have had experiences with cooperative learning—and unfortunately some have learned to sit back and let others in the group do all the work. Teachers need to monitor the groups to make sure all students make an effort to contribute in the group.

—**SANDY SWANSON,** *Menomonee Falls High School*

## Review, Reflect, and Practice

**2** Explain how teachers and peers can jointly contribute to children's learning.

### REVIEW
- What is scaffolding?
- What is a cognitive apprenticeship?
- Is tutoring effective? What are some alternative sources of tutors?
- What is cooperative learning and how might it benefit students? What are some ways to structure it?

### REFLECT
- How would you handle the situation if parents became angry that, because of time allotted to cooperative learning, their children were being allowed less time to learn on an individual basis?

### PRAXIS™ PRACTICE
1. Which of the following is the best example of scaffolding?
   a. Steve gives his friend Vlade the answers to today's homework.
   b. Steve helps his friend Vlade complete today's homework by giving him the least amount of assistance he needs for each question.
   c. Steve helps his friend Vlade complete today's homework by giving him hints to each answer.
   d. Steve tells his friend Vlade that he has to do his homework on his own.
2. Which of the following is an example of a cognitive apprenticeship?
   a. Ms. Notwitzki asks her students lots of questions. If a student does not know the answer to a question, she moves on to another student because she does not want her students to be embarrassed.
   b. Ms. Edgar pays attention to both the verbal and nonverbal cues her students give her regarding their understanding of her lessons. If she asks a student a question, she can determine if the student is thinking or confused. She often gives her students hints to help them answer.

*(continued)*

## Review, Reflect, and Practice

**PRAXIS™ PRACTICE (CONTINUED)**

  c. Ms. Lindell asks her students lots of questions. If a student does not respond immediately to her query, she gives the student the correct answer.

  d. Ms. Samuel lectures her class, and they take notes. She answers any questions that they have at the end of the lesson.

3. Which teacher is using peer tutoring in the most positive way for both the tutor and the student?

  a. Ms. Gasol uses sixth-grade students to tutor her third-grade students in math for 30 minutes, four times each week. She gives each tutor explicit instructions.

  b. Ms. Mathews uses the buddy system in her class. Children choose who they would like to tutor them and what they would like to learn. Generally, they pick a close friend.

  c. Ms. Rankowski selects lower-achieving students from the higher grades to come to her class at least once per week to work with her students. She generally has them do things such as administer spelling.

  d. Ms. Taylor likes to use peer tutoring with her students, especially in math. She has found that often other students can explain things to her students more easily than she can. Therefore, she uses more advanced students in her class to teach those who are struggling with math concepts.

4. Mr. Kotter has assigned the students to work cooperatively on a project about the Civil War. He puts the students into heterogeneous groups of four and gives each group the project guidelines. They are to turn in one project on which they will receive a group grade. He is surprised when some students contribute little to their group's effort. What is Mr. Kotter doing *wrong*?

  a. Mr. Kotter did not include any individual accountability in his assessment.

  b. Mr. Kotter should not give the students a group grade.

  c. Mr. Kotter should not have used heterogeneous groups.

  d. Mr. Kotter should not use cooperative learning in history.

*Please see the answer key at the end of the book.*

## ③ STRUCTURING SMALL-GROUP WORK

| Composing the Group | Team-Building Skills | Structuring Small-Group Interaction |

We have seen that group work has many benefits for students. It requires careful planning on the teacher's part, however. When you structure students' work in small groups, you have to make decisions about how to compose the group, build team skills, and structure group interaction (Bennett & others, 2010; Crooks & others, 2010).

### COMPOSING THE GROUP

Teachers often ask how they should assign students to small groups in their class. The cooperative learning approaches featured in Figure 10.1, shown earlier in this chapter, generally recommend heterogeneous groups with diversity in ability, ethnic background, socioeconomic status, and gender (Johnson & Johnson, 2010). The reasoning behind heterogeneous grouping is that it maximizes opportunities for peer tutoring and support, improves cross-gender and cross-ethnic relations, and ensures that each group has at least one student who can do the work (Kagan, 1992).

**Heterogeneous Ability**    One of the main reasons for using heterogeneous ability groups is that they benefit low-ability students, who can learn from higher-ability students. However, some critics argue that such heterogeneous groupings hold back high-ability students. In most studies, though, high-achieving students perform equally well on achievement tests after working in heterogeneous groups or homogeneous groups (Hooper & others, 1989). In heterogeneous groups, high-ability students often assume the role of "teacher" and explain concepts to other students. In homogeneous groups, high-ability students are less likely to assume this teaching role.

   One problem with heterogeneous groups is that when high-ability, low-ability, and medium-ability students are included, the medium-ability students get left out to some extent; high-ability and low-ability students form teacher-student relationships, excluding medium-ability students from group interaction. Medium-ability students might perform better in groups where most or all of the students have medium abilities.

**Ethnic, Socioeconomic, and Gender Heterogeneity**    One of the initial reasons that cooperative learning groups were formed was to improve interpersonal relations among students from different ethnic and socioeconomic backgrounds. The hope was that interaction under conditions of equal status in cooperative groups would reduce prejudice. However, getting students to interact on the basis of equal status has been more difficult than initially envisioned.

DIVERSITY

   When forming ethnically and socioeconomically heterogeneous groups, it is important to pay attention to a group's composition. One recommendation is to not make the composition too obvious. Thus, you might vary different social characteristics (ethnicity, socioeconomic status, and gender) simultaneously, such as grouping together a middle-income African America female, a White male from a low-income family, and so on. In this way, for example, the White males would not all be from high-income families. Another recommendation is to avoid forming groups that have only one minority student, if at all possible; this avoids calling attention to the student's "solo status."

   In mixed-gender groups, males tend to be more active and dominant. Thus, when mixing females and males, an important task for teachers is to encourage girls to speak up and boys to allow girls to express their opinions and contribute to the group's functioning. A general strategy is to have an equal number of girls and boys. In groups of five or six children in which only one member is a girl, the boys tend to ignore the girl (Webb, 1984).

## TEAM-BUILDING SKILLS

Good cooperative learning in the classroom requires that time be spent on team-building skills. This involves thinking about how to start team building at the beginning of the school year, helping students become better listeners, giving students practice in contributing to a team product, getting students to discuss the value of a team leader, and working with team leaders to help them deal with problem situations.

## TEACHING CONNECTIONS: Best Practices
### Strategies for Developing Students' Team-Building Skills

Here are some guidelines for helping students develop team-building skills (Aronson & Patnoe, 1997):

1. *Don't begin the year with cooperative learning on a difficult task.* Teachers report that academic cooperative learning often works best when students have previously worked together on team-building exercises. A short period each day for several weeks is usually adequate for this team building. Many students have not had much experience in working in cooperative groups so having them engage in team-building exercises helps them to learn how to more effectively interact with each other before they begin trying to work on a difficult group project.

2. *Do team building at the level of the cooperative group (two to six students) rather than at the level of the entire class.* Some students on the team will be more assertive; others will be more passive. The team-building goal is to give all members some experience in being valuable team members, as well as to get them to learn that being cooperative works more effectively than being competitive.

3. *In team building, work with students to help them become better listeners.* Ask students to introduce themselves by name all at the same time to help them see that they have to take turns and listen to each other instead of hogging a conversation. You also can ask students to come up with behavioral descriptions of how they can show others that they are listening. These might include looking directly at the speaker, rephrasing what she just said, summarizing her statement, and so on.

4. *Give students some practice in contributing to a common product as part of team building.* Ask each student to participate in drawing a group picture or writing a group story by passing paper and pen from student to student. Each student's task is to add something to the picture or story as it circulates several times through the team. When the picture or story is finished, discuss each student's contribution to the team. Students will sense that the product is not complete unless each member's contribution is recognized. In Through the Eyes of Teachers, you can read about how a ninth-grade history teacher uses this strategy effectively.

### THROUGH THE EYES OF TEACHERS
#### An Eye-Level Meeting of the Minds

Jimmy Furlow has groups of students summarize textbook sections and put them on transparencies to help the entire

Ninth-grade history teacher Jimmy Furlow converses with a student in his class.

class prepare for a test. Furlow lost both legs in Vietnam but he rarely stays in one place, moving his wheelchair around the room and communicating with students at eye level. When the class completes their discussion of all the points on the overhead, Furlow edits their work to demonstrate concise, clear writing and help students zero in on an important point (Marklein, 1998).

5. *During team building, you may want to discuss the value of having a group leader.* You can ask students to discuss the specific ways a leader should function to maximize the group's performance. Their brainstorming might come up with such characteristics as "helps get the group organized," "keeps the group on task," "serves as liaison between the teacher and the group," "shows enthusiasm," "is patient and polite," and "helps the group deal with disagreements and conflicts." The teacher may select the group leader or students may be asked to elect one.

6. *Work with team leaders to help them deal with problem situations.* For example, some members might rarely talk, one member might dominate the group, members might call each other names, some members might refuse to work, one member might want to work alone, and everyone might talk at once. You can get group leaders together and get them to role-play such situations and discuss effective strategies for handling the problem situation.

## STRUCTURING SMALL-GROUP INTERACTION

One way to facilitate students' work in small groups is to assign students different roles. For example, consider these roles that students can assume in a group (Kagan, 1992):

- Encourager—brings out reluctant students and is a motivator
- Gatekeeper—equalizes participation of students in the group
- Coach—helps with academic content
- Checker—makes sure the group understands the material
- Taskmaster—keeps the group on task
- Recorder—writes down ideas and decisions
- Quiet captain—monitors the group's noise level
- Materials monitor—obtains and returns supplies

Such roles help groups to function more smoothly and give all members of the group a sense of importance. Note that although we just described eight different roles that can be played in groups, most experts, as we noted earlier, recommend that groups not exceed five or six members to function effectively. Some members can fill multiple roles, and all roles do not always have to be filled.

Another way roles can be specialized is to designate some students as "summarizers" and others as "listeners." Researchers have consistently found that summarizing benefits learning more than listening, so if these roles are used, all members should get opportunities to be summarizers (Dansereau, 1988).

To evaluate your attitudes toward social constructivist approaches and whether you are likely to use such strategies when you teach, complete Self-Assessment 10.1.

## TEACHING CONNECTIONS: Best Practices
### Strategies for Structuring Group Work

The Cooperative Learning Center at the University of Minnesota makes the following suggestions for structuring groupwork (Johnson & Johnson, 1989, 1995):

1. *Foster positive interdependence.* Each group member's efforts must be essential to the success of the group. Each member must make a unique contribution to the group.

2. *Students need to promote one another's success.* Group members should support, help, and encourage one another, This is easier done face-to-face than electronically.

3. *Accountability must be at both the individual and group level.* Although the group must be accountable for reaching its goals, each student in the group must also be held accountable for completing his/her share of the work or performing his/her role. One reason many students dislike group work is that they have been "left

holding the bag." Often times one or two students in a group will complete most of the work, leaving them feeling resentful of other group members. Of course, in some cases, one or two students have to take over the group, leaving other group members feeling resentful. Establishing both individual and group accountability can alleviate this situation.

4. *Teach group social skills.* Students who have never worked cooperatively before may not have the requisite skills to do so. For group work to be successful, students need to know how to assume leadership, communicate effectively, and resolve conflicts.

5. *Require group processing.* Groups should discuss how they are progressing toward their goals, the problems they are encountering, and how decisions are being made. By doing so, they may change course and become more effective groups.

# SELF-ASSESSMENT 10.1

## Evaluating My Social Constructivist Experiences

What experiences have you already had with social constructivist thinking and learning? You may have had such experiences in school or in other settings. For each of these settings that you have experienced, record at least one instance in which you can look back and see social constructivist principles at work.

1. Your family:

_____

_____

2. A club or program such as the Scouts:

_____

_____

3. Your K–12 school experience:

_____

_____

4. College:

_____

_____

How do those experiences shape your judgment regarding these ideas for classroom teaching?

1. That thinking should be viewed as located (situated) in social and physical contexts, not only within an individual's mind:

_____

_____

2. Vygotsky's sociocultural cognitive theory:

_____

_____

3. Scaffolding:

_____

_____

4. Peer tutoring:

_____

_____

5. Cooperative learning:

_____

_____

6. Small-group work:

_____

_____

## Review, Reflect, and Practice

**3** Discuss effective decisions in structuring small-group work.

**REVIEW**
- What are some important considerations in placing students in small groups?
- What can teachers do to build team skills within groups?
- What types of role assignments can improve a group's structure?

**REFLECT**
- Suppose you and five other students have decided to form a group to study for a final exam in educational psychology. How would you structure the group? What roles would you want the group to assign?

**PRAXIS™ PRACTICE**

1. Which of the following represents the best practice for forming work groups?
   a. one non-Latino White, high-achieving girl; three African American, middle-achieving boys
   b. one African American, high-achieving boy; two non-Latino White, middle-achieving girls; one Asian American, low-achieving boy
   c. two Asian American, high-achieving boys; two non-Latino White, low-achieving boys
   d. two African American, high-achieving girls; one African American, middle-achieving boy; one African American, low-achieving girl

2. Mr. Fandango decides to work on team building at the beginning of the school year. To this end, he takes his entire class outside and has them create a human knot. They then must work together to untie the "knot." Several students become frustrated and angry during the activity. Mr. Fandango intervenes by encouraging the students to elect a leader and to listen to each other. According to "Teaching Connections: Best Practices and Strategies for Developing Students' Team-Building Skills," what did Mr. Fandango do *incorrectly*?
   a. He did not emphasize the importance of listening skills.
   b. He did not have enough students in the group.
   c. He did not use heterogeneous grouping.
   d. He started with the whole class and a difficult task.

3. George, John, Paul, Cassie, and Mackenzie are working together on a group project involving the Civil War. George is the resident expert on the Civil War. As they work on the project, he answers the other students' questions. John volunteers to get all the supplies that the group needs. The project goes smoothly, and each of the students participates, because Cassie reminds them that everyone's contribution is valuable. During one group work session, the group starts discussing last weekend's football game. Paul says, "Hey guys, we're supposed to be working on this project, you know." After this, the group gets back on task. They become so engrossed in their discussion that they become rather noisy. At this point, Mackenzie reminds her peers to quiet down. Which student took the gatekeeper role?
   a. George
   b. John
   c. Mackenzie
   d. Cassie

*Please see the answer key at the end of the book.*

## 4  SOCIAL CONSTRUCTIVIST PROGRAMS

| Fostering a Community of Learners | Schools for Thought |

Let's explore two programs that systematically incorporate social constructivist philosophies in their efforts to challenge students to solve real-world problems and develop a deeper understanding of concepts. These programs can show you some ways to successfully use social constructivist ideas and techniques in your classroom.

### FOSTERING A COMMUNITY OF LEARNERS

Ann Brown and Joe Campione (1996; Brown, 1997; Campione, 2001) have developed a program called **Fostering a Community of Learners (FCL),** which focuses on literacy development and biology. As currently established, it is set in inner-city elementary schools and is appropriate for 6- to 12-year-old children. Reflection and discussion are key dimensions of the program. In FCL, constructive commentary, questioning, querying, and criticism are the norm rather than the exception. Many of the class activities occur in small groups in which students talk with, try to convince, and challenge each other. Although teachers guide topic selection, an important goal is to gradually turn over responsibility for learning to students (Lehrer & Schauble, 2006). The FCL program emphasizes three strategies that encourage reflection and discussion: (1) the use of adults as role models, (2) children teaching children, and (3) online computer consultation.

**Adults as Role Models**  Visiting experts and classroom teachers introduce the big ideas and difficult principles at the beginning of a unit. The adults demonstrate how to think and self-reflect in the process of identifying topics within a general area of inquiry or reasoning with given information. They continually ask students to justify their opinions and then to support them with evidence, to think of counterexamples of rules, and so on.

For example, one area of biological inquiry used in the FCL program is "Changing Populations." Outside experts or teachers introduce this topic and ask students to generate as many questions about it as possible. The teacher and the students categorize the questions into subtopics such as extinct, endangered, artificial, assisted, and urbanized populations. About six students make up a learning group, and each group takes responsibility for one of the subtopics.

**Children Teaching Children**  Brown (1997) says that children as well as adults enrich the classroom learning experience by contributing their particular expertise. *Cross-age teaching,* in which older students teach younger students, is used. This occurs both face-to-face and via e-mail. Older students often serve as discussion leaders. Cross-age teaching provides students with invaluable opportunities to talk about learning, gives students responsibility and purpose, and fosters collaboration among peers.

FCL uses **reciprocal teaching,** in which students take turns leading a small-group discussion. Reciprocal teaching requires students to discuss complex passages, collaborate, and share their individual expertise and perspectives on a particular topic. Reciprocal teaching can involve a teacher and a student as well as interaction among students.

A modified version of the *jigsaw classroom* (which was described in Chapter 5 and Figure 10.1) also is used. As students create preliminary drafts of reports, they participate in *crosstalk* sessions. These are whole-class activities in which groups periodically summarize where they are in their learning activity and get input from the other groups. *Mini-jigsaws* (small groups) also are used. At both the whole-class level and mini-jigsaw level, if group members can't understand what a student is saying

**Fostering a Community of Learners (FCL)** A social constructivist program that focuses on literacy development and biology. FCL encourages reflection and discussion through the use of adults as role models, children teaching children, and online computer consultation.

**reciprocal teaching** A learning arrangement used by FCL in which students take turns leading a small-group discussion.

A Fostering a Community of Learners (FCL) classroom. *What is the nature of this approach to education?*

or writing about, that student must revise a product and present it again later. Students are then grouped into reciprocal teaching seminars in which each student is an expert on one subtopic, teaches that part to the others, and participates in constructing test questions based on the subunit.

**Online Computer Consultation**   As just noted, FCL classrooms also use e-mail to build community and expertise. Through e-mail, experts provide coaching and advice, as well as commentary about what it means to learn and understand. Online experts function as role models of thinking. They wonder, query, and make inferences based on incomplete knowledge.

At the heart of FCL is a culture of learning, negotiating, sharing, and producing work that is displayed to others. Products of students' work are often in the form of text or talk that includes posters, presentations, written reports, or teaching ideas for working with younger children (Lehrer & Schauble, 2006). The educational experience involves an interpretive community that encourages active exchange and reciprocity. Research evaluation of the FCL approach suggests that it benefits students' understanding and allows a flexible use of content knowledge, resulting in improved achievement in reading, writing, and problem solving (Lehrer & Schauble, 2006). A recent study of fifth- and sixth-grade FCL classrooms revealed that students effectively reasoned and talked about complex biological concepts (Ash, 2008).

Science education experts Richard Lehrer and Laura Schauble (2006) called FCL "a landmark in developmental science education." That said, they also raised several questions about its effectiveness. First, even though many educators agree that shared discourse is an important aspect of classrooms, they caution that it is not clear how to implement this and difficult to gauge its success. Second, in regard to science education, some have suggested FCL may place too much emphasis on reading science texts, integrating text information, and learning *about* science and too little emphasis on *doing* science.

## SCHOOLS FOR THOUGHT

**Schools for Thought (SFT)** is another formal program of social constructivist teaching. Too often students emerge from instruction with only a fragile understanding of the material. For example, students might be able to repeat various scientific

**Thinking Back/Thinking Forward**

The jigsaw classroom involves having students from different cultural backgrounds cooperate by doing different parts of a project to reach a common goal. Chapter 5, p. 159

RESEARCH

**Schools for Thought (SFT)** A social constructivist program that combines aspects of The Jasper Project, Fostering a Community of Learners (FCL), and Computer-Supported Intentional Learning Environments (CSILE).

principles they have been taught in science, but they run into difficulties when they have to explain everyday scientific phenomena. Similarly, in math, students might be good at plugging numbers into formulas but when confronted with variations of these problems be unable to solve them. Thus, many students acquire enough information to pass tests in school but gain no deep understanding of concepts.

TECHNOLOGY

In one effort, SFT has combined aspects of The Jasper Project, Fostering a Community of Learners (FCL), and Computer-Supported Intentional Learning Environments (CSILE) in a school learning environment (Lamon & others, 2006). The Jasper Project, FCL, and CSILE share certain features that allow them to be combined in a school learning environment.

What are the three components of SFT like? The Jasper Project focuses on *The Adventures of Jasper Woodbury,* a multimedia set of 12 math problem-solving adventures, and is an example of problem-based learning (Cognition and Technology Group at Vanderbilt, 1997) (see Figure 10.2). *Jasper*-related projects also have been created for students in science, history, and social studies. We already have described FCL. What characterizes CSILE? In the early 1990s researchers at the Centre for Applied Cognitive Science, in the Ontario Institute for Studies in Education, began applying their work on intentional learning to the development of computer applications to support knowledge building communities (Scardamalia & Bereiter, 1994). Their work led to the development of CSILE, an evolving database application that allows students to collaboratively develop a knowledge base, enter their views and questions, compare perspectives, and reflect on their joint understanding of ideas.

CSILE helps students understand how knowledge is socially constructed and gives them opportunities to reflect on, revise, and transform their thinking. Students in CSILE classrooms performed better on standardized achievement tests of language and mathematics, gave deeper explanations of concepts, were better problem solvers, and had a more positive attitude toward learning than students in traditional classrooms (Scardamalia, Bereiter, & Lamon, 1994).

More recently, CSILE has morphed into a commercial enterprise known as Knowledge Forum (**www.knowledgeforum. com**) and expanded from a K–12 focus to incorporate all kinds of education and training (Bruckman, 2006; Scardamalia & Bereiter, 2006). Knowledge Forum includes knowledge building tools for collaboration, constructing, storing, retrieving, referencing, quoting, and tracking notes, identifying gaps or advances in knowledge, building idea networks, and viewing ideas and idea networks from multiple perspectives.

Knowledge Forum is essentially CSILE online. It provides users with structures and tools to create a knowledge-building community via a local area network, through Internet communications, or using the World Wide Web. Each community creates its own knowledge base in which it can store notes, connect ideas, and build on previous thinking. Users start with an empty knowledge base to which they submit ideas, share information, reorganize the knowledge, and ultimately build understandings. Knowledge Forum makes information accessible from multiple perspectives and from multiple entry points. With it, any number of individuals and groups can share information, launch collaborative investigations, and build networks of new ideas . . . together.

**Curriculum** The three core programs of SFT stress the importance of getting students to think about real-world problems. Problem-based and project-based activities are at the heart of the curriculum. Extended in-depth inquiry in domains such as science, math, and social studies are emphasized. All three programs also incorporate cross-disciplinary inquiry across traditional boundaries. For example, exploring what it means for an animal to be endangered could involve examining problems

"Blueprint for Success"

Christina and Marcus, two students from Trenton, visit an architectural firm on Career Day. While learning about the work of architects, Christina and Marcus hear about a vacant lot being donated in their neighborhood for a playground. This is exciting news because there is no place in their downtown neighborhood for children to play. Recently, several students have been hurt playing in the street. The challenge is for students to help Christina and Marcus design a playground and ballfield for the lot.

"The Big Splash"

Jasper's young friend Chris wants to help his school raise money to buy a new camera for the school TV station. His idea is to have a dunking booth in which teachers would be dunked when students hit a target. He must develop a business plan for the school principal in order to obtain a loan for his project. The overall problem centers on developing this business plan, including the use of a statistical survey to help him decide if this idea would be profitable.

FIGURE **10.2** PROBLEM-SOLVING ADVENTURES IN THE *JASPER* SERIES

A Schools for Thought science classroom at Compton-Drew School in St. Louis.

related to estimating populations, sampling, and other issues usually restricted to mathematics. In the SFT project, curricula are being developed that integrate geography, geology, environmental and physical science, ancient and American history, and language arts and reading.

**Instruction** All three SFT programs involve a change in the classroom instructional climate. In a traditional classroom, students are receivers of information dispensed by teachers, textbooks, and other media; the teacher's role is to give information and mold students' learning. In many traditional schools, what students mainly do is listen, watch, and mimic what teachers and texts tell them to do (Greeno, 2006). In contrast, all three SFT programs provide students with many opportunities to plan and organize their own learning and problem solving. They also encourage students to work collaboratively as they learn and think. Students explore ideas, evaluate information, and consider others' ideas in an ongoing reciprocal interchange with peers, teachers, and experts.

The SFT environments are not simply freewheeling discovery environments. They involve a considerable amount of structure. Teachers and community experts keep learning focused on key principles in the domains being studied, such as mathematics, science, or social science. They monitor and reframe students' self-generated questions and exploration to keep them within the perspective of the key principles. In this manner, they guide the direction of students' inquiry so that students discover the deep concepts of the domain. Still, there is considerable flexibility in how this understanding is achieved and in the nature of the projects undertaken.

**Community** In many schools, classrooms and teachers operate in isolation, not just from each other but from the outside community as well. The Jasper Project, FCL, and CSILE all emphasize the importance of giving students and teachers opportunities to see themselves as part of a team and as members of a larger community. Problems often have a community focus so as to encourage students to think about how learning and problem solving can be used to better understand and improve the world in which we live.

**Technology** The Jasper Project, FCL, and CSILE all use technology to break the isolation of the traditional classroom. They encourage students to communicate electronically with a community of learners beyond the classroom's walls.

TECHNOLOGY

**Assessment** The goals in creating The Jasper Project, FCL, and CSILE were not to improve students' achievement test scores. Assessment in the three programs focuses on achieving authentic performances (such as reading for the purpose of answering research questions, writing to build new knowledge), making assessment coordinate smoothly with learning and instruction, and encouraging students to engage in self-assessment.

## Review, Reflect, and Practice

**④** Describe two social constructivist programs.

**REVIEW**

- What three strategies are embedded in the Fostering a Community of Learners program? What programs are combined in Schools for Thought? What do these programs have in common?

**REFLECT**

- Which of the two social constructivist programs appeals to you the most? Why?

**PRAXIS™ PRACTICE**

1. Which of the following is the best example of Fostering a Community of Learners?
   a. Marks Middle School brings students together to work on math projects. They bring in community members to act as mentors to the students and try to make connections between mathematics and the world in which these rural teens live.
   b. Lincoln Elementary School uses small-group discussions in which students challenge each other's perspectives. They bring in community members to act as mentors to the students. When outside mentors lack the expertise needed, students e-mail outside experts. Older students help younger ones.
   c. Johnson High School uses a hands-on approach to teaching biology. Students complete experiments, dissections, and involve themselves in an environmental project. Students work in small groups on these projects under the guidance of an adult role model.
   d. Luther High School uses a flexible, modular approach to teaching science with extensive opportunities for students to engage in projects that they construct themselves. Students are encouraged to engage in self-reflection and cooperative learning.

2. Mr. Patrick, the principal at Johnson High School, wants to implement Schools for Thought. He works with his teachers to integrate various aspects of the curriculum so that students will understand their interdependence. The teachers develop interdisciplinary units that revolve around projects. In addition, the teachers alter the way in which they teach to become facilitators of learning rather than dispensers of knowledge. What aspect of Schools for Thought has Mr. Patrick neglected?
   a. community
   b. curriculum
   c. discipline
   d. instruction

*Please see the answer key at the end of the book.*

# The Social Constructivist Classroom

Mariana is a new second-grade teacher and full of enthusiasm about her job. She believes that students should be very active in constructing their own knowledge, and that they should work together in doing this. To that end, she has decided that she wants her classroom to be a social constructivist classroom and has made some decisions about some things she wants to do this year with her students.

First, she knows that she will have to provide students with scaffolding when material is new and gradually adjust the amount of help her students receive. She wants to use peer tutoring for this in her class, because she believes that children can often learn more from each other than they can from an adult. So she sets up a system in which the more advanced students in her class help those who are less advanced.

Mariana also likes the idea of cooperative learning. She creates student groups so that they are heterogeneous with regard to ability, gender, ethnicity, and SES. She then assigns roles to each student in a group. Sometimes these roles are things such as coach, encourager, checker, taskmaster, recorder, and materials monitor. She uses this approach for many content areas. Sometimes she uses a jigsaw approach in which each student is responsible for becoming an expert in a particular area and then sharing that expertise with his or her group members. She uses this approach in science and in social studies.

In math, Mariana feels very fortunate that her school has adopted the Everyday Mathematics curriculum. This program makes connections with the real world that she thinks are so important in math instruction. Group work is also stressed.

Mariana hopes that her students and their parents will share her excitement as they "all learn together." However, she soon becomes disappointed. When she groups students, she hears groans of, "Not again," "Why do I have to work with her? She doesn't know anything," "He's too bossy," "I always have to be with him, and then I end up doing everything," "She never lets me do anything but sit there and watch." Parents have gotten in on the act, too. She has received calls and letters from parents who don't understand what she's trying to do. They all seem concerned about test scores and grades rather than what their children are learning together. One parent asked that her child no longer be grouped with another child who is "holding back" her child's learning.

1. What are the issues in this case?
2. What do you think Mariana did incorrectly?
3. What should she do now to recover her constructivist classroom?
4. How can she elicit the cooperation of the parents?
5. Which of the following suggestions would you make to Mariana regarding peer tutoring?
   a. Allow children to choose their partners.
   b. Insist that the more advanced students help those who are less advanced, regardless of parental feelings.
   c. Use cross-age peer tutoring rather than same-age peer tutoring.
   d. Use peer tutors who don't like each other so they won't be tempted to goof around instead of working.
6. Which of the following suggestions would you make to Mariana regarding her use of student groups?
   a. Compose gender-segregated groups to make students more comfortable.
   b. Compose racially segregated groups to make students more comfortable.
   c. Give leadership roles to students who are shy to help draw them out.
   d. Mix up the group composition from time to time so that middle-ability-level students don't get left out.

# Social Constructivist Approaches

**① SOCIAL CONSTRUCTIVIST APPROACHES TO TEACHING:** Compare the social constructivist approach with other constructivist approaches.

| | |
|---|---|
| **Social Constructivism in the Broader Constructivist Context** | Piaget's and Vygotsky's theories are constructivist. Piaget's theory is a cognitive constructivist theory, whereas Vygotsky's is social constructivist. The implication of Vygotsky's model for teaching is to establish opportunities for students to learn through social interactions with others—with the teacher and peers—in constructing knowledge and understanding. In Piaget's view, students construct knowledge by transforming, organizing, and reorganizing previous knowledge and information. In both Piaget's and Vygotsky's models, teachers are facilitators, not directors. Distinctions between cognitive and social constructivist approaches are not always clear-cut. All social constructivist approaches emphasize that social factors contribute to students' construction of knowledge and understanding. |
| **Situated Cognition** | Situated cognition is the idea that thinking occurs (is situated) in social and physical contexts. |

**② TEACHERS AND PEERS AS JOINT CONTRIBUTORS TO STUDENTS' LEARNING:** Explain how teachers and peers can jointly contribute to children's learning.

| | |
|---|---|
| **Scaffolding** | Scaffolding is the technique of providing changing levels of support over the course of a teaching session, with a more skilled individual—a teacher or a more advanced peer of the child—providing guidance to fit the student's current performance. |
| **Cognitive Apprenticeship** | A cognitive apprenticeship involves a novice and an expert. The expert stretches and supports the novice's understanding of and use of a culture's skills. |
| **Tutoring** | Tutoring involves a cognitive apprenticeship between an expert and a novice. Tutoring can take place between an adult and a child or a more skilled child and a less skilled child. Individual tutoring is effective. Classroom aides, volunteers, and mentors can serve as tutors to support teachers and classroom learning. Reading Recovery and Success for All are two examples of effective tutoring programs. In many cases, students benefit more from cross-age tutoring than from same-age tutoring. Tutoring can benefit both the tutee and the tutor. |
| **Cooperative Learning** | Cooperative learning occurs when students work in small groups to help each other learn. Researchers have found that cooperative learning can be an effective strategy for improving students' achievement, especially when group goals and individual accountability are instituted. Cooperative learning works better for complex than simple tasks. It often improves intrinsic motivation, encourages student interdependence, and promotes deep understanding. Cooperative learning approaches include STAD (Student-Teams-Achievement Divisions), the jigsaw classroom (I and II), learning together, group investigation, and cooperative scripting. Such learning approaches generally recommend heterogeneous groupings with diversity in ability, ethnicity, socioeconomic status, and gender. Creating a cooperative community involves developing positive interdependence at a number of levels: a small group within a classroom, the class as a whole, between classrooms, the entire school, between parents and the school, and between the school and the neighborhood. Cooperative learning has a number of strengths, but there also are some potential drawbacks to its use. |

**③ STRUCTURING SMALL-GROUP WORK:** Discuss effective decisions in structuring small-group work.

| | |
|---|---|
| **Composing the Group** | Two strategies in composing a small group are to assign children to heterogeneous groups and to have the group membership reflect diversity in ability, ethnic background, socioeconomic status, and gender. |
| **Team-Building Skills** | Structuring small-group work also involves attention to team-building skills. A good strategy is to spend several weeks at the beginning of the school year on building team skills, helping students become better listeners, and giving them practice in contributing to a team product. Assigning one student in each small group to be a team leader can help to build the team. |
| **Structuring Small-Group Interaction** | A group also can benefit when students are assigned different roles—for example, encourager, gatekeeper, taskmaster, quiet captain, and materials monitor—that are designed to help the group function more smoothly. |

**④ SOCIAL CONSTRUCTIVIST PROGRAMS:** Describe two social constructivist programs.

| | |
|---|---|
| **Fostering a Community of Learners** | Fostering a Community of Learners (FCL) emphasizes (1) using adults as role models, (2) children teaching children, and (3) online computer consultation. |
| **Schools for Thought** | Schools for Thought (SFT) combines activities from three programs: (1) The Jasper Project, (2) Fostering a Community of Learners (FCL), and (3) Computer-Supported Intentional Learning Environments (CSILE). Extended in-depth inquiry is fostered. Teachers guide students in becoming architects of their knowledge. |

# KEY TERMS

social constructivist approach 333
situated cognition 335

cognitive apprenticeship 336
cooperative learning 341

Fostering a Community of Learners (FCL) 352
reciprocal teaching 352

Schools for Thought (SFT) 353

# PORTFOLIO ACTIVITIES

Now that you have a good understanding of this chapter, complete this exercise to expand your thinking.

## Independent Reflection: Evaluating Social Constructivist Experiences

To what extent have you experienced various social constructivist approaches in your education? Think about your different levels of schooling (early childhood, elementary, middle, high school, and college), and evaluate your experience (or lack of experience) with scaffolding, cognitive apprenticeship, tutoring, and cooperative learning. (INTASC: Principles *2, 3, 4, 5, 9*)

## Collaborative Work: Balancing Individual and Group Activities

With four or five other students in the class, discuss how much of the curriculum should include group activities and how much

should involve individual activities at the early childhood, elementary, middle, high school, and college levels. Describe your group's thoughts. Also discuss whether some subject areas might lend themselves better than others to group activities. (INTASC: Principles *1, 3, 4, 5*)

## Research/Field Experience: Practical Applications of Social Constructivism

Beyond a teacher and a room full of students, what resources do the two social constructivist programs that were described in the chapter require? How practical is it to use these programs on a widespread basis? Write your responses. (INTASC: Principles *4, 5, 7*).

*Go to the Online Learning Center for downloadable portfolio templates.*

# STUDY, PRACTICE, AND SUCCEED

Visit www.mhhe.com/santrockep5e to review the chapter with self-grading quizzes and self-assessments, to apply the chapter material to

two more Crack the Case studies, and for suggested activities to develop your teaching portfolio.

## CHAPTER 11

# LEARNING AND COGNITION IN THE CONTENT AREAS

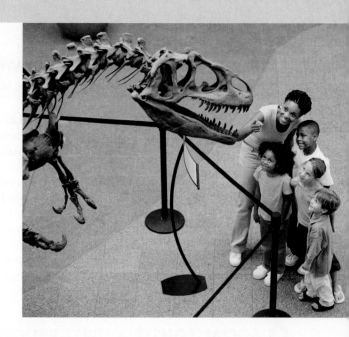

*Meaning is not given to us but by us.*

—Eleanor Duckworth
*Contemporary American Educator*

## Learning **Goals**

**1** Distinguish between expert knowledge and pedagogical content knowledge.

**2** Explain how reading develops, and discuss some useful approaches to teaching reading.

**3** Describe how writing develops, and discuss some useful approaches to teaching writing.

**4** Characterize how mathematical thinking develops, and identify some issues related to teaching mathematics.

**5** Identify some challenges and strategies related to teaching children how to think scientifically.

**6** Summarize how learning in social studies is becoming more constructivist.

# Teaching **Stories**   Wendy Nelson Kauffman

Wendy Nelson Kauffman teaches social studies to tenth- and twelfth-grade students at a Bloomfield, Connecticut, high school. Wendy turned to teaching after a career in journalism that left her feeling unfulfilled. Among the many activities she has students do to improve their thinking and writing skills are

- Writing autobiographies each fall
- Keeping journals all year and writing position papers on historical questions
- Participating in dramatic role-playing
- Carrying out debates and holding "town meetings" to discuss contentious issues such as racial problems
- Interpreting political cartoons and songs
- Making posters

- Engaging in real-world learning experiences—these have included a visit to Ellis Island, after which students acted out immigrant experiences in a school-wide performance, and interviews with retirement home residents about the Great Depression and World War II for an oral history book

In Wendy's words, "Certain skills they have to learn: writing, critical thinking, class participation. If you mix that with something that's fun for them and plays to their strengths, I think it makes it easier for them to do the hard work in class." Wendy also mentors new teachers, about whom she says, "I want them to feel safe, I want them to take risks, I want them to become who they want to be."

_____

(*Source: USA Today,* October 15, 2003.)

# Preview

In previous chapters we described the basic principles of children's learning and cognition. In this chapter we will apply these principles to learning and cognition in five content areas: reading, writing, mathematics, science, and social studies. We begin the chapter by revisiting the concept of expertise and exploring the distinction between expert knowledge and pedagogical content knowledge, the kind of knowledge that teachers like Wendy Nelson Kauffman use to teach effectively.

##  EXPERT KNOWLEDGE AND PEDAGOGICAL CONTENT KNOWLEDGE

In Chapter 8, we discussed the distinction between experts and novices. We saw that sometimes individuals who are experts in the content of a particular area, such as mathematics or biology, aren't good at teaching it in ways that others can effectively learn. These individuals have *expert knowledge* but lack *pedagogical content knowledge.* Let's examine the difference between the two types of knowledge.

**Expert knowledge,** sometimes referred to as *subject matter knowledge,* means excellent knowledge about the content of a particular discipline. Clearly, expert knowledge is important—how can teachers teach students something that they don't understand themselves? However, some individuals with expert knowledge about a particular subject area, such as reading, math, or science, have difficulty understanding the subject matter in a way that allows them to teach it effectively to others. The term *expert blind spots* has been used to describe the gap between what an expert knows and what students know (Nathan & Petrosino, 2003). Too often experts (teachers) don't communicate all of the information and steps necessary for students (novices) to learn something (Bransford, Darling-Hammond, & LePage, 2005).

What teachers need in addition to expert knowledge is **pedagogical content knowledge**—knowledge about how to effectively teach a particular discipline. Both expert knowledge and pedagogical content knowledge are required for being an expert teacher. *Expert teachers* know the structure of their disciplines, and this knowledge gives them the ability to create cognitive road maps that guide the assignments they give to students, the assessments they use to evaluate students' progress, and the types of questions and answers they generate in class (National Research Council,

*What is pedagogical content knowledge? How is it different from expert knowledge?*

**expert knowledge** Also called *subject matter knowledge;* means excellent knowledge about the content of a particular discipline.

**pedagogical content knowledge** Knowledge about how to effectively teach a particular discipline.

**Thinking Back/Thinking Forward**

Teachers can guide students in learning a number of effective strategies and metacognitive strategies for learning. Chapter 8, p. 287

2005). Being an expert teacher in a particular discipline also involves being aware of which aspects of the discipline are especially difficult or easy for students to learn.

In previous chapters, we explored general teaching strategies that are effective across all disciplines. For example, a good teacher in any discipline asks questions that stimulate students' curiosity, encourages students to go beyond the surface of a topic and gain a depth of understanding about a topic, and pays attention to individual variations in students' learning (Borich, 2011; Eby, Herrell, & Jordan, 2011). However, pedagogical content knowledge about particular disciplines goes beyond these general teaching strategies (Cathcart & others, 2011; Fraser-Abder, 2011). We will examine five content areas—reading, writing, mathematics, science, and social studies—and point out effective teaching strategies in each one.

## Review, Reflect, and Practice

**1** Distinguish between expert knowledge and pedagogical content knowledge.

**REVIEW**

- How is expert knowledge different from pedagogical content knowledge?

**REFLECT**

- Have you ever had a teacher who was clearly an expert in his or her discipline but not a good teacher? What pedagogical content knowledge was missing?

**PRAXIS™ PRACTICE**

1. Maria is frustrated with her calculus teacher, a former university math professor. He knows his math but has a difficult time communicating his knowledge to his students. In fact, half the time in class, Maria has no idea what he is talking about. When she asks for help, he is willing to meet with her, but his explanations are no clearer than they are in class. Which statement best characterizes Maria's calculus teacher?
   a. He has both expert knowledge in calculus and pedagogical content knowledge.
   b. He has expert knowledge in calculus but lacks pedagogical content knowledge.
   c. He lacks expert knowledge in calculus but has pedagogical content knowledge.
   d. He lacks both expert knowledge in calculus and pedagogical content knowledge.

*Please see the answer key at the end of the book.*

**2 READING**

| A Developmental Model of Reading | Approaches to Reading | Cognitive Approaches | Social Constructivist Approaches |

Reading expert Steve Stahl (2002) argues that the three main goals of reading instruction should be to help children (1) automatically recognize words, (2) comprehend text, and (3) become motivated to read and appreciate reading. These goals are inter-related. If children cannot recognize words automatically, their comprehension suffers. If they cannot comprehend the text, they are unlikely to be motivated to read it.

Recent analyses by Rich Mayer (2004, 2008) focused on the cognitive processes a child needs to go through in order to read a printed word. In his view, the three processes are as follows:

1. *Being aware of sound units in words,* which consists of recognizing phonemes
2. *Decoding words,* which involves converting printed words into sounds
3. *Accessing word meaning,* which consists of finding a mental representation of a word's meaning

How do children develop the reading skills that Stahl and Mayer describe? What is the best way to teach children to read? How can children construct their reading skills? These are among the main questions that we will examine in our coverage of reading. As we discuss these questions, you will see that teachers play a key role in the development of children's reading skills (Christie, Enz, & Vukevich, 2011; Fox & Alexander, 2011; Tompkins, 2011).

## A DEVELOPMENTAL MODEL OF READING

In one view, reading skills develop in five stages (Chall, 1979). The age boundaries are approximate and do not apply to every child. For example, some children learn to read before they enter first grade. Nonetheless, Chall's stages convey a general sense of the developmental changes involved in learning to read:

DEVELOPMENT

- *Stage 0.* From birth to first grade, children master several prerequisites for reading. Many learn the left-to-right progression and order of reading, how to identify the letters of the alphabet, and how to write their names. Some learn to read words that commonly appear on signs. As a result of watching TV shows such as *Sesame Street* and attending preschool and kindergarten programs, many young children today develop greater knowledge about reading at earlier ages than in the past.
- *Stage 1.* In first and second grade, many children begin to read. They do so by learning to sound out words (that is, translate individual letters or groups of letters into sounds and blend sounds into words). During this stage, they also complete their learning of letter names and sounds.
- *Stage 2.* In second and third grade, children become more fluent at retrieving individual words and other reading skills. However, at this stage, reading is still not used much for learning. The mechanical demands of learning to read are so taxing at this point that children have few resources left over to process the content.
- *Stage 3.* In fourth through eighth grade, children become increasingly able to obtain new information from print. The change from stage 2 to stage 3 involves a shift from "learning to read" to "reading to learn." In stage 3 children still have difficulty understanding information presented from multiple perspectives within the same story. For children who haven't yet learned to read, a downward spiral begins that leads to serious difficulties in many academic subjects.
- *Stage 4.* In the high school years, many students become fully competent readers. They develop the ability to understand material written from many different perspectives. This allows them to engage in sometimes more sophisticated discussions of literature, history, economics, and politics. It is no accident that great novels are not presented to students until high school, because understanding the novels requires advanced reading.

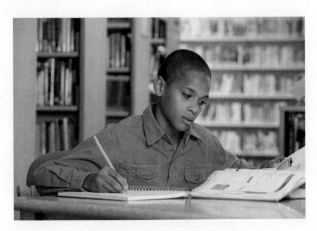

*What are some developmental changes in reading?*

This teacher is helping a student sound out words. Researchers have found that phonics instruction is a key aspect of teaching students to read, especially beginning readers and students with weak reading skills.

---

Thinking Back/Thinking Forward

A number of changes characterize children's language development as they go through infancy, early childhood, middle and late childhood, and adolescence. Chapter 2, p. 59

---

**phonics approach** An approach that emphasizes that reading instruction should teach phonics and its basic rules for translating written symbols into sounds and that early reading instruction should use simplified materials.

**whole-language approach** An approach that stresses that reading instruction should parallel children's natural language learning and that reading materials should be whole and meaningful.

As the previous discussion has implied, *reading* is the ability to understand written discourse. Children cannot be said to read if all they can do is respond to flash cards. Good readers have mastered the basic language rules of phonology, morphology, syntax, and semantics that we discussed in Chapter 2.

## APPROACHES TO READING

What are some approaches to teaching children how to read? Education and language experts continue to debate how children should be taught to read. Currently, debate focuses on the phonics approach versus the whole-language approach (Beatty & Pratt, 2011; Otto, 2010).

The **phonics approach** emphasizes that reading instruction should focus on phonics and basic rules for translating written symbols into sounds. Early reading instruction in this approach involves simplified materials. Only after children have learned the correspondence rules that relate spoken phonemes to the alphabet letters that represent them are they given complex reading materials, such as books and poems (Fox, 2010). A recent study revealed that a computer-based phonics program improved first-grade students' reading skills (Savage & others, 2009).

By contrast, the **whole-language approach** stresses that reading instruction should parallel children's natural language learning. Reading materials should be whole and meaningful. That is, children should be given material in its complete form, such as stories and poems, so that they learn to understand language's communicative function. Reading should be connected with listening and writing skills. Although there are variations in whole-language programs, most share the premise that reading should be integrated with other skills and subjects, such as science and social studies, and that it should focus on real-world material. Thus, a class might read newspapers, magazines, or books, then write about and discuss them. In some whole-language classes, beginning readers are taught to recognize whole words or even entire sentences, and to use the context of what they are reading to guess at unfamiliar words.

Which approach is better? Children can benefit from both approaches, but instruction in phonics needs to be emphasized, especially in kindergarten and the first grade (Cunningham & Allington, 2011; Fox, 2010). A recent study revealed that in a school where students showed high achievement in reading, both phonics and whole language were emphasized (Pressley & others, 2007a). In this study, intensive instruction in phonics improved the reading achievement of students with weak reading skills, whereas more holistic instruction was linked with higher achievement for students with stronger reading skills. As Mayer (2008) and an increasing number of experts in the field of reading now conclude, direct instruction in phonological training is a key aspect of learning to read (Cunningham, 2009; Fox, 2010; Fox & Alexander, 2011).

Conclusions reached by the National Reading Panel (2000) suggest that children benefit from *guided oral* reading—that is, from reading aloud with guidance and feedback. Learning strategies for reading comprehension—such as monitoring one's own reading progress and summarizing—also help children (Fisher, Frey, & Berkin, 2009).

In one study, Michael Pressley and his colleagues (2001) examined literacy instruction in five U.S. classrooms. In the most effective classrooms, teachers exhibited excellent classroom management based on positive reinforcement and cooperation; balanced teaching of skills, literature, and writing; scaffolding and matching of task demands to students' skill level; encouragement of student self-regulation; and strong connections across subject areas. In general, the extensive observations did not support any particular reading approach (such as whole-language or phonics); rather, excellent instruction involved multiple, well-integrated components. An important point in this study is that effective reading instruction involves more than a specific reading approach—it also includes effective classroom management, encouragement of self-regulation, and other components.

Reading, like other important skills, takes time and effort (Jalongo, 2011; Ogle & Beers, 2009). In a national assessment, children in the fourth grade had higher scores on a national reading test when they read 11 or more pages daily for school and homework (National Assessment of Educational Progress, 2000) (see Figure 11.1). Teachers who required students to read a great deal on a daily basis had students who were more proficient at reading than teachers who required little reading by their students.

Reading takes time and effort. *What can you do as a teacher to encourage children to read more books?*

## COGNITIVE APPROACHES

Cognitive approaches to reading emphasize decoding and comprehending words, prior knowledge, and developing expert-reading strategies.

### Decoding and Comprehending Words
At the beginning of our discussion of reading, we described Mayer's (2008) view that decoding words is a key cognitive process in learning to read. The cognitive approach emphasizes the cognitive processes involved in decoding and comprehending words (Gunning, 2010). Important in this regard are certain metacognitive skills and increasing automaticity that is characterized by fluency (Tompkins, 2011).

Metacognition is involved in reading in the sense that good readers develop control of their own reading skills and understand how reading works (Williams & Atkins, 2010). For example, good readers know that it is important to comprehend the "gist" of what an author is saying.

Teachers can help students develop good metacognitive strategies for reading by getting them to monitor their own reading, especially when they run into difficulties in their reading (Fisher, Frey, & Berkin, 2009). Here are some metacognitive strategies that teachers can help students use to improve their reading (Pressley & Harris, 2006):

- Overview text before reading.
- Look for important information while reading and pay more attention to it than other information; ask yourself questions about the important ideas or relate them to something you already know.
- Attempt to determine the meaning of words not recognized (use the words around a word to figure out its meaning, use a dictionary, or temporarily ignore it and wait for further clarification).
- Monitor text comprehension.
- Understand relationships between parts of text.
- Recognize when you might need to go back and reread a passage (you didn't understand it, to clarify an important idea, it seemed important to remember, or to underline or summarize for study).
- Adjust pace of reading depending on the difficulty of the material.

When students process information automatically, they do so with little or no conscious effort (Tompkins, 2011). When word recognition occurs rapidly, understanding

**FIGURE 11.1** THE RELATION OF READING ACHIEVEMENT TO NUMBER OF PAGES READ DAILY

In the recent analysis of reading in the fourth grade in the National Assessment of Educational Progress (2000), reading more pages daily in school and as part of homework assignments was related to higher scores on a reading test in which scores ranged from 0 to 500.

*What characterizes the cognitive approaches to reading?*

of its meaning also often follows in a rapid fashion (Stanovich, 1994). Many beginning or poor readers do not recognize words automatically (Rasinski, Homan, & Biggs, 2009). Their processing capacity is consumed by the demands of word recognition, so they have less capacity to devote to comprehension of groupings of words as phrases or sentences. As their processing of words and passages becomes more automatic, it is said that their reading becomes more fluent (Wolsey & Fisher, 2009). Students' fluency often improves when they (Mayer, 2008) (1) hear others read a passage before and after they read it, which is called *assisted practice;* (2) spend considerable time at reading various passages; and (3) speak with appropriate expression and rhythm in oral reading. A recent study revealed that teachers' knowledge about reading fluency was linked to first-grade students' decoding growth and second-grade students' oral reading fluency growth (Lane & others, 2009).

**Prior Knowledge**   Another emphasis in the cognitive approach to reading is that students' prior knowledge about a topic is related to what they will remember from reading about the topic and their ability to make correct inferences about the material they read (Mayer, 2008). If teachers detect that students don't have adequate knowledge about a topic they are going to read about, what needs to be done? For one, teachers need to evaluate whether the reading material is too difficult for students and should be replaced with something more appropriate for the students' reading level. Also, teachers can provide prereading activities related to the topic.

**Developing Expert-Reading Strategies**   In the cognitive approach, researchers have searched for the underlying cognitive processes that explain reading (Snowling & Gobel, 2011). This search has led to an interest in strategies, especially the strategies of expert readers compared with those of novice readers (Allington, 2009). Researchers advise teachers to guide students in developing good reading strategies.

Michael Pressley and his colleagues (1992) developed the **transactional strategy instruction approach,** a cognitive approach to reading that emphasizes instruction in strategies (especially metacognitive strategies). In their view, strategies control students' abilities to remember what they read. It is especially important to teach students metacognitive strategies to monitor their reading progress. Summarizing is also thought to be an important reading strategy. In the strategy approach, authors of teachers' manuals for subjects other than reading per se are encouraged to include information about the importance of reading strategies, how and when to use particular strategies, and prompts to remind students about using strategies.

## SOCIAL CONSTRUCTIVIST APPROACHES

The social constructivist approaches bring the social aspects of reading to the forefront (Ariza & Lapp, 2011; Hiebert & Raphael, 1996). The contribution of the social context in helping children learn to read includes such factors as how much emphasis the culture places on reading, the extent to which parents have exposed their children to books before they enter formal schooling, the teacher's communication skills, the extent to which teachers give students opportunities to discuss what they have read, and the district-mandated reading curriculum (McGee & Richgels, 2008). Whereas cognitive constructivists emphasize the student's construction of meaning, social constructivists stress that meaning is *socially negotiated.* In other words, meaning involves not only the reader's contribution but also the social context and the purpose for reading (Ariza & Lapp, 2011). Social constructivist approaches emphasize the importance of giving students opportunities for engaging

**Thinking Back/Thinking Forward**

The social constructivist approach emphasizes the social contexts of learning and that knowledge is mutually built and constructed. Chapter 10, p. 333

**transactional strategy instruction approach**
A cognitive approach to reading that emphasizes instruction in strategies, especially metacognitive strategies.

in meaningful dialogue about their reading. One way of doing this is through reciprocal teaching.

**Reciprocal Teaching**   In our discussion of the Fostering a Community of Learners (FCL) program in Chapter 10, we described **reciprocal teaching** in terms of students taking turns leading a small-group discussion. Reciprocal teaching also can involve a teacher and a student. In reciprocal teaching, teachers initially explain the strategies and model how to use them to make sense of the text. Then they ask students to demonstrate the strategies, giving them support as they learn them. As in scaffolding, the teacher gradually assumes a less active role, letting the student assume more initiative. For example, Annemarie Palincsar and Ann Brown (1984) used reciprocal teaching to improve students' abilities to enact certain strategies to improve their reading comprehension. In this teacher-scaffolded instruction, teachers worked

Students engaged in a reciprocal teaching group. *What characterizes reciprocal teaching in reading?*

with students to help them generate questions about the text they had read, clarify what they did not understand, summarize the text, and make predictions.

Research on reciprocal teaching suggests that it is a very effective strategy for improving reading comprehension (Webb & Palincsar, 1996). For example, a recent study examined the influence of reading strategies (summarizing, questioning, clarifying, and predicting) in reciprocal teaching small groups, pairs, and instructor-guided small groups (Sporer, Brunstein, & Kieschke, 2009). Compared to a control group of students who received traditional instruction, students who received strategy instruction achieved higher scores in reading comprehension. Further, students who practiced reciprocal teaching in small groups scored higher on a standardized reading achievement test than students in instructor-guided and traditional instruction groups.

RESEARCH

**School/Family/Community Connections**   From the social constructivist perspective, schools are not the only sociocultural context that is important in reading. Families and communities are also important (Ariza & Lapp, 2011). Of special concern are the language experiences of students from low-income families (Pogrow, 2009). In one research study, on average, young children in welfare homes heard about 600 words an hour, whereas young children in professional families heard about 2,100 words an hour (Hart & Risley, 1995). Also, children in welfare homes received only half as much language experience in their early years as children in middle-income families. And children in high-income families had twice as much language experience as even children in middle-income families.

At-risk students who do not read outside school fall further behind as they go through the elementary school years. Many parents of at-risk students have their own reading difficulties, as well as problems in obtaining books (Gunning, 2010).

*What are some important aspects of social contexts that influence children's reading?*

**reciprocal teaching**  A learning arrangement in which students take turns leading a small-group discussion; can also involve teacher-scaffolded instruction.

## TEACHING CONNECTIONS: Best Practices
### Strategies for Helping Struggling Readers

1. *Focus on phonemic and phonetic awareness in younger students (Wanzek, Dickson, Bursuck, & White, 2000).* Young struggling readers can make tremendous progress through programs that focus on learning letter-sound relationships, which helps with the decoding process that is so important to developing fluency.

2. *Work on comprehension.* Knowing how to decode does not necessarily indicate understanding of what has been read. Practices that facilitate development of comprehension include summarizing and predicting.

3. *Teach specific strategies to promote comprehension and retention of text material.* Around the fourth grade, the focus in reading shifts from learning to read to reading to learn. At this point comprehension is extremely important. Struggling readers will need to learn strategies to facilitate this shift. The PQ4R method (Thomas & Robinson, 1972) discussed in Chapter 8 may be helpful in this regard.

I recently asked teachers how they help students to read more effectively. Following are their responses.

**EARLY CHILDHOOD**   With very young children, it is essential to have a print-rich environment in which they can see words and phrases everywhere. Our classroom  is filled with storybooks, picture dictionaries, magazines, and so on. Also, every object in the classroom is labeled—for example, doors, chairs, windows, and bookshelves, so children associate the word printed on the label with the object. And children's names are printed in many places so that they get used to seeing it in print.

—**VALARIE GORHAM**, *Kiddie Quarters, Inc.*

**ELEMENTARY SCHOOL: GRADES K–5**   I help my second-graders read more effectively by stressing reading for comprehension. That said, I incorporate prereading, during-reading, and postreading comprehension strategies. In  prereading, I state the purpose of the reading and preview pictures, titles, headings, boldface words, and so on. During reading we check the selection for meaning (Does it make sense? Any confusing words?) and reread for understanding. In postreading, we check to see if we know what was read, summarize, and reflect.

—**ELIZABETH FRASCELLA**, *Clinton Elementary School*

**MIDDLE SCHOOL: GRADES 6–8**   One of the best ways to become a better reader is to read! Every time I cover a historical era with my seventh-graders, I also make  them aware of the related books that are available in our school library. Our librarian will pull corresponding books off the shelves and display them for students. Even the most ardent "nonreader" has a book he or she likes; the trick is to find the right book!

—**MARK FODNESS**, *Bemidji Middle School*

**HIGH SCHOOL: GRADES 9–12**   With the way we teach reading in America, it is no wonder many students hate it. We teachers make reading so painful and serious—  for example, we pick apart novels, we quiz and test to death. Teachers need to show students that reading is fun—they should read what students are reading; "sell" the books to students by talking about the most interesting parts; let students see them reading; and be excited and energetic when discussing new books in class.

—**JENNIFER HEITER**, *Bremen High School*

## Review, Reflect, and Practice

**2** Explain how reading develops, and discuss some useful approaches to teaching reading.

**REVIEW**

- What happens at each stage in Chall's developmental model of reading?
- What are some differences between the whole-language approach and the phonics approach to teaching reading? Which approach is better?
- What are the key ideas in cognitive approaches to reading?
- What are the important features of social constructivist approaches to reading?

**REFLECT**

- What would be some of the key considerations in a balanced view of teaching reading?

**PRAXIS™ PRACTICE**

1. Kareem is reading his science text. He is taking notes as he reads to help him remember the information. He has learned much about science from his text this year. For instance, he learned that there are many different kinds of rocks that vary in how they were formed, their hardness, and their color. However, when presented with conflicting views on a scientific matter, Kareem is easily confused. Which of Chall's (1979) developmental stages of reading best characterizes Kareem?
   a. stage 1
   b. stage 2
   c. stage 3
   d. stage 4

2. Which of the following is the best example of the use of the whole-language approach to teaching reading?
   a. Ms. Tillman uses flash cards to help her students develop their sight vocabulary.
   b. Ms. Muhammad's students are immersed in literature. They read various types of literature and write about what they have read.
   c. Ms. Orton uses a phonics workbook to help her students develop their decoding skills.
   d. Ms. Wade's students use a computer game to practice their reading skills. A character says a word, and the student clicks on the correct printed word.

3. Which of the following is the best example of a teacher using a cognitive approach to teaching reading?
   a. Ms. Beckham uses flashcards to help students learn new words and reinforces them with giving candy for correct responses.
   b. Ms. Gomez has her students choose from a variety of books to read. Those students who read a particular book then meet to discuss the book on a regular basis.
   c. Ms. Owen emphasizes the importance of using context clues to help determine the meaning of new words.
   d. Ms. Ronaldo has her students write each word they miss on a spelling pretest five times to help them remember the word.

4. Which of the following is the best example of a teacher using a social constructivist approach to teaching reading?
   a. Ms. Beckham uses flashcards to help students learn new words and reinforces them with giving candy for correct responses.

*(continued)*

## Review, Reflect, and Practice

### PRAXIS™ PRACTICE (CONTINUED)

b. Ms. Gomez has her students choose from a variety of books to read. Those students who read a particular book then meet to discuss the book on a regular basis.

c. Ms. Owen emphasizes the importance of using context clues to help determine the meaning of new words.

d. Ms. Ronaldo has her students write each word they miss on a spelling pretest five times to help them remember the word.

*Please see the answer key at the end of the book.*

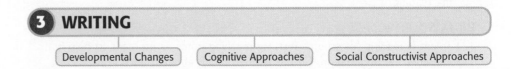

**3** **WRITING**

| Developmental Changes | Cognitive Approaches | Social Constructivist Approaches |

RESEARCH

There are increasing concerns about students' current writing competence (Cunningham & Allington, 2011; Harris & others, 2010). One study revealed that 70 to 75 percent of U.S. students in grades 4 through 12 are low-achieving writers (Persky, Daane, & Jin, 2003). College instructors report that 50 percent of high school graduates are not prepared for college-level writing (Achieve, Inc., 2005).

A recent study of U.S. language arts, social studies, and science high school teachers raises concerns about the quality of writing instruction in U.S. high schools (Kluhara, Graham, & Hawken, 2009). The teachers in this study report that their college teacher education program inadequately prepared them to teach writing in high school. The study also found that writing assignments infrequently involved analysis and interpretation, and that almost 50 percent of teachers did not assign any multiparagraph writing assignments in the span of one month's time. Two-thirds of U.S. students also indicate that their writing assignments total less than one hour per week (Applebee & Langer, 2006).

RESEARCH

As with reading, teachers play a critical role in students' development of writing skills (Cunningham & Cunningham, 2010; De La Paz & McCutchen, 2011; Tompkins, 2011b). The observations of classrooms made by Michael Pressley and his colleagues (2007b) revealed that students became good writers when teachers spent considerable time on writing instruction and were passionate about teaching students to write. Their observations also indicated that classrooms with students who scored high on writing assessments had walls that overflowed with examples of effective writing, whereas it was much harder to find such examples on the walls of classrooms that had many students who scored low on writing assessments.

Our further coverage of writing focuses on these questions: How do writing skills develop? What are cognitive and social constructivist approaches to writing?

### DEVELOPMENTAL CHANGES

DEVELOPMENT

Children's writing emerges out of their early scribbles, which appear at around 2 to 3 years of age. In early childhood, children's motor skills usually become well enough developed for them to begin printing letters and their name (Morrow, 2009). In the United States most 4-year-olds can print their first name. Five-year-olds can reproduce letters and copy several short words. As they develop their printing skills, children gradually learn to distinguish between the distinctive characteristics of letters, such as whether the lines are curved or straight, open or closed, and so on. Through the early elementary grades, many children still continue to reverse letters such as *b* and *d* and *p* and *q*. At this point in development, if other aspects of the child's development are normal, these letter reversals are not a predictor of literacy problems.

As they begin to write, children often invent spellings of words. They usually do this by relying on the sounds of words they hear as clues for how to spell. Teachers and parents should encourage children's early writing without being overly concerned about the proper formation of letters or correct spelling. Such printing errors should be viewed as a natural part of the young child's growth, not scrutinized and criticized. Spelling and printing corrections can be made in positive ways and judiciously enough to avoid dampening early enjoyment and spontaneity in writing.

Like becoming a good reader, becoming a good writer takes many years and lots of practice (Christie, Enz, & Vukelich, 2011; Melzi & Ely, 2009). Children should be given many writing opportunities in the elementary and secondary school years (Cunningham & Cunningham, 2010). As their language and cognitive skills improve with good instruction, so will their writing skills. For example, developing a more sophisticated understanding of syntax and grammar serves as an underpinning for better writing. So do such cognitive skills as organization and logical reasoning. Through elementary, middle, and high school, students develop increasingly sophisticated methods of organizing their ideas. In early elementary school they narrate and describe or write short poems. In late elementary and middle school they move to projects such as book reports that combine narration with more reflection and analysis. In high school they become more skilled at forms of exposition that do not depend on narrative structure (Conley, 2008).

A recent meta-analysis (use of statistical techniques to combine the results of studies) revealed that the following interventions were the most effective in improving fourth-through twelfth-grade students' writing quality: (1) strategy instruction, (2) summarization, (3) peer assistance, and (4) setting goals (Graham & Perin, 2007).

## COGNITIVE APPROACHES

Cognitive approaches to writing emphasize many of the same themes that we discussed with regard to reading, such as constructing meaning and developing strategies (Graham & Olinghouse, 2009). Planning, problem solving, revising, and metacognitive strategies are thought to be especially important in improving students' writing.

**Planning** Planning, which includes outlining and organizing content information, is an important aspect of writing (Tompkins, 2010a,b; Mayer, 2008). Teachers should show students how to outline and organize a paper and give feedback about their efforts. Figure 11.2 provides a model for helping students plan their compositions to meet a deadline.

**Problem Solving** Much of the instruction in writing in schools involves teaching students how to write sentences and paragraphs properly. However, there is more to writing than avoiding run-on sentences or making sure that paragraphs support topic

## THROUGH THE EYES OF STUDENTS

### The Devl and the Babe Goste

Anna Mudd is the 6-year-old author of "The Devl and the Babe Goste." Anna has been writing stories for at least 2 years. Her story includes poetic images, sophisticated syntax, and vocabulary that reflect advances in language development.

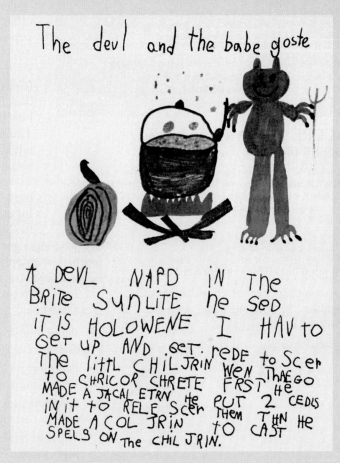

*Source:* "The devl and the babe goste" reprinted by permission of Maryanne Wolf, Ph.D., from Dickinson, D., Wolf, M., & Stotsky, S. (1993). "Words Move": The interwoven development of oral and written language in the school years. In Jean Berko Gleason (Ed.), *The Development of Language,* 3rd ed. New York: Macmillan. pp. 388–390, Ten themes that should be emphasized in courses in the social sciences: From National Council for the Social Sciences, *National Standards for Social Studies Teachers* (2000). © National Council for the Social Studies. Reprinted by permission.

RESEARCH

| | |
|---|---|
| One to two months before the deadline | Select topic. Map ideas. Develop writing plan. Begin to develop a thesis statement. Start research. |
| Two weeks before the deadline | Develop individual sections of paper. Revise with vigor. Complete research. Finalize thesis statement. |
| The week before the deadline | Polish the individual sections of the paper. Create an interesting title. Check references for accuracy. Get some feedback. |
| The night before the deadline | Combine the parts of the paper. Print the final draft. Proofread the paper. Assemble the paper. |

**FIGURE 11.2** A SAMPLE TIMETABLE FOR A WRITING DEADLINE

From John W. Santrock and Jane S. Halonen, Your Guide to College Success: Strategies for Achieving Your Goals, 2nd ed., p. 225. © 2002 Wadsworth, a part of Cengage Learning, Inc. Reproduced by permission. www.cengage.com/permissions

**Thinking Back/Thinking Forward**

Metacognition involves cognition about cognition, or knowing about knowing. Chapter 8, p. 284

RESEARCH

sentences (Cunningham & Allington, 2011; Harris & others, 2010). More fundamentally, writing is a broader sort of problem solving (Mayer, 2008). One psychologist called the problem-solving process in writing "the making of meaning" (Kellogg, 1994).

As problem solvers, writers need to establish goals and work to attain them. It also is helpful to think of writers as constrained by their need for integrated understanding of the subject, knowledge of how the language system works, and the writing problem itself. The writing problem includes the purpose of the paper, the audience, and the role of the writer in the paper to be produced (Flower & Hayes, 1981). A student who is having a problem may be having difficulty with any one of these aspects of writing. Identifying the specific difficulty is the first step in helping the student become a better writer.

**Revising** Revising is a major component of successful writing (Gunning, 2010). Revising involves writing multiple drafts, getting feedback from individuals who are knowledgeable about writing, and learning how to use the critical feedback to improve the writing. It also includes detecting and correcting errors (Ogle & Beers, 2009). Researchers have found that older and more-skilled writers are more likely to revise their writing than younger and less-skilled writers (Hayes & Flower, 1986).

**Metacognition and Strategies** Emphasizing knowledge of writing strategies moves into the area of metacognition, which we discussed in Chapter 8. Monitoring one's writing progress is especially important in becoming a good writer (Harris & others, 2010). This includes being receptive to feedback and applying what one learns in writing one paper to making the next paper better (McKeown & Beck, 2010).

A recent research review revealed that the following are effective writing strategies that should be taught to secondary school students (Graham & Perin, 2007):

- *Prewriting.* A good strategy is to have students engage in prewriting activities that involve generating or organizing ideas for their composition.
- *Planning, revising, and editing.* These are critical skills in becoming a good writer, and students need considerable practice in developing and using them.
- *Summarization.* Teachers need to explicitly and systematically teach students how to summarize the text they write.
- *Sentence combining.* Students need to practice constructing more complex, sophisticated sentences.

## SOCIAL CONSTRUCTIVIST APPROACHES

As in reading, social constructivist approaches emphasize that writing is best understood as being culturally embedded and socially constructed rather than being internally generated.

**The Social Context of Writing** The social constructivist perspective focuses on the social context in which writing is produced (Ariza & Lapp, 2011). Students need to participate in a writing community to understand author-reader relationships and learn to recognize how their perspective might differ from that of others (Hiebert & Raphael, 1996).

Some students bring a rich background of writing experiences and encouragement to write

PEANUTS © United Features Syndicate, Inc.

to the classroom; others do not (Moore-Hart, 2010). In some classrooms the teacher places a high value on writing; in others the teacher treats writing as being less important. A recent study revealed that in a school where students showed high achievement in writing and reading, language arts were given a high priority by the principal and teachers (Pressley & others, 2007b). The principal directed resources toward reading and writing instruction, including a considerable expansion of the number of books in the school's library and encouragement of field trips related to language arts.

**Meaningful Writing and Student-Teacher Writing Conferences** According to the social constructivist approach, students' writing should include opportunities to create "real" texts, in the sense of writing about personally meaningful situations. For example, consider Anthony, whose teacher frequently asks students to write about personal experiences. He wrote about his grandmother's life and death, and his teacher gave him considerable support for writing about this emotional experience. Student-teacher writing conferences play an important support role in helping students become better writers (Moore-Hart, 2010).

**Peer Collaboration and Editing** While working in groups, writers experience the processes of inquiry, clarification, and elaboration that are important in good writing (Webb & Palincsar, 1996). Also, students often benefit from editing other students' writing.

Students frequently bring diverse experiences to bear when they collaborate and coauthor papers. Such rich, shared collaboration can produce new insights into what to write about and how (Harris & others, 2010). By contrast, writing simply to meet the teacher's expectations often produces constrained, imitative, and conforming results. In peer writing groups, teacher expectations are often less apparent. In addition to the benefits of peer collaboration in writing, students' writing often improves when they edit other students' writing.

**School-Community Connections** In the social constructivist approach, it is important to connect students' experiences at school with the world outside the classroom (Combs, 2010). A good strategy is to involve the writing community in your class. Look around your community and think about expert writers you could invite to your classroom to discuss their work. Most communities have such experts, such as journalists and other authors and editors. One of the four most successful middle schools in the United States identified by Joan Lipsitz (1984) built a special Author's Week into its curriculum. Based on students' interest, availability, and diversity, authors are invited to discuss their craft with students. Students sign up to meet individual authors. Before they meet the author, they are required to read at least one of the author's books. Students prepare questions for their author sessions. In some cases, authors come to the class for several days to work with students on their writing projects.

In the course of our discussion of reading and writing, we have described a number of ideas that can be used in the classroom. To evaluate your reading and writing experiences, complete Self-Assessment 11.1.

## THROUGH THE EYES OF STUDENTS

### Writing Self-Evaluations

San Francisco fifth-grade teacher Keren Abra periodically asks her students to evaluate their writing for their writing portfolios. Here are several of her students' comments toward the end of the school year.

> I am in fifth grade right now and I love writing. Anytime that I get to write I will; as far as I can remember I have loved writing. I feel that my writing has developed since fourth grade and I am pleased with my writing. Some authors might not like their writing unlike me; I have *never* thrown away any of my writing. I love to share my writing and give and get ideas from other writers. . . . If I could describe myself as a writer I would say (not to brag) that I was a descriptive, imaginative, captivating writer.

*Michelle*

> I think writing a story is easy because there is so much to write about and if I have to write about a certain thing there are also more things to do with the story. . . . If someone read my writing they would think I probably am a happy and energetic kid. They will think this because most of my stories are upbeat.

*Sarah*

> I feel that when I'm writing I could do better. I could do better especially on spelling. When I was in kindergarten we did not do a lot of writing. When I was in third grade I did not like writing. It was scary learning new things about writing. I'm in fifth grade and I love to write but sometimes it annoys me that I can't spell that well. One thing I like about my writing is the way I put action into all of my work because I love to get excited! I think that if someone were to read my writing uncorrected they would not be able to read it. If it was corrected I think the person would really like my story.

*Janet*

# SELF-ASSESSMENT 11.1
## Evaluating My Reading and Writing Experiences

Regardless of the academic subject or grade you teach, one of your goals should be to help students not only become competent at reading and writing but also enjoy these activities. Think about your own past and current experiences in reading and writing:

1. What made learning to read enjoyable for you?

_____

_____

2. What made learning to read difficult or unenjoyable?

_____

_____

3. How do you feel about reading now?

_____

_____

4. Do you enjoy libraries? Why or why not?

_____

_____

5. Are there reading skills that you still need to improve?

_____

_____

6. What made learning to write enjoyable for you?

_____

_____

7. What made learning to write difficult or unenjoyable?

_____

_____

8. How do you feel about writing now?

_____

_____

9. Are there writing skills that you still need to improve?

_____

_____

Based on your own experience and ideas in this chapter, how could you make learning to read and write more successful and enjoyable for your students?

I recently asked teachers how they help students to improve their writing skills. Following are their responses.

**EARLY CHILDHOOD**   Gradually, preschoolers learn to write. They start with scribbling, then move on to drawing shapes, and then move to writing basic letters. It is important to encourage and support (not correct) children while they learn and practice.

—**HEIDI KAUFMAN,** *Metro West YMCA Child Care and Educational Program*

**ELEMENTARY SCHOOL: GRADES K–5**   One way I help my fifth-graders become better writers is to compose a story myself. I start by showing them how I brainstorm writing ideas and go all the way through to writing the final copy. As I do this, I talk out loud, letting students hear my thought process and thus learn effective writing strategies.

—**CRAIG JENSEN,** *Cooper Mountain Elementary School*

**MIDDLE SCHOOL: GRADES 6–8**   Peer editing is an important part of teaching writing skills. I find it especially important to have my students edit each other's work so that they can pick up any writing errors in a classmate's paper, while learning from studying another student's writing style.

—**CASEY MAASS,** *Edison Middle School*

**HIGH SCHOOL: GRADES 9–12**   Although state standards describe which genres of writing to teach, it is up to the teacher to decide how best to teach them. I take my students through the basic writing phases: brainstorming, prewriting, outlining, first draft, revision, and final draft. I also get my students to think about style by showing them how to replace boring verbs with vivid verbs, or by deleting unnecessary adverbs and adjectives.

—**JENNIFER HEITER,** *Bremen High School*

## TEACHING CONNECTIONS: Best Practices
### Strategies for Incorporating Writing into the Curriculum

You will have many opportunities to incorporate writing into the curriculum. Here are some examples (Bruning & Horn, 2001; Halonen, 2010):

1. *Nurture positive attitudes toward writing.* This can be done by making sure that many writing tasks ensure student success and giving students choices about what they will write. Never give writing assignments as punishment. This only serves to teach students that writing is something you think of as a negative experience, therefore fostering a negative attitude toward writing.

2. *Foster student engagement through authentic writing tasks and contexts.* Encourage students to write about topics of personal interest, have students write for different audiences, and integrate writing into instruction in

other disciplines, such as science, mathematics, and social studies. Students can write letters for a variety of purposes depending on age. Younger students can write letters to family and friends. Older students can write a company or person requesting information. Still older students can write to a company or organization about a particular policy they think should be changed.

3. *Provide a supportive context for writing.* Encourage students to set writing goals, plan how to reach the goals, and monitor their progress toward the goals (see information in Chapter 7 regarding self-regulatory learning). Assist students in creating goals that are neither too challenging nor too simple. Teach writing strategies and monitor their

*(continued)*

## TEACHING CONNECTIONS: Best Practices
### Strategies for Incorporating Writing into the Curriculum

use by students. Give students feedback on their progress toward their writing goals. Encourage students to write the way professional writers do—with successive drafts until they are pleased with their product. Use peers as writing partners in literacy communities. Cross-age letter writing within the school is one way to develop a literacy community. Students in two grades partner as pen-pals and write back and forth throughout the school year.

4. *Have students write to learn.* This can work in any subject area. For example, in biology, after students have studied the adaptation of different species, ask them to write a summary of the main ideas and generate examples not described in class or the text. In addition to fostering writing skills, this is likely to enhance reading comprehension.

5. *Use free-writing assignments.* In free writing, students write whatever they are thinking about. Such assignments are usually unstructured but have time limits—usually five to ten minutes. The point here is not so much *what* students write, but *that* they write. Another option is to give students a topic about which to write for that specified time period. For example, one free-writing assignment in American history might be "Write about the American Revolution for five minutes." Free writing helps students discover new ideas, connections, and questions they might not have generated if they had not had this free-writing opportunity. They can then share these observations with the class to generate further discussion.

6. *Give students creative writing assignments.* These assignments give students opportunities to explore themselves and their world in creative, insightful ways. They might include poetry, short stories, or essays reflecting personal experiences. Younger students might create their own books, complete with illustrations. Blank books are available for purchase, or you could bind them yourself for the students.

7. *Require formal writing assignments.* These involve giving students opportunities to express themselves using an objective point of view, precise writing style, and evidence to support their conclusions. Formal writing helps students learn how to make formal arguments. High school students' formal writing should conform to a specific style manual, such as MLA or APA. For example, high school students might construct a major paper on topics such as "Global Warming: Real Fears or Hype?" or "An In-Depth Examination of Faulkner's Writing Style," or "Why People Are Prejudiced." Such writing projects stimulate students to think analytically, learn how to use

resources, and cite references. Work with students on generating topics for a paper, structuring the paper, using planning and time management skills for completing the paper in a timely manner, drafting and revising, and overcoming spelling and grammatical errors.

8. *Invite writers and authors to visit your classroom.* Look around your community—there likely are some good writers and possibly authors who would be willing to come to your classroom and talk with your students about their work. Contact a local newspaper to see if a journalist or columnist would be willing to talk with your class. People who work in libraries and bookstores likely can give you information about local writers and authors.

## THROUGH THE EYES OF TEACHERS
### Imagine the Possibilities

Beverly Gallagher, a third-grade teacher at Princeton Day School, in New Jersey, created the Imagine the Possibilities program, which brings nationally known poets and authors to her school. She phones each student's parents periodically to describe their child's progress and new interests. She invites students from higher grades to work with small groups in her class so that she can spend more one-on-one time with students. Beverly also created poetry partnerships between eleventh-graders and her third-graders in which the older and younger students collaborate to create poems. Each of her students keeps a writer's notebook to record thoughts, inspirations, and special words that intrigue them. Students get special opportunities to sit in an author's chair, where they read their writing to the class. (Source: *USA Today,* 2000.)

Beverly Gallagher, working with students to stimulate their interest in reading and writing.

## Review, Reflect, and Practice

**3** Describe how writing develops, and discuss some useful approaches to teaching writing.

### REVIEW

- What skills are acquired in writing? At what ages are they commonly acquired?
- What cognitive processes are essential to effective writing?
- What are the key ideas in social constructivist approaches to writing?

### REFLECT

- For the age group and subject you plan to teach, in what ways will the writing assignments you give to students likely be highly structured and specific? In what ways might they be flexible and open-ended?

### PRAXIS™ PRACTICE

1. Which of the following is the best example of developmentally appropriate writing instruction for first-graders?
    a. Ms. Balboa's students are learning how to spell through the use of drill and practice of specific words.
    b. Ms. Donovan carefully corrects students' grammar and spelling errors on their papers and is critical of their errors.
    c. Ms. Figo's students use invented spelling in their work, and she provides them with correct spelling but she does not criticize their efforts.
    d. Ms. Lalas' students practice writing by copying stories that she has written on the blackboard.

2. Ms. Williams emphasizes the importance of prewriting activities to her students. Which aspect of the cognitive approach to writing does she emphasize?
    a. metacognitive strategies
    b. planning
    c. problem solving
    d. revising

3. Which of the following is the best example of a social constructivist approach to writing?
    a. Ms. Reddick's students write reports on various subjects, based on research they have completed.
    b. Ms. Duhon's students write about their own personal experiences and meet with her regularly to discuss their work.
    c. Ms. Williams' students write responses to essay questions about material in their social studies text.
    d. Ms. Randolph's students choose the books they want to read and write book reports about each book that they complete.

*Please see the answer key at the end of the book.*

A major concern in math education is the number of qualified math teachers in middle and high school education in the United States. For example, approximately 50 percent of U.S. students in grades 5 to 12 learn math from teachers who did not major in mathematics or do not have a certificate in the subject—a figure significantly lower than the international average of approximately 70 percent (Augustine & others, 2007). Recall from Chapter 1 that an important aspect of becoming an excellent teacher is to have a high level of knowledge in the subject you teach. Thus, a key agenda for math education in the United States is to increase the percentage of math teachers in middle and high schools who have majored in mathematics in college by actively recruiting more math majors into education programs (National Academies, Advisors to the Nation on Science, Engineering, and Social Policy, 2009).

In our further examination of math education, we will explore these questions: What are some developmental changes in the way children think about mathematics and their math abilities at different grade levels, and how does this affect teaching? What is the biggest controversy in mathematics education today?

## DEVELOPMENTAL CHANGES

DEVELOPMENT

The National Council of Teachers of Mathematics (NCTM, 2000) has described the basic principles and standards for school mathematics at different grade levels. We will survey these for all grade levels, beginning with prekindergarten through grade 2.

**Prekindergarten Through Grade 2**   Children already have a substantial understanding of numbers before they enter first grade (Cross, Woods, & Schweingruber, 2009). Most kindergartners from middle-income families can count past 20, and many can count beyond 100; most can accurately count the number of objects in a set, can add and subtract single digits, and know the relative magnitudes of single-digit numbers (for example, that 8 is greater than 6) (Siegler & Robinson, 1982). However, there is a special concern about young children from economically disadvantaged families who lack opportunities to learn math in early childhood programs or through everyday activities at home and in the community. Leading experts recommend that young children learn two important aspects of math before entering school: (1) basic aspects of numbers and (2) basic aspects of geometry (Cross, Woods, & Schweingruber, 2009). Researchers have found that early number competencies are linked to future math success (Jordan, Glutting, & Ramineni, 2009). In an analysis of six longitudinal studies, school-entry math was one of three key predictors (along with reading and attention skills) of school achievement later in elementary school and middle school (Duncan & others, 2007).

RESEARCH

Building Blocks for Math is a program for developing preschool children's early math skills (SRA/McGraw-Hill, 2010). The program embeds math learning in everyday activities, including circle and story time. Researchers have found that the Building Blocks program is effective in improving young children's math skills (Clements & Sarama, 2008, 2009).

Children enter elementary school with different levels of mathematical understanding. Some children will need additional support for math learning (Cathcart & others, 2011; Edwards, Esmonde, & Wagner, 2011; van de Walle, Karp, & Bay-Williams,

2010). Early assessments should be used to obtain information for teaching and for potential early interventions.

Understanding basic aspects of numbers and geometry are critical in kindergarten through the second grade (NCTM, 2000). For example, at these grade levels, children need to learn the base-10 numeration system. They must recognize that the word *ten* may represent a single entity or 10 separate units (10 ones) and that these representations can be interchanged.

When they go to school, children learn many higher numerical skills (NCTM, 2007a). It is important to be aware that they are often doing something more than simply learning to calculate in a standard way. In fact, what children learn about mathematics and how to solve mathematical problems often reflects independent thinking as well as what they are being "taught." This can be true even in the case of learning the basic "facts" of addition and subtraction, which most of us ultimately memorize.

**Grades 3 Through 5**   Three key themes of mathematics in grades 3 through 5 are as follows:

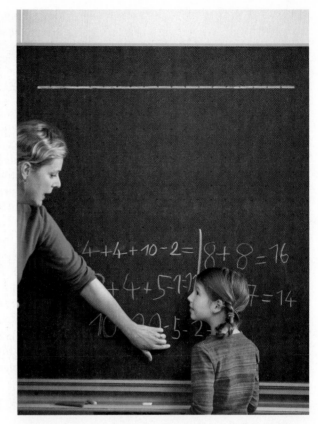

*What are some developmental changes in the basic mathematics principles children need to learn in elementary school?*

- *Multiplicative reasoning.* The emphasis on multiplicative reasoning develops knowledge that children build on as they move to the middle grades, where the focus is on proportional reasoning. In multiplicative reasoning, children need to develop their understanding of fractions as part of a whole and as a division.

- *Equivalence.* The concept of equivalence helps students to learn different mathematical representations and provides an avenue for exploring algebraic ideas.

- *Computational fluency.* Students need to learn efficient and accurate methods of computing that are based on well-understood properties and number relationships. For example, $298 \times 42$ can be thought of as $(300 \times 42) - (2 \times 42)$, or $41 \times 16$ is computed by multiplying $41 \times 8$ to get 328 and then doubling 328 to obtain 656.

**Grades 6 Through 8**   In middle school, students benefit from a balanced mathematics program that includes algebra and geometry. Teachers can help students understand how algebra and geometry are connected. Middle school mathematics also should prepare students to deal with quantitative solutions in their lives outside of school.

Students develop far more powerful mathematical reasoning when they learn algebra. A single equation can represent an infinite variety of situations. Even many students who get *A*'s and *B*'s in algebra classes, however, do so without understanding what they are learning—they simply memorize the equations. This approach might work well in the classroom, but it limits these students' ability to use algebra in real-world contexts (NCTM, 2007b).

**Grades 9 Through 12**   The NCTM (2000) recommends that all students study mathematics in each of the four years of high school. Because students' interests may change during and after high school, they will likely benefit from taking a range of math classes. They should experience the interplay of algebra, geometry, statistics, probability, and discrete mathematics (which involves the mathematics of computers). They should become adept at visualizing,

*What are some developmental changes in the math principles students need to learn in middle school and high school?*

describing, and analyzing situations in mathematical terms. They also need to be able to justify and prove mathematically based ideas (Brahier, 2009; Huetinck & Munshin, 2008).

## CONTROVERSY IN MATH EDUCATION

Educators currently debate whether math should be taught using a cognitive, conceptual, and constructivist approach or a practice, computational approach (Edwards, Esmonde, & Wagner, 2011). Some proponents of the cognitive approach argue against memorization and practice in teaching mathematics. Instead, they emphasize constructivist mathematical problem solving. Others assume that speed and automaticity are fundamental to effective mathematics achievement and argue that such skills can be acquired only through extensive practice and computation. In recent years the constructivist approach has become increasingly popular. In this approach, effective instruction focuses on involving children in solving a problem or developing a concept and in exploring the efficiency of alternative solutions (Bryant & Nunes, 2011).

RESEARCH

A rigorous analysis of research on math instruction programs in elementary schools revealed that only one program had potentially positive effects on math achievement (What Works Clearinghouse, 2007). The program is Everyday Mathematics (Wright Group, 2004, 2007), which includes a comprehensive set of instructions and activities that involve basic math processes and computation as well as critical thinking and problem solving.

## COGNITIVE PROCESSES

In our discussion of developmental changes and the controversy in math education, we mentioned several cognitive processes that help children learn math, such as problem-solving skills, understanding how math concepts are linked, and exploring alternative solutions. The National Research Council (2005) concluded that conceptual understanding, procedural fluency, effective organization of knowledge, and metacognitive strategies are important processes in learning math. A recent study also revealed that working memory and speed of processing information were linked to children's math performance (Swanson & Kim, 2007).

RESEARCH

In our discussion of the controversy in math education, we saw that debate flourishes about whether conceptual understanding or procedural competences should be the main focus in math education. The National Research Council's (2005) conclusion is that both are important. Teaching math with an emphasis only on procedural competency results in students having too little conceptual understanding, and when students have too little knowledge of procedures they often do not solve math problems competently.

As students move through elementary and secondary school and take increasingly complex math courses, new knowledge and competencies must build on, and be integrated with, previous knowledge (Posamentier, Smith, & Stepelman, 2010). By the time students begin solving algebra problems, they must have a network of organized knowledge that they can engage to support new algebraic understanding (Lee, Ng, & Ng, 2009). "The teacher's challenge, then, is to help students build and consolidate prerequisite competencies, understand new concepts in depth, and organize both concepts and competencies in a network of knowledge" (Fuson, Kalchman, & Bransford, 2005, p. 232).

Math instruction that supports students' use of metacognitive strategies also is recommended by the National Research Council (2005). Students can engage in metacognitive self-monitoring to determine

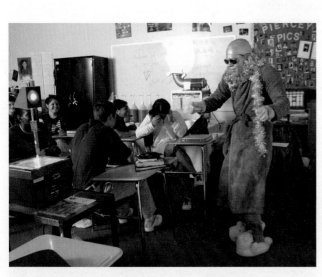

Gary Piercey, who teaches math to high school students in Houston, Texas, makes the classroom an exciting place to be for students. He sometimes dresses up for skits, as in the case shown here in which he plays Freeze, whose evil plans can be foiled only by students being able to successfully solve algebra problems.

their progress in solving individual math problems and their progress in a math course. "Metacognitive functioning is also facilitated by shifting from a focus on answers as just right or wrong to a more detailed focus on 'debugging' a wrong answer, that is, finding where the error is, why it is an error, and correcting it" (Fuson, Kalchman, & Bransford, 2005, p. 239).

Developing some effective general problem-solving strategies can also help students' math learning. Two of these are making a drawing of a situation and asking oneself questions. Students can learn to use these strategies as part of their self-monitoring in math.

## SOME CONSTRUCTIVIST PRINCIPLES

From a constructivist perspective on teaching math (Middleton & Goepfert, 1996), strategies should be used to make math realistic and interesting, students' prior knowledge should be considered, and the math curriculum should be made socially interactive.

**Make Math Realistic and Interesting**   Build your teaching of math around realistic and interesting problems. These problems might involve some kind of conflict, suspense, or crisis that elicits students' interest. The math problem-solving activities might center on the student, community issues, scientific discoveries, or historical events. Math games can provide a motivating context for learning math. Connecting math with other subject areas, such as science, geography, reading, and writing, also is recommended.

**Consider the Students' Prior Knowledge**   In our discussion of cognitive processes, we indicated that building on the student's knowledge is an important aspect of math education (National Research Council, 2005). Evaluate what knowledge the students bring to the unit and the context in which instruction takes place. Make enough information available for students to be able to come up with a method for solving math problems but withhold enough information that students must stretch their minds to solve the problems.

**Make the Math Curriculum Socially Interactive**   Develop math projects that require students to work together to come up with a solution (NCTM, 2007c). Build into the math curriculum opportunities for students to use and improve their communication skills. Generate math projects that engender discussion, argument, and compromise.

## TECHNOLOGY AND MATH INSTRUCTION

One issue in math education is how technology intensive it should be (NCTM, 2007c). The NCTM's *Curriculum and Evaluation Standards* recommends that calculators be used at all levels of mathematics instruction and that some access to computers is also necessary if students are to be adequately educated for future careers. In many school systems, adequate funds for computers is a major issue.

TECHNOLOGY

In contrast to U.S. teachers, Japanese and Chinese teachers do not allow the everyday use of calculators or computers in mathematics classes because they want the students to understand the concepts and operations required to solve problems. Some critics argue that the American emphasis on the early use of these technology aids prevents students from gaining experience in manipulating concrete objects—that they need to learn mathematical concepts (Stevenson, 2001). Only at the high school level, after students have developed a clear understanding of mathematical concepts, are East Asian students allowed to use calculators for solving mathematical problems. In the recent National Assessment of Educational Progress, frequent calculator use in the fourth grade was associated with lower national achievement test scores in mathematics, whereas in the eighth and twelfth

DIVERSITY

**FIGURE 11.3** FREQUENCY OF CALCULATOR USE AT DIFFERENT GRADE LEVELS CORRELATED WITH NATIONAL MATHEMATICS ACHIEVEMENT TEST SCORES

*Note:* Scores on the National Mathematics Achievement Test can range from 0 to 500.

grades, more frequent use of calculators was linked with higher national test scores (see Figure 11.3).

I recently asked teachers to describe their best strategies of teaching math. Following are their responses.

**EARLY CHILDHOOD** For preschoolers, math is a natural. They constantly want to know how much, how long, or is it finished yet. We build on this inquisitiveness  by helping children find the answers for themselves. In the classroom, we have scales for measuring blocks, liquid, counting bears, and more. We measure how tall they are throughout the year and show them in inches and centimeters. We sharpen their counting skills by having them count the number of steps to the bathroom, and have clocks, timers, rulers, calculators, and numbers in numerous places.

—**VALARIE GORHAM,** *Kiddie Quarters, Inc.*

**ELEMENTARY SCHOOL: GRADES K–5** I find that math manipulatives (physical objects used to represent or model a problem situation) are extremely helpful in  teaching my second-graders because they help bring students from concrete thinking to more abstract thinking. Instead of simply memorizing, manipulatives allow students to understand complicated mathematical concepts. This understanding helps them to apply mathematical knowledge to other problems and areas.

—**SUSAN FROELICH,** *Clinton Elementary School*

**MIDDLE SCHOOL: GRADES 6–8** Math skills can be taught through any number of academic disciplines. In social studies, for example, I apply math skills  by having students create timelines, placing historical events in chronological order. Graphing skills are also used when we locate different places on a map.

—**CASEY MAASS,** *Edison Middle School*

**HIGH SCHOOL: GRADES 9–12** As a career and technical education teacher, I make it a point to show students how mathematical skills are applied to real-world situations.  For example, I have my food services students create a gingerbread house in which they use rulers, measurements, and protractors—things some of them have not used since middle school. They also multiply and divide recipes. Having my students develop recipes that sometimes work and sometimes fail (often because of incorrect measurements or division) helps them to see the importance of mastering mathematical skills.

—**SANDY SWANSON,** *Menomonee Falls High School*

## TEACHING CONNECTIONS: Best Practices
### Strategies for Teaching Mathematics

What are some effective strategies for helping your students improve their math skills? Following are some recommendations:

1. *Become more math-proficient yourself.* If you are planning to teach elementary school, chances are you will be teaching math. The more proficient you are in math, the more comfortable you are likely to be teaching it to children. Recent research indicates that math anxiety among female teachers is likely to contribute to math anxiety among their female students (Beilock, Gunderson, Ramirez, & Levine, 2009).

2. *Teach students to become both procedurally and conceptually competent in math.* Students need to develop good computational skills, and they also need to understand math concepts.

3. *Help students to develop good math problem-solving skills.* In working with younger children, in response to their questions about math-related issues, ask them, "How do you think we could figure that out?" Similarly, with older students, allow them to show you how they think a problem should be approached instead of always modeling how to solve a problem. Allow all students to wrestle with real-world math problems.

4. *Encourage students to us metacognitive strategies.* Guide students to monitor their progress in solving math problems and becoming more competent at math. If a student is struggling, consider asking him/her to engage in a "think aloud" strategy while you observe.

Henry Brown.

## THROUGH THE EYES OF TEACHERS
### Never See Failure as Failure

An at-risk student, Henry Brown's life was turned around by middle school teacher Cora Russell, and the experience inspired him to teach. Brown, a recent Florida Teacher of the Year, teaches math at Hallandale Adult Alternative High School. In Brown's view, "Never see failure as failure." Half of the students enter this school with math skills below the fifth-grade level. He believes it is important to teach real-world math skills. In one project, Brown devised a dummy

corporation and had students play different roles in it, learning important math skills as they worked and made decisions in the corporation. He also created Helping Hands, which involves senior citizens in the classroom. (Source: *USA Today,* 2001.)

5. *Make math interesting for students.* For example, using real-world contexts and games can improve many students' motivation for spending more time on math, especially students who are not doing well in math. Using real-world contexts allows you to answer the question heard repeatedly in math classes, "When will I ever use this?"

   To teach both graphing and research skills to young students, you might have them take a survey regarding people's favorite candy, then count and graph the results. They are much more likely to get excited about this than graphing numbers they draw from a book. Partner or small-group games can be used effectively to help students develop automaticity in basic math facts. Most students find this to be much more interesting and enjoyable than traditional drill-and-practice techniques such as timed tests and flashcards.

   With older elementary school students, you might use geography or history as a context for math, having students compute distances traveled by explorers, for instance. Both early and later elementary students benefit from learning how to add, subtract, multiply, and divide money. To do this with younger students, you might have a class store. Older students might set up a monthly budget for a household.

6. *Engage in error analysis.* It is important for you to know, not just that a student made an error on a problem, but where that error occurred and why. Was it a simple computation error or is there a conceptual or procedural misunderstanding? How you address the error instructionally will differ depending on your response to this question. Of course, in order for you to engage in error analysis, your students must show their work.

*(continued)*

## TEACHING CONNECTIONS: Best Practices
### Strategies for Teaching Mathematics

7. *Use technology effectively.* As indicated earlier, some research indicates that use of calculators and computers in math may be best for students if delayed until the middle school years.

8. *Connect with parents.* In Chapter 9, we described Family Math, a program that helps parents experience math with their children in a positive, supportive way. In addition to telling parents about Family Math, consider having Family Math nights, especially at the beginning of the school year. At the Family Math night, offer resources that parents can use at home to help their children learn math more effectively. This is particularly important if

your elementary math curriculum teaches algorithms that differ from those that parents likely learned. Parents cannot help their children if they don't know the algorithms their children are supposed to be using.

9. *If you teach math, one good active step is to join the NCTM and use its resources.* The NCTM has annual conferences, publishes an annual yearbook with stimulating chapters on recent developments in math education, and publishes journals such as *Mathematics Teacher*. For more information about the NCTM, call (800) 235-7566 or go to **www.nctm.org.**

## Review, Reflect, and Practice

**4** Characterize how mathematical thinking develops, and identify some issues related to teaching mathematics.

### REVIEW
- What are some developmental changes in mathematical skills?
- What is the main controversy in math education?
- What are some cognitive processes involving math?
- What are some constructivist principles in learning math?
- What role can technology play in math instruction?

### REFLECT
- Do you think that teachers in Asia are wise not to allow young students to use calculators? Should the United States follow this example?

### PRAXIS™ PRACTICE

1. Ms. Carpenter's students are working on developing an understanding of place value. They are most likely in grade
   a. K–2.
   b. 3–5.
   c. 6–8.
   d. 9–12.

2. Malavi is very fast and accurate at doing multiplication and division. In the controversy on math education, he could be cited as an example of the importance of adopting which of these approaches?
   a. constructivist
   b. practice, computational
   c. conceptual
   d. cognitive

3. Joan is going over her math exam. She is examining her mistakes in an effort to find out what she did wrong. Then she corrects her mistakes and resubmits the exam. Her teacher, Mr. Ewing, allows students to receive credit for

## Review, Reflect, and Practice

**PRAXIS™ PRACTICE (CONTINUED)**

going through this process because he believes it helps students to learn from their errors. This is an example of
  a. algebraic reasoning.
  b. algorithms.
  c. debugging.
  d. rote memorization.

4. Which of the following is the best example of application of constructivist principles to math teaching?
  a. Ms. Carmichael's students complete timed tests of basic math facts.
  b. Ms. Dodge's students play "store," which allows them to add up their purchases, pay for them, and make change.
  c. Ms. Luker's students solve word problems but do not work on computation.
  d. Mr. Pinks' students complete problems on the board so he can determine if they have grasped the concepts.

5. Based on the results of research on calculator use and math achievement, at which of the following grade levels should Ingrid start using a calculator in doing math?
  a. first
  b. third
  c. fifth
  d. eighth

*Please see the answer key at the end of the book.*

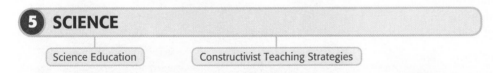

**5  SCIENCE**

Science Education          Constructivist Teaching Strategies

As mentioned in our discussion of math education in the previous section, the National Academies has recently expressed alarm at the shortage of highly qualified middle and high school science teachers (National Academies, Advisors to the Nation on Science, Engineering, and Medicine, 2009). For example, a U.S. high school student has a 70 percent probability of being taught English by a teacher with a degree in English, but only a 40 percent chance of studying chemistry with a teacher who majored in chemistry in college. Thus, an important agenda for U.S. science education is to significantly increase the percentage of science teachers in middle and high school education who have majored in a science area in college (National Academies, Advisors to the Nation on Science, Engineering, and Medicine, 2009).

Our further examination of science focuses on these questions: What are some key ideas in educating students about science? What are some constructivist strategies for teaching science?

> **Thinking Back/Thinking Forward**
>
> Having a deep understanding of subject matter is an important aspect of being a competent teacher. Chapter 1, p. 6

### SCIENCE EDUCATION

Scientists typically engage in certain kinds of thinking and behavior. For example, they regularly make careful observations; collect, organize, and analyze data; measure, graph, and understand spatial relations; pay attention to and regulate their own thinking; and know when and how to apply their knowledge to solve problems (Chapman, 2000).

These skills, which are essential to the practice of science, are not routinely taught in schools, especially elementary schools. As a result, many students are not competent at them. Many scientists and educators argue that schools need to increasingly guide students in learning how to use these skills (Duschi & Hamilton, 2011; Kuhn, 2011; Martin & others, 2009).

Children have many misconceptions that are incompatible with science and reality (Bransford & Donovan, 2005). They may go through mental gymnastics trying to reconcile seemingly contradictory new information with their existing beliefs (Miller, 2000). For example, after learning about the solar system, children sometimes conclude

## TEACHING CONNECTIONS: Best Practices
### Strategies for Teaching Science

Consider adopting the following strategies when teaching science:

1. *Help students learn how to think like scientists.* Create settings in which students are required to make careful observations, work effectively with data, and solve scientific problems. This is likely to look different at different levels of education. Young children, for instance might test how far it is possible to spit a watermelon seed. They could also make and record their observations of natural phenomena, such as pond water viewed with a microscope. Older students might have to generate hypotheses regarding how to best cushion an egg dropped from the roof of the school building so that it doesn't break. They could use their hypotheses to design and construct an egg protection structure and then test these by an adult actually dropping them from the school roof.

2. *Monitor students' misconceptions about science and work with them to develop more accurate conceptions.* Common scientific misconceptions include the cause of our seasons and the phases of the moon.

3. *Guide students in developing inquiry skills.* When teaching inquiry skills, don't leave students completely to their own devices; use guided inquiry.

4. *Make science interesting by giving students opportunities to explore everyday science problems.* Have students generate science questions they would like answered and help them to determine the best way to approach answering their questions. Students can then share their questions and the results of their inquiry.

### THROUGH THE EYES OF TEACHERS
**Dropping an Egg on a Teacher's Head**

Peggy Schweiger uses hands-on projects, such as wiring a doll house and making replicas of a boat for a regatta, to

Peggy Schweiger with a student who is learning how to think and discover how physics works in people's everyday lives.

improve students' understanding of physics. She especially works hard to create projects that will interest both female and male students. According to former student Alison Arnett, 19, "She taught us how to think and learn, not how to succeed in physics class. We were encouraged to stand on desks, tape things to the ceiling, and even drop an egg on her head to illustrate physics—anything to make us discover that we live with physics every day." (Source: *USA Today,* 2001, p. 6.)

that there are two Earths—the seemingly flat world in which they live and the round ball floating in space that their teacher just described.

Good teachers perceive and understand a child's underlying concepts, then use the concepts as a scaffold for learning (Chiapetta & Koballa, 2010; Peters & Stout, 2011). Effective science teaching helps children distinguish between fruitful errors and misconceptions, and detect plainly wrong ideas that need to be replaced by more accurate conceptions (Bransford & Donovan, 2005).

## CONSTRUCTIVIST TEACHING STRATEGIES

Many science teachers help their students construct their knowledge of science through guided discovery (Bass, Contant, & Carrin, 2009; Fraser-Abder, 2011). Constructivist teaching emphasizes that children have to build their own scientific knowledge and understanding with guidance from the teacher. At each step in science learning, they need to interpret new knowledge in the context of what they already understand. Rather than putting fully formed knowledge into children's minds, in the constructivist approach teachers serve as guides and consultants as children construct scientifically valid interpretations of the world and provide them with feedback to help them correct their scientific misconceptions (Abruscato & DeRosa, 2010).

Critics of constructivist approaches argue that too much attention is given to inquiry skills and not enough is given to discipline-specific information. In response, advocates of the constructivist approach to biology argue that it creates more scientifically literate citizens who know how to think in scientific ways rather than just memorize scientific facts (Gallagher, 2007).

Keep in mind, though, that it is important that students not be left completely on their own to construct scientific knowledge independent of *science content.* Students' inquiry should be guided (Magnusson & Palincsar, 2005). Teachers at a minimum should initially scaffold students' science learning, extensively monitor their progress, and ensure that they are learning science content. Thus, in pursuing science investigations, students need to "learn inquiry skills *and* science content" (Lehrer & Schauble, 2006).

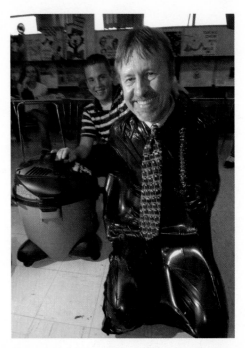

Pete Karpyk, who teaches chemistry in Weirton, West Virginia, uses an extensive array of activities that bring science alive for students. Here he has shrink-wrapped himself to demonstrate the effects of air pressure. He has some students give chemistry demonstrations at elementary schools and has discovered that in some cases students who don't do well on tests excel when they teach children. He also adapts his teaching based on feedback from former students and incorporates questions from their college chemistry tests as bonus questions on the tests he gives his high school students. (Source: Wong Briggs, 2005. p. 6D.)

## Review, Reflect, and Practice

**5** Identify some challenges and strategies related to teaching children how to think scientifically.

**REVIEW**

- What are key ideas in science education?
- What are some constructivist approaches to teaching science?

**REFLECT**

- How effectively did your elementary, middle, and high school teach science to the typical student? If less than perfectly, how could their approach have been improved?

**PRAXIS™ PRACTICE**

1. Which of the following teachers is most likely to be successful in helping students to overcome scientific misconceptions?
    a. Ms. Coster finds out what her students' misconceptions are by carefully asking them questions and then explicitly combats their misconceptions via direct instruction.

*(continued)*

## Review, Reflect, and Practice

**PRAXIS™ PRACTICE (CONTINUED)**

  b. Ms. Quigley uses a science text and carefully tests her students over the content in the text.

  c. Mr. Jones sets up situations in which the students explore materials themselves to discover their misconceptions.

  d. Mr. Foster designs experiences that demonstrate to the students that their misconceptions are incorrect and point out the correct principles.

2. Which of the following is the best example of constructivist teaching strategies in science?

  a. Mr. Ricardo's students study the material in their science tests and take quizzes over each chapter.

  b. Mr. Bunker's students have a "science bee" every Friday. He asks questions, and the students respond. Students who answer wrong are out of the competition.

  c. Ms. Mertz's students perform carefully designed experiments in a few areas that demonstrate scientific principles, helping them to learn in depth and to learn the process of scientific inquiry.

  d. Ms. O'Connor's students keep science notebooks in which they take notes on her presentations, and she gives periodic tests on the material in the notebooks.

*Please see the answer key at the end of the book.*

**6   SOCIAL STUDIES**

What Is Social Studies?        Constructivist Approaches

What is the nature of social studies? What key themes characterize teaching and learning in this subject? How can constructivist approaches be applied to social studies?

## WHAT IS SOCIAL STUDIES?

In general, the field of **social studies,** also called *social sciences,* seeks to promote civic competence. The goal is to help students make informed and reasoned decisions for the public good as citizens of a culturally diverse, democratic society in an interdependent world (Maxim, 2010; Obenchain & Morris, 2011). In schools, the teaching of social studies draws from disciplines such as anthropology, economics, geography, history, law, philosophy, political science, psychology, religion, and sociology (Ellis, 2011; Levstik, 2011; Sunal & Haas, 2011).

Social studies is taught in kindergarten through grade 12 in the United States. In elementary school, children often learn social studies that are integrated across several disciplines. This often takes the form of units constructed around broad themes that are examined in terms of time, continuity, and change. In middle schools and high schools, courses may be either interdisciplinary—such as a history course drawing from geography, economics, and political science—or focused more on a single discipline, such as just history itself (Chapin, 2009).

The National Council for the Social Sciences (2000) emphasizes that 10 themes should be stressed in social sciences:

• *Time, continuity, and change.* Students need to understand their historical roots and locate themselves in time. Knowing how to effectively read about

**social studies** The field that seeks to promote civic competence with the goal of helping students make informed and reasoned decisions for the public good as citizens of a culturally diverse, democratic society in an interdependent world.

and construct the past helps students to explore questions such as these: How am I connected to the past? How can my personal experience be viewed as part of the larger human story across time? This theme typically appears in history courses. Rather than simply teaching history as lists of facts to be memorized, expert history teachers guide students in analyzing and reflecting about historical events, especially encouraging students to think about possible alternative meanings of events and how they might be interpreted in different ways. A number of expert history teachers also get students to engage in debate about the evidence pertaining to a particular historical circumstance.

- *People, places, and environments.* The study of these topics helps students to develop spatial and geographic perspectives on the world. This helps students make informed and competent decisions about the relationship of humans to their environment. In schools this theme usually appears in units and courses linked to geography.

- *Individual development and identity.* A student's personal identity is shaped by culture, groups, and institutions. Students can explore such questions as these: Who am I? How do people learn, think, and develop? How do people meet their needs in a variety of contexts? In schools this theme usually appears in units and courses focused on psychology and anthropology.

- *Individuals, groups, and institutions.* Students need to learn about the ways in which schools, churches, families, government agencies, and the courts play integral roles in people's lives. Students can explore the roles of various institutions in the United States and other countries. In schools this theme typically appears in units and courses on sociology, anthropology, psychology, political science, and history.

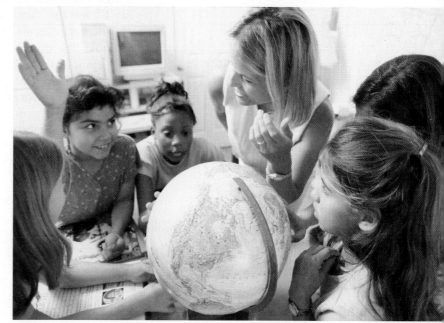

*What knowledge and perspectives do courses in geography help students to develop?*

- *Power, authority, and governance.* Understanding the development of power, authority, and governance in the United States and other parts of the world is essential for developing civic competence. Students can explore such questions as these: What is power, and what forms does it take? How do people gain power, use it, and justify it? How can people keep their government responsive to their needs and interests? How can conflicts within a nation and between nations be resolved? This theme typically appears in units and courses focused on government, political science, history, and other social sciences.

- *Production, distribution, and consumption.* People have needs and desires that sometimes exceed the limited resources that are available to them. As a result, questions such as these are raised: What is to be produced? How is production to be organized? How are goods and services distributed? What is the most effective allocation of production (land, capital, and management)? Increasingly, these questions are global in scope. In schools this theme typically appears in units and courses focused on economics.

- *Science, technology, and society.* Modern life as we know it would be impossible without technology and the science that supports it. However, technology raises many questions: Is new technology always better? How can people effectively cope with rapid technological advances? How are values related to technology? This theme appears in units and courses involving history, geography, economics, civics, and government.

### Thinking Back/Thinking Forward

New advances make it possible for students around the world to communicate through videoconferencing over the Internet. Chapter 5, p. 160

TECHNOLOGY

DIVERSITY

DIVERSITY

- *Global connections.* The realities of increasing interdependence among nations require an understanding of nations and cultures around the world. Conflicts between national and global priorities can involve health care, economic development, environmental quality, universal human rights, and other agendas. This theme typically appears in units and courses involving geography, culture, economics, and other social sciences.

- *Civic ideals and practices.* Understanding civic ideals and the practices of citizenship is important for full participation in society. Students focus on such questions as these: What is civic participation, and how can I be involved? What is the balance between individual needs and community responsibilities? In schools this theme typically appears in units and courses involving history, political science, and anthropology.

- *Culture.* The study of culture prepares students to ask and answer such questions as these: How are cultures similar and different? What is the best way to interact with people who are from cultures that are different from your own? How does religion influence the beliefs of people in different cultures? In schools the theme of culture typically appears in units and courses that focus on geography, history, and anthropology, as well as multicultural topics that cut across the curriculum. We further explore teaching about culture and cultural diversity by examining the study of UN peacekeeping next.

One Canadian middle school social studies teacher developed a project on UN peacekeeping to encourage students to think more deeply and productively about respecting citizens in their own country and about the hardships that people in many countries continue to experience (Welshman, 2000). During the last 50 years, the United Nations has been involved in separating adversaries, maintaining cease-fires, delivering humanitarian relief, helping refugees, and creating conditions that promote democracy. Studying the UN initiatives became a way for students to examine various prosocial values such as kindness, empathy, cooperation, loyalty, equality, and responsibility. In this project, students used a variety of resources, including books and the Internet, over the course of several class periods.

In introducing the UN peacekeeping topic, the teacher asked if any of the students ever had a disagreement with a friend or classmate at school. Students contributed comments, and the teacher said that in many instances it takes a third party to sort things out and help solve the problem. The teacher then shifted attention to how such conflicts also characterize world politics between countries and different ethnic groups. Nations, regions, and small groups of people have disagreements, and there is no teacher present to help cool things down. This is where UN peacekeepers often step in to help solve a particular problem.

Next, students brainstormed about UN peacekeeping, during which they recalled any information they had previously learned about the topic and discussed their ideas with each other. The classroom had a world map on which to identify regions of the world where peacekeeping was taking or had taken place.

Finally, the students were organized into five small groups of five students each to explore questions they had about UN peacekeeping. The first group of students focused on the history of peacekeeping. Questions explored included where the first peacekeeping mission occurred and how peacekeeping has changed since the end of the Cold War. Group 2 expressed an interest in the personal side of peacekeeping. Their questions included how much force peacekeepers can use in a mission and some of the dangers they face. The third group wanted to know about the organization of peacekeeping missions and asked questions such as these: Who provides funding for the mission? How are peacekeepers selected? The fourth group was interested in Canada's role in UN peacekeeping, asking these questions: When did Canada get involved in this? Have any Canadians commanded UN peacekeeping missions? The fifth group was intrigued by why peacekeeping occurs and asked questions such as these: What is the decision-making process like in determining when to form a UN peacekeeping mission? How do people decide on which world problems should be dealt with and which should not? After generating these questions, students researched and presented answers.

## CONSTRUCTIVIST APPROACHES

Many social studies classes continue to be taught in the traditional manner of using a single textbook, with the teacher lecturing and controlling question-and-answer strategies. However, some educators conclude that learning about social studies would benefit from constructivist strategies, such as using varied sources of information, student-generated questions to guide inquiry, and peer collaboration—the strategy used in the UN peacekeeping unit we just discussed. In the constructivist view, students should form their own interpretation of evidence and submit it for review. Allowing them to do so should encourage greater reflection and deeper understanding of social issues (Chapin, 2011).

In the History Alive! program of the Teacher's Curriculum Institute, students work in cooperative groups of four to prepare one student to be the actor in a lively panel debate.

Constructivist approaches also emphasize the meaningfulness of social studies (Beal, Mason-Bolik, & Martorella, 2009; Sunal & Haas, 2011). Students benefit when they find that what they learned in social studies classes is useful both in and outside school. Meaningful learning often takes place when classroom interaction focuses on sustained examination of a few important topics rather than superficial coverage of many.

Constructivist approaches to social studies also stress the importance of thinking critically about values. Ethical dimensions of topics and controversial issues provide an arena for reflective thinking and understanding. Effective teachers recognize opposing points of view, show respect for well-supported positions, have sensitivity to cultural similarities and differences, and demonstrate a commitment to social responsibility. From the constructivist perspective, teachers guide students to consider ethical dimensions of topics and address controversial issues rather than directly telling students what is ethical.

In this chapter, we have explored effective strategies for educating students in a number of content areas. Next, we describe some of the best ways to use technology in these and other content areas.

A wealth of content-specific technology resources is available for teachers. Some are commercial products, others are free.

In English language arts, there are many good programs for beginning readers, such as the *Reader Rabbit* or *Living Books* series. The latter provides software versions of children's literature classics with which young students can read along and interact. For older students, Google Lit Trips (**http://web.mac.com/jburg/ GoogleLit/Home.html**) has sources developed by teachers that allow students to explore many places referenced in literature for all ages. The Gutenberg Project (**www.gutenberg.org**) gives the full texts of thousands of books whose copyright has expired. Many children's authors have Web sites that provide supplementary information about the authors and their books (see, for example, **www.judyblume .com**). There are good supports for writing in most word processors, as well as programs that read written text back to students, such as *Write:OutLoud,* and so help improve their writing.

TECHNOLOGY

Many commercial programs offer students practice in arithmetic and algebra as well as interesting applications that support geometry explorations, such as the *Geometric Supposer.* Symbol-manipulation programs, like Mathematica (**www.wolfram .com/products/mathematica/index.html**) or Maple (**www.maplesoft.com**), allow students to explore algebra and calculus in multiple representations. There are also large repositories of mathematics learning objects (see **www.walterfendt.de/ml4e/** or **www.merlot.org/artifact/BrowseArtifacts.po?catcode=223&browsecat=223&sort= rating**) for supporting the learning of specific mathematical concepts. Also, the *Sim Calc* projects (**www.simcalc.umassd.edu**) provide simulations and activities that run on calculators, computers, and handheld devices; these are designed to help students explore change and variation. And the National Council for Teachers of Mathematics (**www.nctm.org**) provides a variety of digital objects for illustrating mathematical concepts for its members called *Illuminations*.

Technology support for inquiry-based science includes the use of science probes, online access to science expeditions, online interactive activities for students (for example, **www.exploratorium.edu**), and virtual science laboratories such as those freely available at **www.sciencecourseware.org.** The WISE Web site (**http://wise -demo.berkeley.edu**) provides a free online science learning environment with inquiry modules on such topics as global climate change, population genetics, and recycling. Vernier (**www.vernier.com**) and Pasco (**www.pasco.com**) offer a wide variety of hardware and software for supporting hands-on science activities. Online access to science expeditions can be found at Web sites such as the Jason Project (**www.jason.org/public/home/aspx**). There are also good online repositories of learning objects for teaching science including the National Science Foundation's *Digital Library* (**http://nsdl.org**) and the National Science Teachers Association's *SciLinks* (**www.nsta.org/scilinks**).

In social studies, Tom Snyder Productions (**www.tomsnyder.com**) offers a variety of role-playing simulations that introduce students to decision making among competing stakeholders as do *SimCity* and *Civilization* from Aspyr (**www.aspyr.com**) on a grander and more complex scale. My World GIS (**www.myworldgis.org**) is a geographic information system designed for use in educational settings that allows students to explore and analyze geographic data from around the world. There are also incredible sources of original documents (for example, see the Library of Congress *American Memory Collection* [**http://memory.loc.gov/ammem**] or the *Congressional Record,* [**www.gpoaccess.gov/crecord**]), virtual tours of cities all over the world, world newspapers, and collections of maps, including the David Rumsey historical map collection (**www .davidrumsey.com).** Another terrific social studies application is Google Earth (**http://earth.google.com),** which allows students to bring up aerial views of landscapes all over the world at varying degrees of resolution.

Good resources are also available for specialized content areas. For example, the *WebMuseum* is a good source of reproductions for teaching art history, especially the Impressionists. Indeed, museums around the world have good reproductions available. The *Afropop Worldwide* site has a wealth of information about African and world music including music downloads.

And there is much, much more available over the Internet. For example, the WebQuests created by teachers available at **http://webquest.org** can be sorted by topic as can the digital objects available in the MERLOT (**www.merlot.org**) library. In addition, many publishers provide CD-ROMs and online sites for teachers using their texts. A good source for selected commercial software is KidsClick (**www.Kidsclick.com**).

To close our coverage of social studies education, the following comments by former high school history teacher Robert Bain (2005, p. 209) capture many of the

My World GIS allows students to explore geographic information from around the world. Teachers can use My World GIS software to create numerous projects for students.

themes emphasized in this chapter, not only about social science education but also about education in other content areas:

> When my high school students began to study history, they tended to view the subject as a fixed entity, a body of facts that historians retrieved and placed in textbooks (or in the minds of history teachers) for students to memorize. The purpose of history, if it had one, was to somehow inoculate students from repeating past errors. The process of learning history was straightforward and, while not always exciting, relatively simple. Ironically, when I first entered a school to become a history teacher over 30 years ago, I held a similar view, often supported by my education and history courses. . . . I no longer hold such innocent and naive views of learning or teaching history, and I try to disabuse my students of these views as well. Indeed, our experiences in my history courses have taught us that, to paraphrase Yogi Berra, it's not what we know that's the issue, it's what we know for sure that isn't so. . . . Learning and teaching history demands complex thinking by both teachers and students. It centers around interesting, generative, and organizing problems; critical weighing of evidence and accounts; suspension of our views to understand those of others; use of facts, concepts, and interpretations to make judgments; and later, if the evidence persuades, to changes in our views and judgments.

## Review, Reflect, and Practice

**6** Summarize how learning in social studies is becoming more constructivist.

### REVIEW
- What does social studies instruction aim to accomplish? What themes are emphasized by the National Council for the Social Sciences?
- What are some constructivist approaches to teaching social studies?

### REFLECT
- Think about a specific community in which you might teach one day. How might you tailor social studies instruction specifically for those children? How could you make it constructivist?

### PRAXIS™ PRACTICE
1. Mr. Chen wants his students to understand that not all people live in the same way that they do. His students study the ways of life of different people around the world. Which theme of social studies does Mr. Chen emphasize?
   a. culture
   b. civic ideals and practice
   c. power, authority, and governance
   d. production, distribution, and consumption
2. Which is the best example of a constructivist approach to social studies?
   a. Mr. Ewing's students listen to his lectures and take notes on the content covered.
   b. Ms. Drexler's students color and label detailed maps to help them learn geography.
   c. Ms. Byrd's students learn the material in their textbooks and take tests covering the content on a regular basis.
   d. Mr. Jordan presents his students with a controversial issue, which they discuss and debate.

*Please see the answer key at the end of the book.*

# The Constructivist Math Curriculum

Connie teaches fourth grade in a middle-SES school district. Her district has adopted a new K–6 math curriculum for this year based on constructivist principles. In attending the in-service devoted to training teachers in implementing the new curriculum, Connie discovers that many differences exist between what she has been teaching for the past 20 years and this new curriculum. The new curriculum focuses on the use of math in "real life." Instead of endless speed drills, the problems ask the students to think and make connections between their lives at home and what they are doing in math. What drill and practice there is takes place in the context of various games the children play together. Students are allowed, and even taught, to approach problems in a variety of ways rather than focusing on a single algorithm for a particular type of problem. Many of these approaches are completely alien to Connie and, she guesses, to other teachers and parents. "This is going to be a lot of work," she thinks. "I'm going to have to relearn math myself in order to teach this way."

As the school year begins, other teachers begin expressing their concerns over the new curriculum. It is just so different from anything they have ever done in the past. Most of the teachers are managing to stay just a lesson or two ahead of the students. The children in first and second grade seem to love the new math program. They are actively involved during math period, and many of them have said that math is fun. The students in fourth through sixth grade don't appear to be as enthusiastic about the new curriculum, however. Many of them are unable to complete their homework. They can't seem to grasp how to complete problems using the techniques taught in the new curriculum. They constantly fall back on the old algorithms they were taught when they were younger. This is frustrating Connie and her colleagues, as they have worked very hard to master the alternate ways of approaching problems themselves.

To make matters worse, parents are complaining. They can't help their children with their homework because they don't know how to use the new approaches, either. Several have threatened to remove their children from the school and take them "somewhere where they teach normal math." A group of parents will be addressing the board of education regarding this concern at their next meeting.

Adding fuel to the fire is one of the middle school math teachers, who insists that this new curriculum won't give the students the foundation they need for algebra. "They need to develop automaticity with their math facts. That just isn't going to happen with this program. It takes them in too many directions. They'll never make it back to normal in time for algebra."

Proponents answer the middle school teacher by claiming that the new curriculum will actually better prepare the students for higher math because they will have a better conceptual understanding of *why* they are doing things and how the traditional algorithms work. Connie feels caught in the middle. She understands what the curriculum is supposed to do. She even believes it might actually benefit the students in the long run. However, every day she has students in tears in her class because they don't understand what she is asking them to do. She has fielded her share of phone calls from angry parents as well.

1. What are the issues in this case?
2. The students in first and second grade seem to be flourishing in this curriculum, whereas the older students are struggling. Why might this be? Tie your answer to a constructivist principle.
3. How should the teachers address parental concerns regarding the new curriculum?
4. How should they address the concerns of the algebra teacher?
5. What can the teachers do to help their students at this point?

# Learning and Cognition in the Content Areas

**① EXPERT KNOWLEDGE AND PEDAGOGICAL CONTENT KNOWLEDGE:** Distinguish between expert knowledge and pedagogical content knowledge.

Expert knowledge, also called *subject matter knowledge*, involves being an expert regarding the content of a discipline. Pedagogical content knowledge involves knowledge of how to effectively teach a particular discipline. Both are required for being an expert teacher.

**② READING:** Explain how reading develops, and discuss some useful approaches to teaching reading.

**A Developmental Model of Reading**

Chall's model proposes five stages in reading development: (0) from birth to first grade, identify letters of the alphabet and learn to write one's name; (1) in first and second grade, learn to sound out words and complete learning of letter names and sounds; (2) in second and third grade, become more fluent at retrieving individual words and other reading skills; (3) in fourth through eighth grade, increasingly obtain new information from print and shift from "learning to read" to "reading to learn"; and (4) in high school, become a fully competent reader and understand material from different perspectives.

**Approaches to Reading**

Current debate focuses on the phonics approach versus the whole-language approach. The phonics approach emphasizes that reading instruction should focus on phonics and basic rules for translating written symbols into sounds and give children simplified materials for early reading instruction. The whole-language approach stresses that reading instruction should parallel children's natural language learning and give children whole-language materials, such as books and poems. Although both approaches can benefit children, the phonics approach needs to be emphasized, especially in kindergarten and first grade. Research indicates that phonological awareness instruction is most effective when it is combined with letter training and as part of a total literacy program. Effective phonological awareness training mainly involves two skills: blending and segmentation. Children's reading also benefits from guided oral reading and instruction in reading strategies.

**Cognitive Approaches**

Cognitive approaches to reading emphasize decoding and comprehending words, prior knowledge, and developing expert reading strategies. Metacognitive strategies and automatic processes are involved in decoding and comprehending words. Prior knowledge about a topic can help students make correct inferences about material they read. Transactional strategy instruction is one approach to helping students learn to read.

**Social Constructivist Approaches**

Social constructivist approaches to reading stress that the social context plays an important part in helping children learn to read and that meaning is socially negotiated. Reciprocal teaching is a valuable technique in helping students improve their reading. An emphasis on school/family/community connections also reflects the social constructivist perspective.

**③ WRITING:** Describe how writing develops, and discuss some useful approaches to teaching writing.

**Developmental Changes**

Children's writing follows a developmental timetable, emerging out of scribbling. Most 4-year-olds can print their name. Most 5-year-olds can reproduce letters and copy several short words. Advances in children's language and cognitive development provide the foundation for improved writing.

| Cognitive Approaches | Cognitive approaches to writing emphasize many of the same themes as for reading, such as constructing meaning and developing strategies. Planning, problem solving, revising, and metacognitive strategies are thought to be especially important. |

| Social Constructivist Approaches | Social constructivist approaches to writing focus on the social context in which writing is produced. This social context includes the importance of students participating in a writing community to understand author-reader relationships and learn about perspectives of others. Social constructivist approaches to writing include writing of "real texts" about meaningful experiences, teacher-student writing conferences, peer collaboration in writing, and school-community connections. |

## ④ MATHEMATICS: Characterize how mathematical thinking develops, and identify some issues related to teaching mathematics.

| Developmental Changes | Children have a substantial understanding of numerical concepts before they enter first grade. When they go to school, they learn many more advanced kinds of numerical skills. The National Council of Teachers of Mathematics has developed standards for learning mathematics at these grade levels: kindergarten through grade 2 (base-10 numeration system, for example); grades 3 through 5 (multiplicative reasoning, equivalence, and computational fluency); grades 6 through 8 (mathematical reasoning—algebra and geometry); and grades 9 through 12 (interplay of algebra, geometry, statistics, probability, and discrete mathematics). |

| Controversy in Math Education | Currently, there is controversy in math education about whether math should be taught using a cognitive, conceptual, and constructivist approach, or a practice, computational approach. Students need to develop both a conceptual understanding of math and procedural competency in math. |

| Cognitive Processes | Among the cognitive processes involved in math are conceptual understanding, knowledge of math procedures, effective organization of knowledge, and metacognitive strategies. |

| Some Constructivist Principles | Some constructivist principles include making math education more realistic and interesting, making connections to students' prior knowledge, and making the math curriculum socially interactive. |

| Technology and Math Instruction | The NCTM's *Curriculum and Evaluation Standards* recommends that calculators be used at all levels of mathematical instruction and that students' access to computers also is necessary. However, some education experts argue that, as in East Asia, calculators should not be used prior to high school so as to improve students' ability to learn math concepts. |

## ⑤ SCIENCE: Identify some challenges and strategies related to teaching children how to think scientifically.

| Science Education | There is a significant shortage of qualified science teachers in middle and high school education in the United States. Too often, the skills scientists use, such as careful observation, graphing, self-regulatory thinking, and knowing when and how to apply one's knowledge to solve problems, are not routinely taught in schools. Children have many beliefs that are incompatible with science and reality. Good teachers perceive and understand a child's underlying concepts, then use the concepts as a scaffold for learning. |

| Constructivist Teaching Strategies | Constructivist teaching strategies include an emphasis on discovery learning. However, teachers need to supply guidance and feedback, serving as consultants to children as they construct scientifically valid interpretations of the world. Effective science education emphasizes inquiry and science content knowledge. |

- What Is Social Studies?

- Constructivist Approaches

The field of social studies seeks to promote civic competence. In schools, the teaching of social studies draws from disciplines such as anthropology, economics, geography, history, law, philosophy, political science, psychology, religion, and sociology. Ten themes are recommended to be used for units and courses in social studies by the National Council for the Social Sciences: time, continuity, and change; people, places, and environments; individual development and identity; individuals, groups, and institutions; power, authority, and governance; production, distribution, and consumption; science, technology, and society; global connections; civic ideals and practices; and culture.

Many social studies classes continue to be taught in a traditional lecture format, but there is increasing interest in teaching these classes from a constructivist perspective. This perspective emphasizes using varied sources of information, the importance of greater reflection, understanding, meaning, critical thinking about values, and sustained examination of a few important topics rather than superficial coverage of many topics.

## KEY TERMS

expert knowledge  361
pedagogical content
   knowledge  361

phonics approach  364
whole-language
   approach  364

transactional strategy
   instruction approach  366

reciprocal teaching  367
social studies  388

## PORTFOLIO ACTIVITIES

Now that you have a good understanding of this chapter, complete these exercises to expand your thinking.

### Independent Reflection: The Cognitive and Socially Constructive Classroom

For the grade level you plan to teach, create a summary of good ideas for making learning both cognitive and socially constructive. Draw ideas from this and other chapters. Add further ideas of your own. (INTASC: Principles *4, 5*)

### Research/Field Experience: Researching the Nuts and Bolts of Reading

Read about current trends in teaching children to read. Evaluate these trends based on what you've learned in this chapter. Compare current trends with how you were taught to read. Which method

do you think is most effective? Why? What do you think accounts for persistently low reading scores on nationwide standardized tests? (INTASC: Principles *1, 7*)

### Collaborative Work: Taking a Stand in the Math Controversy

There is controversy in math education about whether math should be taught in a constructivist manner or in a more traditional manner. There is also controversy about whether calculators and computers should be used in math instruction in the elementary school years. Get together with several students and evaluate these controversies. Summarize your discussion. (INTASC: Principles *1, 2, 4*)

*Go to the Online Learning Center for downloadable portfolio templates.*

## STUDY, PRACTICE, AND SUCCEED

Visit **www.mhhe.com/santrockep5e** to review the chapter with self-grading quizzes and self-assessments, to apply the chapter material to

two more Crack the Case studies, and for suggested activities to develop your teaching portfolio.

# CHAPTER 12

# PLANNING, INSTRUCTION, AND TECHNOLOGY

*Education is the transmission of civilization.*

—Ariel and Will Durant
*American Authors and Philosophers, 20th Century*

## Learning **Goals**

**1** Explain what is involved in classroom planning.

**2** Identify important forms of teacher-centered instruction.

**3** Discuss important forms of learner-centered instruction.

**4** Summarize how to effectively use technology to help children learn.

# Teaching **Stories**    Lois Guest and Kevin Groves

In Lois Guest's fifth-grade classroom at Hesperian Elementary School in San Lorenzo, California, 30 students are working on their new laptop computers provided by the school district. A month after the computers arrived, outdated encyclopedias sit on shelves, and students no longer have to compete for time in the school's computer lab.

The new laptops mark a monumental shift in Guest's career. She has taught for 35 years at Hesperian Elementary and remembers when slide projectors were the height of high tech. Now, she is building a Web site for her class and learning how to use a digital camera and an optical scanner. Guest says that she is learning a lot about technology and that her students are also teaching

her how to do things on the computer. Ten-year-old Bianca Guitierrez said that she enjoys working on her new laptop computer so much that it makes her look forward to coming to school.

When Kevin Groves took his fifth-grade class on a field trip to a botanical garden, his students insisted that they be allowed to bring their laptops. One of his students, Salvador Mata, spread out on the grass with his mother and explained to her how to make a PowerPoint presentation. His mother is pleased about Salvador learning how to use a computer at such an early age, believing that it will help him get a good job later in his life. Groves commented that he researches every link he puts on his Web site to make sure it is educational and won't lead to something bad for his students.

# Preview

This chapter builds on the learning and cognitive processes we discussed in Chapters 7 through 11 and addresses instructional planning at the level of the overall lesson plan or unit. We explore teacher-centered lesson planning, building on the behavioral principles covered in Chapter 7, and learner-centered lesson planning, building on material covered in Chapters 8 through 11. Finally, we explore important classroom applications of technology, such as use of the Internet.

It has been said that when people fail to plan, they plan to fail. Many successful people attribute their accomplishments to effective planning. Our introduction to planning describes what instructional planning is and the different time frames of planning.

## INSTRUCTIONAL PLANNING

Planning is a critical aspect of being a competent teacher (Burden & Byrd, 2010). **Instructional planning** involves developing a systematic, organized strategy for lessons. Teachers need to decide what and how they are going to teach before they do it. Although some wonderful instructional moments are spontaneous, lessons still should be carefully planned (Eby, Herrell, & Jordan, 2011).

Instructional planning might be mandated by the school in which you teach. Many principals and instructional supervisors require teachers to keep written plans, and you may be asked to submit lesson plans several weeks in advance. When observing classroom teachers, supervisors check to see if the teacher is following the plan. If a teacher is absent, a substitute teacher can follow the plan.

Expectations for teacher planning have increased with the promulgation of state learning standards that specify what students need to know and be able to do (Borich, 2011; Joyce & Weil, 2009). However, these standards usually do not state what the teacher should do in the classroom to reach these standards. When standards are in place, teachers must figure out how to plan and organize their curriculum around the most important dimensions implied by the standards and create a "sequence and

**instructional planning** A systematic, organized strategy for planning lessons.

FRANK AND ERNEST © Thaves/Dist. by United Feature Syndicate, Inc.

set of learning activities for the particular students they teach" (Darling-Hammond & others, 2005, p. 184).

Many planning strategies are organized around four elements: "the nature of the subject matter, the learners, the context, and the teacher's role" (Darling-Hammond & others, 2005, p. 184). One effective planning strategy that many teachers use is *mapping backward* from "goals to desired performances to activities and elements of scaffolding needed to support student progress." In this strategy, then, you begin your planning by thinking about what goals you want your students to reach by the end of the school year and map backward from that point. In one analysis, many experienced teachers described how in the early years of their teaching they lacked a long-term vision in their curriculum planning and strongly urged beginning teachers to think more about the big picture—the key things they want their students to learn that year—and how they can guide their students to get there (Kunzmann, 2003).

Linda Darling-Hammond and her colleagues (2005, pp. 185–186) described some important aspects of curriculum planning:

> Teachers must decide what is important to include, given their goals, and know how to make it accessible to a particular group of students. This requires thinking about how to give students a schema or conceptual map of the domain to be studied (National Research Council, 2000) as well as planning specific activities in light of students' levels of readiness for various kinds of learning experiences. It also requires consideration of the kinds of information, demonstrations, models, inquiry opportunities, discussion, and practice students need over time to understand particular concepts and develop particular skills. . . .

In sum, teachers need to "figure out which things students should do when, in what order, and how" to implement the big picture of their curricular vision.

## TIME FRAMES AND PLANNING

As we just indicated, developing systematic time plans involves knowing what needs to be done and when to do it, or focusing on "task" and "time."

You will need to plan for different time spans, ranging from yearly to daily planning (Eby, Herrell, & Jordan, 2011). If school-wide planning or your own career planning is involved, the time frame likely will be a number of years. Robert Yinger (1980) identified five time spans of teacher planning: yearly planning, term planning, unit planning, weekly planning, and daily planning. Figure 12.1 illustrates these time frames and shows planning for them. Yinger also recommends that teachers attend to four areas when planning: goals, sources of information, the form of the plan, and criteria for the effectiveness of the planning.

Although planning is a key dimension of successful teaching, don't overplan to the point of becoming an automaton. Develop organized plans and try to carry them out, but be flexible; as a year, month, week, or day unfolds, adapt to changing circumstances. A controversial current event or necessary topic might emerge that you

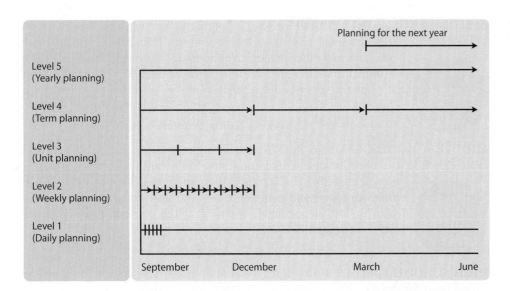

FIGURE **12.1** FIVE TIME SPANS OF TEACHER PLANNING AND THEIR OCCURRENCE OVER THE SCHOOL YEAR

From R. J. Yinger, "A Study of Teacher Planning," *The Elementary School Journal*, Vol. 80, No. 3 (Jan. 1980), p. 113. Copyright © 1980 by The University of Chicago. Reprinted by permission of the University of Chicago Press.

did not originally include. Monitor and rework your plans as the school year goes by to suit these changing circumstances (Cruickshank, Metcalf, & Jenkins, 2009; Roberts, Moore, & Kellough, 2011).

A final comment needs to be made about planning. It is increasingly understood that teachers need to monitor and evaluate their curriculum planning in terms of how well students are making progress toward learning goals as they go through the term (Darling-Hammond & others, 2005). Thus, time for assessment and feedback to students needs to be built into the planning process. We will explore different types of assessment in Chapters 15 and 16.

A final consideration involves how much time schools allot to lesson planning in the United States compared with other countries. Recent cross-cultural comparisons reveal that lesson planning is given a much higher priority in Chinese than American schools (Shen, Zhen, & Poppink, 2007; Shen & others, 2007; Zhao & Ma, 2009). Many American teachers' schedules allow little time for lesson planning, in many cases 30 minutes or less, during the school day. By contrast, Chinese teachers teach only one or two hours a day, in a core subject area, and they spend extensive time on lesson planning: on average about two hours a week of formal collaboration and two hours a week of informational collaboration with colleagues in one core subject area. They also have one to two hours a day to correct homework and classwork, and 30 minutes a day for homework feedback to students.

I recently asked teachers what planning strategies they use to make their teaching more effective. Following are their responses.

*How does time allotted to lesson planning differ in Chinese and American schools?*

**Thinking Back/Thinking Forward**

Think of integrated assessment planning in terms of three time frames: preinstruction, during instruction, and postinstruction. Chapter 16, p. 548

**EARLY CHILDHOOD**  Lesson planning for our preschoolers is done by a team of two at the beginning of the month. The team determines what will be covered by reviewing skills that need to be mastered and implementing appropriate activities. We also incorporate the children's interests in building our plans.

—**VALARIE GORHAM**, *Kiddie Quarters, Inc.*

DIVERSITY

**ELEMENTARY SCHOOL: GRADES K–5** To prepare for my second-grade classes, I plan each week's (and sometimes two weeks') lessons the Thursday before. This way

I can have all copies made, have the necessary materials, and be sure additional materials are available (library books, for example). I then map out the week and check that time is set aside to reteach and reinforce material.

—**Janine Guida Poutre,** *Clinton Elementary School*

**MIDDLE SCHOOL: GRADES 6–8** When planning my lessons, I use the backward design method: I make a list of essential questions that I want my students to know

when they finish the activity. These essential questions go on my whiteboard so that the students are aware of what they are going to learn. By knowing exactly what I want the students to learn, I can plan a successful lesson.

—**Casey Maass,** *Edison Middle School*

**HIGH SCHOOL: GRADES 9–12** I get to school by 6:00 A.M. to plan and lay out what I need for the day. I need quiet time without others around and access to copy machines without a line. By 7:00 A.M. I have my activities for the day laid out and ready to go. Of course, I am a morning person!

—**Sandy Swanson,** *Menomonee Falls High School*

## Review, Reflect, and Practice

**1** Explain what is involved in classroom planning.

**REVIEW**

- What is instructional planning? Why does instruction need to be planned?
- What planning needs to be done related to the use of time?

**REFLECT**

- In your own K–12 experiences, did you ever have a teacher who did not put enough effort into planning? What was that like for students?

**PRAXIS™ PRACTICE**

1. Ms. Swenson is planning for the school year. Which of the following strategies should she follow?
   a. Plan forward, starting with plans for the first week of school.
   b. Map backward, determining the goals she wants her students to reach by the end of the school year.
   c. Not spend too much time in planning but rather get a sense of where her students are in the first month of school.
   d. Engage in circular planning.

2. In planning, Mr. Tomasello considers the objectives established by the district and state-mandated standards and aligns his curriculum to them. After doing this, he considers what he wants to teach, when, based on the sequence that makes the most sense. Finally, he reserves the necessary equipment and requests the appropriate materials to carry out his plans. At what level of planning is Mr. Tomasello most likely to be engaging?
   a. daily
   b. weekly
   c. term
   d. yearly

*Please see the answer key at the end of the book.*

## ② TEACHER-CENTERED LESSON PLANNING AND INSTRUCTION

| Teacher-Centered Lesson Planning | Direct Instruction | Teacher-Centered Instructional Strategies | Evaluating Teacher-Centered Instruction |

Traditionally, the focus in schools has been on teacher-centered lesson planning and instruction. In this approach, planning and instruction are highly structured and the teacher directs students' learning.

## TEACHER-CENTERED LESSON PLANNING

Three general tools are especially useful in teacher-centered planning: behavioral objectives, task analysis, and instructional taxonomies (classifications).

**Behavioral Objectives**    One tool is that of **behavioral objectives,** statements about changes that the teacher wishes to see in students' performance (Borich, 2011). These objectives should be very specific and often have three parts (Mager, 1962):

- *Student's behavior.* Focus on what the student will learn or do.
- *Conditions under which the behavior will occur.* State how the behavior will be evaluated or tested.
- *Performance criteria.* Determine what level of performance will be acceptable.

For example, a teacher might develop a behavioral objective around the idea that the student will describe five causes of the decline of the British Empire (student's behavior). The teacher plans to give the student an essay test on this topic (conditions under which the behavior will occur). And the teacher decides that explaining four or five causes will be acceptable performance (performance criterion).

**Task Analysis**    Another tool of teacher-centered planning is **task analysis,** which focuses on breaking down a complex task that students are to learn into its component parts (Alberto & Troutman, 2009). The analysis can proceed in three basic steps (Moyer & Dardig, 1978):

1. Determine what skills or concepts the student needs to have to learn the task.
2. List any materials that will be required in order to perform the task, such as paper, pencil, and calculator.
3. List all of the components of the task in the order in which they must be performed.

**Instructional Taxonomies**    Instructional taxonomies also aid teacher-centered approaches (Eby, Herrell, & Jordan, 2011; Halawi, McCarthy, & Pires, 2009). A **taxonomy** is a classification system. **Bloom's taxonomy** was developed by Benjamin Bloom and his colleagues (1956). It classifies educational objectives into three domains: cognitive, affective, and psychomotor. Bloom's taxonomy has been used by many teachers in their lesson planning to create goals and objectives (Bart, 2008; Lord & Baviskar, 2007).

**The Cognitive Domain**    Bloom's cognitive taxonomy has six objectives (Bloom & others, 1956):

- *Knowledge.* Students have the ability to remember information. For example, an objective might be to list or describe four main advantages of using a computer for word processing.
- *Comprehension.* Students understand the information and can explain it in their own words. For example, an objective might be to explain or discuss how a computer can effectively be used for word processing.

**behavioral objectives** Statements that communicate proposed changes in students' behavior to reach desired levels of performance.

**task analysis** Breaking down a complex task that students are to learn into its component parts.

**taxonomy** A classification system.

**Bloom's taxonomy** Developed by Benjamin Bloom and colleagues; classifies educational objectives into three domains—cognitive, affective, and psychomotor.

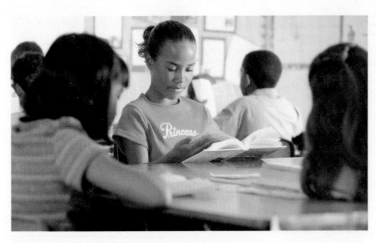

*What objectives are involved in Bloom's cognitive taxonomy?*

- *Application.* Students use knowledge to solve real-life problems. For example, an objective might be to apply what has been learned about using a computer for word processing to how this could be used in various careers.
- *Analysis.* Students break down complex information into smaller parts and relate information to other information. For example, an objective might be to compare one type of word-processing program with another for doing term papers.
- *Synthesis.* Students combine elements and create new information. For example, an objective might be to organize all that has been learned about the use of computers for writing.
- *Evaluation.* Students make good judgments and decisions. For example, an objective might be to critique different word-processing programs or to judge the strengths and weaknesses of a particular word-processing program.

**The Affective Domain**    The affective taxonomy consists of five objectives related to emotional responses to tasks (Krathwohl, Bloom, & Masia, 1964). Each of the following five objectives requires the student to show some degree of commitment or emotional intensity:

- *Receiving.* Students become aware of or attend to something in the environment. For example, a guest comes to class to talk with students about reading. An objective might be for students to listen carefully to the speaker.
- *Responding.* Students become motivated to learn and display a new behavior as a result of an experience. An objective might be for students to become motivated to become better readers as a result of the guest speaker's appearance.
- *Valuing.* Students become involved in, or committed to, some experience. An objective might be for students to value reading as an important skill.
- *Organizing.* Students integrate a new value into an already existing set of values and give it proper priority. An objective might be to have students participate in a book club.
- *Value characterizing.* Students act in accordance with a new value and are firmly committed to it. An objective might be that over the course of the school year, students increasingly value reading.

**The Psychomotor Domain**    Most of us link motor activity with physical education and athletics, but many other subjects, such as handwriting and word processing, also involve movement. In the sciences, for another example, students have to manipulate complex equipment. Also, the visual and manual arts require good hand-eye coordination. Bloom's psychomotor objectives include these:

- *Reflex movements.* Students respond involuntarily, without conscious thought, to a stimulus—for example, blinking when an object unexpectedly hurtles their way.
- *Basic fundamentals.* Students make basic voluntary movements that are directed toward a particular purpose, such as grasping a microscope knob and correctly turning it.
- *Perceptual abilities.* Students use their senses, such as seeing, hearing, or touching, to guide their skill efforts, such as watching how to hold an instrument in science, like a microscope, and listening to instructions on how to use it.
- *Physical abilities.* Students develop general skills of endurance, strength, flexibility, and agility, such as running long distances or hitting a softball.

- *Skilled movements.* Students perform complex physical skills with some degree of proficiency, such as effectively sketching an object or scene.
- *Nondiscussive behaviors.* Students communicate feelings and emotions through bodily actions, such as doing pantomimes or dancing to communicate a musical piece.

Teachers can use Bloom's taxonomies for the cognitive, affective, and psychomotor domains to plan instruction (Borich, 2011). In the past, instructional planning has generally focused on cognitive or behavioral objectives. Bloom's taxonomy provides for a more expansive consideration of skills by including affective and psychomotor domains.

A group of educational psychologists updated Bloom's knowledge and cognitive process dimensions in light of recent theory and research (Anderson & Krathwohl, 2001). In the update, the knowledge dimension has four categories, which lie along a continuum from concrete (factual) to abstract (metacognition):

*How have the objectives been modified in the update of Bloom's cognitive taxonomy?*

- *Factual.* The basic elements students must know to be acquainted with a discipline or solve problems in it (technical vocabulary, sources of information)
- *Conceptual.* The interrelationships among the basic elements within a larger structure that allow them to function together (periods of geological time, forms of business ownership)
- *Procedural.* How to do something, methods of inquiry, and criteria for using skills (skills used in painting with watercolors, interviewing techniques)
- *Metacognitive.* Knowledge of cognition and awareness of one's own cognition (knowledge of outlining and strategies for remembering)

In the update of the cognitive process dimension, six categories lie along a continuum from less complex (remember) to more complex (create):

- *Remember.* Retrieve relevant knowledge from long-term memory. (For example, recognize the dates of important events in U.S. history.)
- *Understand.* Construct meaning from instruction that includes interpreting, exemplifying, classifying, summarizing, inferring, comparing, and explaining. (For example, explain the causes of important eighteenth-century events in France.)
- *Apply.* Carry out or use a procedure in a given situation. (For example, use a law in physics in situations in which it is appropriate.)
- *Analyze.* Break material into its component parts and determine how the parts relate to each other and to overall structure or purpose. (For example, distinguish between relevant and irrelevant numbers in a math word problem.)
- *Evaluate.* Make judgments based on criteria and standards. (For example, detect inconsistencies or fallacies in a product.)
- *Create.* Put elements together to form a coherent or functional whole; reorganize elements into a new pattern or structure. (For example, generate hypotheses to account for an observed phenomenon.)

## DIRECT INSTRUCTION

As we indicated in Chapter 1, **direct instruction** is a structured, teacher-centered approach that is characterized by teacher direction and control, high teacher expectations for students' progress, maximum time spent by students on academic tasks,

**direct instruction** Structured, teacher-centered approach focused on academic activity; characterized by teacher direction and control, high teacher expectations for student progress, and keeping negative affect to a minimum.

- - - - - - - - - - →

Thinking Back/Thinking Forward

A major curriculum controversy is whether teaching should mainly follow a direct instruction or constructivist approach. Chapter 1, p. 6; Chapter 12, p. 432

← - - - - - - - - - -

and efforts by the teacher to keep negative affect to a minimum. The focus of direct instruction is academic activity; nonacademic materials (such as toys, games, and puzzles) tend not to be used; also deemphasized is nonacademically oriented teacher-student interaction (such as conversations about self or personal concerns) (Burden & Byrd, 2010).

Teacher direction and control take place when the teacher chooses students' learning tasks, directs students' learning of the tasks, and minimizes the amount of nonacademic talk. The teacher sets high standards for performance and expects students to reach these levels of excellence.

An important goal in the direct-instruction approach is maximizing student learning time (Coyne & others, 2009; Estes, Mintz, & Gunter, 2011). Time spent by students on academic tasks in the classroom is called *academic learning time*. Learning takes time. The more academic learning time students experience, the more likely they are to learn the material and achieve high standards. The premise of direct instruction is that the best way to maximize time on academic tasks is to create a highly structured, academically oriented learning environment (Cobern & others, 2010; Coyne & others, 2010).

Cross-cultural research about the amount of time students spend on math in different countries, as well as other comparisons across countries, reveals that students in many Asian countries spend more time and effort in learning than do U.S. students. Harold Stevenson, one of the leading experts on children's learning, conducted research on this topic for five decades. In the 1980s and 1990s he turned his attention to discovering ways to improve children's learning by conducting cross-cultural comparisons of children in the United States with children in Asian countries, especially Japan, China, and Taiwan (Stevenson, 1992, 1995, 2000; Stevenson & Hofer, 1999; Stevenson & others, 1990). In Stevenson's research, Asian students consistently outperformed American students in mathematics. Also, the longer students were in school, the wider the gap became—the lowest difference was in first grade, the highest in eleventh grade (the highest grade studied).

To learn more about the reasons for these cross-cultural differences, Stevenson and his colleagues spent thousands of hours observing in classrooms, as well as interviewing and surveying teachers, students, and parents. They found that Asian teachers spent more of their time teaching math than American teachers did. For example, in Japan more than one-fourth of the total classroom time in first grade was spent on math instruction, compared with only one-tenth of the time in U.S. first-grade classrooms. Also, Asian students were in school an average of 240 days a year, compared with 178 days in the United States.

In addition, differences were found between the Asian and American parents. American parents had much lower expectations for the children's education and achievement than did the Asian parents. Also, the American parents were more likely to say that their children's math achievement was due to innate ability; the Asian parents were more likely to say that their children's math achievement was the consequence of effort and training (see Figure 12.2). The Asian students were more likely to do math homework than the American students, and the Asian parents were far more likely to help their children with their math homework than were the American parents (Chen & Stevenson, 1989).

In addition to maximizing student learning time, another emphasis in the direct-instruction approach is keeping negative affect to a minimum. Researchers have found that negative affect interferes with learning

DIVERSITY

RESEARCH

DEVELOPMENT

In Stevenson's research, Asian students scored considerably higher than U.S. students on math achievement tests. *What are some possible explanations for these findings?*

(Merrell & others, 2007). Advocates of direct instruction underscore the importance of keeping an academic focus and avoiding negative affect, such as the negative feelings that can often arise in both the teacher and students when a teacher overcriticizes.

## TEACHER-CENTERED INSTRUCTIONAL STRATEGIES

Many teacher-centered strategies reflect direct instruction. Here we will talk about orienting students to new material; lecturing, explaining, and demonstrating; questioning and discussing; mastery learning; seatwork; and homework.

**Orienting**   Before presenting and explaining new material, establish a framework for the lesson and orient students to the new material: (1) review the previous day's activities; (2) discuss the lesson's objective; (3) provide clear, explicit instructions about the work to be done; and (4) give an overview of today's lesson.

Advance organizers are teaching activities and techniques that establish a framework and orient students to material before it is presented. You can use advance organizers when you begin a lesson to help students see the "big picture" of what is to come and how information is meaningfully connected.

Advance organizers come in two forms: expository and comparative. **Expository advance organizers** provide students with new knowledge that will orient them to the upcoming lesson. The chapter-opening outline and learning goals in each chapter of this book are expository advance organizers. Another way to provide an expository advance organizer is to describe the lesson's theme and why it is important to study this topic. For example, in orienting students to the topic of exploring the Aztec civilization in a history class, the teacher says that they are going to study the Spanish invasion of Mexico and describes who the Aztecs were, what their lives were like, and their artifacts. To heighten student interest, she also says that they will study worlds in collision as Spain's conquistadors were filled with awe at sights of a spectacular Western civilization. There are Mexican American students in her class, and the teacher emphasizes how this information can help everyone in the class understand these students' personal and cultural identity.

**Comparative advance organizers** introduce new material by connecting it with what students already know. For example, in the history class just mentioned, the teacher says that the Spanish invasion of Mexico continued the transatlantic traffic that changed two worlds: Europe and the Americas. She asks students to think about how this discussion of the Aztecs connects with Columbus' journey, which they examined last week.

**Lecturing, Explaining, and Demonstrating**   Lecturing, explaining, and demonstrating are common teacher activities in the direct-instruction approach. Researchers have found that effective teachers spend more time explaining and demonstrating new material than their less effective counterparts do (Rosenshine, 1971).

On some occasions we sit through boring lectures, yet on other occasions we have been captivated by a lecturer and learned a great deal from the presentation. Let's explore some guidelines for when lecturing is a good choice and some strategies for delivering an effective lecture. Here are some goals that lecturing can accomplish:

1. Presenting information and motivating students' interest in a subject
2. Introducing a topic before students read about it on their own, or giving instructions on how to perform a task
3. Summarizing or synthesizing information after a discussion or inquiry
4. Providing alternative points of view or clarifying issues in preparation for discussion
5. Explaining materials that students are having difficulty learning on their own

**FIGURE 12.2** MOTHERS' BELIEFS ABOUT THE FACTORS RESPONSIBLE FOR CHILDREN'S MATH ACHIEVEMENT IN THREE COUNTRIES

In one study, mothers in Japan and Taiwan were more likely to believe that their children's math achievement was due to effort rather than innate ability, whereas U.S. mothers were more likely to believe their children's math achievement was due to innate ability (Stevenson, Lee, & Stigler, 1986). If parents believe that their children's math achievement is due to innate ability and their children are not doing well in math, the implication is that they are less likely to think their children will benefit from putting forth more effort.

From H. W. Stevenson, S. Lee, and J. W. Stigler, "Mathematics Achievement of Chinese, Japanese, and American Children," *Science*, Vol. 231 (Feb. 14, 1986), pp. 693–699 (Figure 6). http://www.sciencemag.org/cgi/content/abstract/231/4739/693. Reprinted with permission from AAAS. Readers may view, browse, and/or download material for temporary copying purposes only, provided these uses are for noncommercial personal purposes. Except as provided by law, this material may not be further reproduced, distributed, transmitted, modified, adapted, performed, displayed, published, or sold in whole or in part, without prior written permission from the publisher.

DIVERSITY

**advance organizers**  Teaching activities and techniques that establish a framework and orient students to material before it is presented.

**expository advance organizers**  Organizers that provide students with new knowledge that will orient them to the upcoming lesson.

**comparative advance organizers**  Organizers that introduce new material by connecting it with the students' prior knowledge.

# TEACHING CONNECTIONS: Best Practices
## Strategies for Lecturing

To ensure success when lecturing, follow these strategies:

1. *Be prepared.* Don't just "wing" a lecture. Spend time preparing and organizing what you will present.

2. *Make the lecture interesting and exciting by keeping it short and interspersing it with questions and activities.* Vary the pace of the lecture by interlacing it with related video clips, demonstrations, handouts, and/or activities for students. Think about what you can say that will motivate students' interest in a topic. Keep in mind the likely attention span of your students, based on their age when planning your lecture. For example, with older children or adolescents, you might lecture for 10 or 15 minutes to provide the background information and framework for a topic, then place students in small discussion groups. With younger children, you might only be able to hold their attention in a lecture format for 5 minutes before needing to move them to another activity.

3. *Follow a designated sequence and include certain key components:*
   - Begin with advance organizers or previews of the topic.
   - Verbally and visually highlight any key concepts or new ideas (like the boldfaced key terms in this book). Use the blackboard, an overhead projector, computer with projector, or another large-display device.
   - Present new information in relation to what students already know about the topic.
   - Periodically elicit student responses to ensure that they understand the information up to that point and to encourage active learning.
   - At the end of the lecture, provide a summary or an overview of the main ideas.
   - Make connections to future lectures and activities.

**Questioning and Discussing** It is necessary but challenging to integrate questions and discussion in teacher-centered instruction (Borich, 2011; Keeling, Polacek, & Ingram, 2009). Teachers should respond to each student's learning needs while maintaining the group's interest and attention. It also is important to distribute participation widely while also retaining the enthusiasm of eager volunteers. An additional challenge is allowing students to contribute while still maintaining the focus on the lesson.

**Mastery Learning** In **mastery learning,** one concept or topic is learned thoroughly before another is introduced. A successful mastery-learning approach involves these procedures (Bloom, 1971; Carroll, 1963):

- Specify the learning task or lesson. Develop precise instructional objectives. Establish mastery standards (this typically is where *A* students perform).

**mastery learning** Involves learning one topic or concept thoroughly before moving on to a more difficult one.

# TEACHING CONNECTIONS: Best Practices
## Strategies for the Effective Use of Questions

Let's examine some effective strategies for using questions in the classroom:

1. *Use fact-based questions as entreés into thinking-based questions.* For example, in teaching a lesson on environmental pollution, the teacher might ask the fact-based question, "What are three types of environmental pollution?" Then she could follow with this thinking-based question, "What strategies can you think of for reducing one of these types of environmental pollution?" Don't

overuse fact-based questions, because they tend to produce rote learning rather than learning for understanding.

2. *Avoid yes/no and leading questions.* Yes/no questions should be used only as a segue into more probing questions. For example, avoid questions like, "Was environmental pollution responsible for the dead fish in the lake?" Keep these questions to a minimum, only occasionally using them as a warm-up for questions such as these: "How did the pollution kill the fish?" "Why do

## TEACHING CONNECTIONS: Best Practices
### Strategies for the Effective Use of Questions

you think companies polluted the lake?" "What can be done to clean up environmental pollution?"

Also avoid asking leading questions such as, "Don't you agree?" or other rhetorical questions such as, "You do want to read more about environmental pollution, don't you?" These types of questions don't produce meaningful responses and simply hand the initiative back to the teacher.

4. *Leave enough time for students to think about answers.* Too often when teachers ask questions, they don't give students enough time to think. In one study, teachers waited less than one second, on the average, before calling on a student to respond (Rowe, 1986)! In the same study, teachers waited only about one second, on the average, for the student to respond before supplying the answer themselves. Such intrusions don't give students adequate time to construct answers. In the same study, teachers were subsequently instructed to wait three to five seconds to allow students to respond to questions. The increased wait time led to considerable improvements in responses, including better inferences about the materials and more student-initiated questions. Waiting three to five seconds or more for students to respond is

not as easy as it might seem; it takes practice. But your students will benefit considerably from having to think and construct responses. Increased wait time increases the likelihood that reflective students (see Chapter 4) will volunteer to answer questions in addition to impulsive students.

5. *Ask clear, purposeful, brief, and sequenced questions.* Avoid being vague. Focus the questions on the lesson at hand. Plan ahead so that your questions are meaningfully tied to the topic. If your questions are long-winded, you run the risk that they will not be understood, so briefer is better. Also plan questions so that they follow a logical sequence, integrating them with previously discussed material before moving to the next topic.

6. *Monitor how you respond to students' answers.* What should you do after a student responds to your question? Many teachers just say, "Okay," or, "Uh-huh" (Sadker, Sadker, & Zittleman, 2010). Instead, use the student's response as a basis for follow-up questions and engage the student or other students in a dialogue. Provide feedback that is tailored to the student's existing level of knowledge and understanding.

7. *Be aware of when it is best to pose a question to the entire class or to a particular student.* Asking the entire class a question makes all students in the class responsible for responding. Asking a specific student a question can make other students less likely to answer it. Some reasons to ask a question to a particular student are (a) to draw an inattentive student into the lesson, (b) to ask a follow-up question of someone who has just responded, and (c) to call on someone who rarely responds when questions are asked to the class as a whole. Don't let a small group of assertive students dominate the responses; talk with them independently about continuing their positive responses without monopolizing class time. One strategy for giving students an equal chance to respond is to pull names from a cookie jar or check names off a class list as students respond (Weinstein & Mignano, 2007).

8. *Encourage students to ask questions.* Praise them for good questions. Encourage them to ask "How?" and "Why?" When students ask a question to which you do not know the answer, be honest with them. Depending on the age of the students and the question asked, you might tell them that you will find out the answer and get back to them (then be sure to do so) or guide them in how they might research the question. Then share the answer with the rest of the class.

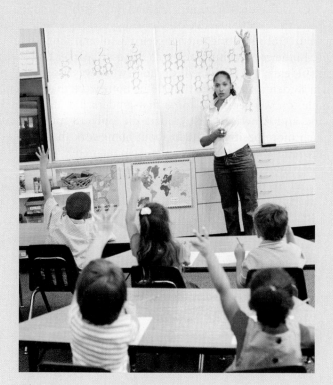

*What are some good teaching strategies for the effective use of questions?*

**For the teacher**

1. Keeping track of what the rest of the class is doing

2. Keeping students on-task

3. Dealing with the varying paces at which students work ("ragged" endings)

4. Selecting or creating seatwork that is clear and meaningful

5. Matching seatwork to students' varying levels of achievement

6. Collecting, correcting, recording, and returning seatwork assignments

**For the student**

1. Completing assigned work on their own

2. Understanding how and when to obtain the teacher's help

3. Understanding the norms for assisting peers

4. Learning how to be effective in obtaining help from peers

**FIGURE 12.3** CHALLENGES OF SEATWORK FOR TEACHERS AND STUDENTS

DIVERSITY

RESEARCH

- Break the course into learning units that are aligned with instructional objectives.

- Plan instructional procedures to include corrective feedback to students if they fail to master the material at an acceptable level, such as 90 percent correct. The corrective feedback might take place through supplemental materials, tutoring, or small-group instruction.

- Give an end-of-unit or end-of-course test that evaluates whether the student has mastered all of the material at an acceptable level.

Mastery learning gets mixed reviews. Some studies indicate that mastery learning is effective in increasing the time that students spend on learning tasks (Lalley & Gentile, 2009), but others find less support for mastery learning (Bangert, Kulik, & Kulik, 1983). Outcomes depend on the teacher's skill in planning and executing the strategy (Joyce & Weil, 2009). One context in which mastery learning might be especially beneficial is remedial reading (Schunk, 2011). A well-organized mastery learning program for remedial reading allows students to progress at their own rates based on their skills, their motivation, and the time they have to learn.

**Seatwork**    Seatwork refers to the practice of having all or a majority of students work independently at their seats. Teachers vary in how much they use seatwork as part of their instruction (Weinstein, 2007). Some teachers use it every day; others rarely use it. Figure 12.3 summarizes the challenges of seatwork for the teacher and the student.

Learning centers are especially good alternatives to paper-and-pencil seatwork. Figure 12.4 provides some suggestions for learning centers. A computer station can be an excellent learning center.

**Homework**    Another important instructional decision involves how much and what type of homework to give students (Demirici, 2011; Xu, 2010). Comments by a leading researcher, Harris Cooper (2006, 2007, 2009), suggest that in the United States homework is the source of more friction between school and home than any other aspect of education. In the cross-cultural research discussed earlier that focused on Asian and American students, the time spent on homework was assessed (Chen & Stevenson, 1989). Asian students spent more time doing homework than American students did. For example, on weekends Japanese first-graders did an average of 66 minutes of homework, and American first-graders did only 18 minutes. Also, Asian students had a much more positive attitude about homework than American students did. And Asian parents were far more likely to help their children with their homework than American parents were.

In a review, Cooper and his colleagues (2006) concluded that overall research indicates there is a positive influence of homework on students' achievement. The

| Science | Social studies | Mathematics | Art | Writing | Computer |
|---|---|---|---|---|---|
| Simple experiments with lab sheets | Recreating items used by different civilizations | Math "challenges" and puzzles | Holiday or thematic projects | Class story writing (e.g., add-on stories) | Content-related programs |
| Observations over time with recording forms | Creating charts or graphs of population trends | Manipulative activities | Crafts related to curriculum studies (quilting, quilling, origami, etc.) | Rewrites of literature | Simulations |
| Exploring properties of objects and classifying them | Map making | | | Writing plays or puppet shows | Story writing |

**FIGURE 12.4** SUGGESTIONS FOR LEARNING CENTERS

research review also indicated that the homework-achievement link is stronger in grades 7 to 12 than in kindergarten to grade 6. In one study, Cooper (1998) collected data on 709 students in grades 2 through 4 and 6 through 12. In the lower grades, there was a significant negative relation between the amount of homework assigned and students' attitudes, suggesting that elementary school children resent having to do homework. But in grades 6 and higher, the more homework students completed, the higher their achievement. It is not clear which was the cause and which the effect, though. Were really good students finishing more assignments because they were motivated and competent in academic subjects, or was completing homework assignments causing students to achieve more? Recent studies of German secondary school students support the general finding that homework assignments are linked to students' achievement gains (Trautwein, 2007; Trautwein & Ludtke, 2007).

A key aspect of the debate about whether elementary school children should be assigned homework is the type of homework assigned (Xu, 2010). What is good homework? Especially for younger children, the emphasis should be on homework that fosters a love of learning and hones study skills. Short assignments that can be quickly completed should be the goal. With young children, long assignments that go uncompleted or completed assignments that bring a great deal of stress, tears, and tantrums should be avoided. Too often teachers assign homework that duplicates without reinforcing material that is covered in class. Homework should be an opportunity for students to engage in creative, exploratory activities, such as doing an oral history of one's family or determining the ecological effects of neighborhood business. Instead of memorizing names, dates, and battles of the Civil War as a homework assignment, students might write fictional letters from Northerners to Southerners, expressing their feelings about the issues dividing the nation. The homework assignments should be linked to the next day's class activities to emphasize to students that homework has meaning and is not just a plot to make them miserable. Homework also should have a focus. Don't ask students to write an open-ended theme from a novel the class is reading. Rather, ask them to select a character and explain why he or she behaved in a particular way.

In Cooper and his colleagues' (2006) review of research, homework began to have a payoff in middle school. How can homework have little or no effect in elementary school yet be so beneficial in middle and high school? In the higher grades, it is easier to assign focused, substantive homework that requires students to integrate and apply knowledge—the type of homework that promotes learning (Corno, 1998). Also, by high school, students have resigned themselves to the routine of homework. Working hard after school and having good study skills are more accepted by middle and high school students than by younger ones.

Some educational psychologists argue that the main reason homework has not been effective in elementary school is that it has focused too much on subject matter and not enough on developing attitudes toward school, persistence, and responsible completion of assignments (Corno, 1998). They stress that it is not homework per se that benefits students but, rather, the opportunities it provides for the student to take responsibility. They think that teachers need to inform parents about guiding their children in these aspects of doing their homework: setting goals, managing their time, controlling their emotions, and checking their work, rather than playing avoidance games or leaving hard work for last. Teachers and parents can use homework in the early grades to help children wrestle with goal setting and follow-through.

Cooper and his colleagues (1989, 2009; Cooper, Robinson, & Patall, 2006; Cooper & Patell, 2007) also have found the following:

- Homework has more positive effects when it is distributed over a period of time rather than done all at once. For example, doing 10 math problems each night for five nights is better than doing 50 over the weekend.

DEVELOPMENT

RESEARCH

*"I don't have my homework because my little brother put a Pop-Tart® in my disk drive!"*

Art Bouthillier, from *Phi Delta Kappan* (February 1997). Reprinted by permission of Art Bouthillier.

- Homework effects are greater for math, reading, and English than for science and social studies.
- For middle school students, one or two hours of homework a night is optimal. High school students benefit from even more hours of homework, but it is unclear what a maximum number of hours ought to be.

Homework can be a valuable tool for increasing learning, especially in middle and high school (Cooper, 2006, 2007, 2009). However, it is important to make homework meaningful, monitor it and give students feedback about it, and involve parents in helping their child with it. A recent study of eighth-grade students taking a French class revealed that when homework involved a low emphasis on drill and practice tasks and teachers placed a high emphasis on students' self-responsibility for their motivation, students put more effort into completing homework assignments and scored higher on a standardized achievement test in French (Trautwein & others, 2009). In another recent study conducted in Germany, the "Big Five" personality factor of conscientiousness (discussed in Chapter 4) was linked with how much effort students put into homework (Trautwein & Ludtke, 2009). Also in this study, boys put more effort into homework in stereotypical "male" school subjects of math and physics, girls in stereotypical "female" subjects of foreign language (in this case, German) and English.

**RESEARCH**

**Thinking Back/Thinking Forward**

The "Big Five" personality factors are openness, conscientiousness, extraversion, agreeableness, and neuroticism (emotional stability). Chapter 4, p. 132

## EVALUATING TEACHER-CENTERED INSTRUCTION

Research on teacher-centered instruction has contributed many valuable suggestions for teaching, including these:

- Be an organized planner, create instructional objectives, and spend initial time orienting students to a lesson.
- Have high expectations for students' progress and ensure that students have adequate academic learning time.
- Use lecturing, explaining, and demonstrating to benefit certain aspects of students' learning.
- Engage students in learning by developing good question-asking skills and getting them involved in class discussion.
- Have students do meaningful seatwork or alternative work to allow individualized instruction with a particular student or a small group.
- Give students meaningful homework to increase their academic learning time and involve parents in students' learning.

Advocates of the teacher-centered approach especially believe that it is the best strategy for teaching basic skills, which involve clearly structured knowledge and skills (such as those needed in English, reading, math, and science). Thus, in teaching basic skills, the teacher-centered approach might consist of a teacher explicitly or directly teaching grammar rules, reading vocabulary, math computations, and science facts.

Teacher-centered instruction has not been without criticism. Critics say that teacher-centered instruction often leads to passive, rote learning and inadequate opportunities to construct knowledge and understanding (McCall, 2007). They also criticize teacher-centered instruction as producing overly structured and rigid classrooms, inadequate attention to students' socioemotional development, external rather than internal motivation to learn, too much reliance on paper-and-pencil tasks, few opportunities for real-world learning, and too little collaborative learning in small groups. Such criticisms are leveled mostly by advocates of learner-centered planning and instruction, which we will turn to next.

## Review, Reflect, and Practice

**2** Identify important forms of teacher-centered instruction.

**REVIEW**

- What are some useful tools in teacher-centered lesson planning?
- What is direct instruction?
- What are some good teacher-centered instructional strategies?
- What are some pros and cons of teacher-centered instruction?

**REFLECT**

- As a student, have you ever wished that a teacher used more (or less) teacher-centered instruction? What lessons can you draw from this for your own work as a teacher?

**PRAXIS™ PRACTICE**

1. Mr. McGregor has assigned his students to write an essay explaining the impact of the use of the atomic bomb during World War II. Which cognitive level of Bloom's taxonomy is best illustrated by this assignment?
   a. analysis
   b. application
   c. comprehension
   d. knowledge

2. A math teacher works with students to solve higher-level problems. The teacher engages the students in discussions of various approaches to solving the problems. The emphasis is on understanding the processes of solving the problems rather than on getting the correct answer. This math class is most typical of instructional methods in
   a. the United States
   b. France
   c. Japan
   d. Germany

3. Ms. Davidson is giving a lecture to introduce her students to a unit on the American Revolution. She begins with a little-known fact to pique her students' interest. She then distributes a brief outline of what her lesson will cover. She lectures from carefully prepared notes, using visual aids to help her students understand the material and keep their interest. Periodically during the lecture she asks questions to make sure her students are attending to, and understanding, the material. She calls on the first person to raise her hand to answer the question. If this person does not answer immediately, she supplies the answer herself so that students will not become confused and the lesson will not drag on. What should Ms. Davidson do differently?
   a. Allow her students more time to answer questions.
   b. Avoid asking questions during the lecture.
   c. Be more spontaneous in her class presentations.
   d. Avoid using distracting visual aids.

4. Ms. Bancroft likes to lecture most of the time, makes sure that her students stay on task when they are in the classroom, and has students do meaningful seatwork. Ms. Bancroft is following which of these approaches?
   a. cognitive constructivist
   b. social constructivist
   c. direct instruction
   d. individualized

*Please see the answer key at the end of the book.*

## ③ LEARNER-CENTERED LESSON PLANNING AND INSTRUCTION

| Learner-Centered Principles | Some Learner-Centered Instructional Strategies | Evaluating Learner-Centered Strategies |
|---|---|---|

Just as the behavioral approaches described in Chapter 7 provide the conceptual underpinnings for teacher-centered lesson planning and instruction, the information-processing and constructivist approaches discussed in Chapters 2, 8, 9, 10, and 11 form the theoretical backdrop for learner-centered lesson planning and instruction. In this section, we will explore the principles and strategies used in learner-centered instruction.

### LEARNER-CENTERED PRINCIPLES

Learner-centered lesson planning and instruction move the focus away from the teacher and toward the student (McCombs, 2010; Mtka & Gates, 2010). In one large-scale study, students' perceptions of a positive learning environment and interpersonal relationships with the teacher—factors associated with learner-centered instruction—were important in enhancing students' motivation and achievement (McCombs, 2001).

Increased interest in learner-centered principles of lesson planning and instruction has resulted in a set of guidelines called *Learner-Centered Psychological Principles: A Framework for School Reform and Redesign* (Presidential Task Force on Psychology and Education, 1992; Work Group of the American Psychological Association Board of Educational Affairs, 1995, 1997). The guidelines were constructed and are now periodically revised by a prestigious group of scientists and educators from a wide range of disciplines and interests. These principles have important implications for the way teachers plan and instruct as they are based on research on the most effective ways children learn.

The Work Group of the American Psychological Association Board of Educational Affairs (1997) stresses that research in psychology relevant to education has been especially informative, including advances in our understanding of cognitive, motivational, and contextual aspects of learning. The work group states that the learner-centered psychological principles it has proposed are widely supported and are being increasingly adopted in many classrooms. The principles emphasize the active, reflective nature of learning and learners. According to the work group, education will benefit when the primary focus is on the learner.

The 14 learner-centered principles can be classified in terms of four main sets of factors: cognitive and metacognitive, motivational and emotional, developmental and social, and individual differences (Work Group of the American Psychological Association Board of Educational Affairs, 1997). Figure 12.5 describes the 14 learner-centered principles.

John Mahoney teaches high school math in Washington, D.C. One of his students, Nicole Williams, says, "He's not going to tell you the answer. He's going to make you think" (Wong Briggs, 2004, p. 6D). *What are some important cognitive and metacognitive factors in learner-centered instruction?*

**Cognitive and Metacognitive Factors**

1. Nature of the learning process
   The learning of complex subject matter is most effective when it is an intentional process of constructing meaning from information and experience.

2. Goals of the learning process
   The successful learner, over time and with support and instructional guidance, can create meaningful, coherent representations of knowledge.

3. Construction of knowledge
   The successful learner can link new information with existing knowledge in meaningful ways.

4. Strategic thinking
   The successful learner can create a repertoire of thinking and reasoning strategies to achieve complex goals.

5. Thinking about thinking
   Higher-order strategies for selecting and monitoring mental operations facilitate creative and critical thinking.

6. Context of learning
   Learning is influenced by environmental factors, including culture, technology, and instructional practices.

**Motivational and Instructional Factors**

7. Motivational and emotional influences on learning
   What and how much is learned is influenced by the learner's motivation. Motivation to learn, in turn, is influenced by the learner's emotional states, beliefs, interests, goals, and habits of thinking.

8. Intrinsic motivation to learn
   The learner's creativity, higher-order thinking, and natural curiosity all contribute to motivation to learn. Intrinsic motivation is stimulated by tasks of optimal novelty and difficulty, relevant to personal interests and providing for personal choice and control.

9. Effects of motivation on effort
   Acquisition of complex knowledge and skills requires extended learner effort and guided practice. Without learners' motivation to learn, the willingness to exert this effort is unlikely without coercion.

**Developmental and Social Factors**

10. Developmental influences on learning
    As individuals develop, there are different opportunities and constraints for learning. Learning is most effective when development within and across physical, cognitive, and socioemotional domains is taken into account.

11. Social influences on learning
    Learning is influenced by social interactions, interpersonal relations, and communication with others.

**Individual Difference Factors**

12. Individual differences in learning
    Learners have different strategies, approaches, and capabilities for learning that are a function of prior experience and heredity.

13. Learning and diversity
    Learning is most effective when differences in learners' linguistic, cultural, and social backgrounds are taken into account.

14. Standards and assessment
    Setting appropriately high and challenging standards and assessing the learner as well as learning progress—including diagnostic, process, and outcome assessment—are integral parts of the learning process.

FIGURE **12.5** LEARNER-CENTERED PSYCHOLOGICAL PRINCIPLES

## SOME LEARNER-CENTERED INSTRUCTIONAL STRATEGIES

We already have discussed a number of strategies that teachers can consider in developing learner-centered lesson plans. These especially include the teaching strategies based on the theories of Piaget and Vygotsky (Chapter 2), constructivist aspects of thinking (Chapters 8 and 9), social constructivist aspects of thinking (Chapter 10), and learning and cognition in the content areas (Chapter 11). To provide you with a further sense of learner-centered strategies that you can incorporate into your lesson planning, we will examine problem-based learning, essential questions, and discovery learning.

**Problem-Based Learning** Problem-based learning emphasizes real-life problem solving (Chapin, 2009; Panasan & Nuangchalerm, 2010). A problem-based curriculum exposes students to the kind of authentic problems that crop up in everyday life. This learner-centered approach involves small-group efforts to identify problems or issues that the students wish to explore, then to locate the necessary materials and resources. Teachers act as guides, helping students to monitor their own problem-solving efforts (Chen, 2010; Donnelly, 2010).

In one example of a problem-based learning project, sixth-grade students explore an authentic health problem in the local community: the causes, incidence, and treatment of asthma and its related conditions (Jones, Rasmussen, & Moffitt, 1997). Students learn how environmental conditions affect their health and share this understanding with others. The project integrates information from many subject areas, including health, science, math, and the social sciences.

In a recent study, 20 eleventh-grade chemistry students were randomly assigned to either a teacher-centered or problem-based learning experience to learn about the effects of temperature, concentration, and pressure on cell potential (Tarhan & Acar, 2007). Interviews with the students following the instruction revealed that the students in both conditions were equally effective in students' understanding of the topic, but that students in the problem-based learning condition were more motivated, self-confident, and interested in solving problems.

**Essential Questions** Questions that reflect the heart of the curriculum, the most important things that students should explore and learn are **essential questions.** For example, in one lesson the initial essential question was, "What flies?" Students explored the question by examining everything from birds, bees, fish, and space shuttles to the notion that time flies and ideas fly. The initial question was followed by other questions, such as, "How and why do things fly in nature?" "How does flight affect humans?" and, "What is the future of flight?"

Essential questions like these perplex students, cause them to think, and provoke their curiosity (Lattimer, 2009). Essential questions are creative choices. With just a slight change, a lackluster question such as, "What was the effect of the Civil War?" can become the thought-provoking question, "Is the Civil War still going on?"

**Discovery Learning** In **discovery learning,** students construct an understanding on their own. Discovery learning stands in contrast to the direct-instruction approach discussed earlier in which the teacher directly explains information to students (Lawson, 2010). In discovery learning, students have to figure out things for themselves. Discovery learning meshes with the ideas of Piaget, who once commented that every time you teach a child something you keep the child from learning.

As teachers began to use discovery learning, they soon found that for it to be effective as a systematic instruction approach it needed to be modified. This led to the development of **guided discovery learning,** in which students are still encouraged to construct their understanding, but with the assistance of teacher-guided questions and directions (Mandrin & Preckel, 2009).

**Thinking Back/Thinking Forward**

Problem-based learning and project-based learning reflect a constructivist approach. Chapter 10, Pp. 335 and 354

RESEARCH

*What are some learner-centered psychological principles?*

**essential questions** Questions that reflect the heart of the curriculum, the most important things that students should explore and learn.

**discovery learning** Learning in which students construct an understanding on their own.

**guided discovery learning** Learning in which students are encouraged to construct their understanding with the assistance of teacher-guided questions and directions.

## TEACHING CONNECTIONS: Best Practices
### Strategies for Using Discovery and Guided Discovery

1. *For either of these strategies to be effective, your instructional objective must be discovery of something important.* Use of guided discovery increases the likelihood that students will discover what it is you want them to discover.

2. *Discovery learning and guided discovery each has its place.* You might use discovery learning with very young children to help them discover the principles of reversibility and conservation, by allowing free exploration of a sand or water table with various sized cups (see Chapter 2). You could also use guided discovery for this by giving children directions to pour water from one cup into another and asking them to note what they see.

   Discovery techniques could be used to help children discover what happens when one mixes primary colors. Using discovery learning, you would allow the children to experiment with this on their own (probably resulting in muddy brown, unless you only give them two colors of paint with which to experiment). Using guided discovery, you would ask the children to mix yellow and blue

and let you know the result. You have now guaranteed some shade of green will emerge.

   You would use guided discovery with older children and adolescents when they conduct science labs for which you have given them directions, thus ensuring the outcome of the experiment and safeguarding your students.

3. *When using guided discovery, make sure you do a trial run, following your own directions exactly as they are written.* Sometimes, given our knowledge, we leave out crucial steps in directions that we perform automatically. This can have unfortunate results—either students will not discover what we want them to discover or some negative side effect (such as a huge mess or the classic, "blowing up the chemistry lab") can happen.

4. *Always conduct a debrief following a discovery learning or guided discovery lesson.* It is important that you check to see that your students discovered what it is you wanted them to discover. This can be done via class discussion or written report

A research review indicated that guided discovery learning was superior to pure discovery learning in every case (Mayer, 2004). In this review, it also was concluded that constructivist learning is best supported by curricular focus than by pure discovery.

## EVALUATING LEARNER-CENTERED STRATEGIES

The learner-centered approach to lesson planning and instruction is positive in many ways (McCombs, 2010; Peters, 2010). The 14 learner-centered principles developed by the American Psychological Association task force can be very helpful in guiding students' learning. These principles encourage teachers to help students actively construct their understanding, set goals and plan, think deeply and creatively, monitor their learning, solve real-world problems, develop more positive self-esteem and control their emotions, be internally motivated, learn in a developmentally appropriate way, collaborate effectively with others (including diverse others), evaluate their learner preferences, and meet challenging standards.

*What is guided discovery learning?*

RESEARCH

   Critics of learner-centered instruction argue that it gives too much attention to the process of learning (such as learning creatively and collaboratively) and not enough to academic content (such as the facts of history) (Hirsch, 1996). Some critics stress that learner-centered instruction works better in some subjects than in others (Feng, 1996). They say that in areas with many ill-defined problems, such as the social sciences and humanities, learner-centered instruction can be effective. However, they believe that in well-structured knowledge domains such as math and science, teacher-centered structure works better. Critics also say that learner-centered instruction is less effective at the beginning level of instruction in a field because students do not have the knowledge to make decisions about what and how they

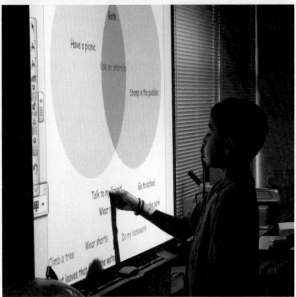

Students using interactive whiteboards at the Research Center for Educational Technology's AT&T classroom at Kent State University.

should learn. And critics stress that there is a gap between the theoretical level of student-centered learning and its actual application (Airasian & Walsh, 1997). The consequences of implementing learner-centered strategies in the classroom are often more challenging than anticipated.

Although we have presented teacher-centered and learner-centered planning and instruction in separate sections, don't think of them as always being either/or approaches. Many effective teachers use some of both in making the classroom a positive learning experience for children (Yeh, 2009). Research on the choice and sequencing of learning activities in the classroom indicates that the use of constructivist and direct-instruction approaches are often more effective than when either approach is used alone (Darling-Hammond & others, 2005).

Consider high school history teacher Robert Bain's (2005) description of how students initially spent time in learner-centered instruction working on constructing accounts of Columbus' voyage to America and struggled with the question of how the anniversaries of the voyage were celebrated. Bain then used teacher-centered direct instruction by lecturing about leading historians' current thinking about the topic. Also, a recent study of a ninth-grade technology-enhanced classroom revealed that both student-centered and teacher-centered instruction promoted students' conceptual understanding and provided students with different opportunities to engage in learning (Wu & Huang, 2007).

*Interactive whiteboards,* a relatively new instructional technology, can be used in both teacher-centered and student-centered instruction (Swan & others, 2009). In many schools they have replaced the traditional blackboard and chalk. This new technology allows teachers and students to interact with content projected from a computer screen onto a whiteboard surface (Torff & Tirotta, 2010). Virtually anything that can be done on a computer can be done on an interactive whiteboard, with the advantage that drawing, marking, and highlighting of computer-based output is supported. A whole class can follow interactions, and lessons can be saved and replayed.

I recently asked teachers to describe their most effective learner-center strategies. Following are their responses.

**EARLY CHILDHOOD**  Learner-centered strategies are common in my preschool classroom. For example, each morning children are given time for free play in which they play dress-up, pretend to cook in a mock kitchen, and build structures using Legos. Through these activities, children not only learn important skills, but they are also instilled with a love of school.

—**MISSY DANGLER,** *Suburban Hills School*

**ELEMENTARY SCHOOL: GRADES K–5**  I use guided discovery learning in almost all of my science classes. The children work in groups, are given guidance at the beginning of the lesson and then assigned a task to do in order to find the answer to a question. When students ask questions, I refer them to an instruction sheet I have given them or ask questions to guide their thinking. If a student asks, "Can we do this?" I reply, "Try it and see!" I also encourage students to count on other members of their group to uncover answers to questions and use phrases such as "Many heads are better than one."

—**JANINE GUIDA POUTRE,** *Clinton Elementary School*

**MIDDLE SCHOOL: GRADES 6–8**   In order to master new vocabulary, I often have my students quiz each other on vocabulary words. It is a noisy activity, but the students love it and learn at the same time.

—**MARGARET REARDON**, *Pocantico Hills School*

**HIGH SCHOOL: GRADES 9–12**   I prefer being the "guide on the side," not the "sage on the stage" when it comes to teaching. I did a writing workshop in which I presented a short mini-lesson each day, and my students chose how to spend the rest of the period. The students set their own goals, and their grade was partly based on achievement of those goals. I conferenced one-on-one with each student daily to monitor how they were doing; students loved the freedom.

—**JENNIFER HEITER**, *Bremen High School*

## TEACHING CONNECTIONS: Best Practices
### Strategies for Using Learner-Centered Instruction

Following are some effective ways to incorporate learner-centered instruction into your teaching:

1. *Become familiar with the learner-centered psychological principles, and incorporate them in your lesson planning and teaching.* Being learner-centered has more to do with matching your instruction to the needs of your students than to using particular techniques.

2. *Focus on the whole child.* Pay attention to motivational and affective factors, and developmental and social factors, in addition to cognitive factors. In Through the Eyes of Teachers, you can read about elementary school science teacher, Luis Recalde, and how he focuses on the whole child and makes learning fascinating for students.

Elementary school science teacher Luis Recalde holds up a seaweed specimen in one of the hands-on, high-interest learning contexts he creates for students.

### THROUGH THE EYES OF TEACHERS
#### Fostering Learning, Unity, and Civic Pride

Luis Recalde, a fourth- and fifth-grade science teacher at Vincent E. Mauro Elementary School, in New Haven, Connecticut, uses every opportunity to make science fascinating and motivating for students to learn. Recalde infuses hands-on science experiences with energy and enthusiasm. To help students get a better sense of what it is like to be a scientist, he brings lab coats to the classroom for students to wear. He holds science fair workshops for teachers and often gives up his vacation time to help students with science projects. He started soccer teams and gardens to foster unity and civic pride among African American and Latino stu-

dents. An immigrant himself, he knows the importance of fostering positive relations among students from different ethnic groups.

3. *Use problem-based learning, essential questions, and guided discovery learning in your teaching.*

4. *Remember that the most effective teachers don't use direct instruction or learner-centered instructional strategies exclusively but rather use both to make the classroom a positive learning experience for students.*

## Review, Reflect, and Practice

**③** Discuss important forms of learner-centered instruction.

### REVIEW

* What is learner-centered lesson planning? Summarize the APA's 14 learner-centered principles.
* How do problem-based learning, essential questions, and discovery learning each embody learner-centered principles?
* What are some pros and cons of learner-centered instruction?

### REFLECT

* As a student, have you ever wished that a teacher would use more (or less) learner-centered instruction? What lessons can you draw from this for your own work as a teacher?

### PRAXIS™ PRACTICE

1. Joan just received a *D* on her science exam. "I knew it," she states, "I've never been any good at science." Which set of factors of the APA's learner-centered principles is best exemplified by Joan's statement?
   a. cognitive and metacognitive
   b. developmental and social
   c. individual differences
   d. motivational and emotional

2. Mr. Williams wants his third-grade students to understand the purpose of blubber in marine mammals. He sets up an experiment for his students using ice water, latex gloves, and lard. First, students put their gloved hands in ice water until they cannot keep them there any longer. Other students time how long they keep their hands submerged. Then, students put their gloved hands in bags of lard and submerge their hands again. Again, other students time how long they keep their hands submerged. All of the students are able to keep their hands in the ice water longer with their hands in the lard than they can when their hands are merely gloved. What learner-centered instructional strategy has Mr. Williams used?
   a. discovery learning
   b. essential questions
   c. guided discovery
   d. problem-based learning

3. Ms. Flanagan, who takes a teacher-centered approach, just observed Mr. Houston's constructivist teaching in his seventh-grade math class. Ms. Flanagan is likely to be most critical of which of the following she observed?
   a. Mr. Houston assigning students homework
   b. Mr. Houston encouraging students to construct their own math problem-solving strategies
   c. Mr. Houston having high expectations for student learning
   d. Mr. Houston using technology to help students learn

*Please see the answer key at the end of the book.*

# 4  TECHNOLOGY AND EDUCATION

| The Technology Revolution and the Internet | Standards for Technology-Literate Students | Teaching, Learning, and Technology |
|---|---|---|

TECHNOLOGY

So far in this chapter we have described many aspects of planning and instruction. In contemporary society, technology plays important roles in planning and instruction (Lever-Duffy & McDonald, 2011; Maloy & others, 2011). Three important ways that technology affects curriculum planning are (1) as a learning goal for students to develop certain technology competencies; (2) as a resource for curriculum planning through the extensive materials that are available on the Internet; and (3) as tools that improve students' ability to learn through techniques such as simulation and visualization in science and text analysis in literature, as well as software that encourages reflection and provides models of good performances (Darling-Hammond & others, 2005).

Technology is such an important theme in education that it is woven throughout this book. In each chapter you come across one or more discussions of technology related to the chapter's contents. For example, you already have studied such topics as technology and children's vocabulary development (Chapter 2), technology connections with students around the world (Chapter 5), computer-supported intentional learning environments (Knowledge Forum) (Chapter 10), and content-specific applications of technology in reading, writing, math, science, and social studies (Chapter 11). Here we will explore the technology revolution and the Internet, standards for technology-literate students, and teaching and learning with technology.

## THE TECHNOLOGY REVOLUTION AND THE INTERNET

Students today are growing up in a world that is far different technologically from the world in which their parents and grandparents were students. If students are to be adequately prepared for tomorrow's jobs, technology must become an integral part of schools and classrooms (de Jong, 2011; Newby & others, 2011; Roblyer & Doering, 2010).

**The Internet**  The **Internet** is a system of computer networks that operates worldwide. As the core of computer-mediated communication, the Internet is playing an important role in the technology revolution, especially in schools (Poteete, 2011). In many cases, the Internet has more current, up-to-date information than textbooks. Nearly 100 percent of public schools in the United States are now connected to the Internet.

However, the Internet did not become the common portal it is today until the introduction of the World Wide Web (the Web). The **Web** is a system for browsing Internet sites. It is named the Web because it is made of many sites linked together. The Web presents the user with documents, called Web pages, full of links to other documents or information systems. Selecting one of these links, the user can access more information about a particular topic. Web pages include text as well as multimedia (images, video, animation, and sound—all of which can be accessed by students with a click on words or images presented on a computer screen). Web indexes and search engines such as Google and Yahoo! can help students find the information they are seeking by examining and collating a variety of sources.

The Internet can be a valuable tool for helping students learn (O'Bannon & Puckett, 2010). However, it has some potential drawbacks. To use it effectively with your students, you will have to know how to use it and feel comfortable with it, as well as have up-to-date equipment and software. In addition, concerns have been raised about students accessing pornographic material and biased Web sites and about the accuracy of information gleaned from the Internet (Brown, Green, &

Thinking Back/Thinking Forward

Technology and children's vocabulary development. Chapter 2, p. 61

Technology connections with students around the world. Chapter 5, p. 160

Computer-supported intentional learning environments. Chapter 10, p. 353

Content-specific applications of technology in reading, writing, math, science, and social studies. Chapter 11, p. 391

A student creating a multimedia program in the Research Center for Educational Technology's AT&T classroom at Kent State University.

**Internet**  The core of computer-mediated communication; a system of computer networks that operates worldwide.

**Web**  A system for browsing Internet sites that refers to the World Wide Web; named the Web because it is comprised of many sites that are linked together.

*"I see what's wrong with your calculator—it's the remote control to your TV."*

John R. Shanks, from *Phi Delta Kappan* (June 1997). Reprinted by permission of John R. Shanks.

### Thinking Back/Thinking Forward

Collaborative learning is reflected in teaching strategies such as the use of cooperative learning and small-group work. Chapter 10, p. 346

### Thinking Back/Thinking Forward

In Fostering a Community of Learners, e-mail is used to build community and expertise. Chapter 10, p. 352

Robinson, 2010). Many of these problems are solved by installing firewalls or blocking software on school servers.

When used effectively, the Internet expands access to a world of knowledge and people that students cannot experience in any other way (Lever-Duffy & McDonald, 2011; Morrison & Lowther, 2010). Here are some effective ways that the Internet can be used in classrooms:

- *Navigating and integrating knowledge.* The Internet has huge databases of information on a vast array of topics that are organized in different ways. As students explore Internet resources, they can work on projects that integrate information from various sources that they could not otherwise access. One way to support such work is through WebQuests (**http://webquest.sdsu.edu**). A WebQuest is an inquiry-oriented activity designed by teachers that maximizes student learning time, emphasizes using information rather than looking for it, and stimulates thinking. WebQuests focus student efforts on doable tasks, provide a set of information resources and guidance for completing those tasks, and frame the work in an integrative context (Segers & Verhoeven, 2009). They help introduce students to Internet searching in meaningful ways.

- *Collaborative learning.* One of the most effective ways to use the Internet in your classroom is through project-centered activities (Ertmer & others, 2009). Indeed, many WebQuests are designed to be collaborative, with roles and tasks assigned to different members of each group. Another collaborative use of the Internet is to have a group of students conduct a survey on a topic, put it on the Internet, and hope to obtain responses from many parts of the world. They can organize, analyze, and summarize the data they receive, then share them with other classes around the world. Another type of collaborative learning project involves sending groups of students on Internet "scavenger hunts" to find information and/or solve a problem.

- *Computer-mediated communications (CMC).* An increasing number of innovative educational projects include the use of computer-mediated communications. For example, there are many online sites (such as **www.studentsoftheworld.info, www.tesol.net/teslpnpl.html**) set up for teachers and students to correspond with "pen pals" around the world. Some of these even provide safe access to more innovative CMC forms such as chats and blogs (such as **www.studentsoftheworld.info**). In Chapter 10, we examined Ann Brown and Joe Campione's (1996) program, Fostering a Community of Learners, in which students communicate with experts via e-mail, giving them access to a wider circle of knowledgeable people. In the Global Lab project (**http://globallab.terc.edu**), a yearlong, interdisciplinary science curriculum for middle school students, students conduct science investigations at their own local "study sites" and then share their findings with students around the country through an Internet discussion board.

- *Improving teachers' knowledge and understanding.* Two excellent Internet resources for teachers are the Educational Resources Information Center (ERIC at **www.eric.ed.gov**) and the Educators' Reference Desk (**www.eduref.org**), which provide free information about a wide range of educational topics. The ERIC database gives abstracts of more than 1 million journal and nonjournal educational papers going back to 1966 and the full text of over 100,000 papers from educational conferences. The Educators' Reference Desk gives easy access to over 2,000 lesson plans and over 3,000 links to online education information. Other excellent Internet resources for teachers include TappedIn (**http://tappedin.org/tappedin**), an online site that brings educators together in learning communities to discuss educational issues and work on collaborative projects, and the PBS TeacherLine (**http://teacherline.pbs.org/teacherline**), which provides both links to teaching resources and online professional development courses for teachers. NASA for educators (**www.nasa.gov/audience/foreducators/index.html**) has an extensive set of resources geared to teachers at all levels and in all subject areas as well as professional development materials to use them effectively.

**Graphics and Presentation**    Graphics software like *PowerPoint* can improve many of the presentations you use in teaching. Such software graphics packages allow you to copy and create images, formulate charts and graphs, set the timing of material, and make excellent visual presentations (Macario, 2010). They can help you organize your content and place it in a dynamic format. However, flashy graphics are no substitute for a well-rehearsed presentation. Text presented on the screens should support material presented orally.

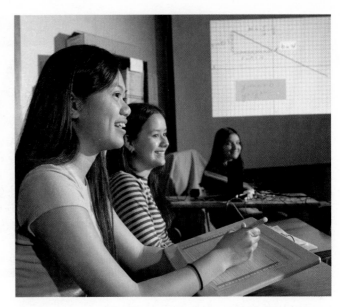

High school students creating a PowerPoint presentation in a math class.

## STANDARDS FOR TECHNOLOGY-LITERATE STUDENTS

Schools must take an active role in ensuring that students become technologically literate. Most national standards recognize this. For example, the National Council of Teachers of English/International Reading Association Standards for the English Language Arts (NCTE/IRA, 1996) include the following: "Students use a variety of technological and information resources (such as libraries, databases, computer networks, and video) to gather and synthesize information and to create and communicate knowledge." Also, a major theme in the National Council for the Social Studies, Curriculum Standards for the Social Studies (NCSS, 1994) is "Science, Technology, and Society."

The International Society for Technology in Education has developed the following six technology standards for students (ISTE, 2007) and teachers (ISTE, 2007).

1. *Creativity and innovation.* Students show creative thinking, construct knowledge, and develop innovative products using technology.

2. *Communication and collaboration.* Students use digital media and contexts to work collaboratively, including at a distance, to improve learning.

3. *Research and information fluency.* Students apply digital tools to gather, evaluate, and use information.

A student creating a bar graph on a computer.

4. *Critical thinking, problem solving, and decision making.* Students engage in critical thinking to plan and carry out research, manage projects, solve problems, and make effective decisions using appropriate technology.

5. *Digital citizenship.* Students improve their understanding of human, societal, and cultural issues involving technology and demonstrate ethical behavior.

6. *Technology operations and concepts.* Students understand technology operations and concepts.

In addition, ISTE provides performance indicators for achieving these standards at four levels: prekindergarten through second grade, grades 3 through 5, grades 6 through 8, and grades 9 through 12. ISTE also includes examples and scenarios to illustrate how technology literacy can be integrated across the curriculum at each of these levels.

DEVELOPMENT

Students at Christopher Maddox High School in Park City, Utah, present a daily, live TV broadcast to more than 1,200 peers and 80 adults. The students create a program that highlights school news and events and have full responsibility for writing scripts, operating cameras, directing segments, and other aspects of producing a TV broadcast.

For example, a curriculum example that effectively uses technology at the first level focuses on animals and their sounds. In Sharon Fontenot's class at Prien Lake Elementary School, students learn to identify polar bears, lions, and other wild animals through images, video clips, and sounds on the *World of Animals* CD-ROM. The teacher models the effective use of technology by creating a tape recording based on information from the CD-ROM and incorporating her own voice to fit the needs of the class. Students practice reading and listening skills by answering questions that encourage them to think about both the science and social living issues related to these animals. Students create their own stories about what they learned using *Kid Pix*, a software program that lets them make their own pictures of the animals, turn them into slide shows, and print out their own books to share with family and friends.

At the second level (grades 3 through 5), a teacher might make extensive use of Internet resources. She could use the Exploring the Environment Web site (**www.cotf.edu/ete**) to access class-tested problem-based learning modules or the Global Learning and Observations for a Better Environment (GLOBE) Web site (**www.globe.gov**) to engage students in making environmental observations around the school, reporting the data to a processing facility through GLOBE, and using global images created from their data to examine local environmental issues.

Population growth and urban planning are the focus of a social studies technology-based learning activity in grades 9 through 12. The activity challenges students to find sources online and elsewhere that describe real-world population dilemmas. The activity can be altered to address different cities and regions worldwide. In small groups in class, students can discuss problems that may occur as a result of a city being heavily populated. They can be asked to project what problems a city such as Tokyo is likely to face in terms of population growth in the year 2050.

ISTE (2007) has created a profile of what characterizes a technology-literate student at prekindergarten through second grade, grades 3–5, grades 6–8, and grades 9–12. Figure 12.6 shows a sampling of these profiles.

These scenarios capture most aspects of the ways in which the Partnership for 21st Century Skills (2010) suggests technology can help teachers and schools look beyond the requirements of the No Child Left Behind legislation to help students develop the knowledge, skills, and attitudes they will need in the coming era. They advocate emphasizing core subjects and learning skills using twenty-first-century tools and content in a twenty-first-century context, and using twenty-first-century assessments to measure those skills.

## TEACHING, LEARNING, AND TECHNOLOGY

A special concern is how technology can be used to improve teaching and learning (Lever-Duffy & McDonald, 2011; Maloy & others, 2011). The Partnership for 21st Century Skills (2010) argues that there is a huge gap between the technology knowledge and skills most students learn in school and the technology knowledge and skills they need in the twenty-first-century workplace. The Partnership emphasizes that schools need to move beyond the emphasis on core content required by the No Child Left Behind legislation and focus more on twenty-first-century themes, including media and technology literacy.

**Using Technology to Improve Students' Understanding**    In line with the thesis of the Partnership for 21st Century Skills (2010), over the last two decades at

| Prekindergarten–Grade 2 | Grades 3–5 | Grades 6–8 | Grades 9–12 |
|---|---|---|---|
| 1. Illustrate and communicate original ideas and stories using digital tools and media-rich resources. | 1. Produce a media-rich digital story about a local event based on first-person interviews. | 1. Describe and illustrate a content-related concept using a model, simulation, or concept-mapping software. | 1. Design, develop, and test a digital learning game to demonstrate knowledge and skills related to curriculum content. |
| 2. Identify, research, and collect data on an environmental issue using digital resources and propose a developmentally appropriate solution. | 2. Use digital-imaging technology to modify or create works of art for use in a digital presentation. | 2. Create original animations or videos documenting school, community, or local events. | 2. Create and publish an online art gallery with examples and commentaries that demonstrate an understanding of different historical periods, cultures, and countries. |
| 3. Engage in learning activities with learners from multiple cultures through e-mail and other electronic means. | 3. Recognize bias in digital resources while researching an environmental issue with guidance from the teacher. | 3. Gather data, examine patterns, and apply information for decision making using digital tools and resources. | 3. Select digital tools or resources to use for a real-world task and justify the selection based on their efficiency and effectiveness. |
| 4. In collaborative group work, use a variety of technologies to produce a digital solution or product in a curriculum area. | 4. Select and apply digital tools to collect, organize, and analyze data to evaluate theories or hypotheses. | 4. Participate in a cooperative learning project in an online learning community. | 4. Employ curriculum-specific simulations to practice critical thinking. |
| 5. Find and evaluate information related to a current or historical person or event using digital resources. | 5. Identify and investigate a global issue and generate possible solutions using digital tools and resources. | 5. Evaluate digital resources to determine the credibility of the author and publisher and the timelines and accuracy of the information. | 5. Identify a complex global issue, develop a systematic plan of investigation, and present innovative sustainable solutions. |

**FIGURE 12.6** A SAMPLING OF ISTE'S (2007) PROFILES FOR TECHNOLOGY-LITERATE STUDENTS AT DIFFERENT GRADE LEVELS

the Educational Technology Center at Harvard University, a number of educators have worked on ways to use technology to improve students' understanding. Martha Stone Wiske has especially been instrumental in creating ways to incorporate technology into classroom contexts that transform student learning. Stone Wiske and her colleagues (2005) recently described how to more effectively use technology to teach for understanding by considering (1) the topics that are worth understanding, (2) what students should understand about such topics, (3) how students develop and demonstrate understanding, (4) how students and teachers assess understanding, and (5) how students and teachers learn together. These five aspects of understanding are based on ideas developed at Harvard by David Perkins, Howard Gardner, and Vito Perrone. Following are Stone Wiske and her colleagues' (2005) views of how to use technology for understanding:

1. *Evaluate which topics are worth understanding.* Technology is especially appropriate for generating worthwhile and interesting learning topics. The Internet provides a wealth of information about virtually every topic imaginable that can be mined to generate new topics or expand what students are studying as part of the curriculum. (O'Bannon & Puckett, 2010). The wide range of information provided by the Internet allows students to learn more about their own interests and ideas and carve a unique pathway in learning about a topic, instead of following cookie-cutter steps from a traditional textbook or workbook (Roblyer & Doering, 2010).

   Stone Wiske and her colleagues (2005) also recommend that technology be used to teach in problem areas that emerge every year. "Examples include heat and temperature or weight and density in science, ratios in mathematics, and stereotypes in history and social studies classes" (p. 28). These topics, which many students

A student creating shapes and patterns on a computer in a Los Angeles elementary school.

struggle to understand, are central to the subject matter and are frequently more easily understood through the use of technology.

2. *Think about what students should understand about a topic.* When teachers consider using technology in the classroom, it is important for them to think about the learning goals they have for their students (Bell & Bull, 2010). Goals might include learning a new concept or applying a key concept to relevant situations. A goal related to technology might be to understand how to find and critically examine information on the Internet that is relevant to a classroom topic. Generating goals in this manner reminds the teacher that "surfing the Web" is "not an end in itself" but rather a way to use "technology to accomplish meaningful work" (Stone Wiske, Franz, & Breit, 2005, p. 44).

3. *Pay attention to how students develop and demonstrate understanding.* Use technology to help students "stretch their minds" and understand something in ways that they never did before. In improving students' understanding, Stone Wiske and her colleagues (2005) recommend that teachers use technology when it can "enhance and enrich their performances of understanding. . . . Word processors, digital audio and video technologies for creating Web sites allow students to express their understanding in a rich variety of media. These technologies also capture student work in forms that can be easily revised, combined, and distributed" (Wiske, Franz, & Breit, 2005, pp. 65–66).

4. *Consider how students and teachers assess learning.* Use ongoing assessment instead of using only a final assessment (Means, 2006). During ongoing assessment, you might guide students in understanding what quality work involves or use peer collaboration to help students analyze and improve their work. A helpful strategy is to also encourage students to assess their own learning progress and to monitor how effectively they are learning. Technology can be used in several ways to effectively assess learning, as follows:

   > Digital technologies, including audio and video recorders and computers, can capture student work in forms that are easy to review. Interactive workspaces and soft ware with multiple windows can help to keep assessment guidelines in view and even offer prompts and reminders. . . . Using networked technologies, students may post their work online where it can be readily reviewed and annotated by multiple advisors, including distant teachers and peers who cannot meet face-to-face. Technologies also provide easy means of preserving digital archives of student work. These may allow teachers and students to create individual portfolios to demonstrate and evaluate a student's work over time. (Wiske, Franz, & Breit, 2005, pp. 84–85)

5. *Reflect on how students and teachers can learn together.* "Networked technologies provide multiple advantages for connecting learners with reflective, collaborative communities. . . ." For example,

   > E-mail permits users to send and receive many-to-many messages and to do so quickly. Students can share information and work with many other students all over the world, exchanging multiple rounds of reflective dialogue. The Web, with digital images, video and audio recordings, and videoconferencing, also allows students and their teachers to publish and collaborate on work, opening up the possibility of communicating with a wide range of audiences outside the classroom. (Wiske, Franz, & Breit, 2005, pp. 100, 102)

In further considering the role of technology in learning, a technology program that is increasingly used in schools is the GenYes program. The goal of the GenYes program is to support the effective integration of technology in teaching and learning (GenYes, 2010). The program, created by Dennis Harper at the Northwest Regional Educational Laboratory, emphasizes that teachers and students are partners in creating lessons that use technology in ways students find meaningful and relevant. GenYes is available for both elementary and secondary school students, who learn by cocreating lessons with teachers and their teachers learn about technology from the students. Instead of teaching technology skills to teachers with the hope that they will use those skills in teaching students, GenYes works with students to help them form productive technology partnerships with their teachers. Students and their teacher-partners learn how to use telecommunication devices, the Internet, presentation tools, and other emerging technologies.

Among the technology units that GenYes students and teachers collaborate on are

- *Online communications,* such as safety, e-mail, forums, blogs, messaging, and collaborative projects
- *Digital media,* such as graphics, animation, and video
- *Digital authoring,* including planning, creating, and delivering multimedia projects
- *Web publishing,* such as how to design and construct Web pages
- *Student leadership and community service*

Students working on a GenYes project. *What are some characteristics of GenYes?*

In addition, a number of mini-units, such as podcasting, digital storytelling, handhelds, and video tutorials can be incorporated in the GenYes class or used by students when they are working on technology projects.

GenYes students are paired, either individually or in teams, with a partner-teacher. Initial meetings are held to determine a curriculum focus that could be enriched by an infusion of technology. The GenYes students are responsible for the nuts and bolts of the technology, and the teacher provides content accuracy and pedagogical strategies. The GenYes program was initiated in Olympia, Washington, in 1996 and is now used in a number of classrooms across the United States. Teachers and students have consistently reported that GenYes has provided them with an excellent opportunity to improve their technology skills. The GenYes program reflects the learner-centered strategies we discussed earlier in this chapter and the social constructivist approach described in Chapter 10.

**Technological Pedagogical Content Knowledge (TPCK)**   The *Technological Pedagogical Content Knowledge (TPCK)* model, created by Matthew Koehler and Punya Mishra (2010; Mishra & Koehler, 2006) that emphasizes the importance of not looking at technology as a stand-alone entity but rather addressing links between technology, content knowledge, and pedagogy (see Figure 12.7). In their view, knowing how to use technology is not sufficient for instructional success in the classroom; you also need to know how to teach it. They argue that teachers who are skilled in all three domains—technology, content knowledge, and pedagogy—have a different level of expertise in teaching a particular topic than a technology expert (a computer scientist, for example), a content knowledge expert in a particular discipline (science, for example), and a pedagogical expert (an experienced educator, for example). TPCK has been adopted by the American Association of Colleges of Teacher Education and sponsored a book by Koehler and Mishra (2010) on the integration of technology, content knowledge, and pedagogy to improve classroom instruction.

**Stages of Integrating Technology into Classroom Teaching** Integrating technology into your classroom teaching often follows the following sequence (Norris & Soloway, 1999):

**Stage 1:** Teacher's awareness that a particular technology exists but hasn't used it; may be avoiding the technology

**Stage 2:** Teacher is currently trying to learn the basic aspects of the technology but often becomes frustrated and still lacks confidence with this technology

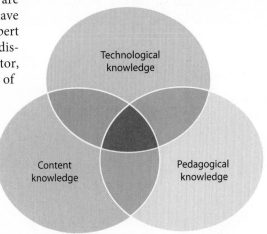

**FIGURE 12.7** TECHNOLOGICAL PEDAGOGICAL CONTENT KNOWLEDGE (TPCK)

# SELF-ASSESSMENT 12.1
## Evaluating My Technology Skills and Attitudes

How good are your technology skills? How positive are your attitudes about using technology and incorporating it into your classroom? For these items, consider the grade and subject(s) you are most likely to teach. Rate yourself from 1 to 5, with 1 = Not like me at all and 5 = Very much like me.

| | 1 | 2 | 3 | 4 | 5 |
|---|---|---|---|---|---|

1. I'm reasonably proficient at using a computer and installing and uninstalling software.

2. I have become comfortable with using a word-processing program.

3. I know when and how to use technology to improve students' understanding.

4. I have ideas for using word processing together with other language learning resources in the classroom.

5. I know how to search efficiently and thoroughly for information that interests me on the Internet.

6. I have ideas about how to use the Internet in my classroom.

7. I'm proficient at using e-mail.

8. I know how to use PowerPoint.

9. I have been part of collaborative learning exercises that involve technology.

10. I can see how collaborative learning can be used with technology in my classroom.

11. I am aware of the sociocultural issues involved in technology and education.

12. I know some good Web sites, journals, and software catalogs that can help me learn how to use technology more effectively in the classroom.

## SCORING AND INTERPRETATION

Look at your scores for each item and evaluate your technology strengths and weaknesses. By the time you step into your classroom for your first day of teaching, make it a goal to be able to confidently rate yourself on each of these items at the level of 4 or 5. On items on which you rated yourself 1, 2, and 3, try to take technology courses at your local college that will improve your knowledge and skills in those areas.

**Stage 3:** Teacher beginning to see how to use a particular technology and thinks about specific situations in which to use it

**Stage 4:** Teacher is gaining confidence in using the technology for certain tasks and feeling more comfortable in using it

**Stage 5:** Teacher now thinks about this technology as something that can help him or her and no longer lacks confidence in using it; perceives that it can be used in a number of instructional contexts

**Stage 6:** Teacher can use this technology as an effective instructional tool across the curriculum to meet instructional objectives

To further evaluate your technology skills and attitudes, complete Self-Assessment 12.1.

I recently asked teachers how they use technology to help students learn. Following are their responses.

**EARLY CHILDHOOD**   Technology helps preschoolers learn music—in addition to listening to music to learn a song, they can also see the written words projected on a screen along with appropriate clip art.

—**Connie Christy,** *Aynor Elementary School (Preschool Program)*

**ELEMENTARY SCHOOL: GRADES K–5**   I often have my fifth-grade students research topics using Google and have them sift through the information. We discuss valid sources and try to determine ones that are questionable.

—**Craig Jensen,** *Cooper Mountain Elementary School*

**MIDDLE SCHOOL: GRADES 6–8**   As a Spanish-language teacher, I devised a plan with a teacher from Chile in which my students e-mailed her students in Spanish. In turn, her students e-mailed mine in English. This bilingual process helped both groups of students learn the respective languages of each country.

—**Margaret Reardon,** *Pocantico Hills School*

**HIGH SCHOOL: GRADES 9–12**   Because kids love technology so much, I like to display notes using PowerPoint slides instead of simply lecturing. Video clips and connection to the Internet are available, so it is easy to display visuals to reinforce topics. I also encourage my students to purchase a flash drive so that their work can be portable and all in one place.

—**Jennifer Heiter,** *Bremen High School*

## TEACHING CONNECTIONS: Best Practices
### Strategies for Choosing and Using Technology in the Classroom

Technology will be a part of your classroom. Here are some guidelines for choosing and using it:

1. *Ask yourself in what way(s) and to what degree the use of technology might enhance student learning.* Not all lessons are enhanced by the use of technology. Others are enhanced greatly.

2. *Choose technology with an eye toward how it can help students actively explore, construct, and restructure information.* Look for software that lets students directly manipulate the information. One review found that students' learning improved when information was presented in a multimedia fashion that stimulated them to actively select, organize, and integrate visual and verbal information (Mayer, 1997). You might want to consult with a school or district media specialist for the soft-

ware that best reflects these characteristics. Two excellent resources for teachers that emphasize the use of technology to improve students' learning and understanding are the Education with New Technologies (ENT) Web site (**http://learnweb.harvard.edu/ent/home/ index.cfm**) and the International Society for Technology in Education (ISTE) Web site (**www.iste.org**). The ENT Web site is especially designed to help you integrate technology into your own classroom. Software catalogs and journals also are good sources.

3. *Look for ways to use technology as part of collaborative and real-world learning.* In Ann Brown and Joe Campione's (1996) words, education should be about "fostering a community of learners." Students often learn

*(continued)*

## TEACHING CONNECTIONS: Best Practices
### Strategies for Choosing and Using Technology in the Classroom

better when they work together to solve challenging problems and construct innovative projects (Hiltz & Goldman, 2005). Think of technologies such as the Web and e-mail as tools for providing students with opportunities to engage in collaborative learning, reaching outside the classroom to include the real world and communicating and possibly collaborating with people in locations that otherwise would be inaccessible to them.

4. *Choose technology that presents positive models for students.* Monitor technology for equity in ethnicity and culture, and be sure that the models presented are positive role models.

5. *Your teaching skills are critical, regardless of the technology you use.* You don't have to worry that technology will replace you as a teacher. Technology becomes effective in the classroom only when you know how to use it, demonstrate it, guide and monitor its use, and incorporate it into a larger effort to develop students who are motivated to learn, actively learn, and communicate effectively. Even the most sophisticated hypermedia will not benefit students much unless you appropriately orient students to it, ask them good questions about the material, orchestrate its use, and tailor it to their needs.

6. *Continue to learn about technology yourself and increase your technological competence.* Digital technology is still changing at an amazing pace. Make it a personal goal to be open to new technology, keep up with technological advances by reading educational journals, and taking courses in educational technology to increase your skills. You will be an important model for your students in terms of your attitude toward technology, your ability to use it effectively yourself, and your ability to communicate how to use it effectively to your students. In a study of computers and education in many countries, the main determinants of effective use of information technology in classrooms were the teacher's competence in using technology and the teacher's positive attitude toward technology (Collis & others, 1996).

RESEARCH

7. *Accept that at times your students will be more facile with new technologies than you are.* This is an opportunity for you to learn from your students and for them to feel wonderful about being able to teach you something. Embrace it—demonstrating the positive attitude discussed above.

## Review, Reflect, and Practice

**4** Summarize how to effectively use technology to help children learn.

### REVIEW
- What characterizes the technology revolution and the Internet?
- What are some standards for technology-literate students?
- What are five things that teachers need to ask when considering the use of technology in the classroom to improve students' understanding?

### REFLECT
- Would one or more of the ways that computers can be used to support learning and instruction be useful to the subject and grade level you plan to teach? How?

### PRAXIS™ PRACTICE
1. Ms. Carlson has her students enrolled in an online history course. This type of distance learning is referred to as
   a. e-mail.
   b. virtual school.
   c. tutorial.
   d. Web enhancement.

## Review, Reflect, and Practice

**PRAXIS™ PRACTICE (CONTINUED)**

2. Mr. Muhammad's eighth-grade history class corresponds via an Internet blog with an eighth-grade class in Spain. They discuss their viewpoints of various aspects of world history. For instance, right now they are discussing the cultural change that occurred in South America as a result of Spanish exploration and conquest. Which answer best describes this activity?
   a. collaborative learning
   b. computer-mediated communication
   c. database searching
   d. WebQuest

3. Mr. Wilson's students are examining various Web sites about world problems. As they examine each one, they are looking at the quality of the information contained on the site, including any forms of cultural, sexual, or political bias. Students will then compile a report of their findings. If Mr. Wilson is following the International Society for Technology in Education Standards, what grades does he most likely teach?
   a. PK–2
   b. 3–5
   c. 6–8
   d. 9–12

4. Which of the following examples best reflects the effective use of technology to promote student understanding?
   a. Roberto is using a classroom computer game to help him learn his multiplication facts. The game presents a fact; he types in an answer. Each correct answer earns points.
   b. Patricia is using her computer's word-processing program to type a paper for her English class after having written it out longhand.
   c. Deshawn is immersed in a computer simulation of the desert ecosystem.
   d. Carmine is texting his best friend during class regarding their plans for the evening.

*Please see the answer key at the end of the book.*

# The Big Debate

Mrs. Rumer was new to teaching third grade at Hillside Elementary School. Before the school year began, she met with other new teachers and their mentors for planning sessions. The administration appeared to be aware of just how much planning was necessary for successful teaching. Mrs. Rumer openly shared her ideas with her mentor, Mrs. Humbolt, and the rest of the group.

"I really want to have a learner-centered classroom," she said. "I'd like to use aspects of problem-based learning, essential questions, and guided discovery. I think the students will learn so much more that way than if I use teacher-centered instruction."

Mrs. Humbolt smiled and said, "Well, they'd probably have more fun, but I doubt that their test scores would reflect much learning at all. We really need to prepare our students to meet state standards, Mrs. Rumer. To do that, you'd better throw in some good old-fashioned direct instruction." Several other teachers readily agreed. One commented, "That constructivist stuff is too much fluff; I want my students to be serious and learn what I teach them." Another said, "I use the computers in the classroom for drilling students to memorize material for the state tests they have to take, sort of like giving them electronic flash cards. I guess that wouldn't fit your scheme."

The other teachers' comments surprised Mrs. Rumer. She had learned in her education courses that learner-centered instruction is supposed to be the best way to teach children. She wanted her students to actively construct their knowledge, not merely have her pour information into their minds. The principal assured her that if she wanted to use a learner-centered approach, she would have that freedom.

With this assurance, Mrs. Rumer began making lists of everything she would have to plan for in order to have an effective learner-centered classroom. She began by going through the district's curriculum guide for third grade. She made lists of all the objectives. Then she went through the learner-centered psychological principles from the APA. After doing this, she realized her job was going to be a daunting one.

1. What are the issues in this case?

2. Where should Mrs. Rumer go from here?

3. How can she take a curriculum that has been taught in a teacher-centered manner and convert it to a learner-centered curriculum? Should she? Why or why not?

4. How can she incorporate technology into the curriculum so that the computers don't become mere electronic flash cards?

5. Which of the following is an activity that would most likely appeal to Mrs. Rumer?
   a. The students will master their basic multiplication facts by completing a worksheet covering them each day.
   b. The students will master their basic multiplication facts by playing multiplication baseball.
   c. The students will master their basic multiplication facts by taking daily timed tests covering them.
   d. The students will master their basic multiplication facts by writing out their multiplication tables repeatedly.

6. Which of the following is an activity that would most likely appeal to Mrs. Rumer's colleagues?
   a. The students will learn the scientific process by completing several experiments.
   b. The students will learn the scientific process by focusing on essential questions in science.
   c. The students will learn the scientific process by reading about it in their science texts and listening to lectures.
   d. The students will learn the scientific process by testing the water in a nearby creek.

# Planning, Instruction, and Technology

**① PLANNING:** Explain what is involved in classroom planning.

**Instructional Planning**

Instructional planning involves developing a systematic, organized strategy for lessons. Planning is critically important to being a competent teacher, and instructional planning may be mandated by schools.

**Time Frames and Planning**

Teachers need to make plans for different time frames, ranging from yearly planning to daily planning. Yinger identified five time frames of teacher planning: yearly, term, unit, weekly, and daily.

**② TEACHER-CENTERED LESSON PLANNING AND INSTRUCTION:** Identify important forms of teacher-centered instruction.

**Teacher-Centered Lesson Planning**

Teacher-centered lesson planning includes creating behavioral objectives, analyzing tasks, and developing instructional taxonomies (classifications). Behavioral objectives are statements that propose changes in students' behavior to reach desired performance levels. Task analysis focuses on breaking down a complex task that students are to learn into its component parts. Bloom's taxonomy classifies educational objectives into cognitive, affective, and psychomotor domains and is used by many teachers to create goals and objectives in lesson planning.

**Direct Instruction**

Direct instruction is a structured, teacher-centered approach that involves teacher direction and control, high expectations for students' progress, maximum time spent by students on academic tasks, and efforts by the teacher to keep negative affect to a minimum. The teacher chooses students' learning tasks and directs students' learning of those tasks. The use of nonacademic materials is deemphasized, as is nonacademically oriented teacher-student interaction.

**Teacher-Centered Instructional Strategies**

Teacher-centered instructional strategies include orienting students to new material; lecturing, explaining, and demonstrating; questioning and discussing; mastery learning (learning one topic or concept thoroughly before moving on to a more difficult one); seatwork (having students work independently at their seats); and homework.

**Evaluating Teacher-Centered Instruction**

Teacher-centered instruction includes useful techniques, and its advocates especially believe it is the best strategy for teaching basic skills such as math computations, grammar rules, and reading vocabulary. Critics of teacher-centered instruction say that by itself it tends to lead to passive rote learning, overly rigid and structured classrooms, inadequate attention to socio-emotional development, external rather than internal motivation, excessive use of paper-and-pencil tasks, too few opportunities for real-world learning, and too little collaborative learning in small groups.

**③ LEARNER-CENTERED LESSON PLANNING AND INSTRUCTION:** Discuss important forms of learner-centered instruction.

**Learner-Centered Principles**

Learner-centered lesson planning and instruction moves the focus away from the teacher and toward the student. The APA's learner-centered psychological principles emphasize the active, reflective nature of learning and learners. The 14 principles involve cognitive and metacognitive

*continued*

factors (the nature of the learning process, goals of the learning process, the construction of knowledge, strategic thinking, thinking about thinking, and the context of learning); motivational and emotional factors (motivational and emotional influences on learning, intrinsic motivation to learn, and effects of motivation on effort); developmental and social factors (developmental influences on learning and social influences on learning); and individual difference factors (individual differences in learning, learning and diversity, and standards and assessments).

Problem-based learning emphasizes real-world problem solving. A problem-based curriculum exposes students to the kind of authentic problems that occur in everyday life. Problem-based learning focuses on small-group discussion rather than lecture. Students identify issues they wish to explore, and teachers act as guides, helping students monitor their problem-solving efforts. Essential questions are questions that engagingly reflect the heart of the curriculum, cause students to think, and motivate their curiosity. Discovery learning is learning in which students construct an understanding on their own. Most discovery-learning approaches today involve guided discovery, in which students are encouraged to construct their understanding with the assistance of teacher-guided questions and directions.

The learner-centered model of planning and instruction has many positive features. The 14 APA learner-centered principles are guidelines that can help teachers develop strategies that benefit student learning (such as encouraging students to actively construct knowledge, think deeply and creatively, be internally motivated, solve real-world problems, and collaboratively learn). Critics argue that learner-centered planning and instruction focus too much on the process of learning and not enough on academic content; are more appropriate for social sciences and humanities than science and math; are not appropriate for beginning instruction when students have little or no knowledge about the topic; and are more challenging to implement than most teachers envision. Keep in mind that although we presented teacher-centered and learner-centered approaches separately, many teachers use aspects of both approaches.

**Some Learner-Centered Instructional Strategies**

**Evaluating Learner-Centered Strategies**

---

**④ TECHNOLOGY AND EDUCATION:** Summarize how to effectively use technology to help children learn.

**The Technology Revolution and the Internet**

The technology revolution is part of the information society in which we now live, and students will increasingly need to have technological skills. Today's technologies can be remarkable tools for motivating students and guiding their learning. The Internet is the core of computer-mediated communication. The Web is a system for browsing Internet sites. The Internet can be an important learning tool in many classrooms. Cautions about Internet use need to be observed.

**Standards for Technology-Literate Students**

The International Society for Technology in Education (ISTE) has established technology standards for students that include using digital technologies to support creativity and innovation, communication and collaboration, problem solving and decision making, and digital citizenship. In addition, ISTE provides performance indicators for achieving these standards at different grade levels.

**Teaching, Learning, and Technology**

Five things teachers need to ask regarding using technology more effectively in the classroom to improve students' learning include considering (1) which topics are worth understanding, (2) what students should understand about such topics, (3) how students develop and demonstrate understanding, (4) how students and teachers assess understanding, and (5) how students and teachers learn together.

# KEY TERMS

# PORTFOLIO ACTIVITIES

Now that you have a good understanding of this chapter, complete these exercises to expand your thinking.

## Research/Field Experience: Instructional Planning in Action

Ask a teacher at the grade level you plan to teach to show you the materials she or he uses in planning lessons, units, the term, and the yearly curriculum for one or more subjects. Create samples for your own later use based on what the teacher shows you. Discuss the importance of planning at each of these levels. (INTASC: Principles *7, 9*)

## Collaborative Work: Evaluating Teacher-Centered and Learner-Centered Classrooms.

With three other students in the class, divide up the work of observing an early childhood, an elementary, a middle school, and a high school classroom. Reconvene after each of you has observed a classroom, and discuss the aspects of teacher-centered and learner-centered approaches the teachers were using. Evaluate how effective the approaches were. Write a comparative analysis. (INTASC: Principles *1, 2, 3, 4, 5, 6, 7, 8, 9*)

## Independent Reflection: Developing a Classroom Technology Plan

Create a written plan for how you might use computers for the subject(s) and grade level you plan to teach. How will you adapt your plan for students with little or no experience with computers? How can your classroom benefit from students with advanced technology skills? (INTASC: Principles *1, 2, 4*)

*Go to the Online Learning Center for downloadable portfolio templates.*

# STUDY, PRACTICE, AND SUCCEED

Visit www.mhhe.com/santrockep5e to review the chapter with self-grading quizzes and self-assessments, to apply the chapter material to two more Crack the Case studies, and for suggested activities to develop your teaching portfolio.

## CHAPTER 13

# MOTIVATION, TEACHING, AND LEARNING

*The art of teaching is the art of awakening the curiosity of young minds.*

—Anatole France
*French Novelist and Poet, 20th Century*

## Chapter **Outline**

## Learning **Goals**

**1** Define motivation, and compare the behavioral, humanistic, cognitive, and social perspectives on motivation.

**2** Discuss the important processes in motivation to achieve.

**3** Explain how relationships and sociocultural contexts can support or undercut motivation.

**4** Recommend how to help students with achievement difficulties.

# Teaching **Stories**   Jaime Escalante

An immigrant from Bolivia named Jaime Escalante became a math teacher at Garfield High School in East Los Angeles, a school largely populated by Latino students from low-income families. When he began teaching at Garfield, many of the students had little confidence in their math abilities, and most of the teachers had low expectations for the students' success. Escalante took it as a special challenge to improve the students' math skills, even enable them to perform well on the Educational Testing Service Advanced Placement (AP) calculus exam.

Jaime Escalante in a classroom teaching math.

The first year was difficult. Escalante's calculus class began at 8 A.M. He told the students the doors would be open at 7 A.M. and that instruction would begin at 7:30 A.M. He also worked with them after school and on weekends. He put together lots of handouts, told the students to take extensive notes, and required them to keep a folder. He gave them a five-minute quiz each morning and a test every Friday. He started with 14 students, but in two weeks the number was cut in half. Only five students lasted through the spring. One of the boys who quit said, "I don't want to come at 7 o'clock. Why should I?"

When Escalante was teaching, on the 5-point AP calculus test (with 5 highest, 1 lowest), a 3 or better meant that a student was performing at a college level and would receive credit for the course at most major universities. The AP calculus scores for Escalante's first five students were two 4's, two 2's, and one 1. This was better than the school had done in the past, but Escalante resolved to do even better.

Three years later, the AP calculus test scores for Escalante's class of 15 students were one 5, four 4's, nine 3's, and one 2. Ten years after Escalante's first class, 151 students were taking calculus in the East Los Angeles high school.

Escalante's persistent, challenging, and inspiring teaching raised Garfield High, a school plagued by poor funding, violence, and inferior working conditions, to seventh place among U.S. schools in calculus. Escalante's commitment and motivation were transferred to his students, many of whom no one had believed in before Escalante came along. Escalante's contributions were portrayed in the film *Stand and Deliver*. Escalante, his students, and celebrity guests also introduce basic math concepts for sixth- to twelfth-grade students on *Futures 1 and 2 with Jaime Escalante,* a PBS series. Escalante has now retired from teaching but continues to work in a consulting role to help improve students' motivation to do well in math and improve their math skills. Escalante's story is a testimony to how one teacher can make a major difference in students' motivation and achievement.

# Preview

In Chapter 12 you learned that motivation is a key component of the American Psychological Association's learner-centered psychological principles. Indeed, motivation is a critical aspect of teaching and learning. Unmotivated students won't expend the necessary effort to learn. As Jaime Escalante's teaching story shows, highly motivated students are eager to come to school and are absorbed in the learning process.

## 1  EXPLORING MOTIVATION

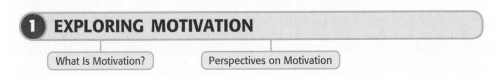

What Is Motivation?        Perspectives on Motivation

A young Canadian, Terry Fox, did one of the great long-distance runs in history (McNally, 1990). Averaging a marathon (26.2 miles) a day for five months, he ran 3,359 miles across most of Canada. What makes his grueling feat truly remarkable is that Terry Fox had lost a leg to cancer before the run, so he was running with the aid of a prosthetic limb. Terry Fox clearly was a motivated person, but exactly what does it mean to be motivated?

## WHAT IS MOTIVATION?

**Motivation** involves the processes that energize, direct, and sustain behavior. Why did Terry Fox do this run? When Terry was hospitalized with cancer, he told himself that if he survived he would do something to help fund cancer research. Thus, the motivation for his run was to give purpose to his life by helping other people with cancer.

Terry Fox's behavior was energized, directed, and sustained. Running across most of Canada, he encountered unforeseen hurdles: severe headwinds, heavy rain, snow, and icy roads. Because of these conditions, he averaged only eight miles a day after the first month, far below what he had planned. But he kept going and picked up the pace in the second month until he was back on track. His example stands as a testimonial to how motivation can help each of us prevail.

Terry Fox's story is portrayed in a good classroom film, *The Power of Purpose*. One sixth-grade teacher showed the film to her class and then asked her students to write down what they learned from it. One student wrote, "I learned that even if something bad happens to you, you have to keep going, keep trying. Even if your body gets hurt, it can't take away your spirit."

Let's look at another example of motivation. Lance Armstrong was an accomplished cyclist when he was diagnosed with testicular cancer in 1996. Chances of his recovery were estimated at less than 50 percent when he began chemotherapy. However, Lance did recover from the cancer and set a goal of winning the three-week, 2,000-plus-mile Tour de France, the world's premier bicycle race and one of the great tests of human motivation in sports. Day after day, Lance trained intensely, keeping the goal of winning the Tour de France in mind. Lance won the Tour de France not once but seven years in a row from 1999 through 2005.

As with Terry Fox's marathon run and Lance Armstrong's winning of the Tour de France, motivation in the classroom involves why students are behaving in a particular way and the extent to which their behavior is energized, directed, and sustained. If students don't complete an assignment because they are bored, lack of motivation is involved. If students encounter challenges in researching and writing a paper, but persist and overcome hurdles, motivation is involved.

## PERSPECTIVES ON MOTIVATION

Different psychological perspectives explain motivation in different ways. Let's explore four of these perspectives: behavioral, humanistic, cognitive, and social.

**The Behavioral Perspective** The behavioral perspective emphasizes external rewards and punishments as keys in determining a student's motivation. **Incentives** are positive or negative stimuli or events that can motivate a student's behavior. Advocates of the use of incentives emphasize that they add interest or excitement to the class and direct attention toward appropriate behavior and away from inappropriate behavior (Emmer & Evertson, 2009).

Incentives that classroom teachers use include numerical scores and letter grades, which provide feedback about the quality of the student's work, and checkmarks or stars for competently completing work. Other incentives include giving students recognition—for example, by displaying their work, giving them a certificate of achievement, placing them on the honor roll, and verbally mentioning their accomplishments. Another type of incentive focuses on allowing students to do something special—such as playing computer games or going on a field trip—as a reward for good work. Shortly, in our discussion of intrinsic and extrinsic motivation, we will look more closely at the issue of whether incentives are a good idea.

**The Humanistic Perspective** The **humanistic perspective** stresses students' capacity for personal growth, freedom to choose their destiny, and positive qualities (such as being sensitive to others). This perspective is closely associated with Abraham

**motivation** The processes that energize, direct, and sustain behavior.

**incentives** Positive or negative stimuli or events that can motivate a student's behavior.

**humanistic perspective** A view that stresses students' capacity for personal growth, freedom to choose their destiny, and positive qualities.

Maslow's (1954, 1971) belief that certain basic needs must be met before higher needs can be satisfied. According to Maslow's **hierarchy of needs,** individuals' needs must be satisfied in this sequence (see Figure 13.1):

- *Physiological.* Hunger, thirst, sleep
- *Safety.* Ensuring survival, such as protection from war and crime
- *Love and belongingness.* Security, affection, and attention from others
- *Esteem.* Feeling good about oneself
- *Self-actualization.* Realization of one's potential

Thus, in Maslow's view, students must satisfy their need for food before they can achieve. His view provides an explanation of why children who come from poor or abusive homes are less likely to achieve in school than children whose basic needs are met.

**Self-actualization,** the highest and most elusive of Maslow's needs, is the motivation to develop one's full potential as a human being. In Maslow's view, self-actualization is possible only after the lower needs have been met. Maslow cautions that most people stop maturing after they have developed a high level of esteem and therefore never become self-actualized. Some characteristics of self-actualized individuals include being spontaneous, problem-centered rather than self-centered, and creative.

The idea that human needs are hierarchically arranged is appealing. However, not everyone agrees with Maslow's ordering of motives. For example, for some students cognitive needs might be more fundamental than esteem needs. Other students might meet their cognitive needs even though they have not experienced love and belongingness.

**FIGURE 13.1** MASLOW'S HIERARCHY OF NEEDS

Abraham Maslow developed the hierarchy of human needs to show how we have to satisfy certain basic needs before we can satisfy higher needs. In the diagram, lower-level needs are shown toward the base of the pyramid, higher-level needs toward the peak.

**The Cognitive Perspective**  According to the cognitive perspective on motivation, students' thoughts guide their motivation. In recent years there has been a tremendous surge of interest in this perspective (Anderman & Dawson, 2011; Elliot & others, 2011), focusing on such ideas as students' internal motivation to achieve, their attributions (perceptions about the causes of success or failure, especially the perception that effort is an important factor in achievement), and their beliefs that they can effectively control their environment. The cognitive perspective also stresses the importance of goal setting, planning, and monitoring progress toward a goal (Urdan, 2010).

Thus, whereas the behavioral perspective sees the student's motivation as a consequence of external incentives, the cognitive perspective argues that external pressures should be deemphasized. Students should be given more opportunities and responsibility for controlling their own achievement outcomes according to this perspective (Ryan & Deci, 2009).

The cognitive perspective on motivation fits with the ideas of R. W. White (1959), who proposed the concept of **competence motivation,** the idea that people are motivated to deal effectively with their environment, to master their world, and to process information efficiently. White said that people do these things because they are internally motivated to interact effectively with the environment. The concept of competence motivation explains why humans are motivated to achieve scientific and technological innovation.

**hierarchy of needs** Maslow's concept that individual needs must be satisfied in this sequence: physiological, safety, love and belongingness, esteem, and self-actualization.

**self-actualization** The highest and most elusive of Maslow's needs; the motivation to develop one's full potential as a human being.

**competence motivation** The idea that people are motivated to deal effectively with their environment, to master their world, and to process information efficiently.

Meredith MacGregor, a senior at Fairview High School in Boulder, Colorado, is an aspiring scientist and one of Colorado's top high school long-distance runners. She has maintained a 4.0 grade point average, participated in a number of school organizations, and cofounded the AfriAid Club. She recently was named a *USA Today* High School Academic All-Star and was awarded the Intel Foundation Young Scientist Award (Wong Briggs, 2007). *What are some factors that likely are involved in Meredith's motivation to achieve?*

**The Social Perspective**   Are you the kind of person who is motivated to be around people a lot? Or would you rather stay home and read a book? The **need for affiliation, or relatedness,** is the motive to be securely connected with other people. This involves establishing, maintaining, and restoring warm, close personal relationships. Students' need for affiliation or relatedness is reflected in their motivation to spend time with peers, their close friendships, their attachment to their parents, and their desire to have a positive relationship with their teachers (Grolnick, Friendly, & Bellas, 2010; Hamm & Zhang, 2010).

Students in schools with caring and supportive interpersonal relationships have more positive academic attitudes and values and are more satisfied with school (Wentzel, 2010). One study revealed that a key factor in students' motivation and achievement was their perception of whether they had a positive relationship with the teacher (McCombs, 2001). In other research, the value that middle school students assigned to math increased when they had a teacher whom they perceived to be high in support (Eccles, 1993).

As you think about the perspectives on motivation, realize that you don't have to adopt just one perspective. All of the perspectives provide information that is relevant to children's education.

## Review, Reflect, and Practice

**①** Define motivation, and compare the behavioral, humanistic, cognitive, and social perspectives on motivation.

**REVIEW**
- What is motivated behavior?
- How would you briefly summarize the four main perspectives on motivation?

**REFLECT**
- Recall a situation in which you were highly motivated to accomplish something.
- How would you describe your motivation in terms of each of the four perspectives?

**PRAXIS™ PRACTICE**

1. Which of the following best exemplifies what motivation is?
   a. Robbie is emotional about the upcoming school year and wants to do well.
   b. Sherrie is energized, sets a high goal for doing well in her English class, persists with considerable effort, and makes an *A* in the class.
   c. Carmello is good at directing his attention to what he wants to accomplish.
   d. Latisha works hard, experiences positive feelings about her academic work, and enjoys working with others.
2. Which of the following best exemplifies the cognitive perspective of motivation?
   a. Mr. Davidson gives his students tickets when he "catches them being good" so that they will continue to behave appropriately.
   b. Mr. McRoberts wants his students to believe they can be successful in anything they try, so he ensures success for those students who work hard.
   c. Ms. Boeteng believes that her students will be more motivated in school if they establish good relationships with both her and with their classmates, so she provides emotional support.
   d. Ms. Pocius keeps a supply of cereal in her desk drawer so that if one of her students is hungry, she can provide food.

*Please see the answer key at the end of the book.*

**need for affiliation, or relatedness** The motive to be securely connected with other people.

## 2 ACHIEVEMENT PROCESSES

| Extrinsic and Intrinsic Motivation | Mastery Motivation and Mindset | Goal Setting, Planning, and Self-Monitoring | Values and Purpose |

| Attribution | Self-Efficacy | Expectations |

The current interest in motivation in school has been fueled by the cognitive perspective and an emphasis on discovering the most important processes involved in students' achievement (Anderman & Anderman, 2010; Winne & Nesbit, 2010). In this section we will study a number of effective cognitive strategies for improving students' motivation to achieve. We'll begin by exploring a crucial distinction between extrinsic (external) and intrinsic (internal) motivation. That will lead us to examine several other important cognitive insights about motivation. Then we will study the role of expectations in students' motivation.

## EXTRINSIC AND INTRINSIC MOTIVATION

**Extrinsic motivation** involves doing something to obtain something else (a means to an end). Extrinsic motivation is often influenced by external incentives such as rewards and punishments. For example, a student may study hard for a test in order to obtain a good grade in the course.

The behavioral perspective emphasizes the importance of extrinsic motivation in achievement; the humanistic and cognitive approaches stress the importance of intrinsic motivation in achievement. **Intrinsic motivation** involves the internal motivation to do something for its own sake (an end in itself). For example, a student may study hard for a test because she enjoys the content of the course.

RESEARCH

Current evidence strongly favors establishing a classroom climate in which students are intrinsically motivated to learn (Ryan & Deci, 2009). For example, a study of third- through eighth-grade students found that intrinsic motivation was positively linked with grades and standardized test scores, whereas extrinsic motivation was negatively related to achievement outcomes (Lepper, Corpus, & Iyengar, 2005). When goals are framed extrinsically, students show a lower level of independent motivation and lower persistence on achievement tasks (Vansteenkiste & others, 2008).

Parental intrinsic/extrinsic motivational practices are also linked to children's motivation. In one study, children had higher intrinsic motivation in math and science from 9 to 17 years of age when their their parents engaged in task-intrinsic practices (encouraging children's pleasure and engagement in learning ) than when their parents engaged in task-extrinsic practices (providing external rewards and consequences contingent on children's performance) (Gottfried & others, 2009).

Students are more motivated to learn when they are given choices, become absorbed in challenges that match their skills, and receive rewards that have informational value but are not used for control. Praise also can enhance students' intrinsic motivation. To see why these things are so, let's first explore four types of intrinsic motivation: (1) self-determination and personal choice, (2) optimal experiences and flow, (3) interest, and (4) cognitive engagement and self-responsibility. Then we'll discuss how extrinsic rewards can either enhance or undermine intrinsic motivation. Next we will identify some developmental changes in intrinsic and extrinsic motivation as students move up the educational ladder. Finally, we will offer some concluding thoughts about intrinsic and extrinsic motivation.

These students were given an opportunity to write and perform their own play. Such types of self-determining opportunities can enhance students' motivation to achieve.

**extrinsic motivation** The external motivation to do something to obtain something else (a means to an end).

**intrinsic motivation** The internal motivation to do something for its own sake (an end in itself).

**Self-Determination and Personal Choice** One view of intrinsic motivation emphasizes self-determination (Deci & Ryan, 2000; Ryan & Deci, 2009). In this view, students want to believe that they are doing something because of their own will, not

# Calvin and Hobbes

by Bill Watterson

CALVIN AND HOBBES © 1991 Watterson. Used by permission of Universal Uclick.

RESEARCH

because of external success or rewards (Vansteenkiste & others, 2009). The architects of self-determination theory, Richard Ryan and Edward Deci (2009) refer to teachers who create circumstances for students to engage in self-determination as *autonomy-supportive teachers.*

Researchers have found that students' internal motivation and intrinsic interest in school tasks increase when students have some choice and some opportunities to take personal responsibility for their learning (Grolnick, Friendly, & Bellas, 2009). In one study, teachers were encouraged to give the students more responsibility for their school programs (deCharms, 1984)—in particular, opportunities to set their own goals, plan how to reach the goals, and monitor their progress toward the goals. Students were given some choice in the activities they wanted to engage in and when they would do them. They also were encouraged to take personal responsibility for their behavior, including reaching the goals that they had set. Compared with a control group, students in this intrinsic motivation/self-determination group had higher achievement gains and were more likely to graduate from high school.

## TEACHING CONNECTIONS: Best Practices
### Strategies for Enhancing Student Self-Determination and Choice

Here are some ways you can promote self-determination and choice in your classroom (Anderman & Anderman, 2010; Brophy, 2004; Reeve, 2004; Ryan & Deci, 2009):

1. Take the time to talk with students and explain why a learning activity is important.

2. Provide students with opportunities to make choices that are meaningful to them. If students are given choices that are personally meaningful to them, they are likely to be more motivated.

3. Work to spark student interest, enjoyment, and sense of challenge. Students are more likely to persist at something in which they are interested, find enjoyable, and challenging. Find ways to tap into this for your students.

4. Be attentive to students' feelings when they are being asked to do something they don't want to do. Accept negative affect from a student and use it to help you structure the learning environment.

5. Manage the classroom effectively, in a way that lets students make personal choices. Let students select topics for book reports, writing assignments, and research projects, and let them decide how they want to report their work—for instance, reporting to you or to the class as a whole, individually, or with a partner.

6. Establish learning centers where students can work individually or collaboratively with other students on different projects and can select their activities from a menu that you have developed.

7. Create self-selected interest groups and let students work on relevant research projects together.

8. Use informational rather than controlling language. When giving students feedback, explain to students what they are doing well and how they are progressing. Look at poor performance as a problem to be solved rather than as a personal deficit in the student.

**Optimal Experiences and Flow**   Mihaly Csikszentmihalyi (1990, 1993; Csikszentmihalyi & Csikszentmihalyi, 2006) has proposed ideas that are relevant to understanding intrinsic motivation after having studied the *optimal experiences* of people for more than two decades. People report that these optimal experiences involve feelings of deep enjoyment and happiness. Csikszentmihalyi uses the term *flow* to describe optimal experiences in life. He has found that flow occurs most often when people develop a sense of mastery and are absorbed in a state of concentration while they engage in an activity. Moreover, he found that flow occurs when individuals are engaged in challenges they find neither too difficult nor too easy. For example, flow is occurring when a student is deeply absorbed in working on a science project that her teacher has structured at a challenging level but not beyond the student's capability. In a recent study, students were less engaged in school classrooms than in other contexts (Shernoff, 2009); that is, they were more engaged when they participated in contexts they found challenging, relevant, and enjoyable. After-school programs, especially those involving organized sports, academic enrichment, and arts enrichment activities, elicited the highest level of engagement.

Perceived levels of challenge and skill can result in different outcomes (see Figure 13.2) (Brophy, 1998). Flow is most likely to occur in areas in which students

|  |  | Students' perceived level of their own skill | |
|---|---|---|---|
|  |  | Low | High |
| Students' perceived level of challenge | Low | Apathy | Boredom |
|  | High | Anxiety | Flow |

**FIGURE 13.2** OUTCOMES OF PERCEIVED LEVELS OF CHALLENGE AND SKILL

## TEACHING CONNECTIONS: Best Practices
### Strategies for Helping Students Achieve Flow

Complex learning environments create the combination of work-like and play-like perceptions characteristic of flow by simultaneously combining many of the following specific instructional elements (Csikszentmihalyi, Rathunde, & Whalen, 1993; Shernoff & Csikszentmihalyi, 2009; Shernoff & Vandell, 2007):

1. *The relevance of the activity is explained to the students.* Use real-world activities of importance to the community or explain the activity's importance to later achievement.

### THROUGH THE EYES OF TEACHERS
#### Turning the Classroom into an Egyptian Tomb, New York City, and Mount Olympus

Rhonda Nachamkin, who teaches first grade at River Eves Elementary School in Roswell, Georgia, has a high-energy style and approaches each unit as if it were a Hollywood production. She turns the classroom into an Egyptian tomb, New York City, or Mount Olympus. She sends parents scurrying to learn who Anubis (Egyptian god) and Prometheus (Greek Titan who stole fire from the gods) were so they can converse about these topics with their 6-year-olds. Rhonda likes to use multiple versions of fairy tales to teach reading, spelling, and analytical concepts. (Source: *USA Today*, 1999.)

Rhonda Nachamkin helps one of her students, Patrick Drones, with his work.

2. *Students are working with materials.* Students are much more likely to be engaged in their learning when they are actively involved in the work through project-based learning, discovery, or guided discovery and interacting with materials.

4. *Good teacher: student rapport has been established and maintained.*

5. *Teachers help students to set proximal goals.* These should be goals for when students can get immediate feedback.

6. *Students are working together.*

7. *Students receive constructive feedback from each other and from the teacher.*

8. *Ideal challenge.* Develop and maintain an optimal match between what you challenge students to do and what their skills are.

9. *Teachers hold high expectations for students.*

10. *Teachers support student autonomy and control over the task.*

11. *Students have perceptions of competence and success.*

are challenged and perceive themselves as having a high degree of skill. When students' skills are high but the activity provides little challenge, the result is boredom. When both the challenge and skill levels are low, students feel apathy. And when students face a challenging task that they don't believe they have adequate skills to master, they experience anxiety.

**Interest** Educational psychologists also have examined the concept of *interest*, which has been proposed as more specific than intrinsic motivation. A distinction has been made between *individual interest*, which is thought to be relatively stable, and *situational interest*, which is believed to be generated by specific aspects of a task activity (Schiefele, 2009). Individual interest might involve whatever math ability a student brings to the course, such as longstanding success in the subject. Situational interest might involve how interesting a particular teacher makes a math class.

Research on interest has focused mainly on how interest is related to learning. Interest is especially linked to measures of deep learning, such as recall of main ideas and responses to more difficult comprehension questions, rather than to surface learning, such as responses to simple questions and verbatim recall of text (Wigfield & others, 2006).

TECHNOLOGY

How can technology be used to stimulate students' interest? *Authentic tasks* approximate the real world or real life as closely as possible, and they can spark students' interest and curiosity. Students often perceive technology-based learning experiences as real-world activities.

Integrating technology into the classroom has clearly been found to increase students' motivation to learn and engagement in learning, especially when it is used to foster authentic learning. For example, researchers have documented improved motivation (Swan & others, 2005), engagement (Silvernail & Lane, 2004), behavior (Apple Computer, 1995), and school attendance (Apple Computer, 1995) among students involved in technology-rich initiatives. In addition, research indicates that such students are better organized and more independent learners (Zucker & McGhee, 2005). Also, research reveals that special needs students can achieve at the same levels as regular students in some situations when using technology (Swan & others, 2006).

*Serious games* are software applications developed using gaming technology and design principles whose primary purpose is for something other than pure entertainment, usually for training or education. The serious games movement in education takes as its framework situated and authentic learning. One example of serious games is *Quest Atlantis* (2009), a National Science Foundation–funded project that uses a three-dimensional multiuser environment to immerse 9- to 12-year-old children in educational tasks. Currently, thousands of registered users from five continents use *Quest Atlantis* in schools. Researchers have found that students who use this game improve their learning over time in science, social studies, and sense of academic efficacy (Barab & others, 2010a,b; Gresalfi & others, 2009).

A computer screen from *Quest Atlantis*. Building on the model of online role-playing games, *Quest Atlantis* combines elements of the commercial gaming world with educational research on motivation and emotion. The core components include a 3D multi-user environment; an unfolding story involving a mythical Council and a set of social commitments; a customizable home page; various trajectories through which the player's character can develop; inquiry learning situations, including quests, missions, simulated worlds; and a global community of 15,000 participants who can log in from five countries.

**Cognitive Engagement and Self-Responsibility** Phyllis Blumenfeld and her colleagues (2006) proposed another variation on intrinsic motivation. They emphasize the importance of creating learning environments that encourage students to become cognitively engaged and take responsibility for their learning. The goal is to get students to become motivated to expend the effort to persist and master ideas rather than doing just enough work to make a passing grade. Especially important is to embed subject matter content and skills learning within meaningful contexts, especially real-world situations that mesh with students' interests.

**Extrinsic Rewards and Intrinsic Motivation**   Now that we have discussed a number of views of intrinsic motivation, let's examine whether classroom rewards might be useful in some situations and whether certain types of rewards might actually increase intrinsic motivation. As we saw in Chapter 7, external rewards can be useful in changing behavior. However, in some situations rewards can undermine learning. In a classic study, students who already had a strong interest in art and did not expect a reward spent more time drawing than did students who also had a strong interest in art but knew they would be rewarded for drawing (Lepper, Greene, & Nisbett, 1973).

However, classroom rewards can be useful (Cameron & Pierce, 2008). Two uses are (1) as an incentive to engage in tasks, in which case the goal is to control the student's behavior, and (2) to convey information about mastery. When rewards are offered that convey information about mastery, students' feelings of competence are likely to be enhanced. Rewards used as incentives lead to perceptions that the student's behavior was caused by the external reward, not by the student's own motivation to be competent.

To better understand the difference between using rewards to control students' behavior and using them to provide information about mastery, consider this example (Schunk, 2011): A teacher puts a reward system in place in which the more work students accomplish, the more points they will earn. Students will be motivated to work to earn points because they are told that the points can be exchanged for privileges. Furthermore, the points provide information about their capabilities—the more points they earn, the more work they know they have accomplished. As they accumulate points, students are more likely to feel competent. In contrast, if points are provided simply for spending time on a task, the task might be perceived as a means to an end. In this case, because the points don't convey anything about capabilities, students are likely to perceive the rewards as controlling their behavior.

Thus, rewards that convey information about students' mastery can increase intrinsic motivation by increasing their sense of competence (Cameron & Pierce, 2008). However, negative feedback, such as criticism, that carries information that students are incompetent can undermine intrinsic motivation, especially if students doubt their ability to become competent (Stipek, 2002).

Judy Cameron (2001) argues that rewards do not always decrease a student's intrinsic motivation. In her analysis of approximately a hundred studies, she found that verbal rewards (praise and positive feedback) can be used to enhance students' intrinsic motivation. She also concluded that when tangible rewards (such as gold stars and money) were offered contingent on task performance or given unexpectedly, intrinsic motivation was maintained. Some critics argue that Cameron's analysis is flawed—for instance, that it does not adequately detect some of the negative effects of rewards on motivation (Deci, Koestner, & Ryan, 2001).

In summary, it is important to examine what rewards convey about competence. When rewards are tied to competence, they tend to promote motivation and interest. When they are not, they are unlikely to raise motivation and may even diminish it once the rewards are withdrawn (Schunk, 2011).

**Developmental Shifts in Intrinsic and Extrinsic Motivation**   Many psychologists and educators stress that it is important for children to develop greater internalization and intrinsic motivation as they grow older (Wigfield, Byrnes, & Eccles, 2006). However, researchers have found that as students move from the early elementary school years to the high school years, their intrinsic motivation decreases (Anderman & Mueller, 2010; Eccles & Roeser, 2010). In one research study, the biggest drop in intrinsic motivation and increase in extrinsic motivation occurred between sixth grade and seventh grade (Harter, 1981). In another study, as students moved from sixth through eighth grade, they increasingly said school was boring and irrelevant (Harter, 1996). In this study, however, students who were intrinsically motivated did much better academically than those who were extrinsically motivated.

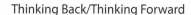

**Thinking Back/Thinking Forward**

One strategy for increasing desirable behaviors is to choose effective reinforcers. Chapter 7, p. 225

DEVELOPMENT

RESEARCH

Why the shift toward extrinsic motivation as children move to higher grades? One explanation is that school grading practices reinforce an external motivation orientation. That is, as students get older, they lock into the increasing emphasis on grades, and their internal motivation drops.

Jacquelynne Eccles and her colleagues (Eccles, 2004, 2007; Eccles & Roeser, 2010; Wigfield, Byrnes, & Eccles, 2006) have identified some specific changes in the school context that help to explain the decline in intrinsic motivation. Middle and junior high schools are more impersonal, more formal, more evaluative, and more competitive than elementary schools. Students compare themselves more with other students because they increasingly are graded in terms of their relative performance on assignments and standardized tests.

Proposing the concept of *person-environment fit*, Eccles (2004, 2007) argues that a lack of fit between the middle school/junior high environment and the needs of young adolescents produces increasingly negative self-evaluations and attitudes toward school. Her research has revealed that teachers became more controlling just at the time when adolescents are seeking more autonomy, and the teacher-student relationship becomes more impersonal at a time when students are seeking more independence from their parents and need more support from other adults. At a time when adolescents are becoming more self-conscious, an increased emphasis on grades and other competitive comparisons only makes things worse.

How might teachers make school more personal for students? Perhaps by getting to know students better and linking their interests to academic content.

Although there is less research on the transition to high school, the existing research suggests that, like the transition to middle school, it can produce similar problems (Eccles, Wigfield, & Schiefele, 1998). High schools often are even larger and more bureaucratic than middle schools. In such schools, a sense of community usually is undermined, with little opportunity for students and teachers to get to know each other. As a consequence, distrust between students and teachers develops easily, and there is little communication about students' goals and values. Such contexts can especially harm the motivation of students who are not doing well academically.

What lessons can be drawn from this discussion? Perhaps the single most important lesson is that middle school and junior high school students benefit when teachers think of ways to make their school settings more personal, less formal, and more intrinsically challenging.

> **Thinking Back/Thinking Forward**
>
> The transition to middle or junior high school can be stressful because it coincides with many other developmental changes. Chapter 3, p. 88

**Some Final Thoughts About Intrinsic and Extrinsic Motivation**   An overwhelming conclusion of motivation research is that teachers should encourage students to become intrinsically motivated. Similarly, teachers should create learning environments that promote students' cognitive engagement and self-responsibility for learning. That said, the real world includes both intrinsic and extrinsic motivation, and too often intrinsic and extrinsic motivation have been pitted against each other as polar opposites. In many aspects of students' lives, both intrinsic and extrinsic motivation are at work (Cameron & Pierce, 2008). Further, both intrinsic and extrinsic motivation can operate simultaneously. Thus, a student may work hard in a course because she enjoys the content and likes learning about it (intrinsic) and to earn a good grade (extrinsic) (Schunk, 2011). Keep in mind, though, that many educational psychologists recommend that extrinsic motivation by itself is not a good strategy.

Our discussion of extrinsic and intrinsic motivation sets the stage for introducing other cognitive processes involved in motivating students to learn. As we explore five additional cognitive processes, notice how intrinsic and extrinsic motivation continue to be important. The five processes are (1) attribution, (2) mastery motivation and mindset; (3) self-efficacy; (4) goal setting, planning, and self-monitoring; and (5) expectations.

# ATTRIBUTION

**Attribution theory** states that individuals are motivated to discover the underlying causes of their own performance and behavior. *Attributions* are perceived causes of outcomes. In a way, attribution theorists say, students are like intuitive scientists, seeking to explain the cause behind what happens (Graham & Williams, 2009; Weiner, 2010). For example, a secondary school student asks, "Why am I not doing well in this class?" or, "Did I get a good grade because I studied hard or because the teacher made up an easy test, or both?" The search for a cause or explanation is most likely to be initiated when unexpected and important events end in failure, such as when a good student gets a low grade. Some of the most frequently inferred causes of success and failure are ability, effort, task ease or difficulty, luck, mood, and help or hindrance from others.

Bernard Weiner (1986, 1992, 2010) identified three dimensions of causal attributions: (1) *locus,* whether the cause is internal or external to the actor; (2) *stability,* the extent to which the cause remains the same or changes; and (3) *controllability,* the extent to which the individual can control the cause. For example, a student might perceive his aptitude as located internally, stable, and uncontrollable. The student also might perceive chance or luck as external to himself, variable, and uncontrollable. Figure 13.3 lists eight possible combinations of locus, stability, and controllability and shows how they match up with various common explanations of failure.

To see how attributions affect subsequent achievement strivings, consider two students, Jane and Susan. Both students fail a math test, but each attributes this negative outcome to a different set of causes (Graham & Weiner, 1996, p. 72):

> When Jane flunks her math test, she searches for the reasons for the failure. Her analysis leads her to attribute the failure to herself, not blaming her teacher or bad luck. She also attributes the failure to an unstable factor—lack of preparation and study time. Thus, she perceives that her failure was due to internal, unstable, and also controllable factors. Because the factors are unstable, Jane has a reasonable expectation that she can still succeed in the future. And because the factors are controllable, she also feels guilty. Her expectations for success enable her to overcome her deflated sense of self-esteem. Her hope for the future results in renewed goal setting and increased motivation to do well on the next test. As a result, Jane seeks tutoring and increases her study time.
>
> When Susan fails the test, she also searches for reasons for the failure. As it happens, her analysis leads her to attribute her failure to internal (lack of ability), stable, and uncontrollable factors. Because Susan perceives the cause of her failure to be internal, her self-esteem suffers. Because it is stable, she sees failure in her future and has a helpless feeling that she can't do anything about her situation. And because it is uncontrollable, she feels ashamed and humiliated. In addition, her parents and teacher tell her that they feel sorry for her but don't provide any recommendations or strategies for success, furthering her belief that she is incompetent. With low expectations of success, low self-esteem, and a depressed mood, Susan decides to drop out of school instead of studying harder.

What are the best strategies for teachers to use in helping students like Susan change their attributions? Educational psychologists often recommend providing students with a planned series of achievement experiences in which modeling, information about strategies, practice, and feedback are used to help them (1) concentrate on the task at hand rather than worrying about failing, (2) cope with failures by retracing their steps to discover their mistake or by analyzing the problem to discover another approach, and (3) attribute their failures to a lack of effort rather than lack of ability (Boekaerts, 2009; Brophy, 2004; Dweck & Elliott, 1983).

The current strategy is not to expose students to models who handle tasks with ease and demonstrate success but rather to expose them to models who struggle to

| Combination of causal attributions | Reason students give for failure |
|---|---|
| Internal-stable-uncontrollable | Low aptitude |
| Internal-stable-controllable | Never study |
| Internal-unstable-uncontrollable | Sick the day of the test |
| Internal-unstable-controllable | Did not study for this particular test |
| External-stable-uncontrollable | School has tough requirements |
| External-stable-controllable | The instructor is biased |
| External-unstable-uncontrollable | Bad luck |
| External-unstable-controllable | Friends failed to help |

**FIGURE 13.3** COMBINATIONS OF CAUSAL ATTRIBUTIONS AND EXPLANATIONS FOR FAILURE

When students fail or do poorly on a test or an assignment, they attribute the outcome to certain causes. The explanation reflects eight combinations of Weiner's three main categories of attributions: locus (internal-external), stability (stable-unstable), and controllability (controllable-uncontrollable).

*Human Motivation: Metaphors, Theories, and Research* by Bernard Weiner, p. 253. Copyright 1992 by Sage Publications Inc Books. Reproduced with permission of Sage Publications Inc Books in the format Textbook via Copyright Clearance Center.

**attribution theory** The theory that individuals are motivated to discover the underlying causes of their own behavior and performance.

**The student:**

- Says "I can't"
- Doesn't pay attention to teacher's instructions
- Doesn't ask for help, even when it is needed
- Does nothing (for example, stares out the window)
- Guesses or answers randomly without really trying
- Doesn't show pride in successes
- Appears bored, uninterested
- Is unresponsive to teacher's exhortations to try
- Is easily discouraged
- Doesn't volunteer answers to teacher's questions
- Maneuvers to get out of or to avoid work (for example, has to go to the nurse's office)

**FIGURE 13.4** BEHAVIORS THAT SUGGEST HELPLESSNESS

Deborah Stipek, *Motivation to Learn*, Table 5.3 "Behaviors Suggesting Learned Helplessness" p. 69, © 2002 by Pearson Education, Inc. Reproduced by permission of Pearson Education, Inc.

Thinking Back/Thinking Forward

Some critics contend that the No Child Left Behind legislation is harmful for students who are gifted and for students' creativity. Chapter 6, p. 207; Chapter 9, p. 313

**helpless orientation** A response to challenges and difficulties in which the individual feels trapped by the difficulty and attributes the difficulty to a lack of ability.

**mastery orientation** A task-oriented response to difficult or challenging circumstances that focuses on learning strategies and the process of achievement rather than the outcome.

**performance orientation** A focus on winning rather than an achievement outcome; success is believed to result from winning.

**mindset** Dweck's concept that refers to the cognitive view individuals develop for themselves; individuals have one of two mindsets: (1) fixed or (2) growth.

overcome mistakes before finally succeeding (Brophy, 2004). In this way, students learn how to deal with frustration, persist in the face of difficulties, and constructively cope with failure.

## MASTERY MOTIVATION AND MINDSET

Becoming cognitively engaged and self-motivated to improve are reflected in adolescents with a mastery motivation (Dweck, 2011; Dweck & Master, 2009). These children also have a growth mindset that they can produce positive outcomes if they put forth the effort.

**Mastery Motivation** Developmental psychologists Valanne Henderson and Carol Dweck (1990) have found that children often show two distinct responses to difficult or challenging circumstances. Children who display mastery motivation are task-oriented; instead of focusing on their ability, they concentrate on learning strategies and the process of achievement rather than the outcome. Those with a **helpless orientation** seem trapped by the experience of difficulty and they attribute their difficulty to lack of ability. They frequently say such things as, "I'm not very good at this," even though they might earlier have demonstrated their ability through many successes. And, once they view their behavior as failure, they often feel anxious, and their performance worsens. Figure 13.4 describes some behaviors that might reflect helplessness (Stipek, 2002).

In contrast, children who have a **mastery orientation** often instruct themselves to pay attention, to think carefully, and to remember strategies that have worked for them in previous situations. They frequently report feeling challenged and excited by difficult tasks, rather than being threatened by them (Anderman & Anderman, 2010).

Another issue in motivation involves whether to adopt a mastery or a performance orientation. Children with a **performance orientation** are focused on winning, rather than on an achievement outcome, and they believe that success results from winning. Does this mean that mastery-oriented children do not like to win and that performance-oriented children are not motivated to experience the self-efficacy that comes from being able to take credit for one's accomplishments? No. A matter of emphasis or degree is involved, though. For mastery-oriented individuals, winning isn't everything; for performance-oriented individuals, skill development and self-efficacy take a backseat to winning.

Recall that the No Child Left Behind (NCLB) Act emphasizes testing and accountability. Although NCLB may motivate some teachers and students to work harder, motivation experts worry that it encourages a performance rather than a mastery motivational orientation on the part of students (Meece, Anderman, & Anderman, 2006).

A final point needs to be made about mastery and performance goals: they are not always mutually exclusive. Students can be both mastery- and performance-oriented, and researchers have found that mastery goals combined with performance goals often benefit students' success (Schunk, 2011).

**Mindset** Carol Dweck's (2006, 2011) most recent analysis of motivation for achievement stresses the importance of children developing a **mindset,** which she defines as the cognitive view individuals develop for themselves. She concludes that individuals have one of two mindsets: (1) *fixed mindset,* in which they believe that their qualities are carved in stone and cannot change; or (2) *growth mindset,* in which they believe their qualities can change and improve through their effort. A fixed mindset is similar to a helpless orientation; a growth mindset is much like having mastery motivation.

In her book, *Mindset,* Dweck (2006) argued that individuals' mindsets influence whether they will be optimistic or pessimistic, shape their goals and how hard they will strive to reach those goals, and affect many aspects of their lives, including

## TEACHING CONNECTIONS: Best Practices
### Strategies for Creating a Mastery-Focused Classroom Goal Structure

Classroom practices can impact the degree to which students adopt a mastery or performance goal orientation. Suggestions for creating a classroom climate conducive to mastery goals are as follows (Ames, 1987, 1992; Meece, 1991; Middleton, & Midgley, 2002; Pintrich & Schunk, 2002)

1. *Focus attention on progress, rather than on performance.* This makes grades secondary to learning. As such, individual performance should be a private matter between teacher and student. This means keeping measures of student performance private.

   **Early elementary**
   - Don't use public star charts to indicate student performance or compliance.
   - Don't put students' names on the board as a punishment.

   **Late elementary**
   - Don't have students grade each others' work.
   - Don't return work in order of grade or announce grades as you return work.
   - Don't ask students to call out grades as you record.

**Middle School/High School**
- Don't publicize an honor roll.
- Don't have assemblies to reward students based on grades.
- Don't post grades.

2. *Communicate to students your goal of their understanding the material, rather than performing well on a test.* Ask students to justify their answers to your questions so that you can monitor understanding and facilitate its development.

3. *Foster a noncompetitive environment.* When students compete with one another, social comparison is inevitable, thus making performance goals more likely.

4. *Use criterion-referenced grading.* Grading should be based on standards, rather than on the bell curve.

5. *Communicate that mistakes are part of the learning process.* Allow students to revise their work when possible.

---

achievement and success in school and sports. Dweck says that mindsets begin to be shaped as children interact with parents, teachers, and coaches, who themselves have either a fixed mindset or a growth mindset. She described the growth mindset of Patricia Miranda:

> [She] was a chubby, unathletic school kid who wanted to wrestle. After a bad beating on the mat, she was told, "You're a joke." First she cried, then she felt: "That really set my resolve . . . I had to keep going and had to know if effort and focus and belief and training could somehow legitimize me as a wrestler." Where did she get this resolve? Miranda was raised in a life devoid of challenge. But when her mother died of an aneurysm at age forty, ten-year-old Miranda . . . [thought] "If you only go through life doing stuff that's easy, shame on you." So when wrestling presented a challenge, she was ready to take it on.
>
> Her effort paid off. At twenty-four, Miranda was having the last laugh. She won a spot on the U.S. Olympic team and came home from Athens with a bronze medal. And what was next? Yale Law School. People urged her to stay where she was already on top, but Miranda felt it was more exciting to start at the bottom again and see what she could grow into this time. (Dweck, 2006, pp. 22–23)

Consider also the powerful role second-grade Chicago teacher Marva Collins has in creating a growth mindset in her students. She tells her students, many of whom are repeating the second grade,

> I know most of you can't spell your name. You don't know the alphabet, you don't know how to read . . . I promise you that you will.

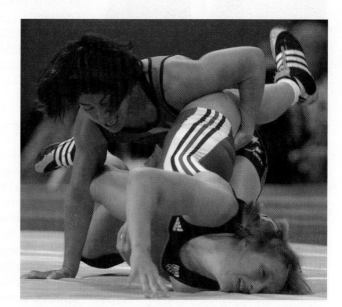

Patricia Miranda (in blue) winning the bronze medal in the 2004 Olympics. *What characterizes her growth mindset, and how is it different from someone with a fixed mindset?*

At a workshop for teachers and board members at Pennington School, Marva Collins encourages a participant as she plays the role of a student.

DIVERSITY

Carol Dweck. *What does she emphasize as the most important aspects of students' achievement?*

RESEARCH

TECHNOLOGY

**self-efficacy** The belief that one can master a situation and produce positive outcomes.

None of you has ever failed. School may have failed you. Well, goodbye to failure, children. Welcome to success. You will read hard books in here and understand what you read. You will write every day. . . . But you must help me to help you. If you don't give anything, don't expect anything. Success is not coming to you, you must come to it. (Dweck, 2006, pp. 188–189)

Her second-grade students usually have to start off with the lowest level of reader available, but by the end of the school year, most of the students are reading at the fifth-grade level. Collins takes inner-city children living in low-income, often poverty, circumstances and challenges them to be all they can be. She won't accept failure by her students and teaches students to be responsible for their behavior every day of their lives. Collins tells students that being excellent at something is not a one-time thing but a habit, that determination and persistence are what move the world, and that thinking others will make you successful is a sure way to fail.

Dweck and her colleagues (Blackwell & Dweck, 2008; Blackwell, Trzesniewski, & Dweck, 2007; Dweck & Master, 2009) recently incorporated information about the brain's plasticity into their effort to improve students' motivation to achieve and succeed. In one study, they assigned two groups of students to eight sessions of either (1) study-skills instruction or (2) study-skills instruction plus information about the importance of developing a growth mindset (called *incremental theory* in the research) (Blackwell, Trzesniewski, & Dweck, 2007). One of the exercises in the growth mindset group was titled, "You Can Grow Your Brain," which emphasized that the brain is like a muscle that can change and grow as it gets exercises and develops new connections. Students were informed that the more you challenge your brain to learn, the more your brain cells grow. Both groups had a pattern of declining math scores prior to the intervention. Following the intervention, the group who only received the study-skills instruction continued to decline but the group that received the combination of study-skills instruction plus the growth mindset emphasis on how the brain develops when it is challenged reversed the downward trend and improved their math achievement.

In other work, Dweck has been creating a computer-based workshop, "Brainology," to teach students that their intelligence can change (Blackwell & Dweck, 2008). Students experience six modules about how the brain works and how the students can make their brain improve. After being tested in 20 New York City schools recently, students strongly endorsed the value of the computer-based brain modules. Said one student, "I will try harder because I know that the more you try the more your brain knows" (Dweck & Master, 2009, p. 137).

## SELF-EFFICACY

In Chapter 7, we introduced Albert Bandura's concept of **self-efficacy,** the belief that one can master a situation and produce positive outcomes. Bandura (1997, 2001, 2009, 2010a) emphasizes that self-efficacy is a critical factor in whether or not students achieve. Self-efficacy has much in common with mastery motivation and intrinsic motivation. Self-efficacy is the belief that "I can"; helplessness, the opposite of mastery, is the belief that "I cannot." Students with high self-efficacy agree with such statements as "I know that I will be able to learn the material in this class" and "I expect to be able to do well at this activity."

Dale Schunk (2011) has applied the concept of self-efficacy to many aspects of students' achievement. In his view, self-efficacy influences a student's choice of activities. Students with low self-efficacy for learning might avoid many learning tasks, especially those that are challenging, whereas students with high self-efficacy eagerly approach these learning tasks. Students with high self-efficacy are more likely to persist with effort at a learning task than are students with low self-efficacy (Schunk & Pajares, 2009). One study revealed that high-self-efficacy adolescents had higher academic aspirations, spent more time doing homework, and were more likely to associate learning activities with optimal experience than their low-self-efficacy counterparts (Bassi & others, 2007). A recent study found that students with high self-efficacy for reading and writing were more likely to adopt a deep, strategy-oriented approach to studying while their low self-efficacy counterparts were more likely to take a surface approach (Prat-Sala & Redford, 2010).

Your self-efficacy as a teacher will have a major impact on the quality of learning that your students experience (Guo & others, 2010). Students learn much more from teachers with a sense of high self-efficacy than from those beset by self-doubts. Teachers with low self-efficacy often become mired in classroom problems and are inclined to say that low student ability is the reason their students are not learning. Low-self-efficacy teachers don't have confidence in their ability to manage their classrooms, become stressed and angered at students' misbehavior, are pessimistic about students' ability to improve, take a custodial view of their job, often resort to restrictive and punitive modes of discipline, and say that if they had it to do all over again they would not choose teaching as a profession.

Efficacious schools are pervaded by high expectations and standards for achievement (Walsh, 2008). Teachers regard their students as capable of high academic achievement, set challenging academic standards for them, and provide support to help them reach these high standards. In contrast, in low-achieving schools not much is expected academically of students, teachers spend less time actively teaching and monitoring students' academic progress, and tend to write off a high percentage of students as unteachable (Brookover & others, 1979). Not surprisingly, students in such schools have low self-efficacy and a sense of academic futility.

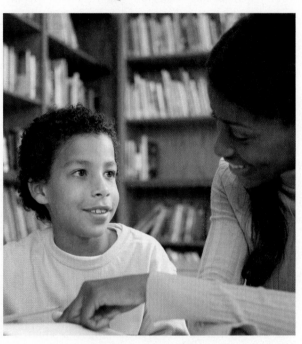

*What characterizes students, teachers, and schools with high self-efficacy?*

**Thinking Back/Thinking Forward**

Bandura's social cognitive theory emphasizes reciprocal links between behavior, environment, and person/cognitive factors Chapter 7, p. 235

## GOAL SETTING, PLANNING, AND SELF-MONITORING

Goal setting is increasingly recognized as a key aspect of achievement (Anderman, 2011; Anderman & Anderman, 2010; Urdan, 2010). Researchers have found that self-efficacy and achievement improve when students set goals that are specific, proximal, and challenging (Bandura, 1997; Schunk, 2011). A nonspecific, fuzzy goal is "I want to be successful." A more concrete, specific goal is "I want to make the honor roll by the end of the semester."

**Long-Term and Short-Term Goals**   Students can set both long-term (distal) and short-term (proximal) goals. It is okay to let students set some long-term goals, such as "I want to graduate from high school" or "I want to go to college," but if you do, make sure that they also create short-term goals as steps along the way. "Getting an A on the next math test" is an example of a short-term, proximal goal. So is "Doing all of my homework by 4 P.M. Sunday." As mentioned earlier, attention should focus mainly on short-term goals, which help students judge their progress better than do long-term goals. David McNally (1990), author of *Even Eagles Need a Push,* advises that when students set goals and plan, they should be reminded to live their lives one day at a time. Have them make their commitments in bite-size chunks. As McNally says, a house is built one brick at a time, a cathedral one stone at a time. The artist paints one stroke at a time. The student should also work in small increments.

**Challenging Goals**   Another good strategy is to encourage students to set challenging goals. A challenging goal is a commitment to self-improvement. Strong interest and involvement in activities is sparked by challenges. Goals that are easy to reach generate little interest or effort. However, goals should be optimally matched

## TEACHING CONNECTIONS: Best Practices
### Strategies for Improving Students' Self-Efficacy

Here are some good strategies for improving students' self-efficacy (Stipek, 2002):

1. *Teach specific strategies.* Teach students specific strategies, such as outlining and summarizing, that can improve their ability to focus on their tasks.

2. *Guide students in setting goals.* Help them create short-term goals after they have made long-term goals. Short-term goals especially help students to judge their progress.

3. *Consider mastery.* Give students performance-contingent rewards, which are more likely to signal mastery, rather than rewards, for merely engaging in a task.

4. *Combine strategy training with goals.* Schunk and his colleagues (Schunk, 2001; Schunk & Rice, 1989; Schunk & Swartz, 1993) have found that a combination of strategy training and goal setting can enhance students' self-efficacy and skill development. Give feedback to students on how their learning strategies relate to their performance.

5. *Provide students with support.* Positive support can come from teachers, parents, and peers. Sometimes a teacher just needs to tell a student, "You can do this." In Through the Eyes of Teachers, Joanna Smith, a high school English teacher, describes how she helps students who struggle with "failure syndrome."

### THROUGH THE EYES OF TEACHERS
#### Helping Students Who Feel Like Failures Gain Confidence

I believe that encouragement can help students overcome "failure syndrome." Students with failure syndrome give up immediately when they sense any difficulty whatsoever. It is easy to feel frustrated when facing these students, but I have found success when I truly reach them. The only way for me to reach individual students is to get to know them and their families by giving journal assignments, choices about books they read, opportunities to tell me about themselves, and by opening myself up to them. These students also need a lot of encouragement. They need to know that you have noticed and are not happy with their failure, and then they need to know you believe in them. Only then will students with failure syndrome perform.

6. *Help students believe in their cognitive abilities* (Anderman & Anderman, 2010). You are likely to have some students in your class who have a history of being unsuccessful in academic settings. Talking to these students about your confidence in their abilities can improve their self-efficacy and help them to become more motivated.

to the student's skill level. If goals are unrealistically high, the result will be repeated failures that lower the student's self-efficacy.

**Personal Goals**    Another good strategy to encourage students in goal-setting is to guide them in developing personal goals about desired and undesired future circumstances (Ford & Smith, 2009). Too often teachers aren't aware of their students' personal goals and what their students hope to attain (Boekaerts, 2009). Personal goals can be a key aspect of students' motivation for coping and dealing with life's challenges and opportunities (Maehr & Zusho, 2009).

DEVELOPMENT

RESEARCH

**Developmental Changes and Goal-Setting**    Unfortunately, many of the changes involved in the transition to middle schools are likely to increase students' motivation to achieve performance goals rather than mastery goals (Anderman & Mueller, 2010; Eccles & Roeser, 2010). Consider that these transitions often include a drop in grades, a lack of support for autonomy, whole-class task organization and between-class ability groupings that likely increase social comparison, concerns about evaluation, and competitiveness.

In one research study, both teachers and students reported that performance-focused goals were more common and task-focused goals less common in middle school than in elementary school classrooms (Midgley, Anderman, & Hicks, 1995). In addition, the elementary school teachers reported using task-focused goals more than middle school teachers did. At both grades, the extent to which the teachers were task-focused was linked with the students' and the teachers' sense of personal efficacy. Not unexpectedly, personal efficacy was lower for the middle school than elementary school participants. Thus, middle school teachers especially need to include task-focused goals in their instruction (Anderman, Austin, & Johnson, 2002). Also, a recent Japanese study revealed that in junior high and high school classrooms in which teachers created a mastery goal structure for their classroom, students were more intrinsically motivated and had a higher academic self-concept; by contrast, in performance-oriented goal structure classrooms students were less intrinsically motivated and had a lower academic self-concept (Murayama & Elliot, 2009).

**Planning and Self-Monitoring**   In Chapter 12 we described the importance of planning for teachers. Planning is also important for students. It is not enough just to get students to set goals. It also is important to encourage them to plan how they will reach their goals. Being a good planner means managing time effectively, setting priorities, and being organized. Give students, especially at the middle school and high school levels, practice at managing their time, setting priorities, and being organized.

## EXPECTATIONS

Expectations can exert a powerful influence on students' motivation. Let's examine student expectations and teacher expectations.

**Students' Expectations**   How hard students will work can depend on how much they expect to accomplish (Cavazos & Cavazos, 2010). If they expect to succeed, they are more likely to work hard to reach a goal than if they expect to fail. Jacquelynne Eccles (1987, 1993) defined expectations for students' success as "beliefs about how well they will do on upcoming tasks, either in the immediate or long-term future" (Wigfield & others, 2006). Three aspects of students' ability beliefs, according to Eccles, are (1) how good they are at a particular activity, (2) how good they are in comparison to other individuals, and (3) how good they are in relation to their performance in other activities.

How hard students work also depends on the value they place on the goal (Wigfield, Tonks, & Klauda, 2009). Indeed, the combination of expectancy and value has been the focus of a number of efforts to better understand students' achievement

RESEARCH

motivation for many decades (Atkinson, 1957; Eccles, 1993, 2007; Feather, 1966). In Jacquelynne Eccles' (1993, 2007) model, "expectancies and values are assumed to directly influence performance, persistence, and task choice. Expectancies and values are . . . influenced by perceptions of competence, perceptions of the difficulty of different tasks, and individuals' goals" (Wigfield & others, 2006, pp. 938–939). In Eccles' view, the culture's achievement orientation also plays a role in influencing students' expectations.

**Teachers' Expectations**   Teachers' expectations influence students' motivation and performance (Anderman & Anderman, 2010; de Boer, Bosker, & van der Werf, 2010; Jussim, Robustelli, & Cain, 2009). "When teachers hold high generalized expectations for student achievement and students perceive

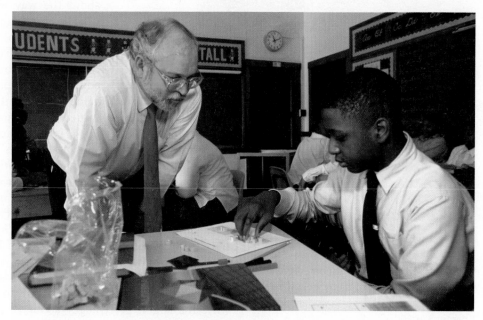

A student and teacher at Langston Hughes Elementary School in Chicago, a school whose teachers have high expectations for students. *How do teachers' expectations influence students' achievement?*

## THROUGH THE EYES OF STUDENTS

### Hari Prabhakar, Student on a Path to Purpose

Hari Prabhakar's ambition is to become an international health expert. Prabhakar graduated from Johns Hopkins University in 2006 with a double major in public health and writing. A top student (3.9 GPA), he took the initiative to pursue a number of activities outside the classroom in the health field. Toward the end of high school, Hari created the Tribal India Health Foundation (**www.tihf.org**), which provides assistance in bringing low-cost health care to rural areas in India. Juggling his roles as a student and as the foundation's director, Prabhakar spent about 15 hours a week leading Tribal India Health. In describing his work, Prabhakar said (Johns Hopkins University, 2006):

> I have found it very challenging to coordinate the international operation. . . . It takes a lot of work, and there's not a lot of free time. But it's worth it when I visit our patients and see how they and the community are getting better.

(*Sources:* Johns Hopkins University, 2006; Lunday, 2006; Marshall Scholarships, 2007; Prabhakar, 2007).

Hari Prabhakar (*in rear*) at a screening camp in India that he created as part of his Tribal India Health Foundation.

**Thinking Back/Thinking Forward**

Character education is a direct approach that involves teaching students basic moral literacy; values clarification emphasizes helping students to clarify what their lives are for and what is worth working for. Chapter 3, p. 100

these expectations, students achieve more, experience a greater sense of self-esteem and competence as learners, and resist involvement in problem behaviors both during childhood and adolescence" (Wigfield & others, 2006, p. 976). In a recent observational study of 12 classrooms, teachers with high expectations spent more time providing a framework for students' learning, asked higher-level questions, and were more effective in managing students' behavior than teachers with average and low expectations (Rubie-Davis, 2007).

Teachers often have more positive expectations for high-ability than for low-ability students, and these expectations are likely to influence their behavior toward them. For example, teachers require high-ability students to work harder than low-ability students, wait longer for them to respond to questions, respond to them with more information and in a more elaborate fashion, criticize them less often, praise them more often, are more friendly to them, call on them more often, seat them closer to the teachers' desks, and are more likely to give them the benefit of the doubt on close calls in grading (Brophy, 2004). An important teaching strategy is to monitor your expectations and be sure to have positive expectations for students with low abilities. Fortunately, researchers have found that with support teachers can adapt and raise their expectations for students with low abilities (Weinstein, Madison, & Kuklinski, 1995).

### VALUES AND PURPOSE

In the discussion of expectations, we indicated that how hard students work is influenced by the value they place on the goal they have set. We also indicated that the culture's achievement orientation influences students' values. Just what are "values"? *Values* are beliefs and attitudes about the way we think things should be. They involve what is important to individuals. Values can be attached to all sorts of things, such as religion, money, sex, helping others, family, friends, self-discipline, cheating, education, career, and so on. In Chapter 3 we described two moral education approaches that emphasize the importance of values in students' development: character education and values clarification.

It is important to note the integral role *purpose* plays in shaping students' values. In his book, *The Path to Purpose: Helping Our Children Find Their Calling in Life* (2008), William Damon defines *purpose* as an intention to accomplish something meaningful to oneself and contribute something to the world beyond the self. Finding purpose involves answering such questions as "*Why* am I doing this? *Why* does it matter? *Why* is it important for me and the world beyond me? *Why* do I strive to accomplish this end?" (Damon, 2008, pp. 33–34).

In interviews with 12- to 22-year-olds, Damon found that only about 20 percent had a clear vision of where they want to go in life, what they want to achieve, and why. The largest percentage—about 60 percent—had engaged in some potentially purposeful activities, such as service learning or fruitful discussions with a career counselor—but still did not have a real commitment or any reasonable plans for

DEVELOPMENT

reaching their goals. And slightly more than 20 percent expressed no aspirations and in some instances said they didn't see any reason to have aspirations.

Damon concludes that most teachers and parents communicate the importance of such goals as studying hard and getting good grades, but rarely discuss what the goals might lead to—what the purpose is for studying hard and getting good grades. Damon emphasizes that too often students focus only on short-term goals and don't explore the big, long-term picture of what they want to do with their life. These interview questions Damon (2008, p. 135) has used in his research are good springboards for getting students to reflect on their purpose:

What's most important to you in your life?

Why do you care about those things?

Do you have any long-term goals?

Why are these goals important to you?

What does it mean to have a good life?

What does it mean to be a good person?

If you were looking back on your life now, how would you like to be remembered?

I recently asked teachers what strategies they use to help students achieve? Following are their responses.

**EARLY CHILDHOOD**   Our preschoolers are given goals to achieve throughout the year. For example, weekly goals are to identify and write a new letter each week.

To motivate children to achieve this goal, we ask them to bring in a special object from home that begins with the letter of the week and share it with the class. The children enjoy the weekly responsibility of bringing in special objects and feel involved in the learning process.

—**Missy Dangler,** *Suburban Hills School*

**ELEMENTARY SCHOOL: GRADES K–5**   I begin the school year by sharing my teaching goals with the students. After that, I ask the children to come up with a list

of their goals for the year, and we display them next to the child's self-portrait. These goals and self-portraits are on display all year, so that we are all reminded of what is important. We also work on classroom rules that support the students' and my goals.

—**Yvonne Wilson,** *North Elementary School*

**MIDDLE SCHOOL: GRADES 6–8**   In this age of testing, it's important to motivate students to learn for learning's sake (not just to do well on a test). With that in mind,

I intentionally identify material that will *not* be included in the assessment process. This material is usually high-interest, trivia, or sometimes a wonderful story relevant to the material. Although this material won't be on the test, my students look forward to learning it.

—**Mark Fodness,** *Bemidji Middle School*

**HIGH SCHOOL: GRADES 9–12**   My high school art students respond best to praise. Everyone loves to hear, "Wow, that looks fantastic; good job!" Another motivator for

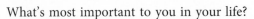

my students is that artworks that are well done may be entered in one of the many contests, shows, and exhibits we enter each year. Having a reward dangling out there is a great motivational tool.

—**Dennis Peterson,** *Deer River High School*

## Review, Reflect, and Connect

**2** Discuss the important processes in motivation to achieve.

**REVIEW**

- What are extrinsic and intrinsic motivation? How are they involved in students' achievement?
- What characterizes attribution theory and an attribution approach to students' achievement?
- How does a mastery orientation compare with a helpless orientation and a performance orientation? Why is a growth mindset important in students' achievement?
- What is self-efficacy? What types of instructional strategies benefit students' self-efficacy?
- How are goal setting, planning, and self-monitoring important in improving students' motivation to achieve?
- How can students' and teachers' expectations affect students' motivation?
- What do values and purpose mean? How can the importance of students developing a purpose be summarized?

**REFLECT**

- Sean and Dave both get cut from the basketball team. The next year, Sean tries out again but Dave does not. What causal attributions (and their effects) could explain the behaviors of these two students?

**PRAXIS™ PRACTICE**

1. Which of the following is the best example of someone who is intrinsically motivated?
   a. Eric is reading the latest Harry Potter book because he wants to become a better reader.
   b. Jordan is reading the latest Harry Potter book because he can't wait to see what happens to Harry and his friends.
   c. Josh is reading the latest Harry Potter book so that he will have read enough pages to qualify for the class pizza party at the end of the month.
   d. Martynas is reading the latest Harry Potter book because his teacher assigned it and he wants to please his teacher.

2. Joan just failed a science test. "I knew it," she says. "I have never been any good at science, and I never will be." Which of the following best characterizes Joan's attribution for her failure?
   a. external-stable-controllable
   b. external-unstable-uncontrollable
   c. internal-stable-controllable
   d. internal-stable-uncontrollable

3. Which of the following is the best example of a performance-goal orientation?
   a. Alicia competes with her best friend to see who can get the higher grade on every test, taking delight in receiving the high score.
   b. Cassandra hates math, does not believe that she can be successful, and gives up at the first sign of struggling.
   c. Ed struggles in math, but wants very much to learn the material, so when he gets stuck on a problem, he asks for help.
   d. Martin does his work as requested and does a fair job on it, but he doesn't really care about his grades or about how much he learns.

## Review, Reflect, and Practice

### PRAXIS™ PRACTICE (CONTINUED)

4. Jacob is struggling in algebra and as a result is experiencing low self-efficacy. Which of the following people would provide the best role model?
   a. David, a local engineer, who tells the class how useful math will be in their futures.
   b. Jamal, a fellow student, who has also struggled in the course but is now grasping the concepts.
   c. Mrs. Jackson, Jacob's algebra teacher, who has always loved math.
   d. Suzanne, a fellow student, who is getting an *A* with minimal effort.

5. Which student has the least appropriate goal?
   a. As Mark is choosing courses for his senior year in high school, he decides to take the more challenging of the two courses his counselor suggested to him.
   b. Sam is taking geometry in his senior year of high school because he has always struggled in math.
   c. Sylvia decides to take advanced-placement calculus in her senior year although she knows it is a difficult course.
   d. Zelda is a capable math student, but she chooses an easy math course in which she is almost certain to get an *A*.

6. Ms. Martin teaches eighth-grade history to an academically diverse class. DeMarcus is a gifted student who has always earned high marks. Joe has a learning disability. Ms. Martin does not believe it would be fair to expect the same performance from Joe as from DeMarcus. However, she knows that Joe can learn the material with proper scaffolding. Because of this, she seats Joe near her desk, praises him when he does something well, and gives him constructive criticism when needed. How are her expectations and behavior likely to affect the achievement of these students?
   a. Her expectations are likely to result in similar achievement from both students.
   b. Her expectations are likely to result in high achievement from DeMarcus and fairly high achievement from Joe.
   c. Her expectations are likely to result in high achievement from Joe and low achievement from DeMarcus.
   d. Her expectations are likely to result in low achievement from both students.

7. Which of the following questions that a teacher poses to a student in her eleventh-grade class best reflects an inquiry about the student's purpose in life?
   a. Why did you not study harder for your test this week?
   b. What's most important to you in your life?
   c. What can you do the rest of the year to get a good grade in this course?
   d. How are you going to improve your chances of becoming a school leader?

*Please see the answer key at the end of the book.*

## 3 MOTIVATION, RELATIONSHIPS, AND SOCIOCULTURAL CONTEXTS

| Social Motives | Social Relationships | Sociocultural Contexts |

In addition to achievement motives, students also have social motives. Our coverage of the social dimensions of motivation focuses on students' social motives, relationships, and sociocultural contexts.

## SOCIAL MOTIVES

**Social motives** are needs and desires that are learned through experiences with the social world. Students' social needs are reflected in their desires to be popular with peers and have close friends and the powerful attraction they feel to someone they love. Though all have a need for affiliation, or relatedness, some have a stronger need than others. Some students like to be surrounded by lots of friends. In middle and high school, some students feel something is drastically missing from their lives if they don't have a girlfriend or boyfriend to date regularly. Others don't have such strong needs for affiliation. They don't fall apart if they don't have several close friends around all day and don't sit in class in an anxious state if they don't have a romantic partner.

Children's social concerns influence their lives at school (Anderman & Anderman, 2010). Every schoolday, students work at establishing and maintaining social relationships. Researchers have found that students who display socially competent behavior are more likely to excel academically than those who do not (Wentzel, 2008). Overall, though, researchers have given too little attention to how students' social worlds are related to their motivation in the classroom.

Both teacher approval and peer approval are important social motives for most students. In the elementary school years, students are motivated to please their parents more than their peers (Berndt, 1979). By the end of elementary school, parent approval and peer approval are about equal in most students' motive systems. By eighth or ninth grade, peer conformity outstrips conformity to parents. By twelfth grade, conformity to peers drops off somewhat as students become more autonomous and make more decisions on their own.

Adolescence can be an especially important juncture in achievement motivation and social motivation (Anderman, 2011; Anderman & Mueller, 2010; Eccles & Roeser, 2010). New academic and social pressures force adolescents toward new roles that involve more responsibility. As adolescents experience more intense achievement demands, their social interests might cut into the time they need for academic matters. Or ambitions in one area can undermine the attainment of goals in another area, as when academic achievement leads to social disapproval. In early adolescence, students face a choice between whether they will spend more of their time pursuing social goals or academic goals. The results of this decision have long-term consequences in terms of how far adolescents will go in their education and the careers they will pursue.

## SOCIAL RELATIONSHIPS

Students' relationships with parents, peers, and friends have a tremendous impact on their lives. Their interactions with teachers, mentors, and others also can profoundly affect their achievement and social motivation.

Research has been conducted on links between parenting and students' motivation (Duchesne & Ratelle, 2010; Pomerantz & Moorman, 2010). Studies have examined family demographic characteristics, child-rearing practices, and provision of specific experiences at home (Eccles, Wigfield, & Schiefele, 1998).

**Demographic Characteristics**    Parents with more education are more likely than less educated parents to believe that their involvement in their child's education is important, to be active participants in their child's education, and to have intellectually stimulating materials at home (Schneider & Coleman, 1993). When parents' time and energy are largely consumed by other concerns or people other than the child, the child's motivation can suffer. Living in a single-parent family, having parents

*What are some aspects of students' social worlds that are linked to their motivation in the classroom?*

DEVELOPMENT

**social motives** Needs and desires that are learned through experiences with the social world.

who are consumed by their work, and living in a large family can undercut children's achievement.

**Child-Rearing Practices**    Even though demographic factors can affect students' motivation, more important are the parents' child-rearing practices (Wigfield & others, 2006). Here are some positive parenting practices that result in improved motivation and achievement:

- Knowing enough about the child to provide the right amount of challenge and the right amount of support
- Providing a positive emotional climate, which motivates children to internalize their parents' values and goals
- Modeling motivated achievement behavior—working hard and persisting with effort at challenging tasks

**Provision of Specific Experiences at Home**    In addition to general child-rearing practices, parents provide various activities or resources at home that may influence students' interest and motivation to pursue various activities over time (Wigfield & others, 2006). For example, reading to one's preschool children and providing reading materials in the home are positively related to students' later reading achievement and motivation (Wigfield & Asher, 1984). Indeed, researchers have found that children's skills and work habits when they enter kindergarten are among the best predictors of academic motivation and performance in both elementary and secondary school (Entwisle & Alexander, 1993). The extent to which parents emphasize academic achievement or sports and provide opportunities and resources for their children to participate in these activities in the elementary school years influence whether the children are likely to continue to choose course work and extracurricular activities consistent with these activities in adolescence (Simpkins & others, 2004). A recent U.S. large-scale longitudinal study revealed that students' achievement was linked to academic resources in their homes (Xia, 2010). In this study, doing homework more frequently, having home Internet access, and owning a community library card were more influential in African American children or children in low-SES families attaining higher achievement than in children from other ethnic and higher SES backgrounds.

**Peers**    Peers can affect a student's motivation in a number of ways (Hamm & Zhang, 2010; Harris, 2010; Winne & Nesbit, 2010). In considering students' achievement, it is important to consider not only academic goals but social goals as well.

Students who are more accepted by their peers and who have good social skills often do better in school and have positive academic achievement motivation. In contrast, rejected students, especially those who are highly aggressive, are at risk for a number of achievement problems, including getting low grades and dropping out of school (Dodge, 2010). A recent study revealed that having aggressive-disruptive friends in adolescence was linked to a lower likelihood of graduating from high school (Veronneau & others, 2008). And, as we saw in Chapter 3, having friends who are academically oriented is linked to higher achievement in adolescence (Crosnoe & others, 2008).

**Teachers**    Teachers play an important role in students' achievement (Friedel & others, 2010; Wentzel, 2009, 2010). When researchers have observed classrooms, they

> **Thinking Back/Thinking Forward**
>
> Family management practices, such as maintaining a structured and organized family environment and effectively monitoring the child's behavior, are positively related to children's grades and self-responsibility. Chapter 3, p. 78

> **Thinking Back/Thinking Forward**
>
> Five different peer statuses of children are popular, average, neglected, rejected, and controversial. Chapter 3, p. 83

RESEARCH

*How might peer relations contribute to students' achievement?*

## FIGURE **13.5** STUDENTS' DESCRIPTIONS OF TEACHERS WHO CARE

| | Teachers who care | Teachers who do not care |
|---|---|---|
| Teaching behaviors | Makes an effort to make class interesting; teaches in a special way | Teaches in a boring way, gets off-task, teaches while students aren't paying attention |
| Communication style | Talks to me, pays attention, asks questions, listens | Ignores, interrupts, screams, yells |
| Equitable treatment and respect | Is honest and fair, keeps promises, trusts me, tells the truth | Embarrasses, insults |
| Concern about individuals | Asks what's wrong, talks to me about my problems, acts as a friend, asks when I need help, takes time to make sure I understand, calls on me | Forgets name, does nothing when I do something wrong, doesn't explain things or answer questions, doesn't try to help me |

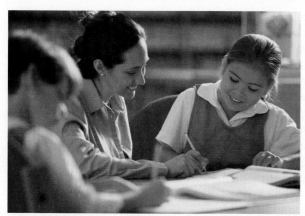

*What role do teachers play in students' motivation?*

RESEARCH

## THROUGH THE EYES OF STUDENTS

### "You Always Manage to Cheer Us Up"

I know our science class sometimes is obnoxious and negative but we really appreciate you. You always manage to cheer us up and treat us like your kids. That shows how much you care about us. If you hadn't been there for me like you were, I probably wouldn't be where I am now. Good luck with all of your other students and I hope they learn as much as I have. I'll miss you next year. Hope to see you around.

*Letter from Jennifer to William Williford, Her Middle School Science Teacher, Perry, Georgia*

have found that effective, engaging teachers not only provide support for students to make good progress, but encourage students to become self-regulated achievers (Pressley & others, 2007a,b). The encouragement takes place in a very positive environment, one in which students are constantly being guided to become motivated to try hard and develop self-efficacy. A recent study revealed that instructional and socioemotional support (as exemplified in attending to students' interest and initiative, providing appropriately challenging learning opportunities, and creating positive social relationships) were linked to first-grade students' achievement (as reflected in meeting reading and math academic standards) (Perry, Donohue, & Weinstein, 2007).

Many children who do not do well in school consistently have negative interactions with their teachers (Stipek, 2002). They are frequently in trouble for not completing assignments, not paying attention, goofing off, or acting out. In many cases, they deserve to be criticized and disciplined, but too often the classroom becomes a highly unpleasant place for them.

Researchers have found that students who feel they have supportive, caring teachers are more strongly motivated to engage in academic work than students with unsupportive, uncaring teachers (Wentzel, 2009, 2010). One researcher examined students' views of the qualities of good relationships with a teacher by asking middle school students questions such as how they knew a teacher cared about them (Wentzel, 1997). As shown in Figure 13.5, students had favorable impressions of teachers who were attentive to them as human beings. Interestingly, students also considered teachers' instructional behaviors in evaluating how much their teachers cared about them. The students said that teachers convey that they care about their students when they make serious efforts to promote learning and have appropriately high standards.

Students' motivation is optimized when teachers provide them with challenging tasks in a mastery-oriented environment that includes good emotional and cognitive support, meaningful and interesting material to learn and master, and sufficient support for autonomy and initiative (Wentzel, 2009). Many researchers conclude that when academic work is meaningful, it sustains students' attention and interest, engages them in learning, and reduces the likelihood that students will feel alienated from school (Blumenfeld, Krajcik, & Kempler, 2006). Also, as we saw in our discussion of Bandura's ideas on self-efficacy earlier in the chapter, the motivation and achievement climate of the entire school affects students' motivation. Schools with high expectations and academic standards, as well as academic and emotional support for students, often have students who are motivated to achieve (Reksten, 2009).

**Teachers and Parents**   In the past, schools have given little attention to how teachers can enlist parents as partners with them in providing opportunities for students to achieve. Currently there is considerable interest in how to accomplish this partnership (Epstein, 2009; Grant & Ray, 2009). When teachers systematically and frequently inform parents of their children's progress and get parents involved in their children's learning, children often reach higher levels of academic achievement (Agnew-Tally & others, 2009; Studer, 2009).

**Thinking Back/Thinking Forward**

Joan Epstein has proposed a number of effective strategies for forging family-school linkages. Chapter 3, p. 80

## SOCIOCULTURAL CONTEXTS

The diversity within ethnic minority groups that we discussed in Chapter 5 is evident in their achievement (Banks, 2010; Ceballo, Huerta, & Ngo, 2010). For example, many Asian American students have a strong academic achievement orientation, but some do not (Lee & Wong, 2009).

DIVERSITY

In addition to recognizing the diversity that exists within every cultural group in terms of their achievement, it also is important to distinguish between difference and deficiency. Too often, the achievements of ethnic minority students—especially African American, Latino, and Native American—have been interpreted in terms of middle-socioeconomic-status White standards as deficits when these students simply are culturally different and distinct.

However, achievement differences are more closely related to socioeconomic status than to ethnicity (Ballentine & Roberts, 2009). Many studies have found that socioeconomic status predicts achievement better than ethnicity (Entwisle, Alexander, & Olson, 2010; Rowley, Kurtz-Costes, & Cooper, 2010). Regardless of their ethnic background, students from middle- and upper-income families fare better than their counterparts from low-income backgrounds in a host of achievement situations—expectations for success, achievement aspirations, and recognition of the importance of effort, for example. An especially important factor in the lower achievement of students from low-income families is lack of adequate resources, such as an up-to-date computer in the home (or even a computer at all) to support students' learning (Schunk, Pintrich, & Meece, 2008).

RESEARCH

Sandra Graham (1986, 1990) has conducted a number of studies that reveal not only a stronger role of socioeconomic status than of ethnicity in achievement but also the importance of studying ethnic minority student motivation in the context of general motivational theory. Her inquiries fall within the framework of attribution theory and focus on the causes African American students identify for their achievement orientation—that is, why they succeed or fail. Graham has found that middle-income African American students, like their White middle-income counterparts, have high achievement expectations and understand that failure is usually due to a lack of effort rather than bad luck.

RESEARCH

A special challenge for many ethnic minority students, especially those living in poverty, is dealing with racial prejudice, conflict between the values of their group versus the majority group, and a lack of high-achieving adults in their cultural group who can serve as positive role models (Murdock, 2009; Murrell, 2009). The lack of high-achieving role models relates to the discussion in Chapter 7, in which we described the importance of increasing the number of mentors in these students' lives. A recent study revealed that perceived racial discrimination by teachers was negatively related to African American and Caribbean adolescents' academic achievement (Thomas & others, 2009).

It is important to further consider the nature of the schools that primarily serve ethnic minority students (Wigfield & others, 2006). More than one-third of African American and almost one-third of Latino students attend schools in the 47 largest city school districts in the United States, compared with only 5 percent of White and 22 percent of Asian

UCLA educational psychologist Sandra Graham is shown talking with adolescent boys about motivation. She has conducted a number of studies which reveal that middle-socioeconomic-status African American students—like their White counterparts—have high achievement expectations and attribute success to internal factors such as effort rather than external factors such as luck.

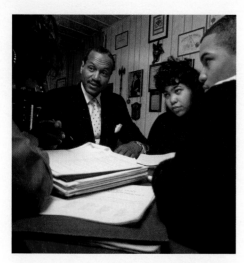

Dr. Henry Gaskins, here talking with three high school students, began an after-school tutorial program for ethnic minority students in 1983 in Washington, D.C. Volunteers like Dr. Gaskins can be especially helpful in developing a stronger sense of the importance of education in ethnic minority adolescents.

American students. Many of these ethnic minority students come from low-income families (more than half are eligible for free or reduced-cost lunches). These inner-city schools are less likely than other schools to serve more advantaged populations or to offer high-quality academic support services, advanced courses, and courses that challenge students' active thinking skills. Even students who are motivated to learn and achieve can find it difficult to perform effectively in such contexts (Hudley, 2009).

A special concern among educators is to find ways to support the achievement efforts of ethnic minority students, many of whom come from low-income backgrounds (Comer, 2010; Rowley, Kurtz-Costes, & Cooper, 2010). In the Teaching Stories segment that opened this chapter, you read about Jaime Escalante, who made a major difference in the motivation of Latino students to learn and excel at math in East Los Angeles.

Another individual who has been exceptional in supporting the motivation of African American students is Henry Gaskins, a physician who began an after-school tutoring program for ethnic minority students in Washington, D.C. For four hours every weeknight and all day on Saturdays, 80 students receive study assistance from Gaskins, his wife, two adult volunteers, and academically talented peers. Those who can afford it contribute $5 to cover the cost of school supplies. In addition to tutoring them in various school subjects, Gaskins helps the tutees learn how to set academic goals and plan how to achieve these goals. Gaskins also encourages students to self-monitor their progress toward the goals. Many of the students being tutored have parents who are high school dropouts and either can't or aren't motivated to help their sons and daughters achieve.

Every community has people like Henry Gaskins who can help provide much needed mentoring and tutoring for students from low socioeconomic backgrounds whose parents cannot help them achieve academically. Many of these potential mentors and tutors from the community have not been contacted by school personnel. If the need exists among your students, make a commitment to scour the community for talented, motivated, and concerned adults like Gaskins, who might only need to be asked to provide mentoring and tutoring support for disadvantaged students.

## Review, Reflect, and Practice

**③** Explain how relationships and sociocultural contexts can support or undercut motivation.

### REVIEW
- What are social motives and the need for affiliation?
- In what ways are students' school performances linked to relationships with parents, peers, friends, and teachers?
- How do ethnicity and socioeconomic status influence motivation to achieve at school?

### REFLECT
- Suppose several children from low-income families in your elementary school classroom are struggling with achieving their potential. How would you work with them to improve their chances of being successful in school?

### PRAXIS™ PRACTICE
1. Which of the following students is most likely to conform to peer expectations for academic achievement?
   a. Patrick, who is in second grade
   b. Ross, who is in fifth grade

## Review, Reflect, and Practice

   c. Sheldon, who is in eighth grade

   d. Rose, who is a senior in high school

2. Which classroom is likely to have the most positive impact on student motivation?

   a. Ms. Davidson is concerned only about her students' academic performance, not their personal lives. Her class is very challenging, though not terribly interesting.

   b. Mr. Nelson works hard to get to know his students on a personal as well as an academic basis. Because he cares so much for them, he makes sure that his class is easy enough for all of his students to do well.

   c. Ms. Pagliuca works hard to get to know her students on a personal as well as an academic basis. She gives her students work that is challenging and interesting.

   d. Mr. Williams' class is very challenging and competitive. His students compete on a daily basis for points.

3. Which of the following students is *least* likely to have a strong achievement motivation?

   a. Lee, an African American student from a middle-income family

   b. Pedro, a Latino student from a middle-income family

   c. Ross, an African-American student from an affluent family

   d. Sean, a White student from a low-income family

*Please see the answer key at the end of the book.*

## 4 EXPLORING ACHIEVEMENT DIFFICULTIES

Achievement problems can surface when students don't set goals, don't plan how to reach them, and don't adequately monitor their progress toward the goals. They also can arise when students are low achievers and have low expectations for success, try to protect their self-worth by avoiding failure, procrastinate, are perfectionists, become overwhelmed by anxiety, or become uninterested or alienated from school. Many of these obstacles to achievement surface during elementary school and then become more pronounced during middle school or high school. We will discuss a number of strategies that teachers, counselors, mentors, and parents can use to help students overcome obstacles to their achievement.

## STUDENTS WHO ARE LOW ACHIEVING AND HAVE LOW EXPECTATIONS FOR SUCCESS

Jere Brophy (1998) provided the following description of low-achieving students with low expectations for success: These students need to be consistently reassured that

| Training method | Primary emphasis | Main goals |
|---|---|---|
| Efficacy training | Improve students' self-efficacy perceptions | Teach students to set and strive to reach specific, proximal, and challenging goals. Monitor students' progress and frequently support students by saying things like "I know you can do it." Use adult and peer modeling effectively. Individualize instruction and tailor it to the student's knowledge and skills. Keep social comparison to a minimum. Be an efficacious teacher and have confidence in your abilities. View students with a failure syndrome as challenges rather than losers. |
| Strategy training | Improve students' domain- and task-specific skills and strategies | Help students to acquire and self-regulate their use of effective learning and problem-solving strategies. Teach students what to do, how to do it, and when and why to do it. |

**FIGURE 13.6** COGNITIVE RETRAINING METHODS FOR INCREASING THE MOTIVATION OF STUDENTS WHO DISPLAY FAILURE SYNDROME

they can meet the goals and challenges you have set for them and that you will give them the help and support they need to succeed. However, they need to be reminded that you will accept their progress only as long as they make a real effort. They might require individualized instructional materials or activities to provide an optimal challenge for their skill level. You should help them set learning goals and give them support for reaching these goals. Also, require them to put forth considerable effort and make progress, even though they might not have the ability to perform at the level of the class as a whole.

**Failure syndrome** refers to having low expectations for success and giving up at the first sign of difficulty. Failure-syndrome students are different from low-achieving students. Low-achieving students fail despite putting forth their best effort whereas failure-syndrome students don't put forth enough effort, often beginning tasks in a halfhearted manner and giving up quickly at the first hint of a challenge. Failure-syndrome students typically have low self-efficacy and a fixed mindset.

A number of strategies can be used to increase the motivation of students who display failure syndrome. Especially beneficial are cognitive retraining methods, such as efficacy retraining and strategy training, which are described in Figure 13.6.

## STUDENTS WHO PROTECT THEIR SELF-WORTH BY AVOIDING FAILURE

Some individuals are so interested in protecting their self-worth and avoiding failure that they become distracted from pursuing goals and engage in ineffective strategies (Assor, Vansteenkiste, & Kaplan, 2009; Covington, 2009). These strategies include the following (Covington & Dray, 2002):

- *Nonperformance.* The most obvious strategy for avoiding failure is to not try. In the classroom, nonperformance tactics include appearing eager to answer a teacher's question but hoping the teacher will call on another student, sliding down in the seat to avoid being seen by the teacher, and avoiding eye contact. These can seem like minor deceptions, but they might portend other, more chronic forms of noninvolvement such as dropping out and excessive absences.

- *Procrastination.* Individuals who postpone studying for a test until the last minute can blame failure on poor time management, thus deflecting attention away from the possibility that they are incompetent. A variation on this theme is for them to take on so many responsibilities that they have an excuse for not doing any one of them in a highly competent manner.

- *Setting unreachable goals.* By setting goals so high that success is virtually impossible, individuals can avoid the implication that they are incompetent, because virtually anyone would fail to reach this goal.

**failure syndrome** Having low expectations for success and giving up at the first sign of difficulty.

Efforts to avoid failure often involve *self-handicapping strategies* (Leondari & Gonida, 2007) such as those just discussed. That is, some individuals deliberately handicap themselves by not making an effort, by putting off a project until the last minute, by fooling around the night before a test, and so on so that if their subsequent performance is at a low level, these circumstances, rather than lack of ability, will be seen as the cause. A recent study revealed that self-regulatory and in-depth learning strategies were negatively linked to students' use of self-handicapping and that surface learning and test anxiety were positively related to their use of self-handicapping (Thomas & Gadbois, 2007).

Here are a few strategies to help students reduce preoccupation with protecting self-worth and avoiding failure (Covington & Teel, 1996):

- Guide students in setting challenging but realistic goals.
- Help students strengthen the link between their effort and self-worth. Tell them to take pride in their effort and warn them to minimize social comparison.
- Encourage students to have positive beliefs about their abilities.

## STUDENTS WHO PROCRASTINATE

Another way that students can fail to reach their potential is to regularly engage in procrastination (Schraw, Wadkins, & Olafson, 2007). A recent meta-analysis of research studies revealed that procrastination is linked to low self-efficacy, low conscientiousness, distractibility, and low achievement motivation (Steel, 2007). Other reasons students procrastinate include (University of Buffalo Counseling Services, 2010) poor time management, difficulty concentrating, fear and anxiety (being overwhelmed by the task and afraid of getting a bad grade, for example), negative beliefs, personal problems (financial problems, problems with a boyfriend or girlfriend, and so on), boredom, unrealistic expectations and perfectionism (believing you must read everything written on a subject before you begin to write a paper, for example), and fear of failure (thinking that if you don't get an *A,* you are a failure, for example).

Procrastination can take many forms, including these (University of Illinois Counseling Center, 1996):

- Ignoring the task with the hope that it will go away
- Underestimating the work involved in the task or overestimating one's abilities and resources
- Spending endless hours on computer games and surfing the Internet
- Substituting a worthy but lower-priority activity, such as cleaning one's room instead of studying
- Believing that repeated minor delays won't hurt
- Persevering on only part of the task, such as writing and rewriting the first paragraph of a paper but never getting to the body of it
- Becoming paralyzed when having to choose between two alternatives—for example, agonizing over whether to do biology homework or English homework first with the outcome that neither is done

## STUDENTS WHO ARE PERFECTIONISTS

As mentioned earlier, perfectionism is sometimes the underlying reason for procrastinating. Perfectionists think that mistakes are never acceptable, that the highest standards of performance always have to be achieved. As indicated in Figure 13.7, healthy achievement and perfectionism differ in a number of ways. Perfectionists are vulnerable to decreased productivity, impaired health, relationship problems, and low self-esteem (Haring, Hewitt, & Flett, 2003). Depression, anxiety, and eating disorders are common outcomes of perfectionism (Rice & others, 2007).

RESEARCH

*And then after high school, I spent twelve years in college and majored in procrastination.*

Ralph Hagen. www.cartoonstock.com

### Perfectionist

Sets standards beyond reach and reason

Is never satisfied by anything less than perfection

Becomes dysfunctionally depressed when experiences failure and disappointment

Is preoccupied with fear of failure and disapproval—this can deplete energy levels

Sees mistakes as evidence of unworthiness

Becomes overly defensive when criticized

### Healthy striver

Sets high standards, but just beyond reach

Enjoys process as well as outcome

Bounces back from failure and disappointment quickly and with energy

Keeps normal anxiety and fear of failure and disapproval within bounds—uses them to create energy

Sees mistakes as opportunities for growth and learning

Reacts positively to helpful criticism

**FIGURE 13.7** DIFFERENCES BETWEEN PERFECTIONISTS AND HEALTHY STRIVERS

## TEACHING CONNECTIONS: Best Practices
### Strategies for Helping Students Conquer Procrastination

Here are some good strategies for helping students reduce or eliminate procrastination:

1. *Get them to acknowledge that procrastination is a problem.* Too often, procrastinators don't face up to their problem. When students admit that they procrastinate, this can sometimes get them to begin thinking about how to solve the problem.

2. *Encourage them to identify their values and goals.* Get them to think about how procrastination can undermine their values and goals.

3. *Help them manage their time more effectively.* Have students make yearly (or term), monthly, weekly, and daily plans. Then help them monitor how they use their time and find ways to use it more wisely.

4. *Have them divide the task into smaller parts.* Sometimes students procrastinate because they view the task as so large and overwhelming that they will never be able to finish it. When this is the case, get them to divide the task into smaller units and set subgoals for completing one unit at a time. This strategy can often make what

seems to be a completely unmanageable task manageable. Interim due dates for smaller units can be very helpful to students prone to procrastination.

5. *Teach students to use behavioral strategies.* Have them identify the diversions that might be keeping them from focusing on the most important tasks and activities. Get them to note when and where they engage in these diversions. Then have them plan how to diminish and control their use. Other behavioral strategies include having students make a contract with you, their parents, or a mentor, or having students engage in self-reinforcement, which gives them an incentive to complete all or part of the task.

6. *Help them learn how to use cognitive strategies.* Encourage students to watch for mental self-seductions that can lead to behavioral diversions, such as "I will do it tomorrow," "What's the problem with watching an hour or two of TV now?" and "I can't do it." Help them learn how to dispute mental diversions. For example, get them to tell themselves, "I really don't have much time left, and other things are sure to come up later," or, "If I get this done, I'll be able to enjoy my time better."

## TEACHING CONNECTIONS: Best Practices
### Strategies for Helping Students Overcome Their Perfectionist Tendencies

Here are some good strategies for guiding students in reducing or eliminating perfectionist tendencies (University of Texas at Austin Counseling and Mental Health Center, 1999):

1. *Have students list the advantages and disadvantages of trying to be perfect.* When students do this, they may discover that the cost of trying to be perfect is too great.

2. *Guide students in becoming more aware of the self-critical nature of all-or-none thinking.* Help students learn how to substitute more realistic, reasonable thoughts for their habitual overly self-critical ones.

3. *Help students become realistic about what they can achieve.* By getting students to set more realistic goals, they will gradually see that "imperfect" outcomes don't lead to the negative consequences they expect and fear.

4. *Talk with students about learning to accept criticism.* Perfectionists frequently view criticism as a personal attack and respond defensively to it. Guide students to become more objective about the criticism and about themselves.

## STUDENTS WITH HIGH ANXIETY

*Anxiety* is a vague, highly unpleasant feeling of fear and apprehension. It is normal for students to be concerned or worried when they face school challenges, such as doing well on a test. Indeed, researchers have found that many successful students have moderate levels of anxiety (Bandura, 1997). However, some students have high levels of anxiety and worry constantly, which can significantly impair their ability to achieve (Rapee, Schniering, & Hudson, 2009).

Some students' high anxiety levels are the result of parents' unrealistic achievement expectations and pressure (Wigfield & others, 2006). For many students, anxiety increases across the school years as they "face more frequent evaluation, social comparison, and (for some) experiences of failure" (Eccles, Wigfield, & Schiefele, 1998, p. 1043). When schools create such circumstances, they likely increase students' anxiety.

A number of intervention programs have been created to reduce high anxiety levels (Wigfield & others, 2006). Some intervention programs emphasize relaxation techniques. These programs often are effective at reducing anxiety but do not always lead to improved achievement. Anxiety intervention programs linked to worrying emphasize modifying the negative, self-damaging thoughts of anxious students by getting them to engage in more positive, task-focused thoughts (Meichenbaum & Butler, 1980). These programs have been more effective than the relaxation programs in improving students' achievement (Wigfield & others, 2006).

## STUDENTS WHO ARE UNINTERESTED OR ALIENATED

Brophy (1998) argues that the most difficult motivation problem involves students who are apathetic, uninterested in learning, or alienated from school learning. Achieving in school is not an important value for them. To reach apathetic students requires sustained efforts to resocialize their attitudes toward school achievement (Murdock, 2009).

I recently asked teachers what strategies they use to help unmotivated students to get motivated. Following are their responses.

**EARLY CHILDHOOD**   Sometimes children become unmotivated because they fear that they will do something wrong or not live up to the teacher's expectations. To combat this issue, we lavish our preschoolers with praise for any and all efforts.

—**MISSY DANGLER,** *Suburban Hills School*

**ELEMENTARY SCHOOL: GRADES K–5**   Unmotivated students are usually motivated by something that holds their interest. I once had a student who was withdrawn and would not participate in group discussions. I later found out about his interest in boats, specifically the *Titanic*. I then incorporated his interests into a few different activities, and he became a different learner. He was more involved in discussions, and his confidence in the group increased as he learned of other students in class who also shared his interests.

—**HEATHER ZOLDAK,** *Ridge Wood Elementary School*

## TEACHING CONNECTIONS: Best Practices
### Strategies to Reach the Uninterested or Alienated

Here are some ways you might be able to reach students who are uninterested or alienated (Brophy, 1998):

1. *Work on developing a positive relationship with the student.* If the uninterested or alienated student doesn't like you, it is hard to get the student to work toward any achievement goals. Show patience, but be determined to help the student, and push for steady progress in spite of setbacks or resistance.

2. *Make school more intrinsically interesting.* To make school more intrinsically interesting for this type of student, find

out the student's interests and if possible include those interests in assignments that you make.

3. *Teach strategies for making academic work more enjoyable.* Help students understand that they are causing their own problems, and find ways to guide them in taking pride in their work.

4. *Consider a mentor.* Think about enlisting the aid of a mentor in the community or an older student you believe the uninterested or alienated student will respect.

**MIDDLE SCHOOL: GRADES 6–8** An important aspect of motivation is to provide challenges for students. For example, I begin my Civil War unit by telling students  that we'll be using this topic as an opportunity to see what it would be like to take a college freshman history course. Even though the material is extensive and more difficult than other units, the average grades on the final exam are higher than any other unit because students are motivated by the challenge of doing college-level work.

—**MARK FODNESS,** *Bemidji Middle School*

**HIGH SCHOOL: GRADES 9–12** Building relationships with students based on their interests is a key to improving their motivation. For example, I recently talked  with a student who didn't show much interest in class but loves clothes. I asked her about an outfit she had on with a cat on it (since I love cats). She explained that the outfit was Baby Phat and brought me all kinds of information on the clothing line and is even trying to get me to wear some of the clothes. More importantly, this student, who showed little interest in class, now participates and turns in assignments that are above average.

—**SANDY SWANSON,** *Menomonee Falls High School*

This chapter has focused on student motivation, but it is important for you to be motivated as a teacher as well. To evaluate your motivation, complete Self-Assessment 13.1.

## Review, Reflect, and Practice

**4** Recommend how to help students with achievement difficulties.

### REVIEW
- How can low-achieving students with low achievement expectations be described, and how can teachers help them?
- What are some strategies students use to protect their self-worth to avoid failure? How can these students be helped?
- What characterizes students who procrastinate, and what are some strategies to help them? What characterizes students who are perfectionists, and how can teachers help students with these tendencies?
- What is anxiety, how does high anxiety interfere with achievement, and what type of programs can benefit students with high anxiety?
- How can teachers help students who are uninterested or alienated?

### REFLECT
- Think about several of your own past schoolmates who showed low motivation in school. Why do you think they behaved the way they did? What teaching strategies might have helped them?

### PRAXIS™ PRACTICE
1. Which of the following students is the best example of failure syndrome?
   a. Andrea, who does not do well in school and rarely tries anymore
   b. Marcy, who works very hard and manages to earn C's
   c. Samantha, who does very well in school but does not try very hard
   d. Vivi, who is never satisfied with her own performance

*(continued)*

# SELF-ASSESSMENT 13.1
## Evaluating My Motivation

Here are 18 statements you can use to analyze your motivational makeup. Rate yourself from 1 (not like me at all) to 5 (very much like me) on each of the statements.

| | 1 | 2 | 3 | 4 | 5 |
|---|---|---|---|---|---|

1. I am aware of the hierarchy of motives in my life and which ones are the most important for me.

2. I am intrinsically motivated.

3. I have high expectations and standards for success.

4. My life has many moments of flow.

5. I am aware of the people in my life who have motivated me the most and what it is they did that motivated me.

6. I make achievement-related attributions that emphasize effort.

7. I have a mastery motivation orientation rather than a helpless or performance orientation.

8. I am motivated to learn and succeed because of my success aspirations, not because I want to protect my self-worth or avoid failure.

9. I have high self-efficacy in general.

10. I have high instructional self-efficacy in terms of my ability as a teacher and in terms of managing my classroom effectively.

11. I regularly set goals, plan how to reach those goals, and systematically monitor my progress toward the goals.

12. I set specific, proximal, and challenging goals.

13. I am a good time manager, regularly doing weekly plans, monitoring my use of time, and making to-do lists.

14. I am good at learning from my mistakes to improve my future success.

15. I don't let anxiety or other emotions get in the way of my motivation.

16. I have a good support system for my motivation and have positive, close relationships with people who can help me sustain my motivation.

17. I do tasks in a timely manner and I don't procrastinate.

18. I'm not a perfectionist.

## SCORING AND INTERPRETATION

Examine the pattern of your responses. If you rated yourself 4 or 5 on each of the items, you likely are getting your motivation to work to your advantage, and you likely will be a positive motivational model for your students. However, for any items on which you rated yourself 3 or below, spend some time thinking about how you can improve those aspects of your motivational life.

## Review, Reflect, and Practice

**PRAXIS™ PRACTICE (CONTINUED)**

2. Scott slides down in his seat to avoid being called on by the teacher. His behavior reflects which of the following in an effort to protect his self-worth by avoiding failure?
   a. failure syndrome
   b. nonperformance
   c. procrastination
   d. setting unreachable goals

3. Which teaching strategy is most likely to help students overcome procrastination?
   a. assigning a large project to be done in parts, with each part due at a different time
   b. assigning many large projects in a semester to ensure that students will have to learn to manage their time
   c. assigning no work that must be done outside class
   d. assigning the writing of a list of all of the things students would rather do than their homework

4. Becky gets very upset when she does not receive full credit on an assignment. She takes particular offense at any critical remarks that are made of her work. Which of the following strategies is most likely to help Becky overcome her perfectionism?
   a. Give Becky lots of constructive feedback, both positive and negative, and allow her to revise her work.
   b. Make sure that Becky is capable of earning full credit on every assignment you give her.
   c. Make sure that Becky is not capable of earning full credit on any assignments you give her so she will get used to it.
   d. Never give Becky any kind of feedback other than a grade, so you don't upset her.

5. Carmella has a great deal of anxiety about school, and it is interfering with her ability to concentrate in school. Which of the following is most likely to help her reduce her anxiety?
   a. helping her to replace her negative, self-damaging thoughts with more positive, task-focused thoughts
   b. encouraging her to set higher goals
   c. guiding her to reduce procrastination
   d. getting her to face the reality that she needs to concentrate better

6. Which of the following is most likely to help a teacher get an uninterested or alienated student to become more motivated to do well in school?
   a. Stress how important going to college is.
   b. Find out the student's interests, and include those in the student's assignments.
   c. Compare the student with other students who are more motivated.
   d. Describe some strategies for reducing perfectionism.

7. Which of the following questions is most likely to get students to reflect on their purpose?
   a. What can you do to get good grades?
   b. What's most important to you in your life?
   c. How can you set better short-term goals?
   d. How can you organize your life better to find more time to study?

*Please see the answer key at the end of the book.*

# The Reading Incentive Program

Catherine teaches second grade in an economically disadvantaged elementary school. Many of her students read below grade level. Some of her students have had little exposure to reading outside school, and most do not choose to read during their free time at school. Knowing that reading skills are important to future success in school, Catherine is justifiably concerned.

In an effort to entice her students to read more, Catherine develops a reading incentive program. She places a large chart on the classroom wall to track student progress. Each time a student completes a book, he tells Catherine, who then places a star next to his name on the chart. Each student who reads five books per month receives a small prize from the class prize box. The student who reads the most books in any given month receives a larger prize. When Catherine tells her students about the new incentive program, they are very excited.

"This is great!" says Joey. "I'm gonna get the most stars!"

"No, you won't," says Peter. "Sami will. She's always got her nose stuck in a book. She's the best reader in the class."

Sami is a very good reader. She is reading well above grade level and generally favors novels from the young adult section of the library. These books are rather lengthy and take her quite some time to finish. However, she really enjoys them. Catherine has brought her several from her own collection as well, since none of her classroom books seem to interest Sami.

The first week of the program is quite exciting. Every day students tell Catherine about the books they have read. The chart begins to fill with stars. By the end of the week, all the students have at least one star next to their name except Sami. During the last week of the month, many students choose reading as a free-time activity. The students are anxious to ensure that they will earn at least one prize, and many are devouring books in anticipation of being the month's "top reader." At the end of the month, 23 of Catherine's 25 students have 5 stars on the chart. The only exceptions are Sami, who has only 1 star, and Michael, who had chicken pox during the month. True to his word, Joey receives the most stars—15. The students excitedly choose their prizes.

The following month, the reading frenzy continues. This time Sami joins her classmates in their accumulation of stars and receives 30, making her the top reader. Joey is right behind her with 25. Every student in the class earns at least 5 stars, entitling all to a prize. Because they are all reading so much, Catherine gives them a Friday afternoon party, at which they watch an animated movie and eat popcorn.

A similar pattern is repeated over the next several months. The star chart fills quickly. Catherine believes that the students are reading enough that they will do quite well on the annual state achievement test. She is thrilled with their progress. She decides that after the test, she will drop the incentive program and just quietly keep track of how much her students read. After doing this, she notices that once again very few students are reading during their free time. Even Sami is no longer reading when she is finished with her other work. Now she draws instead.

1. What are the issues in this case?

2. Analyze the case from the perspective of extrinsic and intrinsic motivation.

3. Analyze the case from a goal-orientation perspective.

4. Why do you think Sami went from receiving 1 star the first month to receiving 30 stars the next? Why does she no longer read in her free time at school?

5. What are the problems with this type of incentive program? How might an incentive program be developed that does not undermine students' motivation to read?

# Motivation, Teaching, and Learning

**1 EXPLORING MOTIVATION:** Define motivation, and compare the behavioral, humanistic, cognitive, and social perspectives on motivation.

> What Is Motivation?

> Perspectives on Motivation

Motivated behavior is behavior that is energized, directed, and sustained.

The behavioral perspective on motivation emphasizes that external rewards and punishments are the key factors that determine a student's motivation. Incentives are positive or negative stimuli or events that can motivate a student's behavior. The humanistic perspective stresses our capacity for personal growth, freedom to choose our own destiny, and our positive qualities. According to Maslow's hierarchy of needs, individuals' needs must be satisfied in this sequence: physiological, safety, love and belonging, esteem, and self-actualization. Self-actualization, the highest and most elusive of the needs Maslow describes, involves the motivation to develop one's full potential as a human being. In the cognitive perspective on motivation, students' thoughts guide their motivation. The cognitive perspective focuses on the internal motivation to achieve; attributions; students' beliefs that they can effectively control their environment; and goal setting, planning, and monitoring progress toward a goal. The cognitive perspective meshes with R. W. White's concept of competence motivation. The social perspective emphasizes the need for affiliation, which is reflected in students' motivation to spend time with peers, their close friendships, attachment to parents, and their desire to have a positive relationship with teachers.

**2 ACHIEVEMENT PROCESSES:** Discuss the important processes in motivation to achieve.

> Extrinsic and Intrinsic Motivation

Extrinsic motivation involves doing something to obtain something else (a means to an end) or to avoid an unpleasant consequence. Intrinsic motivation involves the internal motivation of doing something for its own sake (an end in itself). Overall, most experts recommend that teachers create a classroom atmosphere in which students are intrinsically motivated to learn. One view of intrinsic motivation emphasizes its self-determining characteristics. Giving students some choice and providing opportunities for personal responsibility increase intrinsic motivation. Csikszentmihalyi uses the term *flow* to describe life's optimal experiences, which involve a sense of mastery and absorbed concentration in an activity. Flow is most likely to occur in areas in which students are engaged in challenges that are neither too difficult nor too easy. Interest is conceptualized as more specific than intrinsic motivation, and interest is positively linked to deep learning. It is important for teachers to create learning environments that encourage students to become cognitively engaged and develop a responsibility for their learning. In some situations, rewards can actually undermine learning. When rewards are used, they should convey information about task mastery rather than external control. Researchers have found that as students move from the early elementary school years to high school, their intrinsic motivation drops, especially during the middle school years. The concept of person-environment fit calls attention to the lack of fit between adolescents' increasing interest in autonomy and schools' increasing control, which results in students' negative self-evaluations and attitudes toward school. Overall, the overwhelming conclusion is that it is a wise strategy to create learning environments that encourage students to become intrinsically motivated. However, in many real-world situations, both intrinsic and extrinsic motivation are involved, and too often intrinsic and extrinsic motivation have been pitted against each other as polar opposites.

| Attribution |
| --- |

Attribution theory states that individuals are motivated to discover the underlying causes of their own performance and behavior. Weiner identified three dimensions of causal attributions: (1) locus, (2) stability, and (3) controllability. Combinations of these dimensions produce different explanations of failure and success.

| Mastery Motivation and Mindset |
| --- |

Students with a mastery orientation are challenged and excited by difficult tasks, and concentrate on learning strategies and the achievement process instead of on performance outcome. Students with a helpless orientation feel trapped by difficult tasks, are anxious, and feel they lack ability. Students with a performance orientation are focused on winning, not on achievement outcome. A mastery orientation is preferred over helpless or performance orientations in achievement situations. Mindset is the cognitive view, either fixed or growth, that individuals develop for themselves. Dweck argues that a key aspect of adolescents' development is to guide them in developing a growth mindset. Students with a growth mindset believe they can improve through effort.

| Self-Efficacy |
| --- |

Self-efficacy is the belief that one can master a situation and produce positive outcomes. Bandura stresses that self-efficacy is a critical factor in whether students will achieve. Schunk argues that self-efficacy influences a student's choice of tasks and that low-self-efficacy students avoid many learning tasks, especially those that are challenging. Instructional strategies that emphasize "I can do it" benefit students. Low-self-efficacy teachers become mired in classroom problems. Setting specific, proximal (short-term), and challenging goals benefits students' self-efficacy and achievement.

| Goal Setting, Planning, and Self-Monitoring |
| --- |

Researchers have found that self-efficacy and achievement increase when students set goals that are specific, proximal, and challenging. Personal goals also are an important aspect of students' motivation. Being a good planner helps students manage time effectively, set priorities, and be organized. Giving students opportunities to develop their time management skills likely will benefit their learning and achievement. Self-monitoring is a key aspect of learning and achievement.

| Expectations |
| --- |

Students' expectations for success and the value they place on what they want to achieve influence their motivation. The combination of expectancy and value has been the focus of a number of models of achievement motivation. Teachers' expectations can have a powerful influence on students' motivation and achievement. Teachers often have higher expectations for high-ability students than low-ability students. It is important for teachers to monitor their expectations and to have high expectations for all students.

| Values and Purpose |
| --- |

Values are beliefs and attitudes about the way we think things should be—what is important to an individual. Purpose is an intention to accomplish something meaningful to oneself and contribute something to the world beyond the self. Damon has found that far too few students engage in purposeful reflection about what they want to do with their lives and concludes that parents and teachers need to ask students more questions, especially "why" questions to encourage them to think more deeply about what their purpose is.

## ③ MOTIVATION, RELATIONSHIPS, AND SOCIOCULTURAL CONTEXTS: Explain how relationships and sociocultural contexts can support or undercut motivation.

| Social Motives |
| --- |

Social motives are needs and desires that are learned through experiences with the social world. The need for affiliation, or relatedness, involves the motive to be securely connected with people. Students vary in their need for affiliation—some like to be surrounded by many friends and date regularly; others do not have such strong needs.

| Social Relationships |

In terms of achievement and social motivation, approval from teachers, peers, friends, and parents is important. Peer conformity peaks in early adolescence, a time of important decisions about whether to pursue academic or social motives. Understanding the parent's role in students' motivation focuses on demographic characteristics (such as education level, time spent at work, and family structure), child-rearing practices (such as providing the right amount of challenge and support), and provision of specific experiences at home (such as providing reading materials). Peers can affect students' motivation through social comparison, social competence, peer co-learning, and peer-group influences. Research shows that a teacher's support and caring can play a powerful role in students' motivation. A teacher's instructional style and socioemotional support also can play a role in a student's achievement. An important aspect of student motivation is enlisting parents as partners with you in educating the student.

| Sociocultural Contexts |

Teachers should recognize and value diversity within any cultural group and should be careful to distinguish the influences of socioeconomic status from those of ethnicity. Differences in achievement are more closely linked to socioeconomic status than to ethnicity. The quality of schools for many socioeconomically impoverished students is lower than for their middle-income counterparts. Racial discrimination at school from teachers and peers is linked to a decline in African American middle school students' grades.

## ④ EXPLORING ACHIEVEMENT DIFFICULTIES: Recommend how to help students with achievement difficulties.

| Students Who Are Low Achieving and Have Low Expectations for Success |

A student with low ability and low expectations for success often needs reassurance and support but also needs to be reminded that progress will be acceptable only when considerable effort is put forth. A student with failure syndrome (who has low expectations for success and gives up easily) likely will benefit from cognitive retraining methods such as efficacy training and strategy training.

| Students Who Protect Their Self-Worth by Avoiding Failure |

Students motivated to protect self-worth and avoid failure often engage in one or more of these ineffective strategies: nonperformance, procrastination, or setting unreachable goals. These students likely need guidance in setting challenging but realistic goals, need the link between their effort and self-worth strengthened, and benefit from developing positive beliefs about their abilities.

| Students Who Procrastinate |

Procrastination can take many forms, including ignoring a task with the hope it will go away, underestimating the amount of work a task requires, spending endless hours on distracting activities, and substituting worthwhile but lower-priority activities. Strategies for helping students overcome procrastination include acknowledging they have a procrastination problem, encouraging them to identify their values and goals, helping them manage time more effectively, having them divide the task into smaller parts, and teaching them to use behavioral and cognitive strategies.

| Students Who Are Perfectionists |

Perfectionists think that mistakes are never acceptable and that the highest standards of performance always have to be achieved. Perfectionists are vulnerable to a number of physical and mental health problems. Teachers can help students with perfectionist tendencies by having them list the advantages and disadvantages of trying to be perfect, guiding students to become more aware of the self-critical nature of their all-or-none thinking, helping them become more realistic about what they can achieve, and helping them learn how to accept criticism.

| Students with High Anxiety |

Anxiety is a vague, highly unpleasant feeling of fear and apprehension. High anxiety can result from unrealistic parental expectations. Students' anxiety increases as they get older and face more evaluation, social comparison, and failure (for some students). Cognitive programs that replace students' self-damaging thoughts with positive, constructive thoughts have been more effective than relaxation programs in benefiting student achievement.

Strategies for helping an uninterested or alienated student include establishing a positive relationship with the student, making school more intrinsically interesting, using teaching strategies for making academic work more enjoyable, and considering a mentor in the community or an older student as a support person for the student.

## KEY TERMS

motivation 438
incentives 438
humanistic perspective 438
hierarchy of needs 439
self-actualization 439

competence motivation 439
need for affiliation or
   relatedness 440
extrinsic motivation 441
intrinsic motivation 441

attribution theory 447
helpless orientation 448
mastery orientation 448
performance
   orientation 448

mindset 448
self-efficacy 450
social motives 458
failure syndrome 464

## PORTFOLIO ACTIVITIES

Now that you have a good understanding of this chapter, complete these exercises to expand your thinking.

### Independent Reflection: Motivate, Invigorate, and Innovate Your Students

Design a motivationally rich classroom. What materials would be available? Describe your classroom walls and learning centers. How would teaching proceed? What types of activities would students participate in? Write up your classroom design. (INTASC: Principle 5)

### Collaborative Work: Case Studies in Motivation

With three other students in the class, create a plan to improve the motivation of the following students:

1. 7-year-old Tanya, who has low ability and low expectations for success

2. 10-year-old Samuel, who works overtime to keep his self-worth at a high level but has a strong fear of failure

3. 13-year-old Sandra, who is quiet in the classroom and underestimates her skills

4. 16-year-old Robert, who shows little interest in school and currently lives with his aunt (you have been unable to contact his parents) (INTASC: Principles 2, 3, 5)

### Research/Field Experience: The Face of Student Motivation

Observe a teacher at the grade level you plan to teach, and note the strategies he or she uses to motivate the students. Which strategies are most effective? Least effective? Why do you think this is so? Which students seem particularly difficult to motivate? Why do you think this is so? What would you do differently to foster student motivation in the classroom? (INTASC: Principles 5, 7, 9)

*Go to the Online Learning Center for downloadable portfolio templates.*

## STUDY, PRACTICE, AND SUCCEED

Visit www.mhhe.com/santrockep5e to review the chapter with self-grading quizzes and self-assessments, to apply the chapter material to two more Crack the Case studies, and for suggested activities to develop your teaching portfolio.

# CHAPTER 14

# MANAGING THE CLASSROOM

*Precision in communication is more important than ever in our era of hair-trigger balances, when a false or misunderstood word may create as much disaster as a sudden thoughtless act.*

—James Thurber
*American Essayist and Humorist, 20th Century*

## Learning Goals

**1** Explain why classroom management is both challenging and necessary.

**2** Describe the positive design of the classroom's physical environment.

**3** Discuss how to create a positive classroom environment.

**4** Identify some good approaches to communication for both students and teachers.

**5** Formulate some effective approaches that teachers can use to deal with problem behaviors.

# Teaching **Stories** Adriane Lonzarich

Adriane Lonzarich owns and operates Heartwood, a small preschool in San Mateo, California. In the afternoons she also holds art classes for 5- to 12-year-old children. She talks about her ideas for managing the classroom:

> The most valuable advice I ever received for managing the classroom is to approach a problem or area of difficulty with three questions in this order: (1) Is it the environment? (2) Is it the teacher? (3) Is it the child? For example, if the issue of concern is unfocused energy of the group, I would first ask myself, Is it the environment? Is it overstimulating? Is there not enough to do? Do I need to rearrange the classroom and create more intimate spaces for quiet activity, or do I need to let them have more time outside, and so on? In many cases, I don't need to go on to the next two questions.
>
> Is it the teacher? Am I tired? Nervous? Uninspiring? Have I not taken the time to demonstrate the activities? Have I not been consistent in presenting, monitoring, and enforcing basic classroom rules? Have I not paid enough attention to their needs that day?
>
> Is it the child? If I've addressed all the other possibilities and I'm convinced that the problem is the child's problem, not the environment's or the teacher's, I explore what might be going on. Is anything happening in the child's home that might be causing his or her problems? Is it time for a parent conference? Does the child need help in bonding with a friend? Is the child afraid of failure and avoiding meaningful learning for that reason?
>
> This approach is empowering because it is much easier to change the environment or oneself than to change someone else's behavior. It also is effective because it does not zero in on the problem as the child's until all other avenues have been explored.

# Preview

In educational circles it is commonly said that no one pays attention to good classroom management until it is missing. When classrooms are effectively managed, they run smoothly and students are actively engaged in learning. When they are poorly managed, they can become chaotic settings in which learning is a foreign activity. Our coverage begins by examining why classrooms need to be managed effectively, followed by strategies for designing the classroom's physical environment. Then we discuss the importance of creating a positive environment for learning and ways to be an effective communicator. The chapter concludes with information about what to do when students engage in problem behavior.

Effective classroom management maximizes children's learning opportunities (Evertson & Emmer, 2009). Experts in classroom management report that there has been a change in thinking about the best way to manage classrooms. The older view emphasized creating and applying rules to control students' behavior. The newer view focuses more on students' needs for nurturing relationships and opportunities for self-regulation (Noddings, 2007). Classroom management that orients students toward passivity and compliance with rigid rules can undermine their engagement in active learning, higher-order thinking, and the social construction of knowledge (Jones & Jones, 2010). The new trend in classroom management places more emphasis on guiding students toward self-discipline and less on externally controlling the student (Emmer & Evertson, 2009). Historically in classroom management, the teacher was thought of as a director. In the current, learner-centered trend in

Carmella Williams Scott, a middle school English and law teacher at Fairmont Alternative School in Newman, Georgia, created Juvenile Video Court TV, a student-run judicial system, so that students could experience the "other side of the bench" as a judge, lawyer, bailiff, and camera operator. She especially targeted gang leaders for inclusion in the system because they ran the school. Carmella likes to use meaningful questions to guide students' critical thinking. She believes that mutual respect is a key factor in her success as a teacher and the lack of discipline problems she has in her classes (Wong Briggs, 1999).

DEVELOPMENT

classroom management, the teacher is more of a guide, coordinator, and facilitator (Emmer & Evertson, 2009). The new classroom management model does not mean slipping into a permissive mode. Emphasizing caring and students' self-regulation does not mean that the teacher abdicates responsibility for what happens in the classroom (Larrivee, 2009).

As you explore various aspects of managing the classroom, realize the importance of consulting and working with other staff members on management issues (Shindler, 2010). Also recognize that your class is part of the broader context of school culture and that in such areas as discipline and conflict management your policies will need to reflect and be consistent with the policies of the school and other teachers in the school. We will begin our tour of effective classroom management by exploring how management issues sometimes differ in elementary and secondary classrooms.

## MANAGEMENT ISSUES IN ELEMENTARY AND SECONDARY SCHOOL CLASSROOMS

Elementary and secondary school classrooms have many similar management issues. At all levels of education, good managers design classrooms for optimal learning, create positive environments for learning, establish and maintain rules, get students to cooperate, effectively deal with problems, and use good communication strategies.

However, the same classroom management principles sometimes are applied differently in elementary and secondary schools because these two types of schools are structured differently (Evertson & Emmer 2009; Weinstein, 2007). In many elementary schools, teachers face the challenge of managing the same 20 to 25 children for the entire day. In middle and high schools, teachers face the challenge of managing five or six different groups of 20 to 25 adolescents for about 50 minutes each day. Compared with secondary school students, elementary school students spend much more time with the same students in the small space of a single classroom, and having to interact with the same people all day can breed feelings of confinement and boredom and other problems. However, with 100 to 150 students, secondary school teachers are more likely to be confronted with a wider range of problems than elementary school teachers. Also, because secondary school teachers spend less time seeing students in the classroom, it can be more difficult for them to establish personal relationships with students. And secondary school teachers have to get the classroom lesson moving quickly and manage time effectively, because class periods are so short.

Secondary school students' problems can be more long-standing and more deeply ingrained, and therefore more difficult to modify, than those of elementary

*What are some different management issues in teaching elementary and secondary school students?*

school students. Also in secondary schools, discipline problems are frequently more severe, the students being potentially more unruly and even dangerous. Because most secondary school students have more advanced reasoning skills than elementary school students, they might demand more elaborate and logical explanations of rules and discipline. And in secondary schools, hallway socializing can carry into the classroom. Every hour there is another "settling down" process. Keep in mind these differences between elementary and secondary schools as we further explore how to effectively manage the classroom. As we see next, at both elementary and secondary school levels, classrooms can be crowded, complex, and potentially chaotic.

## THE CROWDED, COMPLEX, AND POTENTIALLY CHAOTIC CLASSROOM

Carol Weinstein and Andrew Mignano (2007) used the title of this section, "The Crowded, Complex, and Potentially Chaotic Classroom," as an alert for potential problems and highlighted Walter Doyle's (1986, 2006) six characteristics that reflect a classroom's complexity and potential for problems:

- *Classrooms are multidimensional.* Classrooms are the setting for many activities, ranging from academic activities, such as reading, writing, and math, to social activities, such as playing games, communicating with friends, and arguing. Teachers have to keep records and keep students on a schedule. Work has to be assigned, monitored, collected, and evaluated. Students have individual needs that are more likely to be met when the teacher takes them into account.

- *Activities occur simultaneously.* Many classroom activities occur simultaneously. One cluster of students might be writing at their desks, another might be discussing a story with the teacher, one student might be picking on another, others might be talking about what they are going to do after school, and so on.

- *Things happen quickly.* Events often occur rapidly in classrooms and frequently require an immediate response. For example, two students suddenly argue about the ownership of a notebook, a student complains that another student is copying her answers, a student speaks out of turn, a student marks on another student's arm with a felt-tip pen, two students abruptly start bullying another student, or a student is rude to you.

- *Events are often unpredictable.* Even though you might carefully plan the day's activities and be highly organized, events will occur that you never expect: a fire alarm goes off, a student gets sick, two students get into a fight, a computer won't work, a previously unannounced assembly takes place, the heat goes off in the middle of the winter, and so on.

- *There is little privacy.* Classrooms are public places where students observe how the teacher handles discipline problems, unexpected events, and frustrating circumstances. Some teachers report that they feel like they are in a "fishbowl," or constantly onstage. Much of what happens to one student is observed by other students, and students make attributions about what is occurring. In one case, they might perceive that the teacher is being unfair in the way she disciplines a student. In another, they might appreciate her sensitivity to a student's feelings.

- *Classrooms have histories.* Students have memories of what happened earlier in their classroom. They remember how the teacher handled a discipline problem earlier in the year, which students have gotten more privileges than others, and whether the teacher abides by his promises. Because the past affects the future, it is important for teachers to manage the classroom today in a way that will support rather than undermine learning tomorrow. This means that

## THROUGH THE EYES OF STUDENTS

### First Week of School

**Sept. 8:** Well now that I know what my teacher is like, I wish I didn't. My best friend Annie got the good teacher, Ms Hartwell. I got the witch Ms. Birdsong. The first thing she did was to read all of her rules to us. It must have taken half an hour. We will never get to do anything fun. Fifth grade is ruined.

**(First Day of Class)**

**Sept. 12:** Ms. Birdsong is still strict but I'm starting to like her better. And she even is beginning to be a little funny sometimes. I guess she's just serious about wanting us to learn.

*Brooke*
*Fifth-Grade Student*
*St. Louis, Missouri*

the first several weeks of the school year are critical for establishing effective management principles.

The crowded, complex nature of the classroom can lead to problems if the classroom is not managed effectively. Indeed, such problems are a major public concern about schools. Year after year, the Gallup Poll has asked the public what they perceive to be the main problems schools face. In the 2004 poll, lack of discipline was rated as the second most important problem, after lack of financial support (Gallup Organization, 2004).

## GETTING OFF TO THE RIGHT START

One key to managing the complexity of the classroom is to make careful use of the first few days and weeks of school. To accomplish this goal, you will need to engage in advanced planning before the school year begins to determine how you are going to manage the classroom on the first day and beyond (Evertson & Poole, 2008; Sterling, 2009). At the beginning of school, you will want to (1) communicate your rules and procedures to the class and obtain student cooperation in following them, and (2) get students to engage effectively in all learning activities.

Taking the time in the first week of school to establish these expectations, rules, and routines will help your class run smoothly and set the tone for developing a positive classroom environment.

## EMPHASIZING INSTRUCTION AND A POSITIVE CLASSROOM CLIMATE

RESEARCH

Contrary to the public's belief that more discipline is the number one need in schools, educational psychology emphasizes the need to develop and maintain a positive classroom environment that supports learning (Jones & Jones, 2010; Williams, 2009). This emphasis involves using preventive, proactive strategies rather than becoming immersed in reactive disciplinary tactics.

In a classic study, Jacob Kounin (1970) was interested in discovering how teachers responded to student misbehaviors. Kounin was surprised to find that effective and ineffective classroom managers responded in very similar ways to the misbehaviors. What the effective managers did far better than the ineffective managers was manage the group's activities. Researchers in educational psychology consistently find that teachers who competently guide and structure classroom activities are more effective than teachers who emphasize their disciplinary role (Brophy, 1996).

Throughout this book we present a vision of students as active learners engaged in meaningful tasks, who think reflectively and critically, and who often interact with other students in collaborative learning experiences. Historically, the effectively managed classroom has been described as a "well-oiled machine," but a more appropriate metaphor for today's effectively managed classroom is a "beehive of activity" (see Figure 14.1) (Randolph & Evertson, 1995). This does not imply that classrooms should be wildly noisy and

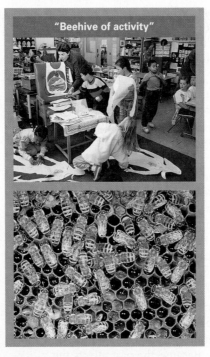

"Well-oiled machine"    "Beehive of activity"

FIGURE **14.1** THE EFFECTIVELY MANAGED CLASSROOM

"Well-oiled machine" or "beehive of activity"?

## TEACHING CONNECTIONS: Best Practices
### Strategies for a Good Beginning of the School Year

Here are some good teaching strategies to adopt for the beginning of the school year (Emmer & Evertson, 2009):

1. *Establish expectations for behavior and resolve student uncertainties.* At the beginning of the school year, students will not be sure what to expect in your classroom. They might have expectations, based on their experiences with other teachers that are different from what your classroom will be like. In the first few days of school, lay out your expectations for students' work and behavior. Don't focus just on course content in the first few days and weeks of school. Be sure to take the time to clearly and concretely spell out class rules, procedures, and requirements so that students know what to expect in your class.

### THROUGH THE EYES OF TEACHERS
#### Establish Yourself in a Positive Manner

My first few days and weeks are highly structured—desks in straight rows, and daily assignments starting with Day One. I try to make the initial environment as businesslike, straightforward, and structured as I possibly can. The games and easy give-and-take come later, after it is firmly established who is in charge of the class, and also if the kids are capable of doing that. Sometimes they aren't.

I'm not saying to scare the kids—they still need to feel safe and comfortable. The main thing is to establish yourself, at least in the minds of the kids, as an organized, confident, firm but fair subject-matter expert.

Someone said the lasting impression is made in the first 15 or 45 seconds of the first introduction. This is true.

2. *Elicit student input into classroom rules.* Allowing students a say in developing classroom rules makes it more likely that they will understand and comply with the rules. Don't worry. They will most likely come up with the same rules that you would have had you chosen to dictate them yourselves. If they don't, it is relatively easy to lead them there.

3. *Make sure that students experience success.* In the first week of school, content activities and assignments should be designed to ensure that students succeed. This helps students develop a positive attitude and provides them with confidence to tackle more difficult tasks later.

4. *Be available and visible.* Show your students that they can approach you when they need information. During seatwork or group work, make yourself available instead of going to your desk and completing paperwork. Move around the room, monitor students' progress, and provide assistance when needed.

5. *Be in charge.* Even if you have stated your class rules and expectations clearly, some students will forget and others will test you to see if you are willing to enforce the rules, especially in the first several weeks of school. Continue to consistently establish the boundaries between what is acceptable and what is not acceptable in your classroom.

6. *Be consistent.* Students need to know what to expect from you. If you are consistent in your expectations and enforcement of rules, they will feel safer and more comfortable.

7. *Establish good rapport with your students.* Respect is reciprocal—students are much more likely to behave respectfully toward you if they believe that you like and respect them. Allowing students to have input into classroom rules is one way to communicate your respect.

chaotic. Rather, students should be actively learning and busily engaged in tasks that they are motivated to do rather than quietly and passively sitting in their seats. Often they will be interacting with each other and the teacher as they construct their knowledge and understanding.

I recently asked teachers how they create a positive classroom environment. Following are their responses.

**EARLY CHILDHOOD** We create positive classrooms for our preschoolers by frequently praising children, speaking with calm voices, following daily schedules, and setting clear rules that are expected to be followed.

—**MISSY DANGLER,** *Suburban Hills School*

**ELEMENTARY SCHOOL: GRADES K–5** To create a positive classroom for my second-graders, I have a banner stretched across one of the walls of my classroom that  reads: "This Is a Positive Learning Area"; this statement is the foundation for everything I do. On the first day of class, I tell the students that they will learn from me, learn from each other, and I will learn from them. I work with them to establish our classroom as a community of learners in order to build feelings of trust, respect, and understanding. With these values in place, academic learning can begin.

—**ELIZABETH FRASCELLA,** *Clinton Elementary School*

**MIDDLE SCHOOL: GRADES 6–8** One of the best ways to create a positive environment for my sixth-graders is to monitor classroom seating arrangements. I recognize who can sit next to each other and who can't. In middle school, when social cliques often form, I change seating arrangements every three weeks or so.

—**MARGARET REARDON,** *Pocantico Hills School*

**HIGH SCHOOL: GRADES 9–12** I create a positive environment by keeping expectations high and consistently enforced. For example, I expect students to turn in their  homework on time. No late work is accepted—however, I do tell students that if they are up late and overwhelmed by an assignment, they can come to me and ask for an extension. I ask that these extensions be the exception, not the rule. My high school students respond well to clear rules and expectations.

—**JOSEPH MALEY,** *South Burlington High School*

## MANAGEMENT GOALS AND STRATEGIES

Effective classroom management has two main goals: to help students spend more time on learning and less time on non-goal-directed activity, and to prevent students from developing academic and emotional problems.

### Help Students Spend More Time on Learning and Less Time on Non-Goal-Directed Activity

In Chapters 12 and 13, we discussed the importance, for both teachers and students, of being a good time manager. Effective classroom management will help you maximize your instructional time and your students' learning time. Carol Weinstein (2007) described the amount of time available for various classroom activities in a typical 42-minute secondary school class over the course of a school year. Actual yearly learning time is only about 62 hours, which is approximately half of the mandated school time for a typical class. Although her time figures are only estimates, they suggest that the hours available for learning are far less than would appear. And as we underscored in Chapter 12, "Planning, Instruction, and Technology," learning takes time.

### Prevent Students from Developing Problems

A well-managed classroom not only fosters meaningful learning but also helps prevent academic and emotional problems from developing (Bloom, 2009; Martinez, 2009). Well-managed classrooms keep students busy with active, appropriately challenging tasks, have activities in which students become absorbed and motivated to learn, and establish clear rules and regulations students must abide by. In such classrooms, students are less likely to develop academic and emotional problems. By contrast, in poorly managed classrooms, students' academic and emotional problems are more likely to fester. The academically unmotivated student becomes even less motivated. The shy student becomes more reclusive. The bully becomes meaner.

**Thinking Back/Thinking Forward**

Managing the classroom includes effective planning and involves knowing what needs to be done and when to do it, or focusing on "task" and "time." Chapter 12, p. 400

## TEACHING CONNECTIONS: Best Practices
### Strategies for Increasing Academic Learning Time

Strategies for increasing academic learning time include maintaining activity flow, minimizing transition time, and holding students accountable (Weinstein, 2007):

1. *Maintain activity flow.* In an analysis of classrooms, Jacob Kounin (1970) studied teachers' ability to initiate and maintain the flow of activity. Then he searched for links between activity flow and students' engagement and misbehavior. He found that some teachers engaged in "flip-flopping"—terminating an activity, starting another, and then returning to the first one. Others were distracted from an ongoing activity by a small event that really did not need attention. For example, in one situation a teacher who was explaining a math problem at the board noticed a student leaning on his left elbow while working on the problem. The teacher went over to the student and told him to sit up straight, interrupting the flow of the class. Some teachers "overdwell" on something that students already understand or go on at length about appropriate behavior. All of these situations—flip-flopping, responding to distractions, and overdwelling—can interrupt the classroom's flow.

2. *Minimize transition time.* In transitions from one activity to another, there is more room for disruptive behavior to occur. Teachers can decrease the potential for disruption during transitions by preparing students for forthcoming transitions, establishing transition routines, and clearly defining the boundaries of lessons. For younger children, playing a short piece of music can help them to know how long they have to transition between activities. Whatever transition routine you choose, establish it early in the academic year and be consistent with it.

3. *Hold students accountable.* If students know they will be held accountable for their work, they are more likely to make good use of class time. Clearly communicating assignments and requirements encourages student accountability. Explain to students what they will be doing and why, how long they will be working on the activity, how to obtain help if they need it, and what to do when they are finished. Helping students establish goals, plan, and monitor their progress also increases students' accountability. And maintaining good records can help you hold students accountable for their performance.

**Managing Instruction**    Classroom management involves not only managing student behaviors but also managing instruction (Jones & Jones, 2010; Savage & Savage, 2009). Ideally, the two go hand in hand—students who are engaged in learning tasks are less likely to develop behavior problems. Recently classroom response systems have been used as part of classroom management. These systems traditionally consist of each of the following: a set of networked, low-cost handheld devices (which may be as simple as a keypad), a computer that is used as a central hub to aggregate student responses, and a whole-class display that shows questions posed to the class and the aggregation of student responses. Each of these components has a key role as teachers pose questions to students, who indicate an answer on their own devices. All answers then appear on the whole-class display in aggregated form, typically as a histogram.

TECHNOLOGY

RESEARCH

Using student response systems, teachers have the ability to pose questions and give practice to whole classes of students, and to gather instant data on all of their students that can be used to quickly assess comprehension. This true, formative assessment enables the teacher to identify students' misconceptions and errors and then correct them immediately. In addition, it encourages active student participation and helps students explore what they know and don't know—and hence take control of their own learning. Most student response systems also produce records of student responses, which can be automatically entered as grades.

Numerous studies show that these relatively simple systems can be effective classroom management tools (Swan & others, 2007; Vahey, Roschell, & Tatar, 2006). Common outcomes include increases in student engagement, teacher awareness of student knowledge, and student understanding of content matter. For example, a recent study found that

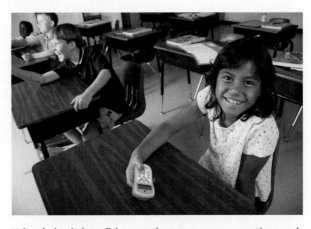

Using their wireless clickers, students can answer questions and record their responses with a simple click of a button. Classroom response systems such as the one shown here are increasingly used in classroom instruction and management.

students scored higher on course exams in an undergraduate educational psychology course when they pressed a button on a handheld device ("clicker") to answer two to four questions projected on a screen in each lecture than students given in-class questions without clickers or students given no in-class questions (Mayer & others, 2009). The researchers concluded that the clicker group was more cognitively engaged in the lecture than the other two groups.

A number of companies offer student response systems. Some of the more popular ones are InterWrite's Personal Response System (**www.gtcocalcomp.com/inter writeprs.htm**), TurningPoint's Audience Response System (**www.turningtechnologies .com/highereducation.htm**), and Quizdom's Student Response System (**www .qwizdom.com/education_ solutions_ applications.htm**).

## Review, Reflect, and Practice

**1** Explain why classroom management is both challenging and necessary.

### REVIEW

- Why must management principles be applied differently to elementary and secondary school classrooms?
- What are six reasons that classrooms are crowded, complex, and potentially chaotic?
- What strategies are most likely to get a school year off to the right start for a teacher?
- What do experts say should be the basic approach to classroom management? What did Kounin find that effective teachers did differently than ineffective teachers did in managing the classroom?
- What are the two main goals of effective classroom management?

### REFLECT

- Which would probably be easier for you to manage—an elementary school classroom or a high school classroom? Why?

### PRAXIS™ PRACTICE

1. Which characteristic of classrooms is best exemplified in the following scenario? Holly and Alex are having a conflict. Holly takes a black permanent marker and makes a large mark on Alex's shirt. Mr. Bronson witnesses the incident and does nothing. Two weeks later, during another conflict, Alex makes a mark on the back of Holly's shirt with a pen. This time Mr. Bronson gives Alex a detention. Alex becomes upset at what he perceives as unfair treatment.
   a. Classrooms are multidimensional.
   b. Classrooms have histories.
   c. There is little privacy.
   d. Things happen quickly.

2. Mr. McClure wants to be certain that his students understand that he has high expectations for them. Therefore, he gives a very difficult exam during the first week of school. Which principle of getting off to the right start did Mr. McClure ignore?
   a. Be available and visible.
   b. Be in charge.

## Review, Reflect, and Practice

**PRAXIS™ PRACTICE (CONTINUED)**

    c. Establish expectations for behavior and resolve student uncertainties.

    d. Make sure that students experience success.

3. Which teacher is most likely to have classroom management problems?

    a. Mr. Knight, who in an effort to keep students from being bored has numerous activities during the period, all of which require transitional time

    b. Mr. Quinn, whose students know that they have to accomplish a significant amount of work during the period that will be collected at the end

    c. Ms. Leifeit, whose students are always actively engaged in activities that require students to work together

    d. Ms. Jefferson, who establishes rules and procedures early in the school year and consistently enforces them

4. Which of the following teachers is likely to be most effective in maximizing academic learning time?

    a. Ms. Chang, who focuses on classroom discipline. Her students are reprimanded each and every time she notices what she perceives to be off-task behavior.

    b. Ms. George, who regularly starts one activity, stops it in favor of another, then returns to the first activity.

    c. Ms. Lange, who informs her students how long they will have to complete an activity, then warns them when there are five minutes left and then plays a certain piece of music during transition time. At the end of the music, the students are to be ready for the next activity.

    d. Ms. Purdy, who requires her students to sit up straight, with both feet on the floor, as a means of gaining their attention.

*Please see the answer key at the end of the book.*

## ② DESIGNING THE PHYSICAL ENVIRONMENT OF THE CLASSROOM

| Principles of Classroom Arrangement | Arrangement Style |

When thinking about effectively managing the classroom, inexperienced teachers sometimes overlook the physical environment. As you will see in this section, designing the physical environment of the classroom involves far more than arranging a few items on a bulletin board.

## PRINCIPLES OF CLASSROOM ARRANGEMENT

Here are four basic principles that you can use when arranging your classroom (Evertson & Emmer, 2009):

- *Reduce congestion in high-traffic areas.* Distraction and disruption can often occur in high-traffic areas. These include group work areas, students' desks, the teacher's desk, the pencil sharpener, bookshelves, computer stations, and storage locations. Separate these areas from each other as much as possible and make sure they are easily accessible.

FIGURE **14.2** VARIATIONS OF CLASSROOM SEATING ARRANGEMENTS

- *Make sure that you can easily see all students.* An important management task is to carefully monitor students. To do this, you will need to be able to see all students at all times. Make sure there is a clear line of sight between your desk, instructional locations, students' desks, and all student work areas. Stand in different parts of the room to check for blind spots.

- *Make often-used teaching materials and student supplies easily accessible.* This minimizes preparation and cleanup time, as well as slowdowns and breaks in activity flow.

- *Make sure that students can easily observe whole-class presentations.* Establish where you and your students will be located when whole-class presentations take place. For these activities, students should not have to move their chairs or stretch their necks. To find out how well your students can see from their locations, sit in their seats in different parts of the room.

## ARRANGEMENT STYLE

In thinking about how you will organize the classroom's physical space, you should ask yourself what type of instructional activity students will mainly be engaged in (whole-class, small-group, individual assignments, and so on). Consider the physical arrangements that will best support that type of activity (Weinstein, 2007).

**Standard Classroom Arrangements** Figure 14.2 shows a number of classroom arrangement styles: auditorium, face-to-face, offset, seminar, and cluster (Renne, 1997). In traditional **auditorium style,** all students sit facing the teacher (see Figure 14.2A). This arrangement inhibits face-to-face student contacts, and the teacher is free to move anywhere in the room. Auditorium style often is used when the teacher lectures or someone is making a presentation to the entire class.

In **face-to-face style,** students sit facing each other (see Figure 14.2B). Distraction from other students is higher in this arrangement than in the auditorium style.

In **offset style,** small numbers of students (usually three or four) sit at tables but do not sit directly across from one another (see Figure 14.2C). This produces less distraction than face-to-face style and can be effective for cooperative learning activities.

In **seminar style,** larger numbers of students (10 or more) sit in circular, square, or U-shaped arrangements (see Figure 14.2D). This is especially effective when you want students to talk with each other or to converse with you.

In **cluster style,** small numbers of students (usually four to eight) work in small, closely bunched groups (see Figure 14.2E). This arrangement is especially effective for collaborative learning activities.

Clustering desks encourages social interaction among students. In contrast, rows of desks reduce social interaction among students and direct students' attention toward the teacher. Arranging desks in rows can benefit students when they are working on individual assignments, whereas clustered desks facilitate cooperative learning. In classrooms in which seats are organized in rows, the teacher is most likely to interact with students seated in the front and center of the classroom (Adams & Biddle, 1970) (see Figure 14.3). This area has been called the "action zone" because students in the front and center locations interact the most with the teacher. For example, they most often ask questions and are most likely to initiate discussion. If you use a row arrangement, move around the room when possible, establish eye contact with students seated outside the "action zone," direct comments to students in the peripheral seats, and periodically have students change seats so that all students have an equal opportunity of being in the front and center seats.

**Personalizing the Classroom** According to classroom management experts Carol Weinstein and Andrew Mignano (2007), classrooms too often resemble motel rooms—pleasant but impersonal, revealing nothing about the people who use the space. Such anonymity is especially true of secondary school classrooms, where six or seven different classes might use the space in a single day. To personalize classrooms, you can post students' photographs, artwork, written projects, charts that list birthdays (of early childhood and elementary school students), and other positive expressions of students' identities. A bulletin board can be set aside for the "student of the week" or be used to display each student's best work of the week, personally chosen by each student.

None of the classrooms we have described will exactly match yours. However, keeping in mind the basic principles we have described should help you create an optimal classroom arrangement for learning.

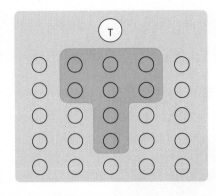

**FIGURE 14.3** THE ACTION ZONE

"Action zone" refers to the seats in the front and center of row arrangement. Students in these seats are more likely to interact with the teacher, ask questions, and initiate discussion than students seated in more peripheral locations.

From Carl H. Rinne, *Excellent Classroom Management*, 1st ed., p. 110. © 1997 Wadsworth, a part of Cengage Learning, Inc. Reproduced by permission. www.cengage.com/permissions

**auditorium style** A classroom arrangement style in which all students sit facing the teacher.

**face-to-face style** A classroom arrangement style in which students sit facing each other.

**offset style** A classroom arrangement style in which small numbers of students (usually three or four) sit at tables but do not sit directly across from one another.

**seminar style** A classroom arrangement style in which large numbers of students (10 or more) sit in circular, square, or U-shaped arrangements.

**cluster style** A classroom arrangement style in which small numbers of students (usually four to eight) work in small, closely bunched groups.

## TEACHING CONNECTIONS: Best Practices
### Strategies for Designing a Classroom Arrangement

Follow these steps to ensure success in designing a classroom arrangement (Weinstein, 2007; Weinstein & Mignano, 2007):

1. *Consider what activities students will be engaging in.* You would not want to use an auditorium style if your students will be primarily engaged in small-group activities, nor would a face-to-face style be ideal for students listening to a lecture.

   If you will be teaching kindergarten or elementary school students, you might need to create settings for reading aloud, small-group reading instruction, sharing time, group math instruction, and arts and crafts. Kindergarten and early elementary classrooms are often designed around learning centers, such as reading, science, building, dramatic play, art, and computers. Many elementary classrooms have a quiet area to which students can go if they feel frustrated, overwhelmed, or just out of sorts.

   A secondary school science teacher might have to accommodate whole-group instruction, "hands-on" lab activities, and media presentations. On the left side of a

sheet of paper, list the activities your students will perform. Next to each activity, list any special arrangements that need to be taken into account—for instance, art and science areas need to be near a sink, and computers need to be near an electrical outlet. Next, William Williford, who teaches science at Perry Middle School in Perry, Georgia, provides a recommendation for classroom arrangement.

## THROUGH THE EYES OF TEACHERS
### Hissing Cockroaches and Minicams

My classroom is set up with tables with about four students per table. This allows for individual or group activities without a lot of transition time or movement. Since my current subject is science, there is an aquarium with fish, a terrarium with a lizard or praying mantis, and a cage with Madagascar hissing cockroaches. There is a table

*(continued)*

# TEACHING CONNECTIONS: Best Practices
## Strategies for Designing a Classroom Arrangement

William Willford, teaching science at Perry Middle School.

with gadgets and mini-experiments. A Minicam may be focused on an earthworm or a spider with the image on the TV as students enter the classroom. The idea is to arrange the classroom so that it promotes inquiry, questioning, and thinking about science.

2. *Draw up a floor plan.* Before you actually move any furniture, draw several floor plans and then choose the one that you think will work the best.

3. *Involve students in planning the classroom layout.* You can do most of your environmental planning before school starts, but once it begins, ask students how they like your arrangement. If they suggest improvements that are reasonable, try them out. Students often report that they want adequate room and a place of their own where they can keep their things.

4. *Try out the arrangement and be flexible in redesigning it.* Several weeks into the school year, evaluate how effective your arrangement is. Be alert for problems that the arrangement might be generating.

5. *As you get to know your students, consider student placement.* Some students have difficulty with certain distractions; some cannot work with particular classmates; others need to sit close to the classroom display (board or screen). When working on arrangements, take these things into account.

## Review, Reflect, and Practice

**2** Describe the positive design of the classroom's physical environment.

**REVIEW**
- What are some basic principles of classroom design and arrangement?
- What are some standard styles of arrangement?

**REFLECT**
- How would you design and arrange your ideal classroom? How would you personalize it?

**PRAXIS™ PRACTICE**

1. Ms. Craig likes her students to work in small groups. Therefore, she arranges her students' desks in small circles or clusters. What is the problem with this arrangement for whole-class presentations?
   a. Ms. Craig will be unable to see all of her students.
   b. Some students will have to turn their chairs to see.
   c. The classroom will be too congested.
   d. There will be blind spots.

2. Mr. James wants his students to be able to talk to each other as well as to him. What type of classroom arrangement is best suited to his needs?
   a. auditorium style
   b. cluster style
   c. offset style
   d. seminar style

*Please see the answer key at the end of the book.*

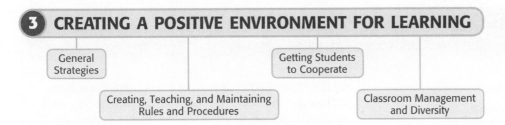

# 3   CREATING A POSITIVE ENVIRONMENT FOR LEARNING

Students need a positive environment for learning. We will discuss some general classroom management strategies for providing this environment, ways to effectively establish and maintain rules, positive strategies for getting students to cooperate, and guidelines for managing diversity in the classroom.

## GENERAL STRATEGIES

General strategies include using an authoritative style and effectively managing classroom activities.

The **authoritative classroom management style** is derived from Diana Baumrind's (1971, 1996) parenting styles, which were discussed in Chapter 3. Like authoritative parents, authoritative teachers have students who tend to be self-reliant, delay gratification, get along well with their peers, and show high self-esteem. An authoritative strategy of classroom management encourages students to be independent thinkers and doers but still involves effective monitoring. Authoritative teachers engage students in considerable verbal give-and-take and show a caring attitude toward them. However, they declare limits when necessary. Authoritative teachers clarify rules and regulations, establishing these standards with input from students.

The authoritative style contrasts with two ineffective strategies: authoritarian and permissive. The **authoritarian classroom management style** is restrictive and punitive. The focus is mainly on keeping order in the classroom rather than on instruction and learning. Authoritarian teachers place firm limits and controls on students and have little verbal exchange with them. Students in authoritarian classrooms tend to be passive learners, fail to initiate activities, express anxiety about social comparison, and have poor communication skills. The **permissive classroom management style** offers students considerable autonomy but provides them with little support for developing learning skills or managing their behavior. Not surprisingly, students in permissive classrooms tend to have inadequate academic skills and low self-control.

Overall, an authoritative style will benefit your students more than authoritarian or permissive styles. An authoritative style will help your students become active, self-regulated learners. A recent study of ninth-grade English classrooms in Singapore revealed that a combination of behavioral control and caring on the part of teachers was linked with positive student outcomes, such as students' engagement in learning, which is consistent with Baumrind's authoritative teaching concept (Nie & Lau, 2009). A recent large-scale study revealed that an authoritative classroom climate (a comibination of structure and the support of caring adults) was linked with school safety, including less bullying and victimization (Gregory & others, 2010). In addition to adopting an authoritative style, the strategies described in the Teaching Connections that follows can benefit your classroom management.

## CREATING, TEACHING, AND MAINTAINING RULES AND PROCEDURES

To function smoothly, classrooms need clearly defined rules and procedures. Students need to know specifically how you want them to behave. Without clearly defined classroom rules and procedures, the inevitable misunderstandings can breed chaos. For example, consider these procedures or routines: When students enter the classroom,

**Thinking Back/Thinking Forward**

In most instances, authoritative parenting is linked with more positive child outcomes than authoritarian, neglectful, or indulgent parenting. Chapter 3, p. 78

RESEARCH

**authoritative classroom management style** A management style that encourages students to be independent thinkers and doers but still provides effective monitoring. Authoritative teachers engage students in considerable verbal give-and-take and show a caring attitude toward them. However, they still set limits when necessary.

**authoritarian classroom management style** A management style that is restrictive and punitive, with the focus mainly on keeping order in the classroom rather than instruction or learning.

**permissive classroom management style** A management style that allows students considerable autonomy but provides them with little support for developing learning skills or managing their behavior.

## TEACHING CONNECTIONS: Best Practices
### Strategies for Being an Effective Classroom Manager

Characteristics of effective classroom managers are that they

1. *Show they are "with it."* Jacob Kounin (1970), whose views were discussed earlier, used the term **withitness** to describe a management strategy in which teachers show students that they are aware of what is happening. These teachers closely monitor students' behavior on a regular basis. This close monitoring allows them to detect inappropriate behavior early, before it gets out of hand. Teachers who are not "with it" are likely to not notice such misbehaviors until they gain momentum and spread.

2. *Cope effectively with overlapping situations.* Kounin observed that some teachers seem to have one-track minds, dealing with only one thing at a time. This ineffective strategy often leads to frequent interruptions in the flow of the class. For example, one teacher was working with a reading group when she observed two boys on the other side of the room hitting each other. She immediately got up, went over to the other side of the room, harshly criticized them, then returned to the reading group. However, by the time she returned to the reading group, the students in the reading group had become bored and were starting to misbehave themselves. In contrast, effective managers were able to deal with overlapping situations in less disruptive ways. For example, in the reading group situation, effective managers quickly responded to students from outside the group who came to ask questions but not in a way that significantly altered the flow of the reading group's activity. When moving around the room and checking each student's seatwork, they kept a roving eye on the rest of the class.

3. *Maintain smoothness and continuity in lessons.* Effective managers keep the flow of a lesson moving smoothly, maintaining students' interest and not giving them opportunities to be easily distracted. Earlier in the chapter, we mentioned some ineffective practices that can disrupt the flow of a lesson, including flip-flopping and overdwelling. Another teacher action that disrupts the lesson's flow is called *fragmentation,* in which the teacher breaks an activity into components even though the activity could be performed as an entire unit. For example, a teacher might individually ask six students to do something, such as get out their art supplies, when all six could be asked to do this as a group.

4. *Engage students in a variety of challenging activities.* Kounin also found that effective classroom managers engaged students in a variety of challenging but not overly hard activities. In these classrooms the students frequently worked independently rather than being directly supervised by a teacher who hovered over them. In Through the Eyes of Teachers, Mark Fodness, an award-wining seventh-grade social studies teacher in Bemidji, Minnesota, gives advice on managing the classroom.

---

## THROUGH THE EYES OF TEACHERS
### Great Teachers Have Few Discipline Problems

The single best method of decreasing undesirable behaviors among students is by increasing the effectiveness of teaching methods. The best teachers have very few discipline problems, not because they are great disciplinarians, but because they are great teachers. To emphasize this point with one of my student teachers, I had her follow our class out the door and into their next classes. She later returned, amazed at what she had seen. Students who she had thought were very well behaved had been off-task or disruptive in other classrooms. In one room, where a substitute teacher was doing his best to fill in, she described students' behavior as "shocking." Yet in another class, where the teacher was presenting a riveting lesson on a novel, the same students once again were well behaved even though the teacher did not seem to be using any specific discipline strategy.

Many first-year teachers and veterans alike identify discipline as their number one teaching challenge. However, the best solution is to use exemplary teaching strategies. I asked my seventh-grade students to identify the characteristics of

Mark Fodness, teaching students in his middle social studies classroom.

teachers who had well-behaved classes. Here is a sample of their responses: well prepared, interesting, funny, organized, fair, caring, nice, and energetic.

are they supposed to go directly to their seats, or may they socialize for a few minutes until you tell them to be seated? When students want to go to the library, do they need a pass? When students are working at their seats, may they help each other, or are they required to work individually?

Both *rules* and *procedures* are stated expectations about behavior (Evertson & Emmer, 2009). *Rules* focus on general or specific expectations or standards for behavior. An example of a general rule is "Respect other persons." An example of a more specific rule is "Cell phones must always be turned off when you are in this classroom." *Procedures,* or routines, also communicate expectations about behavior, but they usually are applied to a specific activity, and their aim is to accomplish something instead of prohibiting a behavior or defining a general standard (Evertson & Emmer, 2009). You might establish procedures for collecting homework assignments, turning in work late, using the pencil sharpener, or using equipment. You can develop procedures for beginning the day (for example, a procedure for "settling in" the classroom—maybe a social item such as a riddle or brief note about school events), leaving the room (for example, to go to the bathroom), returning to the room (such as after lunchtime), and ending the day (for example, clearing off desks and leaving on time).

Rules tend not to change because they address fundamental ways we deal with others, ourselves, and our work, such as having respect for others and their property, and keeping our hands and our feet to ourselves. On the other hand, procedures may change because routines and activities in classrooms change.

What is the best way to get students to learn about rules and procedures? Should the teacher make the rules and procedures, then inform the class about them? Should students be allowed to participate in generating rules and procedures?

Some teachers like to include students in setting rules in the hope that this will encourage them to take more responsibility for their own behavior (Emmer & Evertson, 2009). Student involvement can take many different forms, including a discussion of the reason for having rules and the meaning of particular rules. The teacher might begin by having students discuss why rules are needed and then move on to a number of individual rules. The teacher can clarify the rule by describing, or asking students to describe, the general area of behavior it involves. Students usually can contribute concrete examples of the rule.

Some teachers start off with a whole-class discussion of classroom rules. During the discussion, the teacher and the students suggest possible rules for the classroom, and the teacher records these on an overhead projector, a chalkboard, or a large piece of chart paper. Then, the teacher and students arrange them into broad categories and develop titles for the categories. In some classrooms, this activity is followed by having students role-play each of the rules.

In some schools, students are allowed to participate in setting rules for the entire school. In some cases, student representatives from each room or grade level participate in generating school-wide rules with guidance from teachers and school administrators. However, within individual classrooms, especially in elementary schools, it is uncommon for students to participate in creating rules. Most teachers prefer to create and present their rules, although as indicated earlier, they may encourage discussion of the rules. In secondary schools, especially high schools, greater student contribution to rule setting is possible because of their more advanced cognitive and socioemotional knowledge and skills.

Many effective classroom teachers clearly present their rules to students and give explanations and examples of them. Teachers who set reasonable rules, provide understandable rationales for them, and enforce them consistently usually find that the majority of the class will abide by them.

## GETTING STUDENTS TO COOPERATE

You want your students to cooperate with you and abide by classroom rules without always having to resort to discipline to maintain order (Charles, 2011). How can you

**withitness** A management style described by Kounin in which teachers show students that they are aware of what is happening. Such teachers closely monitor students on a regular basis and thus are able to detect inappropriate behavior early, before it gets out of hand.

## TEACHING CONNECTIONS: Best Practices
### Strategies for Establishing Classroom Rules and Procedures

Here are four principles to keep in mind when you establish rules and procedures for your classroom (Weinstein, 2007, pp. 99–102):

1. *Rules and procedures should be reasonable and necessary.* Ask yourself if the rules and procedures you are establishing are appropriate for this grade level. Also ask yourself if there is a good reason for the rule or procedure. For example, one secondary school teacher has a rule that students must come to class on time. Students are clearly told that if they are late, they will get a detention even on the first violation. She explains the rule to the students at the beginning of the school year and tells them the reason for the rule: if they are late, they might miss important material. Being able to explain the purpose of a rule is particularly important as students move into adolescence and are more likely to question authority as a result of their more advanced cognitive development.

2. *Rules and procedures should be clear and comprehensible.* If you have general rules, make sure that you clearly specify what they mean. For example, one teacher has the rule "Be prepared." Instead of leaving the rule at this general level, the teacher specifies what it means to be prepared and describes specific procedures involving the rule: having your homework, notebook, pen or pencil, and textbook with you every day.

3. *Evaluate whether to let students participate in making classroom rules.* As mentioned earlier, one issue that crops up when establishing classroom rules is whether to let students participate in making them. Involving students in generating classroom rules can increase students' sense of responsibility to abide by them, especially in secondary schools. Some students will suggest ridiculous rules, which you can simply veto. Some teachers like to establish general rules and then ask students to generate specific examples of the rules.

4. *Rules and procedures should be consistent with instructional and learning goals.* Make sure that rules and procedures do not interfere with learning. Some teachers become so concerned about having an orderly, quiet classroom that they restrict students from interacting with each other and from engaging in collaborative learning activities.

5. *Classroom rules should be consistent with school rules.* Know what the school's rules are, such as whether particular behaviors are required in the halls, in the cafeteria, and so on. Many schools have a handbook that spells out what is acceptable and what is not. Familiarize yourself with the handbook. Some teachers go over the handbook with students at the beginning of the school year so that students clearly understand the school's rules regarding absenteeism, truancy, fighting, smoking, substance abuse, abusive language, and so on.

---

get your students to cooperate? There are three main strategies: develop a positive relationship with students, get students to share and assume responsibility, and reward appropriate behavior.

**Develop a Positive Relationship with Students**   When most of us think of our favorite teacher, we think of someone who cared about whether or not we learned. Showing that you genuinely care about students as individuals apart from their academic work helps to gain their cooperation (Jones & Jones, 2010). It is easy to get caught up in the pressing demands of academic achievement and classroom business and ignore the socioemotional needs of students.

One study found that in addition to having effective rules and procedures, successful classroom managers also showed a caring attitude toward students (Emmer, Evertson, Anderson, 1980). This caring was evidenced in part by a classroom environment in which students felt safe and secure and were treated fairly. The teachers were sensitive to their needs and anxieties (for example, they created enjoyable activities the first several days of the school year rather than giving them diagnostic tests), had good communication skills (including listening skills), and they effectively expressed their feelings to students. The classroom atmosphere was relaxed and pleasant. For example, the focus was on academic work, but teachers gave students breaks and allowed them free time to read, use the computer, or draw. Figure 14.4 presents some teaching guidelines for developing a positive relationship with students.

**Thinking Back/Thinking Forward**

Using differential reinforcement to decrease undesirable behavior is a recommended first strategy by applied behavior analysts. Chapter 7, p. 225

## TEACHING CONNECTIONS: Best Practices
### Strategies for Guiding Students to Share and Assume Responsibility

Here are some guidelines for getting students to share and assume responsibility in the classroom (Fitzpatrick, 1993):

1. *Involve students in the planning and implementation of school and classroom initiatives.* This participation helps to satisfy students' needs for self-confidence and belonging.

2. *Encourage students to judge their own behavior.* Rather than pass judgment on students' behavior, ask questions that motivate students to evaluate their own behavior. For example, you might ask, "Does your behavior reflect the class rules?" or, "What's the rule?" Such questions place responsibility on the student. Initially, some students try to blame others or change the subject. In such situations, stay focused and guide the student toward accepting responsibility. Keep in mind that students don't develop responsibility overnight. Many student misbehaviors are ingrained habits that take a long time to break. Be patient one more time than the student expects—difficult to do, but good advice.

3. *Don't accept excuses.* Excuses just pass on or avoid responsibility. Don't even entertain a discussion about excuses. Rather, ask students what they can do the next time a similar situation develops.

4. *Let students participate in decision making by holding class meetings.* In his classic book, *Schools Without Failure,* William Glasser (1969) argued that class meetings can be used to deal with student behavior problems or virtually any issue that is of concern to teachers and students.

---

**Get Students to Share and Assume Responsibility**    Earlier in this chapter we discussed the importance of developing an authoritative atmosphere in the classroom and the issue of whether students should be allowed to participate in establishing class rules. Some experts on classroom management argue that sharing responsibility with students for making classroom decisions increases the students' commitment to the decisions (Blumenfeld, Kempler, & Krajcik, 2006).

**Reward Appropriate Behavior**    We have discussed rewards extensively in Chapter 7, "Behavioral and Social Cognitive Approaches." You might want to read the discussion of rewards in that chapter again, especially the section "Applied Behavior Analysis in Education," and think about how rewards can be used in effectively managing the classroom. The discussion of rewards in Chapter 13, "Motivation, Teaching, and Learning," also is relevant to classroom management, especially the information about rewards and intrinsic motivation. Following are some guidelines for using rewards in managing the classroom.

***Choose Effective Reinforcers***    Find out which reinforcers work best with which students, and individualize reinforcement accordingly. For one student the most effective reward might be praise; for another it might be getting to do a favorite activity. Remember that pleasurable activities often are especially valuable in gaining students' cooperation. You might tell a student, "When you complete your math problems, you can go to the media area and play a computer game."

***Use Prompts and Shaping Effectively***    Remember that if you wait for students to perform perfectly, they might never do so. A good strategy is to use prompts and shape students' behavior by rewarding improvement. Some prompts come in the form of hints or reminders, such as, "Remember the rule about lining up." Recall from Chapter 7 that shaping involves rewarding a student for successive approximations to a specified target behavior. Thus, you might initially reward a student for getting 60 percent of her math problems right, then for 70 percent the next time, and so on.

1. Give a student a friendly "hello" at the door.

2. Have a brief one-on-one conversation about things that are happening in the student's life.

3. Write a brief note of encouragement to the student.

4. Use students' names in class more.

5. Show enthusiasm about being with students (even late in the day, week, or year).

6. Risk more personal self-disclosures, which help students see you as a real person. However, don't cross the line and go too far. Always take into account children's level of understanding and emotional vulnerability in disclosing information about yourself to them.

7. Be an active listener who carefully attends to what the student is saying, even if it is something trivial.

8. Let students know that you are there to support and help them.

9. Keep in mind that developing positive, trusting relationships takes time. This especially is the case for students from high-risk environments who might not initially trust your motives.

FIGURE **14.4** GUIDELINES FOR ESTABLISHING POSITIVE RELATIONSHIPS WITH STUDENTS

Thinking Back/Thinking Forward

It is important to consider what rewards convey about competence. Chapter 13, p. 445

***Use Rewards to Provide Information About Mastery, Not to Control Students'
Behavior*** Rewards that impart information about students' mastery can increase
their intrinsic motivation and sense of responsibility (Vargas, 2009). However,
rewards that are used to control students' behavior are less likely to promote self-
regulation and responsibility. For example, a student's learning might benefit from
the student being selected as student of the week because the student engaged in a
number of highly productive, competent activities. However, the student likely will
not benefit from being given a reward for sitting still at a desk; such a reward is an
effort by the teacher to control the student, and students in heavily controlled learning environments tend to act like "pawns."

DIVERSITY

## CLASSROOM MANAGEMENT AND DIVERSITY

The growing diversity of students makes classroom management more challenging
(Scarlett, Ponte, & Singh, 2009). Children of color, especially African American
and Latino children, and children from low-income backgrounds constitute a disproportionate number of referrals for discipline problems in schools (Fenning &
Rose, 2007). A number of scholars argue that miscommunication between teachers and students and teachers' lack of sensitivity to cultural and socioeconomic
variations in students contribute to this disproportionate number of referrals
(Milner, 2006). Cultural mismatches especially are likely to appear in schools
where the teachers are overwhelmingly from non-Latino White, middle-income
backgrounds and the majority of the students are children of color from low-
income backgrounds.

Geneva Gay (2006, p. 364) recently described such cultural mismatches and how they might be reduced:*

> The commonly held belief that African Americans are disciplined more
> often and more severely because they commit more serious behavior
> infractions is not supported by research findings. Instead, they are pun-
> ished more harshly for relatively minor misconduct (such as defiance,
> disrespect, rudeness, and disobedience) that falls within the purview of
> the interpretive judgments of teachers. This subjective discipline often
> stems from cultural misunderstandings and conflicting expectations
> about how students are supposed to behave in relation to each other,
> and in teaching-learning situations. For example, teachers may consider
> explicit comments from students that their teaching is boring and irrel-
> evant as rude, insulting, and disrespectful. They may be particularly
> incensed by the way some students convey these sentiments. Rather
> than accepting them as useful feedback for improving the quality of
> instruction, teachers may see them as challenges to their authority that
> merit chastisement or even stronger disciplinary action. These tensions
> can be minimized by both teachers and students being more knowl-
> edgeable of each others' cultural styles of communicating, valuing,
> learning, and relating.

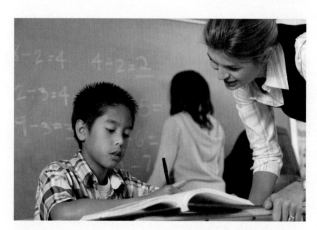

*What are some ways that teachers can engage in culturally
responsive teaching?*

Thinking Back/Thinking Forward

Culturally responsive (or culturally relevant) teaching seeks to make connections with the learner's cultural background. Chapter 1, p. 9; Chapter 5, p. 157

Engaging in such culturally responsive teaching and demonstrating sensitivity to
cultural and socioeconomic variations in students can help teachers to reduce discipline problems in their classroom (Gollnick & Chinn, 2009). An increasing number
of programs reveal that showing greater cultural sensitivity to socioculturally diverse
students benefits these students when they are at risk for academic and emotional
problems (Milner, 2006).

---

*Geneva Gay, "Connections between Classroom Management and Culturally Responsive Teaching," in *Handbook
of Classroom Management: Research, Practice, and Contemporary Issues,* ed. C. M. Evertson and C. S. Weinstein,
p. 364. Copyright 2006 by Taylor & Francis Group LLC—Books. Reproduced with permission of Taylor & Francis
Group LLC—Books in the format Textbook via Copyright Clearance Center.

## Review, Reflect, and Practice

**3** Discuss how to create a positive classroom environment.

### REVIEW

- What are some general strategies for creating a positive environment for learning?
- What are some hallmarks of good classroom rules?
- What are the best approaches in getting students to cooperate?
- What is important for teachers to know about classroom management and diversity?

### REFLECT

- In your classroom, what standards of "good" behavior would be nonnegotiable? Would you be flexible about some things? Explain.

### PRAXIS™ PRACTICE

1. Ms. Rockefeller has high expectations for her students' behavior. She is rather harsh with punishments when they do not live up to these expectations and accepts no explanations for noncompliance. Her standard response to excuses is, "I don't want to hear it. You broke the rules. You know the consequences." Which management style does Ms. Rockefeller exemplify?
   a. authoritative
   b. authoritarian
   c. permissive
   d. neglectful

2. Which of the following is the best example of a clearly stated classroom procedure?
   a. Keep your hands to yourself.
   b. Put all homework in the homework folder when you come in.
   c. Respect other people's property.
   d. Stay in your seat unless you have permission to get up.

3. Which teacher is most likely to gain the cooperation of students in following classroom rules and procedures?
   a. Ms. Benes and her students developed a list of rules and procedures at the beginning of the school year; however, she does not enforce the rules and procedures she has established. There are no reinforcements for proper behavior and no consequences for inappropriate behavior.
   b. Ms. Costanza wants her classroom to be very orderly. As a result, she punishes students for the slightest infractions.
   c. Ms. Kramer's students participated in the development of classroom rules. They all agreed that each rule was necessary and that the procedures would make things run more smoothly. When students disobey a rule, she asks them if their behavior is appropriate.
   d. Ms. Peterman has a long list of rules and procedures for students to follow. For instance, when they come in the classroom, they are to first put their homework in the proper folder, then change into their P.E. shoes. If students do these things in the opposite order, they are reprimanded.

4. During a class discussion in social sciences, a male African American high school student says that Mr. Smith, a non-Latino White teacher, doesn't seem to understand the difficulties and discrimination that many ethnic minority

*(continued)*

## Review, Reflect, and Practice

**PRAXIS™ PRACTICE (CONTINUED)**

groups have experienced. Which of the following is the most appropriate response of the non-Latino White teacher?

a. Ignore what the student said rather than reinforcing what was said

b. Tell the student that he seems to be overreacting

c. Say that he appreciates the student's contribution to the discussion and that he hopes to better understand such difficulties and discrimination

d. State that he doesn't appreciate the student's lack of respect for his knowledge

*Please see the answer key at the end of the book.*

## 4    BEING A GOOD COMMUNICATOR

Speaking Skills          Listening Skills          Nonverbal Communication

Managing classrooms and constructively resolving conflicts require good communication skills. Three key aspects of communication are speaking skills, listening skills, and nonverbal communication.

## SPEAKING SKILLS

You and your students will benefit considerably if you have effective speaking skills and you work with your students on developing their speaking skills (DeVito, 2011; Hogan & others, 2011; Zarefsky, 2011). Let's first explore some strategies for speaking with your class.

**Speaking with the Class and Students**    In speaking with your class and students, one of the most important things to keep in mind is to clearly communicate information (German & others, 2010; Grice & Skinner, 2010; Pearson & others, 2011). *Clarity* in speaking is essential to good teaching.

Some good strategies for speaking clearly with your class include the following (Florez, 1999):

1. Selecting vocabulary that is understandable and appropriate for the level of your students

2. Speaking at an appropriate pace, neither too rapidly nor too slowly

3. Being precise in your communication and avoiding vagueness

4. Using good planning and logical thinking skills as underpinnings of speaking clearly with your class

**Barriers to Effective Verbal Communication**    Barriers to effective verbal communication include the following (Gordon, 1970):

- *Criticizing.* Harsh, negative evaluations of another person generally reduce communication. An example of criticizing as the term is used here is telling a student, "It's your own fault you flunked the test; you should have studied." Instead of criticizing, you can ask students to evaluate why they did not do well on a test and try to get them to arrive at an attribution that reflects lack of effort as the reason for the poor grade.

- *Name-calling and labeling.* These are ways of putting down the other person. Students engage in a lot of name-calling and labeling. They might say to another student, "You are a loser," or "You are stupid." Monitor students' use of such name-calling and labeling. When you hear this type of statement, intervene and talk with them about considering other students' feelings.

- *Advising.* As used here, the term means talking down to others while giving them a solution to a problem. For example, a teacher might say, "That's so easy to solve. I can't understand why . . ."

- *Ordering.* Commanding another person to do what you want is often not effective because it creates resistance. For example, a teacher might yell at a student, "Clean up this space, right now!" A calm instruction, "Remember the rule of cleaning things up when we are finished," works better.

- *Threatening.* Threats are intended to control the other person by verbal force. As an extreme example, a teacher might say, "If you don't listen to me, I'm going to make your life miserable here." Obviously, a better strategy is to approach the student calmly and talk with her about the need for listening better.

- *Moralizing.* This means preaching to the student about what he should do in a condemning fashion, as in, "You know you should have turned your homework

## THROUGH THE EYES OF STUDENTS

### Forensics Teacher Tommie Lindsey's Students

Tommie Lindsey teaches competitive forensics (public speaking and debate) at Logan High School in Union City, California. Forensics classes in most U.S. schools are mainly in affluent areas, but most of Lindsey's students come from impoverished or at-risk backgrounds. His students have won many public speaking honors.

The following comments by his students reflect Lindsey's outstanding teaching skills:

> He's one of the few teachers I know who cares so much. . . . He spends hours and hours, evenings, and weekends, working with us.
>
> —Justin Hinojoza, 17

> I was going through a tough time. . . . Mr. Lindsey helped me out. I asked how I could pay back and and he said, "Just help someone the way I helped you."
>
> —Robert Hawkins, 21

> This amazing opportunity is here for us students and it wouldn't be if Mr. Lindsey didn't create it.
>
> —Michael Joshi, 17

Tommie Lindsey, working with his students on improving their public speaking and debate skills.

As a ninth-grade student, Tommie Lindsey became a public speaker. He says that his English teacher doubted his ability, and he wanted to show her how good he could be at public speaking, preparing a speech that received a standing ovation. Lindsey remembers, "She was expecting me to fail, and I turned the tables on her. . . . And we do that with our forensic program. When we started, a lot of people didn't believe our kids could do the things they do."

For his outstanding teaching efforts, Tommie Lindsey was awarded a prestigious McArthur Fellowship in 2005. (Source: Seligson, 2005.)

Giving students opportunities to practice their speaking skills is a vastly underutilized aspect of elementary and secondary education. Fear of speaking in front of a group is consistently listed as the number one fear of adults. *How do you think you can help your students become more effective speakers?*

in on time; you ought to feel ashamed." Moralizing increases students' guilt and anxiety. A better strategy in this example would be to avoid words such as *should* and *ought,* instead inquiring why the homework was not turned in on time.

**Giving an Effective Speech**   Not only will you be speaking in your class every day to your students in both formal and informal ways, but you also will have opportunities to give talks at educational and community meetings. Knowing some good strategies for giving a speech can significantly reduce your anxiety and help you deliver an effective speech (Griffin, 2011; Hasling, 2010; Nelson, Pearson, & Titworth, 2011).

Also, what you learn about giving an effective speech can be passed on to your students. Reflecting on our experiences as students, most of us can remember few opportunities to give talks in class unless we took a specific class in speech. Your students can be given speaking opportunities not only through formal presentations, but also by participating in panel discussions and debates. All these activities give students opportunities to improve their speaking, organizational, and thinking skills (Coopman & Lull, 2011; Lucas, 2009; Simonds, Hunt, & Simonds, 2010).

Here are some guidelines for delivering a speech that can benefit students as well as teachers (Alverno College, 1995):

- *Connect with the audience.* Talk directly to the audience; don't just read your notes or recite a memorized script.
- *State your purpose.* Keep this focus throughout the talk.
- *Effectively deliver the speech.* Use eye contact, supportive gestures, and effective voice control.
- *Use media effectively.* Certain media can help the audience grasp key ideas and vary the pace of the talk.

## LISTENING SKILLS

Effectively managing your classroom will be easier if you and your students have good listening skills. Listening is a critical skill for making and keeping relationships (Beebe, Beebe, & Redman, 2011; Berko, Wolvin, & Wolvin, 2010; Brownell, 2010). If you are a good listener, students, parents, other teachers, and administrators will be drawn to you. If your students are good listeners, they will benefit more from your instruction and will have better social relationships. Poor listeners "hog" conversations. They talk "to" rather than "with" someone. Good listeners actively listen (Lane, 2010; West & Turner, 2011). They don't just passively absorb information. **Active listening** means giving full attention to the speaker, focusing on both the intellectual and the emotional content of the message.

**active listening** A listening style that gives full attention to the speaker and notes both the intellectual and emotional content of the message.

PEANUTS © United Features Syndicates, Inc.

Some good active listening strategies follow:

- Pay careful attention to the person who is talking, including maintaining eye contact.
- Paraphrase.
- Synthesize themes and patterns.
- Give feedback in a competent manner.

## NONVERBAL COMMUNICATION

In addition to what you say, you also communicate by how you fold your arms, cast your eyes, move your mouth, cross your legs, or touch another person. Indeed, many communication experts maintain that most interpersonal communication is nonverbal (Burgoon, Guerrero, & Floyd, 2010; Stewart, 2009). Even a person sitting in a corner, silently reading, is nonverbally communicating something, perhaps that he wants to be left alone. And when you notice your students blankly staring out the window, it likely indicates that they are bored. It is hard to mask nonverbal communication. Recognize that it can tell you how others really feel.

Let's further explore nonverbal communication by examining facial expressions, personal space, and silence. People's faces disclose emotions and telegraph what really matters to them (Adams & Galanes, 2009; Leathers & Eaves, 2008; Verderber, Verderber, & Sellnow, 2011). A smile, a frown, a puzzled look all communicate.

Each of us has a personal space that at times we don't want others to invade. Not surprisingly, given the crowdedness of the classroom, students report that having their own space where they can put their materials and belongings is important to them. Make sure that all students have their own desks or spaces. Tell students that they are entitled to have this individual space, and that they should courteously respect other students' space.

In our fast-paced, modern culture we often act as if there is something wrong with anyone who remains silent for more than a second or two after something is said to them. In Chapter 12, we indicated that after asking a question of students, many teachers rarely remain silent long enough for students to think reflectively before giving an answer. By being silent, a good listener can observe the speaker's eyes, facial expressions, posture, and gestures for communication; think about what the other person is communicating; and consider what the most appropriate response

**Thinking Back/Thinking Forward**

Waiting three to five seconds or more after asking a question can often produce better student responses. Chapter 12, p. 409

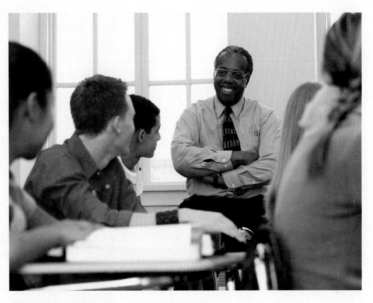

*How would you describe the nonverbal behaviors of the teachers and the students in these two photographs?*

# SELF-ASSESSMENT 14.1
## Evaluating My Communication Skills

Good communication skills are critical for effectively managing a classroom. Read each of the statements and rate them on a scale from 1 (very much unlike me) to 5 (very much like me).

1. I know the characteristics of being a good speaker in class and with students.

2. I am good at public speaking.

3. I do not tend to dominate conversations.

4. I talk "with" people, not "to" people.

5. I don't criticize people very much.

6. I don't talk down to people or put them down.

7. I don't moralize when I talk with people.

8. I'm good at giving my full attention to someone when they are talking with me.

9. I maintain eye contact when I talk with people.

10. I smile a lot when I interact with people.

11. I know the value of silence in communication and how to practice it effectively.

| 1 | 2 | 3 | 4 | 5 |
|---|---|---|---|---|
|   |   |   |   |   |
|   |   |   |   |   |
|   |   |   |   |   |
|   |   |   |   |   |
|   |   |   |   |   |
|   |   |   |   |   |
|   |   |   |   |   |
|   |   |   |   |   |
|   |   |   |   |   |
|   |   |   |   |   |
|   |   |   |   |   |

## SCORING AND INTERPRETATION

Look over your self-ratings. For any items on which you did not give yourself a 4 or 5, work on improving these aspects of your communication skills. Both you and your students will benefit.

is. Of course, silence can be overdone and is sometimes inappropriate (Lustig & Koester, 2010; Wood, 2011). It is rarely wise to listen for an excessive length of time without making some verbal response.

We have discussed a number of communication skills that will help you manage your classroom effectively. To evaluate your communication skills, complete Self-Assessment 14.1.

I recently asked teachers to describe communication skills that have been effective in their classrooms. Following are their responses.

**EARLY CHILDHOOD**   At our preschool, we communicate in such a way that children know what they *can do,* not what they can't. For example, instead of telling children to "keep quiet," we tell them to "use their listening ears."

—**HEIDI KAUFMAN,** *MetroWest YMCA Child Care and Educational Program*

**ELEMENTARY SCHOOL: GRADES K–5**   I use a lot of call and response methods to get my second-graders' attention. For example, I say, "One, two, three, eyes on me," and the children respond, "One, two, eyes on you." On the first day of school, they are taught to stop what they are doing when they hear me say this and turn to me for new instructions or information.

—**JANINE GUIDA POUTRE,** *Clinton Elementary School*

**MIDDLE SCHOOL: GRADES 6–8**   One of the keys to communicating effectively is good listening skills. I teach my students to have respect for speakers by having them clear their desk of everything on it whenever someone, teacher or student, is presenting. This strategy assures that the class is listening and respecting the person making a presentation rather than doodling in notebooks or reading.

—**MARK FODNESS,** *Bemidji Middle School*

**HIGH SCHOOL: GRADES 9–12**   I show my students the importance of being an effective communicator by giving them a complicated set of directions verbally (such as how to properly fold a dinner napkin) and then asking them to do the task without talking to anyone or asking questions. After this activity, I hold a discussion on why it was impossible to do the task given the ineffective communication of instructions. This activity quickly shows students the value of communicating effectively.

—**SANDY SWANSON,** *Menomonee Falls High School*

## Review, Reflect, and Practice

**4** Identify some good approaches to communication for both students and teachers.

**REVIEW**

- What are some barriers to effective speech? What are some principles of good speech? What is active listening, and what can teachers and students do to develop active listening skills?
- What are some important aspects of nonverbal communication for teachers to understand?

**REFLECT**

- What are your own communication strengths and weaknesses? What might you do to improve them?

**PRAXIS™ PRACTICE**

1. Ms. Carmichael is upset with Zack, one of her fifth-grade students, because he has not turned in his homework for the third time in the past week. She is discussing the situation with him, trying to express the importance of turning in assignments on time. Which of the following is likely to be her best response to the situation?
   a. "Okay, Zack, you may turn it in tomorrow."
   b. "What is wrong with you, Zack? This is the third time in a week! I know you can do the work. Are you just plain lazy? Is that it? This is getting ridiculous. Do you want to fail?"
   c. "Zack, I know you can do the work. Are you trying to make things more difficult for me by not turning it in?"
   d. "Zack, I can't possibly assess your understanding of the material when you don't turn in your work. This can't continue. Please get it to me by the end of the day, and no more late work."

*(continued)*

## Review, Reflect, and Practice

### PRAXIS™ PRACTICE (CONTINUED)

2. Edward and James are having a discussion about the best way to engage their students' interest in American history. Which of the following best exemplifies active listening?
   a. As Edward speaks about the importance of integrating electronic media into their courses, James interrupts with an argument that primary sources are much more useful and accurate.
   b. As Edward speaks about the importance of integrating electronic media into their courses, James makes a rude noise and tells him that is a bunch of nonsense.
   c. As Edward speaks, James maintains eye contact and nods occasionally. However, James is really planning how he will counter Edward's assertion that electronic media will engage the students.
   d. As Edward speaks, James maintains eye contact, nods his head occasionally, and leans forward. When Edward has finished, James says, "So what you're saying is that if we used more electronic media, the kids would be more interested, right?"

3. As Edward is speaking about the importance of integrating electronic media into their American history courses, James checks his watch, looks toward the door, and drums his fingers on the desk. What message is James communicating?
   a. interest
   b. disdain
   c. anxiety
   d. boredom

*Please see the answer key at the end of the book.*

## 5 DEALING WITH PROBLEM BEHAVIORS

Management Strategies          Dealing with Aggression

No matter how well you have planned and created a positive classroom environment, problem behaviors will emerge. It is important that you deal with them in a timely, effective manner.

## MANAGEMENT STRATEGIES

Classroom management experts Carolyn Evertson and Edward Emmer (2009) distinguish between minor and moderate interventions for problem behaviors. The following discussion describes their approach.

**Minor Interventions**   Some problems require only minor interventions. These problems involve behaviors that, if infrequent, usually don't disrupt class activities and learning. For example, students might call out to the teacher out of turn, leave their seats without permission, engage in social talk when it is not allowed, or eat candy in class. When only minor interventions are needed for problem behaviors, these strategies can be effective (Evertson & Emmer, 2009, pp. 188–190):

- "*Use nonverbal cues.* Make eye contact with the student and give a signal such as a finger to the lips, a head shake, or a hand signal to issue a desist."

- *Keep the activity moving.* Sometimes transitions between activities take too long, or a break in activity occurs when students have nothing to do. In these situations, students might leave their seats, socialize, crack jokes, and begin to get out of control. A good strategy is not to correct students' minor misbehaviors in these situations but rather start the next activity in a more timely fashion. By effectively planning the day, you should be able to eliminate such long transitions and gaps in activity.

- *Move closer to students.* When a student starts misbehaving, simply moving near the student will often cause the misbehavior to stop.

- *"Redirect the behavior."* If students get off-task, let them know what they are supposed to be doing. You might say, "Okay, remember, everybody is supposed to be working on math problems."

- *"Provide needed instruction."* Sometimes students engage in minor misbehaviors when they haven't understood how to do the task they have been assigned. Unable to effectively do the activity, they fill the time by misbehaving. Solving this problem involves carefully monitoring students' work and providing guidance when needed.

- *Directly and assertively tell the student to stop.* Establish direct eye contact with the student, be assertive, and tell the student to stop the behavior. "Keep your comments brief and monitor the situation until the student complies. Combine this strategy with redirection to encourage desirable behavior."

- *"Give the student a choice."* Place responsibility in the student's hands by telling him that he has a choice of either behaving appropriately or receiving a negative consequence. Be sure to tell the student what the appropriate behavior is and what the consequence is for not performing it.

Carolyn Evertson (*center,* in red, shown in a COMP classroom), a leading expert on classroom management, created COMP, a classroom management program, with Evelyn Harris. COMP includes many of the themes we have emphasized in developing a positive environment for learning. COMP emphasizes supporting students' learning and guiding students in taking responsibility for their own decisions, behavior, and learning. COMP also includes strategies for problem prevention, management and instruction integration, student involvement, and professional collaboration among teachers. The program is implemented through training workshops, classroom application, and collaborative reflection. Research has revealed that COMP results in positive changes in teacher and student behavior (Evertson & Harris, 1999).

A helpful strategy is to plan ahead for how you will handle such behavior problems once they occur. A recent study of elementary schools in Australia revealed that minor forms of student misbehavior were a common concern of teachers, that teachers were spending considerable time on behavior management issues, and that planning ahead for how to handle such problems was linked to lower stress for the teachers (Clunies-Ross, Little, & Kienhuis, 2008).

**Moderate Interventions**   Some misbehaviors require a stronger intervention than those just described—for example, when students abuse privileges, disrupt an activity, goof off, or interfere with your instruction or other students' work. Here are some moderate interventions for dealing with these types of problems (Evertson & Emmer 2009, pp. 177–178):

- *"Withhold a privilege or a desired activity."* Inevitably, you will have students who abuse privileges they have been given, such as being able to move around the classroom or to work on a project with friends. In these cases, you can revoke the privilege.

- *"Isolate or remove students."* In Chapter 7 we discussed the time-out, which involves removing a student from positive reinforcement. If you choose to use a time-out, you have several options. You can (1) keep the student in the classroom but deny her access to positive reinforcement, (2) take the student outside the activity area or out of the classroom, or (3) place the student in

*"How come when you say we have a problem, I'm always the one who has the problem?"*

George Abbott from *Phi Delta Kappan*, vol. 74, no. 2 (October 1992), p. 171. Reprinted by permission of George Abbott.

a time-out room designated by the school. If you use a time-out, be sure to clearly identify the student's behavior that resulted in the time-out, such as, "You are being placed in time-out for 30 minutes because you punched Derrick." If the misbehavior occurs again, reidentify it and place the student in time-out again. After the time-out, don't comment on how well the student behaved during the time-out; just return him to the activity that was interrupted.

- *Impose a penalty.* A small amount of repetitious work can be used as a penalty for misbehavior. In writing, a student might have to write an extra page; in math, a student might have to do extra problems; in physical education, a student might have to run an extra lap. The problem with penalties is that they can harm the student's attitude toward the subject matter.

  Students also can be made to serve a detention for their misbehaviors, at lunch, during recess, before school, or after school. Teachers commonly assign detentions for goofing off, wasting time, repeating rule violations, not completing assignments, and disrupting the class. Some detentions are served in the classroom; some schools have a detention hall where students can be sent. If the detention occurs in your classroom, you will have to supervise it. The length of the detention should initially be short, on the order of 10 to 15 minutes, if the misbehavior is not severe. As when using the time-out, you will need to keep a record of the detention.

**Using Others as Resources** Among the people who can help you get students to engage in more-appropriate behavior are peers, parents, the principal or counselor, and mentors.

**Peer Mediation** Peers sometimes can be very effective at getting students to behave more appropriately. Peer mediators can be trained to help students resolve quarrels and change undesirable behaviors. For example, if two students have started to argue with each other, an assigned peer mediator can help to mediate the dispute, as described later in the chapter when we discuss conflict resolution.

**Parent-Teacher Conference** You can telephone the student's parents or confer with them in a face-to-face conference. Just informing them can sometimes get the student to improve behavior. Don't put the parents on the defensive or suggest that you are blaming them for their child's misbehavior in school. Just briefly describe the problem and say that you would appreciate any support that they can give you.

**Enlist the Help of the Principal or Counselor** Many schools have prescribed consequences for particular problem behaviors. If you have tried unsuccessfully to deal with the behavior, consider asking the school's administration for help. This might involve referring the student to the principal or a counselor, which may result in a detention or warning to the student, as well as a parent conference with the principal. Letting the principal or counselor handle the problem can save you time. However, such help is not always practical on a regular basis in many schools.

**Find a Mentor** Earlier we underscored the importance of students having at least one person in their life who cares about them and supports their development. Some students, especially those from high-risk impoverished backgrounds, do not have that one person. A mentor can provide such students with the guidance they need to reduce problem behaviors (Lindley, 2009; Rowley, 2009). Look around the community for potential mentors for students in high-risk, low-income circumstances.

I recently asked teachers how they handle student misbehavior in their classrooms. Following are their responses.

**EARLY CHILDHOOD**   We teach our preschoolers that misbehavior always brings a consequence. We first speak to students about why the behavior is wrong and ways  to conduct themselves next time. We also send notes home to parents when misbehavior occurs. A student will be placed in time-out as a last resort.

—**Missy Dangler,** *Suburban Hills School*

**ELEMENTARY SCHOOL: GRADES K–5**   I make it a point to call every parent during the first month of school to establish a nonthreatening rapport and to have a  good-natured telephone call be the first communication of the year between us. During the call, I introduce myself, say something positive about his or her child, and ask the parent if he or she has any questions for me. If and when there is a call to be made to a parent for student misbehavior, I have already made positive contact with the parent, and the parent may be more willing to help with the problem.

—**Janine Guida Poutre,** *Clinton Elementary School*

**MIDDLE SCHOOL: GRADES 6–8**   If a student presents a problem that may cause harm to other classmates, either remove that student or remove the entire class. Students look to adults for safety.

—**Felicia Peterson,** *Pocantico Hills School*

**HIGH SCHOOL: GRADES 9–12**   I treat all of my students with respect, even the ones that are misbehaving. For example, when I see signs of misbehavior, I meet with the student individually outside of class and say something like "I get distracted when you talk to Sally while I'm speaking. Could you work on that for me? I don't want to stop class, because I think that would be embarrassing for you." Most students are receptive to the respect that I give them in these situations.

—**Joseph Maley,** *South Burlington High School*

## DEALING WITH AGGRESSION

Violence in schools is a major, escalating concern. In many schools, it now is common for students to fight, bully other students, or threaten each other and teachers verbally or with a weapon. These behaviors can arouse your anxiety and anger, but it is important to be prepared for their occurrence and handle them calmly. Avoiding an argument or emotional confrontation will help you to solve the conflict.

**The Scope of Aggression and School Violence**   A recent national study of almost 3,500 U.S. schools revealed that aggression and school violence are serious concerns. In the 2007–2008 school year, schools reported the following (Neiman, DeVoe, & Chandler, 2009):

RESEARCH

- The rate of violent incidents per 1,000 students was higher in middle schools (41 incidents) than in elementary schools (26 incidents) or high schools (22 incidents).

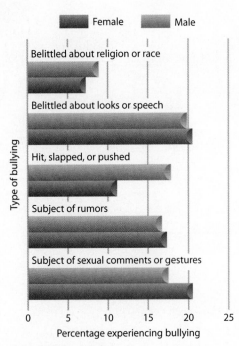

**FIGURE 14.5** BULLYING BEHAVIORS AMONG U.S. YOUTH

This graph shows the types of bullying most often experienced by U.S. youth. The percentages reflect the extent to which bullied students said that they had experienced a particular type of bullying. In terms of gender, note that when they were bullied, boys were more likely to be hit, slapped, or pushed than girls were.

RESEARCH

- Almost 50 percent of schools reported at least one student threat of physical attack without a weapon, and almost 10 percent of schools had such a threat with a weapon.
- Approximately 13 percent of city schools indicated they have had at least one gang-related crime, a higher percentage than reported by suburban (5 percent), town (5 percent), or rural (3 percent) schools.
- Almost 20 percent of city schools reported that student disrespect for teachers (other than verbal abuse) occurred daily or at least once a week, higher than reported by suburban (9 percent), town (11 percent), or rural (5 percent) schools.
- About 25 percent of schools report that the reason they have difficulty reducing or preventing crime in a major way is the lack of or inadequate alternative placements or programs for disruptive students.

Let's now explore different types of aggressive behavior problems and teacher strategies for how to effectively deal with them.

**Fighting** Classroom management experts Carolyn Evertson and Edmund Emmer (2009) recommend the following in dealing with students who are fighting. In elementary school, you can usually stop a fight without risking injury to yourself. If for some reason you cannot intervene, immediately get help from other teachers or administrators. When you intervene, give a loud verbal command: "Stop!" Separate the fighters, and as you keep them separated, tell other students to leave or return to what they are doing. If you intervene in a fight that involves secondary school students, you will probably need the help of one or two other adults. Your school likely will have a policy regarding fighting. If so, you should carry it out and involve the principal and/or parents if necessary.

Generally, it is best to let the fighters have a cooling-off period so that they will calm down. Then meet with the fighters and get their points of view on what precipitated the fight. Question witnesses if necessary. Have a conference with the fighters, emphasizing the inappropriateness of fighting, the importance of taking each other's perspective, and the importance of cooperation.

**Bullying** Significant numbers of students are victimized by bullies (Kaiser & Rasminsky, 2009; Vernberg & Biggs, 2010). In a national survey of more than 15,000 sixth- through tenth-grade students, nearly one of every three students said that they had experienced occasional or frequent involvement as a victim or perpetrator in bullying (Nansel & others, 2001). In this study, bullying was defined as verbal or physical behavior intended to disturb someone less powerful. As shown in Figure 14.5, being belittled about looks or speech was the most frequent type of bullying.

Who is likely to be bullied? In the study just described, boys and younger middle school students were most likely to be affected (Nansel & others, 2001). Children who said they were bullied reported more loneliness and difficulty in making friends, while those who did the bullying were more likely to have low grades and to smoke and drink alcohol. Researchers have found that anxious, socially withdrawn, and aggressive children are often the victims of bullying (Hannish & Guerra, 2004). Anxious and socially withdrawn children may be victimized because they are nonthreatening and unlikely to retaliate if bullied, whereas aggressive children may be the targets of bullying because their behavior is irritating to bullies (Rubin, Bukowski, & Parker, 2006).

Social contexts also influence bullying (Faris, 2009; Schwartz & others, 2010). Recent research indicates that 70 to 80 percent of victims and their bullies are in the same school classroom (Salmivalli & Peets, 2009). Classmates are often aware of bullying incidents and in many cases witness bullying. The larger social context of the peer group plays an important role in bullying (Salmivalli & Peets, 2009). In many cases, bullies torment victims to gain higher status in the peer group, and they need others to witness their power displays. Many bullies are not rejected by the peer group. In one study, bullies were only rejected by peers for whom they were a potential threat (Veenstra & others, 2010). In another study, bullies often affiliated with each other or in some cases maintained their position in the popular peer group (Wivliet & others, 2010).

What are the outcomes of bullying? Bullies and victims are characterized by a number of negative developmental outcomes (Arseneault & others, 2008). A recent meta-analysis of 33 studies revealed a small but significant link between peer victimization and lower academic achievement (Nakamoto & Schwartz, 2010). A recent study indicated that bullies and their victims in adolescence were more likely to experience depression and engage in suicide ideation and attempt suicide than their counterparts who were not involved in bullying (Brunstein & others, 2007). Recently, bullying has been linked to these suicides: An 8-year-old jumped out of a two-story building in Houston; a 13-year-old girl hanged herself in Houston; and teenagers harassed a girl so mercilessly that she killed herself in Massachusetts (Meyers, 2010). Another study revealed that bullies, victims, or those who were both bullies and victims also had more health problems (such as headaches, dizziness, sleep problems, and anxiety) than their counterparts who were not involved in bullying (Srabstein & others, 2006).

RESEARCH

An increasing number of prevention/intervention programs have been developed to reduce bullying (Biggs & Vernberg, 2010; Guerra & Williams, 2010; Singh, Orpinas, & Horne, 2010; Swearer, Espelage, & Napolitano, 2009). How can bullying be reduced? A research review revealed mixed results for school-based intervention (Vreeman & Carroll, 2007). Such interventions vary greatly, ranging from involving the whole school in an antibullying campaign to individualized social-skills training. Following are two of the most promising school-based bullying intervention programs:

- *Olweus Bullying Prevention.* Created by Dan Olweus, this program focuses on 6- to 15-year-olds, with the goal of decreasing opportunities and rewards for bullying. School staff are instructed in ways to improve peer relations and make schools safer. A large study of 2,500 students in 42 schools in Norway found that the Olweus program was effective in reducing bullying (Olweus, 1994). Information on how to implement the program can be obtained from the Center for the Study and Prevention of Violence at the University of Colorado (**www.colorado.edu/cspv/blueprints**).

*What are some strategies for reducing bullying?*

- *Bully-Proofing Your School.* This program is tailored for students in kindergarten through the eighth grade and offers a school-wide approach and a teacher curriculum for reducing bullying. It emphasizes how to recognize bullying behavior and quickly respond to it and how to develop students' communication skills in conflict situations. Intervention methods are provided, school posters related to bullying are available, and a parent's guide helps involve parents in effective ways to reduce bullying. Recent research indicates that this program is effective in reducing bullying (Beran & Tutty, 2002; Plog, Epstein, & Porter, 2004). Information about the Bully-Proofing Your School program is available at **www.sopriswest.com.**

There is increasing concern about *cyberbullying,* which occurs when a child or adolescent is tormented, threatened, harassed, or humiliated by another child or adolescent on the Internet (Hinduja & Patchin, 2009). There has been a substantial increase in youth harassment and cyberbulling on the Internet in recent years (Palfrey & others, 2009; Uhls & Greenfield, 2009). A recent survey found that bullying and harassment, both online and offline—most frequently by peers—were the most frequent threats that adolescents said they face (Palfrey & others, 2009). In a recent study of fifth- to eighth-grade students, some of the students said they consider online bullying as more serious than traditional bullying, especially when the identity

TECHNOLOGY

RESEARCH

## TEACHING CONNECTIONS: Best Practices
### Strategies for Reducing Bullying

Here are some suggestions to reduce bullying (Cohn & Canter, 2003; Hyman & others, 2006; Limber, 1997, 2004; Milsom & Gallo, 2006; Wright, 2004):

1. *Confront a bully in a firm manner.* It is usually a good idea to confront the bully in private when possible. If you need to confront the bully in public (classroom or playground when other students are present), approach the bully, describe what you saw, explain why it is not acceptable, and impose a consequence. A warning, time-out, apology to victim, and loss of privileges are possible consequences.

2. *Get older peers to serve as monitors for bullying and to intervene when they see it taking place.* Choose students who command respect from their peers when selecting these monitors.

3. *Be aware that bullying often occurs outside the classroom, so you may not actually see it taking place. Also, many victims of bullying don't report the bullying to*

*adults.* Unsupervised areas such as the playground, bus, and school corridors are common places where students are bullied. Be a presence in the halls during high-traffic times to help reduce the likelihood of bullying.

4. *If you observe bullying in your classroom or in other locations, you will need to make a decision about whether it is serious enough to report to school authorities or parents.* If you observe a student engaging in bullying on multiple occasions, set up a conference with the bully's parents and ask for their help in stopping the bullying.

5. *Get together with other teachers and the school administration to develop school-wide rules and sanctions against bullying and post them throughout the school.*

6. *Learn more about bullying.* For more information regarding bullying and how to prevent it, consult this Web site. In addition to information for teachers, there is information for students, parents, and administrators. **http://stopbullyingnow.hrsa.gov/adults/teachers-corner.aspx**

of the bully is unknown (Mishna, Saini, & Solomon, 2009). To learn more about helping students prevent cyberbullying, see the Web site of Stop Cyberbullying (2010) (**www.stopcyberbullying.org/**).

**Defiance or Hostility Toward the Teacher**   Edmund Emmer and Carolyn Evertson (2009) discussed the following strategies for dealing with students who defy you or are hostile toward you. If students get away with this type of behavior, it likely will continue and even spread. Therefore, try to defuse the event by keeping it private and handling the student individually, if possible. If the defiance or hostility is not extreme and occurs during a lesson, try to depersonalize it and say that you will deal with it in a few minutes to avoid a power struggle. At an appropriate later time, meet with the student and spell out any consequence the misbehavior might merit.

In extreme and rare cases, students will be completely uncooperative, in which case you should send another student to the office for help. In most instances, though, if you stay calm and don't get into a power struggle with the student, the student will calm down, and you can talk with the student about the problem.

## Review, Reflect, and Practice

**5** Formulate some effective approaches that teachers can use to deal with problem behaviors.

### REVIEW

- What are some minor and moderate interventions for managing problem behaviors in the classroom environment? Who else can help?
- What can the teacher do about fighting, bullying, and defiance? What are some effective school-based bullying intervention programs?

## Review, Reflect, and Practice

### REFLECT

- How worried are you about problem behaviors among the students you plan to teach? In view of your own current skills, personality, and values, what steps could you take now to prepare yourself for dealing with them?

### PRAXIS™ PRACTICE

1. Mr. Martin is telling his students how to complete their assignment for tomorrow. While he talks, Sally and Shelly are discussing their after-school plans. Mr. Martin should
   a. interrupt his instruction to say, "Listen up, girls, or you'll be spending your after-school hours with me."
   b. interrupt his instructions to ask, "Is there something that you would like to share with the class, girls?"
   c. keep talking, but look directly at Sally and Shelly; if that doesn't work, slowly approach them.
   d. stop his instructions and wait silently for the girls to stop talking, while looking directly at them, then say, "Thank you, ladies."

2. Ken is a fifth-grade student who is not well liked by his peers. They tease him about the way he looks, the way he dresses, his lack of coordination, and his lack of emotional self-regulation. The bulk of this takes place on the playground during recess. The teasing often reduces Ken to tears, which seems to add fuel to the fire. Which of the following is most likely to reduce this bullying behavior?
   a. in-school suspensions for the bullies
   b. isolating Ken from his peers so he does not have to deal with the bullying
   c. removing the bullies' recess privileges
   d. social-skills training for both the bullies and Ken

   *Please see the answer key at the end of the book.*

# The Chatty Student

Ms. Welch was a new middle school language-arts teacher. Prior to beginning her new position, she developed a classroom management plan that mirrored the code of conduct for the school. She expected the students to behave respectfully toward her and toward their classmates. She also expected them to respect school property and the learning environment. In addition, she expected them to keep their hands, feet, and possessions to themselves. Minor behavioral infractions were to result in a verbal warning. Further infractions would net more severe consequences in steps: a detention, a referral to the office, and a call to the students' parents. Ms. Welch was pleased with her management plan. She distributed it to students on the first day of class. She also distributed it to parents at the annual Back-to-School Night during the first week of school.

Darius, a student in one of Ms. Welch's seventh-grade classes, was what Ms. Welch termed "chatty." He was very social and spent much of his class time talking to other students rather than working. Ms. Welch tried moving him to different parts of the room and tried seating him next to students to whom she had never seen him talk, neither of which decreased his chattiness. He simply made new friends and continued chatting, sometimes disrupting the class in the process. She tried seating him next to girls, and this seemed to make things even worse.

Darius was very bright in addition to being very social. Although he was only in seventh grade, he was taking algebra with a group of mathematically advanced eighth-grade students. This was something of an anomaly in this school; in fact, it had never been done previously. The algebra teacher, Ms. Zaccinelli, and Darius had a good relationship. He never disrupted her class or misbehaved in any way in her class. Ms. Zaccinelli was amazed to hear that Darius did not always behave appropriately in his other classes.

Ms. Zaccinelli served as Ms. Welch's mentor. She had helped Ms. Welch write her classroom management plan and served as a sounding board when she had difficulties. At one point when Ms. Welch was discussing her eighth-grade classes, Ms. Zaccinelli referred to inclusion in the eighth-grade algebra class as "a privilege, not a right." She further told Ms. Welch that she expected her students to behave appropriately at all times.

The next day, Darius was especially talkative in class. Ms. Welch asked him to stop talking. He did, but he resumed his chatter within five minutes. When he began talking again, Ms. Welch took him aside and told him loudly, "That's it, Darius. I'm going to have you removed from algebra class. You know taking that class is a privilege, not a right."

Darius was stunned. He sat quietly for the rest of the period but did not participate. He made no eye contact with Ms. Welch or any other students. The rest of the day was something of a blur to him. He had no idea how he would explain this to his parents.

When Darius told his mother he was going to be removed from algebra for his behavior in language arts, she immediately went to see Ms. Welch. She tried to tell Ms. Welch that to remove Darius from algebra would be to deny him the free and appropriate public education to which he (and all other students) was entitled. Ms. Welch held her ground and insisted that she could and would have his placement altered.

1. What are the issues in this case?
2. Is removal from algebra class an appropriate consequence for Darius? Why or why not?
3. Do you think removal from algebra class would have a positive effect on Darius' behavior? Why or why not?
4. What impact do you think this would have on his motivation in school?
5. How do you think this situation will impact the relationship between Ms. Welch and Darius?
6. What do you think Darius' mother will do now?
7. How do you think Ms. Zaccinelli will react when she hears about the situation?
8. How do you think the principal will react?
9. What should Ms. Welch do?
10. How would Ms. Welch's strategy of moving Darius to quiet him be characterized?
    a. This is an example of a minor intervention.
    b. This is an example of a moderate intervention.
    c. This is an example of a severe intervention.
    d. This is an example of an effective intervention.
11. Which of the following is likely to be the most effective way for Ms. Welch to deal with Darius' chatty behavior?
    a. Make Darius write out a page of the dictionary.
    b. Put tape over Darius' mouth.
    c. Isolate Darius from his peers for the remainder of the period.
    d. Send Darius to the office for the principal to discipline.

# Managing the Classroom

**1** **WHY CLASSROOMS NEED TO BE MANAGED EFFECTIVELY:** Explain why classroom management is both challenging and necessary.

### Management Issues in Elementary and Secondary School Classrooms

Many management issues are similar across elementary and secondary school classrooms. However, certain differences in elementary and secondary classrooms require differences in management. Elementary school teachers often see the same 20 to 25 students all day long; secondary school teachers see 100 to 150 students about 50 minutes a day. Confinement, boredom, and interaction with the same people all day in elementary school can create problems. Secondary school teachers have to get the lesson moving quickly. They also might see a greater range of problems, and their students can have more long-standing problems that are more difficult to modify. These problems can be more severe than those of elementary school students. Secondary school students might demand more elaborate and logical explanations of rules and discipline.

### The Crowded, Complex, and Potentially Chaotic Classroom

Six reasons that classrooms are crowded, complex, and potentially chaotic are (1) multidimensionality, (2) simultaneous activities going on, (3) events occurring at a rapid pace, (4) often unpredictable events, (5) lack of privacy, and (6) classroom histories.

### Getting Off to the Right Start

Good strategies for getting off to the right start are to (1) establish expectations for behavior and resolve student uncertainties, (2) make sure that students experience success, (3) be available and visible, and (4) be in charge.

### Emphasizing Instruction and a Positive Classroom Climate

The focus in educational psychology used to be on discipline. Today it is on developing and maintaining a positive classroom environment that supports learning. This involves using proactive management strategies rather than being immersed in reactive discipline tactics. Historically, the well-managed classroom was conceptualized as a "well-oiled machine," but today it is more often viewed as a "beehive of activity." Kounin found that good classroom managers effectively manage the group's activities.

### Management Goals and Strategies

Goals and strategies include (1) helping students spend more time on learning and less time on non-goal-directed activity (maintain activity flow, minimize transition times, and hold students accountable) and (2) preventing students from developing academic and emotional problems.

**2** **DESIGNING THE PHYSICAL ENVIRONMENT OF THE CLASSROOM:** Describe the positive design of the classroom's physical environment.

### Principles of Classroom Arrangement

Basic principles of effective design of the classroom's physical environment include (1) reducing congestion in high-traffic areas, (2) making sure that you can easily see all students, (3) making often-used teaching materials and student supplies easily accessible, and (4) making sure that all students can see whole-class presentations.

### Arrangement Style

Classroom arrangement styles include auditorium, face-to-face, offset, seminar, and cluster. It is important to personalize the classroom and become an environmental designer who considers what activities students will be engaging in so as to draw up a floor plan, involve students in classroom design, and try out the arrangement and be flexible in redesigning it.

## ❸ CREATING A POSITIVE ENVIRONMENT FOR LEARNING: Discuss how to create a positive classroom environment.

**General Strategies**

Use an authoritative style of classroom management rather than an authoritarian or permissive style. The authoritative style involves considerable verbal give-and-take with students, a caring attitude toward students, and limits on student behavior when necessary. Authoritative teaching is linked with competent student behavior. Also, being sensitive to ethnic and socioeconomic variations in students is an important aspect of managing the classroom effectively. Kounin's work revealed other characteristics that were associated with effective classroom management: exhibiting withitness, coping with overlapping situations, maintaining smoothness and continuity in lessons, and engaging students in a variety of challenging activities.

**Creating, Teaching, and Maintaining Rules and Procedures**

Distinguish between rules and procedures, and consider the appropriateness of including students in the discussion and generation of rules. Classroom rules should be (1) reasonable and necessary, (2) clear and comprehensible, (3) consistent with instructional and learning goals, and (4) consistent with school rules.

**Getting Students to Cooperate**

Getting students to cooperate involves (1) developing a positive relationship with them, (2) getting them to share and assume responsibility (involve students in the planning and implementation of school and classroom initiatives, encourage them to judge their own behavior, don't accept excuses, and give the self-responsibility strategy time to work), and (3) rewarding appropriate behavior (choose effective reinforcers, use prompts and shaping effectively, and use rewards to provide information about mastery).

**Classroom Management and Diversity**

The increasing diversity of students makes managing the classroom more complex. Too often teachers are not knowledgeable about the cultural background of their students and as a consequence miscommunicate with them. Cultural mismatches may especially occur in schools in which the teachers are overwhelmingly non-Latino White and the students are mainly from ethnic minority groups. Engaging in culturally responsive teaching can help teachers reduce discipline problems in the classroom.

## ❹ BEING A GOOD COMMUNICATOR: Identify some good approaches to communication for both students and teachers.

**Speaking Skills**

Some barriers to effective speech include being imprecise and vague, using poor grammar, using vocabulary inappropriate for the students' level, and speaking too quickly or too slowly. You and your students will benefit considerably if you have effective speaking skills and if you work with your students on developing their speaking skills. Speaking effectively with the class and students involves being a clear communicator, connecting with the audience, using media effectively, and avoiding barriers to verbal communication such as criticizing, name-calling, ordering, and threatening. Both teachers and students can benefit from knowing how to give speeches effectively.

**Listening Skills**

Active listening occurs when a person gives full attention to the speaker, focusing on both the intellectual and the emotional content of the message. Some good active listening strategies are to (1) pay careful attention to the person who is talking, including maintaining eye contact; (2) paraphrase; (3) synthesize themes and patterns; and (4) give feedback in a competent manner.

**Nonverbal Communication**

A number of communication experts stress that the majority of communication is nonverbal rather than verbal. It is hard to mask nonverbal communication, so a good strategy is to recognize that nonverbal communication usually reflects how a person really feels. Nonverbal communication involves facial expressions and eye communication, touch, space, and silence.

**5  DEALING WITH PROBLEM BEHAVIORS:** Formulate some effective approaches that teachers can use to deal with problem behaviors.

Management Strategies

Interventions can be characterized as minor or moderate. Minor interventions involve using nonverbal cues, keeping the activity moving, moving closer to students, redirecting the behavior, giving needed instruction, directly and assertively telling the student to stop the behavior, and giving the student a choice. Moderate interventions include withholding a privilege or a desired activity, isolating or removing students, and imposing a penalty or detention. A good management strategy is to have supportive resources. These include using peers as mediators, calling on parents for support, enlisting the help of a principal or counselor, and finding a mentor for the student.

Dealing with Aggression

Violence is a major, escalating concern in schools. Be prepared for aggressive actions on the part of students so that you can calmly cope with them. Try to avoid an argument or emotional confrontation. Helpful guidelines for dealing with fighting, bullying, and defiance or hostility toward the teacher include developing and posting school-wide rules and sanctions against bullying, defusing the hostile event by keeping it private and handling the student individually, and if needed sending another student to the office for help. Two school-based bullying intervention programs are Olweus Bullying Prevention and Bully-Proofing Your School.

## KEY TERMS

auditorium style  486
face-to-face style  486
offset style  486
seminar style  486

cluster style  486
authoritative classroom
    management style  489

authoritarian classroom
    management style  489
permissive classroom
    management style  489

withitness  490
active listening  498

## PORTFOLIO ACTIVITIES

Now that you have a good understanding of this chapter, complete these exercises to expand your thinking.

### Collaborative Work: Creating Classroom Rules

List the rules you feel your students must follow. Describe how you might react when students break these rules. Then get together with three or four of your classmates and discuss each other's lists. Revise your rules based on their feedback. (INTASC: Principle 5)

### Independent Reflection: Cultivating Respectful Student-Teacher Relationships

How self-disclosing and open should teachers be with students? It is important for teachers to develop positive relationships with students, but is there a point at which teachers become too close with

their students? Write a personal reflection on this issue, incorporating thoughts about how it might relate to your future work as a teacher. (INTASC: Principle 6)

### Research/Field Experience: Researching School Discipline Policies

Interview school counselors at an elementary, a middle, or a high school. Ask them to describe the discipline policies at their schools and to evaluate how well they work. Also ask them to describe the most difficult student problem they have ever dealt with. Write up that problem as a case study. (INTASC: Principles 5, 9)

*Go to the Online Learning Center for downloadable portfolio templates.*

## STUDY, PRACTICE, AND SUCCEED

Visit www.mhhe.com/santrockep5e to review the chapter with self-grading quizzes and self-assessments, to apply the chapter material to

two more Crack the Case studies, and for suggested activities to develop your teaching portfolio.

# CHAPTER 15

# STANDARDIZED TESTS AND TEACHING

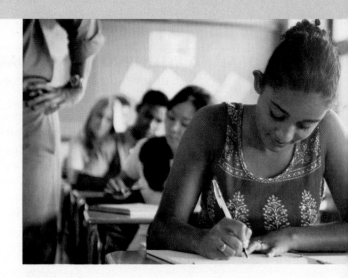

*People do not have equal talents. But all individuals should have an equal opportunity to develop their talents.*

—John F. Kennedy
*U.S. President, 20th Century*

## Chapter **Outline**

### The Nature of Standardized Tests

Standardized Tests and Their Purposes
Criteria for Evaluating Standardized Tests

### Aptitude and Achievement Tests

Comparing Aptitude and Achievement Tests
Types of Standardized Achievement Tests
High-Stakes State Standards-Based Tests
Standardized Tests of Teacher Candidates

### The Teacher's Roles

Preparing Students to Take Standardized Tests
Understanding and Interpreting Test Results
Using Standardized Test Scores to Plan and Improve Instruction

### Issues in Standardized Tests

Standardized Tests, Alternative Assessments, and High-Stakes Testing
Diversity and Standardized Testing

## Learning **Goals**

**1** Discuss the nature and purpose of standardized tests as well as the criteria for evaluating them.

**2** Compare aptitude and achievement tests, and describe different types of achievement tests as well as some issues involved in these tests.

**3** Identify the teacher's roles in standardized testing.

**4** Evaluate some key issues in standardized testing.

# Teaching **Stories**   Barbara Berry

Barbara Berry teaches French and humanities at Ypsilanti High School in Ypsilanti, Michigan, where she also is chairperson of the foreign languages department. She offers this story related to standardized tests:

> I had a fourth-year French student who was a wonderful student and clearly had a gift for languages. A minority student, she had been recruited by a major state university and offered a "full-ride" scholarship, provided she met certain requirements on the Scholastic Assessment Test (SAT). She took the test and did well on the verbal part but not well enough on the math part to meet the scholarship requirements. She was taking her fourth year of math classes and receiving above-average grades but said she just didn't like math and didn't understand it.
>
> Although I was teaching French at the time, I knew that I enjoyed math and had done well in school and on standardized tests. I knew that the SAT math section includes a lot of algebra. I offered to tutor her before she retook the SAT. She accepted the offer. I obtained some algebra materials from the math department to help work with her. Mostly, though, she worked on her own, reading the book and doing problems, only coming to me when she encountered problems. We met about once a week. About six weeks later, she retook the test and improved her math SAT score by 110 points. She got the scholarship.
>
> I did not teach this student much math, although I did help her work through some of the more difficult problems. What I did most to help her were two things: (1) I communicated my own enthusiasm for math and expressed confidence in her ability to do it, and (2) I focused her efforts on the material that the test assesses. Since we related so well with each other in my French class, I felt that I could help her feel better about her ability to do math.

# Preview

As Barbara Berry's story shows, standardized tests can have a major impact on students' lives. They are widely used to evaluate students' learning and achievement. Despite their increasing use to compare students' performance in different schools, districts, states, and countries, they are not without controversy. We begin our discussion in this chapter by examining some basic ideas about standardized tests and then distinguish between aptitude and achievement tests. Next we explore what your role as a teacher is likely to be in regard to standardized testing and conclude the chapter by describing several important issues in standardized testing.

**1  THE NATURE OF STANDARDIZED TESTS**

Standardized Tests and Their Purposes       Criteria for Evaluating Standardized Tests

Chances are you have taken a number of standardized tests. In kindergarten you may have taken a school readiness test, in elementary school some basic-skills or achievement tests, and in high school the SAT or ACT test for college admission. But what does it mean to say that a test is "standardized"? And what purpose is served by standardized testing?

## STANDARDIZED TESTS AND THEIR PURPOSES

**Standardized tests** have uniform procedures for administration and scoring and often allow a student's performance to be compared with the performance of other students at the same age or grade level on a national basis. Standardized tests can serve a number of purposes:

- *Provide information about students' progress.* Standardized tests are a source of information about how well students are performing. Students in one class might get *A*'s but perform at a mediocre level on a nationally standardized test, and students in another class might get *B*'s yet do extremely well on the same nationally standardized test. Without an external, objective marker such as a standardized test, individual classroom teachers have difficulty knowing

**standardized tests** Tests that have uniform procedures for administration and scoring and often allow a student's performance to be compared with the performance of other students at the same age or grade level on a national basis.

*What are some of the most important purposes of standardized tests?*

DEVELOPMENT

Thinking Back/Thinking Forward

Teachers need to integrate assessment in their planning. Chapter 16, p. 548

how well their students are performing compared with students elsewhere in the state or nation. Standardized tests also are used to show growth in achievement across months or years.

- *Diagnose students' strengths and weaknesses.* Standardized tests also can provide information about a student's learning strengths or weaknesses. Different subscale scores can be compared to show strengths and weaknesses, and individually administered tests can be used to pinpoint the student's learning weaknesses.

- *Provide evidence for placement of students in specific programs.* Standardized tests can be used to make decisions about whether a student should be allowed to enter a specific program. In elementary school a standardized test might be used to provide information for placing students in different reading groups. In high school a standardized test might be used to determine which math classes a student should take. In some cases standardized tests are used along with other information to evaluate whether a student might be allowed to skip a grade or to graduate. Students also might take standardized tests to determine their suitability for particular careers. One type of standardized test—the *benchmark*, or *interim assessment*—is given quarterly to help teachers determine the areas of achievement that need further instruction.

- *Provide information for planning and improving instruction.* In conjunction with other information about students, scores from standardized tests can be used by teachers in making decisions about instruction. For example, students' scores on a standardized test of reading skills administered at the start of the school year can help teachers determine the level at which they need to gear their reading instruction. Students' scores on a standardized test at the end of the year might show teachers about how effective their reading instruction has been, information that can be used to continue similar instruction or modify it accordingly.

- *Contribute to accountability.* Schools and teachers are increasingly being held accountable for students' learning. Although this is controversial, standardized tests are being used to determine how effectively schools are using tax dollars (Nitko & Brookhart, 2011; Yell & Dragsow, 2009). In Texas, principals can lose their jobs if their school's standardized test scores don't measure up. In Maryland, schools that don't do well forfeit thousands of dollars in reward money. Interest in accountability has led to the creation of **standards-based tests,** which assess skills that students are expected to have mastered before they can be promoted to the next grade or permitted to graduate. Schools that use standards-based tests often require students who do not pass the tests to attend special programs in the summer that will help them reach the minimum level of competency required by the school system. **High-stakes testing** is using tests in a way that will have important consequences for the student, affecting decisions such as whether the student will be promoted to the next grade or be allowed to graduate. Later in the chapter, we will discuss state-mandated tests, which are increasingly being used to make such "high-stakes" decisions.

An important theme throughout this chapter is that a standardized test should not be the only method for evaluating a student's learning. Nor should standardized tests by themselves be considered sufficient information in holding schools accountable for students' learning (Brookhart, 2008).

## CRITERIA FOR EVALUATING STANDARDIZED TESTS

**standards-based tests** Tests that assess skills that students are expected to have mastered before they can be promoted to the next grade or permitted to graduate.

**high-stakes testing** Using tests in a way that will have important consequences for the student, affecting such decisions as whether the student will be promoted or be allowed to graduate.

Among the ways to evaluate standardized tests are to understand whether the test is norm-referenced or criteria-referenced, and the extent to which the test score is valid, reliable, and fair. Let's begin our discussion by examining norm-referenced and criterion-referenced tests.

**Norm-Referenced and Criterion-Referenced Tests**    Standardized tests can be norm-referenced or criterion-referenced. A **norm group** is the group of individuals previously tested that provides a basis for interpreting a test score. Thus, in **norm-referenced tests** a student's score is interpreted by comparing it with how others (the norm group) performed.

The norm-referenced test is said to be based on *national norms* when the norm group consists of a nationally representative group of students. For example, a standardized test for fourth-grade science knowledge and skills might be given to a national sample of fourth-grade students. The scores of this representative sample of thousands of fourth-grade students become the basis for comparison. A norm group should include students from urban, suburban, and rural areas; different geographical regions; private and public schools; boys and girls; and different ethnic groups. Based on an individual student's score on the standardized science test, the teacher can determine whether a student is performing above, on a level with, or below a national norm (Gregory, 2011; Gronlund & Waugh, 2009). The teacher also can see how the class as a whole is performing in relation to the general population of students.

Unlike norm-referenced tests, **criterion-referenced tests** are standardized tests in which the student's performance is compared with established criteria or standards (McMillan, 2011). State standardized tests are typically criterion-referenced tests that do not use norms. For example, state criterion-referenced tests might assess whether a student has attained a level of achievement termed "proficient," or reached a certain percentage level, such as answering 80 percent of the items correctly. These levels of achievement are set by the state and used to determine annual yearly progress (AYP) for No Child Left Behind requirements. Criterion-referenced tests are designed to assess students' skills and knowledge in specific areas, such as English, math, and science.

**Validity, Reliability, and Fairness**    Whether the standardized test is norm-referenced or criterion-referenced, three important ways to evaluate the test are whether it is valid, reliable, and fair. Let's examine a standardized test's validity first.

*Validity*    Traditionally, validity has been defined as the extent to which a test measures what it is intended to measure. However, an increasing number of assessment experts in education argue that it is not just the characteristics of the test itself that should be judged valid or invalid but also the inferences that are made about the test scores (McMillan, 2011). Thus, **validity** involves the extent to which a test measures what it is intended to measure and whether inferences about the test scores are accurate and appropriate.

In terms of the test characteristics themselves—the substance of the test—three types of validity can be described: content validity, criterion validity, and construct validity. A valid standardized test should have good **content validity,** which is the test's ability to sample the content that is to be measured. This concept is similar to *content-related evidence.* For example, if a standardized fourth-grade science test purports to assess both content information and problem-solving skills, then the test should include items that measure content information about science and items that measure problem-solving skills.

Another form of validity is **criterion validity,** which is the test's ability to predict a student's performance as measured by other assessments or criteria. How might criterion validity be assessed for the standardized science test? One method is to get a representative sample of fourth-grade teachers to evaluate the competence of the students in their science classes and then compare those competence ratings with the students' scores on the standardized tests. Another method is to compare the scores of students on the standardized test with the scores of the same students on a different test that was designed to test the same material.

Criterion validity can be either concurrent or predictive (Oosterhof, 2009). **Concurrent validity** is the relation between the test's scores and other criteria that

**norm group**  The group of individuals previously tested that provides a basis for interpreting a test score.

**norm-referenced tests**  Standardized tests in which a student's score is interpreted by comparing it with how others (the norm group) performed.

**criterion-referenced tests**  Standardized tests in which the student's performance is compared with established criteria.

**validity**  The extent to which a test measures what it is intended to measure and whether inferences about the test scores are accurate and appropriate.

**content validity**  A test's ability to sample the content that is to be measured.

**criterion validity**  A test's ability to predict a student's performance as measured by other assessments or criteria.

**concurrent validity**  The relation between a test's scores and other criteria that are currently (concurrently) available.

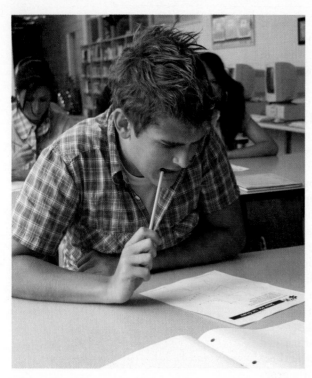

*If it is stated that a test is valid and reliable, what does that mean? What are some different types of validity and reliability?*

**predictive validity** The relation between test scores and the student's future performance.

**construct validity** The extent to which there is evidence that a test measures a particular construct. A construct is an unobservable trait or characteristic of a person, such as intelligence, learning style, personality, or anxiety.

**reliability** The extent to which a test produces a consistent, reproducible score.

**test-retest reliability** The extent to which a test yields the same performance when a student is given the same test on two occasions.

**alternate-forms reliability** Reliability judged by giving different forms of the same test on two different occasions to the same group of students to determine how consistent their scores are.

**split-half reliability** Reliability judged by dividing the test items into two halves, such as the odd-numbered and even-numbered items. The scores on the two sets of items are compared to determine how consistently the students performed across each set.

are currently (concurrently) available. For example, does the standardized fourth-grade science test correspond to students' grades in science this semester? If it does, we say that test has high concurrent validity. **Predictive validity** is the relation between test scores and the student's future performance. For example, scores on the fourth-grade science test might be used to predict how many science classes different students will take in high school, whether middle school girls are interested in pursuing a science career, or whether students will win an award in science at some point in the future.

A third type of validity is **construct validity,** the extent to which there is evidence that a test measures a particular construct. A *construct* is an unobservable trait or characteristic of a person, such as intelligence, creativity, learning style, personality, or anxiety. Construct validity is the broadest of the types of validity we have discussed and can include evidence from concurrent and predictive validity (Green & Johnson, 2010). Judgments about construct validity might also rely on a description of the development of the test, the pattern of the relations between the test and other significant factors (such as high correlations with similar tests and low correlations with tests measuring different constructs), and any other type of evidence that contributes to understanding the meaning of test scores. Because a construct typically is abstract, a variety of evidence may be needed to determine whether a test validly measures a particular construct.

Earlier we indicated that we should consider not only the substance of the test in determining validity but also whether inferences about the test scores are accurate (McMillan, 2011). Let's look at an example of how this might work. A school superintendent decides to use test scores from a standardized test given to students each spring as an indicator of teacher competence. In other words, the test scores are being used to *infer* whether teachers are competent. These are the validity questions in this situation: How reasonable is it to use standardized test scores to measure teacher competence? Is it actually true (accurate) that teachers whose students score high are more competent than teachers whose students score low?

***Reliability*** The extent to which a test produces a consistent, reproducible score is its **reliability.** To be called reliable, scores must be stable, dependable, and relatively free from errors of measurement (Lodico, Spaulding, & Voegtle, 2011; Musial & others, 2009). Reliability can be measured in several ways, including test-retest reliability, alternate-forms reliability, and split-half reliability.

**Test-retest reliability** is the extent to which a test yields the same performance when a student is given the same test on two occasions. Thus, if the standardized fourth-grade science test is given to a group of students today and then given to them again a month later, the test would be considered reliable if the students' scores were consistent across the two testings. There are two negative features of test-retest reliability: students sometimes do better the second time they take the test because of their familiarity with it, and some students may have learned information in the time between the first test and the second test that changes their performance.

**Alternate-forms reliability** is determined by giving different forms of the same test on two different occasions to the same group of students and observing how consistent the scores are. The test items on the two forms are similar but not identical. This strategy eliminates the likelihood that students will perform better on the second test administration due to their familiarity with the items, but it does not eliminate the possibility of a student's increase in knowledge and increased familiarity with the testing procedures and strategies.

**Split-half reliability** involves dividing the test items into two halves, such as the odd-numbered and even-numbered items. The scores on the two sets of items are compared to determine how consistently the students performed across each set. When split-half reliability is high, we say that the test is *internally consistent*. For example, on the standardized fourth-grade science test, the students' scores on the odd-numbered and even-numbered items could be compared. If they scored similarly on the two sets of items, we could conclude that the science test had high split-half reliability.

Reliability is influenced by a number of errors in measurement (Popham, 2011). A student can have adequate knowledge and skill, yet still not perform consistently across several tests because of a number of internal and external factors. Internal factors include health, motivation, and anxiety. External factors include inadequate directions given by the examiner, ambiguously created items, poor sampling of information, and inefficient scoring. When students perform inconsistently across the same or similar tests of their knowledge and skill, careful analysis should be made of internal and external factors that may have contributed to the inconsistency.

Validity and reliability are related (Anderman & Anderman, 2010). A test score that is valid is reliable, but a test score that is reliable is not necessarily valid. People can respond consistently on a test, but the test might not be measuring what it purports to measure. To understand this, imagine that you have three darts to throw. If all three fall close together, you have reliability. However, you have validity only if all three hit the bull's-eye.

***Fairness and Bias***   Fair tests are unbiased and nondiscriminatory (McMillan, 2011). They are not influenced by factors such as gender, ethnicity, or subjective factors such as the bias of a scorer. When tests are fair, students have the opportunity to demonstrate their learning so that their performance is not affected by their gender, ethnicity, disability, or other factors unrelated to the purpose of the test.

An unfair test is a test that puts a particular group of students at a disadvantage (Green & Johnson, 2010). This often occurs when there is something about the test that makes it more difficult for students with certain characteristics. For instance, suppose a test that is supposed to assess writing skills asks students to write a short story about a boy who practices very hard to be good in football and makes the team. Clearly, this type of item will be easier for boys than girls because boys are generally more familiar with football, so the test will be unfair to girls as an assessment of their writing skills. Consider also an item that might be used to assess reading comprehension. The reading passage is about a sailing experience. Thus, students who have had experience in sailing are likely to have an easier time reading and understanding the passage than those who have not. It is impossible to completely eliminate all unfair aspects of a test for every student, but test-makers can do much to create tests that are as fair as possible.

For students with disabilities, fairness often requires adaptations in administering the test. Many of the adaptations depend on the particular disability (Friend, 2011; Rosenberg, Westling, & McLesky, 2011). The goal is to lessen the negative influence of the disability on the trait being tested. For example, for students with a hearing disability, be sure that the directions are written; for students with a visual problem, be sure that directions are given orally.

> **Thinking Back/Thinking Forward**
>
> Establishing high-quality assessments that are valid, reliable, and fair is an important goal for teachers when they contruct tests to evaluate students' learning and achievement. Chapter 16, p. 552

## Review, Reflect, and Practice

**1** Discuss the nature and purpose of standardized tests as well as the criteria for evaluating them.

**REVIEW**

- What is meant by a standardized test? What are the uses of standardized tests?
- What are norm-referenced and criterion-referenced tests? Why are validity, reliability, and fairness important in judging the quality of a standardized test?

*(continued)*

## Review, Reflect, and Practice

### REFLECT

• Give an example of test scores that are reliable but not valid.

### PRAXIS™ PRACTICE

1. Which of the following is the best example of using the results of a standardized test to provide information for planning and improving instruction?
   a. At Lincoln Elementary School, students take a standardized achievement test each year to help determine who is in need of specialized services.
   b. At Jefferson Elementary School, teacher salary increases are based in part on student performance on the state-mandated standardized test.
   c. Mr. Whitney uses the results of the social studies portion of the state-mandated standardized achievement test to help him to see how well his instruction is working to help his students meet state standards in history.
   d. Ms. Walker uses the results of a standardized reading test to place her students into small instructional reading groups. She gives the same test several times throughout the school year to gauge progress and regroup students.

2. Which of the following is the best example of the predictive validity of a test?
   a. Students who score well on the ACT taken in their junior year in high school tend to do better in their first year of college than those who score poorly.
   b. The reading portion of a standardized test is supposed to measure both reading comprehension and vocabulary knowledge. It contains a section related to vocabulary and a reading passage with questions that follow.
   c. Students who do well on the state-mandated standardized test also do well on a nationally normed standardized test.
   d. Students who do well on the reading section of the state-mandated standardized test also get good grades in reading.

*Please see the answer key at the end of the book.*

## 2 APTITUDE AND ACHIEVEMENT TESTS

Comparing Aptitude and Achievement Tests

Types of Standardized Achievement Tests

High-Stakes State Standards-Based Tests

Standardized Tests of Teacher Candidates

There are two main types of standardized tests: aptitude tests and achievement tests. First we will define and compare these types of tests, then examine different types of achievement tests. Next we'll describe high-stakes state standards-based tests, as well as standardized tests of teacher candidates.

## COMPARING APTITUDE AND ACHIEVEMENT TESTS

An **aptitude test** is designed to predict a student's ability to learn a skill or accomplish something with further education and training. Aptitude tests include general mental ability tests such as the intelligence tests (Stanford-Binet, Wechsler scales, and so on) that we described in Chapter 4, "Individual Variations." They also include tests used to predict success in specific academic subjects or occupational areas. For example, one aptitude test might be given to students to predict their future success

---

**Thinking Back/Thinking Forward**

Controversy characterizes what intelligence is and how to assess it. Chapter 4, p. 122

**aptitude test** A type of test that is used to predict a student's ability to learn a skill or accomplish something with further education and training.

in math, whereas another might be given to predict whether they are likely to do well in sales or medicine.

An **achievement test** is intended to measure what the student has learned or what skills the student has mastered (Gregory, 2011). However, the distinction between aptitude and achievement tests is sometimes blurred. Both types of tests assess a student's current status, the questions they use are often quite similar, and usually the results of the two kinds of tests are highly correlated.

The SAT that you may have taken as part of your admission to college is usually described as an aptitude test, but the SAT can be either an aptitude test or an achievement test depending on the purpose for which it is used. If it is used to predict your success in college, it is an aptitude test. If it is used to determine what you have learned (such as vocabulary, reading comprehension, and math skills), it is an achievement test.

## TYPES OF STANDARDIZED ACHIEVEMENT TESTS

There are numerous types of standardized achievement tests. One common way to classify them is as survey batteries, specific subject tests, or diagnostic tests.

**Survey Batteries**   A *survey battery* is a group of individual subject-matter tests designed for a particular level of students. Survey batteries are the most widely used national norm-referenced standardized tests (McMillan, 2008a). Some common batteries are the California Achievement Tests, Iowa Tests of Basic Skills, Metropolitan Achievement Tests, and Stanford Achievement Test Series.

Many survey batteries also contain a number of subtests within a subject area. For example, the Metropolitan Achievement Tests include reading as one of the subject areas at each level. The reading subtests on the Metropolitan Tests include vocabulary, word recognition, and reading comprehension.

In their early years, survey batteries consisted of multiple-choice items to assess the student's content knowledge. However, recent editions have increasingly included open-ended items that evaluate the student's thinking and reasoning skills.

**Tests for Specific Subjects**   Some standardized achievement tests assess skills in a particular area such as reading or mathematics. Because they focus on a specific area, they usually assess the skill in a more detailed, extensive way than a survey battery. Two examples of specific area tests that involve reading are the Woodcock Reading Mastery Tests and the Gates-McKillop-Horowitz Reading Diagnostic Test. Some standardized subject-area tests cover such topics as chemistry, psychology, or computer science—topics that are not included in survey batteries.

**Diagnostic Tests**   As we said earlier, diagnosis is an important function of standardized testing. *Diagnostic testing* consists of a relatively in-depth evaluation of a specific area of learning. Its purpose is to determine the specific learning needs of a student so that those needs can be met through regular or remedial instruction. Reading and mathematics are the two areas in which standardized tests are often used for diagnosis.

Test publishers of all national norm-referenced standardized achievement tests claim that their tests can be used for diagnosis (McMillan, 2008a). However, for a test to be effective in diagnosis it should have several test items for each skill or objective that is measured, and many of these national tests fall short in this regard.

## HIGH-STAKES STATE STANDARDS-BASED TESTS

As the public and government have demanded increased accountability of how effectively schools are educating our nation's children, state standards-based tests have taken on a more powerful role (Green & Johnson, 2010; McMillan, 2011).

**achievement test** A test that measures what the student has learned or what skills the student has mastered.

States have mandated tests for many years, but their emphasis has recently changed. Prior to the 1990s their content was not closely linked with what was actually taught and learned in the classroom. The early state-mandated assessments simply provided an overall view of how students in a state were performing in certain subject areas, especially reading and mathematics.

In the 1990s efforts began to connect state-mandated testing to state-endorsed instructional objectives. Most states already have identified or are in the process of identifying objectives that every student in the state is expected to achieve. These objectives—often called standards—form the basis not only for these mandated standards-based tests but also for such activities as teacher education and curriculum decisions. Teachers are strongly encouraged to incorporate these objectives into their classroom planning and instruction. In many states, the objectives are reflected in the achievement tests that are given to every student in the state. Many school districts use pacing guides for curriculum to ensure that all students are adequately prepared for the state-mandated tests.

**The Format of State Standards-Based Tests** State standards-based tests contain mostly or soley multiple-choice items. These types of items, however, do not support or promote constructivist learning. When constructivist-based assessments are included, they typically involve short-answer items or writing prompts. Very few states include a portfolio as part of their assessment. Almost all states use criterion-referenced scoring, which means that the student's score is evaluated against predetermined standards.

**Possible Advantages and Uses of High-Stakes Testing** Many policymakers argue that high-stakes state standards-based testing will have a number of positive effects:

- Improved student performance
- More time teaching the subjects tested
- High expectations for all students
- Identification of poorly performing schools, teachers, and administrators
- Improved confidence in schools as test scores increase

The widest uses of these tests for guiding the progress of individual students have to do with decisions regarding remediation, promotion, and graduation. *Remediation* consists of assigning students who do not do well on the tests to special classes. Such remediation usually occurs after school, on Saturday, or during the summer. Currently 13 states require and fund remediation strategies to help low-performing students reach state standards.

Many endorsers of state standards-based tests argue that students should not be promoted to the next grade without reaching a certain standard of performance on the tests. In this regard, the goal is to end *social promotion* (promotion based on the idea that students should not be left behind their age-mates). Currently test-based promotion policies have been instituted in nine states.

State standards-based tests are also being used to determine whether a student should be allowed to graduate from high school in many states. Such a decision can have a major impact on a youth's future.

In addition, state standards-based tests are used to make decisions about school and staff accountability (McMillan, 2008b). Holding schools accountable means using test scores to place the schools in designated categories, such as watch/warning (which is publicly reported and implies that improvement is expected); probation (which usually requires the school to submit a comprehensive reform plan); failing/in crisis (which requires serious outside assistance in developing an improvement plan); accredited, accredited with warning, and nonaccredited. This puts considerable pressure on schools to do everything possible to obtain passing scores.

**Criticism of State Standards-Based Tests**   Critics of the state standards-based tests argue that they lead to these negative consequences (McMillan, 2002):

- *Dumbing down the curriculum with greater emphasis on rote memorization than on problem-solving and critical-thinking skills.* In one analysis, most state tests focused on less demanding knowledge and skills rather than more complex cognitive skills (Quality Counts, 2001). This narrows the curriculum and focuses it more on lower-order cognitive skills. Adhering to a test-driven curriculum often means superficial coverage of topics.

- *Teaching to the test.* Teachers increasingly teach knowledge and skills that are to be covered on the state tests (Stiggins, 2008). They spend inordinate amounts of time on testlike activities and practice tests, with less time for actual teaching of important content and skills.

- *Discrimination against low-socioeconomic-status (SES) and ethnic minority children.* This results when disproportionate percentages of these children do not meet the state standards, while higher-SES and non-Latino White students do. Researchers have found that students who are placed in the lowest tracks or remedial programs—disproportionately low-income and minority students—are most likely to experience subsequent inferior teaching and reduced achievement (Cooper & Sherk, 1989; Oakes, 1990). There is evidence that high-stakes state standards-based testing that rewards or sanctions schools based on average student scores can create incentives for pushing low-scorers into special education, holding them back a grade and encouraging them to drop out of school so that the schools' average scores will look better (Darling-Hammond, 2001).

- *Narrowing the curriculum.* Because of the potential negative consequence of poor performance on state-mandated tests many schools limit the curriculum to only what is covered on the test. In some cases, nontested subjects such as foreign language or art are deemphasized.

For these reasons and others, the American Psychological Association, the American Educational Research Association, and the National Council on Measurement in Education have issued standards for the use of tests, noting that test scores are too limited and unstable to be used as the sole source of information for any major decision about student placement or promotion. Test scores should always be used in combination with other sources of information about student achievement when making important decisions about students (National Research Council, 2001).

RESEARCH

Because high-stakes state standards-based testing is relatively new, there is little systematic research on its consequences (McMillan, 2011). However, there are some serious concerns about the way high-stakes testing currently is structured. One concern involves the validity of the inferences that can be drawn from the results (National Research Council, 2001). Just documenting higher test scores does not mean that education has improved. Indeed, if the tests are assessing the wrong skills or are flawed, it could mean just the opposite. As yet, we do not know if the high-stakes testing is causing students to be better prepared for college and the workplace.

Yet another concern is the extent to which high-stakes testing is useful for improving teaching and learning—the ultimate goal of educational reforms (Stiggins, 2008). Most current high-stakes tests provide very limited information for teachers and administrators about why students do not perform well or how they can modify instruction to improve student achievement. Most of the high-stakes tests provide only general information about where a student stands relative to peers (such as scoring at the 63rd percentile) or whether the students have not performed well in certain domains (such as performing below the basic level in mathematics). Such tests do not provide information about whether students are using misguided strategies to solve problems or which concepts in a domain students do not understand. In sum, most current high-stakes tests do not provide information about the types of interventions that would improve students' performance or even yield information about their strengths and weaknesses.

## THROUGH THE EYES OF STUDENTS

### It's as if a Test Score Is All There Is to a Person

Spend enough time in school and you start to think that standardized tests are the only things that matter in life. My standardized test scores are disappointing, but I take pride in being in the top 4 percent of my class. I have a 4.0 GPA. If I can pull off those kinds of grades in tough classes—including three Advanced Placement courses—I'm forced to wonder, what do these tests really prove?

It's as if a test score is all there is to a person. I enjoy all kinds of creative writing, and I spend long nights trying to *understand* school subjects, rather than just memorize formulas. But none of this matters for standardized tests.

*Tania Garcia*
**Twelfth-Grade Student**
**Oakland High School**
**Oakland, California**

**Thinking Back/Thinking Forward**

Because of NCLB, standards-based instruction has become a major issue in U.S. education. Chapter 1, p. 10

RESEARCH

**No Child Left Behind** In Chapter 1 we described the No Child Left Behind (NCLB) Act, the federal government's legislation that was signed into law in 2002. NCLB is the U.S. government's effort to hold schools and school districts accountable for the success or failure of their students. The legislation shifts responsibility to the states, with states being required to create their own standards for students' achievement in mathematics, English/language arts, and science. Reading and math assessments in grades 3 to 8 were required through 2006. Then, beginning in the 2007–2008 school year, science assessments were made in elementary, middle, and high schools. The goal by 2014 is that every U.S. student will test to proficiency in core math and literacy skills (Shaul, 2007). A recent analysis concluded that such an ambitious goal will not be met and that if NCLB is reauthorized it should include more reasonable improvement targets (Stecher & Vernez, 2010).

States are required to create an accountability system that ensures students are making adequate annual progress in the subject areas just mentioned (Yell & Drasgow, 2009). Schools that fail to make *adequate yearly progress (AYP)* for two consecutive years are labeled "underperforming." Underperforming schools are to be given special help, but they must give parents the option of moving their children to a better-performing school. If underperforming schools don't improve after four years, states are required to implement major staff and curriculum changes in the schools, and if progress is not made after five years, states must close the schools. A difficulty in achieving AYP is that it must be achieved not only for the entire school but for certain subgroups of students as well, including those who are economically disadvantaged, students from ethnic minority groups, students with disabilities, and students with limited English proficiency (Hallahan, Kauffman, & Pullen, 2009). A recent analysis revealed that approximately one-third of public schools did not make adequate yearly progress in the 2008–2009 school year (Dietz, 2010).

Also as part of the NCLB legislation, states and districts are required to provide report cards that show a school's performance level, so that the public is aware of which schools are underperforming. Another aspect of the NCLB legislation is that all teachers now are required to be "highly qualified," which means being licensed and having an academic major in the field in which they are teaching. Schools are required to notify parents if a teacher is not "highly qualified." A recent analysis revealed considerable variability across states in what constitutes a highly qualified teacher (Birman & others, 2007). The percentage of teachers who fell into the "not highly qualified category" was higher for special education teachers, teachers of limited English proficiency students, middle school teachers, and teachers in high-poverty and high ethnic minority schools.

Each state is allowed to have different criteria for what constitutes passing or failing grades on tests designated for NCLB inclusion. This had led to a number of problems (Stecher & Vernez, 2010). For example, an analysis of NCLB data indicated that almost every fourth-grade student in Mississippi knows how to read but only half of Massachusetts's students do (King, 2007). When these students take a common assessment, Massachusetts students' achievement is much higher than Mississippi students' achievement. Clearly, Mississippi's standard for passing the reading test are far below that of Massachusetts. In the recent analysis of state-by-state comparisons, many states have taken the safe route and are keeping the passing bar low. Thus, while one of NCLB's goals was to raise standards for achievement in U.S. schools, apparently allowing states to set their own standards likely has lowered achievement.

A number of criticisms of NCLB have been made (Anderman & others, 2010; Green & Johnson, 2010; McMillan, 2011). Some critics even say that the NCLB legislation will do more harm than good (Lewis, 2007).

One widely adopted criticism stresses that using a single score from a test as the sole indicator of students' and teachers' progress and competence represents a very narrow aspect of students' and teachers' skills. This criticism is similar to the one leveled at IQ testing, described in Chapter 4. To more accurately assess student progress and achievement, many psychologists and educators argue that a number of measures should be used—including tests, quizzes, projects, portfolios, and classroom observations—rather than a single score on a single test.

Also, the tests schools are using to assess achievement and progress as part of NCLB don't measure such important skills as creativity, motivation, persistence, flexible thinking, and social skills (Stecher & Vernez, 2010). Critics point out that teachers and schools are spending far too much class time "teaching only to the test" by drilling students and having them memorize isolated facts at the expense of more student-centered constructivist teaching that focuses on higher-level thinking skills, which students need for success in life (McKim, 2009).

By permission of Marshall Ramsey and Creators Syndicate, Inc.

Another criticism is that the increased cost of carrying out standardized testing on a statewide basis, including creating tests, administering them, scoring them, and reporting their results to the federal government, comes at a time when most states are facing budget crunches (Lewis, 2007). Having to spend so much more money on testing means that some existing resources and programs in other areas will have to be trimmed or eliminated.

Yet another criticism of NCLB is that high-stakes testing encourages test score inflation (Koretz, 2008), in which scores rise over the course of several years but do not reflect actual improvements in student learning.

One goal of NCLB is to close the ethnic achievement gap that characterizes lower achievement by African American and Latino students and higher achievement by Asian American and non-Latino White students (Forte, 2010). However, leading expert Linda Darling-Hammond (2007) recently concluded that NCLB has failed to reach this goal. She criticizes NCLB for inappropriate assessment of English language learners and students with special needs, strong incentives to exclude low-achieving students from school to achieve test score targets, and the continued shortage of highly qualified teachers in high-need schools. While some progress has been made inequities still exist in high-poverty and high-minority schools in which too often students are taught by inexperienced, unqualified, or out-of-field teachers (Bumgardner, 2010).

Other criticisms of NCLB were described in Chapters 6, 9, and 13. Recall that some individuals are concerned that in the era of NCLB policy there is a neglect of students who are gifted in the effort to raise the achievement level of students who are not doing well (Clark, 2008; Cloud, 2007). So, too, is there mounting concern that NCLB legislation has harmed the development of students' creative thinking by focusing attention on the memorization of content (Beghetto & Kaufman, 2009). And there is concern that the NCLB policy encourages a performance rather than a mastery orientation to achievement (Meece, Anderman, & Anderman, 2006).

Despite such criticisms, the U.S. Department of Education is committed to implementing NCLB, and schools are making accommodations to meet the requirements of this law (Parkay & Stanford, 2010; Taylor & others, 2010). Indeed, most educators support the importance of high expectations and high standards of excellence for students and teachers (Anderman & Anderman, 2010). At issue, however, is whether the tests and procedures mandated by NCLB are the best ones for achieving these high standards (Yell & Drasgow, 2009).

The growing emphasis on accountability and data-driven decision making occasioned by the NCLB legislation has prompted educators to think differently about how standardized assessments and resulting data can inform classroom instruction

DIVERSITY

**Thinking Back/Thinking Forward**

Criticisms of NCLB include neglect of children who are gifted, harm of children's development of creative thinking skills, and encouragement of a performance rather than a mastery achievement motivation. Chapter 6, p. 207; Chapter 13, p. 448

"I Know no child is supposed to be left behind, but they might make an exception in your case."

Dan Rosandich. www.cartoonstock.com

A New Mexico teacher using a handheld computer in student assessment.

TECHNOLOGY

RESEARCH

and ultimately affect student achievement. Educators across the country, therefore, are working hard to develop strategies that provide standardized test data to stakeholders at all levels of the educational system and offer teachers technical assistance to administer assessments and use results effectively. Increasingly, districts and schools are turning to technology-based applications.

A good example is the state of New Mexico's early literacy program. A recipient of a federal Department of Education Reading First grant, the state recognized that Reading First offered them not only a unique opportunity to support literacy instruction, but also a way to collect and use data in a standardized fashion. State education officials contracted with Wireless Generation, a company that provides mobile software for early literacy assessments and that allows teachers to use handheld computers to administer assessments, record student data, then upload that assessment data to a desktop computer and to a Web site where it is immediately made available in graphic form. This lets teachers view a student's assessment results, as well as individual student data in relation to previous assessments or assessment data from other students in the same classroom. While several assessments reside on the handhelds, the state required that the participating teachers administer the Dynamic Indicators of Basic Early Literacy Skills, also known as the DIBELS (Good & Kaminski, 2003) to all of their students during three assessment windows throughout the school year—fall, winter, and spring.

Researchers found many benefits for the handheld computers in the program (Hupert & Heinze, 2006). Teachers reported that the use of handhelds was much more efficient. They said it was much easier to bring the handheld around with them to administer the DIBELS. Also, the results were instantly uploaded in contrast to having to reenter pencil and paper data. This led to a second benefit: instantaneous feedback—teachers immediately saw results in a variety of formats for both individual students and their entire class. These first two benefits, in turn, led to several others, including shaping professional development opportunities to address perceived problems, strengthening home-school communications in that teachers could immediately report on student achievement, and enhancing the use of data to drive instruction.

The success of New Mexico's Reading First project has led several other states (Florida, Oklahoma, and Ohio), the Bureau of Indian Affairs, and school districts, such as those of Chicago and New York City, to contract with Wireless Generation to supply participating teachers with handhelds to administer the DIBELS.

I recently asked teachers about their opinions on the NCLB Act. Following are their responses.

**EARLY CHILDHOOD** Our preschool receives state funding so that financially disadvantaged children receive a quality preschool experience that their parents would

not otherwise be able to afford. The No Child Left Behind Act is controversial and continues to be hotly debated; however, no matter what your opinion is, unless educational opportunities are created for the least financially able, the American educational system will never be equal for all. Everyone deserves a chance to shine, and a quality preschool education is a start.

—**VALARIE GORHAM**, *Kiddie Quarters, Inc.*

**ELEMENTARY SCHOOL: GRADES K–5** The NCLB Act is an idealistic approach to measuring student growth and teacher effectiveness. Just as no one program works in

every classroom, we cannot expect all children to meet the same standards regardless of their background or experiences. The stress of having to meet state benchmarks and increase scores on state and/or national tests has taken a toll on veteran teachers. For us, teaching is no longer fun—we are now required to teach so many test-specific skills that we are unable to instill a lifelong love of learning in our students.

—**KAREN PERRY**, *Cooper Mountain Elementary School*

**MIDDLE SCHOOL: GRADES 6–8**   NCLB is a typical example of how the education "pendulum" swings too far in any given direction. Although testing is important,  NCLB makes testing the ultimate measuring tool. Many students who do not excel at reading or math (or who struggle with standardized tests) are seen as failures, as are the schools they attend. Ironically, these students and schools spend so much time trying to remediate for the tests that they are not allowed to explore other options in which the student might thrive.

—**MARK FODNESS,** *Bemidji Middle School*

**HIGH SCHOOL: GRADES 9–12**   I find it somewhat ridiculous that teachers are graded by how well their students do. Are dentists judged by how many patients have zero cavities? On the other hand, NCLB does hold teachers accountable and raises the bar. In that sense, it is beneficial.

—**JENNIFER HEITER,** *Bremen High School*

**National Assessment and World-Class Standards**   In addition to state assessments required by the NCLB Policy, U.S. students are assessed periodically on standardized tests at national and international levels.

*National Assessment*   The federal government also is involved in standardized testing through the National Assessment of Educational Progress (NAEP). The NAEP is a census-like assessment of students' skills and achievement in subject areas such as reading, writing, math, science, and history. Recent findings from the NAEP (2009) reveal the following:

- Math scores for fourth- and eighth-grade students increased 16 points for fourth-grade students from 1996 to 2009 and 13 points for eighth-grade students across this time period (on a scale of 0 to 500 points).
- Science scores for fourth-grade students showed only a slight increase from 1996 to 2005 (from 147 to 151 on a 300-point scale); there was no change in science scores of eighth-grade students across this time frame; and science scores for twelfth-grade students declined from 150 to 147 over this time period.
- Reading scores for fourth-grade and eighth-grade students increased only slightly, by 4 points, from 1992 to 2009 on a scale of 0 to 500 points.

RESEARCH

DEVELOPMENT

Thus, in recent years, the greatest improvement in the core subject areas of math, science, and reading in U.S. schools have been achieved in math, with science scores showing little or no improvement and even declining for twelfth-grade students.

The federal government argues that increasing national test scores assessed by NAEP indicate that the NCLB policy is succeeding. Improving math scores support this conention; however, only slight progress has been made in reading, and, depending on the grade level, only slight progress or even a decline in science scores have occurred since NCLB was introduced in 2002.

*International Assessments*   National assessment of students is part of an effort to get U.S. students to measure up to, and eventually set the standard for, world-class achievement in education. How are U.S. students faring versus students in other countries? Recent international assessments of student achievement in reading, math, and science include (1) Progress in International Reading Study (PIRLS), which assesses fourth-grade students' reading achievement every five years (first assessment in 2001); (2) Program for International Assessment (PISA), which tests reading, math,

DIVERSITY

RESEARCH

Recent international comparisons indicate that students in many East Asian countries have significantly higher math and science achievement scores on standarized tests than U.S. students. Shown here is a five-year girl from China working on complex math problems on a blackboard in her home.

and science achievement of 15-year-old students every three years (first assessment in 2000); (3) Trends in International Mathematics and Science Study (TIMSS), which assesses math and science achievement of fourth-grade students every four years (first assessment in 1995) (National Center for Health Statistics, 2009).

In reading, in 2006, the average U.S. fourth-grade student's reading score (540) was slightly above the PIRLS average score of 500 but below the scores of 10 of 45 countries (Mullis & others, 2007). From 2001 to 2006, fourth-grade U.S. students' reading achievement scores showed no change. Fourth-grade students in the Russian Federation had the highest reading scores in 2006 as well as showing the greatest increase in reading scores from 2001 to 2006. Fourth-grade students in Hong Kong and Singapore showed similar increases.

In math, in 2006, U.S. 15-year-old students' average math score (474) was below the average math score of students in the 30 countries in the PISA assessment, placing U.S. students in the bottom quarter of participating countries. There was no change in U.S. 15-year-olds' math scores from 2003 to 2006. Fifteen-year-olds in Chinese Taipei, Finland, Korea, and Hong Kong had the highest math scores.

Also in math, in 2007, TIMSS results for U.S. fourth- and eighth-grade students' scores (529 and 508, respectively) were above the average of 500. Fourth-grade students in 8 of 35 countries scored higher than their U.S. counterparts; highest math scores were attained by East Asian countries, with Hong Kong fourth-graders having the highest scores. The average fourth-grade math score in 2007 was slightly higher (11 points) than in 1995. However, in several countries, dramatic improvement occurred over this time period—fourth-graders in Singapore improved by 63 points, in Latvia by 56 points, and in Iran by 55 points.

In science, in the 2006 PISA assessment, U.S. 15-year-old students scored below the average (489, with the average being 500), placing the U.S. students in the bottom one-third of students in the international comparisons (National Center for Education Statistics, 2007). Countries with the highest science scores for 15-year-olds in the 2006 assessment were Finland, Canada, and Japan.

In the 2007 TIMMS science assessment, both fourth- and eighth-grade U.S. students were above the international average in science (539 for fourth-graders and 520 for eighth-graders, with 500 being the average score). As in math comparisons, East Asian countries such as Singapore, Chinese Taipei, and Japan scored the highest on the international science comparisons. There was no change from 1995 to 2007 in U.S. fourth- and eighth-grade students' science scores in the TIMMS assessment.

Clearly, these international assessments indicate that the United States still has considerable room for progress in the reading, math, and science achievement of elementary and secondary school students. Especially disconcerting is the lack of substantial improvement in scores by U.S. students in most areas and at different grade levels in recent years.

## STANDARDIZED TESTS OF TEACHER CANDIDATES

Not only do students have to take standardized tests, but, as you are likely aware, so do teacher candidates. Many teacher candidates are required to take some version of the PRAXIS™ tests or a test created by an individual state.

**The PRAXIS™ Tests and State Tests for Teachers**   Most states now require teacher candidates to take a licensing exam. In some cases this involves one or more PRAXIS™ tests published by Educational Testing Service or a test that is used only by a particular state. A recent count indicated that 43 states now use PRAXIS™ tests (Hack, 2008). The tests used by states for licensing of teacher candidates assess (1) basic skills, or general academic ability; (2) subject-matter knowledge (such as math, English, science, or social studies); and/or (3) pedagogical knowledge. In many cases, there is little consistency across states in which specific tests are used.

The PRAXIS™ tests consist of PRAXIS I™, PRAXIS II™, and PRAXIS III™. The PRAXIS I™ test is a preliminary screening of basic skills that is often taken early in an undergraduate program or before a student is formally admitted to a teacher certification program.

PRAXIS II™ tests are essentially exit exams that typically are taken in the junior or senior year of undergraduate school to ensure that students know their specialty content areas and/or effective pedagogy before being awarded a preliminary teaching certificate (Shorall, 2009). The PRAXIS II™ tests cover four main categories: (1) organizing content knowledge for student learning, (2) creating an environment for student learning, (3) teaching for student learning, and (4) teacher professionalism. They use a case-study approach to measure students' pedagogical knowledge. The PRAXIS II™ tests are oriented toward specific age groups (elementary school—K–6; middle school—grades 5–9; and secondary school—grades 7–12).

PRAXIS III™ tests are assessments of classroom teaching performance. They are typically administered during the first year of teaching and can be used as part of a licensing decision. PRAXIS III™ tests include essays, oral response tests, listening tasks, portfolio reviews, video stimuli, and in-class observation.

Criticisms of the current PRAXIS™ and state licensure tests for teacher candidates have been made. Three such criticisms follow (Darling-Hammond & Baratz-Snowden, 2005, pp. 61–62):

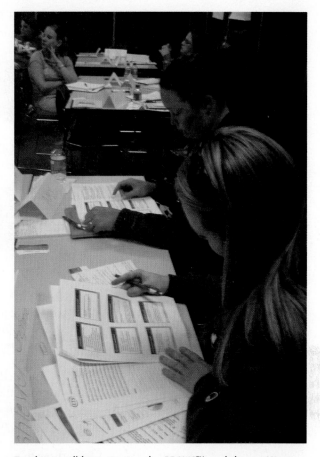

Teacher candidates at a two day PRAXIS™ workshop at Western Kentucky University—Elizabethtown. *What are some characteristics of the PRAXIS™ tests?*

- Tests assess *"low-level or marginally relevant knowledge and skills"* rather than *"deep knowledge of subject matter and actual teaching skills."*

- *The cutoff scores for the tests sometimes are low or not enforced.* If states are experiencing a shortage of teachers, "they often waive the testing requirement" and hire individuals who have failed the test.

- *There is a lack of consistency across states that has restricted teacher mobility.* This is especially a problem because some states have teacher surpluses, others teacher shortages.

DEVELOPMENT

I recently asked teachers about their experiences with the standardized tests for teacher certification. Following are their responses.

**EARLY CHILDHOOD**   Preschool teachers do not need to pass state-standardized tests. There are, however, certificate programs for those who choose to teach young children.

—**VALARIE GORHAM,** *Kiddie Quarters, Inc.*

**ELEMENTARY SCHOOL: GRADES K–5**   I honestly don't remember much about the test I took because it was over 19 years ago. What I do remember is that it was rigorous, and that I reviewed all I could think of in math, reading, and writing before the test. I also thought about and reflected on my education and what kind of philosophy I wanted to adopt as a teacher.

—**CRAIG JENSEN,** *Cooper Mountain Elementary School*

**MIDDLE SCHOOL: GRADES 6–8** Taking the PRAXIS™ test was an extremely intense and stressful time for me. For the PRAXIS™ II, I bought a study guide. I worked with the guide for about two weeks before the test, which prepared me—however, the test was still difficult because either you know the information or you don't.

—CASEY MAASS, *Edison Middle School*

**HIGH SCHOOL: GRADES 9–12** When taking these types of tests, it is important to be able to write with a clock blinking on the computer screen. I practiced for this particular scenario by playing video games so I got used to performing under the pressure of a blinking clock.

—SANDY SWANSON, *Menomonee Falls High School*

**The Call for a National Test for Teacher Candidates** Currently no national test is required for teacher candidates, but the call for one has been made. The National Academy of Education, which is made up of a distinguished group of educators, prepared *A Good Teacher in Every Classroom* (Darling-Hammond & Baratz-Snowden, 2005). The report states that the national test should assess a common core of knowledge for professional preparation, including how to create learning opportunities that make subjects accessible to all students. The National Academy of Education also recommended that the test results should be incorporated into state licensing requirements: Such a test, like those used to certify doctors, lawyers, and architects, should demonstrate not only what teachers *know* about their subjects and how to teach them but also what they can *do* in the classroom—for example, whether they can plan and implement lessons to teach standards, evaluate students' needs and design instruction to meet them, use a variety of teaching strategies, and maintain a purposeful, productive classroom. Fortunately, assessments that use videotapes of teaching and teachers' and students' work samples to evaluate what teachers actually do in the classroom have been developed by the National Board for Professional Teaching Standards (for use in certifying veteran accomplished teachers) and by states such as Connecticut for use in licensing beginning teachers (Darling-Hammond & Baratz-Snowden, 2005, pp. 62–63).

## Review, Reflect, and Practice

**2** Compare aptitude and achievement tests, and describe different types of achievement tests as well as some issues involved in these tests.

### REVIEW
- How can aptitude and achievement tests be compared?
- What are survey batteries, specific subject tests, and diagnostic tests?
- What are some possible advantages to high-stakes state standards-based testing, and what are some ways their results are being used? What are some criticisms of high-stakes state standards-based testing?
- How can standardized tests of teachers be characterized?

# Review, Reflect, and Practice

## REFLECT

- What value do you see in the No Child Left Behind legislation? What problems? Should No Child Left Behind legislation be abolished or retained? Explain.

## PRAXIS™ PRACTICE

1. Which of the following would be an appropriate use of an aptitude test?
   a. Josh takes a standardized test to help determine whether he is likely to be successful in medical school.
   b. Pete takes a standardized test to help determine what he has learned in his teacher preparation program.
   c. Stan takes a standardized test to determine to what degree he has met state mathematics standards.
   d. Penelope takes a standardized test to determine if she can graduate from high school.

2. Ms. Jerovitz is reviewing the results of a standardized achievement test her students have taken. She carefully examines and charts the scores on each of the subtests included in the test. She has scores in mathematical reasoning, computation, vocabulary, reading comprehension, spelling, science, and social studies. What type of test did her students most likely take?
   a. diagnostic test
   b. aptitude test
   c. intelligence test
   d. survey battery

3. Ms. Comer is frustrated by the state standards-based tests she must give to her third-grade students. State funding for the district is now tied to performance on these tests. As a result, Ms. Comer and other teachers are under pressure from the administration and board of education to ensure that all students meet state standards. Which of the following is the most likely outcome of this scenario?
   a. Ms. Comer and other teachers will become better teachers so that their students will achieve at higher levels.
   b. Ms. Comer and other teachers will begin to teach only the things that will be covered on the state standards-based test, thus narrowing the curriculum and student learning opportunities.
   c. Ms. Comer and other teachers will ignore the pressure from administrators and the board of education, continue to teach as they always have, and hope for the best.
   d. Ms. Comer and other teachers will spend more time enriching their curriculum so that students will achieve at higher levels.

4. Sally is nervous about the test she will be taking as part of the teacher certification process. The test will cover information regarding educational psychology and child development. Which test is Sally most likely taking?
   a. PRAXIS I™
   b. PRAXIS II™
   c. PRAXIS III™
   d. National Teacher Certification Test

*Please see the answer key at the end of the book.*

## 3 THE TEACHER'S ROLES

| Preparing Students To Take Standardized Tests | Understanding and Interpreting Test Results | Using Standardized Test Scores to Plan and Improve Instruction |

The teacher's roles in standardized testing include preparing students for the test, understanding and interpreting test results, and communicating test results to parents. Teachers also use test scores to plan and improve instruction.

## PREPARING STUDENTS TO TAKE STANDARDIZED TESTS

All students need the opportunity to do their best. One way to do this is to make sure that students have good test-taking skills (McMillan, 2011). You should communicate a positive attitude about the test to students. Explain the test's nature and purpose and describe it as an opportunity and a challenge rather than an ordeal. Avoid saying anything that can cause students to get nervous about the test. If you observe that anxiety in some students may hinder their performance, consider having a counselor talk with them about ways to reduce their test anxiety. Also, use challenging tasks that require critical thinking rather than the "drill and kill" approach that emphasizes rote memorization (Green & Johnson, 2010).

Here are some "don'ts" regarding teachers preparing students for standardized tests (McMillan, 2002): don't teach to the test, don't use the standardized test format for classroom tests, don't describe tests as a burden, don't tell students that important decisions will be made solely on the results of a single test, don't use previous forms of the same test to prepare students, and don't convey a negative attitude about the test.

I recently asked teachers how they prepare students for standardized tests. Following are their responses.

**EARLY CHILDHOOD**   A standard test is administered to our preschool children twice per school year. In September, it measures how much they know; in the spring, it measures how much they have learned. The test is hands-on; children manipulate materials and answer questions aloud. There is no preparation for this test.

—**VALARIE GORHAM,** *Kiddie Quarters, Inc.*

**ELEMENTARY SCHOOL: GRADES K–5**   We practice on sample tests, discussing the kinds of questions that will appear on the test, strategies for answers, and general good attitudes for test taking (for example, don't rush, read the whole question). We also reorganize the desks so that students get used to the testing configuration. I have students stretch, take deep breaths, and wriggle their fingers in order to warm up for the test. I also make a few cheerful comments before the test to relax them.

—**KEREN ABRA,** *Convent of the Sacred Heart Elementary School*

**MIDDLE SCHOOL: GRADES 6–8**   As a social studies teacher, I assist the language-arts and reading teachers in preparing students for the standardized exam by helping students build their writing skills. I assign essays after each unit and teach students to prepare the essays in the same way that they will need to do on the state test. The social studies department in my district meets monthly with the language-arts department so that we can work together to raise test scores.

—**CASEY MAASS,** *Edison Middle School*

## TEACHING CONNECTIONS: Best Practices
### Strategies for Improving Students' Test-Taking Skills

Here are some important test-taking skills that you might want to discuss with your students (Gronlund, 2009):

1. *Read the instructions carefully.*

2. *Read the items carefully.*

3. *Keep track of the time and work quickly enough to finish the test.*

4. *Skip difficult items and return to them later.*

5. *Make informed guesses instead of omitting items, if scoring favors doing so.*

6. *Eliminate as many items as possible on multiple-choice items.*

7. *Follow directions carefully in marking the answer (such as darkening the entire space).* Make sure students know how to do this by modeling a sample answer for them.

8. *Check to be sure that the appropriate response was marked on the answer sheet.*

9. *Go back and check answers if time permits.*

In Through the Eyes of Teachers, Marlene Wendler, a fourth-grade teacher in New Ulm, Minnesota, describes her experiences with standardized tests that her students take.

### THROUGH THE EYES OF TEACHERS
**Make Sure You Evaluate Your Students on More than Just Tests**

Standardized tests are just one very small, isolated picture of a child. A much fuller "video" comes from daily observations. Do not unfairly label a child based on a test. Rarely or never during the school year do my students encounter fill-in-the-oval items like those on standardized tests. Therefore, to be fair, before standardized testing I give them examples similar to the format of the test. If adults take a test with a special format, they prepare themselves by practicing in that format. Why should it be any different for children?

**HIGH SCHOOL: GRADES 9–12**   In addition to going over the standard test-taking strategies, we also stress the importance of eating a filling breakfast the day of the test and getting a good night's sleep the night before the test.

—**JENNIFER HEITER,** *Bremen High School*

## UNDERSTANDING AND INTERPRETING TEST RESULTS

Knowledge of some basic descriptive statistics will help you interpret standardized tests. Your ability to understand and interpret standardized tests will come in handy when you have parent-teacher conferences regarding children in your class. We will discuss these basic statistics as well as some ways that test results are commonly reported.

**Understanding Descriptive Statistics**   Our primary focus here is on **descriptive statistics,** which are mathematical procedures used to describe and summarize data (information) in a meaningful way. We will study frequency distributions, measures of central tendency, measures of variability, and the normal distribution.

**Frequency Distributions**   The first step in organizing data involves creating a **frequency distribution,** a listing of scores, usually from highest to lowest, along with the number of times each score appears. Imagine that a test was given and 21 students received the following scores on the test: 96, 95, 94, 92, 88, 88, 86, 86, 86, 86, 84, 83, 82, 82, 82, 78, 75, 75, 72, 68, and 62. Figure 15.1a shows a frequency distribution for these scores. Frequency distributions often are presented graphically. For example, a **histogram** is a frequency distribution in the form of a graph. Vertical bars represent the frequency of scores per category. Figure 15.1b shows a histogram for the 21 scores. A histogram often is called a *bar graph*. Notice in the histogram

**descriptive statistics** Mathematical procedures that are used to describe and summarize data (information) in a meaningful way.

**frequency distribution** A listing of scores, usually from highest to lowest, along with the number of times each score appears.

**histogram** A frequency distribution in the form of a graph.

(a) Frequency Distribution

| Score | Frequency |
|-------|-----------|
| 96 | 1 |
| 95 | 1 |
| 94 | 1 |
| 92 | 1 |
| 88 | 2 |
| 86 | 4 |
| 84 | 1 |
| 83 | 1 |
| 82 | 3 |
| 78 | 1 |
| 75 | 2 |
| 72 | 1 |
| 68 | 1 |
| 62 | 1 |

(b) Histogram

FIGURE **15.1**  A FREQUENCY DISTRIBUTION AND HISTOGRAM

that the horizontal axis (the *x*-axis) indicates the obtained scores and the vertical axis (the *y*-axis) indicates how often each score occurs.

Although representing a group of scores graphically can provide insight about students' performance, so can some statistical techniques that represent scores numerically. These techniques involve the concepts of central tendency and variability, each of which we will discuss.

***Measures of Central Tendency***    A measure of **central tendency** is a number that provides information about the average, or typical, score in a set of data. There are three primary measures of central tendency: mean, median, and mode. The **mean** is the numerical average of a group of scores, commonly labeled as $\overline{X}$ or $M$ by statisticians. The mean is computed by adding all the scores and then dividing the sum by the number of scores. Thus, the mean for the 21 students' test scores above is 1,740/21 = 82.86. The mean often is a good indicator of the central tendency of a group of scores.

The **median** is the score that falls exactly in the middle of a distribution of scores after they have been arranged (or ranked) from highest to lowest. In our example of 21 test scores, the median is the 11th ranked score (10 above, 10 below it), so the median is 84.

The **mode** is the score that occurs most often. The mode can be determined easily by looking at the frequency distribution or histogram. In our example of 21 scores, the mode is 86 (the score occurring most often—four times). The mode is most revealing when its value is much more frequent than the other values or scores. For example, in the 21 scores in our example, if 15 of the 21 scores had been the same,

**central tendency** A number that provides information about the average, or typical, score in a set of data.

**mean** The numerical average of a group of scores.

**median** The score that falls exactly in the middle of a distribution of scores after they have been arranged (or ranked) from highest to lowest.

**mode** The score that occurs most often.

MISS PEACH. By permission of Mell Lazarus and Creators Syndicate, Inc.

then the mode probably would be the best measure of central tendency for the data. In this case, the mean and median would be less meaningful.

A set of scores may have more than one mode. For example, in our example of 21 students taking a test, if four students had scored 86 and four students had scored 75, then the set of scores would have two modes (86 and 75). A set of scores with two modes is called a *bimodal distribution*. It is possible for a set of scores to have more than two modes, in which case it is called a *multimodal distribution*.

**Measures of Variability**　In addition to obtaining information about the central tendency of a set of scores, it also is important to know about their variability. **Measures of variability** tell us how much the scores vary from one another. Two measures of variability are range and standard deviation.

The **range** is the distance between the highest and lowest scores. The range of the 21 students' test scores in our example is 34 points (96 − 62 = 34). The range is a rather simple measure of variability and it is not used often. The most commonly used measure of variability is the standard deviation.

The **standard deviation** is a measure of how much a set of scores varies on the average around the mean of the scores. In other words, it reveals how closely scores cluster around the mean (Frey, 2005). The smaller the standard deviation, the less the scores tend to vary from the mean. The greater the standard deviation, the more the scores tend to spread out from the mean. Calculating a standard deviation is not very difficult, especially if you have a calculator that computes square roots. To calculate a standard deviation, follow these four steps:

1. Find the mean of the scores.
2. From each score, subtract the mean, then square the difference between the score and the mean. (Squaring the scores will eliminate any minus signs that result from subtracting the mean.)
3. Add the squares, then divide that sum by the number of scores.
4. Compute the square root of the value obtained in step 3. This is the standard deviation.

The formula for these four steps is

$$\sqrt{\frac{\Sigma(\chi - \overline{\chi})^2}{N}}$$

where $\chi$ = the individual score and $\overline{\chi}$ = the mean, $N$ = the number of scores, and $\Sigma$ means "the sum of." Applying this formula to the test scores of the 21 students,

1. We already computed the mean of the scores and found that it was 82.86.
2. Subtract 82.86 from the first score: 96 − 82.86 = 13.14. Square 13.14 to get 172.66. Save the value, and go on to do the same for the second score, the third score, and so on.
3. Add the 21 scores to get 1,543.28. Divide the sum by 21: 1,543.28/21 = 73.49.
4. Find the square root of 73.49. The result is 8.57, the standard deviation.

Calculators are very helpful in computing a standard deviation. To evaluate your knowledge of and skills in computing the various measures of central tendency and variability we have described, complete Self-Assessment 15.1.

Mastering these kinds of descriptive statistics is useful not only for classroom work but also for understanding research results. The standard deviation is a better measure of variability than the range because the range represents information about only two bits of data (the highest and lowest scores), whereas the standard deviation represents combined information about all the data. It also usually is more helpful to know how much test scores are spread out or clustered together than to know the highest and lowest scores. If a teacher gives a test and the standard deviation turns out to be very low, it means the scores tend to cluster around the same value. That

*"Tonight, we're going to let the statistics speak for themselves."*

© Edward Koren/The New Yorker Collection/
www.cartoonbank.com

**measures of variability** Measures that tell how much scores vary from one another.

**range** The distance between the highest and lowest scores.

**standard deviation** A measure of how much a set of scores varies on the average around the mean of the scores.

# SELF-ASSESSMENT 15.1
## Evaluating My Knowledge of and Skills in Computing Measures of Central Tendency and Variability

Examine each of these statements and place a check mark next to the statement if you feel confident of your knowledge of the concept and your skill in computing the measure or using the instrument.

_____ I know what a frequency distribution is.
_____ I can describe what a histogram is and know how to create one.
_____ I understand what a mean is and know how to compute it.
_____ I understand what a median is and know how to calculate it.
_____ I know what a mode is and am aware of how to compute it.
_____ I know what a range is and how to arrive at it.
_____ I can discuss what a standard deviation is and know how to compute it.
_____ I have a good calculator and know how to use it to compute basic descriptive statistics.

For any items that you did not check off, go back and study the concept again. If you are still not confident about computing the various measures, seek additional help from a college instructor, a math-skills tutor (many colleges have these available for students), or a capable friend. Practice the calculations in order to absorb the concepts.

could mean that everyone in the class learned the material equally well, but it more likely suggests that the test was too easy and is not discriminating very effectively between students who mastered the material and those who did not.

***The Normal Distribution*** In a **normal distribution,** most of the scores cluster around the mean. The farther above or below the mean we travel, the less frequently each score occurs. A normal distribution also is called a *normal curve, bell-shaped curve,* or *bell curve.* Many characteristics, such as human intelligence measured by intelligence tests, athletic ability, weight, and height, follow or approximate a normal distribution. Normal distributions are useful to know about because when testing a large number of students with a good standardized test, the graph of resulting scores will tend to resemble a normal curve (Bart & Kato, 2008).

We presented the normal distribution for standardized testing of intelligence in Chapter 4. Here we provide a more detailed description of the normal distribution, including some important characteristics (see Figure 15.2). First, the normal distribution is symmetrical. Because of this symmetry, the mean, median, and mode are identical in a normal distribution. Second, its bell shape shows that the most common scores are near the middle. The scores become less frequent the farther away from the middle they appear (that is, as they become more extreme). Third, the normal distribution incorporates information about both the mean and the standard deviation. The area on the normal curve that is 1 standard deviation above the mean and 1 standard deviation below it represents 68.26 percent of the scores. At 2 standard deviations above and below the mean, 95.42 percent of the scores are represented. Finally, at 3 standard deviations above and below the mean, 99.74 percent of the scores are included. If we apply this information to the normal distribution of IQ scores in the population, 68 percent of the population has an IQ between 85 and 115, 95 percent an IQ between 70 and 130, and 99 percent between 55 and 145.

**Interpreting Test Results** Understanding descriptive statistics provides the foundation for effectively interpreting test results. A **raw score** is the number of items the student answered correctly on the test. Raw scores, by themselves, are not very useful because they don't provide information about how easy or difficult the test was or how the student fared compared with other students. Test publishers usually provide teachers

**normal distribution** *A bell-shaped curve* in which most of the scores are clustered around the mean; the farther above or below the mean that we travel, the less frequently each score occurs.

**raw score** The number of items the student answered correctly on the test.

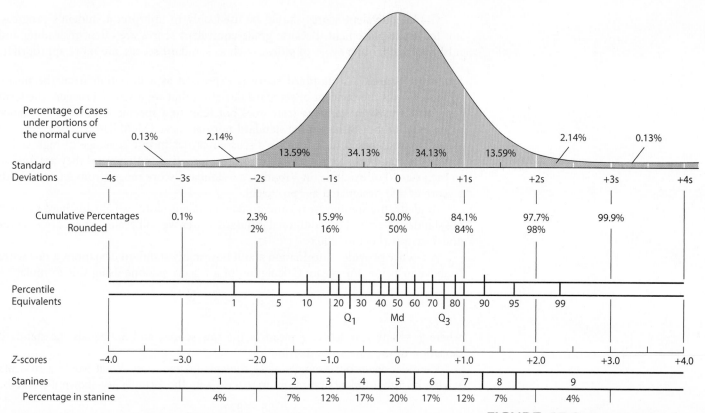

FIGURE **15.2** SOME COMMONLY REPORTED TEST SCORES BASED ON THE NORMAL CURVE

with many different kinds of scores that go beyond raw scores. These include percentile-rank scores, stanine scores, grade-equivalent scores, and standard scores.

***Percentile-Rank Scores***   A **percentile-rank score** reveals the percentage of the distribution that lies at or below the score. It also provides information about the score's position in relation to the rest of the scores. Percentile ranks range from 1 to 99. If a student has a percentile rank of 81 on a test, it means that the student performed as well as or higher on the test than 81 percent of the sample who made up the norm group. Note that percentiles do not refer to percentages of items answered correctly on the test. Percentile rank for standardized tests is determined by comparison with the norm group distribution. Different comparison groups may be used in computing percentile ranks, such as urban norms or suburban norms.

***Stanine Scores***   A **stanine score** describes a student's test performance on a nine-point scale ranging from 1 to 9. Scores of 1, 2, and 3 are usually considered to be below average; 4, 5, and 6 average; and 7, 8, and 9 above average. As in the case of a student's percentile rank score, a stanine score in one subject area (such as science) can be compared with the student's stanine score in other areas (such as math, reading, and social studies).

A stanine refers to a specific percentage of the normal curve's area. The correspondence between a stanine score and a percentile-rank score is shown in Figure 15.3. A stanine score provides a more general index of a student's performance, whereas a percentile rank score yields a more precise estimation.

***Grade-Equivalent Scores***   A **grade-equivalent score** indicates a student's performance in relation to grade level and months of the school year, assuming a 10-month school year, to the norm group. Thus, a grade-equivalent score of 4.5 refers to fourth grade, fifth month in school. A grade equivalent of 6.0 stands for the beginning of the sixth grade. In some test reports, a decimal is omitted so that 45 is the same as 4.5 and 60 is the same as 6.0.

| Stanine Score | Percentile Rank Score |
|:---:|:---:|
| 9 | 96 or Higher |
| 8 | 89–95 |
| 7 | 77–88 |
| 6 | 60–76 |
| 5 | 40–59 |
| 4 | 23–39 |
| 3 | 11–22 |
| 2 | 4–10 |
| 1 | Below 4 |

FIGURE **15.3** THE RELATION BETWEEN STANINE SCORE AND PERCENTILE-RANK SCORE

**percentile-rank score**  The percentage of a distribution that lies at or below the score.

**stanine score**  A nine-point scale that describes a student's performance.

**grade-equivalent score**  A score that indicates a student's performance in relation to grade level and months of the school year, assuming a 10-month school year.

Grade-equivalent scores should be used only to interpret a student's progress, not for grade placement. Because grade-equivalent scores are often misleading and misinterpreted, other types of scores, such as standard scores, are more appropriate.

***Standard Scores*** A **standard score** is expressed as a deviation from the mean, which involves the concept of standard deviation that we discussed earlier. The term *standard* as used in *standard score* does not refer to a specific level of performance or expectation but rather to the standard normal curve (McMillan, 2011). Scores on state standards-based tests that we discussed earlier in our coverage of high-stakes testing are standard scores derived from raw score distributions, and they are unique to each state. For example, in Virginia, the standard score ranges from 0 to 600, with a score of 400 designated as "proficient."

Actually, the stanine scores and grade-equivalent scores we already have profiled are standard scores. Two additional standard scores we will evaluate here are *z*-scores and *T*-scores (Peyton, 2005).

A ***z*-score** provides information about how many standard deviations a raw score is above or below the mean. Calculation of a *z*-score is done using this formula:

$$z\text{-score} = \frac{\chi - \bar{\chi}}{SD}$$

where $\chi$ = any raw score, $\chi$ mean of the raw scores, and *SD* equals the standard deviation of the raw score distribution.

Consider again our example of 21 students taking a test. What would a student's *z*-score be if the student's raw score were 86? Using the formula just shown it would be

$$\frac{86 - 82.6}{8.57} = .37$$

Thus, the raw score of 86 is .37 of a standard deviation above the mean. The *z*-score mean is 0 and the standard deviation is 1.

In addition to showing a student's relative placement on a test, standard scores also allow for comparisons across different types of tests. For example, a student may score 1 standard deviation above the mean on a math test and 1 standard deviation below the mean on a reading test. Comparisons of raw scores don't always allow for such comparisons.

***Don't Overinterpret Test Results*** Use caution in interpreting small differences in test scores, especially percentile-rank and grade-equivalent test scores. All tests have some degree of error. A good strategy is to think of a score not as a single number but as a location in a band or general range. Small differences in test scores are usually not meaningful.

Some test reports include percentile bands, a range of scores (rather than a single score) expressed in percentiles, such as 75th to 85th percentile for an obtained score of 80. This is referred to as the *standard error of measurement.* The Metropolitan Achievement Tests use percentile bands in reporting scores. A percentile rank of 6 to 8 points or a two- to five-month grade-equivalence difference between two students rarely indicates any meaningful difference in achievement.

When considering information from a standardized test, don't evaluate it in isolation (Neukrug & Fawcett, 2006). Evaluate it in conjunction with other information you know about the student and your classroom instruction. Most manuals that accompany standardized tests warn against overinterpretation.

## USING STANDARDIZED TEST SCORES TO PLAN AND IMPROVE INSTRUCTION

Teachers can use standardized test scores from the end of the previous year in planning their instruction for the next year and as a way to evaluate the effectiveness of

**standard score** A score expressed as a deviation from the mean; involves the standard deviation.

**z-score** A score that provides information about how many standard deviations a raw score is above or below the mean.

instruction after content and skills have been taught (McMillan, 2007). Any use of standardized test results should be made in conjunction with information from other sources.

Prior to instruction, standardized test results may provide an indication of the general ability of the students in the class. This can help the teacher select the appropriate level of instruction and materials to begin the school year. A standardized test should not be used to develop a very low or very high expectation for a student or the entire class. Expectations should be appropriate and reasonable. If the results of a reading readiness test suggest that the class overall lacks appropriate reading skills, the teacher needs to carefully select reading materials that the students will be able to understand.

A very recent development involves test publishers and school districts developing items that correspond to the standards in state tests, then allowing schools or teachers to pull from an item bank to "test" progress toward meeting the standard, typically at each nine weeks of the school year (McMillan, 2007). The intent is to provide an evaluation of student learning that can be used to plan subsequent teaching weekly or monthly. Usually these "benchmark" or "interim" tests are online, and information about them can be found on the Web sites of major testing companies, such as Educational Testing Service.

Standardized tests are sometimes used in grouping students. In cooperative learning, it is common to group students so that a wide range of abilities is reflected in the group. However, a single test score or single test should not be used by itself for any instructional purpose. It always should be used in conjunction with other information.

The subscales of tests (such as in reading and math) can be used to pinpoint strengths and weaknesses of incoming students in particular subject areas. This can help teachers to determine the amount of instruction to give in different areas. If students' achievement is considerably lower than what is expected on the basis of ability testing, they may need further testing, special attention, or counseling.

## TEACHING CONNECTIONS: Best Practices
### Strategies for Communicating Test Results to Parents

Here are some good strategies for communicating test results to parents (McMillan, 1997):

1. *Don't report the test scores in isolation.* Report the scores in the context of the student's overall work and performance on other classroom assessments. This will help keep parents from placing too much importance on a score from a single standardized test.

2. *Try to use easy-to-understand language when you describe the students' test results to parents.* Don't get caught up in using obscure test language. Report the information in your own words.

3. *Let parents know that the scores are approximate rather than absolute.* You might say something about how various internal and external factors can affect students' test scores.

4. *Recognize that percentile scores or bands are the easiest set of scores for parents to understand.* Be sure to help parents understand the difference between percentile and percentage.

5. *Prior to the conference, spend some time familiarizing yourself with the student's test report.* Make sure you know how to interpret each score you report to parents. It is not a good idea just to show parents the numbers on a test report. You will need to summarize what the scores mean. Parents of early elementary students are likely to have the most questions because they are likely to have the least experience dealing with standardized test scores. Allow plenty of time to review and explain the scores.

6. *Be ready to answer questions that parents might have about their child's strengths, weaknesses, and progress.* Most standardized tests don't measure progress. However, you can apprise parents of progress their student is making.

7. *Rather than talking "to" or lecturing parents, talk "with" them in a discussion format.* After you have described a test result, invite them to ask questions that will help you to further clarify for them what the test results mean.

Standardized tests administered after instruction can be used to evaluate the effectiveness of instruction and the curriculum. Students should score well in the areas that have been emphasized in instruction. If they do not, then both the test itself and the instruction need to be analyzed to determine why this is the case.

In using standardized tests to plan and improve instruction—we emphasize again—it is important not to use a single test or test score to make decisions. Placement decisions in particular should be made on the basis of information from multiple sources, including prior teachers' comments, grades, systematic observations, and further assessments. It also is very important to (1) guard against using a single test to develop an expectation for a student's ability and (2) make sure that the student's test scores reflect a fair assessment.

There likely will be times as a teacher when you will need to communicate test results that involve statistics to parents. In Teaching Connections, you can read about some strategies for communicating effectively with parents about test results.

## Review, Reflect, and Practice

**3** Identify the teacher's roles in standardized testing.

### REVIEW

- What are effective ways to prepare students for standardized tests?
- What roles do frequency distributions, measures of central tendency and variability, and normal distributions play in describing standardized test results? What are some different types of scores? How should scores be evaluated?
- How can standardized tests be used in planning and improving instruction?

### REFLECT

- Considering the grade level and subject(s) that you plan to teach, how might standardized test results be useful to you in your instructional planning?

### PRAXIS™ PRACTICE

1. Mark, Jenny, Nicole, and Chris are all taking the SAT this year. Which student is preparing the most wisely?
   a. Chris, who has taken a test-taking skills test every year throughout high school
   b. Jenny, who has consistently taken relatively easy high school courses, and has gotten straight *A*'s
   c. Mark, who has enrolled in a specialized, expensive SAT preparation program
   d. Nicole, who has taken a rigorous high school program of studies, and has reviewed some of the math she took in her early high school years

2. Ms. Scott has just received the standardized test scores for her class. As she reviews each of them, she notices that Pete scored at the 98th percentile on the reading portion of this nationally normed test. What does this mean?
   a. Pete did better than all but 2 percent of the norm group on the test.
   b. Pete's score is 1 standard deviation above the mean score of the norm group.
   c. Pete got 98 percent of the answers correct on the reading portion of the test.
   d. Pete's score is 3 standard deviations above the mean score of the norm group.

3. Which of the following is an example of best practices in using the results of standardized tests to plan and improve instruction?
   a. Ms. Carter uses her students' standardized test scores to determine their placement in her class.

## Review, Reflect, and Practice

### PRAXIS™ PRACTICE (CONTINUED)

b. Mr. Peabody decides that the standardized test scores are invalid when his students do not do well in an area he emphasized in class.

c. Mr. Lemhert looks at the standardized test scores of each student and uses the information to help him identify relative strengths and weaknesses.

d. Ms. Ziegler uses her students' standardized test scores to explain their classroom performance to their parents.

*Please see the answer key at the end of the book.*

## ④ ISSUES IN STANDARDIZED TESTS

| Standardized Tests, Alternative Assessments, and High-Stakes Testing | Diversity and Standardized Testing |
|---|---|

As we have already mentioned, standardized testing is controversial. One debate concerns how standardized tests stack up against alternative methods of assessment, especially in high-stakes state standards-based testing. Another is about whether standardized tests discriminate against ethnic minority students and students from low-income backgrounds.

## STANDARDIZED TESTS, ALTERNATIVE ASSESSMENTS, AND HIGH-STAKES TESTING

As we will explain in greater detail in Chapter 16, alternative assessments include assessments of student performance, such as assessments of oral presentations, real-world problem solving, projects, and portfolios (systematic and organized collections of the student's work that demonstrate the student's skills and accomplishments) (Burke, 2010). Which is the best way to assess student performance—standardized tests that mainly rely on multiple-choice questions, or alternative assessments?

Some experts argue that performance tests should be used, either instead of standardized tests that mainly include multiple-choice questions or at least as part of the student's total assessment (Wiggins, 1992). The argument is that performance assessment is more meaningful, involves higher-level thinking skills, and fits better with current educational reform that emphasizes constructivist and social constructivist learning. In Kentucky and Vermont, the inclusion of problem solving in mathematics and the written communication of mathematical ideas on state-mandated tests led teachers to work more on these areas in their math instruction. However, use of performance assessments for large-scale assessments can be problematic because their reliability can be low, the amount of time and energy required is often too extensive, and performance assessments don't typically address a wide range of learning outcomes.

Standardized tests are especially helpful in providing information about comparability from a "big picture" perspective. Comparing their class with the one down the hall won't give teachers the information they need about where their students stand compared with the broader population of students. Standardized tests can provide better information about "big picture" questions: Are my fourth-grade students learning basic math? Can my seventh-grade students read at a predefined level of competency?

At the same time, teachers are urged to scrupulously avoid any misuses of tests or test results and to educate themselves about tests so that they understand their

---

**Thinking Back/Thinking Forward**

A trend in alternative assessment is to increasingly use authentic assessment that approximates the real world or real life as closely as possible. Chapter 16, p. 564

Thinking Back/Thinking Forward

Creating culture-fair tests is very difficult, so difficult that Robert Sternberg concludes that there are no culture-fair tests, only culture-reduced tests. Chapter 4, p. 123

capabilities and limitations, not asking tests to do more than they can or are intended to do. They also say a standardized test should be only one of a number of assessments used to evaluate students.

## DIVERSITY AND STANDARDIZED TESTING

Earlier in the chapter we raised the issue of fairness in standardized testing (McMillan, 2011). And in Chapter 4, we discussed issues related to diversity and assessment. A special concern is cultural bias in tests and the importance of creating culturally responsive tests for diagnostic and instructional purposes (Banks, 2010; Nieto, 2010). Because of the potential for cultural bias in standardized tests, it is important to assess students using a variety of methods. As indicated earlier, some assessment experts emphasize that performance and portfolio assessments reduce some of the inequity that characterizes standardized tests for ethnic minority students and students from low-income backgrounds (Stiggins, 2008).

In sum, portfolio assessment holds promise by focusing instruction on higher-level thinking skills, providing useful feedback to teachers about students' thinking skills, and emphasizing real-world problem solving (Burke, 2010). However, portfolio assessment is not currently used as part of NCLB or other large-scale standardized testing. As indicated earlier, using portfolio and performance assessment as part of large-scale standardized testing can be problematic.

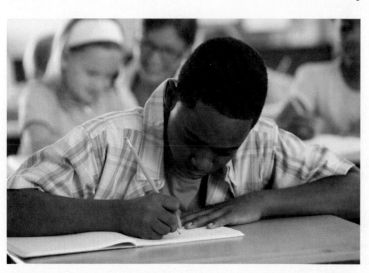

*How might standardized tests discriminate against ethnic minority students?*

DIVERSITY

### Review, Reflect, and Practice

**4** Evaluate some key issues in standardized testing.

**REVIEW**

- Why is it argued that performance assessments should accompany standardized tests in high-stakes testing? What are some problems in using performance assessments as part of large-scale standardized testing?
- What characterizes concern about diversity and standardized tests?

**REFLECT**

- In what situations would you rather be tested with standardized testing? With performance assessments? Why?

**PRAXIS™ PRACTICE**

1. Which of the following is the best example of a performance test used to issue a driver's license?
   a. a road test
   b. a written test covering the rules of the road
   c. a vision test
   d. a computerized test covering the meaning of road signs
2. What is a good test strategy to avoid cultural bias?
   a. Use a single, good standardized test to control for extraneous influences.
   b. Assess students using a variety of methods.
   c. Assume that ethnic differences are due to heredity.
   d. Avoid using portfolios for assessment purposes.

*Please see the answer key at the end of the book.*

# The Standardized Test Pressure

Ms. Pryor teaches third grade at Pulaski Elementary School in Steelton. In her state, third grade is the first grade at which students are tested using the state-wide standardized test. The test, given in March of each year, is supposed to measure how well the school is doing at meeting state standards in math, science, reading, writing, and social studies. This test yields individual, classroom, school, and district scores, and compares these to state averages. The state uses district-level scores to address school funding. Schools that have a large percentage of students who do not meet or exceed state standards run the risk of losing a portion of their funding. In recent years, the Steelton School District has broadened the purpose of the state-mandated tests to include how well an individual teacher is doing at helping the students to meet state standards. Student scores have become part of the teacher-evaluation process. Steelton teachers receive merit points based on the percentage of their class that meets or exceeds state standards. Those with more merit points are given greater consideration if they request an in-district transfer, reimbursement for attending conferences, or release time for other development activities. Ms. Pryor has always received merit points for her students' performance on this test.

In addition to the state test, the district uses a nationally normed test to assess achievement. This test yields individual scores as they relate to national norms. These scores are reported as percentile-rank scores and grade-equivalent scores. This test is generally given near the beginning of the school year. The district uses the results of these tests to identify students in need of special education services or enrichment programs.

Ms. Pryor is not thrilled about giving her students so many standardized tests. She says, "Sometimes it seems all we do is prepare for these tests and take them." However, she makes sure she has taught her students appropriate test-taking strategies. She also tries to give her students some experiences that mirror the standardized tests, such as filling in bubbles on answer sheets, and having limited time in which to complete tests. She carefully goes over tests from previous years and uses them to write lesson plans. She is certain to have covered everything covered on previous state tests prior to the test in March, leaving the "fun stuff" for the end of the school year. The week before state testing, Ms. Pryor sends notes home to parents asking them to ensure that their children get adequate sleep and eat breakfast during testing weeks. After all, student performance on these tests impacts how the school is perceived and whether or not Ms. Pryor will receive merit points.

In the past, some groups of students have been excused from state testing. These students included those with learning disabilities and those who were not proficient at English. However, this year the rules have changed. The state now mandates that all students be tested regardless of ability or primary language. This concerns Ms. Pryor. If these students are included in the state testing, it is rather unlikely that all of her class will meet or exceed state standards, resulting in no merit points for Ms. Pryor.

After receiving the results of the nationally normed tests, Ms. Pryor devises a strategy to ensure that more of her students will meet or exceed state standards on the state test in the spring. She begins by looking at her students' national percentile scores. She separates the students into three groups—those who scored above the 60th percentile, those who scored between the 40th and 60th percentiles, and those who scored below the 40th percentile. Her reasoning is that those who scored above the 60th percentile will meet state standards with no problem. In fact, many of them probably already have met state standards for third grade, given their grade-equivalent scores on the national test. She needn't worry about this group. Those who scored below the 40th percentile are not likely to meet state standards no matter what she does. Some may come close, but the return on her effort is not likely to be great. That leaves the middle group. She reasons that if she works intensively with this group, she has a chance of helping them to meet state standards—and that if they do, she will meet her goal in terms of merit points.

1. What testing issues are evident in this case?

2. What does Ms. Pryor do correctly in terms of preparing her students to take standardized tests?

3. What does Ms. Pryor do incorrectly in terms of preparing her students to take standardized tests?

4. What does it mean if a student's national percentile-rank score is 60?
   a. The student got 60 percent of the items correct.
   b. The student scored as well as or better than 60 percent of the students in the norm group.
   c. The student scored as well as or worse than 60 percent of the students in the norm group.
   d. The student scored as well as or better than 60 percent of the students in his class.

5. When Ms. Pryor uses percentile-rank scores on the nationally normed achievement test to evaluate likely performance on the state-mandated test, what is she likely expecting from the nationally normed test?
   a. She expects the nationally normed test to have predictive ability for the state-mandated test.
   b. She expects the nationally normed test to have concurrent validity.
   c. She expects the nationally normed test to have test-retest reliability.
   d. She expects the nationally normed test to have split-half reliability.

6. In what ways is it evident that the state-mandated test is a high-stakes test?

7. Why do you think Ms. Pryor decided only to concentrate her efforts at the middle of her class?

8. To what extent do you agree with her strategy? Why?

# Reach Your **Learning Goals**

## Standardized Tests and Teaching

**① THE NATURE OF STANDARDIZED TESTS:** Discuss the nature and purpose of standardized tests as well as the criteria for evaluating them.

Standardized Tests and
Their Purposes

Standardized tests have uniform procedures for administration and scoring. Many standardized tests allow a student's performance to be compared with the performance of other students at the same age or grade level on a national basis. The purposes of standardized tests include providing information about students' progress, diagnosing students' strengths and weaknesses, providing evidence for placement of students in specific programs, providing information for planning and improving instruction, and contributing to accountability. Interest in accountability has led to the creation of state standards-based high-stakes benchmark testing. Important decisions about students should be made not on the basis of a single standardized test but rather on the basis of information from a variety of assessments.

Criteria for Evaluating
Standardized Tests

The most important ways to evaluate standardized tests involve whether they are norm-referenced or criterion-referenced, and the extent to which they yield valid, reliable, and fair scores. Norm-referenced tests involve comparing a student's performance with a group of individuals previously tested that provides a basis for interpreting the student's score. National norms are based on a nationally representative group of students. Criterion-referenced tests are standardized tests in which the student's performance is compared to established criteria rather than norms. State standardized tests are typically criterion-referenced, and criterion-referenced tests are designed to assess skills and knowledge in specific areas, such as English, math, and science. Validity is the extent to which a test measures what it is intended to measure and the extent to which inferences about test scores are accurate and appropriate. Three important types of validity are content validity, criterion validity (which can be either concurrent or predictive), and construct validity. Reliability is the extent to which a test produces a consistent, reproducible measure of performance. Reliable measures are stable, dependable, and relatively free from errors of measurement. Reliability can be measured in several ways, including test-retest reliability, alternate-forms reliability, and split-half reliability. Fair tests are unbiased and nondiscriminatory, uninfluenced by irrelevant factors such as gender, ethnicity, or bias on the part of the scorer.

**② APTITUDE AND ACHIEVEMENT TESTS:** Compare aptitude and achievement tests, and describe different types of achievement tests as well as some issues involved in these tests.

Comparing Aptitude and
Achievement Tests

An aptitude test predicts a student's ability to learn, or what the student can accomplish with further education and training. An achievement test measures what the student has learned, or the skills the student has mastered. Aptitude tests include general mental ability tests, such as intelligence tests, and specific tests used to predict success in an academic subject or occupational area. The SAT test can be used as either an aptitude test or as an achievement test.

Types of Standardized
Achievement Tests

Standardized achievement tests include survey batteries (individual subject-matter tests that are designed for a particular level of students), specific subject tests (to assess a skill in a more detailed, extensive way than a survey battery), and diagnostic tests (given to students to pinpoint specific learning needs so those needs can be met with regular or remedial instruction).

| High-Stakes State Standards-Based Tests | Some possible advantages of high-stakes state standards-based testing are improved student performance; more time teaching subjects being tested; high expectations for all students; identification of poorly performing schools, teachers, and administrators; and improved confidence in schools as test scores improve. High-stakes state standards-based tests are being used in decisions about remediation, promotion, and graduation. They are criticized for "dumbing down" and narrowing the curriculum, promoting rote memorization, encouraging teachers to "teach to the test," and discriminating against students from low-income and minority backgrounds. National assessment of educational progress is periodically assessed in the United States, and only slight improvements have been made in recent years by U.S. elementary and secondary school students in reading, math, and science. International comparisons on standardized tests show that U.S. students have considerable room for improvement in reading, math, and science achievement, especially in comparison to students in a number of East Asian countries. |

| Standardized Tests of Teacher Candidates | Most teacher candidates have to take one or more standardized tests as part of licensure to teach in a particular state. Many states use one or more of the PRAXIS™ tests created by Educational Testing Service, although some states create their own test. Criticisms of the current tests of teacher candidates have been made, and a call for a national test of teacher candidates has been made. |

## 3 THE TEACHER'S ROLES: Identify the teacher's roles in standardized testing.

| Preparing Students to Take Standardized Tests | Make sure that students have good test-taking skills; communicate a positive attitude about the test to students; describe the test as an opportunity, not an ordeal; and avoid saying anything to raise students' anxiety. |

| Understanding and Interpreting Test Results | Descriptive statistics are math procedures used to describe and summarize data in a meaningful way. A frequency distribution is a listing of scores, usually from highest to lowest, along with the number of times each score appears. A histogram is one way that frequency distribution information can be presented. Measures of central tendency include the mean, median, and mode. Measures of variability tell how much scores vary and include the range and standard deviation. The normal distribution is also called a bell-shaped curve, in which most scores cluster around the mean. A normal distribution is symmetrical and incorporates information about both the mean and the standard deviation. A raw score is the number of items a student gets right on a test, which typically is not as useful as many other types of scores. Percentile-rank scores reveal the percentage of the distribution that lies at or below the particular score. Stanine scores describe a student's performance on a nine-point scale ranging from 1 to 9. Grade-equivalent scores indicate a student's performance in relation to grade level and months of the school year. Standard scores are expressed as a deviation from the mean and involve the concept of standard deviation ($z$-scores are examples of standard scores). Avoid overinterpreting test results. A good strategy is to think of a score not as a single score but as being located in a band or general range. Don't evaluate standardized test results in isolation from other information about the student, such as classroom performance and the nature of instruction. |

| Using Standardized Test Scores to Plan and Improve Instruction | Standardized test scores can be used to plan and improve instruction either prior to instruction or after instruction. They sometimes are used in grouping students, but it is important to guard against unrealistic expectations for students based on standardized test scores. The subscales of tests can be used to pinpoint students' strengths and weaknesses in particular subject areas, which can help teachers determine the amount of instruction to give in different areas. Standardized tests should always be used in conjunction with other information about students and the appropriateness and fairness of the tests evaluated. |

**ISSUES IN STANDARDIZED TESTS:** Evaluate some key issues in standardized testing.

> **Standardized Tests, Alternative Assessments, and High-Stakes Testing**

There is disagreement about the value of standardized tests versus alternative assessments such as performance tests and portfolio assessments. When used correctly, standardized tests have value but provide only part of the assessment picture and do have limits. Some assessment experts and teachers emphasize that high-stakes state standards-based testing should include more alternative assessments. However, using performance assessments in large-scale standardized testing can be problematic.

> **Diversity and Standardized Testing**

Cultural bias is of special concern in standardized testing. Some assessment experts believe that performance assessments have the potential to reduce bias in testing.

## KEY TERMS

standardized tests 515
standards-based tests 516
high-stakes testing 516
norm group 517
norm-referenced tests 517
criterion-referenced tests 517
validity 517
content validity 517
criterion validity 517

concurrent validity 517
predictive validity 518
construct validity 518
reliability 518
test-retest reliability 518
alternate-forms
   reliability 518
split-half reliability 518
aptitude test 520

achievement test 521
descriptive statistics 533
frequency distribution 533
histogram 533
central tendency 534
mean 534
median 534
mode 534
measures of variability 535

range 535
standard deviation 535
normal distribution 536
raw score 536
percentile-rank score 537
stanine score 537
grade-equivalent score 537
standard score 538
z-score 538

## PORTFOLIO ACTIVITIES

Now that you have a good understanding of this chapter, complete these exercises to expand your thinking.

### Independent Reflection: Find a Frequency Distribution

Create a frequency distribution and histogram for the following scores: 98, 96, 94, 94, 92, 90, 90, 88, 86, 86, 86, 82, 80, 80, 80, 80, 80, 78, 76, 72, 70, 68, 64. (INTASC: Principle 8)

### Collaborative Work: Calculate and Interpret Test Results

With a partner in your class, calculate the mean, median, and mode of the 23 scores just listed. Compute the range and standard deviation for these scores. What do these figures mean? (INTASC: Principle 8)

### Research/Field Experience: What Do the Critics Say About Standardized Testing?

In a short essay, evaluate each of the following criticisms of standardized tests. State whether you agree with the criticism and then explain your reasoning. (1) High-stakes multiple-choice tests will lead to a "dumbing down" of teaching and learning. (2) Establishing national tests will undermine new educational programs at the state and local levels. (INTASC: Principle 8)

*Go to the Online Learning Center for downloadable portfolio templates.*

## STUDY, PRACTICE, AND SUCCEED

Visit www.mhhe.com/santrockep5e to review the chapter with self-grading quizzes and self-assessments, to apply the chapter material to two more Crack the Case studies, and for suggested activities to develop your teaching portfolio.

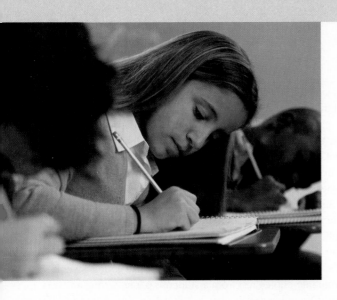

## CHAPTER 16

# CLASSROOM ASSESSMENT AND GRADING

*I call my tests "opportunities" to give students
a different way of thinking about them.*

—Bert Moore
*Contemporary American Psychologist*

## Chapter Outline

## Learning Goals

**1** Discuss the classroom as an
assessment context.

**2** Provide some guidelines for
constructing traditional tests.

**3** Describe some types of alternative
assessments.

**4** Construct a sound approach
to grading.

# Teaching **Stories**  Vicky Farrow

Vicky Farrow is a former high school teacher who currently teaches educational psychology at Lamar University in Beaumont, Texas. She reflects on the ongoing process of assessment in the classroom and what to do and what not to do in constructing tests:

Assessment is an ongoing process. It is more than giving tests or assigning grades. It is everything a teacher does to determine if his or her students are learning. It may be asking students questions, monitoring their understanding as you circulate through the room during an activity, and noticing the frown on the face of a student who is confused or the smile of a student who has grasped the concept. Without this ongoing assessment, a teacher can never know if instruction is effective or needs to be modified. Done effectively, assessment provides a teacher with valuable information for providing an optimal learning experience for every child.

When you do give tests, every item on a test should relate back to the objectives. This helps the teacher avoid "gotcha" questions—those questions that may be trivial or unimportant to the intended learning outcomes. If it is not important enough to spend valuable class time on, it probably is not important enough to test the student over.

Be careful that test items are written at an appropriate level. The test should be testing students' understanding of the unit content, not their reading skills (unless, of course, it is reading skills that are being tested). I remember as a student taking an analogies test that was intended to assess my ability to identify relationships between concepts. However, the vocabulary was so difficult that I missed some items because the words were too difficult for that level of schooling.

If an essay question is on an examination, write a model answer *before* grading the exam. Would you make your answer key for a multiple-choice test from a student's paper, wrong answers and all? Of course not! It does not make any more sense to do that with an essay item. If an essay item is well written and a model answer is constructed in advance, the grade a student receives will more accurately reflect the level of that student's understanding of the material being tested.

# Preview

Assessment of students' learning has recently generated considerable interest in educational circles. This interest has focused on such issues as the extent to which teachers should incorporate state standards into their teaching and assessment, as well as the degree to which teachers should use traditional tests or alternative assessments. Our coverage of classroom assessments begins with an examination of the varied features of the classroom as an assessment context. Then we contrast traditional tests and alternative assessments, followed by a discussion of the role of grading in education.

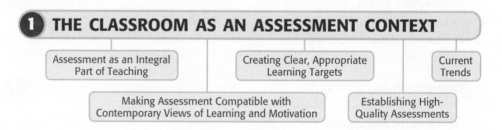

**1 THE CLASSROOM AS AN ASSESSMENT CONTEXT**

Assessment as an Integral Part of Teaching

Creating Clear, Appropriate Learning Targets

Current Trends

Making Assessment Compatible with Contemporary Views of Learning and Motivation

Establishing High-Quality Assessments

When you think of assessment, what comes to mind? Probably tests. However, as we discuss the classroom as a context for assessment, you will discover that contemporary assessment strategies involve far more than testing.

## ASSESSMENT AS AN INTEGRAL PART OF TEACHING

Teachers spend more time in assessment than you might imagine. In one analysis they spent 20 to 30 percent of their professional time dealing with assessment matters (Stiggins, 2001). And that time allocation for assessment was made before the introduction of No Child Left Behind (NCLB) legislation in 2002 (discussed in Chapter 15), which mandates states to test students' achievement to determine if they are making adequate yearly progress. The high-stakes testing required by NCLB has meant that teachers have to integrate this testing in their assessment planning (Cizek, 2010;

| Preinstruction | During instruction (formative assessment) | Postinstruction (summative assessment) |
| --- | --- | --- |
| Do my students have the prerequisite knowledge and skills to be successful? | Are students paying attention to me? | How much have my students learned? |
| What will interest my students? | Are students understanding the material? | What should I do next? |
| What will motivate my students? | To which students should I direct questions? | Do I need to review anything the class didn't understand? |
| How long should I plan to cover each unit? | What type of questions should I ask? | What grades should I give? |
| What teaching strategies should I use? | How should I respond to student questions? | What should I tell my students? |
| How should I grade students? | When should I stop lecturing? | How should I change my instruction next time? |
| What type of group learning should I use? | Which students need extra help? | Do the test scores really reflect what my students know and can do? |
| What are my learning objectives or targets? | Which students should be left alone? | Is there anything that students misunderstood? |

**FIGURE 16.1** TEACHER DECISION MAKING BEFORE, DURING, AND AFTER INSTRUCTION

These are questions a teacher can answer to improve assessment before, during, and after instruction.

*Essential Assessment Concepts for Teachers and Administrators* by James H. McMillan, p. 3 (Figure 1.1). Copyright 2001 by Corwin Press, Inc. Reproduced with permission of Sage Publications Inc. Books in the format Textbook via Copyright Clearance Center.

Popham, 2011). For example, many teachers spend considerable time prepping students for such tests.

With so much time spent on assessment, it should be done well (Green & Johnson, 2010; Nitko & Brookhart, 2011). Assessment expert James McMillan (2011) stresses that competent teachers frequently evaluate their students in relation to learning goals and adapt their instruction accordingly. Assessment not only documents what students know and can do but also affects their learning and motivation. These ideas represent a change in the way assessment is viewed, away from the concept that assessment is an isolated outcome done only after instruction is finished and toward the concept of integrating assessment with instruction (Andrade & Cizek, 2010).

Think of integrating instruction and assessment in terms of three time frames: preinstruction, during instruction (formative), and postinstruction (summative) (O'Shea, 2009). The Standards for Teacher Competence in Educational Assessment, developed jointly in the early 1990s by the American Federation of Teachers, National Council on Measurement in Education, and National Education Association, describe the teacher's responsibility for student assessment in these three time frames (see Figure 16.1).

**Preinstruction Assessment** Imagine that you want to know how well your students can solve a certain level of math problem before you begin formal instruction on a more advanced level. You might look at your students' prior grades and their scores on standardized math tests, as well as observe your students for several days to see how well they perform. These assessments are designed to answer this question: what math skills are my students able to demonstrate? If the results of your assessment indicate that students lack prerequisite knowledge and skills, you will decide to begin with materials that are less difficult for them. If they do extremely well on your preinstruction assessment, you will move your level of instruction to a higher plane. Without this preinstructional assessment, you run the risk of having a class that is overwhelmed (if your instruction level is too advanced) or bored (if your instruction level is too low).

Much of preinstructional assessment is informal observation (Forgarty & Kerns, 2010). In the first several weeks of school, you will have numerous opportunities to observe students' characteristics and behavior. Be sensitive to whether a student is shy or outgoing, has a good or weak vocabulary, speaks and listens effectively, is considerate of others or is egocentric, engages in appropriate or inappropriate behavior, and so on. Also focus on the student's nonverbal behavior for cues that might reveal nervousness, boredom, frustration, or a lack of understanding.

In preinstructional assessments, guard against developing expectations that will distort your perception of a student. It is virtually impossible not to have expectations about students. Because teacher expectations are potentially powerful influences on student learning, some teachers don't even want to look at a student's prior grades or standardized test scores. Whether you do or do not examine such assessment information, work on making your expectations realistic. If you err, err in the direction of having overly positive expectations for students.

A good strategy is to treat your initial impressions of students as hypotheses to be supported or modified by subsequent observation and information. Some of your initial observations will be accurate; others will need to be revised. As you try to get a sense of what your students are like, refrain from believing hearsay information, from making enduring judgments based on only one or two observations, and from labeling the student (Airasian & Russell, 2008).

Some teachers also administer diagnostic pretests in subject areas to examine a student's level of knowledge and skill. And many schools are increasingly collecting samples of students' work in portfolios, which can accompany a student from grade to grade. The portfolios provide teachers with a far more concrete, less biased set of information to evaluate than other teachers' hearsay comments. We will describe portfolios in much greater depth later in the chapter.

**Assessment During Instruction** One of the most significant trends in classroom assessment is the increasing use of **formative assessment,** which is assessment during the course of instruction rather than after it is completed. Formative assessment has become a buzzword with its emphasis on assessment *for* learning rather than assessment *of* learning (Andrade & Cizek, 2010; William, 2010). An important aspect of being an effective teacher is assessing students' understanding—formative assessment is extremely important in this regard. Your ongoing observation and monitoring of students' learning while you teach informs you about what to do next (Davidson & Feldman, 2010). Assessment during instruction helps you set your teaching at a level that challenges students and stretches their thinking. It also helps you to detect which students need your individual attention.

Assessment during instruction takes place at the same time as you make many other decisions about what to do, say, or ask next to keep the classroom running smoothly and help students actively learn. It requires listening to student answers, observing other students for indications of understanding or confusion, framing the next question, and looking around the class for misbehavior (McMillan, 2010). Simultaneously, the teacher needs to monitor the pace of the activity, which students are being called on more or less frequently, answer quality, and the sequence of content. With small groups, the teacher might need to be aware of several different activities simultaneously.

Oral questions are an especially important aspect of assessment during instruction. Some teachers ask as many as 300 to 400 questions a day, not only to stimulate students' thinking and inquiry but also to assess their knowledge and skill level.

When you ask questions, remember to avoid overly broad, general questions; involve the whole class in questioning instead of calling on the same students all of the time; allow sufficient "wait time" after asking a question; probe students' responses

**Thinking Back/Thinking Forward**

Reading and mathematics are the two areas in which standardized tests are often used for diagnostic purposes. Chapter 15, p. 521

*What is formative assessment? Why is it such an important aspect of assessment?*

**formative assessment** Assessment during the course of instruction rather than after it is completed.

with follow-up questions; and highly value students' own questions (Airasian & Russell, 2008).

An increasing trend in formative assessment is to get students to assess their own progress on a day-to-day basis (Andrade, 2010). An important goal of student self-assessment is for students to become deeply involved in evaluating their schoolwork so they can more quickly determine how they are progressing. Encouraging students to assess their own progress also can increase their self-confidence and motivation to learn. Getting students to be reflective and monitor their own progress is a key aspect of student self-assessment. Self-monitoring relates to our discussion of self-regulation in Chapter 7 and our coverage of metacognition in Chapter 8. One of the biggest challenges in incorporating student self-assessment in classroom assessment is getting students used to doing it (Andrade, 2010). A good teaching strategy is to create student self-assessment worksheets, checklists, and other prepared material to facilitate their evaluation of their progress.

Providing effective feedback is an essential aspect of formative assessment and has always been an integral aspect of good teaching (Enger & Yager, 2010). The idea is to not only continually assess students as they learn but to provide informative feedback so that students' focus is appropriate. Researchers have found that positive feedback during formative assessment increases students' self-regulation of learning (Davis & McGowen, 2007). As part of providing feedback in formative assessment, instructional "correctives" are used to help students make progress. The idea is that there is assessment, feedback, and then more instruction (McMillan, 2010). Among the important aspects of feedback in formative assessment is that it should be immediate, specific, and individualized. Figure 16.2 describes some do's and don'ts in giving praise as a part of feedback.

**Postinstruction Assessment** Also called *formal assessment,* **summative assessment** is assessment after instruction is finished, with the purpose of documenting student performance. Assessment after instruction provides information about how well your students have mastered the material, whether students are ready for the next unit, what grades they should be given, what comments you should make to parents, and how you should adapt your instruction (McMillan, 2011).

## MAKING ASSESSMENT COMPATIBLE WITH CONTEMPORARY VIEWS OF LEARNING AND MOTIVATION

Throughout this book we have encouraged you to view students as active learners who discover and construct meaning and to help them set goals, plan, and reach goals; associate and link new information with existing knowledge in meaningful ways; think reflectively, critically, and creatively; develop self-monitoring skills; have positive expectations for learning and confidence in their skills; be enthusiastically and internally motivated to learn; apply what they learn to real-world situations; and communicate effectively.

Assessment plays an important role in effort, engagement, and performance (Hammerman, 2009). Your informal observations can provide information about how motivated students are to study a subject. If you have a good relationship with the student, direct oral questioning in a private conversation can often produce valuable insight about the student's motivation. In thinking about how assessment and motivation are linked, ask yourself if your assessments will encourage students to become more meaningfully involved in the subject matter and more intrinsically motivated to study the topic (Chang, 2007). Assessments that are challenging but fair should increase students' enthusiasm for learning. Assessments that are too difficult will lower students' self-esteem and self-efficacy, as well as raise their anxiety. Assessing students with measures that are too easy will bore them and not motivate them to study hard enough.

**Thinking Back/Thinking Forward**

High-achieving students are often self-regulatory learners. Chapter 7, p. 243

Metacognitive regulation involves learning a number of strategies that result in solutions to learning problems; monitoring how well one is performing on a task is an important aspect of metacognition. Chapter 8, p. 287

**Do**

Focus on specific accomplishments.

Attribute success to effort and ability.

Praise spontaneously.

Refer to prior achievement.

Individualize and use variety.

Give praise immediately.

Praise correct strategies leading to success.

Praise accurately with credibility.

Praise privately.

Focus on progress.

**Don't**

Focus on general or global achievement.

Attribute success to luck or other's help.

Praise predictably.

Ignore prior achievement.

Give the same praise to all students.

Give praise much later.

Ignore strategies and focus only on outcomes.

Praise for undeserving performance.

Praise publicly.

Focus solely on current performance.

**FIGURE 16.2** DO'S AND DON'TS OF USING PRAISE WHEN GIVING FEEDBACK DURING FORMATIVE ASSESSMENT

J. H. McMillan, *Classroom Assessment,* Table 5.5 "Do's and Don'ts of Effective Praise" p. 143, © 2007 by Pearson Education, Inc. Reproduced by permission of Pearson Education, Inc.

**Thinking Back/Thinking Forward**

Teachers' expectations play an important role in students' achievement. Chapter 13, p. 453

**summative assessment** Assessment after instruction is finished to document student performance; also called *formal assessment.*

Susan Brookhart (1997, 2008) developed a model of how classroom assessment helps motivate students. She argues that every classroom environment hosts a series of repeated assessment events. In each assessment event, the teacher communicates with the students through assignments, activities, and feedback about performance. Students respond according to their perceptions of these learning opportunities and how well they think they will be able to perform. Brookhart argues that this view of classroom assessment suggests that teachers should evaluate students using a variety of performances, especially performances that are meaningful to students.

Similarly, many other classroom assessment experts emphasize that if you think motivated, active learning is an important goal of instruction, you should create alternative assessments that are quite different from traditional tests, which don't evaluate how students construct knowledge and understanding, set and reach goals, and think critically and creatively (McMillan, 2011; Stiggins, 2008). Later in the chapter we will explore how alternative assessments can be used to examine these aspects of students' learning and motivation.

## CREATING CLEAR, APPROPRIATE LEARNING TARGETS

Tying assessment to current views on learning and motivation also involves developing clear, appropriate learning goals, or targets. A *learning target* consists of what students should know and be able to do. You should establish criteria for judging whether students have attained the learning target (McMillan, 2011). Figure 16.3 provides some examples of unit learning targets.

## ESTABLISHING HIGH-QUALITY ASSESSMENTS

Another important goal for the classroom as an assessment context is achieving high-quality assessment. Like standardized testing, assessment reaches a high level of quality when it yields reliable and valid information about students' performance. High-quality assessments also are fair (McMillan, 2008).

> **Thinking Back/Thinking Forward**
>
> A current trend in alternative assessment is to require students to solve some type of authentic problem or to complete a project or demonstrate a skill rather than take a formal test. Chapter 16, p. 563

**FIGURE 16.3** EXAMPLES OF UNIT LEARNING TARGETS

Students will be able to explain how various cultures are different and how cultures influence people's beliefs and lives by answering orally a comprehensive set of questions about cultural differences and their effects.

Students will demonstrate their knowledge of the parts of a plant by filling in words or a diagram for all parts studied.

Students will demonstrate their understanding of citizenship by correctly identifying whether previously unread statements about citizenship are true or false. A large number of items is used to sample most of the content learned.

Students will be able to explain why the American Constitution is important by writing an essay that indicates what would happen if we abolished our Constitution. The papers would be graded holistically, looking for evidence of reasons, knowledge of the Constitution, and organization.

Students will show that they know the difference between components of sentences by correctly identifying verbs, adverbs, adjectives, nouns, and pronouns in seven of eight long, complex sentences.

Students will be able to multiply fractions by correctly computing eight of ten fraction problems. The problems are new to the students; some are similar to "challenge" questions in the book.

Students will be able to use their knowledge of addition, subtraction, division, and multiplication to solve word problems that are similar to those used in the sixth-grade standardized test.

Students will demonstrate their understanding of how visual art conveys ideas and feelings by correctly indicating, orally, how examples of art communicate ideas and feelings.

**Validity**    As indicated in Chapter 15, *validity* refers to the extent to which assessment measures what it is intended to measure and the appropriateness of inferences from and uses of the information (McMillan, 2011). *Inferences* are conclusions that teachers draw from information.

You can't assess everything a student learns. Therefore, your assessment of a student will necessarily be a sample of the student's learning. The most important source of information for validity in your classroom, then, will be *content-related evidence,* the extent to which the assessment reflects what you have been teaching (McMillan, 2011).

Adequately sampling content is clearly an important goal of valid assessment. You need to use your best professional judgment when sampling content; thus, for example, you wouldn't want to use just one multiple-choice question to assess a student's knowledge of a chapter on geography. An increasing trend is to use multiple methods of assessment, which can provide a more comprehensive sampling of content. Accordingly, the teacher might assess students' knowledge of the geography chapter with some multiple-choice questions, several essay questions, and a project to complete. Always ask yourself whether your assessments of students are adequate samples that accurately reflect their knowledge and understanding.

Linking instruction and assessment in the classroom leads to the concept of **instructional validity:** the extent to which the assessment is a reasonable sample of what actually went on in the classroom (McMillan, 2011). For example, a classroom assessment should reflect both what the teacher taught and students' opportunity to learn the material. Consider a math class in which the teacher gives students a test on their ability to solve multiplication problems. For instructional validity, it is important that the teacher competently instructs students in how to solve the problems and gives them adequate opportunities to practice this skill beforehand.

An important strategy for validity in classroom assessment is to systematically link learning targets, content, instruction, and assessment (McMillan, 2011). Imagine that you are a science teacher and that one of your learning targets is to get students to think more critically and creatively in designing science projects. Ask yourself what content is important to achieve this learning target. For instance, will it help students to read biographies of famous scientists that include information about how they came up with their ideas? Also ask yourself what learning targets you will emphasize in instruction. For your target regarding students' science projects, it will be important for you to carry through in your instruction on the theme of helping students to think critically and creatively about science.

**Reliability**    As noted in Chapter 15, *reliability* is the extent to which a test produces consistent, reproducible scores. Reliable scores are stable, dependable, and relatively free from errors of measurement (Gregory, 2011; Lodico, Spaulding, & Voegtle, 2011). Consistency depends on circumstances involved in taking the test and student factors that vary from one test to another (McMillan, 2011).

Reliability is not about the appropriateness of the assessment information but is about determining how consistently an assessment measures what it is measuring (Suen, 2008). If a teacher gives students the same test in a math class on two occasions and the students perform in a consistent manner on the tests, this indicates that the test was reliable. However, the consistency in students' performance (with high-scorers being high both times the test was given, middle-scorers performing similarly across the two assessments, and low-scorers doing poorly on both assessments) says nothing about whether the test actually measured what it was designed to measure (for example, being an accurate, representative sample of questions that measured the math content that had been taught). Thus, reliable assessments are not necessarily valid.

Reliability is reduced by errors in measurement. A student can have adequate knowledge and skill and still not perform consistently across several assessments because of a number of factors. Internal factors can include health, motivation, and

**instructional validity** The extent to which the assessment is a reasonable sample of what went on in the classroom.

anxiety. External factors can include inadequate directions given by the teacher, ambiguously created items, poor sampling of information, and inefficient scoring of the student's responses. For example, a student might perform extremely well on the first test a teacher gives to assess the student's reading comprehension but considerably lower on the second test in this domain. The student's lack of knowledge and skill could be the reason for the low reliability across the two assessments, but the low reliability also could be due to any number of measurement errors. In classroom assessment there typically is no statistical measure of reliability. Rather, teachers rely on their observations and judgments about whether possible influences of error have occurred.

**Fairness**   High-quality classroom assessment is not only valid and reliable but also fair (McMillan, 2011). Assessment is fair when all students have an equal opportunity to learn and demonstrate their knowledge and skill. Also, assessment is fair when teachers have developed appropriate learning targets, provided competent content and instruction to match those targets, and chosen assessments that reflect the targets, content, and instruction.

Assessment bias includes offensiveness and unfair penalization (Popham, 2011). Assessment is offensive to a subgroup of students when negative stereotypes of that subgroup are included in the test. For example, consider a test in which the items portray males in high-paying and prestigious jobs (doctors and business executives) and females in low-paying and less prestigious jobs (clerks and secretaries). Because some females taking the test likely will be offended by this gender inequality, and appropriately so, the stress this creates may produce a less successful outcome for females on the test.

An assessment also may be biased if it unfairly penalizes a student based on the student's group membership, such as ethnicity, socioeconomic status, gender, religion, and disability. For example, consider an assessment that focuses on information that students from affluent families are far more likely to be familiar with than students from low-income families (Popham, 2011). Suppose a teacher decides to see how well students can collaboratively solve problems in groups, and the content of the problem to be discussed is a series of locally presented operas and symphonies likely to have been attended only by those who can afford the high ticket prices. Even if the affluent students didn't attend these musical events themselves, they may have heard their parents talk about them. Thus, students from low-income families might perform less effectively on the collaborative problem-solving exercise pertaining to musical events not because they are less skilled at such problem solving but because they are unfamiliar with the events.

Some assessment experts believe it is important to create a philosophy of *pluralistic assessment,* which includes being responsive to cultural diversity in the classroom and at school (Payne, 1997). This usually includes performance assessments during instruction and after instruction.

Geneva Gay (1997, pp. 215–216, 218) evaluated the role of ethnicity and culture in assessment and recommended a number of culturally responsive strategies in assessing students. She advocates (1) modifying the Eurocentric nature of current U.S. instruction and achievement assessments, (2) using a wider variety of assessment methods that take into account the cultural styles of students of color, (3) evaluating students against their own records, and (4) assessing students in ways that serve culturally appropriate diagnostic and developmental functions.

Achievement assessments "are designed to determine what students know. Presumably they reflect what has been taught in schools." Gay argues that "although progress has been made in the last three decades to make school curricula more inclusive of ethnic and cultural diversity, most of the knowledge taught, and consequently the achievement tests, continue to be Eurocentric." She points out that even mastery of skills tends to be "transmitted through Eurocentric contexts. For instance, achievement tests may embed skills in scenarios that are not relevant to the cultural

DIVERSITY

**Thinking Back/Thinking Forward**

Validity, reliability, and fairness not only are important aspects of teacher-constructed tests but also are important aspects of standardized tests. Chapter 15, p. 517

backgrounds and life experiences of students of color," as when a teacher asks "immigrant students from the Caribbean who have never experienced snow to engage in problem solving" by evaluating the challenges and dilemmas presented by a blizzard—the students might have the problem-solving skill to respond to this request, but their unfamiliarity with cold winters can interfere with their ability to perform the task effectively.

This does not mean that students of color should not be assessed or that they should not be expected to meet high achievement standards. They should. However, "to avoid perpetuating educational inequality through assessment procedures, these students should not always be expected to demonstrate" knowledge and skills in terms of contexts with which they are not familiar. A good strategy is to use a variety of assessment methods to ensure that no single method gives an advantage to one ethnic group or another. These methods should include socioemotional measures as well as measures of academic content. Teachers also should carefully observe and monitor students' performance for verbal and nonverbal information in the assessment context.

Gay stresses that assessment should always "serve diagnostic and developmental functions and be culturally responsible. . . . Narrative reports, developmental profiles, student-teacher-parent conferences, and anecdotal records should always be included in reporting students' progress."

## CURRENT TRENDS

Here are some current trends in classroom assessment (Hambleton, 1996; McMillan, 2011; National Research Council, 2001):

- *Using at least some performance-based assessment.* Historically, classroom assessment has emphasized the use of **objective tests** such as multiple-choice, which have relatively clear, unambiguous scoring criteria. In contrast, **performance assessments** require students to create answers or products that demonstrate their knowledge or skill. Examples of performance assessment include writing an essay, conducting an experiment, carrying out a project, solving a real-world problem, and creating a portfolio (Stiggins, 2008).

- *Examining higher-level cognitive skills.* Rather than assess only content knowledge, as many objective tests do, a current trend is to evaluate a student's higher-level cognitive skills, such as problem solving, critical thinking, decision making, drawing of inferences, and strategic thinking.

- *Using multiple assessment methods.* In the past, assessment meant using a test—often a multiple-choice test—as the sole means of assessing a student. A current trend is to use multiple methods to assess students. Thus, a teacher might use any number of these methods: a multiple-choice test, an essay, an interview, a project, a portfolio, and student evaluations of themselves. Multiple assessments provide a broader view of the child's learning and achievement than a single measure.

- *Using more multiple-choice items to prepare students for taking high-stakes state standards-based tests.* Just when a trend in assessment that was more compatible with cognitive, constructivist, and motivational approaches (performance assessment, use of portfolios, and student self-assessment) had developed, teachers returned to using objective formats for assessment—in many cases more than before. In assessment expert James McMillan's (2007, p. 19) view, many teachers need to balance the demands of tests mandated by No Child Left Behind "with what they know about best practices of teaching and assessment that maximize student learning and motivation. Clearly, classroom assessment must be considered in the current climate that emphasizes high-stakes testing."

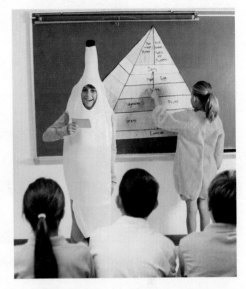

The two students here are demonstrating their knowledge and understanding of nutrition. *What are some other examples of performance assessment?*

**Thinking Back/Thinking Forward**

Complex cognitive processes include reasoning, critical thinking, decision making, problem solving, and creative thinking. Chapter 9, p. 301

**objective tests** Tests that have relatively clear, unambiguous scoring criteria, usually multiple-choice tests.

**performance assessment** Assessment that requires creating answers or products that demonstrate knowledge and skill; examples include writing an essay, conducting an experiment, carrying out a project, solving a real-world problem, and creating a portfolio.

TECHNOLOGY

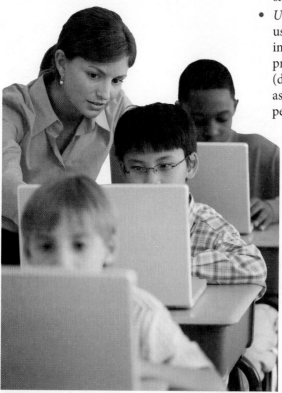

*What are some ways that computers are being used in the assessment of students?*

- *Having high performance standards.* Another trend is the demand for high performance standards, even world-class performance standards, for interpreting educational results. Some experts say that world-class performance standards are driving contemporary classroom assessment by providing goals, or targets, to attain (Taylor, 1994). However, questions arise about who should set these standards and whether they should be set at all.

- *Using computers as part of assessment.* Traditionally, computers have been used to score tests, analyze test results, and report scores. Today computers increasingly are being used to construct and administer tests, as well as to present different assessment formats to students in a multimedia environment (de Jong, 2011; Newby & others, 2011). With coming advances in technology, assessment practices are likely to be very different from traditional paper-and-pencil tests.

Many school systems are turning to *Web-based assessment*—assessment available on the Internet—because of its potential for greater accuracy and cost reduction (Lever-Duffy & McDonald, 2011; Maloy & others, 2011). A number of testing firms, including Educational Testing Service, are developing tests to be administered on computers in the classroom, school, or district, but those are not Web-based assessments. If an assessment is Web-based, students use a computer and the assessment takes place on the Internet (Newby & others, 2011).

Some of the best Web-based assessments can be easily adapted to the curriculum you use in your classroom. Certain assessments focus on recording and evaluating student behavior, others involve academic progress, and still others include all of these areas. The best Web-based assessments let teachers "develop their own tests or forms and usually include a databank of questions or other assessment tools. Most are aligned with various state and national standards," or No Child Left Behind standards.

Trends in assessment also include emphasizing integrated rather than isolated skills, involving students in all aspects of assessment, giving students more feedback, and making standards and criteria public rather than private and secretive.

## Review, Reflect, and Practice

**1** Discuss the classroom as an assessment context.

**REVIEW**

- Describe assessment before, after, and during instruction.
- How can assessment be brought into line with contemporary views of learning and motivation?
- What are learning targets?
- What standards can be used to judge the quality of classroom assessments?
- What are some current trends in assessing students' learning?

**REFLECT**

- Think of one of the better teachers that you had as a K–12 student. In retrospect, how would you describe the teacher's classroom as an "assessment context"?

## Review, Reflect, and Practice

### PRAXIS™ PRACTICE

1. Which of the following is the best example of formative assessment?
   a. Mr. Harrison's students write a paper at the conclusion of a unit of instruction. This allows him to assess to what degree his students understand the content of the unit.
   b. Mr. Shockey asks his students open-ended questions during instruction. This way he can determine to what degree his students understand the content of his lesson.
   c. Ms. Manning plays a game of *Jeopardy!* at the end of her unit of instruction to assess student understanding of the content of the unit.
   d. Ms. Walker gives her students a brief assessment prior to beginning a unit of instruction, so she knows what her students are already capable of doing. This allows her to gear her instruction to her students' zones of proximal development.

2. Which of the following assessments will most likely enhance student motivation to study and learn?
   a. Mr. Ditka assigns his students a project that requires knowledge from the unit of instruction to complete successfully.
   b. Mr. Payton gives periodic tests that are easy enough for all of his students to earn high scores if they have attended class.
   c. Mr. Rivera puts two or three tricky questions in each test so he can determine which of his students read the items carefully before responding.
   d. Mr. Singletary constructs very challenging exams to ensure that only those students who have studied the material carefully will be successful.

3. Ms. Ramirez has assigned her students to analyze the water in a nearby stream, determine the level of pollution in the stream, and develop a solution to the pollution problem. What type of learning target has she created?
   a. affect
   b. knowledge
   c. product
   d. reasoning

4. Ms. Vick has created an assessment to measure the degree to which her students have mastered the content of her unit on the U.S. Constitution. Included in the test are items about the Bill of Rights, other constitutional amendments, the American Revolution, and World War II. What is the best description of this assessment?
   a. It is likely to yield both valid and reliable scores.
   b. The scores are unlikely to be valid or reliable.
   c. While the scores may be reliable, they will not be valid.
   d. While the scores may be valid, they will not be reliable.

5. Ms. Krzyzewski is teaching a science unit on anatomy. Students have been studying the anatomy of various animals. Which of the following is the best example of a performance assessment of this material?
   a. Students answer oral questions regarding the structures present in different animals.
   b. Students write an essay comparing and contrasting the anatomy of frogs and pigs.
   c. Students dissect animals and identify their anatomical parts.
   d. Students take a multiple-choice test covering the material in the unit.

*Please see the answer key at the end of the book.*

## ② TRADITIONAL TESTS

Selected-Response Items   Constructed-Response Items

Traditional tests are typically paper-and-pencil tests in which students select from choices, calculate numbers, construct short responses, or write essays. Our coverage of traditional tests focuses on two main types of item formats in assessment: (1) selected-response items and (2) constructed-response items.

### SELECTED-RESPONSE ITEMS

**Selected-response items** have an objective format that allows students' responses to be scored quickly. A scoring key for correct responses is created and can be applied by an examiner or by a computer. Multiple-choice, true/false, and matching items are the most widely used types of items in selected-response tests.

**Multiple-Choice Items**   A **multiple-choice item** consists of two parts: the stem plus a set of possible responses. The *stem* is a question or statement. Incorrect alternatives are called *distractors*. The student's task is to select the correct choice from among the distractors—for example:

> What is the capital of Vermont? (Stem)
> a. Portland (Distractor)
> b. Montpelier (Answer)
> c. Boston (Distractor)
> d. Weston (Distractor)

Students below the fourth grade probably should answer questions on the test page rather than on a separate answer sheet. Young elementary school students tend to respond slowly and lose their place easily when they have to use a separate answer sheet (Sax, 1997). Using a separate answer sheet with older students often reduces scoring time because the answers usually can fit on only one page. Many school districts have commercially printed answer sheets that teachers can order for their

**selected-response items** Test items with an objective format in which student responses can be scored quickly. A scoring guide for correct responses is created and can be applied by an examiner or a computer.

**multiple-choice item** An objective test item consisting of two parts: a stem plus a set of possible responses.

## TEACHING CONNECTIONS: Best Practices
### Strategies for Writing Multiple-Choice Items

Some good strategies for writing high-quality multiple-choice items include the following (Gronlund & Waugh, 2009; McMillan, 2011; Sax, 1997):

1. *Write the stem as a question.*

2. *Give three or four possible alternatives from which to choose.*

3. *State items and options positively when possible.* Elementary school students especially find negatives confusing. If you use the word *not* in the stem, *italicize,* print it in all capital letters, or underline it—for example:

   Which of the following cities is *not* in New England?

   a. Boston

   b. Chicago

   c. Montpelier

   d. Providence

4. *Include as much of the item as possible in the stem, thus making the stem relatively long and the alternatives relatively short*—for example:

   Which U.S. president wrote the Gettysburg Address?

   a. Thomas Jefferson

   b. Abraham Lincoln

   c. James Madison

   d. Woodrow Wilson

5. *Alternatives should grammatically match the stem so that answers are grammatically correct.* Otherwise

# TEACHING CONNECTIONS: Best Practices
## Strategies for Writing Multiple-Choice Items

students can eliminate options simply based on grammar. For example, the first item is better than the second:

Orville and Wilbur Wright became famous because of which type of transportation?

a. airplane

b. automobile

c. boat

d. train

Orville and Wilbur Wright became famous because of an

a. airplane

b. automobile

c. boat

d. train

6. *Write items that have a clearly defensible correct or best option.* Unless you give alternative directions, students will assume that there is only one correct or best answer to an item.

7. *Vary the placement of the correct option.* Students who are unsure of an answer tend to select the middle options and avoid the extreme options. Alphabetizing response choices (by the first letters in the response) will help to vary the placement of the correct option.

8. *Beware of cues in the length of the options.* Correct answers tend to be longer than incorrect ones because of the need to include specifications and qualifications that make it true. Lengthen the distractors (incorrect responses) to approximately the same length as the correct answer.

9. *Don't expect students to make narrow distinctions among answer choices.* For example, the first item in the following example is better than the second:

The freezing point of water is

a. 25°F

b. 32°F

c. 39°F

d. 46°F

The freezing point of water is

a. 30°F

b. 31°F

c. 32°F

d. 33°F

10. *Do not overuse "None of the above" and "All of the above."* Also avoid using variations of "a. and b." or "c. and d. but not a."

11. *Don't use the exact wording in a textbook when writing a question.* Struggling students might recognize the correct answer but not really understand its meaning.

12. *Write at least some items that encourage students to engage in higher-level thinking.* As we indicated earlier in the chapter, a current trend is to use more multiple-choice items in classroom assessment because of the demands imposed on teachers by high-stakes state standards-based tests. An important issue in the return to using more multiple-choice items is the cognitive level demanded by the items. Many teachers report that they use "higher-level" test items, but in reality they mainly are lower-level recall and recognition items (McMillan, 2011).

How can you write higher-level thinking multiple-choice items? Here are some recommendations (Center for Instructional Technology, 2006):

- Don't write more than three or four items a day that involve higher-level thinking, because they are more difficult to write and take more time than simple, straightforward items.

- Write one or two items after a class (a good idea for writing any test items) and then simply assemble them at a later time when making up a test.

- Use some analogy-based items (see the discussion of analogies in Chapter 9). An example of a multiple-choice item using an analogy is

  Bandura is to social cognitive theory as _____ is to social constructivist theory:

  a. Piaget

  b. Siegler

  c. Vygotsky

  d. Skinner

- Write some case-study items. You already have encountered many of these in this textbook. Many of the PRAXIS™ Practice features at the end of main sections in a chapter and all of the Crack the Case multiple-choice items at the end of chapters involve case studies.

- Write items in which students have to select what is missing or what needs to be changed in a scenario you provide.

**Strengths**

1. Both simple and complex learning outcomes can be measured.

2. The task is highly structured and clear.

3. A broad sample of achievement can be measured.

4. Incorrect alternatives provide diagnostic information.

5. Scores are less influenced by guessing than true/false items.

6. Scoring is easy, objective, and reliable.

**FIGURE 16.4** STRENGTHS AND LIMITATIONS OF MULTIPLE-CHOICE ITEMS

Norman E. Gronlund, *Assessment of Student Achievement*, "Strengths and Limitations of multiple-choice items" p. 60, © 1998. Reproduced by permission of Pearson Education, Inc.

**Strengths**

1. The item is useful for outcomes where there are only two possible alternatives (for example, fact or opinion, valid or invalid).

2. Less demand is placed on reading ability than in multiple-choice items.

3. A relatively large number of items can be answered in a typical testing period.

4. Scoring is easy, objective, and reliable.

**Limitations**

1. It is difficult to write items at a high level of knowledge and thinking that are free from ambiguity.

2. When a statement indicates correctly that a statement is false, that response provides no evidence that the student knows what is correct.

3. No diagnostic information is provided by the incorrect answers.

4. Scores are more influenced by guessing than with any other item type.

**FIGURE 16.5** STRENGTHS AND LIMITATIONS OF TRUE/FALSE ITEMS

Norman E. Gronlund, *Assessment of Student Achievement*, "Strengths and limitations of true/false items" p. 79, © 1998. Reproduced by permission of Pearson Education, Inc.

**Limitations**

1. Constructing good items is time consuming.

2. It is frequently difficult to find plausible distractors.

3. The multiple-choice format is ineffective for measuring some types of problem solving and the ability to organize and express ideas.

4. Score can be influenced by reading ability.

classes. If you hand-score multiple-choice tests, consider preparing a scoring stencil by cutting or punching holes in the answer sheet in the locations of the correct answers.

For most classroom requirements, simply count the number of answers marked correctly. Some teachers penalize students for guessing by deducting for wrong answers, but assessment experts say that this probably is not worth the extra bother and frequently leads to mistakes in scoring (Sax, 1997). Strengths and limitations of multiple-choice items are listed in Figure 16.4.

**True/False Items** A true/false item asks a student to mark whether a statement is true or false—for example:

Montpelier is the capital of Vermont.          True    False

The ease with which true/false items can be constructed has a potential drawback. Teachers sometimes take statements directly from a text or modify them slightly when making up true/false items. Avoid this practice, because it tends to encourage rote memorization with little understanding of the material.

The strengths and limitations of true/false items are described in Figure 16.5.

**Matching Items** Used by many teachers with younger students, matching requires students to connect one group of stimuli correctly with a second group of stimuli (Hambleton, 1996). Matching is especially well suited for assessing associations or links between two sets of information. In a typical matching format, a teacher places a list of terms on the left side of the page and a description or definition of the terms on the right side of the page. The student's task is to draw lines between the columns that correctly link terms with their definitions or descriptions. In another format, a space is left blank next to each term, in which the student writes the correct number or letter of the description/definition. When using matching, limit the number of items to be matched to no more than eight or ten. Using no more than five or six items per set is a good strategy.

Matching tests are convenient for teachers in that (1) their compact form requires little space, thus making it easy to assess quite a lot of information efficiently, and (2) they can be easily scored by using a correct-answer template (Popham, 2008).

But matching tests may tend to ask students to connect trivial information. Also, most matching tasks require students to connect information they have simply memorized, although items can be constructed that measure more complex cognitive skills.

## CONSTRUCTED-RESPONSE ITEMS

**Constructed-response items** require students to write out information rather than select a response from a menu. Short-answer and essay items are the most commonly used forms of traditional constructed-response items. In scoring, many constructed-response items require judgment on the part of the examiner.

**Short-Answer Items** A **short-answer item** is a constructed-response format in which students are required to write a word, a short phrase, or several sentences in response to a task. For example, a student might be asked, "Who discovered penicillin?" The short-answer format allows recall and could provide a problem-solving assessment of a wide range of material. The disadvantages of short-answer questions are that (1) they can require judgment to be scored and (2) they typically measure rote learning.

# TEACHING CONNECTIONS: Best Practices
## Strategies for Scoring Essay Questions

Here are some good strategies for scoring essays (Sax, 1997):

1. *Outline a plan for what constitutes a good or acceptable answer prior to administering or scoring students' responses* (McMillan, 2011). Essays can be scored holistically or analytically. *Holistic scoring* means making an overall judgment about the student's answer and giving it a single number or letter. You might make this judgment based on your overall impression of the essay or on several criteria that you have generated. Holistic scoring is often used when essays are long. *Analytic scoring* means scoring various criteria separately, then adding up the points to produce an overall score for the essay. Analytic scoring can be time-consuming, so avoid having more than three or four criteria for an essay.

2. *Devise a method by which you can score the essays without knowing which students wrote them.* You might do this by having students write their name beside a number on a separate sheet, then write only their number on the essay. When you record the grade, you can match up the student's number and name. This reduces the chance that your positive or negative expectations for the student will enter into your evaluation of the responses.

3. *Evaluate all answers to the same questions together.* Read and score all students' responses to one item before moving on to the next item. It is easier for you to remember the criteria for evaluating an answer to a single essay item than to remember the criteria for all essay

items. Also, if you read all of one student's responses together, your evaluation of the first few items will tend to influence your evaluation of the remaining items.

4. *Decide on a policy for handling irrelevant or incorrect responses.* Some students try to bluff their way through essays. Other students write everything they know about a topic without taking the time to zero in on what the item is asking for. Still other students might use poor grammar, misspell words, or write illegibly. Decide ahead of time whether and how much you will penalize such responses. Clearly communicate this to the students beforehand.

5. *If possible, reread papers before handing them back to students.* This helps you guard against any flaws or oversights in your scoring.

6. *Write comments on the paper.* An essay, especially a long one, with only a number or letter grade on it does not give adequate feedback to a student. And if you only circle or correct spelling errors and grammar, you are not giving students insight about the content of their essay responses. A good strategy is to write a number of brief comments at appropriate places throughout the essay, such as "Expand this idea more," "Unclear," or "Needs an example," in addition to making overall comments about the essay at its beginning or end. Include positive comments as well, such as "Interesting idea," or "Good connection."

---

Sentence completion is a variation of the short-answer item in which students express their knowledge and skill by completing a sentence. For example, a student might be asked to complete this sentence stem: The name of the person who discovered penicillin is _____.

**Essays** An **essay item** allows students more freedom of response to questions but requires more writing than other formats. Essay items are especially good for assessing students' understanding of material, higher-level thinking skills, ability to organize information, and writing skills. Here are some examples of high school essay questions:

What are the strengths and weaknesses of a democratic approach to government?
Describe the main themes of the novel you just read.
Argue that the United States is a gender-biased nation.

Essay items can require students to write anything from a few sentences to several pages. In some cases teachers ask all students to answer the same essay question(s). In others, teachers let students select from a group of items the item(s) they want to write about, a strategy that makes it more difficult to compare different students' responses. Suggestions for writing good essay items include these (Sax, 1997):

- *Specify limitations.* Be sure to specify the length of the desired answer and the weight that will be given to each item in determining scores or judgments.

**constructed-response items** Items that require students to write out information rather than select a response from a menu.

**short-answer item** A constructed-response format in which students are required to write a word, a short phrase, or several sentences in response to a task.

**essay items** Items that require more writing than other formats but allow more freedom of response to questions.

**Strengths**

1. The highest level of learning outcomes (analysis, synthesis, evaluation) can be measured.

2. The integration and application of ideas can be emphasized.

3. Preparation time is usually less than for selection-type formats.

**Limitations**

1. Achievement may not be adequately sampled due to the time needed to answer each question.

2. It can be difficult to relate essay responses to intended learning outcomes because of freedom to select, organize, and express ideas.

3. Scores are raised by writing skill and bluffing, and lowered by poor handwriting, misspelling, and grammatical errors.

4. Scoring is time consuming, subjective, and possibly unreliable.

**FIGURE 16.6** STRENGTHS AND LIMITATIONS OF ESSAY QUESTIONS

Norman E. Gronlund, *Assessment of Student Achievement*, "Strengths and limitations of essay questions" p. 103, © 1998. Reproduced by permission of Pearson Education, Inc.

- *Structure and clarify the task.* Make clear what they are supposed to write about. A poorly worded item is "Who was George Washington?" This could be answered in six words: "First president of the United States." In cases like this, ask yourself what more you want the student to tell. The following more-structured essay item requires more thinking on the part of the student:

  Discuss several events in the life of George Washington that confirm or disprove the claim that "he never told a lie." Use the events to support a claim of your own about how truthful Washington was.

- *Ask questions in a direct way.* Don't get too tricky. You might hear the term *rubric* used in regard to scoring students' responses on essays and other tests. In this context, rubric simply means a scoring system. Figure 16.6 lists some strengths and limitations of essay questions.

## Review, Reflect, and Practice

**2** Provide some guidelines for constructing traditional tests.

### REVIEW

- What are some important ideas to remember when creating multiple-choice, true/false, and matching items?
- What are constructed-response items and how do short-answer items differ from essay items?

### REFLECT

- Why do you think traditional testing has survived so long in K–12 classrooms?

### PRAXIS™ PRACTICE

1. Mr. Brown, a college instructor, includes the following item in a test about the impact of the family on children: "What parenting style does Homer Simpson exhibit?" Mr. Brown's possible answers are "authoritative," "authoritarian," "neglectful," and "permissive." Which of the following is the most appropriate criticism of Mr. Brown's question and answers?
   a. It is too easy to eliminate options because they are not all parenting styles.
   b. Parenting style has nothing to do with the impact of family on children.
   c. The question is biased in favor of people who watch *The Simpsons*.
   d. There is more than one clearly correct response.

2. Mr. Dent has just returned Marcia's graded essay to her. Notations of spelling and grammar errors, and the grade, 42/50—B, are all he has written on the test. What is the most appropriate criticism of this assessment?
   a. An essay should never be worth this many points on a test.
   b. Essays should not be graded numerically.
   c. There are no comments to help Marsha see where she did well and where she lost points.
   d. Spelling and grammar errors should not be marked on an essay.

*Please see the answer key at the end of the book.*

## ③ ALTERNATIVE ASSESSMENTS

| Trends in Alternative Assessment | Performance Assessment | Portfolio Assessment |

There are alternatives to the traditional assessments that we just discussed (Green & Johnson, 2010; Nitko & Brookhart, 2011). Let's examine some trends in this regard.

## TRENDS IN ALTERNATIVE ASSESSMENT

One current trend is to require students to solve some type of authentic problem or to perform in terms of completing a project or demonstrating other skills outside the context of a test or an essay (Gallavan, 2009). Another trend is to have students create a learning portfolio to demonstrate what they have learned (Badgett & Christmann, 2009a,b). Such alternative assessments are needed to make instruction compatible with contemporary views of learning and motivation.

Alternative assessments offer students more choices than they would have in taking a test or writing an essay (Salend, 2010). Consider several alternative assessments that a middle school language-arts teacher devised (Combs, 1997). She gave students a menu of options to choose from that included book reports, artwork, videos, and models. For example, in a unit on mystery, students might choose to write a report on an author of mystery stories, write an original mystery, make a children's mystery book, or conduct an interview with a private investigator. Each of these options came with a detailed set of instructions and a scoring guide for quality control. Figure 16.7 shows the directions and scoring guide for alternative assessments that focus on the Middle Ages and family history.

**Middle Ages option model**

Directions:
Make a model of a creature or character from the Middle Ages. Write a one-half to one page description of your character (tell who or what it is and its importance in the Middle Ages). Your model must portray the creature or character through the use of appropriate costume, props, or other attributes.

Scoring Guide

| | |
|---|---|
| 25 | Model portrays the character or creature and time period through the use of attire, props, and other attributes |
| 10 | Artistic quality |
| 15 | Model shows evidence of effort |
| 50 | A one-half to one page written description of the character is included |

**Family history option: family tree poster**

Directions:

Make a poster of your family tree, going back at least three generations. Provide as much information about the family members as possible, including, but not limited to, birthdate, death date (if not living), occupation, place of birth, accomplishments, and so on. In addition, provide at least two anecdotes about your family's history (for example, how they came to live in our town, special notoriety, honors, awards, medals). You must *write out* your family tree! (You may not make a copy of a commercially prepared family tree and paste it on the poster.) Make your poster attractive and neat!

Scoring Guide

| | |
|---|---|
| 25 | Family tree includes at least three generations prior to you |
| 25 | In addition to names, most entries include information such as birth, death, and place of birth |
| 25 | Poster includes at least two anecdotes about interesting or well-known family members |
| 15 | Poster is neatly and attractively typed or written by you |
| 10 | Mechanics, spelling, usage |

FIGURE **16.7** EXAMPLES OF ALTERNATIVE ASSESSMENT IN A MIDDLE SCHOOL LANGUAGE-ARTS CLASS

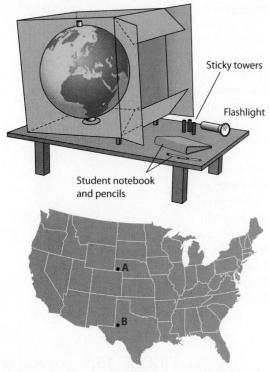

**(a)** The equipment consists of a spinning Earth globe inside a carton box, three sticky towers, and a flashlight; the students stick Towers A and B at two specific U.S. locations on the globe and are told what Tower C's shadow looks like when it is noon for Towers A and B. They have to find out where in the U.S. Tower C is. The solution requires modeling the sunlight by using the flashlight to project the towers' shadows onto the globe.

Sticky towers

Flashlight

Student notebook and pencils

**(b)** Draw a dot on this map to show where you think Tower C is. How did you figure out where Tower C is?

**(c)**

| Observation/results | score |
|---|---|
| Tower C is in eastern United States | 1 |
| Tower C is in northeastern United States | 1 |
| Tower C is somewhere between Pennsylvania and Maine | 1 |

| Data gathering/modeling | | score |
|---|---|---|
| Flashlight Position | Points flashlight at Equator | 2 |
| Flashlight Motion | Moves flashlight from E to W | 2 |
| Globe Rotation | Rotates globe<br>Rotates globe from W to E | 1<br>2 |
| Towers | Moves Tower C around on the map/globe until shadow is matched | 1 |
| | Moves Tower C around on the map/globe in the E/NE region until shadow is matched | 2 |
| Shadows | Uses shadows of Towers A and B as reference | 1 |

**(b)** The response format involves having students record in notebooks their solutions, the actions they carried out, and the reasoning behind their actions.

**(c)** Students' performances are scored for the accuracy of their results and the accuracy of their modeling, reasoning, and observations.

**FIGURE 16.8** A PERFORMANCE-BASED ASSESSMENT IN SCIENCE: DAYTIME ASTRONOMY

**Authentic assessment** means evaluating a student's knowledge or skill in a context that approximates the real world or real life as closely as possible. Traditional assessment has involved the use of paper-and-pencil tests that are often far removed from real-world contexts. An increasing trend is to assess students with items that more closely reflect reality (Burke, 2010). In some circles, the terms *performance assessment* and *authentic assessment* have been used interchangeably. However, not all performance assessments are authentic (McMillan, 2011).

Critics of authentic assessment argue that such assessments are not necessarily superior to more conventional assessments such as multiple-choice and essay tests (Terwilliger, 1997). They say that the proponents of authentic assessment rarely present data in support of the validity of authentic assessments. They also point out that authentic assessments don't adequately examine knowledge and basic skills.

## PERFORMANCE ASSESSMENT

Moving from traditional assessment with objective tests to performance assessment has been described as going from "knowing" to "showing" (Burz & Marshall, 1996). Performance assessments include what is commonly thought of as students' actual performances (such as in dance, music, art, and physical education), as well as papers, projects, oral presentations, experiments, and portfolios (Gronlund & Waugh, 2009). Figure 16.8 shows an example of a performance assessment in science (Solano-Flores & Shavelson, 1997).

**authentic assessment** Evaluating a student's knowledge or skill in a context that approximates the real world or real life as closely as possible.

Some disciplines, such as art, music, and physical education, have been using performance assessments for many years. The major change in performance assessment has involved introducing these forms of assessment into the traditional "academic areas."

**Features of Performance Assessment**    Performance assessments often include an emphasis on "doing" open-ended activities for which there is no correct, objective answer and that may assess higher-level thinking. Performance assessment tasks sometimes also are realistic. Evaluating performance often includes direct methods of evaluation, self-assessment, assessment of group performance as well as individual performance, and an extended period of time for assessment (Hambleton, 1996).

Traditional tests emphasize what students know. Performance assessments are designed to evaluate what students know and can do. In many cases, there is no correct, objective answer. For example, there is no one "correct answer" when a student gives a talk in class, creates a painting, performs a gymnastic routine, or designs a science project. Many performance assessments give students considerable freedom to construct their own responses rather than narrowing their range of answers. Although this makes scoring more difficult, it provides a context for evaluating students' higher-level thinking skills, such as the ability to think deeply about an issue or a topic (Stiggins, 2008).

Performance assessments use direct methods of evaluation, such as evaluating writing samples to assess writing skills and oral presentations to assess speaking and judging oral presentations to assess speaking skills (Gallavan, 2009). Observing a student give an oral presentation is a more direct assessment than asking the student a series of questions about speaking skills on a paper-and-pencil test.

Some performance assessments also involve having students evaluate their own performance. This emphasis shifts responsibility away from teachers and places it more squarely on the student's shoulders. Rubrics are useful aids to students in conducting self-assessments. For example, students might be required to evaluate a scrapbook that they have created (Goodrich, 1997). One criterion for evaluation might be "Gives enough details?" with the following possible responses: excellent ("Yes, I put enough details to give the reader a sense of time, place, and events"), good ("Yes, I put in some details, but some key details are missing"), minimal ("No, I did not put in enough details but did include a few"), and inadequate ("No, I had almost no details").

Some performance assessments evaluate how effectively a group of students perform, not just how the students perform individually. Thus, a group of students might be assigned to create a science project rather than having each student do a project individually. Evaluation of the student can include both the individual's contribution and the group's product. Group projects are often complex and allow for the assessment of cooperative skills, communication skills, and leadership skills.

Finally, as we noted, performance assessments may take place over an extended period of time (Gallavan, 2009). In traditional assessment, assessment occurs in a single time frame. For example, a teacher gives a multiple-choice test and students are allowed an hour to take it. By contrast, it is not unusual for performance assessments to involve sustained work over days, weeks, and even months. For example, a student might be evaluated once a month on the progress he is making on a science project, then receive a final evaluation when the project is completed (Hammerman, 2009).

**Guidelines for Performance Assessment**    Guidelines for performance assessment cover four general issues (Airasian & Russell, 2008): (1) establishing a clear purpose, (2) identifying observable criteria, (3) providing an appropriate setting, and (4) judging or scoring the performance.

*What might be some guidelines for creating performance criteria for evaluating the art creations of these elementary school students?*

Make sure that any performance assessment has a clear purpose and that a clear decision can be made from the assessment. The purposes can be diverse: to assign a grade, to evaluate a student's progress, to recognize the important steps in a performance, to generate products to be included in a learning portfolio, to provide concrete examples of students' work for admission to college or other programs, and so forth.

**Performance criteria** are specific behaviors that students need to perform effectively as part of the assessment. Establishing performance criteria helps the teacher go beyond general descriptions (such as "Do an oral presentation" or "Complete a science project") in specifying what the student needs to do (Easton, 2007). As guidelines, they direct the teacher's observations to be more systematic and focused rather than haphazard. Moreover, communicating these performance criteria to students at the beginning of instruction lets them know how to focus their learning.

Once you have clearly outlined the performance criteria, it is important to specify the setting in which you will observe the performance or product. You may want to observe behaviors directly in the regular flow of classroom activity, in a special context you create in the classroom, or in a context outside the classroom. As a rule of thumb, it is a good idea to observe the student on more than one occasion, because a single performance might not fairly represent the student's knowledge or skill.

Finally, you will need to score or rate the performance. *Scoring rubrics* involve the criteria that are used to judge performance, what the range in the quality of the performance should look like, what score should be given and what that score means, and how the different levels of quality should be described and differentiated from one another (Larkin, 2008).

In preparing a rubric, you may want to do the following (Re: Learning by Design, 2000):

1. *Include a scale of possible points to be assigned in scoring work.* High numbers usually are assigned to the best work. Scales typically use 4, 5, or 6 as the highest score, down to 1 or 0 for the lowest score.

2. *Provide descriptors for each performance criteria to increase reliability and avoid biased scoring.*

3. *Decide whether the rubric will be generic, genre-specific, or task-specific.* If generic, the rubric can be used to judge a broad performance, such as communication or problem solving. If genre-specific, the rubric applies to a more specific type of performance, such as an essay, a speech, or a narrative as a form of communication; open-ended or closed-end problems as kinds of problems solved. A task-specific rubric is unique to a single task, such as a single math problem or a speech on a specific topic.

4. *Decide whether the rubric should be longitudinal.* This type of rubric assesses progress over time toward mastery of educational objectives. One strategy for developing rubrics is to work backward from *exemplars*—examples of student work (McMillan, 1997, p. 218). "These exemplars can be analyzed to determine what descriptors distinguish them. The examples can also be used as *anchor* papers for making judgments, and can be given to students to illustrate the dimensions." An *anchor* is a sample of work or performance used to set the specific performance standard for a rubric level. Thus, attached to a paragraph describing a six-level performance in writing might be two or three samples of writing to illustrate several levels (Re: Learning by Design, 2000). Figure 16.9

**performance criteria** Specific behaviors that students need to perform effectively as part of an assessment.

| Criteria | Greater ← Quality → Lesser | | | |
|---|---|---|---|---|
| **Purposes** | The report explains the key purposes of the invention and also points out less obvious ones. | The report explains all of the key purposes of the invention. | The report explains some of the purposes of the invention but misses key purposes. | The report does not refer to the purposes of the invention. |
| **Features** | The report details both key and hidden features of the invention and explains how they serve several purposes. | The report details the key features of the invention and explains the purposes they serve. | The report neglects some of the features of the invention or the purposes they serve. | The report does not detail the features of the invention or the purposes they serve. |
| **Critique** | The report discusses the strengths and weaknesses of the invention, and suggests ways that it can be improved. | The report discusses the strengths and weaknesses of the invention. | The report discusses either the strengths or weaknesses of the invention, but not both. | The report does not mention the strengths or weaknesses of the invention. |
| **Connections** | The report makes appropriate connections between the purposes and features of the invention and many different kinds of phenomena. | The report makes appropriate connections between the purposes and features of the invention and one or two phenomena. | The report makes unclear or inappropriate connections between the invention and other phenomena. | The report makes no connections between the invention and other things. |

FIGURE **16.9**  SCORING RUBRIC FOR A REPORT ON AN INVENTION

*Note:* A teacher might assign each of the columns a score and/or label, such as column 1: 4 (Excellent), column 2: 3 (Good), column 3: 2 (Minimal), and column 4: 1 (Inadequate).

shows a scoring rubric for scoring a report on an invention. Figure 16.10 indicates the importance of clarity in creating rubrics.

**Evaluating Performance Assessment**  Many educational psychologists support the increased use of performance-based assessment (Gallavan, 2009; Stiggins, 2008). They contend that performance assessments involve students more in their learning, encourage higher-level thinking skills, can measure what is really important in the curriculum, and can tie assessment more to real-world, real-life experiences.

However, "although support for performance-based assessment is high in many parts of the United States and Canada, effective implementation" faces several hurdles (Hambleton, 1996, p. 903). Performance assessments often "take considerably more

**Criterion: gains audience's attention**
**Quality**

Greater → → Lesser

| (a) | Creative beginning | Boring beginning | No beginning |
|---|---|---|---|
| (b) | Gives details or an amusing fact, a series of questions, a short demonstration, a colorful visual or a personal reason for why they picked the topic | Gives a one- or two-sentence introduction, then starts the speech | Does not attempt to gain the audience's attention, just starts the speech |

FIGURE **16.10**  CREATING CLARITY IN A RUBRIC FOR ONE DIMENSION OF AN ORAL PRESENTATION

The descriptions on top (a) are rather vague and do not clearly specify what students need to do to be evaluated very positively on the criterion. The descriptions on the bottom (b) provide more detailed specifications of how the criterion will be rated, a recommended strategy.

## TEACHING CONNECTIONS: Best Practices
### Strategies for Developing Scoring Rubrics

Here are some good strategies for incorporating scoring rubrics in performance assessments (Goodrich, 1997; McMillan, 2011; Re: Learning by Design, 2000):

1. *Match the type of rating with the purpose of the assessment.* If your purpose is global and you need a general judgment, use a holistic scale. If your purpose is to provide specific feedback on different aspects of a performance, use a more analytical approach.

2. *Share the criteria with students prior to instruction.* This encourages students to incorporate the descriptions as standards to guide their work. You might ask older students to use the same rubric you will use to self-evaluate their work, increasing the likelihood that they will attend to the rubric.

3. *Build your rubrics from the top, starting from a description of an exemplary performance.* Even if no student can perform at an exemplary level, the rubric should be built from a picture of excellence to establish an anchor for scoring. A good strategy is to use two or three examples of excellence rather than a single example so that students are not limited in their thinking about what an excellent performance is. After you have described the best level of quality, describe the worst; then fill in the middle levels.

4. *Carefully construct the rubric language for each criterion or score.* Use words such as *excellent* and *good,* and carefully describe what each term means. Typically, you will have a paragraph for each criterion or score that includes concrete indicators of when the criterion or score has been met.

5. *Make rubrics more authentic.* Criteria should validly, not arbitrarily, distinguish different degrees of performance. For example, criteria often used in assessing writing in large-scale performance tests include organization, usage/word choice, focus, sentence construction, mechanics, and voice. However, the following criteria are more authentic in that they relate more clearly to the impact of the writing (and they include the previously mentioned criteria without restricting the writer to conventions and rules): clarity, memorability, persuasiveness, and enticingness.

6. *Show students models.* Let students examine examples of work that meets expectations and work that does not. Identify what is good or bad about the models.

7. *Take appropriate steps to minimize scoring error.* A scoring system should be objective and consistent. Some types of errors in particular should be avoided in scoring rubrics. The most common errors involve personal bias and halo effects of the person making the judgment. *Personal bias* occurs when teachers tend to give students higher scores (such as mostly 5 and 6 on a one- to six-point scale), lower scores (1 or 2), or scores in the middle (3 or 4). A *halo effect* occurs when a teacher's general impression of the student influences the score given on a particular performance.

---

time to construct, administer, and score than objective tests." Also, many performance tests do not meet the standards of validity and reliability advocated by many educational psychologists. Moreover, the research base for performance tests is not well established.

Still, even the strongest supporters of traditional tests acknowledge that these tests do not measure all of what schools expect students to learn (Hambleton, 1996). Although planning, constructing, and scoring performance tests is challenging, teachers should make every effort to include performance assessments as an important aspect of their teaching (Stiggins, 2008).

I recently asked teachers how they use performance assessment in the classroom. Following are their responses.

**EARLY CHILDHOOD**    Most of the assessments in early childhood classrooms are based on a performance assessment model. Teachers observe and record informa-

tion that the child presents as part of play and participation in classroom activities. For example, a teacher might date a paper that a child used to write her full phone number for the first time, demonstrating the knowledge of identity, ability to write the specific numbers, sequencing, memory, and more. This piece of information would be kept in the child's portfolio record to be shared with the family as part of the assessment process.

—**HEIDI KAUFMAN,** *Metro West YMCA Child Care and Educational Program*

**ELEMENTARY SCHOOL: GRADES K–5** I set up an assignment that students prepare in class and for homework. For example, they can memorize and perform a poem or write and perform a speech about a human rights activist. I assess the student's performance, research, content, language, effort, and care.

—**KEREN ABRA,** *Convent of the Sacred Heart Elementary School*

**MIDDLE SCHOOL: GRADES 6–8** One project I give my students is a decades project. The students get to choose a decade that interests them and present their findings to the class. They can do this like a news report and dress up like people from that decade. They can also bring in music from their decade and mementoes as well. This is a lot of fun and a great learning experience for students.

—**CASEY MAASS,** *Edison Middle School*

**HIGH SCHOOL: GRADES 9–12** In sophomore English, students give four speeches. One demonstrates a method, one uses PowerPoint as a visual aid, one shares a personal story, and one is videotaped and reflected on formally. We also do extemporaneous speeches where a student will choose a topic and speak for two minutes. Speeches are often very stressful for many high school students, but I usually see growth with each speech.

—**JENNIFER HEITER,** *Bremen High School*

## PORTFOLIO ASSESSMENT

Interest in portfolio assessment has increased dramatically in recent years (Oosterhof, 2009). Portfolios represent a significant departure from traditional tests of learning (Enger & Yager, 2010). Figure 16.11 summarizes the contrast between portfolios and traditional testing.

A **portfolio** consists of a systematic and organized collection of a student's work that demonstrates the student's skills and accomplishments. A portfolio is a purposeful collection of work that tells the story of the student's progress and achievements. It is much more than a compilation of student papers stuffed into a manila folder or a collection of memorabilia pasted into a scrapbook. To qualify for inclusion in a portfolio, each piece of work should be created and organized in a way that demonstrates progress and purpose. Portfolios can include many different types of work, such as writing samples, journal entries, videotapes, art, teacher comments, posters, interviews, poetry, test results, problem solutions, recordings of foreign language communication, self-assessments, and any other expression of the student that the teacher believes demonstrates the student's skills and accomplishments (Green & Johnson, 2010). Portfolios can be collected on paper, in photographs, and on audiotape, videotape, computer disk, or CD-ROM. Assessment expert Joan Herman (1996) says that portfolio assessment has become increasingly popular because it is a natural way to integrate instruction and assessment.

Four classes of evidence that can be placed in students' portfolios are artifacts, reproductions, attestations, and productions (Barton & Collins, 1997). *Artifacts* are

**portfolio** A systematic and organized collection of a student's work that demonstrates the student's skills and accomplishments.

| Traditional tests | Portfolios |
|---|---|
| • Separate learning, testing, and teaching | • Link assessment and teaching to learning |
| • Fail to assess the impact of prior knowledge on learning by using short passages that are often isolated and unfamiliar | • Address the importance of the student's prior knowledge as a critical determinant to learning by using authentic assessment activities |
| • Rely on materials requesting only literal information | • Provide opportunities to demonstrate inferential and critical thinking that are essential for constructing meaning |
| • Prohibit collaboration during the assessment process | • Represent a collaborative approach to assessment involving both students and teachers |
| • Often treat skills in isolated contexts to determine achievement for reporting purposes | • Use multifaceted activities while recognizing that learning requires integration and coordination of communication skills |
| • Assess students across a limited range of assignments that may not match what students do in classrooms | • Represent the full range of instructional activities that students are doing in their classrooms |
| • Assess students in a predetermined situation where the content is fixed | • Can measure the student's ability to perform appropriately in unanticipated situations |
| • Assess all students on the same dimensions | • Measure each student's achievements while allowing individual differences |
| • Address only achievement | • Address improvement, effort, and achievement |
| • Seldom provide vehicles for assessing students' abilities to monitor their own learning | • Implement self-assessment by having students monitor their learning |
| • Are mechanically scored or scored by teachers who have little input into the assessment | • Engage students in assessing their progress and/or accomplishments and establishing on-going learning goals |
| • Rarely include items that assess emotional responses to learning | • Provide opportunities to reflect upon feelings about learning |

FIGURE **16.11** CONTRASTING TRADITIONAL TESTS AND PORTFOLIOS

documents or products such as student papers and homework that are produced during normal academic work in the classroom. *Reproductions* consist of documentation of a student's work outside the classroom, such as special projects and interviews. For example, a student's description of an interview with a local scientist in the community about the scientist's work is a reproduction. *Attestations* represent the teacher's or other responsible persons' documentation of the student's progress. For example, a teacher might write evaluative notes about a student's oral presentation and place them in the student's portfolio. *Productions* are documents the student prepares especially for the portfolio. Productions consist of three types of materials: goal statements, reflections, and captions. Students generate goal statements about what they want to accomplish with their portfolio, write down their reflections about their work and describe their progress, and create captions that describe each piece of work in the portfolio and its importance.

**Using Portfolios Effectively** Effective use of portfolios for assessment requires (1) establishing the portfolio's purpose, (2) involving the student in decisions about it, (3) reviewing the portfolio with the student, (4) setting criteria for evaluation, (5) scoring and judging the portfolio, and (6) student self-reflection.

***Establishing Purpose*** Portfolios can be used for different purposes (Green & Johnson, 2010; Popham, 2011). Two broad types of purpose are to document growth and to show best work. A **growth portfolio** consists of the student's work produced over an extended time frame (throughout the school year or even longer) to reveal the student's progress in meeting learning targets. Growth portfolios also are sometimes referred to as *developmental portfolios*. They are especially helpful in

**growth portfolio** A portfolio of work produced over an extended time frame (throughout the school year or longer) to reveal the student's progress in meeting learning targets.

providing concrete evidence of how much a student has changed or learned over time. As students examine their portfolios, they can see for themselves how much they have improved. One example of a growth portfolio is the Integrated Language Arts Portfolio used in the elementary school grades in Juneau, Alaska (Arter, 1995). It is designed to replace report cards and grades as a way to demonstrate growth and accomplishments. Growth is tracked along a developmental continuum for levels of skills in reading, writing, speaking, and listening. A student's status on the continuum is marked at several designated times during the year. Samples of the student's work are used as the basis for judgments about the student's developmental level.

A **best-work portfolio** showcases the student's most outstanding work. Sometimes it even is called a *showcase portfolio* (Green & Johnson, 2010). Best-work portfolios are more selective than developmental portfolios and usually include the student's latest product. They are especially useful for parent-teacher conferences, students' future teachers, and admission to higher education levels.

*Passportfolios,* or *proficiency portfolios,* are sometimes used to demonstrate competence and readiness to move on to a new level of work (Lankes, 1995). For example, the Science Portfolio is an optional aspect of the Golden State Evaluation in California (California State Department of Education, 1994). It is produced during a year of science and contains a problem-solving investigation, a creative expression (presenting a scientific idea in a unique and original manner), a "growth through writing" section that demonstrates progress over time in understanding a concept, and a written self-reflection. The Central Park East Secondary School in New York City uses portfolios to determine graduation eligibility. Students are required to complete 14 portfolios that demonstrate their competence in areas such as science and technology, ethics and social issues, community service, and history (Gold & Lanzoni, 1993).

***Involving Students in Selecting Portfolio Materials*** Many teachers let students make at least some of the decisions about the portfolio's contents. When students are allowed to choose the contents for their own portfolios, a good strategy is to encourage self-reflection by having them write a brief description of why they chose each piece of work (Airasian & Russell, 2008).

***Reviewing with Students*** Explain to students at the beginning of the year what portfolios are and how they will be used. You also should have a number of student-teacher conferences throughout the year to review the student's progress and help her plan future work for the portfolio (McMillan, 2011).

***Setting Criteria for Evaluation*** Clear and systematic performance criteria are essential for effectively using portfolios. Clear learning targets for students make developing performance criteria much easier. Ask yourself what knowledge and skills you want your students to have. This should be the focus of your teaching and your performance criteria.

***Scoring and Judging*** It takes considerable time to score and judge portfolios (Airasian & Russell, 2008). Teachers must evaluate not only each individual item but also the portfolio as a whole. When the portfolio's purpose is to provide descriptive information about the student for the teacher at the next grade level, no scoring or summarizing of the portfolio might be necessary. However, when its purpose is to diagnose, reflect improvement, provide evidence for effective instruction, motivate students to reflect on their work, or give grades to students, summary scoring and judgments are needed. Checklists and rating scales are commonly used for this purpose. As with other aspects of portfolio assessment, some teachers give students the opportunity to evaluate and critique their own work.

**best-work portfolio** A portfolio that showcases the student's most outstanding work.

**Evaluating the Role of Portfolios in Assessment** Learning portfolios have several strengths: Their comprehensive nature captures the complexity and completeness of the student's work and accomplishments. They provide opportunities for encouraging student decision making and self-reflection. They motivate students to think critically and deeply. And they provide an excellent mechanism for evaluating student progress and improvement (Musial & others, 2009).

Learning portfolios also have several weaknesses: They take considerable time to coordinate and evaluate. Their complexity and uniqueness make them difficult to evaluate, and their reliability is often much lower than that of traditional tests. Also, their use in large-scale assessments (such as state-wide evaluation) is expensive. However, even with these weaknesses in mind, most educational psychology experts and educational organizations, such as the National Education Association, support the use of portfolios.

I recently asked teachers how they use portfolios in their classroom. Following are their responses.

**EARLY CHILDHOOD** We use portfolios to collect specific work done by our children—such as sample writing and pictures—three times during the year. We arrange these portfolios similarly so that we can assess and compare the child's development over the year. Parents are shown the portfolios during conferences to demonstrate how their child has progressed. We also use portfolios as a tool to assess possible developmental delays.

—**VALARIE GORHAM,** *Kiddie Quarters, Inc.*

**ELEMENTARY SCHOOL: GRADES K–5** My fourth-graders do a "Best Work" writing portfolio and a "Draft" writing portfolio. The process of gathering materials for both of these portfolios takes roughly five weeks, with writing lessons mixed in. By the end of the year, students see their writing progress by examining both their Draft and Best Work portfolios.

—**SHANE SCHWARZ,** *Clinton Elementary School*

**MIDDLE SCHOOL: GRADES 6–8** I have my students keep portfolios with their tests, quizzes, reports, projects, essays, and other important assignments. A key part of the portfolio process is when I instruct students to take their portfolios home, evaluate their work with their parents or guardians, and then come back to school with a set of goals to improve their work in class.

—**CASEY MAASS,** *Edison Middle School*

**HIGH SCHOOL: GRADES 9–12** I use portfolios for my work-experience students. Four times a year, they include evaluations from supervisors at their job assignments, their own reflections on the job itself, completed job applications, and feedback on interviews that they have gone on. I encourage students to assemble their portfolios professionally for use when seeking their next job.

—**SANDY SWANSON,** *Menomonee Falls High School*

Now that you've read about many types of assessment, this is a good time to think about what your classroom assessment philosophy will be. Self-Assessment 16.1 gives you this opportunity.

# SELF-ASSESSMENT 16.1
## Planning My Classroom Assessment Practices

With the subject matter and grade level at which you plan to teach in mind, examine the following list of assessments that we have discussed in this chapter. Rate each of the assessments on this scale: 1 = I don't plan to use this at all, 2 = I plan to use this occasionally, 3 = I plan to use this moderately, 4 = I plan to use this often, and 5 = This will be one of the most important assessments I will use.

| | 1 | 2 | 3 | 4 | 5 |
|---|---|---|---|---|---|
| 1. Informal observations in preinstructional assessment | | | | | |
| 2. Structured exercises in preinstructional assessment | | | | | |
| 3. Observation during instruction | | | | | |
| 4. Questions during instruction | | | | | |
| 5. Student self-assessment | | | | | |
| 6. Assessments of students' motivation, effort, and participation | | | | | |
| 7. True/false items | | | | | |
| 8. Multiple-choice items | | | | | |
| 9. Matching | | | | | |
| 10. Short-answer items | | | | | |
| 11. Essays | | | | | |
| 12. Authentic assessment | | | | | |
| 13. Experiments | | | | | |
| 14. Projects | | | | | |
| 15. Oral presentations | | | | | |
| 16. Interviews | | | | | |
| 17. Performances | | | | | |
| 18. Exhibitions | | | | | |
| 19. Portfolios | | | | | |

Look back through your responses and then use this information to help you formulate your classroom assessment philosophy here. If you need more space, do this outside the book or on the student Web site.

_____

_____

_____

_____

_____

_____

## Review, Reflect, and Practice

**③** Describe some types of alternative assessments.

**REVIEW**

- What makes an assessment "authentic"? What are some criticisms of authentic assessments?
- What are some features of performance assessment? What are some guidelines for using them?
- What is a portfolio, and how can portfolios be used in assessment? What are some strengths and weaknesses of portfolios?

**REFLECT**

- Suppose that you were teaching this course in educational psychology. How would you go about creating rubrics for assessing answers to the preceding three items?

**PRAXIS™ PRACTICE**

1. Nicole has just been told that as part of her teacher certification process, there will be a performance assessment. Which of the following is the best performance assessment of Nicole's teaching skills?
   a. a multiple-choice exam
   b. an essay exam
   c. an exam based on case studies
   d. direct observation of classroom teaching

2. Kyle is working on his portfolio for journalism class. Included in the portfolio are his teacher's evaluation notes regarding articles he has written for the school newspaper. These notes are examples of which of the following:
   a. artifacts
   b. attestations
   c. productions
   d. reproductions

*Please see the answer key at the end of the book.*

## ④ GRADING AND REPORTING PERFORMANCE

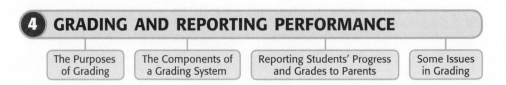

| The Purposes of Grading | The Components of a Grading System | Reporting Students' Progress and Grades to Parents | Some Issues in Grading |

**Grading** means translating descriptive assessment information into letters, numbers, or other marks that indicate the quality of a student's learning or performance.

### THE PURPOSES OF GRADING

Grading is carried out to communicate meaningful information about a student's learning and achievement (Green & Johnson, 2010). In this process, grades serve four basic purposes (Airasian & Russell, 2008):

- *Administrative.* Grades help determine students' class rank, credits for graduation, and whether a student should be promoted to the next grade.

**grading** Translating descriptive assessment information into letters, numbers, or other marks that indicate the quality of a student's learning or performance.

- *Informational.* Grades can be used to communicate with students, parents, and others (such as admissions officers for subsequent schooling) about a student's work. A grade represents the teacher's overall conclusion about how well a student has met instructional objectives and learning targets.
- *Motivational.* Many students work harder because they are extrinsically motivated by a desire for high grades and a fear of low grades.
- *Guidance.* Grades help students, parents, and counselors to select appropriate courses and levels of work for students. They provide information about which students might require special services and what levels of future education students will likely be able to handle.

## THE COMPONENTS OF A GRADING SYSTEM

Grades reflect teachers' judgments. Three main types of teacher judgments underlie a teacher's grading system (Airasian & Russell, 2008): (1) What standard of comparison will I use for grading? (2) What aspects of students' performance will I use to establish grades? and (3) How will I weight different kinds of evidence in giving grades?

**Standards of Comparison**   A student's performance can be graded by comparing it with the performance of other students or to predefined standards of performance.

**Comparing Performance Across Students**   The system of **norm-referenced grading** is based on comparison of a student's performance with that of other students in the class or of other classes and other students. In such a system, students get high grades for performing better than most of their classmates or low grades for performing worse. Norm-referenced grading is commonly referred to as *grading on the curve.* The grading scale determines what percentages of students get particular grades. In most instances the scale is created so that the largest percentage of students get *C*'s.

This is a typical breakdown of grades: 15 percent *A*'s, 25 percent *B*'s, 40 percent *C*'s, 15 percent *D*'s, and 5 percent *F*'s. In assigning grades, instructors often look for gaps in the range of scores. If six students score 92 to 100 and ten students score 81 to 88, and there are no scores between 88 and 92, the teacher would assign a grade of *A* to the 92 to 100 scores and a *B* to the 81 to 88 scores. Norm-referenced grading has been criticized for reducing students' motivation, increasing their anxiety, increasing negative interactions among students, and hindering learning. Consequently, norm-referenced grading is not widely used.

**Comparing Performance with a Predetermined Standard**   In **criterion-referenced grading** students receive a certain grade for a certain level of performance regardless of any comparison with the work of other students. Sometimes called *absolute grading,* criterion-referenced grading is based on the proportion of points attained on a test or the level of mastery reached in a performance skill, such as giving an oral presentation and meeting all the predetermined criteria. This grading system is recommended over norm-referenced grading.

In theory, the standard established is supposed to be absolute, but in practice it doesn't always work out that way (McMillan, 2011). For example, a school system often develops a grading system that goes something like this: *A* = 94 to 100 percent correct, *B* = 87 to 93 percent, *C* = 77 to 86 percent, *D* = 70 to 76 percent, and *F* = below 70 percent. Although this system is absolute in the sense that every student must get 94 points to get an *A* and every student who does not get at least 70 points gets an *F,* teachers and classrooms vary enormously in what constitutes enough mastery of material to get a 94, an 87, a 77, or a 70. One teacher might give very hard tests, another very easy tests.

*"Your grading curve and my learning curve don't intersect."*

Dave Carpenter from *Phi Delta Kappan* (1997). Reprinted with permission of Dave Carpenter.

**norm-referenced grading** A grading system based on a comparison of a student's performance with that of other students in the class or of other classes and other students.

**criterion-referenced grading** A grading system based on a certain grade for a certain level of performance regardless of any comparison with the work of other students.

Many teachers use different cutoff scores than the ones just mentioned. Some teachers argue that low grades discourage student motivation and refuse to give *D*'s or *F*'s; others won't fail students unless their scores fall below 50.

*Standards-based grading* is a recent development based on criterion-referenced grading. It involves basing grading on standards that students are expected to achieve in a course (Guskey & Bailey, 2010). In some cases, national associations such as the National Council of Teachers of Mathematics (NCTM) have developed standards for student achievement. Consequently, in one form of standards-based grading, a mathematics teacher, for example, might tie students' grades to how well their performance meets these national standards.

*Rubrics* are often are used in standards-based grading to indicate the degree to which students have met standards, and grades are based on what level of the rubric is reached (McMillan, 2011). For example, grades might be assigned based on these categories: below basic, basic, proficient, and advanced.

**Aspects of Performance**   Over the course of a grading period, students will likely have created many products that can be evaluated and used as a basis for grading. These can include test and quiz results as well as various alternative assessments such as oral reports, projects, interviews, and homework. Increasingly, portfolios are used as the complete collection of materials to be graded or a portion of the work on which an overall grade is based. Some educators argue that grades should be based only on academic performance. In the view of other educators, grades should be based mainly on academic performance, but teacher ratings of motivation, effort, and participation can be factored in as well.

Many teachers use tests as the main, or even sole, basis for assigning grades. However, many assessment experts recommend basing an overall grade on a series of tests and other types of assessments (McMillan, 2011). Thus, a semester grade in geography might be based on two major tests and a final, eight quizzes, homework, two oral reports, and a project. Basing a grade on a series of tests and different types of assessment helps to balance out students' strengths and weaknesses, as well as compensate for a poor performance or two because of internal and external sources of measurement error.

Some educators advocate factoring characteristics such as motivation, effort, and participation into grades, especially by giving borderline students a plus or minus. Thus, a teacher might convert a student's B to a B+ if the student was highly motivated, put forth considerable effort, and actively participated in the class—or to a B− if the student was poorly motivated, made little effort, and did not actively participate. However, other educators believe that grades should be based only on academic performance. One of the problems with including factors such as effort in grades is the difficulty in determining the reliability and validity of effort. Measures of effort or improvement can be made more systematic and reliable by developing scoring rubrics and examples (McMillan, 2011).

**Weighting Different Kinds of Evidence**   You will need to determine how much weight to give the different components of a student's grade. For example, the teacher might arrive at a weighting system that looks something like this:

| | |
|---|---|
| Major tests (2): | 20 percent |
| Final test: | 25 percent |
| Quizzes: | 20 percent |
| Homework: | 5 percent |
| Oral report: | 10 percent |
| Project: | 20 percent |

Many teachers don't use homework as a component for a grade. One reason for this is that when a student's grade depends on homework or other work done outside class, parents might be tempted to do their child's work to ensure a high grade. Another reason is that including homework as a component of grading favors students from better home environments. As with other aspects of classroom assessment, your judgment is involved in how you synthesize information to arrive at a student's grade. If a student fails to turn in a certain number of homework assignments, some teachers lower the student's grade.

## REPORTING STUDENTS' PROGRESS AND GRADES TO PARENTS

Grades are the most common method of informing parents about a child's progress and performance in the classroom (Guskey & Bailey, 2010). Especially important in reporting students' progress is the report card.

**The Report Card**　The report card is a standard method of reporting students' progress and grades to parents (McMillan, 2011). The form of judgments on report cards varies from one school system to another, and, in many cases, from one grade level to another. Some report cards convey letter grades (typically *A, B, C, D,* and *F,*

*"How much to shred a report card?"*
© Martha F. Campbell. Reprinted by permission.

---

## TEACHING CONNECTIONS: Best Practices
### Strategies for Parent-Teacher Conferences Related to Grades and Assessment

Here are some good strategies for meeting with parents about their child's progress and grades (Payne, 1997):

1. *Be prepared.* Review the student's performance prior to the meeting with parents. Think about what you are going to say to the parents. Have examples of the student's work to show parents.

2. *Be positive.* Even if the student has performed poorly, try to find at least some areas to discuss in which the student has performed well. This does not mean glossing over and ignoring a student's lack of achievement; it means including positive areas in addition to the negative ones. If you need to discuss negatives, try the "sandwich approach" of starting and ending on a positive note, with any negative statements between.

3. *Be objective.* Even as you provide positive aspects of the student's record to communicate to parents, also be objective and honest about what needs to improve. Don't give parents false hopes if the student has low ability in a particular subject area.

4. *Practice good communication skills.* Good communication means being an active listener and giving parents adequate opportunities to contribute to the conversation. Make sure that parents and students understand your grading criteria. In Through the Eyes of Teachers, Lynn Ayres, an English teacher at East Middle School, Ypsilanti, Michigan, provides her thoughts about this topic.

### THROUGH THE EYES OF TEACHERS
#### Some Grading Strategies

I think it is extremely important that parents and students clearly know what is expected of students if they are to succeed in my class. I try to help students understand that they are in control of the grade they get. If students think a grading system is capricious or unknowable, it creates frustration, anxiety, and is of little use in motivating students. By getting them to see that their grades are in their own hands, I move to the position of "facilitator" in the classroom. The students see me as someone who is there to *help* them achieve rather than someone who sits in judgment of their work and gives them a grade.

5. *Don't talk about other students.* The focus of the parent-teacher conference should be on the parent's child. Don't compare the child with other students. Respect confidentiality.

6. *Be punctual.* Start and end each conference on time. If you need more time to discuss a particular student, set up a follow-up appointment. This will keep things flowing and will avoid the problem of parents congregating in the hall listening to what you are saying about another student.

*"I don't know why you're so surprised by his poor grades. Every day you asked him what he did at school, and every day he answered, 'Nothing.'"*

© Art Bouthillier. Reprinted with permission.

sometimes also allowing pluses and minuses). Some report cards convey numerical scores (such as 91 in math, 85 in English, and so on). Other report cards have a pass/fail category in one or more subjects. Yet other report cards have checklists indicating skills or objectives the student has attained. Some report cards have categories for affective characteristics, such as effort, cooperation, and other appropriate and inappropriate behaviors.

Checklists of skills and objectives are mainly used in elementary schools or kindergartens. In the higher elementary school grade levels and secondary schools, letter grades are mainly used, although these might be accompanied by other information such as written comments.

**Written Progress Reports**   Another reporting strategy is to provide parents with a weekly, biweekly, or monthly report of the student's progress and achievement (McMillan, 2011). These written reports can include the student's performance on tests and quizzes, projects, oral reports, and so on. They also can include information about the student's motivation, cooperation, and behavior, as well as suggestions for how parents can help students improve their performance.

**Parent-Teacher Conferences**   Parent-teacher conferences are another way to communicate information about grades and assessment. Such conferences are both a responsibility and an opportunity (Stiggins, 2008). Parents have a right to know how their child is doing in school and how their child might improve. Conferences provide an opportunity for giving parents helpful information about how they can be partners with you in helping the child learn more effectively.

## SOME ISSUES IN GRADING

Should a zero be given to a missed assignment or paper? Should teachers go strictly by the numbers when assigning a grade? Should grading be abolished? Is there too much grade inflation? These are important issues that concern many educators today.

**Should a Missed Assignment or Paper Receive a Zero?**   One grading issue is whether a student should be given a zero for a missed assignment or paper. Including a zero with other scores badly skews the mean of the scores. Many experts on assessment recommend not using a zero in this manner because it weights the assignment or paper more than what was intended in that the interval between 0 and 65 or 70 is more than the intervals between the scores for other grades (McMillan, 2011). Using a score of 60 for a missed assignment or paper is considered more reasonable.

**Should Teachers Go Strictly by the Numbers in Grading?**   One concern about grading is that too many teachers engage in "mindless" number crunching, which is now more likely to occur with grading software available. No matter how objective the process is for averaging scores and grades, grading remains a matter of professional judgment (O'Connor, 2009). Going strictly by the numbers can result in a grade that is not consistent with the actual knowledge and skill of the student, especially if pulled down by minor assignments and homework or a later paper. In the end, it is important for teachers to be confident that the grade they give reflects what the student knows, understands, and is able to do in relation to standards of performance (McMillan, 2011).

**Should Grading Be Abolished?**   Occasionally there are calls to abandon grades, usually based on the belief that evaluation of students is necessary but that competitive grading deemphasizes learning in favor of judging. Critics of grading argue that it discourages the vast majority of students, especially those who receive below-average grades. The critics often call for more constructive evaluation that would encourage students to engage in maximum effort by underscoring their strengths, identifying concrete ways for them to improve, and providing positive feedback (Culbertson & Jalongo, 1999). Critics of grading also point out that the practice often motivates students to study only the material that will be on the test.

As classroom assessment experts Peter Airasian and Michael Russell (2008) concluded, grades are powerful symbols in our society that are taken seriously by students, teachers, and the public. Regardless of whether you like the way grading is currently conducted—and even if you think it should be eliminated—in the foreseeable future it is important for you to take grading your students seriously and do it in a way that is fair to your students. Never use grades to reward or punish students because you like them or don't like them. Always base students' grades on how well they have learned the subject matter, based on objective evidence of learning.

**Is There Too Much Grade Inflation?**   Some teachers do not like to give low grades because they point out that they diminish the student's motivation to learn. However, some critics argue that grade inflation, especially in the form of giving high grades for mediocre performance, provides students with a false belief that they are learning and achieving more than they actually are. The result is that many students discover that they can perform well below their ability and still achieve high grades (Guskey & Bailey, 2010). A rising tide of grade inflation has occurred (Olenik, 2009). In 2003, 42 percent of U.S. college-bound seniors had an *A* average compared with 28 percent in 1989, but the average scores of the students on college admissions tests in 2003 were lower than in 1989 (College Board, 2004).

## Review, Reflect, and Practice

 Construct a sound approach to grading.

### REVIEW
- What are the purposes of grading?
- What types of judgments underlie a teacher's grading system? Comment about each type. What are some choices in reporting students' progress to parents? What are some issues in grading?

### REFLECT
- What criteria would you adopt for deciding whether a teacher is doing an excellent job in grading?

### PRAXIS™ PRACTICE
1. Amaal brings home her school report card. On the card are letter grades indicating that Amaal has earned an *A* in math, reading, and social studies, and a *B* in science and P.E. Her parents look over her grades, sign the card, and return it to the school. What purpose did these grades serve?
   a. administrative
   b. guidance
   c. informational
   d. motivational

*(continued)*

## Review, Reflect, and Practice

**PRAXIS™ PRACTICE (CONTINUED)**

2. Mr. Walker teaches algebra. On the first day of class, he tells students that of the 25 students in the class, 5 will receive *A*'s, 6 will receive *B*'s, 7 will receive *C*'s, 4 will receive *D*'s, and 3 will receive *F*'s. What type of grading system is Mr. Walker using?
   a. criterion-referenced
   b. norm-referenced
   c. standards-based
   d. weighted

3. Isabella brings home her quarterly school report card. On the card are letter grades indicating that Isabella has earned an *A* in math, language arts, and social studies, and a *B* in science and P.E. Which of the following is a valid criticism of such a grading system?
   a. It gives parents too much information about the student's performance.
   b. It is too specific.
   c. Letter grades are unfair.
   d. It does not provide enough information to allow parents to evaluate their child's performance.

4. Ms. Gregory and Ms. Templeton are discussing grading issues. Which of the following comments made by Ms. Gregory and Ms. Templeton is the *least* likely to be supported by educational psychologists?
   a. Many students are being rewarded with high grades for mediocre performance.
   b. In the last several decades, grades have been increasing while SAT scores have been going down.
   c. Some teachers don't like to give low grades because they believe the low grades decrease students' motivation.
   d. Grades should be abolished.

*Please see the answer key at the end of the book.*

# The Project

Mr. Andrews generally was using traditional, multiple-choice tests in his sixth-grade class on ancient history, but the students seemed bored with studying for these tests and with his lectures. Therefore, for the unit on ancient Mesopotamia, he decided to allow the students to complete a project instead of taking a test. He gave these choices:

- Construct a test covering the chapter on Mesopotamia.
- Create a game about Mesopotamia.
- Create a diorama about Mesopotamia.
- Write a play about life in Mesopotamia.
- Create artifacts from Mesopotamia that an archaeologist might find.

Mr. Andrews' co-teacher, Ms. Benjamin, told the children that they could not use a computer to complete their projects.

Sally decided to write a test for her project. She carefully read the chapter and constructed questions as she went along. She used short-answer questions because she was worried about constructing good multiple-choice questions. It had been her experience that the distractors used in these questions were often confusing. She felt the same way about true/false questions. She wanted to make her questions as clear as possible because she didn't want her classmates mad at her when they took her test.

Sally carefully printed each question because of the ban on using a computer. She then created a key, which she intended to use to grade her classmates' tests. The final product consisted of 25 short-answer questions. She was very proud of her work the day she turned it in.

Mr. Andrews looked at her test and told her, "This isn't acceptable. Why didn't you type it?"

"Ms. Benjamin told us we couldn't use computers."

"That isn't what she meant. She meant you couldn't use the Internet," responded Mr. Andrews. "Take it home and type it. Turn it in tomorrow."

Sally left the room very upset. She took her test home and carefully typed both the test and the key. She turned them in the next day. Three days later, Sally received these marks:

Content: **B** Did not include a question on religion (actually Sally did have a question regarding polytheism). Should have included a variety of question types, such as multiple-choice, matching, and true/false.

Mechanics: **A** Nicely typed. Correct spelling used.

Accuracy: **B**

Effort: **C**

**Overall Grade C**

Sally was upset with her grade. "A C for effort?! I worked really hard on this! I even had to do it twice, 'cause of stupid Ms. Benjamin!" She took her grade sheet and test home and showed it to her mother. Sally's mother was equally upset, particularly about the low grade for effort. She called Mr. Andrews, asking to see the guidelines for the project and the grading rubric. Mr. Andrews was unable to provide either. She asked him the difference between content and accuracy. He could not tell her. She also asked him how he had measured effort, to which he responded, "I consider what I expect from students and then what they give me."

"So you're telling me that you graded content three times. Once you gave her a B, once a B, and once a C, right?"

Mr. Andrews did not know how to respond to her question.

1. What are the issues involved in this situation?
2. What did Mr. Andrews do wrong?
3. How should he have gone about developing his alternative assessments?
4. How should he have developed his grading guide?
5. What do you think of the practice of including an effort grade on students' projects? Why?

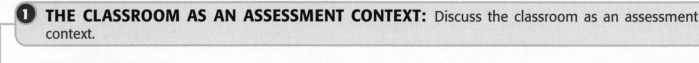
## Classroom Assessment and Grading

**1** **THE CLASSROOM AS AN ASSESSMENT CONTEXT:** Discuss the classroom as an assessment context.

### Assessment as an Integral Part of Teaching

Preinstruction assessment, assessment during instruction, and postinstruction assessment should be integral to teaching. Much of preinstruction assessment involves informal observations, which require interpretation. In informal observations, watch for nonverbal cues that give insights about the student. Structured exercises also can be used in preinstruction assessment. Guard against expectations that will distort your perception of a student. Treat your initial perceptions as hypotheses to be confirmed or modified by subsequent observation and information. Some teachers also administer pretests in subject areas. An increasing trend is to examine students' learning portfolios from previous grades. Formative assessment is assessment during instruction with an emphasis on assessment *for* learning instead of assessment *of* learning. An increasing trend is to have students engage in self-assessment of their progress on a day-to-day basis as part of formative assessment. Summative assessment, or formal assessment, is assessment after instruction is finished in order to document student mastery of the material, whether students are ready for the next unit, how your teaching should be adapted, and what grades the students should get.

### Making Assessment Compatible with Contemporary Views of Learning and Motivation

To bring assessment into line with contemporary views of motivation and learning, it is important to focus on the following: active learning and constructing meaning; the use of planning and goal setting; reflective, critical, and creative thinking; positive student expectations for learning and confidence in skills; degree of motivation; the ability to apply what is learned to real-world situations; and effective communication. Consider the role that assessment (especially alternative assessment) plays in effort, engagement, and performance.

### Creating Clear, Appropriate Learning Targets

A learning target, much like an instructional objective, consists of what students should know and be able to do.

### Establishing High-Quality Assessments

High-quality assessments are valid, reliable, and fair. Validity is the extent to which an assessment measures what it is intended to measure, as well as how accurate and useful a teacher's inferences are. Reliability is the extent to which assessments produce consistent, reproducible scores. Assessment is fair when all students have an equal opportunity to learn and demonstrate their knowledge and skills. A pluralistic assessment philosophy, including being sensitive to cultural diversity, also contributes to fairness.

### Current Trends

Current trends in assessment include using at least some performance-based assessments, examining higher-level skills, using multiple assessment methods, having high performance standards, and using computers as a part of assessment. Other trends focus on assessing an integration of skills, giving students considerable feedback, and making standards and criteria public.

**2** **TRADITIONAL TESTS:** Provide some guidelines for constructing traditional tests.

### Selected-Response Items

A multiple-choice item has two parts: a stem and a number of possible options or alternatives. Incorrect alternatives are called distractors. True/false items are easy to construct but can encourage rote memorization. Matching items often are used with younger students.

| Constructed-Response Items |

Constructed-response items require students to write out information rather than select it from a menu. Short-answer and essay items are the most commonly used constructed- response items. Short-answer items require students to write a word, a short phrase, or several sentences in response to a task and often encourage rote memorization. Essay questions allow students more freedom of response than the other item formats. Essay questions are especially good for assessing students' understanding, higher-level thinking skills, organizational skills, and writing skills.

## 3 ALTERNATIVE ASSESSMENTS: Describe some types of alternative assessments.

| Trends in Alternative Assessment |

Authentic assessment is evaluating a student's knowledge or skill in a context that approximates the real world or real life as closely as possible. Critics argue that authentic assessments are not necessarily better than more conventional assessments, that there are few data to support their validity, and that they don't adequately examine knowledge and basic skills.

| Performance Assessment |

Performance assessments of higher-level thinking often emphasize "doing," open-ended activities for which there is no one correct answer. The tasks are sometimes realistic, and many, but not all, performance assessments are authentic (approximate the real world or real life). Evaluating performance often includes direct methods of evaluation, self-assessment, assessment of group performance as well as individual performance, and an extended period of time. There are four main guidelines in using performance assessments: (1) establishing a clear purpose, (2) identifying observable criteria, (3) providing an appropriate setting, and (4) judging or scoring the performance.

| Portfolio Assessment |

A portfolio is a systematic and organized collection of a student's work to demonstrate skills and accomplishments. Four classes of evidence can be included: artifacts, reproductions, attestations, and productions. Using a portfolio for assessment requires (1) establishing the portfolio's purpose, (2) involving the student in decisions about it, (3) reviewing the portfolio with the student, (4) setting criteria for evaluation, and (5) scoring and judging the portfolio. Two broad types of purposes of portfolios are to document growth through a growth portfolio and to showcase the student's most outstanding work through a best-work portfolio. Learning portfolios have strengths—such as capturing the complexity and completeness of the student's work and accomplishments, as well as encouraging student decision making and self-reflection—and weaknesses—such as the time required to coordinate and evaluate them and the difficulty in evaluating them.

## 4 GRADING AND REPORTING PERFORMANCE: Construct a sound approach to grading.

| The Purposes of Grading |

Grading purposes include administrative (help determine students' class rank, credits); informational (communicate with parents, teachers, students); motivational (students' desire for higher grades); and guidance (select appropriate courses and levels for students).

| The Components of a Grading System |

Three main types of teacher judgments underlie a grading system: (1) standard of comparison to use for grading (norm-referenced or criterion-referenced—criterion-referenced grading is recommended over norm-referenced); (2) aspects of students' performance (a good strategy is to base an overall grade on a series of assessments, including tests and other assessments); and (3) weighting of different kinds of evidence (judgment is involved in how teachers synthesize information to arrive at a student's grade).

| Reporting Students' Progress and Grades to Parents |

Report cards are the standard method of reporting. Checklists of skills and objectives are sometimes used in kindergarten and elementary school. Letter grades are standard in the higher elementary grades and secondary schools. Reporting also includes written progress reports and parent-teacher conferences.

Issues in grading include (1) whether teachers should assign a zero for a missed assignment or paper; (2) whether teachers should go strictly by the numbers in grading; (3) whether grading should be abolished (although the form of grading might change in the future, judgments about students' performance will still be made and communicated to students, parents, and others); and (4) whether grade inflation is a problem.

# KEY TERMS

formative assessment 550
summative assessment 551
instructional validity 553
objective tests 555
performance assessment 555

selected-response items 558
multiple-choice item 558
constructed-response
   items 560
short-answer item 560

essay items 561
authentic assessment 564
performance criteria 566
portfolio 569
growth portfolio 570

best-work portfolio 571
grading 574
norm-referenced grading 575
criterion-referenced
   grading 575

# PORTFOLIO ACTIVITIES

Now that you have a good understanding of this chapter, complete these exercises to expand your thinking.

## Collaborative Work: Develop an Assessment Plan

Get together with a classmate who plans to teach the same subject(s) and grade level. Select a subject and construct a plan for assessment throughout the course. (INTASC: Principles *1, 8*)

## Independent Reflection: State Your Views on Assessment

Think about the following statements and decide whether you agree or disagree with each. Then explain your position.

1. Multiple-choice tests should not be used to assess students' learning.

2. A teacher should never use a single measure to assess learning.

3. Performance-based assessment is too subjective.

(INTASC: Principle *8*)

## Research/Field Experience: Balancing Traditional and Alternative Assessments

Consider a course you took in grade school or high school in which your performance was assessed using traditional methods. In a brief position statement, explain how students in that case could have been evaluated using alternative assessments or some combination of traditional and alternative assessments. What would have been gained (or lost) by using alternative assessments? (INTASC: Principle *8*)

*Go to the Online Learning Center for downloadable portfolio templates.*

# STUDY, PRACTICE, AND SUCCEED

Visit **www.mhhe.com/santrockep5e** to review the chapter with self-grading quizzes and self-assessments, to apply the chapter material to two more Crack the Case studies, and for suggested activities to develop your teaching portfolio.

# Glossary

## A

**accommodation** Piagetian concept of adjusting schemas to fit new information and experiences.

**achievement test** A test that measures what the student has learned or what skills the student has mastered.

**action research** Research used to solve a specific classroom or school problem, improve teaching and other educational strategies, or make a decision at a specific level.

**active listening** A listening style that gives full attention to the speaker and notes both the intellectual and emotional content of the message.

**advance organizers** Teaching activities and techniques that establish a framework and orient students to material before it is presented.

**algorithms** Strategies that guarantee a solution to a problem.

**alternate-forms reliability** Reliability judged by giving different forms of the same test on two different occasions to the same group of students to determine how consistent their scores are.

**altruism** An unselfish interest in helping another person.

**amygdala** The seat of emotions in the brain.

**analogy** A correspondence in some respects between otherwise dissimilar things.

**androgyny** The presence of positive masculine and feminine characteristics in the same individual.

**applied behavior analysis** Application of the principles of operant conditioning to change human behavior.

**aptitude test** A type of test that is used to predict a student's ability to learn a skill or accomplish something with further education and training.

**articulation disorders** Problems in pronouncing sounds correctly.

**Asperger syndrome** A relatively mild autism spectrum disorder (ASD) in which there is relatively good verbal language, mild nonver-bal language problems, a restricted range of interests and relationships, and frequent repetitive routines.

**assimilation** Piagetian concept of the incorporation of new information into existing knowledge (schemas).

**associative learning** Learning that two events are connected (associated).

**Atkinson-Shiffrin model** A model of memory that involves a sequence of three stages: sensory memory, short-term memory, and long-term memory.

**attention deficit hyperactivity disorder (ADHD)** A disability in which children consistently show one or more of the following characteristics over a period of time: (1) inattention, (2) hyperactivity, and (3) impulsivity.

**attention** The focusing of mental resources.

**attribution theory** The theory that individuals are motivated to discover the underlying causes of their own behavior and performance.

**auditorium style** A classroom arrangement style in which all students sit facing the teacher.

**authentic assessment** Evaluating a student's knowledge or skill in a context that approximates the real world or real life as closely as possible.

**authoritarian classroom management style** A management style that is restrictive and punitive, with the focus mainly on keeping order in the classroom rather than instruction or learning.

**authoritarian parenting** A restrictive and punitive parenting style in which there is little verbal exchange between parents and children; associated with children's social incompetence.

**authoritative classroom management style** A management style that encourages students to be independent thinkers and doers but still provides effective monitoring. Authoritative teachers engage students in considerable verbal give-and-take and show a caring attitude toward them. However, they still set limits when necessary.

**authoritative parenting** A positive parenting style that encourages children to be inde-pendent but still places limits and controls on their actions; extensive verbal give-and-take is allowed; associated with children's social competence.

**autism spectrum disorders (ASD)** Also called *pervasive developmental disorders,* they range from the severe disorder labeled *autistic disorder* to the milder disorder called *Asperger syndrome.* Children with these disorders are characterized by problems in social interaction, verbal and nonverbal communication, and repetitive behaviors.

**autistic disorder** A severe autism spectrum disorder (ASD) that has its onset in the first three years of life and includes deficiencies in social relationships, abnormalities in communication, and restricted, repetitive, and stereotyped patterns of behavior.

**automaticity** The ability to process information with little or no effort.

## B

**backward-reaching transfer** Occurs when the individual looks back to a previous situation for information to solve a problem in a new context.

**behavioral objectives** Statements that communicate proposed changes in students' behavior to reach desired levels of performance.

**behaviorism** The view that behavior should be explained by observable experiences, not by mental processes.

**belief perseverance** The tendency to hold on to a belief in the face of contradictory evidence.

**best-work portfolio** A portfolio that showcases the student's most outstanding work.

**between-class ability grouping (tracking)** Grouping students based on their ability or achievement.

**"Big Five" factors of personality** Openness, conscientiousness, extraversion, agreeableness, and neuroticism (emotional stability).

**Bloom's taxonomy** Developed by Benjamin Bloom and colleagues; classifies educational objectives into three domains—cognitive, affective, and psychomotor.

# C

**care perspective** A moral perspective that focuses on connectedness and relationships among people; Gilligan's approach reflects a care perspective.

**case study** An in-depth look at an individual.

**central tendency** A number that provides information about the average, or typical, score in a set of data.

**centration** Focusing, or centering, attention on one characteristic to the exclusion of all others; characteristic of preoperational thinking.

**cerebral palsy** A disorder that involves a lack of muscle coordination, shaking, or unclear speech.

**character education** A direct approach to moral education that involves teaching students basic moral literacy to prevent them from engaging in immoral behavior and doing harm to themselves or others.

**children who are gifted** Children with above-average intelligence (usually defined as an IQ of 130 or higher) and/or superior talent in some domain such as art, music, or mathematics.

**chunking** Grouping, or "packing," information into "higher-order" units that can be remembered as single units.

**classical conditioning** A form of associative learning in which a neutral stimulus becomes associated with a meaningful stimulus and acquires the capacity to elicit a similar response.

**cluster style** A classroom arrangement style in which small numbers of students (usually four to eight) work in small, closely bunched groups.

**cognitive apprenticeship** A relationship in which an expert stretches and supports a novice's understanding and use of a culture's skills.

**cognitive behavior approaches** Changing behavior by getting individuals to monitor, manage, and regulate their own behavior rather than letting it be controlled by external factors.

**cognitive moral education** An approach to moral education based on the belief that students should value things such as democracy and justice as their moral reasoning develops; Kohlberg's theory has served as the foundation for many cognitive moral education efforts.

**collectivism** A set of values that support the group.

**comparative advance organizers** Organizers that introduce new material by connecting it with the students' prior knowledge.

**competence motivation** The idea that people are motivated to deal effectively with their environment, to master their world, and to process information efficiently.

**concept map** A visual presentation of a concept's connections and hierarchical organization.

**concepts** They group objects, events, and characteristics on the basis of common properties.

**concrete operational stage** Piaget's third cognitive developmental stage, occurring between about 7 to 11 years of age. At this stage, the child thinks operationally, and logical reasoning replaces intuitive thought but only in concrete situations; classification skills are present, but abstract problems present difficulties.

**concurrent validity** The relation between a test's scores and other criteria that are currently (concurrently) available.

**confirmation bias** The tendency to search for and use information that supports our ideas rather than refutes them.

**conservation** The idea that some characteristic of an object stays the same even though the object might change in appearance; a cognitive ability that develops in the concrete operational stage, according to Piaget.

**constructed-response items** Items that require students to write out information rather than select a response from a menu.

**constructivist approach** A learner-centered approach to learning that emphasizes the importance of individuals actively constructing knowledge and understanding with guidance from the teacher.

**construct validity** The extent to which there is evidence that a test measures a particular construct. A construct is an unobservable trait or characteristic of a person, such as intelligence, learning style, personality, or anxiety.

**content validity** A test's ability to sample the content that is to be measured.

**continuity-discontinuity issue** The issue regarding whether development involves gradual, cumulative change (continuity) or distinct stages (discontinuity).

**contracting** Putting reinforcement contingencies into writing.

**control group** The group whose experience is treated in every way like the experimental group except for the manipulated factor.

**conventional reasoning** The second, or intermediate, level in Kohlberg's theory of moral development. At this level, individuals abide by certain standards (internal), but they are the standards of others such as parents or the laws of society (external). The conventional level consists of two stages: mutual interpersonal expectations, relationships, and interpersonal conformity (stage 3) and social systems morality (stage 4).

**convergent thinking** Thinking with the aim of producing one correct answer. This is usually the type of thinking required on conventional intelligence tests.

**cooperative learning** Learning that occurs when students work in small groups to help each other learn.

**corpus callosum** Where fibers connect the brain's left and right hemispheres.

**correlational research** Research that describes the strength of the relation between two or more events or characteristics.

**creativity** The ability to think about something in novel and unusual ways and come up with unique solutions to problems.

**criterion-referenced grading** A grading system based on a certain grade for a certain level of performance regardless of any comparison with the work of other students.

**criterion-referenced tests** Standardized tests in which the student's performance is compared with established criteria.

**criterion validity** A test's ability to predict a student's performance as measured by other assessments or criteria.

**critical thinking** Thinking reflectively and productively and evaluating the evidence.

**cross-cultural studies** Studies that compare what happens in one culture with what happens in one or more other cultures; they provide information about the degree to which people are similar and to what degree behaviors are specific to certain cultures.

**cue-dependent forgetting** Retrieval failure caused by a lack of effective retrieval cues.

**culture-fair tests** Tests of intelligence that are intended to be free of cultural bias.

**culture** The behavior patterns, beliefs, and all other products of a particular group of people that are passed on from generation to generation.

# D

**decay theory** The theory that new learning involves the creation of a neurochemical *memory trace,* which will eventually disintegrate. Thus, decay theory suggests that the passage of time is responsible for forgetting.

**decision making** Evaluating alternatives and making choices among them.

**declarative memory** The conscious recollection of information, such as specific facts or events that can be verbally communicated.

**deductive reasoning** Reasoning from the general to the specific.

**deep/surface styles** Involve whether students approach learning materials in a way that helps them understand the meaning of the materials (deep style) or to learn only what needs to be learned (surface style).

**dependent variable** The factor that is measured in an experiment.

**descriptive statistics** Mathematical procedures that are used to describe and summarize data (information) in a meaningful way.

**developmentally appropriate practice** Education based on knowledge of the typical development of children within an age span (age appropriateness) as well as the uniqueness of the child (individual appropriateness).

**development** The pattern of biological, cognitive, and socioemotional processes that begins at conception and continues through the life span. Most development involves growth, although it also eventually involves decay (dying).

**differentiated instruction** Involves recognizing individual variations in students' knowledge, readiness, interests, and other characteristics, and taking these differences into account when planning curriculum and engaging in instruction.

**difficult child** A temperament style in which the child tends to react negatively, cries frequently, engages in irregular routines, and is slow to accept new experiences.

**direct instruction** Structured, teacher-centered approach focused on academic activity; characterized by teacher direction and control, high teacher expectations for student progress, and keeping negative affect to a minimum.

**direct instruction approach** A structured, teacher-centered approach characterized by teacher direction and control, high teacher expectations for students' progress, maximum time spent by students on academic tasks, and efforts by the teacher to keep negative affect to a minimum.

**discovery learning** Learning in which students construct an understanding on their own.

**divergent thinking** Thinking with the aim of producing many answers to the same question. This is characteristic of creativity.

**divided attention** Concentrating on more than one activity at a time.

**Down syndrome** A genetically transmitted form of mental retardation due to an extra (47th) chromosome.

**dual-process model** States that decision making is influenced by two systems, one analytical and one experiential, which compete with each other; in this model, it is the experiential system—monitoring and managing actual experiences—that benefits adolescent decision making.

**dyscalculia** Also known as *developmental arithmetic disorder,* this learning disability involves difficulty in math computation.

**dysgraphia** A learning disability that involves difficulty in handwriting.

**dyslexia** A severe impairment in the ability to read and spell.

# E

**early-later experience issue** The issue of the degree to which early experiences (especially infancy) or later experiences are the key determinants of the child's development.

**easy child** A temperament style in which the child is generally in a positive mood, quickly establishes regular routines, and easily adapts to new experiences.

**ecological theory** Bronfenbrenner's theory that consists of five environmental systems: microsystem, mesosystem, exosystem, macrosystem, and chronosystem.

**educational psychology** The branch of psychology that specializes in understanding teaching and learning in educational settings.

**elaboration** The extensiveness of information processing involved in encoding.

**emotional and behavioral disorders** Serious, persistent problems that involve relationships, aggression, depression, fears associated with personal or school matters, and other inappropriate socioemotional characteristics.

**emotional intelligence** The ability to perceive and express emotion accurately and adaptively, to understand emotion and emotional knowledge, to monitor one's own and others' emotions and feelings, to discriminate among them, and to use this information to guide one's thinking and action.

**empowerment** Providing people with intellectual and coping skills to succeed and make this a more just world.

**encoding specificity principle** The principle that associations formed at the time of en-

coding or learning tend to be effective retrieval cues.

**encoding** The process by which information gets into memory.

**English as a second language (ESL)** A widely used term for bilingual education programs and classes that teach English to students whose native language is not English.

**epilepsy** A neurological disorder characterized by recurring sensorimotor attacks or movement convulsions.

**episodic memory** The retention of information about the where and when of life's happenings.

**equilibration** A mechanism that Piaget proposed to explain how children shift from one stage of thought to the next. The shift occurs as children experience cognitive conflict, or disequilibrium, in trying to understand the world. Eventually, they resolve the conflict and reach a balance, or equilibrium, of thought.

**essay items** Items that require more writing than other formats but allow more freedom of response to questions.

**essential questions** Questions that reflect the heart of the curriculum, the most important things that students should explore and learn.

**ethnicity** A shared pattern of characteristics such as cultural heritage, nationality, race, religion, and language.

**ethnographic study** In-depth description and interpretation of behavior in an ethnic or a cultural group that includes direct involvement with the participants.

**executive attention** Involves action planning, allocating attention to goals, error detection and compensation, monitoring progress on tasks, and dealing with novel or difficult circumstances.

**experimental group** The group whose experience is manipulated in an experiment.

**experimental research** Research that allows the determination of the causes of behavior; involves conducting an experiment, which is a carefully regulated procedure in which one or more of the factors believed to influence the behavior being studied is manipulated and all others are held constant.

**expert knowledge** Also called *subject matter knowledge;* means excellent knowledge about the content of a particular discipline.

**expository advance organizers** Organizers that provide students with new knowledge that will orient them to the upcoming lesson.

**expressive language** The ability to use language to express one's thoughts and communicate with others.

# F

**face-to-face style** A classroom arrangement style in which students sit facing each other.

**failure syndrome** Having low expectations for success and giving up at the first sign of difficulty.

**far transfer** The transfer of learning to a situation that is very different from the one in which the initial learning took place.

**fixation** Using a prior strategy and thereby failing to examine a problem from a fresh, new perspective.

**fluency disorders** Disorders that often involve what is commonly referred to as "stuttering."

**formal operational stage** Piaget's fourth cognitive developmental stage, which emerges between about 11 and 15 years of age; thought is more abstract, idealistic, and logical in this stage.

**formative assessment** Assessment during the course of instruction rather than after it is completed.

**forward-reaching transfer** Occurs when the individual looks to apply learned information to a future situation.

**Fostering a Community of Learners (FCL)** A social constructivist program that focuses on literacy development and biology. FCL encourages reflection and discussion through the use of adults as role models, children teaching children, and online computer consultation.

**frequency distribution** A listing of scores, usually from highest to lowest, along with the number of times each score appears.

**fuzzy trace theory** States that memory is best understood by considering two types of memory representations: (1) verbatim memory trace and (2) fuzzy trace, or gist. In this theory, older children's better memory is attributed to the fuzzy traces created by extracting the gist of information.

# G

**gender identity** The sense of being male or female, which most children acquire by the time they are 3 years old.

**gender role** A set of expectations that prescribes how females or males should think, act, and feel.

**gender schema theory** States that gender typing emerges as children gradually develop gender schemas of what is gender-appropriate and gender-inappropriate in their culture.

**gender stereotypes** Broad categories that reflect impressions and beliefs about what behavior is appropriate for females and males.

**gender** The characteristics of people as males and females.

**gender typing** Acquistion of a traditional masculine or feminine role.

**goodness of fit** The match between a child's temperament and the environmental demands the child must cope with.

**grade-equivalent score** A score that indicates a student's performance in relation to grade level and months of the school year, assuming a 10-month school year.

**grading** Translating descriptive assessment information into letters, numbers, or other marks that indicate the quality of a student's learning or performance.

**gratitude** A feeling of thankfulness and appreciation, especially in response to someone doing something kind or helpful.

**growth portfolio** A portfolio of work produced over an extended time frame (throughout the school year or longer) to reveal the student's progress in meeting learning targets.

**guided discovery learning** Learning in which students are encouraged to construct their understanding with the assistance of teacher-guided questions and directions.

# H

**helpless orientation** A response to challenges and difficulties in which the individual feels trapped by the difficulty and attributes the difficulty to a lack of ability.

**heuristics** Strategies or rules of thumb that can suggest a solution to a problem but don't ensure that it will work.

**hidden curriculum** Dewey's concept that every school has a pervasive moral atmosphere even if it does not have a program of moral education.

**hierarchy of needs** Maslow's concept that individual needs must be satisfied in this sequence: physiological, safety, love and belongingness, esteem, and self-actualization.

**high-road transfer** The transfer of learning from one situation to another that is conscious and effortful.

**high-stakes testing** Using tests in a way that will have important consequences for the stu-

dent, affecting such decisions as whether the student will be promoted or be allowed to graduate.

**hindsight bias** The tendency to falsely report, after the fact, that we accurately predicted an event.

**histogram** A frequency distribution in the form of a graph.

**hostile environment sexual harassment** Occurs when students are subjected to unwelcome sexual conduct that is so severe, persistent, or pervasive that it limits the students' ability to benefit from their education.

**humanistic perspective** A view that stresses students' capacity for personal growth, freedom to choose their destiny, and positive qualities.

**hypothetical-deductive reasoning** Piaget's formal operational concept that adolescents can develop hypotheses to solve problems and systematically reach (deduce) a conclusion.

# I

**identity achievement** The identity status in which individuals have explored meaningful alternatives and made a commitment.

**identity diffusion** The identity status in which individuals have neither explored meaningful alternatives nor made a commitment.

**identity foreclosure** The identity status in which individuals have made a commitment but have not explored meaningful alternatives.

**identity moratorium** The identity status in which individuals are in the midst of exploring alternatives but have not yet made a commitment.

**impulsive/reflective styles** Also referred to as *conceptual tempo*, they involve a student's tendency either to act quickly and impulsively or to take more time to respond and reflect on the accuracy of the answer.

**incentives** Positive or negative stimuli or events that can motivate a student's behavior.

**inclusion** Educating children with special education needs full-time in the regular classroom.

**independent variable** The manipulated, influential, experimental factor in an experiment.

**individualism** A set of values that give priority to personal rather than to group goals.

**individualized education plan (IEP)** A written statement that spells out a program specifically tailored for the student with a disability.

**Individuals with Disabilities Education Act (IDEA)** This act spells out broad mandates for services to all children with disabilities, including evaluation and determination of eligibility, appropriate education and an individualized education plan (IEP), and education in the least restrictive environment (LRE).

**inductive reasoning** Reasoning from the specific to the general.

**indulgent parenting** A parenting style of involvement but few limits or restrictions on children's behavior; linked with children's social incompetence.

**information-processing approach** A cognitive approach in which people manipulate information, monitor it, and strategize about it. Central to this approach are the cognitive processes of memory and thinking.

**instructional planning** A systematic, organized strategy for planning lessons.

**instructional validity** The extent to which the assessment is a reasonable sample of what went on in the classroom.

**intelligence** Problem-solving skills and the ability to adapt to and learn from experiences.

**intelligence quotient (IQ)** A person's mental age (MA) divided by chronological age (CA), multiplied by 100.

**interference theory** The theory that we forget not because we actually lose memories from storage but because other information gets in the way of what we are trying to remember.

**Internet** The core of computer-mediated communication; a system of computer networks that operates worldwide.

**intrinsic motivation** The internal motivation to do something for its own sake (an end in itself).

**intuitive thought substage** The second substage of preoperational thought, lasting from about 4 to 7 years of age. Children begin to use primitive reasoning and want to know the answer to all sorts of questions. They seem so sure about their knowledge in this substage but are unaware of how they know what they know.

# J

**jigsaw classroom** A classroom in which students from different cultural backgrounds cooperate by doing different parts of a project to reach a common goal.

**Joplin plan** A standard nongraded program for instruction in reading.

**justice perspective** A moral perspective that focuses on the rights of the individual; Kohlberg's theory is a justice perspective.

# L

**laboratory** A controlled setting from which many of the complex factors of the real world have been removed.

**language** A form of communication, whether spoken, written, or signed, that is based on a system of symbols.

**language disorders** Significant impairments in receptive or expressive language.

**lateralization** The specialization of functions in each hemisphere of the brain.

**learning and thinking styles** Individuals' preferences in how they use their abilities.

**learning** A relatively permanent influence on behavior, knowledge, and thinking skills that comes about through experience.

**learning disability** A child with a learning disability has difficulty in learning that involves understanding or using spoken or written language, and the difficulty can appear in listening, thinking, reading, writing, and spelling. A learning disability also may involve difficulty in doing mathematics. To be classified as a learning disability, the learning problem cannot be primarily the result of visual, hearing, or motor disabilities; mental retardation; emotional disorders; or due to environmental, cultural, or economic disadvantage.

**least restrictive environment (LRE)** A setting that is as similar as possible to the one in which children who do not have a disability are educated.

**levels of processing theory** The theory that processing of memory occurs on a continuum from shallow to deep, with deeper processing producing better memory.

**long-term memory** A type of memory that holds enormous amounts of information for a long period of time in a relatively permanent fashion.

**low-road transfer** The automatic, often unconscious, transfer of learning to another situation.

# M

**mastery learning** Involves learning one topic or concept thoroughly before moving on to a more difficult one.

**mastery orientation** A task-oriented response to difficult or challenging circumstances that focuses on learning strategies and the process of achievement rather than the outcome.

**means-end analysis** A heuristic in which one identifies the goal (end) of a problem, assesses the current situation, and evaluates what needs to be done (means) to decrease the difference between the two conditions.

**mean** The numerical average of a group of scores.

**measures of variability** Measures that tell how much scores vary from one another.

**median** The score that falls exactly in the middle of a distribution of scores after they have been arranged (or ranked) from highest to lowest.

**memory span** The number of digits an individual can report back without error in a single presentation.

**memory** The retention of information over time, which involves encoding, storage, and retrieval.

**mental age (MA)** An individual's level of mental development relative to others.

**mental processes** Thoughts, feelings, and motives that cannot be observed by others.

**mental retardation** A condition with an onset before age 18 that involves low intelligence (usually below 70 on a traditional individually administered intelligence test) and difficulty in adapting to everyday life.

**mental set** A type of fixation in which an individual tries to solve a problem in a particular way that has worked in the past.

**metacognition** Cognition about cognition, or "knowing about knowing."

**metalinguistic awareness** Knowledge of language.

**mindfulness** Means being alert, mentally present, and cognitively flexible while going through life's everyday activities and tasks. Mindful students maintain an active awareness of the circumstances in their lives.

**mindset** Dweck's concept that refers to the cognitive view individuals develop for themselves; individuals have one of two mindsets: (1) fixed or (2) growth.

**mixed methods research** Involves research that blends different research designs and/or methods.

**mode** The score that occurs most often.

**Montessori approach** An educational philosophy in which children are given considerable freedom and spontaneity in choosing activities and are allowed to move from one activity to another as they desire.

**moral development** Development with respect to the rules and conventions of just interactions between people.

**morphology** Refers to the units of meaning involved in word formation.

**motivation** The processes that energize, direct, and sustain behavior.

**multicultural education** Education that values diversity and includes the perspectives of a variety of cultural groups on a regular basis.

**multiple-choice item** An objective test item consisting of two parts: a stem plus a set of possible responses.

**myelination** The process of encasing many cells in the brain with a myelin sheath that increases the speed at which information travels through the nervous system.

# N

**naturalistic observation** Observation in the real world rather than a laboratory.

**nature-nurture issue** Issue that involves the debate about whether development is primarily influenced by nature (an organism's biological inheritance) or nurture (environmental experiences).

**nature-nurture issue** Nature refers to an organism's biological inheritance, nurture to environmental influences. The "nature" proponents claim biological inheritance is the most important influence on development; the "nurture" proponents claim environmental experiences are the most important.

**near transfer** The transfer of learning to a situation that is similar to the one in which the initial learning took place.

**need for affiliation, or relatedness** The motive to be securely connected with other people.

**negative reinforcement** Reinforcement based on the principle that the frequency of a response increases because an aversive (unpleasant) stimulus is removed.

**neglectful parenting** A parenting style of uninvolvement in which parents spend little time with their children; associated with children's social incompetence.

**neo-Piagetians** Developmental psychologists who believe that Piaget got some things right but that his theory needs considerable revision; emphasize how to process information through attention, memory, and strategies.

**network theories** Theories that describe how information in memory is organized and connected; they emphasize nodes in the memory network.

**nondeclarative memory** Procedural knowledge in the form of skills and cognitive operations. Nondeclarative memory cannot be consciously recollected, at least not in the form of specific events or facts.

**nongraded (cross-age) program** A variation of between-class ability grouping in which students are grouped by their ability in particular subjects regardless of their age or grade level.

**normal distribution** A *bell-shaped curve* in which most of the scores are clustered around the mean; the farther above or below the mean that we travel, the less frequently each score occurs.

**normal distribution** A symmetrical distribution, with a majority of scores falling in the middle of the possible range of scores and few scores appearing toward the extremes of the range.

**norm group** The group of individuals previously tested that provides a basis for interpreting a test score.

**norm-referenced grading** A grading system based on a comparison of a student's performance with that of other students in the class or of other classes and other students.

**norm-referenced tests** Standardized tests in which a student's score is interpreted by comparing it with how others (the norm group) performed.

# O

**objective tests** Tests that have relatively clear, unambiguous scoring criteria, usually multiple-choice tests.

**observational learning** Learning that involves acquiring skills, strategies, and beliefs by observing others.

**offset style** A classroom arrangement style in which small numbers of students (usually three or four) sit at tables but do not sit directly across from one another.

**operant conditioning** Also called *instrumental conditioning,* this is a form of learning in which the consequences of behavior produce changes in the probability that the behavior will occur.

**organization** Piaget's concept of grouping isolated behaviors into a higher-order, more smoothly functioning cognitive system; the grouping or arranging of items into categories.

**orthopedic impairments** Restricted movements or lack of control of movements, due to muscle, bone, or joint problems.

**overconfidence bias** The tendency to have more confidence in judgment and decisions than we should have, based on probability or past experience.

# P

**participant observation** Observation conducted at the same time the teacher-researcher is actively involved as a participant in the activity or setting.

**pedagogical content knowledge** Knowledge about how to effectively teach a particular discipline.

**percentile-rank score** The percentage of a distribution that lies at or below the score.

**performance assessment** Assessment that requires creating answers or products that demonstrate knowledge and skill; examples include writing an essay, conducting an experiment, carrying out a project, solving a real-world problem, and creating a portfolio.

**performance criteria** Specific behaviors that students need to perform effectively as part of an assessment.

**performance orientation** A focus on winning rather than an achievement outcome; success is believed to result from winning.

**permissive classroom management style** A management style that allows students considerable autonomy but provides them with little support for developing learning skills or managing their behavior.

**personality** Distinctive thoughts, emotions, and behaviors that characterize the way an individual adapts to the world.

**person-situation interaction** The view that the best way to conceptualize personality is not in terms of personal traits or characteristics alone, but also in terms of the situation involved.

**phonics approach** An approach that emphasizes that reading instruction should teach phonics and its basic rules for translating written symbols into sounds and that early reading instruction should use simplified materials.

**phonology** A language's sound system.

**portfolio** A systematic and organized collection of a student's work that demonstrates the student's skills and accomplishments.

**positive reinforcement** Reinforcement based on the principle that the frequency of a response increases because it is followed by a rewarding stimulus.

**postconventional reasoning** The third and highest level in Kohlberg's theory of moral development. At this level, morality is more internal. The postconventional level consists of two stages: social contract or utility and individual rights (stage 5) and universal ethical principles (stage 6).

**pragmatics** The appropriate use of language in different contexts.

**preconventional reasoning** The lowest level in Kohlberg's theory. At this level, morality is often focused on reward and punishment. The two stages in preconventional reasoning are punishment and obedience orientation (stage 1) and individualism, instrumental purpose, and exchange (stage 2).

**predictive validity** The relation between test scores and the student's future performance.

**prefrontal cortex** The highest level in the frontal lobes; involved in reasoning, decision making, and self-control.

**prejudice** An unjustified negative attitude toward an individual because of the individual's membership in a group.

**Premack principle** The principle that a high-probability activity can serve as a reinforcer for a low-probability activity.

**preoperational stage** The second Piagetian stage, lasting from about 2 to 7 years of age, symbolic thought increases, but operational thought is not yet present.

**problem-based learning** Learning that emphasizes authentic problems like those that occur in daily life.

**problem solving** Finding an appropriate way to attain a goal.

**program evaluation research** Research designed to make decisions about the effectiveness of a particular program.

**project-based learning** Students work on real, meaningful problems beyond those of everyday life and create tangible products.

**prompt** An added stimulus or cue that is given just before a response, thus increasing the likelihood the response will recur.

**prototype matching** Deciding if an item is a member of a category by comparing it with the most typical item(s) of the category.

**Public Law 94-142** The Education for All Handicapped Children Act, which required that all students with disabilities be given a free, appropriate public education and which provided the funding to help implement this education.

**punishment** A consequence that decreases the probability that a behavior will occur.

## Q

**qualitative research** Involves obtaining information using descriptive measures such as interviews, case studies, personal journals and diaries, and focus groups but not statistically analyzing the information.

**quantitative research** Employs numerical calculations in an effort to discover information about a particular topic.

**quid pro quo sexual harassment** Occurs when a school employee threatens to base an educational decision (such as a grade) on a student's submission to unwelcome sexual conduct.

## R

**random assignment** In experimental research, the assignment of participants to experimental and control groups by chance.

**range** The distance between the highest and lowest scores.

**rapport talk** The language of conversation and a way of establishing connections and negotiating relationships; more characteristic of females than males.

**raw score** The number of items the student answered correctly on the test.

**receptive language** The reception and understanding of language.

**reciprocal teaching** A learning arrangement used by FCL in which students take turns leading a small-group discussion; can also involve teacher-scaffolded instruction.

**rehearsal** The conscious repetition of information over time to increase the length of time it stays in memory.

**reinforcement (reward)** A consequence that increases the probability that a behavior will occur.

**reliability** The extent to which a test produces a consistent, reproducible score.

**report talk** Talk that gives information; more characteristic of males than females.

**response cost** Taking a positive reinforcer away from an individual.

## S

**scaffolding** A technique that involves changing the level of support for learning. A teacher or more-advanced peer adjusts the amount of guidance to fit the student's current performance.

**schedules of reinforcement** Partial reinforcement timetables that determine when a response will be reinforced.

**schema** Information—concepts, knowledge, information about events—that already exists in a person's mind.

**schemas** In Piaget's theory, actions or mental representations that organize knowledge.

**schema theories** Theories based on the premise that when we construct information, we fit it into information that already exists in our mind.

**Schools for Thought (SFT)** A social constructivist program that combines aspects of The Jasper Project, Fostering a Community of Learners (FCL), and Computer-Supported Intentional Learning Environments (CSILE).

**script** A schema for an event.

**selected-response items** Test items with an objective format in which student responses can be scored quickly. A scoring guide for correct responses is created and can be applied by an examiner or a computer.

**selective attention** Focusing on a specific aspect of experience that is relevant while ignoring others that are irrelevant.

**self-actualization** The highest and most elusive of Maslow's needs; the motivation to develop one's full potential as a human being.

**self-efficacy** The belief that one can master a situation and produce positive outcomes.

**self-esteem** Also called *self-image* and *self-worth,* the individual's overall conception of herself or himself.

**self-instructional methods** Cognitive behavior techniques aimed at teaching individuals to modify their own behavior.

**self-regulatory learning** The self-generation and self-monitoring of thoughts, feelings, and behaviors in order to reach a goal.

**semantic memory** An individual's general knowledge about the world, independent of the individual's identity with the past.

**semantics** The meaning of words and sentences.

**seminar style** A classroom arrangement style in which large numbers of students (10 or more) sit in circular, square, or U-shaped arrangements.

**sensorimotor stage** The first Piagetian stage, lasting from birth to about 2 years of age, in which infants construct an understanding of the world by coordinating sensory experiences with motor actions.

**sensory memory** Memory that holds information from the world in its original form for only an instant.

**serial position effect** The principle that recall is better for items at the beginning and the end of a list than for items in the middle.

**seriation** A concrete operation that involves ordering stimuli along some quantitative dimension.

**service learning** A form of education that promotes social responsibility and service to the community.

**shaping** Teaching new behaviors by reinforcing successive approximations to a specified target behavior.

**short-answer item** A constructed-response format in which students are required to write a word, a short phrase, or several sentences in response to a task.

**short-term memory** A limited-capacity memory system in which information is retained at least 30 seconds unless it is rehearsed, in which case it can be retained longer.

**situated cognition** The idea that thinking occurs (is situated) in social and physical contexts.

**slow-to-warm-up child** A temperament style in which the child has a low activity level, is somewhat negative, and displays a low intensity of mood.

**social cognitive theory** Bandura's theory that social and cognitive factors, as well as behavior, play important roles in learning.

**social constructivist approach** Approach that emphasizes the social contexts of learning and the idea that knowledge is mutually built and constructed. Vygotsky's theory exemplifies this approach.

**social motives** Needs and desires that are learned through experiences with the social world.

**social studies** The field that seeks to promote civic competence with the goal of helping students make informed and reasoned decisions for the public good as citizens of a culturally diverse, democratic society in an interdependent world.

**socioeconomic status (SES)** A grouping of people with similar occupational, educational, and economic characteristics.

**specific language impairment (SLI)** Involves problems in language development that are not accompanied by other obvious physical, sensory, or emotional problems; in some cases, the disorder is called *developmental language disorder*.

**speech and language disorders** A number of speech problems (such as articulation disorders, voice disorders, and fluency disorders) and language problems (difficulties in receiving information and expressing language).

**splintered development** The circumstances in which development is uneven across domains.

**split-half reliability** Reliability judged by dividing the test items into two halves, such as the odd-numbered and even-numbered items. The scores on the two sets of items are compared to determine how consistently the students performed across each set.

**standard deviation** A measure of how much a set of scores varies on the average around the mean of the scores.

**standardized tests** Tests with uniform procedures for administration and scoring. They assess students' performance in different domains and allow a student's performance to be compared with the performance of other students at the same age or grade level on a national basis.

**standards-based tests** Tests that assess skills that students are expected to have mastered before they can be promoted to the next grade or permitted to graduate.

**standard score** A score expressed as a deviation from the mean; involves the standard deviation.

**stanine score** A nine-point scale that describes a student's performance.

**stereotype threat** The anxiety that one's behavior might confirm a negative stereotype about one's group.

**strategy construction** Creation of a new procedure for processing information.

**subgoaling** The process of setting intermediate goals that place students in a better position to reach the final goal or solution.

**summative assessment** Assessment after instruction is finished to document student performance; also called *formal assessment*.

**sustained attention** Maintaining attention over an extended period of time; also called vigilance.

**symbolic function substage** The first substage of preoperational thought, occurring between about 2 to 4 years of age; the ability to represent an object not present develops and symbolic thinking increases; egocentrism is present.

**syntax** The ways that words must be combined to form acceptable phrases and sentences.

**systematic desensitization** A method based on classical conditioning that reduces anxiety by getting the individual to associate deep relaxation with successive visualizations of increasingly anxiety-provoking situations.

# T

**task analysis** Breaking down a complex task that students are to learn into its component parts.

**taxonomy** A classification system.

**teacher-as-resesarcher** Also called teacher-researcher, this concept involves classroom teachers conducting their own studies to improve their teaching practice.

**temperament** A person's behavioral style and characteristic ways of responding.

**test-retest reliability** The extent to which a test yields the same performance when a student is given the same test on two occasions.

**theory of mind** Awareness of one's own mental processes and the mental processes of others.

**thinking** Manipulating and transforming information in memory, which often is done to form concepts, reason, think critically, make decisions, think creatively, and solve problems.

**time-out** Removing an individual from positive reinforcement.

**transactional strategy instruction approach** A cognitive approach to reading that emphasizes instruction in strategies, especially metacognitive strategies.

**transfer** Applying previous experiences and knowledge to learning or problem solving in a new situation.

**transitivity** The ability to reason and logically combine relationships.

**triarchic theory of intelligence** Sternberg's view that intelligence comes in three main forms: analytical, creative, and practical.

# V

**validity** The extent to which a test measures what it is intended to measure and whether inferences about the test scores are accurate and appropriate.

**values clarification** An approach to moral education that emphasizes helping people clarify what their lives are for and what is worth working for; students are encouraged to define their own values and understand the values of others.

**voice disorders** Disorders producing speech that is hoarse, harsh, too loud, too high-pitched, or too low-pitched.

# W

**Web** A system for browsing Internet sites that refers to the World Wide Web; named the Web because it is comprised of many sites that are linked together.

**whole-language approach** An approach that stresses that reading instruction should parallel children's natural language learning and that reading materials should be whole and meaningful.

**within-class ability grouping** Placing students in two or three groups within a class to take into account differences in students' abilities.

**withitness** A management style described by Kounin in which teachers show students that they are aware of what is happening. Such teachers closely monitor students on a regular basis and thus are able to detect inappropriate behavior early, before it gets out of hand.

**working memory** A three-part system that holds information temporarily as a person performs a task. A kind of "mental workbench" that lets individuals manipulate, assemble, and construct information when they make decisions, solve problems, and comprehend written and spoken language.

# Z

**zone of proximal development (ZPD)** Vygotsky's term for the range of tasks that are too difficult for children to master alone but that can be mastered with guidance and assistance from adults or more-skilled children.

**z-score** A score that provides information about how many standard deviations a raw score is above or below the mean.

# PRAXIS™ Practice Answer Key

## CHAPTER 1

**Historical Background**
1. b
2. c

**Effective Teaching**
1. d
2. b

**Research in Educational Psychology**
1. a
2. d
3. c

## CHAPTER 2

**An Overview of Child Development**
1. d    3. a
2. c    4. d

**Cognitive Development**
1. b
2. d
3. c

**Language Development**
1. a
2. b
3. b

## CHAPTER 3

**Contemporary Theories**
1. b
2. c

**Social Contexts of Development**
1. b
2. d
3. a

**Socioemotional Development**
1. c
2. b

## CHAPTER 4

**Intelligence**
1. c    3. d
2. b    4. b

**Learning and Thinking Styles**
1. a
2. d

**Personality and Temperament**
1. b
2. b

## CHAPTER 5

**Culture and Ethnicity**
1. c    3. a
2. c    4. c

**Multicultural Education**
1. d    3. a
2. d    4. a

**Gender**
1. c    4. a
2. c    5. a
3. b

## CHAPTER 6

**Children with Disabilities**
1. c    5. c
2. b    6. b
3. a    7. b
4. b    8. d

**Educational Issues Involving Children with Disabilities**
1. b
2. c

**Children Who Are Gifted**
1. a
2. a
3. b

## CHAPTER 7

**What Is Learning?**
1. b
2. b

**Behavioral Approach to Learning**
1. d
2. b

**Applied Behavior Analysis in Education**
1. a    3. d
2. a    4. d

**Social Cognitive Approaches to Learning**
1. b    3. a
2. a    4. d

## CHAPTER 8

**The Nature of the Information-Processing Approach**
1. b
2. a
3. a

**Attention**
1. a
2. a

**Memory**
1. a    3. a
2. b    4. d

**Expertise**
1. b
2. a
3. b

**Metacognition**
1. d
2. c
3. a

## CHAPTER 9

**Conceptual Understanding**
1. b
2. c

**Thinking**
1. d    3. a
2. c    4. a

**Problem Solving**
1. b    3. b
2. a    4. a

**Transfer**
1. b
2. c

## CHAPTER 10

### Social Constructivist Approaches to Teaching

1. a
2. b

### Teachers and Peers as Joint Contributors to Students' Learning

1. b     3. a
2. b     4. a

### Structuring Small-Group Work

1. b
2. d
3. d

### Social Constructivist Programs

1. b
2. a

## CHAPTER 11

### Expert Knowledge and Pedagogical Content Knowledge

1. b

### Reading

1. c     4. c
2. c     5. b
3. b

### Writing

1. c
2. b
3. b

### Mathematics

1. a     4. b
2. b     5. d
3. c

### Science

1. d
2. c

### Social Studies

1. a
2. d

## CHAPTER 12

### Planning

1. b
2. d

### Teacher-Centered Lesson Planning and Instruction

1. a     3. a
2. c     4. c

### Learner-Centered Lesson Planning and Instruction

1. d
2. c
3. b

### Technology and Education

1. b     3. c
2. b     4. a

## CHAPTER 13

### Exploring Motivation

1. b
2. b

### Achievement Processes

1. b     5. d
2. d     6. b
3. a     7. b
4. b

### Motivation, Relationships, and Sociocultural Contexts

1. c
2. c
3. d

### Students with Achievement Problems

1. a     5. a
2. b     6. b
3. a     7. b
4. a

## CHAPTER 14

### Why Classrooms Need to Be Managed Effectively

1. b     3. a
2. d     4. c

### Designing the Physical Environment of the Classroom

1. b
2. d

### Creating a Positive Environment for Learning

1. b
2. b
3. c

### Being a Good Communicator

1. d
2. d
3. d

### Dealing with Problem Behaviors

1. c
2. d

## CHAPTER 15

### The Nature of Standardized Tests

1. b
2. a

### Aptitude and Achievement Tests

1. a     3. b
2. d     4. b

### The Teacher's Roles

1. d
2. a
3. c

### Issues in Standardized Tests

1. a
2. b

## CHAPTER 16

### The Classroom as an Assessment Context

1. b     4. c
2. a     5. c
3. d

### Traditional Tests

1. c
2. c

### Alternative Assessments

1. d
2. b

### Grading and Reporting Performance

1. c     3. d
2. b     4. d

# References

## A

**ABC News.** (2005). *Larry Page and Sergey Brim.* Retrieved December 12, 2005, from http://abcnews.go.com?Entertainment/12/8/05

**Abruscato, J. A., & DeRosa, D. A.** (2010). *Teaching children science* (7th ed.). Boston: Allyn & Bacon.

**Academic Software.** (1996). *Adaptive Device Locator System* [computer program]. Lexington, KY: Author.

**Acar, O., Turkmen, L., & Roychoudhury, A.** (2010). Student difficulties in socio-scientific argumentation and decision-making research findings: Crossing the borders of two research lines. *International Journal of Science Education, 32,* 1191–1206.

**Achieve, Inc.** (2005). *Rising to the challenge: Are high school graduates prepared for college and work?* Washington, DC: Author.

**ACSD.** (2009). *Classroom management that works.* Upper Saddle River, NJ: Prentice Hall.

**Adams, G. R.** (2008). Erikson's theory of psychosocial development. In N. J. Salkind (Ed.), *Encyclopedia of educational psychology.* Thousand Oaks, CA: Sage.

**Adams, K. L., & Galanes, G. J.** (2009). *Communicating in groups* (7th ed.). New York: McGraw-Hill.

**Adams, R., & Biddle, B.** (1970). *Realities of teaching.* New York: Holt, Rinehart & Winston.

**Agnew-Tally, J., Mott, D., Brooks, S., & Thornburg, K.** (2009). Teacher as a family resource and advocate. In K. B. Grant & J. A. Ray (Eds.), *Home, school, and community collaboration.* Thousand Oaks, CA: Sage.

**Ahrons, C.** (2007). Introduction to the special issue on divorce and its aftermath. *Family Process, 46,* 3–6.

**Airasian, P., & Walsh, M. E.** (1997, February). Constructivist cautions. *Phi Delta Kappan,* pp. 444–450.

**Airasian, P. W., & Russell. M. K.** (2008). *Classroom assessment* (6th ed.). New York: McGraw-Hill.

**Alberto, P. A., & Troutman, A. C.** (2009). *Applied analysis for teachers* (8th ed.). Upper Saddle River, NJ: Prentice Hall.

**Alexander, P., & Mayer, R.** (Eds.) (2011). *Handbook of research on learning and instruction.* New York: Routledge.

**Alexander, P. A.** (2003). The development of expertise. *Educational Researcher, 32,* (8), 10–14.

**All Kinds of Minds** (2005). *Learning Base: Self-regulating learning.* Retrieved August 15, 2009, from www.allkingsofminds.org/learning.

**Allen, B.** (2008). Head Start. In N. J. Salkind (Ed.), *Encyclopedia of educational psychology.* Thousand Oaks, CA: Sage.

**Allensworth, E., & Nagako, J.** (2010). Grade retention, student achievement, and high school dropout: Results of the Chicago School Project. In J. Meece & J. Eccles (Eds.), *Handbook of schools, schooling, and human development.* New York: Routledge.

**Allington, R. L.** (2009). *What really matters in fluency.* Boston: Allyn & Bacon.

**Alloway, T. P., Gathercole, S. E., & Elliott, J.** (2010, in press). Examining the link between working memory behavior and academic attainment in children with ADHD. *Developmental Medicine and Child Neurology.*

**Alverno College.** (1995). *Writing and speaking criteria.* Milwaukee, WI: Alverno Productions.

**Alyahri, A., & Goodman, R.** (2008). Harsh corporal punishment of Yemeni children: Occurrence, type, and associations. *Child Abuse and Neglect, 32,* 766–773.

**Amabile, T. M.** (1993). [Commentary]. In D. Goleman, P. Kaufman, & M. Ray, (Eds.), *The creative spirit.* New York: Plume.

**Amabile, T. M., & Hennesey, B. A.** (1992). The motivation for creativity in children. In A. K. Boggiano & T. S. Pittman (Eds.), *Achievement and motivation.* New York: Cambridge University Press.

**Amadieu, F., van Gog, T., Paas, F., Tricot, A., & Marine, C.** (2009). Effects of prior knowledge and concept-map structure on disorientation, cognitive load, and learning *Learning and Instruction, 19,* 376–386.

**Amato, P. R., & Dorius, C.** (2010). Fathers, children, and divorce. In M. E. Lamb (Ed.), *The role of the father in child development* (5th ed.). New York: Wiley.

**American Association on Mental Retardation, Ad Hoc Committee on Terminology and Classification.** (1992). *Mental retardation* (9th ed.). Washington, DC: Author.

**Ames, C.** (1987). The enhancement of student motivation. In M. L. Maehr & D. A. Kleiber (Eds.). *Advances in motivation and achievement* (Vol. 5, pp. 123–148). Greenwich, CT: JAI Press.

**Ames, C.** (1992). Achievement goals and the classroom motivational climate. In D. H. Schunk & J. L. Meece (Eds.), *Student perceptions in the classroom* (pp. 327–348). Hillsdale, NJ: Erlbaum.

**Anastasi, A., & Urbino, S.** (1997). *Psychological testing* (11th ed.). Upper Saddle River, NJ: Prentice-Hall.

**Anderman, E. M.** (2011, in press). Adolescence. In K. Harris, S. Graham, & T. Urden (Eds.), *APA handbook of educational psychology.* Washington, DC: American Psychological Association.

**Anderman, E. M., & Anderman, L. H.** (2010). *Classroom motivation.* Upper Saddle River, NJ: Merrill.

**Anderman, E. M., Anderman, L. H., Yough, M. S., & Gimbert, B. G.** (2010). Value-added models of assessment: Implications for motivation and accountability. *Educational Psychologist, 45,* 123–137.

**Anderman, E. M., Austin, C. C., & Johnson, D. M.** (2002). The development of goal orientation. In A. Wigfield & J. S. Eccles (Eds.), *Development of achievement motivation.* San Diego: Academic Press.

**Anderman, E. M., & Dawson, H.** (2011). Learning and motivation. In P. A. Alexander & R. E. Mayer (Eds.), *Handbook of research on learning and instruction.* New York: Routledge.

**Anderman, E. M., & Mueller, C.** (2010). Middle school transitions and adolescent development: Disentangling psychological, social, and biological effects. In J. Meece &

J. Eccles (Eds.), *Handbook of research on schools, schooling, and human development.* New York: Psychology Press.

**Anderman, E. M., & Murdock, T. B.** (Eds.). (2007). *Psychology of academic cheating.* San Diego: Academic Press.

**Anderson, B. M., & others** (2009, in press). Examination of associations of genes in the serotonin system to autism. *Neurogenetics.*

**Anderson, D. R., Lorch, E. P., Field, D. E., Collins, P. A., & Nathan, J. G.** (1985, April). *Television viewing at home: Age trends in visual attention and time with TV.* Paper presented at the meeting of the Society for Research in Child Development, Toronto.

**Anderson, J. R.** (2009). Context theory of classification learning. In D. Shanks (Ed.), *Psychology of learning.* Thousand Oaks, CA: Sage.

**Anderson, L. W., & Krathwohl, D. R.** (Eds.). (2001). *A taxonomy for learning, teaching, and assessing.* New York: Longman.

**Anderson, N. B., & Shames, G. H.** (2011). *Human communication disorders* (8th ed.). Boston: Allyn & Bacon.

**Andersson, U.** (2010, in press). The contribution of working memory capacity to foreign language comprehension in children. *Memory.*

**Andrade, H., & Cizek, G. J.** (Eds.). (2010). Handbook of formative assessment. New York: Routledge.

**Andrade, H. L.** (2010). Students as the definitive source of formative assessment: Academic self-assessment and the self-regulation of learning. In H. L Andrade & G. J. Cisek (Eds.), *Handbook of formative assessment.* New York: Routledge.

**Ang, S. Y., & Lee, K.** (2010). Exploring developmental differences in visual short-term memory and working memory. *Developmental Psychology, 46,* 279–285.

**Ansary, N. S., & Luthar, S. S.** (2009). Distress and academic achievement among adolescents of affluence: A study of externalizing and internalizing problem behaviors and school performance. *Development and Psychopathology, 21,* 319–341.

**Apple Computer.** (1995). Changing the conversation about teaching, learning and technology: A report on 10 years of ACOT research. Retrieved April 8, 2005, from http://images.apple.com/education/k12/leadership/acot/pdf/10yr.pdf

**Applebee, A. & Langer, J.** (2006). The partnership for literacy: A study of professional development, instructional change and stu-

dent growth. Retrieved August 5, 2008, from http://cela.albany.edu/publication/IRAResearch.

**Arends, R. I.** (2004). *Learning to teach* (6th ed.). New York: McGraw-Hill.

**Ariza, E.N.W., & Lapp, S. I.** (2011). *Literacy, language, and culture.* Boston: Allyn & Bacon.

**Aronson, E. E.** (1986, August). *Teaching students things they think they already know about: The case of prejudice and desegregation.* Paper presented at the meeting of the American Psychological Association, Washington, DC.

**Aronson, E. E., Blaney, N., Sephan, C., Sikes, J., & Snapp, M.** (1978). *The jigsaw classroom.* Thousand Oaks, CA: Sage.

**Aronson, E. E., & Patnoe, S.** (1997). *The jigsaw classroom* (2nd ed.). Boston: Addison-Wesley.

**Aronson, J.** (2002). Stereotype threat: Contending and coping with Unnerving Expectations. *Improving academic achievement.* San Diego: Academic Press.

**Arsenealut, L., Milne, B. J., Taylor, A., Adams, F., Delgado, K., Caspi, A., & Moffit, T. E.** (2008). Being bullied as an environmentally mediated contributing factor to children's internalizing problems: A study of twins discordant for victimization. *Archives of Pediatric and Adolescent Medicine, 162,* 145–150.

**Arter, J.** (1995). *Portfolios for assessment and instruction.* ERIC Document Reproduction Service No. ED388890.

**Arthur, J.** (2008). Traditional approaches to character education in Britain and America. In L. Nucci & D. Narvaez (Eds.), *Handbook of moral and character education.* Clifton, NJ: Psychology Press.

**Asa, I. K., & Wiley, J.** (2008). Hindsight bias in insight and mathematical problem solving: Evidence of different reconstruction mechanisms for metacognitive versus situational judgments. *Memory and Cognition, 36,* 822–837.

**Ashcraft, M. H., & Radvansky, G. A.** (2010). *Cognition* (5th ed.). Upper Saddle River, NJ: Prentice Hall.

**Asher, S. R., & McDonald, K. L.** (2009). The behavioral basis of acceptance, rejection, and perceived popularity. In K. H. Rubin, W. M., Bukowski, & B. Laursen (Eds.), *Handbook of peer interactions, relationships, and groups.* New York: Guilford.

**Asian, A., Zellner, M., & Bauml, K. H.** (2010, in press). Working memory capacity predicts listwise directed forgetting in adults and children. *Memory.*

**Assaf, M. A.** (2009). Teaching and thinking: A literature review of the teaching of thinking skills. Retrieved August 17, 2009, from www.eric.ed.gov ERIC #ED505029.

**Assor, A., Vansteenkiste, M., & Kaplan, A.** (2009). Identified versus introjected approach and introjected avoidance motivations in school and sports: The limited benefits of self-worth strivings. *Journal of Educational Psychology, 101,* 482–497.

**Atkinson, J. W.** (1957). Motivational determinants of risk-taking behavior. *Psychological Review, 64,* 359–372.

**Atkinson, J. W., Blackwell, L. S., Trzesniewski, K. H., & Dweck, C. S.** (2007). Implicit theories of intelligence predict achievement across an adolescent tradition: A longitudinal study and an intervention. *Child Development, 78,* 246–263.

**Atkinson, R. C., & Shiffrin, R. M.** (1968). Human memory: A proposed system and its control processes. In K. W. Spence & J. T. Spence (Eds.), *The psychology of learning and motivation, Vol. 2.* San Diego: Academic Press.

**Augustine, N. R. & others** (2007). *Rising above the gathering storm: Energizing and employing America for a brighter economic future.* Washington, DC: National Academies Press.

**Austin, V. L., & Sciarra, D. T.** (2010). *Children and adolescents with emotional disorders.* Upper Saddle River, NJ: Merrill.

# B

**Baars, B. J., & Gage, N. M.** (Eds.) (2010). *Cognition, brain, and consciousness* (2nd ed.). New York: Elsevier.

**Babbie, E. R.** (2011). *The basics of social research* (5th ed.). Boston: Cengage.

**Baddeley, A.** (2000). Short-term and working memory. In E. Tulving & F.I.M. Craik (Eds.), *The Oxford handbook of memory.* New York: Oxford University Press.

**Baddeley, AD.** (2007). *Working memory, thought and action.* Oxford: Oxford University Press.

**Baddeley, A. D., Eysenck, M., & Anderson, M. C.** (2009). *Memory.* New York: Psychology Press.

**Badget, J. L., & Christmann, E. P.** (2009a). *Designing elementary instruction and assessment.* Thousand Oaks, CA: Corwin.

**Badgett, J. L., & Christmann, E. P.** (2009b). *Designing middle and high school instruction and assessment.* Thousand Oaks, CA: Corwin.

**Bain, R. B.** (2005). "They thought the world was flat?": Applying the principles of *How People Learn* in teaching high school history. In M. S. Donovan & J. D. Bransford (Eds.). *How students learn.* Washington, DC: National Academies Press.

**Baker, D. F.** (2010). Enhancing group decision making: An exercise to reduce shared information bias. *Journal of Management Education, 34,* 249–279.

**Ballentine, J. H., & Roberts, K. A.** (2009). *Our social world* (2nd ed.). Thousand Oaks, CA: Sage.

**Bandura, A.** (1965). Influence of models' reinforcement contingencies on the acquisition of imitative responses. *Journal of Personality and Social Psychology, I,* 589–596.

**Bandura, A.** (1986). *Social foundations of thought and action.* Englewood Cliffs, NJ: Prentice Hall.

**Bandura, A.** (1997). *Self-efficacy: The exercise of control.* New York: W. H. Freeman.

**Bandura, A.** (2001). Social cognitive theory. *Annual Review of Psychology, Vol. 51.* Palo Alto, CA: Annual Reviews.

**Bandura, A.** (2009). Social and policy impact of social cognitive theory. In M. Mark, S. Donaldson, & B. Campbell (Eds.) *Social psychology and program/policy evaluation.* New York: Guilford.

**Bandura, A.** (2010a), Self-efficacy. In D. Matsumoto (Ed.) *Cambridge dictionary of psychology.* Cambridge: Cambridge University Press.

**Bandura, A.** (2010b). Vicarious learning. In D. Matsumoto (Ed.) *Cambridge dictionary of psychology.* Cambridge: Cambridge University Press.

**Bandura, A.** (2010c). Self-reinforcement. In D. Matsumoto (Ed.) *Cambridge dictionary of psychology.* Cambridge: Cambridge University Press.

**Bangert, K., Kulik, J., & Kulik, C.** (1983). Individualized systems of instruction in secondary schools. *Review of Educational Research, 53,* 143–158.

**Banich, M. T., & Caccamise, D.** (Eds.) (2010). *Generalization of knowledge.* New York: Psychology Press.

**Banks, J. A.** (2003). *Teaching strategies for ethnic studies* (7th ed.). Boston: Allyn & Bacon.

**Banks, J. A.** (2006). *Cultural diversity and education* (5th ed.). Boston: Allyn & Bacon.

**Banks, J. A.** (2008). *Introduction to multicultural education* (4th ed.). Boston: Allyn & Bacon.

**Banks, J. A.** (Ed.) (2010). *The Routledge international companion to multicultural education.* New York: Routledge.

**Banks, J. A., & others** (2005). Teaching diverse learners. In L. Darling-Hammond & J. Bransford (Eds.), *Preparing teachers for a changing world.* San Francisco: Jossey-Bass.

**Banks, J. A., Cochran-Smith, M., Moll, L., Richert, A., Zeichner, K., LePage, P., Darling-Hammond, L., Duffy, H., & McDonald, M.** (2005). Teaching diverse learners. In L. Darling-Hammond & J. Bransford (Eds.), *Preparing teachers for a changing world.* San Francisco: Jossey-Bass.

**Barab, S. A., Scott, B., Siyahhan, S. Goldstone, R., Ingram-Goble, A., Zuiker, S., & Warren, S.** (2010 in press). Transformational play as a curricular scaffold: Using videogames to support science education. *Journal of Science Education and Technology.*

**Barbarin, O., Mercado, M., & Jigjidsuren, D.** (2010). Development of tolerance and respect for diversity in children in the context of immigration. In E. L. Grigorenko & R. Takanishi (Eds.), *Immigration, diversity, and education.* New York: Routledge.

**Barbarin, O. A., & Miller, K.** (2009). Developmental science and early education: An introduction. In O. A. Barbarin & B. H. Wasik (Eds.), *Handbook of child development and early education.* New York: Guilford.

**Barbarin, O. A., & Odom, E.** (2009). Promoting social acceptance and respect for cultural diversity in young children: Learning from developmental research. In O. A. Barbarin & B. H. Wasik (Eds.), *Handbook of child development and early education.* New York: Guilford.

**Barber, B., Stone, M., & Eccles, J.** (2010). Protect, prepare, support, and engage: The roles of school-based extracurricular in students' development. In J. Meece & J. Eccles (Eds.), *Handbook of schools, schooling, and human development.* New York: Routledge.

**Baron-Cohen, S.** (2008). Autism, hypersystemizing, and truth. *Quarterly Journal of Experimental Psychology, 61,* 64–75.

**Baron-Cohen, S., Golan, O., Chapman, E., & Granader, Y.** (2007). Transported to a world of emotion. *The Psychologist, 20,* 76–77.

**Barron, A. E., Dawson, K., & Yendol-Hoppey, D.** (2009). Peer coaching and technology integration: An evaluation of the Microsoft Peer Coaching Program. *Mentoring and Tutoring: Partnership in Learning, 17,* 83–102.

**Bart, W. M.** (2008). *Educational psychology.* Thousand Oaks, CA: Sage.

**Bart, W. M., & Kato, K.** (2008). Normal curve. In N. J. Salkind (Ed.), *Encyclopedia, of educational psychology.* Thousand Oaks, CA: Sage.

**Bart, W. M., & Peterson, D. P.** (2008). Stanford-Binet test. In N. J. Salkind (Ed.), *Encyclopedia of educational psychology.* Thousand Oaks, CA: Sage.

**Bartlett, J.** (2010, January). *Personal conversation.* Richardson, TX: Department of Psychology, University of Texas at Dallas.

**Barton, J., & Collins, A.** (1997). Starting out: Designing your portfolio. In J. Barton & A. Collins (Eds.), *Portfolio assessment: A handbook for educators.* Boston: Addison-Wesley.

**Bass, J. E., Contant, T. L., & Carin, A. A.** (2009). *Activities for teaching science as inquiry* (7th ed.). Boston: Allyn & Bacon.

**Bassi, M., Steca, P., Della Fave, A., & Caprara, G. V.** (2007). Academic self-efficacy beliefs and quality of experience on learning. *Journal of Youth and Adolescence, 36,* 301–312.

**Bates, J. E.** (2008). Unpublished review of Santrock, J. W. *Children* (11th ed.). New York: McGraw-Hill.

**Bauer, P. J.** (2009). Neurodevelopmental changes in infancy and beyond: Implications for learning and memory. In O. A. Barbarin & B. H. Wasik (Eds.), *Handbook of child development and early education.* New York: Guilford.

**Bauerlein, M.** (2008). *The dumbest generation: How the digital age stupefies young Americans and jeopardizes our future (Or, don't trust anyone under 30).* New York: Tarcher.

**Baumeister, R. F., Campbell, J. D., Krueger, J. I., & Vohs, K. D.** (2003). Does high self-esteem cause better performance, interpersonal success, happiness, or healthier lifestyles? *Psychological Science in the Public Interest, 4*(1), 1–44.

**Baumrind, D.** (1971). Current patterns of parental authority. *Developmental Psychology Monographs, 4* (1, pt. 2).

**Baumrind, D.** (1996, April). Unpublished review of J. W. Santrock's *Children* (5th ed.). New York: McGraw-Hill.

**Beal, C., Mason-Bolick, C. H., & Martorella, P. H.** (2009). *Teaching social studies in middle and secondary schools* (5th ed.). Boston: Allyn & Bacon.

**Beatty, J. J., & Pratt, L.** (2011). *Early childhood language arts* (5th ed.). Boston: Allyn & Bacon.

**Beck, I. L., McKeown, G. M., Sinatra, K. B., & Loxterman, J. A.** (1991). Revising social studies texts from a text-processing perspective:

Evidence of improved comprehensibility. *Reading Research Quarterly, 26,* 251–276.

**Bednar, R. L., Wells, M. G., & Peterson, S. R.** (1995). *Self-esteem* (2nd ed.). Washington, DC: American Psychological Association.

**Beebe, S. A., Beebe, S. J., & Redmond, M. V.** (2011). *Interpersonal communication* (6th ed.). Boston: Allyn & Bacon.

**Beghetto, R. A., & Kaufman, J. C.** (Eds.), (2010, in press). *Nurturing creativity in the classroom.* New York: Cambridge University Press.

**Begley, S., & Interlandi, J.** (2008, June 2). The dumbest generation? Don't be dumb. *Newsweek.* Retrieved July 22, 2008, from www.newsweek.com/id/138536/

**Beilock, S. L., Rydell, R. J., & McConnell, A. R.** (2007). Stereotype threat and working memory: Mechanisms, alleviation, and spill-over. *Journal of Experimental Psychology: General, 136,* 256–276.

**Bell, L., & Bull, G. L.** (2010). *Teaching with digital video.* Eugene, OR: ISTE.

**Bell, M. A., Greene, D. R., & Wolfe, C. D.** (2010). Psychobiological mechanisms of cognition-emotion integration in early development. In S. D. Calkins & M. A. Bell (Eds.), *Child development at the intersection of cognition and emotion.* New York: Psychology Press.

**Bell, S.** (2010). Project-based learning for the 21st century: Skills for the future. *Clearing House: A Journal of Educational Strategies, 83,* 39–43.

**Bem, S. L.** (1977). On the utility of alternative procedures for assessing psychological androgyny. *Journal of Consulting and Clinical Psychology, 45,* 196–205.

**Bender, H. L., Allen, J. P., McElhaney, K. B., Antonishak, J., Moore, C. M., Kello, H. O., & Davis, S. M.** (2007). Use of harsh physical discipline and developmental outcomes in adolescence. *Development and Psychopathology, 19,* 227–242.

**Bennett, C. I.** (2011). *Comprehensive multicultural education* (7th ed.). Boston: Allyn & Bacon.

**Bennett, J., Hogarth, S., Lubben, F., Campbell, B., & Robinson, A.** (2010). Talking science: The research evidence on the use of small group discussions in science teaching. *International Journal of Science Education, 32,* 69–95.

**Bensley, D. A., Crowe, D. S., Bernhardt, P., Buckner, C., & Allman, A. L.** (2010). Teaching and assessing critical thinking skills for argument analysis in psychology. *Teaching of Psychology, 37,* 91–96.

**Benson, P. L., Scales, P. C., Hamilton, S. F., & Sesma, A.** (2006). Positive youth development. In W. Damon & R. Lerner (Eds.), *Handbook of child psychology* (6th ed.). New York: Wiley.

**Beran, T. N., & Tutty, L.** (2002). *An evaluation of the Bully Proofing Your School Program.* Unpublished manuscript, Calgary: RESOLVE, Alberta, CAN.

**Berecz, J. M.** (2009). *Theories of personality.* Boston: Allyn & Bacon.

**Bereiter, C., & Scardamalia, M.** (2006). Education for the knowledge age: Design-centered models of teaching and instruction. In P. A. Alexander & P. H. Winne (Eds.), *Handbook of educational psychology* (2nd ed.). Mahwah, NJ: Erlbaum.

**Berine-Smith, M., Patton, J. R., & Kim, S. H.** (2006). *Mental retardation* (7th ed.). Upper Saddle River, NJ: Prentice Hall.

**Berk, L. E.** (1994). Why children talk to themselves. *Scientific American, 271* (5), 78–83.

**Berk, L. E., & Spuhl, S. T.** (1995). Maternal interaction, private speech, and task performance in preschool children. *Early Childhood Research Quarterly, 10,* 145–169.

**Berko, J.** (1958). The child's learning of English morphology. *Word, 14,* 150–177.

**Berko, R. M., Wolvin, A. D., & Wolvin, D. R.** (2010). *Communicating* (11th ed.). Boston: Allyn & Bacon.

**Berko Gleason, J.** (2009). The development of language: An overview. In J. Berko Gleason & N. Ratner (Eds.), *The development of language* (7th ed.). Boston: Allyn & Bacon.

**Berko Gleason, J., & Ratner, N. B.** (Eds.), (2009). *The development of language* (7th ed.). Boston: Allyn & Bacon.

**Berkowitz, M. W., Battistich, V. A., & Bier, M.** (2008). What works in character education: What is known and what needs to be known. In L. Nucci & D. Narvaez (Eds.), *Handbook of moral and character education.* Clifton, NJ: Psychology Press.

**Berman, R. A.** (2010). Developing linguistic knowledge and language use across adolescence. In E. Hoff & M. Shatz (Eds.), *Blackwell handbook of language development.* New York: Wiley.

**Berndt, T. J.** (1979). Developmental changes in conformity to peers and parents. *Developmental Psychology, 15,* 608–616.

**Berninger, V. W.** (2006). A developmental approach to learning disabilities. In W. Damon & R. Lerner (Eds.), *Handbook of child psychology* (6th ed.). New York: Wiley.

**Berninger, V. W., Raskind, W., Richards, T., Abbott, R., & Stock, P.** (2008). A multidisci-

plinary approach to understanding developmental dyslexia within working-memory architecture: Genotypes, phenotypes, brain, and instruction. *Developmental Neuropsychology, 33,* 707–744.

**Bernstein, L., Rappaport, C. D., Olsho, L, Hunt, D., & Levin, M.** (2009). Impact of evaluation of the U.S. Department of Education's student mentoring program: Final report. NCEE 2009-4047. Available on ERIC as document # ED504310.

**Best, D. L.** (2010). Gender. In M. H. Bornstein (Ed.), *Handbook of developmental cultural science.* New York: Psychology Press.

**Betts, J., McKay, J., Maruff, P., & Anderson, V.** (2006). The development of sustained, attention in children: The effect of age and task load. *Child Neuropsychology, 12,* 205–221.

**Bialystok, E.** (1997). Effects of bilingualism and biliteracy on children's emerging concepts of print. *Developmental Psychology, 33,* 429–440.

**Bialystok, E.** (2001). Metalinguistic aspects of bilingual processing. *Annual Review of Applied Linguistics, 21,* 169–181.

**Bialystok, E.** (2007). Acquisition of literacy in preschool children: A framework for research. *Language Learning, 57,* 45–77.

**Bialystok, E., & Craik, F. I. M.** (2010). Cognitive and linguistic processing in the bilingual mind. *Current Directions in Psychological Science, 19,* 19–23.

**Biggs, B. K., & Vernberg, E. M.** (2010). Future directions. In E. M. Vernberg & B. K. Biggs (Eds.), *Preventing and treating bullying and victimization.* New York: Oxford University Press.

**Bill and Melinda Gates Foundation.** (2008). *Report gives voice to dropouts.* Retrieved July 5, 2008. From www.gatesfoundation.org/ UnitedStates/Education/Transforming -HighSchools/Related...

**Birman, B. F., Le Floch, K. C., Klekotka. A., Ludwig, M., Taylor, J., Walters, K., Wayne, A., & Yoon, K-S.** (2007). State and local implementation of the "No Child Left Behind Act." In *Volume II—Teacher quality under "NCLB": Interim report.* Jessup. MD: U.S. Department of Education.

**Bjorklund, D.** (2005). *Children's thinking* (4th ed.). Belmont, CA: Wadsworth.

**Bjorklund, D. F.** (2011, in press). Cognitive development: An overview. In P. D. Zelazo (Ed.), *Oxford handbook of developmental psychology.* New York: Oxford University Press.

**Bjorklund, D. F., & Rosenbaum, K.** (2000). Middle childhood: Cognitive development.

In A. Kazdin (Ed.), *Encyclopedia of psychology*. Washington, DC, & New York: American Psychological Association and Oxford University Press.

**Blackhurst, A. E.** (1997, May/June). Perspectives on technology in special education. *Teaching Exceptional Children*, pp. 41–47.

**Blackwell, L. S., & Dweck, C. S.** (2008). *The motivational impact of a computer-based program that teaches how the brain changes with learning*. Unpublished manuscript, Department of Psychology, Stanford University, Palo Alto, CA.

**Blackwell, L. S., Trzesniewski, K. H., & Dweck, C. S.** (2007). Implicit theories of intelligence predict achievement across an adolescent tradition: A longitudinal study and an intervention. *Child Development, 78*, 246–263.

**Blair, M., & Somerville, S. C.** (2009). The importance of differentiation in young children's acquisition of expertise. *Cognition, 112*, 259–280.

**Blakemore, J. E. O., Berenbaum, S. A., & Liben, L. S.** (2009). *Gender development*. New York: Psychology Press.

**Blakemore, S-J., & Choudhury, S.** (2006). Brain development during puberty: State of the science. *Developmental Science, 9*, 11–14.

**Block, J. H., & Block, J.** (1980). The role of ego-control and ego-resiliency in the organization of behavior. In W. A. Collins (Ed.), *Minnesota symposium on child psychology, Vol. 13*. Minneapolis: University of Minnesota Press.

**Bloom, B.** (1985). *Developing talent in young people*. New York: Ballantine.

**Bloom, B., & Dey, A. N.** (2006). Summary health statistics for U.S. children: National Health Interview survey, 2004. *Vital Health Statistics, 227*, 1–85.

**Bloom, B. S.** (1971). Mastering learning. In J. H. Block (Ed.), *Mastery learning*. New York: Holt, Rinehart & Winston.

**Bloom, B. S., Engelhart, M. D., Frost, E. J., Hill, W. H., & Krathwohl, D. R.** (1956). *Taxonomy of educational objectives*. New York: David McKay.

**Bloom, L.** (1998). Language acquisition in its developmental context. In W. Damon (Ed.), *Handbook of child psychology, Vol. 2* (5th ed.). New York: Wiley.

**Bloom, L. A.** (2009). *Classroom management*. Upper Saddle River, NJ: Prentice Hall.

**Blumenfeld, P., Krajcik, J., & Kempler, T.** (2006). Motivation in the classroom. In W. Damon & R. Lerner (Eds.), *Handbook of child psychology* (6th ed.). New York: Wiley.

**Blumenfeld, P. C., Kempler, T. M., & Krajcik, J. S.** (2006). Motivation and cognitive engagement in learning environments. In R. K. Sawyer (Ed.), *Cambridge handbook of learning sciences*. New York: Cambridge University Press.

**Blumenfeld, P. C., Pintrich, P. R., Wessles, K., & Meece, J.** (1981, April). *Age and sex differences in the impact of classroom experiences on self-perceptions*. Paper presented at the biennial meeting of the Society of Research in Child Development, Boston.

**Bodrova, E., & Leong, D. J.** (2007). *Tools of the mind* (2nd ed.). Upper Saddle River, NJ: Prentice Hall.

**Boekaerts, M.** (2009). Goal-directed behavior in the classroom. In K. R. Wentzel & A. Wigfield (Eds.), *Handbook of motivation at school*. New York: Routledge.

**Bonifacci, P., Giombini, L., Bellochhi, S., & Contento, S.** (2010, in press). Speed of processing, anticipation, inhibition, and working memory in bilinguals. *Developmental Science*.

**Bonney, C., & Sternberg, R. J.** (2011). Learning to think critically. In P. A. Alexander & R. E. Mayer (Eds.), *Handbook of research on learning and instruction*. New York: Routledge.

**Bordin, I. A., Duarte, C. S., Peres, C. A., Nascimento, R., Curto, B. M., & Paula, C. S.** (2009). Severe physical punishment: Risk of mental health problems for poor urban children in Brazil. *Bulletin of the World Health Organization, 87*, 336–344.

**Borich, G. D.** (2011). *Effective teaching methods* (7th ed.). Boston: Allyn & Bacon.

**Bornstein, M. H.** (Ed.) (2010). *Handbook of cultural developmental science*. New York: Psychology Press.

**Borrero, C. S. W., & others** (2010). Concurrent reinforcement schedules for problem behavior and appropriate behavior: Experimental applications of the matching law. *Journal of the Experimental Analysis of Behavior, 93*, 455–469.

**Boutot, E. A., & Myles, B. S.** (2011). *Autism spectrum disorders*. Upper Saddle River, NJ: Merrill.

**Bowman-Perrott, L.** (2009). Classwide peer tutoring: An effective strategy for students with emotional and behavioral disorders. *Intervention in School and Clinic, 44*, 259–267.

**Boyles, N. S., & Contadino, D.** (1997). *The learning differences sourcebook*. Los Angeles: Lowell House.

**Brahier, D. J.** (2009). *Teaching secondary and middle school mathematics* (3rd ed.). Boston: Allyn & Bacon.

**Brainerd, C. J., Forrest, T. J., Karibian, D., & Reyna, V. F.** (2006). Fuzzy-trace theory and memory development. *Developmental Psychology, 42*, 962–979.

**Brainerd, C. J., & Gordon, L. L.** (1994). Development of verbatim and gist memory for numbers. *Developmental Psychology, 30*, 163–177.

**Brams, H., Mao, A. R., & Doyle, R. L.** (2009). Onset of efficacy of long-lasting psychostimulants in pediatric attention-deficit/hyperactivity disorder. *Postgraduate Medicine, 120*, 69–88.

**Brans, R. G., & others** (2010). Brain plasticity and intellectual ability are influenced by shared genes. *Journal of Neuroscience, 30*, 5519–5524.

**Bransford, J., Barron, B., Pea, R., Meltzoff, A., Kuhl, P., Bell, P., Stevens, R., Schwartz, D., Vye, N., Reeves, B., Roschelle, J., & Sabelli, N.** (2006). Foundations and opportunities for an interdisciplinary science. In R. K. Sawyer (Ed.), *The Cambridge handbook of the learning sciences*. New York: Cambridge University Press.

**Bransford, J., Darling-Hammond, L., & LePage, P.** (2005). Introduction. In L. Darling-Hammond & J. Bransford (Eds.), *Preparing teachers for a changing world*. New York: Jossey-Bass.

**Bransford, J., Derry, S., Berliner, D., Hammerness, K., & Beckett, K. L.** (2005). Theories of learning and their role in teaching. In L. Darling-Hammond & J. Bransford (Eds.), *Preparing teachers for a changing world*. San Francisco: Jossey-Bass.

**Bransford, J. D., & Donovan, M. S.** (2005). Scientific inquiry and *How People Learn*. In M. S. Donovan & J. D. Bransford (Eds.), *How students learn*. Washington, DC: National Academies Press.

**Bransford, J. D., & Stein, B. S.** (1993). *The IDEAL problem solver*. New York: W. H. Freeman.

**Bredekamp, S.** (2011). *Effective practices in early childhood education*. Upper Saddle River, NJ: Merrill.

**Brewer, M. B., & Campbell, D. I.** (1976). *Ethnocentrism and intergroup attitudes*. New York: Wiley.

**Bridgeland, J. M., Dilulio, J. J., & Wulsin, S. C.** (2008). *Engaged for success*. Washington, DC: Civic Enterprises.

**Briggs, T. W.** (1999, October 14). Honorees find keys to unlocking kids' minds. Retrieved March 10, 2000, from www.usatoday.com/education

**Brodkin, A.** (2009). Commentary in What you should do when you suspect child abuse. Retrieved August 15, 2009, from http://content.scholastic.com/browse/article .jsp?id4435

**Brody, N.** (2000). Intelligence. In A. Kazdin (Ed.), *Encyclopedia of psychology.* Washington, DC, & New York: American Psychological Association and Oxford University Press.

**Brody, N.** (2007). Does education influence intelligence? In P. C. Kyllonen, R. D. Roberts, & L. Stankov (Eds.), *Extending intelligence.* Mahwah, NJ: Erlbaum.

**Bronfenbrenner, U.** (1995). Developmental ecology through space and time: A future perspective. In P. Moen, G. H. Elder, & K. Luscher (Eds.), *Examining lives in context.* Washington, DC: American Psychological Association.

**Bronfenbrenner, U.** (2000). Ecological theory. In A. Kazdin (Ed.), *Encyclopedia of psychology.* Washington, DC, & New York: American Psychological Association and Oxford University Press.

**Bronfenbrenner, U., & Morris, M. A.** (2006). The ecology of developmental processes. In W. Damon & R. Lerner (Eds.), *Handbook of child psychology* (6th ed.). New York: Wiley.

**Bronstein, P.** (2006). The family environment: Where gender socialization begins, In J. Worell & C. D. Goodheart (Eds.), *Handbook of girls' and women's psychological health.* New York: Oxford University Press.

**Brookhart, S. M.** (1997). A theoretical framework for the role of classroom assessment in motivating student effort and achievement. *Applied Measurement in Education, 10,* 161–180.

**Brookhart, S. M.** (2008). *Assessment and grading in classrooms.* Upper Saddle River, NJ: Prentice Hall.

**Brookover, W. B., Beady, C., Flood, P., Schweitzer, U., & Wisenbaker, J.** (1979). *School social systems and student achievement: Schools make a difference.* New York: Praeger.

**Brooks, J. G., & Brooks, M. G.** (1993). *The case for constructivist classrooms.* Alexandria, VA: Association for Supervision and Curriculum Development.

**Brooks, J. G., & Brooks, M. G.** (2001). *In search of understanding: The case for constructivist classrooms.* Upper Saddle River, NJ: Merrill.

**Brophy, J.** (1996). *Teaching problem students.* New York: Guilford.

**Brophy, J.** (1998). *Motivating students to learn.* New York: McGraw-Hill.

**Brophy, J.** (2004). *Motivating students to learn* (2nd ed.). Mahwah, NJ: Erlbaum.

**Brown, A. H., Green, T. D., & Robinson, L. K.** (2010). *Security vs. access.* Eugene, OR: ISTE.

**Brown, A. L.** (1997). Transforming schools into communities of thinking and learning about serious matters. *American Psychologist, 52,* 399–413.

**Brown, A. L., & Campione, J. C.** (1996). Psychological learning theory and the design of innovative environments. In L. Schuable & R. Glaser (Eds.), *Contributions of instructional innovation to understanding learning.* Mahwah, NJ: Erlbaum.

**Brownell, J.** (2010). *Listening* (4th ed.). Upper Saddle River, NJ: Allyn & Bacon.

**Bruckman, A.** (2006). Learning in online communities. In R. K. Sawyer (Ed.), *Cambridge handbook of learning sciences.* New York: Oxford University Press.

**Bruning, R., & Horn, C.** (2001). Developing motivation to write. *Educational Psychologist, 35,* 25–37.

**Brunstein Klomek, A., Marrocco, F., Kleinman, M., Schofeld, I. S., & Gould, M. S.** (2007). Bullying, depression, and suicidality in adolescents. *Journal of the American Academy of Child and Adolescent Psychiatry, 46,* 40–49.

**Bryant, J. A.** (2007). *The children's television community.* Mahwah, NJ: Erlbaum.

**Bryant, J. B.** (2009). Language in social contexts: Communication competence in the preschool years. In J. Berko Gleason & N. Ratner (Eds.), *The development of language* (7th ed.). Boston: Allyn & Bacon.

**Bryant, P., & Nunes, T.** (2011). Children's understanding of mathematics. In U. Goswami (Ed.), *Wiley-Blackwell handbook of childhood cognitive development.* New York: Wiley.

**Buckner, J. C., Mezzacappa, E., & Beardslee, W. R.** (2009). Self-regulation and its relations to adaptive functioning in low income youths. *American Journal of Orthopsychiatry, 79,* 19–30.

**Bumgardner, S.** (2010). The equitable distribution of high-quality teachers. *District Administration, 46,* 45–47.

**Burden, P. R., & Byrd, D. M.** (2010). *Methods for effective teaching* (5th ed.). Boston: Allyn & Bacon.

**Burgoon, J. K., Guerrero, L. K., & Floyd, K.** (2010). *Nonverbal communication.* Boston: Allyn & Bacon.

**Burke, K.** (2010). *How to assess authentic learning* (5th ed.). Thousand Oaks, CA: Sage.

**Burkham, D. T., Lee, V. E., & Smerdon, B. A.** (1997). Gender and science learning early in high school: Subject matter and laboratory experiences. *American Educational Research Journal, 34,* 297–331.

**Burnette, J.** (1998). Reducing the disproportionate representation of minority students in special education. *ERIC/OSEP Digest, No. E500.*

**Burz, H. L., & Marshall, K.** (1996). *Performance-based curriculum for mathematics: From knowing to showing.* ERIC Document Reproduction Service No. ED400194.

**Buss, D. M.** (2008). *Evolutionary psychology* (3rd ed.). Boston: Allyn & Bacon.

## C

**Caldwell, S.** (2010). *Statistics unplugged* (3rd ed.). Boston: Cengage.

**California State Department of Education.** (1994). *Golden State examination science portfolio.* Sacramento: California State Department of Education.

**Cameron, J. R.** (2001). Negative effects of reward on intrinsic motivation—A limited phenomenon. *Review of Educational Research, 71,* 29–42.

**Cameron, J. R., & Pierce, D.** (2008). Intrinsic versus extrinsic motivation. In N. J. Salkind (Ed.), *Encyclopedia of educational psychology.* Thousand Oaks, CA: Sage.

**Campbell, B.** (2008). *Handbook of differentiated instruction using the multiple intelligences: Lesson plans and more.* Boston: Allyn & Bacon.

**Campbell, D. E.** (2010). *Choosing democracy: A practical guide to multicultural education* (4th ed.). Boston: Allyn & Bacon.

**Campbell, D. T., & LeVine, D. T.** (1968). Ethnocentrism and intergroup relations. In R. Abelson & others (Eds.), *Theories of cognitive consistency.* Chicago: Rand McNally.

**Campbell, L., Campbell, B., & Dickinson, D.** (2004). *Teaching and learning through multiple intelligence* (3rd ed.). Boston: Allyn & Bacon.

**Campione, J.** (2001, April). *Fostering a Community of Learners.* Paper presented at the meeting of the American Educational Research Association, Seattle.

**Cardelle-Elawar, M.** (1992). Effects of teaching metacognitive skills to students with low mathematics ability. *Teaching and Teacher Education, 8,* 109–121.

**Carnegie Council on Adolescent Development.** (1995). *Great transitions.* New York: Carnegie Foundation.

**Carnegie Foundation** (1989). *Turning points: Preparing youth for the 21st century.* New York: Author.

**Carota, F., Posada, A., Harquel, S., Delpuech, C., Bertrand, O., & Sirigu, A.** (2010, in press). Neural dynamics of intention to speak. *Cerebral Cortex.*

**Carpendale, J. I., & Chandler, M. J.** (1996). On the distinction between false belief understanding and subscribing to an interpretive theory of mind. *Child Development. 67,* 1686–1706.

**Carpenter, M.** (2011). Social cognition and social motivations in infancy. In U. Goswami (Ed.), *Wiley-Blackwell handbook of childhood cognitive development* (2nd ed.). New York: Wiley Blackwell.

**Carrell, S. E., Malmstrom, F. V., & West, J. E.** (2008). Peer effects in academic cheating. *Journal of Human Resources, 43,* 173–207.

**Carretti, B., Borella, E., Cornodli, C., & De Beni, R.** (2009). Role of working memory in explaining the performance of individuals with specific reading comprehension difficulties: A meta-analysis. *Learning and Individual Differences, 19,* 246–251.

**Carroll, J.** (1993). *Human cognitive abilities.* Cambridge, UK: Cambridge University Press.

**Carroll, J. B.** (1963). A model of school learning. *Teachers College Record, 64,* 723–733.

**Carter, N., Prater, M. A., & Dyches, T. T.** (2009). *What every teacher should know about: Adaptations and accommodation for students with mild to moderate disabilities.* Upper Saddle River. NJ: Prentice Hall.

**Case, R.** (2000). Conceptual structures. In M. Bennett (Ed.), *Developmental psychology.* Philadelphia Psychology Press.

**Cathcart, G., Pothier, Y. M., Vance, J. H., & Bezuk, N. S.** (2011). *Learning mathematics in elementary and middle schools* (5th ed.). Boston: Allyn & Bacon.

**Cavazos, A. G., & Cavazos, J.** (2010). Understanding the experiences of Latina/o students: A qualitative study for change. *American Secondary Education, 38,* 95–109.

**Caviness, L. B.** (2008). Brain-relevant education. In N. J. Salkind (Ed.), *Encyclopedia of educational psychology.* Thousand Oaks, CA: Sage.

**Ceballo, R., Huerta, M., & Ngo, Q. E.** (2010). Schooling experiences of Latino students. In J. Meece & J. Eccles (Eds.), *Handbook of research on schools, schooling, and human development.* New York: Routledge.

**Ceci, S. J., & Williams, W. M.** (1997). Schooling, intelligence, and income. *American Psychologist, 52,* 1051–1058.

**Center for Instructional Technology.** (2006). Writing multiple-choice questions that demand critical thinking. Retrieved January 12, 2006, from http://cit.necc.mass .edu/atlt/TestCritThink.htm

**Centers for Disease Control and Prevention** (2010). *Autism spectrum disorders.* Atlanta: Author.

**Cervone, D., & Pervin, L. A.** (2010). *Personality* (11th ed.). New York: Wiley.

**Chall, J. S.** (1979). The great debate: Ten years later with a modest proposal for reading stages. In L. B. Resnick & P. A. Weaver (Eds.), *Theory and practice of early reading.* Mahwah, NJ: Erlbaum.

**Chance, P.** (2009). *Learning and behavior* (6th ed.). Boston: Cengage.

**Chang, M-M.** (2007). Enhancing web-based language learning through self-assessment. *Journal of Computer Assisted Learning, 23,* 187–196.

**Chao, R. K.** (2005, April). *The importance of guan in describing the parental control of immigrant Chinese.* Paper presented at the meeting of the Society for Research in Child Development, Atlanta.

**Chao, R. K.** (2007, March). *Research with Asian Americans: Looking back, moving forward.* Paper presented at the meeting of the Society for Research in Child Development, Boston.

**Chapin, J. R.** (2009). *Elementary social studies* (7th ed.). Boston: Allyn & Bacon.

**Chapman, J. W., Tunmer, W. E., & Prochnow, J. E.** (2001). Does success in the Reading Recovery program depend on developing proficiency in phonological-processing skills? A longitudinal study in the whole language instructional context. *Scientific Studies of Reading, 15,* 141–176.

**Chapman, O. L.** (2000). Learning science involves language, experience, and modeling. *Journal of Applied Developmental Psychology, 21,* 97–108.

**Charles, C. M.** (2011). *Building classroom discipline* (10th ed.) Boston: Allyn & Bacon.

**Charney, R. S.** (2005). *Exploring the first "R": To reinforce.* Retrieved on October 26, 2006 from www.nea.org/classmanagement/ifc050201.html

**Chen, C., & Stevenson, H. W.** (1989). Homework: A cross-cultural comparison. *Child Development, 60,* 551–561.

**Chen, C-H.** (2010). Promoting college students' knowledge acquisition and ill-structured problem solving: Web-based integration and procedure prompts. *Computers & Education, 55,* 292–303.

**Chen, Z-Y.** (2009a). Parenting style. In D. Carr (Ed.), *Encyclopedia of the life course and human development.* Boston: Gale Cengage.

**Chen, Z-Y.** (2009b). Parent-child relationships, childhood, and adolescence. In D. Carr (Ed.), *Encyclopedia of the life course and human development.* Boston: Gale Cengage.

**Chess, S., & Thomas, A.** (1977). Temperamental individuality from childhood to adolescence. *Journal of Child Psychiatry, 16,* 218–226.

**Chi, M. T. H.** (1978). Knowledge structures and memory development. In R. S. Siegler (Ed.), *Children's thinking: What develops?* Hillsdale, NJ: Erlbaum.

**Chi, M. T. H, & Brem, S. K.** (2009). Contrasting Ohlsson's resubsumption theory with Chi's categorical shift theory. *Educational Psychologist, 44,* 58–63.

**Chiapatta, E. L., & Koballa, T. R.** (2010). *Science instruction in the middle and secondary schools* (7th ed.). Boston: Allyn & Bacon.

**Children's Defense Fund.** (1992). *The state of America's children.* Washington, DC: Author.

**Childstats.gov** (2009). *Poverty.* Retrieved November 16, 2009, from www.childstats .gov/americaschildren/index.3.asp

**Chomsky, N.** (1957). *Syntactic structures.* The Hague: Mouton.

**Christie, J., Enz, B. J., & Vukelich, C.** (2011). *Teaching language and literacy* (4th ed.). Boston: Allyn & Bacon.

**Cicchetti, D., & Toth, S. L.** (2011). Child maltreatment: The research imperative and the exploration of results to clinical contexts. In B. Lester & J. D. Sparrow (Eds.), *Nurturing children and families.* New York: Wiley.

**Cizek, G. J.** (2010). An introduction to formative assessment: History, characteristics, and challenges. In H. Andrade & G. J. Cizek (Eds.), *Handbook of formative assessment.* New York: Routledge.

**Clark, B.** (2008). *Growing up gifted* (7th ed.). Upper Saddle River, NJ: Prentice Hall.

**Clark, K. B., & Clark, M. P.** (1939). The development of the self and the emergence of racial identification in Negro preschool children. *Journal of Social Psychology, 10,* 591–599.

**Clark, L.** (Ed.). (1993). *Faculty and student challenges in facing cultural and linguistic diversity.* Springfield, IL: Charles C Thomas.

**Clarke-Stewart, A.** (2006). What have we learned: Proof that families matter, prospects for future research, and policies for families and children. In A. Clarke-Stewart & J. Dunn (Eds.), *Families count.* New York: Cambridge University Press.

**Clements, D. H., and Sarama, J.** (2008). Experimental Evaluation of the Effects of a Research-Based Preschool Mathematics Curriculum. *American Educational Research Journal, 45,* 443–494.

**Clements, D. H., and Sarama, J.** (2009). *Learning and teaching early math: The learning trajectories approach.* New York: Routledge.

**Cloud, J.** (2007, August 27). Failing our geniuses. *Time,* 40–47.

**Clunies-Ross, P., Little, E., & Kienhuis, M.** (2008). Self-reported and actual use of proactive and reactive management strategies and their relationship with teacher stress and school behavior. *Educational Psychology, 28,* 693–710.

**Cobern, W. W., & others** (2010). Experimental comparison of inquiry and direct instruction in science. *Research in Science and Technological Education, 28,* 81–96.

**Cognition and Technology Group at Vanderbilt.** (1997). *The Jasper Project.* Mahwah, NJ: Erlbaum.

**Cohn, A., and Canter, A.** (2003). *Bullying: Facts for schools and parents.* Washington, DC. National Association of School Psychologists.

**Colangelo, N., & Davis, G. A.** (2003). *Handbook of gifted education* (3rd ed.). Boston: Allyn & Bacon.

**Colangelo, N. C., Assouline, S. G., & Gross, M. U. M.** (2004). *A nation deceived: How schools hold back America's brightest students.* Retrieved October 16, 2006, from http://nationdeceived.org/

**Colby, A., Kohlberg, L., Gibbs, J., & Lieberman, M.** (1983). A longitudinal study of moral judgment. *Monograph: The Society for Research in Child Development, 48* (21, Serial No. 201).

**Cole, M.** (2006). Culture and cognitive development in phylogenetic, historical, and ontogenetic perspective. In W. Damon & R. Lerner (Eds.), *Handbook of child psychology* (6th ed.). New York: Wiley.

**Coley, R.** (2001). *Differences in the gender gap: Comparisons across/racial/ethnic groups in the United States.* Princeton, NJ: Educational Testing Service.

**College Board** (2004). *2003 college-bound seniors: Tables and related items.* Princeton, NJ: College Board.

**Collins, M.** (1996, winter). The job outlook for '96 grads. *Journal of Career Planning,* pp. 51–54.

**Collis, B. A., Knezek, G. A., Lai, K. W., Miyashita, K. T., Pelgrum, W. J., Plomp, T., & Sakamoto, T.** (1996). *Children and computers in school.* Mahwah, NJ: Erlbaum.

**Colom, R., & others** (2009). Gray matter correlates of fluid, crystallized, and spatial intelligence. *Intelligence, 37,* 124–135.

**Combs, D.** (1997, September). Using alternative assessment to provide options for student success. *Middle School Journal,* pp. 3–8.

**Combs, M.** (2010). *Readers and writers in the primary grades.* Boston: Allyn & Bacon.

**Comer, J. P.** (1988). Educating poor minority children. *Scientific American, 259,* 42–48.

**Comer, J. P.** (2004). *Leave no child behind.* New Haven, CT: Yale University Press.

**Comer, J. P.** (2006). Child development: The underweighted aspect of intelligence. In P. C. Kyllonen, R. D. Roberts, & L. Stankov (Eds.), *Extending intelligence.* Mahwah, NJ: Erlbaum.

**Comer, J. P.** (2010). Comer School Development Program. In J. Meece & J. Eccles (Eds.), *Handbook of research on schools, schooling, and human development.* New York: Routledge.

**Conley, M. W.** (2008). *Content area literacy: Learners in context.* Boston: Allyn & Bacon.

**Cook, T. D., Deng, Y., & Morgano, E.** (2007). Friendship influences during early adolescence: The special role of friends' grade point average. *Journal of Research on Adolescence, 17,* 325–356.

**Cooper, E., & Sherk, J.** (1989). Addressing urban school reform: Issues and alliances, *Journal of Negro Education, 58,* 315–331.

**Cooper, H.** (1989). Synthesis of research on homework. *Educational Leadership, 47* (3), 85–91.

**Cooper, H.** (1998, April). *Family, student, and assignment characteristics of positive homework experiences.* Paper presented at the meeting of the American Educational Research Association, San Diego.

**Cooper, H.** (2006). *The battle over homework.* Thousand Oaks, CA: Corwin.

**Cooper, H.** (2007). *The battle over homework: Common ground for administrators, teachers, and parents* (3rd ed). Thousand Oaks. CA: Corwin Press.

**Cooper, H.** (2009). Homework. In T. Bidell (Ed.). *Chicago Companion to the Child.* Chicago: University of Chicago Press.

**Cooper, H., & Patall, E. A.** (2007). Homework. In S. Mathison & E. W. Ross (Eds.), *Battleground schools* (pp. 319–326). Westport, CT: Greenwood Press.

**Cooper, H., Robinson, J. C., & Patall, E. A.** (2006). Does homework improve academic achievement? A synthesis of research. 1987–2003. *Review of Educational Research, 76,* 1–62.

**Cooper, S. M., McLoyd, V., Wood, D., & Hardaway, C.** (2008). The mental health consequences of racial discrimination for African American adolescents. In S. Quintana and C. McKown (Eds.), *Handbook of race, racism and the developing child.* New York: Wiley.

**Copeland, L.** (2003, December). Science teacher just wanted to do some good, and he has. *USA Today.* Retrieved December 12, 2003, from www.usatoday.com/news/education/2003-12-30-laster-usal_x.htm

**Copeland, S. R., & Luckasson, R.** (2008). Mental retardation. In N. J. Salkind (Ed.), *Encyclopedia of educational psychology.* Thousand Oaks, CA: Sage.

**Corno, L.** (1998, March 30). Commentary. *Newsweek,* p. 51.

**Cosmides, L.** (2011). Evolutionary psychology. *Annual Review of Psychology, Vol. 62.* Palo Alto, CA: Sage.

**Cossentino, J.** (2008). Montessori schools. In N. J. Salkind (Ed.), *Encyclopedia of educational psychology.* Thousand Oaks, CA: Sage.

**Coté, J. E.** (2009). Identity formation and self-development in adolescence. In R. M. Lerner & L. Steinberg (Eds.), *Handbook of adolescent psychology* (3rd ed.). New York: Wiley.

**Council of Chief State School Officers.** (2005). *Marilyn Jachetti Whirry.* Retrieved on February 8, 2006 from www.cesso.org

**Council for Exceptional Children.** (1998). *CEC's comments on the proposed IDEA regulations.* Washington, DC: Author.

**Courage, M. L., & Richards, J. E.** (2008). Attention. In M. M. Haith & J. B. Benson (Eds.), *Encyclopedia of infant and early childhood development.* Oxford, UK: Elsevier.

**Covington, M. V.** (2009). Self-worth theory: Retrospection and prospects. In K. R. Wentzel & A. Wigield (Eds.), *Handbook of motivation at school.* New York: Routledge.

**Covington, M. V., & Dray, E.** (2002). The development course of achievement motivation: A need-based approach. In A. Wigfield & J. S. Eccles (Eds.), *Development of achievement motivation.* San Diego: Academic Press.

**Covington, M. V., & Teel, K. T.** (1996). *Overcoming student failure.* Washington, DC: American Psychological Association.

**Cowan, N., & Alloway, T.** (2009). The development of working memory in childhood. In M. Carriage & N. Cowan (Eds.), *The development of memory in infancy and childhood*. Clifton, NJ: Psychology Press.

**Cowan, N., & others** (2010). Seven-year-olds allocate attention like adults unless working memory is overloaded. *Developmental Science, 13,* 120–133.

**Coyne, M. D., & others** (2009). Direction instruction of comprehension: Instructional examples from intervention research on listening and reading comprehension. *Reading & Writing Quarterly, 25,* 221–245.

**Coyne, M. D., McCoadch, D. B., Loftus, S., Zipoli, R., & Kapp, S.** (2010). Direct vocabulary instruction in kindergarten: Teaching for breadth versus depth. *Elementary School Journal, 110,* 1–18.

**Craik, F. I. M., & Lockhart, R. S.** (1972). Levels of processing: A framework for memory research. *Journal of Verbal Learning and Verbal Behavior, 11,* 671–684.

**Crick, N. R., Murray-Close, D., Marks, P. E. L., & Mohajeri-Nelson, N.** (2009). Aggression and peer relationships in school-age children: Relational and physical aggression in group and dyadic contexts. In K. H. Rubin, W. M. Bukowski, & B. Laursen (Eds.), *Handbook of peer interactions, relationships, and groups*. New York: Guilford.

**Crooks, C. V., Chiodo, D., Thomas, D., & Hughes, R.** (2010). Strengths-based programming for First Nations youth: Building engagement through healthy relationships and leadership skills. *International Journal of Mental Health and Addiction, 8,* 160–173.

**Crosnoe, R., Riegle-Crumb, C., Field, S., Frank, K., & Muller, C.** (2008). Peer group contexts of girls' and boys' academic experiences. *Child Development, 79,* 139–155.

**Cross, C. T., Woods, T. A., & Schweingruber, H.** (Eds.) (2009). *Mathematics learning in early childhood: Paths toward excellence and equity*. Washington, DC: National Academies Press.

**Crouter, A. C.** (2006). Mothers and fathers at work. In A. Clarke-Stewart & J. Dunn (Eds.), *Families count*. New York: Cambridge University Press.

**Crowley, K., Callahan, M. A., Tenenbaum, H. R., & Allen, E.** (2001). Parents explain more to boys than to girls during shared scientific thinking. *Psychological Science, 12,* 258–261.

**Cruickshank, D. R., Metcalf, K. M., & Jenkins, D. B.** (2009). *The act of teaching* (5th ed.). Boston: Allyn & Bacon.

**Csikszentmihalyi, M.** (1990). *Flow*. New York: Harper & Row.

**Csikszentmihalyi, M.** (1993). *The evolving self*. New York: Harper & Row.

**Csikszentmihalyi, M.** (1996). *Creativity*. New York: HarperCollins.

**Csikszentmihalyi, M.** (2000). Creativity: An interview. In A. Kazlin (Ed.). *Encyclopedia of psychology*. Washington, DC, & New York: American Psychological Association and Oxford University Press.

**Csikszentmihalyi, M., & Csikszentmihalyi, I. S.** (Eds.). (2006). *A life worth living*. New York: Oxford University Press.

**Csikszentmihalyi, M., Rathunde, K., & Whalen, S.** (1993). *Talented teenagers: The roots of success and failure*. Cambridge, UK: Cambridge University Press.

**Culbertson, L. D., & Jalongo, M. R.** (1999). "But what's wrong with letter grades?" Responding to parents' questions about alternative assessments. *Childhood Education, 75,* 130–135.

**Cummings, E. M., & Merrilees, C. E.** (2009). Identifying the dynamic processes underlying links between marital conflict and child adjustment. In M. S. Schulz, P. K. Kerig, M. K. Pruett, & R. D. Parke (Eds.), *Feathering the nest*. Washington, DC: American Psychological Association.

**Cunningham, P. M.** (2009). *Phonics they use* (5th ed.). Boston: Allyn & Bacon.

**Cunningham, P. M., & Allington, R. L.** (2011). *Classrooms that work: They can all read and write* (5th ed.). Boston: Allyn & Bacon.

**Cunningham, P. M., & Cunningham, J. W.** (2010). *What really matters in writing*. Boston: Allyn & Bacon.

**Curran, K., DuCette, J., Eisenstein, J., & Hyman, I. A.** (2001, August). *Statistical analysis of the cross-cultural data: The third year*. Paper presented at the meeting of the American Psychological Association, San Francisco, CA.

**Curtis, M. E., & Longo, A. M.** (2001, November). *Teaching vocabulary development to adolescents to improve comprehension*. Retrieved April 26, 2006, from www.readingonline.org/articles/curtis

**D**

**Dahl, R. E.** (2004). Adolescent brain development: A period of vulnerabilities and opportunities. *Annals of the New York Academy of Sciences, 1021,* 1–22.

**Daley, D.** (2006). Attention deficit hyperactivity disorder: A review of the essential facts. *Child: Care, Health, and Development, 32,* 193–204.

**Damon, W.** (2008). *The path to purpose: Helping our children find their calling in life*. New York: Free Press.

**Daniels, H.** (2011). Vygotsky and psychology. In U. Goswami (Ed.), *Wiley-Blackwell handbook of childhood cognitive development* (2nd ed.). New York: Wiley Blackwell.

**Danielson, C.** (2010). *Pathways to teaching series: Teaching methods*. Upper Saddle River, NJ: Merrill.

**Dansereau, D. F.** (1988). Cooperative learning strategies. In C. E. Weinstein, E. T. Goetz, & P. A. Alexander (Eds.), *Learning and study strategies*. Orlando, FL: Academic Press.

**Darling-Hammond, L.** (2001, August). *What's at stake in high-stakes testing?* Paper presented at the meeting of the American Psychological Association, San Francisco.

**Darling-Hammon, L.** (2007). *Race, Ethnicity, and education. 10,* 245–260.

**Darling-Hammond, L., Banks, J., Zumwalt, K., Gomez, L., Sherin, M. G., Griesdorn, J., & Finn, L-E.** (2005). Educational goals and purposes: Developing a curricular vision for education. In L. Darling-Hammond & J. Bransford (Eds.), *Preparing teachers for a changing world*. San Francisco: Jossey-Bass.

**Darling-Hammond, L., & Baratz-Snowden, J.** (Eds.). (2005). *A good teacher in every classroom: Preparing the highly qualified teachers our children deserve*. San Francisco: Jossey-Bass.

**Darling-Hammond, L., & Bransford, J.** (Eds.). (2005). *Preparing teachers for a changing world*. San Francisco: Jossey-Bass.

**Darragh, J. C.** (2010). *Introduction to early childhood education: Equity and inclusion*. Upper Saddle River, NJ: Merrill.

**Davidson, D.** (1996). The effects of decision characteristics on children's selective search of predecisional information. *Acta Psychologica, 92,* 263–281.

**Davidson, J., & Davidson, B.** (2004). *Genius denied: How to stop wasting our brightest young minds*. New York: Simon & Schuster.

**Davidson, J. & Feldman, J.** (2010). Formative assessment applications culminating demonstrations of mastery. In H. Andrade & G. J. Cizek (Eds.) *Handbook of formative assessment*. New York: Routledge.

**Davies, J., & Brember, I.** (1999). Reading and mathematics attainments and self-esteem in years 2 and 6—an eight-year cross-sectional study. *Educational Studies, 25,* 145–157.

**Davis, G. A., Rimm, S. B., & Siegle, D.** (2011). *Education of the gifted and talented* (6th ed.). Upper Saddle River, NJ: Merrill.

**Davis, G. E., & McGowen, M. A.** (2007). Formative feedback and the mindful teaching of mathematics. *Australian Senior Mathematics Journal, 21,* 19–29.

**de Boer, H., Bosker, R. J., & van der Werf, M. P. C.** (2010). Sustainability of teacher expectation bias effects on long-term student performance. *Journal of Educational Psychology, 102,* 168–179.

**De Feyter, J. J., & Winsler, A.** (2010). Disentangling nativity status, race/ethnicity, and country of origin in predicting the school readiness of young immigrant children. In E. L. Grigorenko & R. Takanishi (Eds.), *Immigration, diversity, and education.* New York: Routledge.

**de Haan, M., & Gunnar, M. R.** (Eds.) (2009). *Handbook of social developmental neuroscience.* New York: Guilford.

**de Jong, T.** (2011, in press). Instruction based on computer instruction. In P. A. Alexander & R. E. Mayer (Eds.), *Handbook of research on learning and instruction.* New York: Routledge.

**De La Paz, S., & McCutchen, D.** (2011, in press). Learning to write. In P. A. Alexander & R. E. Mayer (Eds.), *Handbook of research on learning and instruction.* New York: Routledge.

**De Smet, M., Van Keer, H., De Wever, B., & Valcke, M.** (2010). Cross-age peer tutors in asynchronous discussion groups: Exploring the impact of three types of tutor training on patterns in tutor support and on tutor characteristics. *Computers and Education, 54,* 1167–1181.

**Deary, I. J., Penke, L., & Johnson, W.** (2010). The neuroscience of human intelligence differences. *Nature Review: Neuroscience, 11,* 201–211.

**Deary, I. J., Strand, S., Smith, P., & Fernandes, C.** (2007). Intelligence and educational achievement. *Intelligence, 35,* 13–21.

**deCharms, R.** (1984). Motivation enhancement in educational settings. In R. Ames & C. Ames (Eds.), *Research on motivation in education, Vol. 1.* Orlando: Academic Press.

**Deci, E. I., Koestner, R., & Ryan, R. M.** (2001). Extrinsic rewards and intrinsic motivation in education: Reconsidered once again. *Review of Educational Research, 71,* 1–28.

**Delisle, J. R.** (1987). *Gifted kids speak out.* Minneapolis: Free Spirit Publishing.

**DeLoache, J. S., Simcock, G., & Macari, S.** (2007). Places, trains, and automobiles— and tea sets. *Developmental Psychology, 43,* 1579–1586.

**Demetriou, A., Mouyi, A., & Spanoudis, G.** (2011). The development of mental processing. In R. M. Lerner & W. F. Overton (Eds.), *Handbook of life-span development.* New York: Wiley.

**Demirici, N.** (2010). Web-based vs. paper-based homework to evaluate students' performance in introductory physics course and students' perceptions: two years experience. *International Journal on E-Learning, 9,* 27–49.

**Dempster, F. N.** (1981). Memory span: Sources of individual and developmental differences. *Psychological Bulletin, 89,* 63–100.

**Derman-Sparks, L., & the Anti-Bias Curriculum Task Force.** (1989). *Anti-bias curriculum.* Washington, DC: National Association for the Education of Young Children.

**DeRosier, M. E., & Marcus, S. R.** (2005). Building friendships and combating bullying: Effectiveness of S. S. GRIN at one-year follow-up. *Journal of Clinical Child and Adolescent Psychology, 34,* 140–150.

**DeVito, J. A.** (2011). *Interpersonal messages* (2nd ed.). Boston: Allyn & Bacon.

**Dewey, J.** (1933). *How we think.* Lexington, MA: D. C. Health.

**DeZolt, D. M., & Hull, S. H.** (2001). Classroom and school climate. In J. Worell (Ed.), *Encyclopedia of women and gender.* San Diego: Academic Press.

**Diamond, A., Barnett, W. S., Thomas, J., & Munro, S.** (2007). Preschool program improves cognitive control. *Science, 318,* 1387–1388.

**Diamond, A., Casey, B. J., & Munakata, Y.** (2011). *Developmental cognitive neuroscience.* New York: Oxford University Press.

**Diaz, C.** (1997). Unpublished review of J. W. Santrock's *Educational psychology.* New York: McGraw-Hill.

**Diaz-Rico, L. T., & Weed, K. Z.** (2010). *Crosscultural, language, and academic development* (4th ed.). Boston: Allyn & Bacon.

**Dickinson, D.** (1998). *How technology enhances Howard Gardner's eight intelligences.* Retrieved Feruary 15, 2002, from www.america-tomorrow.com/ati/nhl80402.htm

**Diesendruck, G.** (2010). Mechanisms of word learning. In E. Hoff & M. Shatz (Eds.), *Blackwell handbook of language development.* New York: Wiley.

**Dietz, S.** (2010). *How many schools have not made adequate yearly progress under the No Child Left Behind Act?* Washington, DC: Center on Education Policy.

**Dishion, T. J., & Piehler, T. F.** (2009). Deviant by design: Peer contagion in development, interventions, and schools. In K. H. Rubin, W. M. Bukowski, & B. Laursen (Eds.), *Handbook of peer interactions, relationships, and groups.* New York: Guilford.

**Dixon, M. L., Zelazo, P. D., & De Rosa, E.** (2010). Evidence for intact memory-guided attention in school-aged children. *Developmental Science, 13,* 161–169.

**Dodge, K. A.** (2010). *Current directions in child psychopathology.* Boston: Allyn & Bacon.

**Dodge, K. A., Coie, J. D., & Lynam, D. R.** (2006). Aggression and antisocial behavior in youth. In W. Damon & R. Lerner (Eds.), *Handbook of child psychology* (6th ed.). New York: Wiley.

**Domina, T.** (2009). Parental involvement in education. In D. Carr (Ed.), *Encyclopedia of the life course and human development.* Boston: Gale Cengage.

**Domjan, M.** (2010). *The principles of learning and behavior* (6th ed.). Belmont, CA: Wadsworth.

**Donnelly, R.** (2010). Harmonizing technology with interaction in blended problem-based learning. *Computers & Education, 54,* 350–359.

**Downing, K., Kwong, T., Chan, S-W., Lam, T-F., & Downing, W-K.** (2009). Problem-based learning and the development of meta-cognition. *Higher Education, 57,* 609–621.

**Doyle, W.** (1986). Classroom organization and management. In M. C. Wittrock (Ed.), *Handbook of research on teaching* (3rd ed.). New York: Macmillan.

**Doyle, W.** (2006). Ecological approaches to classroom management. In C. M. Evertson & C. S. Weinstein (Eds.), *Handbook of classroom management.* Mahwah, NJ: Erlbaum.

**Drummond, R. J., & Jones, K. D.** (2010). *Assessment procedures for counselors and helping professionals* (7th ed.). Upper Saddle River, NJ: Prentice Hall.

**Dubois, D. L., & Karcher, M. J.** (Eds.) (2006). *Handbook of youth mentoring.* Thousand Oaks, CA: Sage.

**Dubow, E. F., Huesmann, L. R., & Greenwood, D.** (2007). Media and youth socialization. In J. E. Grusec & P. D. Hastings (Eds.), *Handbook of socialization.* New York: Guilford.

**Duchesne, S., & Ratelle, C.** (2010). Parental behaviors and adolescents' achievement goals at the beginning of middle school: Emotional problems as potential mediators. *Journal of Educational Psychology 102*, 497–507.

**Duncan, G. J., & others** (2007). School readiness and later achievement. *Developmental Psychology, 43*, 1428–1446.

**Dunkelberger, M.** (2008). Speech disabilities. In N. J. Salkind (Ed.). *Encyclopedia of educational psychology.* Thousand Oaks, CA: Sage.

**Dunlap, G., Iovannone, R., Wilson, K. J., Kincaid, D. K., & Strain, P.** (2010). Preventteach-reinforce: A standardized model of school-based behavioral intervention. *Journal of Positive Behavior Interventions, 12*, 9–22.

**Durrant, J. E.** (2008). Physical punishment, culture, and rights: Current issues for professionals. *Journal of Developmental and Behavioral Pediatrics, 29*, 55–66.

**Durston, S.** (2010, in press). Imaging genetics in ADHD. *Neuroimage.*

**Durston, S., & Casey, B. J.** (2006). What have we learned about cognitive development from neuroimaging. *Neuropsychologia, 44*, 2149–2157.

**Durston, S., Davidson, M. C., Tottenham, N. T., Galvan, A., Spicer, J., Fossella, J. A., & Casey, B. J.** (2006). A shift from diffuse to focal cortical activity with development. *Developmental Science, 9*, 1–8.

**Duschi, R., & Hamilton, R.** (2011). Learning science. In P. A. Alexander & R. E. Mayer (Eds.), *Handbook of research on learning and instruction.* New York: Routledge.

**Dweck, C. S.** (2006). *Mindset.* New York: Random House.

**Dweck, C. S.** (2011, in press). Social development. In P. Zelazo (Ed.), *Oxford handbook of developmental psychology.* New York: Oxford University Press.

**Dweck, C. S., & Elliott, E.** (1983). Achievement motivation. In P. Mussen (Ed.), *Handbook of child psychology, Vol. 4* (4th ed.). New York: Wiley.

**Dweck, C. S., & Master, A.** (2009). Selftheories and motivation: Students' beliefs about intelligence. In K. R. Wentzel & A. Wigfield (Eds.), *Handbook of motivation at school.* New York: Routledge.

# E

**Eagle, J. W., & Oeth, J.** (2008). Parentteacher conferences. In N. J. Salkind (Ed.), *Encyclopedia of educational psychology.* Thousand Oaks, CA: Sage.

**Eagly, A. H.** (2001). Social role theory of sex differences and similarities. In J. Worell (Ed.), *Encyclopedia of women and gender.* San Diego: Academic Press.

**Eagly, A. H.** (2010, in press). The his and hers of prosocial behavior: An examination of the social psychology of gender. *American Psychologist.*

**Eagly, A. H., & Crowley, M.** (1986). Gender and helping behavior: A meta-analytic review of the social psychological literature. *Psychological Bulletin, 100*, 283–308.

**Eagly, A. H., & Steffen, V. J.** (1986). Gender and aggressive behavior: A meta-analytic review of the social psychological literature. *Psychological Bulletin, 100*, 309–330.

**Eagly, A. H, & Wood, W.** (2011, in press). Gender roles in a biosocial world. In P. van Lange, A. Kruglanski, & E. T. Higgins (Eds.), *Handbook of theories in social psychology.* Thousand Oaks, CA: Sage.

**Easton, L. B.** (2007). Walking our walk about standards. *Phi Delta Kappan, 88*, 391–394.

**Eby, J. W., Herrell, A. L., & Jordan, M. L.** (2011). *Teaching in elementary school: A reflective action approach* (6th ed.). Boston: Allyn & Bacon.

**Eccles, J. S.** (1987). Gender roles and women's achievement-related decisions. *Psychology of Women Quarterly. 11*, 135–172.

**Eccles, J. S.,** (1993). School and family effects on the ontogeny of children's interests, self-perceptions, and activity choice. In J. Jacobs (Ed.), *Nebraska symposium on motivation, 1992; Developmental perspectives on motivation.* Lincoln. NB: University of Nebraska Press.

**Eccles, J. S.** (2004). School, academic motivation, and stage-environment fit. In R. Lerner & L. Steinberg (Eds.), *Handbook of adolescent psychology* (2nd ed.). New York: Wiley.

**Eccles, J. S.** (2007). Families, schools, and developing achievement-related motivations and engagement. In J. E. Grusec & P. D. Hastings (Eds.), *Handbook of socialization.* New York: Guilford.

**Eccles, J. S., & Roeser, R. W.** (2009). Schools, academic motivation, and stage-environment fit. In R. M. Lerner & L. Steinberg (Eds.), *Handbook of adolescent psychology* (3rd ed.). New York: Wiley.

**Eccles, J. S., & Roeser, R.** (2010). Schools, academic motivation, and stage-environment fit. In J. Meece & J. Eccles (Eds.), *Handbook of research on schools, schooling, and human development.* New York: Routledge.

**Eccles, J. S., Wigfield, A., & Schiefele, U.** (1998). Motivation to succeed. In W. Damon (Ed.), *Handbook of child psychology, Vol. 4* (5th ed.). New York: Wiley.

**Echevarria, J. L., & Graves, A.** (2011). *Sheltered content instruction: Teaching English Language Learners with diverse abilities* (4th ed.). Boston: Allyn & Bacon.

**Educational Cyber Playground.** (2006). *Ringleader Alan Haskvitz.* Retrieved July 1, 2006, from http://www.edu-cyberpg.com/ringleaders/al.html

**Educational Testing Service.** (2002). *Differences in the gender gap.* Princeton: Author.

**Edwards, A. R., Esmonde, I., & Wagner, J. F.** (2011, in press). Learning mathematics. In P. A. Alexander & R. E. Mayer (Eds.), *Handbook of research on learning and instruction.* New York: Routledge.

**Eisenberg, N.** (2010). Emotion regulation in children. *Annual Review of Clinical Psychology, Vol. 6.* Palo Alto, CA: Annual Reviews.

**Eisenberg, N., & others** (2010). Relations of temperament to maladjustment and ego resiliency in at-risk children. *Social Development, 19*, 577–600.

**Eisenberg, N., Fabes, R. A., & Spinrad, T. L.** (2006). Prosocial development. In W. Damon & R. Lerner (Eds.), *Handbook of child psychology* (6th ed.). New York: Wiley.

**Eisenberg, N., Morris, A. S., McDaniel, B., & Spinrad, T. L.** (2009). Moral cognitions and prosocial responding in adolescence. In R. M. Lerner & L. Steinberg (Eds.), *Handbook of adolescent psychology* (3rd ed.). New York: Wiley.

**Eisenberger, R.** (2009). Commitment, choice, and self-control. In D. Shanks (Ed.), *Psychology of learning.* Thousand Oaks, CA: Sage.

**Eisenhower Foundation** (2010). *Quantum Opportunities program.* Retrieved June 26, 2010 from http://www.eisenhowerfoundation.org/qop.php

**El-Fishawy, P., & State, M. W.** (2010). The genetics of autism: Key issues, recent findings, and clinical implications. *Psychiatric Clinics of North America, 33*, 83–105.

**Elkind, D.** (1976). *Child development and education: A Piagetian perspective.* New York: Oxford University Press.

**Elkind, D.** (1978). Understanding the young adolescent. *Adolescence, 13*, 127–134.

**Elliot, A. J., Conroy, D. E., Barron, K. E., & Murayama, K.** (2011). Achievement motives and goals: A developmental analysis. In R. M. Lerner, A. Freund, & M. Lamb (Eds.), *Handbook of life-span development.* New York: Wiley.

**Ellis, A. K.** (2011). *Teaching and learning elementary social studies* (9th ed.). Boston: Allyn & Bacon.

**Ellis, S., Klahr, D., & Siegler, R. S.** (1994, April). *The birth, life, and sometimes death of good ideas in collaborative problem-solving.* Paper presented at the meeting of the American Educational Research Association, New Orleans.

**Emmer, E. T., & Evertson. C.** (2009). *Classroom management for middle and secondary teachers* (8th ed.). Boston: Allyn & Bacon.

**Emmer, E. T., Evertson, C. M., & Anderson, L. M.** (1980). Effective classroom management at the beginning of the school year. *Elementary School Journal, 80,* 219–231.

**Enger, S. K., & Yager, R. E.** (2010). *Assessing student understanding in science* (2nd ed.). Thousand Oaks, CA: Corwin.

**Engler, B.** (2009). *Personality theories* (8th ed.). Belmont, CA: Wadsworth.

**Enright, M. S., Schaefer, L. V., Schaefer, P., & Schaefer, K. A.** (2008). Building a just adolescent community. *Montessori Life, 20,* 36–42.

**Entwisle, D. R., & Alexander, K. L.** (1993). Entry into the school: The beginning school transition and educational stratification in the United States. *Annual Review of Sociology, 19,* 401–423.

**Entwisle, D. R., Alexander, K. L., & Olson, L.** (2010). The long reach of socioeconomic status in education. In J. Meece & J. Eccles (Eds.), *Handbook of research on schools, schooling, and human development.* New York: Routledge.

**Epstein, J.** (1998, April). *Interactive homework: Effective strategies to connect home and school.* Paper presented at the meeting of the American Educational Research Association meeting, San Diego.

**Epstein, J. L.** (2001). *School, family, and community partnerships.* Boulder, CO: Westview Press.

**Epstein, J. L.** (2009). *School, family, and community partnerships* (3rd ed.) Thousand Oaks, CA: Corwin Press.

**Ericsson, K. A., Krampe, R. T., & Tesch-Romer, C.** (1993). The role of deliberate practice in acquisition of expert performance. *Psychological Review, 100,* 363–406.

**Ericsson, K. A., Krampe, R. T., & Tesch-Romer, C.** (2009). Three aspects of cognitive development. In D. Shanks (Ed.), *Psychology of learning.* Thousand Oaks, CA: Sage.

**Erikson, E. H.** (1968). *Identity: Youth and crisis.* New York: W. W. Norton.

**Ertmer, P., & others** (2009). Facilitating technology-enhanced problem-based learning (PBL) in the middle school curriculum: An examination of how and why teachers

adapt. *Journal of Interactive Learning Research, 20,* 35–54.

**Estes, T. H., Mintz, S. L., & Gunter, M. A.** (2011). *Instruction: A model's approach* (6th ed.). Boston: Allyn & Bacon.

**Evans, G. W.** (2004). The environment of childhood poverty. *American Psychologist, 59,* 77–92.

**Evans, G. W., & English, K.** (2002). The environment of poverty: Multiple stressor exposure, psychophysiological stress, and socioeconomic disadvantage. *Child Development, 73,* 1238–1248.

**Evans, G. W., & Kim, P.** (2007). Childhood poverty and health: Cumulative risk exposure and stress dysregulation. *Psychological Science, 18,* 953–957.

**Evans, J. L.** (2009). The emergence of language: A dynamical systems account. In E. Hoff & M. Shatz (Eds.), *Blackwell handbook of language development* (2nd ed.). New York: Wiley.

**Evertson, C., & Emmer, E. T.** (2009). *Classroom management for elementary teachers* (8th ed.). Boston: Allyn & Bacon.

**Evertson, C. M., & Harris, A. H.** (1999). Support for managing learning-centered classrooms: The classroom organization and management program. In H. J. Freiberg (Ed.), *Beyond behaviorism: Changing the classroom management paradigm.* Boston: Allyn & Bacon.

**Evertson, C. M., & Poole, I. R.** (2008). Proactive classroom management. In T. Good (Ed.), *Twenty-first century education: A reference handbook.* Los Angeles, CA: Sage.

## F

**Fabiano, G. A., & others** (2009). A meta-analysis of behavioral treatments for attention deficit/hyperactivity disorder. *Clinical Psychology Review, 29,* 129–140.

**Faraone, S. V., & Mick, E.** (2010). Molecular genetics of attention deficit hyperactivity disorder. *Psychiatric Clinics of North America, 33,* 159–180.

**Faris, R.** (2009). Bullying and peer victimization. In D. Carr (Ed.), *Encyclopedia of the life course and human development.* Boston: Gale Cengage.

**Farrington, D. P.** (2009). Conduct disorder, aggression, and delinquency. In R. M. Lerner & L. Steinberg (Eds.), *Handbook of adolescent psychology* (3rd ed.). New York: Wiley.

**Feather, N. T.** (1966). Effects of prior success and failure on expectations of success

and subsequent performance. *Journal of Personality and Social Psychology, 3,* 287–298.

**Feeney, S., Moravcik, E., Nolte, S., & Christensen, D.** (2010). *California version of who am I in the lives of children* (8th ed.). Upper Saddle River, NJ: Prentice Hall.

**Feinberg, M. E., & Kan, M. L.** (2008). Establishing family foundations: Intervention effects on coparenting, parent/infant well-being, and parent-child relations. *Journal of Family Psychology, 22,* 253–263.

**Feng, Y.** (1996). Some thoughts about applying constructivist theories to guide instruction. *Computers in the Schools, 12,* 71–84.

**Fenning, P., & Rose, J.** (2007). Overrepresentation of African American students in exclusionary discipline: The role of school policy. *Urban Education, 42,* 536–559.

**Fenzel, L. M., Blyth, D. A., & Simmons, R. G.** (1991). School transitions, secondary. In R. M. Lerner, A. C. Petersen, & J. Brooks-Gunn (Eds.), *Encyclopedia of adolescence, Vol. 2.* New York: Garland.

**Fernell, E., & others** (2010). Developmental profiles in preschool children with autism spectrum disorders referred for intervention. *Research in Developmental Disabilities, 31,* 790–799.

**Finn, B.** (2008). Framing effects on meta-cognitive monitoring and control. *Memory and Cognition, 36,* 813–821.

**Fiori, M.** (2009). A new look at emotional intelligence: A dual-process framework. *Personality and Social Psychology Bulletin, 13,* 21–44.

**Fischer, K. W., & Immordino-Yang, M. H.** (2008). Introduction: The fundamental importance of the brain and learning for education. In *The Jossey-Bass reader on the brain and learning.* San Francisco: Jossey-Bass.

**Fischoff, B., Bruine de Bruin, W., Parker, A. M., Millstein, S. G., & Halpernelsher, B. L.** (2010). Adolescents' perceived risk of dying. *Journal of Adolescent Health, 46,* 265–269.

**Fisher, D., Frey, N., & Berkin, A.** (2009). *Good habits, great readers.* Boston: Allyn & Bacon.

**Fitzpatrick, J.** (1993). *Developing responsible behavior in schools.* South Burlington, VT: Fitzpatrick Associates.

**Flavell, J. H.** (2004). Theory-of-mind development: Retrospect and prospect. *Merrill-Palmer Quarterly, 50,* 274–290.

**Flavell, J. H., Friedrichs, A., & Hoyt, J.** (1970). Developmental changes in memorization processes. *Cognitive Psychology, 1,* 324–340.

Flavell, J. H., Green, F. L., & Flavell, E. R. (1995). The development of children's knowledge about attentional focus. *Developmental Psychology, 31,* 706–712.

Flavell, J. H., Miller, P. H., & Miller, S. (2002). *Cognitive development* (4th ed.). Upper Saddle River. NJ: Prentice Hall.

Flick, G. L. (2011). *Understanding and managing emotional and behavior disorders in the classroom.* Upper Saddle River, NJ: Merrill.

Florence, N. (2010). *Multiculturalism 101.* New York: McGraw-Hill.

Florez, M. A. C. (1999). Improving adult English language learners' speaking skills. *ERIC Digest,* EDO-LE-99-01, 1–5.

Flower, L. S., & Hayes, J. R. (1981). Problem-solving and the cognitive processes in writing. In C. Frederiksen & J. F. Dominic (Eds.), *Writing: The nature, development, and teaching of written communication.* Mahwah, NJ: Erlbaum.

Flynn, J. R. (1999). Searching for justice: The discovery of IQ gains over time. *American Psychologist, 54,* 5–20.

Flynn, J. R. (2007). The history of the American mind in the 20th century: A scenario to explain gains over time and a case for the irrelevance of g. In P. C. Kyllonen, R. D. Roberts, & L. Stankov (Eds.), *Extending intelligence.* Mahwah, NJ: Erlbaum.

Fogarty, R. (Ed.). (1993). *The multiage classroom.* Palatine, IL: IRI/Skylight.

Fogarty, R. J., & Kerns, G. M. (2010). *Informative assessment.* Thousand Oaks, CA: Corwin.

Follari, L. (2011). *Foundations and best practices in early childhood education* (2nd ed.). Upper Saddle River, NJ: Merrill.

Forget-Dubois, N., Dionne, G., Lemelin, J-P., Perusse, D., Tremblay, R. E., & Boivin, M. (2009). Early child language mediates the relation between home environment and school readiness. *Child Development, 80,* 736–749.

Fox, B. J. (2010). *Phonics and structural analysis for the teacher of reading* (10th ed.). Boston: Allyn & Bacon.

Fox, E., & Alexander, P. A. (2011, in press). Learning to read. In P. A. Alexander & R. E. Mayer (Eds.), *Handbook of research on learning and instruction.* New York: Routledge.

Fraser-Abder, P. (2011). *Teaching budding scientists.* New York: Allyn & Bacon.

Frederikse, M., Lu, A., Aylward, E., Barta, P., Sharma, T., & Perlsons, G. (2000). Sex differences in inferior lobule volume in schizophrenia. *American Journal of Psychiatry, 157,* 422–427.

Fredricks, J. A. (2008). Extracurricular activities. In N. J. Salkind (Ed.), *Encyclopedia of educational psychology.* Thousand Oaks, CA: Sage.

Frey, B. (2005). Standard deviation. In S. W. Lee (Ed.), *Encyclopedia of school psychology.* Thousand Oaks. CA: Sage.

Friedel, J. M., Cortina, K. S., Turner, J. C., & Midgley, C. (2010). Changes in efficacy beliefs in mathematics across the transition to middle school: Examining the effects of perceived teacher and parent goal emphases. *Journal of Educational Psychology, 102,* 102–114.

Friedman, N. P., Haberstick, B. C., Willcutt, E. G., Miyake, A., Young, S. E., Corley, R. P., & Hewitt, J. K. (2007). Greater attention problems during childhood predict poorer executive functioning in late adolescence. *Psychological Science, 18,* 893–900.

Friend, M. (2008). *Special education* (2nd ed.). Boston: Allyn & Bacon.

Friend, M. (2011). *Special education* (3rd ed.). Upper Saddle River, NJ: Merrill.

Froh, J. J., Yurkewicz, C., & Kashdan, T. B. (2009). Gratitude and subjective well-being in early adolescence: Examining gender differences. *Journal of Adolescence.*

Frydenberg, E. (2008). *Adolescent coping.* Clifton, NJ: Psychology Press.

Fuchs, D., Fuchs, L. S., & Burish, P. (2000). Peer-assisted strategies: An empirically-supported practice to promote reading. *Learning Disabilities Research and Practice, 9,* 203–212.

Fuchs, D., Fuchs, L. S., Mathes, P. G., & Simmons, D. C. (1997). Peer-assisted learning strategies: Making classrooms more responsive to diversity. *American Educational Research Journal, 34,* 174–206.

Fuligni, A., Hughes, D. L., & Way, N. (2009). Ethnicity and immigration. In R. M. Lerner & L. Steinberg (Eds.), *Handbook of adolescent psychology* (3rd ed.). New York: Wiley.

Furth, H. G., & Wachs, H. (1975). *Thinking goes to school.* New York: Oxford University Press.

Fuson, K. C., Kalchman, M., & Bransford, J. D. (2005). Mathematical understanding: An introduction. In M. S. Donovan & J. D. Bransford (Eds.). *How students learn.* Washington, DC: National Academies Press.

## G

Galambos, N. L., Berenbaum, S. A., & McHale, S. M. (2009). Gender development in adolescence. In R. M. Lerner & L. Steinberg (Eds.), *Handbook of adolescent psychology.* New York: Wiley.

Gallagher, J. J. (2007). *Teaching science for understanding.* Upper Saddle River, NJ: Prentice Hall.

Gallagher, K. C., & Sylvester, P. R. (2009). Supporting peer relationships in early education. In O. A. Barbarin & B. H. Wasik (Eds.), *Handbook of child development and early education.* New York: Guilford.

Gallavan, N. P. (2009). *Developing performance-based assessments, grades 6–12.* Thousand Oaks, CA: Corwin.

Gallup Organization. (2004). *Gallup Poll: The public's attitudes toward schools.* Princeton, NJ: Author.

Galotti, K. M., Kozberg, S. F., & Gustafon, M. (2009). Goal-setting and decision-making by at-risk youth. *Prevention Researcher, 16* (2). 17–20.

Gambrell, L. B., Malloy, J. A., & Anders-Mazzoni, S. (2007). Evidence-based best practices for comprehensive literacy instruction. In L. B. Gambrell, L. M. Morrow, & M. Presley (Eds.), *Best practices in literacy instruction.* New York: Guilford.

Gambrell, L. B., Morrow, L. M., & Pressley, M. (Eds.). (2007). *Best practices in literacy instruction.* New York: Guilford.

Gandara, P. (2002). *Peer group influence and academic aspirations across cultural/ethnic groups of high school students.* Santa Cruz, University of California, Center for Research on Education, Diversity & Excellence.

GarageBand. (2008). Retrieved January 16, 2008, from www.apple.com/ilife/garageband/

Gardner, H. (1983). *Frames of mind.* New York: Basic Books.

Gardner, H. (1993). *Multiple intelligences.* New York: Basic Books.

Gardner, H. (1998). Multiple intelligences: Myths and messages. In A. Woolfolk (Ed.), *Readings in educational psychology* (2nd ed.). Boston: Allyn & Bacon.

Gardner, H. (2002). The pursuit of excellence through education. In M. Ferrari (Ed.), *Learning from extraordinary minds.* Mahwah, NJ: Erlbaum.

Gardner, M., & Steinberg, L. (2005). Peer influence and risk taking, risk preference, and psychology, *Developmental Psychology, 41,* 625–635.

Gargiulo, R. M. (2009). *Special education in contemporary society.* Thousand Oaks, CA: Sage.

Garmon, A., Nystrand, M., Berends, M., & LePore, P. C. (1995). An organizational analysis of the effects of ability grouping. *American Educational Research Journal, 32,* 687–715.

**Gates, W.** (1998, July 20). Charity begins when I'm ready [interview]. *Fortune* magazine.

**Gathercole, V. C. M., & Hoff, E.** (2010). Input and the acquisition of language: Three questions. In E. Hoff & M. Shatz (Eds.), *Blackwell handbook of language development.* New York: Wiley.

**Gauvain, M.** (2008). Vygotsky's sociocultural theory. In M. M. Haith & J. B. Benson (Eds.), *Encyclopedia of infant and early childhood development.* Oxford, UK: Elsevier.

**Gauvain, M., & Parke, R. D.** (2010). Socialization. In M. H. Bornstein (Ed.), *Handbook of developmental cultural science.* New York: Psychology Press.

**Gay, G.** (1997). Educational equality for students of color. In J. A. Banks & C. M. Banks (Eds.), *Multicultural education* (3rd ed). Boston: Allyn & Bacon.

**Gay, G.** (2006). Connections between classroom management and culturally responsive teaching. In C. M. Evertson & C. S. Weinstein (Eds.), *Handbook of classroom management.* Mahwah, NJ: Erlbaum.

**Gazzaniga, M. S.** (Ed.) (2010). *The cognitive neurosciences* (4th ed.). New York: Cambridge University Press.

**Geake, J.** (2010). Neuromythologies in education. In P. Howard-Jones (Ed.), *Education and neuroscience.* New York: Psychology Press.

**Gelman, R.** (1969). Conservation acquisition: A problem of learning to attend to relevant attributes. *Journal of Experimental Child Psychology, 7,* 67–87.

**Gelman, S. A.** (2009). Learning from others: Children's construction of concepts. *Annual Review of Psychology, Vol. 60.* Palo Alto, CA: Annual Reviews.

**Gelman, S. A., & Opfer, J. E.** (2004). Development of the animate-inanimate distinction. In U. Goswami (Ed.), *Blackwell handbook of childhood cognitive development.* Malden, MA: Blackwell.

**Gen Yes** (2010). Retrieved January 14, 2010, from http: genyes.com

**German, K. M., Gronbeck, B. E., Ehninger, D., & Monroe, A. H.** (2010). *Principles of public speaking* (17th ed.). Boston: Allyn & Bacon.

**Gerrard, M., Gibbons, F. X., Houlihan, A. E., Stock, M. L., & Pomery, E. A.** (2008). A dual-process approach to health risk decision-making. The prototype-willingness model. *Developmental Review, 28,* 29–61.

**Ghetti, S., Castelli, P., & Lyons, K. E.** (2010). Knowing about *not* remembering: Developmental dissociations in lack-of-memory monitoring. *Developmental Science, 4,* 611–621.

**Gibbs, J. C.** (2010). *Moral development and reality* (2nd ed.). Boston: Allyn & Bacon.

**Giedd, J. N.** (2008). The teen brain: Insights from neuroimaging. *Journal of Adolescent Medicine, 42,* 335–343.

**Giedd, J. N., Lalonde, F. M., Celano, M. J., White, S. L., Wallace, G. L., Lee, N. R., & Lenroot, R. K.** (2009). Anatomical brain magnetic imaging of typically developing children and adolescents. *Journal of the American Academy of Child and Adolescent Psychiatry, 48,* 465–470.

**Gill, D. L.** (2001). Sports and athletics. In J. Worell (Ed.), *Encyclopedia of women and gender.* San Diego: Academic Press.

**Gilligan, C.** (1982). *In a different voice.* Cambridge, MA: Harvard University Press.

**Gilligan, C.** (1992, May). *Joining the resistance: Girls' development in adolescence.* Paper presented at the symposium on development and vulnerability in close relationships, Montreal, Quebec.

**Gilligan, C.** (1998). *Minding women: Reshaping the education realm.* Cambridge, MA: Harvard University Press.

**Gilligan, C., Spencer, R., Weinberg, M. K., & Bertsch, T.** (2003). On the listening guide: A voice-centered relational model. In P. M. Carnic & J. E. Rhodes (Eds.), *Qualitative research in psychology.* Washington, DC: American Psychological Association.

**Ginsburg-Block, M.** (2005). Peer tutoring. In S. W. Lee (Ed.), *Encyclopedia of school psychology.* Thousand Oaks, CA: Sage.

**Given, L. M.** (2008). Qualitative research methods. In N. J. Salkind (Ed.), *Encyclopedia of educational psychology.* Thousand Oaks, CA: Sage.

**Glascher, J., & others** (2009). Lesion mapping of cognitive abilities linked to intelligence. *Neuron, 61,* 681–691.

**Glascher, J., & others** (2010). Distributed neural system for general intelligence revealed by lesion mapping. *Proceedings of the National Academy of Sciences USA, 107,* 4705–4709.

**Glasgow, N. A., & Hicks, C. D.** (2009). *What successful teachers do.* Thousand Oaks, CA: Sage.

**Glasser, W.** (1969). *Schools without failure.* New York: Harper & Row.

**Goffin, S. G., & Wilson, C. S.** (2001). *Curriculum models and early childhood education.* Upper Saddle River, NJ: Prentice Hall.

**Gogtay, N., & Thompson, P. M.** (2010). Mapping gray matter development: Implications for typical development and vulnerability to psychopathology. *Brain and Cognition, 72,* 6–15.

**Gold, J., & Lanzoni, M.** (Eds.). (1993). [Video] *Graduation by portfolio—Central Park East Secondary School.* New York: Post Production, 29th St. Video, Inc.

**Goldberg, W. A., & Lucas-Thompson, R.** (2008). Maternal and paternal employment, effects. In M. M. Haith & J. B. Benson (Eds.), *Encyclopedia of infant and early childhood development.* Oxford, UK: Elsevier.

**Goldman-Rakic, P.** (1996). *Bridging the gap.* Presentation at the workshop sponsored by the Education Commission of the States and the Charles A. Dana Foundation, Denver.

**Goldsmith, H. H.** (2011). Human development: Biological and genetic processes in development. *Annual Review of Psychology, Vol. 62.* Palo Alto, CA: Annual Reviews.

**Goleman, D.** (1995). *Emotional intelligence.* New York: Basic Books.

**Goleman, D., Kaufman, P., & Ray, M.** (1993). *The creative spirit.* New York: Plume.

**Gollnick, D. M., & Chinn, P. C.** (2009). *Multicultural education in a pluralistic society* (8th ed.). Boston: Allyn & Bacon.

**González, N., & Moll, L. C., & Amanti, C.** (Eds.). (2005). *Funds of knowledge: Theorizing practices in households, communities, and classrooms.* Mahwah, NJ: Erlbaum.

**Good, R. H., & Kaminski, R. A.** (2003). Dynamic indicators of basic early literacy skills (6th ed.). Longmont, CO: Sopris West Educational Services.

**Goodlad, S., & Hirst, B.** (1989). *Peer tutoring: A guide to learning by teaching.* New York: Nichols.

**Goodnow, J. J.** (2010). Culture. In M. H. Bornstein (Ed.), *Handbook of developmental cultural science.* New York: Routledge.

**Goodrich, H.** (1997). Understanding rubrics. *Educational Leadership, 54,* 14–17.

**Gordon, T.** (1970). *Parent effectiveness training.* New York: McGraw-Hill.

**Goswami, U.** (2010). Reading, dyslexia, and the brain. In P. Howard-Jones (Ed.), *Education and neuroscience.* New York: Psychology Press.

**Goswami, U.** (2011). Inductive and deductive reasoning. In U. Goswami (Ed.), *Wiley-Blackwell handbook of childhood cognitive development.* New York: Wiley.

**Gottfried, A. E., Marcoulides, G. A., Gottfried, A. W., & Oliver, P. H.** (2009). A latent curve model of motivational practices and developmental decline in math and science academic intrinsic motivation. *Journal of Educational Psychology, 101,* 729–739.

Graham, S. (1986, August). *Can attribution theory tell us something about motivation in Blacks?* Paper presented at the meeting of the American Psychological Association, Washington, DC.

Graham, S. (1990). Motivation in African Americans. In G. L. Berry & J. K. Asamen (Eds.), *Black students*. Newbury Park, CA: Sage.

Graham, S. (2005, February 16). Commentary in *USA Today,* p. 2D.

Graham, S., & Olinghouse, N. (2009). Learning and teaching writing. In E. Anderman & L. Anderman (Eds.), *Psychology of classroom learning*. Boston: Gale Cengage.

Graham, S., & Perin, D. (2007). A meta-analysis of writing instruction for adolescent students. *Journal of Educational Psychology, 99,* 445–476.

Graham, S., & Weiner, B. (1996). Theories and principles of motivation. In D. C. Berliner & R. C. Calfee (Eds.), *Handbook of educational psychology*. New York: Macmillan.

Graham, S., & Williams, C. (2009). An attributional approach to motivation in school. In K. Wentzel & A. Wigfield (Eds.), *Handbook of motivation at school*. New York: Routledge.

Grant, K. B., & Ray, J. A. (Eds.) (2009). *Home, school, and community collaboration*. Thousand Oaks, CA: Sage.

Gratz, R. R., & Bouton, P. J. (1996). Erikson and early childhood educators. *Young Children, 51,* 74–78.

Gray, J. (1992). *Men are from Mars, women are from Venus*. New York: HarperCollins.

Graziano, A. M., & Raulin, M. L. (2010). *Research methods* (7th ed.). Boston: Allyn & Bacon.

Graziano, P., Keane, S. P., & Calkins, S. D. (2007). Cardiac vagal regulation and early peer status. *Child Development, 78,* 264–278.

Gredler, M. (2009). *Learning and instruction* (6th ed.). Upper Saddle River, NJ: Merrill.

Gredler, M. E. (2009). Hiding in plain sight: The stages of mastery/self-regulation in Vygotsky's cultural-historical theory. *Educational Psychologist, 44,* 1–19.

Green, S. K., & Johnson, R. L. (2010). *Assessment is essential*. New York: McGraw-Hill.

Greenfield, P. P. M. Suzuki, L. K., & Rothstein-Fisch, C. (2006). Cultural pathways through human development. In W. Damon & R. Lerner (Eds.), *Handbook of child psychology* (6th ed.). New York: Wiley.

Greeno, J. S. (2006). Learning in activity. In R. K. Sawyer (Ed.), *The Cambridge handbook of learning sciences*. New York: Oxford University Press.

Greenough, W. T. (1997, April 21). Commentary in article, "Politics of biology." *U.S. News & World Report,* p. 79.

Greenough, W. T. (2000). Brain development. In A. Kazdin (Ed.), *Encyclopedia of psychology*. Washington, DC, & New York: American Psychological Association and Oxford University Press.

Gregory, A., Cornell, D., Fan, X., Sheras, P., Shih, T-H., & Huang, F. (2010). Authoritative school discipline: High school practices associated with lower bullying and victimization. *Journal of Educational Psychology, 102,* 483–496.

Gregory, R. J. (2011). *Psychological testing* (6th ed.). Upper Saddle River, NJ: Pearson.

Gresalfi, M., Barab, S. A., Siyahhan, S., & Christensen, T. (2009). Virtual worlds, conceptual understanding, and me: Designing for consequential engagement. *On the Horizon, 17* (1), 21–34.

Grice, G. L., & Skinner, J. F. (2010). *Mastering public speaking* (7th ed.). Boston: Allyn & Bacon.

Griffin, C. L. (2011). *Invitation to speak handbook*. Boston: Cengage.

Grigorenko, E. L., & Takanishi, R. (Eds.) (2010). *Immigration, diversity, and education*. New York: Routledge.

Grindstaff, K., & Richmond, G. (2008). Learners' perceptions of the roles of peers in a research experience: Implications for the apprenticeship process, scientific inquiry, and collaborative work. *Journal of Research in Science Teaching, 45,* 251–272.

Grolnick, W. S., Friendly, R. W., & Bellas, V. M. (2009). Parenting and children's motivation at school. In K. R. Wentzel & A. Wigfield (Eds.), *Handbook of motivation at school*. New York: Routledge.

Gronlund, N. E. (2009). *Assessment of student achievement* (8th ed.). Boston: Allyn & Bacon.

Gronlund, N. E., & Waugh, C. K. (2009). *Assessment of student achievement* (9th ed.). Upper Saddle River, NJ: Prentice Hall.

Grusec, J. E. (2009). Unpublished review of J. W. Santrock's *Child Development,* (13th ed.). New York: McGraw-Hill.

Grusec, J. E. (2011). Human development: Development in the family. *Annual Review of Psychology, Vol. 62.* Palo Alto, CA: Annual Reviews.

Grusec, J. E. (2011). Socialization processes in the family: Social and emotional development. *Annual Review of Psychology, Vol. 62.* Palo Alto, CA: Annual Reviews.

Guastello, D. D., & Guastello, S. J. (2003). Androgyny, gender role behavior, and emotional intelligence among college students and their parents. *Sex Roles, 49,* 663–673.

Guerra, N. G., & Williams, K. R. (2010). Implementing bullying prevention in diverse settings: Geographic, economic, and cultural influences. In E. M. Vernberg & B. K. Biggs (Eds.), *Preventing and treating bullying and victimization*. New York: Oxford University Press.

Guilford, J. P. (1967). *The structure of intellect*. New York: McGraw-Hill.

Gunning, T. G. (2010). *Creating literacy instruction for all students* (7th ed.). Boston: Allyn & Bacon.

Guo, Y., Piasta, S. B., Justice, L. M., & Kaderavek, J. N. (2010). Relations among preschool teachers' self-efficacy, classroom quality, and children's language and literacy gains. *Teaching and Teacher Education, 26,* 1094–1103.

Gur, R. C., & others (1995). Sex differences in regional cerebral glucose metabolism during a resting state. *Science, 267,* 528–531.

Gurwitch, R. H., Silovksy, J. F., Schultz, S., Kees, M., & Burlingame, S. (2001). *Reactions and guidelines for children following trauma/disaster*. Norman, OK: Department of Pediatrics, University of Oklahoma Health Sciences Center.

Guskey, T. R., & Bailey, J. H. (2010). *Developing standards-based report cards*. Thousand Oaks, CA: Corwin.

Gustafsson, J.-E. (2007). Schooling and intelligence: Effects of track of study on level and profile of cognitive abilities. In P. C. Kyllonen, R. D. Roberts, & L. Stankov (Eds.), *Extending intelligence*. Mahwah, NJ: Erlbaum.

Gutherie, C. (2010). Towards greater learner control: Web supported project-based learning. *Journal of Information Systems Education, 21,* 121–130.

Hack, T. (2008). PRAXIS. In N. J. Salkind (Ed.), *Encyclopedia of educational psychology*. Thousand Oaks, CA: Sage.

Hacker, D., Dunlosky, J., & Graesser, A. (Eds.). (2009). *Handbook of metacognition in education*. New York: Psychology Press.

**Hagen, J. W., & Lamb-Parker, F. G.** (2008). Head Start. In M. M. Haith & J. B. Benson (Eds.), *Encyclopedia of infant and early childhood development*. Oxford, UK: Elsevier.

**Hakuta, K.** (2000). Bilingualism. In A. Kazdin (Ed.), *Encyclopedia of psychology*. Washington, DC, and New York: American Psychology Association and Oxford University Press.

**Hakuta, K.** (2001, April 5). *Key policy milestones and directions in the education of English language learners*. Paper prepared for the Rockefeller Foundation Symposium, Leveraging change: An emerging framework for educational equity, Washington, DC.

**Hakuta, K.** (2005, April). *Bilingualism at the intersection of research and public policy*. Paper presented at the meeting of the Society for Research in Child Development, Atlanta.

**Hakuta, K., Butler, Y. G., & Witt, D.** (2000). *How long does it take English learners to attain proficiency?* Berkeley, CA: The University of California Linguistic Minority Research Institute Policy Report 2000–1.

**Halawi, L., McCarthy, R. V., & Pires, S.** (2009). An evaluation of e-learning on the basis of Bloom's taxonomy: An exploratory study. *Journal of Education for Business, 84,* 374–380.

**Hale-Benson, J. E.** (1982). *Black children: Their roots, culture, and learning styles*. Baltimore: The Johns Hopkins University Press.

**Halford, G. S.** (2008). Cognitive developmental theories. In M. M. Haith & J. B. Benson (Eds.), *Encyclopedia of infant and early childhood development*. Oxford, UK: Elsevier.

**Halford, G. S., & Andrews, G. S.** (2011). Information-processing models of cognitive development. In U. Goswami (Ed.), *Wiley-Blackwell handbook of childhood cognitive development*. New York: Wiley.

**Hall, G. N.** (2010). *Multicultural psychology* (2nd ed.). Upper Saddle River, NJ: Prentice Hall.

**Hall, L .J.** (2009). *Autism spectrum disorders: From therapy to practice*. Boston: Allyn & Bacon.

**Hallahan, D. P., & Kauffman, J. M.** (2006). *Exceptional learners* (10th ed.). Boston, Allyn & Bacon.

**Hallahan, D. P., Kauffman, J. M., & Pullen, P. C.** (2009). *Exceptional learners* (11th ed.) Boston Allyn & Bacon.

**Halonen, J.** (2010). Express yourself. In J. W. Santrock & J. Halonen, *Your guide to college success* (6th ed.). Belmont, CA: Wadsworth.

**Halpern, D. F., Benbow, C. P., Geary, D. C., Gur, R. C., & Hyde, J. S.** (2007). The science of sex differences in science and mathematics, *Psychological Science in the Public Interest, 8,* 1–51.

**Halpern-Felsher, B.** (2009). Adolescent decision making: An overview. *Prevention Researcher, 16,* 3–7.

**Hambleton, R. K.** (1996). Advances in assessment models, methods, and practices. In D. C. Berliner & R. C. Calfee (Eds.), *Handbook of educational psychology*. New York: Macmillan.

**Hamilton, S. F., & Hamilton, M. A.** (2004). Contexts for mentoring: Adolescent-adult relationships in workplaces and communities. In R. Lerner & L. Steinberg (Eds.), *Handbook of adolescent psychology* (2nd ed.). New York: Wiley.

**Hamm, J. V., & Zhang, L.** (2010). The multilevel nature of adolescent peer relations in ethnically diverse schools. In J. Meece & J. Eccles (Eds.), *Handbook of research on schools, schooling, and human development*. New York: Routledge.

**Hammerman, E.** (2009). *Formative assessment strategies for enhanced learning in science, K–8*. Thousand Oaks, CA: Corwin Press.

**Hammerness, K., Darling-Hammond, L., Grossman, P., Rust, F., & Shulman, L.** (2005). How teachers learn and develop. In L. Darling-Hammond & J. Bransford (Eds.), *Preparing teachers for a changing world*. San Francisco: Jossey-Bass.

**Han, W-J.** (2009). Maternal employment. In D. Carr (Ed.). *Encyclopedia of the life course and human development*. Boston: Gale Cengage.

**Hanania, R., & Smith, L. B.** (2010). Selective attention and attention switching: Towards a unified developmental approach. *Developmental Science, 13,* 622–635.

**Hannish, L. D., & Guerra, N. G.** (2004). Aggressive victims, passive victims, and bullies: Development continuity or developmental change? *Merrill-Palmer Quarterly, 50,* 17–38.

**Haring, M., Hewitt, P. L., & Flett, G. L.** (2003). Perfectionism and quality of intimate relationships. *Journal of Marriage and the Family, 65,* 143–158.

**Harris, D. N.** (2010). How do school peers influence student educational outcomes? Theory and evidence from economics and other social sciences. *Teachers College Record, 112,* 1163–1197.

**Harris, K. R., Graham, S., Brindle, M., & Sandmel, K.** (2010). Metacognition and children's writing. In D. J. Hacker, J. Dunlosky, & A. C. Graesser (Eds.), *Handbook of metacognition in education*. Mahwah, NJ: Erlbaum.

**Harris, K. R., Graham, S., Mason, L., & Friedlander, B.** (2008). *Powerful writing strategies for all students*. Baltimore, MD: Brookes.

**Harris, K. R., Graham, S., & Urdan, T.** (Eds.) (2011, in press). *APA handbook of educational psychology*. Washington, DC: American Psychological Association.

**Harris, P. L.** (2006). Social cognition. In W. Damon & R. Lerner (Eds.), *Handbook of child psychology* (6th Ed.). New York: Wiley.

**Hart, B., & Risley, T. R.** (1995). *Meaningful differences*. Baltimore: Paul H. Brookes.

**Hart, C. H., Yang, C., Charlesworth, R., & Burts, D. C.** (2003, April). *Early childhood teachers' curriculum beliefs, classroom practices, and children's outcome: What are the connections?* Paper presented at the biennial meeting of the Society for Research in Child Development, Tampa, FL.

**Hart, D., Matsuba, M. K., & Atkins, R.** (2008). The moral and civic effects of learning to serve. In L. Nucci & D. Narvaez (Eds.), *Handbook of moral and character education*. Clifton, NJ: Psychology Press.

**Harter, S.** (1981). A new self-report scale of intrinsic versus extrinsic orientation in the classroom: Motivational and informational components. *Developmental Psychology, 17,* 300–312.

**Harter, S.** (1996). Teacher and classmate influences on scholastic motivation, self-esteem, and level of voice in adolescents. In J. Juvonen & K. R. Wentzel (Eds.), *Social motivation*. New York: Cambridge University Press.

**Harter, S.** (2006). The Self. In W. Damon & R. Lerner (Eds.), *Handbook of Child Psychology* (6th ed.) New York: Wiley.

**Hartshorne, H., & May, M. S.** (1928–1930). *Moral studies in the nature of character: studies in deceit, Vol. 1; Studies in self-control, Vol. 2; Studies in the organization of character, Vol. 3*. New York: Macmillan.

**Hartup, W. W.** (1983). The peer system. In P. H. Mussen (Ed.), *Handbook of child psychology, Vol. 4* (4th ed.). New York: Wiley.

**Hasling, J.** (2010). *The audience, the message the speaker* (8th ed.). New York: McGraw-Hill.

**Hastings, P. D., Utendale, W. T., & Sullivan, C.** (2007). The socialization of prosocial development. In J. E. Grusec & P. D. Hastings (Eds.). *Handbook of socialization*. New York: Guildford.

Hayes, J. R., & Flower, L. S. (1986). Writing research and the writer. *American Psychologist, 41,* 1106–1113.

Healey, J. F. (2009). *Race, ethnicity, and class* (5th ed.). Thousand Oaks, CA: Sage.

Heath, S. B. (1989). Oral and literate traditions among Black Americans living in poverty. *American Psychologist, 44,* 367–373.

Heaven, P. C., & Ciarrochi, J. (2008). Parental styles, conscientiousness, and academic performance in high school: A three-wave longitudinal study. *Personality and Social Psychology Bulletin, 34,* 451–461.

Heit, E. (2008). Properties of inductive reasoning. In J. E. Adler & L. J. Rips (Eds.), *Reasoning.* New York: Cambridge University Press.

Heller, C., & Hawkins, I. (1994). Spring, Teaching tolerance. *Teachers College Record.* p. 2.

Heller, K. W., Forney, P. E., Alberto, P. A., Bet, S. E., & Schwartzman, M. N. (2009). *Understanding physical, health, and multiple disabilities* (2nd ed.). Boston: Allyn & Bacon.

Henderson, V. L., & Dweck, C. S. (1990). Motivation and achievement. In S. S. Feldman & G. R. Elliott (Eds.), *At the threshold: The developing adolescent.* Cambridge, MA: Harvard University Press.

Hendricks, C. C. (2009). *Improving schools through action research.* Upper Saddle River, NJ: Prentice Hall.

Herman, J. (1996). Commentary in "The latest on student portfolios." *NEA Today, 15* (4), 17.

Hernandez, D. J., Denton, N. A., & Macartney, S. E. (2010). Children of immigrants and the future of America. In E. L. Grigorenko & R. Takanishi (Eds.), *Immigration, diversity, and education.* New York: Routledge.

Herrera, S. G., & Murry, K. G. (2011). *Mastering ESL and bilingual methods* (2nd ed.). Boston: Allyn & Bacon.

Hertzog, N. B. (1998, January/February). Gifted education specialist. *Teaching Exceptional Children,* pp. 39–43.

Hetherington, E. M. (1995, March). *The changing American family and the well-being of others.* Paper presented at the meeting of the Society for Research in Child Development, Indianapolis.

Hetherington, E. M. (2006). The influence of conflict, marital problem solving, and parenting on children's adjustment in nondivorced, divorced, and remarried families. In A. Clarke-Stewart & J. Dunn (Eds.), *Families count.* New York: Oxford University Press.

Hiebert, E. H., & Raphael, T. E. (1996). Psychological perspectives on literacy and extensions to educational practice. In D. C. Berliner & R. C. Calfee (Eds.), *Handbook of educational psychology.* New York: Macmillan.

Higgins, A., Power, C., & Kohlberg, L. (1983, April). *Moral atmosphere and moral judgment.* Paper presented at the biennial meeting of the Society for Research in Child Development, Detroit.

Hilgard, E. R. (1996). History of educational psychology. In D. C. Berliner & R. C. Calfee (Eds.), *Handbook of educational psychology.* New York: Macmillan.

Hiltz, S. R., & Goldman, R. (Eds.) (2005). *Learning together online.* Mahwah, NJ: Erlbaum.

Hinduja, S., & Patchin, S. (2009). *Bullying beyond the schoolyard.* Thousand Oaks. CA: Corwin Press.

Hirsch, E. D. (1996). *The schools we need: And why we don't have them.* New York: Doubleday.

Hocutt, A. M. (1996). Effectiveness of special education: Is placement the critical factor? *Future of Children, 6* (1), 77–102.

Hodapp, R. M., & Dykens, E. M. (2006). Mental retardation. In W. Damon & R. Lerner (Eds.), *Handbook of child psychology* (6th ed.). New York: Wiley.

Hoeksema, E., & others (2010, in press). Enhanced neural activity in frontal and cerebellar circuits after cognitive training in children with attention deficit hyperactivity disorder. *Human Brain Mapping.*

Hoekstra, R. A., Happe, F., Baron-Cohen, S., & Ronald, A. (2010, in press). Limited genetic covariance between autistic traits and intelligence: Findings from a longitudinal twin study. *American Journal of Medical Genetics, B. Neuropsychiatric Genetics.*

Hoffman, B., & Schraw, G. (2009). The influence of self-efficacy and working memory capacity on problem-solving efficiency. *Learning and Individual Differences, 19,* 91–100.

Hogan, J. M., Andrews, P. H., Andrews, J. R., & Williams, G. (2011). *Public speaking* (2nd ed.). Boston: Allyn & Bacon.

Hollingworth, L. S. (1916). Sex differences in mental tests. *Psychological Bulletin, 13,* 377–383.

Holzman, L. (2009). *Vygotsky at work and play.* Oxford. UK: Routledge.

Homa, D. (2008). Long-term memory. In N. J. Salkind (Ed.), *Encyclopedia of educational psychology.* Thousand Oaks, CA: Sage.

Hooper, S., Ward, T. J., Hannafin, M. J., & Clark, H. T. (1989). The effects of aptitude composition on achievement during small group learning. *Journal of Computer-Based Instruction, 16,* 102–109.

Horowitz, E. K. (2008). *Becoming a language teacher.* Boston: Allyn & Bacon.

Horowitz, F. D. (2009). Introduction: A developmental understanding of giftedness and talent. In F. D. Horowitz, R. F. Subotnik, & D. J. Matthews (Eds.), *The development of giftedness and talent across the life span.* Washington, DC: American Psychological Association.

Horowitz, F. D., Darling-Hammond, L., Bransford, J., Comer, J., Rosebrock, K., Austin, K., & Rust, F. (2005). Educating teachers for developmentally appropriate practice. In L. Darling-Hammond & J. Bransford (Eds.), *Preparing teachers for a changing world.* San Francisco: Jossey-Bass.

Howard-Jones, P. (Ed.) (2010). *Education and neuroscience.* New York: Psychology Press.

Howe, M. J. A., Davidson, J. W., Moore, D. G., & Sloboda, J. A. (1995). Are there early childhood signs of musical ability? *Psychology of Music, 23,* 162–176.

Howe, W. A. (2010). Unpublished review of Santrock's *Educational Psychology* (5th ed.) New York: McGraw-Hill.

Howell, D. C. (2010). *Statistical methods for psychology* (7th ed.). Boston: Cengage.

Howes, C., & Ritchie, S. (2002). *A matter of trust: Connecting teachers and learners in the early childhood classroom.* New York: Teachers College Press.

Howlin, P., Magiati, I., & Charman, T. (2009). Systematic review of early intensive behavioral interventions with autism. *American Journal on Intellectual and Developmental Disabilities, 114,* 23–41.

Hudley, C. (2009). Academic motivation and achievement of African American youth. In H. A. Neville, B. M. Tynes, & S. O. Utley (Eds.), *Handbook of African American psychology.* Thousand Oaks, CA: Sage.

Huetinck, L., & Munshin, S. N. (2008). *Teaching mathematics in the 21st century* (3rd ed.). Boston: Allyn & Bacon.

Humphrey, N., Curran, A., Morris, E., Farrell, P., & Woods, K. (2007). Emotional intelligence and education: A critical review. *Educational Psychology, 27,* 235–254.

Hung, W. (2009). The 9-step problem design process for problem-based learning. *Educational Research Review, 4,* 118–141.

Hunt, E. (2006). Expertise, talent, and social encouragement. In K. A. Ericsson, N. Charness, P. J. Feltovich, & R. R. Hoffman (Eds.),

*The Cambridge handbook of expertise and expert performance.* New York: Cambridge University Press.

**Hunt, E. B.** (1995). *Will we be smart enough? A cognitive analysis of the coming work force.* New York: Russell Sage.

**Hunt, R. R., & Ellis, H. C.** (2004). *Fundamentals of cognitive psychology* (7th ed.), New York: McGraw-Hill.

**Hunt, R. R., & Kelly, R. E. S.** (1996). Accessing the particular from the general: The power of distinctiveness in the context of organization. *Memory and Cognition, 24,* 217–225.

**Hupert, N., & Heinze, J.** (2006). Results in the Palms of their hands: Using handheld computers for data-driven decision making in the classroom. In M. van't Hooft & K. Swan (Eds.), *Ubiquitous computing in education: Invisible technology, visible results.* Mahwah, NJ: Erlbaum.

**Huston, A. C., & Bentley, A. C.** (2010). Human development in societal context. *Annual Review of Psychology, Vol. 61.* Palo Alto, CA: Annual Reviews.

**Huston, A. C., & Ripke, M. N.** (2006). Experiences in middle childhood and children's development. In A. C. Huston & M. N. Ripke (Eds.), *Developmental contexts in middle childhood.* New York: Cambridge University Press.

**Huttenlocher, P. R., & Dabholkar, A. S.** (1997). Regional differences in synaptogenesis in human cerebral cortex. *Journal of Comparative Neurology, 37(2),* 167–178.

**Huurre, T., Junkkari, H., & Aro, H.** (2006). Long-term psychosocial effects of parental divorce: A follow-up study from adolescence to adulthood. *European Archives of Psychiatry and Clinical Neuroscience, 256,* 256–263.

**Hybels, S., & Weaver, R. L.** (2009). *Communicating effectively* (9th ed.). New York: McGraw-Hill.

**Hyde, J. S.** (2007). *Half the human experience* (7th ed.). Boston: Houghton Mifflin.

**Hyde, J. S., Lilndberg, S. M., Linn, M. C., Ellis, A. B., & Williams, C. C.** (2008). Gender similarities characterize math performance. *Science, 321,* 494–495.

**Hyman, I., Eisenstein, J., Amidon, A., & Kay, B.** (2001, August 28). An update on the cross-cultural study of corporal punishment and abuse. In F. Farley (Chair), *Cross cultural aspects of corporal punishment and abuse: A research update.* Symposium presented at the 2001 Annual Convention of the American Psychological Association, San Francisco, CA.

**Hyman, I., Kay, B., Tabori, A., Weber, M., Mahon, M., & Cohen, I.** (2006). Bullying: Theory, research, and interventions. In C. M. Evertson & C. S. Weinstein (Eds.), *Handbook of classroom management: Research, practice, and contemporary issues.* Mahwah, NJ: Erlbaum.

**Hyson, M., Copple, C., & Jones, J.** (2006). Early childhood development and education. In W. Damon & R. Lerner (Eds.). *Handbook of child psychology* (6th ed.). New York: Wiley.

**I**

**Intercultural Development Research Association.** (2010). *Coca-Cola Valued Youth Program.* Retrieved January 4, 2010, from www.idra.org/Coca-Cola_Valued_Youth_Program.html/

**International Montessori Council.** (2006). *Much of their success on Prime-Time Television.* Retrieved March 24, 2006, from www.Montessori.org/enews/barbara_walters.html

**International Society for Technology in Education.** (2007). *National educational technology standards for students* (2nd ed.). Eugene. OR: Author.

**Irvine, J. J.** (1990). *Black students and school failure.* New York: Greenwood Press.

**Irvine, S. H., & Berry, J. W.** (Eds.) (2010, in press). *Human abilities in cultural contexts.* New York: Cambridge University Press.

**Ise, E., & Schulte-Korne, G.** (2010, in press). Spelling deficits in dyslexia: Evaluation of an orthographic spelling training. *Annals of Dyslexia.*

**J**

**Jackson, S. L.** (2011). *Research methods* (2nd ed.). Boston: Cengage.

**Jackson-Newsom, J., & Shelton, T. L.** (2010). How the timing and quality of early experiences influence the development of brain architecture. *Developmental Psychobiology, 52,* 295–297.

**Jaeggi, S. M., Berman, M. G., & Jonides, J.** (2009). Training attentional processes. *Trends in Cognitive Science, 13,* 191–192.

**Jallifar, A.** (2010). The effect of cooperative learning techniques on college students' reading comprehension. *System, 38,* 96–108.

**Jalongo, M. R.** (2011). *Early childhood language arts* (5th ed.). Boston: Allyn & Bacon.

**James, W.** (1890). *Principles of psychology.* New York: Dower.

**James, W.** (1899/1993). *Talks to teachers.* New York: W. W. Norton.

**Jenkins, J., & Jenkins, L.** (1987). Making peer tutoring work. *Educational Leadership, 44,* 68–74.

**Jenkins, J. M., & Astington, J. W.** (1996). Cognitive factors and family structure associated with theory of mind development in young children. *Developmental Psychology, 32,* 70–78.

**Jenson-Campbell, L. A., & Malcolm, K. T.** (2007). The importance of conscientiousness in adolescent interpersonal relationships. *Personality and Social Psychology Bulletin, 33,* 368–383.

**Jimerson, S. R.** (2009). High school dropout. In D. Carr (Ed.), *Encyclopedia of the life course and human development.* Boston: Gale Cengage.

**John-Steiner, V.** (2007). Vygotsky on thinking and speaking. In H. Daniels, J. Wertsch, & M. Cole (Eds.), *The Cambridge companion to Vygotsky.* New York: Cambridge University Press.

**Johns Hopkins University** (2006). *Research: Tribal connection.* Retrieved January 31, 2008, from http://www.krieger.jhu.edu/research/spotlight/prabhakar.html

**Johnson, A. P.** (2010). *Making connections in elementary and middle school social studies.* Thousand Oaks, CA: Sage.

**Johnson, D. R., & Johnson, F. P.** (2010). *Joining together* (10th ed.). Upper Saddle River, NJ: Prentice Hall.

**Johnson, D. W., & Johnson, R. T.** (1989). *Cooperation and competition: Theory and research.* Edina, MN: Interaction Book Company.

**Johnson, D. W., & Johnson, R. T.** (1995, February). Why violence prevention programs don't work—and what does. *Educational Leadership, 63–68.*

**Johnson, D. W., & Johnson, R. T.** (1995). *Teaching students to be peacemakers* (3rd ed.). Edina, MN: Interaction Book Company.

**Johnson, D. W., & Johnson, R. T.** (2002). *Multi-cultural and human relations.* Boston: Allyn & Bacon.

**Johnson, M. H., Grossmann, T., and Cohen-Kadosh, K.** (2009). Mapping functional brain development: Building a social brain through Interactive Specialization. *Developmental Psychology, 45,* 151–159.

**Johnson, R. S., Mims-Cox, J. S., & Doyle-Nichols, A.** (2010). *Developing portfolios in education.* Thousand Oaks, CA: Sage.

**Johnson-Laird, P. N.** (2008). Mental models and deductive reasoning. In J. E. Adler & L. J.

Rips (Eds.), *Reasoning*. New York: Cambridge University Press.

**Jonassen, D. H.** (2006). *Modeling with technology: Mindtools for conceptual change.* Columbus, OH: Merrill/Prentice-Hall.

**Jonassen, D. H.** (2010). *Mindtools.* Retrieved February 11, 2010, from http://web.missouri .edu/jonassend/mindtools.html

**Jonassen, D. H., & Grabowski, B. L.** (1993). *Handbook of individual differences, learning, and instruction.* Mahwah, NJ: Erlbaum.

**Jones, B. F., Rasmussen, C. M., & Moffitt, M. C.** (1997). *Real-life problem solving.* Washington, DC: American Psychological Association.

**Jones, V., & Jones, L.** (2010). *Comprehensive classroom management* (9th ed.). Upper Saddle River, NJ: Merrill.

**Jordan, N. C., Glutting, J., & Ramineni, C.** (2010). The importance of number sense to mathematics achievement in first and third grades. *Learning and Individual Differences, 20,* 82–88.

**Josephson Institute of Ethics.** (2008). *The ethics of American youth 2008.* Los Angeles: Josephson Institute.

**Joyce, B. R., & Weil, M.** (2009). *Models of teaching* (8th ed.). Boston: Allyn & Bacon.

**Juang, L. P., & Syed, M.** (2010). Family cultural socialization practices and ethnic Identity-related experiences. *Developmental Psychology, 46,* 208–219.

**Jurecic, A.** (2006). Mindblindness: Autism, writing, and the problem of empathy. *Literature and Medicine, 25,* 1–23.

**Jussim, I., Robustelli, S. L., & Cain, T. R.** (2009). Teacher expectations and self-fulfilling prophecies. In K. R. Wentzel & A. Wigfield (Eds.), *Handbook of motivation at school.* New York: Routledge.

# K

**Kagan, J.** (1965). Reflection-impulsivity and reading development in primary grade children. *Child Development, 36,* 609–628.

**Kagan, J.** (2002). Behavioral inhibition as a temperamental category. In R. J. Davidson, K. R. Scherer, & H. H. Goldsmith (Eds.), *Handbook of affective sciences.* New York: Oxford University Press.

**Kagan, J.** (2010). Emotions and temperament. In M. H. Bornstein (Ed.), *Handbook of developmental cultural science.* New York: Psychology Press.

**Kagan, S.** (1992). *Cooperative learning.* San Juan Capistrano, CA: Resources for Teachers.

**Kagitcibasi, C.** (2007). *Family, self, and human development across cultures.* Mahwah, NJ: Erlbaum.

**Kail, R. V.** (2007). Longitudinal evidence that increases in processing speed and working memory enhance children's reasoning. *Psychological Science, 18,* 312–313.

**Kaiser, B., & Rasminsky, J.** (2009). *Challenging behavior in elementary and middle school.* Upper Saddle River, NJ: Prentice Hall.

**Kamii, C.** (1985). *Young children reinvent arithmetic: Implications of Piaget's theory.* New York: Teachers College Press.

**Kamii, C.** (1989). *Young children continue to reinvent arithmetic.* New York: Teachers College Press.

**Kamps, D. M., & others** (2008). The efficacy of ClassWide peer tutoring in middle schools. *Education and Treatment of Children, 31,* 119–152.

**Kanter, D. E.** (2010). Doing the project and learning the content: Designing project-based science curricula for meaningful understanding. *Science Education, 94,* 525–551.

**Kaplan, H. B.** (2009). Self-esteem. In D. Carr (Ed.), *Handbook of the life course and human development.* Boston: Gale Cengage.

**Kar, N.** (2009). Psychological impact of disasters on children: Review of assessment and interventions. *World Journal of Pediatrics, 5,* 5–11.

**Karniol, R., Grosz, E., & Schorr, I.** (2003). Caring, gender-role orientation, and volunteering. *Sex Roles, 49,* 11–19.

**Karsenty, R.** (2010). Nonprofessional mathematics tutoring for low-achieving students in secondary schools: A case study. *Educational Studies in Mathematics, 74,* 1–21.

**Kasari, C., & Lawton, K.** (2010). New directions in behavioral treatment of autism spectrum disorders. *Current Opinion in Neurology, 23,* 137–143.

**Katz, L.** (1999). Curriculum disputes in early childhood education. *ERIC Clearinghouse on Elementary and Early Childhood Education,* Document EDO-PS-99-13.

**Kaufman, J. C., & Sternberg, R. J.** (Eds.) (2010, in press). *Cambridge handbook of creativity.* New York: Cambridge University Press.

**Kauffman, J. M., & Hallahan, D. P.** (2005). *Special education: What it is and why we need it.* Boston: Allyn & Bacon.

**Kauffman, J. M., & Landrum, T. J.** (2009). *Characteristics of emotional and behavioral disorders of children and youth* (9th ed.). Boston: Allyn & Bacon.

**Kauffman, J. M., McGee, K., & Brigham, M.** (2004). Enabling or disabling? Observations on changes in special education. *Phi Delta Kappan, 85,* 613–620.

**Kaufman, S. B., & Sternberg, R. J.** (2008). Conceptions of giftedness. In S. I. Pfeiffer (Ed.), *Handbook of the gifted & talented: A psychological approach.* New York: Kluwer.

**Kazdin** (Ed.), *Encyclopedia of psychology.* Washington, DC, & New York: American Psychological Association and Oxford University Press.

**Keating, D. P.** (1990). Adolescent thinking. In S. S. Feldman & G. R. Elliott (Eds.), *At the threshold: The developing adolescent.* Cambridge, MA: Harvard University Press.

**Keating, D. P.** (2009). Developmental science and giftedness: An integrated life-span framework. In F. D. Horowitz, R. F. Subotnik, & D. J. Matthews (Eds.), *The development of giftedness and talent across the life span.* Washington, DC: American Psychological Association.

**Keeling, E. L., Polacek, K. M., & Ingram, E. L.** (2009). A statistical analysis of student questions in a cell biology laboratory. *American Society for Cell Biology, 8,* 131–139.

**Kellogg, R. T.** (1994). *The psychology of writing.* New York: Oxford University Press.

**Kellough, R. D., & Carjuzaa, J. D.** (2009). *Teaching in the middle and secondary schools* (9th ed.). Boston: Allyn & Bacon.

**Kelly, S.** (2008). Tracking. In N. J. Salkind. (Ed.), *Encyclopedia of educational psychology.* Thousand Oaks, CA: Sage.

**Kensinger, E. A., & Choi, E. S.** (2009). When side matters. Hemispheric processing and the visual specificity of emotional memories. *Journal of Experimental Psychology: Learning, Memory, and Cognition, 35,* 247–253.

**Keogh, B. K.** (2003). *Temperament in the classroom.* Baltimore: Brookes.

**Keramti, M.** (2010). Effect of cooperative learning on academic achievement of physics course. *Journal of Computers in Mathematics and Science Teaching, 29,* 155–173.

**Kerschreiter, R., Schulz-Hardt, S., Mojzisch, A., & Frey, D.** (2008). Biased information search in homogeneous groups: Confidence as a moderator for the effect of anticipated task requirements. *Personality and Social Psychology Bulletin, 34,* 679–691.

**Kessels, U., & Hannover, B.** (2008). When being a girl matters less: Accessibility of gender-related self-knowledge in single-sex and coeducational classes and its impact on students' physics-related self-concept of ability.

*British Journal of Educational Psychology, 78,* 273–289.

**Kim, S. Y., Su, J., Yancura, L., & Yee, B.** (2009). Asian American and Pacific Islander families. In N. Tewari & A. Alvarez (Eds.) *Asian American Psychology.* Clifton, NJ: Psychology Press.

**King, L.** (2007, June 7). The standards complaint. *USA Today,* p. 11D.

**Kinshuk, T. L., & McNab, P.** (2006). Cognitive trait modeling: The case of inductive reasoning ability. *Innovations in Education and Teaching, 43,* 151–161.

**Kitayama, S.** (2011). Psychology and culture: Cross-country or regional comparisons. *Annual Review of Psychology, Vol. 62.* Palo Alto, CA: Annual Reviews.

**Kivel, P.** (1995). *Uprooting racism: How White people can work for racial justice.* Philadelphia: New Society.

**Klein, S. B.** (2009). *Learning* (5th ed.). Thousand Oaks, CA: Sage.

**Klimstra, T., Hale, W., Raaijmakers, Q., Branje, S., & Meeus, W.** (2009). Maturation of personality in adolescence. *Journal of Personality and Social Psychology, 96* (4), 898–912.

**Kluhara, S. A., Graham, S., & Hawken, L. S.** (2009). Teaching writing to high school students: A national survey. *Journal of Educational Psychology, 101,* 136–160.

**Knopik, V. S.** (2009). Maternal smoking during pregnancy and child outcomes: Real or spurious effect? *Developmental Neuropsychology, 34,* 1–36.

**Knox, M.** (2010). On hitting children: A review of corporal punishment in the United States. *Journal of Pediatric Health Care, 24,* 103–107.

**Koehler, M.J., & Mishra, P.** (2010). Introducing technological pedagogical content knowledge (TPCK), AACTE's Committee on Innovation and Technology (Eds.), *The handbook of technological pedagogical content knowledge for educators.* New York, NY: Routledge.

**Kohen, D. E., Leventhal, T., Dahinten, V. S., & McIntosh, C. N.** (2008). Neighborhood disadvantage: Pathways of effects for young children. *Child Development, 79,* 156–169.

**Kohlberg, L.** (1976). Moral stages and moralization: The cognitive-developmental approach. In T. Lickona (Ed.), *Moral development and behavior.* New York: Holt, Rinehart & Winston.

**Kohlberg, L.** (1986). A current statement of some theoretical issues. In S. Modgil & C. Modgil (Eds.), *Lawrence Kohlberg.* Philadelphia: Falmer.

**Kopp, C. B.** (2009). Emotion-focused coping in young children: Self and self-regulatory processes. *New Directions in Child and Adolescent Development, 124,* 33–46.

**Kopp, C. B.** (2011). Socioemotional development in the early years. *Annual Review of Psychology, Vol. 62.* Palo Alto, CA: Annual Reviews.

**Koppelman, K., & Goodhart, L.** (2011). *Understanding human differences* (3rd ed.). Boston: Allyn & Bacon.

**Koretz, D.** (2008). *Measuring up: What educational testing really tells us.* Cambridge, MA: Harvard University Press.

**Kostelnik, M. J., Soderman, A. K., & Whiren, A. P.** (2011). *Developmentally appropriate curricula* (5th ed.). Upper Saddle River, NJ: Merrill.

**Kounin, J. S.** (1970). *Discipline and management in classrooms.* New York: Holt, Rinehart & Winston.

**Kozol, J.** (1991). *Savage inequalities.* New York: Crown.

**Kozol, J.** (2005). *The shame of the nation.* New York: Crown.

**Kraft, M. A.** (2010). From ringmaster to conductor: 10 simple techniques can turn an unruly class into a productive one. *Phi Delta Kappan, 91,* 44–47.

**Krajcik, J. S., & Blumenfeld, P. C.** (2006). Project-based learning. In R. K. Sawyer (Ed.), *The Cambridge handbook of learning sciences.* New York: Oxford University Press.

**Krathwohl, D. R., Bloom, B. S., & Masia, B. B.** (1964). *Taxonomy of educational objectives. Handbook II: Affective domain.* New York: David McKay.

**Kretuzer, L. C., & Flavell, J. H.** (1975). An interview study of children's knowledge about memory. *Monographs of the Society for Research in Child Development, 40* (1, Serial No. 159).

**Kuder, S. J.** (2009). *Teaching students with language and communication disabilities* (3rd ed.). Boston: Allyn & Bacon.

**Kuhn, D.** (2009). Adolescent thinking. In R. M. Lerner & L. Steinberg (Eds.), *Handbook of adolescent psychology* (3rd ed.). New York: Wiley.

**Kuhn, D.** (2011). What is scientific thinking and how does it develop? In U. Goswami (Ed.), *Wiley-Blackwell handbook of childhood cognitive development.* New York: Wiley.

**Kuhn, D., & Franklin, S.** (2006). The second decade: What develops (and how)? In W. Damon & R. Lerner (Eds.), *Handbook of child psychology* (6th ed.). New York: Wiley.

**Kuhn, D., Katz, J., & Dean, D.** (2004). Developing reason. *Thinking & Reasoning, 10* (2), 197–219.

**Kuhn, D., Weinstock, M., & Flaton, R.** (1994). How well do jurors reason? Competence dimensions of individual variation in a juror reasoning task. *Psychological Science, 5,* 289–296.

**Kumar, D. D.** (2010). Approaches to interactive video anchors in problem-based science learning. *Journal of Science Education and Technology, 19,* 13–19.

**Kunzmann, R.** (2003). From teacher to student: The value of teacher education for experienced teachers. *Journal of Teacher Education, 54,* 241–253.

# L

**Ladd, G. W., Birch, S. H., & Buhs, E. S.** (1999). Children's social and scholastic lives in kindergarten: Related spheres of influence? *Child Development, 70(6),* 1373–1400.

**Lalley, J. P., & Gentile, J. R.** (2009). Classroom assessment and grading to assure mastery. *Theory Into Practice, 48,* 28–35.

**Lamon, M., Secules, T., Petrosino, A. J., Hackett, R., Bransford, J. D., & Goldman, S. R.** (1996). Schools for thought. In L. Schauble & R. Glaser (Eds.), *Innovations in learning.* Mahwah, NJ: Erlbaum.

**Landa, S.** (2000, Fall). If you can't make waves, make ripples. *Intelligence Connections Newsletter of the ASCD, X (No. 1),* 6–8.

**Lane, H. B. & others** (2009). Teacher knowledge about reading fluency and indicators of students' fluency growth in Reading First schools. *Reading & Writing Quarterly, 25,* 57–86.

**Lane, S. D.** (2010). *Interpersonal communication* (2nd ed.). Boston: Allyn & Bacon.

**Langdon, H.** (2011). Bilingual language acquisition and learning. In S. Levey & S. Pollirstok (Eds.), *Language development: Understanding language diversity in the classroom.* Thousand Oaks, CA: Sage.

**Langer, E.** (2005). *On becoming an artist.* New York: Ballantine.

**Langer, E. J.** (1997). *The power of mindful learning.* Reading, MA: Addison-Wesley.

**Langer, P.** (2009). Situated learning: What ever happened to educational psychology? *Educational Psychology Review, 21,* 181–192.

**Langston, W.** (2011). *Research methods laboratory manual for psychology* (3rd ed.). Boston: Cengage.

**Lankes, A. M. D.** (1995). *Electronic portfolios: A new idea in assessment.* ERIC Document Reproduction Service No. ED390377.

**Lansford, J. E., Dishion, T. J., & Dodge, K. A.** (2010, in press). Deviant peer clustering and influence within public school settings: Inadvertent negative outcomes from traditional professional practices. In M. R. Shinn, H. M. Walker, & G. Stoner (Eds.), *Interventions for achievement and behavior in a three-tier model including response to intervention.* Bethesda, MD: National Association for School Psychologists Press.

**Larkin, M. J.** (2008). Rubrics. In N. J. Salkind (Ed.), *Encyclopedia of educational psychology.* Thousand Oaks, CA: Sage.

**Larrivee, B.** (2009). *Authentic classroom management.* Upper Saddle River, NJ: Prentice Hall.

**Larsen, R. J., & Buss, D. M.** (2010). *Personality psychology* (4th ed.). New York: McGraw-Hill.

**Larson, R., Wilson, S., & Rickman, A.** (2009). Globalization, societal change, and adolescence across the world. In R. M. Lerner & L. Steinberg (Eds.), *Handbook of adolescent psychology* (3rd ed.). New York: Wiley.

**Larson, R. W.** (2007). Development of the capacity for teamwork in youth development. In R. K. Silbereisen & R. M. Lerner (Eds.), *Approaches to positive youth development.* Thousand Oaks, CA: Sage.

**Larson, R. W., & Verma, S.** (1999). How children and adolescents spend time across the world: Work, play, and developmental opportunities. *Psychological Bulletin, 125,* 701–736.

**Larzelere, R. E., & Kuhgn, B. R.** (2005). Comparing child outcomes of physical punishment and alternative discipline tactics: A meta-analysis. *Clinical Child and Family Psychology Review, 8,* 1–37.

**Lattimer, H.** (2009). Challenging history: Essential questions in the social studies classroom. *School Education, 72,* 326–329.

**Lau, W. W. F., & Yuen, A. H. K.** (2010). Promoting conceptual change of learning sorting algorithm through the diagnosis of mental models: The effect of gender and learning styles. *Computers & Education, 54,* 275–288.

**Lawson, A. E.** (2010). Basic inferences of scientific reasoning, argumentation, and discovery. *Science Education, 94,* 336–364.

**Lawson, A. E.** (2010). *Teaching inquiry science in middle and secondary schools.* Thousand Oaks, CA: Sage.

**Laxman, K.** (2010). A conceptual framework mapping the application of information search strategies to well and ill-structured problem solving. *Computers & Education, 55,* 513–526.

**Lazar, L., & others** (1982). Lasting effects of early education. *Monographs of the Society for Research in Child Development, 47.*

**Leaper, C., & Brown, C. S.** (2008). Perceived experiences with sexism among adolescent girls. *Child Development, 79,* 685–704.

**Leaper, C., & Smith, T. E.** (2004). A meta-analytic review of gender variations in children's language use: talkativeness, affiliative speech, and assertive speed. *Developmental Psychology, 40,* 993–1027.

**Leary, M. R.** (2008). *Introduction to behavioral research* (5th ed.). Upper Saddle River, NJ: Pearson.

**Leathers, D., & Eaves, M. H.** (2008). *Successful nonverbal communication* (4th ed.). Boston: Allyn & Bacon.

**Lee, C. D., & Slaughter-Defoe, D.** (1995). Historical and sociocultural influences of African American education. In J. A. Banks, & C. M. Banks (Eds.), *Handbook of research on multicultural education.* New York: Macmillan.

**Lee, K., Ng, E. L., & Ng, S. F.** (2009). The contributions of working memory and executive functioning to problem representation and solution generation in algebraic word problems. *Journal of Educational Psychology, 101,* 373–387.

**Lee, S. J.** (2009). Behind the model-minority stereotype: Voices of high- and low-achieving Asian American students. *Anthropology and Education, 25,* 413–429.

**Lee, S. J., & Wong, A. N.** (2009). The model minority and the perceptual foreigner: Stereotypes of Asian Americans. In N. Tewari & A. Alvarez (Eds.), *Asian American Psychology.* Clifton, NJ: Psychology Press.

**Lehr, C. A., Hanson, A., Sinclair, M. F., & Christensen, S. I.** (2003). Moving beyond dropout prevention towards school completion. *School Psychology Review, 32,* 342–364.

**Lehrer, R., & Schauble, L.** (2006). Scientific thinking and science literacy: Supporting developmental change in learning contexts. In W. Damon & R. Lerner (Eds.), *Handbook of child psychology* (6th ed.). New York: Wiley.

**Leonard, L. B.** (2007). Processing limitations and the grammatical profile of children with specific language impairment. *Advances in Child Development and Behavior, 35,* 135–171.

**Leondari, A., & Gonida, E.** (2007). Predicting academic self-handicapping in different age groups: The role of personal achievement goals and social goals. *British Journal of Educational Psychology, 77,* 595–611.

**Lepper, M. R., Corpus, J. H., & Iyengar, S. S.** (2005). Intrinsic and extrinsic orientations in the classroom: Age differences and academic correlates. *Journal of Educational Psychology, 97,* 184–196.

**Lepper, M. R., Greene, D., & Nisbett, R.** (1973). Undermining children's intrinsic interest with intrinsic rewards: A test of the overjustification hypothesis. *Journal of Personality and Social Psychology, 28,* 129–137.

**Lerner, R. M., Boyd, M., & Du, D.** (2008). Adolescent development. In I. B. Weiner & C. B. Craighead (Eds.), *Encyclopedia of psychology* (4th Ed.). New York: Wiley.

**Lesaux, N., & Siegel, L.** (2003). The development of reading in children who speak English as a second language. *Developmental Psychology, 39,* 1005–1019.

**Lesser, G.** (1972). Learning, teaching, and television production for children: The experience of *Sesame Street. Harvard Educational Review, 42,* 232–272.

**Leventhal, T., Dupere, V., & Brooks-Gunn, J.** (2009). Neighborhood influences on adolescent psychology. In R. M. Lerner & L. Steinberg (Eds.), *Handbook of adolescent psychology* (3rd ed.). New York: Wiley.

**Lever-Duffy, J., & McDonald, J. B.** (2011). *Teaching and learning with technology* (4th ed.). Boston: Allyn & Bacon.

**Levin, J.** (1980). *The mnemonics '80s: Keywords in the classroom.* Theoretical paper No. 86. Wisconsin Research and Development Center for Individualized Schooling, Madison.

**Levin, J., & Fox, J. A.** (2011). *Elementary statistics in social research* (3rd ed.). Upper Saddle River, NJ: Pearson.

**Levin, J., & Nolan, J.** (2007). *Principles of classroom management* (5th ed.). Boston: Allyn & Bacon.

**Levine, L. N., & McCloskey, M. L.** (2009). *Teaching learners of English in mainstream classrooms.* Boston: Allyn & Bacon.

**Levstik, L.** (2011). Learning history. In P. A. Alexander & R. E. Mayer (Eds.), *Handbook of research on learning and instruction.* New York: Routledge.

**Levy, F.** (2009). Dopamine vs noradrenaline: Inverted-U effects and ADHD theories. *Australian and New Zealand Journal of Psychiatry, 43,* 101–108.

**Lewis, A. C.** (2007). Looking beyond NCLB. *Phi Delta Kappan, 88,* 483–484.

**Li, P.** (2009). What's in a lexical system? Discovering meaning through an interactive eye. In V. C. M. Gathercole (Ed.), *Routes to language: Essays in honor of Melissa Bowerman*. New York: Psychology Press.

**Liben, L. S.** (1995). Psychology meets geography: Exploring the gender gap on the national geography bee. *Psychological Science Agenda, 8,* 8–9.

**Liben, L. S.** (2009). Giftedness during childhood: The spatial-graphic domain. In F. D. Horowitz, R. F. Subotnik, & D. J. Matthews (Eds.), *The development of giftedness and talent across the life span*. Washington, DC: American Psychological Association.

**Lidz, J.** (2010). The abstract nature of syntactic representations: Consequences for a theory of learning. In E. Hoff & M. Shatz (Eds.), *Blackwell handbook of language development* (2nd ed.). New York: Wiley.

**Limber, S. P.** (1997). Preventing violence among school children. *Family Futures, 1,* 27–28.

**Lindblad, F., & Hjern, A.** (2010). ADHD after fetal exposure to maternal smoking. *Nicotine and Tobacco Research, 12,* 408–415.

**Lindley, F.** (2009). *The portable mentor* (2nd ed.). Thousand Oaks, CA: Corwin Press.

**Lipsitz, J.** (1984). *Successful schools for young adolescents*. New Brunswick, NJ: Transaction Books.

**Litt, J., Taylor, H. G., Klein, N., & Hack, M.** (2005). Learning disabilities in children with very low birthweight: Prevalence, neuropsychological correlates, and educational interventions. *Journal of Learning Disabilities, 38,* 130–141.

**Litton, E. F.** (1999). Learning in America: The Filipino-American sociocultural perspective. In C. Park & M. M. Chi (Eds.), *Asian-American education: Prospects and challenges*. Westport, CT: Bergin & Garvey.

**Liu, K. Y., King, M., & Bearman, P. S.** (2010). Social influence and the autism epidemic. *American Journal of Sociology, 115,* 1387–1434.

**Lockl, K., & Schneider, W.** (2007). Knowledge about the mind: Links between theory of mind and later metamemory. *Child Development, 78,* 147–167.

**Lodico, M. G., Spaulding, D. T., & Voegtle, K. H.** (2011). *Methods in educational research* (2nd ed.). New York: Wiley.

**Logan, J.** (1997). *Teaching stories*. New York: Kodansha International.

**Lord, T., & Baviskar, S.** (2007). Moving students from information recitation to information understanding: Exploiting Bloom's taxonomy in creating science questions.

*Journal of College Science Teaching, 36,* 40–44.

**Lubinski, D.** (2009). Exceptional cognitive ability: The phenotype. *Behavior Genetics, 39,* 350–358.

**Luders, E., Narr, K. L., Thompson, P. M., & Toga, A. W.** (2009). Neuroanatomical correlates of intelligence. *Intelligence, 37,* 156–163.

**Lunday, A.** (2006). *Two Homewood seniors collect Marshall, Mitchell scholarships.* Retrieved January 31, 2008, from http://www.jhu.edu/~gazette/2006/04dec06/04schol.html

**Luria, A., & Herzog, E.** (1985, April). *Gender segregation across and within settings.* Paper presented at the biennial meeting of the Society for Research in Child Development, Toronto.

**Lustig, M. W., & Koester, J.** (2010). *Intercultural competence* (6th ed.). Upper Saddle River, NJ: Allyn & Bacon.

**Luthar, S. S.** (2006). Resilience in development: A synthesis of research across five decades. In D. Cicchetti & D. J. Cohen (Eds.), *Developmental psychopathology (Vol. 3): ME LOOK UPRisk, disorder, and adaptation* (2nd ed.). Hoboken, NJ: Wiley.

**Luthar, S. S., & Goldstein. A. S.** (2008). Substance use and related behaviors among suburban late adolescents: The importance of perceived parent containment. *Development and Psychopathology, 20,* 591–614.

**Lyon, T. D., & Flavell, J. H.** (1993). Young children's understanding of forgetting over time. *Child Development, 64,* 789–800.

## M

**Macario, J.** (2010). *Graphic design essentials.* Upper Saddle River, NJ: Prentice Hall.

**Maccoby, E. E.** (1998). *The two sexes: Growing up apart, coming together*. Cambridge, MA: Harvard University.

**Maccoby, E. E.** (2007). Historical overview of socialization research and theory. In J. E. Grusec & P. D. Hastings (Eds.), *Handbook of socialization*. New York: Guilford.

**Maccoby, E. E., & Jacklin, C. N.** (1974). *The psychology of sex differences*. Palo Alto, CA: Stanford University Press.

**MacGeorge, E. L.** (2004). The myth of gender cultures: Similarities outweigh differences in men's and women's provisions of and responses to supportive communication. *Sex Roles, 50,* 143–175.

**Mader, S. S.** (2011). *Biology* (2nd ed.). New York: McGraw-Hill.

**Madole, K. L., Oakes, L. M., & Rakison, D. H.** (2010, in press). Information processing approaches to infants' developing representations of dynamic features. In L. Oakes, C. Cashon, M. Casasola, & D. Rakison (Eds.), *Infant perception and cognition*. New York: Oxford University Press.

**Maehr, M. L., & Zusho, A.** (2009). Goal-directed behavior in the classroom. In K. Wentzel & A. Wigfield (Eds.), *Handbook of motivation at school*. New York: Routledge.

**Mael, F. A.** (1998). Single-sex and coeducational schooling: Relationships to socioemotional and academic development. *Review of Educational Research, 68* (2), 101–129.

**Mager, R.** (1962). *Preparing instructional objectives* (2nd ed.). Palo Alto, CA: Fearon.

**Magnusson, S. J., & Palinscar, A. S.** (2005). Teaching to promote the development of scientific knowledge and reasoning about light at the elementary school level. In *How students learn*. Washington, DC: National Academies Press.

**Mahoney, J., Parente, M. E., & Zigler, E.** (2010). After-school program engagement and in-school competence: Program quality, content, and staffing. In J. Meece & J. Eccles (Eds.), *Handbook of schools, schooling, and human development*. New York: Routledge.

**Mahoney, J. L., Vandell, D. L., Simpkins, S., & Zarrett, N.** (2009). Adolescent out-of-school activities. In R. M. Lerner & L. Steinberg (Eds.), *Handbook of adolescent psychology* (3rd ed.). New York: Wiley.

**Maier, S. F., & Seligman, M. E. P.** (2009). Fears, phobias, and preparedness: Toward an evolved module of fear and fear learning. In D. Shanks (Ed.), *Psychology of learning*. Thousand Oaks, CA: Sage.

**Maloy, R. W., Verock-O'Loughlin, R-E., Edwards, S. A., & Woolf, B. P.** (2011). *Transforming learning with new technologies*. Boston: Allyn & Bacon.

**Mandler, G.** (1980). Recognizing: The judgment of previous occurrence. *Psychological Review, 87,* 252–271.

**Mandrin, P-A., & Preckel, D.** (2009). Effect of similarity-based guided discovery learning on conceptual performance. *School Science and Mathematics, 109,* 133–145.

**Manis, F. R., Keating, D. P., & Morrison, F. J.** (1980). Developmental differences in the allocation of processing capacity. *Journal of Experimental Child Psychology, 29,* 156–169.

**Marcia, J. E.** (1980). Identity in adolescence. In J. Adelson (Ed.), *Handbook of adolescent psychology*. New York: Wiley.

**Marcia, J. E.** (1998). Optimal development from an Eriksonian perspective. In H. S. Friedman (Ed.), *Encyclopedia of mental health, Vol. 2*. San Diego: Academic Press.

**Marinas, T., & van der Lely, H. K.** (2007). On-line processing of wh- questions in children with G-SLI and typically developing children. *International Journal of Language and Communication Disorders, 42*, 557–582.

**Marion, M. C.** (2010). *Introduction to early childhood education*. Upper Saddle River, NJ: Prentice Hall.

**Marshall Scholarships.** (2007). *Scholar profiles: 2007*. Retrieved January 31, 2008, from http://www.marshallscholarship.org/profles2007.html.

**Martin, C. L., & Ruble, D. N.** (2010). Patterns of gender development. *Annual Review of Psychology, Vol. 31*. Palo Alto, CA: Annual Reviews.

**Martin, J. F.** (2009). The goal of long division. *Teaching Children Mathematics, 15*, 482–487.

**Martin, J. L.** (2008). Peer sexual harassment: finding voice, changing culture—an intervention strategy for adolescent females. *Violence Against Women, 14*, 100–124.

**Martin, R., Sexton, C., Franklin, T., Gerlovich, J., & McElroy, D.** (2009). *Teaching science for all children* (5th ed.). Boston: Allyn & Bacon.

**Martinez, M. E.** (2010). *Learning and cognition: The design of the mind*. Upper Saddle River, NJ: Merrill.

**Martinez, S.** (2009). A system gone berzerk: How are zero-tolerance policies affecting schools? *Preventing School Failure, 53*, 153–158.

**Marton, F., Hounsell, D. J., & Entwistle, N. J.** (1984). *The experience of learning*. Edinburgh: Scottish Academic Press.

**Marzano, R. J., & Pickering, D. J.** (2007). The case for and against homework. *Educational Leadership, 64*, 74–79.

**Mashburn, A. J., Pianta, R. C., Hamre, B. K., Downer, J. T., Barbarin, O. A., Bryant, D., & others** (2008). Measures of classroom quality in prekindergarten and children's development of academic, language, and social skills. *Child Development, 79*, 732–749.

**Maslow, A. H.** (1954). *Motivation and personality*. New York: Harper & Row.

**Maslow, A. H.** (1971). *The farther reaches of human nature*. New York: Viking Press.

**Mathematica** (2008). Retrieved January 16, 2008, from www.wolfram.com/products/mathematica/index.html

**Mathes, P. G., Torgesen, J. K., & Allor, J. H.** (2001). The effects of peer-assisted literacy strategies for first-grade readers with and without additional computer-assisted instruction in phonological awareness. *American Educational Research Journal, 38*, 371–410.

**Matthews, D. J.** (2009). Developmental transitions in giftedness and talent: Childhood into adolescence. In F. D. Horowitz, R. F. Subotnik, & D. J. Matthews (Eds.), *The development of giftedness and talent across the life span*. Washington, DC: American Psychological Association.

**Matusov, E., Bell, N., & Rogoff, B.** (2001). Schooling as a cultural process: Working together and guidance by children from schools differing in collaborative practices. Unpublished manuscript, Department of Psychology, University of California at Santa Cruz.

**Maxim, G. W.** (2010). *Dynamic social studies for constructivist classrooms* (9th ed.). Boston: Allyn & Bacon.

**Mayer, R. E.** (1997). Multimedia learning: Are we asking the right questions? *Educational Psychologist, 32*, 1–19.

**Mayer, R. E.** (2004). Should there be a three-strike rule against pure discovery learning? *American Psychologist, 59*, 14–19.

**Mayer, R. E.** (2004). Teaching of subject matter. *Annual Review of Psychology, 55*, Palo Alto, CA: Annual Review, 5.

**Mayer, R. E.** (2008). *Learning and instruction* (2nd ed.). Upper Saddle River, NJ: Prentice Hall.

**Mayer, R. E.** (2009). *Multimedia learning* (2nd ed). New York: Cambridge University Press.

**Mayer, R. E.** (2010). *Current research: Richard E. Mayer*. Retrieved February 10, 2010, from /www.psych.ucsb.edu/people/faculty/mayer/research/research.php

**Mayer, R. E., Stull, A., DeLeeuw, K., Ailmeroth, K., Bimber, B., Chun, D., Bulger, M., Campbell, J., Knight, & Zhang, M.** (2009). Clickers in college classrooms: Fostering learning with questioning methods in large lecture classes. *Contemporary Educational Psychology, 34*, 51–57.

**McBurney, D. H., & White, T. L.** (2010). *Research methods* (8th ed.). Boston: Cengage

**McCall, A.** (2007). Supporting exemplary social studies teaching in elementary schools. *Social Studies, 97*, 161–167.

**McClelland, M. M., Ponitz, C. C., Messersmith, E. E., & Tominey, S. S.** (2011). Self-regulation: The integration of cognition and emotion. In R. M. Lerner & W. F. Overton (Eds.), *Handbook of life-span development, Vol. 1*. New York: Wiley.

**McCombs, B. L.** (2001, April). *What do we know about learners and learning? The learner-centered framework*. Paper presented at the meeting of the American Educational Research Association, Seattle.

**McCombs, B. L.** (2010). Learner-centered practices: Providing the context for positive learner development. In J. Meece & J. Eccles (Eds.), *Handbook of research on schools, schooling, and human development*. New York: Routledge.

**McCrae, R. R., & Costa, P. T.** (2006). Cross-cultural perspectives on adult personality trait development. In D. K. Mroczek & T. D. Little (Eds.), *Handbook of personality development*. Mahwah, NJ: Erlbaum.

**McDonald, B. A., Larson, C. D., Dansereau, D., & Spurlin, J. E.** (1985). Cooperative dyads: Impact on text learning and transfer. *Contemporary Educational Psychology, 10*, 369–377.

**McDuffle, K. A., Mastropieri, M. A., & Scruggs, T. E.** (2009). Differential effects of peer tutoring in co-taught and non-co-taught classes: Results for content learning and student-teacher interactions. *Exceptional Children, 75*, 493–510.

**McGee, L. M., & Richgels, D. J.** (2008). *Literacy's beginnings: Supporting young readers and writers* (5th ed.). Boston: Allyn & Bacon.

**McKay, R.** (2008), Multiple intelligences. In N. J. Salkind (Ed.), *Encyclopedia of educational psychology*. Thousand Oaks, CA: Sage.

**McKeown, M., & Beck, I. L.** (2010). The role of metacognition in understanding and supporting reading comprehension. In D. J. Hacker, J. Dunlosky, & A. C. Graesser (Eds.), *Handbook of metacognition in education*. New York: Psychology Press.

**McKim, B.** (2009). The road less traveled. *Phi Delta Kappan, 89*, 298–299.

**McLean, K. C., & Breen, A. V.** (2009). Processes and content of narrative identity development in adolescence: Gender and well-being. *Developmental Psychology, 45*, 702–710.

**McLoyd, V. C., Kaplan, R., Purtell, K. M., Bagley, E., Hardaway, C. R., & Smalls, C.** (2009). Poverty and socioeconomic disadvantage in adolescence. In R. M. Lerner & L. Steinberg (Eds.), *Handbook of adolescent psychology* (3rd ed.). New York: Wiley.

**McMaster, K. L., Kung, S., Han, I., & Cao, M.** (2008). Peer-assisted learning strategies:

A "Tier 1" approach to promoting English learners' response to intervention. *Exceptional Children, 74,* 194–204.

**McMillan, J.** (2010). The practical implications of educational aims and contexts for formative assessment. In H. Andrade & G. J. Cizek (Eds.), *Handbook of formative assessment.* New York: Routledge.

**McMillan, J. H.** (1997). *Classroom assessment.* Boston: Allyn & Bacon.

**McMillan, J. H.** (2002). *Essential assessment concepts for teachers and administrators.* Thousand Oaks, CA: Corwin Press.

**McMillan, J. H.** (2007). *Classroom assessment* (4th ed.). Boston: Allyn & Bacon.

**McMillan, J. H.** (2008a). *Educational research: Fundamentals for the consumer* (5th ed.). Boston: Allyn & Bacon.

**McMillan, J. H.** (2008b). *Assessment essentials for standards-based education* (2nd ed.). Thousand Oaks, CA: Corwin.

**McMillan, J. H.** (2011). *Classroom assessment* (5th ed.). Boston: Allyn & Bacon.

**McMillan, J. H., & Schumacher, S.** (2010). *Research in education: Evidence-based inquiry* (7th ed.). Upper Saddle River, NJ: Merrill.

**McMillan, J. H., & Wergin, J. F.** (2010). *Understanding and evaluating educational research* (4th ed.). Upper Saddle River, NJ: Merrill.

**McNally, D.** (1990). *Even eagles need a push.* New York: Dell.

**Means, B.** (2006). Prospects for transforming schools with technology-supported assessment. In R K. Sawyer (Ed.), *The Cambridge handbook of the learning sciences.* New York: Cambridge University Press.

**Meeece, J. L.** (1991). The classroom context and students' motivational goals. In M. L. Maehr & P. R. Pintrich (Eds.), *Advances in motivation and achievement* (Vol. 7, pp. 261–285).

**Meece, J. L., Anderman, E. M., & Anderman, L. H.** (2006). Classroom goal structure, student motivation, and academic achievement. *Annual Review of Psychology, Vol. 57.* Palo Alto, CA: Annual Reviews.

**Meece, J. L., & Eccles, J.** (Eds.) (2010). *Handbook of research on schools, schooling, and human development.* New York: Routledge.

**Meichenbaum, D., & Butler, L.** (1980). Toward a conceptual model of the treatment of test anxiety: Implications for research and treatment. In I. G. Sarason (Ed.), *Test anxiety.* Mahwah, NJ: Erlbaum.

**Meichenbaum, D., Turk, D., & Burstein, S.** (1975). The nature of coping with stress.

In I. Sarason & C. Spielberger (Eds.), *Stress and anxiety*: Washington, DC: Hemisphere.

**Melzi, G., & Ely, R.** (2009). Language development in the school years. In J. Berko Gleason & N. B. Ratner (Eds.), *The development of language* (7th ed.). Boston: Allyn & Bacon.

**Merenda, P.** (2004). Cross-cultural adaptation of educational and psychological testing. In R. K. Hambleton, P. F. Merenda, & C. D. Spielberger (Eds.), *Adapting educational and psychological tests for cross-cultural assessment.* Mahwah, NJ: Erlbaum.

**Merrell, K. W., Carrizales, D., Feuerborn, L., Gueldner, B. A., & Tran, O. K.** (2007). *Strong kids—grades 6–8: A social and emotional learning curriculum.* Baltimore: Brookes.

**Mertler, C. A., & Charles, C. M.** (2011). *Introduction to education research* (7th ed.). Boston: Allyn & Bacon.

**Metzger, M.** (1996, January). Maintaining a life. *Phi Delta Kappan, 77,* 346–351.

**Meyers, J.** (2010, April 1). Suicides open eyes to bullying. *Dallas Morning News,* pp. 1A–2A.

**Mezzacappa, E.** (2004). Alerting, orienting, and executive attention: Developmental properties and socio-demographic correlates in an epidemiological sample of young, urban children. *Child Developmesnt, 75,* 1–14.

**Michaels, S.** (1986). Narrative presentations: An oral presentation for literacy with first graders. In J. Cook-Gumperz (Ed.), *The social construction of literacy.* New York: Cambridge University Press.

**Middleton, J., & Goepfert, P.** (1996). *Inventive strategies for teaching mathematics.* Washington, DC: American Psychological Association.

**Middleton, M. J. & Midgley, C.** (2002). Beyond motivation: Middle school students' perceptions of press for understanding in math. *Contemporary Educational Psychology, 27,* 373–391.

**Midgley, C., Anderman, E., & Hicks, L.** (1995). Differences between elementary school and middle school teachers and students: A goal theory approach. *Journal of Early Adolescence, 15,* 90–113.

**Miller, C. F., Lurye, L. E., Zusuls, K. M., & Ruble, D. N.** (2009). Accessibility of gender stereotype domains: Developmental and gender differences in children. *Sex Roles, 60,* 870–881.

**Miller, G. A.** (1956). The magical number seven, plus or minus two: Some limits on

our capacity for information processing. *Psychological Review, 48,* 337–442.

**Miller, J. E.** (2008). Gifted and talented education. In N. J. Salkind (Ed.), *Encyclopedia of educational psychology.* Thousand Oaks. CA: Sage.

**Miller, K. F.** (2000). Representational tools and conceptual change: The young scientist's tool kit. *Journal of Applied Developmental Psychology, 21,* 21–25.

**Miller, P. H.** (2011). Piaget's theory: Past, present, and future. In U. Goswami (Ed.), *Wiley-Blackwell handbook of childhood cognitive development* (2nd ed.). New York: Wiley Blackwell.

**Miller, S. R., Tserakhava, V., & Miller, C. J.** (2010, in press). "My child is shy and has no friends: What does parenting have to do with it?" *Journal of Youth and Adolescence.*

**Miller, T. W., Nigg, J. T., & Faraone, S. V.** (2007). Axis I and II comorbidity in adults with ADHD. *Journal of Abnormal Psychology, 116,* 519–528.

**Miller-Jones, D.** (1989). Culture and testing. *American Psychologist, 44,* 360–366.

**Mills, B., Reyna, V., & Estrada, S.** (2008). Explaining contradictory relations between risk perception and risk taking. *Psychological Science, 19,* 429–433.

**Mills, D., & Mills, C.** (2000). *Hungarian kindergarten cirriculum translation.* London: Mills Production.

**Mills, G. E.** (2011). *Action research* (4th ed.). Boston: Allyn & Bacon.

**Milner, H. R.** (2006). Preservice teachers' learning about cultural and racial diversity. *Urban Education, 41* (4), pp. 343–375.

**Milsom, A., & Gallo, L. L.** (2006). Bullying in middle schools: Prevention and intervention. *Middle School Journal, 37,* 12–19.

**Minuchin, P. P., & Shapiro, E. K.** (1983). The school as a context for social development. In P. H. Mussen (Ed.), *Handbook of child psychology, Vol. 4* (4th ed.). New York: Wiley.

**Mishna, F., Saini, M., & Solomon, S.** (2009). Ongoing and online: Children's and youth's perceptions of cyber bullying. *Children and Youth Services Review, 31,* 1222–1228.

**Mishra, P., & Koehler, M. J.** (2006). *Technological Pedagogical Content Knowledge: A new framework for teacher knowledge. Teachers College Record, 108,* 1017–1054.

**Mitchell, M. L., & Jolley, J. M.** (2010). *Research designs explained* (7th ed.). Belmont, CA: Wadsworth.

**Moll, L. C., & González, N.** (2004). Engaging life: A funds of knowledge approach to multicultural education. In J. A. Banks & C. A. M. Banks (Eds.), *Handbook of research on multicultural education* (2nd ed.). San Francisco: Jossey-Bass.

**Monaco, T.** (2008). The application of molecular genetics to the study of specific language impairment. In C. Norbury, B. Tomblin, & D. Bishop (Eds.), *Understanding developmental language disorders in children.* Milton Park, UK: Routledge.

**Moon, S. M.** (2008). Personal and social development. In K. A. Karnes & K. R. Stephens (Eds.), *Achieving excellence: Educating the gifted and talented.* Upper Saddle River, NJ: Prentice Hall.

**Moore-Hart, M. A.** (2010). *Teaching writing in diverse classrooms* (10th ed.). Boston: Allyn & Bacon.

**Moore Partin, T. C., Robertson, R. E., Daniel, M., Oliver, R. M., & Wehby, J. H.** (2010). Using teacher praise and opportunities to promote appropriate student behavior. *Preventing School Failure, 54,* 172–178.

**Moran, S., & Gardner, H.** (2006). Extraordinary achievements. In W. Damon & R. Lerner (Eds.), *Handbook of child psychology* (6th ed.). New York: Wiley.

**Moreno, R.** (2009). Constructing knowledge with an agent-based instructional program: A comparison of cooperative and individual meaning making. *Learning and Instruction, 19,* 433–444.

**Morra, S., Gobbo, C., Marini, Z., & Sheese, R.** (2008). *Cognitive development: Neo-Piagetian perspectives.* Mahwah, NJ: Erlbaum.

**Morrison, G. R., & Lowther, D. L.** (2010). *Integrating computer technology into the classroom* (4th ed.). Boston: Allyn & Bacon.

**Morrison, G. S.** (2011). *Fundamentals of early childhood education* (6th ed.). Upper Saddle River, NJ: Merrill.

**Morrow, L.** (2009). *Literacy development in the early years* (7th ed.). Boston: Allyn & Bacon.

**Moyer, J. R., & Dardig, J. C.** (1978). Practical task analysis for teachers. *Teaching Exceptional Children, 11,* 16–18.

**Mtka, P., & Gates, P.** (2010). Developing learner-centered education among secondary trainee teachers in Malawai: The dilemma of appropriation and application. *International Journal of Educational Development, 30,* 396–404.

**Mullis, I. V. S., Martin, M. O., Kennedy, A. M., & Foy, P.** (2007). *IEA's progress in international reading literacy study in primary school in 40 countries.* Chestnut Hill, MA: TIMSS & PIRLS International Study Center, Boston College.

**Murayama, K., & Elliott, A. J.** (2009). The joint influence of personal achievement goals and classroom goal structures on achievement-relevant outcomes. *Journal of Educational Psychology, 101,* 432–447.

**Murdock, T. B.** (2009). Achievement motivation in racial and ethnic context. In K. R. Wentzel & A. Wigfield (Eds.), *Handbook of motivation at school.* New York: Routledge.

**Murrell, P. C.** (2009). Identity, agency, and culture: Black achievement and educational attainment. In L. C. Tillman (Ed.), *The SAGE handbook of African American education.* Thousand Oaks, CA: Sage.

**Musial, D., Nieminen, G., Thomas, J., & Burke, K.** (2009). *Foundations of meaningful educational assessment.* New York: McGraw-Hill.

**Myers, D. G.** (2010). *Psychology* (9th ed). New York: Worth.

**Myerson, J., Rank, M. R., Raines, F. Q., & Schnitzler, M. A.** (1998). Race and general cognitive ability: The myth of diminishing returns in education. *Psychological Science, 9,* 139–142.

# N

**Naigles, L. R., & Swensen, L. D.** (2010). Syntactic supports for word learning. In E. Hoff & M. Shatz (Eds.), *Blackwell handbook of language development* (2nd ed.). New York: Wiley.

**Nakamoto, J., & Schwartz, D.** (2010). Is peer victimization associated with academic achievement? A meta-analytic review. *Social Development, 19,* 221–242.

**Nansel, T. R., Overpeck, M., Pilla, R. S., Ruan, W. J., Simons-Morton, B., & Scheldt, P.** (2001). Bullying behaviors among U.S. youth: Prevalence and association with psychosocial adjustment. *Journal of the American Medical Association, 285,* 2094–2100.

**Narváez, D., & Lapsley, D.** (Eds.). (2009). Personality, identity, and character: An interdisciplinary future. New York: Cambridge University Press.

**Narváez, D., Lynchard, N., Vaydich, J., & Mattan, B.** (2008, March). *Cheating, explicit recognition, implicit evaluation, moral judgment and honor code training.* Paper presented at the annual meeting of the Society for Research in Adolescence, Chicago.

**Nash, J. M.** (1997, February 3). Fertile minds. *Time,* pp. 50–54.

**Nathan, M. J., & Petrosino, A. J.** (2003). Expert blind spot among preservice teachers. *American Educational Research Journal, 40* (4), 905–928.

**National Academies, Advisors to the Nation on Science, Engineering, and Medicine.** (2009). *Rising above the gathering storm: Two years later.* Washington, DC: National Academies Press.

**National Assessment of Educational Progress.** (2000). *Reading achievement.* Washington in National Center for Education Statistics.

**National Assessment of Educational Progress.** (2005). *The nation's report card.* Washington, DC: U.S. Department of Education.

**National Assessment of Educational Progress.** (2007). *The nation's report card.* Washington, DC: National Center for Education Statistics.

**National Assessment of Educational Progress.** (2009). *The nation's report card 2009.* Washington, DC: U.S. Department of Education.

**National Association for the Education of Young Children.** (1996). NAEYC position statement: Responding to linguistic and cultural diversity—Recommendations for effective early childhood education. *Young Children, 51,* 4–12.

**National Association for the Education of Young Children.** (2009). *Developmentally appropriate practice in early childhood programs serving children from birth through age 8.* Washington, DC: NAEYC.

**National Center for Education Statistics.** (2003). Digest of Education Statistics, Table 52. Washington, DC: Author.

**National Center for Education Statistics.** (2006). *Children with disabilities in public schools.* Washington, DC: U.S. Department of Education.

**National Center for Education Statistics.** (2007). *The condition of education, 2007.* Washington, DC: U.S. Department of Education.

**National Center for Education Statistics.** (2007). *Highlights from PISA 2006: Performance of U.S. 15-year-old students in science and mathematics literacy in an international context.* Washington, DC: U.S. Department of Education.

**National Center for Education Statistics.** (2007). *Students with disabilities indicator 31,*

(p. 68). Washington. DC: U.S. Department of Education.

**National Center for Educational Statistics.** (2008). *Children and youth with disabilities in public schools.* Washington, DC: U.S. Department of Education.

**National Center for Education Statistics.** (2008a). *School Dropouts.* Washington, DC: U.S. Department of Education.

**National Center for Education Statistics.** (2009). *Comparative indicators of education in the United States and other G-8 countries: 2009.* Washington, DC: U.S. Department of Education.

**National Center for Learning Disabilities.** (2006). *Learning disabilities.* Retrieved March 6, 2006, from http://www.ncld.org/

**National Council for the Social Studies.** (1994). *Expectations of excellence: Curriculum standards for social studies.* Waldorf, MD: NCSS.

**National Council for the Social Studies.** (2000). *National standards for social studies teachers.* Baltimore: Author.

**National Council of Teachers of English/ International Reading Association** (1996). *Standards for the English Language Arts.* Urbana, IL: NCTE/IRA.

**National Council of Teachers of Mathematics.** (2000). *Principles and standards for school mathematics.* Reston, VA: NCTM.

**National Council of Teachers of Mathematics.** (2007a). *Navigating through number & operations in grades 3–5.* Reston, VA: NCTM.

**National Council of Teachers of Mathematics.** (2007b). *Mathematics teaching today: Professional standards for teaching mathematics, revision.* Reston, VA: NCTM.

**National Council of Teachers of Mathematics.** (2007c). *Making sense of mathematics: Children sharing and comparing solutions to challenging problems.* Reston, VA: NCTM.

**National Institutes of Health.** (1993). *Learning disabilities* NIH publication (No. 93–3611). Bethesda, MD: Author.

**National Reading Panel.** (2000). *Teaching children to read.* Washington, DC: National Institute of Child Health and Human Development.

**National Research Council.** (1999). *How people learn.* Washington, DC: National Academic Press.

**National Research Council.** (2000). *How people learn.* Washington, DC: National Academy Press.

**National Research Council.** (2001). *Knowing what students know.* Washington, DC: National Academies Press.

**National Research Council** (2005). *How students learn.* Washington, DC: National Academies Press.

**Neiman, S., DeVoe, J. F., & Chandler, K.** (2009). *Crime, violence, discipline, and safety in U.S. public schools.* Washington, DC: U.S. Department of Education.

**Nelson, C. A.** (2011). Brain development and behavior. In A. M. Rudolph, C. Rudolph, L. First, G. Lister, & A. A. Gersohon (Eds.), *Rudolph's pediatrics* (22nd ed.). New York: McGraw-Hill.

**Nelson, P. E., Pearson, J. C., & Titsworth, S.** (2011). *iSpeak* (3rd ed.). New York: McGraw-Hill.

**Neugarten, B. L.** (1988). *Policy issues for an aging society.* Paper presented at the meeting of the American Psychological Association, Atlanta.

**Neuhaus, E., Beauchaine, T. P., & Bernier, R.** (2010). Neurobiological correlates of social functioning in autism. *Clinical Psychology Review, 30,* 733–748.

**Neukrug, E. S., & Fawcett, R. C.** (2006). *Essentials of testing and assessment.* Belmont, CA: Wadsworth.

**Neukrug, E. S., & Fawcett, R. C.** (2010). *Essentials of testing and assessment* (2nd ed.). Boston: Cengage.

**Newby, T. J., Stepich, D., Lehman, J., Russell, J. D., & Leftwich, A. T.** (2011). *Educational technology for teaching and learning* (4th ed.). Boston: Allyn & Bacon.

**NICHD Early Child Care Research Network** (2005). Predicting individual differences in attention, memory, and planning in first graders from experiences at home, child care, and school. *Developmental Psychology, 41,* 99–114.

**NICHD Early Child Care Research Network** (2009). Family-peer linkages: The meditational role of attentional processes. *Social Development, 18,* 875–895.

**Nichols, J. D., & Miller, R. B.** (1994). Co-operative learning and student motivation. *Contemporary Educational Psychology, 19,* 167–178.

**Nie, Y., & Lau, S.** (2009). Complementary roles of care and behavioral control in classroom management: The self-determination theory perspective. *Contemporary Educational Psychology, 34,* 185–194.

**Nieto, S.** (2010). Multicultural education in the United States: Historical realities, ongoing challenges, and transformative possibilities. In J. A. Banks (Ed.), *The Routledge international companion to multicultural education.* New York: Routledge.

**Nikola-Lisa, W., & Burnaford, G. E.** (1994). A mosaic: Contemporary schoolchildren's images of teachers. In P. B. Joseph & G. E. Burnaford (Eds.), *Image of schoolteachers in twentieth century America.* New York: St. Martin's Press.

**Nintendo Wii.** (2008). Retrieved January 16, 2008, from http://www.nintendo.com/wii

**Nippold, M. A.** (2009). School-age children talk about chess: Does knowledge drive syntactic complexity? *Journal of Speech, Language, and Hearing Research., 38,* 131–142.

**Nitko, A. J., & Brookhart, S. M.** (2011). *Educational assessment of students* (6th ed.). Boston: Allyn & Bacon.

**Noddings, N.** (2007). *When school reform goes wrong.* New York: Teachers College Press.

**Noddings, N.** (2008). Caring and moral education. In L. Nucci & D. Narvaez (Eds.), *Handbook of moral and character education.* Clifton, NJ: Psychology Press.

**Noftle, E. E., & Fleeson, W.** (2010). Age differences in big five behavior averages and variabilities across the adult life span: Moving beyond retrospective, global summary accounts of personality. *Psychology and Aging, 25,* 95–107.

**Noftle, E. E., & Robins, R. W.** (2007). Personality predictors of academic outcomes: Big five correlates of GPA and SAT scores. *Journal of Personality and Social Psychology, 93,* 116–130.

**Nolen-Hoeksema, S.** (2011). *Abnormal psychology* (5th ed.). New York: McGraw-Hill.

**Norbury, C., Tomblin, B., & Bishop, D.** (Eds.). (2008). *Understanding developmental language disorders in children.* Milton Park, UK: Routledge.

**Norris, K. & Soloway, E.** (1999). Teachers & technology: A snapshot survey. University of North Texas, Texas Center for Educational Technology.

**Nucci, L.** (2006). Education for moral development. In M. Killen & J. Smetana (Eds.), *Handbook of moral development.* Mahwah, NJ: Erlbaum.

**Nusbaum, M., Alvarez, C., McFarlane, A., Gomez, F., Claro, S., & Radovic, D.** (2009). Technology as small group face-to-face collaborative learning. *Computers and Education, 52,* 147–153.

**Oakes, J.** (1990). *Multiplying inequalities: The effects of race, social class, and tracking on opportunities to learn mathematics and science.* Santa Monica: The RAND Corporation.

**Oakes, L., Cashon, C., Casasola, M., & Rakison, D.** (2010, in press). *Infant perception and cognition.* New York: Oxford University Press.

**O'Bannon, B. W., & Puckett, K.** (2010). *Preparing to use technology* (2nd ed.). Boston: Allyn & Bacon.

**Obenchain, K. M., & Morris, R. V.** (2011). *50 social studies strategies for K-8 classrooms* (3rd ed.). Boston: Allyn & Bacon.

**O'Connor, K.** (2009). *How to grade for learning, K–12.* Thousand Oaks, CA: Corwin.

**Ogbu, J., & Stern, P.** (2001). Caste status and intellectual development. In R. J. Sternberg & E. L. Grigorenko (Eds.), *Environmental effects on cognitive abilities.* Mahwah, NJ: Erlbaum.

**Ogle, D., & Beers, J. W.** (2009). *Engaging in the language arts.* Boston: Allyn & Bacon.

**Olenik, A.** (2009). Does education corrupt? Theories of grade inflation. *Educational Research Review, 4,* 156–164.

**Olsen, M., & Hergenhahn, B. R.** (2011). *Introduction to theories of personality* (8th ed.). Upper Saddle River, NJ: Pearson.

**Olson, M., & Hergenhahn, B. R.** (2009). Introduction to theories of learning (8th ed.). Upper Saddle River, NJ: Prentice-Hall.

**Olweus, D.** (1994). Bullying at school: Basic facts and effects of a school-based intervention program. *Journal of Child Psychology and Psychiatry, 33* (7), 1171–1190.

**Oosterhof, A.** (2009). *Developing and using classroom assessments* (4th ed.). Upper Saddle River, NJ: Prentice Hall.

**Ornstein, P. A., Coffman, J. L., & Grammer, J. K.** (2007, April). Teachers' memory-relevant conversations and children's memory performance. In P. A. Ornstein & F. J. Morrison (Chairs), *The impact of the classroom context on children's cognitive development: Memory, mathematics, and literacy.* Symposium conducted at the biennial meeting of the Society for Research in Child Development, Boston, MA.

**Ornstein, P. A., Coffman, J. L., & Grammer, J. K.** (2009). Learning to remember. In O. A. Barbarin & B. H. Wasik (Eds.), *Handbook of child development and early education.* New York: Guilford.

**Ornstein, P. A., Coffman, J., McCall, L., Grammer, J., & San Souci, P.** (2010). *Linking the classroom context and the development of children's memory skills.* In J. Meece & J. Eccles (Eds.), *Handbook of research on schools, schooling, and human development.* Oxford, UK: Routledge.

**Ornstein, P. A., & Light, L. L.** (2010). Memory development across the lifespan. In

W. F. Overton & R. M. Lerner (Eds.), *Handbook of Life-span Development.* New York: Wiley.

**O'Shea, M.** (2009). *Assessment throughout the year.* Upper Saddle River, NJ: Merrill.

**Osofsky, J. D.** (Ed.). (2007). *Young children and trauma.* New York: Guilford.

**Ostrov, J. M., Keating, C. F., & Ostrov, J. M.** (2004). Gender differences in preschool aggression during free play and structured interactions: An observational study. *Social Development, 13,* 255–277.

**Otten, L. J., Henson, R. N., & Rugg, M. D.** (2001). Depth of processing effects on neural correlates of memory encoding. *Brain, 124,* 399–412.

**Otto, B. W.** (2010). *Language development in early childhood* (3rd ed.). Upper Saddle River, NJ: Prentice Hall.

**Owens, R. E.** (2010). *Language disorders* (5th ed.). Boston: Allyn & Bacon.

## P

**Paivio, A.** (1971). *Imagery and verbal processes.* Fort Worth, TX: Harcourt Brace.

**Paivio, A.** (1986). *Mental representations: A dual coding approach.* New York: Oxford University Press.

**Palfrey, J., Sacco, D. T., Boyd, D., Debones, L., & Tatlock, J.** (2009). *Enhancing child safety and online technologies.* Cambridge, MA: Berkman Center for Internet Safety, Harvard University.

**Palincsar, A. S., & Brown, A. L.** (1984). Reciprocal teaching of comprehension-fostering and comprehension-monitoring activities. *Cognition and Instruction, 1,* 117–175.

**Pan, B. A., & Uccelli, P.** (2009). Semantic development. In J. Berko Gleason & N. Ratner (Eds.), *The development of language* (7th ed.). Boston: Allyn & Bacon.

**Panasan, M., & Nuangchalerm, P.** (2010). Learning outcomes of project-based and inquiry-based learning activities. *Journal of Social Sciences, 6,* 252–255.

**Pang, V. O.** (2005). *Multicultural education.* (3rd ed.). New York: McGraw-Hill.

**Papageorgi, I., & others** (2010). Perceptions and predictions of expertise in advanced musical learners. *Psychology of Music, 38,* 31–66.

**Papert, S.** (1980). *Mindstorms, children, computers, and powerful ideas.* New York: Basic Books.

**Parens, E., & Johnston, J.** (2009). Facts, values, and attention-deficit hyperactivity

disorder (ADHD): An update on the controversies. *Child and Adolescent Psychiatry and Mental Health, 3,* 1.

**Parkay, F. W., & Stanford, B. H.** (2010). *Becoming a teacher* (8th ed.). Upper Saddle River, NJ: Pearson.

**Partnership for 21st Century Skills.** (2008). Retrieved January 16, 2008, from www.21stcenturyskills.org/

**Partnership for 21st Century Skills.** (2010). *Learning for the 21st Century.* Retrieved January 15, 2010 from www.21stcentury-skills.org.

**Paus, T.** (2009). Brain development. In R. M. Lerner & L. Steinberg (Eds.), *Handbook of adolescent psychology* (3rd ed.). New York: Wiley.

**Paus, T., Toro, R., Leonard, G., Lerner, J. V., Lerner, R. M., Perron, M., Pike, G. B., Richer, L., Steinberg, L., Veillete, S., & Pausova, Z.** (2008). Morphological properties of the action-observation cortical network in adolescents with low and high resistance to peer influence. *Social Neuroscience, 3,* 303–316.

**Pavlov, I. P.** (1927). *Conditioned reflexes.* New York: Dover.

**Pawan, F.** (2008). Content-area teachers and scaffolded instruction for English Language Learners. *Teaching and Teacher Education: An International Journal of Research and Studies, 24,* 1450–1462.

**Payne, D. A.** (1997). *Applied educational assessment.* Belmont, CA: Wadsworth.

**Pearce, J. M., & Hall, G.** (2009). A model for stimulus generalization: Pavlovian conditioning. In D. Shanks (Ed.), *Psychology of learning.* Thousand Oaks, CA: Sage.

**Pearson, J. C., Nelson, P. E., Titsworth, S., & Harter, L.** (2011). *Human communication* (4th ed.). New York: McGraw-Hill.

**Pennington, B. F., & Bishop, D. V. M.** (2009). Relations among speech language, and reading disorders. *Annual Review of Psychology,* Vol. 60. Palo Alto, CA: Annual Reviews.

**Perry, K. E., Donohue, K. M., & Weinstein, R. S.** (2007). Teaching practices and the promotion of achievement and adjustment in first grade. *Journal of School Psychology, 45,* 269–292.

**Perry, N. E., Turner, J. C., & Meyer, D. K.** (2006). Classrooms as contexts for motivating learning. In P. A. Alexander & P. H. Winne (Eds.), *Handbook of educational psychology* (2nd ed.). Mahwah, NJ: Erlbaum.

**Persky, H. R., Daane, M. C., & Jin, Y.** (2003). *The nation's report card: Writing 2002.* Washington. DC: U.S. Department of Education.

**Peters, E. E.** (2010). Shifting to a student-centered science classroom: An exploration of teacher and student changes in perceptions and practices. *Journal of Science and Teacher Education, 21,* 329–349.

**Peters, J. M., & Stout, D. L.** (2011). *Science in elementary education* (11th ed.). Boston: Allyn & Bacon.

**Peterson, E. R., Rayner, S. G., & Armstrong, S. J.** (2009). Researching the psychology of cognitive style and learning style: Is there really a future? *Learning and Individual Differences, 19,* 518–523.

**Peterson, G. B.** (2008). Shaping. In N. J. Salkind (Ed.). *Encyclopedia of educational psychology.* Thousand Oaks, CA: Sage.

**Pham, A. V., & Carlson, J. S.** (2008). Family influences. In N. J. Salkind (Ed.), *Encyclopedia of educational psychology.* Thousand Oaks, CA: Sage.

**Phan, M. L., & Vicario, D. S.** (2010). Hemispheric differences in processing of vocalizations depend on early experience. *Proceedings of the National Academy of Sciences USA, 107,* 2301–2306.

**Philipsen, N. M., Johnson, A. D., & Brooks-Gunn, J.** (2009). Poverty, effects on social and emotional development. *International Encyclopedia of Education* (3rd ed.). St. Louis: Elsevier.

**Phillips, D. A., & Lowenstein, A.** (2011). Early care, education, and development. *Annual Review of Psychology, Vol. 62.* Palo Alto, CA: Annual Reviews.

**Phye, G. D., & Sanders, C. E.** (1994). Advice and feedback: Elements of practice for problem solving. *Contemporary Educational Psychology, 19,* 286–301.

**Piaget, J.** (1954). *The construction of reality in the child.* New York: Basic Books.

**Piaget, J., & Inhelder, B.** (1969). *The child's conception of space.* New York: Norton.

**Pianta, R. C., Belsky, J., Vandergrift, N., Houts, R., & Morrison, F. J.** (2008). Classroom effects on children's achievement trajectories in elementary school. *American Educational Research Journal, 45*(2), 365–397.

**Pintrich, P. R., & Schunk, D. H.** (2002). *Motivation in education: Theory, research, and applications* (2nd ed.). Upper Saddle River, NJ: Merrill/Prentice Hall.

**Pipe, M-E., & Salmon, K.** (2009). Memory development and the forensic context. In M. Courage & N. Cowan (Eds.), *The development of memory in infancy and childhood.* New York: Psychology Press.

**Pipkin, C. S., Vollmer, T. R., & Sloman, K. N.** (2010). Effects of treatment integrity

failures during differential reinforcement of alternative behavior: A translational model. *Journal of Applied Behavior Analysis, 43,* 43–70.

**Plano Clark, V. L., & Creswell, J. W.** (2010). *Understanding research: A consumer's guide.* Boston: Allyn & Bacon.

**Plog, A., Epstein, L., & Porter, W.** (2004, April). *Implementation fidelity: Lessons learned from the Bully-Proofing Your School Program.* Paper presented at the meeting of the National School Psychologists Association, Dallas, TX.

**Plomin, R., DeFries, J. C., McClearn, G. E., & McGuffin, P.** (2009). *Behavioral genetics* (5th ed.). New York: Worth.

**Pogrow, S.** (2009). Accelerate the learning of 4th and 5th graders born into poverty. *Phi Delta Kappan, 90,* 408–412.

**Pollack, W.** (1999). *Real boys.* New York: Owl Books.

**Pomerantz, E., & Moorman, E.** (2010). Parents' involvement in children's schooling: A context for children's development. In J. Meece & J. Eccles (Eds.), *Handbook of schools, schooling, and human development.* New York: Routledge.

**Ponitz, C. C., McCelland, M. M., Martinez, J. S., & Morrison, F. J.** (2009). A structured observation of behavioral self-regulation and its contribution to kindergarten outcomes. *Developmental Psychology, 45,* 605–619.

**Popham. W. J.** (2008). *Classroom assessment* (5th ed.). Boston: Allyn & Bacon.

**Popham, W. J.** (2011). *Classroom assessment* (6th ed.). Boston: Allyn & Bacon.

**Posamentier, A. S., Smith, B. S., & Stepelman, J.** (2010). *Teaching secondary mathematics* (8th ed.). Boston: Allyn & Bacon.

**Posner, M. I., & Rothbart, M. K.** (2007). *Educating the human brain.* Washington, DC: American Psychological Association.

**Poteete, H.** (2011). *Kids, computers, and learning.* Eugene, OR: ISTE.

**Prabhakar, H.** (2007). Hopkins Interactive Guest Blog: *The public health experience at Johns Hopkins.* Retrieved January 31, 2008, from http://hopkins.typepad.com/guest/2007/03/the_public_heal.html

**Prat-Sala, M., & Redford, P.** (2010). The interplay between motivation, self-efficacy, and approaches to studying. *British Journal of Educational Psychology, 80,* 283–305.

**Preiss, D., & Sternberg, R. J.** (Eds.). (2010). *From genes to context: New discoveries about learning from educational research and their applications.* New York: Springer.

**Presidential Task Force on Psychology and Education.** (1992). *Learner-centered psychological principles: Guidelines for school redesign and reform* (draft). Washington, DC: American Psychological Association.

**Pressley, M.** (1983). Making meaningful materials easier to learn. In M. Pressley & J. R. Levin (Eds.), *Cognitive strategy research: Educational applications.* New York: Springer-Verlag.

**Pressley, M.** (2007). Achieving best practices. In L. B. Gambrell, L. M. Morrow, & M. Pressley (Eds.), *Best practices in literary instruction.* New York: Guilford.

**Pressley, M., Allington, R., Wharton-McDonald, R., Block, C. C., & Morrow, L. M.** (2001). *Learning to read: Lessons from exemplary first grades.* New York: Guilford.

**Pressley, M., Borkowski, J. G., & Schneider, W.** (1989). Good information processing: What it is and what education can do to promote it. *International Journal of Educational Research, 13:* 857–867.

**Pressley, M., Cariligia-Bull, T., Deane, S., & Schneider, W.** (1987). Short-term memory, verbal competence, and age as predictors of imagery instructional effectiveness. *Journal of Experimental Child Psychology, 43,* 194–211.

**Pressley, M., Dolezal, S. E., Raphael, L. M., Welsh, L. M., Bogner, K., & Roehrig, A. D.** (2003). *Motivating primary grades teachers.* New York: Guilford.

**Pressley, M., & Harris, K. R.** (2006). Cognitive strategies instruction: From basic research to classroom instruction. In P. A. Alexander & P. H. Winne (Eds.), *Handbook of educational psychology* (2nd ed.). Mahwah, NJ: Erlbaum.

**Pressley, M., & Hilden, K.** (2006). Cognitive strategies. In W. Damon & R. Lerner (Eds.), *Handbook of child psychology* (6th ed.). New York: Wiley.

**Pressley, M., Levin, J. R., & McCormick, C. B.** (1980). Young children's learning of a foreign language vocabulary: A sentence variation of the keyword. *Contemporary Educational Psychology, 5,* 22–29.

**Pressley, M., & McCormick, C. B.** (2007). *Child and adolescent development for educators.* New York: Guilford.

**Pressley, M., Mohan, L., Fingeret, L., Reffitt, K., & Raphael Bogaert, L.** (2007b). Writing instruction in engaging and effective elementary settings. In S. Graham, C. A. MacArthur, & J. Fitzgerald (Eds.), *Best practices in writing instruction.* New York: Guilford.

**Pressley, M., Mohan, L., Raphael, L. M., & Fingeret, L.** (2007a). How does Bennett

Woods Elementary School produce such high reading and writing achievement? *Journal of Educational Psychology, 99*, 221–240.

**Pressley, M., Raphael, L., Gallagher, D., & DiBella, J.** (2004). Providence-St. Mel School: How a school that works for African-American students works. *Journal of Educational Psychology, 96*, 216–235.

**Pressley, M., Schuder, T., SAIL Faculty and Administration, German, J., & El-Dinary, P. B.** (1992). A researcher-educator collaborative interview study of transactional comprehension strategies instruction. *Journal of Educational Psychology, 84*, 231–246.

**Pressley, M., Wharto-McDonald, R., Allington, R., Block, C. C., Morrow, H. L., Tracey, D., Baker, K., Brooks, G., Cronin, J., Nelson, E., & Woo, D.** (2001). A study of effective first grade literacy instruction. *Scientific Studies of Reading, 15*, 35–58.

**Pretz, J. E.** (2008). Intuition versus analysis: Strategy and experience in complex everyday problem solving. *Memory and Cognition, 36*, 554–566.

**Prinsen, F. R., Volman, M. L. L., Terwel, J., & van den Eeden, P.** (2009). Effects on participation of an experimental CSCL-program to support elaboration: Do all students benefit? *Computers and Education, 52*, 113–125.

**Prinstein, M. J., Rancourt, D., Guerry, J. D., & Browne, C. B.** (2009). Peer reputations and psychological adjustment. In K. H. Rubin, W. M. Bukowksi, & B. Laursen (Eds.), *Handbook of peer interactions, relationships, and groups.* New York: Guilford.

**Pruett, M. K., & Barker, R.** (2009a). Children of divorce: New trends and ongoing dilemmas. In J. Bray (Ed.), *Family Handbook of Psychology.* Washington DC.: American Psychological Association.

**Pruett, M. K., & Barker, R.** (2009b). Influencing co-parenting effectiveness after divorce: What works and how it works. In M. Schulz, P. Kerig, M. K. Pruett, & R. Parke (Eds.), *Feathering the nest: Couple relationships, couples' interventions and children's development.* Washington DC: American Psychological Association.

**Pryor, J. H., Hurtado, S., DeAngelo, L., Sharkness, J., Romero, L. C., Korn, W. S., & Tran, S.** (2008). *The American freshman: National norms fall 2008.* Los Angeles: Higher Education Research Institute, UCLA.

**PSU** (2006). Anchored instruction. Retrieved January 6, 2006, from www.ed.psu.edu/nasa/achrtxt.html

**Putallaz, M., Grimes, C. L., Foster, K. J., Kupersmidt, J. B., Clie, J. D., & Dearing, K.** (2007). Overt and relational aggression and victimization: multiple perspectives within the school setting. *Journal of School Psychology, 45*, 523–547.

## Q

**Quality Counts.** (2001). *A better balance: Standards, tests, and the tools to succeed.* Bethesda, MD: Education Week on the Web.

**Quiamzade, A., Mugny, G., & Darnon, C.** (2009). The coordination of problem solving strategies: When low competence sources exert more influence on task processing than high competence sources. *British Journal of Social Psychology, 48*, 159–182.

**Quinn, P. C.** (2009). Concepts are not just for objects: Categorization of spatial relation information by infants. In D. H. Rakison & L. M. Oakes (Eds.), *Early category and concept development.* New York: Oxford University Press.

**Quinn, P. C.** (2011). Born to categorize. In U. Goswami (Ed.), *Wiley-Blackwell handbook of childhood cognitive development.* New York: Wiley.

## R

**Rabiner, D. L., Murray, D. W., Skinner, A. T., & Malone, P. S.** (2010). A randomized trial of two promising computer-based interventions for students with attention difficulties. *Journal of Abnormal Child Psychology, 52*, 856–871.

**Racine, T. P.** (2011). The development of representation and concepts. In R. M. Lerner & W. F. Overton (Eds.), *Handbook of life-span development, Vol. 1.* New York: Wiley.

**Raffaelli, M., & Ontai, L. L.** (2004). Gender socialization in Latino families: Results from two retrospective studies. *Sex Roles, 50*, 287–299.

**Rait, S., Monsen, J. J., & Squires, G.** (2010). Cognitive behavior therapies and their implications for applied educational psychology. *Educational Psychology in Practice, 26*, 105–122.

**Rakoczy, H., Warneken, F., & Tomasello, M.** (2007). "This way!", "No! That way!"—3-year-olds know that two people can have mutually incompatible desires. *Cognitive Development, 22*, 47–68.

**Ramey, C. T., Bryant, D. M., Campbell, F. A., Sparling, J. J., & Wasik, B. H.** (1988). Early intervention for high-risk children. The Carolina Early Intervention Program. In

R. H. Price, E. L. Cowen, R. P. Lorion, & J. Ramos-McKay (Eds.), *14 ounces of prevention.* Washington, DC: American Psychological Association.

**Ramey, S. L., Ramey, C. T., & Lanzi, R. G.** (2009). Early intervention: Background, research findings, and future directions. In J. W. Jacobson, J. A. Mulick, & J. Rojahn (Eds.). *Handbook of Intellectual and Developmental Disabilities.* New York: Springer.

**Randolph, C. H., & Evertson, C. M.** (1995). Managing for learning: Rules, roles, and meanings in a writing class. *Journal of Classroom Instruction, 30*, 17–25.

**Rapee, R. M., Hudson, J. L., & Schiering, C. A.** (2009). Anxiety disorders during childhood and adolescence: origins and treatment. *Annual Review of Clinical Psychology, 5.* Palo Alto, CA: Annual Reviews.

**Rapee, R. M., Schniering, C. A., & Hudson, J. L.** (2009). Anxiety disorders in children and adolescence. *Annual review of clinical psychology, Vol. 5.* Palo Alto, CA: Annual Reviews.

**Rasinski, T., Homan, T., & Biggs, S.** (2009). Fluency in learning to read for meaning: Going beyond repeated readings. *Reading & Writing Quarterly, 25*, 192–204.

**Ratner, N. B.** (2009). Atypical language development. In J. Berko Gleason (Ed.), *The development of language* (7th ed.). Boston: Allyn & Bacon.

**Rayner, S. G. & Peterson, E. R.** (2009). Re-affirming style as an individual difference—Toward a global paradigm or knowledge diaspora? In L. F. Zhang & R. J. Sternberg (Eds.), Perspectives on the nature of intellectual styles. New York: Springer.

**Re: Learning by Design.** (2000). *Design resource center.* Re: Learning by Design. Retrieved July 16, 2002, from http://www .relearning.org

**Redelmeier, D. A.** (2005). Improving patient care: The cognitive psychology of missed diagnoses. *Annals of Internal Medicine, 142*, 115–120.

**Reed, D. D., Luiselli, J. K., Morizio, L. C., & Child, S. N.** (2010). Sequential modification and the identification of instructional components occasioning self-injurious behavior. *Child & Family Behavior Therapy, 32*, 1–16.

**Reed, S. K.** (2010). *Cognition* (8th ed.). Boston: Cengage.

**Regalado, M., Sareen, H., Inkelas, M., Wissow, L. S., & Halfon, N.** (2004). Parents' discipline of young children: Results from the National Survey of Early Childhood Health. *Pediatrics, Supplement, 113*, 1952–1958.

**Reid, G., Fawcett, A., Manis, F., & Siegel, L.** (2009). *The SAGE handbook of dyslexia.* Thousand Oaks, CA: Sage.

**Reksten, L. E.** (2009). *Sustaining extraordinary student achievement.* Thousand Oaks, CA: Corwin Press.

**Renne, C. H.** (1997). *Excellent classroom management.* Belmont, CA: Wadsworth.

**Renzulli, J. S.** (1998). A rising tide lifts all ships: Developing the gifts and talents of all students. *Phi Delta Kappan, 80,* 1–15.

**Rescorla, R. A.** (2009). A theory of Pavlovian Conditioning: Variations in the effectiveness of reinforcement and nonreinforcement. In D. Shanks (Ed.), *Psychology of learning.* Thousand Oaks, CA: Sage.

**Reyna, V., & Farley, F.** (2006). Risk and rationality in adolescent decision-making. Implications for theory, practice, and public policy. *Psychological Science in the Public Interest, 7,* 1–44.

**Reyna, V. F., & Rivers, S. F.** (2008). Current theories of risk and rational decision making *Developmental Review, 28,* 1–11.

**Rhodes, J. E., & Lowe, S. R.** (2009). Mentoring in adolescence. In R. M. Lerner & L. Steinberg (Eds.), *Handbook of adolescent psychology* (3rd ed.). New York: Wiley.

**Ricco, R. B.** (2011). The development of deductive reasoning across the life span. In R. M. Lerner & W. F. Overton (Eds.), *Handbook of life-span development. Vol. 1.* New York: Wiley.

**Rice, K. G., Leever, B. A., Noggle, C. A., & Lapsley, D. A.** (2007). Perfectionism and depressive symptoms in early adolescence. *Psychology in the Schools. 44,* 139–156.

**Rips, L. J.** (2008). Logical approaches to human deductive reasoning. In J. E. Adler & L. J. Rips (Eds.). *Reasoning.* New York: Cambridge University Press.

**Ritchart, R., Turner, T., & Hadar, L.** (2009). Undercovering students' thinking about thinking using concept maps. *Metacognition and Learning, 4,* 145–159.

**Ritchie, S., Maxwell, K. L., & Bredekamp, S.** (2009). Rethinking early schooling: Using developmental science to transform children's early school experiences. In O. A. Barbarin & B. H. Wasik (Eds.), *Handbook of child development and early education.* New York: Guilford.

**Rittle-Johnson, B.** (2006). Promoting transfer: Effects of self-explanation and direct instruction. *Child Development, 77,* 1–15.

**Rivera, L. M.** (2010). Acculturation. In J. G. Ponterotto & others (Eds.), *Handbook of multicultural counseling.* Thousand Oaks, CA: Sage.

**Roberts, B. W., Jackson, J. J. Fayard, J. V. Edmonds, G., & Meints, J.** (2009). Conscientiousness. In M. Leary & R. Hoyle (Eds.), *Handbook of individual differences in social behavior.* New York: Guilford.

**Roberts, B. W., Wood, D., & Caspi, A.** (2008 press). Personality development. In O. P. John, R. W. Robins, & L. A. Pervin (Eds.), *Handbook of personality* (3rd ed.). New York: Guilford.

**Roberts, R. L., Moore, K. M., & Kellough, R. D.** (2011). *Resource guide for elementary school teaching* (7th ed.). Boston: Allyn & Bacon.

**Robins, R. W., Trzesniewski, K. H., Tracey, J. L., Potter, J., & Gosling, S. D.** (2002). Age differences in self-esteem from age 9 to 90. *Psychology and Aging, 17,* 423–434.

**Robinson, N. M.** (2008). The social world of gifted children and youth. In S. I. Pfeiffer (Ed.), *Handbook of giftedness in children.* New York: Springer.

**Roblyer, M. D., & Doering, A. H.** (2010). *Integrating educational technology into teaching* (5th ed.). Boston: Allyn & Bacon.

**Rodriquez, E. T., Tamis-LeMonda, C. S., Spellman, M. E., Pan, B. A., Riakes, H., Lugo-Gil, J., & Luze, G.** (2009, in press). The formative role of home literacy experiences across the first three years of life in children from low-income families. *Journal of Applied Developmental Psychology.*

**Rogoff, B.** (2003). *The cultural nature of human development.* New York: Oxford University Press.

**Rogoff, B., Moore, L., Najafi, B., Dexter, A., Correa-Chavez, M., & Solis, J.** (2007). Children's development of cultural repertoires through participation in everyday routines and practices. In J. E. Grusec & P. D. Hastings (Eds.), *Handbook of socialization.* New York: Guilford.

**Rogoff, B., Turkanis, C. G., & Barlett, L.** (Eds.). (2001). *Learning together. Children and adults in a school community.* New York: Oxford University Press.

**Rohrbeck, C. A., Ginsburg-Block, M. D., Fantuzzo, J. W., & Miller, T. R.** (2003). Peer-assisted learning interventions with elementary school students: A meta-analytic review. *Journal of Educational Psychology, 95,* 240–257.

**Rondou, P., Haegeman, G., & Van Craenenbroeck, K.** (2010, in press). The dopamine D4 receptor: biochemical and signaling properties. *Cellular and Molecular Life Sciences.*

**Rosch, E. H.** (1973). On the internal structure of perceptual and semantic categories. In T. E. Moore (Ed.), *Cognition and the acquisition of language.* New York: Academic Press.

**Roscoe, R. D., & Chi, M. T. H.** (2008). Tutor learning: The role of explaining and responding to questions. *Instructional Science, 36,* 321–350.

**Rosenberg, M. S., Westling, D. L., & McLeskey, J.** (2011). *Special education for today's teachers* (2nd ed.). Upper Saddle River, NJ: Merrill.

**Rosenblum, S., Aloni, T., & Josman, N.** (2010). Relationships between handwriting performance and organizational abilities among children with and without dysgraphia: A preliminary study. *Research in Developmental Disabilities, 31,* 502–509.

**Rosenshine, B.** (1971). *Teaching behaviors and student achievement.* London: National Foundation for Educational Research.

**Rosenzweig, M. R., & Bennett, E. L.** (2009). The role of deliberate practice in the acquisition of expert performance. In D. Shanks (Ed.), *Psychology of learning.* Thousand Oaks, CA: Sage.

**Rothbart, M. K.** (2004). Temperament and the pursuit of an integrated developmental psychology. *Merrill-Palmer Quarterly, 50,* 492–505.

**Rothbart, M. K.** (2007). Temperament, development, and personality. *Current Directions in Psychological Science, 16,* 207–212.

**Rothbart, M. K., & Bates, J. E.** (2006). Temperament. In W. Damon & R. Lerner (Eds.), *Handbook of child psychology* (6th ed.). New York: Wiley.

**Rowe, M.** (1986). Wait time: Slowing down may be a way of speeding up! *Journal of Teacher Education, 37,* 43–50.

**Rowley, J. B.** (2009). *Becoming a high-performance mentor.* Thousand Oaks, CA: Corwin Press.

**Rowley, S., Kurtz-Costes, B., & Cooper, S. M.** (2010). The role of schooling in ethnic minority achievement and attainment. In J. Meece & J. Eccles (Eds.), *Handbook of research on school, schooling, and human development.* New York: Routledge.

**Rubie-Davies, C. M.** (2007). Classroom interactions: Exploring the practices of high- and low-expectation teachers. *British Journal of Educational Psychology, 77,* 289–306.

**Rubin, K. H., Bukowski, W., & Parker, J.** (2006). Peer interactions, relationships, and groups. In W. Damon & R. Lerner (Eds.), *Handbook of child psychology* (6th ed.). New York: Wiley.

**Rubin, K. H., & Coplan, R. J. (Eds.)** (2010). *The development of shyness and social withdrawal.* New York: Guilford.

**Rueda, R., & Yaden, D. B.** (2006). The literacy education of linguistically and culturally diverse young children: An overview of outcomes, assessment, and large-scale interventions. In B. Spodek & O. N. Saracho (Eds.), *Handbook of research on the education of young children.* Mahwah, NJ: Erlbaum.

**Rumberger, R. W.** (1995). Dropping out of middle school: A multilevel analysis of students and schools. *American Education Research Journal, 3,* 583–625. New York: Wiley.

**Runco, M. & Spritzker, S. (Eds.)** (2011, in press). Encyclopedia of Creativity. New York. Elsevier.

**Rushton, J. P., & Ankney, C. D.** (2009). Whole brain size and general mental ability: A review. *International Journal of Neuroscience, 119,* 691–731.

**Ryan, K., & Cooper, J. M.** (2010). *Those who can, teach* (12th ed.). Boston: Cengage.

**Ryan, R. M., & Deci, E. L.** (2009). Promoting self-determined school engagement, motivation, learning, and well-being. In K. R. Wentzel & A. Wigfield (Eds.). *Handbook of motivation at school.* New York: Routledge.

**Rykhlevskaia, E., Uddin, L. Q., Kondos, L., & Menon, V.** (2010, in press). Neuroanatomical correlates of developmental dyscalculia: Combined evidence from morphometry and tractography. *Frontiers in Human Neuroscience.*

**Ryum, T., Stiles, T. C., Svartberg, M., & McCullough, L.** (2010). The effects of therapist competence in assigning homework in cognitive therapy with cluster C personality disorders: Results from a randomized controlled trial. *Cognitive and Behavioral Practice, 17,* 283–289.

## S

**Saarni, C.** (1999). *The development of emotional competence.* New York: Guilford.

**Saarni, C., Campos, J., Camras, L. A., & Witherington, D.** (2006). Emotional development. In W. Damon & R. Lerner (Eds.), *Handbook of child psychology* (6th ed.).

**Sabers, D. S., Cushing, K. S., & Berliner, D. C.** (1991). Differences among teachers in a task characterized by simultaneity, multi-dimensionality, and immediacy. *American Educational Research Journal, 28,* 63–88.

**Sachs, J.** (2009). Communication development in infancy. In J. Berko Gleason & N. B. Ratner (Eds.), *The development of language* (7th ed.). Boston: Allyn & Bacon.

**Sackett, P. R., Borneman, M. J., & Connelly, B. S.** (2009). Responses to issues raised about validity, bias, and fairness in high-stakes testing. *American Psychologist, 64,* 285–287.

**Sadker, D. M., Sadker, M. P., & Zittleman, K. R.** (2010). *Teachers, schools, and society* (9th ed.). New York: McGraw-Hill.

**Sadker, M. P., & Sadker, D.** (1994). *Failing at fairness: How America's schools cheat girls.* New York: Scribners.

**Sadker, M. P., & Sadker, D. M.** (2005). *Teachers, schools, and society* (7th ed.). New York: McGraw-Hill.

**Saenz, L. M., Fuchs, L. S., & Fuchs, D.** (2005). Peer-assisted learning strategies for English language learners with learning disabilities. *Exceptional Children. 71,* 231–247.

**Saifer, S.** (2007, August 29). *Tools of the Mind—A Vygotskian-inspired early childhood curriculum.* Paper presented at the 17th Annual Conference of the European Early Childhood Education Research Association, Prague.

**Salend, S. J.** (2010). *Classroom testing and assessment for all students.* Thousand Oaks, CA: Corwin.

**Salmivalli, C., & Peets, K.** (2009). Bullies, victims, and bully–victim relationships in middle childhood and adolescence. In K. H. Rubin, W. M. Bukowski, & B. Laursen (Eds.), *Handbook of peer interactions, relationships, and groups.* New York: Guilford.

**Salomon, G., & Perkins, D.** (1989). Rocky roads to transfer: Rethinking mechanisms of a neglected phenomenon. *Educational Psychologist, 24,* 113–142.

**Salovy, P., & Mayer, J. D.** (1990). Emotional intelligence. *Imagination, Cognition, and Personality, 9,* 185–211.

**Sanger, M. N.** (2008). What we need to prepare teachers for the moral nature of their work. *Journal of Curriculum Studies, 40,* 169–185.

**Sanson, A. V., & Rothbart, M. K.** (1995). Child temperament and parenting. In M. H. Bornstein (Ed.), *Handbook of parenting.* Mahwah, NJ: Erlbaum.

**Sanson, A. V., & Rothbart, M. K.** (2002). Child temperament and parenting. In M. H. Bornstein (Ed.), *Handbook of parenting.* Mahwah, NJ: Erlbaum.

**Santrock, J. W., & Halonen, J. A.** (2009). *Your guide to college success* (6th ed.). Belmont, CA: Wadsworth.

**Savage, R. S., Abrami, P., Hipps, G., & Deault, L.** (2009). A randomized controlled trial study of the ABRACADABRA reading intervention program in grade 1. *Journal of Educational Psychology, 101,* 590–604.

**Savage, T. V., & Savage, M. K.** (2009). *Successful classroom management and discipline.* Thousand Oaks, CA: Sage.

**Sax, G.** (1997). *Principles of educational and psychological measurement and evaluation* (4th ed). Belmont, CA: Wadsworth.

**Scanlon, D. M., Anderson, K. L., & Sweeney, J. M.** (2010). *Early intervention for reading difficulties: The interactive strategies approach.* New York: Guilford.

**Scardamalia, M., & Bereiter, C.** (1994). Computer support for knowledge-building communities. *Journal of the Learning Sciences, 3* (3), 265–283.

**Scardamalia, M., & Bereiter, C.** (2006). Knowledge building: theory, pedagogy, and technology. In R. K. Sawyer (Ed.), *Cambridge handbook of learning sciences.* New York: Oxford University Press.

**Scardamalia, M., Bereiter, C., & Lamon, M.** (1994). The CSILE Project: Trying to bring the classroom into the world. In K. McGilly (Ed.), *Classroom lessons.* Cambridge, MA: MIT Press.

**Scarlett, W. G., Ponte, I. C., & Singh, J. P.** (2009). Approaches to behavior and classroom management. Thousand Oaks, CA: Sage.

**Scarr, S., & Weinberg, R. A.** (1983). The Minnesota Adoption Studies: Genetic differences and malleability. *Child Development, 54,* 253–259.

**Schacter, D. L.** (2001). *The seven sins of memory.* Boston: Houghton Mifflin.

**Schaie, K. W.** (2010). Adult intellectual abilities. *Corsini encyclopedia of psychology.* New York: Wiley.

**Schaie, K. W.** (2011, in press). *Developmental influences on adult intellectual development.* New York: Oxford University Press.

**Schauble, L., Beane, D. B., Coates, G. D., Martin, L. M. W., & Sterling, P. V.** (1996). Outside classroom walls: Learning in informal environments. In L. Schauble & R. Glaser (Eds.), *Innovations in learning.* Mahwah, NJ: Erlbaum.

**Schiefele, U.** (2009). Situational and individual interest. In K. R. Wentzel & A. Wigfield (Eds.), *Handbook of motivation at school.* New York: Routledge.

**Schmader, T., Forbes, C. E., Zhang, S., & Mendes, W. B.** (2009). A metacognitive perspective on cognitive deficits experienced in intellectually threatening environments. *Personality and Social Psychology Bulletin, 35,* 584–596.

Schmidt, J. A. (2011, in press). Flow in Education. In B. McGaw, E. Baker, P. P. Peterson (Eds.), *International Encyclopedia of Education,* (3rd ed.). London, Elsevier.

Schmidt, J., Shumow, L., & Kackar, H. (2007). Adolescents' participation in service activities and its impact on academic, behavioral, and civic outcomes. *Journal of Youth and Adolescence, 36,* 127–140.

Schnaar, R. L., & Lopez, P. H. (2009, in press). Myelin-associated glycoprotein and its axonal receptors. *Journal of Neuroscience Research.*

Schneider, B., & Coleman, J. S. (1993). *Parents, their children, and schools.* Boulder, CO: Westview Press.

Schneider, M., Dunton, G. F., Cooper, D. M. (2008). Physical activity and physical self-concept among sedentary adolescent females: An intervention study. *Psychology of Sport and Exercise, 9,* 1–14.

Schneider, W. (2004). Memory development in childhood. In U. Goswami (Ed.), *Blackwell handbook of childhood cognitive development.* Malden, MA: Blackwell.

Schneider, W. (2011). Memory development in childhood. In U. Goswami (Ed.), *Wiley-Blackwell handbook of childhood cognitive development* (2nd ed.). New York: Wiley Blackwell.

Schneider, W., & Bjorklund, D. F. (1998). Memory. In W. Damon (Ed.), *Handbook of child psychology* (5th ed.). New York: Wiley.

Schneider, W., & Pressley, M. (1997). *Memory development between 2 and 20* (2nd ed.). Mahwah, NJ: Erlbaum.

Schraw, G., Wadkins, T., & Olafson, L. (2007). Doing the things we do: A grounded theory of academic procrastination. *Journal of Educational Psychology, 99,* 12–25.

Schrum, L., & Berenfeld, B. (1997). *Teaching and learning in the information age: A guide to telecommunications.* Boston: Allyn & Bacon.

Schultz, D. P., & Schultz, S. E. (2009). *Theories of personality* (9th ed.). Belmont, CA: Wadsworth.

Schunk, D. H. (2001). Social cognitive theory and self-regulated learning. In B. J. Zimmerman & D. H. Schunk (Eds.), *Self-regulated learning and achievement* (2nd ed.). Mawah, NJ: Erlbaum.

Schunk, D. H. (2008). *Learning theories: An educational perspective* (5th ed.). Upper Saddle River, NJ: Prentice Hall.

Schunk, D. H. (2011, in press). *Learning theories: An educational perspective* (6th ed.). Upper Saddle River, NJ: Prentice Hall.

Schunk, D. H., & Pajares, F. (2009). Self-efficacy theory. In K. R. Wentzel & A. Wigfield (Eds.), *Handbook of motivation at school.* New York: Routledge.

Schunk, D. H., Pintrich, P. R., & Meece, J. L. (2008). *Motivation in education: Theory, research, and applications* (3rd ed). Upper Saddle River, NJ: Prentice Hall.

Schunk, D. H., & Rice, J. M. (1989). Learning goals and children's reading comprehension. *Journal of Reading Behavior, 23,* 351–364.

Schunk, D. H., & Swartz, C. W. (1993). Goals and progressive feedback: Effects on self-efficacy and writing achievement. *Contemporary Educational Psychology, 18,* 337–354.

Schunk, D. H., & Zimmerman, B. J. (2006). Competence and control beliefs: Distinguishing the means and ends. In P. A. Alexander & P. H. Winne (Eds.), *Handbook of educational psychology* (2nd ed.). Mahwah, NJ: Erlbaum.

Schwartz, D., Kelly, B. M., Duong, M., & Badaly, D. (2010). Contextual perspective on intervention and prevention efforts for bully/victim problems. In E. M. Vernberg & B. K. Biggs (Eds.), *Preventing and treating bullying and victimization.* New York: Oxford University Press.

Schwartz, D. L., Bransford, J. D., & Sears, D. (2005). Efficiency and innovation in transfer. In J. Mestre (Ed.), *Transfer of learning: Research and perspectives.* Greenwich, CT: Information Age Publishing.

Schweinhart, L. J., Montie, J., Xiang, Z., Barnett, W. S., Belfield, C. R., & Nores, M. (2005). *Lifetime effects: The High/Scope Perry Preschool study through age 40.* Ypsilanti, MI: High/Scope Press.

Sears, D. A. (2006, June). Effects of innovation versus efficiency tasks on recall and transfer in individual and collaborative learning contents. In Proceedings of the 7th International Conference on Learning Sciences, pp. 681–687.

Sears, D. A. (2008). Unpublished review of J. W. Santrock's, *Educational Psychology* (4th ed.). New York: McGraw-Hill.

Seaton, E. K., Yip, T., & Sellers, R. M. (2009). A longitudinal examination of racial identity and racial discrimination among African American adolescents. *Child Development, 80,* 406–417.

Segers, E., & Verhoeven, L. (2009). Learning in a sheltered environment: The use of WebQuests. *Learning and Instruction, 19,* 423–432.

Selfhout, M., & others (2010). Emerging late adolescent friendship networks and Big Five personality traits: a social network approach. *Journal of Personality, 78,* 509–538.

Sensenbaugh, R. (1995). Reading Recovery. *ERIC Clearinghouse on Reading, English, and Communication Digest, No. 106.*

Serra, M. J., & Metcalfe, J. (2009). Effective implementation of metacognition. In D. J. Hacker, J. Dunlosky, & A. C. Graesser (Eds.), *Handbook of metacognition in education.* New York: Psychology Press.

Shalev, R. S. (2004). Developmental dyscalculia. *Journal of Child Neurology, 19,* 765–771.

Shanks, D. (Ed.). (2009). *Psychology of learning.* Thousand Oaks, CA: Sage.

Sharan, S. (1990). Cooperative learning and helping behavior in the multi-ethnic classroom. In H. C. Foot, M. J. Morgan, & R. H. Shute (Eds.), *Children helping children.* New York: Wiley.

Sharan, S., & Sharan, S. (1992). *Expanding cooperative learning through group investigation.* New York: Teachers College Press.

Sharan, S., & Shaulov, A. (1990). Cooperative learning, motivation to learn, and academic achievement. In S. Sharan (Ed.), *Cooperative learning.* New York: Praeger.

Shatz, M. (2010). On the development of the field of language. In E. Hoff & M. Shatz (Eds.), *Blackwell handbook of language development.* New York: Wiley.

Shaul, M. S. (2007). *No Child Left Behind Act: States face challenges measuring academic growth that education's initiatives may help address.* Washington, DC: Government Accountability Office.

Shaw, P., Eckstrand, K., Sharp, W., Blumenthal, J., Lerch, J. P., Greenstein, D., Clasen, L., Evans, A., Giedd, J., & Rapoport, J. L. (2007). Attention-deficit/hyperactivity disorder is characterized by a delay in cortical maturation. *Proceedings of the National Academy of Sciences, 104* (49), 19649–19654.

Shaywitz, S. E., Morris, R., & Shaywitz, B. A. (2008). The education of dyslexic children from childhood to young adulthood. *Annual Review of Psychology, 59.* Palo Alto, CA: Annual Reviews.

Shea, S. E., & Coyne, L. W. (2008). Parenting styles. In N. J. Salkind (Ed.), *Encyclopedia of educational psychology.* Thousand Oaks, CA: Sage.

Shen, J., Poppink, Cui, Y., & Fan, G. (2007). Lesson planning: A practice of professional responsibility and development. *Educational Horizons, 85,* 248–258.

**Shen. J., Zhen, J., & Poppink, S.** (2007). Open lessons: A practice to develop a learning community for teachers. *Educational Horizons, 85,* 181–191.

**Shen, Y., & others** (2010). Clinical genetic testing for patients with autism spectrum disorders. *Pediatrics, 125,* e727–e735.

**Shernoff, D. J.** (2001). *The experience of student engagement in high school classrooms: A phenomenological perspective.* Unpublished doctoral dissertation, University of Chicago.

**Shernoff, D. J.** (2009, April). *Flow in educational contexts: Creating optimal learning environments.* Paper presented at the meeting of the Society for Research in Child Development, Denver.

**Shernoff, D. J., & Csikszentmihalyi, M.** (2009). Flow in schools: Cultivating engaged learners and optimal learning environments. In R. C. Gilman, E. S. Heubner & M. J. Furlong (Eds.), *Handbook of Positive Psychology in Schools* (pp. 131–145). New York: Routledge.

**Shernoff, D. J., Csikszentmihalyi, M., Schneider, B., & Shernoff, E. S.** (2003). Student engagement in high school classrooms from the perspective of flow Theory. *School Psychology Quarterly, 18*(2), 158–176.

**Shernoff, D. J., & Hoogstra, L.** (2001). Continuing Motivation beyond the High School Classroom. *New Directions for Child and Adolescent Development, 93,* 73–87.

**Shernoff, D. J., & Vandell, D. L.** (2007). Engagement in after-school program activities: Quality of experience from the perspective of participants. *Journal of Youth and Adolescence, 36,* 891–903.

**Shields, P. M., & others** (2001). *The status of the teaching profession 2001.* Santa Cruz, CA: The Center for the Future of Teaching and Learning.

**Shields, S. A.** (1991). Gender in the psychology of emotion: A selective research review. In K. T. Strongman (Ed.), *International review of studies on emotion, Vol. 1.* New York: Wiley.

**Shindler, J.** (2010). *Transformative classroom management.* San Francisco: Jossey-Bass.

**Shiraev, E., & Levy, D.** (2007). *Cross-cultural psychology* (3rd ed.). Belmont, CA: Wadsworth.

**Shiraev, E., & Levy, D. A.** (2010). *Cross-cultural psychology* (4th ed.). Boston: Allyn & Bacon.

**Shirts, R. G.** (1997). *BAFA, BAFA, a cross-cultural simulation.* Del Mar, CA: SIMILE II.

**Shonkoff, J. P.** (2010). Building a new biodevelopmental framework to guide the future of early childhood policy. *Child Development, 81,* 357–367.

**Shorall, C.** (2009). *What every teacher should know about the Praxis II test* (3rd Ed.). Upper Saddle River, NJ: Prentice Hall.

**Short, E. L., & others** (2010). Counseling immigrants and refugees. In J. G. Ponterotto & others (Eds.), *Handbook of multicultural counseling* (3rd ed.). Thousand Oaks, CA: Sage.

**Shwalb, D. W., & others** (2010). East and Southeast Asia: Japan, South Korea, Vietnam, and Indonesia. In M. H. Bornstein (Ed.), *Handbook of developmental cultural science.* New York: Psychology Press.

**Siegal, M., & Surian, L.** (2010). Conversational understanding in young children. In E. Hoff & M. Shatz (Eds.), *Blackwell handbook of language development.* New York: Wiley.

**Siegel, L. S.** (2003). Learning disabilities. In I. B. Weiner (Ed.), *Handbook of psychology Vol. 7.* New York: Wiley.

**Siegler, R. S.** (1998). *Children's thinking* (3rd ed.). Upper Saddle River, NJ: Prentice Hall.

**Siegler, R. S.** (2002). Microgenetic studies of self-explanation. In N. Garnott & J. Parziale (Eds.), *Microdevelopment: A process-oriented perspective for studying development and learning.* New York: Cambridge University Press.

**Siegler, R. S.** (2007). Cognitive variability. *Developmental Science, 10,* 104–109.

**Siegler, R. S.** (2009). Improving preschoolers' number sense using information-processing theory. In O. A. Barbarin & B. H. Wasik (Eds.), *Handbook of child development and early education.* New York: Oxford University Press.

**Siegler, R. S., & Robinson, M.** (1982). The development of numerical understandings. In H. W. Reese & L. P. Litsitt (Eds.), *Advances in child development and behavior, Vol. 12.* New York: Academic Press.

**Silva, C.** (2005, October 31). When teen dynamo talks, city listens. *Boston Globe,* pp. BI, B4.

**Silvernail, D. L., & Lane, D. M. M.** (2004). *The impact of Maine's one-to-one laptop program on middle school teachers and students.* (Report #1). Gorham, ME: Maine Education Policy Research Institute, University of Southern Maine Office.

**Simonds, C. J., Hunt, S. K., & Simonds, B. K.** (2010). *Public speaking.* Boston: Allyn & Bacon.

**Simons, J., Finlay, B., & Yang, A.** (1991). *The adolescent and young adult fact book.* Washington, DC: Children's Defense Fund.

**Simos, P. G., & others** (2007). Altering the brain circuits for reading through intervention: A magnetic source imaging study. *Neuropsychology, 21,* 485–496.

**Simpkins, S. D., Fredricks, J. A., Davis-Kean, P. E., & Eccles, J. S.** (2004). Healthy mind, healthy habits: The influence of activity involvement in middle childhood. In A. C. Huston & M. N. Ripke (Eds.), *Middle childhood: Contexts of development,* New York: Cambridge University Press.

**Singh, A. A., Orpinas, P., & Horne, A. M.** (2010). Empowering schools to prevent bullying: A holistic approach. In E. Vernberg & B. K. Biggs (Eds.), *Preventing and treating bullying and victimization.* New York: Oxford University Press.

**Skiba, T., Tan, M., Sternberg, R. J., & Grigorenko, E. L.** (2010, in press). Roads not taken, new roads to take: Looking for creativity in the classroom. In J. Kaufman & R. Beghetto (Eds.), *Creativity in classrooms.* New York: Springer.

**Skidmore, D.** (2009). Race and special education. In P. Hick & G. Thomas (Eds.), *Inclusion and diversity in education.* Thousand Oaks, CA: Sage.

**Skinner, B. F.** (1938). *The behavior of organisms.* New York: Appleton-Century-Crofts.

**Skinner, B. F.** (1954). The science of learning and the art of teaching. *Harvard Educational Review, 24,* 86–97.

**Skinner, B. F.** (1957). *Verbal behavior.* New York: Appleton-Century-Crofts.

**Skinner, B. F.** (1958). Teaching machines. *Science, 128,* 969–977.

**Slavin, R. E.** (1995). *Cooperative learning: Theory, research, and practice* (2nd ed.). Boston: Allyn & Bacon.

**Slavin, R. E.** (2011). Instruction based on cooperative learning. In P. A. Alexander & R. E. Mayer (Eds.), *Handbook of research on learning and instruction.* New York: Routledge.

**Slavin, R. E., Madden, N. A., Chambers, B., & Haxby, B.** (2009). *2 million children* (2nd ed.). Thousand Oaks, CA: Sage.

**Slavin, R. E., Madden, N. A., Dolan, L. L., & Wasik, B. A.** (1996). *School: Success for all.* Newbury Park, CA: Corwin Press.

**Smith, D. D., & Tyler, N. C.** (2010). *Introduction to special education* (7th ed.). Upper Saddle River, NJ: Merrill.

**Smith, J. B.** (2009). High school organization. In D. Carr (Ed.), *Encyclopedia of the life* *course and human development.* Boston: Gale Cengage.

**Smith, R. L., Rose, A. J., & Schwartz-Mette, R. A.** (2010). Relational and overt aggression in childhood and adolescence: Clarifying mean-level gender differences and associations with peer acceptance. *Social Development, 19,* 243–269.

**Smoll, F. L., & Schutz, R. W.** (1990). Quantifying gender differences in physical performance: A developmental perspective. *Developmental Psychology, 26,* 360–369.

**Smyth, M. M., Collins, A. F., Morris, P. E., & Levy, P.** (1994). *Cognition in action* (2nd ed.). Hove, UK: Erlbaum.

**Snell, M. E., & Janney, R. E.** (2005). *Practices for inclusive schools: Collaborative teaming* (2nd ed.). Baltimore: Brookes.

**Snow, C. E., & Kang, J. Y.** (2006). Becoming bilingual, biliterate, and bicultural. In W. Damon & R. Lerner (Eds.), *Handbook of child psychology* (6th ed.). New York: Wiley.

**Snow, R. E., Como, L., & Jackson, D.** (1996). Individual differences in affective and conative functions. In D. C. Berliner & R. C. Calfee (Eds.), *Handbook of educational psychology.* New York: Macmillan.

**Snowling, M. J., & Gobel, S. M.** (2011). Reading development and dyslexia. In U. Goswami (Ed.), *Wiley-Blackwell handbook of childhood cognitive development.* New York: Wiley.

**Solano-Flores, G., & Shavelson, R. J.** (1997, Fall). Development of performance assessments in science: Conceptual, practical, and logistical issues. *Educational Measurement,* pp. 16–24.

**Soto, C. J., John, O. P., Gosling, S. D., & Potter, J.** (2008). The development of psychometrics of big five reports: acquiescence, factor structure, coherence, and differentiation from ages 10 to 20. *Journal of Personality and Social Psychology, 94,* 718–737.

**Sousa, D. A.** (1995). *How the brain learns: A classroom teacher's guide.* Reston, VA: National Association of Secondary School Principals.

**Spence, J. T., & Buckner, C. E.** (2000). Instrumental and expressive traits, trait stereotypes, and sexist attitudes: What do they signify? *Psychology of Women Quarterly, 24,* 44–62.

**Spence, J. T., & Helmreich, R.** (1978). *Masculinity and femininity: Their psychological dimensions.* Austin: University of Texas Press.

**Spiegler, M. D., & Guevremont, D. C.** (2010). *Contemporary behavior therapy* (5th ed.). Boston: Cengage.

**Sporer, N., Brunstein, J. C., & Kieschke, U.** (2009). Improving students' reading comprehension skills: Effects of strategy instruction and reciprocal teaching. *Learning and Instruction, 19,* 272–286.

**Spring, J.** (2010). *Deculturalization and the struggle for equality* (6th ed.). New York: McGraw-Hill.

**SRA/McGraw-Hill** (2010). *SRA Real Math Building Blocks PreK.* New York: McGraw-Hill.

**Srabstein, J. C., McCarter, R. J., Shao, C., & Huang, Z. J.** (2006). Morbidities associated with bullying behaviors in adolescents: School-based study of American adolescents. *International Journal of Adolescent Medicine and Health, 18,* 587–596.

**Sroufe, L. A.** (2007). Commentary: The place of development in developmental psychology. In A. S. Masten (Ed.), *Multilevel dynamics in developmental psychology.* Mahwah, NJ: Erlbaum.

**Sroufe, L. A., Cooper, R. G., DeHart, G., and Bronfenbrenner, U.** (1992). *Child development: Its nature and course* (2nd ed.). New York: McGraw-Hill.

**Stahl, G.** (2010). The generalization of group knowledge by a virtual math team. In M. T. Banich & D. Cassamise (Eds.), *Generalization of knowledge.* New York: Psychology Press.

**Stahl, S.** (2002, January). *Effective reading instruction in the first grade.* Paper presented at the Michigan Reading Recovery conference. Dearborn, MI.

**Stake, R. E.** (2010). *Qualitative research.* New York: Guilford Press.

**Stangor, C.** (2011). *Research methods for the behavioral sciences* (4th ed.). Boston: Cengage.

**Stanovich, K. E.** (1994). Romance and reality. *Reading Teacher, 47,* 280–291.

**Stanovich, K. E.** (2010). *How to think straight about psychology* (9th ed.). Boston: Allyn & Bacon.

**Staudt, M.** (2010). Brain plasticity following early life brain injury: Insights from neuuroimaging. *Seminars in Perinatology, 34,* 87–92.

**Stecher, B. M., & Vernez, G.** (2010). *Reauthorizing "No Child Left Behind": Facts and recommendations.* Pittsburgh: Rand Corporation.

**Steel, P.** (2007). The nature of procrastination: A meta-analytic and theoretical review of quintessential self-regulatory failure. *Psychological Bulletin, 133,* 65–94.

**Steele, C. M., & Aronson, J. A.** (2004). Stereotype threat does not live by Steele and Aronson (1995) alone. *American Psychologist, 59,* 47–48.

**Steinberg, L.** (2004). Risk taking in adolescence: What changes, and why? *Annals of the New York Academy of Sciences, 1021,* 59–60.

**Steinberg, L.** (2008). A social neuroscience perspective on adolescent risk-taking. *Developmental Review, 28,* 78–106.

**Steinberg, L.** (2009). Adolescent development and juvenile justice. *Annual Review of Clinical Psychology, Vol. 5.* Palo Alto, CA: Annual Reviews.

**Steinberg, L., Cauffman, E., Woolard, J., Graham, S., & Banich, M.** (2009). Are adolescents less mature than adults? Minors' access to abortion, the juvenile death penalty, and the alleged APA "flip-flop." *American Psychologist, 64,* 583–594.

**Stephens, J. M.** (2008). Cheating. In N. J. Salkind (Ed.), *Encyclopedia of educational psychology.* Thousand Oaks, CA: Sage.

**Sterling, D. R.** (2009). Classroom management: Setting up the classroom for learning. *Science Scope, 32,* 29–33.

**Sternberg, R. J.** (1986). *Intelligence applied.* Fort Worth, TX: Harcourt Brace.

**Sternberg, R. J.** (2004). Individual differences in cognitive development. In P. Smith & C. Hart (Eds.), *Blackwell handbook of cognitive development.* Malden, MA: Blackwell.

**Sternberg, R. J.** (2009). *Cognitive psychology* (5th ed.). Boston: Cengage.

**Sternberg, R. J.** (2009). Leadership and giftedness. In B. MacFarlane & T. Stambaugh (Eds.), *Leading change in gifted education* (pp. 513–526). Waco, TX: Prufrock.

**Sternberg, R. J.** (2010a). Intelligence. In B. McGaw, P. Peterson, & E. Baker (Eds.), *The International Encyclopedia of Education* (3rd ed.). New York: Elsevier.

**Sternberg, R. J.** (2010b). The triarchic theory of successful intelligence. In B. Kerr (Ed.), *Encyclopedia of giftedness, creativity, and talent.* Thousand Oaks, CA: Sage.

**Sternberg, R. J.** (2010c, in press). The dark side of creativity and how to combat it. In D. Cropley, A. Cropley, J. Kaufman, & M. Runco (Eds.), *The dark side of creativity.* New York: Cambridge University.

**Sternberg, R. J.** (2011a, in press). Individual differences in cognitive development. In U. Goswami (Ed.), *Blackwell handbook of childhood cognitive development.* Malden, MA: Blackwell.

**Sternberg, R. J.** (2011b, in press) Intelligence. In B. McGaw, P. Peterson, & E. Baker (Eds.). *International encyclopedia of education* (3rd ed.). New York: Elsevier.

Sternberg, R. J. (2011c, in press). Personal wisdom in the balance. In M. Ferrari & N. Weststrate (Eds.), *Personal wisdom*. New York: Springer.

Sternberg, R. J. (2011d, in press). Intelligence in cultural context. In M. Gelfand, C-Y Chiu, & Y-Y Hong (Eds.), *Advances in cultures and psychology, Vol. 2*. New York: Oxford University Press.

Sternberg, R. J., & Ben-Zeev, T. (2001). *Complex cognitive processes*. New York: Oxford University Press.

Sternberg, R. J., & Grigorenko, E. L. (2008). Ability testing across cultures. In L. Suzuki (Ed.), *Handbook of multicultural assessment* (3rd ed.). New York: Jossey-Bass.

Sternberg, R. J., Jarvin, L., & Grigorenko, E. L. (2009). *Teaching for intelligence, creativity, and success*. Thousand Oaks, CA: Corwin.

Sternberg, R. J., Jarvin, L., & Grigorenko, E. L. (2011, in press). *Explorations of the nature of giftedness*. New York: Cambridge University Press.

Sternberg, R. J., Jarvin, L., & Reznitskaya, A. (2011, in press). Teaching for wisdom through history: Infusing wise thinking skills in the school curriculum. In M. Ferrari & N. Weststrate (Eds.), *Personal wisdom*. New York: Springer.

Sternberg, R. J., & Spear-Swerling, P. (1996). *Teaching for thinking*. Washington, DC: American Psychological Association.

Sternberg, R. J., & Williams, W. M. (1996.) *How to Develop Student Creativity*. Alexandria, VA.: ASCD.

Stevenson, H. W. (1992, December). Learning from Asian schools. *Scientific American*, pp. 6, 70–76.

Stevenson, H. W. (1995). Mathematics achievement of American students: First in the world by 2000? In C. A. Nelson (Ed.), *Basic and applied perspectives in learning, cognition, and development*. Minneapolis: University of Minnesota Press.

Stevenson, H. W. (2000). Middle childhood: Education and schooling. In A. Kazdin (Ed.). *Encyclopedia of psychology*. Washington, DC, & New York: American Psychological Association and Oxford University Press.

Stevenson, H. W. (2001). *Commentary on NCTM standards*. Department of Psychology, University of Michigan, Ann Arbor.

Stevenson, H. W., & Hofer, B. K. (1999). Education policy in the United States and abroad: What we can learn from each other. In G. J. Cizek (Ed.), *Handbook of educational policy*. San Diego: Academic Press.

Stevenson, H. W., Lee, S., Chen, C., Stigler, J. W., Hsu, C., & Kitamura, S. (1990). Contexts of achievement. *Monographs of the Society for Research in Development, 55* (Serial No. 221).

Stevenson, H. W., Lee, S., & Stigler, J. W. (1986). Mathematics achievement of Chinese, Japanese, and American children. *Science, 231*, 693–699.

Stewart, J. (2009). *Bridges not walls: A book about interpersonal communication* (10th ed.). New York: McGraw-Hill.

Stiggins, R. (2008). *Introduction to student-involved assessment for learning* (5th ed.). Upper Saddle River, NJ: Prentice Hall.

Stiggins, R. J. (2001). *Student-involved classroom assessment* (3rd ed.). Upper Saddle River, NJ: Prentice Hall.

Stipek, D. (2005, February 16). Commentary in *USA TODAY*, p. 1D.

Stipek, D. J. (2002). *Motivation to learn* (4th ed.). Boston: Allyn & Bacon.

Stipek, D. J., Feiler, R., Daniels, D., & Milburn, S. (1995). Effects of different instructional approaches on young children's achievement and motivation. *Child Development, 66*, 209–223.

Stoel-Gammon, C., & Sosa, A. V. (2010). Phonological development. In E. Hoff & M. Shatz (Eds.), *Blackwell handbook of language development* (2nd ed.). New York: Wiley.

Stolzer, J. M., (2009). Attention deficit/hyperactivity disorder. In D. Carr (Ed.), *Encyclopedia of the life course and human development*. Boston: Gale Cengage.

Stop Cyberbullying. (2010). Retrieved July 31, 2010, from www.stopcyberbullying.com

Strasburger, V. C., Wilson, B. J., & Jordan, A. (2008). *Children, adolescents, and the media*. Thousand Oaks, CA: Sage.

Straus, M. A. (1991). Discipline and deviance: Physical punishment of children and violence and other crimes in adulthood. *Social Problems, 38*, 133–154.

Stray, L. L., Ellertsen, B., & Stray, T. (2010, in press). Motor function and methylphenidate effect in children with attention deficit hyperactivity disorder. *Acta Pediatrica*.

Strenze, T. (2007). Intelligence and socioeconomic success: A meta-analytic review of longitudinal research. *Intelligence, 35*, 401–426.

Studer, J. (2009). Teacher as family communication facilitator. In K. B. Grant & J. A. Ray (Eds.), *Home, school, and community collaboration*. Thousand Oaks, CA: Corwin Press.

Suen, H. K. (2008). Measurement. In N. J. Salkind (Ed.), *Encyclopedia of educational psychology*. Thousand Oaks, CA: Sage.

Sunal, C. S., & Haas, M. E. (2011). *Social studies for the elementary and middle grades: A constructivist approach* (4th ed.). Boston: Allyn & Bacon.

Suyemoto, K. L. (2009). Multiracial Asian Americans. In N. Tewari & A. Aluarez (Eds.), *Asian American psychology*. New York: Psychology Press.

Swan, K., Cook, D., Kratcoski, A., Lin, Y., Schenker, J., & van't Hooft, M. (2006). Ubiquitous computing: Rethinking teaching, learning and technology integration. In S. Tettegah & R. Hunter (Eds.), *Educational and technology: Issues and applications, policy, and administration*. New York: Elsevier.

Swan, K., Kratcoski, A., Schenker, J., & van't Hooft, M. (2009). Interactive whiteboards and student achievement. In M. Thomas and E. C. Schmid (Eds.), *Interactive whiteboards for education and training: Emerging technologies and applications*. Hershey, PA: IGI Global.

Swan, K., Kratcoski, A., van't Hooft, M., Campbell, D., & Miller, D. (2007). Technology support for whole group engagement: A pilot study. *Advanced Technologies for Learning. 4* (2), 68–73

Swan, K., van't Hooft, M., Kratcoski, A., & Unger, D. (2005). Uses and effects of mobile computing devices in K-8 classrooms: A preliminary study. *Journal of Research on Technology and Education, 38* (1), 99–112.

Swanson, D. P. (2010). Adolescent psychosocial processes: Identity, stress, and competence. In D. P. Swanson, M. C. Edwards, & M. B. Spencer (Eds.), *Adolescence: Development in a global era*. San Diego: Academic Press.

Swanson, H. L. (1999). What develops in working memory? A life-span perspective. *Developmental Psychology, 35*, 986–1000.

Swanson, L., & Kim, K. (2007). Working memory, short-term memory, and naming speed as predictors of children's mathematical performance. *Intelligence, 35*, 151–168.

Swearer, S. M., Espelage, D. L., & Napolitano, S. A. (2009). *Bullying prevention and intervention*. New York: Guilford.

**T**

Tager-Flusberg, H., & Zukowski, A. (2009). Putting words together. Morphology and syntax in the preschool years. In J. Berko Gleason & N. Ratner (Eds.), *The development of language* (7th ed.). Boston: Allyn & Bacon.

**Tamis-LeMonda, C., & McFadden, K. E.** (2010). The United States of America. In M. H. Bornstein (Ed.), *Handbook of developmental cultural science.* New York: Psychology Press.

**Tang, Y-Y., & Posner, M. I.** (2009). Attention training and attention state training. *Trends in Cognitive Science, 13,* 222–227.

**Tannen, D.** (1990). *You just don't understand!* New York: Ballantine.

**Tarhan, L., & Acar, B.** (2007). Problem-based learning in an eleventh-grade chemistry class: "Factors affecting cell potential." *Research in Science & Technological Education, 25,* 351–369.

**Taylor, C.** (1994). Assessment of measurement or standards: The peril and the promise of large-scale assessment reform. *American Educational Research Journal, 32,* 231–262.

**Taylor, J., Stecher, B., O'Day, J., Naftel, S., & Le Floch, K.** (2010). *State and local implementation of the "No Child Left Behind Act." Volume IX—Accountability under "NCLB": Final Report.* Washington, DC: U.S. Department of Education.

**Taylor, L. S., & Whittaker, C. R.** (2009). *Bridging multiple worlds* (2nd ed.). Boston: Allyn & Bacon.

**Taylor, R. L., Brady, M., & Richards, S. B.** (2005). *Mental retardation.* Boston: Allyn & Bacon.

**Taylor, R. L., Smiley, L., & Richards, S. B.** (2009). *Exceptional students.* New York: McGraw-Hill.

**Tenenbaum, H. R., Callahan, M., Alba-Speyer, C., & Sandoval, L.** (2002). Parent-child science conversations in Mexican descent families: Educational background, activity, and past experience as moderators. *Hispanic Journal of Behavioral Science, 24,* 225–248.

**Tennyson, R., & Cocchiarella, M.** (1986). An empirically based instructional design theory for teaching concepts. *Review of Educational Research, 56,* 40–71.

**Terman, D. L., Larner, M. B., Stevenson, C. S., & Behrman, R. E.** (1996). Special education for students with disabilities: Analysis and recommendations. *Future of Children, 6* (1), 4–24.

**Terman, L.** (1925). *Genetic studies of genius. Vol. 1: Mental and physical traits of a thousand gifted children.* Stanford, CA: Stanford University Press.

**Terwilliger, J.** (1997). Semantics, psychometrics, and assessment reform: A close look at "authentic" assessments. *Educational Researcher, 26,* 24–27.

**Tewari, N., & Aluarez, A.** (Eds.) (2009). *Asian American Psychology.* New York: Psychology Press.

**Thomal, E. L. & Robinson, H. A.** (1972). *Improving reading in every class: A sourcebook for teachers.* Boston, MA: Allyn & Bacon.

**Thomas, A., & Chess, S.** (1991). Temperament in adolescence and its functional significance. In R. M. Lerner, A. C. Petersen, & J. Brooks-Gunn (Eds.), *Encyclopedia of adolescence, Vol. 2.* New York: Garland.

**Thomas, C. R., & Gadbois, S. A.** (2007). Academic self-handicapping: The role of self-concept clarity and students' learning strategies. *British Journal of Educational Psychology, 77,* 109–119.

**Thomas, J. R., & Thomas, K. T.** (1988). Developmental gender differences in physical activity. *Quest, 40,* 219–229.

**Thomas, O. N., Caldwell, C. H., Fiason, N., & Jackson, J. S.** (2009). Promoting academic achievement: The role of racial identity in buffering perceptions of teacher discrimination on academic achievement among African American and Caribbean Black adolescents. *Journal of Educational Psychology, 101,* 420–431.

**Thomas, R. M.** (2005). *Teacher doing research.* Boston: Allyn & Bacon.

**Thomas, V., Ray, K., & Moon, S. M.** (2007). Counseling gifted individuals and their families: A systems perspective. In S. Mendaglio & J. Peterson (Eds.). Counseling the gifted. Waco, TX: Prufroc Press.

**Thompson, R. A.** (2009). Unpublished review of J. W. Santrock's *Life-Span Development* (13th ed.). New York: McGraw-Hill.

**Thompson, R. A., & Goodman, M.** (2009). Development of self, relationships, and socioemotional competence: Foundations for early school success. In O. A. Barbarin & B. H. Wasik (Eds.), *Handbook of child development and early education.* New York: Guilford.

**Thurston, A., & others** (2010). Cooperative learning in science: Follow-up from primary to high school. *International Journal of Science Education, 32,* 501–522.

**Thurston, A., Duran, D., Cunningham, E., Blanch, S., & Topping, K.** (2009). International on-line reciprocal peer tutoring to promote modern language development in primary schools. *Computers and Education, 53,* 462–472.

**Toga, A., & Mazziotta, J.** (Eds.) (2011). *Brain mapping.* New York: Elsevier.

**Tomlinson, C. A.** (2006). *An educator's guide to differentiating instruction.* Boston: Houghton Mifflin.

**Tomoda, A., Suzuki, H., Rabi, K., Sheu, Y. S., Polcari, A., & Teicher, M. H.** (2009). Reduced prefrontal cortical gray matter volume in young adults exposed to harsh corporal punishment. *NeuroImage, 47* (Suppl. 2), S66–S71.

**Tompkins, G. E.** (2011). *Literacy in the early grades* (3rd ed.). Boston: Allyn & Bacon.

**Torff, B., & Tirotta, R.** (2010). Interactive whiteboards produce small gains in elementary students' self-reported motivation in mathematics. *Computers & Education, 54,* 379–383.

**Towsend, M., & Konold, T. R.** (2010). Measuring early literacy skills: A latent variable investigation of the phonological awareness literacy screening for preschool. *Journal of Psychoeducational Assessment, 28,* 115–128.

**Trautwein, U.** (2007). The homework-achievement relation reconsidered: Differentiating homework time, homework frequency, and homework effort. *Learning and Instruction, 17,* 372–388.

**Trautwein, U., & Ludtke, O.** (2007). Students' self-reported effort and time on homework in six school subjects: Between-students differences and within-students differences. *Journal of Educational Psychology, 99,* 432–444.

**Trautwein, U., & Ludtke, O.** (2009). Predicting homework motivation and homework effort in six school subjects: The role of person and family characteristics, classroom factors, and school track. *Learning and Instruction, 19,* 243–258.

**Trautwein, U., Niggli, A., Schnyder, I., & Ludtke, O.** (2009). Between-teacher differences in homework assignments an the development of students' homework effort, homework emotions, and achievement. *Journal of Educational Psychology, 101,* 176–189.

**Triandis, H. C.** (2007). Culture and psychology: A history of their relationship. In S. Kitayama & D. Cohen (Eds.), *Handbook of cultural psychology.* New York: Guilford.

**Tripp, G., & Wickens, J. R.** (2009). Neurobiology of ADHD. *Neuropharmacology.*

**Trzesniewski, K. H., Donnellan, M. B., Moffit, T. E., Robins, R. W., Poulton, R., & Caspi, A.** (2006). Low self-esteem during adolescence predicts poor health, criminal behavior, and limited income prospects during adulthood. *Developmental Psychology, 42,* 381–390.

**Tsal, Y., Shalev, L., & Mevorach, C.** (2005). The diversity of attention deficits in ADHD. *Journal of Learning Disabilities, 38,* 142–157.

**Tsang, C. L.** (1989). Bilingual minorities and language issues in writing. *Written Communication, 9* (1), 1–15.

**Tulving, E.** (2000). Concepts of memory. In E. Tulving & F. I. M. Craik (Eds.), *The Oxford handbook of memory*. New York: Oxford University Press.

**Turnbull, A. P., Turnbull, R., & Wehmeyer, M. L.** (2010). *Exceptional lives* (6th ed.). Upper Saddle River, NJ: Merrill.

**Turnbull, H. R., Huerta, N., & Stowe, M.** (2009). *What every teacher should know about: The Individuals with Disabilities Education Act as amended in 2004* (2nd ed.). Upper Saddle River. NJ: Prentice Hall.

**Turrigiano, G.** (2010). Synaptic homeostasis. *Annual Review of Neuroscience, Vol. 33.* Palo Alto, CA: Annual Reviews.

# U

**Uhls, Y. T., & Greenfield, P. M.** (2009). *Adolescents and electronic communication: Risks, benefits, and ideas for parenting.* Retrieved July 31, 2010, from www.education.com

**Ullman, J. G.** (2005). *Making technology work for learners with special needs.* Boston: Allyn & Bacon.

**Umana-Taylor, A. J., Gonzales-Backen, M. A., & Guimond, A. B.** (2009). Latino adolescents' ethnic identity: Is there a developmental progression and does growth in ethnic identity predict growth in self-esteem? *Child Development, 80,* 391–405.

**Umbreit, J., Ferro, J., Liaupsin, C. J., & Lane, K. I.** (2007). *Functional behavioral assessment and function-based intervention.* Upper Saddle River. NJ: Prentice Hall.

**University of Buffalo Counseling Services.** (2009). *Procrastination.* Buffalo, NY: Author.

**University of Illinois Counseling Center.** (1996). *Overcoming procrastination.* Urbana-Champaign. IL: Department of Student Affairs.

**University of Texas at Austin Counseling and Mental Health Center.** (1999). *Coping with perfectionism.* Austin, TX: Author.

**Urdan, T.** (2010). Classroom goal structures, motivation, and learning. In J. Meece & J. Eccles (Eds.), *Handbook of research on schools, schooling and human development.* New York: Routledge.

**USA Today.** (1999). All-USA TODAY Teacher Team. Retrieved January 15, 2004, from www.usatoday.com/news/education/1999

**USA Today.** (2000, October 10). All-USA first teacher team. Retrieved November 15, 2004, from http://www.usatoday.com/life/teacher/teach/htm

**USA Today.** (2001, October 10). All-USA first teacher team. Retrieved November 20, 2004, from http://www.usatoday.com/news/education2001

**USA Today.** (2003, October 15). From kindergarten to high school, they make the grade. Retrieved on April 22, 2006, from www.usatoday.com/news/education/2003-10-15-2003-winners

**U.S. Department of Education.** (2000). *To assure a free and appropriate education of all children with disabilities.* Washington, DC: U.S. Office of Education.

**U.S. Office for Civil Rights.** (2008). *Sexual harassment.* Retrieved July 16, 2008, from www.ed.gov/about/offices/list/ocr/qa-sexharass.html

**U.S. Office of Education.** (1998). *The benchmark study.* Washington, DC: Office of Education & Minority Affairs.

**U.S. Office of Education.** (1999). *Elementary and secondary school compliance reports.* Washington, DC: U.S. Government Printing Office.

# V

**Van Buren, E., & Graham, S.** (2003). *Redefining ethnic identity: Its relationship to positive and negative school adjustment outcomes for minority youth.* Paper presented at the meeting of the Society for Research in Child Development, Tampa.

**van de Walle, J. A., Karp, K. S., & Bay-Williams, J. M.** (2010). *Elementary and Middle School Mathematics* (7th ed.). Boston: Allyn & Bacon.

**van der Stel, M., & Veenam, M. V. J.** (2010). Development of metacognitive skillfulness: A longitudinal study. *Learning and Individual Differences, 20,* 220–224.

**van Ettinger-Veenstra, H. M., & others** (2010). Right-hemispheric brain activation correlates to language performance. *Neuroimage, 49,* 3481–3488.

**van Rooij, S. W.** (2009). Scaffolding project-based learning with the project management body of knowledge. *Computers & Education, 52,* 210–219.

**Vahey, P., Roschelle, J., & Tatar, D.** (2006). Moving between the private and the public in the mathematics classroom with handheld technology. In M. van't Hooft & K. Swan (Eds.), *Ubiquitous computing.* New York: Psychology Press.

**Vallone, R. P., Griffin, D. W., Lin, S., & Ross, L.** (1990). Overconfident prediction of future actions and outcomes by self and others. *Journal of Personality and Social Psychology, 58,* 582–592.

**Vansteenkiste, M., Sierens, E., Soenens, B., Luyckx, K., & Lens, W.** (2009). Motivational profiles from a self-determination perspective: The quality of motivation matters. *Journal of Educational Psychology, 101,* 671–688.

**Vansteenkiste, M., Timmermans, T., Lens, W., Soenens, B., & Van den Broeck, A.** (2008). Does extrinsic goal framing enhance extrinsic goal-oriented individuals' learning and performance? An experimental test of the match perspective versus self-determination theory. *Journal of Educational Psychology, 100,* 387–397.

**Vargas, J.** (2009). *Behavior analysis for effective teaching.* New York: Routledge.

**Veenman, M. V. J.** (2011). Learning to self-monitor and self-regulate. In P. A. Alexander & R. E. Mayer (Eds.), *Handbook of research on learning and instruction.* New York: Routledge.

**Veenstra, A., Lindenberg, S., Munniksma, A., & Dijkstra, J. K.** (2010). The complex relationship between bullying, victimization, acceptance, and rejection: Giving special attention to status, affection, and sex differences. *Social Development, 19,* 480–486.

**Verderber, R. F., Verderber, K. S., & Sellnow, D. D.** (2011). *Communicate!* (13th ed.). Boston: Cengage.

**Vernberg, E. M., & Biggs, B. K.** (2010). Preventing and treating bullying and victimization: An evidence-based approach. In E. M. Vernberg & B. K. Biggs (Eds.), *Preventing and treating bullying and victimization.* New York: Oxford University Press.

**Veronneau, M-H., Vitaro, F., Pedersen, S., & Tremblay, R. E.** (2008). Do peers contribute to the likelihood of secondary graduation among disadvantaged boys? *Journal of Educational Psychology, 100,* 429–442.

**Veselka, L., Schermer, J. A., Petries, K. V., & Vernon, P. A.** (2009). Evidence for a heritable general factor of personality in two studies. *Twin Research and Human Genetics, 12,* 254–260.

**Vreeman, R. C., & Carroll, A. E.** (2007). A systematic review of school-based interventions to prevent bullying. *Archives of Pediatric and Adolescent Medicine, 161,* 78–88.

**Vygotsky, L. S.** (1962). *Thought and language.* Cambridge, MA: MIT Press.

# W

**Wagner, R. K., & Sternberg, R. J.** (1986). Tacit knowledge and intelligence in the everyday world. In R. J. Sternberg & R. K. Wagner (Eds.), *Practical intelligence.* Cambridge, UK: Cambridge University Press.

**Walker, L. J., & Frimer, J. A.** (2011, in press). The science of moral development. In M. K. Underwood & L. H. Rosen (Eds.), *Social development*. New York: Guilford.

**Waller, R. D., & Higbee, T. S.** (2010). The effects of fixed-time escape on inappropriate and appropriate classroom behavior. *Journal of Applied Behavior Analysis, 43,* 149–153.

**Walsh, J.** (2008). Self-efficacy. In N. J. Salkind (Ed.), *Encyclopedia of educational psychology*. Thousand Oaks, CA: Sage.

**Wang, Q., & Pomerantz, E. M.** (2009). The motivational landscape of early adolescence in the United States and China: A longitudinal study. *Child Development, 86,* 1272–1287.

**Wanzek, J., Dickson, S., Bursuck, W. D., & White, J. M.** (2000) Teaching phonological awareness to students at risk for reading failure: An analysis of four instructional programs. *Learning disabilities research and practice, 15*(4), 226–239.

**Wargo, E.** (2009). *Adolescents and risk: Helping young people make better choices.* Retrieved August 19, 2009 from www.human.cornell.edu/che/HD/Outreach_extension/index.com

**Warrington, M., & Younger, M.** (2003). "We decided to give it a twirl": Single-sex teaching in English comprehensive schools. *Gender and Education, 15,* 339–350.

**Webb, J. T., Gore, J. L., Mend, E. R., & DeVries, A. R.** (2007). *A parent's guide to gifted children.* Scottsdale. AZ: Great Potential Press.

**Webb, L. D., Metha, A., & Jordan, K. F.** (2010). *Foundations of American education* (6th ed.). Upper Saddle River, NJ: Merrill.

**Webb, N. M.** (1984). Sex differences in interaction and achievement in cooperative small groups. *Journal of Educational Psychology, 76,* 33–34.

**Webb, N. M., & Palincsar, A. S.** (1996). Group processes in the classroom. In D. C. Berliner & R. C. Calfee (Eds.), *Handbook of educational psychology.* New York: Macmillan.

**Webster, N. S., & Worrell, F. C.** (2008). Academically talented adolescents' attitudes toward service in the community. *Gifted Child Quaterly, 52,* 170–179.

**Weiler, J.** (1998). Success for All. *ERIC/CUE Digest, No. 139.*

**Weiner, B.** (1986). *An attributional theory of motivation and emotion.* New York: Springer.

**Weiner, B.** (1992). *Human motivation: Metaphors, theories, and research.* Newbury Park, CA: Sage.

**Weiner, B.** (2010). The development of an attribution-based theory of motivation: A history of ideas. *Educational Psychologist, 45,* 28–36.

**Weinstein, C. S.** (2007). *Middle and secondary classroom management* (3rd ed.). Boston: McGraw-Hill.

**Weinstein, C. S., & Mignano, A.** (2007). *Elementary classroom management* (4th ed.). Boston: McGraw-Hill.

**Weinstein, R. S.** (2004). *Reaching higher: The power of expectations in schooling* (Paperback edition). Cambridge, MA: Harvard University Press.

**Weinstein, R. S., Madison, S. M., & Kuklinski, M. R.** (1995). Raising expectations in schooling: Obstacles and opportunities for change. *American Educational Research Journal, 32* (1), 121–159.

**Weiss, H. B., Kreider, H., Lopez, M. E., & Chatman, C. M.** (2010). *Preparing educators to engage families.* Thousand Oaks, CA: Sage.

**Wellman, H. M.** (2011). Developing a theory of mind. In U. Goswami (Ed.), *Wiley-Blackwell handbook of childhood cognitive development.* New York: Wiley.

**Wellman, H. M., Cross, D., & Watson, J.** (2001). Meta-analysis of theory-of-mind development: The truth about false belief. *Child Development, 72,* 655–684.

**Welsh, J. A., Nix, R. L., Blair, C., Bierman, K. L., & Nelson, K. E.** (2010). The development of cognitive skills and gains in academic school readiness for children from low-income families. *Journal of Educational Psychology, 102,* 43–53.

**Welshman, D.** (2000). *Social studies resources.* St. Johns, Newfoundland: Leary Brooks Jr. High School.

**Wenglinsky, H.** (2002). The link between teacher classroom practices and student academic performance. *Education Policy Analysis Archives, 10,* 12.

**Wentzel, K. R.** (1997). Student motivation in middle school: The role of perceived psychological caring. *Journal of Educational Psychology, 89,* 411–419.

**Wentzel, K. R.** (2008). Social competence, sociocultural contexts, and school success. In C. Hudley & A. E. Gottfried (Eds.). *Academic motivation and the culture of school in childhood and adolescence.* New York: Oxford University Press.

**Wentzel, K .R.** (2009). Students' relationships with teachers as motivational contexts. In K. R. Wentzel & A. Wigfield (Eds.), *Handbook of motivation at school.* New York: Routledge.

**Wentzel, K. R.** (2010). Teacher-student relationships and school adjustment. In J. Meece & J. Eccles (Eds.), *Handbook of research on schools, schooling, and human development.* New York: Routledge.

**Wentzel, K. R., Barry, C. M., & Caldwell, K. A.** (2004). Friendships in middle school: Influences on motivation and school adjustment. *Journal of Educational Psychology, 96,* 195–203.

**Wentzel, K. R., & Erdley, C. A.** (1993). Strategies for making friends: Relations to social behavior and peer acceptance in early adolescence. *Developmental Psychology, 29,* 819–826.

**Wentzel, K. R., & Watkins, D. E.** (2011). Instruction based on peer interaction. In P. A. Alexander & R. E. Mayer (Eds.), *Handbook of research on learning and instruction.* New York: Routledge.

**West, R., & Turner, L. H.** (2011). *Understanding interpersonal communication* (2nd ed.). Boston: Cengage.

**What Works Clearinghouse** (2007). *Elementary school math.* Rockville, MD: Author.

**What Works Clearinghouse** (2007a). *Reading Recovery.* Rockville, MD: Author.

**What Works Clearinghouse** (2007b). *Peer-Assisted Learning Strategies.* Rockville, MD: Author.

**What Works Clearinghouse** (2009, August). *Success for All.* Washington, DC: Institute of Education Sciences. Also available on ERIC, #ED506157.

**Wheelock, A.** (1992). *Crossing the tracks: How "untracking" can save America's schools.* New York: New Press.

**White, R., & Dinos, S.** (2010). Investigating the impact of mediated learning experiences on cooperative peer communication during group initiatives. *Journal of Experimental Education, 32,* 226–238.

**White, R. W.** (1959). Motivation reconsidered: The concept of confidence. *Psychological Review, 66,* 297–333.

**Whitehead, K. A., Ainsworth, A. T., Wittig, M. A., & Gadino, B.** (2009). Implications of ethnic identity exploration and ethnic identity affirmation and belonging for intergroup attitudes among adolescents. *Journal of Research on Adolescence, 19,* 123–135.

**Whitescarver, K.** (2006, April). *Montessori rising: Montessori education in the United States, 1955-presented.* Paper presented at the meeting of the American Education Research Association, San Francisco.

**Wigfield, A., & Asher, S. R.** (1984). Social and motivational influences on reading. In

P. D. Pearson, R. Barr, M. L. Kamil, & P. Mosenthal (Eds.), *Handbook of reading research*. New York: Longman.

**Wigfield, A., Byrnes, J. P., & Eccles, J. S.** (2006). Developing during early adolescence. In P. A. Alexander & P. H. Winne (Eds.), *Handbook of educational psychology* (2nd ed.). Mahwah, NJ: Erlbaum.

**Wigfield, A., Eccles, J. S., Schiefele, U., Roeser, R., & Davis-Kean, P.** (2006). Development of achievement motivation. In W. Damon & R. Lerner (Eds.), *Handbook of child psychology* (6th ed.). New York: Wiley.

**Wigfield, A., Tonks, S., & Klauda, S. L.** (2009). Expectancy-value theory. In K. R. Wentzel & A. Wigfield (Eds.), *Handbook of motivation at school*. New York: Routledge.

**Wiggins, G.** (1992, May). Creating tests worth taking. *Educational Leadership*, pp. 26–33.

**Wildman, T. M.** (2008). Learning. In. N. J. Salkind (Ed.), *Encyclopedia of educational psychology*. Thousand Oaks, CA.: Sage.

**William, D.** (2010). An integrative summary of the research literature and implications for a new theory of formative assessment. In H. Andrade & G. J. Cisek (Eds.), *Handbook of formative assessment*. New York: Routledge.

**Williams, J. P., & Atkins, J. G.** (2009). The role of metacognition in teaching reading comprehension to primary students. In D. J. Hacker, J. Dunlosky, & A. C. Graesser (Eds.), *Handbook of metacognition in education*. New York: Psychology Press.

**Williams, K. C.** (2009). *Elementary classroom management*. Thousand Oaks, CA: Sage.

**Williams, R. B.** (2007). *Cooperative learning: A standard for high achievement*. Thousand Oaks, CA: Corwin.

**Willingham, D. T.** (2008). Critical thinking: Why is it so hard to teach? *Arts Education Policy Review, 109* (4), 21–29.

**Winn, I. J.** (2004). The high cost of uncritical teaching. *Phi Delta Kappan, 85*, 496–497.

**Winne, P. H.** (2001). Self-regulated learning viewed from models of information processing. In B. J. Zimmerman & D. H. Schunk (Eds.), *Self-regulated learning and academic achievement*. Mahwah, NJ: Erlbaum.

**Winne, P. H.** (2005). Key issues in modeling and applying research on self-regulated learning. *Applied Psychology: An International Review, 54*, 232–238.

**Winne, P. H., & Nesbit, J. C.** (2010). The psychology of academic achievement. *Annual Review of Psychology, Vol. 61*. Palo Alto, CA: Annual Reviews.

**Winner, E.** (1986, August). Where pelicans kiss seals. *Psychology Today*, pp. 24–35.

**Winner, E.** (1996). *Gifted children: Myths and realities*. New York: Basic Books.

**Winner, E.** (2000). The origins and ends of giftedness. *American Psychologist, 55*, 159–169.

**Winner, E.** (2006). Development in the arts. In W. Damon & R. Lerner (Eds.), *Handbook of child psychology* (6th ed.). New York: Wiley.

**Winner, E.** (2009). Toward broadening our understanding of giftedness: The spatial domain. In F. D. Horowitz, R. F. Subotnik, & D. J. Matthews (Eds.), *The development of giftedness and talent across the life span*. Washington, DC: American Psychological Association.

**Winsler, A., Carlton, M. P., & Barry, M. J.** (2000). Age-related changes in preschool children's systematic use of private speech in a natural setting. *Journal of Child Language, 27*, 665–687.

**Wisenthal, P.** (2010, January 8–10). 5 great websites that let your kids get creative. *USA Weekend*, p. 4

**Wiske, S., Franz, K. R., & Breit, L.** (2005). *Teaching for understanding with technology*. New York: Wiley.

**Witelson, S. F., Beresh, H., & Kigar, D. L.** (2006). Intelligence and brain size in 100 postmortem brains: sex, lateralization and age factors. *Brain, 129*, 386–398.

**Witelson, S. F., Kigar, D. L., & Harvey, T.** (1999). The exceptional brain of Albert Einstein. *The Lancet, 353*, 2149–2153.

**Wittmer, D. S., & Honig, A. S.** (1994). Encouraging positive social development in young children. *Young Children, 49*, 4–12.

**Witvliet, M., & others** (2010). Peer group affiliation in children: The role of perceived popularity, likeability, and behavioral similarity in bullying. *Social Development, 19*, 285–303.

**Wolsey, T. D., & Fisher, D.** (2009). *Learning to predict and predicting to learn*. Upper Saddle River, NJ: Prentice Hall.

**Wong Briggs, T.** (1999, October 14). *Honorees find keys to unlocking kids' minds*. Retrieved March 10, 2000, from www.usatoday.com/education

**Wong Briggs, T.** (2004, October 14). Students embrace vitality of *USA Today's* top 20 teachers. *USA Today*, p. 7D.

**Wong Briggs, T.** (2005). Math teacher resets the learning curve. Retrieved March 6, 2006,

from www.usatoday.com/news/education/2005-04-05-math-teacher_x.htm

**Wong Briggs, T.** (2005, October 13). *USA Today's* 2005 All-USA Teacher Team. *USA Today*, p. 6D.

**Wong Briggs, T.** (2007, October 18). An early start for learning. *USA Today*, p. 6D.

**Wood, J. T.** (2011). *Communication mosaics* (6th ed.). Boston: Cengage.

**Work Group of the American Psychological Association Board of Educational Affairs.** (1995). *Learner-centered psychological principles: A framework for school redesign and reform* (draft). Washington, DC: American Psychological Association.

**Work Group of the American Psychological Association Board of Educational Affairs.** (1997). *Learner-centered psychological principles: A framework for school reform and redesign*. Washington, DC: American Psychological Association.

**Wray-Lake, L., Crouter, A. C., & McHale, S. M.** (2010). Developmental patterns in decision-making autonomy across middle childhood and adolescence: European American parents' perspectives. *Child Development, 81*, 636–651.

**Wright Group** (2004). *Everyday math* (2nd ed.). New York: McGraw-Hill.

**Wright Group** (2007). *Everyday math* (3rd ed.). New York: McGraw-Hill.

**Wright, J.** (2004). *Preventing classroom bullying: What teachers can do*. Retrieved January 16, 2010, from www.intervention-central.org

**Wright, R. J.** (2011). *Introduction to school counseling*. Thousand Oaks, CA: Sage.

**Write:Outloud** (2009). Retrieved January 16, 2009 from *USA Today* www.donjohnston.com/products/write_outloud/index.html

**Wu, H-K., & Huang, Y-L.** (2007). Ninth-grade student engagement in teacher-centered and student-centered technology-enhanced learning environments. *Science Education, 91*, 727–749.

# X

**Xia, N.** (2010). *Family factors and student outcomes*. Unpublished doctoral dissertation, RAND Corporation, Pardee RAND Graduate School, Pittsburgh.

**Xu, J.** (2010). Homework purposes reported by secondary school students: A multilevel analysis. *Journal of Educational Research, 103*, 171–182.

## Y

**Yeh, Y-C.** (2009). Integrating e-learning into the direction-instruction model to enhance the effectiveness of critical-thinking instruction. *Instructional Science, 37,* 185–203.

**Yell, M. L., & Drasgow, E.** (2009). *What every teacher should know about No Child Left Behind* (2nd ed.). Upper Saddle River, NJ: Prentice Hall.

**Yinger, R. J.** (1980). Study of teacher planning. *Elementary School Journal, 80,* 107–127.

**Yoo, H. C., Burrola, K., & Steger, M. F.** (2010). A preliminary report on a new measure: Internalization of the model minority myth measure (IM-4) and its psychological correlates among Asian American college students. *Journal of Counseling Psychology, 57,* 114–127.

**Yu, W-F., She, H-C., & Lee, Y-M.** (2010). The effects of Web-based/non-Web-based problem-solving instruction and high/low achievement on students' problem-solving ability and biology achievement. *Innovations in Education and Teaching International, 47,* 187–199.

## Z

**Zarefsky, D.** (2011). *Public speaking* (6th ed.). Boston: Allyn & Bacon.

**Zelazo, P. D., & Lee, W. S. C** (2011). Brain development: An overview. In R. M. Lerner & W. F. Overton (Ed.), *Handbook of life-span development, Vol.1.* New York: Wiley.

**Zhang, L-F., & Sternberg, R. J.** (2011, in press). Learning in cross-cultural perspective. In T. Husen & T. N. Postlethwaite (Eds.), *International encyclopedia of education* (3rd ed.). New York: Elsevier.

**Zhao, D., & Ma, Y.** (2009). A qualitative study on primary school mathematics lesson evaluation. *Frontiers of Education in China, 4,* 506–525.

**Zhou, M., & others** (2010). Forebrain overexpression of CK1delta leads to down-regulation of dopamine receptors and altered locomotor activity reminiscent of ADHD. *Proceeding of the National Academy of Sciences, 107,* 4401–4406.

**Zhou, Q., Lengua, L. J., & Wang, Y.** (2009). The relations of temperament reactivity and effortful control to children's adjustment problems in the United States and China. *Developmental Psychology, 45,* 724–239.

**Zhou, Z., Siu, C. R., & Xin, T.** (2009). Promoting cultural competence in counseling Asian American children and adolescents. *Psychology in the Schools, 46,* 290–298.

**Zigler, E. F., & Finn-Stevenson, M.** (1999). Applied developmental psychology. In M. H. Bornstein & M. E. Lamb (Eds.), *Developmental psychology* (4th ed.). Mahwah, NJ: Erlbaum.

**Zigler, E. F., & Styfco, S. J.** (2010). *The hidden history of Head Start.* New York: Oxford University Press.

**Zimmerman, B. J., Bonner, S., & Kovach, R.** (1996). *Developing self-regulated learners.* Washington, DC: American Psychological Association.

**Ziol-Guest, K. M.** (2009). Child custody and support. In D. Carr (Ed.), *Encyclopedia of the life course and human development.* Boston: Gale Cengage.

**Zoo Cams Worldwide** (2008). Retrieved January 16, 2008, from www.zoos-worldwide.de/zoocam.html

**Zosuls, K. M., Lurye, L. E., & Ruble, D. N.** (2008). Gender: Awareness, identity, and sterotyping. In M. M. Haith & J. B. Benson (Eds.), *Encyclopedia of infancy and early childhood.* Oxford, UK: Elsevier.

**Zucker, A. A., & McGhee, R.** (2005) *A study of one-to-one computer use in mathematics and science instruction at the secondary level in Henrico County Public Schools.* Washington, DC: SRI International.

**Zydney, J. M.** (2010). The effect of multiple scaffolding tools on students' understanding, consideration of different perspectives, and misconceptions of a complex problem. *Computers and Education, 54,* 360–370.

# Credits

## TEXT AND LINE ART

### Chapter 1

p. 2, Teaching Stories, Margaret Metzger: From Margaret Metzger, "Maintaining a Life," *Phi Delta Kappan,* vol. 77 (January 1996), pp. 346–351. Reprinted by permission of the author. Figure 1.1: From "Students say: What makes a good teacher?" *Schools in the Middle,* vol. 6, no. 5 (May/June 1997), p. 16 (Tables 1 and 2). Copyright 1997 National Association of Secondary School Principals. www.principals.org. Reprinted with permission. Figure 1.2: Kevin Crowley, Maureen A. Callanan, Harriet R. Tenenbaum, and Elizabeth Allen, "Parents explain more to boys than girls during shared scientific thinking," *Psychological Science,* 12, no. 3, pp. 258–261 (Figure 1b), copyright © 2001 by Association for Psychological Science. Reprinted by Permission of SAGE Publications. Figure 1.3: John W. Santrock, *Life-Span Development,* 10th ed., Figure 2.9, p. 62. Copyright © 2006 by The McGraw-Hill Companies, Inc. Reprinted with permission of The McGraw-Hill Companies.

### Chapter 2

Figure 2.1: Line art from John W. Santrock, *Life-Span Development,* 10th ed., Figure 1.8, p. 20. Copyright © 2006 by The McGraw-Hill Companies, Inc. Reprinted with permission of The McGraw-Hill Companies. Figure 2.5: John W. Santrock, *Essentials of Life-Span Development,* 1st ed., Figure 9.3. Copyright © 2008 by The McGraw-Hill Companies, Inc. Reprinted with permission of The McGraw-Hill Companies. Figure 2.10 a&b: From *The Symbolic Drawings of Young Children.* Reprinted by permission of Dr. Dennie Palmer Wolf. Figure 2.11: From John W. Santrock, *Psychology,* 7th ed. Copyright © 2003 by The McGraw-Hill Companies, Inc. Reprinted with permission of The McGraw-Hill Companies. Figure 2.13b: John W. Santrock, *Essentials of Life-Span Development,* 1st ed., Figure 5.5.

Copyright © 2008 by The McGraw-Hill Companies, Inc. Reprinted with permission of The McGraw-Hill Companies. Figure 2.14: John W. Santrock, *Children,* 7th ed., Figure 13.1. Copyright © 2003 by The McGraw-Hill Companies, Inc. Reprinted with permission of The McGraw-Hill Companies. Figure 2.16: Bodrova, E., & Leong, D. J. (2001). *Tools of the Mind: A Case Study of Implementing the Vygotskian Approach in American Early Childhood and Primary Classrooms.* Geneva, Switzerland: International Bureau of Education, UNESCO, Figure 7 (p. 36), Figure 9 (p. 38). Figure 2.18: From Jean Berko, "The Child's Learning of English Morphology," *Word,* vol. 14 (1958), p. 154. By permission of Jean Berko Gleason.

### Chapter 3

Figure 3.3: John W. Santrock, *Life-Span Development,* 10th ed., Figure 9.8. Copyright © 2006 by The McGraw-Hill Companies, Inc. Reprinted with permission of The McGraw-Hill Companies. Figure 3.5: National Center for Education Statistics, 2007. Figure 3.6: From Robins, R. W., Trzesniewski, K. H., Tracy, J. L., Gosling, S. D., & Potter, J. (2002). Global self-esteem across the life span. *Psychology and Aging,* 17, 423–434 (Fig. 1, p. 428). Copyright © 2002 by the American Psychological Association. Adapted with permission. Figure 3.7: From John W. Santrock, *Life-Span Development,* 10th ed. Copyright © 2006 by The McGraw-Hill Companies, Inc. Reprinted with permission of The McGraw-Hill Companies.

### Chapter 4

p. 111, Teaching Stories, Shiffy Landa: From Shiffy Landa, "If you can't make waves, make ripples," *Intelligence Connections: Newsletter of the ASCD,* Vol. X, No. 1 (Fall 2000), pp. 6–8. Reprinted by permission of Thomas R. Hoerr, Ph.D., Head of School, New City School, St. Louis. www.newcityschool.org. Figure 4.1: John W. Santrock, *Life-Span Development,*

10th ed., Figure 10.6. Copyright © 2006 by The McGraw-Hill Companies, Inc. Reprinted with permission of The McGraw-Hill Companies. Figure 4.4: John W. Santrock, *Children,* 9th ed., Figure 6.6. Copyright © 2007 by The McGraw-Hill Companies, Inc. Reprinted with permission of The McGraw-Hill Companies. Figure 4.5: from Ulric Neisser, "The Increase in IQ Scores from 1932–1997." Reprinted by permission of the author.

### Chapter 5

Figure 5.2: National Assessment of Educational Progress (2005). pp. 173–174, Through the Eyes of Teachers: Reprinted by permission of Kodansha America, LLC. Excerpted from *Teaching Stories* by Judy Logan published by Kodansha America, Inc. (1999).

### Chapter 6

Figure 6.1: National Center for Education Statistics (2008). *Children and youth with disabilities in public schools.* Washington DC: U.S. Department of Education.

### Chapter 7

p. 217, Teaching Stories, Ruth Sidney Charney: From Charney, Ruth Sidney. (2005). Using language to encourage and empower children, Part 2: Exploring the first 'R': To reinforce. EducationWorld.com. Retrieved from http://www.education-world.com/a_curr/columnists/charney/charney004b.shtml. Reprinted by permission of Education World. Figure 7.5: John W. Santrock, *Psychology,* 7th ed., Figure 7.9. Copyright © 2003 by The McGraw-Hill Companies, Inc. Reprinted with permission of The McGraw-Hill Companies. Figure 7.6: After Irwin Hyman, *Statistical Analysis of the Cross-Cultural Data: The Third Year.* Paper presented at the meeting of the American Psychological Association, San Francisco, 2001. Reprinted by permission of Irwin Hyman. Figure 7.7: John W. Santrock, *Psychology,* 7th ed., Figure 12.6 (p. 487). Copyright © 2003 by The McGraw-

Hill Companies, Inc. Reprinted with permission of The McGraw-Hill Companies. p. 244, Self-Assessment 7.2, Self-Monitoring: From Zimmerman, B. J., Bonner, S., & Kovach, R. (1996). *Developing self-regulated learners: Beyond achievement to self-efficacy.* Washington, DC: American Psychological Association (Exhibit 1, p. 28). Copyright © 1996 by the American Psychological Association. Reprinted with permission. Figure 7.11: From Zimmerman, B. J., Bonner, S., & Kovach, R. (1996). *Developing self-regulated learners: Beyond achievement to self-efficacy.* Washington, DC: American Psychological Association (Figure 1, p. 11). Copyright © 1996 by the American Psychological Association. Adapted with permission.

### Chapter 8

Figure 8.1: From John W. Santrock, *Psychology,* 7th ed. Copyright © 2003 by The McGraw-Hill Companies, Inc. Reprinted with permission of The McGraw-Hill Companies. Figure 8.2: Reprinted from *Contemporary Educational Psychology,* vol. 5, no. 1, M. Pressley, J. R. Levin, and C. B. McCormick, "Young Children's Learning of a Foreign Language Vocabulary: A Sentence Variation of the Keyword Method," pp. 22–29, Copyright 1980, with permission from Elsevier. Figure 8.3: Reprinted from *Journal of Experimental Child Psychology,* vol. 43, no. 2, M. Pressley, T. Cariligia-Bull, S. Deane, and W. Schneider, "Short-Term Memory, Verbal Competence, and Age as Predictors of Imagery Instructional Effectiveness," pp. 194–211, Copyright 1987, with permission from Elsevier. Figure 8.5: John W. Santrock, *Psychology,* 7th ed., Figure 8.8 (p. 314). Copyright © 2003 by The McGraw-Hill Companies, Inc. Reprinted with permission of The McGraw-Hill Companies. Figure 8.6: From Swanson, H. L. (1999). What develops in working memory? A life span perspective. *Developmental Psychology,* 35, 986–1000 (Table 1, p. 990). Copyright © 1999 by the

American Psychological Association. Adapted with permission. Figure 8.7: John W. Santrock, *Psychology,* 7th ed., Figure 8.5 (p. 312). Copyright © 2003 by The McGraw-Hill Companies, Inc. Reprinted with permission of The McGraw-Hill Companies. Figure 8.8: John W. Santrock, *Psychology,* 7th ed., Figure 8.9 (p. 316). Copyright © 2003 by The McGraw-Hill Companies, Inc. Reprinted with permission of The McGraw-Hill Companies. Figure 8.9: Laura A. King, *The Science of Psychology: An Appreciative View,* 1st ed., Figure 8.10. Copyright © 2008 by The McGraw-Hill Companies, Inc. Reprinted with permission of The McGraw-Hill Companies. Figure 8.10: Adapted from Bennet B. Murdock, Jr., *Human Memory: Theory and Data.* Potomac, MD: Lawrence Erlbaum Associates, 1974. Figure 8.11: From John W. Santrock, *Life-Span Development,* 6th ed. Copyright © 1997 by The McGraw-Hill Companies, Inc. Reprinted with permission of The McGraw-Hill Companies. Figure 8.12: After M. T. H. Chi, "Knowledge structures and memory development," in R. S. Siegler, ed., *Children's Thinking.* Hillsdale, NJ: Lawrence Erlbaum, 1978. Figure 8.13: From Frederick Reif, "Cognitive Mechanisms Facilitating Human Problem Solving in a Realistic Domain: The Example of Physics," printed at the University of California at Berkeley, October 19, 1979. Reprinted by permission of the author. Figure 8.14: H. M. Wellman, D. Cross, and J. Watson, "Meta-Analysis of Theory-of-Mind Development: The Truth about False Belief," *Child Development,* vol. 72, no. 3 (May/June 2001), p. 662 (Figure 2A). Copyright © 2001 The Society for Research in Child Development, Inc. Reprinted by permission of John Wiley & Sons, Inc. http://www3.interscience.wiley.com/journal/117957161/home

## Chapter 9

p. 295, Teaching Stories, Marilyn Whirry: Council of Chief State School Officers. (2000). Description of 2000 National Teacher of the Year Marilyn Jachetti Whirry. Washington, DC: Author. http://www.ccsso.org/Projects/national_teacher_of_the_year/national_teachers/156.cfm. Used by permission of the Council of Chief State School Officers. Figure 9.1: From DeLoache, J. S., Simcock, G., & Macari, S. (2007). Planes, trains, automobiles—and tea sets: Extremely intense interests in very young children. *Developmental Psychology,*

*43,* 1579–1586 (Figure 2, p. 1583). Copyright © 2007 by the American Psychological Association. Reprinted with permission. Figure 9.3: From John W. Santrock, *Psychology,* 5th ed. Copyright © 1997 by The McGraw-Hill Companies, Inc. Reprinted with permission of The McGraw-Hill Companies. Figure 9.5: Adapted from Richard I. Arends, *Learning to Teach,* 6th ed., Table 11.1 (p. 406). Copyright © 2004 by The McGraw-Hill Companies, Inc. Reprinted with permission of The McGraw-Hill Companies.

## Chapter 11

p. 361, Teaching Stories, Wendy Nelson Kauffman: From "USA Today's 2003 All-USA Teacher Team," *USA Today,* October 16, 2003. p. 371: "The devl and the babe goste" reprinted by permission of Maryanne Wolf, Ph.D., from Dickinson, D., Wolf, M., & Stotsky, S. (1993). "Words Move": The interwoven development of oral and written language in the school years. In Jean Berko Gleason (Ed.), *The Development of Language,* 3rd ed. New York: Macmillan. pp. 388–390, Ten themes that should be emphasized in courses in the social sciences: From National Council for the Social Sciences, *National Standards for Social Studies Teachers* (2000). © National Council for the Social Studies. Reprinted by permission.

## Chapter 12

Figure 12.3: From Carol Simon Weinstein and Andrew J. Mignano, Jr., *Elementary Classroom Management,* 2nd ed. Copyright © 1997 by The McGraw-Hill Companies, Inc. Reprinted with permission of The McGraw-Hill Companies. Figure 12.4: From Carol Simon Weinstein and Andrew J. Mignano, Jr., *Elementary Classroom Management,* 2nd ed. Copyright © 1997 by The McGraw-Hill Companies, Inc. Reprinted with permission of The McGraw-Hill Companies. Figure 12.5: John W. Santrock and Steven R. Yussen, *Child Development: An Introduction,* 3rd ed., Figure 17.1. Copyright © 1987 by The McGraw-Hill Companies, Inc. Reprinted with permission of The McGraw-Hill Companies. Figure 12.6: *National Educational Technology Standards for Students,* Second Edition © 2007 ISTE® (International Society for Technology in Education), www.iste.org. All rights reserved. pp. 425–426: From Martha Stone Wiske, with Kristi Rennebohm

Franz and Lisa Breit, *Teaching for Understanding with Technology.* Copyright © 2005 by John Wiley & Sons, Inc. Reproduced with permission of John Wiley & Sons, Inc.

## Chapter 13

Figure 13.2: From Jere Brophy, *Motivating Students to Learn.* Copyright © 1998 by The McGraw-Hill Companies, Inc. Reprinted with permission of The McGraw-Hill Companies. p. 447: From S. Graham and B. Weiner, "Theories and Principles of Motivation," in *Handbook of Educational Psychology,* ed. David Berliner and R. C. Calfee. New York: Macmillan Library Reference, 1996, p. 72. Figure 13.6: From Jere Brophy, *Motivating Students to Learn.* Copyright © 1998 by The McGraw-Hill Companies, Inc. Reprinted with permission of The McGraw-Hill Companies.

## Chapter 14

Figure 14.4: From Carol Simon Weinstein, *Secondary Classroom Management.* Copyright © 1996 by The McGraw-Hill Companies, Inc. Reprinted with permission of The McGraw-Hill Companies. p. 494: Geneva Gay, "Connections between Classroom Management and Culturally Responsive Teaching," in *Handbook of Classroom Management: Research, Practice, and Contemporary Issues,* ed. C. M. Evertson and C. S. Weinstein, p. 364. Copyright 2006 by Taylor & Francis Group LLC—Books. Reproduced with permission of Taylor & Francis Group LLC—Books in the format Textbook via Copyright Clearance Center. Figure 14.5: From Tonja R. Nansel et al., "Bullying Behaviors among U.S. Youths: Prevalence and Association with Psychosocial Adjustment," *Journal of the American Medical Association,* Vol. 285 (2001), pp. 2094–2100.

## Chapter 16

Figure 16.7: Reprinted with permission from National Middle School Association. From Combs, D. (1997, September). Using alternative assessment to provide options for student success. *Middle School Journal,* p. 5 (Figure 1). Figure 16.8: G. Solano-Flores and R. J. Shavelson, "Development of Performance Assessments in Science: Conceptual, Practical, and Logistical Issues," *Educational Measurement: Issues and Practice,* vol. 16, no. 3 (Sept. 1997), p. 17 (Figure 1). Copyright © 1997 National Council on Measurement in

Education. Reprinted by permission of John Wiley & Sons, Inc. http://www3.interscience.wiley.com/journal/118495101/home. Figure 16.9: From Heidi Goodrich, "Understanding Rubrics," *Educational Leadership,* Vol. 54, No. 4 (1997), Figure 1. Reprinted by permission of the author. Figure 16.10: From Heidi Goodrich, "Understanding Rubrics," *Educational Leadership,* Vol. 54, No. 4 (1997), Figure 3. Reprinted by permission of the author. Figure 16.11: From Nancy Jean Johnson and Leonie Marie Rose, *Portfolios.* Lanham, MD: Rowman & Littlefield Education, 1997. Reprinted by permission of the publisher.

## PHOTO

### Chapter 1

p. 1: Ariel Skelley/Blend Images/Getty Images; p. 3: (left to right): © Brown Brothers; Columbia University Archives, Columbia University in the City of New York; Archives of the History of American Psychology, University of Akron; p. 4: (top): Courtesy of Kenneth Clark; p. 4 (bottom left): Prints and Photographs Collection CN10383, Center for American History, University of Texas at Austin; p. 4 (bottom right): © Archives of the History of American Psychology, University of Akron; p. 5: © 2007, USA TODAY, Reprinted with permission; p. 7: Image Source/Getty Images; p. 8: © Davis Turner; p. 9: Blend Images/Getty Images; p. 10: BananaStock/age fotostock; p. 13: © Alan Marler; p. 17: Courtesy of Steven and Cindi Binder; p. 18: BananaStock/age fotostock

### Chapter 2

p. 28: Design Pics Inc./Alamy; p. 31 (left to right): © Brand X Pictures/PunchStock; © Digital Vision; Laurence Mouton/Photoalto/PictureQuest; © Stockbyte; Getty Images/SW Productions; p. 35: © Photo Researchers; p. 36: ER Productions/Getty Images; p. 37 (top): ER Productions/Getty Images; (bottom): © A. Glauberman/Photo Researchers; p. 38: (top): © David Grugin Productions, Inc. Reprinted by permission; p. 38 (bottom): Image courtesy of Dana Boatman, Ph.D., Department of Neurology, John Hopkins University, reprinted with permission from *The Secret Life of the Brain,* Joseph Henry Press; p. 39 (top): Corbis/age fotostock; (bottom): Rubberball Productions/Getty Images;

## Chapter 14

p. 476: Creatas/PunchStock; p. 478 (top): © Michael A. Schwarz Photography; p. 478 (bottom left): © Pixland/PunchStock; (bottom right): © Echo/Getty Images; p. 480 (clockwise): © Spencer Grant/Photo Edit; © Elizabeth Crews; © Rick Raymond/Stone/Getty Images; © David Young-Wolff/Photo Edit;

p. 483: Courtesy of eInstruction; p. 488: © William Williford, Perry Middle School, Perry, GA; p. 490: © Mark Fodness; p. 494: Comstock/PictureQuest; p. 497: © Tommie Lindsey; p. 498: © RF/Corbis; p. 499 (left): Tim Pannell/Corbis; (right): © Photodisc/PunchStock; p. 503: Courtesy of Department of Teaching and Learning, Peabody College,

Vanderbilt University; p. 507: Digital Vision/Getty Images

## Chapter 15

p. 514: Comstock Select/Corbis; p. 516: Stretch Photography/Getty Images; p. 518: Radius Images/Corbis; p. 526: Photo courtesy of Martha McArthur, Reading First Program, NM; p. 528: © iStockphoto.com/Jorge

Delgado; p. 529: Used with permission from WKU-Elizabethtown/Radcliff/Fort Knox; p. 542: Comstock Images/Getty Images

## Chapter 16

p. 547: Corbis/age fotostock; p. 550: © Image Source/Alamy; p. 555: Randy Faris/Corbis; p. 556: © Superstock RF; p. 566: BananaStock/age fotostock

# Name Index

# Subject Index

in Piaget's theory, 52
teaching strategies for, 63–65
in Vygotsky's theory, 52
language disorders, 193
lateralization of brain, 37
Latinos. *See also* diversity; ethnicity
achievement and, 461–462
diversity in, 148
ethnic identity of, 95–96
gender and, 170
high school drop-out rate of, 89
increase in U.S., 148
intelligence tests and, 123
NCLB Act and, 525
parenting styles of, 79
learner-centered approach
discovery learning in, 416
essential questions in, 416
evaluating, 417–418
principles of, 414–415
problem-based learning in,
320, 416
teaching strategies for, 418–419
learning. *See also specific approaches*
approaches to, 218–219
classroom assessment compatibility
with, 551–552
defined, 217
distributing and consolidating,
279–280
expertise and, 277–281
scope of, 217–218
learning and thinking styles,
129–131, 137
learning disabilities, 182–184, 185
learning together approach, 343
least restrictive environment (LRE),
200–201
lecturing, 407, 408
legal issues for children with disabilities,
199–202
lesson planning. *See* instructional
planning
levels of processing theory, 264
life-span theory, 73–76
listening skills, 498–499
literacy in early childhood, 61–62
long-term goals, 451
long-term memory, 268–270
Lorge-Thorndike Intelligence
Tests, 114
low-road transfer, 325
low vision, 192

**M**

macrosystem, 72
mastery learning, 408, 410
mastery motivation, 448
mastery orientation, 448, 449
mathematics, 378–385
Asian and U.S. education compared,
406, 408
calculator use in, 381–382
children with disabilities and, 183
cognitive processes of, 380–381

constructivist principles for, 381, 394
controversy in education, 380
developmental changes in, 378–380
in Gardner's frames of mind, 116
gender and skills in, 166–167
international assessments, 528
NAEP findings, 527
teaching strategies for, 382–384
technology for instruction in,
381–382
technology resources for, 391–392
mean, 534
meaning
reading and, 366–367
as socially negotiated, 366
social studies and, 391
writing and, 373
means-end analysis, 318
measures of variability, 535–536
median, 534
memory, 263–276
Atkinson-Shiffrin model, 268–269
declarative, 269
defined, 263
encoding of, 263–266
episodic, 270
forgetting, 272–273
fuzzy trace theory of, 271
long-term, 268–270
mnemonic strategies, 274–275
network theories of, 270
procedural, 269
retrieval of, 263, 271–272
schema theories of, 270–271
self-assessment, 281
semantic, 270
sensory, 266
short-term, 266–269
storage of, 263, 266–271
strategies for improving, 273–275
working, 266–268
memory span, 266, 267
mental age (MA), 112
mental processes, 218
mental retardation, 189–191
mental set, 319
mentors, 239, 337–338, 340, 504
mesosystem, 72
metacognition, 284–290
defined, 256
developmental changes in,
285–287
Good Information-Processing
model, 287
in learner-centered approach, 415
learning and, 284–285
mathematics and, 380–381
as mechanism of change, 256
metamemory, 285
reading and, 365
strategies and metacognitive
regulation, 287–289
teaching strategies for, 288
theory of mind, 285–287
metacognitive knowledge, 284
metalinguistic awareness, 63
metamemory, 285

metaphor, 63
microsystem, 72
middle and late childhood. *See also*
elementary school
attention in, 259
brain development in, 36
concrete operational stage, 41,
44–45, 46
as development period, 31
Gardner's frames of mind in, 118
industry versus inferiority
stage, 74, 75
language development in, 62–63
preoperational stage, 41–44, 45
theory of mind in, 286
middle school. *See also* adolescence;
teaching strategies
classroom management in, 478–479
effective schools, 88
identity versus identity confusion
stage, 75
mathematics in, 379
performance assessment in, 569
reading in, 363
shortage of math and science teachers
in, 378, 385
standards for technology-literate
students, 424, 425
transition to, 88
milestones. *See also* stages
of development
adolescence, 31, 35, 36–37, 38, 63
in attention focus and control,
258–259
brain development, 35–37
early childhood, 30–31, 60–62
infancy, 30, 60
language development, 60, 62–63
in mathematics, 378–380
middle and late childhood, 31, 36,
62–63
in reading, 363
in theory of mind, 286–287
in writing, 370–371
mindblindness, 285
mindfulness, 303–304
mindset, 448–450
minor interventions, 502–503
minorities. *See* culture; diversity;
ethnicity; socioeconomic
status (SES)
mixed methods research, 21
mnemonic strategies, 274–275
mode, 534–535
modeled demonstrations, 237
moderate interventions, 503–504
Montessori approach, 85–87
moral development, 96–103
cheating, 99–100
defined, 97
domains of, 97
Kohlberg's theory of, 97–99
moral education and, 100–102
prosocial behavior, 100, 101, 103
teaching strategies for, 103
moral education, 100–102, 158
morphology, 58, 60

motivation, 437–450, 457–461
behavioral perspective on, 438
classroom assessment compatibility
with, 551–552
cognitive perspective on, 439
competence, 439
cooperative learning and, 342
defined, 438
for expertise, 282
extrinsic, 441, 445–446
failure syndrome and, 464
humanistic perspective on, 438–439
incentives for, 438
intrinsic, 441–446
in learner-centered approach, 415
mastery, 448
in observational learning, 237
as problem-solving obstacle, 319
self-assessment, 469
skills of teachers, 8
social motives, 458
social perspective on, 440
social relationships and, 458–461
teachers' affect on, 460
teachers' need for, 10–12, 13
teaching strategies for, 442, 443
multicultural education, 154–164
characteristics of multicultural
schools, 155–156
culturally relevant teaching, 157–158
defined, 154–155
empowering students, 157
improving ethnic relations, 159–161
issues-centered education, 158
teaching strategies for, 156, 162
multiple-choice items, 558–560
multiple intelligences theories,
114–121
comparison of, 120
emotional intelligence, 120
evaluating, 120–121
Gardner's frames of mind, 115–120
Sternberg's triarchic theory, 115
multiplicative reasoning, 379
musical skills, 116, 117
myelination, 35

**N**

national assessment, 527
naturalistic observation, 15
naturalist skills, 116, 117
nature-nurture issue
defined, 32
evaluating, 33
giftedness and, 205
intelligence and, 122–123, 125
language development and, 59
overview, 32
near transfer, 325
negative affectivity, 134
negative reinforcement, 222–223, 227
neglected children, 83
neglectful parenting, 78
neo-Piagetians, 50
network theories of memory, 270